P9-DYZ-930

International Directory of
COMPANY
HISTORIES

International Directory of
COMPANY
HISTORIES

VOLUME 93

Editor

Jay P. Pederson

ST. JAMES PRESS
A part of Gale, Cengage Learning

GALE
CENGAGE Learning™

Detroit • New York • San Francisco • New Haven, Conn • Waterville, Maine • London

International Directory of Company Histories, Volume 93

Jay P. Pederson, Editor

Project Editor: Miranda H. Ferrara

Editorial: Virgil Burton, Donna Craft, Louise Gagné, Peggy Geeseman, Julie Gough, Linda Hall, Lauren Haslett, Sonya Hill, Lauren Haslett, Keith Jones, Lynn Pearce, Holly Selden, Justine Ventimiglia

Production Technology Specialist: Mike Weaver

Imaging and Multimedia: Lezlie Light

Composition and Electronic Prepress: Gary Leach, Evi Seoud

Manufacturing: Rhonda Dover

Product Management: David Forman

Cover Photograph: Astor Theatre, New York City, c. 1936. Courtesy Library of Congress, Prints & Photographs Division, FSA/OWI Collection, reproduction number LC-USZ62-74610.

For product information and technology assistance, contact us at **Gale Customer Support, 1-800-877-4253.** For permission to use material from this text or product, submit all requests online at **www.cengage.com/permissions.** Further permissions questions can be emailed to **permissionrequest@cengage.com**

While every effort has been made to ensure the reliability of the information presented in this publication, Gale, a part of Cengage Learning, does not guarantee the accuracy of the data contained herein. Gale accepts no payment for listing; and inclusion in the publication of any organization, agency, institution, publication, service, or individual does not imply endorsement of the editors or publisher. Errors brought to the attention of the publisher and verified to the satisfaction of the publisher will be corrected in future editions.

EDITORIAL DATA PRIVACY POLICY: Does this product contain information about you as an individual? If so, for more information about our editorial data privacy policies, please see our Privacy Statement at www.gale.cengage.com.

Gale
27500 Drake Rd.
Farmington Hills, MI, 48331-3535

LIBRARY OF CONGRESS CATALOG NUMBER 89-190943
ISBN-13: 978-1-55862-614-0
ISBN-10: 1-55862-614-X

This title is also available as an e-book
ISBN-13: 978-1-4144-2977-9   ISBN-10: 1-4144-2977-0
Contact your Gale, a part of Cengage Learning sales representative for ordering information.

BRITISH LIBRARY CATALOGUING IN PUBLICATION DATA
International directory of company histories, Vol. 93
Jay P. Pederson
33.87409

Printed in the United States of America
1 2 3 4 5 6 7 12 11 10 09 08

Contents

Preface

The St. James Press series *The International Directory of Company Histories* (*IDCH*) is intended for reference use by students, business people, librarians, historians, economists, investors, job candidates, and others who seek to learn more about the historical development of the world's most important companies. To date, *IDCH* has covered over 9,075 companies in 93 volumes.

INCLUSION CRITERIA

Most companies chosen for inclusion in *IDCH* have achieved a minimum of US$25 million in annual sales and are leading influences in their industries or geographical locations. Companies may be publicly held, private, or nonprofit. State-owned companies that are important in their industries and that may operate much like public or private companies also are included. Wholly owned subsidiaries and divisions are profiled if they meet the requirements for inclusion. Entries on companies that have had major changes since they were last profiled may be selected for updating.

The *IDCH* series highlights 25% private and nonprofit companies, and features updated entries on approximately 35 companies per volume.

ENTRY FORMAT

Each entry begins with the company's legal name; the address of its headquarters; its telephone, toll-free, and fax numbers; and its web site. A statement of public, private, state, or parent ownership follows. A company with a legal name in both English and the language of its headquarters country is listed by the English name, with the native-language name in parentheses.

The company's founding or earliest incorporation date, the number of employees, and the most recent available sales figures follow. Sales figures are given in local currencies with equivalents in U.S. dollars. For some private companies, sales figures are estimates and indicated by the abbreviation *est.* The entry lists the exchanges on which the company's stock is traded and its ticker symbol, as well as the company's NAIC codes.

Entries generally contain a *Company Perspectives* box which provides a short summary of the company's mission, goals, and ideals; a *Key Dates* box highlighting milestones in the company's history; lists of *Principal Subsidiaries*, *Principal Divisions*, *Principal Operating Units*, *Principal Competitors*; and articles for *Further Reading*.

American spelling is used throughout *IDCH*, and the word "billion" is used in its U.S. sense of one thousand million.

SOURCES

Entries have been compiled from publicly accessible sources both in print and on the Internet such as general and academic periodicals, books, and annual reports, as well as material supplied by the companies themselves.

CUMULATIVE INDEXES

IDCH contains three indexes: the **Index to Companies**, which provides an alphabetical index to companies discussed in the text as well as to companies profiled, the **Index to Industries**, which allows researchers to locate companies by their principal industry, and the **Geographic Index**, which lists companies alphabetically by the country of their headquarters. The indexes are cumulative and specific instructions for using them are found immediately preceding each index.

SUGGESTIONS WELCOME

Comments and suggestions from users of *IDCH* on any aspect of the product as well as suggestions for companies to be included or updated are cordially invited. Please write:

The Editor
International Directory of Company Histories
St. James Press
Gale, Cengage Learning
27500 Drake Rd.
Farmington Hills, Michigan 48331-3535

St. James Press does not endorse any of the companies or products mentioned in this series. Companies appearing in the *International Directory of Company Histories* were selected without reference to their wishes and have in no way endorsed their entries.

Notes on Contributors

M. L. Cohen
Novelist, business writer, and researcher living in Paris.

Jeffrey L. Covell
Seattle-based writer.

Ed Dinger
Writer and editor based in Bronx, New York.

Jodi Essey-Stapleton
Writer based in Illinois.

Robert Halasz
Former editor in chief of *World Progress* and *Funk & Wagnalls New Encyclopedia Yearbook*; author, *The U.S. Marines* (Millbrook Press, 1993).

Frederick C. Ingram
Writer based in South Carolina.

Kathleen Peippo
Minnesota-based writer.

Nelson Rhodes
Editor, writer, and consultant in the Chicago area.

Carrie Rothburd
Writer and editor specializing in corporate profiles, academic texts, and academic journal articles.

David E. Salamie
Part-owner of InfoWorks Development Group, a reference publication development and editorial services company.

Daniel Patrick Thurs
Writer and researcher specializing in issues related to science and technology.

Mary Tradii
Colorado-based writer.

Frank Uhle
Ann Arbor-based writer; movie projectionist, disc jockey, and staff member of *Psychotronic Video* magazine.

List of Abbreviations

¥ Japanese yen
£ United Kingdom pound
$ United States dollar

A

AB Aktiebolag (Finland, Sweden)
AB Oy Aktiebolag Osakeyhtiot (Finland)
A.E. Anonimos Eteria (Greece)
AED Emirati dirham
AG Aktiengesellschaft (Austria, Germany, Switzerland, Liechtenstein)
aG auf Gegenseitigkeit (Austria, Germany)
A.m.b.a. Andelsselskab med begraenset ansvar (Denmark)
A.O. Anonim Ortaklari/Ortakligi (Turkey)
ApS Amparteselskab (Denmark)
ARS Argentine peso
A.S. Anonim Sirketi (Turkey)
A/S Aksjeselskap (Norway)
A/S Aktieselskab (Denmark, Sweden)
Ay Avoinyhtio (Finland)
ATS Austrian shilling
AUD Australian dollar
ApS Amparteselskab (Denmark)
Ay Avoinyhtio (Finland)

B

B.A. Buttengewone Aansprakeiijkheid (Netherlands)
BEF Belgian franc

BHD Bahraini dinar
Bhd. Berhad (Malaysia, Brunei)
BRL Brazilian real
B.V. Besloten Vennootschap (Belgium, Netherlands)

C

C.A. Compania Anonima (Ecuador, Venezuela)
CAD Canadian dollar
C. de R.L. Compania de Responsabilidad Limitada (Spain)
CEO Chief Executive Officer
CFO Chief Financial Officer
CHF Swiss franc
Cia. Companhia (Brazil, Portugal)
Cia. Compania (Latin America (except Brazil), Spain)
Cia. Compagnia (Italy)
Cie. Compagnie (Belgium, France, Luxembourg, Netherlands)
CIO Chief Information Officer
CLP Chilean peso
CNY Chinese yuan
Co. Company
COO Chief Operating Officer
Coop. Cooperative
COP Colombian peso
Corp. Corporation
C. por A. Compania por Acciones (Dominican Republic)
CPT Cuideachta Phoibi Theoranta (Republic of Ireland)

CRL Companhia a Responsabilidao Limitida (Portugal, Spain)
C.V. Commanditaire Vennootschap (Netherlands, Belgium)
CZK Czech koruna

D

D&B Dunn & Bradstreet
DEM German deutsche mark
Div. Division (United States)
DKK Danish krone
DZD Algerian dinar

E

EC Exempt Company (Arab countries)
Edms. Bpk. Eiendoms Beperk (South Africa)
EEK Estonian Kroon
eG eingetragene Genossenschaft (Germany)
EGMBH Eingetragene Genossenschaft mit beschraenkter Haftung (Austria, Germany)
EGP Egyptian pound
Ek For Ekonomisk Forening (Sweden)
EP Empresa Portuguesa (Portugal)
E.P.E. Etema Pemorismenis Evthynis (Greece)
ESOP Employee Stock Options and Ownership
ESP Spanish peseta
Et(s). Etablissement(s) (Belgium,

France, Luxembourg)
eV eingetragener Verein (Germany)
EUR euro

F

FIM Finnish markka
FRF French franc

G

G.I.E. Groupement d'Interet Economique (France)
gGmbH gemeinnutzige Gesellschaft mit beschraenkter Haftung (Austria, Germany, Switzerland)
G.I.E. Groupement d'Interet Economique (France)
GmbH Gesellschaft mit beschraenkter Haftung (Austria, Germany, Switzerland)
GRD Greek drachma
GWA Gewerbte Amt (Austria, Germany)

H

HB Handelsbolag (Sweden)
HF Hlutafelag (Iceland)
HKD Hong Kong dollar
HUF Hungarian forint

I

IDR Indonesian rupiah
IEP Irish pound
ILS new Israeli shekel
Inc. Incorporated (United States, Canada)
INR Indian rupee
IPO Initial Public Offering
I/S Interesentselskap (Norway)
I/S Interessentselskab (Denmark)
ISK Icelandic krona
ITL Italian lira

J

JMD Jamaican dollar
JOD Jordanian dinar

K

KB Kommanditbolag (Sweden)
KES Kenyan schilling
Kft Korlatolt Felelossegu Tarsasag (Hungary)
KG Kommanditgesellschaft (Austria, Germany, Switzerland)
KGaA Kommanditgesellschaft auf

Aktien (Austria, Germany, Switzerland)
KK Kabushiki Kaisha (Japan)
KPW North Korean won
KRW South Korean won
K/S Kommanditselskab (Denmark)
K/S Kommandittselskap (Norway)
KWD Kuwaiti dinar
Ky Kommandiitiyhtio (Finland)

L

LBO Leveraged Buyout
Lda. Limitada (Spain)
L.L.C. Limited Liability Company (Arab countries, Egypt, Greece, United States)
L.L.P. Limited Partnership (United States)
L.P. Limited Partnership (Canada, South Africa, United Kingdom, United States)
Ltd. Limited
Ltda. Limitada (Brazil, Portugal)
Ltee. Limitee (Canada, France)
LUF Luxembourg franc

M

mbH mit beschraenkter Haftung (Austria, Germany)
Mij. Maatschappij (Netherlands)
MUR Mauritian rupee
MXN Mexican peso
MYR Malaysian ringgit

N

N.A. National Association (United States)
NGN Nigerian naira
NLG Netherlands guilder
NOK Norwegian krone
N.V. Naamloze Vennootschap (Belgium, Netherlands)
NZD New Zealand dollar

O

OAO Otkrytoe Aktsionernoe Obshchestve (Russia)
OHG Offene Handelsgesellschaft (Austria, Germany, Switzerland)
OMR Omani rial
OOO Obschestvo s Ogranichennoi Otvetstvennostiu (Russia)
OOUR Osnova Organizacija Udruzenog Rada (Yugoslavia)

Oy Osakeyhtî (Finland)

P

P.C. Private Corp. (United States)
PEN Peruvian Nuevo Sol
PHP Philippine peso
PKR Pakistani rupee
P/L Part Lag (Norway)
PLC Public Limited Co. (United Kingdom, Ireland)
P.L.L.C. Professional Limited Liability Corporation (United States)
PLN Polish zloty
P.T. Perusahaan/Perseroan Terbatas (Indonesia)
PTE Portuguese escudo
Pte. Private (Singapore)
Pty. Proprietary (Australia, South Africa, United Kingdom)
Pvt. Private (India, Zimbabwe)
PVBA Personen Vennootschap met Beperkte Aansprakelijkheid (Belgium)

Q

QAR Qatar riyal

R

REIT Real Estate Investment Trust
RMB Chinese renminbi
Rt Reszvenytarsasag (Hungary)
RUB Russian ruble

S

S.A. Société Anonyme (Arab countries, Belgium, France, Jordan, Luxembourg, Switzerland)
S.A. Sociedad Anónima (Latin America [except Brazil], Spain, Mexico)
S.A. Sociedades Anônimas (Brazil, Portugal)
SAA Societe Anonyme Arabienne (Arab countries)
S.A.C. Sociedad Anonima Comercial (Latin America [except Brazil])
S.A.C.I. Sociedad Anonima Comercial e Industrial (Latin America [except Brazil])
S.A.C.I.y.F. Sociedad Anonima Comercial e Industrial y Financiera (Latin America [except Brazil])

S.A. de C.V. Sociedad Anonima de Capital Variable Mexico)

SAK Societe Anonyme Kuweitienne (Arab countries)

SAL Societe Anonyme Libanaise (Arab countries)

SAO Societe Anonyme Omanienne (Arab countries)

SAQ Societe Anonyme Qatarienne (Arab countries)

SAR Saudi riyal

S.A.R.L. Sociedade Anonima de Responsabilidade Limitada (Brazil, Portugal)

S.A.R.L. Société à Responsabilité Limitée (France, Belgium, Luxembourg)

S.A.S. Societá in Accomandita Semplice (Italy)

S.A.S. Societe Anonyme Syrienne (Arab countries)

S.C. Societe en Commandite (Belgium, France, Luxembourg)

S.C.A. Societe Cooperativa Agricole (France, Italy, Luxembourg)

S.C.I. Sociedad Cooperativa Ilimitada (Spain)

S.C.L. Sociedad Cooperativa Limitada (Spain)

S.C.R.L. Societe Cooperative a Responsabilite Limitee (Belgium)

Sdn. Bhd. Sendirian Berhad (Malaysia)

SEK Swedish krona

SGD Singapore dollar

Sdn. Bhd. Sendirian Berhad (Malaysia)

S.L. Sociedad Limitada (Latin America (except Brazil), Portugal, Spain)

S/L Salgslag (Norway)

S.N.C. Société en Nom Collectif (France)

Soc. Sociedad (Latin America (except Brazil), Spain)

Soc. Sociedade (Brazil, Portugal)

Soc. Societa (Italy)

S.p.A. Società per Azioni (Italy)

Sp. z.o.o. Spólka z ograniczona odpowiedzialnoscia (Poland)

S.R.L. Sociedad de Responsabilidad Limitada (Spain, Mexico, Latin America [except Brazil])

S.R.L. Società a Responsabilità Limitata (Italy)

S.R.O. Spolecnost s Rucenim Omezenym (Czechoslovakia

S.S.K. Sherkate Sahami Khass (Iran)

Ste. Societe (France, Belgium, Luxembourg, Switzerland)

Ste. Cve. Societe Cooperative(Belgium)

S.V. Samemwerkende Vennootschap (Belgium)

S.Z.R.L. Societe Zairoise a Responsabilite Limitee (Zaire)

T

THB Thai baht

TND Tunisian dinar

TRL Turkish lira

TWD new Taiwan dollar

U

U.A. Uitgesloten Aansporakeiijkheid (Netherlands)

u.p.a. utan personligt ansvar (Sweden)

V

VAG Verein der Arbeitgeber (Austria, Germany)

VEB Venezuelan bolivar

VERTR Vertriebs (Austria, Germany)

VND Vietnamese dong

V.O.f. Vennootschap onder firma (Netherlands)

VVAG Versicherungsverein auf Gegenseitigkeit (Austria, Germany)

W–Z

WA Wettelika Aansprakalikhaed (Netherlands)

WLL With Limited Liability (Bahrain, Kuwait, Qatar, Saudi Arabia)

YK Yugen Kaisha (Japan)

ZAO Zakrytoe Aktsionernoe Obshchestve (Russia)

ZAR South African rand

ZMK Zambian kwacha

ZWD Zimbabwean dollar

A. O. Smith Corporation

11270 West Park Place
P.O. Box 245008
Milwaukee, Wisconsin 53224-9508
U.S.A.
Telephone: (414) 359-4000
Fax: (414) 359-4064
Web site: http://www.aosmith.com

Public Company
Incorporated: 1904 as A. O. Smith Company
Employees: 18,000
Sales: $2.16 billion (2006)
Stock Exchanges: New York
Ticker Symbol: AOS
NAIC: 333319 Other Commercial and Service Industry Machinery Manufacturing; 335228 Other Major Household Appliance Manufacturing; 335312 Motor and Generator Manufacturing; 333996 Fluid Power Pump and Motor Manufacturing

■■■

A. O. Smith Corporation is a manufacturer specializing in water heaters and electric motors. The company's Water Products unit accounts for nearly 60 percent of revenues and makes both residential and commercial water heaters, as well as large-volume copper-tube boilers. The remaining sales are generated by the Electrical Products unit, producer of motors for air conditioners, furnaces, refrigerators, microwave ovens, garage door openers, and pumps used in home water systems, swimming pools, spas, and hot tubs. Over its long history, A.

O. Smith has evolved from a small bicycle parts factory to a specialized manufacturer of motors and water heating products. For a long period the company was a much more diversified manufacturer, with such additional product lines as automotive structural components, fiberglass piping systems, livestock feed storage systems, and storage tanks. Most of these businesses were divested in the late 20th century or early in the 21st.

EARLY DECADES: FROM BABY CARRIAGE PARTS TO AUTO FRAMES

Although A. O. Smith was incorporated in 1904, the company traces its history back to the mid-19th century, when Charles Jeremiah (C. J.) Smith immigrated from England to the United States. The journeyman metal tradesman ventured all the way to Milwaukee, Wisconsin, and, after being self-employed for a decade, went to work for the Milwaukee Railroad Shop. As a highly skilled workman, he made a good living, but went back into business for himself in 1874, when he opened a machine shop and began manufacturing baby carriage parts. Two of Smith's four sons, Charles S. and George H., joined the family firm in the mid-1880s.

The increasing popularity of bicycles prompted C. J. Smith and Sons to branch out into the bicycle industry in 1889. By 1895, it was the largest manufacturer of steel bicycle parts in the United States. The patriarch called in his eldest son, Arthur O. (A. O.), an architectural engineer specializing in large buildings, to help build a five-story factory for the growing family business. After two years of close work with his father, A. O. decided to join the company permanently as treasurer. By then, C. J. Smith and Sons had declared itself the largest manufacturer of component bicycle parts in the world.

Increasing overcapacity in that industry and the advent of the automobile brought another change to C.J. Smith and Sons. In 1899 the family sold its business to the Federal Bicycle Corporation of America, a then-legal monopoly known as the "Bicycle Trust." A. O. retained management of the Milwaukee (or "Smith Parts") Branch of the Trust. Arthur Smith indulged his personal interest in the composition and manufacture of automobile frames with two years of "tinkering" that culminated in the sale of his first automotive frame to the Peerless Motor Car Co. in 1902. Word of his frame, which was lighter, stronger, more flexible, and less expensive than conventional ones, spread quickly: by the following year, Smith had contracts with six major automobile manufacturers.

COMPANY'S INCORPORATION IN 1904

A. O. Smith quit Federal in 1903, bought the Smith Parts Co. from his former employer, and incorporated it as A. O. Smith Company in 1904. The company's sales totaled $375,733 and profits topped $100,000 that first year. Unfortunately, patriarch C. J. Smith also passed away in 1904.

In April 1906 Henry Ford contracted with A. O. Smith for frames. At the time, the company was producing only ten pressed steel frames a day. Ford needed 10,000 frames in four months, a tenfold increase in the prevailing production rate. Realizing that adding workers and space would only consume valuable time in

training and construction, Smith looked for ways to increase efficiency through technological improvements. He and his team of engineers retooled existing presses to produce two corresponding halves of an auto frame simultaneously and arranged the presses to form a continuous assembly line. The delivery of 10,000 A. O. Smith frames that August helped Ford introduce his popularly priced Model N late in 1906 and attracted more automobile manufacturers to the supplier. Because A. O. Smith soon found itself turning away business, it built a new, larger headquarters on 135 acres on the outskirts of Milwaukee to accommodate demand. By the end of the decade, A. O. Smith was manufacturing 110,000 frames per year, over 60 percent of the auto industry's requirements.

Three years later, when A. O. Smith died, his son Lloyd Raymond (Ray) was made president. Ray's was not just a dynastic leadership, however. Both A. O. and L. R. Smith were later inducted into the Automotive Hall of Fame and the Wisconsin Business Hall of Fame. The 23-year-old former company secretary had previously proposed manufacturing improvements that multiplied A. O. Smith's production rate seven times: by 1916, the company was manufacturing 800,000 frames per year, half the auto industry's needs. Called "decisive, restless and a profound thinker" by corporate historians, Ray Smith also propelled the family company into new ventures. Smith bought a license to manufacture "The Motor Wheel," a small gas engine that could be attached to a bicycle's rear wheel to make a "motorbike." The company sold 25,000 of the vehicles nationwide from 1914 to 1919, and even applied the technology to a small wooden "sports car" called the Smith Flyer.

L. R. Smith's reluctance to pay for the marketing support necessary to maintain such products' popularity, combined with the fact that the United States was thoroughly embroiled in World War I, brought diversification to a halt in 1919. A. O. Smith manufactured hollow-steel artillery vehicle poles and bomb casings for the war effort. By war's end, the company was producing 6,500 bomb casings per day, thanks to a welding breakthrough that produced stronger bonds in less time.

THE MECHANICAL MARVEL

Throughout the war years, a team of Smith's best engineers formulated a revolutionary plan to automate the company's frame production process. Although expensive—construction consumed $6 million by 1920—the "Mechanical Marvel" they created produced 7,200 frames on two 180-man shifts per day. The machines performed 552 separate functions, including

---

KEY DATES

■

1874: Charles Jeremiah Smith opens a machine shop in Milwaukee to make baby carriage parts.

1889: C. J. Smith and Sons branches out into the bicycle industry.

1895: Company is the largest maker of steel bicycle parts in the United States.

1899: C. J. Smith and Sons is sold to Federal Bicycle Corporation and operates as the Smith Parts branch.

1902: Arthur O. Smith, son of C. J., sells his first automotive frame.

1904: A. O. Smith buys Smith Parts and incorporates it as A. O. Smith Company.

1910: Company has grown to become the largest auto frame maker in North America.

1921: Company's frame production process is automated through the construction of the Mechanical Marvel.

1936: A. O. Smith develops an affordable, durable, glass-lined water heater.

1940: Company diversifies into electric motors through the purchase of Sawyer Electrical Manufacturing Company.

1949: Harvestore glass-lined silos are introduced.

1959: A. O. Smith establishes glass fiber division, which begins making fiberglass pipe and fittings.

1972: Water heater division begins its first European operation in the Netherlands.

1986: Small motor division of Westinghouse Electric Corporation is acquired.

1997: UPPCO, Incorporated, maker of electric motors, is acquired; automotive products business is sold to Tower Automotive, Inc.

1998: A. O. Smith acquires the domestic compressor motor business of General Electric Company.

1999: The fractional horsepower motors business of MagneTek, Inc., is acquired.

2000: Fiberglass pipe business is sold to Varco International Inc.

2001: Company sells its storage tank unit to CST Industries, Inc., and concentrates solely on electric motors and water heaters; water heater business is nearly doubled by the acquisition of State Industries, Inc.

2006: A. O. Smith becomes North America's top manufacturer and marketer of residential and commercial water heaters through the acquisition of GSW Inc.

---

forming, trimming, and riveting. It took A. O. Smith 15 years to recoup its investment in the Mechanical Marvel (which was designated a National Historic Mechanical Engineering Landmark in 1979), but the plant ran practically without stop until 1958.

The Mechanical Marvel marked only the beginning of an enterprising decade, during which the company's 500-person engineering department developed new applications for the welding process formulated during World War I. A welded coupling designed to link seamless steel casings for oil drilling rigs soon became a petroleum industry standard. High pressure tanks for gasoline refineries developed by A. O. Smith could withstand three times the pressure of customary tanks. Engineers also modified those tanks for use in the paper, chemical refining, and other industries by adding an anticorrosive, stainless-steel liner to the tanks. During

the 1920s, A. O. Smith also originated the large-diameter, high-pressure pipe that launched the natural gas transmission industry and made natural gas a viable alternative to coal and oil. The company captured every order for large diameter pipe in the country. As the authority in this industry, Smith had to send its own employees out to weld pipeline installations around the world.

A. O. Smith was thus well positioned when the stock market crash of October 1929 ushered in the Great Depression. It had a two-year backlog of pipe orders and a dominant position in its other markets. As auto sales fell from 4.4 million in 1929 to less than two million in 1931, however, the company was forced to cut employment by 10 percent at its main plant. In 1930 sales plummeted from $57 million to $9 million, and the company suffered an operating loss of $5 million the following year. L. R. brought in an outsider, William C. Heath, to play "bad cop." Heath cut executive salaries by 50 percent and reduced the operating staff by one-fourth, but even these measures did not bring the company into the black. In May 1932, 3,000 employees, almost half the total company's payroll, were laid off. Corporate historians noted that "Demand for frames was so low, supervisors painted them by hand to save the expense of starting the automatic equipment."

A. O. Smith's "savior" came from a highly unlikely source: the December 1933 repeal of Prohibition. The end of that "noble experiment" brought the nation's brewing capital, Milwaukee, back to life, and A. O. Smith used its technical creativity to profit from the rebirth. The company quickly introduced a steel beer barrel with a special liner that protected the beer from metallic migration. The new keg's quick acceptance enabled A. O. Smith to recall 450 laid-off workers. The company also developed an innovative process to fuse glass to the interior of 35,000 gallon tanks that resulted in the superior cleanliness demanded by the brewing industry.

EXPANSION INTO WATER
HEATERS (1936) AND ELECTRIC
MOTORS (1940)

Ray Smith left day-to-day management of the company to Heath after suffering a heart attack in 1934. Heath led the company to apply its glass-and-steel fusing process in A. O. Smith's first mass consumer product, the water heater. Before the product's introduction, most homeowners had to replace their all-steel water heaters often because of corrosion, or spend prohibitive amounts on stainless-steel ones. Although A. O. Smith developed its affordable, durable, glass-lined model in 1936 and was able to mass-produce it by 1939, world war interrupted the company's plans a second time.

Smith began to expand through acquisitions before World War II, purchasing Smith Meter Co., a Los Angeles firm that produced petroleum line-measuring devices in 1937. The company diversified into electric motors with the 1940 acquisition of Los Angeles-based Sawyer Electrical Manufacturing Company and Whirl-A-Way Motors in Dayton, Ohio. By the end of the 1950s, A. O. Smith had expanded its electric motor product line into new applications, such as residential air conditioning compressors.

By the time the United States entered World War II in 1941, A. O. Smith had already submitted proposals for aerial bombs made of welded pipe, won the government contracts, and built a factory to produce them. The company's engineers developed better, lower-cost

propeller blades and manufactured landing gear for B-17 "Flying Fortress" and B-29 "Super Fortress" fighter bombers. The company was such a vital wartime supplier that Adolf Hitler targeted it in an unexecuted invasion of the United States.

The investment of over $50 million in new plants and equipment before 1950 propelled A. O. Smith to unprecedented success in the booming postwar American economy. As new housing starts jumped to 4,000 per day and auto production soared to one million a month, the company was poised to prosper. Volume at the centrally located Kankakee, Illinois, water heater plant built in 1947 doubled twice before 1950, with the help of retail giant Sears, Roebuck and Co., which sold A. O. Smith water heaters under a private label. Monthly production approached 50,000 units by the mid-1950s. A. O. Smith had also entered the commercial water heater market in 1948 through the acquisition of Toledo, Ohio-based Burkay Company. In addition, A. O. Smith supplied all of Chevrolet's automotive frames during the 1950s, when that make was the most popular in the United States. The contract helped establish A. O. Smith as the largest independent supplier of chassis frames to the auto industry in the postwar era. Petroleum pipeline sales also recovered quickly and Smith formed a joint venture with steelmaker ARMCO to create a pipe factory in Texas close to customers.

FURTHER DIVERSIFICATION IN
POSTWAR ERA

Diversification continued under Heath in the postwar era, with the development in 1949 of Harvestore glass-lined silos that were filled from the top, emptied from the bottom, and were dark-colored to prevent wintertime freezing of the feed stored inside. After a slow start, the silos were well accepted by U.S. farmers, and the company offered them overseas in Germany and the United Kingdom beginning in the 1960s. A. O. Smith started exploring the fiberglass industry in 1953 in cooperation with the Dow Chemical Company, forming a glass fiber division in 1959 (forerunner of Smith Fiberglass Products). The company soon developed fiberglass pipe and fittings for special niche applications in oil fields, and later made fiberglass Corvette Sting Ray bodies.

Diversification was accompanied by rationalization. When A. O. Smith's patent on the glass-lined water heater expired in 1955 and competition was opened, Smith eased out of the private-label segment, and scaled back efforts in the residential market to concentrate on the commercial segment with its leading Burkay brand. The company also phased out pressure containers and the glass-lined beer tank business by the early 1960s. A. O. Smith's own success thwarted some of its business interests. The completion of the U.S. Transcontinental Pipeline System significantly reduced the demand for pipe, eventually forcing the company to sell its steel pipe business in Texas to its partner, ARMCO. Despite these withdrawals from certain markets, sales at A. O. Smith increased from $190 million in 1946 to $280 million by 1960.

A. O. Smith's automotive division endured several upheavals throughout the 1960s and 1970s that threatened its existence. The proliferation of car models in the 1960s challenged Smith's adaptive ability and compelled it to retool from riveted frames to more adaptable welded frames. During this same period, 45 percent of U.S. auto production converted to unitized frame construction, effectively eliminating the need for a conventional frame. General Motors Corporation's decision to stick with the tried-and-true isolated frame construction kept the automotive division afloat for the time being.

L. B. "Ted" Smith was elected chairman and chief executive officer and Urban Kuechle became president in 1967. The team sought out new businesses to replace the ones that had been eliminated. In 1969 alone, A. O. Smith acquired Layne & Bowler Pump company in Los Angeles, Bull Motors of the United Kingdom, and a majority interest in Armor Elevator, the sixth largest elevator manufacturer in the United States. The company also pushed its international growth, forming a Mexican affiliate to manufacture auto frames, Canadian and Dutch water heater subsidiaries, and a consumer products division in Japan. Successive earnings records in 1968 and 1969 seemed to affirm the acquisition spree; sales climbed as well, from $355 million in 1969 to $600 million in 1973.

1970–89: OVERCOMING NUMEROUS DIFFICULTIES

Unfortunately, the ensuing decade ushered in a myriad of problems that impaired A. O. Smith. The government wage and price freeze mandated in 1971 squeezed profit margins, and the Arab oil embargo that started in 1973 forever harmed sales of full-size, gas-consuming cars, which constituted the majority of Smith's remaining frame market. Labor unrest also plagued many Smith divisions. A ten-month strike at Armor Elevator, which had just completed two years of acquisitions, crippled that subsidiary in 1972. The following year saw strikes at plants in Pennsylvania and Kentucky and the first labor halt at the Milwaukee factory in its 100-year history.

In 1972 the water heater division began its first European operation, in Veldhoven, Netherlands. L. B. Smith and President Jack Parker divested Armor Elevator, Bull Motors, and Meter Systems in 1975. After the strikes were settled and the government lifted the wage and price freeze, inflation set in. Still, A. O. Smith began to recover in the last half of the decade, winning a new contract with General Motors and expanding the Harvestore and Electrical Products divisions. Sales increased $100 million from 1976 to 1977 and profits were also on the rise.

However, General Motors' 1980 announcement that it would convert all of its production to front-wheel drive, unitized body autos threatened the survival of the $270 million automotive segment of A. O. Smith's $836 million business. Luckily, the massive automaker took more than eight years to phase out full-framed vehicles (A. O. Smith delivered its last Cadillac frame in 1990), and A. O. Smith used that time to transform its automotive division. Automotive, which had made truck frames since 1905, shifted its primary focus to the expanding market for trucks, vans, and sport-utility vehicles (SUVs), winning contracts with Ford, Chrysler, and General Motors in 1980 alone. By 1985, light truck frames were the corporation's single largest product line. Smith also won a contract to produce components for the critically acclaimed and top-selling Ford Taurus in the early 1980s.

The company would meet other challenges under the leadership of Tom Dolan, who became president in 1982 and advanced to chairman and CEO upon the retirement of L. B. Smith. Pressures from auto manufacturers, who were themselves influenced by intense foreign competition, spurred A. O. Smith to simultaneously reduce costs and increase quality. It was no simple task for the automotive division, which was then characterized by hostility between labor and management and 20 percent defect rates. Management embarked on a three-stage strategy to increase employee involvement through quality circles, labor-management task forces, and cooperative work teams. Although the plan initially met resistance from union leaders, six years of gradual change yielded impressive results: the productivity growth rate doubled in 1988 and defects were reduced to 3 percent. The work teams also enabled A. O. Smith to save money by drastically reducing the ratio of foremen to workers from 1-to-10 in 1987 to 1-to-34 in 1988.

During this period of cultural revolution, A. O. Smith was hit hard by recessions in 1980 and 1982. Hundreds of workers were laid off as auto sales fell to their lowest levels in 20 years. The company slashed capital spending and expenses, cut officer salaries by 10 percent, and let one-fourth of the corporate staff go. Even more layoffs were necessary later in the decade, as the company trimmed net employment from a high of 12,300 in 1986 to 9,400 in 1990.

The farming crisis that occurred at this same time reduced the Harvestore subsidiary's sales from $140 million in 1979 to $21 million by 1984. The division shuttered two plants and consolidated all operations at the main DeKalb, Illinois, plant. A. O. Smith eventually shifted the subsidiary's focus to municipal water storage tanks and sold Harvestore's U.K. subsidiary. Although its revenues remained small, Harvestore did eventually return to profitability.

A. O. Smith's problems compounded in the late 1970s and early 1980s, as competition in the water heater industry exposed internal problems. Inefficient plants cost the Water Products Division $10 million in 1981 alone. The subsidiary closed high-cost factories in Newark, California, and Kankakee, Illinois, and opened more efficient plants in South Carolina and Mexico, and other cost-cutting measures helped it achieve profitability in 1983 after four successive years of losses. Continuing efforts helped the division become one of A. O. Smith's most consistently profitable divisions, setting profit records in 1986, 1988, and 1990.

A. O. Smith's electric motors division was one of the corporation's few consistently bright spots in the 1980s. Despite fairly intense competition, the subsidiary was able to establish operations in Mexico and even acquire a primary competitor's small motor business (that of Westinghouse Electric Corporation, purchased in 1986). The unit set a profit record of $45 million in 1985. Smith's fiberglass business had also recovered from the shocks of the previous decade to set four successive years of record profits beginning in 1987.

SURPASSING $1 BILLION IN SALES

Despite an inconsistent earnings record in the 1980s (the company achieved only two successive profitable years during the decade), A. O. Smith had managed to pay cash dividends on its common stock every year since 1940. Having endured a grueling six years at the company's helm and achieving several of his goals, Tom Dolan retired from the chief executive office in 1988. Robert J. O'Toole assumed that office, adding the chairmanship in 1991. He directed the company's implementation of "just-in-time" delivery of automotive products through the construction of five regional assembly plants in close proximity to customers. Although the firm recorded a net loss in 1992, its return to profitability the following year coincided with a general

economic recovery in the United States.

Sales rose steadily into the mid-1990s as the company was well-positioned to benefit from the explosive growth in sales of SUVs and light trucks. The company's automotive operation also sought new business with Japanese automakers, opening a sales and engineering office in Yokohama in 1993 and landing a major contract with Nissan for the manufacture of structural components for pickup trucks. In December 1995 A. O. Smith doubled the revenues of its storage tank business and entered the bulk dry storage market through the acquisition of Parsons, Kansas-based Peabody TecTank Inc. That same year, the company launched three joint ventures in China, one of which would make A. O. Smith the first U.S. company to manufacture water heaters in that rapidly developing country. Overall company revenues increased from $915.8 million in 1991 to $1.54 billion in 1995.

Despite the sales gains and steady profitability enjoyed by A. O. Smith in the mid-1990s, the company's automotive unit was under pressure to further ratchet up investments to maintain a competitive position. The difficulty was that every time an automaker began work on a new car or truck model, manufacturers of the frames had to spend $30 million to $50 million to retool their plants. A. O. Smith also did not have the financial resources to grow its automotive unit through acquisitions. After reviewing its strategic options, the company decided to make the dramatic move of selling the automotive unit, which had the additional disadvantage of operating in a low-growth, cyclical industry.

In April 1997 the unit was sold to Tower Automotive, Inc., of Minneapolis for $710 million. The deal allowed A. O. Smith to virtually extinguish its long-term debt, buy back some of its stock, and concentrate on its key remaining units: electric motors, water heaters, industrial storage tanks, and fiberglass pipe. The company also still had its agricultural storage tank operation, Harvestore, but had decided, in the face of numerous lawsuits and class-action suits alleging that Harvestore had sold farmers defective silos, to sell the unit. A sale did not immediately materialize, however.

1997–2001: SERIES OF ACQUISITIONS AND DIVESTMENTS

Part of the proceeds from the automotive divestment were slated for acquisitions to build up the remaining units. Before the deal with Tower Automotive had even been completed, in fact, A. O. Smith had finished its first such acquisition, a $60.9 million deal for UPPCO,

Incorporated, a manufacturer of subfractional horsepower electric motors based in Monticello, Indiana. Such motors were used in a variety of applications, including bathroom and range hood fans, microwave ovens, frost-free refrigerators, dishwashers, and humidifiers. In July 1998 A. O. Smith paid $125.6 million for the domestic compressor motor business of General Electric Company. Based in Scottsville, Kentucky, the GE unit had annual sales of about $130 million for its compressors that were used primarily in residential and commercial air conditioning units and in commercial refrigeration units. This acquisition made the electric motors unit the largest A. O. Smith unit in terms of revenues.

In August 1999, A. O. Smith made its third motor acquisition in as many years when it bought the electric motors unit of Nashville-based MagneTek, Inc., for $244.6 million, the company's largest acquisition to date. The MagneTek unit, which had 1998 revenues of about $367 million, produced fractional horsepower motors for pools, spas, and air conditioners. Through this series of acquisitions, A. O. Smith was able to increase its sales of electric motors from the $340 million level of 1996 to $884.2 million by 2000. Meantime, the company began manufacturing residential water heaters in Nanjing, China, in 1998, having bought out its joint-venture partner. By 1999 it had achieved $13 million in sales of A. O. Smith brand water heaters in that country.

Rounding out the company's whirlwind transformation were the divestments of the fiberglass pipe and storage tank businesses. In December 2000 A. O. Smith sold the fiberglass business to Varco International Inc., while the storage tank unit was sold to the newly formed CST Industries, Inc., in January 2001. Cash proceeds from the sales were about $63 million. These latest divestments were designed to allow the company to concentrate on its two main businesses, electric motors and water heaters, and to serve as a consolidator within those industries. Under the continued leadership of O'Toole, A. O. Smith had begun the new century as a radically different company from what it had been less than a decade earlier, and as a much stronger company as well.

EARLY 21ST CENTURY: CONCENTRATING ON WATER HEATERS AND ELECTRIC MOTORS

During the first half of 2001 A. O. Smith suffered from a significant drop in the sales of electric motors because of the economic downturn, prompting a workforce reduction of 1,000 and a shifting of some production from the United States to Mexico. Plants in Indiana, Virginia, and Tennessee were shut down, and the production from those plants was moved to facilities in Monterrey and Juárez. In October of that same year, after earnings in the third quarter had plunged by 95 percent, A. O. Smith announced plans to cut a further 1,300 jobs in its electric motors division and transfer more of its manufacturing operations to Mexico. The difficulties in the motors division pushed net earnings down 50 percent for the full year of 2001, while sales fell 7.8 percent to $1.15 billion.

In December 2001 A. O. Smith gained its first motor manufacturing operation in Asia via the $3.3 million purchase of Shenzhen Speeda Industrial Co., Ltd., a producer of subfractional horsepower electric motors based in Shenzhen, China. In a much larger deal completed that same month, the company nearly doubled the size of its water heater business by acquiring State Industries, Inc., for $117.2 million, including the assumption of $56.3 million in debt. A private firm based in Ashland City, Tennessee, and founded in 1948, State was a producer of both residential and commercial water heaters that had garnered fiscal 2000 sales of roughly $325 million. State had a strong position in the retail market through a longstanding arrangement to provide private-label water heaters to Sears as well as an exclusive licensing arrangement with Maytag Corporation through which it produced high-end water heaters under the Maytag brand. State's retail strength complemented A. O. Smith's traditionally robust position in the wholesale channel.

In addition to its main manufacturing facility in Ashland City and a smaller pump tank plant in Charlotte, North Carolina, State had a wholly owned subsidiary, APCOM Inc., with plants in Franklin and Cookeville, Tennessee. A. O. Smith entered the water heater component business through its ownership of APCOM, producer of heating elements, thermostats, drain valves, and other components. Another consequence of the State acquisition occurred in 2002, when A. O. Smith moved the headquarters of its Water Products division to Ashland City. In May of that year, the company completed a secondary public offering of 4.7 million shares of common stock at $28.25 per share. The $127.5 million in net proceeds was used to pay down debt, including that incurred through the State purchase.

By 2003 A. O. Smith had completed the realignment of its motor manufacturing operations launched two years earlier. In addition to this shift of production to Mexico, the company also gained two more Chinese motor manufacturers. In a December 2002 acquisition, A. O. Smith purchased Jiangsu Changheng Group Co.

Ltd. of Changzhou, China, a producer of fractional horsepower air conditioning motors. The following November, the company acquired Taicang Special Motor Co., Ltd., of Suzhou, China, a manufacturer of hermetic motors for commercial air conditioning equipment. During this same period, residential water heater production in North America was consolidated within the plants in Ashland City and Juárez, Mexico.

Late in 2005, a year in which net earnings totaled $46.5 million on sales of $1.69 billion, A. O. Smith spent $17.9 million on its fourth acquisition of a Chinese electric motor manufacturer. Yueyang Zhong-min Special Electrical Machinery Co., Ltd., based in Yueyang City, Hunan Province, produced hermetic motors used in commercial air conditioning and refrigeration compressors. At the end of the year O'Toole retired from his position as chairman and CEO, ending his 42-year career at A. O. Smith. The new chairman and CEO was Paul W. Jones, who had joined the company in January 2004 as president and COO. Prior to joining A. O. Smith, Jones had headed U.S. Can Company, Inc.

2006 ACQUISITION OF GSW

In April 2006 A. O. Smith completed the largest acquisition in its history, one that propelled the firm into a position as North America's top manufacturer and marketer of residential and commercial water heaters. The purchase of GSW Inc. for approximately $340 million in cash added almost $360 million to the company's sales in 2006, past the $2 billion mark. Headquartered in Oakville, Ontario, GSW included both Canadian and U.S. subsidiaries, with the U.S. unit based in Johnson City, Tennessee.

In addition to increasing the overall size of A. O. Smith's water heater business, the deal significantly strengthened its position in the Canadian residential market, broadened the firm's access to the Canadian commercial market, and further bolstered its retail channel of distribution. In regard to the latter, GSW's U.S. subsidiary was the exclusive supplier of Whirlpool brand residential water heaters to home improvement retail giant Lowe's Companies, Inc. GSW also had a building products subsidiary that produced vinyl rainware systems, but A. O. Smith divested this operation in December 2006. That year A. O. Smith maintained its record of paying cash dividends on its common stock every year since 1940.

The year 2006 was also noteworthy for the continued growth of the firm's Chinese water heater business, which enjoyed a revenue increase of 40 percent to more than $120 million. While A. O. Smith's overseas success continued in 2007, the crisis in the housing market back home began dragging down its domestic business in both water heaters and electric motors. By October, the company had begun trimming inventory and moving more quickly to pass on rising material costs, and it also announced another restructuring of its array of manufacturing facilities. Residential electric motor plants in Scottsville, Kentucky; Mebane, North Carolina; and Budapest, Hungary, were slated for closure with the production shifting to plants in Mexico and China. Although it was impossible to predict the length and depth of the U.S. housing downturn, A. O. Smith certainly faced a challenging business environment over the near term.

April Dougal Gasbarre
Updated, David E. Salamie

PRINCIPAL SUBSIDIARIES

American Appliance Mfg. Corp.; AOS Holding Company; A. O. Smith International Corporation; American Water Heater Holdings, Inc.; Flame Guard Water Heaters, Inc.; GSW Holdings, Inc.; GSW Industries Inc.; American Water Heater Company; State Industries, Inc.; A. O. Smith Holdings (Barbados) SRL; Winston Park Insurance Company Ltd. (Barbados); A. O. Smith Enterprises Ltd. (Canada); A. O. Smith (China) Investment Co., Ltd.; A. O. Smith (China) Water Heater Co., Ltd.; A. O. Smith Electrical Products (Changzhou) Co., Ltd. (China); A. O. Smith Electrical Products (Shenzhen) Co., Ltd. (China); A. O. Smith Electrical Products (Suzhou) Co., Ltd. (China); A. O. Smith Electrical Products (Taizhou) Co., Ltd. (China); A. O. Smith Electrical Products (Yueyang) Co., Ltd. (China); A. O. Smith L'eau chaude S.a.r.l. (France); A. O. Smith Warmwasser-Systemtechnik GmbH (Germany); A. O. Smith Electrical Products Limited Liability Company (Hungary); A. O. Smith Water Heating Private Limited (India); A. O. Smith Electric Motors (Ireland) Ltd.; A. O. Smith Holdings (Ireland) Ltd.; IG-Mex, S. de R.L. de C.V. (Mexico); Motores Electricos de Juarez, S. de R.L. de C.V. (Mexico); Motores Electricos de Monterrey, S. de R.L. de C.V. (Mexico); Productos de Agua, S. de R.L. de C.V. (Mexico); Productos Electricos Aplicados, S. de R.L. de C.V. (Mexico); A. O. Smith Electrical Products B.V. (Netherlands); A. O. Smith Holdings B.V. (Netherlands); A. O. Smith International Holdings B.V. (Netherlands); A. O. Smith Products v.o.f. (Netherlands); A. O. Smith Water Products Company, B.V. (Netherlands); A. O. Smith Electrical Products (S.E.A.) Pte Ltd. (Singapore); A. O. Smith Electrical Products Limited (U.K.).

PRINCIPAL OPERATING UNITS

Electrical Products Company; Water Products Company.

PRINCIPAL COMPETITORS

Emerson Electric Co.; Regal Beloit Corporation; Paloma Co., Ltd.; Bradford White Corporation; Lochinvar Corporation; Haier Group Company; Indesit Company; Tecumseh Products Company; Baldor Electric Company.

FURTHER READING

"A. O. Smith Buys American Water Heater Parent," *Contractor,* May 2006, pp. 1, 8.

"A. O. Smith: 'Safe' Diversification That Is Endangering Profits," *Business Week,* September 21, 1981, pp. 82+.

"A. O. Smith to Acquire State Industries," *Contractor,* October 2001, p. 1.

Content, Thomas, "A. O. Smith to Buy Tennessee Company," *Milwaukee Journal Sentinel,* September 18, 2001, p. 2D.

Derus, Michele, "Housing Slump Hurts A. O. Smith Outlook," *Milwaukee Journal Sentinel,* October 17, 2007, p. D1.

Fauber, John, "Analysts Question A. O. Smith Cost Cuts," *Milwaukee Journal,* May 22, 1991, p. C8.

Gallagher, Kathleen, "A. O. Smith's Motor Business Starting to Purr," *Milwaukee Journal Sentinel,* June 18, 2000, p. 45D.

Gores, Paul, "A. O. Smith Sells Off Fiberglass Pipe Division," *Milwaukee Journal Sentinel,* December 12, 2000, p. 2D.

Hawkins, Lee, Jr., "A. O. Smith Plans to Buy MagneTek Motor Business," *Milwaukee Journal Sentinel,* June 29, 1999, p. 1D.

————, "A. O. Smith to Cut Jobs, Consolidate As Earnings Fall 96%," *Milwaukee Journal Sentinel,* October 18, 2001, p. 3D.

————, "A. O. Smith to Sell Off Division," *Milwaukee Journal Sentinel,* January 22, 2000, p. 1D.

————, "Unit of A. O. Smith Divested," *Milwaukee Journal Sentinel,* December 19, 2000, p. 1D.

Hoerr, John, "The Cultural Revolution at A. O. Smith," *Business Week,* May 29, 1989, pp. 66, 68.

Johnson, Robert, "The Rust Bowl: A. O. Smith Sets Diversity As New Goal," *Wall Street Journal,* June 27, 1984.

Lazo, Shirley A., "Revived A. O. Smith Rewards Its Holders," *Barron's,* April 4, 1994, p. 47.

Mullins, Robert, "'New' Smith Seeks Wall Street Attention," *Business Journal-Milwaukee,* September 19, 1997, pp. 23+.

Petersen, Chris, "Built on Innovation," *U.S. Business Review,* March 2006, pp. 49–50.

Savage, Mark, "A. O. Smith Buys Motor Unit from General Electric," *Milwaukee Journal Sentinel,* May 14, 1998, p. 1D.

Spivak, Cary, "A. O. Smith to Use Cash from Deal for Acquisitions," *Milwaukee Journal Sentinel,* February 2, 1997, p. 1D.

Spivak, Cary, and Lee Hawkins, Jr., "A. O. Smith Sells Unit Here," *Milwaukee Journal Sentinel,* January 28, 1997, p. 1D.

Stavro, Barry, "Framed," *Forbes,* June 4, 1984, pp. 66+.

"Tower Automotive to Pay $625 Million for A. O. Smith Unit," *Wall Street Journal,* January 28, 1997, p. A6.

Wright, Charles S., and Roger S. Smith, *"A Better Way": The History of A. O. Smith Corporation,* 2nd ed., Milwaukee: A. O. Smith Corporation, 1995, 95 p.

Abbott Laboratories

———— ▪ ————

100 Abbott Park Road
Abbott Park, Illinois 60064-6400
U.S.A.
Telephone: (847) 937-6100
Fax: (847) 937-9555
Web site: http://www.abbott.com

Public Company
Incorporated: 1900 as Abbott Alkaloidal Company
Employees: 65,000
Sales: $22.48 billion (2006)
Stock Exchanges: New York Chicago London Swiss Boston Philadelphia
Ticker Symbol: ABT
NAIC: 325412 Pharmaceutical Preparation Manufacturing; 325411 Medical and Botanical Manufacturing; 325413 In-Vitro Diagnostic Substance Manufacturing; 339113 Surgical Appliance and Supplies Manufacturing; 311514 Dry, Condensed, and Evaporated Dairy Product Manufacturing; 541710 Research and Development in the Physical, Engineering, and Life Sciences

■ ■ ■

Abbott Laboratories is one of the oldest and most successful pharmaceutical and medical product companies in the United States. The company's pharmaceuticals business, which generates around 55 percent of overall annual revenues, is led by its blockbuster rheumatoid-arthritis drug Humira. Other key Abbott drugs include AIDS treatments Kaletra and Norvir; Depakote, prescribed for epilepsy and bipolar disorder; TriCor, a cholesterol-management drug; the antibiotic Biaxin; and Synthroid, used in the treatment of hypothyroidism. Abbott's nutritional products business, responsible for 19 percent of revenues, produces such well-known brands as Similac infant formula and Ensure adult nutritional supplements. Another 18 percent of sales stem from Abbott's diagnostic products business, specializing in blood analyzers and equipment to detect and monitor infections and diseases. The company's vascular products business, generator of 5 percent of revenues, concentrates on devices used in the treatment of vascular disease, most notably drug-coated heart stents. Abbott's annual research and development budget exceeds $2.2 billion, with areas of emphasis including AIDS/antivirals, anti-infectives, diabetes, immunology, neuroscience, oncology, pain care, and vascular medicine.

EARLY DECADES

Abbott Laboratories has its origin in the late 19th century in a small pharmaceutical operation run from the kitchen of a Chicago physician named Wallace Calvin Abbott. As did other physicians of the time, Dr. Abbott commonly prescribed morphine, quinine, strychnine, and codeine (all of which were liquid alkaloid extracts) for his patients. Because they existed only in a liquid form, these drugs were prone to spoilage over time, mitigating their effectiveness as treatments. In 1888 Dr. Abbott heard that a Belgian surgeon had developed alkaloids in solid form. Alkaloid pills soon became available in Chicago, but Dr. Abbott was dis-

COMPANY PERSPECTIVES

Today's Abbott is a uniquely well-balanced company, with leadership positions in each of three great and essential businesses: medical products, nutritional products and pharmaceuticals. We've built a rich and varied portfolio to increase our range of opportunities and limit risk to our overall performance. We've strengthened that base with a heightened emphasis on technological innovation, developed both within and outside of Abbott.

satisfied with their quality, and he decided to manufacture his own.

Dr. Abbott began to advertise his products to other doctors in 1891. So successful was his business that he eventually sold shares to other doctors and incorporated his operation in 1900 as the Abbott Alkaloidal Company. By 1905, annual sales had grown to $200,000. Ten years later, the company changed its name to Abbott Laboratories. During World War I, Abbott's company was essential to the medical community, as several important drugs, manufactured exclusively by German companies, were no longer available in the United States. Abbott developed procaine, a substitute for the German novocaine, and barbital, a replacement for veronal.

After the war, Abbott continued to concentrate on the research and development of new drugs. In 1921 the company established a laboratory in Rocky Mount, North Carolina, which developed a number of new drugs, including sedatives, tranquilizers, and vitamins. Even after Dr. Abbott's death that year, the company continued to invest heavily in new product development and aggressive marketing campaigns. The company went public in 1929 with a listing on the Chicago Stock Exchange. Two years later, Abbott expanded outside the United States for the first time with the establishment of an affiliate in Montreal, Canada.

DeWitt Clough was named president of the company in 1933, ending a period of somewhat stale communal leadership. A more dynamic character than any since Dr. Abbott, Clough is best remembered for the inauguration of the company magazine, *What's New?* The publication had such a positive impact on worker morale and public opinion that several of Abbott's competitors started similar publications. In 1936 Abbott began its long-term association with anesthetics when it introduced sodium pentothal, which had been

developed by Abbott scientists Ernest Volwiler and Donalee Tabern (who in 1986 were named to the U.S. Inventors Hall of Fame for this discovery).

During World War II, Abbott once again played an important role in battlefield and hospital healthcare. By this time, American pharmaceutical companies such as Abbott were much less dependent on Germany's companies, particularly the IG Farben, a conglomeration of the world's most advanced drug manufacturers. After the war, much of the IG Farben's research was turned over to American manufacturers. Abbott, however, had little to gain from this information; it was already a worthy competitor on its own.

ANTIBIOTICS, CYCLAMATE, SIMILAC

After the departure of DeWitt Clough in 1945, Abbott shifted its attention to the development of antibiotics. The company developed the antibiotic erythromycin, which, introduced under the brand names Erythrocin and E.E.S. in 1952, constituted a significant portion of Abbott's prescription drug sales for several decades, even after the expiration of its 17-year patent. Sales of the drug increased dramatically when it was found to be an effective treatment for Legionnaire's disease.

Abbott stumbled onto a lucrative new product when one of its researchers accidentally discovered that a chemical with which he had been working had a sweet taste. The chemical, a cyclamate, could be used as an artificial sweetener. Initially, from 1950, it was marketed to diabetics, but in the 1960s, as Americans became more health and diet conscious, it was increasingly used as a sugar substitute in a wide variety of foods.

In 1964 Abbott completed the first major acquisition in company history when it purchased Columbus, Ohio-based M&R Dietetic Laboratories. M&R was the manufacturer of Similac baby formula and over the succeeding decades, as the company's Ross Products Division, formed the basis for Abbott's market-leading infant and adult nutritionals business.

DIVERSIFICATION AND CRISES

By the mid-1960s, Abbott had gone several years without a major breakthrough in research, and none was projected at any time in the immediate future. Then, in 1967, Edward J. Ledder was named president of the company. He advocated a reduction in Abbott's emphasis on pharmaceuticals by diversifying into other fields. In the years that followed, Abbott introduced an array of consumer products, including Pream nondairy creamer, Glad Hands rubber gloves, Faultless golf balls,

KEY DATES

1888: Dr. Wallace Calvin Abbott begins manufacturing alkaloid pills.

1900: Abbott incorporates his firm as Abbott Alkaloidal Company.

1915: Company changes its name to Abbott Laboratories.

1929: Abbott goes public with a listing on the Chicago Stock Exchange.

1936: Company introduces the anesthetic sodium pentothal.

1952: Company launches a new antibiotic, Erythrocin.

1964: Abbott acquires M&R Dietetic Laboratories, maker of Similac baby formula.

1967: New President Edward J. Ledder begins a diversification into consumer products, including Sucaryl, a cyclamate sugar substitute.

1970: FDA bans the sale of cyclamates.

1971: Abbott is forced to recall 3.4 million bottles of intravenous solution.

1977: Company forms joint venture with Takeda Chemical Industries, Ltd., of Japan called TAP Pharmaceuticals Inc.

1985: Abbott develops the first diagnostic test for AIDS.

1987: Abbott's Hytrin is approved by the FDA for the treatment of hypertension.

1990: Clarithromycin, an antibiotic, is introduced.

1996: Abbott acquires MediSense, Inc., a maker of blood-testing devices for diabetics.

1999: Abbott agrees to pay a $100 million fine relating to quality control problems at its medical test kit plants; company enters the vascular market with the purchase of suture maker Perclose, Inc.

2000: FDA approves the AIDS drug Kaletra.

2001: The Knoll Pharmaceutical Co. unit of BASF AG is acquired for $6.9 billion in cash.

2002: Abbott secures FDA approval for the rheumatoid-arthritis drug Humira, gained via the Knoll purchase.

2004: Company solidifies its position in glucose monitoring with the acquisition of Thera-Sense, Inc.; Abbott's hospital products business is spun off into the newly independent Hospira, Inc.

2006: Abbott acquires the vascular business of Guidant Corporation for $4.1 billion and Kos Pharmaceuticals, Inc., for $3.8 billion.

and Sucaryl, the cyclamate sugar substitute. In an effort to ensure the success of Abbott's consumer product line, Ledder placed Melvin Birnbaum, a highly experienced and able manager he had hired away from Revlon, in charge of the division. Ledder's policy of diversification laid the groundwork for more flexible corporate strategies. No longer exposed exclusively within the pharmaceuticals market, Abbott was able to cross-subsidize failing operations until they could be rehabilitated.

Despite this flexibility, Abbott soon realized new obstacles to its growth. The company's hospital products competed in a limited, institutional market. New drugs had greater profit margins but were subject to government approval procedures that kept companies waiting for several years before they could market their discoveries. Consumer products, on the other hand, involved more expensive marketing and generated less profit than pharmaceuticals. Unable to increase profits

without substantial risk, Abbott's management decided to maintain the strategies that were in place.

Cyclamate sales had grown so dramatically that by 1969 they accounted for one-third of Abbott's consumer product revenues, or about $50 million. The increasing popularity of cyclamates as an ingredient in diet foods, however, led the Food and Drug Administration (FDA) to conduct an investigation of possible side effects from their overuse. The FDA's research was widely criticized as "fragmentary" and "fatally flawed," but it was nonetheless used as evidence that cyclamates were carcinogenic. The market collapsed in August 1970 when the FDA banned domestic sales of cyclamates. Abbott, which overnight had suffered the loss of one of its most profitable operations, protested the ban, but was unable to reverse the decision. Although the company continued to petition the FDA, subsequent studies confirmed that metabolization of cyclamates can lead to chromosome breakage and bladder cancer.

Less than a year after cyclamates were banned, Abbott was forced to recall 3.4 million bottles of intravenous solution. The bottles were sealed with a varnished paper called Gilsonite, which, it was discovered, harbored bacteria. The contamination was discovered only when healthcare workers noticed and then investigated the high incidence of infection in patients who had been administered Abbott's intravenous solutions. The Centers for Disease Control linked the contaminated solutions to at least 434 infections and 49 deaths. With sales down from $17.9 million to $3 million, Abbott's share price began to fall. Abbott moved quickly to replace its Gilsonite seals with synthetic rubber, but the company was unable to regain its leadership of the intravenous market. Litigation resulted in the company eventually pleading no contest to a charge of conspiracy and paying a fine.

REFOCUSING ON PHARMACEUTICALS, NUTRITIONALS, AND DIAGNOSTIC EQUIPMENT

The crises of the early 1970s left the company's upper echelon of management weakened and vulnerable to criticism. Although Edward Ledder was recognized for the success of his diversification program (and largely excused for his inability to prevent either the cyclamate ban or the intravenous solution crisis), conditions were obviously ripe for the expression of talent by a new manager. Robert Schoellhorn, a veteran of the chemical industry, was just such a manager. His efforts as a vice-president in the hospital products division at Abbott resulted in a revenue increase of 139 percent for that division between 1974 and 1979. He correctly predicted that the next most profitable trend in healthcare would be toward cost-effective analysis and treatment. Schoellhorn was later promoted to president and chief operating officer of the company. Meantime, in 1977 Abbott entered into a joint venture with Takeda Chemical Industries, Ltd., of Japan called TAP Pharmaceuticals Inc. for the codevelopment and comarketing of pharmaceuticals.

Abbott Laboratories registered an annual sales growth rate of 15.5 percent and an earnings growth rate of 16.5 percent by 1979. This expansion was attributed by financial analysts to the company's increased productivity, reduced costs, expansion into foreign markets, and greater involvement in hospital nutritionals and diagnostic testing equipment. The company also introduced three new drugs in 1979: Depakene, an anticonvulsant; Tranxene, a mild tranquilizer; and Abbokinase, a treatment for blood clots in the lungs. All three products were the direct result of the company's increased investment in research and development in the mid-1970s.

Utilizing its knowledge of intravenous solution production, vitamin therapy, and infant formula, Abbott developed a comprehensive nutritional therapy program to speed the recovery of hospital patients and thereby reduce medical care costs. In the 1980s, as many as 65 percent of all hospital patients suffered from some form of malnutrition, so Abbott was highly successful in marketing their program. Another advantage of adult nutritional products was that they had a place in the growing home care market.

Abbott had similar success marketing its lines of diagnostic equipment. Electronic testing devices developed by Abbott proved more accurate than manual procedures. In order to strengthen the technical end of its diagnostic equipment research, Abbott hired two top executives away from Texas Instruments to head the division.

Schoellhorn, who advanced to chairperson and chief executive officer in 1979, continued to emphasize investment in pharmaceutical research and development in the 1980s. Seven new drugs introduced in 1982 accounted for 17 percent of sales in 1985. Foreign operations also remained extremely important to Abbott, and the company had more than 75 foreign subsidiaries and manufacturing facilities in more than 30 countries. Schoellhorn continued to support Ledder's original diversification policy. The introduction of Murine eye-care products and Selsun Blue dandruff shampoo served to expand the domestic consumer product line and promised to provide earning stability in the event of a downturn in any of the company's other markets.

FIRST DIAGNOSTIC TEST FOR AIDS, 1985

Schoellhorn was also credited with promoting Abbott's emphasis on diagnostic equipment, especially blood analyzers. These devices were increasingly used to detect legal and illegal substances in the bloodstream. Abbott led the trend, developing the first diagnostic tests for acquired immune deficiency syndrome (AIDS), in 1985, and hepatitis. The company's "Vision" blood analyzer fit on a desktop and performed 90 percent of typical blood tests within eight minutes. By the end of the 1980s, sales of blood analysis devices represented a billion-dollar business, and medical diagnostic products (at $2.3 billion per year) constituted nearly half of Abbott's annual sales. Meanwhile, in the pharmaceuticals arena, Abbott in 1987 received FDA approval for a new drug called Hytrin for the treatment of hypertension. Hytrin was approved in 1993 for the treatment of noncancerous enlarged prostate.

Schoellhorn was widely praised as the driving force behind Abbott's phenomenal growth during the 1980s, when sales nearly tripled, profits doubled, and the pharmaceutical company rose to 90th from 197th on *Fortune*'s list of the world's top 500 companies. The leader's aggressive management style, however, often led to conflict. Over the course of the 1980s, three presidents—James L. Vincent (1981), Kirk Raab (1985), and Jack W. Schuler (1989)—quit. In December 1989 Abbott's board of directors unseated Schoellhorn, who in turn sued the company for his job. Abbott accused Schoellhorn of misappropriation of company assets and "fraudulent conduct," adding that the former CEO exercised stock options worth $9.3 million within days of his release. Schoellhorn was succeeded by Vice-Chairman Duane L. Burnham.

LATE-CENTURY PHARMACEUTICAL INTRODUCTIONS

Unlike many of its competitors (including Merck, SmithKline Beecham, and Eli Lilly), Abbott did not acquire a drug distribution manager in the early 1990s. Instead, the company plowed funds into research and development (R&D). R&D outlays rose from 5.2 percent of sales in 1982 to more than 10 percent of sales by 1994; by the latter year, R&D expenditures neared $1 billion. That year marked the company's 23rd consecutive earnings lift and helped Abbott's stock hold its value better than most competitors in the uncertain healthcare environment of the early 1990s.

Among key developments in the early 1990s was the introduction in 1990 of clarithromycin, an antibiotic developed as a successor to Abbott's erythromycin. Marketed in the United States under the name Biaxin, clarithromycin was useful in the treatment of common upper respiratory ailments such as the flu as well as other types of infections. It quickly became Abbott's flagship pharmaceutical—eventually achieving $1 billion in annual sales—remaining so into the early 21st century.

New product introductions continued in the middle years of the decade. In 1994 Abbott introduced sevoflurane, an inhalation anesthetic that soon gained popularity because of its wide range of uses. The following year, TAP, the joint venture with Takeda Chemical, received FDA approval for Prevacid, an ulcer treatment (sales of Prevacid reached $1.3 billion by 1998). In 1996 FDA clearance was granted for Norvir, a protease inhibitor for the treatment of HIV and AIDS.

LATE-CENTURY ACQUISITION HITS AND ONE NEAR-MISS

Despite these R&D successes, Abbott's earnings were failing to increase at the high-double-digit rate that they had in the 1980s, and the company was beginning to face the risk of being gobbled up by a larger rival in the rapidly consolidating healthcare industry of the 1990s. Shrugging off the conservative management of the early 1990s, Abbott moved aggressively in the second half of the decade to expand via acquisition and thereby stave off being acquired itself. In 1996 Abbott bolstered its diagnostics division through the $867 million purchase of MediSense, Inc., a Waltham, Massachusetts-based maker of blood-testing devices for diabetics. This was the company's first major deal since the 1964 acquisition of M&R Dietetic Laboratories. In 1997 Abbott spent about $200 million for certain intravenous product lines of Sanofi Pharmaceuticals, Inc., the U.S. unit of France's Sanofi S.A. Included in this deal was Carpujet, an injectable drug-delivery system based on preloaded, single-dose syringes. Also in 1997, Abbott suffered a potential setback when Takeda Chemical did not renew a ten-year contract that gave Abbott the right of first refusal to distribute Takeda's new drugs in the United States via the TAP venture. Takeda had decided to set up its own sales and marketing organization in the United States. By this time TAP was generating annual sales in excess of $2 billion, primarily from the marketing of Prevacid and Lupron, a prostate-cancer drug.

By 1997 Abbott had doubled its sales and earnings since Burnham had taken over from the ousted Schoellhorn. In early 1998 Burnham announced that he would retire in 1999. At the beginning of that year, Miles D. White, who had been a senior vice-president in charge of the diagnostics division, took over as CEO. Later in 1999, White was named chairman as well. During the leadership transition period in 1998, Abbott acquired Murex Technologies Corporation, a maker of diagnostics products, for $234 million. Abbott's appetite for growth increased exponentially with the announcement in June 1999 of a deal to acquire ALZA Corporation for $7.3 billion in stock. ALZA was a leading producer of advanced drug-delivery systems and had a solid pipeline of new pharmaceuticals under development. The Federal Trade Commission (FTC), however, raised antitrust concerns about the merger, and when the two sides were unable to reach an agreement with the FTC, they called off the merger in December. Another possible factor in the collapse of the deal was the decline in Abbott's stock price following the company's agreement in November to pull 125 types of medical-diagnostic test kits off the U.S. market and to pay a $100 million civil penalty to the U.S. government. Since 1993 the FDA had been issuing warnings to Abbott regarding quality control deficiencies at its test kit plants, with the market withdrawal and payment of the fine being the outcome of this process. The FDA also cited poor manufacturing controls as the reason for its halting the sales of Abbott's clot-dissolving agent Abbokinase in early 1999.

In the meantime, Abbott managed to complete two smaller acquisitions in 1999. It acquired Perclose, Inc., a maker of sutures used to close arteries during angioplasty procedures, for about $600 million in stock. This deal marked the company's entrance into the vascular products sector. Abbott also paid $217 million in cash to Glaxo Wellcome Inc. for five anesthesia products.

EARLY 21ST CENTURY: KALETRA, KNOLL, HUMIRA

In January 2000 Abbott sold its agricultural products business to Sumitomo Chemical Co., Ltd., and for the first time in decades, Abbott was a pure healthcare firm. In April of that year Abbott began marketing Biaxin XL, a new once-daily formulation of its flagship Biaxin antibiotic. The FDA in September 2000 granted expedited approval to Kaletra, a second-generation AIDS medication developed by Abbott. Kaletra had the potential to overtake the top AIDS drug, Pfizer Inc.'s Viracept, because it had fewer side effects. It also appeared that patients did not develop resistance to Kaletra over time, as happened with most other AIDS drugs, including Viracept. Kaletra did in fact turn into a blockbuster, and the world's top-selling protease inhibitor, with global sales reaching $1 billion by 2005.

In March 2001 Abbott completed a major acquisition, purchasing the Knoll Pharmaceutical Co. unit of German chemical giant BASF AG for $6.9 billion in cash. This deal, Abbott's largest to that time, added to the company's pharmaceutical lineup Meridia, an obesity drug with annual sales of about $400 million, and Synthroid, a $150 million thyroid drug. It also enabled the company to substantially increase its pharmaceutical R&D budget to more than $1.5 billion in 2001. Most importantly, the product pipeline was bolstered with the addition of a drug then called D2E7, a rheumatoid arthritis treatment that Knoll was in the process of developing. Abbott gained FDA approval for this drug in 2002, and it was launched under the brand name Humira. A European debut followed in 2003. Humira turned into another Abbott blockbuster, as global sales passed $1 billion by 2005 and then $2 billion just a year later, making it the company's top-selling product of all time. Aiding this skyrocketing rise were the subsequent approvals for Humira to treat other diseases, including psoriatic arthritis and Crohn's disease.

In another 2001 acquisition, Abbott bolstered its diagnostic products business with the $362 million purchase of Vysis, Inc., of Downers Grove, Illinois. Vysis produced test kits that analyzed patients' genetic material for such things as the recurrence of bladder cancer. In another embarrassing episode for Abbott, the TAP Pharmaceutical Products joint venture in late 2001 pleaded guilty to conspiring to violate federal law and agreed to pay a settlement of $875 million in a case involving allegations that TAP employees had given doctors improper inducements to prescribe the prostate-cancer drug Lupron. Three years later, TAP agreed to pay an additional $150 million to resolve civil lawsuits that had been filed in regard to the marketing and pricing of Lupron.

Abbott Laboratories continued its deal making in 2002 with the divestment of the Selsun Blue dandruff shampoo and Murine and Clear Eyes eye-care product brands. The company's vascular products business received another boost with the purchase of the cardiovascular-stent business of the U.K. firm Biocompatibles International plc for $234.5 million. During the year the FDA approved Abbott's Synthroid thyroid medication decades after it had been first marketed but also determined that the company's diagnostic-equipment plant near Chicago still failed to meet manufacturing standards, thwarting Abbott's plans to resume selling the scores of diagnostic test kits that it had been forced to pull from the market in 1999. In October 2002 the company launched an effort to streamline its global manufacturing operations that involved a reduction in the workforce of more than 2,000, or about 3 percent, and a pretax charge of $174 million. The charge reduced Abbott's net earnings for the year to $2.79 billion, while revenues reached a record $17.68 billion.

In July 2003 a subsidiary of Abbott pleaded guilty to a federal felony charge of obstructing a criminal investigation of an alleged scheme to defraud the government's Medicare and Medicaid health-insurance programs. Abbott agreed to pay more than $600 million in criminal and civil fines and payments as part of its plea. In December 2003 the FDA finally gave Abbott a green light to resume selling its full array of diagnostic tests in the United States. The lengthy regulatory dispute cost the company hundreds of millions of dollars in lost sales, and Abbott ended up paying more than $225 million in fines and related costs.

2004 FORWARD: MORE WHEELING AND DEALING

In 2004 Abbott, still under the leadership of White, continued its wheeling and dealing. On the acquisition side, the largest deal was the purchase of TheraSense, Inc., for around $1.2 billion in cash. This purchase substantially strengthened Abbott's position in the glucose-monitoring portion of the diagnostic products market. TheraSense, based in Alameda, California, was a rapidly growing and innovative producer of blood glucose self-monitoring systems. The acquisition propelled the revenues of Abbott's diabetes care unit past the $1 billion mark by 2005. In the meantime, Abbott in the spring of 2004 spun off its slow-growing hospital products business to shareholders, creating the newly independent, publicly traded Hospira, Inc. The divested business, which had generated about 13 percent of Abbott's 2003 revenues of $19.68 billion, or roughly $2.5 billion, concentrated on medication delivery systems, critical care devices, and specialty injectable pharmaceuticals.

The tremendous growth in the sales of Humira helped push Abbott's revenues to $22.34 billion by 2005. Although Humira was far from reaching its peak sales, Abbott was under pressure to find new blockbusters in anticipation of this inevitable occurrence. Significant setbacks in its pharmaceutical pipeline in 2005 cast doubt about Abbott's future. High hopes for Simdax, a heart medication, were dampened when medical studies questioned its efficacy. In addition, in October 2005 the FDA rejected Abbott's application to sell Xinlay, an experimental drug for treating prostate cancer.

In the wake of these disappointments, Abbott turned acquisitive once again. Seeking to bolster its medical device side to compensate for the struggles in pharmaceutical development, the company purchased the vascular business of Guidant Corporation for approximately $4.1 billion in cash in April 2006. The divestment of this business had been a regulatory requirement of Boston Scientific Corporation's acquisition of Guidant. The deal made Abbott the third largest player in the global vascular care market. A key device acquired from Guidant was a drug-coated heart stent called Xience. Abbott gained regulatory approval to begin selling this device in Europe later in 2006, and then in November 2007 the FDA granted approval for the commencement of U.S. sales. Xience had the potential for global annual sales well in excess of $1 billion.

Abbott also used the acquisition route to prop up its drug pipeline, spending $3.8 billion in cash for Kos Pharmaceuticals, Inc. in December 2006. Acquiring the Cranbury, New Jersey, company provided a particular boost to Abbott in the area of cholesterol medications. Abbott had grown TriCor, used to lower blood fats called triglycerides, into a $900-million-plus drug since

its 1998 introduction. The Kos purchase brought into the Abbott stable Niaspan, used to raise levels of HDL (so-called good cholesterol) and Advicor, a drug combining Niaspan with lovastatin, a drug used to lower levels of LDL, or bad cholesterol.

In early 2007 Abbott reached an agreement to sell its diagnostics products division to General Electric Company for $8.13 billion. Abbott aimed to shed a slower-growth, lower-margin business and focus more of its attention and resources on the high-risk, high-reward areas of pharmaceutical and vascular-care device development. The deal collapsed, however, in July 2007 when the two sides were unable to agree on final terms.

During this same period, Abbott was the recipient of a great deal of negative publicity concerning controversial actions it was alleged to have taken in the marketing and selling of its AIDS drugs. Most notably, a page-one story in a January 2007 issue of the *Wall Street Journal* contended that Abbott had quintupled the price of its AIDS drug Norvir, which was used in combination with drugs from other companies, as part of a strategy to persuade patients to drop Norvir and switch to Abbott's combination pill Kaletra. Lawsuits were soon filed charging Abbott with abusing its monopoly position in the AIDS drug market. Later in 2007 the company broke an industry taboo by suing a French AIDS group that had launched a cyber attack on its web site.

Despite the failed divestment of the diagnostics unit and the controversies swirling around the company's AIDS medications, Abbott's prospects appeared bright. Sales of Humira were still growing strongly and were expected to top $3 billion in 2007. In addition, the FDA's approval of Xience late in 2007 paved the way for this stent to become the next blockbuster in the Abbott portfolio.

April Dougal Gasbarre
Updated, David E. Salamie

PRINCIPAL SUBSIDIARIES

Abbott Bioresearch Center, Inc.; Abbott Cardiovascular Inc.; Abbott Diabetes Care Inc.; Abbott Diabetes Care Sales Corporation; Abbott Health Products, Inc.; Abbott Home Infusion Services of New York, Inc.; Abbott International LLC; Abbott Laboratories Inc.; Abbott Laboratories International Co.; Abbott Laboratories Pacific Ltd.; Abbott Laboratories (Puerto Rico) Incorporated; Abbott Laboratories Services Corp.; Abbott Molecular Inc.; Abbott Pharmaceutical Corporation; Abbott Point of Care Inc.; Abbott Spine Inc.; Abbott Vascular Inc.; Advanced Cardiovascular Systems,

Inc.; Aeropharm Technology, LLC; AVI Corp.; Bioabsorbable Vascular Solutions, Inc.; BioDisplay Technologies, Inc.; CG Nutritionals, Inc.; Gene-Trak, Inc.; Gene-Trak Systems Industrial Diagnostics Corp.; Guidant Endovascular Solutions, Inc.; IEP Pharmaceutical Devices, LLC; IMTC Technologies, Inc.; Integrated Vascular Systems, Inc.; Knoll Pharmaceutical Company; Kos Life Sciences, Inc.; Kos Pharmaceuticals, Inc.; Murex Diagnostics, Inc.; Natural Supplement Association, Incorporated; S&G Nutritionals Inc.; Solartek Products, Inc.; Spine Next America Corp.; Swan-Myers, Incorporated; Tobal Products Incorporated; Vectoris Corporation; Woodside Biomedical, Inc.; X Technologies Inc.; ZonePerfect Nutrition Company; Abbott Laboratories Argentina, S.A.; Abbott Australasia Pty. Limited (Australia); EAS Australia Pty Ltd.; Abbott Gesellschaft m.b.H. (Austria); Abbott Laboratories (Bangladesh) Ltd. (85%); Abbott S.A. (Belgium); Abbott Vascular International BVBA (Belgium); Abbott Laboratorios do Brasil Ltda. (Brazil); Abbott Laboratories, Limited (Canada); Abbott Point of Care Canada Limited; Abbott Laboratories de Chile Limitada; Abbott Laboratories Trading (Shanghai) Co., Ltd. (China); Guidant International Trading (Shanghai) Co. (China); Shanghai Abbott Pharmaceutical Co., Ltd. (China; 75%); Abbott Laboratories de Colombia, S.A.; Abbott Laboratories d.o.o. (Croatia); Abbott Laboratories s.r.o. (Czech Republic); Abbott Laboratories A/S (Denmark); Abbott Laboratorios del Ecuador Cia. Ltda.; Abbott Limited Egypt; Abbott, S.A. de C.V. (El Salvador); Abbott OY (Finland); Abbott France S.A.S.; Abbott GmbH & Co. KG (Germany); Abbott Laboratories (Hellas) S.A. (Greece); Abbott Laboratorios, S.A. (Guatemala); Abbott Laboratories Limited (Hong Kong); Abbott Laboratories (Hungary) Health Products and Medical Equipment Trading and Servicing Limited Liability Company; Abbott India Limited (61.7%); P. T. Abbott Indonesia; Abbott Laboratories, Ireland, Limited; Abbott S.p.A. (Italy); Abbott Japan K.K.; Abbott Japan Co., Ltd.; Abbott Korea Limited; Abbott Laboratories Baltics (Latvia); Abbott Middle East S.A.R.L. (Lebanon); Abbott Laboratories (Malaysia) Sdn. Bhd.; Abbott Laboratories de Mexico, S.A. de C.V.; Abbott Laboratories (Mozambique), Limitada; Abbott B.V. (Netherlands); Abbott Laboratories B.V. (Netherlands); Abbott Nederland C.V. (Netherlands); Abbott Laboratories (N.Z.) Limited (New Zealand); EAS Asia/Pacific Limited (New Zealand); Abbott Norge AS (Norway); Abbott Laboratories (Pakistan) Limited (77.9%); Abbott Laboratories, C.A. (Panama); Abbott Laboratorios S.A. (Peru); Abbott Laboratories (Philippines); Abbott Laboratories Poland Sp.z.o.o.; Abbott Laboratorios, Limitada (Portugal); Abbott Laboratories (Singapore) Private Limited; Abbott Laboratories Slovakia s.r.o.; Abbott Laboratories d.o.o. (Slovenia); Abbott Laboratories South Africa (Proprietary) Limited; Abbott Laboratories, S.A. (Spain); Abbott Scandinavia A.B. (Sweden); Abbott AG (Switzerland); Abbott Laboratories S.A. (Switzerland); Abbott Laboratories Tanzania Limited; Abbott Laboratories Limited (Thailand); Abbott Laboratuarlari Ithalat Ihracat Ve Tecaret Limited Sirketi (Turkey); Abbott Diabetes Care Limited (U.K.); Abbott Laboratories Limited (U.K.); Abbott Vascular Devices Limited (U.K.); Experimental and Applied Sciences UK Limited; Knoll Pharmaceuticals Unlimited (U.K.); TheraSense UK Limited; Abbott Laboratories Uruguay S.A.; Abbott Laboratories, C.A. (Venezuela).

PRINCIPAL COMPETITORS

Merck & Co., Inc.; Sanofi-Aventis; Roche Holding Ltd.; Pfizer Inc.; AstraZeneca PLC; Johnson & Johnson; Boston Scientific Corporation; Novartis AG; Bristol-Myers Squibb Company; Eli Lilly and Company; GlaxoSmithKline plc; Schering-Plough Corporation; Bayer AG; Nestlé S.A.; Royal Numico N.V.

FURTHER READING

"Abbott: Profiting from Products That Cut Costs," *Business Week,* June 18, 1984, pp. 56+.

Arndt, Michael, "Diagnosis: Shrewd Moves," *Business Week,* January 29, 2007, p. 76.

"Baby Bottle Battle," *Forbes,* November 28, 1988, pp. 222+.

Barrett, Amy, and Richard A. Melcher, "Drugmaker, Heal Thyself," *Business Week,* October 11, 1999, pp. 88+.

Bennett, Johanna, "Abbott Labs Pumps Up Its Product Line," *Barron's,* April 2, 2007, p. 43.

Benoit, Ellen, "Abbott Laboratories: Room at the Top," *Financial World,* October 17, 1989, p. 28.

Berss, Marcia, "Aloof but Not Asleep," *Forbes,* August 29, 1994, pp. 43–44.

Bleiberg, Robert M., "Abbott and Costello: The Ban on Cyclamates Is a Comedy—or Tragedy—of Errors," *Barron's,* October 9, 1978, p. 7.

"Bob Schoellhorn Is Refusing to Go Quietly," *Business Week,* March 26, 1990, pp. 34+.

Burton, Thomas M., "Abbott Laboratories and Alza Call Off Their Deal," *Wall Street Journal,* December 17, 1999, p. B10.

———, "Abbott Labs to Buy BASF Unit for $6.9 Billion," *Wall Street Journal,* December 15, 2000, pp. A3, A12.

———, "Abbott Says Wait for Drugs Will Be Worth It," *Wall Street Journal,* May 30, 2003, p. B2.

———, "Abbott's White Wins CEO Job," *Wall Street Journal,* September 16, 1998, p. A3.

———, "Abbott to Pay $100 Million in Fine to United States," *Wall Street Journal,* November 3, 1999, p. A3.

————, "Abbott to Purchase TheraSense," *Wall Street Journal,* January 14, 2004, p. B4.

————, "Abbott to Spin Off Hospital Products in a Shift of Focus," *Wall Street Journal,* August 25, 2003, p. B5.

————, "Federal Judge Clears Abbott in Formula Case: Bid Process for Infant Food Is Called 'Questionable,' but Oversight Is Faulted," *Wall Street Journal,* June 1, 1994, p. A3.

Burton, Thomas M., and Patricia Callahan, "Abbott Unit Is Guilty in Liquid-Nutrient Case," *Wall Street Journal,* July 24, 2003, p. A8.

Burton, Thomas M., Geeta Anand, and Gardiner Harris, "FDA Hits Abbott Labs, Schering," *Wall Street Journal,* May 16, 2002, p. A3.

Carreyrou, John, "New Regimen: Inside Abbott's Tactics to Protect AIDS Drug," *Wall Street Journal,* January 3, 2007, p. A1.

Carreyrou, John, and Avery Johnson, "Abbott Breaks with Industry, Sues AIDS Group," *Wall Street Journal,* June 18, 2007, p. B1.

Carter, Kim, "Abbott Laboratories Betting Its Future on the Development of New Products," *Modern Healthcare,* November 7, 1986, pp. 138+.

Chase, Brett, "Can Abbott Be the Next J&J?" *Crain's Chicago Business,* April 18, 2005, p. 1.

Colias, Mike, "Abbott Faces Stent Squeeze," *Crain's Chicago Business,* July 10, 2006, p. 2.

————, "Can Abbott Restock Its Cabinet?" *Crain's Chicago Business,* May 29, 2006, p. 4.

Dooren, Jennifer Corbett, and Avery Johnson, "Abbott Stent Gets Panel Backing Despite Clot Worries," *Wall Street Journal,* November 30, 2007, p. B3.

Hamilton, David P., "Abbott Enters Arthritis-Drug War with FDA Approval of Humira," *Wall Street Journal,* January 2, 2003, p. D4.

Jarvis, Lisa, "Abbott Labs to Eliminate 2,000 Jobs and Streamline Its Operations," *Chemical Market Reporter,* October 14, 2002, p. 2.

Johnson, Avery, "Abbott Buys Kos, Pays Premium to Boost Pipeline," *Wall Street Journal,* November 7, 2006, p. A3.

————, "Abbott Makeover Stirs Attention of Investors," *Wall Street Journal,* January 19, 2007, p. A11.

Klein, Sarah A., "Abbott Deal on TAP Will Please Investors," *Crain's Chicago Business,* April 23, 2001, p. 4.

————, "Abbott Lifeline: Drug Pipeline," *Crain's Chicago Business,* March 22, 2004, p. 3.

————, "Abbott's Biotech Biz Gets a Booster Shot: Picking Up Keys to State-of-the-Art Lab in BASF Deal," *Crain's Chicago Business,* January 1, 2001, p. 4.

————, "Abbott's Biotech Search: Counting on Partnerships, Wonder Drugs," *Crain's Chicago Business,* March 4, 2002, p. 4.

————, "Medicine Man: Pushing His Scientists to Do No Less Than Solve the Remaining Mysteries of Medicine, CEO Miles White Has Reshaped Abbott Labs—but Not Without Controversy," *Crain's Chicago Business,* January 13, 2003, p. 1.

————, "Restocked Product Pipeline Invigorating Abbott," *Crain's Chicago Business,* September 4, 2000, p. 4.

Kogan, Herman, *The Long White Line: The Story of Abbott Laboratories,* New York: Random House, 1963, 309 p.

Loftus, Peter, "Abbott Charges Offset Humira Sales," *Wall Street Journal,* October 18, 2007, p. C8.

Merrion, Paul, "Nestlé Sours Baby Formula for Abbott," *Crain's Chicago Business,* June 13, 1988.

Miller, James P., "Abbott Labs Agrees to Purchase Alza," *Wall Street Journal,* June 22, 1999, p. A3.

————, "Abbott Ousts Schoellhorn As Chairman, Drawing Lawsuit by Embattled Official," *Wall Street Journal,* March 12, 1990, p. B6.

Oloroso, Arsenio, Jr., "Abbott's Prescription for Sluggish Drug Biz Pays Off," *Crain's Chicago Business,* October 21, 1991, p. 3.

————, "Abbott's Tough Rx: Buy or Risk Being Bought," *Crain's Chicago Business,* March 2, 1998, p. 3.

————, "Abbott Tries Costly Growth Drug: M&A," *Crain's Chicago Business,* April 8, 1996, p. 4.

————, "New CEO Poised to Rev Up Sleepy Abbott's Strategy," *Crain's Chicago Business,* September 21, 1998, p. 4.

Pratt, William D., *The Abbott Almanac: 100 Years of Commitment to Quality Health Care,* Elmsford, N.Y.: Benjamin, 1987, 224 p.

Salwan, Kevin G., "Infant-Formula Firms Rigged Bids, U.S. Says," *Wall Street Journal,* June 12, 1992, p. A3.

Somasundaram, Meera, "Abbott Set to Stock Medicine Cabinet: Drug Giant Expected to Shop for Mid-Sized Rivals," *Crain's Chicago Business,* February 1, 1999, p. 1.

Tatge, Mark, "Medicine Show," *Forbes,* March 19, 2001, pp. 70, 72.

Twitchell, Evelyn Ellison, "Full Medicine Chest: Abbott Labs Is a Bargain, Assuming It Cleans House," *Barron's,* June 24, 2002, p. T6.

ABC Learning Centres Ltd.

43 Metroplex Avenue
Murarrie, Queensland 4172
Australia
Telephone: (+61 617) 39062000
Fax: (+61 617) 39082577
Web site: http://www.childcare.com.au

Public Company
Incorporated: 1988
Employees: 8,000
Sales: AUD 1.7 billion ($1.2 billion) (2007)
Stock Exchanges: Australian
Ticker Symbol: ABS
NAIC: 624410 Child Day Care Services

■ ■ ■

ABC Learning Centres Ltd. is the world's largest operator of child-care facilities. The Australian company, that market's leader, has built up an international portfolio of more than 2,200 centers. While Australia remains a major market for the company, accounting for nearly 1,100 of its day-care centers, ABC has moved aggressively into the U.S. market. Starting from 2004, the company has made a series of acquisitions, including La Petite Academy Inc., Tutor Time Learning Centers, The Children's Courtyard, and Childtime Childcare Inc., among others. In 2007, the company's child-care operations had topped 1,030 centers. ABC is also present in New Zealand, where it operates 104 centers, and has targeted the United Kingdom for growth. In 2006 and 2007 the company bought Busy Bees Group Ltd. and

Leapfrog Nurseries Group. With more than 120 centers in operation in the United Kingdom, the company has become that market's leader as well. ABC Learning has also been developing plans to expand its operations beyond the preschool market to include the operation of private elementary schools. The company is led by cofounder Eddy Groves, CEO, and wife Le Neve Groves, who serves as the company CEO in charge of education. ABC Learning is listed on the Australian Stock Exchange and posted revenues of nearly AUD 1.7 billion ($1.2 billion) in 2007.

FROM MILKMAN TO CHILD-CARE SPECIALIST IN 1988

ABC founder Eddy Groves had established himself as one of Australia's most promising young entrepreneurs when he entered the child-care business in 1988. The Canadian-born, Queensland-raised Groves had started his career as a bank clerk in the early 1980s, but soon set his sights on building his own business. As he told the *Financial Times:* "I was studying accounting but it just wasn't for me. I needed something that could generate more money than a normal job."

Groves, then 19, saw potential in the milk delivery sector. In 1985, he acquired a van and a contract to distribute milk for Queensland dairy producer Pauls. Groves quickly built that business into the largest Pauls distributorship in the Queensland region. By age 22, Groves himself was driving about in his first Ferrari.

By then, Groves had set his eye on his next fortune. Groves's wife, Le Neve, with a background in early childhood education, provided the inspiration for

COMPANY PERSPECTIVES

Our dream is to improve human life by providing the best care in the world. We will achieve this because we love what we do. We love to continually raise the standard of service to our communities, colleagues and stakeholders. We love that we are united to develop tailored care and educational services that enhance people's life long learning. We love to approach everything with a profound and personal respect for the individual. We love to champion the overall health and well being of everyone. We love to pursue everything with relentless honesty and integrity. We love that our "spirit of fun" runs as deep as our "spirit of competition." We love to create safe and dynamic environments that everyone can enjoy. We love to innovate so we never ever have to follow others. We love that we attract, motivate and retain outstanding people.

Groves's new venture. In 1988, the couple acquired a former church hall and opened their first child-care center in Brisbane. The Groveses quickly opened several more child-care centers through the end of the decade, establishing ABC Learning Centres.

While Le Neve Groves completed her Ph.D. in education, Eddy Groves had recognized the strong potential for the private child-care market. At the time, the operation of child-care facilities in Australia remained largely in the nonprofit sphere, supported by government subsidies. Yet Groves foresaw the coming boom in demand for child care. As he explained to the *Financial Times:* "With land and housing prices going up so much, families need to have two incomes to survive. Childcare is really not a discretionary spend. Parents need to have care if they are going to work."

BUILDING THE NETWORK TO LOWER COSTS

Groves understood that, with more centers in operation, he could reduce costs for each individual center. Savings were generated by centralizing administrative and other back office functions. The greater purchasing power of the larger network of child-care centers enabled the company to negotiate more favorable pricing on items ranging from food to furniture to electricity. These cost reductions helped the ABC centers remain competitive,

despite the generous subsidies that allowed nonprofit centers to charge lower fees.

By 1996, ABC operated 18 centers, enough to place at the top of the country's nascent private child-care industry. The relatively small size and steady cash flow of the business allowed the company to focus on developing the professionalism of its network. As such, the company invested in furnishing its centers with state-of-the-art equipment. The company also introduced such features as staff uniforms. In order to ensure the supply of trained personnel, ABC set up its own training academy, ABC Early Childhood Training College in 1995. That operation later became known as the National Institute of Early Childhood Education.

ABC's early development placed the company in a strong position to capitalize on a major event in the Australian child-care market. In 1997, the conservative-oriented Australian government moved to abolish the subsidies for nonprofit day-care centers. Instead, the government decided to provide child-care payments directly to families. The ending of subsidies became the signal for the start of ABC's spectacular growth into the new century.

ABC launched a new and more ambitious expansion program. The new phase of the group's expansion was based in part on the acquisition of properties in prime locations. At the same time, the company targeted the acquisition of single day-care centers and smaller child-care networks. The strong cash flow from the group's existing operations provided the funding for its expansion. That cash flow also played a prominent role in consolidating the company's position as industry leader, as it provided the company with the means to remain at the cutting edge of child-care technologies and furnishings.

TAKING CHILD CARE PUBLIC IN 2001

By 1999, ABC's network had topped 30 centers. Just two years later, the company numbered 50 centers, including 12 outside of the Queensland region. In that year, ABC prepared its public offering, listing its shares on the Australian Stock Exchange. The listing gave the company access to a new pool of capital, setting its growth into overdrive. Over the next several years, the company nearly doubled its network each year, building to 94 centers in 2002, then to 192 centers in 2003, and to more than 325 in 2004.

These figures did not include another lucrative area pioneered by the company—the corporate day-care market. More and more of Australia's larger corporations had begun offering day-care services to their

KEY DATES

1988: Eddy and Le Neve Groves found ABC Learning Centres in Brisbane, Australia.

1995: ABC establishes its own training academy, later called National Institute of Early Childhood Education.

1997: End of government subsidies to nonprofit day-care centers signals start of new growth in the Australian private day-care sector.

2001: ABC goes public with listing on Australian Stock Exchange.

2004: Company acquires Peppercorn and Child Care Centres Australia, becoming world's largest publicly listed day-care specialist; first foreign expansion occurs with entry into New Zealand.

2006: ABC enters U.S. market with $160 million acquisition of Learning Care Group; company acquires Busy Bees group in United Kingdom.

2007: ABC becomes U.K. market leader with acquisition of Leapfrog nurseries group; company acquires La Petite Academy in United States, adding 650 centers in 36 states.

TARGETING THE UNITED STATES AND BEYOND IN 2005

ABC's dominance of the Australian market limited its future growth prospects there. At the same time, the company faced growing criticism of the corporatization of the country's child-care market. With few legislative barriers to entry into the market, the country had seen the emergence of a number of highly aggressive players. Many of these, such as Bambuu, had little to no background in child care. Their purely speculative interest in the sector raised alarm among many industry observers.

By the middle of the first decade of the 2000s, an increasing number of reports of poor and even unsafe conditions at many corporate-owned centers had brought scrutiny on the industry. The industry was also accused of exploiting its workforce, offering poor wages and low levels of training. ABC, as market leader, inevitably became a target of industry watchdogs. Yet the company was able to point to its extremely low employee turnover rate—less than 8 percent per year—to set itself apart from its rivals. The company's commitment to maintaining the standards of its facilities was also seen in the more than AUD 160 million spent on refurbishments and upgrades of its network during the first half of the 2000s.

ABC tested the international waters during this time as well, establishing its first foreign operations in New Zealand. By 2007, the company operated more than 100 centers in that country. By then, however, ABC had gained a position as a leader in the world's largest day-care market, the United States.

ABC's entry into the United States came in early 2006, when the company paid nearly $160 million to acquire the Learning Care Group, the NASDAQ-listed operator of more than 460 centers in 25 states. By the end of the year, the company had completed another significant acquisition, of Children's Courtyard, for $66 million. That Texas-based operation added another 74 centers to the group. At the same time, the company entered an agreement, through Tutor Time, its U.S.-based subsidiary, to acquire 17 centers in California.

U.K. LEADER IN 2007

Back at home, ABC took out another major rival with the acquisition of Hutchison's Childcare Services for AUD 96.2 million. Yet ABC had begun scouting out new horizons for its growth. The U.K. market naturally attracted the company's attention. ABC's entry into that market was completed by December 2006 when it agreed to pay £77 million ($140 million) to buy the Busy Bees group. That acquisition gave the company a

employees. Many of these corporations turned to third-party providers, such as ABC, rather than develop and operate their own centers. ABC established a dedicated division to serve this market. The company quickly grew into the segment's leader.

A major milestone in ABC's growth came in 2004, when the company negotiated a merger with its leading rival in Australia, Peppercorn and Child Care Centres Australia, in a deal worth AUD 375 million. The merger doubled ABC's child-care network. The company was not only the largest operator of child-care centers in Australia, but it also claimed the lead as the world's largest publicly listed day-care specialist.

By 2005, ABC claimed 20 percent of the total Australian day-care market. The company continued to make new acquisitions at home. In March 2006, for example, the company spent AUD 142 million to acquire Kids Campus from the Bambuu diamond mining group. Yet the company's interest had increasingly turned to the international market.

base of 46 child-care centers across the United Kingdom. It also gave ABC control of the Busy Bee voucher operation, which enabled large companies to subsidize employees' child-care expenses.

Within months after its entry into the United Kingdom, ABC had claimed the market's leadership. In August 2007, ABC agreed to pay just over £31 million ($55 million) to take over the struggling Leapfrog nursery network owned by Nord Anglia Education. The purchase, completed in October 2007, gave the company control of the 88 Leapfrog centers, placing firmly as the top operator in the United Kingdom.

The Groves sold another 12 percent of their stake in ABC to Temasek, the Singapore government's investment arm, raising fresh capital for the group's expansion. The share sale left the couple with an 8 percent stake, worth AUD 270 million, of the company they had founded. Following the sale, the company announced its interest in expanding its operations into the Singapore market before the end of the decade.

ABC's North American operations in the meantime had taken a major step forward. In January 2007, the company agreed to pay $330 million to acquire Chicago-based La Petite Academy Inc. The purchase gave ABC control of an additional 650 centers located in 36 states, for a total of nearly 98,000 places. An important component of the La Petite Academy acquisition was that it enabled ABC to expand its operations beyond the preschool sector, targeting an age range from six weeks to 12 years old. The company also boosted its position in New Zealand in 2007, acquiring Forward Steps Holdings, an operator of 49 child-care centers. With more than 2,250 day-care centers in four countries, ABC had grown into the world's largest day-care specialist.

M. L. Cohen

PRINCIPAL SUBSIDIARIES

A.B.C. Corporate Care Pty Ltd; A.B.C. Developmental Learning Centres Pty Ltd; A.B.C. Early Childhood Training College Pty Ltd; A.B.C. USA Holdings Pty Ltd; ABC Developmental Learning Centres (NZ) Ltd (New Zealand); Busy Bees Group Limited (U.K.); Child Care Centres Australia Ltd; Childtime Childcare, Inc. (U.S.A.); Forward Steps Holdings Limited (New Zealand); FutureOne Pty Ltd; Kids Campus Limited; La Petite Academy Inc. (U.S.A.); Learning Care Group, Inc. (U.S.A.); Peppercorn Management Group Ltd; Premier Early Learning Centres Pty Ltd; The Children's Courtyard LLP (U.S.A.); Tutor Time Learning Centers LLC (U.S.A.).

PRINCIPAL COMPETITORS

L.P.A. Holding Corp.; ServiceMaster Co.; KinderCare Learning Centers Inc.; Knowledge Learning Corp.; Bright Horizons Family Solutions Inc.; Studentsamskipnaden I Trondheim; National Pediatric Support Services Inc.; Kidicorp Group Ltd.

FURTHER READING

"Australian Child Care Group Purchases 74 More US Centres," *Community Action*, August 21, 2006, p. 8.

"Australia's ABC Learning Acquires UK Nurseries Group," *AsiaPulse News*, September 19, 2007.

"Australia's 'Child Care Wal-Mart' Heading for Canada, Expert Says," *Community Action*, October 24, 2005, p. 1.

Cratchley, Drew, "ABC Learning Grabs 17 Centres in US," *Sydney Morning Herald*, June 21, 2006.

Lambert, Emily, "Babysitting Bonanza," *Forbes Global*, October 15, 2007, p. 28.

Marsh, Virginia, "Talent for Nurturing Fledgling Entrepreneurship," *Financial Times*, December 7, 2006, p. 9.

"Millions Milked," *Business Review Weekly*, November 17, 2003.

Moulds, Josephine, "Busy Bees Buzz In for Leapfrog Nursery," *Daily Telegraph*, August 14, 2007, p. 6.

Rush, Emma, and Christian Downie, "ABC Learning Centres: A Case Study of Australia's Largest Child Care Corporation," *Australia Institute*, June 2006.

Administración Nacional de Combustibles, Alcohol y Pórtland

Paysandú y Avenida del Liberador
P.O. Box 1090
Montevideo, 11100
Uruguay
Telephone: (598 2) 902-0608
Fax: (598 2) 902-1136
Web site: http://www.ancap.com.uy

State-Owned Company
Founded: 1931
Employees: 2,667
Sales: $1.8 billion (2006)
NAIC: 111332 Grape Vineyards; 111930 Sugarcane Farming; 221210 Natural Gas Distribution; 311311 Sugarcane Mills; 312140 Distilleries; 324110 Petroleum Refineries; 324191 Petroleum Lubricating Oil and Grease Manufacturing; 327310 Cement Manufacturing; 447190 Other Gasoline Stations; 483111 Deep Sea Freight Transportation; 486210 Pipeline Transportation of Natural Gas

■ ■ ■

Administración Nacional de Combustibles, Alcohol y Pórtland, or National Administration of Fuels, Alcohol and Portland Cement, a public body, is the largest commercial and industrial enterprise in Uruguay. Its principal activities are to import and refine crude oil and its derivatives; manufacture and sell liquid, semiliquid, and gaseous petroleum-based fuels; import, manufacture, and sell lubricants; and manufacture and sell Portland cement, the kind normally used in construction. It also produces, imports and exports, distributes, and sells alcohol, sugar, and molasses, plus their derivatives and subproducts, and distributes chemical solvents. Through subsidiaries and affiliated enterprises, ANCAP also is engaged in a number of related activities in Argentina, including ownership of a gas pipeline, exploration and exploitation of oil and gas deposits, fuel distribution, and the manufacture of chemical solvents. ANCAP is an autonomous public body with its own budget and a publicly appointed board of directors responsible for the management of the enterprise.

THE ESTABLISHMENT OF ANCAP: 1931

The creation of ANCAP was in the context of a society oriented toward welfare-state socialism. ANCAP was established in 1931 after a protracted struggle, mainly by the Colorado Party, to break what amounted to a monopoly on the manufacture of distilled liquors held by Pedro Meillet y Cia., which was blamed for stagnant production. The new enterprise was not engaged in the business of making or selling wine or beer. It was, however, also authorized to manufacture cement exclusively, thereby ending the monopoly held by Compañia Uruguaya de Cemento Pórtland, a subsidiary of Lone Star Cement Co. This company was unpopular because the cement it made was sold abroad, where the proceeds remained, while cement needed in Uruguay had to be imported.

ANCAP also received the exclusive right to import crude oil, to refine it into petroleum products, and to

COMPANY PERSPECTIVES

■

Our Mission: To secure for the nation its supplies of energy products and to provide Portland cement and alcohols, all conforming to regional standards of quality and the needs of our customers/users. We are oriented to the continuous improvement of efficiency and competitiveness, we foster integral development and participation of personnel, we act with social and environmental responsibility, and we are committed to the trust that our enterprise generates.

distribute these products. A refinery, yet to be built, was mandated to produce at least half the gasoline consumed in Uruguay. At the time four foreign corporations— Standard Oil Company of New Jersey (Esso), Royal Dutch/Shell Group (Shell), the Texas Corporation (Texaco), and Atlantic Refining Company—were engaged in these activities in Uruguay, through subsidiaries. The nation did not have, and still does not have, producing oilfields. It was felt that Uruguay, for reasons of national security, must have control of the industry. There was also a prevailing sentiment that a public monopoly would result in lower fuel prices.

Under the enabling legislation, ANCAP and other autonomous public bodies were to be governed by a seven-member board of directors, with employment in each based on party affiliation. The proportion was a formula established by the results for the Colorado and (opposition) Blanco parties in the prior national election. "Jobs were being created and these jobs would be doled out not on the basis of merit or institutional need," wrote Martin Weinstein in his history of Uruguay, "and not even in fact by the two traditional parties as corporate entities, but by specific factions of each party. The agreement was quickly dubbed the Pacto de Chinchulín—the Pork Barrel Pact." However, AN-CAP was not perceived as corrupt. In a 2002 article for the business magazine *AméricaEconomía,* Gustavo Stok wrote, "In contrast to the majority of state enterprises in the region, [Uruguay's public enterprises] have been historically an example of correct administration."

MEETING THE NATIONAL NEED FOR PETROLEUM PRODUCTS: 1937–61

ANCAP began its life without an oil refinery and under a boycott from the expelled oil companies. It began importing petroleum products from the Soviet Union in

1934. Near the end of 1935, however, Uruguay broke relations with the U.S.S.R., under pressure from neighboring countries, which accused the Soviets of organizing subversion from their offices in Montevideo. Consequently, Uruguay had to make peace with its former suppliers, and in 1936, legislation was adopted allowing reentry of the expelled four. A five-year agreement signed in 1938 gave them the right to bring in half of Uruguay's crude oil in their own ships, at prices they established. The oil would be refined by ANCAP, but the companies were given the right to distribute and sell petroleum products, with fixed quotas for each product. This agreement was periodically renewed.

Among ANCAP's first acts was to purchase two ships and to begin work on a refinery in Montevideo. This facility, built by U.S.-based Foster Wheeler Corp., was completed in 1937. ANCAP had installed three fuel storage tanks near Paysandú to make supplies available to the region north of Río Negro. Also in 1937, the agency was authorized to import and sell solid as well as liquid and gaseous petroleum-based fuels. However, repeated exploration and drilling failed, then and later, to find commercial deposits of petroleum.

After the opening of the refinery, petroleum derivatives instantly became Uruguay's second largest manufacturing sector, albeit trailing well behind the leader, food products. The capacity of the refinery was periodically increased, and the output of fuels grew more than tenfold between 1937 and 1956. ANCAP also made good the expectation of its supporters that it would reduce costs. The price of gasoline fell 4 percent between 1932 and 1947, while the amount consumed grew 54 percent. By 1949 ANCAP's oil refinery had more than tripled in capacity. Two oil tankers had been acquired from the United States, and others were chartered from abroad, to assure self-sufficiency of crude oil supply. In 1951 ANCAP began producing industrial lubricants, asphalt, and liquid petroleum gas. The refinery was expanded and modernized again in 1961, when it reached more than 16 times the capacity of the original facility.

RUM, CEMENT, AND OTHER PRODUCTS: 1937–67

ANCAP's scope of operations grew in 1957 with the inclusion of the Institute of Industrial Chemistry, formerly under the direction of the Ministry of Industry and Commerce. The addition of the institute brought ANCAP into the manufacture of basic products for agriculture and animal husbandry, such as chemical fertilizers and pesticides. This activity had ceased by 1983, however.

KEY DATES

1931: Administración Nacional de Combustibles, Alcohol y Pórtland (ANCAP) is established.

1936: Foreign companies regain a role in supplying ANCAP with crude oil and distributing refined products.

1937: ANCAP opens its own oil refinery and establishes a company for making Portland cement.

1942: ANCAP establishes a company to make rum.

1951: ANCAP begins producing industrial lubricants, asphalt, and liquid petroleum gas.

1961: The oil refinery has reached more than 16 times the capacity of the original facility.

1981: ANCAP's workforce has fallen almost by half since 1969 because of economy measures.

1990: Private concessionaires are allowed to compete with ANCAP service stations.

1998: ANCAP establishes a joint venture with Argentina's leading cement producer.

1999: ANCAP controls a struggling chain of service stations in Argentina.

2003: Uruguay's voters reject legislation that would allow ANCAP to take on foreign partners.

2005: Venezuela pledges to meet ANCAP's petroleum needs for the next 25 years.

ANCAP established Compañía Nacional de Cementos S.A. in 1937, with headquarters in Pan de Azúcar. This company achieved a significant price reduction in Portland cement and added plants in Minas and Paysandú. It was able not only to supply Uruguay but also to gain a market in Argentina, Paraguay, and Brazil. All official bodies were required to obtain coal and Portland cement through ANCAP, which imported the coal.

ANCAP's own barges and tankers hauled oil and cement from Montevideo to river ports such as Salto and Paysandú. Its cement division was said by the U.S. program Alliance for Progress to be among the better-managed public enterprises in Latin America. The Minas plant was about an hour's drive from the capital. Limestone deposits near Paysandú, where the second plant opened, were considered plentiful enough to furnish the nation's cement plants with clay for another century.

With regard to alcoholic beverages, ANCAP promoted Uruguayan-made *caña,* a white rum drink made with molasses imported from Argentina and crude sugar from Peru or Brazil. Compañía Azucanería Artigas S.A. was established for this purpose in 1942 and opened a mill the following year. ANCAP had begun the first cultivation of sugarcane in Uruguay, irrigating the fields. In 1948 it purchased 10,000 hectares (about 25,000 acres) for further sugarcane plantations. Eventually ANCAP became self-sufficient in molasses. It had also begun to produce grappa, a kind of brandy, from the grapes of Uruguayan, Argentine, and Chilean wineries and was also planning to make cognac from local grapes. The enterprise purchased a vineyard for this purpose in 1946. A curiosity was ANCAP's MacPay whisky, a uniquely Uruguayan brand. Agricultural stations, sometimes irrigated, were established for the cultivation of grain as well as sugarcane. A modern grain distillery was opened in 1949 in Paysandú.

A LARGER ROLE FOR PRIVATE ENTERPRISE: 1970–99

With the rapid rise of world petroleum prices in the 1970s, the share of crude oil in Uruguay's imports rose from one-fifth to one-third of the total. This decade, and the early 1980s, were hard years for the national economy, and ANCAP as well as other public entities were called on to make economies. The number of AN-CAP employees, which peaked at 11,773 in 1969, had fallen to almost half that figure by 1981. Private enterprises were allowed to compete in the area of chemical products made by the enterprise. This was also true for cement, although ANCAP cement still maintained priority in the area of public works. Private companies were also allowed to compete for waterborne transportation of ANCAP's raw materials and finished goods.

With the collapse of the Soviet Union at the end of the 1980s, the political climate in Latin America, including Uruguay, further turned against statism as exemplified by public bodies such as ANCAP and toward privatization and the development of free markets. Private concessionaires were allowed to operate ANCAP service stations in 1989.

ANCAP's cement operations were soon facing stiff competition from the local affiliate of a Spanish company and experiencing the problem of disposing of growing overproduction. Despite stepped up export volume, almost all to Argentina, the surplus, by 1997, reached one-seventh of production. Consequently, in 1998 ANCAP signed a ten-year pact with Loma Negra C.I.A.S.A., Argentina's leading cement producer. They established a joint venture, Cementos del Plata S.A., to help ANCAP sell more cement in Argentina as well as Uruguay and to upgrade ANCAP's production plants.

With regard to alcoholic beverages, ANCAP prepared for increased competition by signing an agreement in 1999 with Scotland's Morrison Bowmore Distillers, a subsidiary of Japan's Suntory Ltd., to create a joint venture named AMBD S.A. This company was created to open new markets for ANCAP's high-end whiskies. CABA S.A. was established in 2000 as an ANCAP subsidiary dedicated to the production and commercialization of alcohol and alcoholic beverages. The Uruguayan government toyed with the idea of getting the state out of the alcohol business but was unable to find a prospective buyer who would make what it considered an adequate offer.

FALLING VICTIM TO
ARGENTINA'S MELTDOWN:
1998–99

ANCAP's oil refinery presented a bigger problem: it once again needed to be increased in size in order to produce fuels more economically to compete within Mercosur—the customs union that took in Argentina, Brazil, Paraguay, and Uruguay. Petrouruguay S.A. had been established in Argentina in 1991, with ANCAP as majority shareholder, to seek and exploit oil and gas deposits outside Uruguay. A gas pipeline linking Argentine and Uruguay ports was subsequently built. In 1998 ANCAP signed a long-term pact with Sol Petróleo S.A., an Argentine company controlled by Bermuda-based Phoebius Energy Ltd. Under the terms, ANCAP would sell petroleum-based products in Argentina through Sol Petróleo's network of service stations, mostly in the Buenos Aires metropolitan area. ANCAP took a one-third stake in the joint venture, Ancsol S.A., investing $30 million.

The agreement soon foundered. The partners had underestimated the difficulty of gaining market share in Argentina's rapidly deteriorating economic climate. Sol Petróleo went bankrupt in 1999. It was replaced by Petrolera del Conosur S.A., with ANCAP holding 77 percent of the stock through Ancsol. In 2000 this company had 220 service stations in Argentina, but only 2 percent of the national market. It also owned what had been Sol Petróleo's petrochemical plant. (In Uruguay, an ANCAP subsidiary administered 214 of the nation's 524 service stations.)

Mindful that ANCAP would, in theory, have to open up its protected markets by 2006 to Mercosur competition, Uruguay's Congress passed a bill in 2002 that would further authorize the enterprise to enter into joint ventures with foreign partners. The legislation also stripped ANCAP of its monopolies on the import and export of crude oil and the refining of crude oil into petroleum products. This attracted the attention of several foreign oil companies, including Shell and ChevronTexaco Corporation, but, in a 2003 referendum, Uruguay's voters nullified the legislation by a 5 to 3 margin.

By this time Argentina's economy had collapsed, leaving in its wake a heap of defaulted debt and a devaluation of its peso, previously tied to the U.S. dollar, to only about 30 cents. The government placed a ceiling on crude oil prices that kept gasoline and other fuel prices low, meaning—since ANCAP paid for the crude oil for its refinery at higher international prices—that the enterprise was losing money on everything it sold in Argentina. Petrolera del Conosur lost about $18 million in 2003 alone. For the first time ever, ANCAP itself lost money in 2006. Its net loss was $4.19 million on operating revenues of $1.8 billion, of which sales abroad accounted for 8 percent.

VENEZUELA TO THE RESCUE:
2005–07

In 2005 ANCAP looked to oil-rich Venezuela for help. Following several agreements with the Uruguayan government, President Hugo Chávez declared that Venezuela's state-owned oil producer, Petróleos de Venezuela S.A. (PDVSA), would guarantee to supply Uruguay's needs for petroleum for the next 25 years. One accord called for Venezuela to double the capacity of the La Teja refinery, which would have to be adapted to accommodate PDVSA's heavy, high-sulfur "sour" crude oil. ANCAP announced in 2007 that it would spend $180 million to build three additional plants at the La Teja complex. One would reduce the sulfur content of gasoline. The second would do the same for liquid petroleum gas. The third would liquefy the extracted sulfur for use in fertilizers.

Another agreement called for the refurbishing of an ANCAP cement plant that would export the product to Venezuela under favorable terms. A third earmarked funds for the improvement of an ANCAP plant that would send alcohol to Venezuela for use as fuel. Venezuela strengthened its ties with ANCAP in 2006, the year it was admitted to Mercosur, when a PDVSA subsidiary in Argentina purchased 46 percent of Petrolera del Conosur, reducing ANCAP's share to the same 46 percent.

In 2007 ANCAP bought 90 of ChevronTexaco's Texaco-brand service stations in Uruguay, giving it a majority of the nation's service stations. Yet the rapid rise of world oil prices in 2007 was taking its toll on ANCAP's resources. The enterprise was hoping for a price break from Venezuela while paying three-quarters in cash and financing the remainder over 15 years, at 2 percent annual interest. It was expecting to pay $1 billion for crude oil during the year.

Robert Halasz

PRINCIPAL SUBSIDIARIES

Ancsol S.A.; Carboclor S.A. (Argentina; 74%); Distribuidora Uruguaya de Combustibles S.A.; Petrouruguay S.A. (Argentina; 97%).

PRINCIPAL DIVISIONS

Environment, Industrial Scarcity and Quality Management; Fuels and Lubricants; Natural Gas; Portland Cement.

FURTHER READING

Gutiérrez, Fernando, "Sol Petróleo con poca nafta," *Apertura,* October 1999, pp. 34–37.

Jacob, Raúl, *Breve historia de la industria en Uruguay,* Montevideo: Fundación de Cultura Universitaria, 1979, 153 p.

Lebel, Oscar, *ANCAP: Una visión geopolítica del Uruguay en el mundo del petróleo,* Montevideo: Cauce Editorial, 2003, 111 p.

Rebella, Jorge, "Market Formula," *Business Latin America,* June 22, 1998, p. 2.

———, "State Affair," *Business Latin America,* May 18, 1998, p. 6.

Silva, Pablo, "ANCAP en un período de transición," *Política Economía,* July 2000, pp. 26–30.

Sintesís histórica de la ingenería en el Uruguay, Montevideo: Asociación de inginieros del Uruguay, 1949, pp. 207–15.

Solari, Aldo, and Rolando Franco, *Las empresas públicas en el Uruguay,* Montevideo: Fundación de Cultura Universitaria, 1983, 130 p.

Stok, Gustavo, "A medio gas," *AméricaEconomía,* June 28–July 11, 2002, p. 32.

———, "Tango uruguayo," *AméricaEconomía,* January 21–February 17, 2005, pp. 34–35.

Vasquez, Patricia I., "Uruguayans Reject Privatization of Oil Sector," *Oil Daily,* December 10, 2003.

Weinstein, Martin, *Uruguay: Democracy at the Crossroads,* Boulder, Colo.: Westview Press, 1988, p. 31.

Wertheim, Howard, "Venezuela's Chavez Using Oil for Influence in S. America," *Oil & Gas Journal,* September 5, 2005, pp. 28–29.

Willis, Jean L., *Historical Dictionary of Uruguay,* Metuchen, N.J.: Scarecrow Press, 1974, pp. 4–5.

Agilent Technologies Inc.

5301 Stevens Creek Boulevard
Santa Clara, California 95051
U.S.A.
Telephone: (408) 345-8886
Toll Free: (877) 424-4536
Fax: (408) 345-8474
Web site: http://www.agilent.com

Public Company
Incorporated: 1999
Employees: 18,700
Sales: $5.42 billion (2007)
Stock Exchanges: New York
Ticker Symbol: A
NAIC: 334413 Semiconductor and Related Device Manufacturing; 334290 Other Communications Equipment Manufacturing; 334513 Instruments and Related Products Manufacturing for Measuring, Displaying, and Controlling Industrial Process Variables

■ ■ ■

Agilent Technologies Inc. is the world's leading supplier of electronic test and measurement equipment. Its life sciences and chemical analysis unit manufactures laboratory equipment and other scientific instruments. It serves customers in more than 110 countries, including such global giants as Cisco, Dow Chemical, Glaxo-SmithKline, Intel, Merck, and Samsung.

SPIN OFF FROM HEWLETT-PACKARD: 1999

In March 1999, Hewlett-Packard (HP), originally founded in 1938 by Stanford University–trained electrical engineers Dave Packard and Bill Hewlett, announced a strategic realignment that would allow it to concentrate on its computer, printing, and software businesses. Hewlett-Packard would continue as a computing and imaging company and include all of HP's computing, printing, and imaging businesses, while Agilent Technologies Inc. would consist of HP's Test and Measurement, Semiconductor Products, Life Sciences, and Chemical Analysis divisions. In November 1999, Agilent Technologies, its name a combination of "agile" and the technological-sounding "ent," began business as a company with $8 billion in sales, or about 15 percent of HP's annual revenue.

In the area of testing and measurement, Agilent provided companies in the communications, electronics, semiconductor, and related industries with standard and customized test and measurement solutions. In the field of semiconductors, it was a supplier of semiconductor components, modules, and assemblies for high-performance communications infrastructure, computing devices, and mobile information appliances. Agilent's healthcare solutions were focused on electro-medical clinical measurement and diagnostic solutions. Its chemical analysis business provided analytical instrument systems that enabled customers to identify, quantify, analyze, and test the properties of substances and products down to the atomic level.

Agilent began business with about 43,000 employees, approximately one-third of HP's workforce. It also took with it about one-third of HP's Laboratories, which it renamed Agilent Technologies Laboratories. At its helm was Edward W. Barnholt as president and CEO. Barnholt, known to employees as Ned, frequently invoked the company's connection to HP. He saw the new company as heir to Hewlett and Packard's vision, true keepers of the "HP way," as described in the 1995 book *The HP Way;* HP was an organization based upon "participatory management," one in which workers gave their best toward a common purpose in return for being treated honestly and listened to. To this model Barnholt added three values: speed, accountability, and focus. He instituted a pay-for-performance plan for managers and retrained all 6,000 of them to make better and faster decisions.

Barnholt defined the company's vision, direction, and strategy; recruited a management team; and convinced financial analysts to purchase stock. Agilent held its initial public offering (IPO) on November 18, 1999, selling approximately 65 million shares, or 15 percent of Agilent's stock, at $30 a piece. HP retained the other 85 percent. It distributed the remaining shares of Agilent stock to HP shareholders in June 2000, which made Agilent a fully independent company. Wall Street reacted favorably to the IPO, sending the stock up from its initial offering price of $30 a share to $42.44 on the first day. By year's end, that price had reached $79.25 as the market realized that Agilent's future was tied to the growth of the communications industry, specifically to the Internet, and that networks and devices were going to require more and more test equipment.

2000: AN INDEPENDENT COMPANY

Throughout 2000, Agilent introduced new products and hustled to meet orders. It also added manufacturing capacity in communications to address the strong demand for its products in those areas. By November 2000, Agilent employed 47,000 people. Its Semiconductor Products Group carved out a position for itself as one of the few chip makers to achieve strong growth in its communications and life sciences businesses. The life sciences business, part of its Chemical Analysis Group, grew about 20 percent. By 2001, 90 percent of Agilent's $2.2 billion semiconductor revenue derived from its communications segment.

However, falling orders for healthcare products during fiscal 2000 led to the layoff of about 650 workers in Agilent's Healthcare Solutions Group, and toward the end of the year, the company announced that it would sell its healthcare products business to Royal Philips Electronics N.V. for about $1.7 billion. Agilent also sold its Automation Integration Software (AIS) business to Verano. The strategy of selling its unprofitable businesses enabled it to focus on the faster-growing markets for communications and measurement equipment.

For the fiscal year ending October 31, 2000, Agilent's sales of communications test equipment rose 55 percent, making it the company's fastest-growing business. Companies such as Cisco Systems Inc. and AT&T Corp. used Agilent products to test their communications network equipment, and the company formed a key partnership with wireless chip maker Qualcomm Inc., which included the incorporation of Agilent's RFIC (radio frequency integrated circuit) test equipment with Qualcomm's RF chips. Other alliances existed with Alcatel, Rosetta Inpharmatics Inc., PE Biosystems Group, Xilinx Inc., American Healthways, ST-Microelectronics, Extended Systems Inc., and Adeptec Inc.

Agilent also engaged in a series of acquisitions throughout 2000 to complement and stretch its various businesses. These included the Silicon Valley Networking Lab, Inc., which provided a range of testing services and products to network equipment manufacturers, communications service providers, and system integrators; J&W Scientific, which became part of its chemical analysis business; American Holographic Inc., a manufacturer of holographic diffraction gratings and spectral sensor modules; Zymed Inc., a provider of cardiac analysis solutions; SAFCO Technologies, a subsidiary of Salient 3 Communications Inc. and a supplier of planning, measurement, analysis, and predictive software systems for the wireless industry; and the eCamera business unit of PhotoAccess.com Corp. Agilent also acquired Digital Technology Inc., a developer of network-protocol test solutions, and Objective Systems Integrators, whose communications test software helped Internet sites and e-commerce systems provide more reliable service.

<table>
<tr><td colspan="2" align="center">

KEY DATES
■
</td></tr>
</table>

1947: Hewlett-Packard Company incorporates on August 18.
1966: HP Laboratories is established.
1999: Hewlett-Packard creates Agilent Technologies Inc.; Agilent holds its initial public offering.
2000: Agilent becomes a fully independent company; it divests its Healthcare Solutions Group and sells its healthcare products and its Automation Integration Software (AIS) businesses.
2001: The company lays off 8,000 employees.
2002: The company launches Agilent Technologies Shanghai Co. Ltd., a joint venture with Shanghai Precision and Scientific Instrumentation Co.
2003: Agilent lays off another 4,000 employees; company collaborates with the China Integrated Circuit Design Center to establish Beijing's first system-on-a-chip engineering testing center.
2005: Bill Sullivan replaces Ned Barnholt as president and CEO; the company forms Agilent Technologies China Holding Co.
2006: Agilent sells its Semiconductor Products Group and spins off its system-on-a-chip and memory test business.

2001–02: DEALING WITH A DOWNTURN

Then came 2001 and, despite $10.8 billion in revenues, problems. Hammered by the ailing economy and the downfall in the telecoms (once the big buyers of chips, electronic components, and testing and measurement devices), Agilent's orders were down 40 to 60 percent for the year. Early in 2001, employees and executive level managers agreed to a 10 percent cut in pay until October, but in August the company had to face the fact that it had overhired from 1999 to 2000. It laid off 4,000 employees that summer and another 4,000 in December. In early 2003 another 4,000 workers were let go.

The company dealt with letting its people go "the HP way." It peppered employees with information and enlisted them in the effort to cut costs. It sent its managers to workshops to learn how to lay people off with honesty, an open door, and a willingness to answer questions. Barnholt was honest about the mistakes his company had made and his intention not to make them a second time around. "I think we did overhire, like most companies, back in the 1999–2000 time frame, and we need to recognize that we are in a cyclical business," he confessed in a 2002 *Northern Colorado Business Report*. Barnholt also said that his company had to be careful about rehiring as things turned around. "My goal is that as we do hire, we will look first to the people who left." In spite, or perhaps, because of its track record with layoffs, the company made *Fortune* magazine's "Most Admired Companies" list in 2002.

Agilent also canceled some research and development and marketing and sales activities and outsourced some of its manufacturing as part of its cutbacks. Throughout most of 2002, business remained flat while the communications market remained weak and the optical test market, which accounted for anywhere from 25 to 10 percent of Agilent's business, was a long way from recovering. Revenues dropped to $8.4 billion. The company's response was to accelerate its semiconductor product development and to switch its research and development efforts to close-to-market areas.

Agilent also began to focus its expansion efforts on China. Narrowing its strategic focus, it launched a joint venture with Shanghai Precision and Scientific Instrumentation Co., called Agilent Technologies Shanghai Co. Ltd., in 2002 to provide a software application development center for all of Agilent's business groups, including communications and semiconductor industries. In 2003, Agilent also collaborated with the China Integrated Circuit Design Center to establish Beijing's first system-on-a-chip engineering testing center.

2003–07: FOCUSING ON ELECTRONIC MEASUREMENT

Despite such realignment, in early 2003, Agilent was still posting losses. Revenues dropped again to $6 billion for the year, and the company cut its workforce by 4,000 for a third time and closed a manufacturing plant. Hoping to create new opportunities, it went after the camera-in-a-cell-phone market with a new family of camera module products called sensors that could record and transmit a photographic image over a cellular phone network. That spring, in a surprising move, it put itself in competition with IBM Microelectronics and Fujitsu; as design opportunities for single-use chips were declining, it began shopping its ASIC (application-specific integrated circuit) sockets to large original equipment manufacturers. Also in 2003, Agilent partnered with Anite Technologies to develop test solutions for wireless device manufacturers and network operators.

Despite a 30 percent decline in revenues to $7.2 billion in 2004, Agilent returned to profitability after three years of losses. Still a market leader in almost all optical test segments from lab to field, it commanded the largest optical test market share overall. The company began to aggressively market its trade-up programs for next-generation products among customers. The 2004 surge in cellphone popularity, primarily in the area of cellphone gaming, was good news for Agilent, whose test sets were used to test 70 percent of the wireless phones produced worldwide. As the number of application makers increased dramatically with the increase in games, services, and video and phone products, manufacturers required the test sets to confirm how well their components received or transmitted data at different speeds and frequencies, as well as how well a device captured a network signal as it moved farther from a cell tower.

Agilent also developed a comprehensive infrared hardware and software platform in 2004 and then partnered with Link Evolution Corp., a wireless communications software development company, to collaborate on developing an infrared financial messaging-compliant smart solution for the Japanese infrared mobile payment market. In a separate partnership, it targeted the automotive mobile phone and lighting markets with Lumileds Lighting to develop new light-emitting diodes that same year.

The following year, China's growing market continued to attract Agilent's attention and investment dollars. It formed Agilent Technologies China Holding Co. to consolidate its China-based enterprises and a joint venture with Qianfeng Electronics Corporation as a first step toward introducing its third-generation wireless telecom technology there. At home, Agilent partnered with Asylum Research to collaborate on technologies and applications in the area of nanotechnology measurements. It acquired Molecular Imaging, manufacturer of nanotechnology-measurement tools, such as modular atomic force microscopes.

CONSOLIDATING AND REORGANIZING FOR THE 21ST CENTURY

In 2005, Agilent was the world's largest electronic measurement company with about 20,000 employees internationally and about $5.1 billion in revenue. Like many other tech firms, however, Agilent was still engaged in a long process of reassessment after the tech bubble burst in 2000. Although initially slow in making changes, Agilent's efforts were surpassing those being made by the rest of the industry by 2005. Still Sonoma County's largest high-tech employer despite four years

of downsizing, Agilent cut back further in 2005, divesting itself of its nonprimary businesses to focus on its growing measurement business. It sold its Semiconductor Products Group to Kohlberg Kravis Roberts & Co. and Silver Lake Partners for $2.7 billion and announced it would spin off its system-on-a-chip and memory test business in 2006. It also sold its stake in its joint venture Lumileds Lighting to develop new light-emitting diodes. Another major component in its plan to meet the demands of the new century involved a shift in leadership. In 2005, Bill Sullivan replaced Ned Barnholt as president and CEO.

Between 2001 and 2006, Agilent had shifted most of its Sonoma County manufacturing to Asian countries. However, in 2007, the company decided to expand its presence in northern California and launched a $200 million company-wide effort to upgrade domestic facilities. Intent on providing "excellent work environments that support innovation," Agilent had invested in remodeling part of its Liberty Lake facility and upgrading its Fountaingrove campus to develop a series of low-cost spectrum analyzers for cellphones and wireless devices in 2005. In 2007, the company focused on making its Loveland, Colorado, facility the hub for the company's Operations Support Systems Group, part of its testing and measurements business. Rounding out Agilent's California facilities was Santa Rosa, where it developed wireless test and measurement instruments for aerospace and military communications.

Indeed, the company always kept one eye on future expansion. Although Agilent decided in 2005 to consolidate its northern Colorado employees from a number of locations into a single building in Loveland, it noted the presence of empty land near the site and the possibility of future construction. It also continued to engage in strategic acquisitions. Already involved in nanotechnology, it increased its presence in the life sciences sector with the 2007 acquisition of Stratagene, which developed research products and diagnostic equipment, and Velocity 11, a maker of automated and robotic life sciences laboratory equipment. Such moves seemed likely to help the company become an important player in the 21st century.

Carrie Rothburd

PRINCIPAL SUBSIDIARIES

Yokogawa Analytical Systems.

PRINCIPAL COMPETITORS

Affymetrix, Inc.; Anritsu Corporation; Ansoft Corporation; Applied Biosystems Group; Applied Materials,

Inc.; Fluke Corporation; GE Healthcare; IBM Software; Invitrogen Corporation; JDS Uniphase Corporation; Keithley Instruments Inc.; LeCroy Corporation; National Instruments Corporation; PerkinElmer, Inc.; Rohde & Schwarz GmbH & Co. KG; Tektronix, Inc.; Teradyne, Inc.; Varian, Inc.; Waters Corporation.

FURTHER READING

"Barnholt Steers Agilent Technologies Toward Profit," *Northern Colorado Business Report,* May 31, 2002, p. A12.

Bastian, Kristen S., "Consolidation at Agilent, HP Translates into 'Opportunity,'" *Northern Colorado Business Report,* November 25, 2005, p. A1.

——, "Loveland to Become Agilent Hub," *Northern Colorado Business Report,* September 16, 2005, p. 1.

"Communicating Under Pressure: Agilent Technologies CEO Receives IABC 2003 EXCEL Award," *Communication World,* August 1, 2003, p. 36.

Riply, Richard, "Agilent Rides Cellular Surge," *Journal of Business,* February 12, 2004, p. A1.

Roth, Daniel, "How to Cut Pay, Lay Off 8,000 People, and Still Have Workers Who Love You," *Fortune,* February 4, 2002, p. 62.

Souza, Crista, "Agilent Unlocks ASIC Vault and Enters Merchant Market," *EBN,* April 29, 2003, p. 1.

Sperling, Ed, and Jeff Chappell, "Biggest Test; The Back Page; Interview of Agilent Technologies CEO Ned Barnholt," *Electronic News,* November 25, 2002, p. 22.

AIR PARTNER

Air Partner PLC

—■—

Platinum House
Gatwick Road
Crawley, RH10 9RP
United Kingdom
Telephone: (+44 1293) 844 888
Toll Free: (888) AIR-PARTNER (888-247-7278)
Fax: (+44 1293) 539 263
Web site: http://www.airpartner.com

Public Company
Incorporated: 1961 as Airways Training Ltd.
Employees: 250
Sales: £185.78 million (2007)
Stock Exchanges: London
Ticker Symbol: AIP
NAIC: 481211 Nonscheduled Chartered Passenger Air
Transportation; 481212 Nonscheduled Chartered
Freight Air Transportation

■ ■ ■

Air Partner PLC is the world's leading broker of aircraft charters. Every year it handles thousands of transactions for commercial planes ranging from business aircraft to jumbo jets. Its largest projects involve mustering dozens of airliners to ferry thousands of delegates to international product launches.

Air Partner's commercial division accounts for a majority of revenues. Much of the rest comes from private jets, with freight providing a small but growing percentage of sales. The company is also developing travel, emergency planning, and flight support businesses.

With approximately two-dozen offices in the United Kingdom and abroad, Air Partner is able to cover most of the globe on short notice. Clients include celebrities, large corporations, and government agencies. The company has responded to market developments by bringing out its own "JetCard" program, offering prepaid access to private aircraft on an hourly basis.

FOUNDING IN 1961

Air Partner PLC traces its origins to 1961, when Tony Mack, Sr., launched Airways Training Ltd., a commercial flying school for ex-RAF pilots at London's Gatwick Airport. Mack was a veteran of the Berlin Airlift and had flown international charters for Skyways Ltd. and Air Safaris Ltd. According to *Air Transport World*, his original investment was just £100.

The pilot training led to some air taxi work to keep the company's aircraft busy on the weekends. In the 1960s, the school owned a half-dozen light planes of the type made by Piper and Beagle Aircraft, available for £15 an hour. The fleet grew slowly over the next couple of decades, at one point including a BAe 146 commuter jet. However, in 1983 the company sold its planes to focus on brokering.

Tony Mack, Jr., son of the company founder, told the *Sunday Times* the business really took off after they began chartering other people's aircraft, an innovation for which he himself is credited. Many privately owned planes typically spent most of their time parked on the

---

COMPANY PERSPECTIVES

Air Partner is a world-class company; it provides every type of aircraft, for every conceivable mission, in every part of the planet. No other company does what we do. Our reputation for absolute discretion, reliability and innovation has been forged over almost 50 years.

---

tarmac, and increasing their utilization unlocked a tremendous amount of value. This new business was launched in 1970 as Air London Ltd. Leadership of the company passed to the founder's son in 1979. He had spent most of his career working for his father's business, apart from a brief stint in banking.

AN INTERNATIONAL CORPORATION

Air London began the 1980s with revenues of £1 million, according to Britain's *Financial Times*. In 1986 the company moved from Gatwick's original building to Mack House. During the year it also made an acquisition, buying Merlin Aviation. By 1987 annual sales were up to £5 million. Clients included celebrities, large corporations, and government agencies.

The company offered some shares to the public on the Unlisted Securities Market in November 1989. Revenues were up to £10 million. There were then just 20 employees. It snagged a listing on the London Stock Exchange in 1995. The parent company, Air London plc, was renamed Air Partner in 1999. Revenues were £74 million in the 2000 fiscal year.

Increasing profits allowed the company to bankroll new international offices. It set up its first foreign subsidiary, Paris-based Air Partner International SARL, in 1994. It originally held a majority interest in the unit, with the rest held by Claude Giunta, a veteran of Air France's charter business.

A German unit was established in mid-1997. Air Partner Inc., the U.S. subsidiary, opened in Fort Lauderdale, Florida, in September 1997. It originally focused on serving the local cruise lines. By 2007, the company had 21 offices around the world.

As it grew geographically, the firm also expanded its range of services into virtually every aspect of civil aviation. A freight division was formed in 1998. Air Partner developed a specialty in evacuating corporate personnel from far-flung places whenever trouble emerged. This work came to the fore during the Gulf

War. The company formalized its emergency evacuation service in 1999.

AN EVOLVING MARKET

Air Partner faced a rising challenge from fractional ownership programs, which were essentially timeshares for jets. In the mid-1990s the company was part of its own joint ownership scheme, the Jet Network Company Ltd. (JetCo); this, however, proved short-lived. Several years later, in 2001, Air Partner participated in another program with British Airways that offered part owners the option of connecting flights in their own jets to the carrier's scheduled flights. This, too, was soon shuttered.

The company remained largely aloof of the fractional ownership model led by such companies as NetJets, Inc. In most cases, Air Partner maintained, it was better to charter a jet than own one. Fractional ownership was more of a "status symbol," sniffed Air Partner Managing Director David Savile. The company responded to developments in the market by bringing out its own "JetCard" membership program in July 2006. This offered prepaid access to private aircraft on an hourly basis.

STILL CLIMBING

The argument for chartering seemed to get even better after the turn of the millennium. The September 11, 2001, terrorist attacks on the United States left many people wary of flying with strangers at all, at least temporarily. The security measures and long lines that followed led to a further degradation of the commercial flying experience. There was also increased work related to military operations in the Middle East, which helped turnover peak at £191 million in 2004.

While private jet travel seemed an efficient and productive option for traveling businesspeople, in the age of Sarbanes-Oxley, it could be more embarrassing than ever to have ownership of private jets on the balance sheet. Air Partner was not limited to executive jets when it came to serving the corporate world. It had developed a particular specialty in carrying thousands of delegates to international product launches, projects that could require chartering dozens of airliners. It also put together transportation to bankers squeezing in as many destinations as possible during the lead-ins to initial public offerings.

In October 2006 business-jet operator and management company Gold Air International Ltd. was acquired from Gold Group for £4.4 million. Gold Air had annual sales of about £11 million. It had been launched by brothers David and Ralph Gold in 1985. At the time of

KEY DATES

1961: Tony Mack, Sr., launches a commercial flying school for ex-RAF pilots.

1970: Mack forms the Air London Ltd. charter brokering business.

1989: Air London becomes a public company.

1994: Air Partner SARL is established in Paris as company's first international subsidiary.

1995: Shares are listed on the London Stock Exchange.

1997: Subsidiaries are established in the United States and Germany.

1998: Freight Division is launched.

1999: Parent company is renamed Air Partner; emergency evacuation service is launched.

2006: Business-jet operator and management company Gold Air International is acquired.

the acquisition Gold Air had several of its own executive jets, most of them brand new, with another two on order. The purchase brought Air Partner back into the operation of its own commercial flights for the first time since 1983. Air Partner's revenues rose by a third in the 2007 fiscal year, reaching £185.8 million. The company that had been launched with £100 46 years earlier now had a market capitalization of more than £100 million.

Frederick C. Ingram

PRINCIPAL SUBSIDIARIES

Air Partner International SAS (France; 55%); Air Partner International GmbH (Germany); Air Partner Inc. (U.S.A.); Air Partner Switzerland AG; Air Partner Travel Consultants Limited; Air Partner Srl (Italy); Air Partner Leasing Pty Limited (Australia).

PRINCIPAL DIVISIONS

Commercial Jets; Private Jets; Freight.

PRINCIPAL OPERATING UNITS

Air Partner Austria; Air Partner Benelux; Air Partner Dubai; Air Partner France; Air Partner Germany; Air Partner Hungary; Air Partner India; Air Partner Italy; Air Partner Japan; Air Partner Spain; Air Partner Sweden; Air Partner Switzerland; Air Partner UK; Air Partner USA.

PRINCIPAL COMPETITORS

European Aviation Group; FlightTime; NetJets Inc.; PrivateAir Group.

FURTHER READING

"Air London Sets Up Two New Subsidiaries," *Reuters News,* August 23, 1994.

"Air Partner (AIP)," *Investors Chronicle,* April 13, 2007.

Bennett, Neil, "Air London International—USM Debut," *Times* (London), November 6, 1989.

Boschat, Nathalie, "Europe Stk Focus: Air Partner Getting Small Boost from War," *Dow Jones International News,* April 26, 1999.

Bray, Roger, "Private Aircraft in the Mainstream; Business Travel Jets: A Deal Between BA and a Charter Broker May Popularise Corporate Jets," *Financial Times* (London), Inside Track Sec., May 1, 2001, p. 15.

Bryant, Chris, "Jet Propulsion," *Financial Times* (London), Companies UK Sec., August 9, 2007, p. 21.

Cohen, Amon, "Corporate Customers' Loyalty Holding Firm: Charter Brokers," *Financial Times* (London), Survey—Corporate Aviation, December 12, 2001, p. 2.

Done, Kevin, "Air Partner Builds Up Jet-for-Leisure Business," *Financial Times* (London), Smaller Companies UK Sec., April 7, 2006, p. 21.

———, "Air Partner Enters Private Jet Market with Gold Air Deal," *Financial Times* (London), Companies UK Sec., October 12, 2006, p. 26.

———, "Air Partner in Jets for Leisure Challenge," *Financial Times* (London), Companies UK Sec., May 3, 2006, p. 20.

———, "Air Partner Soars on Strong Demand," *Financial Times* (London), Companies International Sec., October 12, 2007, p. 16.

———, "Business Aircraft Charter Orders Point to Recovery," *Financial Times* (London), Companies UK Sec., October 10, 2003, p. 25.

———, "Charter Switches Boost Air Partner," *Financial Times* (London), Companies & Finance UK & Ireland Sec., October 11, 2002, p. 25.

———, "City Rediscovers the Joy of the Private Jet," *Financial Times* (London), Smaller Companies UK Sec., October 7, 2004, p. 28.

———, "Demand for Emergency Rescues Lifts Air Partner," *Financial Times* (London), Companies & Finance UK Sec., April 17, 2002, p. 24.

———, "Strong Charter Demand Sees Air Partner Rising Rapidly," *Financial Times* (London), Companies UK Sec., April 5, 2007, p. 18.

———, "US Contracts Help to Lift Air Partner," *Financial Times* (London), Companies International Sec., April 8, 2005, p. 23.

Gimbel, Florian, "Global 'Hotspots' a Boon for Air Partner," *Financial Times* (London), Companies & Finance UK & Ireland Sec., October 20, 2000, p. 27.

"Government to Take Over Beagle for £1m.; First Fully Nationalized Air Building Firm," *Times* (London), December 13, 1966, p. 10.

Gunnion, Stephen, "Air Partner Gains Altitude As Demand for Charters Grows," *Investors Chronicle,* August 9, 2007.

Kavanagh, Paul, "Sky Is the Limit As Air London Spreads Its Wings," *Sunday Times,* February 8, 1998.

Kingsley-Jones, Max, "Charter House: Air London Is One of the Largest Business Air-Charter Brokers," *Flight International,* August 14, 1996.

Lee, John "Blue Skies Beckon for Air Charter Broker; My Portfolio: Profits Are Poised to Take Off at Air Partners As It Continues to Expand," *Financial Times* (London), Equity Markets Sec., November 11, 2000, p. 3.

Levere, Jane L., "A Way Around Air Rage: The Charter Flight," *New York Times,* November 26, 2000, p. BU9.

Morais, Richard C., "Flight to Safety," *Forbes,* May 29, 2000, p. 166.

"Pilots 'Wait a Month' for Flying Tests; Shortage of Examiners May Cut B.E.A. Recruiting," *Times* (London), March 6, 1967, p. 3.

Prynn, Jonathan, "Air London Aims to Fly High in US," *Evening Standard,* April 29, 1998, p. D34.

Reed, Arthur, "Busy Broker," *Air Transport World,* January 1, 1999.

Rigby, Elizabeth, "Air Partner's Business Takes Off," *Financial Times* (London), Companies & Finance UK & Ireland Sec., October 11, 2001, p. 24.

Sarsfield, Kate, "VIP 747 Sale Fills Concorde Niche," *Flight International,* November 21, 2000, p. 31.

Shelley, Toby, "Air Partner Hit by Pre-War Lull," *Financial Times* (London), Companies & Finance UK & Ireland Sec., January 8, 2003, p. 22.

"Smaller Companies: Analysis: Air London Rides the Gulf War Tail Wind—With Prestigious Customers Including the MOD and the UN, Air London Seems Capable of Prospering Whether World Air Travel Is Flying High or Down in the Dumps," *Investors Chronicle,* November 1, 1991, p. 64.

Smith, Alison, "Air Partner Expands with Rapid Evacuation Wing," *Financial Times* (London), Companies & Finance UK Sec., April 20, 2000, p. 26.

Steiner, Rupert, "Flying Start for Charter Chief Who Was Born in a Hangar," *Sunday Times,* Bus. Sec., April 20, 1997.

Tieman, Ross, "Demand 'Still Reasonably Firm': Flexible Chartered Services in Europe Have Seen a Welcome Increase in Recent Weeks," *Financial Times* (London), FT Report—European Corporate Aviation 2003, May 7, 2003, p. 2.

————, "How to Set Up a Whistle-Stop Tour: Up to 40 International Meetings in Six Days," *Financial Times* (London), FT Report—European Corporate Aviation 2003, May 7, 2003, p. 2.

————, "Launches Help Keep the Fleets Flying and Afloat; Charter Market: Flexibility, Safety and Privacy Are Winning Charters, Says Ross Tieman," *Financial Times* (London), FT Report—Corporate Aviation, October 8, 2003, p. 3.

"Tip of the Week: Air London International—On Board with Air London—If You Have the Stomach for a Bumpy Ride, Air Charter Broker Air London International Could Be Just the Ticket; Its Shares Are a Buy in the Long Term," *Investors Chronicle,* November 8, 1996, p. 66.

Voyle, Susanna, "Air Partner Wants to Be the Flexible Friend of the World's Jet Set," *Financial Times,* Companies & Finance UK and Ireland Sec., August 5, 1999, p. 23.

AirAsia Berhad

———— ■ ————

Mezzanine Floor, LCC Terminal Jalan KLIA S3
Southern Support Zone, Kuala Lumpur
International Airport
Sepang, Selangor Darul Ehsan 64000
Malaysia
Telephone: (+603) 8660 4330
Fax: (+603) 8775 4373
Web site: http://www.airasia.com

Public Company
Incorporated: 1996 as AirAsia Berhad
Employees: 3,000
Sales: $458 million (2007)
Stock Exchanges: Malaysia
Ticker Symbol: AIRASIA 5099
NAIC: 481111 Scheduled Passenger Air Transportation;
481112 Scheduled Freight Air Transportation;
561510 Travel Agencies

■ ■ ■

AirAsia Berhad claims the title of Asia's first low-cost carrier. Using a business model pioneered by Southwest Airlines in the United States and Ryanair and easyJet in Europe, AirAsia does away with amenities such as frequent flier miles in favor of low fares. It boasts the lowest operating costs in the industry.

Based in Kuala Lumpur, Malaysia, the airline flies a fleet of five-dozen aircraft to more than 70 destinations in Southeast Asia. In 2006 about 18 million passengers traveled via AirAsia, including joint ventures in Thailand and Indonesia. Another affiliate, AirAsia X, was

established in 2007 to apply the no-frills ethic to long-haul flights.

RELAUNCH AS NO FRILLS AIRLINE IN 2001

AirAsia Berhad was but a tiny airline when an investment group acquired it in 2001. Its new leader, Tony Fernandes, would take AirAsia to unprecedented heights by restyling it as a no frills airline.

Born in Malaysia to an Indian father, Fernandes attended boarding school in the United Kingdom and studied at the London School of Economics. He worked in high level accounting positions at Virgin Communications London and Warner Music International London before returning home in 1992 to lead Warner's operations, first in Malaysia and later the entire ASEAN region.

An article on EasyJet plc got Fernandes thinking about launching his own budget airline. This U.K. carrier had stormed the European market by applying the low-cost business model that had brought Southwest Airlines such success in the United States. Ireland's Ryanair was another popular exemplar of the concept; its operations chief, Conor McCarthy, was hired to run things at AirAsia.

Fernandes felt certain Asia was ripe for the low-cost, low-fare formula, but there were skeptics. According to *Air Transport World*, some industry observers were dubious since Hong Kong-based Cathay Pacific and Singapore Airlines had reputations as two of the most efficient carriers in the world.

COMPANY PERSPECTIVES

∎

AirAsia strives to maximize profit and provide low fares and quality service. The airline has optimized costs by operating a faster turnaround time, improving aircraft utilization and crew efficiency, providing a "no frills" service, using one type of aircraft to save training costs, all of which result in savings which are passed back to consumers in the form of low fares.

Fernandes was not deterred. He formed a holding company called Tune Air Sdn Bhd, and entered the airline business by buying a tiny, struggling carrier called AirAsia. He acquired it for little more than a song: one Malaysian ringgit (a little more than an American quarter dollar), plus assumed debt of $11 million (MYR 40 million; this was only half of the total net liabilities). The DRB-HICOM auto manufacturing group was the seller in the deal, which closed in December 2001.

AirAsia had originally been launched in November 1996 and had operated under the name Pacific Eagle Airlines. It flew charter routes to international vacation spots, beginning with Pattaya, Thailand. However, at the time it was controlled by Malaysian government interests and prevented from competing directly with newly privatized flag carrier Malaysia Airlines (MAS). Ambitious expansion plans were dashed by the Asian financial crisis of the late 1990s.

AirAsia already operated two of the Boeing 737s that had become the standard low-cost carrier workhorse. Fernandes added another 737 when the carrier was relaunched; keeping to a single aircraft reduced maintenance and training expenses.

The reborn carrier was an instant success, thanks to its extremely low fares. Passage on the Kuala Lumpur–Penang route could be had for MYR 39 ($10), less than half what MAS was asking and a little less than bus fare for the equivalent journey.

RAPID GROWTH

AirAsia carried 611,000 passengers in its first full fiscal year. Within three years it was carrying nearly three million people a year. As it grew, it opened a training center to maintain its flow of flight crews, and to train pilots for other airlines.

Tune Air, AirAsia's holding company, sold stakes in the airline in its first few years of ownership in order to finance the acquisition of new aircraft, one or two at a time. By June 2003, the once worthless company was valued at $100 million, given the 26 percent stake acquired by foreign investors for $26 million (MYR 99 million).

In spite of its youth, or perhaps because of it, AirAsia was a quite innovative airline. In August 2003 it became the first to book tickets via mobile phone text messages. Another unique initiative was inserting advertisements in its annual reports.

EXPANDING TERRITORY

AirAsia was unable to immediately fly into Singapore, but in late 2003 started a service to a city just inside Malaysia's border with its neighbor. In fact this town, Senai, was designated a second hub for AirAsia.

The company expanded into other countries in 2004 by setting up joint ventures with local partners. These were executed via its AirAsia International Limited (AAIL) subsidiary. The first, which began flying in January 2004, brought AirAsia into Thailand. It was a 49 percent partner in the venture with Shin Corporation. It launched with just a pair of planes but grew rapidly, adding international flights to Singapore and Macau, a center for tourism and gambling on the coast of southern China. AirAsia's enterprise in Indonesia took over an existing operation, PT AWAIR. AirAsia bought a 49 percent holding in it in November 2004 and refashioned it as a low-cost carrier within a month.

2004 INITIAL PUBLIC OFFERING

The company went public in November 2004 in an offering that raised MYR 717 million. This was a bit less than planned, but respectable given the state of the world airline industry, which was beleaguered by record fuel prices. It was also one of the largest Malaysian initial public offerings (IPOs) to date. The offering placed 30 percent of shares on the market and lowered Tune Air's stake to about 45 percent.

In December 2004, AirAsia strayed from its loyalty to the Boeing 737 by ordering up to 80 of Airbus's midsize A320 model. The reason was mainly due to lower cost. A global lull in the aviation business attributed to SARS and the war in Iraq kept aircraft prices down, intensifying the pricing pressure on manufacturers. The original order was quickly expanded to 100; AirAsia made a similarly large order just three years later.

KEY DATES
■

1996: AirAsia is launched in Malaysia as a small, alternative airline.

2001: Tony Fernandes acquires AirAsia, relaunches it as a privately owned, low-cost carrier.

2003: AirAsia is first airline to book tickets via mobile phone text messages.

2004: AirAsia forms local ventures in Thailand and Indonesia, holds public offering.

2007: A second airline, AirAsia X, begins long-haul flights, starting with a Malaysia-Australia route.

AIRASIA X

AirAsia had come a long way as a strictly short-haul carrier. In January 2007 it announced plans to tackle the long-haul market. It was aiming to extend its reach as far as the United Kingdom by the end of 2008. The plans for long-haul routes were a departure from the typical low-cost carrier business model, and they were being handled by a separate company, Fly Asian Xpress (FAX).

FAX had been formed in 2006 to take over some regional routes once operated by Malaysia Airlines, which was undergoing a massive restructuring. FAX attracted substantial venture capital interest. Fernandes owned half the stock; one of the minority shareholders was none other than legendary globetrotter Sir Richard Branson.

Fernandes was involved in a number of other side ventures besides AirAsia X. By 2008, his Tune Air Sdn Bhd holding company was involved in hotels, music, credit cards, and education, each project operating with a no-frills ethic, which Fernandes described in Malaysia's *Business Times* as "low price but of high quality and taking out things one [doesn't] really want."

There was more to AirAsia X than the long-haul flights themselves. Fernandes was attempting to forge marketing links with other low-cost carriers such as Ryanair and easyJet. This had the potential, observed *Airline Business,* of creating the first international alliance of budget airlines. However, the others first had to take him up on the deal, which, as originally envisioned, offered merely exchanged website links, rather than the seamless integrated travel experience of the major world airline cliques. "I don't think you'll ever see a Star Alliance of budget airlines," said Fernandes.

The long-haul idea had been Fernandes's original plan for AirAsia before he bought it in 2001. However, advisers convinced him to focus instead on the local market. Just a few years later, the new long-haul, low-cost concept was no longer unique: a handful of new budget airlines were trying their wings from bases in Asia and Australia.

ROOM TO GROW

The growth of open skies in the ASEAN (Association of Southeast Asian) countries and an increasingly affluent customer base were expected to bode well for the region's airlines, particularly low-cost carriers, noted *BusinessWeek.* AirAsia's massive aircraft orders put it in good stead as the industry began to show signs of recovery. Other, less ambitious carriers were finding their growth constrained by a lack of new aircraft on the market. AirAsia was looking to establish more joint ventures in Vietnam and the Philippines. Another area with growth potential was increasing use of the cargo space inside the company's aircraft.

Frederick C. Ingram

PRINCIPAL SUBSIDIARIES

AirAsia Go Holiday Sdn Bhd; Crunchtime; AirAsia International Limited (99.8%); AirAsia Mauritius; AirAsia Philippines; AirAsia (B) Sdn Bhd.

PRINCIPAL COMPETITORS

Tiger Airways Pte Ltd; Malaysian Airline System Berhad; Singapore Airlines Limited.

FURTHER READING

"AirAsia Goes on Offensive," *Airline Business,* December 1, 2003, p. 27.

"AirAsia IPO Falls Below Expectations," *Airfinance Journal,* November 2004, p. 13.

"AirAsia to Gain from MAS Revamp," *Flight International,* April 4, 2006.

Ballantyne, Tom, "Eagle Lands in MAS' Lair," *Airline Business,* November 1996, p. 18.

———, "Malay Duo to Share Routes," *Airline Business,* June 1997, p. 22.

Barrie, Douglas, "Regional Ramp-Up: Frontrunner in Asia's Low-Cost Realm Set to Name Its Narrow-Body Choice," *Aviation Week & Space Technology,* December 6, 2004, pp. 48+.

"Beginner's Luck: Asian Start-Ups Are Finding It Difficult to Find Fleet Financing; As More Airlines Are Muscling In on the Lucrative Asian Markets, This Is Set to Become Much Worse," *Airfinance Journal,* June 2005, pp. 28–30.

Chu, Jeff, "The $3 Flight; Tony Fernandes Had No Aviation Experience When He Founded His No-Frills Carrier, AirAsia. It's Now Among the Fastest-Growing Airlines in the World," *Condé Nast Portfolio,* November 2007, pp. 86–94.

Doebele, Justin, "Proletariat Capitalist," *Forbes,* June 18, 2007, p. 128.

Done, Kevin, "AirAsia Chief Spreads His Wings," *FT.com,* October 28, 2007.

——, "AirAsia X Locks Up More Funds," *FT.com,* October 28, 2007.

Fernandez, Francis, "AirAsia May Buy More Planes to Meet Seat Demand," *Business Times* (Malaysia), July 28, 1999.

Ganesan, Vasantha, "Fernandes Gets in Tune with the Market," *Business Times* (Malaysia), December 26, 2007.

Gupta, Ritesh, "Eastern Star; Company Overview," *Airfinance Journal,* November 1, 2006.

Ionides, Nicholas, "AirAsia Raises $227m in Share Sale As It Prepares to Renew Its Fleet," *Flight International,* November 9, 2004, p. 25.

——, "Man of the Moment," *Airline Business,* April 1, 2004, p. 27.

Ionides, Nicholas, and Brendan Sobie, "About Turn for AirAsia As It Expands into the Long Haul," *Airline Business,* January 22, 2007.

Jayasankaran, S., and Cris Prystay, "Fare Fight: Upstart Shakes Up the Clubby World of Asian Flying," *Wall Street Journal Europe,* July 20, 2004, p. A1.

Knibb, David, "Seconds Out, MAS Doubts," *Airline Business,* August 1994, p. 16.

"Malaysia's No-Frills AirAsia Ready for IPO Take-Off This Month," *Euroweek,* October 15, 2004, p. 25.

"The Mêlée in Malaysia," *Aircraft Economics,* May/June 2005, pp. 14, 16.

"New Owners for Thai AirAsia," *Airline Business,* April 1, 2006.

Perrett, Bradley, "X Marks the Spot," *Aviation Week & Space Technology,* January 8, 2007, pp. 34+.

Saywell, Trish, and Scott Newman, "No Frills, Smaller Bills," *Far Eastern Economic Review,* July 10, 2003, pp. 32+.

Shameen, Assif, "Asia Takes Flight on Low-Cost Carriers; Taking a Cue from Ryanair and EasyJet, Budget Fliers Such As AirAsia and Tiger Are Opening Up the Skies over India, China, and Southeast Asia," *Business Week Online,* October 2, 2006.

Sritama, Suchat, "AirAsia X in It for the Long Haul," *Nation* (Thailand), August 11, 2007.

"Taking the Long View," *Airline Business,* January 22, 2007.

Thomas, Geoffrey, "AirAsia's New Worlds," *Air Transport World,* April 2007, pp. 24–28.

——, "In Tune with Low Fares in Malaysia; Former Music Executive Tony Fernandes Appears to Have Hit the Right Chord with AirAsia," *Air Transport World,* May 2003, pp. 45–46.

——, "Revolution Deferred but Not Denied; After Years of Defying Trends in the US and Europe, the Asia/Pacific Region Has Climbed Aboard the Budget Airline Revolution Train," *Air Transport World,* August 2004, pp. 28–30.

"Tune Air Aiming to Recapitalize AirAsia," *Airline Industry Information,* December 14, 2001.

Almost Family, Inc.

■

9510 Ormsby Station Road, Suite 300
Louisville, Kentucky 40223
U.S.A.
Telephone: (502) 891-1000
Toll Free: (800) 845-6987
Fax: (502) 891-8067
Web site: http://www.almostfamily.com

Public Company
Incorporated: 1985 as Caretenders Health Corp.
Employees: 3,200
Operating Revenues: $91.8 million (2007)
Stock Exchanges: NASDAQ
Ticker Symbol: AFAM
NAIC: 813319 Other Social Advocacy Organizations; 621610 Home Health Care Services; 624120 Services for the Elderly and Persons with Disabilities; 624190 Other Individual and Family Services

■ ■ ■

Almost Family, Inc., home health nursing services provides an alternative to nursing home care to senior citizens in nine states: Florida, Kentucky, Ohio, Connecticut, Massachusetts, Alabama, Indiana, Illinois, and Missouri. It operates through two segments: its Medicare-certified visiting nurse program, known as Caretenders, and its in-home personal care, housekeeping, and medical escort services. Chairman and CEO William Yarmuth and his wife, Senior Vice-President Mary Yarmuth, own about 22 percent of the company.

Approximately 92 percent of the visiting nurse program revenues come from Medicare.

SEARCHING FOR AN IDENTITY: 1976–92

In 1976, Linda Mudd formed Caretenders, a personal care service company based in Louisville, Kentucky, with the help of William Yarmuth, a young stockbroker at Olmstead Bros. Three years later, Olmstead was sold to J. C. Bradford & Co., and Yarmuth, who had made the move from Olmstead, invested in Caretenders along with three of his siblings. Yarmuth went on to serve on Caretenders' board of directors and then became president of the company in 1981, at which point Caretenders had annual revenues of about $1 million. In 1982, Caretenders established its home health division and gained Medicare certification.

By 1991, Caretenders had revenues of $26 million. That year the company changed its name not once, but twice; it became Senior Service Corporation after merging with a parent company of the same name. Kenneth Hamlet was chairman and chief executive officer and William Yarmuth president. As Senior Service Corporation, the company established an adult care division and extended its operations to Maryland and Connecticut. It held its initial public offering (IPO) on the NASDAQ where it listed as SENR.

The second name change took place in December 1991, by which point the company offered home health services in Kentucky, Alabama, Indiana, Virginia, and Massachusetts, having purchased Care Services Inc. of Richmond, Virginia, and Metro Home Care of

Louisville. The board of directors voted to call the company Caretenders HealthCorp (listed as CTND), with Kenneth Hamlet as chairman and chief executive, and set up a subsidiary called Almost Family that operated adult day-care centers in Maryland and Connecticut. Each of these centers provided care for an average of 60 persons per day. In 1992, William Yarmuth replaced Kenneth Hamlet as chairman and chief executive officer of Caretenders Healthcorp as well as continuing on as the company's president.

ESTABLISHING A VISION FOR "ONE-STOP-SHOPPING": 1992

Known for being persistent and competitive, William Yarmuth had attended the University of Pennsylvania and Wharton School of Finance before becoming a stockbroker. However, he had been exposed to the world of business from his childhood; his father, Stanley Yarmuth, had transformed National Industries, a holding company, from a venture with fewer than $1 million in annual sales into the 371st largest public company worldwide with annual revenue of $807 million in 1975.

Yarmuth wanted the company "to be considered a leader and a major player in the home-health care industry," according to the text of a 1992 *Business First—Louisville* article. He intended the company to develop the then-fledgling industry of adult day care in the United States by providing services for people with memory problems, Alzheimer's disease, or other dementias; for people recovering from strokes, heart attacks, or accidents; for people who needed help with eating, bathing, or other activities of daily living; and for people who had developmental disabilities.

One of the strategies that Yarmuth established to distinguish his company from others in its field was to provide comprehensive services, so-called one-stop shopping or home healthcare for seniors or those with disabilities. The goal was to offer a broad array of services in easy-to-reach locations within communities both to help individuals and families manage chronic illness and to prevent premature admission to nursing homes. According to Yarmuth in the 1992 article

mentioned above, "That's where home health care has to go. Everybody's looking to make things as simple as possible."

FINDING A WAY TO GROW: 1992–98

Caretenders continued to expand within Maryland and Connecticut and to extend its reach along the East Coast throughout the early 1990s. However, its steady growth in numbers was not paralleled by comparable growth in revenues. Despite sales of $42.1 million for fiscal 1991, the company had not turned a profit since 1987. Thus, in 1993, the company sold its Healthcare Review Corp. subsidiary to National Health Services, Inc. Healthcare Review provided utilization review services, preapproval of hospital stays, and monitoring of care.

The sale of Healthcare Review enabled Caretenders to concentrate on its home healthcare and adult day-care programs at a time when the in-home care market was providing ample opportunities for growth. Home healthcare companies could benefit from the ongoing aging of the American population, pressure by insurance companies to move healthcare outside of hospitals, and better technology that allowed patients to stay at home. In fiscal 1993 alone, for example, Caretenders tallied up 100,000 home nursing service visits in seven states. In 1994, there were nine Almost Family day-care centers on the East Coast, and Caretenders had plans to increase that number to 70 centers nationwide by 1997.

During the following two years, 1994 and 1995, Caretenders partnered with Columbia/HCA Healthcare Corp., selling two home healthcare agencies to the latter. The agreement provided for Columbia to oversee the company's nursing operations for five years with Caretenders continuing to manage the agencies. However, in 1998 Columbia sold the agencies, and Caretenders sought recovery of lost income through litigation. Columbia paid Caregivers $1.5 million for breach of contract.

Meanwhile, during the second half of the 1990s, Caretenders kept on growing. In 1995, it opened an Almost Family adult day-care center in Louisville and one in Indianapolis. The company's revenues reached $60.8 million in 1995 and began to climb steadily. By 1996, Caretenders was in the midst of an aggressive growth period. Beginning in March of that year, the company opened five and acquired two new home care operations and opened one day-care center. Revenues for the year totaled $76 million. By 1997, there were 20 Almost Family adult day-care centers in seven states. In 1998, with 21 Almost Family facilities, Caretenders had

KEY DATES

1976: Caretenders begins operation in Louisville, Kentucky, as a personal care service company.

1981: William Yarmuth becomes president of Caretenders.

1982: Caretenders establishes its home health division and gains Medicare certification.

1985: The company incorporates.

1991: Caretenders merges with and changes its name to Senior Service Corporation; the company is listed on the NASDAQ as SENR; Caretenders sets up Almost Family with Kenneth Hamlet as chairman and chief executive.

1992: William Yarmuth replaces Kenneth Hamlet as chairman and chief executive.

1998: Caretenders purchases Metro Home Care and Visiting Nurse Association of Palm Beach County.

2000: Company changes its name to Almost Family, Inc.

2005: Company sells its adult day-care division to Active Services, Inc.; acquires three visiting nurse operations in Florida.

2006: Company acquires all the home health agencies owned by Mederi, Inc.

become the nation's largest operator of adult day-care centers. It served 1,100 clients daily with meals, transportation, onsite nurses, and recreational activities.

ENSURING GROWTH AS ALMOST FAMILY: 1998–2007

Nationally, home health totaled 3 percent of total healthcare expenditures or about $36 billion in 1996. In response, Caretenders strategically focused on the home health side of its business, primarily in Florida, during the remainder of the 1990s. In 1998, it purchased Metro Home Care, a large Florida provider of home healthcare that had entered Chapter 11 reorganization due to financial difficulties related to its non-Medicare services. It also purchased Visiting Nurse Association of Palm Beach County.

Despite changes to Medicare, occurring from October 1997 through October 1999, Almost Family's revenues increased impressively. Medicare first rolled payments back to 1993 levels and, then beginning in 1999, started paying the industry a flat fee for a specific

diagnosis. After suffering losses in 1999 and 2000, Almost Family experienced positive earnings on revenues of $49.6 million in 2001, $85.8 million in 2002, $83.3 million in 2003, and $86.8 million in 2004.

After changing its name to Almost Family in 2000 (its visiting nurse services continued to operate as Caretenders), the company embarked on a series of purchases to ensure ongoing growth. It bought Medlink of Ohio, a provider of home health services, in 2002. From 2004 to 2005, it purchased three Florida-based home health agencies. In 2006, it purchased the 21 Medicare-certified home health agencies located in Florida, Missouri, and Illinois of Mederi, Inc., one of Florida's oldest and best-known companies in the home healthcare field. In 2007, it acquired BayCare HomeCare's home health agency in Jacksonville, Florida, and all of the four Medicare-certified home health agencies owned and operated by Quality of Life Holdings, Inc.

FOCUSING ON MEDICARE REVENUES: 2005–07

During this same period, the company decided to sell its adult day-care division, which accounted for about two-thirds of its business, to Active Services Inc. of Alabama. Although attendance at the company's 19 day-care centers in Ohio, Maryland, Connecticut, Massachusetts, Alabama, and Indiana had increased, the revenues generated by each patient had declined due to declining reimbursement rates. The sale took place in 2005, leaving Almost Family with two divisions, its visiting nurse program and its personal care unit, which provided in-home custodial care services.

This move better prepared Almost Family to focus on its goal of increasing Medicare revenues to two-thirds of its total by 2010. By 2006, 52 percent of Almost Family's sales derived from visiting nurse/home healthcare revenue, of which Medicare paid 93 percent. Personal care was responsible for the remaining 48 percent of revenue, with 72 percent of that coming from Medicare. Despite the fact that in mid-2006 Medicare issued another challenge to home healthcare providers when it repealed its already implemented pay increase of 3 percent retroactively to January 1, 2006, the company had profits on revenues of $84.8 million that year.

As a company heavily dependent on government reimbursement for services, Almost Family had the dual task of waging an ongoing educational campaign with state and federal officials to maintain or increase payment for its services and of increasing its volume of patients while controlling expenses. In 2007, debt free, with cash to spare and few publicly traded rivals, Almost Family appeared to be "positioned to take advantage of first the growth in the senior population and the desire of people to remain in their homes and be independent," as Yarmuth had forecast in 2002 in a *Business First* article.

Carrie Rothburd

PRINCIPAL SUBSIDIARIES

Adult Day Care of America, Inc.; Adult Day Care of Maryland, Inc.; HHJC Holdings, Inc.; National Health Industries, Inc.; Pro-Care Home Health of Broward, Inc.

PRINCIPAL COMPETITORS

Amedisys, Inc.; Gentiva Health Services, Inc.; National Healthcare Corporation; Option Care, Inc.

FURTHER READING

Benmour, Eric, "Caretenders Bets on Future Earnings with Growth Spurt," *Business First—Louisville,* September 9, 1996, p. 1.

——, "Yarmuth Carries on Father's Business Prowess: Builds Caretenders into $40 Million Company," *Business First—Louisville,* May 25, 1992, p. 22.

Butgereit, Betsy, "Home Health Care Changes Medicare Funding Cuts, New Rules Could Mean Fewer Patient Services," *Birmingham (Ala.) News,* December 1, 1997, p. 1D.

Eckhouse, John, "Day Care Isn't Just for Kids: Centers for Adults Are Seen As a Big Business Opportunity," *San Francisco Chronicle,* October 2, 1992, p. B1.

Gordon, Jennifer, "Almost Family Inches Forward with Its Growth Plans," *Business First—Louisville,* December 27, 2002, p. 6.

American Oriental Bioengineering Inc.

308 Xuefu Rd.
Nangang District
Harbin, 150086
China
Telephone: (+86 0451) 8666 6601
Fax: (+86 0451) 8669 0967
Web site: http://www.bioaobo.com

Public Company
Incorporated: 1994 as Harbin Three Happiness Bioengineering Co., Ltd.; 2002 as American Oriental Bioengineering Inc.
Employees: 750
Sales: $110.18 million (2006)
Stock Exchanges: New York
Ticker Symbol: AOB
NAIC: 325412 Pharmaceutical Preparation Manufacturing

∎∎∎

Despite its name, American Oriental Bioengineering Inc. (AOBO) is neither American nor a bioengineering company. Rather, the Harbin, China-based company is focused on developing and marketing plant-based nutritional supplements, over-the-counter pharmaceuticals, and related nutraceuticals. The company produces more than 20 products, developed according to traditional Chinese medicine methods. These include its Cease Eurenesis Soft Gel tablets, used for the treatment of bedwetting and incontinence; ginseng and other tablets; Shuanghuanglian injection powders used for the long-term treatment of respiratory and related ailments; and over-the-counter (OTC) Jinji preparations for the treatment of endometriosis and menopause symptoms. The company's nutraceuticals line focuses on development of soybean peptide-based preparations, and includes beverages, capsules, powders, and other nutritional supplements.

Established in 1994 as Harbin Three Happiness Bioengineering Ltd., AOBO has combined organic growth with a strong acquisition program. Since 2003, the company has completed six major acquisitions, each of which has served to extend the company's product families, as well as expand its manufacturing base. The company operates two factories in Harbin and a third in Hezhou. AOBO has also developed a strong distribution base, with a network of 30 sales offices providing direct sales to more than 100,000 points of sale, including pharmacies, hospitals, retail shops, and other resellers. AOBO is led by founder Shujun (Tony) Liu, a former commander of the People's Liberation Army, with ongoing ties to the Chinese government, including the country's FDA equivalent. AOBO is listed on the New York Stock Exchange under the symbol AOB.

MURKY BEGINNINGS IN 1994

If American Oriental Bioengineering Inc. (AOBO) appeared to be a legitimate company with a viable product line by 2007, the company's origins remained quite murky. Although the company traced its operations back to 1970, its actual beginnings occurred only in 1994. In that year, Shujun (Tony) Liu founded Harbin Three Happiness Bioengineering Ltd., in Harbin, in

---

China's Heilongjiang Province. Liu was joined by Jun Min, Yanchun Li, Binsheng Li, and others. Many of the company's cofounders had been members of the Heilongjiang Province government, and remained in executive positions within the company into the 2000s.

Despite calling itself a bioengineering company, Harbin Three Happiness's product line appeared to consist primarily of a beverage product, composed of honey, marine plants, and herbs. That beverage was launched as a nutritional beverage in 1995, and was granted recognition as a health product in 1996. By the beginning of the 2000s, the company had also begun to market its Cease Enuresis Soft Gel formulation, a herbal formulation marketed as a means of alleviating bedwetting and incontinence.

In the meantime, Liu himself had been conducting a side project in conjunction with Harbin Medical University. That project investigated the development of commercially viable products based on soybean protein peptides. The project included a team of more than 20 scientists, and developed its own manufacturing facilities with a production capacity of 1,000 tons per year. By 2002, AOBO had launched its first products based on protein peptides, marketed as nutritional supplements. These and its earlier products were modest successes for the company. By 2001, the company posted revenues of nearly $6 million.

REVERSE TAKEOVER IN 2001

Into the beginning of the 2000s, Harbin Three Happiness remained a clearly China-based and China-focused company. In 2001, however, Harbin Three Happiness performed a reverse takeover of a U.S.-based shell company, a publicly listed penny stock known as Internet Golf Company. That company, ostensibly involved in the development and promotion of online golf tournaments, had itself been founded only in 1999. Yet in May of that year, Internet Golf completed its own reverse takeover of a publicly listed company, Champion Ventures.

Champion Ventures' origins reached back to its founding in Nevada in 1970. Over the next two decades, Champion had been involved in a number of industries including mining. At the time of its merger

with Internet Golf, however, Champion had been dormant for several years. Champion and Internet Golf both had connections to Paul Metzinger, a businessman who had already faced scrutiny from the Securities and Exchange Commission (SEC).

Among other things, Metzinger had been accused of conducting so-called pump and dump strategies. This consisted of creating publicly listed companies that seized on up-and-coming business trends. These companies then paid, often with shares, third-party and Internet-based analysts and publicists to tout up the company's stock to the investment community. As the company's stock rose, its founders were then able to sell their shares at a profit.

A key feature of many of these companies was the absence of any product or revenue-generating operations. Internet Golf appeared to be such a company. An earlier company founded by Metzinger, Intercell, never launched a marketable product, despite having raised significant venture capital. Another Metzinger company, Nanopierce Technologies, purported to be developing a fixing technology for semiconductors which, despite the company's name, had nothing to do with the highly trendy nanotechnology. Into the middle of the first decade of the 2000s, this Metzinger company remained without a truly viable product.

Following its merger with Internet Golf, Harbin Three Happiness became the main subsidiary of a newly formed holding company, American Oriental Bioengineering Inc. (AOBO), which maintained its listing on the New York Stock Exchange. Certain features of the company raised concerns from the outset. For one, the company remained associated with Metzinger, through its agreement to maintain Patricia Johnston, involved in a number of Metzinger vehicles, as a consultant for the company for a three-year period.

For another, AOBO, despite its name, appeared neither to be involved in bioengineering nor to have any operations in the United States. Finally, AOBO continued to associate with questionable partners, such as Mid-Continental Securities and CEOcast. Both companies had been controlled and/or operated by people convicted of fraud by the SEC.

BUYING A PRODUCT LINE IN 2002

If AOBO's choice of associates remained questionable, the company nonetheless set out to develop its product line in earnest starting from 2002. Acquisitions formed the heart of this effort. The first of these was of the soybean peptide project developed by Jiu in partnership with Harbin Medical University. AOBO agreed to pay

KEY DATES

1994: Shujung (Tony) Liu leads creation of Harbin Three Happiness Bioengineering Co., which launches a nutritional beverage the following year.

2002: Company completes reverse takeover of U.S.-based, publicly listed shell company Internet Golf, changing name to American Oriental Bioengineering Inc.; acquires soybean protein peptide project operated by Liu.

2004: American Oriental acquires HSPL as part of shift to plant-based pharmaceuticals sector.

2006: Stock is listed on New York Stock Exchange; company acquires GLP and HQPL, extending distribution reach to 100,000 points of sale.

2007: Company acquires CCXA and Boke, adding more than 100 new products.

$3.3 million to acquire the project and its manufacturing facilities in August 2002. The company then began marketing an expanded line of protein peptide supplements.

Jiu's connection with the Heilongjiang government provided the company with its next acquisition opportunities. In 2004, the company purchased Heilongjiang Sonhuajiang Pharmaceutical Ltd. (HSPL), paying $7.2 million. The acquisition of government-owned HSPL gave the company a new line of injectable Shuanghuanglian Lyophilized Powder. Developed in 1997, the HSPL product had captured a 50 percent share of the Chinese market for injectable Shuanghuanglian-based powders. This product represented AOBO's first true extension from the sphere of plant-based nutritional supplements to that of plant-based pharmaceutical products. The injectable powder product, used for the treatment of respiratory illnesses, also provided a strong boost to the company's revenues. By the end of that year, the company's sales had jumped to nearly $32 million.

Although the Cease Enuresis Soft Gel had been counted as part of the company's product portfolio in its 2002 prospectus, the company counted 2004 as the product's official launch. As part of that launch, the company gained Chinese FDA approval to market the bedwetting product as a first-grade medicine. By 2005, the company had developed a skin patch variant of the Cease Enuresis formulation. In that year, AOBO shifted its stock listing to the American Stock Exchange.

NEW ACQUISITIONS IN 2006

The Heilongjiang government provided the company with a new acquisition in 2006. In July of that year, AOBO agreed to pay $4 million to acquire Heilongjiang Qitai Pharmaceutical Company Ltd. (HQPL). That company held a pharmaceutical distribution license, and also operated a wholesale exchange for Chinese herbal medicines and products. The addition of HQPL boosted AOBO's reach to more than 100,000 points-of-sale across China.

The HQPL purchase came on the heels of another significant acquisition—Guangxi Lingfeng Pharmaceutical Company Ltd. (GLP). That company marketed the highly popular Jinji line of traditional gynecological medicines, adding a total of 70 products and sales of $10 million to AOBO's operations and strong operations in southern China. The company paid a total of $24 million in cash and shares for GLP.

By the end of 2006, AOBO's total sales had soared to $110 million. At the same time, its plant-based pharmaceutical line had become its largest revenue generator, accounting for nearly 70 percent of sales. By then, the company's total product line numbered more than 100 products that had been approved by the Chinese FDA for OTC sales.

AOBO's fast-growing operations enabled the company to shift its stock listing to the New York Stock Exchange's main board in 2006. By then, too, the company appeared to have shed most of the more dubious associations of its past.

The company continued seeking new acquisitions through 2007. In September of that year, the company paid $28.5 million to buy the Changchun Xinan Pharmaceutical Group Company (CCXA). That acquisition added another 100 products to the group's portfolio, including the popular Nubao premenstrual syndrome formulation and Nanboa, a sexual stimulant for men.

The CCXA acquisition was followed just one month later by the purchase of Guangxi Boke Pharmaceutical Company Limited (Boke). At $36.5 million, the purchase represented the company's largest to date. The addition of Boke further broadened the group's range of OTC medicines, adding such specialties as nasal congestion treatments, sore throat lozenges, and dandruff treatments. Boke also brought the company its own national distribution network. By the end of that year, AOBO counted 30 sales and distribution offices throughout China. With revenues expected to top $160 million at the end of 2007, AOBO appeared to have come into its own as a viable contender for China's booming traditional medicines market.

M. L. Cohen

PRINCIPAL SUBSIDIARIES

American Oriental Bioengineering (H.K.) Limited; Bestkey International Limited; Goware Holding Limited; Guangxi Ling Feng Pharmaceutical Company Limited; Harbin Three Happiness Bioengineering Co. Ltd.; Heilongjiang Qitai Pharmaceutical Limited; Heilongjiang Songhuajiang Pharmaceutical Limited; Yield Chance Limited.

PRINCIPAL COMPETITORS

Shandong Huaxin Pharmaceutical Company Ltd.; Shandong Sanzhu Pham. Group Imp. and Exp. Co.; Zhejiang Hengdian Imp and Exp Company Ltd.; Henan Pharmaceutical Company Ltd.; Hebei Jiheng Chemical Company Ltd.; AstraZeneca China Ltd.; Bayer (China) Ltd.; Guangdong Zhaoqing Star Lake Biotechnology Company Ltd.; Shanxi Jinxin Double Crane Pharmaceutical Company Ltd.; Hunan Guhan Group Company Ltd.

FURTHER READING

"AOBO Acquires Soybean Protein Peptide Operation," *Manufacturing Chemist,* December 2002, p. 30.

"AOBO Completes Soy Protein Project Buy," *Nutraceuticals International,* February 2003.

"AOBO: Deal to Supply Soy Products to Japan," *Nutraceuticals International,* May 2003.

"Chinese Biotech Firm Acquires Heilongjiang Songhuajiang Pharmaceutical," *Biotech Week,* December 1, 2004, p. 54.

"Double-Digit Revenue, Income Growth Expected by Chinese Biotech Firm," *Biotech Week,* June 9, 2004, p. 40.

"Fifteen Soft Gel Clinics to Begin Operations in 2003," *Biotech Week,* February 19, 2003, p. 15.

Norton, Leslie P., "Chinese Medicine Show," *Barron's,* June 25, 2007.

American Restaurant Partners, L.P.

3020 North Cypress Road, Suite 100
Wichita, Kansas 67226
U.S.A.
Telephone: (316) 634-1190
Fax: (316) 634-1662

Public Company
Incorporated: 1987
Sales: $130 million (2006 est.)
Stock Exchanges: Pink Sheets
Ticker Symbol: XXMUT
NAIC: 722211 Limited-Service Restaurants

∎ ∎ ∎

Based in Wichita, Kansas, American Restaurant Partners, L.P. owns and operates more than 130 Pizza Hut restaurants franchised from YUM! Brands, located in seven states, mostly in Montana, Oklahoma, and Texas. Many of the restaurants also offer carryout and delivery services. An affiliated company, Restaurant Management Co., also owns and operates 20 Long John Silver's stores, and ten Kentucky Fried Chicken restaurants, as well as some dual-brand units with YUM! operations. Although American Restaurant Partners is a public company, its shares available on a Pink Sheet basis, it is mostly owned by Chairman and Chief Executive Officer Hal W. McCoy, Sr., and his son, Hal W. McCoy, Jr., who serves as the company's president.

FOUNDER WORKED FOR PIZZA HUT: 1971

After graduating from the University of Oklahoma in 1967, Hal McCoy moved to Wichita to take a position with IBM as a systems engineer and marketing representative. In 1971 he went to work for Wichita-based Pizza Hut, which had been established a dozen years earlier by brothers Dan and Frank Carney. The chain started out as a single pizza parlor but after just one year in business, Pizza Hut began to franchise, spreading the brand across the country. In 1966 the company had 145 franchise units and was reaching out to Canada, prompting the opening of a home office in Wichita. By the end of the decade units were open or under construction in Mexico, Germany, and Australia. By 1971 Pizza Hut numbered 1,000 units, making it the largest pizza chain in the world. To better manage its far-flung empire, Pizza Hut began improving its operations, and McCoy was at the center of much of it. At first he worked in the data processing department, part of an effort to merge the different accounting systems used by companies acquired by Pizza Hut and to provide management with relevant data for strategic decision making, beyond the numbers that could be combed from the annual report that had previously been the basis for long-term business planning. In addition, Pizza Hut became more dependent on marketing in order to continue the chain's growth, and McCoy was among a small group of people that formed the nucleus of a marketing department in the early 1970s.

McCoy also became a Pizza Hut franchisee, operating a unit in Missouri that he acquired in 1971. Three years later, however, Pizza Hut was a public company

KEY DATES

1974: Hal McCoy, Sr., forms Restaurant Management Company to franchise Pizza Hut stores.
1975: Long John Silver's joins corporate holdings.
1987: American Restaurant Partners is formed to take business public.
1996: Interest is purchased in Oklahoma Magic, L.P.
1998: Company delists from American Stock Exchange.
2003: Winny Enterprises is acquired.

and under the auspices of the Securities and Exchange Commission, which ruled that headquarters' personnel such as McCoy were no longer permitted to own franchises. McCoy complied by selling his Missouri restaurant, but soon regretted the decision and began questioning whether he wanted to continue working at Pizza Hut's home office. "The choice became clear to me," he told *Restaurant Business* in a 1981 profile. "I felt the best thing for me and for my family would be to be at the franchising end of the business, not in headquarters." Thus, he resigned his position and formed Restaurant Management Company to operate as a Pizza Hut franchisee.

ADDITION OF LONG JOHN SILVER'S FRANCHISES: 1975

McCoy quickly expanded Restaurant Management Company. Not only did he open Pizza Hut units in Wyoming and Montana, in 1975 he diversified his operations further by becoming a franchisee of the Long John Silver's chain, one of the first companies to award franchises according to the ADI (area of dominant influence) method. McCoy received the rights to Tucson, Albuquerque, and Phoenix. Pizza and seafood proved to be a good mix, as poor conditions in one were offset by better conditions in the other. In 1975, for example, the price of fish soared, but because beef prices remained stable Restaurant Management was able to weather the tough times visited upon seafood restaurants because of a strong Pizza Hut business. The down cycle for Long John Silver's lasted from 1976 to 1978, and it was Mc-Coy's team that instituted many of the changes that would revitalize the concept, among other things improving food presentation, replacing benches with cushioned booths, adding plants, and hiring hostesses to make the atmosphere more friendly. Thus, when Pizza Hut was to experience some of its own difficulties, the

improved Long John Silver's operations were able to keep Restaurant Management profitable.

Beyond diversification, there were operational reasons for bringing Long John Silver's into the fold. According to *Restaurant Business,* McCoy's "management philosophy dictates that he never wants his divisional operations chiefs to be more than one step removed from his store managers. He needed another franchise concept to develop in order to maintain that position." McCoy explained that he wanted division managers "to be intimately familiar with the problems faced by the manager in an individual unit. If the operations chain of command gets too far away from the store level, that's when the problems start." As a result of this approach, he was able to develop a well-run operation and minimize turnover. However, in order to retain talented managers, he needed to provide opportunities for further career growth. The addition of a new franchise concept helped to increase those opportunities. At the start of the 1980s, Restaurant Management became a franchisee in a third restaurant concept, Grandy's Country Cookin, a quick-serve chain launched in Dallas in 1973 that served homestyle fare, such as fried chicken, country steaks, and catfish.

By the end of 1980, Restaurant Management operated 28 Pizza Huts, 24 Long John Silver's, and six Grandy's. Together they generated sales of $21 million. Over the next several years the company grew at a steady clip, both through the development of new stores and through acquisitions, so that by the summer of 1987 Restaurant Management was operating 47 Pizza Huts in Colorado, Georgia, Montana, Texas, and Wyoming. The company's portfolio also included a combined 41 Long John Silver's and Grandy's restaurants.

FORMATION OF AMERICAN RESTAURANT PARTNERS: 1987

In order to pay down $4.1 million in debt incurred from the acquisition of 21 Pizza Hut stores as well as to have additional funds available to develop new stores, McCoy decided to make a public equity offering by selling units in a new limited partnership, American Restaurant Partners L.P., which was formed in Delaware in April 1987 to acquire the assets of Restaurant Management Co. With Milwaukee-based Brunt Ellis & Loewi acting as underwriter, American Restaurant Partners completed an initial public offering of 800,000 partnership units in August 1987, netting nearly $7 million. The units then began trading on the American Stock Exchange. Regardless of the formal change in ownership, McCoy remained in charge of the business, becoming president of American Restaurant Partners.

The company's Pizza Hut holdings grew to 64 units over the next four years, making it the ninth largest Pizza Hut franchisee. With the Pizza Hut units leading the way American Restaurant Partners posted total revenues of $33.4 million in 1991 and net income of $1.4 million. A 65th Pizza Hut unit was added in 1992, but the company soon chose to sell seven North Texas Stores in order to pare down debt and free up money to expand its pizza delivery business as well as to open a new unit in Waco, Texas, a high-growth market.

HAL MCCOY, JR., JOINS COMPANY: 1992

It was also in 1992 that Hal McCoy, Jr., joined his father at American Restaurant Partners, having tried his hand at entrepreneurship and learning something of the restaurant franchisee business on his own. While studying business administration at the University of Kansas, he started a successful T-shirt company. He was then sitting in on a meeting with his father in 1990 when American Partners considered divesting four underperforming Texas Pizza Hut stores. The younger McCoy decided to buy them and formed CenTex Pizza Partners, L.P. to own and operate the stores. He turned around the units, sold CenTex back to American Partners in 1993, and joined his father's management team in Wichita.

The sale of seven Pizza Hut units helped to boost net income to more than $3.4 million in 1992 on sales of $34.6 million. The company enjoyed modest growth over the next three years, topping the $40 million mark in revenues in 1995, when the company also posted net income of $2.5 million. New products, in particular the introduction of Stuffed Crust Pizza, were instrumental in driving sales. The company's Pizza Hut holdings totaled 60 stores, 25 of which were located in Texas, 17 in Montana, eight each in Georgia and Wyoming, and two in Louisiana.

In 1996 American Restaurant Partners acquired a 45 percent stake and Restaurant Management Co. purchased a 29.25 percent interest in Oklahoma Magic, L.P., a new company that owned and operated 27 Pizza Hut units in Oklahoma. Two years later, American Restaurant Partners increased its position to 60 percent and Restaurant Management Co. to 39 percent, giving McCoy-controlled partnerships almost complete ownership of the Oklahoma operation. The debt taken on to make the original purchase, however, adversely impacted the bottom line for American Restaurant Partners in 1997, as well as the loss of income from the closing of five restaurants during the year. As a result, sales dipped from $40.4 million in 1996 to $39 million in 1997, while net income fell from $1.6 million in 1996 to a

net loss of almost $2 million in 1997. In November of that year the partnership elected to be delisted from the American Stock Exchange and limited the trading of its units. In order to continue to be taxed as a partnership rather than a corporation, the company maintained a Qualified Matching Service, which connected individuals interested in buying units with people looking to sell.

In 1998, American Restaurant Partners closed single units in Louisiana and Texas while opening a new store in Montana, so that by the end of 1998 the company's Pizza Hut holdings numbered 89 stores in six states. The company also continued to operate 20 Long John Silver's restaurants. Sales totaled $43.5 million for the year, resulting in net income of $808,000, a significant improvement over the loss the company reported the year before. American Restaurant Partners closed the 1990s by selling a Texas Pizza Hut and closing another unit in Oklahoma, reducing the number of stores to 87. Nevertheless, revenues soared to $57.8 million, driven by the introduction of the 16-inch Big New Yorker Pizza early in the year, and net income improved to $1.3 million in 1999.

GROWTH IN THE NEW CENTURY

At the start of the new century Hal McCoy, Jr., assumed a greater role in the running of American Restaurant Partners, taking over as president while his father remained chief executive and chairman. The company enjoyed steady growth in revenues in the 2000s, increasing to $70 million in 2002, again driven by successful product introductions, such as The Insider Pizza in the fourth quarter of 2000, Twisted Crust Pizza in the second quarter of 2001, and the P'Zone, unveiled early in 2002.

In order to expand its slate of Pizza Hut units, American Restaurant partners relied more on acquisitions than new store openings in the new century. "Our business has tended to grow by buying failing companies and turning them around. There isn't much territory left for us to build," Hal McCoy, Jr., explained to the *Wichita Eagle* in a 2007 interview, adding "There are a few people in the Pizza Hut business that have the ability to acquire other companies, and we are one of them. We basically wait until the deals are right in the markets we want to be in." One of those opportunities arose in 2003 when Winny Enterprises, Inc., was acquired, adding 13 Pizza Hut restaurants in Colorado, bringing the total number of units in the system, less one closing in Oklahoma, to 100. The rights to open additional Pizza Hut units in several Colorado counties were also acquired. Two years later another 42 restaurants were added in Austin, Texas. After winnowing out some of the units, American Restaurant Partners' Pizza Hut holdings numbered 135 units by 2007 and announced sales were in the $130 million range.

Ed Dinger

PRINCIPAL SUBSIDIARIES

Mountain View Pizza, LLC.; Oklahoma Magic, L.P.

PRINCIPAL COMPETITORS

Domino's Pizza, Inc.; Papa John's International, Inc.; Pizza Inn, Inc.

FURTHER READING

Farrell, Kevin, "Hal McCoy: A Hands-on Management Style Gives This Young Franchisee the Foundation to Expand and Diversify," *Restaurant Business,* July 1, 1981, p. 118.

"Franchisee Sells 7 Units to Pizza Hut," *Nation's Restaurant News,* October 19, 1992, p. 14.

Jeffrey, Don, "Pizza Hut Franchisee to Go Public with Partnership," *Nation's Restaurant News,* July 13, 1987, p. 94.

"Northern Colorado Pizza Huts Change Hands," *Greeley Tribune,* November 26, 2003.

Pearce, Dennis, "Wichita, Ka., Pizza Hut Operator Lost $1.6 Million in 1997," *Wichita Eagle,* February 18, 1998.

"Pizza Hut Licensee Adds 2 More Units, Shuffles Executives," *Nation's Restaurant News,* May 10, 1993, p. 96.

Voorhis, Dan, "A Conversation with … Hall McCoy II," *Wichita Eagle,* July 22, 2007, p. 3C.

AROTECH

Arotech Corporation

■

1229 Oak Valley Drive
Ann Arbor, Michigan 48108
U.S.A.
Telephone: (734) 761-5836
Toll Free: (800) 281-0356
Fax: (734) 761-5368
Web site: http://www.arotech.com

Public Company
Incorporated: 1990 as Electric Fuel Corporation
Employees: 342
Sales: $43.12 million (2006)
Stock Exchanges: NASDAQ Tel Aviv
Ticker Symbol: ARTX
NAIC: 332995 Other Ordnance and Accessories
Manufacturing; 334511 Search, Detection, Naviga-
tion, Guidance, Aeronautical, and Nautical System
and Instrument Manufacturing; 335311 Power,
Distribution, and Specialty Transformer Manu-
facturing; 335911 Storage Battery Manufacturing;
335912 Primary Battery Manufacturing; 335999
All Other Miscellaneous Electrical Equipment and
Component Manufacturing; 336111 Automobile
Manufacturing; 511210 Software Publishers

■ ■ ■

Arotech Corporation is a holding company with
interests in high-tech niches, mostly related to defense
and law enforcement. With operations in the United
States and Israel, Arotech focuses on three main areas:
advanced batteries; simulators; and body and vehicle

armor. Formerly known as Electric Fuel Corporation,
the company first tied its fortunes to the electric vehicle
concept, then to long-lasting alternative power packs for
mobile phones and other portable electronic devices using its distinctive zinc-air batteries. After 9/11, the
company shifted its emphasis to the military and
homeland defense, acquiring armor and simulator
companies. It did continue to research electric vehicle
power, however.

INVENTING BATTERIES FOR
ELECTRIC VEHICLES

Electric Fuel Corporation was incorporated in Delaware
in late 1990, but most of its operations were through a
subsidiary, Electric Fuel Limited, based in the ancient
city of Jerusalem, Israel. Yehuda Harats was named the
company's president and CEO in May 1991. Revenues
were $1.5 million in 1992 and $3.7 million the next
year.

The company's mission was to make a battery for
electric vehicles. California and some European
countries were then pushing for automobile manufacturers to introduce emissions-free models, opening the door
for the prospect of a large market if a practical electric
vehicle (EV) could be produced. Electric Fuel settled
upon a technology suggested by ex-Soviet émigré
scientists, the zinc-air battery. While not rechargeable,
zinc-air batteries could theoretically drive all day before
being swapped for fresh ones. In effect, electric cars
would be refueled with new zinc-air cells, rather than
gasoline. The spent batteries, arranged in easily replace-

COMPANY PERSPECTIVES

Arotech Corporation provides quality defense and security products for the military, law enforcement and homeland security markets, including advanced zinc-air and lithium batteries and chargers, multimedia interactive simulators/trainers and lightweight vehicle armoring.

able cassettes, would then be remanufactured at a dedicated facility powered by off-peak electricity.

The fuel would be fresh batteries, rather than gasoline. Electric Fuel maintained its technology was less toxic than other brands of zinc-air batteries, developed for hearing aids (which contained mercury). As a bonus, the manufacturing cost was more in line with traditional lead-acid batteries than newer types such as nickel-cadmium. The list of attributes went on and on. Unlike traditional car batteries, zinc-air cells did not lose much of their capacity in cold weather. In addition, while some newer technologies could be extremely hazardous in the event of an accident, potentially spewing out boiling acid upon vehicle occupants, Electric Fuel's cells were relatively inert. This latter quality later proved attractive to designers of military equipment concerned about the potential of exacerbating battle damage.

Since the zinc-air concept required some infrastructure, it was initially pitched to operators of large fleets. Early interest came from Germany, where in the mid-1990s Deutsche Bundespost Postdienst, the country's post office, launched a test of 64 electric vehicles (Mercedes Benz vans and Opel postal station wagons) powered by Electric Fuel's technology. Swedish utility company Vattenfall AB, the Swedish post office, and South African electric company Escom later joined the test. Around the same time, Italy's Edison SpA was trying out the batteries in small cars.

Electric Fuel established partnerships with companies in Italy and Germany to build regeneration facilities for its zinc-air systems. It also established a $2 million production facility in Jerusalem to make the battery packs. The United States eventually followed suit, announcing an electric city bus test involving Electric Fuel, General Electric Co., and Volvo AB in 2000.

NEW MARKETS

Revenues grew from $4.4 million in 1995 to $5.4 million in 1996. Electric Fuel had begun to develop products for niche markets outside the EV world. The company found a use for its zinc-air batteries in locator beacons for aviation. A similar marine product followed. In 1996 Electric Fuel launched a product built around a different chemistry: lifejacket lights with water-activated magnesium-cuprous chloride batteries. Electric Fuel also applied its energy to an array of demanding military applications, such as batteries for torpedoes and for field radios.

The company had about 200 employees in the late 1990s, most of them at the operation in Israel. Revenues were down to $2.7 million by 1999, and the company posted a loss of nearly $7 million. Seeking bigger markets, in 1998 Electric Fuel also began adapting its technology to products for consumer use. In the growing market for portable electronic devices, alkaline batteries had been eclipsed by NiMH (nickel metal hydride) ones, which were more powerful and rechargeable. Electric Fuel's zinc acid batteries were not meant to be reused, but they could last as much as five times longer, or up to a month of normal cellphone use. The company believed there was a niche for them among travelers and others seeking convenience.

Electric Fuel produced the zinc-air batteries by hand at a plant in Beit Shemesh, Israel. It was making them by hand as late as 2000, an expensive process. It then bought a plant in Israel, Tadiran Batteries Ltd., to get its manufacturing automated. The factory purchase was worth $52 million in stock; Electric Fuel's share price was soaring based on investor enthusiasm for its consumer electronics gambit.

The company's Instant Power Charger, a portable backup powerpack for mobile phones and PDAs, appeared in the U.S. and U.K. markets by 2001. Unfortunately, they failed to catch on with the consumer market, and retail sales were wrapped up at the end of 2002. The number of employees had peaked at 150, but three dozen were given the pink slip following the end of the consumer business.

CORPORATE CHANGES

Robert S. Ehrlich succeeded Yehuda Harats as president and CEO in October 2002. Ehrlich had been board chairman since January 1993, and also served as chief financial officer from May 1991 to October 2002. Before coming to Electric Fuel, Erlich had been chairman of PSC Inc., a New York manufacturer of scanning equipment. It was a challenging time to be handed the reins. Electric Fuel lost $18 million in 2002.

Electric Fuel had become a public company in March 1994, offering shares at $12.50 each, trading under the ticker symbol EFCX. The company became

KEY DATES

1990: Electric Fuel Corporation is formed; most operations are in Israel.

1994: Electric Fuel has initial public offering.

1995: Zinc-air battery regeneration station opens in Bremen, Germany, during electric vehicle test.

1998: Company applies its technology to military products.

2000: Electric Fuel brings disposable cellphone batteries to market but they fail to catch on with consumers.

2002: Acquisitions of MDT Armor and IES Interactive Training Inc. expand company's security and defense offerings.

2003: Company changes name to Arotech Corporation.

2004: Arotech makes three acquisitions, moves headquarters from New York to Ann Arbor, Michigan.

teries were not rechargeable, they could be recycled in an environmentally safe manner. In addition, unlike most city buses, this one did not leave behind a cloud of diesel smoke everywhere it went.

Arotech had a milestone year in 2004. Revenues reached $50 million. Although the net loss was nearly unchanged at $9 million, the company reported its first positive cash flow. Arotech also bought three companies, bolstering each of its three main product lines. One of the acquisitions led to a new home for Arotech's corporate headquarters.

FAAC Corporation of Ann Arbor, Michigan, produced simulators for private and public sector clients. The company had been formed in 1971 by Gene Jordan. It was profitable on annual revenues of $15 million. Arotech bought the company for $14 million in February 2004, then moved both its New York City corporate headquarters and its Colorado-based IES Interactive Training Inc. subsidiary to Ann Arbor.

The other two acquisitions also built upon existing businesses. Israel's Epsilor Electronic Industries, Ltd., sold lithium batteries and chargers to markets in the Middle East, Europe, and Asia. Armour of America, Incorporated of Auburn, Alabama, made a wide range of military armor, from aviation armor to a ballistic personal flotation device.

Arotech's revenues slipped to $49 million in 2005. A net loss of $24 million was blamed largely on the devalued armor business. The loss narrowed to $15.6 million in 2006 as revenues dipped to $43 million. As the company struggled to maintain its listing on the NASDAQ, it announced it was entering the military vehicle market in India via a joint venture between its MDT Armor unit and local defense and automotive interests.

known as Arotech Corporation in 2003 (ticker symbol ARTX), with the Electric Fuel name living on through an Alabama-based subsidiary. Right before going public, Arotech merged with one of its principal shareholders, Advanced Materials Technologies, Inc. (Amtec).

REFOCUSING ON DEFENSE

Arotech refocused on defense and homeland security products during the War on Terror. A couple of acquisitions in the second half of 2002 brought the company a couple of new military-oriented product lines. MDT Armor made light armor while IES Interactive Training Inc. provided training simulators for clients ranging from NASA to the FBI.

The net loss was halved to about $9 million in 2003. During the year Arotech began supplying a unique type of battery to the U.S. military. These zinc-air cells were intended for a single use in field radios and lasted six times longer than lithium batteries. These were made at the company's plant in Auburn, Alabama. The fighting in Iraq also brought a large demand for armored vehicles, another new business for Arotech. However, the company had a hard time making money in this arena.

Arotech had not given up on electric vehicles, and in September 2003 demonstrated a transit bus powered by zinc-air cells in Albany, New York. Although its bat-

Frederick C. Ingram

PRINCIPAL SUBSIDIARIES

FAAC Incorporated; IES Interactive Training, Inc.; Armour of America; MDT Protective Industries, Ltd. (Israel; 75.5%); MDT Armor Corporation (88%); Epsilor Electronic Industries, Ltd. (Israel); Electric Fuel Battery Corporation; Electric Fuel (E.F.L.) Ltd. (Israel).

PRINCIPAL DIVISIONS

Battery and Power Systems; Simulation, Training and Consulting; Armoring.

PRINCIPAL COMPETITORS

Rayovac Corporation; Armor Holdings, Inc.; Brentronics Inc.; AEA Technology plc; Ultralife Batteries, Inc.; Saft S.A.

FURTHER READING

Blackburn, Nicky, "Arotech Subsidiary IES Wins $2m. FBI Contract," *Jerusalem Post,* Econ. Sec., June 10, 2003, p. 9.

————, "Innovations: Test Drive an All-Electric Bus," *Jerusalem Post,* Econ. Sec., September 16, 2001, p. 11.

Brown, Warren, "Automakers Being Driven to High-Tech Extremes; Down the Road, Hybrid Alternatives to Traditional Engines," *Washington Post,* February 28, 1998, p. H1.

"CEO Interview: Yehuda Harats, Electric Fuel Corporation," *Wall Street Transcript,* May 3, 1999.

"CEO Interview: Yehuda Harats, Electric Fuel Ltd.," *Wall Street Transcript,* June 1, 1998.

"CEO/Company Interview: Yehuda Harats, Electric Fuel Corp.," *Wall Street Transcript,* June 12, 2000.

Choi, Audrey, "Electric Fuel of Israel Poised to Draw Two More European Concerns to Project," *Wall Street Journal,* May 30, 1995, p. B5.

————, "Israeli Battery Maker Lands Contract with STN Atlas," *Wall Street Journal Europe,* June 28, 1995, p. 9.

Cohn, Lynne M., "Zinc Power Cell Shows Promise," *American Metal Market,* August 1993, p. 7.

"Company Interview: Robert S. Ehrlich, Arotech Corporation," *Wall Street Transcript,* January 26, 2004.

Dietderich, Andrew, "Arotech Given Conditions to Keep Its Listing on the Nasdaq; Military Supplier Gets July 6 Deadline," *Crain's Detroit Business,* May 22, 2006, p. 4.

————, "Faac Owners Sell for $14m," *Crain's Detroit Business,* February 9, 2004, p. 7.

"Edison SpA EV Tests Underway," *Battery & EV Technology,* May 1, 1996.

Eisenstein, Paul A., "No-Emission Vehicle Depends on Battery," *Washington Times,* March 10, 1995, p. E13.

"Electric Fuel Aims for Zero Emissions," *Battery & EV Technology,* September 1, 1995.

"Electric Fuel Building $2M Zinc-Air Battery Pack Production Facility," *Alternative Energy Network Online Today,* February 2, 1995.

"Electric Fuel Corp. President Says Electric Vehicles Can Operate Effectively in Cold Weather," *PR Newswire,* October 13, 1994.

"Electric Fuel Raises $2.85m. in Placement," *Jerusalem Post,* Econ. Sec., December 29, 1999, p. 12.

"Electric Fuel Shares Soar on US Program," *Jerusalem Post,* Econ. Sec., February 23, 2000, p. 12.

Feder, Barnaby J., "Almost an Energy Alternative; Fuel Cells Hold Promise, but Problems Remain," *New York Times,* May 27, 2000, p. C1.

Gerstenfeld, Dan, "Electric Fuel: Sales to Triple in 2000; Large-Scale Sales of Cellphone Batteries Seen Starting in Second Half," *Jerusalem Post,* Econ. Sec., January 27, 2000, p. 13.

"Israeli Company Makes Fuel Cell/Battery Hybrid," *Electric Vehicles Energy Network Online Today,* June 12, 1996.

Marcus, Amy Dockser, Gabriella Stern, and Brandon Mitchener, "Driving Force: Israel Is Becoming High-Tech Frontier for the Auto Industry—Dead Sea Magnesium Plant and a Zinc-Air Battery Draw Germans and U.S.—Search for 'Three-Quart Car,'" *Wall Street Journal,* August 22, 1996, p. A1.

Marriott, Michel, "New Cellular Phone Batteries Are Called Tough but Gentle," *New York Times,* March 4, 1999, p. G3.

Miller, Stephen C., "A Battery Recharges the Remote Road Warrior," *New York Times,* April 12, 2001, p. G3.

Pope, Gregory T., and Philip Chien, "Zinc-Air Batteries Made Easy," *Popular Mechanics,* April 1995, p. 22.

Roosevelt, Ann, "Arotech Unit Forms Armored Vehicle Joint Venture in India," *Defense Daily International,* February 3, 2006.

Sandler, Neal, "Israel's Electric Fuel Buys Koor Factory," *Daily Deal,* March 15, 2000.

Stub, Zev, "Electric Fuel Lays Off 40," *Jerusalem Post,* Econ. Sec., October 22, 2002, p. 9.

Tuckey, Bill, "Still Dreaming of the Electric Alternative," *Age* (Melbourne, Australia), March 8, 1995, p. 45.

Wald, Matthew L., "Coaxing More Miles from the Electric-Car Battery," *New York Times,* July 11, 1993, p. F9.

Wilson, Jim, and Louis M. Brill, "Zinc-Air Battery Climbs the Alps," *Popular Mechanics,* January 1997, p. 14.

Woodruff, David, "A Big Charge for Electric Vehicles?" *Business Week,* November 18, 1996, p. 102.

Xundu, Xolani, "Fleets Could Pioneer Use of Electric Vehicles," *Business Day* (South Africa), November 1, 1999, p. 4.

"Zinc Fuel-Cell Bus to Be Demonstrated in Albany," *Business Review* (Albany, N.Y.), September 24, 2003.

Assured Guaranty Ltd.

30 Woodbourne Avenue
Hamilton, HM 08
Bermuda
Telephone: (+441) 2964004
Fax: (+441) 2963379
Web site: http://www.assuredguaranty.com

Public Company
Incorporated: 2003
Employees: 126
Sales: $322.1 million (2006)
Stock Exchanges: New York
Ticker Symbol: AGO
NAIC: 524126 Direct Property and Casualty Insurance
  Carriers

■ ■ ■

Bermuda-based Assured Guaranty Ltd. is one of the world's leading providers of reinsurance, credit enhancement, and related insurance and financial services to the global insurance market. Assured Guaranty develops credit derivatives, financial guarantees, and related financial support products designed to improve the credit ratings of debt obligations. The company provides insurance backing for primary insurance companies, banks, and other credit institutions in the event of nonpayment of loans, mortgages, and other credit. Assured Guaranty operates in four primary business areas: Financial Guaranty Direct, serving banks and other credit institutions; Financial Guaranty Reinsurance, serving the insurance market; Mortgage Guaranty, which develops guaranties specifically to mortgage lenders; and Other, which includes the company's operations in trade credit reinsurance, title reinsurance, and equity layer credit protection. Assured Guaranty is the holding company for three main subsidiaries. Assured Guaranty Corp. operates in the United States and has secured licenses to operate in all 50 states, as well as in Washington, D.C., and in Puerto Rico. This subsidiary supplies the public finance, mortgage, and structured finance and credit sectors. From the United Kingdom, Assured Guaranty (UK) Ltd. provides reinsurance and credit guaranty services throughout the United Kingdom and European Union. The company's reinsurance operations are grouped under Assured Guaranty Re Ltd., based in Bermuda. A spinoff of Bermuda's ACE Limited, Assured Guaranty is listed on the New York Stock Exchange and holds triple A ratings from Standard & Poor's and Fitch Ratings, and Aaa status from Moody's Investors Service. The company posted revenues of $322.1 million in 2006.

ACE ORIGINS IN 1986

Assured Guaranty stemmed from the operations of ACE Limited. That company was formed in 1985 as a partnership among a group of nearly 35 *Fortune* 500 companies in order to develop excess liability coverage. Founded in Hamilton, Bermuda, ACE wrote its first policy that same year. By 1986, the company had also launched a financial guaranty arm, called ACE Guaranty Re. Registered in Maryland and headquartered in Bermuda, ACE Guaranty Re served as an underwriter

<table>
<tr><td>

COMPANY PERSPECTIVES

Assured Guaranty, through its subsidiaries, is a leading provider of financial guaranty and credit enhancement products to investors, financial institutions and other participants in the global capital markets.

</td></tr>
</table>

for the U.S. insurance market. The company's first policy was issued in 1988.

For most of the next decade, ACE's insurance guarantee operations focused especially on the reinsurance market. During this period, ACE itself grew strongly. In 1987, for example, the company took over Corporate Officers & Directors Assurance Ltd., or CODA. This allowed ACE to launch a diversification of its insurance products. Into the early 1990s, ACE entered the markets for satellite, excess property, and aviation insurance, among others. The acquisition of CI-GNA Corporation in 1999 in particular helped ACE expand to a global level. In this way, ACE became one of only a few insurance groups capable of providing insurance products and services across the world.

ACE also continued to expand its reinsurance operations. In 1994, for example, the company launched the internationally operating Assured Guaranty Re Overseas Ltd., based in Bermuda. The company also made a number of acquisitions through the 1990s. The company added Financial Lines in 1995, bolstering its strategic and alternative risk products. In 1996, the company bought Tempest Re. That company, also based in Bermuda, allowed ACE to expand its operations into the catastrophe reinsurance sector. This move was reinforced by the creation of Sovereign Risk Insurance Ltd. The joint venture, formed in partnership with Risk Capital Re and XL Insurance Company, focused on providing political risk insurance and reinsurance in 1997.

By the end of the decade, the company's catastrophe operations had expanded to include CAT Limited, acquired in 1998. In that year, also, the company expanded its political risk business through an alliance with the World Bank Group's Multilateral Investment Guarantee Agency. The agreement called for the company to provide treaty reinsurance policies for the agency's own political risk activities. ACE also expanded its financial guaranty operations at the end of the decade. This came through another acquisition, of Capital Re Corporation, in 1999.

PRIMARY FOCUS

Through the previous decade, ACE's Assured Guaranty operations had focused especially on the reinsurance market. With the new century, however, the company began shifting its focus to building up its operations in the primary financial guarantee segment. A major reason for this conversion was the desire by Assured Guaranty and ACE to boost their ratings from the primary credit rating groups in order to compete with its more established, AAA-rated rivals.

As part of this process, Assured Guaranty shed a number of its existing operations while also trimming its staff. Into the early 2000s, the company worked on narrowing its range to a focus on the financial and mortgage guaranty insurance market, on the one hand, and the financial guaranty reinsurance segment on the other.

The company's progress was reflected in the change of name of its U.S. operation, from ACE Guaranty Re to ACE Guaranty Corp., in 2003. ACE Guaranty Corp. was then placed under a new holding company, called AGC Holdings Ltd. The new company also took over the rest of ACE's financial guaranty operations, including ACE Capital Re International.

The restructuring came as the lead-in to the next step in ACE's attempt to increase the rating of its financial guaranty business. In April 2004, ACE spun off Assured Guaranty as a separate company, listing its shares on the New York Stock Exchange. The listing raised nearly $1 billion for the company, while reducing ACE's own holding to just 35 percent.

EARNING ITS TRIPLE-A RATING

Following the spinoff, Assured Guaranty moved to expand its international reach. The company opened its London subsidiary in 2004, gaining authorization from the U.K. government in July of that year. The new subsidiary permitted Assured Guaranty to expand its operations throughout the European Union. Assured Guaranty (UK) Ltd., as the company was called, issued its first policy in 2005.

The United States, however, remained the company's primary market. With its initial public offering (IPO) successfully completed, the company set out to procure licenses for operating in all 50 states. The process was not as smooth as the company might have hoped. In California, for example, the company's former operations in the credit market prevented it from entering that state. Yet, after a lobbying effort that reportedly cost the company nearly $100,000, the state of California drafted new legislation that paved the way for

KEY DATES

1985: ACE Limited is established in Bermuda.
1986: ACE Limited founds reinsurance subsidiary Ace Guaranty Re, focused on U.S. market.
1988: ACE Guaranty Re issues first policy.
1994: Company founds international operation, ACE Guaranty Overseas, based in Bermuda.
1999: ACE acquires Capital Re Corporation and begins refocusing ACE Guaranty from reinsurance to primary guaranty sector.
2003: ACG Holding is formed to take over ACE's financial guaranty businesses, including Capital Re and ACE Guaranty Re, which is renamed Assured Guaranty Corp.
2004: ACE spins off 65 percent of ACG Holding, which lists on New York Stock Exchange as Assured Guaranty Ltd.; company opens London subsidiary, Assured Guaranty (UK) Ltd.
2007: Assured Guaranty agrees to provide reinsurance for $29 billion in financial guaranty contracts held by Ambac.

The continuing crisis in the sector made Assured Guaranty a still more attractive partner as the year drew to a close. In mid-December, the company announced that it had reached an agreement to reinsure about $29 billion of the financial guaranty contracts held by bond insurance giant Ambac Financial Group. That company had been threatened with a ratings downgrade. In exchange, Ambac agreed to provide Assured Guaranty additional reinsurance contracts over the next three years. Assured Guaranty appeared on its way to establishing itself among the major players of the world's financial guaranty markets.

M. L. Cohen

PRINCIPAL SUBSIDIARIES

Assured Guaranty (UK) Ltd.; Assured Guaranty Corp. (U.S.A.); Assured Guaranty Finance Overseas Ltd.; Assured Guaranty Re Ltd.; Assured Guaranty US Holdings Inc.

PRINCIPAL COMPETITORS

Ambac Assurance Corporation; Financial Guaranty Insurance Company; Financial Security Assurance Inc.; MBIA Insurance Corporation; XL Capital Assurance Inc.; CDC IXIS; Radian Reinsurance Inc.; RAM Reinsurance Company Ltd.; XL Financial Assurance Ltd.; Channel Reinsurance Ltd.; BluePoint Re Ltd.

FURTHER READING

"ACE Raises $882 Million in Assured Guaranty IPO," *Business Insurance,* April 26, 2004, p. 1.

"Ambac, Assured Guaranty Strike $29 Billion Reinsurance Deal," *Seeking Alpha,* December 14, 2007.

"Assured Guaranty Ltd. Announces Authorization of Insurance Subsidiary in the United Kingdom," *Business Wire,* July 27, 2004.

"Assured Guaranty Spin-off Not Enough for Top Rating," *Reactions,* June 2004, p. 51.

Chang, Helen, "Bond Insurance: N.Y.-Based Assured Guaranty Receives License to Operate in California," *Bond Buyer,* January 13, 2005, p. 7.

"Fitch Assigns 'AAA' IFS Rating to Assured Guaranty Corp.," *Business Wire,* April 14, 2005.

Hanson, Matthew, "Assured's Parent Company Reveals $221M Pretax Unrealized Loss," *Bond Buyer,* October 24, 2007, p. 4.

———, "FSA, Assured Buck Subprime Trend: Amid Credit Crisis, Both Enjoy Boost," *Bond Buyer,* November 27, 2007, p. 1.

Assured Guaranty's gaining a license there. By 2007, the company had successfully gained licenses for all 50 states, as well as for the District of Columbia and for Puerto Rico.

Assured Guaranty also began to make progress in its ratings. The company gained its first AAA rating from Standard and Poor's, albeit with a negative outlook. By 2005, however, the company gained an AAA rating from Fitch Ratings, while also seeing its rating upgraded at both Standard & Poor's and Moody's Investors Service. Nonetheless, the latter agency remained less enthusiastic over Assured Guaranty, and only raised its rating of the company to AAa into 2007.

Assured Guaranty's limited exposure to the subprime loan market, which collapsed in 2007, helped raise the company's profile that year. Assured Guaranty had focused its U.S. business primarily on the credit-card and accounts receivable securities market. With its competitors suffering from the ongoing crisis in the U.S. housing market, Assured Guaranty's own fortunes rose. By July 2007, the company received its coveted AAA rating from Moody's. This in turn helped the company boost its market share through the end of the year.

————, "Moody's Gives Aaa to Assured Guaranty: Firm Becomes 7th Gilt-Edged Insurer," *Bond Buyer,* July 13, 2007, p. 1.

Johnson, Matthew, "Bond Insurers: Assured Guaranty Reports 6% Drop in Profit As It Marks Year Since IPO," *Bond Buyer,* May 9, 2005, p. 6.

Meyers, Maxwell, "Assured Guaranty Raises Estimated Katrina Exposure to $220 Million," *Bond Buyer,* September 21, 2005, p. 6.

Saskal, Rich, "ACE's Assured Lobbying," *Bond Buyer,* June 18, 2004, p. 35.

ATMI, Inc.

———————————■———————————

7 Commerce Drive
Danbury, Connecticut 06810
U.S.A.
Telephone: (203) 794-1100
Fax: (203) 792-8040
Web site: http://www.atmi.com

Public Company
Incorporated: 1986 as Advanced Technology Materials,
Inc.
Employees: 806
Sales: $325.91 million (2006)
Stock Exchanges: NASDAQ
Ticker Symbol: ATMI
NAIC: 325131 Inorganic Dye and Pigment
Manufacturing; 541710 Research and Development
in the Physical Sciences and Engineering

■ ■ ■

ATMI, Inc., is a leading producer of materials, materials packaging, and materials delivery systems used in the production of microelectronic devices, particularly semiconductors. The company's products, the materials used in the production of integrated circuits, enable chip makers to keep pace with the rapid advancements in production technology. ATMI serves semiconductor and flat-panel-display manufacturers, counting nearly every major producer in the world as a customer. A major focus of ATMI is using copper interconnects, as opposed to the more common aluminum interconnects, to increase the speed, stability, and size reduction of chips.

ORIGINS

During its first decade of business, ATMI operated as Advanced Technology Materials, Inc., a company established by five entrepreneurs. Of the five founders, three remained with the company during its inaugural decade, Ward C. Stevens, Duncan W. Brown, and Gene Banucci. Each of the principal founders worked for a New Jersey-based chemical manufacturer named American Cyanamid Company before launching their entrepreneurial effort. Stevens, who served as Advanced Technology's vice-president during its formative years, worked as a materials scientist and project leader at American Cyanamid. Brown, also an Advanced Technology vice-president, functioned as a research chemist at American Cyanamid. Both Stevens and Brown made vital contributions to Advanced Technology's founding and its development, but their influence paled in comparison to what their American Cyanamid colleague brought to the table.

Banucci left a lasting imprint on ATMI. He helped found the company, presided over its transition from Advanced Technology to ATMI, orchestrated a series of acquisitions and divestitures, and served as the company chief executive officer and chairman for two decades. Banucci earned his undergraduate degree in chemistry from Beloit College and his doctorate in organic chemistry from Wayne State University. After school, he spent a decade at General Electric Company, serving in various management capacities at the company's corporate research and development center and its GE

Plastics division. At American Cyanamid, Banucci served as a director of the company's chemical research division, leading more than 400 scientists and engineers in new product research and development who generated more than $1 billion in annual revenues for American Cyanamid. As part of his duties at the New Jersey-based company, Banucci oversaw the discovery of new specialty chemical and materials technology, managing efforts that led to new business ventures. In 1986, he left the company to launch his own venture, teaming with Stevens, Brown, and two other scientists to form Advanced Technology.

Advanced Technology was established to focus on semiconductor materials used in chemical vapor deposition (CVD) processes. In the CVD process, wafers (the base material of semiconductors) were placed in a reaction chamber and subjected to a gas or vaporized liquid material along with a form of energy, such as heat or plasma. The energy introduced into the reactor caused the decomposition of the gas or vaporized liquid, leaving a thin film of material deposited on the surface of the wafer. The process, one of several ways to deposit materials on wafers, was instrumental in the fabrication of semiconductors.

NAME CHANGE TO ATMI IN 1997

Advanced Technology converted to public ownership seven years after it was formed, completing its initial public offering (IPO) of stock in 1993. The next significant corporate milestone was the company's name change four years later, a change that drew its impetus from two transactions completed in 1997. In April, Advanced Technology purchased Austin, Texas-based

Advanced Delivery & Chemical Systems, a company with manufacturing facilities in Burnet, Texas, and Anseong, South Korea. The acquisition, an all-stock deal valued at $92 million, combined ATMI's major strength, its technology, with Advanced Delivery's major strength, its manufacturing and distribution capabilities. A little more than a month later, Advanced Technology announced another all-stock deal, the $78 million purchase of Lawrence Semiconductor Laboratories. Based in Mesa, Arizona, Lawrence Semiconductor specialized in the production of epitaxial thin silicon films by CVD, generating more than $20 million in annual revenue.

The company, known as ATMI after the transactions in 1997, embarked on an acquisition spree after buying Advanced Delivery and Lawrence Semiconductor. Within the next six years, ATMI would absorb more than a dozen companies, seeking to become a "one-stop" provider of all specialty materials needed to make semiconductors. Banucci looked to add to the company's capabilities in providing the specialty materials and compounds to produce chips, and he looked to build ATMI's capabilities in providing equipment services. For the latter, Banucci began acquiring companies with expertise in cleaning up contaminates released in the chip-making process, a consequence of manufacturers' need to use caustic chemicals to scrub chip surfaces clean.

ACQUISITIONS

As the acquisition campaign progressed, ATMI's talents broadened and its list of subsidiaries grew. In April 1998, the company reached an agreement to acquire NOW Technologies Inc., a $15-million-in-sales company that became an ATMI subsidiary. Based in Bloomington, Minnesota, NOW was a manufacturer and distributor of semiconductor materials packaging systems based on its patented NOWPak system, a product that had a broad range of uses in the packaging of advanced photoresist materials.

In 1999, Banucci set his sights on three companies, completing deals that expanded ATMI's capabilities. In May, the company signed an agreement to acquire Advanced Chemical Systems International, Inc., a specialist in photolithography chemicals that generated roughly $17 million in annual sales. The purchase of the Milpitas, California-based company provided entry into the photolithography and chemical mechanical polishing (CMP) materials field, complementing ATMI's strengths in CVD, ion implant materials, and specialty materials packaging.

In October, the company signed an agreement to buy Newform N.V., a Belgium-based provider of high-

KEY DATES

1986: Advanced Technology Materials, Inc., is founded by former American Cyanamid Co. executives.
1993: Advanced Technology completes its initial public offering of stock.
1997: Advanced Technology changes its name to ATMI, Inc.
2000: After a series of acquisitions, ATMI's revenues reach $300 million.
2004: A year of divestitures eliminates ATMI's equipment services business.
2006: ATMI celebrates its 20th anniversary.

purity, ultra-clean packaging to the semiconductor and pharmaceutical industries. Before the end of the year, Banucci completed his third acquisition, buying Buffalo Grove, Illinois-based MST Analytics Inc., a maker of semiconductor gas monitoring systems. "MST has two primary product lines, both of which are excellent strategic fits for ATMI," an ATMI executive explained in a December 19, 1999, interview with *Microtechnology News.* "MST's gas sensing products monitor the toxic gases widely used in manufacturing semiconductors on both a fabwide and personal basis."

CRISIS AT THE START OF THE NEW CENTURY

As ATMI entered the 21st century, the strategy of developing into a more comprehensive competitor in its industry was producing encouraging financial results. Revenues in 2000 leaped 48 percent, jumping to $300 million. Quickly, however, market conditions soured, stripping the company of its vitality. "The semiconductor industry's worst-in-its-lifetime downturn, dissipated consumer demand, and the national recession all combined to create a difficult economic scenario," an ATMI executive explained in a January 30, 2002, interview with *PR Newswire.* Revenues fell 29 percent to $213.5 million in 2001, but more alarming was the severe decline in profits. After posting $43.7 million in net income in 2000, ATMI announced a $9.7 million net loss in 2001, a dismal effort that left a lasting impression on Banucci.

ATMI's financial health worsened before it improved. In 2002, when revenues slipped to $136.9 million, the company posted a staggering $30.7 million loss. The year proved to be the nadir of ATMI's free-

fall—losses were reduced to $9.9 million in 2003, as revenues increased to $171.6 million—but once conditions improved, Banucci began to develop plans for sweeping changes. He remembered the bad times and vowed never to fall victim to the cyclicality of the semiconductor industry.

STRATEGIC CHANGES

ATMI's corporate profile was about to undergo significant change. In 2003, the company operated in two segments, materials and technologies. The materials segment, which provided ultra-pure materials used in semiconductor manufacturing and delivery and packaging systems, generated 64 percent of the company's annual revenue. The technologies segment generated 36 percent of ATMI's annual volume, a percentage generated by sensing and abatement equipment used to treat effluent gases and warn factory workers of gas leaks. After the financial debacle in the early 2000s, Banucci decided to shed the company's technologies businesses, which had produced some of the worst financial losses during the downturn, and to focus entirely on creating compounds and specialty materials. The change in strategy signaled the beginning of a divestiture program, one that would rid the company of money-losing operations and direct all its resources on its fastest-growing business.

A FOCUS ON COPPER

Although selling businesses occupied much of the company's attention midway through the decade, ATMI did complete several acquisitions, particularly in the area of copper interconnects. Banucci saw copper as ATMI's future. Compared to aluminum, copper conducted electricity more easily and possessed superior capacity for miniaturization, enabling semiconductor manufacturers to keep pace with Moore's law, which holds that the number of a chip's transistors will double every 24 months. Historically, manufacturers had been able to increase the capabilities of chips by continually refining their design and improving the precision of the tools used to build integrated circuits, but Banucci believed future advancements in the capabilities of chips would rely on specialty materials, specifically copper, to make increasingly sophisticated chips. In his mind, aluminum-based chips could not be made small enough or work fast enough to perform the tasks that would be demanded of chips in the future. The widespread use of copper (only 5 percent of the chips produced in 2004 contained copper) had been held in check because it was four times more difficult than aluminum to embed in a chip, but analysts were predicting 35 percent of chips would contain copper by the end of the decade.

DIVESTITURE OF ONE-THIRD OF ATMI: 2004

As ATMI invested heavily in copper-related technologies, the company began shedding its unwanted operations. The divestitures were made in 2004, beginning with the sale of its gallium nitride business in March to Durham, North Carolina-based Cree, Inc., "The sale of our gallium nitride business is the first element of the planned disposition of ATMI's six technologies businesses," Banucci said in a March 25, 2004, interview with *PR Newswire*. In May, the company sold its life safety sensors business to City Technology, Ltd. The following month ATMI sold its fabrication services business to Materials Support Resources Inc., a sale that included operations in Arizona, New Mexico, Texas, Oregon, and Ireland. In July, the company divested its specialty silicon epitaxial services unit, selling the business to one of its major customers, International Rectifier Corporation. The final two divestitures were made in August, when the company's Emosyn smart card business was sold, and in December, when its environmental treatment systems business was sold.

As the divestiture program was winding down, Banucci announced he was scaling back his responsibilities at ATMI. In November 2004, he announced he was stepping down as chief executive officer, but staying on as chairman. His restructuring efforts nearly completed, Banucci decided to focus his energies on strategy, investor relations, and governance, paving the way for the promotion of Doug Neugold to the position of chief executive officer. A 20-year veteran of the electronics industry, Neugold joined ATMI in 1998, becoming the company's president two years later. In 2003, he added the title of chief operating officer.

WELL POSITIONED FOR FUTURE GROWTH

In the wake of the divestitures, ATMI performed admirably, recording substantial increases in its financial totals. The gains ensured that the company's 20th anniversary was an event to be celebrated. The company's discontinued operations generated revenues of $71.8 million in their last year as part of ATMI, but the absence of the business volume was hardly missed. Revenues increased from $246.2 million in 2004 to $281.7 million in 2005 before reaching $325.9 million in the company's 20th year of business. Far more impressive were the increases in profits during the period. After posting a $9.9 million loss in 2003, ATMI surged into the black, generating $31.5 million in net income in 2004. By 2006, the company's net income had increased to $39.9 million. In the years ahead,

ATMI hoped to continue to benefit from its sharpened strategic focus and from its investment in copper interconnects. The company's materials appeared in 70 percent of all chips that contained copper, leaving ATMI poised to reap the rewards of the industry's increased use of copper in the future.

Jeffrey L. Covell

PRINCIPAL SUBSIDIARIES

Advanced Technology Materials, Inc.; Epitronics Corporation; ATMI Ecosys Corporation; Advanced Delivery & Chemical Systems Nevada, Inc.; Advanced Delivery & Chemical Systems Holdings, LLC; Advanced Delivery & Chemical Systems Operating, LLC; Advanced Delivery & Chemical Systems Manager, Inc.; ATMI Materials, Ltd.; ATMI Korea Co. Ltd.; ATMI UK Limited; ATMI Packaging, Inc.; ATMI International Holdings, Inc.; ATMI Taiwan Holdings, Inc.; ATMI Belgium Holdings, Inc.; ATMI Belgium, LLC; ATMI Packaging N.V. (Belgium); ATMI International Trading Co. Ltd. (China); ATMI Japan KK; ATMI Taiwan Co. Ltd.; ATMI GmbH (Germany); ATMI Pte. Ltd. (Singapore); ATMI Fab Services Ireland, Ltd. (Ireland); ATMI Acquisition BVBA (Belgium).

PRINCIPAL COMPETITORS

E.I. du Pont de Nemours and Company; Air Products and Chemicals, Inc.; Rohm and Haas Company.

FURTHER READING

"ATMI Acquires ESC Inc.," *Fairfield County Business Journal*, August 11, 2003, p. 5.

"ATMI Acquires NOW," *Semiconductor Industry & Business Survey*, April 27, 1998.

"ATMI Buying Epitronics, Guardian," *Electronic News (1991)*, December 4, 1995, p. 62.

"ATMI Buys MST Analytics Sensors," *Microtechnology News*, December 19, 1999.

"ATMI to Acquire Newform," *Electronic News (1991)*, October 18, 1999, p. 6.

"CEO to Step Down at Danbury, Conn.-based Microchip Supplier ATMI Inc.," *Hartford Courant*, November 17, 2004.

Fasca, Chad, "ATMI, ADCS Plan $92M Merger," *Electronic News (1991)*, April 14, 1997, p. 1.

———, "ATMI Buys Lawrence for $78M," *Electronic News (1991)*, May 26, 1997, p. 4.

Lubanko, Matthew, "Danbury, Conn.-based Materials Company to Split into Two Parts," *Hartford Courant*, April 25, 2004.

Tortoriello, Richard, "Riding a Chip Rebound with ATMI," *Business Week Online*, March 25, 2003.

Axsys Technologies, Inc.

175 Capital Boulevard, Suite 103
Rocky Hill, Connecticut 06067
U.S.A.
Telephone: (860) 257-0200
Fax: (860) 594-5750
Web site: http://www.axsys.com

Public Company
Incorporated: 1959 as Vernitron Corporation
Employees: 765
Sales: $156.35 million (2006)
Stock Exchanges: NASDAQ
Ticker Symbol: AXYS
NAIC: 333314 Optical Instrument and Lens Manu- facturing

∎ ∎ ∎

Axsys Technologies, Inc., is a producer of high performance optics and other components for advanced aerospace, surveillance, and electronics applications. Known as Vernitron Corporation before 1996, in its first few decades the company specialized in electric motors and precision screws and branched out into the medical and scientific industries. Since the September 11, 2001, terrorist attacks on the United States (9/11), Axsys has focused on optics found in many of the latest targeting and surveillance systems. One of its loftiest projects involves supplying optics for the James Webb Space Telescope.

ORIGINS

Vernitron Corporation, the precursor of Axsys Technologies, Inc., was launched in New York in 1959 by Bernard Levine, who served as its chairman and president. After working for Bendix Aviation, one of many aerospace contractors in the area, Levine formed Vernitron with a couple of fellow alumni from Cooper Union, the arts and science college where he had earned his electrical engineering degree.

Vernitron made electrical and electronic components, including motors. Within a few years it expanded its product line through acquisition. The company made one of its first major buys in 1965, spending $1 million on Jaymax Precision Products, Inc. Jaymax, formed a year before Vernitron, was a maker of precision nuts, bolts, and other metal parts. It was based in Prospect, Connecticut. Jaymax was later renamed Vernitron Precision Products Inc. and was ultimately sold in the late 1970s.

There were other acquisitions in the 1960s. Vernitron was in the medical equipment market by 1969, when it bought Allied Plasma Corp. and International Bio-Science Corp., lumping them into newly formed Allied Bio-Science Inc.

CHANGES AT THE TOP

Originally incorporated in New York, Vernitron was reorganized as a Delaware corporation in 1968. By this time, its shares were trading on the American Stock Exchange.

The company's ten-year anniversary was accompanied by changes in the executive ranks. Dr. Leslie

K. Gulton, who had previously launched a metal alloys business, became Vernitron's chairman in 1969. Herman S. Nathanson was named president and CEO of the company in 1970 and the next year added the position of chairman as well. Levine remained as chief financial officer until his retirement in 1984. The company's chief engineer, Albert Diamond, was named president in 1984.

Vernitron revenues were up about $20 million a year at the end of the 1970s. The company had made a number of acquisitions in the last years of the decade. TRW Inc.'s IRC Potentiometer business was acquired in 1977 for $4 million. In 1979 the company acquired Better Built Machinery Corp., a manufacturer of washers and dryers. It also added Aladdin Industries Inc.'s electronics division. Vernitron continued the buying spree into 1980, when it bought McGraw-Edison Co.'s Brevel Motors division. Brevel had annual sales of $20 million and supplied small commercial and industrial motors.

M&A ACTIVITY

Vernitron grew to 2,800 employees and sales of nearly $150 million by the mid-1980s. However, it was beginning to lose money. In late 1986 Vernitron was acquired for about $80 million by an investment group led by Stephen W. Bershad (via newly formed SB Holding Corporation). Bershad became CEO.

More intense merger and acquisition activity followed a couple of years later. In December 1988, Verni-tron launched a hostile takeover bid for Connecticut-based rival Kollmorgen Corp. Kollmorgen's 1987 revenues of $301 million were three times those of Vernitron at the time.

This effort dragged on for years, with a chronicle of lawsuits and poison pills being played out in business headlines. Vernitron originally offered $20 per share, or $203 million. After finally winning an agreement to buy Kollmorgen for $25 a share, or $320 million, in September 1989, Vernitron backed out on news of a heavy quarterly loss by its takeover target. Not content to let matters rest, in May 1990 Vernitron offered a new bid at $15 a share but this was rebuffed. CEO Stephen Bershad described the adventure to the *New York Times* as a "disaster." According to the *Washington Post*, the failed bid cost the company $20 million in all.

Revenues were about $60 million in the mid-1990s, when there were 600 employees, but rose to $91 million in 1996. The company had several plants scattered across the United States and outsourced some work to a facility in Mexico.

LOOKING TO OPTICS FOR GROWTH

In 1996 Vernitron bought Precision Aerotech, a manufacturer of laser scanners, optics, bearings, and other precision machined parts. It was based in La Jolla, California.

A couple of strategic acquisitions in the same year bolstered Vernitron's aerospace optics business. The Speedring companies made optics for forward-looking infrared (FLIR) devices, used in military targeting systems, and commercial space projects, and were also involved in optical scanning. This was bolstered with the acquisition of the beryllium business of Lockheed Martin Corporation soon after.

The company was renamed Axsys Technologies, Inc., in December 1996 while its ticker symbol changed from VRNT to AXYS. Its common shares had been trading on the NASDAQ since 1991.

FIBER AUTOMATION FORAY

Axsys opened a fiber automation plant in Pittsburgh in February 2001. This made equipment for producing fiber-optic components for the telecom market. After an unprofitable year and a half, it was sold to Vista, California's Palomar Technologies.

With the fiber automation sale, Axsys abandoned the telecom business to focus on its traditional strengths. It restructured into three business lines in March 2002:

KEY DATES

1959: Vernitron Corporation is founded by Bernard Levine.
1965: Vernitron buys Jaymax Precision Products, Inc.
1978: Jaymax is sold in a leveraged buyout.
1986: Investment group led by Stephen Bershad acquires Vernitron.
1988: Vernitron launches failed takeover bid for rival Kollmorgen Corp.
1991: Company lists shares on the NASDAQ.
1996: Vernitron is renamed Axsys Technologies, Inc.
2004: Infrared specialist Telic Optics is acquired.
2007: Stabilized camera system manufacturer Cineflex LLC is acquired.

weapons guidance optics and machined parts, precision bearings, and optical test scanning equipment. One divestment of 2002 was Teletrac, a small manufacturer of data storage testing equipment.

AN EYE ON DEFENSE AFTER 9/11

Axsys bought Telic Optics, Inc., of North Billerica, Massachusetts, in 2004 in a deal worth up to $18 million. Telic was a specialist in infrared optics with military and homeland security applications.

Axsys began working on the James Webb Space Telescope (JWST) in 2004. It was supplying beryllium segments for its giant mirror as a subcontractor to Ball Aerospace and Technology Corporation; Northrop Grumman was the prime contractor. The JWST, the replacement for the Hubble, was scheduled for deployment in 2013; Axsys was expected to complete its work on the mirror segments several years before that.

The acquisitions continued in 2005 with the $60 million purchase of Diversified Optical Products Inc. (DiOP). Based in Salem, New Hampshire, DiOP produced infrared camera systems for the defense and homeland security fields. It had annual revenues in excess of $20 million and employed 120 people. The next year, Axsys acquired a former Teradyne Inc. plant in Nashua, New Hampshire, as a new home for DiOP and Telic Optics.

By this time, Axsys was organized into two main groups. The Optical Systems Group accounted for 83 percent of Axsys's total revenues of $156 million in 2006. The rest came from the Distributed Products

Group, which supplied precision bearings, bushings, and related subassemblies. Revenues had doubled since 2002, when sales were about $80 million.

ACQUISITION OF CINEFLEX IN 2007

Stabilized camera system manufacturer Cineflex LLC of Van Nuys, California, was acquired in 2007. Cineflex was well known in the entertainment business; in addition to playing a prominent role in aerial cinematography, its equipment had been used to televise the pursuit of O. J. Simpson's white Ford Bronco live to a national audience in 1994. Cineflex had been owned by helicopter services entrepreneur Alan Purwin (via Helinet Aviation Services LLC) since 2003 and was drawing increasing interest in its technology for use in military applications. The deal was worth up to $69 million if Cineflex met certain revenue goals.

Frederick C. Ingram

PRINCIPAL SUBSIDIARIES

Precision Aerotech, Inc.; Speedring, Inc.; Speedring Systems, Inc.; Axsys IR Systems, Inc.

PRINCIPAL DIVISIONS

Optical Systems Group; Distributed Products Group.

PRINCIPAL COMPETITORS

Excel Technology, Inc.; ROFIN-SINAR Technologies Inc.; Janos Technology, Inc.; Agilent Technologies Inc.; GSI Group, Inc.; MRC Optics.

FURTHER READING

"Axsys Adds N.H.-Based IR Surveillance System Firm in $60M Buy," *Mass High Tech: Journal of New England Technology,* March 21, 2005, http://www.bizjournals.com/masshightech/stories/2005/03/21/daily15.html.

"Axsys Tech to Consolidate Operations in New Hampshire," *Boston Business Journal,* May 8, 2006, http://www.bizjournals.com/boston/stories/2006/05/08/daily2.html.

Bramlet, Christina R., and John M. Jordan, "Going Where No Toolholder Has Gone Before," *Modern Machine Shop,* September 2006, pp. 110–14.

Chavtal, Kris, "Kollmorgen Gives in to Vernitron—Finally," *Electronic Buyers' News,* May 8, 1989, p. 3.

Davis, Christopher, "Working for a Big Firm, Feeling Like a Start-Up," *Pittsburgh Business Times,* May 31, 2002, http://

www.bizjournals.com/pittsburgh/stories/2002/06/03/focus2.html.

Destefani, Jim, "Stability and Precision," *Manufacturing Engineering* 135 (4), October 2005, pp. 57–60, 62, 64.

Gilpin, Kenneth N., "Vernitron Promotes Officer to President," *New York Times,* Financial Desk, August 13, 1984.

Guzzo, Maria, "California Company Buys Axsys Fiber Automation," *Pittsburgh Business Times,* November 7, 2002, http://www.bizjournals.com/pittsburgh/stories/2002/11/04/daily56.html.

Levine, Bernard, "Kollmorgen Losses End Vernitron Deal," *Electronic News,* September 25, 1989, p. 1.

Mastandrea, John, "Kollmorgen Moves to Halt Vernitron," *Fairfield County Business Journal,* February 13, 1989, p. 1.

———, "Kollmorgen Spurns Merger Proposal," *Fairfield County Business Journal,* January 9, 1989, p. 1.

———, "Vernitron Makes $20-a-Share Bid for Stamford-Based Kollmorgen," *Fairfield County Business Journal,* December 26, 1988, p. 1.

Norris, Floyd, "The Bitter Fight for Kollmorgen," *New York Times,* Financial Desk, May 16, 1990.

Resende, Patricia, "Axsys Closes Down Its Automation Group," *Mass High Tech: The Journal of New England Technology,* October 21, 2002, http://www.bizjournals.com/masshightech/stories/2002/10/21/daily37.html.

Riley-Katz, "From Hollywood to the War on Terror; Defense Firm Buys Helicopter Camera Used to Film 'Planet Earth,'" *Los Angeles Business Journal,* June 11, 2007, pp. 1, 47.

Saxon, Wolfgang, "Bernard Levine, an Industrialist and Cooper Union Trustee, 68," *New York Times,* June 29, 1993.

Sloan, Allan, "In the World of Takeovers, Let the Preferred Stockholders Beware," *Washington Post,* July 30, 1991, p. E3.

Sloane, Leonard, "Bateman Eichler Planning to Sell Vernitron and Frigitronics Stock," *New York Times,* August 5, 1977, p. 66.

———, "Gulton Is Elected by Vernitron; He Left Company He Founded," *New York Times,* December 9, 1969, p. 101.

Soule, Alexander, "Optical Gear Maker Axsys Sells Subsidiary," *Mass High Tech: The Journal of New England Technology,* April 29, 2002, http://www.bizjournals.com/masshightech/stories/2002/04/29/daily41.html.

"Vernitron Corporation and Jaymax Precision Products," *New York Times,* November 6, 1965, p. 39.

Wax, Alan J., "Ex-Vernitron Execs Allowed to Resume Doing Business," *Newsday,* August 27, 1986, p. 41.

———, "Investment Group Makes $75M Offer for Vernitron," *Newsday,* September 27, 1986, p. 13.

Zielenziger, David, "Kollmorgen Control War Heats Up," *Electronic Engineering Times,* January 30, 1989, p. 41.

———, "Raid for Kollmorgen Turns Nasty," *Electronic Engineering Times,* March 6, 1989, p. 10.

AZZ Incorporated

—■—

1300 South University Drive
University Centre 1, Suite 200
Fort Worth, Texas 76107
U.S.A.
Telephone: (817) 810-0095
Fax: (817) 336-5354
Web site: http://www.azzincorporated.com

Public Company
Incorporated: 1956 as Aztec Manufacturing Co.
Employees: 1,301
Sales: $260.3 million (2007)
Stock Exchanges: New York
Ticker Symbol: AZZ
NAIC: 335122 Commercial, Industrial, and Institutional Electric Lighting Fixture Manufacturing; 332812 Metal Coating, Engraving (Except Jewelry and Silverware), and Allied Services to Manufacturers

■ ■ ■

A New York Stock Exchange–listed company based in Fort Worth, Texas, AZZ Incorporated divides its business into two segments: Electrical and Industrial Products, and Galvanizing Services. The activities of the former unit is conducted through seven subsidiaries located in Massachusetts, Mississippi, Missouri, Oklahoma, South Carolina, and Texas. Serving the power generation and transmission industry, petrochemical companies, and other industrial customers, AZZ products include electrical power distribution enclosures, tubular goods, air-insulated and gas insulated bus duct systems, relay control systems, electrical switchgear, and specialty industrial lighting components. AZZ's Galvanizing Services unit bathes steel in molten zinc to protect it from corrosion, serving fabricators and manufacturers in such industries as telecommunications, transportation, petrochemical, construction, and agriculture. AZZ maintains 14 hot dip plants spread across the southern United States and portions of the Midwest.

FORMATION OF AZTEC MANUFACTURING IN 1956

AZZ was founded as Aztec Manufacturing Co. in 1956 by five oilfield service company executives, including L. C. Martin, who would lead the company for half a century. Martin was 29 years old at the time, an employee for a Halliburton unit. He invested $5,000, his life savings, for 5,000 shares of Aztec and assumed the position of chief engineer for the new oilfield pump manufacturer. Aztec's timing proved unfortunate, however, its management team failing to recognize the impact of a 1954 Supreme Court ruling that resulted in natural gas being controlled at the well head and drastically cutting the need for pumping units, the expected lifeblood of the company. On the verge of failure after just one year, Aztec was rescued by a business it had launched to generate sales while it geared up to turn out pumps: finishing the ends of oilfield tubing. Because these tubing capabilities were in place, Aztec was able to take advantage of the emerging demand for thin tubing, known in the industry as "macaroni."

Earlier in the 1950s, Humble Oil & Refining, an early incarnation of Exxon, pioneered a method of tapping oil and gas from multiple points at the same wellhead using thin tubing. Steel mills were willing to produce the product, but opted not to add capacity to finish the tubing for an industry that everyone assumed offered limited growth potential. Aztec was able to step into the breach and began finishing macaroni tubing, which, as it turned out, was used in the one kind of drilling that would prosper during a 16-year drilling slump that ensued. By the time other companies recognized the opportunity presented by macaroni tubing, Aztec had staked out a dominant market position and earned a solid reputation in the oil industry, which preferred to rely on proven suppliers. The price of tubing meant little in terms of the millions of dollars spent to drill a well; it was reliability that counted, and Aztec was the proven company in the field.

TAKEN PUBLIC: 1960

Aztec went public in 1959, and continued to grow into the 1960s. Flush with cash, the company began to pursue diversification in 1963. A year later, Martin took over as chief executive officer, the last of the five founders to be involved with Aztec: three had sold out while another had passed away. It was at this stage that the foundation was laid for AZZ's galvanizing business, albeit in a roundabout way. Martin paid $65,000 in 1966 for an Oklahoma highway sign manufacturer. Because of weather, the signs were galvanized. Unlike macaroni tubing, the highway sign business was highly competitive and the Oklahoma unit in time became a disappointment. In 1975 Aztec stopped making signs, but Martin wisely retained the galvanizing part of the business.

Nevertheless, galvanizing services were still a minor sideline for Aztec in the early 1970s. Following an extended slump, drilling began to increase in 1972, prompting Martin to borrow $1 million to build a new tubing plant. The 1973–74 oil embargo served to create a boom in domestic drilling, essentially forcing Aztec to expand in order to protect its market position. Martin correctly assessed the situation and borrowed more money to further increase the company's tubing capacity and was able to take advantage of exploding demand in 1978, leading Aztec to double its workforce.

OILFIELD BUSINESS PEAKING: 1982

Again Martin looked to take advantage of good times to branch out into a new area, drill pipe, but rather than compete with well-established manufacturers he opted on the far less crowded rental niche. Yet just as quickly as the drilling boom had begun it came to an end. Fortunately, Aztec's tubing business took less of a hit during the 1979 downturn, helping the company to wait out a short-lived drilling lull. As the company entered the 1980s, business was once again thriving. The peak came in 1982 when revenues reached $60 million and it appeared that Aztec was well on its way to attaining $100 million, a level that Martin hoped to hit by 1986. However, another, deeper slump would visit the oil industry and derail his plans.

As the oil business suffered, Aztec saw its revenues shrink to $10.5 million in 1986. In response, Aztec began to beef up its galvanizing operations. In March, Mississippi's Automatic Processing Inc. was acquired for $1.7 million. Later in the month another hot-dip galvanizing plant was bought in Waskom, Texas, bringing the total number of Aztec plants to five. Martin also looked for other lines of business to pursue. In December 1986 the company paid $560,000 to acquire Parks Machine Co., a Fort Worth manufacturer of hose fittings and charge casings needed to hold explosive charges used in oil and gas drilling. Although these products had been generally immune to the cyclical nature of the oil and gas industry, they did not provide Aztec with the kind of business line Martin believed was necessary.

While the search for an alternative business continued in the second half of the 1980s, Aztec added several more galvanizing plants, which became the company's mainstay. In 1988 Martin attended an electrical power seminar in California, triggering an interest in power generation. As he had done in the past, Martin looked for an angle, finally settling on industrial applications in the electrical products field. A search for suitable acquisitions lasted until 1990 when Aztec found a pair of affordable companies. In March 1990 Aztec paid $3.4 million in cash and assumed $300,000 in liabilities to pick up Rig-A-Lite, Inc., maker of lighting systems. A unit of Fort Worth-based Kendavis Industries, it became available when the parent

KEY DATES

■

1956: Aztec Manufacturing Co. is founded as oil-field services company.
1959: Company goes public.
1964: Cofounder L. C. Martin is named CEO.
1966: Company enters galvanizing business.
1986: Company is devastated by oilfield slump.
1990: Company enters electrical products field.
1997: Aztec is listed on New York Stock Exchange.
2000: Aztec changes name to AZZ Incorporated.
2001: Martin retires as CEO.
2003: Martin retires as chairman.

company went bankrupt because of the oil industry collapse. Another opportunistic acquisition was completed in September 1990 when Aztec paid $2.8 million in cash and assumed $3.1 million in liabilities for The Calvert Company, a manufacturer of electrical buses that was on the block because no one in the family of its aging founder was willing to run the company.

Aztec's new electrical business did well, but Martin was unable to find any more acquisition prospects. In the meantime, Parks Machine, which was losing money, was shut down in 1992, further reducing Aztec's commitment to the oilfield services industry, which supplied just one-tenth of the company's revenues. Moreover, the recession of the early 1990s also adversely affected the galvanizing unit. To help build its electrical products unit, Aztec hired the investment banking division of Dallas-based NationsBank, and in a matter of months it had ten prospects to consider. One of those leads resulted in the 1993 acquisition of Atkinson Industries, Inc., a manufacturer of power distribution equipment, for $6.3 million and $800,000 in liabilities.

As the economy began to recover, so too did the galvanizing business, prompting Aztec to ramp up production. In early 1994 a sixth plant was added with the $2.4 million purchase of Alabama-based Gulf Coast Galvanizing Inc. Later in the year Aztec opened a seventh plant in Phoenix, Arizona. Total revenues for Aztec increased from $30.8 million in fiscal 1993 to $40.8 million in fiscal 1994, while net income improved from $1.1 million to $2.2 million. Aztec enjoyed steady growth over the next few years and continued to make acquisitions as opportunities arose, buying Prairie Grove, Arkansas-based Arkansas Galvanizing, Inc., for $4.2 million in cash and $800,000 in liabilities in 1996 and New Orleans–area Hobson Galvanizing a year later for $3.9 million. Also in 1997 Aztec acquired Beaumont,

Texas-based International Galvanizers, Inc., for $1.65 million, and reached an agreement on the purchase of Texarkana, Texas-based Drill Pipe Industries, Inc.

NEW YORK STOCK EXCHANGE LISTING: 1997

Sales reached $57.7 million and net income increased to more than $4.3 million in fiscal 1997. During the year Aztec also gained a listing on the New York Stock Exchange. Aztec continued to operate in three business segments—oilfield tubing, electrical products, and galvanizing services—in fiscal 1998, when the company posted record results, finally eclipsing the marks set 16 years earlier. Aztec netted $7.2 million on sales of almost $75.5 million in fiscal 1998. More importantly, the company's oilfield tubing business accounted for only about 10 percent of revenues. Aztec elected to focus more attention on its galvanizing business and the company was reorganized into two business segments: Manufactured Products, which included electrical and tubular products, and Services, which contained the galvanizing operations. Fiscal 1999 also saw the acquisition of Drilling Rig Electrical System Inc. (DRES-CO), a Houston maker of electrical systems for oilfield drilling and barges, and the $13 million purchase of West-borough, Massachusetts-based ABB Power T&D's compressed gas insulation transmission bus duct division, which did business as CGIT Westboro Inc. For the fiscal year, Aztec recorded revenues of $80.9 million and net income of nearly $5 million.

NEW CENTURY, NEW NAME

Aztec changed its name to AZZ Inc. in the summer of 2000, part of an effort to recast the company's brand to open up new opportunities. The company continued to grow through strategic acquisitions, in February of that year paying $10.6 million for Westside Coating Services, Inc., of Baton Rouge, Louisiana, adding its 11th galvanizing plant. AZZ also pursued internal growth, completing a major expansion of its bus duct manufacturing facility in 2000, an investment made to take advantage of growing demand in power generation that in turn increased the market for AZZ's bus duct product line. In addition, AZZ introduced a new product offering during the year, retail lighting, another growth area.

Revenues improved to $92.5 million in fiscal 2000, and then increased another 31.2 percent to $121.4 million in fiscal 2001. Net income totaled $7 million in 2000 and grew to $8.2 million a year later. AZZ also invested in a pair of November acquisitions to help maintain momentum. Central Electric Company of Fulton, Missouri, a manufacturer of specialty switchgear products, power center enclosures, relay panels, and non-segregated bar bus equipment, was acquired for $17 million in cash, another $1.8 million in stock, and the assumption of $10 million in liabilities. On the same day, AZZ closed on another acquisition, spending $15.4 million for Carter & Crawley, Inc., a Greenville, South Carolina, provider of electrical engineering services, process control systems, relay control panels, and installation services.

On his way to finally reaching a long-coveted goal of growing the company he cofounded to the $100 million mark, Martin in 2001 turned over the CEO position to David H. Dingus, who had served as president and chief operating officer since 1998. Martin stayed on as chairman of the board for another two years, then retired when Dr. H. Kirk Downey succeeded him as chairman.

AZZ enjoyed two years of strong growth, increasing revenues to $183.4 million in fiscal 2003 while posting net income of $8.6 million, but economic conditions soured in 2004, hurting the all-important industrial and manufacturing sector, which became price sensitive. Although AZZ experienced a drop in sales to $136.2 million it was able to post its 17th consecutive profitable year, netting $4.3 million. Business rebounded in fiscal 2005 and AZZ increased revenues to $152.4 million and net income to $4.8 million. Sales grew another 23 percent to $187.2 million in fiscal 2006, and net income jumped 63 percent to $7.8 million. AZZ returned to the acquisition trail in October 2006, paying $12.15 million in cash for the three galvanizing plants operated by Witt Industries, Inc. Having turned the corner, AZZ again enjoyed record results in fiscal 2007, increasing revenues 39 percent to $260.3 million, and net income increased 176 percent to $21.6 million.

The company set an even higher pace through the first half of fiscal 2008.

Ed Dinger

PRINCIPAL SUBSIDIARIES

Aztec Industries, Inc.; The Calvert Company, Inc.; Arbor-Crowley, Inc.; Gulf Coast Galvanizing; Arkglav Inc.; Arizona Galvanizing, Inc.; Hobson Galvanizing, Inc.; CGIT Westboro, Inc.; Westside Galvanizing Services, Inc.; Central Electric Company; Carter and Crawley, Inc.; Atkinson Industries, Inc.; Witt Galvanizing - Cincinnati, Inc.; Witt Galvanizing - Muncie, Inc.; Witt Galvanizing - Plymouth, Inc.

PRINCIPAL COMPETITORS

Genlyte Group, Inc.; Xenonics Holdings Inc.; Tri-Lite Inc.

FURTHER READING

Berman, Phyllis, "'Close to the Vest,'" *Forbes*, April 27, 1981, p. 102.

Francis, Robert, "Aztec, Starting over Again, Diversifies into New Areas," *American Metal Market*, December 29, 1986, p. 6.

Fuquay, Jim, "Co-Founder of Crowley, Texas, Manufacturing to Retire," *Fort Worth Star-Telegram*, January 31, 2001.

———, "Significant Shifts in Direction Were Key to 1991 Sales Growth," *Fort Worth Star-Telegram*, April 13, 1992, p. 15D.

———, "Triumph over Trouble," *Fort Worth Star-Telegram*, June 16, 1997, p. 18.

Knights, Mikell, "Aztec Buys Galvanizing Plant," *American Metal Market*, January 12, 1994, p. 4.

Sapino, Brenda, "Aztec Acquiring Fifth Facility for Galvanizing," *American Metal Market*, March 18, 1986, p. 7.

Smith, Jack Z., "Acquisition Would Satisfy Aztec's Itch to Grow," *Fort Worth Star-Telegram*, August 31, 1992, p. 1.

Banco de Crédito del Perú

Calle Centenario 158
Lima, 12
Peru
Telephone: (51 1) 313-2000
Fax: (51 1) 313-2353
Web site: http://www.viabcp.com

Wholly Owned Subsidiary of Credicorp Ltd.
Founded: 1888
Employees: 10,771
Total Assets: PEN 33.71 billion ($10.55 billion) (2006)
NAIC: 522110 Commercial Banking; 522210 Credit Card Issuing; 522291 Consumer Lending; 523110 Investment Banking and Securities Dealing; 523120 Securities Brokerage; 523920 Portfolio Management; 523930 Investment Advice; 523991 Trust, Fiduciary and Custody Activities

■ ■ ■

Banco de Crédito del Perú (BCP) is Peru's largest commercial bank. Unusually for contemporary Latin America, where banking is dominated by outside financial institutions, it remains Peruvian-owned. While primarily commercial in focus, its activities include investment and retail banking. It ranks first among Peruvian banks in total assets, total loans, deposits, and shareholders' equity, and it has the largest branch network of any commercial bank in Peru. As a full service bank, it offers such products to its customers as custody and trust, research, advice, brokerage, and asset management. BCP is the largest unit in Credicorp Ltd.,

the Bermuda-based holding company that is Peru's largest financial services corporation.

BANCO ITALIANO: 1888–1942

BCP was founded in 1888 as Banco Italiano by Italian citizens residing in Lima and Callao (Lima's port); the company had seven employees by the following year. The fledgling bank financed small Italian-owned ventures in Peru, particularly food businesses. By 1909 it had four branches, a mortgage section, two insurance companies, and other subsidiaries. The bank was the first in Peru to provide short-term loans, extending them in 1918 to cotton growers against the year's crop. In the 1920s it became Peru's leading bank (other than the central bank). By the end of 1940 the bank was in 43 cities besides Lima, and there were 59 customer offices.

Originally the directors of Banco Italiano were almost always merchants, but by the 1930s a mix of agriculturists and ranchers, merchants, industrialists, financiers, and property holders were on the board. Among them were Luis Nicolini, member of a family that remains an economic power in Peru, and Federico Milne, who with Nicolini was owner of the major processor of local grains.

With World War II underway and Italy allied with Germany, Peru (likely prodded by the United States) grew concerned about Banco Italiano's perceived Axis ties, and legislation adopted in 1941 forced it to change its name to Banco de Crédito del Perú the following year.

CONTINUING UNDER ITALIAN CONTROL: 1942–79

Although bearing a new name, BCP remained controlled by the Banca Comerciale Italiana, acting through a French subsidiary, Banque Sudameris et Italianne pour l'Amérique de Sud (renamed Banque Sudameris in 1978). Although BCP's chairman was a Peruvian, the general director and the most important managers were Italian. BCP built a new headquarters in central Lima in 1958 and had 123 offices two years later.

The next major event in the history of Banco de Crédito del Perú was a result of the military coup of 1968, which brought to power in Peru a group of intensely nationalistic army officers. A decree aimed concretely at BCP established a ceiling of one-third of the commercial banking sector that any single bank could hold, in terms of total obligations on reserve in national money. The military also looked with suspicion on the domination of BCP by Banque Sudameris et Italianne, which held 48 percent of the shares. This participation fell to 20 percent in 1971, when a decree limited shareholding in a Peruvian company by foreign enterprises to one-fifth of the stock. Nevertheless, Italians continued to run the bank until nearly the end of the decade.

The end of Italian dominance in Banco de Crédito's affairs was largely the work of the Romero group. Its 19th century founder, Calixto Santos Romero y Hernández, left Spain at the age of 14 and came to Peru after arriving successively in Cuba, Bolivia, and Chile. He established C. Romero y Cía., a commercial enterprise, in Piura in 1886. His chief business at first was the export of Panama hats. Financed by cotton growers, Romero next established a ginning business. By 1922 the Romeros were cotton growers themselves, often taking control of property when loans by them could not be repaid. By 1940 the family was a major power whose holdings included a rice mill and enterprises turning out a variety of other foodstuffs, textiles, hardware, and general machinery. The Romeros also sold imported cars and trucks.

The Romero family group, with others, founded Banco Continental in 1951 and was its chief shareholder until 1964, when Chase Manhattan Bank purchased majority control. Banco Continental was expropriated by the military government in 1970. By this time, however, the Romeros, who had held shares in Banco Italiano since 1918, had set their sights on BCP. Dionisio Romero Seminario, a grandson of Calixto, joined the board of directors in 1966. During the next two years BCP acquired two smaller banks, Banco Gibson S.A. and Banco Unión.

UNDER THE ROMERO FAMILY GROUP: 1979–90

The Romeros, with their allies, held about one-third of BCP's shares in 1979, when they wrested control of the bank from the Italians and made Dionisio Romero Seminario the president, or chairman, of the board. The Romero family, and allied family business groups, wanted credits from the bank to finance imports of raw materials for industrial production or to finance sales of the products that their enterprises offered to consumers. The Romeros' chief allies were the Brescia, Ruffo, Nicolini, and Luis Barchero families.

Sudameris sold the majority of its shares in Banco de Crédito in 1984 to Uebersee Bank AG, which held 13.6 percent of the stock in 1987. The Romero family group held 14.14 percent. Sudameris still had 4.86 percent. Some 6,225 smaller shareholders held 38 percent. The BCP of the 1980s was, among other things, a merchant bank—that is, one that made investments on its own account—with many holdings in real estate and manufacturing firms. It built a new $40 million headquarters about 12 miles from central Lima; although only eight stories high, the building was clad in black and white marble and blue crystal glass imported from Europe. There were two branches abroad: in New York City and Nassau, Bahamas. The bank also had $350 million in deposits in Atlantic Security Bank and Atlantic Security Financial Services, both of them located in the Cayman Islands.

The 1980s were a period of great political and economic distress in Peru. The nation's financial institutions, already mainly under state control, became even more so as the government tried to deal with its debts and runaway inflation by nationalizing even more banks. By 1987 state institutions held 84 percent of financial assets and nongovernment commercial banks only 11 percent. Of the latter, BCP remained by far the biggest, with 45 percent of the total assets in this shrinking sector. When the government of President Alan García attempted to nationalize BCP that year, the majority shareholders forestalled the action by selling a controlling interest to the employees and transferring management to them. After market-friendly Alberto

KEY DATES

1888: Banco Italiano, the predecessor of Banco de Crédito del Perú (BCP), is founded.

1909: The bank's holdings include four branches and two insurance companies.

1920s: Banco Italiano has become Peru's largest private bank.

1942: With World War II underway, the bank changes its name to Banco de Crédito del Perú.

1958: BCP moves into new headquarters in central Lima.

1979: The Romero family group takes control of BCP.

1993: BCP acquires control of Banco Popular de Bolivia.

1995: BCP becomes a subsidiary of Bermuda-based Credicorp Ltd.

2002: BCP purchases a competitor, Banco Santander Hispano-Perú.

Fujimori assumed the presidency in 1990, the Romeros again reestablished their holding and direction of the bank.

One bright spot in the dismal picture during this period was Banco de Crédito's leasing contracts with businesses seeking to purchase buildings, vehicles, or equipment. These transactions remained free of government regulation and were more profitable than conventional loans. BCP's finance company was the nation's leading lessor. In 1988 the bank connected almost all its offices to a central computer in Lima and installed an extensive network of ATMs.

A LIBERALIZED OPERATING CLIMATE: 1990–2000

Under Fujimori, the economic climate changed markedly in the early 1990s. Two of Banco de Crédito's main competitors were privatized, and foreign financial institutions began buying Peruvian banks. In the liberalized business climate, corporations were able to find alternative means of financing. Accordingly, Peruvian banks, notorious for rude treatment of individual customers and open for as few as two and a half hours per working day, displayed new interest in retail banking, offering such products as mortgages, personal loans, guaranteed checks, automatic tellers, credit cards, and electronically linked branch banking. BCP joined in this effort but remained more cautious than others in extending personal loans, despite the high margin of profit, for fear of default.

During the early 1990s Banco de Crédito established a brokerage and securities management subsidiary named Credibolsa Sociedad Agento de Bolsa S.A. and a pension fund management subsidiary called Inversiones Crédito del Perú that took a 20 percent stake in the pension fund AFP Unión. In 1993 BCP acquired a majority share in Banco Popular de Bolivia, that nation's second largest lender, renaming it Banco de Crédito de Bolivia. The following year BCP established Credifondo S.A. Sociedad de Administradora de Fondo, a subsidiary dedicated to the promotion of mutual funds.

Banco de Crédito itself became a subsidiary in 1995, when its management established the Credicorp holding company. Although Credicorp was registered in Bermuda and listed on the New York (as well as Lima) Stock Exchange, its headquarters remained in Lima. In 1995 or 1996 BCP established Crédito Leasing S.A. for financial leasing products. The bank's subsidiaries in 1998, besides Credibolsa, Credifondo, and Crédito Leasing, included Solución Financiera de Crédito del Perú S.A., a consumer finance company.

BCP itself had 29 percent of deposits and 23 percent of all assets in Peru's banking system in 1998, more than any other bank. Lending to big corporations was, and had long been, the source of its strength. It also sought business from small and medium sized companies and to extend its retail banking activities, but it was not willing to make loans to customers of dubious creditworthiness. The bank invested heavily in central risk evaluation systems so that loans to individual customers would be approved only after being thoroughly analyzed by objective data. Even so, BCP experienced a deterioration in its loan portfolio between 1997 and 2000, a period in which its net income fell by more than two-thirds.

BCP IN THE EARLY 21ST CENTURY

By 2001, however, a resurgent Banco de Crédito was considered sound enough to warrant the highest investment-grade rating in issuing $100 million of seven-year bonds. The key to this rating, far above that of the Peru government's own, was BCP's leading share in remittances made by Peruvians abroad. BCP agreed to divert these funds into a trust account.

Banco de Crédito, in 2002, purchased Banco Santander Hispano-Perú for $50 million. In 2005 it paid $353.8 million for the loan portfolio of Bank

Boston N.A. and the loan portfolio of Peruvian nationals with Fleet Boston N.A. BCP had survived Peru's political and economic troubles and remained in Peruvian hands, while its two main rivals, Banco Wiese and Banco Continental, had been purchased by foreign financial companies. It accounted, in 2006, for 82.2 percent of Credicorp's total assets, 69.7 percent of Credicorp's total revenues that year, and 88.3 percent of the holding company's net income, which came to a record $247.8 million and constituted a 28.6 percent return on equity.

Besides leading all other Peruvian banks in loans, assets, and deposits, Banco de Crédito was the largest mortgage lender in Peru and, in addition, had issued 378,677 credit cards. It also had the largest commercial bank network in Peru, with 237 offices, and was operating a branch in Panama and an agency in Coral Gables, Florida. Dionisio Romero was chairman and chief executive officer of both Credicorp and BCP. Luis Nicolini was deputy chairman. While the Romero family remained the chief shareholder, pension funds were collectively more important, holding at least 25 percent of Credicorp's shares. Credicorp owned 86 percent of BCP's shares in 2005.

Much of the credit for Banco de Crédito's continued dominance of commercial banking in Peru went to Raimundo Morales, its general manager from 1990 to 2007. Under his guidance, by 2003 BCP's assets had grown more than twelvefold. Interviewed for *LatinFinance's* 15th anniversary issue, Morales, who saw the bank's future as a regional bank, said, "Eventually we have to be present in different markets. I think we will keep seeing more of a globalized world as economies keep opening up and financial and trade flows increase with free trade agreements in the Americas. Many of the countries have dollar-based economies and eventually we will end up with one currency in the Americas."

Robert Halasz

PRINCIPAL SUBSIDIARIES

Banco de Crédito de Bolivia (Bolivia; 96%); Credibolsa Sociedad Agento de Bolsa S.A.; Credifondo S.A. Sociedad Administradora de Fondo; Crédito Leasing S.A.

PRINCIPAL OPERATING UNITS

Capital Markets Group; Retail Banking Group; Service Banking Group; Wholesale Banking Group.

PRINCIPAL COMPETITORS

Banco Internacional del Perú S.A.A.; BBVA Banco Continental; Scotiabank Perú S.A.A.

FURTHER READING

Campbell, Monica, "Rolling with the Punches," *Banker,* July 2003, pp. 114–16.

Field, Graham, *Peru: An Economy for the 21st Century,* London: Euromoney, 1999, pp. 83–84.

Kilby, Paul, "Where Credit Is Due," *LatinFinance,* October 1996, pp. 36–38.

Malpica Silva Santiestaban, Carlos, *El poder económico en el Perú,* Lima: Perugraph Editores, 1989, Vol. 1, pp. 59–82.

Quiroz, Alfonso W., *Banqueros en conflicto,* Lima: Universidad del Pacífico, 1989, pp. 183–89.

Reaño Álvarez, Germán, and Enrique Vásquez Huamán, *El grupo Romero,* Lima: Universidad de Pacífico, 1988, 176 p.

Rivas Gómez, Victor, *Historia financiera del Perú 1960–1990,* Lima: Universidad de San Martín de Porres, 1997, Vol. 2, pp. 405, 409, 427.

———, *Perú en el umbral del siglo XXI,* Lima: Universidad de San Martín de Porres, 2000, pp. 295 and 309–10.

Salmon, Felix, "Latin America: Banco de Crédito del Peru," *Euromoney,* June 2001, p. 106.

Swafford, David, "Best Bank in Peru: Banco de Credito del Peru," *LatinFinance,* October 1997, p. 56.

"VICTOR Raimundo Morales," *LatinFinance,* July 2003, p. 61.

Zuckerman, Sam, "Coup de Garcia for Peru's Banks," *Euromoney,* September 1987, pp. 320–22.

Belvedere S.A.

10 Ave. Charles Jaffelin
Beaune, F-21200
France
Telephone: (+33 03) 80 22 93 83
Fax: (+33 03) 80 22 93 84
Web site: http://www.belvedere.fr

Public Company
Incorporated: 1991 as France Euro Agro
Employees: 1,965
Sales: EUR 889.8 million ($1.13 billion) (2006)
Stock Exchanges: Euronext Paris
Ticker Symbol: 60873
NAIC: 312130 Wineries; 312140 Distilleries

■ ■ ■

Belvedere S.A. is a fast-growing France-based spirits group with a strong presence in the Eastern European market. In Poland, the company is the single largest producer and distributor of vodka, through its premium Sobieski and other local and regional brands. Sobieski, created by the company at the end of the 1990s, is also one of the world's top ten premium vodka brands. The company acquired four distilleries during the privatization of Poland's state-owned distilleries in the early 2000s; the company acquired a fifth, in Vilnius, Lithuania, and also owns two wineries in Bulgaria. Since the middle of the first decade of the 2000s, however, Belvedere has developed a two-pronged strategy of expanding its geographic focus while building its brand portfolio beyond the white spirits category. Acquisitions are helping to drive this strategy. Notably, in 2006 the company acquired Marie Brizard International, one of France's oldest producers and distributors of cordials, liqueurs, and other spirits. The company bought the Danska vodka brand, the fourth largest selling vodka in the duty-free channel, the following year. These acquisitions complement the group's entry in the French wine market, through its purchase of Provence-based Chateau d'Esclans. The company also owns the William Pitt brand, the leading Scotch whiskey brand in France. As part of its geographic expansion, Belvedere has entered the United States, acquiring production facilities and founding a distribution subsidiary, Imperial Brands, Inc., in Florida. Belvedere is listed on the Euronext Paris stock exchange, and is led by cofounders, principal shareholders, and, respectively, chairman and managing director, Jacques Rouvroy and Krzysztof Trylinski. The company had sales of EUR 889.8 million ($1.13 billion) in 2006.

MARKETING IDEA IN 1993

In 1991, Jacques Rouvroy, a graduate of France's École de Commerce, teamed up with Krzysztof Trylinski, a popular Polish athlete then residing in France, to form a company importing French wines to Poland and Czechoslovakia. Rouvroy and Trylinski founded France Euro Agro that year, along with a Czech subsidiary and a subsidiary in Poland, France Vins Company. Euro Agro soon began to diversify into the wider spirits category.

In 1992, however, Rouvroy and Trylinski hit upon a new idea. With the collapse of the Communist regime

KEY DATES

1991: Jacques Rouvroy and Krzysztof Trylinski found France Euro Agro to import French wine to Poland.

1993: Company develops marketing concept featuring high-end decorated bottles for Polish vodkas, including Belvedere Brand, then expands concept to international level.

1997: Company changes name to Belvedere S.A. and lists stock on Paris Stock Exchange.

1998: Belvedere launches Sobieski vodka brand and creates distribution network in Poland.

2001: Company sells rights to Belvedere and begins acquiring privatized distilleries in Poland, becoming leading vodka group in that country.

2006: Belvedere diversifies portfolio and geographic focus with acquisition of Marie Brizard International.

2007: Company founds U.S. distribution subsidiary and launches Sobieski brand there.

and the introduction of the free market, Polish consumers had begun to show an interest in branded goods, especially in luxury products and brands. Rouvroy and Trylinski recognized an opportunity to extend their own business in wine and spirit. Specifically Euro Agro targeted the market for vodkas, the best-selling spirit in Poland. That country was also one of the world's single largest vodka markets, trailing only Russia and the United States.

Euro Agro's idea was to create a line of premium vodkas packaged in high-end bottles decorated with Polish national symbols. The bottles were designed and produced in France, and imported to Poland to be filled by a local brewery there. In this way, the company was able to overcome the steep import duties placed on foreign spirits brands in order to protect the local market.

During the Soviet era, the Polish vodka market had been entirely controlled by the state, with production completed through a network of 11 distilleries. In 1991, as a partial reform of the market, the government restructured its distillery network into 11 independently operating distilleries, or Polmos, which remained controlled by the government. Euro Agro's Polish partner began making the rounds of the distilleries seeking a partner for the company. In 1993, the company

reached an agreement with Polmos Zyrardow, one of the smallest of the distilleries.

BELVEDERE SUCCESS

Zyrardow at the time had no viable brands of its own, and was struggling for its survival. The agreement with Euro Agro quickly became a strong partnership, as the two companies became determined to produce a high-quality, high-end vodka. The distillery soon succeeded in developing a light-flavored vodka, positioned between the flavor of Absolut and the more full-flavored Polish vodkas such as the Wyborowa brand. Yet the new vodka's success lay as much in Euro Agro's bottle designs. The first of these also became one of the companies' most emblematic, featuring a window overlooking Belvedere, the Polish presidential mansion and one of the symbols of the recent revolution. Other designs featured Chopin and the Krakow Cathedral.

The unusual bottles helped the new vodka brand, called Belvedere, gain instant notoriety in Poland. Despite being priced at two and even two-and-a-half times that of competing vodkas, the Belvedere brand became one of the highest-selling in the country. As Rouvroy explained to the *Wall Street Transcript:* "People went crazy for these new products, because for the first time ever, they had an opportunity to find on their markets, an upmarket product that looked like a Western product, but had strong features of the Polish and Czechoslovakian local culture."

The bottles also quickly found international success. Part of this came as a result of chance. One of the first shops to feature the bottles was a small duty-free store in Warsaw's Okecie Airport. The vodka became a popular souvenir item for foreign visitors, and before long demand grew beyond Poland. The success of these bottles led Euro Agro to roll out its bottling concept to other markets. Starting in 1994, the company added operations with local distilleries in China, Japan, Greece, Russia, Bulgaria, Belorussia, Croatia, and Yugoslavia, as well as markets in Latin America. While vodka remained the group's primary market in Eastern Europe, Euro Agro's bottles elsewhere contained the local white spirits favorite, such as ouzo in Greece, tequila in Mexico, pisco in Chile, and white rum in the Caribbean.

In support of its growing operations the company beefed up its logistics end, creating a dedicated subsidiary based in Germany. In France, the company formed a subsidiary, Mad Sarl, which became responsible for its glass purchases, as well as overseeing its bottle decorations subcontractors.

Among the company's international customers, meanwhile, was the wife of former presidential aide

Zbigniew Brzezinski, who ordered several cases of the vodka for an art exhibition in New York City. In this way, the Belvedere brand gained almost instant access into U.S. high society. Attracted by the brand's success, Phillips Millennium Beverages (PMB), a drinks distributor in the United States, approached the Zyrardow distillery with an offer to become the Belvedere brand's U.S. representative.

BECOMING A CASE STUDY IN 1998

Belvedere hit the U.S. market with a bang in 2005. Within two years, the number of cases sold had jumped from just 100,000 cases the first year to more than 1.2 million. The Belvedere brand quickly emerged as the top-selling premium vodka brand in the United States.

Nonetheless, the Polish market remained Euro Agro's primary source of revenues. In the late 1990s, the company moved to respond to a number of significant changes in that market, notably, the upcoming end of protective import duties, and the coming privatization of its distilleries. The former promised an onslaught of new competition in the vodka market, as foreign brands were able to compete on an equal basis. In response, the company decided to develop its own distribution operations in Poland to ensure its own brands' viability. At the same time, the privatization of the industry gave the company the opportunity to move from being essentially a marketing company to becoming a full-fledged drinks producer.

In order to finance its new strategy, the company went public in 1997, listing its shares on the Paris stock exchange. For the offering, the company changed its name, adopting the name of its most successful brand to become Belvedere S.A. Over the next year, Belvedere's stock rose strongly, from FRF 125 at the time of the offering, to more than FRF 1,400.

Belvedere's ambitions quickly ran into a major hurdle, as PMB attempted to gain control of the Belvedere brand. The company found itself vulnerable because of an earlier mix-up in the registration of the Belvedere brand and its bottle design. As a result, in 1996, the company and the Zyrardow distillery had reached an agreement in which the then-Euro Agro was given ownership of the Belvedere brand and bottle design, while Zyrardow was granted a free and permanent license to produce the vodka, distributed in the Belvedere bottle.

Belvedere found itself under attack by PMB. At first, PMB attempted to register the Belvedere brand as its own in 29 different countries. When Belvedere successfully countered that effort, Phillips Millennium launched an all-out assault on the French group in an effort to void the 1996 agreement made between Euro Agro and the Zyrardow distillery.

PMB began lobbying members of the Polish government, including reportedly giving $10,000 to a charity run by the country's president. Part of PMB's strategy involved discrediting Belvedere itself. For this, PMB hired the Edelman public relations firm to launch a negative publicity campaign. A centerpiece of that campaign was the creation of a web site claiming that Belvedere was under investigation by the COB, the French equivalent of the Securities and Exchange Commission. As a result, Belvedere's stock crashed, and the company's survival was threatened.

The attack, and Belvedere's ultimately successful defense, represented the first time the Internet had been used as a tool to attack a quoted French company, and soon became a case study presented at business schools in the country. Belvedere ultimately agreed to sell the Belvedere brand to PMB for a total of $22 million. The COB later exonerated Belvedere of any wrongdoing, and instead fined PMB for its attempt to defame the company. (As a footnote, in 2007, the Belvedere Vodka brand, acquired by the LVMH luxury group, found itself under attack by a California winery that claimed to have owned the Belvedere brand for more than 35 years.)

CHANGING COURSE FOR THE NEW CENTURY

Faced with its difficulties surrounding the Belvedere brand and the attack by PMB, another company might have found itself out of business. Yet, if Belvedere ultimately agreed to sell its namesake brand, it was because the company had moved on to something bigger.

In the midst of its battle with PMB, Belvedere had recognized the need to adapt to the future liberalization of the Polish vodka market. The company recognized the need to create a new midrange vodka brand that could position itself as a direct rival to the foreign brands soon to enter Poland. For this, the company developed Vodka Sobieski, named after King Jan Sobieski III, a legendary figure in Polish history. Produced at the Zyrardow distillery, the new brand was supported by a major advertising campaign, featuring the well-known French actor Jean Reno. Instead of using etched bottles, the Sobieski brand was packaged in more standard bottles. This enabled the company to market the brand at an affordable price.

Polish national pride helped with the rest. Within a month of its launch Sobieski had sold 500,000 bottles.

The brand quickly became one of the top-selling vodka brands in Poland. At the same time, with a new strong brand in the company's portfolio, the investment community once again embraced the company's stock, which recovered its former levels by the year 2000.

The success of Sobieski also enabled Belvedere to position itself as one of the frontrunners in the privatization of Poland's vodka industry. Belvedere first acquired a 45 percent stake in the small Alco Pegro distillery in 2001. By the end of 2002, the company had bought the larger Starogard distillery in Gdansk and the Polmos Krakow distillery. A fourth Polish distillery, Polmos Lancut, was acquired in 2004. By then, the company had also bought a distillery in Lithuania, Vilnius Degtine. By the end of its acquisition drive, Belvedere had become the largest single vodka company in Poland, with its flagship Sobieski brand, and a portfolio of ten major regional brands.

Belvedere was primarily refocused on the Polish market, which accounted for 92 percent of its sales of EUR 349 million in 2003. The company added a new subsidiary, importing Bulgarian wine into Poland, meeting new success notably through the acquisition of the rights to use the well-known Sofia brand in 2003. By mid-decade, Belvedere had also acquired two wine estates in that country, and had begun developing its own premium quality wines.

EXPANDING THE PORTFOLIO IN 2006

Belvedere failed in its attempt to buy Poland's largest distillery. As a result, the company later lost its leadership position in the market, becoming only the second largest vodka seller. Instead, Belvedere once again adapted its strategy, and focused on broadening its operations, both geographically, and toward a more diversified drinks portfolio.

The company quickly achieved both, when it reached an agreement to acquire Marie Brizard International at the end of 2005. Marie Brizard was one of France's oldest drinks groups, founded in 1795. The purchase not only gave Belvedere the perennially strong Marie Brizard cordials brand, it also added brands including William Peel, the number one Scotch whiskey brand in France; Old Lady's, the country's second largest gin brand; and San José Tequila, the leading tequila brand. The Marie Brizard purchase also included a soft drinks component, including the Pulco fruit syrups brand; this was sold in 2007 in order to pay off debts taken on by the acquisition.

Belvedere continued targeting add-on acquisitions. The company acquired Chateau d'Esclans, a Provence-based vineyard, in 2006. Also that year, Belvedere targeted the duty-free market, acquiring the Danzka vodka brand from Absolut-owner V&S. The acquisition gave the company the fourth largest selling duty-free vodka brand, and an entry point for a wider rollout of its portfolio in the duty-free channel.

The strength of the Sobieski brand in the meantime encouraged the company to make a new attempt to the enter the U.S. market. The company began building a base of operations in Florida in 2007, buying Florida Distillers, a producer of bulk and branded beverages, as well as vinegar and other products with four production facilities. Belvedere then created a dedicated U.S. distribution subsidiary, Imperial Brands, in order to launch Sobieski in the United States.

For this, the company positioned Sobieski as an inexpensive alternative to the highly expensive super premium category, suggesting "It's time vodka drinkers knew the truth about vodka. ... In essence, they are paying for fancy packaging and bloated marketing costs." An interesting twist, considering that just such marketing lay behind Belvedere's initial success. Yet Belvedere had successfully transitioned itself from a mere marketer to a fast-growing, diversified wine and spirits group in the new century.

M. L. Cohen

PRINCIPAL SUBSIDIARIES

Belvedere Czeska; Belvedere Distribution (Bulgaria); Belvedere Logistik (Germany); Chais Beaucairois Sas; Cognac Gautier Sa; Euro-Agro Warszawa (Poland); Imperial Brands, Inc. (U.S.A.); Magichesky Kristall (Russia; 50%); Marie Brizard & Roger International Sa; Menada Vineyards (Bulgaria); Sakar Vineyards (Bulgaria); Sci Roger; Sobieski USA; Tianjin Belvedere International Trade Co. Ltd. (China); Vilnius Degtine (Lithuania); William Pitters International Sas.

PRINCIPAL COMPETITORS

Christian Dior S.A.; LVMH Moët Hennessy Louis Vuitton SA; Suntory Ltd.; Pernod Ricard S.A.; Maxxium Worldwide B.V.; Diageo Scotland Ltd.; V&S Vin & Sprit AB; Remy Cointreau S.A.; Champagne Moët and Chandon SCS.

FURTHER READING

"A Fondaudege, la Peur du Drame," *Sud Ouest*, December 14, 2007.

"Belvedere Bids to Buy Out Marie Brizard Shareholders," *just-drinks.com*, April 20, 2006.

"Belvedere Closes Marie Brizard Soft Drink Sales," *just-drinks. com,* September 25, 2007.

"Belvedere Declares US Vodka War with Sobieski Launch," *just-drinks.com,* September 26, 2007.

"Belvedere Opens Bulgarian Winery," *Just-drinks.com,* September 5, 2007.

"Belvedere Pleased with Year So Far, on Acquisition Trail," *just-drinks.com,* November 16, 2007.

"Déménagement de Marie Brizard: 80% des Salariés ne Suivraient pas," *Les Echos,* December 14, 2007.

"France's Belvedere Purchases 77.6% Stake in Polmos Krakow Spirits for PLN 16.4 Mln," *Poland Business News,* November 6, 2002.

"Interview: Jacques Rouvroy," *Wall Street Transcript,* October 1999.

"Les Familles Fondatrices Retrouvent le Controle du Groupe," *Les Echos,* August 1, 2007.

Mathieu, Gilles, "Belvédère's Offre 69.3% de Marie Brizard," *Le Bien Public,* December 28, 2005.

"Sweden's V&S Group Sells Florida Distillers to French Spirits Group Belvedere," *Nordic Business Report,* February 1, 2007.

Bio-Rad Laboratories, Inc.

1000 Alfred Nobel Drive
Hercules, California 94547
U.S.A.
Telephone: (510) 724-7000
Fax: (510) 741-5817
Web site: http://www.bio-rad.com

Public Company
Incorporated: 1957
Employees: 5,400
Sales: $1.27 billion (2006)
Stock Exchanges: American
Ticker Symbol: BIO
NAIC: 334516 Analytical Laboratory Instrument Manufacturing; 325413 In-Vitro Diagnostic Substance Manufacturing; 325998 All Other Miscellaneous Chemical Product Manufacturing

■ ■ ■

Bio-Rad Laboratories, Inc., sells more than 8,000 products and systems used to separate chemical and biological materials, a process that enables researchers to identify, analyze, and purify components. The company serves 70,000 customers involved in life sciences research, healthcare, and analytical chemistry, selling its products in more than 30 countries. Bio-Rad divides its business into two operating segments, Life Sciences and Clinical Diagnostics. Through its Life Sciences segment, the company supplies reagents, instruments, and software to aid in the study of the characteristics, behavior, and structure of living organisms. Through its Clinical Diagnostics segment, Bio-Rad develops tests and test kits that are used to detect, identify, and measure substances in blood or other body fluids and tissues. The division's chemicals and instruments are used to detect and monitor a variety of diseases such as anemia, diabetes, and acquired immune deficiency syndrome (AIDS). Although publicly held, Bio-Rad is tightly controlled by the Schwartz family, who wield 90 percent of the company's stock voting power.

BERKELEY IN THE FIFTIES

Bio-Rad was founded by two University of California at Berkeley scientists, David Schwartz and his wife Alice Schwartz. Their entrepreneurial effort began in a surplus military structure, an austere setting for a business that a half-century later would generate more than $1 billion in revenue annually. Remarkably, the husband-and-wife team would witness the full maturation of their business, leaving a lasting mark on Bio-Rad and factoring as the dominant personalities during the company's first 50 years in business.

David, a chemist, and Alice, a biochemist, began their professional careers in Berkeley. They began by doing scientific work for other firms on a contract basis, functioning essentially as freelance chemists. In the course of their work, the pair developed new products and tools to facilitate their research, which soon led them to the realization that their colleagues, other researchers, might benefit from their discoveries. The idea became the motivation for starting a business, a company they named Bio-Rad Laboratories, Inc.

If the journey is indeed the reward, we are fortunate to be traveling during an auspicious time in the field of healthcare. On this path, each point along the way represents a step of hope, each advancement a higher quality of life for patients. Today, with the promise of genetic discovery and improved diagnostic techniques, this pathway is offering new routes to successful outcomes. At Bio-Rad, we are an integral part of this journey, helping researchers and diagnosticians continually reach innovative and important milestones for improving the way diseases are understood, managed, and, in some cases, completely eradicated.

David and Alice Schwartz established their business in 1952 and incorporated it five years later. Initially, they housed Bio-Rad in a Quonset hut, the type of temporary quarters widely used during World War II. The prefabricated, corrugated steel structure sat behind Spenger's fish emporium in Berkeley, where the two scientists focused their efforts on the study of proteins. The success of their work would eventually enable the Schwartzes to replace their Quonset with a corporate headquarters spread across an 80-acre site, replete with multistory, modern office buildings.

From the start, the two entrepreneurs were developing custom methods to separate proteins from each other. By isolating proteins, the molecules could be tested by researchers to determine which function each protein performed. Although complex, the process could be simplified into three steps: separation, purification, and analysis. The Schwartzes and the rest of Bio-Rad's staff would use the same basic process for the next five decades.

Bio-Rad recorded slow but steady growth during its first years in business. The company generated $55,000 in revenue during its first year, and would wait nearly 15 years before reaching the $1-million-in-sales mark. During this initial phase, the company limited its involvement to the life sciences sector, developing and producing specialty chemicals used in biochemical, pharmaceutical, and other life sciences research applications. The company began packaging a variety of tests and shipping them to other laboratories. Financial totals increased as its roster of products increased, as did the financial totals for most companies, but for Bio-Rad, a company that eventually depended on thousands of

products, it took a while for its research and development efforts to reach critical mass.

ENTRY INTO CLINICAL DIAGNOSTICS IN 1967

A turning point in terms of the company's pace of growth occurred during the late 1960s. Bio-Rad, dependent entirely on life sciences work, added a second segment to its operations. In 1967, the Schwartzes collaborated with a researcher from their alma mater and developed a thyroid diagnostic test, which marked the beginning of Bio-Rad's involvement in the clinical diagnostics field. Through its clinical diagnostics segment, which relied on the same basic separation techniques used by its life sciences segment, Bio-Rad developed and manufactured automated test systems and test kits. The systems and kits were used by hospitals and clinical laboratories to assist physicians in diagnosing and monitoring their patients.

By the time Bio-Rad made its first foray into the clinical diagnostics field, its operations were open to public scrutiny. Few industry observers chose to take more than a cursory look at the company, however. The Schwartzes took their company public in 1966, which ordinarily would have raised the business's profile, but Bio-Rad remained in the shadows. The type of business the company was in was partly responsible for its relative anonymity. The company made the tools, instruments, and tests that enabled other researchers to complete high-profile work. "It's not sexy," a Bio-Rad senior executive remarked in a January 11, 1997, interview with the *San Francisco Business Times*. "We aren't going to be the ones curing cancer. Hopefully, we'll be supplying the tools."

Bio-Rad also maintained a low profile because its stock was thinly traded. David and Alice Schwartz owned more than 60 percent of the company's controlling stock (an interest that would increase to 90 percent in later years), leaving the couple in firm command of the company. "Schwartz totally controls the company," an industry observer noted in the December 6, 1991, edition of the *San Francisco Business Times*. "There's no way anyone can force him to do anything he doesn't want to do." Bio-Rad, except for a few occasions, flew under the business press's radar, quietly developing into an industry stalwart.

ANALYTICAL INSTRUMENTS BECOMING THE THIRD SEGMENT

Bio-Rad added a second operating segment during the 1960s, and it added a third operating segment in the

1970s. The company diversified into clinical diagnostics through internal means, but it would develop a third business arm through external means. Acquisitions paved Bio-Rad's entry into the analytical instruments field. The company purchased Block Engineering in 1978 and Polaron Equipment Limited in 1982, giving it the foundation for developing instruments used in industrial and scientific research. The company's products in its third operating segment included spectrometer systems, analytical and measuring instrument systems, and semiconductor measurement instruments, products that were sold to government agencies, research institutions, and industrial companies. Bio-Rad's Analytical Instruments segment received a boost to its stature with a third acquisition, the purchase of Vickers Instruments in 1989.

AN INTERNATIONAL PROFILE

The year Bio-Rad acquired Vickers Instruments, its sales reached $236 million, representing an average 20 percent annual increase each year for the previous quarter-century. Alice Schwartz had retired from active duty a decade earlier (she remained a Bio-Rad director), but David Schwartz continued to guide the company on a day-to-day basis, serving as chairman and chief executive officer. He presided over a company that had

recorded substantial growth not only financially but in other areas as well. The expansion of the company's product line—Bio-Rad was selling more than 4,500 different products by the beginning of the 1990s—had fueled the company's geographic march. The company relied on markets outside North America for 60 percent of its annual sales, maintaining sales and manufacturing offices in Brussels, Paris, Vienna, Tokyo, Beijing, and Hong Kong, as well as elsewhere.

Bio-Rad made headlines on several occasions, shedding the veil that surrounded its operations to enjoy brief moments in the limelight. In 1995, the company's research into genetics attracted widespread interest during the trial of O. J. Simpson. In 1997, a technique the company developed to inject DNA into sheep cells enabled the birth of Dolly, the first cloned lamb. Bio-Rad tools were used to help identify the *E. coli* bacteria strain. Its Helios Gene Gun was used in research for vaccines to combat AIDS, hepatitis, and other infectious diseases. The attention the company would receive would only heighten in the coming years.

A MAD COW MASTER

In 1999, Bio-Rad spent $210 million to acquire a French company named Pasteur Sanofi Diagnostics. Included in the acquisition was a test for bovine spongiform encephalopathy, or BSE, a disease known worldwide as "mad cow disease." The first human case of mad cow disease occurred in 1996; by the beginning of 2001, 96 people, mostly Britons, had died or were dying from the brain-eating disease. Bio-Rad jumped into the market with its acquired test, beginning sales in November 2000 of its proprietary Platelia-BSE. Bio-Rad was one of only three companies licensed to market a test for BSE, and the first established name (the other two firms were private, European companies) to enter the market. Within a short time, Bio-Rad captured more than two-thirds of the market for BSE test kits, the type of accomplishment that earned the attention of Wall Street. By 2002, the company's stock value had nearly doubled.

Although the increasing value of Bio-Rad shares was gratifying, particularly to the Schwartzes who owned much of the company's stock, the attention received from its involvement in the BSE crisis exaggerated the importance of mad cow to the company. Bio-Rad dominated the market, but sales collected from test kits amounted to only 10 percent of its total revenue volume. The company made the majority of its money by selling thousands of products developed to assist in the research of scores of applications. The sense of what drove the company forward was ingrained in the leader appointed as chief executive officer in 2003, the first change in Bio-Rad's leadership in 50 years.

NEW LEADERSHIP IN 2003

When David Schwartz finally relinquished the duties of chief executive officer, he passed the responsibilities to familiar hands, his son, Norman Schwartz. The younger Schwartz was no newcomer to the company, having joined Bio-Rad 29 years earlier, in 1974, when he began serving in a variety of managerial capacities for the company. Under the tutelage of his father, Schwartz served as corporate treasurer, general manager of the company's U.K.-based manufacturing operations, manager of its Japanese subsidiary, and as head of Bio-Rad's Life Sciences Group, a position he held when the company completed the purchase of Pasteur Sanofi Diagnostics.

The company's involvement in BSE-related business deepened in 2003 when the specter of a contaminated beef supply spread to the United States. In December, a cow in Washington State was diagnosed with mad cow disease, triggering calls for the U.S. Department of Agriculture (USDA) to implement widespread screening of U.S. cattle. In response, Bio-Rad, which sold more BSE test kits in Europe and Japan than any other company, applied for USDA licensure in January 2004. In March 2004, the company became one of the first companies to gain federal approval for a mad cow test kit.

A PROMISING FUTURE

As Bio-Rad prepared for the future, it could also look forward to a wealth of business opportunities arising from the sequencing of the human genome. The mapping of genes revealed vital information about the chemical composition of the body's proteins, which participated in every process within the body's cells, but it offered scant information about the specific roles each protein played. Determining each protein's function, a field known as proteomics, was Bio-Rad's specialty, the same sort of work David and Alice Schwartz were doing in their Quonset hut during the early 1950s. By understanding each protein's function, drug discovery and development efforts for the spectrum of human illnesses promised to improve dramatically. The demand for aid in advancing the field of proteomics put Bio-Rad in an enviable position, ensuring that the company, as it had for five decades, would continue to play a pivotal role in scientific discovery. "The biggest challenge is really making choices," Norman Schwartz explained in a March 4, 2002, interview with *Investor's Business Daily.* "We have so many opportunities, so many interesting

areas to explore. Our biggest challenge is trying to focus in on the best opportunities."

Jeffrey L. Covell

PRINCIPAL SUBSIDIARIES

Bio-Rad Laboratories Pty. Limited (Australia); Bio-Rad Laboratories Ges.m.b.H. (Austria); Bio-Rad Laboratories S.A.-N.V. (Belgium); Research Specialties for Laboratories N.V. (Belgium); Bio-Rad Laboratorios Brasil Ltda. (Brazil); Bio-Metrics Properties, Limited; Bio-Rad Laboratories (Israel) Inc.; Bio-Rad Pacific Limited; Blackhawk Biosystems, Inc.; Bio-Rad Laboratories (Canada) Limited; Bio-Rad Laboratories (Shanghai) Limited (China); Bio-Rad spol. sr.o. (Czech Republic); Bio-Rad Export, Inc.; Bio-Metrics Ltd.; Bio-Rad Holdings LLC; MJ Bioworks, Inc.; Bio-Rad Laboratories APS (Denmark); Bio-Rad France Holding; Bio-Rad France Holding 2; Bio-Rad Pasteur (France); ADIL Instruments SAS (France); Bio-Rad Laboratories SAS (France); Bio-Rad Verdot SAS (France); Bio-Rad SNC (France); Bio-Rad Laboratories G.m.b.H. (Germany); Bio-Rad Laboratories E.P.E. (Greece); Bio-Rad Hungary Trading Ltd.; IMV Medical Information Division, Inc.; Bio-Rad Laboratories (India) Private Limited; Bio-Rad Haifa Ltd. (Israel); Bio-Rad Laboratories S.r.l. (Italy); Nippon Bio-Rad Laboratories K.K. (Japan); Bio-Rad Fujirebio Inc. (Japan); Bio-Rad Korea Limited; International Marketing Ventures, Limited; MJ Research, Inc.; Bio-Rad, S.A. (Mexico); Bio-Rad Laboratories B.V. (Netherlands); Bio-Rad Polska Sp. z o.o. (Poland); Bio-Rad Laboratoires-Aparelhos e Reagentes Hospitalares, LDA (Portugal); Bio-Rad Labortorii OOO (Russia); Bio-Rad Laboratories (Singapore) Pte. Limited; Bio-Rad Laboratories (Pty) Limited (South Africa); Bio-Rad Laboratories S.A. (Spain); Bio-Rad Laboratories AB (Sweden); Bio-Rad Laboratories AG (Switzerland); Bio-Rad Laboratories Limited (Thailand); Bio-Rad Ltd. (U.K.); Bio-Rad Laboratories Europe Limited (U.K.); Bio-Rad Laboratories Limited (U.K.); PB Diagnostics Ltd. (U.K.); MJ Geneworks, Inc.

PRINCIPAL DIVISIONS

Life Sciences; Clinical Diagnostics.

PRINCIPAL COMPETITORS

GE Healthcare Bio Sciences; Invitrogen Corporation; Applera Corporation; Abbott Laboratories; Roche Diagnostics Corporation.

FURTHER READING

"Bio-Rad," *San Francisco Business Times,* March 21, 1988, p. 35.

"Bio-Rad Signs Definitive Agreement to Acquire Diamed," *Internet Wire*, May 16, 2007.

Hemmila, Donna, "Adding to Its Toolbox: Bio-Rad Going Shopping Again," *San Francisco Business Times*, July 11, 1997, p. 3.

Lamb, Celia, "Maker of Clinical Devices Is Sold to Biotech Giant," *Sacramento Business Journal*, August 24, 2001, p. 5.

Lau, Gloria, "Bio-Rad Laboratories Inc.," *Investor's Business Daily*, February 28, 2001, p. A12.

Ortiz, Jon, "Hercules, Calif., Lab Wins FDA Approval of Quick Test for Mad Cow Disease," *Sacramento Bee*, March 19, 2004.

"A 'Rad' Firm: Bio-Rad Laboratories Inc. Says Its Success in the Healthcare Industry Stems from Strong Customer Relationships Based on R&D and New Technology," *US Business Review*, June 2006, p. 230.

Rauber, Chris, "High-Tech Outfit Tends Low Profile," *San Francisco Times*, December 6, 1991, p. 1.

Reeves, Amy, "Bio-Rad Laboratories Inc.," *Investor's Business Daily*, March 4, 2002, p. A9.

Silber, Judy, "Hercules, Calif.-based Biotech Firm Reports Profits Nearly Triple," *Contra Costa Times*, May 2, 2001.

Tansey, Bernadette, "Protein a Healthy Research Model," *San Francisco Chronicle*, August 22, 2006, p. E1.

Biomet, Inc.

56 East Bell Drive
Post Office Box 587
Warsaw, Indiana 46581-0587
U.S.A.
Telephone: (574) 267-6639
Toll Free: (800) 348-9500
Fax: (574) 267-8137
Web site: http://www.biomet.com

Private Company
Incorporated: 1977
Employees: 4,254
Sales: $2.11 billion (2007)
NAIC: 339112 Surgical and Medical Instrument Manufacturing; 339113 Surgical Appliance and Supplies Manufacturing; 339114 Dental Equipment and Supplies Manufacturing

■■■

Biomet, Inc., is one of the largest U.S. manufacturers of orthopedic medical devices and supplies. Biomet and its subsidiaries design, develop, manufacture, and market products used primarily by orthopedic specialists in surgical and non-surgical therapy, including reconstructive implants and artificial joints, fixation devices, electrical bone growth stimulators, orthopedic support devices, operating room supplies, general surgical instruments, bone cements, and bone substitutes. Acquired by a consortium of private-equity firms in September 2007, Biomet distributes its products in more than 100 countries around the world.

Located in Warsaw, Indiana, Biomet is part of a seemingly average midwestern community with a population of less than 30,000. What makes Warsaw unique, however, is its reputation as a high-tech hotbed of orthopedic equipment industry innovation. Recognized as the birthplace of the business—industry leaders Depuy Inc. and Zimmer Holdings, Inc., started operations there in 1885 and 1926, respectively—the northern Indiana town is home to three of the four largest orthopedic supplies companies in the world. It is from this pool of longstanding talent that Biomet emerged.

VENTURING TO CREATE A BETTER ORTHOPEDIC EQUIPMENT COMPANY

Dane A. Miller, Jerry L. Ferguson, M. Ray Harroff, and Niles L. Noblitt were all employed in Warsaw's diverse orthopedic equipment industry in the mid-1970s. While working for different companies, they became acquainted with each other through their business dealings. As early as 1975 the four had shared their dissatisfaction with what they viewed as a stifling corporate culture within the industry, but it was not until the late 1970s that they decided to do something about it.

Ranging in age from only 27 to 39, the four entrepreneurs quit their jobs in early 1978 to start Biomet, Inc. (though the entity had been incorporated late in 1977). The company name combined "bio," referring to the body, and "met," referring to metallurgical implants. The group pooled $130,000 of its own money, received a $500,000 loan from the Small Business Administration, and secured a $100,000 line of

COMPANY PERSPECTIVES

Established in 1977, Biomet, Inc., is a family of companies that has enjoyed steady growth at levels exceeding market expansion. Biomet's sales performance demonstrates a responsive, customer-oriented approach to the health care market. Even in a dynamic, cost-conscious environment, Biomet thrives by strengthening its commitment to innovation and partnership.

Biomet prides itself on its unconventional profile: *the responsiveness and innovation of a small company, with the resources and market presence of a large company.*

credit from a local bank. By taking suggestions from surgeons and emphasizing short product development cycles, they believed they could improve upon artificial joint implant designs offered by the companies they abandoned. Their diverse experience in marketing, engineering, and finance could be parlayed into a formidable force in the orthopedic implants industry. Notably, Miller, who would become Biomet's CEO, brought a Ph.D. in biochemical engineering to the table.

With good reason, critics of the new venture wondered about the timing of the start-up. Shortly before the friends left their safe corporate jobs, amendments to the federal Food and Cosmetics Act placed squelching legislation on the artificial implants industry. Indeed, many industry participants believed that new safety regulations and product liability hazards had made the implant business too risky. "People laughed at us for starting up a new company after the new device legislation went into effect," Miller recalled in *Indiana Business.* "[Getting the company started] was traumatic. In retrospect, it was a lot more traumatic than it seemed at the time."

Despite hardship, Biomet was able to find a role in the marketplace as a developer and marketer of orthopedic products, contracting with independent manufacturing shops to make its implants. In its first year of operation the company developed a breakthrough titanium "total hip replacement" implant, the first of which was implanted in Miller's grandmother. Total hip replacement devices and the use of titanium both became industry standards by the late 1980s. Although Biomet had only $17,000 in sales dur-

ing its first year of operation and lost a total of $63,000, by 1980 the struggling enterprise was turning a meager profit.

Unfortunately, Miller and his three partners realized that they were essentially training the manufacturing shop operators to build and sell Biomet-inspired products to their competitors. Unable to locate financing for their own manufacturing program to overcome this dilemma, the Biomet founders considered selling the fledgling business. The company was saved, however, by two brothers from Kalamazoo, Michigan—Kenneth and Jerry Miller (no relation to Dane Miller)—who provided $500,000 in venture capital in return for one-third ownership of the business. Thus the Biomet team found itself in the manufacturing business.

Biomet's second major product innovation occurred in 1980, when it introduced the metal-backed acetabular cup. It was a device used in total joint replacement that increased the longevity of implant-to-bone stem attachments. "That was one example of how we took an opportunity, responded to it quickly, and then took it to the market," Miller related in *Indiana Business.* The company broke new ground again in 1983 with its development of a high-tech knee implant system that allowed a surgeon to align ligaments precisely, ensuring that the joint worked properly. The invention was held up for several years, however, because of technical problems and FDA approval. In the meantime, Biomet solidified its financial position via an October 1982 initial public offering (IPO) of stock on the NASDAQ over-the-counter market. The IPO raised $1.43 million through the sale of 110,000 shares at $13 apiece.

Breakthroughs such as the acetabular cup and titanium hip replacements were central to the momentum Biomet was gaining during the early 1980s. Likewise, aggressive marketing and innovative delivery systems placed the company on the forefront of customer service and cost-containment. Contradicting their detractors, the Biomet management team slowly boosted annual company revenues and profits. By 1984 annual sales had grown to $10.6 million and earnings topped a healthy $1.6 million.

UNIQUE CORPORATE CULTURE

Aside from innovations in product development, marketing, and operations, Biomet founders attributed much of their success to a unique corporate culture that bred creativity and achievement. The company was founded on a premise of risk-taking and teamwork, and

KEY DATES

1977: Dane A. Miller, Jerry L. Ferguson, M. Ray Harroff, and Niles L. Noblitt found Biomet, Inc.

1982: Biomet goes public with an initial public offering of stock on the NASDAQ.

1984: Company completes its first acquisition, Orthopedic Equipment Company.

1988: Electro-Biology, Inc., producer of bone growth stimulation devices, is acquired.

1990: Acquisition of Arrow Surgical Technologies Inc. leads to the formation of arthroscopy subsidiary Arthrotek, Inc. (later Biomet Sports Medicine, Inc.).

1998: Biomet and Merck KGaA form a European orthopedic products joint venture.

1999: Dental implant maker Implant Innovations International Corporation (3i) is acquired.

2001: Company revenues reach $1 billion.

2004: Biomet buys out Merck's interest in the companies' European joint venture and also enhances its position in the spinal market via the purchase of Interpore International, Inc.

2006: Miller resigns as company CEO.

2007: Biomet is taken private via a buyout by a private-equity consortium that includes the Blackstone Group, Goldman Sachs Capital Partners, Kohlberg Kravis Roberts & Co., and Texas Pacific Group.

maintained a very loose structure. Biomet developed only one organizational chart during its early history, and that was created only to please a potential lender. "We try to avoid a lot of structure. ... Whoever is there to make a decision makes it," CEO Miller stated in *Indiana Business*.

In addition to its unorthodox organization, the company prospered by shattering many business school myths that Miller believed were a hindrance to other corporations. While many organizations relied on detailed planning to reach their goals, for example, Biomet spent about 1 percent of its time planning and the rest of the time implementing and monitoring results. "Too much planning sometimes keeps a company from responding to a world that is changing around it," Miller explained in the *Elkhart (Indiana) Truth*. Another myth, according to Miller, was that a company should set a goal and not let anything interfere with the

accomplishment of that mission. "One thing you have to let get in the way from time to time is reality," he said.

Also a part of Biomet's management strategies was intimate worker involvement in, and employee reliance on, the company's performance. All employees were stockholders, either through stock options or by way of a benefit plan. Moreover, half of senior management's compensation was directly dependent on Biomet's financial performance. Miller set the example for his employees by accepting a comparatively conservative compensation package. In fact, Miller was cited in *Business Week* during 1992 for giving shareholders more for their money than any other CEO surveyed: he received only $712,000 between 1989 and 1991 while shareholders garnered huge returns. In the *Indianapolis Business Journal,* Miller declared, "I'd have to admit that if my board came to me and said, 'We're cutting your salary to zero,' I'm having enough fun that I'd come into work anyway."

FIRST ACQUISITIONS

Indeed, if Miller's job satisfaction was any reflection of the company's performance during the mid- to late 1980s, he was a very happy man. After posting its $1.6 million profit in 1984, Biomet entered a sustained period of steady, rapid growth that soon earned the company international recognition within the industry. An October 1983 secondary stock offering raised an additional $11.9 million that funded the firm's first acquisition. In May 1984 Biomet acquired Orthopedic Equipment Company, a manufacturer based in nearby Bourbon, Indiana, for $8.4 million, boosting its revenues for 1985 more than 300 percent. Sales continued to swell through 1988, when the company purchased New Jersey-based Electro-Biology, Inc. (EBI), developer and producer of devices that stimulate bone growth, for $25.8 million. As a result of this important acquisition, Biomet's 1989 revenues leapt to $136 million, of which one-third was contributed by EBI.

Even by the mid-1980s, Biomet's success had earned the company a lofty position in the hierarchy of Warsaw's orthopedic supplies business. Biomet was still dwarfed by Zimmer and Depuy, but its rapid growth and unique products garnered the company third place in the local industry, making Biomet a competitive force that could not be ignored. All three major producers credited the local community with supplying a high-quality, hardworking supply of labor that helped to ensure their success. The region also provided an excellent location for distribution and offered fantastic land prices, cost-of-living advantages, and a high quality of life.

INTERNATIONAL EXPANSION EFFORTS

While grateful to the community, by the late 1980s Biomet had begun to branch out from its native turf. Not only was the company seeking domestic growth, but Biomet management was fully committed to an international expansion effort that was expected to carry the corporation into the 21st century. In fact, Biomet had been chasing international business since its early years. By the early 1990s, international sales represented about 25 percent of the company's revenues and comprised more than 30 percent of its annual growth.

The success of Biomet's important international business reflected the drive and initiative of Chuck Niemier, senior vice-president of international operations. Niemier was a 24-year-old accountant at an outside audit firm when he was introduced to Miller and the small Biomet team. "I think because of my hairline, he thought I was older," recalled Niemier in *Indiana Business*. Miller liked Niemier, and was able to lure him to Biomet with an offer of $26,000 per year and a chance to own some Biomet shares.

Niemier played an early role in developing Biomet's international expansion, which entailed delivering cutting-edge implant products to overseas buyers. During the 1980s and early 1990s, the company expanded into Europe, South America, Japan, the Middle East, the Soviet Union, and other regions. In those countries where Biomet maintained manufacturing facilities, including Germany and England, a direct sales force was established; in other countries it worked through dealer organizations. Niemier benefited from Biomet's flat organizational structure and decentralized decision-making process. The Berlin Wall had barely fallen, for example, before Biomet acquired a successful German orthopedics firm, Berlin-based Effner GmbH, purchased in March 1991. The acquisition of Effner, coupled with the August 1990 purchase of Arrow Surgical Technologies Inc., formed the nucleus for Arthrotek, Inc., Biomet's arthroscopy subsidiary.

Not all of Biomet's international deals played out so nicely, however. When the company received a multimillion-dollar order for trauma products from Iraq in the early 1990s, for instance, Biomet managers were excited. Several months later, though, Iraq invaded Kuwait, providing insight into Iraq's giant order and ending Biomet's dealings with the aggressor nation. Likewise, Biomet invested in several ventures in the Soviet Union during the early 1990s, only to have that market dry up as a result of inner political turmoil. Regardless of minor setbacks, international growth remained a priority for the company going into the mid-1990s. Biomet was operating in about 100 countries by 1992.

Augmenting rising international sales in the late 1980s and early 1990s were continued product and manufacturing innovations that kept Biomet on the leading edge of the industry. In 1989, for example, Biomet technicians began using computer-aided-design (CAD) systems to create three-dimensional images of diseased and damaged joints. When integrated into the production process, the CAD systems allowed Biomet to customize artificial joints for individual patients. The company also became involved in advanced research projects related to bone-growth protein, flexible carbon-fiber implants, and the use of naturally occurring soft tissue to lubricate artificial joints.

REPUTATION AS A SOLID GROWTH STOCK

By the early 1990s, Biomet's stellar rise had earned the company a reputation on Wall Street as a solid growth stock. In 1992, for example, *USA Today* listed Biomet as one of "the hot stocks to watch in the 1990s." Although the 30 percent growth rate in the company's stock price enjoyed by shareholders during the late 1980s and early 1990s had subsided by 1993, it continued to outperform many of its competitors and was considered a good, long-term purchase by a number of analysts. Biomet's ascension was aided by its string of acquisitions, including the July 1992 purchase of Jacksonville, Florida-based Walter Lorenz Surgical, Inc., a leading producer of craniomaxillofacial products for oral surgeons.

Furthermore, Biomet's profit growth continued unabated in the early 1990s and was even accelerating going into the mid-1990s. Sales jumped 22 percent in 1993 to $335 million, and net income ballooned to $64 million. These figures represented five-year compound annual revenue growth of 28 percent in the reconstructive device segment (56 percent of Biomet sales) and 17 percent in the EBI division (25 percent of sales); the remaining revenue was generated from the operations of Arthrotek and Walter Lorenz Surgical as well as the sale of fixation and trauma devices, orthopedic support devices, and operating room supplies.

Aside from sales and stock statistics, Miller and the Biomet managed team looked to another, less tangible measure of their company's success: its victories in helping people to lead better lives. "I believe as we look back 10 years, the evolution of orthopedics has led to the rehabilitation of America," Miller explained in *Indiana Business.* "Ten years ago, if you were incapacitated with a bad knee or hip, you were in bed for the rest of your life. ... In the last ten years, the tools and products have been developed to allow ... patients to live a normal life."

By the beginning of 1993, Miller and Noblitt were the only Biomet founders left at the company, although Ferguson returned late that year after leaving in the mid-1980s to open a classic car dealership (Harroff departed in the early 1980s and bought a golf course). They and other company leaders had ambitious plans for the future, including development of new high-tech products, aggressive global growth, and diversification into new technologies and markets. In the meantime Biomet's entrepreneurial atmosphere and quick-response management structure were retained, owing to the success of such technological breakthroughs as the Maxim, a cutting-edge knee implant introduced in 1993 that significantly boosted profits from the fast-growing knee replacement market. The Maxim in fact became Biomet's biggest new product introduction to that time. Products such as the Maxim cemented Biomet's reputation as a customer-oriented supplier of leading edge, low-cost, high-performance orthopedic devices.

ROUNDING OUT THE CENTURY WITH FURTHER GROWTH INITIATIVES

In the mid-1990s, while contending with pricing pressures stemming from the trend toward managed health insurance plans, most notably HMOs, Biomet continued to pursue growth. In November 1994 the company acquired Kirschner Medical Corporation for $38.9 million. Kirschner, a firm with annual sales of $70 million based in Timonium, Maryland, specialized in joint replacements for hips, knees, and shoulders plus spinal implants and fracture fixation products. Kirschner also had a soft-goods division offering products used for musculoskeletal orthopedic support or in postoperative treatments, such as braces, supports, splints, and cast materials. In 1996 Biomet strengthened its position in Europe through the establishment of Biomet Europe. This unit coordinated sales, development, and manufacturing operations in Germany, Spain, and the United Kingdom and sales centers in France and Italy. That year, when sales and profits both increased for the 18th consecutive year, Biomet paid a dividend to its shareholders for the first time, signaling a shift to a more mature phase in the company's development. By 1997, its 20th anniversary year, Biomet had seen its

sales reach $580.3 million, while net income that year grew another 13 percent, to $106.5 million.

At the beginning of 1998 Biomet and German pharmaceutical giant Merck KGaA formed a joint venture that combined Biomet's European operations with Merck's biomaterials division, which encompassed orthopedic products and biological agents and also ranked as Europe's leading seller of bone cement. The joint venture, which was headquartered in the Netherlands and had its research base in Darmstadt, Germany, started off with annual sales of roughly $200 million, which translated into a European market share of around 10 percent.

While keeping alert for acquisition and joint venture opportunities, Biomet continued to introduce innovative new products. During fiscal 1998 the company became the first in its field to introduce a minimally invasive partial knee implant. The Repicci II Unicondylar Knee System was designed specifically for people whose osteoarthritis was confined to one compartment of the knee. The system typically required a smaller surgical incision, which reduced blood loss and resulted in a shorter recovery time with less pain in comparison with total knee replacement surgery. In many cases, the Repicci system enabled the surgery to be performed on an outpatient basis. The system had been developed in conjunction with a surgeon, Dr. John Repicci.

Fiscal 1999 saw Biomet's string of consecutive years of net profit growth end at 20 due to a special charge of $55 million the company recorded after losing a breach-of-contract lawsuit brought by Orthofix SRL. A jury had ruled in Orthofix's favor regarding its contention that a Biomet subsidiary had breached an agreement to distribute Orthofix's external fixation devices. Damages of nearly $50 million had been awarded. The special charge reduced Biomet's net income for 1999 to $125 million, which was down slightly from the $127.9 million of the previous year. Sales for 1999 jumped more than 17 percent, hitting $827.9 million.

The most significant event of 1999, however, occurred in December when Biomet acquired Implant Innovations International Corporation, known as 3i, in a stock swap valued at approximately $175 million, Biomet's largest acquisition to that date. Based in Palm Beach Gardens, Florida, 3i was a world leader in dental reconstructive implants, which were an alternative to crowns and bridges for dental patients. Its revenues of around $70 million made 3i the second largest player in the U.S. dental implant sector and the third largest in the world.

CONTINUING EXPANSION IN THE EARLY 21ST CENTURY

Biomet followed up the 3i deal with another acquisition completed in September 2000. That month the company acquired, through its EBI subsidiary, Biolectron, Inc., based in Allendale, New Jersey. Biolectron produced external electrical devices for the stimulation of bone growth for spinal fusion and for long bone fractures, as well as a bone tunneling product used to reattach soft tissue to bone in arthroscopy procedures. The acquired company had generated sales of $26 million in 1999. The continuing rollout of new products coupled with the acquisitions of 3i and Biolectron propelled Biomet's sales past the $1 billion mark for 2001. Sales for the year increased 12 percent, to $1.03 billion, while net income increased 14 percent to a record $197.5 million.

Strategic alliances were another important avenue for Biomet growth. In August 2001 the company entered into an agreement with Organogenesis, Inc., of Canton, Massachusetts, that granted Biomet the right to globally develop and market orthopedic and periodontal products stemming from Organogenesis' FortaFlex bioengineered matrix technology. The first fruit from this alliance was the launch in 2002 of the CuffPatch rotator cuff product used for repairing tendons and ligaments of the shoulder. In February 2002 Biomet entered into an alliance with Hollywood, Florida-based Z-KAT, Inc., for the codevelopment and distribution of image-guided surgical applications in all of Biomet's business sectors.

In March 2004 Biomet bought out Merck's interest in the companies' European joint venture in a $300 million cash deal. By this time the venture was generating annual revenues of around $370 million. Although the deal provided Biomet with increased flexibility to pursue acquisitions in Europe, the company's next purchase occurred back home. In June 2004 Biomet enhanced its position in the spinal market by acquiring Interpore International, Inc., of Irvine, California, for $266 million in cash. Interpore, which had net sales of $67.5 million in 2003, specialized in spinal implant products, orthobiologic products, and minimally invasive surgery products. Interpore's product line included stainless-steel screws, rods, and plates for spinal implants as well as a kit to inject bone cement for the treatment of compression fractures. By 2005 Biomet's expansion efforts had added up to revenues of $1.88 billion, the 27th straight year of record sales. Net income for the year amounted to $351.6 million, an increase of 8 percent over 2004.

2006 FORWARD: NEW LEADERSHIP, NEW OWNERSHIP

In March 2006 Miller resigned suddenly and unexpectedly after apparently clashing with the board of directors over the company's rather lackluster performance over the preceding year. Biomet had fallen short of Wall Street expectations several times during that period. While cofounder Noblitt remained chairman of the board, Daniel P. Hann was named interim president and CEO as a search for a permanent successor was launched. Hann had joined Biomet in 1989 and had most recently served as senior vice-president, general counsel, and secretary. Miller was given much credit for spearheading Biomet's remarkable development into one of the leaders of the orthopedic device industry during his nearly 30 years at the helm.

Shortly after Miller's resignation, Biomet hired Morgan Stanley to evaluate possible "strategic alternatives" at a time when rumors were spreading about a sale of the company. In November 2006 Biomet entered into preliminary talks with U.K. rival Smith & Nephew plc about a possible merger, but the negotiations failed to lead to a deal. Private-equity firms then came to the fore as the most likely buyers, and in December 2006 Biomet agreed to be acquired by a consortium that included affiliates of the Blackstone Group, Goldman Sachs Capital Partners, Kohlberg Kravis Roberts & Co., and Texas Pacific Group. Miller was also an additional investor in the consortium. At the time the deal was announced, the consortium and Biomet had settled on a price of $44 per share, or a total of $10.9 billion.

In February 2007, while the takeover was still pending, Jeffrey R. Binder was appointed president and CEO. Binder was an orthopedic industry veteran who most recently had served in a senior management position at Abbott Laboratories. Around this same time, several company subsidiaries began operating under new monikers as additional emphasis was placed on the Biomet brand: Arthrotek was renamed Biomet Sports Medicine, Inc.; Implant Innovations, Inc., became Biomet 3i, Inc.; and Walter Lorenz Surgical adopted the name Biomet Microfixation, Inc. Revenues for the fiscal year ending in May 2007, the firm's final year as a public company, totaled $2.11 billion. Although sales had increased just 4 percent over fiscal 2006, this still marked the 29th consecutive year of record revenues.

After several large shareholders expressed their opposition to the $44 per share takeover price, the private-equity consortium in June 2007 increased its offer by 4.5 percent to $46 a share, or $11.4 billion. Shareholders accepted this sweetened offer, and the deal was consummated in September 2007. A new board of directors was seated that included representatives of the private-equity firms that composed the consortium, along with Binder, who was named chairman while remaining president and CEO, and cofounder Miller.

Just days after being taken private, Biomet was one of five orthopedic device makers to enter into a $311 million settlement with the U.S. government relating to a probe of allegations that the firms had paid kickbacks to surgeons to use their products. Biomet's portion of the settlement amounted to $26.9 million, and all the companies agreed to abide by new standards for consulting agreements with surgeons and to be monitored for 18 months to ensure that they were following the new standards. In October 2007 it was revealed that the Securities and Exchange Commission was investigating Biomet and several of its competitors for possible violations of the Foreign Corrupt Practices Act in connection with their sales practices in foreign countries.

Despite these clouds that hung over the orthopedic device industry, demographics boded well for the future success of Biomet and its competitors. The enormous baby boom generation was just entering the age range at which degenerative joint disease becomes increasingly common, setting the stage for increased demand for Biomet's replacement knees and hips and other orthopedic devices. In addition, younger patients were beginning to seek treatment earlier in the disease process in part because the devices were constantly being improved to last longer. Every year, Biomet introduced dozens of new products to maintain its position as one of a handful of major manufacturers of orthopedic devices.

Dave Mote
Updated, David E. Salamie

PRINCIPAL SUBSIDIARIES

Biomet Biologics, Inc.; Biomet Manufacturing Corp.; Biomet Microfixation, Inc.; Biomet Orthopedics, Inc.; Biomet Sports Medicine, Inc.; Biomet 3i, Inc.; EBI, L.P.; Biomet Europe B.V. (Netherlands).

PRINCIPAL COMPETITORS

Zimmer Holdings, Inc.; DePuy Inc.; Stryker Corporation; Smith & Nephew plc; Synthes, Inc.

FURTHER READING

"Biomet: Wall Street Likes What It Sees," *Indiana Business Magazine,* April 1985, p. 55.

Bray, Chad, and Jon Kamp, "Orthopedic Firms Settle Kickback Probe," *Wall Street Journal,* September 28, 2007, p. B4.

Carey, Susan, and Jonathan Vuocolo, "Biomet Agrees to Be Acquired for $10.9 Billion," *Wall Street Journal,* December 19, 2006, p. C4.

Cassak, David, "Biomet Goes Solo in Europe," *In Vivo,* February 2004.

———, "Biomet's Contrarian Conservatism," *In Vivo,* May 1999, pp. 48–50.

———, "Biomet's Rebirth?" *In Vivo,* September 2007.

Ellis, James E., "Biomet Should Boom As Baby Boomers Get Older," *Business Week,* July 27, 1987, p. 77.

Green, Lisa, "Biomet Acquiring N.J. Firm," *Fort Wayne (Ind.) Journal Gazette,* September 26, 2000, p. 5B.

Howey, Brian, "Biomet: Bringing R&D to Market," *Indiana Business Magazine,* May 1988, pp. 72+.

Hubbard, Richard F., and Jeffrey L. Rodengen, *Biomet Inc.: From Warsaw to the World,* Fort Lauderdale, Fla.: Write Stuff Enterprises, 2002, 144 p.

Kaelble, Steve, "International Business Person of the Year," *Indiana Business Magazine,* October 1992, pp. 17+.

Kamp, Jon, "Biomet Co-founder, CEO Retires," *Wall Street Journal,* March 28, 2006, p. B11.

———, "New Buyout Offer for Biomet Is Now Sweeter and Tender," *Wall Street Journal,* June 8, 2007, p. C3.

———, "SEC Targets Sales of Devices for Orthopedics," *Wall Street Journal,* October 15, 2007, p. B9.

Karkaria, Urvaksh, "Biomet Pays $300 Million for Venture in Europe," *Fort Wayne (Ind.) Journal Gazette,* December 19, 2003, p. 8B.

———, "Biomet to Buy Spinal Implant Maker," *Fort Wayne (Ind.) Journal Gazette,* March 9, 2004, p. 7B.

Ketzenberger, Jolene, "Future Looks Rosy for Maker of Joint Replacements," *Indianapolis Business Journal,* May 26, 2003, pp. 16B–17B.

Kurowski, Jeff, "Biomet Blossoms from Warsaw Roots," *South Bend (Ind.) Tribune Business Weekly,* September 30, 1996, p. 10.

———, "Indiana Business's Industrialist of the Year: Dane Miller, CEO, Biomet," *Indiana Business Magazine,* December 1989, pp. 8+.

Lee, Daniel, "Private Equity Group Will Acquire Biomet," *Indianapolis Star,* December 19, 2006, p. C1.

Lee, Daniel, and Jeff Swiatek, "U.S. Probe Targeting Three Orthopedics Firms in State," *Indianapolis Star,* June 27, 2006.

Margolis, Jay, "Biomet Signs Merger Deal with Kirschner," *Fort Wayne (Ind.) Journal Gazette,* July 19, 1994, p. C1.

Miller, Jim, "Biomet Founder Recalls Years Filled with 'Sheer Excitement,'" *Elkhart (Ind.) Truth,* October 29, 1992.

Panzica, Lisa, "Getting a Knee Up on the Competition," *South Bend (Ind.) Tribune Business Weekly,* September 22, 1993, p. 14.

Peterson, Kimberly, "Chief Tapped for Transition," *Fort Wayne (Ind.) Journal Gazette,* March 5, 2007, p. 1C.

Ronco, Ed, "Biomet Chief Steps Down," *South Bend (Ind.) Tribune,* March 28, 2006.

———, "Biomet Names New Chief," *South Bend (Ind.) Tribune,* February 27, 2007.

————, "Biomet Will Go Private," *South Bend (Ind.) Tribune,* July 13, 2007.

————, "Shake-up Ends Biomet Probe," *South Bend (Ind.) Tribune,* April 3, 2007.

Russell, John, "Foreign Sales of Orthopedics Investigated," *Indianapolis Star,* October 13, 2007, p. C1.

Schroeder, Michael, "Private Group Acquires Biomet," *Fort Wayne (Ind.) Journal Gazette,* December 19, 2006, p. 1A.

————, "Shareholders OK Biomet Sale," *Fort Wayne (Ind.) Journal Gazette,* July 13, 2007, p. 1A.

Shankle, Greta, "FDA Proposes Stiffening Regulation of the Medical Device Industry," *Indianapolis Business Journal,* January 10, 1994, p. 11A.

Slater, Sherry, "Warsaw Firms Fined by Feds," *Fort Wayne (Ind.) Journal Gazette,* September 28, 2007, p. 1A.

Theobald, Bill, "CEO's Personality Pushes Biomet to Forefront," *Indianapolis Star,* July 11, 2004.

The Boston Symphony
Orchestra Inc.

·

301 Massachusetts Avenue
Boston, Massachusetts 02115
U.S.A.
Telephone: (617) 266-1492
Toll Free: (888) 266-7575
Web site: http://www.bso.org

Nonprofit Company
Incorporated: 1981
Operating Revenues: $80.2 million (2008)
NAIC: 711100 Performing Arts Companies

∎∎∎

The Boston Symphony Orchestra Inc. is a nonprofit organization that administers the programs of the Boston Symphony Orchestra (BSO), one of the world's premiere orchestras, performing in its permanent venue, Symphony Hall. The company is known for its Boston Pops programs performed from May to July as well as the December holiday season, featuring a combination of classical music and Broadway tunes. The 11 principals of the BSO also comprise the Boston Symphony Chamber Players, who tour during the Boston Pops season. BSO caters to the young people of the Boston area through its Boston Symphony Youth Concerts and Boston Symphony Education and Community Outreach. In July and August, BSO makes its home at the Tanglewood Music Center, performing outdoors. Members of the orchestra serve on the faculty of Tanglewood's summer institute for young instrumentalists, singers, composers, and conductors.

Another outgrowth is the Tanglewood Festival Chorus, which also serves as the official chorus of the BSO, and on occasion joins the orchestra on its tours. All told, the orchestra presents more than 250 concerts each year.

19TH-CENTURY ORIGINS

The founder of the Boston Symphony Orchestra was Henry Lee Higginson, New York–born in 1834 but a member of an old-line New England family. He returned to Boston in time to receive his education at the venerable Boston Latin School and then remained to attend Harvard College, graduating in 1855. He developed a passion for music and moved to Vienna to study to be a musician for two and a half years. Although he came to realize that as a pianist he would never rise above talented amateur, his enthusiasm for music was left unabated. Higginson served in the Civil War and was discharged in 1864 after being wounded and rising to the rank of major, and for the rest of his life he would be known as Major Higginson. After the war, following failures in the oil and cotton industries, he became a banker by default, taken in by the family firm of Lee, Higginson & Company, where he was eventually named a partner; he made his fortune from investments in Bell Telephone Company, railroads, and the companies that would combine to become General Electric.

Higginson's enthusiasm for music did not wane, however, and he was a frequent audience member at Boston's "The Music Hall," established in 1852 and host to many touring European orchestras. He desired to improve the state of music in Boston and began to develop a dream of creating a full-size symphony orchestra comprised of top-notch international musicians. With considerable wealth at his disposal Higginson established the city's first symphony orchestra in 1881, making Boston Music Hall the company's primary performance space, the first concert held on October 22 of that year. The annual budget at this stage was $115,000 with Higginson footing the $50,000 deficit.

BOSTON POPS ROOTS

Serving as conductor for that first performance was German-born Georg Henschel, who during his three years with BSO established a professional bearing for the young company. His successor, Austrian Wilhelm Gericke, built upon this foundation and began arranging for performances in New York and elsewhere. In 1885 he established the "Promenade Concerts," summer concerts in a lighter vein intended to keep orchestra members employed year-round, and which in time evolved into the present-day Boston Pops program. The foundation of BSO's youth program was also laid by Gericke with the first Boston Symphony Youth Concert held in 1888. Poor health forced Gericke to step down in 1889 but three years later he returned to serve as the company's conductor for an eight-year stint.

Higginson, as BSO's chief benefactor, recognized that the orchestra would eventually need to find a new venue. While a fixture in the city, the Music Hall was considered to be a drafty firetrap. In preparation, Higginson and some friends bought a parcel of land, three-quarters of an acre in size, located in a section of town that at the time was remote. More importantly, the price tag, $170,000, was reasonable. A year later plans to build a new hall were hastened when it was announced that the city intended to construct an elevated railroad line and the Music Hall was in the direct path. Although the plan never came to fruition, it spurred the building of a new home for the orchestra. In 1893 Higginson led a group that recruited investors for a new corporation to raise $400,000 and build the hall.

Higginson was overly optimistic in predicting that the new hall would open in October 1894. In fact, seven years would elapse. Chosen to design the building was Harvard graduate architect Charles Follen McKim, one of the founding partners of the well-respected New York architectural firm of McKim, Mead & White. Higginson's influence on what was to become Symphony Hall was not to be discounted, however. He made it clear from the start that the hall should seat fewer than the Music Hall's 2,600 and that the stage had to be large enough to accommodate 90 musicians. He also suggested certain architectural details, which for the most part McKim accommodated. In the end, however, the stage was a bit cramped and more seats, 2,625, were included.

What would set Symphony Hall apart from other auditoriums would be its superb acoustics, the credit belonging to Wallace Clement Sabine, a Harvard physics professor McKim hired to apply the science of acoustics to the building of an auditorium for the first time. Using the old Boston Music Hall and The Leipzig Gerwandhaus as models, the designers took pains to find the right shape for Symphony Hall to achieve balance between the number of seats, the sound, and the sightlines. It was in order to achieve superior acoustics, in fact, that the stage was smaller than Higginson had hoped. The stage walls were also sloped inward to help project the sound to the audience, and side balconies were kept shallow to prevent the sound being trapped. Even what appeared to be mere decorations—the recesses of the coffered ceiling and niches featuring replicas of Greek and Roman statues on the three walls encompassing the audience—actually helped to evenly distribute the sound. Sabine was also responsible for a unique heating and ventilation system that quietly dispensed heated air through the ceiling that was drawn down and out through vents in the floor.

OPENING OF SYMPHONY HALL: 1900

The final drawings for Symphony Hall were delivered in March 1988 and ground was soon broken. The auditorium was supposed to take the name Boston Music Hall, but since the orchestra's former home had managed to survive the wrecker's ball and was being renovated by a new owner that name was not available. Symphony Hall was not actually the new hall's chosen name, but one that gained common usage and acceptance. The building, budgeted at $200,000, in the end cost $583,000, while a mortgage of $325,000 was also taken on the land. Symphony Hall's inaugural concert was held on October 15, 1900.

KEY DATES

1881: Henry Lee Higginson founds Boston Symphony Orchestra.
1885: First "Promenade" concert is offered.
1900: Symphony Hall opens.
1917: Orchestra makes first RCA recording.
1940: Berkshire Music Center is founded.
1952: Orchestra takes first international tour.
1960: Ford Foundation provides matching grant.
1979: Orchestra visits People's Republic of China.
1992: Orchestra tours South America for first time.
2004: James Levine becomes orchestra's first U.S.-botn music director.

With Gericke having resigned, Higginson launched an exhaustive search for a new music director in 1906, finally settling on another German conductor, Karl Muck, who would serve as BSO's conductor from 1906 until 1908 and then return in 1912 for a six-year stint. In 1915 he took the BSO on its first cross-country trip, the orchestra performing 13 concerts at the Panama-Pacific Exposition in San Francisco. He also conducted the orchestra when it made its first recordings for Victor Talking Machine Company (RCA) in 1917. His time with the company ended in comic opera fashion, however. Muck, a highly loyal German, ran afoul of the U.S. government through intercepted love letters to a 20-year-old woman with whom the 59-year-old, married conductor was having an affair. The letters, later disclosed by the *Boston Post*, also revealed a disdain for his patrons. In one, Muck wrote, "I am on my way to the concert hall to entertain the crowds of dogs and swine who think that because they pay the entrance fee they have the right to dictate to me my selections. I hate to play for this rabble. ... [In] a very short time our gracious Kaiser will smile on my request and recall me to Berlin. ... Our Kaiser will be prevailed upon to see the benefit to the Fatherland of my obtaining a divorce and making you my own." The U.S. Department of Justice apparently thought Muck was as much of a spy as he was a philanderer. He was arrested while at the podium during a rehearsal of the orchestra, held in custody for a 30-hour train ride to Georgia, and interned as an enemy alien until eventually being deported to Germany.

DEATH OF HIGGINSON: 1918

Higginson remained loyal to Muck until the end. By this time Higginson was aging and his health failing. He turned over control of BSO to a board of trustees and

passed away in November 1918 at the age of 83. The board soon had to contend with musicians seeking higher pay and threatening to unionize in 1920. Many of them then went on strike, leading to the BSO launching its first endowment campaign to meet their financial demands.

After Muck, the BSO eschewed German-inspired music in favor of French-oriented material conducted by Henri Rabaud and his successor, Pierre Montreux. Many French musicians were hired as well. The trend continued even when Russian-born Serge Koussevitzky assumed the baton in 1924. Koussevitzky served as conductor for 22 years and then in the new post of music director from 1947 until 1949. During his quarter-century at the helm, the BSO enjoyed a number of advances. In January 1926 the orchestra performed its first live radio concert. A number of radio broadcasts were to follow over the years until October 1935 when regular live BSO broadcasts were begun. It was also under Koussevitzky that Arthur Fiedler, in 1930, began his 50-year tenure as conductor of the Boston Pops. In 1936 Koussevitzky took the orchestra to the Berkshires for summer concerts and the following summer BSO began its long-term residence at Tanglewood. A firm believer in the education of young musicians, Koussevitzky in 1940 founded the Berkshire Music Center, which later took the name Tanglewood Music Center.

FIRST INTERNATIONAL TOUR: 1952

Succeeding Koussevitzky as music director in 1949 was German-born Charles Munch. Under his leadership, the BSO made its first international tour in 1952, performing in 11 cities, including London, Berlin, and Paris. A second international tour followed in 1959, during which the BSO became the first Western orchestra to tour the Soviet Union. Munch also maintained Koussevitzky's commitment to the work of contemporary composers. In the 1955–56 season, the BSO commissioned new works from 13 composers to help commemorate its 75th anniversary.

Despite its endowment, after Higginson the BSO relied on the generosity of old-line Boston families to underwrite its annual deficit from 1920 to 1960 and did not seek corporate donations. However, as operating expenses began to mount and it took on new endeavors, including the most ambitious touring schedule of any U.S. orchestra, the company either had to reduce its activities or seek new sources of funding to make up the annual deficit that totaled between $300,000 and $400,000. The first outside money was received from the Ford Foundation in the form of a matching grant in 1960. Further money was raised from Boston's nouveau riche. The new funds would help to support the 1960 tour to the Far East and the 1964 creation of the Boston Symphony Chamber Players. In the early 1970s BSO developed a new corporate fund-raiser that also increased the profile of BSO in the business community, Presidents at Pops, which begat a holiday version, Christmas at Pops. The $32 million that would be raised over the next 20 years would be used to fund community outreach and education programs.

In 1973, 37-year-old Seiji Ozawa became BSO's 13th music director. The former artistic director at Tanglewood, Ozawa would begin an unprecedented 29-year tenure leading the company. He maintained the orchestra's international reputation and continued BSO's history of touring. In 1978 the orchestra visited Japan and the following year toured the People's Republic of China, where its members also conducted classes. In 1992 the orchestra paid its first visit to South America.

Ozawa also continued BSO's commitment to living composers. For the orchestra's 100th anniversary season, 1980–81, he commission 12 new works. He expanded the orchestra's recording activities, and took steps to put the organization on a more solid financial footing. When he took charge the company's endowment was less than $10 million. By the end of the century it would top $200 million. In the late 1990s BSO hired Sametz Blackstone Associates to revamp its subscription campaign. Not only would the organization increase its subscription rates, more importantly it would be successful in adding new subscribers under the age of 35, key to the orchestra's long-term health.

OZAWA ANNOUNCING RETIREMENT: 1999

In the summer of 1999, the 63-year-old Ozawa announced that he would leave the orchestra following the 2002 season and assume control of the Vienna State Opera. With ample time to recruit a new music director, the BSO trustees finally settled on American James Levine, the longtime artistic director of New York's Metropolitan Opera, one of the world's most celebrated conductors, and the recipient of numerous honors. Given Levine's extensive commitments—in addition to the Met he held a conductorship with the Munich Philharmonic and made regular appearances at many other musical capitals, including Bayreuth, Berlin, and Salzburg, as well as directing the financially successful Three Tenor recitals—significant lead time was required.

In October 2001 Levine accepted the BSO post while keeping his position at the Met. For the BSO it was the first time that an American would serve as its music director. For Levine, the appointment, according to the *New York Times,* gave him "control of his own symphony orchestra and an exalted musical pulpit that he has long sought, associates said. The music directorship of the Boston ensemble also carries with it the prestige of directing the annual festival at Tanglewood."

In October 2004 Levine conducted the BSO for the first time as music director, leading Mahler's Eighth Symphony. He would offer the audience a blend of orchestral, operatic, and choral classics as well as new works commissioned from major American composers, ensuring that the BSO would remain vital in the years to come. To stay current the orchestra also began offering video podcasts of its Boston Pops and Tanglewood concerts, thus enhancing its outreach to audiences around the world. In addition, Levine maintained the company's commitment to touring. In 2007 he led the orchestra on a two-month European tour. The company also continued to secure new sources of funding. In late 2007 the BSO secured a seven-figure donation to the Tanglewood summer music festival, the undisclosed amount of money spread over five years.

Ed Dinger

PRINCIPAL SUBSIDIARIES

Boston Pops; Boston Symphony Chamber Players; Tanglewood Summer Music Festival.

PRINCIPAL COMPETITORS

New York Philharmonic; Chicago Symphony Orchestra; Philadelphia Orchestra; Cleveland Orchestra.

FURTHER READING

Blumenthal, Ralph, "James Levine to Take Post in Boston," *New York Times,* October 27, 2001, p. A9.

———, "Ozawa to Quit Boston Symphony," *New York Times,* June 23, 1999.

Clendinen, Dudley, "A 'Different' Boston Symphony Marks a Century," *New York Times,* October 23, 1981.

"A Cultural Institution Finds Strength in Unity," *Entertainment Marketing Letter,* March 15, 2003, p. 1.

Horowitz, Joseph, "Finding a New Music Director the Old-Fashioned Way," *New York Times,* October 8, 2000, p. AR42.

———, "A Plain Home with a Sense of Place," *New York Times,* October 8, 2000, p. AR33.

Joyce, Michael, "'Presidents at Pops' Sets Pace for Corporate Support of Arts," *Boston Business Journal* June 8, 2001, p. 63.

Symphony Halls: The First 100 Years, Boston: Boston Symphony Orchestra, Inc., 2000, p. 120.

Tommasini, Anthony, "A Last Bow, to Polite Applause," *New York Times,* March 31, 2002, p. AR1.

————, "What Boston Job Means to Levine's Musical Legacy," *New York Times,* October 30, 2001, p. E1.

Wakin, Daniel J., "A Sponsor for Tanglewood," *New York Times,* December 1, 2007.

Brother's
Brother Foundation

1200 Galveston Avenue
Pittsburgh, Pennsylvania 15233
U.S.A.
Telephone: (412) 321-3160
Fax: (412) 321-3325
Web site: http://www.brothersbrother.org

Nonprofit Company
Incorporated: 1964
Employees: 10
Operating Revenues: $322 million (2007 est.)
NAIC: 813219 Other Grantmaking and Giving Services

■ ■ ■

Brother's Brother Foundation (BBF) is a Pittsburgh, Pennsylvania-based nonprofit corporation that is regarded as one of the world's most efficient charities. According to the *Chronicle of Philanthropy,* BBF is the sixth largest U.S.-based international charity. The organization does little fund-raising, concentrating most of its efforts on collecting in-kind donations from companies, individuals, and the U.S. government and distributing them to about 120 countries around the world. Because of its international focus, BBF is little known in its home country, but its operation is a fixture at the top of *Forbes* magazine's annual ratings of effective and efficient charities. BBF's activities are threefold. Its medical program, the heartbeat of the organization, distributes medicines, supplies, and equipment wherever they are needed. In addition, BBF regularly provides requested medical supplies and surgical instruments for

mission teams to underserved populations. The Humanitarian Program at BBF is charged with responding to natural and manmade disasters, whether they result from earthquakes, floods, hurricanes, or the problems caused by the mismanagement of natural resources, war, economic upheaval, or political crises. In addition, BBF's Educational Program, started by Tobie Hingson, wife of founder Dr. Robert A. Hingson, has worked with publishers to fight illiteracy by providing over 60 million books in the last half-century and other educational materials to schools and libraries in less developed and developing countries around the world. BBF is headed by Luke Hingson, the son of the organization's founder, who was better known as the inventor of the jet injection method for mass immunization, the "peace gun" that laid the foundation for BBF. Dr. Hingson never sought a patent on the device, contending that it belonged to mankind.

BIRTH AND MATURATION OF FOUNDER

Robert Hingson was born in 1913 in Anniston, Alabama, and raised in nearby Oxford where he came to empathize with the area's African American population, which suffered greatly from disease, leading to unnecessarily shortened lives. This experience inspired him to become a doctor, and after earning an undergraduate degree from the University of Alabama in 1935, he enrolled at the Emory University School of Medicine in Atlanta. After graduating three years later he interned at the U.S. Marine Hospital on Staten Island, New York. It was here that an incident led to his quest to develop the jet injector. A shipyard worker was admitted to the

COMPANY PERSPECTIVES

The mission of Brother's Brother Foundation (BBF) is to promote international health and education through the efficient and effective distribution and provision of donated medical, educational, agricultural and other resources. All BBF programs are designed to fulfill its mission by connecting people's resources with people's needs.

hospital with an odd ailment: While delivering diesel oil to a ship through a high pressure hose, the man collapsed and was sent to the hospital with an injured hand. Hingson was baffled by the discolored hand, but as soon as he made an incision and a tablespoon of black oil oozed out, he realized that the substance had been forced through the skin through high pressure, leaving no apparent hole. Further investigation revealed that there was a small rupture in the high pressure hose at the shipyard. Hingson was thus inspired to develop a device that could inject medicine using high pressure.

The jet injector took shape over several years, however. By 1939 war was developing in both Europe and the Far East, and believing that it was only a matter of time before he would be inducted into the military, Hingson joined the U.S. Public Health Service. When full-fledged war broke out in Europe later in the year, Hingson was assigned to a hospital ship in the North Atlantic.

In the fall of 1939 Hingson experienced a major turning point in his life. He was dispatched to Finland aboard a Coast Guard ship to minister to U.S. Treasury Secretary Henry Morgenthau, who had been sent as an envoy to Nazi Germany's Adolf Hitler in a last-minute bid to stave off war. On the return home, Morgenthau suffered from severe migraine headaches. Hingson was able to successfully treat Morgenthau, who was so grateful he asked the young doctor if there was any way he could return the favor. Hingson indicated that he hoped to further his graduate education. True to his word, Morgenthau arranged a coveted slot for Hingson at the Mayo Clinic, where he studied anesthesiology, a field that until that time had been given scant attention, considered more of a chore to delegate to nurses.

POSTWAR ADVANCES IN JET INJECTION

After the United States' entry into World War II in late 1941, Hingson returned to the Staten Island Marine Hospital, and in 1943 he was transferred to the Pennsylvania Hospital in Philadelphia to establish an obstetric analgesia service. In the final year of the war, 1945, he was assigned to the University of Tennessee School of Medicine, where he established the university's anesthesiology department while combating the unusually high infant mortality rate. A man of incredible energy, Hingson was still able to find time to work with a mechanical engineer to develop the jet injector, what he called the "hydrospray," using it on himself and cadavers to work out the kinks. A workable version of the gun using carbon dioxide was ready in 1946, and proved itself treating lepers in a Louisiana hospital. Because the leprosy drug had to be injected every four hours and the patients' skin was sore and the nerves inflamed from the disease, jet injection was a godsend.

Over the next decade, Hingson continued to perfect the jet injector yet still found time for other endeavors. After retiring as a public health officer in 1951 he became the first professor of anesthesiology at Western Reserve University School of Medicine as well as director of anesthesia at the University Hospital of Cleveland. Here he pioneered epidural anesthesia in order to deaden pain in the pelvic area of women giving birth, a significant improvement over the practice of giving women general anesthesia, which may have relieved the mother's pain but sedated the baby. Hingson also developed a portable anesthesia machine, the so-called Western Reserve Midget, capable of delivering short-term, general anesthesia, and later adapted as a ventilator, used to resuscitate firefighters, military personnel, and rescue workers.

What Hingson found to be especially beneficial about the jet injector was that unlike a needle and syringe it did not frighten children. As a result, it was an ideal way to quickly dispense vaccinations to large numbers of children. In 1956 Hingson was able to apply this production-line approach to Salk vaccine when he and his team immunized 300,000 patients in Cleveland, Ohio. This success led to the perfection of the jet injector and set the stage for a 1958 medical mission survey made in association with the Baptist World Alliance. The 16 members of the group, including six doctors, surveyed 100 hospitals in 35 countries in Europe, Asia, and Africa. They also distributed $100,000 worth of donated medical supplies and used injector guns to deliver more than 90,000 vaccinations, while the doctors performed 120 operations. Hingson's wife, in the meantime, visited local schools, where she found books were in short supply, a discovery that would lead to BBF's book program.

KEY DATES

1958: Organization is founded in Cleveland, Ohio, as My Brother's Keeper by Dr. Robert Hingson.
1968: Headquarters are moved to Pittsburgh, Pennsylvania.
1974: Hingson's son, Luke, joins organization.
1980: Luke Hingson succeeds father as foundation leader.
1996: Robert Hingson dies.
2000: Foundation moves into new facility.
2002: Donations distributed reach $1 billion mark.
2006: Donations distributed reach $2 billion mark.

In truth, the 1958 trip was revelatory on many levels. Hingson told the *Pittsburgh Post-Gazette* that at the time, "We had terrible misinformation from officials who said there's no need to take the polio vaccine to Africa because the people there are so dirty it would be a waste of time." Hingson witnessed scenes of horrible deprivation, of abject poverty, hunger, and rampant disease. "In Liberia," he recalled, "there were only two doctors for the entire population of 2 million. One was in jail and the other was in Yale and the whole health of a nation was left to a dentist."

STARTING A FOUNDATION: 1958

When Hingson returned from the survey, he traveled to Washington, D.C., to report his findings to a group that included members of Congress as well as President Dwight D. Eisenhower. Maintaining that it would take a week to catalog the problems he witnessed, he said that what the people needed could be summed up with the letter *S:* shots, shoes, screen, soup, sanitation, and schools. Once those were provided, the religious Hingson said the people would be ready for salvation. He then lectured widely, leading to donations in kind and money, and the 1958 creation of a nonsectarian humanitarian organization that took the name My Brother's Keeper, the goal to leverage the United States' large medical resources to meet the health needs of less developed and developing countries around the world. The name was changed later in 1958 after a Nigerian medical student objected, saying "We don't need a keeper; we need a brother." Hence, the organization became Brother's Brother Foundation.

Hingson continued to hold his positions at Case Western and the University Hospital of Cleveland while growing BBF, his children often helping him. His son Luke began working for the organization at the age of five and as a teenager operated the slide projector while his father delivered lectures at churches, synagogues, and businesses after a full day at the hospital. At the same time, Hingson had the ear of presidents. In 1962 he persuaded President John F. Kennedy to provide BBF with a ship supplied with vaccine, medical supplies, and seeds to make a trip to Liberia to combat a smallpox epidemic. It was also this mission that developed a problem that turned out to be a blessing in disguise. As Hingson prepared to stockpile smallpox vaccine for the trip, a smallpox case was reported in New York, prompting Governor Nelson Rockefeller to commandeer two-thirds of Hingson's smallpox vaccine. While onboard ship to Liberia, Hingson conducted some experiments and discovered that the jet injector was more effective than even he had realized. Only 1 percent of the amount of vaccine delivered by syringe was actually necessary for the jet injection method. Thus, he had an ample supply of vaccine and was able to inoculate more than 800,000 Liberians during the next four months.

HINGSON DEVOTING HIMSELF TO BBF FULL-TIME: 1973

Hingson left Cleveland for Pittsburgh, Pennsylvania, in 1968 to become a professor at University of Pittsburgh Medical Center and director of anesthesia at Magee-Women's Hospital in nearby Oakland, and took BBF with him. As it turned out, the move was the best thing that could have happened to the foundation. The city embraced BBF, which thrived because of the generosity of the community. BBF grew large enough that in 1973, after his youngest son, Luke, graduated from college, Hingson resigned his medical positions in order to devote all of his time to running the foundation. The decision represented a financial hardship, his salary dropping from $53,000 a year to $10,000.

By this time, the focus of BBF began to change, in large part because of the success of the inoculation program in the countries the organization visited. Medical education was emphasized and in the 1970s BBF changed course again when some of the countries that had been recipients of the inoculation program were struck by natural disasters, including an earthquake in Nicaragua and a hurricane in Honduras. BBF took advantage of the resources it already had in place in order to distribute medical supplies, laying the foundation for the organization's disaster relief program. Moreover, BBF remained involved once the immediate crisis was over in Honduras, and for the first time donated seeds to an agricultural community.

During the 1970s Luke Hingson joined his father full-time with BBF. More than once he had delayed his college education to help with BBF, periodically working in the field starting in 1966, eventually serving in 30 countries. He finally graduated from Tufts University in 1974 and went to work for BBF as associate director. At the time, BBF shipped 12 containers of medical supplies annually, a number that would steadily grow over the years. Essentially, the foundation collected donated supplies until a container was filled, then shipped it and began filling a new container. By the early 1980s BBF was shipping 20 to 30 containers of medical supplies and other goods each year. The organization's book program also took a decided turn in 1980. Established by Hingson's wife, the program had always distributed used books, but now the foundation began forging ties with publishers to send new books, starting with medical texts but soon branching out to include textbooks and professional titles. A system was developed to allow recipients to request specific titles, and BBF contacted publishers to see if they would be willing to donate those books.

FAILING HEALTH FORCING HINGSON'S RETIREMENT: 1980

Hingson's health began to fail and after suffering his fourth heart attack he turned over the reins of BBF in 1980 to Luke Hingson, who became executive director. Two years later he became president. Robert Hingson remained BBF's medical director and continued to travel widely and promote the organization through lectures. He was also able to trade on his good name to scare up donations for the foundation. Robert Hingson would live until 1996, passing away at the age of 83 in Florida. He received numerous awards for his work, and over the years virtually every country he worked in bestowed upon him their highest humanitarian honor. He never regretted eschewing the high salary he could have earned in private practice or the riches that could have been made from the patent of the injector jet, telling the *Atlanta Constitution* in 1987, "My spirit is at such peace that I live like a millionaire spiritually."

BBF was left in good hands with Luke Hingson, who led a small staff in the organization's cramped Pittsburgh offices, 15,000 square feet rented out of a warehouse. The organization continued to expand its activities, so that by 1990 BBF was shipping 200 containers of supplies a year. It also continued to find a way to make do with limited resources. The organization's annual budget at mid-decade was $40 million and less than 1 percent was spent on administration and fund-raising. While most chief executives at top charities were paid more than $100,000 in salary,

Luke Hingson earned just $49,000. The organization's humanitarian efforts in the former Yugoslavia in 1994 reflected its frugality. BBF secured the donation of $13 million in medicine from pharmaceutical companies and then arranged free shipping by planes and ships to Croatia, where the Ministry of Health and others agreed to distribute the supplies.

In 2000 BBF was able to buy a facility to accommodate its administrative offices and serve as a warehouse, paying $450,000 for a 27,000-square-foot former factory. Rather than spend an additional $70,000 to install an elevator for its third-floor offices, however, BBF elected to save the money and instead placed folding chairs at each landing of the stairs to accommodate weary travelers.

BBF reached a significant milestone in mid-2002, when it surpassed the $1 billion mark in distributed donations. For the year, the organization donated about $160 million in materials and supplies, a significant improvement over the $94 million the previous year. What took 44 years to accomplish, the first $1 billion, took just four years to duplicate as BBF enjoyed tremendous growth in the early 2000s. Donated materials and supplies grew to $265 million in 2006. BBF shipped over $320 million of donated goods in 2007 including 2.5 million bottles of medicine, 2.8 million books and 200,000 pairs of shoes. Another $2 million in cash gifts covered the foundation's overhead, processing, shipping, and other costs. While the mission remained the same, BBF continued to change with the times. With the economies of Eastern Europe improving and with China's booming, resources were shifted increasingly to Africa. In addition, BBF took advantage of new technologies to remain vital. "It is much easier to communicate with people you want to help because of telephone systems, the Internet, international travel," Luke Hingson told the *Pittsburgh Tribune-Review* in 2006. "You can do a better, faster job of discussing what people need on the other side."

Ed Dinger

PRINCIPAL COMPETITORS

AmeriCares Foundation, Inc.; Feed the Children, Inc.; MAP International; World Vision International, Inc..

FURTHER READING

Barrett, William P., "Your Charity Dollars at Work (Brother's Brother Foundation)," *Forbes,* December 10, 2007, p. 180.

Beasley, David, "Retired Doctor Still Invents Ways to Keep Busy," *Atlanta Constitution,* July 13, 1987, p. D1.

Burgess, Kelly D., "Brother's Brother Gives Aid to the Needy Overseas," *Pittsburgh Post-Gazette,* June 2, 1999, p. B3.

Certo, Tracy Herbst, "Since '58, Foundation Has Extended Helping Hand Worldwide," *Pittsburgh Post-Gazette,* March 14, 1993, p. J1.

Levin, Steve, "Brother's Brother Gifts Nearing $1 Billion Mark," *Pittsburgh Post-Gazette,* June 19, 2002, p. B5.

Rosenberg, Henry, "Robert Andrew Hingson, M.D.: OB Analgesia Pioneer (1913–1996)," *ASA Newsletter,* September 1999.

Spice, Byron, "Dr. Robert A. Hingson, Armed with Peace Gun, He Ministered to World," *Pittsburgh Post-Gazette,* October 12, 1996, p. A1.

Zlatos, Bill, "Brother's Brother Reaches $1 Billion Mark," *Pittsburgh Tribune-Review,* December 9, 2006.

Buffets Holdings, Inc.

1460 Buffet Way
Eagan, Minnesota 55121-1133
U.S.A.
Telephone: (651) 994-8608
Toll Free: (800) 871-0956
Fax: (651) 365-2356
Web site: http://www.buffet.com

Private Company
Incorporated: 1983 as Buffets, Inc.
Employees: 38,000
Sales: $1.39 billion (2007)
NAIC: 722211 Limited-Service Restaurants; 722110
    Full-Service Restaurants

■ ■ ■

The second largest company in the family dining segment of the U.S. restaurant industry, Buffets Holdings, Inc., is the nation's largest operator of buffet-style restaurants, with around 650 eating establishments in 42 states. Nearly all of these are company-owned outlets, with only about 20 franchised locations. The vast majority of the units are operated under one of four names: Old Country Buffet, HomeTown Buffet, Ryan's, or Fire Mountain. These buffet-style restaurants feature a "scatter system" with several separate food islands or counters rather than the straight-line system typical of most buffets. Buffets Holdings was taken private in October 2000 in a management-led buyout backed by the New York-based private equity firm Caxton-Iseman Capital,

LLC. Caxton-Iseman continues to maintain a stake in Buffets of 77.4 percent.

INSTANTLY SUCCESSFUL BEGINNINGS

Buffets was founded by Roe Hatlen in 1983. Hatlen, a veteran of the restaurant industry, had spent nine years with International King's Table, Inc., an Oregon-based chain whose revenues were boosted to an annual $40 million with Hatlen's help. In 1982 Hatlen moved to Minnesota, where he took an executive position at the publicly held Pizza Ventures chain of restaurants. After only eight months at Pizza Ventures, however, he was let go when the company was acquired and reorganized by Godfather's Pizza.

During this time, Hatlen contacted his friend and former colleague at King's Table, C. Dennis Scott, an experienced restaurant operator responsible for running 22 King's Table restaurants. Hatlen persuaded Scott to leave the financial security of King's Table to pursue a new restaurant venture.

Hatlen and Scott decided to open a buffet-style operation, which they expected to prove economical both for themselves and their customers. Without wait-staff and bartenders, the buffet would necessitate a lower payroll than more formal operations and might appeal to customers who preferred not to pay gratuities.

The partners divided responsibilities along the lines of their expertise, with Hatlen handling financial matters and Scott overseeing the details of restaurant management. Hatlen was able to purchase Pizza

Ventures' discarded computer system for five cents on the dollar and tapped his network of acquaintances in the restaurant business for investment capital, amassing about $750,000 by the time Buffets, Inc., was incorporated on October 13, 1983.

Scott planned the restaurant's offerings, designing a series of menus that centered on typical U.S. favorites, such as fried chicken, baked fish, and hamburgers. With particular attention to the value-conscious diner, he made sure that each meal included salad and dessert. Also featured were pasta dishes and other fare that could be prepared fresh in small batches throughout the day by cooks rather than by highly trained and expensive chefs.

With a staff of 29, Old Country Buffet opened in March 1984 in a small strip mall on the outskirts of Minneapolis. There, customers encountered a plain but comfortable decor, a buffet station with lines at either end, affording the customer a view of all food items, and a generous and varied menu. Customers prepaid the fixed rate before lining up at the buffet.

The restaurant was an instant success. Hatlen and Scott's initially cautious projections for sales of $1 million during its first year were doubled by the end of 1984. By October 1985, nine Old Country Buffet restaurants were in operation around Wisconsin, Illinois, and Minnesota, requiring a total of 687 employees and netting sales of $59.5 million. Moreover, several investors were encouraging Buffets, Inc., to go public, which it did that year with an initial offering of 525,000 shares.

RAPID EXPANSION

The cash flow generated by the offering allowed the company to expand over the next few years. By 1987, the Old Country Buffet chain had grown to include 11 restaurants in Minnesota, seven in Wisconsin, four in Illinois, and the remainder in new territories, including Missouri, Nebraska, Pennsylvania, and Oklahoma.

Public recognition of Old Country Buffet steadily increased. Moreover, *Restaurants and Institutions,* a food industry trade magazine, praised the chain as "shipshape" and "financially responsible." The reviewer

also observed that buffets were beginning to offer strong competition to the country's cafeterias.

While buffets and cafeterias offered similar menus, the buffet featured a fixed-rate policy, which proved less costly to the customer than the pay-per-item policy common in cafeterias. Moreover, buffets began to offer an alternative to the standard straight-line cafeteria layout. In 1989 Old Country Buffet restaurants adopted a new "scatter system" layout that featured individual food islands throughout, a system that hastened the self-service process and thereby allowed each restaurant to accommodate more customers. The number of restaurants in the chain rose to 70 by the beginning of 1990.

Buffets also became known for providing employment opportunities in the early 1990s, when economic recession led to high unemployment rates on a national level. During this time, Buffets placed a series of newspaper advertisements targeting potential managers seeking long-term employment. Emphasizing the rapid growth and continued success of Buffets, the copy received widespread attention and garnered the company the *Personnel Journal's* Vantage Award for 1989.

In an effort to maintain employees knowledgeable in food production and personnel management, and to help curb its high employee turnover rate, Buffets opened a training center for managers at their Eden Prairie headquarters in Minnesota. There, employees underwent five weeks of seminars and three weeks of hands-on training in the headquarters restaurant.

Though at least 75 percent of Buffets employees were on part-time schedules in the early 1990s, graduates of the eight-week program helped establish a solid managerial framework in almost all Old Country Buffets. Each restaurant retained two managers: one associate manager and one general manager in charge of operations. To maximize the profitability of each unit, the company based 50 percent of the general manager's annual salary on the profitability of his or her establishment.

In addition to enhancing the company's workforce, founder Hatlen also focused on procuring new restaurant locations left by unsuccessful retailers, whose incomplete leases gave him considerable negotiating power with desperate landlords. These lower rents helped make 1990 the seventh record year for earnings; sales soared 26 percent to $145.2 million, up from 1989's total of $115.4 million.

By 1991, Buffets operated a total of 110 restaurants, including those under the direction of two new subsidiaries. Gateway Buffets, acquired in 1989, came with a purchase price of $1.9 million. Evergreen

KEY DATES

1983: Buffets, Inc., is founded by Roe Hatlen.

1985: Company goes public.

1989: "Scatter system" buffet format is introduced.

1996: HomeTown Buffet is acquired.

2000: Company is taken private via a management-led buyout backed principally by Caxton-Iseman Capital, LLC; Buffets Holdings is formed as a new holding company.

2006: Ryan's Restaurant Group, Inc., is acquired.

2008: Burdened by a high debt load and hurt by an economic slowdown, Buffets files for Chapter 11 bankruptcy protection.

Buffets was purchased for $1.7 million from C. Dennis Scott, who had left the company in 1990.

Firmly established as a leader in the restaurant industry, the company earned its fifth accolade from *Forbes* magazine as one of the 200 best small companies in the United States in 1992. Buffets' gross sales for 1992 reached $247.5 million, a figure that was bolstered one year later when the company discontinued its policy of serving free meals to employees. Charging employees $2 per meal, Buffets' added $300,000 to the sales total. Overall sales reached $334.9 million in 1993, an increase of 35 percent over 1992.

1996 ACQUISITION OF HOMETOWN

Buffets entered the mid-1990s as a 180-unit chain, with plans for continuing rapid expansion. By mid-1996 there were more than 250 Old Country Buffet restaurants. There was also a significant challenger to Buffets in the form of HomeTown Buffet Inc. of San Diego, which had been founded by C. Dennis Scott in 1991. By mid-1996 Scott's company operated 74 HomeTown Buffets, a format that used the scatter system pioneered by Buffets, and two Original Roadhouse Grills (steakhouses where entrees were ordered from a menu and prepared at an "on-display" grill); and franchised 19 HomeTown Buffets. For 1995, HomeTown reported earnings of $6.6 million on revenues of $152.4 million.

In June 1996, then, Buffets announced that it would acquire HomeTown Buffet, in a stock and debt transaction valued at about $190 million when it was consummated in September 1996. The merger made good geographic sense, as the strongest markets for Old

Country Buffet were in the Midwest and Southeast while HomeTown had the majority of its units on the West Coast. The deal also reunited the cofounders of Buffets, with Hatlen continuing as chairman and CEO and Scott serving as vice-chairman. Buffets' headquarters remained in Eden Prairie. At year-end 1996, Buffets owned or franchised a total of 270 restaurants.

The acquisition resulted in some difficulties for Buffets as merger costs were larger than expected and merger savings did not materialize as fast as anticipated. Despite impressive revenues of $750.7 million for 1996, Buffets suffered a net loss of $7.2 million as a result of asset impairment and site closing costs and merger charges totaling $49.6 million. Weak performances at 38 units led to the asset impairment costs and the closing of three restaurants, while the merger charges stemmed in part from the shuttering of five units because of their proximity to other units and from the closure of the San Diego headquarters of HomeTown Buffet. In another follow-up to the merger, during 1997 Buffets converted more than two dozen Old Country Buffets to Home-Town Buffets; such conversions were said to increase sales at stagnating units.

Buffets was back on track in the late 1990s, posting net income of $28.6 million in 1997 and $39.4 million in 1998, on revenues of $808.5 million and $868.9 million, respectively. In 1998 the company increased the number of company-owned restaurants from 360 to 386. Part of this increase came from the acquisition of 11 eating establishments from Country Harvest Buffet Restaurants, Inc., for $5.6 million. Ten of these units were subsequently converted to the company's buffet format with one of them converted to an Original Roadhouse Grill.

Buffets also began testing two new restaurant formats, both of which were buffets with a twist. The PizzaPlay format offered Italian food and pizza served buffet style along with nonfood entertainment, including big screen televisions for sporting events, televisions showing children's cartoons, and a game area. This format was received lukewarmly by customers, and was abandoned during 1999. The second test format was called Country Roadhouse Buffet and Grill and its feature attraction was a display grill as part of its buffet. Both the Original Roadhouse Grill and the Country Roadhouse Buffet and Grill formats were performing well enough to be slated for expansion in 2000. In April 1999 Buffets purchased an 80 percent stake in Tahoe Joe's, Inc., the operator of two Tahoe Joe's Famous Steakhouses in California, thereby moving further into the nonbuffet sector. The company broke ground in late 1998 on a new headquarters located in Eagan, Minnesota, and it moved into the building in March 2000.

TAKEN PRIVATE IN 2000

In the spring of 2000 Hatlen handed over his CEO duties to Kerry Kramp, who had been company president. Hatlen continued serving as chairman. Kramp had helped Scott found HomeTown Buffet and played an instrumental role in the integration of that company into Buffets. At the time of the leadership changeover, Buffets was on a financial roll. It was in the midst of the most successful quarter in company history and achieved 12 consecutive quarters of comparable-store sales increases and improvements in profits.

Wall Street, however, seemed to be ignoring these achievements at a time when the dot-com bubble had not yet fully burst. Frustrated that the company stock was trading at the bottom end of the restaurant sector, Buffets' top management engineered a buyout that took the company private in October 2000. The management group was backed by Caxton-Iseman Capital, LLC, a private-equity firm based in New York City. On completion of the $643 million buyout, through which investors received $13.85 per share for their holdings, Caxton-Iseman held about 77 percent of the shares of a new holding company called Buffets Holdings, Inc., while roughly 7 percent was held by another New York equity firm, Sentinel Capital Partners, L.P., and managers of Buffets, including Kramp and Hatlen, secured the remaining 16 percent. Kramp continued to serve as CEO, while Hatlen was named vice-chairman. Taking over the chairmanship was Frederick J. Iseman, president of Caxton-Iseman.

The year 2000 was also noteworthy as the firm's first with revenues in excess of $1 billion, although the buyout that year saddled the firm with more than $400 million in debt, nearly ten times the previous level. Buffets attempted to whittle away at this burden over the next few years by shutting down a number of underperforming restaurants and selling its 13 Original Roadhouse restaurants in 2003. In August 2003 Buffets acquired the 20 percent of Tahoe Joe's it did not already own. Later that year, one in which same-store sales were on the decline, Buffets upgraded the menus at its core Old Country and HomeTown restaurants, using television ads to tout the new entree and dessert offerings.

Primarily because of the divestment of Original Roadhouse and the closure of 15 other buffet restaurants during the year, Buffets' revenues for the fiscal year ending in June 2004 fell 4.3 percent, to $942.8 million. Same-store sales for the year increased 1.3 percent, a gain mainly attributable to price increases as guest traffic actually fell. Kramp left the company in November 2004, and Hatlen reassumed the CEO position for the following year. In November 2005 R.

Michael Andrews was promoted from CFO to CEO. Prior to joining Buffets in February 2004, Andrews had served as CFO of Don Pablo's Restaurants and of the parent company of Jekyll & Hyde Clubs.

TAKEOVER OF RYAN'S IN 2006

Throughout 2005 and continuing into 2006 Buffets struggled with depressed guest traffic and soft sales. Its customers, who tended to come from the lower income brackets, were under increasing economic pressure, including higher gas prices, and they appeared to be opting for the less expensive offerings of such fast-food chains as McDonald's Corporation. Early in 2006 Caxton-Iseman began exploring a sale of Buffets but reversed course when a new opportunity arose. Ryan's Restaurant Group, Inc., was put up for sale, and Caxton-Iseman engineered the purchase of Ryan's by Buffets for $834 million in cash, a deal that closed in November 2006.

Ryan's, based in Greer, South Carolina, operated around 330 grill-buffet restaurants mainly under the Ryan's and Fire Mountain names. The geographic fit with Buffets was highly complementary, as Buffets' units were concentrated primarily in the Upper Midwest and West and Ryan's were in the Midwest and South. The combination made Buffets Holdings the largest operator of buffet-style restaurants in the United States, surpassing previous leader Golden Corral Corporation, with more than 650 restaurants in 42 states.

The takeover of Ryan's, however, pushed Buffets' debt up to an even more burdensome level of more than $800 million. Furthermore, while Buffets was able to report record revenues of $1.39 billion for fiscal 2007, it also posted a net loss that year of $105.5 million. This loss stemmed at least in part from declining same-store sales at both the Buffets and Ryan's restaurants as the chains' core customers remained under financial pressure in a worsening economic environment. By November 2007 Buffets had announced that it intended to sell the 11-unit Tahoe Joe's chain, while at the same time Moody's Investors Service was reporting that Buffets was likely to default on its loans. Later in the month Buffets said that it had hired an investment bank to provide advice on the company's capital structure and its business plan, and it also appointed Steven R. Layt as COO. Layt had more than 19 years of restaurant industry experience, his last post being at the Pizza Hut unit of Yum! Brands Inc. In January 2008 the financially troubled Buffets was forced to file for Chapter 11 bankruptcy protection. Its restaurants remained open as the company worked to reduce its debt and began reviewing underperforming locations for possible closure.

Gillian Wolf
Updated, David E. Salamie

PRINCIPAL SUBSIDIARIES

Buffets, Inc.; Ryan's Restaurant Group, Inc.

PRINCIPAL COMPETITORS

Golden Corral Corporation; CBRL Group, Inc.; Denny's Corporation; Metromedia Restaurant Group; Brinker International, Inc.; Darden Restaurants, Inc.; Waffle House, Inc.; VICORP Restaurants, Inc.; IHOP Corp.; Shoney's North America Corporation.

FURTHER READING

Brickley, Peg, "Buffets Files for Chapter 11 As Diners Curb Spending," *Wall Street Journal,* January 23, 2008, p. B3B.

Brumback, Nancy, "Buffeted by Change," *Restaurant Business,* January 1, 1997, pp. 53–54+.

"Buffets Buyout of Ryan's Increases Loss; Company to Sell Tahoe Joe's," *Nation's Restaurant News,* November 19, 2007, p. 10.

"Buffets, Inc. Planning Its Biggest Expansion Ever During 1991," *Wall Street Journal,* November 16, 1990.

"Buffets Inc. Profits Jump Despite Slowed Economy," *Nation's Restaurant News,* September 9, 1991.

"Buffets Serves Up Big Plate of Earnings As Takeover Nears," *Nation's Restaurant News,* August 21, 2000, p. 12.

Carlino, Bill, "Buffets Inc. Purchases Rival HomeTown Buffet," *Nation's Restaurant News,* June 17, 1996, p. 1.

Cebrzynski, Gregg, "Buffets Inc. Promotes Menu Upgrade at Old Country, Home Town Restaurants," *Nation's Restaurant News,* October 27, 2003, p. 14.

"Corporate Performance: Buffets," *Fortune,* February 12, 1990, p. 118.

Crecca, Donna Hood, "C. Dennis Scott," *Nation's Restaurant News,* January 1997, pp. 194, 196.

Dunnavant, Keith, "End of the Line," *Restaurant Business,* February 10, 1992, p. 44.

Farkas, David, "Eating It Up," *Chain Leader,* March 2001, pp. 56–58, 60.

Fiedler, Terry, "Really Cookin'," *Minnesota Business Journal,* March 1986, p. 20.

Lockyer, Sarah E., "Buffets Inc. Set to Become Buffet Leader with Ryan's Group Purchase," *Nation's Restaurant News,* August 7, 2006, pp. 1, 103.

———, "Ryan's Shareholders Agree to $876M Buffets Buyout," *Nation's Restaurant News,* October 16, 2006, p. 14.

Marcial, Gene G., "Buffets to Make Your Mouth Water," *Business Week,* July 1, 1996, p. 91.

Martin, Richard, "Old Country Buffet Parent Loses Recipe Lawsuit," *Nation's Restaurant News,* October 24, 1994, p. 3.

McKinney, Matt, "Buffets Inc. to Double in Merger," *Minneapolis Star Tribune,* July 27, 2006, p. 1D.

Meeks, Fleming, and R. Lee Sullivan, "If at First You Don't Succeed," *Forbes,* November 9, 1992, p. 172.

Meyers, Mike, "Buffets Inc. Off the Table: Chain Sold to N.Y. Investment Company," *Minneapolis Star Tribune,* June 6, 2000, p. 1D.

"Old Country Buffet Plans to Sell 525,000 Shares," *Nation's Restaurant News,* October 7, 1985.

Papiernik, Richard L., "Buffets Eyes Two Test Concepts to Replace Tired Units," *Nation's Restaurant News,* March 9, 1998, pp. 6, 11, 52.

———, "Buffets Hones Margins and Marketing into a Profitable Edge," *Nation's Restaurant News,* August 24, 1998, pp. 11, 22, 24.

———, "Buffets Inc. Engine Is Back on Track, Pulling Its Load," *Nation's Restaurant News,* March 1, 1999, pp. 11, 81.

Papiernik, Richard L., and Amy Spector, "Buffets' Pending Buyout Has Investors Questioning Sale," *Nation's Restaurant News,* June 19, 2000, pp. 4, 11, 28.

Peterson, Susan E., "Buffets, HomeTown to Merge," *Minneapolis Star Tribune,* June 5, 1996, p. 1D.

Phelps, David, "A 'More Knowledgeable' Buffets Turns Optimistic," *Minneapolis Star Tribune,* June 23, 1997, p. 1D.

Schafer, Lee, "Salad Days: Buffets Inc. Is Ten Years Old, but Still Fresh Under CEO Roe Hatlen," *Corporate Report Minnesota,* June 1, 1994, p. 32.

Walkup, Carolyn, "Kerry Kramp," *Nation's Restaurant News,* September 22, 2003, pp. 68, 70.

Waters, C. Dickinson, "Buffets Inc. Eschews Glamour in Lieu of Profits," *Nation's Restaurant News,* May 22, 2000, p. 14.

Weleczi, Ruth, "Buffets, Inc.," *Minneapolis-St. Paul City Business,* June 24, 1991, p. 31.

BVR Systems (1998) Ltd.

16 Hamelacha Street
Afek Industrial Park
Rosh Ha'ayin, 48091
Israel
Telephone: (+972-3) 9008000
Fax: (+972-3) 9008080
Web site: http://www.bvr.co.il

Public Company
Incorporated: 1998 as BVR Systems (1998) Ltd.
Employees: 80
Sales: $10.1 million (2006)
Stock Exchanges: OTC Bulletin Board
Ticker Symbol: BVRSF.OB
NAIC: 332995 Other Ordnance and Accessories Manufacturing; 333319 Other Commercial and Service Industry Machinery Manufacturing; 334419 Other Electronic Component Manufacturing; 334511 Search, Detection, Navigation, Guidance, Aeronautical, and Nautical System and Instrument Manufacturing; 336413 Other Aircraft Parts and Auxiliary Equipment Manufacturing; 511210 Software Publishers; 541511 Custom Computer Programming Services

■ ■ ■

BVR Systems (1998) Ltd. is an Israel-based producer of simulators and defense electronics. Traditionally centered in aviation, the company has applied its technology to naval and land warfare simulation. Leading aviation products include the Ehud air combat maneuvering instrument (ACMI), Advanced Trainer Avionics Suite (ATAS), In-Flight Electronic Warfare Simulator (IF-EWS), Embedded Virtual Avionics (EVA) system, and Naval Combat Maneuvering Instrumentation (NCMI) system.

Europe is BVR's largest market, accounting for 45 percent of 2006 sales. Its products are also popular in Asia, another area where space limitations make BVR's air combat simulation systems attractive. The 2006 purchase of Blue Ridge Simulation of Virginia seemed likely to finally get the company noticed by the U.S. Department of Defense. The company is majority owned by Chun Holdings, a partnership led by BVR Systems Chairman Aviv Tzidon.

FORMATION OF BVR TECHNOLOGIES: 1986

BVR Systems (1998) Ltd. is a spinoff of BVR Technologies Ltd., which was formed in 1986 by Yaron Sheinman and Aviv Tzidon, a couple of former pilots for the Israel Defense Forces. The two had previously tried their hand as aviation industry consultants before launching their own company.

The flight simulator market seemed like a promising area. The massive, custom-built devices of the day cost tens of millions of dollars and consumed so much electricity they required dedicated power supplies and cooling systems. Still, training in simulators was still much less costly, and safer, than using actual jets, guaranteeing demand well into the future.

As the *Jerusalem Post* noted, the company found a way to make F-16 simulators for a fraction of the cost

COMPANY PERSPECTIVES

BVR Systems (1998) Ltd. is a world leader in the development, manufacture and delivery of training and simulation turnkey projects for the military and civil markets. BVR offers highly efficient and cost-effective integrated solutions for air, sea and land forces, and has provided outstanding products to our international customer base since 1987. BVR's products cover the principal training areas of live/embedded, virtual and constructive training. BVR is focused on the delivery of training solutions for joint force, on-board training and distributed simulation systems. BVR Systems—delivering to our customers today, the training systems of tomorrow.

using PC components. It then applied its methods to a variety of other air-, ground- and sea-based weapons systems simulators. Sales boomed and BVR Technologies held an initial public offering (IPO), allowing it to reward its underpaid employees in the manner of a textbook high-tech success story.

BVR's PC-based approach was widely copied, however. After years of double-digit growth, revenues peaked at nearly $17 million in 1994 before slipping by a third the next year. The company then had about 100 employees.

SAFER AIR COMBAT TRAINING

BVR introduced one of its most successful products around 1992. Called the Ehud air combat maneuvering instrument (ACMI), this was a unique suite of instruments and computers carried in a pod underneath the wing of a fighter aircraft. It could be used to electronically simulate dogfights, including missile launches, while providing important safety-enhancing features, such as collision warnings. The system was named after Ehud Falk, one of Sheinman's colleagues who had died several years earlier in a midair collision on an air combat training course.

Previous ACMI systems developed decades earlier had required expensive, ground-based emitters to keep track of planes taking part in the training missions. GPS technology allowed BVR to do away with the ground station, offering potential savings of millions of dollars.

Boosted by the Ehud, BVR's sales took off, nearly doubling in 1996 to $20 million. A half-dozen Asian

and European countries had adopted the Ehud, although the U.S. market remained an impenetrable fortress to the relatively small, foreign company.

1998 BVR SYSTEMS SPINOFF

BVR Technologies had also developed extensive civilian businesses. Subsidiaries called Nexus and EVR were formed to tackle private sector markets. Nexus specialized in wireless products, while EVR produced networked video game software (through its own Netgame Ltd. and Real Time Synthesized Entertainment Technology Ltd. subsidiaries). BVR soon reduced its stakes in Nexus and EVR.

BVR Systems (1998) Ltd. was then launched to take over the military side of things, with the original BVR Technologies serving as a holding company. The spinoff was completed at the end of October 1998. The newly created company started out trading on the NASDAQ Small-Cap Market (ticker symbol BVRSF).

BVR Technologies cofounder Aviv Tzidon was the first chairman and CEO at BVR Systems. Yaron Sheinman took over Tzidon's CEO duties at BVR Technologies, where he remained chairman as well.

ADVANCED TRAINER AVIONICS SUITE (ATAS)

In 1999 BVR Systems released another revolutionary new product, the Advanced Trainer Avionics Suite (ATAS). This was a pod of avionics gear that allowed less expensive trainer aircraft to simulate top-of-the-line fighters.

In spite of the promising new offering, BVR Systems' shares lost most of their value in the tech slowdown of 2000. Political unrest in Israel did not help; nor did a squabble with MLM Systems Engineering & Integration, a division of Israel Aircraft Industries, Ltd. (IAI), which was BVR's partner in building and marketing the Ehud. (This dispute was ultimately resolved after two years in August 1999 when BVR agreed to transfer some technology to IAI in exchange for royalties.) Elisra Electronic Systems began building up a majority holding in BVR during this time. Elisra's main shareholder was Israeli defense contractor Koor Industries.

CRISIS AND CHANGE

Revenues exceeded $28 million in 2002, but the company was losing money badly: $6 million a year at that point. BVR Systems' shares were delisted from the NASDAQ in early 2003. Nevertheless, BVR Systems

KEY DATES

1986: Former Israel Defense Forces (IDF) pilots Yaron Sheinman and Aviv Tzidon form BVR Technologies to produce flight simulators.

1992: Ehud air combat maneuvering instrument (ACMI) debuts.

1998: BVR Technologies spins off military and aviation businesses into BVR Systems (1998) Ltd.

1999: Advanced Trainer Avionics Suite (ATAS) is launched; Koor Industries invests in company through Elisra Systems.

2003: Aviv Tzidon's Chun Holdings buys out Koor's shares after they collapse in value.

2006: Virginia's Blue Ridge Simulation is acquired, enhancing BVR's prospects in the U.S. defense market.

still had its believers, including the Boeing Company, which chose it as its partner in bidding on a $270 million contract to build air combat trainers for the U.S. military. They did not win that one, but BVR Systems was part of a successful Lockheed Martin Corporation bid to produce a simulator for Israel's new F-16I aircraft.

Toward the end of the year, the company laid off half its 160 employees. Revenues were less than $15 million for 2003. As BVR Systems teetered on the brink of closure, another round of layoffs followed, lowering the total head count to fewer than 100.

Israel Aerospace Industries Ltd. (IAI) had made an offer to buy BVR Systems but later changed its mind. Instead, Chun Holdings, led by BVR cofounder Aviv Tzidon, bought out Koor's stake. The deal valued BVR Systems at about $2 million.

There were also changes at former parent company BVR Technologies, which sold the last of its holdings and merged into TechnoCross Ltd. in 2003. It took the name Technoprises Ltd. the next year.

U.S. ACQUISITION IN 2006

The United States, the largest defense market in the world, remained almost completely out of reach until 2006, when BVR Systems announced it was buying Blue Ridge Simulation, Inc. (BRS). Based in Leesburg, Virginia, BRS specialized in making PC-based simulators to train radar operators for the Department of Defense and the private sector.

In addition to access to the U.S. market, BVR Systems was interested in the purchase as a means to become more competitive by simply growing in size, recently promoted President and CEO Ilan Gillies told *Israel Business Arena*. The cash and stock deal was worth up to $5 million, and was made possible by a new investment from a group led by Nir Dor, former CEO of bottled water manufacturer Eden Springs Ltd.

After seven years in the red, BVR Systems had managed to break even in 2005 on revenues of $19.2 million. However, sales slipped to $10.1 million in 2006 as the company posted a net loss of $2.2 million. By this time, the workforce was down to about 80 employees. A pipeline of new products gave the faithful new hope that BVR would soon reap real profits from the simulated training environment.

UNVEILING OF EVA

BVR unveiled its most advanced product, the Embedded Virtual Avionics (EVA) system, in early 2006. EVA simulated the radar and weapons systems of specific fighter aircraft, including ground mapping radar. By extending the useful training capabilities of lower cost trainer aircraft, it promised to save up to a million dollars off the cost of training each pilot.

BVR was also upgrading its offerings in other spheres. The company's latest generation of the Naval Combat Maneuvering Instrumentation (NCMI) system could exchange data with other ships and with BVR's air combat training systems, facilitating war games involving hundreds of real or simulated ships and planes.

In September 2007 BVR Systems announced plans to add a new dimension to its training simulators by incorporating voice analysis technology from Nemesyco Ltd., a high-tech start-up based in Netanya, Israel. Layered voice analysis (LVA) promised to reveal the emotional state of pilots to instructors in live simulations or debriefing.

Frederick C. Ingram

PRINCIPAL SUBSIDIARIES

BVR-S Pacific PTE (Singapore); Blue Ridge Simulation, Inc. (U.S.A.).

PRINCIPAL COMPETITORS

CAE Inc.; Cubic Corporation; L-3 Communications Holdings, Inc.; Elbit Systems Ltd.; Lockheed Martin Corporation; Thales.

FURTHER READING

"Air Combat Training Heat Up over Asia," *Defense Update,* November 22, 2007.

"Aviv Tzidon to Fire Half BVR Employees," *Asia Africa Intelligence Wire,* November 26, 2003.

Bennett, Magnus, "BVR Systems to Provide Simulator to Israeli Air Force," *Aerospace Daily & Defense Report,* September 8, 2005, p. 5.

Blackburn, Nicky, "BVR Systems Sees Profits Again in 2000," *Jerusalem Post,* Econ. Sec., February 21, 2000, p. 17.

————, "BVR Systems Wins $43m. Korean Contract," *Jerusalem Post,* Econ. Sec., December 14, 1999, p. 12.

————, "Making It Big in a Troubled Defense Industry," *Jerusalem Post,* Econ. Sec., July 17, 1997, p. 13.

Dupont, Jean, "Le simulateur qui traque le stress," *Air & Cosmos,* October 19, 2007, p. 30.

Gerstenfeld, Dan, "Koor Invests Another $19m. in BVR Systems," *Jerusalem Post,* Econ. Sec., August 6, 1999, p. 9A.

Gordon, Buzzy, "Troubled BVR Shuffles Top Execs," *Jerusalem Post,* Econ. Sec., December 18, 2000, p. 17.

Greenberg, Shlomo, "BVR—The Long Wait," *Israel Business Arena,* March 28, 2006.

Habib, Shiri, "Simulating Take Off," *Israel Business Arena,* May 11, 2006.

Horesh, Shira, "BVR Wins $12m Contract for Naval Training System," *Israel Business Arena,* September 11, 2006.

Hughes, David, "A Growing Market Is Emerging," *Aviation Week & Space Technology,* December 12, 2005.

"IAI Withdraws Bid for BVR Systems," *Asia Africa Intelligence Wire,* November 3, 2003.

Kessner, B. C., "Boeing Awards BVR Contract for Korean F-15K Combat Training Systems," *Defense Daily International,* October 15, 2004.

————, "BVR to Acquire Blue Ridge Simulation, Gain U.S. Foothold," *Defense Daily International,* February 24, 2006.

Laing, Yehezkel, "Boeing Awards BVR Contract for Korean F-15K Combat Training Systems," *Defense Daily International,* October 15, 2004.

————, "BVR Teams Up with Boeing in Bid for $270m. US Air-Combat Training Contract," *Jerusalem Post,* Econ. Sec., February 14, 2003, p. 10A.

Nassie, Jonathan, "The Feud That Cost BVR a Year and a Half," *Ha'aretz,* October 20, 1999.

Penney, Stewart, "Defence—France Acquires BVR Systems Training System," *Flight International,* January 1, 2000, p. 20.

Rodan, Steve, "BVR to Complete Spin-Off of BVR Systems," *Jerusalem Post,* Econ. Sec., October 23, 1998, p. 10.

Shlomo, Gil, "BVR Systems Posts First Profit in 7 Years," *Israel Business Arena,* March 6, 2006.

Camargo Corrêa S.A.

Rua Funchal 160, Vila Olimpia
São Paulo, São Paulo 04551-903
Brazil
Telephone: (55 11) 3841-5884
Fax: (55 11) 3841-5157
Web site: http://www.camargocorrea.com.br

Private Company
Incorporated: 1939 as Construtora Camargo & Companhia Limitada—Engenheirs e Construtores
Employees: 35,542
Sales: BRL $10.07 billion ($4.82 billion) (2006)
NAIC: 111110 Soybean Farming; 112111 Beef Cattle Ranching and Farming; 221111 Hydroelectric Power Generation; 221112 Fossil Fuel Electric Power Generation; 221113 Nuclear Electric Power Generation; 221310 Sewage Treatment Facilities; 237120 Oil and Gas Pipeline and Related Structures; 237130 Highway, Street, and Bridge Construction; 313210 Broadwoven Fabric Mills; 316219 Other Footwear Manufacturing; 324110 Petroleum Refineries; 327310 Cement Manufacturing; 488119 Other Airport Operations; 488210 Support Activities for Rail Transportation; 488310 Port and Harbor Operations; 541620 Environmental Consulting Services; 551112 Offices of Other Holding Companies

■ ■ ■

Camargo Corrêa S.A. is the holding company for one of the largest industrial groups in Brazil. Founded by a man with two burros and a wagon, it grew to become a giant construction company, whose works included power plants throughout the nation, subways, airports, highways, and other public works projects, including construction of what became Brazil's spanking new capital, Brasília. It has since become a conglomerate with holdings in companies producing petroleum products, metals, textiles, and footwear as well as making cement and operating and maintaining roads and electric utilities. Other activities include engineering and environmental services. The sprawling family-owned private group even includes cattle ranches and a soybean growing plantation. It is also active in other South American countries and sees its future in doing as much business internationally as within Brazil.

RISING FROM POVERTY: 1930–50

Sebastião Ferraz de Camargo Penteado was born into poverty. The eldest of the ten children of a farmer in the state of São Paulo, he began working at the age of six and never received schooling beyond the third grade. After running a street stall, he rose to become a coffee broker but lost everything in the depression that followed the 1929 Wall Street stock market crash. With a beat up cart and two burros, he started a small earth moving and road paving business in 1930. Its first important government contract was for an eight-mile stretch of highway. Yet working for the state government was at times a hazardous enterprise, especially when it began making payment in bonds that were almost without value on the market.

In 1936 Camargo joined with Silvio Brandt Corrêa

to open a civil engineering office in São Paulo. They incorporated the business in 1939 as Construtora Camargo & Companhia Limitada—Engenheiros e Construtores, a construction company engaged in developing railroads and highways in São Paulo. This company later changed its name to Camargo Corrêa Engenharia e Construções S.A. During the 1950s it changed its name again, to Construções e Comércio Camargo Corrêa S.A. (CCCC). Its real growth began in this decade, as Brazil's leaders shook off the doldrums stemming from the Great Depression and World War II and bankrolled vast infrastructure projects.

INFRASTRUCTURE PROJECTS: 1950–90

For the first time Camargo Corrêa was able to import the kind of heavy machinery and equipment it needed to win big contracts. None was more spectacular than the ones for Brasília, the capital city built on an unpopulated plateau in the interior of a country whose people had always clustered along the Atlantic coast. The area was so bereft of infrastructure that CCCC's cement was, at first, transported to the construction site by air. Work on the city began in 1957. It was dedicated in 1960 according to a futuristic plan and linked to São Paulo and Rio de Janeiro by newly constructed roads and rail as well as by an airport.

By this time Camargo Corrêa, prescient in judging hydroelectric power to be the wave of the future, had built two such plants. Projects of the 1960s included the Presidente Dutra and Jupiá power plants as well as the Castelo Branco highway. In 1968 CCCC entered the cement business with the establishment of Camargo Corrêa Cimentos S.A. (Cauê).

Camargo Corrêa's annual revenue reached $376 million in 1973. The projects on which it worked during the 1970s included the airport at Manaus, the city in the heart of the Amazon; the São Paulo subway; the

bridge-and-road link between Rio de Janeiro and suburban Nitarói, the Trans-Amazon Highway, and the Itaipu and Guri hydroelectric plants, the latter in Venezuela. In 1977 CCCC won a big contract to build the hydroelectric facilities for the Tucurí dam in the eastern Amazon. This would provide electricity for the exploitation of Brazil's largest known concentration of minerals, about 175 miles to the south. One of the world's largest hydroelectric complexes and the largest ever built in a tropical rain forest, Tucurí was not completed until about 1989. It was the biggest work in concrete ever made in Brazil: eight million cubic meters.

Among the clients for Tucurí's power was Alcoa, Inc., the world's largest aluminum producer, which was the largest participant in a consortium building an alumina and aluminum plant in São Luis, an Atlantic port connected to the mineral concentration by a new electrified railway. Camargo Corrêa, in 1983, acquired a 36 percent stake in Alcoa's Brazilian subsidiary for $220 million. In the previous year CCCC had been the most profitable Brazilian company owned by Brazilians rather than foreigners. Its revenues reached $1.14 billion in that year.

Other company achievements of the 1980s included the construction of the Cumbica airport and the Bandeirantes and Ayrton Serna highways. By 1987 Camargo Corrêa was a behemoth, composed of 33 companies engaged not only in civil construction, mining and quarrying, and engineering, but also such activities as forestry and banking. Sebastião Camargo was now a billionaire. Called "China" for what John Barnham, in a *Fortune* article, called "his inscrutable manner and vaguely Oriental features," Camargo was an insider within Brazil's power elite who kept a low profile. Although nearing age 80, he gave no indications of retiring and kept close tabs on company executives, flying into even remote encampments on a moment's notice.

TRANSITION TO PROFESSIONALLY MANAGED CONGLOMERATE: 1987–98

As Camargo neared his inevitable passing, the question of succession became a pressing concern. The founder of the business had three daughters and no son. He elevated his three sons-in-law to high positions in 1987 but seemingly was unable to decide which one would be his heir. In 1989 he chose a company executive as president of CCCC but resumed the position himself within two years. After absenting himself for medical treatment in the United States in 1992, he chose to turn over administration of the enterprise to existing executives. Camargo died in 1994. Two years later, the

KEY DATES

1930: Sebastião Camargo starts an earth moving and road paving business.

1936: Camargo and his partner open the business that later becomes Camargo Corrêa.

1968: Already a construction giant, Camargo Corrêa enters the cement business.

1977: Company begins work on the largest hydroelectric power project in a tropical rain forest.

1982: Company annual revenue passes $1 billion, and Camargo is himself a billionaire.

1996: Camargo Corrêa S.A. is founded as the company for the conglomerate's holdings.

2003: The company takes control of SP Alpargatas, and, with Alpergatas, of Santista Têxtil.

2006: Camargo Corrêa is the holding company for 19 diverse companies.

company board, which included the three sons-in-law, chose an outsider, Alciades Tápias, an executive of Banco Bradesco (Brazil's leading bank) to lead the company. He presided over a reorganization that established Camargo Corrêa S.A. as the holding company for the enterprise's far flung endeavors.

A flurry of activity followed the changing of the guard. Camargo Corrêa Energia S.A., established in 1997, joined with Bradesco and the Votarantim family group that year to purchase a 30-year renewable concession to operate Cia. Paulista de Força & Luz, a newly privatized company in the state of São Paulo. Engaged in both generating and distributing electricity, CPFL Energia became the leading investor in electrical energy in Brazil. Camargo Corrêa Desenvolvimento Inmobiliário S.A. (CCDI) was established as the holding company's arm for real estate development, while CAVO Serviçoes e Meio Ambiente became the company for environmental services, including industrial waste management. On the other hand, Camargo Corrêa sold a stake in the private bank it controlled, Banco Geral do Comércio, to Banco Santander Brasil for $220 million, then sold its shares in Santander for $214 million.

Founded in 1998, Camargo Corrêa Transportes S.A. (CCT) was the subsidiary administering the parent company's concessions for some of the highways privatized in the 1990s. It held one-sixth of Camargo Corrêa Rodavias (CCR), the largest private operator of roads in Latin America. In 2002 CCR road concessions reached

one-seventh of the national total. Another fledgling Camargo Corrêa company was Camargo Corrêa Metais S.A. (CCM). Located next to the Tucurí power station, CCM made metallic silicates for industry, civil construction, and medical devices; aluminum alloys for motor vehicles and ships; and auto wheels, computer chips, digital watches, and electronic equipment in general. Ninety percent of its output was being exported. This company was sold in 2007 to Globe Specialty Metals Inc. for about $38 million.

TEXTILES, FOOTWEAR, CEMENT, AND MORE: 1988–2007

Camargo Corrêa had been engaged in the textile field since 1948, by means of Cia. Jauense Industrial. By 1988 it held a one-third stake in one of Brazil's foremost textile and footwear manufacturers, São Paulo Alpargatas S.A. Acting in concert with his former colleagues at Bradesco, which held a one-fifth share of the company, Tápias ousted the firm's longtime chief. In 2003 Camargo Corrêa took majority control of SP Alpargatas by purchasing Bradesco's shares and also, in combination with Alpargatas, became full owners of Santista Têxtil S.A. by purchasing the 55 percent stake held by Bradesco and the Bunge group. Santista was one of the largest denim manufacturers in the world.

In the first decade of the 21st century, SP Alpargatas proved a smashing success, particularly because of the worldwide popularity of its Haviana flip-flop sandals. Camargo Corrêa held a 43 percent stake in the company in 2006. Santista Têxtil ranked second in Brazil in jeans production but was being hit hard by Chinese competition in textiles. In 2006 it was merged into Tavex Algodonera S.A., a big Spanish producer of denim that also owned the Spanish retail chain Zara and the Italian luxury jeans brand Diesel. As a result of the merger, Camargo Corrêa had a 46 percent stake in Tavex.

Camargo Corrêa Cimentos, or Cauê, was best known for its white cement, which led other producers in this segment. In the concrete market, Cauê differed from its rivals by offering a system for tracking cement mixers by satellite so that customers could go online to order the product. However, it held only 8 percent of the national cement market and, in the judgment of the holding company's management, needed to grow to remain viable. Accordingly, in 2005, Camargo Corrêa purchased Loma Negra C.I.A.S.A., which was producing almost half of Argentina's cement, for $1.02 billion. (It also thus acquired Ferrosur, an Argentine rail cargo line 80 percent owned by Loma Negra.) The parent company's bottom line for this purchase had been buttressed by its 2003 sale of its 41 percent share in Alcoa Aluminio S.A. for $410.9 million in Alcoa, Inc., stock.

Also under the holding company's umbrella were Morro Vermelho Táxi Aéreo, which had five airplanes for outside clients as well as the conglomerate's own needs, and Arrossensal Agropecuário e Industrial S.A., which was growing soybeans on 6,480 hectares (about 16,000 acres) and also operating two cattle ranches. In addition, Camargo Corrêa held a 6 percent stake in Usinas Siderúrgicas de Minas Gerais S.A. (Usiminas), Brazil's leading manufacturer of flat steel; a 4 percent stake in the holding company controlling Brazil's second largest bank, Banco Itaú; and a 2 percent share in Alcoa, Inc.

ENGINEERING, CONSTRUCTION, AND MANAGEMENT

Engineering and construction remained at Camargo Corrêa's heart. Among the achievements of the 1990s was the building of a gas pipeline between Brazil and Bolivia. Projects underway in 2005 included the part of a highway from the Atlantic to Pacific coasts running from the westernmost part of Amazonian Brazil to three ports in southern Peru and a stretch of highway between Brazil and Bolivia. The firm had won a contract to repair a Venezuelan dam and even had its eye on business in Africa.

By 2007 the firm had won several highway infrastructure contracts in South Africa, Angola, and Mozambique. It was also the lead contractor in the construction of a new São Paulo subway line and was a contractor and investor in the Campos Novos hydroelectric project in southern Brazil. Furthermore, it was lead contractor for the construction of a 300-kilometer (185-mile) stretch of the InterOceanic Highway passing through the Andes Mountains of southern Peru. In addition, it was engaged in lighter construction than its previous work, building facilities such as retail stores, supermarkets, and hospitals.

Looming over all these activities was CCCC, which operated in synergy with the other business units of the group as the manager and integrating link for the implementation of projects, from conception to operation, involving all technical and financial aspects. Under its umbrella were six hydroelectric stations, providing half of all hydroelectric power in Brazil, and five other power plants, one of them nuclear. It also operated and maintained four big airports; three port terminals; several railroad and subway lines; an oil refinery; oil and gas pipelines and offshore platforms; and water and sewage treatment plants. CCCC also included a unit that studied engineering projects, made technical assess-

ments, and acted as consultant, and another that specialized in implementing solutions for electricity substations. Its 16 subsidiaries included 13 Camargo Corrêa units in other countries: nine in South America, three in Africa, and Camargo Corrêa USA.

CHARTING A COURSE FOR THE 21ST CENTURY

Since 1999 Camargo Corrêa had been under the direction of Raphael Antonio Nogueira de Freitas, but he was due to step down in 2006. The question of succession set off jockeying by several veteran executives, each of whom was presiding over a different area of the holding company. Finally, the contest narrowed down to José Édison Barros Franco of the cement area, representing tradition, and Marcelo Araújo of footwear and textiles, representing modernization. Ultimately, the decision rested with the three daughters of Sebastião Camargo, who were represented on the board by their husbands. The choice was an outsider, Vitor Sarquís Hallack, known for his diplomatic skills in bringing together antagonistic business groups.

Hallack inherited management of a conglomerate composed of 19 companies and no core business. Energy, engineering and construction, and footwear accounted for slightly more than half of Camargo Corrêa's revenues in 2005 in almost equal shares. Cement and textiles also had significant shares of the holding company's revenues, followed by steel and silicon metals and trailed by highway concessions and environmental engineering. Hallack's chief goal was to consolidate the process of internationalization to raise the group's revenues in foreign currency from 15 percent to 50 percent by 2012. He would have to shuttle between the three families participating in the family-owned company that in turn controlled Camargo Corrêa, although several of the companies in which the conglomerate held stakes, directly or indirectly, were publicly traded, among them Alpargatas, CCDI, CCR, CPFL, and Tavex.

Robert Halasz

PRINCIPAL SUBSIDIARIES

Camargo Corrêa Cimentos S.A.; Camargo Corrêa Desenvolvimento Imobiliário S.A.; Camargo Corrêa Energia S.A.; Camargo Corrêa Transportes S.A.; CAVO Serviços e Meio Ambiente S.A.; Construções e Comércio Camargo Corrêa S.A.

PRINCIPAL COMPETITORS

Construtora Andrade Gutierrez S.A.; Construtora Norberto Oderbrecht S.A.; Duratex S.A.; Electropaulo Metropolitana Electricidade de São Paulo S.A.; Grendine S.A.; Holcim Brasil S.A. Vicunha Têxtil S.A.

FURTHER READING

"The Bank to Beat in Brazil," *Global Finance,* June 1998, pp. 38–39.

Barham, John, "The Man Who Built Brazil," *Fortune,* October 12, 1987, p. 185.

"Camargo montou um império com o trabalho," *O Estado de São Paulo,* August 28, 1994, p. B13.

Carvalho, Denise, "Difícil sucessão na Camargo," *Exame,* May 24, 2006, p. 75.

———, "O diplomata da Camargo Corrêa," *Exame,* December 6, 2006, pp. 46–48.

Charters, Ann, "Brazil Builds Northern Powerhouse," *Financial Times,* January 11, 1985, p. 4.

Duggan, Patrice, "Sebastião Camargo," *Forbes,* October 15, 1987, p. 157.

Pastor, Luzia, "O sucesso das 'ravianas,'" *Exame Melhores e Maiores,* July 2006, pp. 170, 172.

Rosa, Maria Alice, and Jane Soares, "Cimento Online," *Exame Melhores e Maiores,* July 2004, pp. 224–25.

Schexnayder, C. J., "Brazil's Local Contractor Giant Reaches Out to Spur Growth," *ENR,* February 26, 2007, pp. 17–19.

Schexnayder, Cliff, "South American Project Stretches Ocean to Ocean," *ENR,* January 1/8, 2007, pp. 16–18.

Stok, Gustavo, "El Nuevo Estilo Camargo Corrêa," *AméricaEconomía,* December 15, 2005, pp. 25–26.

Whitley, Andrew, "Brazilian Group Buys into Local Alcoa Subsidiary," *Financial Times,* November 7, 1983, p. 18.

Cardtronics, Inc.

3110 Hayes Road, Suite 300
Houston, Texas 77082
U.S.A.
Telephone: (281) 596-9988
Toll Free: (800) 786-9666
Fax: (281) 596-9984
Web site: http://www.cardtronics.com

Public Company
Incorporated: 1989 as Cardpro, Inc.
Employees: 278
Sales: $293.6 million (2006)
Stock Exchanges: NASDAQ
Ticker Symbol: CATM
NAIC: 541512 Computer Systems Design Services

■■■

Cardtronics, Inc., is the largest, non-bank automated-teller-machine (ATM) operator in the world. The company's network comprises more than 30,000 ATMs in the United States, the United Kingdom, and Mexico. Domestically, Cardtronics has ATMs in all 50 states. Internationally, it operates through Bank Machine Limited, which manages more than 1,700 ATMs throughout Great Britain, and through Cardtronics Mexico, which manages more than 700 ATMs in Mexico. Cardtronics owns roughly half of the ATMs it has in service and operates the balance of its fleet under management agreements with merchants, who own the ATMs. For the ATMs it owns, Cardtronics is responsible for all aspects of operation, including procuring cash, supplies, and telecommunications, as well as routine maintenance. For the merchant-owned ATMs, Cardtronics provides transaction processing services and connection to electronic-funds-transfer networks. The company has merchant agreements with dozens of companies, including Sears, Roebuck and Co., Walgreen Co., Costco Wholesale Corp., Target Corp., The Kroger Co., Chevron Corp., and ExxonMobil Corp. Cardtronics also operates through branding agreements with banks, including JPMorgan Chase & Co., HSBC Holdings PLC, and Sovereign Bancorp, Inc. Through its subsidiary Allpoint, Cardtronics operates the largest surcharge-free network of ATMs in the United States.

FAILURE PRECEDING SUCCESS

At age 53, Ralph Clinard decided to strike out on his own and become an entrepreneur. Disaster soon followed, shattering what had been decades of financial stability for the former Exxon executive. Born in Springfield, Tennessee, in 1933, Clinard earned his undergraduate degrees in mathematics and mechanical engineering from Muskingum College and Penn State University, respectively. Shortly after graduation in 1957, Clinard settled in Houston, Texas, and joined Exxon, where he would remain for the next 29 years. Clinard's years at Exxon gave him structure, stability, and financial success, all of which he threw away when he decided to be his own boss.

Clinard left Exxon in 1986, opting for early retirement. He decided to use his savings to launch a career as a restaurateur and real estate investor. He

COMPANY PERSPECTIVES

Cardtronics was founded on one central belief: that people are at their best when they are striving to exceed accomplishments of the past. We take seriously our commitment to our customers and shareholders to pursue higher standards of service and performance in all that we do every day. Today, under the leadership of CEO Jack Antonini, Cardtronics is one of the world's leading ATM providers. As an organization, we strive to provide innovative solutions for our customers, and for the industry as a whole. To be a leader is to be involved and responsive. Cardtronics will continue to be just that in the rapidly changing electronic transactions market. You can be sure that Cardtronics will be attuned to new technology, innovation, and increased functionality—for the company, for our customers and for the future of the industry.

opened a posh French restaurant in Houston, La Bonne Auberge, that he remembered fondly in a March 21, 2006, interview with *ATM Marketplace.* "We had one of the city's finest French restaurants," he said. "Our chef used to cook for King Hussein." He also related why his upscale restaurant quickly foundered. "The oil business went into a steep decline," he explained. "Suddenly, there weren't many people who could go out and pay for French food." Deteriorating economic conditions cost Clinard everything: La Bonne Auberge closed, the mortgages on his real estate ventures foreclosed, and he found himself $200,000 in debt to the Internal Revenue Service. Within three years, he lost more than $1 million.

FROM CREDIT CARD MACHINES TO DEBIT CARD MACHINES

Clinard, the financially secure former Exxon executive, transmogrified into a destitute 59-year-old, stuck in a financial quagmire. He needed to get back to work, and he found inspiration for his second career while liquidating his restaurant equipment. The sale of a credit card terminal and printer back to its original owner led Clinard to Houston-based Southwest Merchant Services, a company that provided credit card merchant services. Clinard began working for the firm, but soon his entrepreneurial inclinations sparked another bold move.

"After about two months," Clinard recalled in an August 24, 2001, interview with the *Houston Business Journal,* "I realized I could do this myself, so I began working out of my home and borrowed money from my family to get the business started."

The business Clinard started was Cardpro, Inc., the predecessor to Cardtronics. He began in 1989, working alone at home, spending his time making sales calls and building a customer base. After several years, he backed away from marketing and selling credit machines, lured by the earning potential in a relatively new sector of the financial services industry: debit card machines. To make his way into the field, Clinard called upon the skills he learned at Penn State, where he had earned his degree in mechanical engineering. He began designing and building a scrip machine, an inexpensive precursor to ATMs. Unlike ATMs, which dispensed cash, scrip machines dispensed a receipt that could be redeemed for cash. A customer using a scrip machine in a convenience store, for instance, could use the voucher to obtain cash from the store's clerk. Clinard, whose design work eventually garnered him a patent for his scrip machine, began marketing the simple cash-ticket machines to small, independent convenience store owners in the greater Houston area. One customer at a time, one location at a time, Clinard began building a new business foundation for Cardpro.

Clinard made the defining move that would turn Cardpro into Cardtronics as the tenth anniversary of his second entrepreneurial venture neared. The success of Clinard's scrip machine business enabled him to repay the Internal Revenue Service. He also was able to repay his family, who had provided the start-up capital for Cardpro. Financially, Clinard was back on his feet, but the comfort of stability after the despair of the late 1980s did not breed complacency. Clinard saw greater profits in the non-bank ATM business, a business whose entry barriers had been removed when Visa and Master-Card eliminated their bans on surcharge fees in 1996. He leaped at the chance to enter the fray and began selling ATMs.

Cardpro had roughly 900 of its scrip machines in operation when Visa and MasterCard made their decision. "Coincidentally," Clinard said in his *ATM Marketplace* interview, "that same year was when I decided, 'If I'm going to be successful in this business, I want to get some talent in here.' So I brought in a lot of bright people and gave them stock in the company to join forces with me. That amounted to about 25 percent of the company. It's probably one of the best things I ever did to make this company successful."

KEY DATES

1989: Ralph Clinard begins selling credit card machines.

1997: After recording moderate success in selling scrip machines, Clinard begins selling ATMs.

2001: Clinard's company, Cardpro, changes its name to Cardtronics.

2003: Jack Antonini is appointed president and chief executive officer.

2004: After acquiring E*Trade Financial's ATM network, Cardtronics ranks as the largest, non-bank operator in the United States.

2005: Cardtronics expands overseas for the first time, acquiring England-based Bank Machine Ltd.

2006: Cardtronics enters Mexico by purchasing CCS Mexico.

2007: The purchase of 7-Eleven's ATM network makes Cardtronics the largest operator in the world.

TWO GENERATIONS OF CLINARDS

One of the employees who joined in the first big increase in Cardpro's payroll was Clinard's son, Michael Clinard. The younger Clinard, a 1990 graduate of Howard Payne University, had spent the previous six years serving as chief operating officer of Worldwide Cellular, Inc., gaining experience in corporate planning, strategic business development, marketing, operations, and automation design. When he joined Cardpro as the company's new chief operating officer, Clinard urged his father to expand the business. Cardpro had never strayed too far from the greater Houston area, but Clinard realized the company could easily expand into other markets. "We had a great business model," he said in an August 24, 2001, interview with the *Houston Business Journal.* "When we started mail-outs to Austin, San Antonio, Dallas, Atlanta, Arkansas, and Florida, we were immediately successful."

1997–2001: ONE STEP AT A TIME

There were two distinct periods of growth for the Clinards' business during the ensuing decade. When Michael Clinard joined the company, it embarked on its first, genuine expansion campaign, looking to build its presence in other markets. It did so gradually and steadily, preferring to broaden its network one location at a time, the same measured approach employed by Ralph Clinard when he began deploying scrip machines. Despite the methodical pace of expansion, the company grew into one of the largest ATM operators in the United States within a short period. By 2001, the company had more than 5,000 ATMs operating in 49 states, 1,200 of which were located in the Houston area. The total was sufficient to make Cardpro one of the five largest, non-bank competitors in the country. Annual sales reflected the impressive rise through the industry's ranks, reaching $26.7 million in 2000, an exponential leap from the $1.3 million generated in 1996. The growth also was sufficient to earn praise from *Inc.* magazine, which selected the company as one of the 500 fastest-growing, privately held companies in the United States in 2001.

CARDPRO BECOMES CARDTRONICS: 2001

The progress achieved during the 1997–2001 period made Cardpro a legitimate national competitor, but far greater growth was to be recorded in the years to follow. Cardpro began its second period of expansion under a new name, adopting the Cardtronics corporate title in 2001. The year also marked a significant change in its strategy. Instead of expanding store by store, the Clinards began acquiring batches of ATMs, executing their strategy far more aggressively. In October 2001, for instance, the new personality of the company was on display. Cardtronics took over ownership and management of 1,100 ATMs owned by McLane Company Inc., a food distributor owned by Wal-Mart Stores Inc. Less than a week later, the company announced a long-term agreement with SSP/Circle K to install and service 335 ATMs located in Circle K convenience stores in Texas and Oklahoma. Instead of courting individual store owners, Cardtronics was pursuing merchant accounts, seeking to become the dominant competitor in its industry. "Our vision," Ralph Clinard declared in an October 23, 2001, interview with *American Banker,* "is to become the nation's largest and most well-regarded independent sales organization specializing in ATM products and services."

JACK ANTONINI TAKES THE HELM IN 2003

As Cardtronics marched forward, a change in leadership occurred, but the new blood at headquarters did not signal a change in the company's expansion strategy. In 2003, Ralph Clinard retired, handing his duties as president and chief executive officer to Jack Antonini. A graduate of Ferris State University, Antonini was a banking and electronic payment services veteran capable of and willing to make Ralph Clinard's vision a reality.

Cardtronics achieved great strides under the leadership of Antonini, becoming a dominant global force. In 2003, several months after acquiring 938 ATMs located in Winn-Dixie stores in the southeastern United States, Antonini brokered a deal to purchase 1,704 ATMs from American Express Co. The acquisition vaulted Cardtronics ahead of American Express in the national rankings, making Cardtronics the third largest deployer of ATMs in the country, trailing only industry leader eFunds Corp. and runner-up E*Trade Financial Corp. In June 2004, Antonini reached the top of the industry rankings by signing an agreement with his closest rival. E*Trade Financial agreed to sell substantially all its assets in E*Trade Access, its ATM subsidiary, to Cardtronics. The acquisition more than doubled the number of cash machines under Cardtronics' control, giving it a network of more than 25,000 ATMs and making it the largest, non-bank operator of ATMs in the United States.

EXPANSION OVERSEAS IN 2005

After climbing to the top of its industry, there was no hint Cardtronics was scaling back its expansion efforts. The company had signed merchant agreements with Albertsons, Barnes & Noble, Chevron, Costco, Sears, Target, and a bevy of others, which it coupled with branding agreements with banks, an area of focus in the years after it became the largest operator in the United States. More noticeable to industry observers than bank-branding agreements were the company's first steps overseas. In May 2005, Cardtronics announced the acquisition of Bank Machine Ltd., a Hertfordshire, England-based ATM deployer. Bank Machine, which became a subsidiary of Cardtronics, operated roughly 1,000 ATMs throughout Great Britain in shopping centers, convenience stores, pubs, and post offices. Next, in early 2006, Cardtronics completed another international acquisition, purchasing CCS Mexico, an operator of 300 ATMs that the company renamed Cardtronics Mexico. At roughly the same time the company entered Mexico, it strengthened its business on the home front with the addition of a third branded subsidiary. Cardtronics acquired Allpoint, the operator of the largest surcharge-free ATM network in the United States.

WORLD DOMINATION AND A PUBLIC DEBUT IN 2007

As Cardtronics' 20th anniversary neared, two major events grabbed the attention of the business press. In July 2007, the company's acquisition campaign netted the ultimate prize. Cardtronics acquired the entire ATM network owned by 7-Eleven Inc., a transaction that included approximately 3,500 ATMs and 2,000 kiosks, known as Vcoms, that allowed customers to cash checks, pay bills, purchase money orders, and transfer money. The acquisition, valued at $135 million, made Cardtronics the largest, non-bank owner of ATMs in the world.

Within a decade, Cardtronics became the global leader in its industry. The company's next move was to sell its towering stature on Wall Street. The company initially had intended to make its public debut in 2004, when it filed for an initial public offering (IPO) of stock with the Securities and Exchange Commission. Cardtronics canceled its IPO plans in 2005, but in the wake of the 7-Eleven deal it was ready for another attempt. In September 2007, the company filed for an IPO and completed the offering in December 2007, when it sold 12 million shares at $10 per share, raising net proceeds of approximately $110 million. A new era had begun, one that promised to include new challenges as Cardtronics sought to remain the global leader, satisfy shareholders, and continue to expand in the years ahead.

Jeffrey L. Covell

PRINCIPAL SUBSIDIARIES

Cardtronics GP, Inc.; Cardtronics LP, Inc.; Cardtronics LP; Cardtronics Holdings, LLC; Cardtronics Limited (U.K.); Bank Machine (Acquisitions) Limited (U.K.); Bank Machine Limited (U.K.); ATM National, LLC; ATM Ventures, LLC; Cardtronics Mexico, S.A. de C.V.

PRINCIPAL COMPETITORS

Bank of America Corporation; U.S. Bancorp; PNC Corp.; TRM Corp.; The Royal Bank of Scotland Group PLC; Society of Lloyd's; Cardpoint PLC.

FURTHER READING

Bills, Steve, "Cardtronics' IPO Plan Seen As Consolidation Precursor," *American Banker,* September 11, 2007, p. 17.

Breitkopf, David, "Cardtronics Buys Allpoint to Diversify," *American Banker,* January 31, 2006, p. 1.

———, "Deals and a Demise Lift Cardtronics in ATM Field," *American Banker,* October 23, 2001, p. 10.

———, "7-Eleven's Deal Hands ATM Fleet to Cardtronics," *American Banker,* June 7, 2007, p. 1.

"Building Momentum," *American Executive,* July 2006, p. 158.

"Cardtronics Acquires Bank Machine Ltd. in the U.K.," *PrimeZone Media Network,* May 18, 2005.

"Cardtronics Inks ATM Branding Deal with PNC Bank," *National Petroleum News,* March 2005, p. 35.

"E*Trade Agrees to Sell Most of Its ATM Subsidiary to Cardtronics for $106 Million," *Cardline,* June 4, 2004, p. 1.

Gibson, Kevin, "Who's Who: Ralph Clinard," *ATM Marketplace,* March 21, 2006.

Roberts, Ed, "Cardtronics Acquires 7-Eleven's 5,500 ATMs," *Credit Union Journal,* June 11, 2007, p. 1.

Wolfe, Daniel, "7-Eleven Acquires Amex's Remaining ATMs," *American Banker,* August 18, 2004, p. 5.

Wollam, Allison, "Credit to the Trade," *Houston Business Journal,* August 24, 2001, p. 17.

CareerBuilder, Inc.

—■—

200 North LaSalle Street, Suite 1100
Chicago, Illinois 60631
U.S.A.
Telephone: (773) 527-3600
Toll Free: (800) 638-4212
Fax: (772) 399-6313
Web site: http://www.careerbuilder.com

Private Company
Incorporated: 1995 as NetStart, Inc.
Employees: 1,800
Sales: $672 million (2007 est.)
NAIC: 561310 Employment Placement Agencies

■ ■ ■

CareerBuilder, Inc., is an Internet recruitment company that currently runs the largest online job site and manages job listings for a large network of web sites, including MSN, and newspapers around the nation. Career-Builder also provides tools for employers and aspiring employees to manage recruitment materials, including resumes.

STARTING NETSTART: 1995–96

CareerBuilder began doing business in 1995 as NetStart, Inc. NetStart was founded in Reston, Virginia, by Robert J. McGovern, a longtime executive in the computer industry, who had formerly worked for Hewlett-Packard and then at a software development company called Legent Corp. As McGovern later recalled, the initial idea of beginning a company focused on online job recruitment came to him while he was vacationing on a Delaware beach in the summer of 1994. "By the third day of the vacation, I was typing up the business plan," McGovern recounted in a 1996 *Washington Post* article. "By the fourth day, it wasn't a vacation anymore."

Eventually, McGovern received a generous buyout when Legent was sold to Computer Associates International. He used these funds to help him begin NetStart. The company was initially a modest enterprise. During its first year, it consisted of McGovern and five software engineers. Like many other young start-ups, NetStart initially lacked any tangible product. Nevertheless, McGovern's efforts attracted outside investment. A California-based venture capital firm called New Enterprise Associates contributed funds. In 1996, NetStart received $5 million from 21st Century Internet Venture Partners.

By that year, however, NetStart did have something to sell. Its TeamBuilder software, which sold for about $5,000, enabled human resources staff, rather than information technology (IT) experts, to manage online job listings and the recruitment data received from applicants. About 30 companies were using TeamBuilder at the end of the year. NetStart also worked to develop its CareerBuilder.com web site. Meanwhile, the company itself was growing. It employed around 25 people and had opened a second office across the country in San Francisco. It had further plans to open another office in New York, as well as three more, and to increase its sales force fourfold.

COMPANY PERSPECTIVES

We are changing the way companies around the world recruit their most important asset: their people. Our mission is to be the global leader in online recruitment advertising by being an employee-driven, customer-focused organization that provides the best rate of return to our shareholders.

CREATING AND ESTABLISHING CAREERBUILDER: 1997–99

In 1997, NetStart released TeamBuilder 2.1 and launched TeamBuilder Online. It also achieved revenues of $7 million. However, it was through CareerBuilder.com, which included job listings and, unlike many other recruitment sites, tools for managing application materials such as resumes, that the company made a name for itself. In fact, at the beginning of the year, NetStart renamed itself CareerBuilder. It also extended the CareerBuilder brand by inaugurating the CareerBuilder Network along with 16 online partners, including American Banker Online, Yahoo!, AOL Digital Cities, Hispanic Online, Black Enterprise Online, and Women's Connection Online. Two more partners eventually joined the network, which grew to include job listings from over 800 employers. CareerBuilder.com itself reached the 1,000 customer mark.

Over the next several years, the CareerBuilder Network grew dramatically. In 1999, the company joined with NBC Interactive Neighborhood to create the NBC CareerBuilder Career Center. It also reached an agreement with Lycos Network to give CareerBuilder.com a prominent place on Lycos's sites, especially those that reached out to the IT industry. One of the company's main objectives was to replace massive job boards with sites limited by geography, profession, and diversity. It was named among the "Best of the Web: Jobs" category by *U.S. News & World Report* in 1999. A September 7, 2000, press release depicted CareerBuilder as offering the "industry's most targeted recruiting results." Toward that end, it entered into partnerships with Medical Economics CareerPulse, a site devoted to the medical industry, and QuestiLink Technology Inc., an online source aimed at manufacturing professionals and engineers.

CareerBuilder's success included an initial public offering (IPO) of stock in the spring of 1999. The company's fortunes initially inspired high hopes among investors, but within weeks, its stock began to decline in value, partly due to a general downturn in tech stocks and partly because of the large number of Internet recruiting firms. One analyst noted in a 2000 issue of *Editor and Publisher* magazine that there were "too many players [in the online recruitment industry] to get the awareness of the limited audience." Some investors still expressed optimism about CareerBuilder. One observer in a 2000 *Washington Post* article considered it "the fastest-growing and smartest and most media-savvy" among its competitors. Nevertheless, by the spring of 2000, its stock had plummeted in value and McGovern was himself bothered by what he saw as investor apathy.

VIRTUAL AND REAL WORLD SUCCESS: 1999–2001

At the beginning of the 21st century, the company continued to expand its presence on the Internet. Between 2000 and 2001, it forged relationships with a variety of online partners that gave employers access to specific populations of potential job seekers, including those in the IT and healthcare industries. CareerBuilder also established an agreement with YAPA.com, a site focused on young professionals. It also sought to reach out to college students through such web portals as College Central Network and CollegeClub.com, the most visited online college-focused site. In addition, it established links with BlackVoices.com and with QuickHire, which focused on recruitment for federal, state, and local government agencies.

Likewise, the company sought opportunities to develop its online infrastructure. In 2000, it announced an arrangement with Brainbench to deploy software to evaluate the skills of potential employees and with EzeeNet to help automate its job listing process. The company's efforts bore fruit. By May 2000, the number of visitors to the CareerBuilder Network surpassed two million per month, making it the second online recruiting source to achieve that milestone. In 2001, it included over 100 partners, drew more than 5.5 million visitors per month, and listed upwards of 300,000 jobs from 25,000 employers. CareerBuilder.com attracted attention as well.

The period also witnessed a variety of other successes for the company. It received its first patent in 1999. Its number of employees grew to 120. It also benefited from a $17.8 million investment from Microsoft and an agreement to incorporate CareerBuilder's job listings on the MSN network. Finally, CareerBuilder inaugurated its first national multimedia ad campaign, focused on the question: "Where is your future?" Its revenues had risen to $14.9 million, although like many other startups, it had yet to make a profit. Nevertheless, in 2000, it announced a "Hit the Road to Success" bus

KEY DATES

1995: Robert J. McGovern starts NetStart, Inc.
1996: NetStart opens a second office in San Francisco; the company develops its CareerBuilder.com web site.
1997: NetStart changes its name to CareerBuilder.
1998: CareerBuilder partners with Narrative Communications Corp.
1999: Company holds initial public offering; joins with NBC Interactive Neighborhood to create the NBC CareerBuilder Career Center, reaches an agreement with Lycos Network to give CareerBuilder.com a prominent place on Lycos's sites.
2000: Company announces agreements with Brainbench and with EzeeNet; merges with an online recruitment firm called CareerPath; Tribune Co. and Knight-Ridder Inc. each buy a 47 percent stake in the company.
2002: CareerBuilder merges with Headhunter; Robert J. Montgomery succeeds McGovern as chief executive.
2004: Matt Ferguson becomes president and CEO; Montgomery becomes chairman of the board.
2007: MSN acquires a stake in the company.

tour, which planned to visit over 40 college campuses in 13 states to spread the word about the company.

MERGERS AND ACQUISITIONS: 2000–02

CareerBuilder experienced another major shift in 2000. Media giants Tribune Co. and Knight-Ridder Inc. completed a $200 million deal to each purchase a 47 percent stake in the company, leaving McGovern with the remaining 6 percent, in September. Tribune and Knight-Ridder also merged CareerBuilder with another acquisition of theirs, an online recruitment firm called CareerPath that had been formed in 1995 by a group of newspapers including the *New York Times* and the *Washington Post.* McGovern became CEO of the combined company, which took the CareerBuilder name. The new CareerBuilder also promised to be able to list jobs from over 100,000 companies and to contain information on 1.5 million job seekers.

"What we're going to do," McGovern asserted in a 2000 *Information Week* article, "is combine our online job services with their online job services to take on the No. 1 player in the market," which was at that time Monster.com. CareerBuilder's association with Tribune and Knight-Ridder also gave the company access to nearly three dozen major newspapers in most of the largest metropolitan markets in the country, making it a hybrid between print and online sources and allowing clients to post job listings in a single newspaper, on the paper's web site, or on one of the specialized sites in the CareerBuilder Network. In 2001, CareerBuilder expanded its relationship with newspapers although a deal with Belo Inc., which owned the *Dallas Morning News* and DallasNews.com.

The company's stock price leapt upward at the news of the purchase. Hopes that the company would make a profit by the end of 2000 also increased. However, not everyone was happy. Some investors filed a lawsuit trying to stop the sale to Tribune and Knight-Ridder based on a concern that company insiders who approved the sale stood to make a profit while ordinary stockholders, who were receiving a price far below that at which many had originally purchased stock in the company's IPO, stood to lose money.

In 2002, CareerBuilder underwent a further and much more dramatic change when it merged with Headhunter, another online recruitment firm that had a particularly strong presence in the healthcare industry and among staffing agencies. This combination followed a similar consolidation between Monster.com and HotJobs and created what McGovern characterized in a 2001 article in Canada's *Globe and Mail* as a "Pepsi-Coke challenge" between Monster and CareerBuilder. Unlike the merger with CareerPath, however, and even though the new company continued to hold the CareerBuilder name, it was Headhunter's software and practices, both technical and business, that were adopted. Meanwhile, McGovern and his leadership team left the company and were replaced with executives from Headhunter, including Robert M. Montgomery, Jr., who succeeded McGovern as CEO.

Plans to re-create CareerBuilder as Monster's main competitor, however, met with a major setback at the end of 2001. At the last moment, Yahoo! purchased HotJobs out from under Monster.com. This was doubly a challenge to CareerBuilder, first because Yahoo! was already a significant member of the CareerBuilder Network. Ultimately, Yahoo! severed that connection in April 2002. Second, and contrary to expectation, CareerBuilder took up third place in the online recruitment market behind Monster and Yahoo! Instead of battling for leadership, the company found itself fighting with Yahoo! for the number two spot.

OUSTING MONSTER AS NUMBER ONE: 2002–07

In other ways, too, 2002 proved to be a difficult year for CareerBuilder. It cut 30 percent of its 420 employees, a move that reflected staff cuts at Knight-Ridder. Belo Inc. also ended its relationship with the company, complaining that it was promoting the CareerBuilder brand over individual newspaper brands. However, there were positive developments as well. CareerBuilder hoped to gain ground by seeking more relationships with small to midsize newspapers. It was aided in this goal when Gannett Co. bought a 30 percent stake in the company for $93.3 million, bringing with it more than 90 newspapers, television stations, and the *USA Today* web site.

In 2003, the company achieved two important successes. It replaced Monster as the provider of job listings for AOL, a move that helped it to enhance its presence on the Internet. It reached a similar deal with MSN. The next year, user traffic on its sites more than doubled, allowing the company to capture at least 45 percent of the online recruitment market, more than any other competitor. In June 2005, it recorded 16.6 million visitors to the CareerBuilder Network, placing it ahead of Yahoo! and Monster, listed one million jobs, and featured 11 million resumes. The next year it became the largest online recruitment site in terms of revenue. Meanwhile, the CareerBuilder Network continued to grow, including 1,100 partners by 2006 and relationships with 172 newspapers, and reaching 40 percent of the country.

There were changes within the company, too. In 2004, Matt Ferguson became president and CEO while Bob Montgomery became chairman of the board of directors. CareerBuilder sought to raise its public profile as well. In 2005, it began an extremely successful multimedia ad campaign, including a series of television ads featuring an office full of chimps and the tagline "a better job awaits." CareerBuilder also began building international relationships. In 2003, it established links with international web sites in the United Kingdom, Italy, Spain, Ireland, France, Latin America, Singapore, India, Malaysia, Philippines, Belgium, Netherlands, and Australia. In 2005, it reached an agreement with TimesJobs.com, the online arm of The Times of India Group, the largest Indian media company.

By 2007, challenges did remain for CareerBuilder, particularly from a new generation of job sites that focused on particular industries and areas. However, the company continued to show signs of success and hints of a bright future. MSN acquired a 4 percent stake in the company, and the partnership with MSN was expanded and extended until 2013. CareerBuilder also extended the "viral" advertising campaign begun with Monk-e-Mail in 2006, which allowed people to send talking-chimp e-mail messages to friends, by inaugurating Age-o-Matic, a feature that allowed users to age pictures of their friends by 50 years. Meanwhile, revenues rose and, eventually, there was again talk of another public stock offering at some point in the future.

Daniel Patrick Thurs

PRINCIPAL COMPETITORS

Monster; Yahoo! HotJobs; craigslist, inc.

FURTHER READING

Chandrasekaran, Rajiv, "Tapping into a Web of Aspirations; NetStart Helps Firms with Online Job Hunts," *Washington Post,* December 30, 1996, p. F13.

Joyce, Amy, and Peter Behr, "CareerBuilder of Reston Sells for $200 Million," *Washington Post,* July 18, 2000, p. E01.

Joyner, Tammy, "Deal to Create No. 2 Online Recruiting Firm," *Atlanta Journal-Constitution,* August 25, 2001, p. 1E.

Knight, Jerry, "Washington Investing; IPO Investors Are Losers in Buyouts," *Washington Post,* July 24, 2000, p. F07.

"Knight Ridder, Tribune Target Online Recruiting; Competition for Classified Advertising Starting to Heat Up," *Florida Times-Union,* July 18, 2000, p. F2.

Leibovich, Mark, "Making the Job Search Profitable; CareerBuilder, a Top Online Employment Service, Is About to Go Public," *Washington Post,* April 5, 1999, p. F05.

Leonard, Bill, "Major Online Boards Jockey for Position," *HR-Magazine,* October 1, 2003, p. 32.

Mearle, Renae, "CareerBuilder Alters Focus; Online Job Site Deepens Ties with Newspapers," *Washington Post,* January 2002, p. E01.

———, "CareerBuilder Left in Doubt," *Washington Post,* December 28, 2001, p. E01.

"Media Giants Tackle Monsters," *Information Week,* July 24, 2000, p. 149.

Moses, Lucia, "KR, Tribune Bid to Create a Classified Powerhouse," *Editor & Publisher Magazine,* July 24, 2000, p. 7.

"United States: Report on Business," *Globe and Mail,* August 27, 2001, p. B8.

CARUS PUBLISHING
Cricket Magazine Group • Cobblestone Publishing • Cricket Books

Carus Publishing Company

·

140 South Dearborn, Suite 1450
Chicago, Illinois 60603
U.S.A.
Telephone: (312) 701-1720
Toll Free: (800) 821-0115
Fax: (312) 701-1728
Web site: http://www.cricketmag.com

Private Company
Founded: 1973
Employees: 130
Sales: $15.7 million (2007)
NAIC: 511120 Periodical Publishers

■ ■ ■

Much like the lovable insects that inhabit the pages of its literary magazines, Carus Publishing Company holds a small but important place in the immense landscape of children's publishing. Issues concerning literacy and the importance of quality children's literature have long been a major factor in the company's business. From the debut of *Cricket* magazine in 1973 to operations spanning three divisions—Cricket Magazine Group, Cobblestone Publishing, and Cricket Books—three decades later, the enterprise has attracted and nurtured millions of young readers. Dodging the attempts of early critics to squash its publishing success, Carus Publishing Company, founded by the Carus family, has left an indelible mark on the field of children's literature.

GERMAN ROOTS

Carus Publishing Company is the literal and figurative offspring of the intricate merger of science, arts, and education, with roots in Germany. In 1852 Paul Carus was born in Germany. He later earned a doctorate in philosophy and classical philology (the scientific study of texts) and began a writing career. In 1876 he began teaching in a military academy, but his liberal religious views clashed with the school's more conservative ideals. Concerned about censorship and in a quest for freedom of expression, Carus moved to England where he wrote poetry and learned to speak and write English. Subsequently he was offered a job in the United States to edit a German American journal. He immigrated to New York and stayed there for a few years. In 1887 Edward Hegeler, another German immigrant, offered him an editing job in La Salle, Illinois, a small town about 100 miles southwest of Chicago.

Hegeler, a metallurgical engineer, was also interested in philosophy and religion. He had immigrated from Germany to Illinois to begin a zinc-smelting business. He later founded the *Open Court Magazine* to promote his ideas about the relationship between scientific study and religion, culture, and philosophy. Hegeler initially offered Carus a job to translate German articles into English. Soon after, Carus became editor of *Open Court* and published his first article, "The Harmony of the Spheres." Within a year, Carus married Hegeler's daughter, Mary.

The Carus-Hegeler family and their descendants continued to manage the chemical and publishing busi-

COMPANY PERSPECTIVES

Cricket Magazine Group began with the launch of *Cricket* in 1973. Marianne Carus, founder and editor-in-chief, was determined to create a literary children's magazine that would appeal to a child's intellect and imagination. She insisted upon publishing only the highest quality children's literature and selected world-class illustrators to produce the art accompanying the stories. Cricket Books is a division of Carus Publishing and brings the same high quality and standards of excellence to its books for children and young adults as Open Court brings to academic scholarship, the Cricket Magazine Group to children's magazines, and Cobblestone Publishing to educational nonfiction magazines and books. Publishing picture books, chapter books, poetry, nonfiction, and novels for children and young adults, Cricket Books, together with its Marcato imprint, will make young people fall in love with books and reading.

nesses throughout the late 19th and early 20th centuries. In 1921, one of the children, Dr. Edward Hegeler Carus, married. His son, Blouke, followed in his great-grandfather's scientific footsteps and became an electrical engineer with an interest in chemistry and foreign languages. Blouke went to the University of Freiburg in Germany to continue his studies and met Marianne, a German native. Marianne and Blouke eventually married, studied French literature and art history at the Sorbonne in Paris, and moved back to Illinois to run the Carus family businesses (Carus Chemical Company and Open Court Publishing). In 1962 Blouke and Open Court Publishing Company developed a breakthrough reading and language arts program for kindergarten through sixth-grade students (this phonics-based reading program eventually led to the *Basic Readers,* a K–6 reading and writing program launched several years later).

About the same time, Marianne and Blouke had children of their own. When their oldest child began to read, they became disappointed in the quality and content of available children's books. In the hopes of finding compelling and educational literature, Marianne tracked down classic children's stories in *St. Nicholas,* a 1930s magazine edited by acclaimed American author Mary Mapes Dodge. *St. Nicholas,* however, was out of print, and Marianne and Blouke decided to start a magazine of their own, following in *St. Nicholas's* literary tradition.

BUGS IN THE BIG CITY

In the early 1970s the Carus family business was enjoying success in the elementary school market through its Open Court Publishing Company. In 1971 Blouke Carus and a group of educators developed the *Basic Readers,* a new basal reading program based on classic literature from authors such as William Shakespeare, Aristotle, Robert Frost, and Langston Hughes, and from *Grimm's Fairy Tales.* Children learned how to read and think at the same time. It was this same concept the Caruses hoped to instill in their new magazine venture. With high hopes and a bit of naïveté, the couple jumped feet first into the sea of children's literature, when there were nearly 85 children's magazines in publication at the time.

Their first plea for acceptance and exposure came in the form of a launching party at the St. Moritz Hotel in New York City. They invited publishers, agents, editors, critics, authors, and illustrators. The evening hit a high point when author Isaac Bashevis Singer, who later won the Nobel Prize for literature, amused the audience with witty anecdotes about why he liked children. Singer commented on how children could "sin without making long and boring confessions," and how they did not "feel guilty for being healthy, beautiful and charming." The New York publishing world was soon aware of this new children's publication called *Cricket.* Its pilot issue, in 1973, featured Arnold Lobel's "Frog and Toad" story and Sid Fleischman's "McBroom the Rainmaker." Both stories went on to become timeless, award-winning classics, as did many other works published in *Cricket.*

By 1974 the company had grown to six employees and maintained its production and editing in La Salle. Carus hired Clifton Fadiman (a former *New Yorker* book reviewer) as senior editor and designer John Grandits. Manuscripts from many well-known authors, including Singer, continued to roll in. Although many critics predicted a short life for this chirping insect and recommended a stylized, colorful redesign of the original black anatomically correct bug appearing on its pages, *Cricket* had nearly 100,000 subscribers by 1976 while preserving its black bug. The original bug was drawn by author/illustrator Trina Schart Hyman (Cricket's newly hired art director), whose design was prompted by Marianne Carus's fondness of the storytelling cricket in Singer's *A Day of Pleasure.*

During the next decade, the company ventured overseas. In response to British readers who requested a magazine in England, *Cricket and Company* was launched in 1976. While 45,000 young British readers were happy, publication and advertising costs became too costly. Fourteen months later the British division ceased production. In 1988 Marianne and Blouke Carus crossed the ocean again, this time to Norway for the biannual International Board on Books for Young People Congress, where they met an editorial director of children's magazines at Bayard Press in France. Bayard published 14 children's magazines and from them the Caruses garnered ideas for a new magazine geared toward readers younger than *Cricket*'s targeted six-through 12-year-olds. After purchasing a few stories and art from Bayard, *Cricket* was ready to welcome a new friend.

INSECTS GALORE, 1990 TO 2000

From 1990 to 2000 Carus more than doubled its insect collection and readership. After a brief encounter with Bayard Press, Carus unveiled *Cricket*'s friend, *Ladybug,* a magazine intended for two- to seven-year-old readers in 1990. In addition to high-quality short stories, *Ladybug* featured colorful illustrations by award-winning artists and activities to promote reading. Within two years *Ladybug* had amassed 130,000 paid subscriptions while *Cricket* had a paid circulation of 110,000 readers. In 1992 both magazines charged $29.97 for an annual subscription.

For the next several years, Carus Publishing experienced many changes in its business. In 1994 the company launched *Spider,* for six- to nine-year-olds, and *Babybug,* board-book magazines for six-month- to two-year-olds. Two years later, in 1996, SRA/McGraw-Hill, a division of the McGraw-Hill Company, paid $31.2 million in cash for the assets of Open Court Publishing, Carus's textbook publishing division. Textbooks generated more than $20 million in sales for Open Court but the company could not compete with rivals in the educational publishing marketplace. André Carus, Blouke's son who had taken over as chief executive of the Carus Publishing empire, arranged a licensing deal with McGraw-Hill to publish academic and trade books under an Open Court imprint. The other operating division of Carus Publishing, "bug magazines" as Marianne Carus called them, enjoyed continued success, reaching 330,000 subscriptions in 1996.

While agreements were ironed out with McGraw-Hill in 1996, other Carus collaborations were in the works. Aiming to inspire children's knowledge and enthusiasm for science while continuing the guiding Carus mission to promote reading, Cricket Magazine Group struck a deal with the Smithsonian Institution to publish *Muse* in 1997 for nine- to 14-year-olds, *Click* in 1998 for three- to seven-year-olds, and *Ask* in 2002 for seven- to ten-year-olds. These publications featured nonfiction articles rich in the Smithsonian's research on topics such as travel, genetics, ancient world history, and architecture. The magazines also included something *Cricket* readers were not accustomed to: advertising. Cricket received a percentage of the ads sold by the Smithsonian; both companies shared the start-up costs. In 1996 Carus Publishing earned about $12 million in annual revenue.

For the remainder of the 1990s Carus Publishing continued to grow. In 1998, responding to requests from longtime and graduating readers of *Cricket,* Carus began *Cicada,* a magazine for readers 14 years and older. Also in 1998, Carus ventured into the book publication market, forming an alliance with Front Street Books, a

North Carolina-based independent publisher. The new book division, Cricket Books, targeted beginning and middle-grade readers. With plans to release six book titles by the end of 1999 and 12 per year thereafter, Carus Publishing was operating in the black and set to tackle the new challenges of a new millennium.

BEYOND THE BUG

By 2000 Carus Publishing had cornered the high-quality children's magazine market, with seven magazines and a book division. Plans for expansion were still underway, however. As the new century began, one of the first journeys Carus took was a venture into children's magazines focusing on the histories and cultures of the world and the United States. The ideal companion turned out to be Cobblestone Publishing, which had been producing history magazines for children since 1980. Cobblestone became a nonfiction magazine division of Carus and with it came seven publications: *Cobblestone, Faces, Dig, Odyssey, Calliope, Footsteps,* and *Appleseeds.* It was a natural union of two companies known for their passion to provoke thought and discourse through fun children's reading.

The same year, Marc Aronson, who had been senior editor for Holt Books for Young Readers, joined the editing staff at Cricket Books and started a line of books specifically for teenagers. The name of the new division, Marcato Books, was chosen to represent a musical term meaning "with a distinct accent," reflecting Aronson's interest in music and his vision for the line of books. Aronson stayed on as editor of the book division for four years.

As Carus Publishing and its literary insects were weaving a metaphorical worldwide web, the company also crept into the virtual world of the Internet. The company went online with cricketmag.com in 1997. Marketing Director Jeanne Kerl told *Forbes* in a Fall 2000 Supplement, "We see the Web site as a way for kids to find great Web links, listen to songs featured in our magazines, and even to work on crossword puzzles. Parents and teachers can find reading recommendations activities for the family." With this move, the company began to overcome its reliance on traditional modes of communication and advertising.

Prior to the web site, Carus had used only direct-mail subscription sales, placed ads in upscale publications such as the *New Yorker,* and put ads on local classical and public radio stations. The web site opened a world of opportunities to reach the company's targeted audience while keeping tabs on a tight advertising budget. Carus allocated only 5 percent of its advertising dollars to ads featured on web sites outside of cricketmag.com and found they spent less than traditional print advertising.

Thirty years after its inception, it was clear Marianne Carus's *Cricket* was invincible. Pleased with its ongoing success, in 2003 Carus edited *Celebrate Cricket,* an illustrated book reminiscing about the company's beginnings and including recollections by the publisher's impressive roster of writers and illustrators including William Saroyan, James Herriot, and Jane Yolen. Two years later, in 2005, in an effort to remain competitive in the multibillion-dollar children's publishing market, Carus Publishing moved its executives and employees away from small-town Illinois to Chicago where they hoped to attract more talented publishing professionals.

Despite its primary competitors having higher recorded revenues (*Highlights for Children* at $100 million and *Weekly Reader* reaching $21.8 million), Carus Publishing's $15.7 million in revenue in 2007 was a proud achievement, as the company maintained its focus of providing a superior product to discriminating readers. Marianne Carus, who was 70 years old and still editor-in-chief of *Cricket,* wrote in *Celebrate Cricket* that the company's guiding mission had always been "to create in children a love of reading by sustaining a lively, witty, and cheerful tone and a sense of humor."

Jodi Essey-Stapleton

PRINCIPAL DIVISIONS

Cobblestone Publishing; Cricket Books; Cricket Magazine Group.

PRINCIPAL COMPETITORS

American Girl, Inc.; Disney Publishing Worldwide; Highlights for Children, Inc.; National Geographic Society; Weekly Reader Corporation.

FURTHER READING

Borden, Jeff, "Cricket Publisher Makes Leap into Science-Education Venture," *Crain's Chicago Business,* December 9, 1996, p. 6.

Carus, Marianne, ed., *Celebrate Cricket,* Chicago: Cricket Books, 2003.

"Front Street and Cricket Announce Joint Venture," *Publishers Weekly,* March 2, 1998, p. 16.

Hechinger, Fred, "About Education; Magazines for Children Address Serious Topics," *New York Times,* June 11, 1985, p. C7.

Knutson, Carol, "Jumping (Virtual) Hurdles," *Forbes,* Fall 2000 Supplement, p. 83.

Milliot, Jim, "McGraw-Hill Cos. Buys Open Court Text Division," *Publishers Weekly,* March 25, 1996, p. 12.

O'Brien, Ken, "Roots of Carus Corp. Reach Back to Germany," *Chicago Tribune,* October 23, 1994, p. 3.

Smith, Wes, "Keeping the Right Chemistry Carus' Corporate Collection Ranges from Potassium Permanganate to Marty the Inchworm," *Chicago Tribune,* June 21, 1992, p. 1.

Trohan, Walter, "Johnny Can Read, If It's Readable," *Chicago Tribune,* December 1, 1971, p. 10.

Cash Systems, Inc.

7350 Dean Martin Drive, Suite 309
Las Vegas, Nevada 89139
U.S.A.
Telephone: (702) 987-7169
Toll Free: (877) 987-7171
Fax: (702) 987-7168
Web site: http://www.cashsystemsinc.com

Public Company
Incorporated: 1983 as Cameron Resources, Inc.
Employees: 289
Sales: $96.03 million (2006)
Stock Exchanges: NASDAQ
Ticker Symbol: CKNN
NAIC: 541512 Computer Systems Design Services

■ ■ ■

Cash Systems, Inc., is a leading provider of cash-access products and related services to the gaming industry. The company provides three primary services to casinos that enable their guests to obtain cash. Cash Systems facilitates credit and debit card advances, automated-teller-machine (ATM) withdrawals, and check-cashing services. The company operates in approximately 135 casinos and at 25 retail locations, deriving roughly 60 percent of its business from casinos operated by Native American tribes. Cash Systems maintains offices in Las Vegas, Nevada; Burnsville, Minnesota; and San Diego, California.

ORIGINS

Early in adulthood, Craig Potts set his sights on the gaming industry, adopting his father's career interest as his own. Potts' father owned a business that provided check-cashing services to casinos, a service Potts intended to offer, as well as others, through his own company. Before he could begin to court casinos as customers, however, Potts needed to establish himself as an entrepreneur, something he started to do when he was 24 years old. In 1997, he teamed up with Christopher Larson, also 24 years old, and began earning the financial clout to pave his entry into the casino business.

The two Cash Systems founders, both Minnesota residents, demonstrated impressive business skills from the start. They borrowed $25,000 and purchased five ATMs, installing the machines in service stations and supermarkets in the Minneapolis–St. Paul area. By doing so, the two young entrepreneurs drew a battle line, squaring off against two massive, Minneapolis-based financial holding companies, U.S. Bancorp and TCF Financial Corp., the main competitors in the area. "I thought I could provide customers with better service and higher commission than TCF and U.S. Bank," Potts explained in an August 31, 2003, interview with the *Star Tribune.*

FOUNDERS TURN TO CASINOS

Potts' customers, store operators, evidently agreed with his self-appraisal. By the end of 1999, Cash Systems had ATMs installed in approximately 125 locations. Annual revenues nearly reached $2 million. The company's net income climbed into the six-figure range. It was an encouraging, profitable start for the entrepreneurial neophytes, but in their minds the deployment of ATMs merely was a means to an end. Potts and Larson had something else in mind, a business plan that needed the profits from the ATM business to reach its execution stage. When Larson talked to the *Star Tribune* on August 31, 2003, he referred to the financial results recorded in 1999, saying, "that wasn't a lot of profit, but it was enough to leverage into the bank loans we needed to move into the casino market," before adding, "which is where we wanted to go all along."

Potts and Larson switched their focus. The change in strategy found them butting against new competitors, but Potts, for the second time, was undaunted by the presence of larger adversaries. "There were three big competitors in the casino market," he said in his interview with the *Star Tribune*, "and I thought their cash-advance systems were slow and inflexible, hard for guests to use." His riposte to the established market leaders could not be made without considerable investment, however. Potts saw deficiencies in technology and planned to beat his competition by developing superior technology. Cash Systems spent nearly $2 million developing more powerful, feature-filled software for use in casinos, focusing its efforts on a credit card system.

The investment into software development became the linchpin of Cash Systems' success. The proprietary software made the task of obtaining cash far easier for casino guests, who were able to gain authorization to access their accounts without having to know their personal identification number (PIN). For obvious reasons, casino operators wanted their guests to have access to cash as easily as possible, but the main reason Cash Systems' software proved to be a commercial success had little to do with it being user-friendly. The product offered by Potts and Larson became com-

mercially successful because it gave casino operators important data about their guests, including name, address, telephone number, and transaction history, on a real-time basis. Information critical to developing marketing programs that previously had only been available through weekly or monthly updates was available instantly. The superior technology was a magnet for customers, drawing casino operators to the Burnsville, Minnesota, company headed by Potts and Larson.

Cash Systems made the first sale of its new system in October 2000. Canterbury Park, a horse-racing track and casino in Shakopee, Minnesota, and the Jackpot Casino in Morton, Minnesota, became the company's first gaming customers. Additional contracts soon followed, fueling revenue growth from $1.9 million in 2000 to $7.9 million in 2001. Once Potts, who served as president and chief executive officer, and Larson, who served as chief financial officer, realized they had developed a successful business model they took the next logical step: turn to Wall Street for the capital to finance their company's rapid expansion.

PUBLIC COMPANY IN 2001

The route the founders took to convert their burgeoning business into a publicly traded company was chosen for its speed. It also gave Cash Systems the odd incorporation date of 1983, back when Potts and Larson were ten years old. Rather than wade through the process of completing an initial public offering (IPO) of stock, the founders opted to merge with a publicly traded corporate shell, a so-called blank-check company. They chose a Utah-based company incorporated in June 1983 named Cameron Resources, Inc., which changed its name to Unicom, Inc., in 1989 and to Unistone, Inc., in 1998. The company was formed to participate in the mineral, oil, and gas business, but it never found its footing, existing as a company with no assets and no employees when Cash Systems merged into it in October 2001, thereby becoming a publicly traded company. "This is a very exciting and significant milestone for Cash Systems as we take the important step of becoming a fully reporting publicly traded company," Potts said in a statement published in the October 12, 2001, issue of *Finance and Commerce Daily*. "Our primary objective will be to devote all our resources to rapidly expanding Cash Systems' share of the casino cash-access industry."

CASH-ADVANCE SERVICE FUELING GROWTH

Cash Systems flourished in its role as a cash-access provider. Potts earned recognition for determining the

1997: Craig Potts and Christopher Larson begin installing ATMs in Minnesota.
2000: After developing software, the founders enter the cash-access market, targeting casinos.
2001: Cash Systems merges with a publicly traded corporate shell, thereby becoming a publicly traded company.
2005: Michael D. Rumbolz is appointed president and chief executive officer.
2006: Cash Systems acquires Indian Gaming Services, gaining contracts with 11 casinos.

needs and desires of casino operators and developing products and services that fulfilled their expectations. As more customers flocked to Cash Systems, its revenues swelled, increasing to $15.3 million 2002 before more than doubling to $32.7 million in 2003, when the company had contracts with 120 casinos and racetracks in 21 states and four Caribbean countries.

Driving the company's sales growth was its credit/debit card cash-advance (CCCA) service, which accounted for 70 percent of its revenue in 2003. For a credit card cash-advance, gaming patrons typically paid a fee of 7 percent of the sum they obtained. For debit card withdrawals considered to be CCCA transactions, patrons paid a fixed fee of $1.95 plus 2 percent of the amount withdrawn. Cash Systems depended on ATM cash withdrawals for 20 percent of its revenue, a service that entailed installing ATMs and processing the ATM transactions. The company collected a fixed fee charged for each transaction. Check-cashing services generated 10 percent of Cash Systems' revenue. The company offered two types of service, either providing a software system that ensured the availability of a patron's funds or providing the service at a booth located in the casino, which was staffed by Cash Systems employees. For its check-cashing service, the company collected a variable fee depending on the amount of the check.

A FAILED ACQUISITION IN 2003

For a brief period, it looked as if Cash Systems was going to record a sizable increase in its financial totals. In mid-2003, the company announced it had agreed to acquire Chex Services Inc., a company that provided CCCA, ATM, and check-cashing services to several Native American–owned casinos. Cash Systems brokered the deal with Chex Services' parent company, Engle-

wood, Colorado-based Equitex, Inc. Cash Systems agreed to a $4 million, all-stock deal, which was expected to add $20 million to the company's annual revenue volume and $1.5 million in annual profits, but negotiations with Equitex soon turned hostile. Cash Systems terminated the agreement in December 2003, alleging Equitex had accepted a competing offer from another company. Equitex disagreed, claiming Cash Systems owed it $50,000 for terminating the agreement. Months of legal wrangling ensued, but the matter was eventually resolved through an out-of-court settlement in April 2004.

A NEW LEADER IN 2005

As Cash Systems matured into a market leader, the company underwent a change in management. For undisclosed reasons, Potts resigned from the company at the end of 2004. He was replaced on the first day of 2005 by Michael D. Rumbolz, who became Cash Systems' new chief executive officer. The year also marked the relocation of the company's main offices from Burnsville to Las Vegas.

Potts, the inexperienced yet confident young entrepreneur, was replaced by a seasoned veteran. Rumbolz, who served as chairman of the Nevada Gaming Control Board during the 1980s, earned his bachelor's degree from the University of Nevada–Las Vegas. He earned his law degree from the University of California's Gould School of Law. After completing his education, Rumbolz set up his own legal practice, practiced law for several years, and earned the esteem of the legal community. In 1983, Rumbolz was appointed chief deputy attorney general for Nevada. Next, he held various executive positions at Trump Hotels & Casino Resorts, served as director of corporate development for Circus Circus Enterprises Inc., and presided as president and chief executive officer of Anchor Gaming. After leaving Anchor Gaming in 2000, Rumbolz became vice-chairman of Casino Data Systems Inc.

In the capable hands of Rumbolz, Cash Systems continued to record robust growth. Rumbolz negotiated his first deal in November 2005, when Cash Systems agreed to acquire Indian Gaming Services from Borrego Springs Bank, a bank owned by the Viejas Band of Kumeyaay Indians. Indian Gaming Service provided CCCA, ATM, and check-cashing services to 11 casinos. The acquisition was completed in February 2006.

A decade after Potts and Larson acquired five ATMs to pave their entry into the casino market, Cash Systems stood as a national leader. From $48.4 million in 2004, sales increased to $63.1 million in 2005 before leaping to $96 million in 2006. The company entered 2007 with its systems installed at 135 gaming locations, each offering casino operators and their guests a wealth of cash-access options. Cash Systems marketed "all in 1" ATMs, which conducted ATM and CCCA transactions. "Cashclub," another service offered by the company, enabled patrons to receive funds for CCCA and check-cashing transactions directly from an ATM, eliminating the need for guests to visit the casino cage to obtain their cash. The company sold its "powercash" system, which enabled players to access funds from their enrolled credit cards without leaving a gaming device, such as a slot machine. Cash Systems offered "table-cash," a wireless, cash-on-demand system that supported a full range of payment methods.

As Cash Systems looked to the future, its success hinged on its ability to effectively wed new technology with customer service. To retain its market share, the company needed to devise new ways to give casino operators and their guests safe, reliable, and speedy access to account information and account funds. For the short-term at least, Rumbolz figured as the executive to lead the company forward. In 2007, he signed a two-year contract renewal with Cash Systems. "I'm excited by the progress we have made at the company and with our new product development," he noted in a March 7, 2007, company press release. "I look forward to continuing to work with our board and our strategic partners to create long-term shareholder value."

Jeffrey L. Covell

PRINCIPAL SUBSIDIARIES

Cash Systems of Canada, Inc.

PRINCIPAL COMPETITORS

Global Cash Access, Inc.; Global Payments, Inc.; Fidelity National Information Services, Inc.

FURTHER READING

Allen, Mike, "Bank Sells Gaming Arm," *San Diego Business Journal,* November 21, 2005, p. 28.

Brus, Brian, "Cash Systems Inks Contract with Creek Nation of Oklahoma," *Journal Record,* September 12, 2005.

"Cash Systems Agrees to Buy Chex Services," *Cardline,* July 25, 2003, p. 1.

"Cash Systems, Inc. Gets GLI Approval for Powercash," *Wireless News,* November 20, 2007.

"Cash Systems Launches Smart Processing Solutions," *CNW Group,* October 11, 2006.

"Cash Systems Secures New Contract," *Wireless News,* February 24, 2007.

"Cash Systems Secures New Contract," *Wireless News,* September 22, 2007.

"Chex Service, Cash Systems Settle Their Lawsuits," *Cardline,* April 23, 2004, p. 1.

Lindenmayer, Isabelle, "New Chief Executive for Cash Systems," *American Banker,* December 27, 2004, p. 6.

"Minneapolis-Based Cash Systems Completes Reorganization Agreement," *Finance and Commerce Daily Newspaper,* October 13, 2001.

Youngblood, Dick, "Cash Dealings," *Star Tribune,* August 31, 2003, p. 3D.

Central Florida
Investments, Inc.

5601 Windhover Drive
Orlando, Florida 32819-7914
U.S.A.
Telephone: (407) 351-3350
Fax: (407) 352-8935
Web site: http://www.westgateresorts.com

Private Company
Incorporated: 1970
Employees: 4,000
Sales: $297.6 million (2006 est.)
NAIC: 531390 Other Activities Related to Real Estate;
813990 Other Similar Organizations (Except Business, Professional, Labor, and Political Organizations)

■ ■ ■

Central Florida Investments, Inc. (CFI), is an Orlando, Florida-based private company owned by CEO David A. Siegel, one of the leaders of the "vacation ownership" industry. Still known to most people as timeshares, vacation ownership is shared ownership of a resort condominium that gives the participants a long-term right to use the property for a specified time each year. CFI operates mostly through subsidiary Westgate Resorts, the world's third largest timeshare company as well as the largest privately held company in the industry. All told, Westgate owns and manages about 30 resorts accounting for 10,000 timeshare units. In addition to its flagship property, Westgate Vacation Villas, located near Walt Disney World in Orlando, the company operates in such locales as Miami Beach and Daytona Beach, Florida; Myrtle Beach, South Carolina; Williamsburg, Virginia; Gatlinburg, Tennessee; Branson, Missouri; Robinsonville, Mississippi; Park City, Utah; Mesa, Arizona; Anaheim, California; and Las Vegas, Nevada. Resort ownership has also led CFI to become involved in related businesses, including hotels, travel services, insurance, restaurants, and magazines. In addition, CFI holds interests in oil, cattle, and Internet companies.

FOUNDER, DEPRESSION-ERA BORN

David Siegel, born in the mid-1930s, started CFI in 1970 in his garage as a real estate development firm. The son of a grocery store owner, Siegel grew up in Indianapolis, then moved to Miami. After high school he studied TV and radio repair and started a small business by bringing in equipment for his instructors to repair. He soon quit his studies to open a repair shop, putting his former teacher to work for him. "Over the next decade," according to a *Forbes* profile, "Siegel hopped around a lot. He tried his luck in Hollywood, returned to Florida to become a deputy sheriff, attended the University of Miami, joined the U.S. Air Force Reserve to avoid being drafted and started several businesses (three of which failed)." After a year of active duty in the Air Force, Siegel suffered a number of reversals in his career: a new TV repair business was closed after his manager was shot and killed in the store, and a furniture store fell victim to the riots that plagued inner cities in 1968.

COMPANY PERSPECTIVES

We provide affordable luxury vacations with first-class accommodations to our owners and guests.

FOUNDING OF CFI: 1970

Starting from scratch once again, Siegel tried his hand at telephone land sales, and was fired from one job because he deviated from the script. He reached a turning point in 1970 when he relocated to Orlando and divorced his first wife to marry his high school sweetheart, Bettie. He was at the right place at the right time. Orlando, founded in 1840 near a fort built during the Seminole Wars, had grown into a major citrus producing area by the early 1900s. It then enjoyed a major building boom in the 1920s, but that paled in comparison to what would take place a half-century later, spurred by the construction of Disney World. Media mogul Walt Disney had reinvented the amusement park in the 1950s with the opening of the 400-acre Disneyland in Anaheim, California, and in 1964 began quietly buying land in the Orlando area in order to build a theme park on a much grander scale. Although Disney would die in late 1966, his brother Roy a year later broke ground on the so-called Florida Project that took the name Walt Disney World in honor of the man who conceived the idea.

The opening of Walt Disney World in 1971 led to a major building boom, as hotels, motels, resorts, tourist attractions, and all manner of related businesses were constructed to take advantage of the popular Disney park, which would grow further with additional Disney sites. By setting up his real estate business in Orlando a year before Walt Disney World opened its gates, Siegel was well positioned to prosper. He also proved to be a shrewd player in the real estate field. Soon after starting his business he sold a 1.25-acre parcel of land to a woman for $5,000, convincing her that nearby land advertised for $500 an acre in a brochure she carried was cheap because it was swampland. He then wasted little time in snapping up all of this land, nearly 1,300 acres, for $640,000, despite not having enough money in the bank to cover his $25,000 deposit check. He visited area banks door-to-door until he was able to obtain a loan to keep the deposit check from bouncing, and then lined up a private investor to cover the balance.

ACQUISITION OF MYSTERY FUN HOUSE: 1976

Siegel grew rich off this cache of property and used some of the money to acquire hotels and apartments. He turned his attention to the growing tourism business in 1976 by buying Mystery Fun House, a second-tier attraction on Orlando's International Drive, a stretch that over the years would become home to a number of attractions and restaurants. Siegel became involved in the timeshare business in 1980 when one day, according to *Forbes,* "a man offered to pay him double the market value for 10 acres of the grove, explaining that he wanted to develop a timeshare business on it. Siegel demurred—and instead built his own timeshare villa." It opened in 1982 as Westgate Vacation Villas, so named because it was located close to Disney World's west gate. Selling timeshares out of a tent on the property he grew rich enough to retire at the age of 50. Yet retirement would prove to be little more than a theme for his 50th birthday party, as he continued to grow Westgate, which *Florida* magazine predicted in 1986 would one day emerge as the largest timeshare resort in the world.

Westgate was Siegel's flagship property, but it was just one of a number of assets owned by Siegel's Central Florida Investments holding company. By the early 1990s they included Mystery Fun House, the Everything by Water swimsuit store, the Hotel Royal Plaza in Lake Buena Vista, and a carpet manufacturer, Tapis Royale. Siegel was also interested in investing in a Major League Baseball franchise that he and a number of other businessmen tried to bring to Orlando during this time. However, timeshares were at the heart of CFI's and Siegel's interests.

Timeshares had developed a less than savory reputation, with many properties proving to be little more than motel conversions that failed to live up to the expectations of customers and offered virtually no resale value. Moreover, an odd dance also developed between timeshare salespeople and prospective buyers. In order to lure prospects, timeshare operators offered gifts, such as tickets to Disney World and the other Orlando attractions, if they would take a tour of a property and sit through a presentation. Many of them were "grazers," people who were determined not to buy and were simply enduring the sales pitch in order to receive the gift package at the end. Because the promotions were costly, the timeshare operators brought pressure to bear on prospects, pretending that they were being given a special deal and sometimes seeking to humiliate them into buying, to "crispy-fry" them in the parlance of timeshare sales agents. They would then "hammer" the check, quickly taking it to the bank for certification to prevent a stop payment lest buyer's remorse set in.

KEY DATES

1970: David Siegel founds company.
1976: Mystery Fun House opens in Orlando.
1982: Westgate Vacation Villas opens near Walt Disney World.
1996: Westgate Miami Beach opens.
1999: Westgate Smoky Mountain Resort opens.
2004: Grand Vista Resorts is acquired.
2005: Partnership with Planet Hollywood is formed to build Las Vegas tower.

The timeshare industry, especially in Florida, began to clean up its act in the 1990s and rebuilt its image, due in large part to the participation of Disney and Marriott International in the industry. With timeshares' rehabilitation CFI enjoyed strong growth as well. In 1995 the company looked to south Florida, opening Westgate Miami Beach. A year later Westgate Daytona Beach was added, as was the massive Westgate Lakes Resorts & Spa, which in short order became the world's second largest timeshare resort. Another area resort opened in 1997, Westgate Towers, built in the shadow of Walt Disney World Resort. By this point CFI was doing more than $300 million in annual sales, making it one of central Florida's largest private companies.

CONTROVERSIAL 1997 DIVORCE SIDETRACKS CFI

Yet with wealth and success came controversy for Siegel. In 1997 he began divorce proceedings, after moving out of his home in July 1996, eventually marrying for a third time to a former Mrs. Florida. However, his wife of 26 years, Bettie, was half-owner of CFI and the settlement over the property proved contentious and crippled CFI because she refused to authorize loans that were needed to keep the business growing unless she received a $200 million settlement. The divorce disrupted CFI operations in other ways as well. Chief Financial Officer R. Alan Rainey was fired shortly after giving testimony in a deposition that was unhelpful to Siegel. Rainey then sued Siegel and CFI for a year's salary plus legal costs, contending that Siegel asked that he withhold CFI financial records from his wife and make false statements to her attorneys about the financial state of CFI. Rainey had been appointed by Siegel to serve on a three-person strategy team for the divorce settlement, along with CEO Ronald A. Leventhal, the brother of Siegel's first wife, and corporate counsel Michael E. Marder. Rainey urged Siegel to accept the $200 million

settlement, the largest of its kind in Florida history, and in late 1997 Siegel finally agreed.

The matter did not end there, however. A year later, in October 1998, Siegel attempted to have the settlement overturned, claiming that he had been tricked by Rainey and Leventhal, whom he said inflated CFI's profits in fiscal 1997 by nearly $70 million, this distortion resulting in a higher than necessary settlement figure. By this time Leventhal had left CFI to start his own timeshare company, Tempus Resorts International Ltd., taking with him about two dozen Westgate managers as well as hiring Rainey. Earlier in 1998 Siegel had filed a $2.89 million civil lawsuit against Levanthal, his wife, who at one time managed Mystery Fun House, and Levanthal's son, Roger Farwell, a former CFI vice-president of sales and marketing. Siegel accused them of soliciting timeshare locations for themselves, starting in the summer of 1997, while still in the employ of CFI, and also meeting with potential lenders and investors to set up Tempus, which was already incorporated by the time Leventhal resigned in November 1997. The suit also alleged the trio forged checks and documents. In the end, Siegel was unsuccessful in his attempts (a second effort failed in 2001) to change his divorce settlement, although he ultimately reached a settlement with Leventhal. His fight with Rainey, on the other hand, continued through the fall of 2007.

The late 1990s brought other legal entanglements for Siegel and CFI. In 1999 timeshare consultant and former CFI executive Jose Franco sued Siegel for $3.1 million, contending that Siegel acquired the assets from a pair of marketing companies he owned but neglected to pay for them and then fired him. Also during this time CFI was one of a number of timeshare companies, including Tempus, which were being investigated for discriminating against foreign nationals that they believed were less likely to purchase timeshares because of the economic conditions of their native countries. Off-premises contacts, known in the business as OPCs, were paid a commission to cajole people into attending a timeshare sales presentation. Yet because the lure of free theme-park tickets was expensive, on top of the OPC commission that was paid whether a sale ever resulted or not, timeshare companies instructed OPCs to screen out people who were perceived to be doubtful buyers.

Despite these legal distractions, CFI continued to grow through the rest of the 1990s and into the new century. In 1997 the company became involved in magazines, publishing the first issue of *I Love Orlando*. The following year, in order to keep driving sales, Westgate Resorts opened a new state-of-the-art 210,000-square-foot call center in Ocoee, Florida. CFI expanded beyond Florida in 1999 when it opened Westgate Smoky Mountain Resort at the entrance to the Great Smoky Mountains National Park in Gatlinburg, Tennessee. At the same time, CFI did not neglect its core Orlando operation. In 1999 it opened Westgate Town Center, part of a major new expansion of Westgate Vacation Villas that would add 3,000 new units.

NEW CENTURY, NEW PROPERTIES

CFI also began to look westward. In 2000 the company began construction on Westgate Park City Resorts & Spa in Park City, Utah, which opened two years later. In 2001 Westgate Flamingo Bay was opened in Las Vegas, and CFI grew through acquisition as well that year, acquiring the 1,600-acre River Ranch resort near Lake Wales, Florida, which a year later reopened as Westgate River Ranch. Other acquisitions followed in 2002: Miami's Coral Sands, renamed Westgate South Beach, and Haines City, Florida's Grenelefe Golf & Tennis Resort, located near Westgate River Ranch. In 2003, CFI purchased the Ramada Plaza Hotel & Inn gateway in the Orlando area along with Leisure Resorts Orlando. In the meantime, several internally developed properties opened, including Westgate Blue Tree Resort in Lake Buena Vista, Florida, in 2002; and Westgate Palace in Orlando and Westgate Historic Williamsburg in Williamsburg, Virginia, both in 2003. The early 2000s also saw the closing of Mystery Fun House after a quarter-century under CFI ownership. The attraction simply could not compete against the large theme parks that were doing a better job of keeping tourists on their property and a host of new, more exciting attractions that populated International Drive.

Additional acquisitions were completed in 2004. The Holiday Inn Hotel in Myrtle Beach, South Carolina, was brought into the fold in 2004. Grand Vista Resorts was also acquired, adding properties in Branson and Springfield, Missouri; Tunica, Mississippi; and Mesa, Arizona. CFI expanded its print offerings in 2005, publishing the first issues of *I Love Vacations* and *I Love Las Vegas*. In 2007, Westgate Smoky Mountain added a major new attraction, a 60,000-square-foot indoor waterpark, Wild Bear Falls. Also in 2007, CFI broke ground on Westgate Garden Walks at Anaheim in Anaheim, California, and Westgate Myrtle Beach. Also

in the works was a major project with Planet Hollywood to build a new Las Vegas resort and casino, Planet Hollywood Towers by Westgate Resorts, a 2,853-unit tower. The partnership was announced in 2005 but the project was delayed as the price tag tripled the original estimate. Nevertheless, it was scheduled to open in 2009. It was a project that Siegel believed would be a major turning point in CFI's history. "Once the Westgate name is on top of the 50-story icon property," he told *Forbes*, "we will be a brand, and it will give us more credibility."

Ed Dinger

PRINCIPAL SUBSIDIARIES

Westgate Resorts; Westgate Restaurant Group.

PRINCIPAL COMPETITORS

Interval International, Inc.; Marriott Vacation Club International; Sunterra Corporation.

FURTHER READING

Finkelstein, Alex, "A Business Divided: Siegels Split Properties," *Orlando Business Journal*, October 31, 1997, p. 4.

———, "Caught in the Cross Fire," *Orlando Business Journal*, October 3, 1997, p. 4.

———, "Developer Sues Former Salesman over 'Extortion,'" *Orlando Business Journal*, July 17, 1992, p. 1.

———, "Round Two: Local Time Share Titans Heading Back to Court," *Orlando Business Journal*, October 30, 1998, p. 8.

———, "Siegel, Friends and Family Back to Orange Circuit Court," *Orlando Business Journal*, February 26, 1999, p. 13.

———, "Siegel Spat: All in the Family," *Orlando Business Journal*, March 13, 1998, p. 3.

Guzman, Rafer, "Time Share Sues to Block Investigation," *Wall Street Journal*, September 29, 1999, p. F1.

———, "Time Shares Shun Tourists Based on Their Nationality," *Wall Street Journal*, July 21, 1999, p. F1.

Hetzer, Barbara, and Edward C. Baig, "Timeshares: Their Time Has Come," *Business Week*, April 14, 1997, p. 108.

Kroll, Luisa, "Pet Projects," *Forbes*, October 15, 2007, p. 96.

Rowe, Megan, "The High-Volume Vacation Biz," *Lodging Hospitality*, August 1998, p. 64.

Channel Four Television Corporation

124 Horseferry Road
London, SW1P 2TX
United Kingdom
Telephone: (+44 020) 7396 4444
Fax: (+44 020) 7306 8697
Web site: http://www.channel4.com

State-Owned Company
Incorporated: 1981
Employees: 917
Sales: £936.9 million ($1.89 billion) (2006)
NAIC: 515120 Television Broadcasting

∎ ∎ ∎

Channel Four Television Corporation (also referred to as Channel 4) is one of the United Kingdom's fastest-growing broadcasting corporations. The company is owned by the British government. Unlike its BBC counterparts, however, Channel Four operates on a commercial, for-profit basis. As such, the company receives no funding from the British government. Channel Four was the United Kingdom's first "publisher/broadcaster." Rather than produce its own programs, the company purchases programming from independent studios in the United Kingdom and worldwide. Once primarily known as a "minority" programmer, Channel Four has adopted a more popular programming style in the 2000s. Among the company's biggest successes has been its broadcasts of the highly popular *Big Brother* series. The company also operates a film production wing, FilmFour, known for such films as *Four Weddings*

and a *Funeral* and *The Crying Game,* among others. Although the Channel 4 station remains the company's core operation, the company has embraced the free-to-air digital television market. The company's digital stations include E4, More4, and Film4. In 2007, the company announced plans to launch a music channel in partnership with EMAP. The company also operates the 4oD video-on-demand services and the FourDocs broadband service, both through its web site. Channel Four has also been preparing an entry into radio broadcasting, through the 4 Digital Group consortium, in partnership with EMAP and others. That group expects to launch ten digital radio stations in 2008. Channel Four is led by Chairman Luke Johnson and Managing Director Andy Duncan. The company posted revenues of £936.9 million ($1.9 billion) in 2006.

THE UNITED KINGDOM'S FOURTH STATION IN 1981

The United Kingdom had just three television stations at the beginning of the 1980s. These included the two state-owned and funded BBC (British Broadcasting Corporation) channels, and a single ITV (Independent Television) channel. All three stations had been launched by the middle of the 1950s. At the same time, plans were made to launch a second independent station. In the 1960s, the country's network of television transmitters added the frequency allotment for the projected channel. By the 1970s the first television sets appeared with settings for the fourth channel, then referred to as ITV/IBA 2. Yet the station itself failed to materialize, in part because of the reigning conflict

Channel Four Television Corporation

COMPANY PERSPECTIVES

The Channel's primary purpose is the fulfilment of its public service remit, which was most recently defined in the 2003 Communications Act. This states that "the public service remit for Channel 4 is the provision of a broad range of high quality and diverse programming which, in particular: (a) demonstrates innovation, experiment and creativity in the form and content of programmes; (b) appeals to the tastes and interests of a culturally diverse society; (c) makes a significant contribution to meeting the need for the licensed public service channels to include programmes of an educational nature and other programmes of educative value; and (d) exhibits a distinctive character."

As a publisher-broadcaster, Channel 4 does not produce its own programmes but commissions them from more than 300 independent production companies across the U.K., a far greater number than any other broadcaster, including the whole of the BBC. It works very closely with the independent production sector, and invests heavily in training and talent development throughout the industry.

between the government's desire to limit commercial television broadcasts in the country.

The passage of the Broadcasting Act of 1981 set in motion the development of the future Channel 4. The new legislation created something of a hybrid between the public service model of the BBC stations and the commercially oriented model of ITV. The new channel was to remain a state-owned corporation with a clear public-service commitment. Specifically, the company was established to "appeal to tastes and interests not generally catered to (by other channels), encourage innovation and experiment and be distinctive." In this way, the channel was expected to appeal to "minority" interests, as opposed to the more mainstream offerings of the ITV station. Yet Channel Four Television Company was placed under the Independent Broadcast Authority (IBA), and not the BBC. In this way, Channel 4 was expected to generate its own funding through sales of advertisements.

Channel 4 did not, however, have control of its own advertising sales. Instead, that role was given to ITV, which provided the new broadcaster with its

advertising. Channel Four was then provided funding through those revenues. This system enabled the group to carry out its mandate to provide alternative programming, as it was relieved of commercial pressures to develop more popular programming. On the other hand, the system meant that the company did not necessarily receive all of the revenues due to it.

Another important characteristic of the new television entity was its classification as a "publisher-broadcaster." This reflected the requirement that the company source all of its programming from third parties. In this way, Channel 4 singlehandedly stimulated the growth of the independent production industry in the United Kingdom.

Channel 4's official launch came on November 4, 1982. The company's first program, the game show *Countdown,* also became its longest-running, and remained in production into the 2000s. Because the channel's frequency allotment had been in place for nearly two decades, Channel 4 immediately became available on a national scale. In this way the channel provided coverage across nearly all of the United Kingdom. The exception to this was in Wales, which saw the creation of its own fourth channel.

TOWARD THE MAINSTREAM FROM 1993

Under Managing Director Jeremy Isaacs, the company developed a strong reputation as an alternative broadcaster. As Isaacs explained to *Campaign:* "We were encouraged by an Act of Parliament to pursue innovation and experiment and we just gave the nod to things that wouldn't have previously got on British television." Many of the channel's broadcasts inspired controversy. These included the Red Triangle art-house film series, labeled as "pornographic" by some reviewers. Channel 4 also inspired the ire of self-proclaimed public decency advocate Mary Whitehouse.

Yet Channel 4 was also noted for the high quality of much of its programming during the Isaacs era. This included the launch of the popular *Brookside* soap opera series. Also under Isaacs, Channel 4 launched the Films on Four broadcasts of independent films. These included the highly praised *Angel* by Neil Jordan.

The next phase in Channel 4's development came under Isaacs' successor, Michael Grade, who took over as managing director in 1988. Grade was charged with increasing Channel 4's commercial focus in order to allow the company to become more fully self-sufficient. As a result, the company began to develop a more mainstream approach to its broadcasts. Part of this process included acquiring the rights to popular U.S.

KEY DATES

1982: Channel Four Television Company becomes the United Kingdom's fourth television broadcaster.
1993: Channel Four Corporation is created as an independent state-owned broadcaster.
1998: First digital channel, Film4, is launched.
2000: Company creates 4Ventures and launches second digital channel, E4.
2004: Under new Managing Director Andy Duncan, Channel Four converts digital channels to free-to-air model, and enters radio broadcasting.
2007: Company begins development of music channel in partnership with EMAP.

shows. In this way, Channel 4 premiered such series as *Friends* and *ER* for the British market.

The company's reliance on ITV for its advertising sales and its funding presented a major restriction for Channel 4's growth. The radical reorganization of the British television sector, launched with the Broadcasting Act of 1990, began a new era of self-sufficiency for the company. The new legislation dismantled the IBA, which was replaced by the Independent Television Commission (ITC, later itself replaced by Ofcom), opening the way for a whole new range of broadcasters to enter the U.K. market. At the same time, Channel 4 became a fully independent entity, changing its name to Channel Four Corporation.

Channel 4 became responsible for its own advertising sales. The move toward full independence began in 1992. As Andy Barnes, the company's first sales director, explained to *Campaign:* "When I arrived at Channel 4 there was no sales department, no desks, no lights. We had a year to prepare for selling our own airtime. Channel 4 felt, quite rightly, that it was being undersold and could make more money in the open marketplace. ITV only sold it to a level of 14 percent of its own channel. The worst percentage we've since got was an 18.5 percent share in 1993. It is currently 20.4 percent and this in an environment with many more competitors."

Channel 4's sales force came into service in January 1993. The effort was a quick success, and by 1996 the company booked record profits of £134 million. Yet the company remained hampered by a commitment to return a proportion of its profits to ITV; in that year,

the payment topped £87 million. These payments were finally phased out in 1998.

NO LONGER A "MINORITY CHANNEL" FROM 1998

The arrival of Michael Jackson as head of Channel 4 heralded a new era for the broadcaster. Jackson turned the company more firmly toward the mainstream market, declaring that Channel 4 was no longer a "minority channel." The company also faced into the rising competition presented by the growing numbers of satellite and digital broadcasters. As part of this effort, the company launched its own digital stations. The first of these, Film4, took over from the popular Films on Four series, and began broadcasting on a pay-per-view basis in 1998. The company's next digital station, E4, launched in 2001. The new station was also made available on a subscriber basis. Both stations were placed under a new subsidiary, 4 Ventures Limited, created in 2000.

Yet these efforts came at a cost to the company, which slumped into losses at the beginning of the new decade. By the end of the 2001 year, the company's losses topped £28 million. Jackson left the company that year, replaced by Mark Thompson, formerly an executive with the BBC. Thompson launched a widespread cost-cutting effort, including the shedding of 200 jobs. Also under the ax was Channel 4's film production division. That division had been unable to extend its string of successful hit films, including *Four Weddings and a Funeral* and *The Crying Game,* into the new century.

Thompson soon succeeded in returning Channel 4 to profitability. Under his direction, the channel also successfully fought off the challenge for market share from its younger rival, Channel 5. A reshuffling of the channel's programming proved a key point in the channel's new success, including acquiring the rights to such hit American series as *Sex and the City* and *The Simpsons.* Yet one of the most important factors behind the company's resurgence was its broadcasts of the hugely successful *Big Brother* reality television program. *Big Brother* became a major franchise for the company, with new seasons continuing to appear through the first decade of the 2000s, as well as a number of spinoff series, including *Celebrity Big Brother.* The success with reality television led Channel 4 to launch other reality-based series, including *Wife Swap.*

By the middle of the first decade of the 2000s, Channel 4 had shed its longtime image as the smallest of the public broadcasters. The company faced criticism, however, for its reliance on such "populist" programming, with some observers opining that the company no longer served its purpose by offering a true difference in its broadcasts. Part of the answer to this came with the passage of the Communications Act of 2003. Under this new legislation, the company was granted more freedom in its programming choices.

CONVERTING TO THE DIGITAL ERA

Mark Thompson left Channel 4 in 2004 to take up the top job at the BBC, having restored the company to profitability and boosting revenues past £700 million. Controversy surrounded his replacement, Andy Duncan, whose previous career as a head marketer for Unilever earned him the nickname the "margarine man." Yet, as *Marketing* reported: "Duncan's two years in charge of Channel 4 have seen more launches and initiatives than any of the preceding 21 since its launch."

Among the major moves made by Duncan was the transformation of its digital channels into the advertising-supported free-to-air format. The company also rolled out a new channel, More4, as well as the FourDocs broadband-based simulcast service, and web-based video-on-demand services. In 2007, the company then teamed up with the EMAP media group to begin preparing the launch of its own music channel.

Duncan also led Channel 4 into radio broadcasting. In 2005, the company acquired majority control of Oneword, a talk-based digital radio station. The company also led the formation of the 4 Digital Group, a consortium including EMAP and UTV, among others, which successfully bid for one of two national digital radio licenses. The consortium began preparations to launch ten digital radio stations, including Channel 4 Radio and E4 Radio, among others. By 2006, the consortium had already made available the podcast-based 4radio service. Full rollout of the digital radio operations was expected for 2008.

Nonetheless, Channel 4's future remained clouded by the coming switchover to digital broadcasting. Channel 4's analog-based transmissions had long played a key role in its ability to compete against the onslaught of rival broadcasters. The company appealed to Ofcom to provide the company with funding similar to that given

to the BBC. As Chairman Luke Johnson threatened in the company's 2006 annual report: "In coming years we shall be forced to steadily reduce our output of public service broadcasting, and focus more and more of our schedule on strictly commercial shows, unless we receive help in kind." Channel 4's status as a state-owned, commercially driven broadcaster nonetheless made it unique in the British television landscape.

M. L. Cohen

PRINCIPAL SUBSIDIARIES

4 Ventures Ltd.; Channel Four International Ltd.; Film-Four Ltd.; Oneword Radio Ltd.

PRINCIPAL COMPETITORS

British Sky Broadcasting Group PLC; British Broadcasting Corp.; Reuters Group P.L.C.; Virgin Media Ltd.; ITV PLC; Channel Four Television Corp.; United Business Media PLC; London Weekend Television Ltd.; ITV Meridian Ltd.; Channel 5 Broadcasting Ltd.

FURTHER READING

Beale, Claire, "Michael Jackson Channel 4's Champion," *Campaign,* May 1, 1998, p. 30.

Carter, Ben, and John Cheves, "Expanding the Family," *New Media Age,* June 12, 2003, p. 20.

"Channel 4 Cashes In on Youth Market with £70m Profit," *Sunday Business,* May 15, 2005.

Darby, Ian, "Is Channel 4 Showing Its Age?" *Campaign,* November 8, 2002, p. 22.

Hargrave, Sean, "Strategic Play—Channel 5: Upwardly Mobile," *New Media Age,* March 17, 2005, p. 20.

Hodgson, Jessica, "UK's Channel 4 Television Goes Back to Its Roots," *Sunday Business,* January 11, 2005.

"Lifeline—Channel 4," *Campaign,* November 12, 2004, p. 11.

Mistry, Tina, "Channel 4's Quiet Man Faces a Battle for Change," *Campaign,* May 27, 1994, p. 16.

"Taking C4 into the Future—Andy Duncan, Chief Executive, Channel 4," *Marketing,* July 26, 2006, p. 20.

Wilkinson, Amanda, "Down to Business at C4," *Marketing Week,* July 8, 2004, p. 26.

Chello Zone Ltd.

105–109 Salisbury Road
London, NW6 6RG
United Kingdom
Telephone: (+44 20) 7328-8808
Fax: (+44 20) 7624-3652
Web site: http://www.zonevision.co.uk

Private Company
Incorporated: 1991 as Zonevision Ltd.
Sales: $70 million (2007 est.)
NAIC: 512191 Teleproduction and Other Postproduction Services

■ ■ ■

Chello Zone Ltd. is a major developer of television programming. The company develops, produces, broadcasts, and distributes a bouquet of themed television channels. The U.K.-based company's programming operations focus on developing highly specialized and niche formats that, as the company puts it, "respond to gaps in the media market." Among the company's offerings are flagship Zone Reality (formerly known as Reality TV), which features unscripted and reality-based programming; Zone Romantica, which features telenovelas, soap operas, and other drama and variety programming designed to appeal to a largely female audience; JimJam, a children's oriented channel; and Zone Europe, specializing in European-made commercial films. Other Zone channels include the Extreme Sports Channel, Zone Horror, Zone Thriller, and Club Zone.

Zone has long been one of the most international of television programmers, having been founded to provide U.K.-made television programs for the Eastern European market. In 2007, the company's programming reached more than 126 countries, and was available in 24 languages. The company operates its own network of production studios providing voice-over, dubbing, subtitling, and other localization services for its own and other television programming. The company operates studios in the United Kingdom, Poland, Romania, Russia, Hungary, Croatia, Bulgaria, Slovenia, and Serbia. These studios support channel representation, the group's other major area of operation for Chello Zone. The company acts as a representative for more than 28 channels, including MTV and VH1, Discovery, Animal Planet, Cartoon Network, and Turner Broadcasting's TCM, negotiating carriage deals, and providing localization, marketing, administration, and other management support services. This division is especially active in the Eastern European and Middle East regions. Founded as Zone Vision in 1991, Chello Zone has been 90 percent owned by Chellomedia, the content division of Liberty Global, since 2005. The company changed its name to Chello Zone in 2007. Founder Chris Wronski remains the company's chairman, while Dermot Short serves as company CEO.

SELLING MUSIC PROGRAMMING TO EASTERN EUROPE IN 1991

Polish-born Chris Wronski immigrated to the United Kingdom at the beginning of the 1980s. Then 20 years old, Wronski received training from the Overseas Film

COMPANY PERSPECTIVES
Chello Zone is a leading international broadcaster and distributor of thematic television channels, reaching more than 300 million homes worldwide. With hard-hitting documentaries, real life drama, lifestyle television and cutting edge movies, its channels offer something for everyone.

School in London's Barbican district. Wronski's interest in music led him into managing bands and operating a small music studio by the end of the 1980s. At the same time, Wronski had also been involved in organizing concerts and music festivals.

The beginning of the 1990s provided a fertile period for Wronski's future business interest. The collapse of Communism and the end of the Soviet domination of Eastern Europe introduced a surge of interest in Western music, films, and television broadcasts. At the same time, the arrival of new satellite broadcasting technologies promised not only wider distribution possibilities, but heightened demand for the programming to fill their channels.

Wronski spotted an opportunity to use his contacts in the British music industry to sell music television programming to Polish broadcasters. In 1991, he founded Zone Vision for that purpose; the company quickly became an important intermediary for music and sports events programming in Poland, and soon throughout Eastern Europe.

In 1992, Wronski was joined in the business by Chris Sharp, who became one of the company's shareholders and later served as both chief programming officer and general manager. Sharp brought his own programming sales experience to the company, starting with a stint at The Music Channel in 1986, followed by Super Channel, and finally at the Music Box channel in 1989. At the Music Box, Sharp took over direction of the channel's international programming distribution operations.

Zone Vision's success helped position the company as one of a very small number of intermediaries covering the Central and Eastern European broadcasting market. The company's operations took a new direction early on when MTV approached it to act as its representative in these markets.

MEDIA INTERMEDIARY IN THE MID-NINETIES

The deal with MTV came at an important moment for the company, which then consisted of Wronski, Sharp, and one other partner. The company incorporated, as Zone Vision Limited, in 1994. In that year, the company's annual revenues topped $500,000. Yet the market for music festival broadcasts had already peaked. Wronski recognized that the company's focus had to shift to providing broader television content.

Zone Vision proved highly successful in expanding the MTV brand across the Eastern European markets. The company also developed experience in localizing the popular channel's programming. Before long the company had built a network of recording and production studios, where it offered services including dubbing, voice-overs, and subtitling, as well as developing localized content.

The company's success with MTV attracted the attention of other broadcasters eager to expand their own operations into the Eastern markets. The company quickly signed up a number of major channels, including VH1, Discovery, Animal Planet, Eurosport, Hallmark, and the British Broadcasting Corporation. Channel representation remained an important part of the company's operations, and by the midpoint of the first decade of the 2000s Zone provided representation to more than 30 top channels.

ADDING A PROGRAMMING WING

Through the 1990s and into the next decade, Zone supported its growing operations through the creation of a network of branch offices. These appeared in most of the region's capital cities, including Warsaw, Budapest, Prague, and Sofia. The company also became active in the former Soviet Union as well, adding offices in Moscow and Kiev. By 1999, the company operated nine offices throughout the Central European zone.

By then, the company had begun developing its own programming operations. Zone Vision's entry into this side of the television broadcasting market appeared a natural extension of its business, particularly its robust localization and production studio operations. At the same time, the steady expansion of satellite technologies provided space for an ever increasing number of channels.

Zone Vision recognized the possibility of creating its own range of channels. For this, the company targeted niche and specialty markets that remained underdeveloped, and which also allowed the company to avoid direct competition with the programming of its

KEY DATES

1991: Chris Wronski, a native of Poland, founds Zone Vision in London to begin selling music programming to the Eastern European television broadcast market.

1994: Company incorporates as Zone Vision Limited, and launches channel representation operations with deal to introduce MTV into Eastern European market.

1998: Company begins television programming operations, creating its first channel, Romantica.

1999: Reality TV, Le Cinema (later Europa Europa) and Private Blue channels are launched.

2001: Advent International invests $12 million into company.

2003: Company enters U.S. market with deal to broadcast Reality TV on DISH Network.

2005: Liberty Global acquires 90 percent stake in Zone Vision.

2007: Company changes name to Chello Zone Limited.

channel representation customers. In particular, the company spotted the potential for introducing the telenovela, a type of television soap opera highly popular in Latin American markets, to an Eastern European audience.

The company began buying the rights to popular telenovelas, and began producing localized versions for broadcast on its first channel, Romantica, launched in Poland in 1998. The strong success of the channel led the company to prepare a wider rollout throughout the region. By 1999, the company had prepared the launch of Russian and Romanian versions of Romantica as well. Rather than rely solely on the telenovela format, however, the company began broadening Romantica's range of programming to include variety and other programming to appeal to a largely female audience.

Romantica attracted attention beyond the Eastern European market, and by March 1999 the company had signed a deal with Israel's DBS to launch versions of Romantica in Hebrew, Arabic, and Russian there. The company also had developed a number of other successful channels by then. These included the adult-oriented Private Blue and Le Cinema, later known as Europa Europa, which was dedicated to broadcasting European-produced films.

Zone Vision continued to work with other broadcasters as well. In 1999, the company formed a partnership with E! Entertainment Television Networks to launch a localized version of the E! channel for Polish, Russian, and Romanian markets. Yet the company's own production efforts remained central to its growth strategy.

REALITY FLAGSHIP IN 1999

The success of a new generation of so-called reality programs gave the company a new idea at the end of the 1990s. In 1999, Zone Vision launched a channel dedicated to this type of programming, called Reality TV. Formed as a joint venture with United Pan-Europe Communications, the new channel became the company's most successful, and served as a flagship for its entry into a number of new markets into the 2000s. Reality TV especially enabled the company to expand beyond its core Eastern European markets, and by 2000 the company had placed the channel, along with Private Blue, in the United Kingdom. By 2001, the company had also launched its first operations, starting with Reality TV in the South American broadcast market as well.

In order to fuel its further development plans, which included the launch of a new channel concept called Speed TV, Zone Vision began seeking new investment capital. In May 2001, the company sold shares to investment group Advent International in exchange for $12 million, a deal that valued the company at $100 million.

CRACKING THE UNITED STATES IN 2003

As part of the Advent investment, Wronski moved into the chairman's position, while the company's day-to-day operations were placed under new CEO Dermot Short. Short had helped found Discovery Networks Europe in the 1990s, helping to expand its operations to a total viewership potential of more than 92 million viewers. Soon after his arrival at Zone Vision, Short led the company on an ambitious growth strategy.

A centerpiece of the company's new strategy was the company's decision to enter the U.S. market, starting from 2003. Once again, Reality TV played the role of company flagship, and by September 2003 the company announced it had reached a deal with Echostar's DISH Network to begin broadcasting a localized version of the channel to the U.S. market.

The successful entry into the United States encouraged the company to seek new frontiers for its programming. Zone Vision targeted entry into Asia, specifically the Japanese, Chinese, and Indian markets. The company quickly reached a deal to launch Reality TV in India as part of the Zee-Turner offering. The company also launched negotiations to acquire blocks of programming in China as well.

NEW OWNERS AND NEW NAME FOR THE NEW CENTURY

By 2005, Zone Vision had expanded its total viewership from just seven million to more than 150 million subscribers around the world. The company prepared to move to the next level. For this, the company sought a major partner, and in 2005 agreed to sell nearly 90 percent of its shares to global cable television giant Liberty Global Inc. Wronski nonetheless remained onboard as chairman of the company, which was placed under Liberty Global's own programming arm, Chellomedia.

The acquisition by Liberty Global enabled the company to transform itself once again; by 2007 the company's total subscriber base topped 350 million worldwide, with broadcasts in more than 125 countries, and in 24 different languages.

The company launched a rebranding exercise, which included changing its own name, at first to Zone Media, and finally, in October 2007, to Chello Zone Ltd. At the same time, the company rebranded its growing list of channels, most adopting the Zone brand.

Chello Zone had continued to roll out new channels in the meantime. In 2006, for example, the company launched a children's television format, Jim-Jam, featuring such series and characters as *Bob the Builder, Barney and Friends, Pingu, Fireman Sam,* and others. The company also created Zone Horror, which began broadcasting in the Netherlands and the United Kingdom; Zone Thriller in the United Kingdom, and Zone Fantasy, which launched on the Sky Italia platform in 2006. Chello Zone had successfully transformed itself from its focus on the Eastern European market into one of the world's most dynamic television programmers.

M. L. Cohen

PRINCIPAL COMPETITORS

British Broadcasting Corporation; Pinewood Shepperton plc; HIT Entertainment Limited; VTR plc; Central European Media Enterprises Ltd.; SMG Productions Limited; Aardman Animations Ltd.; Ginger Television Productions Limited.

FURTHER READING

"Asia's Television Industry Is Talking About ... Rebranding Strategy for Zone Vision," *Television Asia,* July–August 2006, p. 6.

Carugati, Anna, "Zone Vision's Chris Wronski," *Worldscreen,* April 2005.

Clarke, Steve, "Dutch Land Horror," *Daily Variety,* October 31, 2006, p. 6.

———, "UK Channel Outfit Looks to New Ideas and Asia to Stay in the Zone," *TV International,* November 21, 2003, p. 10.

Forrester, Chris, "Europe's Zone Vision Eyes More Countries," *Multichannel News,* May 8, 2000, p. 166.

Jaffe, Joshua, "Zone Vision Attracts $12M in First Round," *Daily Deal,* May 10, 2001.

Meils, Cathy, "Zone Vision Expands East Euro Operation," *Variety,* March 8, 1999, p. 56.

Szalai, Georg, "Liberty's China TV Picture Clearer," *Hollywood Reporter,* June 24, 2005, p. 12.

"Zone Vision Channels Broaden Their Outlook," *Television Business International,* May 1, 2004.

"Zone Vision Launches Channels in Russia, Renews MTV Contract," *Television Europe,* January 2001, p. 7.

"Zone Vision's Reality TV Cracks the US Market," *Television Business International,* September 1, 2003.

"Zonemedia Programming Heads for Global TV Distribution Platform Joost," *M2 Presswire,* June 6, 2007.

Chesapeake Corporation

James Center II
1021 East Cary Street
P.O. Box 2350
Richmond, Virginia 23218-2350
U.S.A.
Telephone: (804) 697-1000
Fax: (804) 697-1199
Web site: http://www.cskcorp.com

Public Company
Incorporated: 1918
Employees: 5,553
Sales: $995.4 million (2006)
Stock Exchanges: New York
Ticker Symbol: CSK
NAIC: 322212 Folding Paperboard Box Manufacturing; 322213 Setup Paperboard Box Manufacturing; 322214 Fiber Can, Tube, Drum, and Similar Products Manufacturing; 322215 Nonfolding Sanitary Food Container Manufacturing; 326160 Plastics Bottle Manufacturing; 332115 Crown and Closure Manufacturing; 322299 All Other Converted Paper Product Manufacturing

∎ ∎ ∎

Once a broader-based paper and packaging company, Chesapeake Corporation between 1997 and 2001 transformed itself into a global specialty packaging firm. Roughly 84 percent of revenues are generated by the company's paperboard packaging operations, which specialize in such areas as folding cartons, spirally wound composite tubes, leaflets, and labels. Chesapeake's paperboard packaging is used in pharmaceutical and healthcare products and such branded products as alcoholic beverages, confectioneries, food, and tobacco. The balance of sales are derived from plastic packaging, including containers, bottles, preforms, and closures, and these products are used to package agrochemicals, specialty chemicals, and food and beverage items. Although still based in Virginia, where it was founded in 1918, Chesapeake derives only a little more than 5 percent of its revenues from its home country. The United Kingdom, where around half of sales originate, is by far the company's largest market, followed by Germany (13%), Ireland (9%), France (8%), Belgium (5%), and South Africa (4%).

EARLY HISTORY

Elis Olsson, a Swedish-born papermaker, was a recognized pioneer in the industry when he moved his family from Quebec to Virginia in 1918. Olsson had become director of a corporation he organized with the help of a Norwegian shipping financier, Christoffer Hannevig. Olsson had helped to develop the first kraft process mill in Canada. Kraft paper is the heavy brown paper produced from unbleached pulp that is used for such items as grocery bags. Another of Olsson's technical innovations was the first commercial paper mill boiler to use wastewood and bark for fuel. He also engineered the first modern chemical recovery boiler. When Olsson first moved to West Point, the paper industry was in its infancy.

Chesapeake Corporation began via an agreement to lease the assets of Chesapeake Pulp & Paper Company, a

COMPANY PERSPECTIVES

Our strategy is to focus our financial, capital and human resources in the markets that are aligned with customers that have special packaging requirements and desire innovative packaging solutions.

subsidiary of Fox Paper Company, based in Ohio. Included with the leased assets was a sulfate mill in West Point that dated to 1914. The company had not proven profitable and the assets were leased with an option to buy, as the original owners wished to withdraw from the operation. Upon his arrival, Olsson quickly invested in plant improvements; pulp and board mills had deteriorated throughout the United States during World War I. Olsson also put his technical skills to use, revamping the tricky sulfate process that produced paper from pine.

Chesapeake was profitable by 1921, but president Hannevig's shipping empire went under and he resigned from the company. Olsson thus sought both financial backing and a new company president. It was hard to find supportive investors in the shaky postwar climate, but H. Watkins Ellerson, president of one of Chesapeake's pulp customer companies, agreed to back the enterprise and serve as president of a reorganized Chesapeake. Olsson became vice-president, but for all practical purposes he ran the company. One of the first decisions of the restructured corporation was to buy the West Point mill instead of leasing. In 1922 bonds were issued to cover the purchase price, as well as the cost of needed plant improvements.

By 1926 Chesapeake was producing kraft paper, market pulp, crude turpentine, and boxboard on an average of 85 tons a day. It paid its first dividends the same year, a tradition uninterrupted except by the Great Depression. In 1929 Olsson was named president; he remained a leader in the company for the next 30 years, 14 of them as chairman of the board.

The 1930s were a time of growth for Chesapeake, despite the Depression. In 1932 Chesapeake became the second company in Virginia to hire a professional forester and begin a program of reforestation. Reforestation had been a company undertaking since 1922. As orders dropped off during the Depression, salaries and wages were cut. Nonetheless, Chesapeake's earnings reached the million-dollar mark for the first time in 1934. Chesapeake worked with Camp Manufacturing Company to erect and operate a pulp and paper mill in

Franklin, Virginia, in 1936. The new mill was named Chesapeake-Camp Corporation at the time; its name later changed to Union Camp Corporation. Chesapeake eventually sold its interest in the mill.

In 1941 the company name was changed to The Chesapeake Corporation of Virginia. Its stock was offered on the New York Stock Exchange for the first time in 1944. During the labor shortage of World War II, Chesapeake maintained its production levels with the help of women—who worked at office jobs, as well as at cutting pulp wood in the forests—and German and Italian prisoners. In 1945 Olsson became company chairman. His son, Sture Olsson, assumed the position of president of the company in 1951.

ENTERING PACKAGING IN THE POSTWAR YEARS

Having entered the corrugated container industry in 1946 via the purchase of a 50 percent stake in Long Island, New York-based Interstate Container Corporation, Chesapeake acquired two box and container companies in 1961: Baltimore Paper Box Company and Miller Container Corporation. Miller went on to become the Roanoke division of Chesapeake Packaging Company. Between 1962 and 1964, Chesapeake invested $21 million into an expansion program that included its second paper machine and a new power plant. In 1967 Scranton Corrugated Box Company, Inc., was acquired. It became the Scranton division of Chesapeake Packaging Company.

In 1968 Sture Olsson resigned as president to serve as chairman of the board; Lawrence Camp was named president and CEO. That same year, Chesapeake acquired the Binghamton Container Company, now a division of the Chesapeake Packaging Company. The company's next major acquisition came in 1977 when it purchased a packaging company that eventually became the Louisville and St. Anthony divisions of Chesapeake Packaging Company.

DECENTRALIZATION AND RESTRUCTURING

The 1980s were a time of great growth and change for Chesapeake. During this decade it vaulted to a position as a *Fortune* 500 company and instituted a policy of decentralization. Changes commenced with the election of J. Carter Fox as president and CEO of Chesapeake. Only 41 years old at the time, he was the youngest CEO in the industry. Fox had moved up the ranks at Chesapeake. He first worked as a summer maintenance helper while still in school, then joined the company

KEY DATES

1918: Chesapeake Corporation is founded to lease and operate a kraft pulp mill in West Point, Virginia.

1944: Company's stock is listed on the New York Stock Exchange.

1946: Chesapeake enters the corrugated container business.

1987: Headquarters are relocated from West Point to Richmond, Virginia.

1994: Sales of packaging exceed that of Chesapeake's founding business, kraft products, for the first time.

1997: Chesapeake exits from the kraft products sector with the sale of its founding West Point mill, four corrugated container plants, and related assets to St. Laurent Paperboard Inc.

1999: U.K.-based Field Group plc, a leading European specialty packaging firm, is acquired; Chesapeake divests its building products business and most of its timberlands; company combines its commercial tissue operations with those of Georgia-Pacific Corporation, creating a joint venture in which Chesapeake holds a 5 percent stake; Chesapeake receives $755 million in cash as part of the Georgia-Pacific deal.

2000: Company acquires Boxmore International PLC, a specialty packaging firm based in Belfast, Northern Ireland.

2001: Chesapeake sells most of its remaining U.S.-based businesses, completing its shift to specialty paperboard and plastic packaging.

2005: Pharmaceutical leaflet maker Arlington Press of Lake Success, New York, is acquired.

full-time in 1963 as a project accountant. As president and CEO, Fox reorganized the company's management structure. By putting managers in charge of operating units, the company was better able to focus on niche markets. The company was also restructured to reflect its four core business segments: treated wood, point-of-sale displays, table napkins, and brown and white linerboard boxes. Fox also oversaw trimming of the company, unloading unprofitable units such as plywood and sawmill plants.

In 1981 Chesapeake opened its first wood-treating plant in Pocomoke City, and a new wastewood-fueled boiler went online at West Point. The new boiler helped to cut oil consumption by about 5 percent of total energy consumed. Chesapeake's energy program was often ahead of the industry in its utilization of residual and self-generated sources of energy. About this time, Chesapeake wrapped up a $51 million capital improvement program at West Point that was designed, among other advances, to allow the company to bear a greater wood inventory at the mill, thus minimizing its reliance on outside woodyards. In order to meet production demands, the company's sawmill and plywood plants were supplied primarily by contract loggers who harvested wood off private and company-controlled timberlands. These timberlands were in the Blue Ridge Mountains of Virginia and North Carolina, as well as in parts of Maryland and Delaware. In 1982 about 75 percent of the raw material used to produce needed pulpwood and chips came from southern pine. Because the company had experienced four serious wood shortages between 1968 and 1982, management of the woodlands was critical. Decentralization helped to minimize the shortages, as an area manager was designated to oversee and coordinate land management, acquisition, and wood procurement.

Decentralization began in earnest in 1983, when the company was divided into three investment centers. Chesapeake was one of the few pulp and paper companies in the United States to make expansion plans in 1983. The industry was still recovering from the recession and prices for key pulp and paper products were just beginning to bounce back.

In order to utilize the valuable company-owned land in Delaware, Maryland, and Virginia, Delmarva Properties, Inc., was established in 1983. Delmarva concentrated on developing various residential, recreational, commercial, and industrial lots on some of the properties too valuable to manage as timberlands. Chesapeake also modernized its West Point mill via a $73 million expansion project; this included a major revamp of the mill's roll handling system to reduce paperwork and order error and make inventory more accurate. The improved system was in place by 1984. Chesapeake acquired its tenth container plant, Color-Box, Inc., of Indiana, that same year. It also purchased a wood-treating plant near Fredericksburg, Virginia. The company's name was shortened during this period to Chesapeake Corporation from The Chesapeake Corporation of Virginia.

In an interview in *Pulp and Paper* magazine in 1984, Chesapeake president and CEO Fox said that the company's small size worked to its advantage. The company could manufacture different special market products to suit individual customer needs. "Only in this way can we hope to successfully compete with some of our competitors who in many cases are much larger firms with far greater financial reserves than Chesapeake," said Fox. Another of the company's advantages, he said, was that "Chesapeake has the closest linerboard mill to the northeastern U.S. market, and we can offer overnight service to the New York City area."

FURTHER EXPANSION AND DIVERSIFICATION EFFORTS

It was during this time that Chesapeake began plumping up its capacity to produce linerboard through expansions and upgrades. It also expanded its production of market pulp. Both these product lines were hard hit in 1982 and 1983. To counterbalance the dip in sales, Chesapeake negotiated a multiyear labor agreement that lowered wages and reduced staff by 5 percent. The amount spent on capital improvements was justified by the fact that the company had only one mill and had to keep it running efficiently. In 1985 the company acquired Wisconsin Tissue Mills Inc., of Wisconsin and Plainwell Paper Co., Inc., of Michigan, deals that enabled Chesapeake to diversify into commercial tissue and fine paper, respectively. Prices for pulp and linerboard, however, continued to be depressed.

In 1986 Chesapeake completed the conversion of its paper machine at West Point and began production of a new product: corrugating medium. This enabled the company to offer its customers a uniform, high-quality linerboard. The company's new high-speed Tri-Kraft linerboard machine was the first of its kind in North America, using multi-ply technology to produce linerboard and thus producing a sheet with superior strength and uniformity. Start-up costs affected the company's earnings for that year, but ultimately the gamble paid off. When Chesapeake began offering white linerboard instead of the common brown, sales dramatically increased. Companies preferred the white because logos and advertising could be clearly read from them.

In 1987 the company moved its corporate headquarters from West Point to the James Center in downtown Richmond. According to Fox, this was done so that paper-mill staff there could operate as independently as the other decentralized operations. A $160 million expansion was approved to add a fourth paper machine to the Wisconsin Tissue facilities. This project, completed in 1990, boosted that mill's production capacity by more than 70 percent. Chesapeake also acquired Distinctive Printing and Packaging Co., thus expanding its point-of-sale display business.

In 1988 Chesapeake's earnings rose 71 percent, in large part because of the boom in sales of white corrugated boxes. Chesapeake Packaging Company was reorganized to better handle the national sales of point-of-sale display. The company also continued its acquisition of other properties with the purchase in 1988 of a wood-treating plant in Holly Hill, South Carolina, followed shortly by the acquisition of Displayco Midwest Inc.

In 1991 Chesapeake combined with Toronto-based StakeTech to form a $2.5 million venture called Recoupe Recycling Technologies to market a "steam explosion" system of paper recycling. Using basic pressure cooker technology, the system saved water and energy and produced more uniform pulp than other processes. Sales for that year declined a bit; the recession, low demand, and continued pricing pressures were cited. Chesapeake underwent another management restructuring that year, with Paul Dresser becoming chief operating officer.

Pulp market prices dipped in 1992, costing the company about $2 million in the fourth quarter alone. The year was a disappointing one, although the company held a 20 percent share of the mottled white linerboard market that year, a business that was still growing at a rate of 7 percent a year. Chesapeake was also doing well in the areas of commercial tissue and point-of-sale corrugated displays.

LATE-CENTURY EMPHASIS ON SPECIALTY PACKAGING

Through a detailed reassessment of corporate strategy undertaken in 1992, Chesapeake determined that specialty packaging would be the fastest area of company growth. The company thus began to expand its packaging operations, which accounted for 29 percent of sales in 1993 but would account for almost half by 1998. In addition to the faster growth projected for the specialty packaging sector, that segment of the paper industry was less prone to economic swings and less capital intensive than other industry sectors, particularly the kraft products area. Chesapeake's first major move in building up its packaging operations came in January 1994, when it acquired Lawless Holding Corp., owner of Lawless Container Corp. and six plants in western New York and Ohio. Through this acquisition packaging became, in 1994, the company's largest business segment in terms of sales for the first time.

In April 1994 Sture Olsson retired after 26 years as chairman; Fox added the chairmanship to his duties as president and CEO. Paul A. Dresser, Jr., was named president in April 1995 but resigned a year later, with Fox reassuming that title.

Despite the decreasing importance of kraft products in its overall business mix, Chesapeake felt the full effects of the commodity pricing cycle in 1995 and 1996, with the "up" year of 1995 leading to record net sales of $1.23 billion and net income of $93.4 million, and the "down" year that followed leading to declines in these figures to $1.16 billion and $30.1 million, respectively. During 1996, Chesapeake expanded internationally for the first time, acquiring display and packaging operations in France and Canada and a tissue converting facility in Mexico.

1997–2001: THOROUGHLY TRANSFORMED THROUGH SERIES OF TRANSACTIONS

The most dramatic event in the transformation of Chesapeake came in May 1997 when the company sold its West Point kraft products mill, four corrugated container plants, and other related assets to St. Laurent Paperboard Inc. for about $500 million. The exit from kraft products left Chesapeake with two primary sectors, specialty packaging and tissue, along with a much smaller forest products/land development sector. In August 1997 Thomas H. Johnson was named president and CEO of Chesapeake, with Fox remaining chairman. Johnson had previously served as president and CEO of Atlanta-based Riverwood International Corp., a privately held packaging company. In April 1998 Fox retired, with longtime board member Harry H. Warner taking over as chairman. Also that year, Chesapeake added to its packaging operations through the acquisition of Denver-based Capitol Packaging Corporation, a specialty packaging company; and of Utica, New York-based Rock City Box Company, Inc., a manufacturer of corrugated containers, trays, and pallets, and wood and foam packaging products.

A dizzying series of transactions thoroughly transformed Chesapeake in 1999. In March of that year, following a bidding war with Shorewood Packaging Corporation, Chesapeake paid approximately $373 million to acquire U.K.-based Field Group plc, a leading European specialty packaging firm. Field was the number one European supplier of cartons, leaflets, and labels for pharmaceutical and healthcare products, held a leading position in Europe in packaging for branded confectionary and spirits products, and was also one of Europe's largest suppliers of tobacco packaging. Its annual sales were approximately $400 million. Later in the year Chesapeake bolstered Field through the acquisition of Berry's Limited, one of the largest suppliers of printed pharmaceutical leaflets and self-adhesive labels in Ireland. In October 1999 Chesapeake further expanded its point-of-sale display business by purchasing

Consumer Promotions International, Inc., a firm based in Mount Vernon, New York, with annual sales of $50 million.

On the divestment side, Chesapeake in 1999 sold its building products business to a subsidiary of St. Laurent Paperboard and 278,000 acres of timberland in Virginia, Maryland, and Delaware to Hancock Timber Resource Group, a subsidiary of John Hancock Mutual Life Insurance Company. Combined cash proceeds from these sales totaled approximately $185 million. In October 1999 Chesapeake and Georgia-Pacific Corporation combined their commercial tissue operations into a joint venture. The venture, named Georgia-Pacific Tissue, LLC, was 95 percent owned by Georgia-Pacific and 5 percent by Chesapeake and was managed by Georgia-Pacific. As part of the deal, Chesapeake received $755 million in cash from Georgia-Pacific. Through these moves Chesapeake was almost entirely focused on one sector: specialty packaging. The cash generated from these transactions went toward debt reduction and stock repurchases in addition to providing funding for acquisitions.

In November 1999 Shorewood Packaging made an offer to buy Chesapeake for $700 million, a move that prompted Chesapeake to launch a $480 million counteroffer for Shorewood. Chesapeake's bid for Shorewood, a specialty packaging concern based in Shorewood, New York, eventually turned hostile, but a protracted battle ended in February 2000 when Shorewood agreed to be acquired by International Paper Company in a deal later valued at around $640 million. As this battle played out, Chesapeake successfully completed another important European acquisition. In a February 2000 deal valued at roughly $319 million, the company acquired Boxmore International PLC, a company based in Belfast, Northern Ireland, specializing in folding cartons, leaflets, labels, and plastic containers for pharmaceutical and healthcare, food and beverage, and agrochemical products.

Chesapeake followed up the Boxmore deal with two more 2000 purchases. In March, the company gained its first foothold in the North American specialty packaging sector via the acquisition of Green Printing Company, Inc., of Lexington, North Carolina. Then in October, Chesapeake purchased First Carton Group Limited for $69 million plus the assumption of $50 million in debt. First Carton produced food and beverage cartons at six locations in the United Kingdom and Germany and had sales of $120 million in 1999.

In 2001 Chesapeake completed its transformation into a specialty paperboard and plastic packaging specialist by selling most of its U.S.-based businesses. The company sold its stake in the Georgia-Pacific Tissue joint venture to Georgia Pacific for $237 million, its Chesapeake Packaging corrugated packaging subsidiary to Temple-Inland Inc. for $120 million, and its point-of-purchase display business to CorrFlex Graphics, LLC, for approximately $37 million.

A NEW CHESAPEAKE

By 2002 Chesapeake was generating 95 percent of its revenues of $822.2 million from specialty packaging. Its U.S.-based land development business was responsible for the balance. Its only other U.S. operations were the Green Printing subsidiary and the corporate headquarters in Richmond. Europe was by far the firm's largest market as 56 percent of 2002 revenues originated in the United Kingdom, while Germany and France contributed 9 percent each. Over the next several years, Chesapeake incrementally built on its new platform.

In 2002, in addition to unveiling a number of new products, the company expanded plants in Westport, Ireland, and Oss, Netherlands. Production also began at new plastic packaging plants in the African island republic of Mauritius and in Kunshan, China, near Shanghai. Chesapeake also streamlined its European manufacturing network by closing a plant in Congleton, England, and consolidating two plants in Scotland into one. In 2003 two new plants were completed in Germany, one located in Melle focusing on confectionery packaging and the other sited in Delmenhorst designed to serve tobacco customers in central and Eastern Europe.

In September 2005 Chesapeake significantly increased its profile at home by acquiring Arlington Press for $65.8 million. Based in Lake Success, New York, Arlington was the leading supplier of pharmaceutical leaflets in North America and was thus perfectly complementary with the firm's existing European-based operations. Johnson, who had led Chesapeake through its transformation, retired in November 2005. The new CEO was Andrew J. Kohut, who was promoted from the position of president, having moved up through the ranks since joining the company in 1979.

Kohut immediately began implementing a cost-cutting program in reaction to pricing pressures within certain areas of the paperboard packaging market and increasing pension and benefit costs. With a goal of achieving annual pretax savings of $25 million, Chesapeake by the end of 2006 had shut down plants in Birmingham and Bedford, England, and in Ezy sur Eure, France; and sold its luxury packaging business based in France and its plastic packaging operation in Northern Ireland. These actions resulted in a collective workforce reduction of 10 percent, or approximately 600 employees.

At the same time this restructuring was launched, Chesapeake took an after-tax goodwill impairment charge of $311.7 million that took into account the challenging marketplace environment as well as the analysis of the company's operations that had led to the restructuring. This charge was largely responsible for the company's $314.3 million net loss for 2005. Chesapeake remained in the black in 2006, suffering a net loss of $39.6 million on sales of $995.4 million. Affecting results that year were an after-tax goodwill impairment charge of $14.3 million and an after-tax restructuring charge of $27.4 million. Despite the loss, Chesapeake paid a dividend to its shareholders for the 73rd consecutive year.

Through the first nine months of 2007, net sales were up 7 percent but Chesapeake was still operating in the red. Needing funds to invest in growth initiatives and also to strengthen its balance sheet, mainly by reducing debt, the company in 2007 suspended payment of quarterly cash dividends. Among the initiatives launched that year, Chesapeake entered into a joint venture with the Hungarian pesticide maker Chemark Termelő és Kereskedő Kft. to manufacture and market plastic agrochemical containers. It also restructured its global operations into three divisions: pharmaceutical and healthcare packaging, branded products packaging, and plastic packaging. In October 2007 Chesapeake beefed up its Asia-Pacific operations by opening a new 36,000-square-foot plant in Kunshan, China, designed for the production of pharmaceutical paperboard packaging.

Carol I. Keeley
Updated, David E. Salamie

PRINCIPAL SUBSIDIARIES

Field Group plc (U.K.); Boxmore Plastics Limited (Ireland); Chesapeake Asia-Pacific Limited (Hong Kong).

PRINCIPAL DIVISIONS

Pharmaceutical and Healthcare Packaging; Branded Products Packaging; Plastic Packaging.

PRINCIPAL COMPETITORS

MeadWestvaco Corporation; Amcor Limited; RPC Group Plc; Nampak Ltd.; Algroup International Werbeträger Vertriebs-GmbH; Mayr-Melnhof Karton AG;

Van Genechten Packaging; Cardinal Health, Inc.; Copapharm Europe SCRL; PharmaPact Ltd.; Constar International Inc.; Huhtamäki Oyj; Paradigm Packaging.

FURTHER READING

Abbott, Rodney, "First in Its Field," *Packaging Today International,* January 2003, p. 13.

Betts, Dickey, "Air-Assisted Separation, New Skim Tank Ups to Yield at Chesapeake," *Pulp and Paper,* August 1982, pp. 86–89.

Blackwell, John Reid, "Chesapeake Corp. Acquires N.Y. Supplier of Leaflets," *Richmond (Va.) Times-Dispatch,* August 6, 2005, p. C1.

———, "Chesapeake Cuts Corporate Staff," *Richmond (Va.) Times-Dispatch,* October 4, 2001, p. B10.

———, "Chesapeake Sells Display Businesses," *Richmond (Va.) Times-Dispatch,* October 2, 2001, p. C1.

———, "Chesapeake to Sell Most U.S.-Based Businesses; New Emphasis: Specialty Packaging," *Richmond (Va.) Times-Dispatch,* January 13, 2001, p. A1.

———, "Company to Sell Display Business," *Richmond (Va.) Times-Dispatch,* April 24, 2001, p. C8.

———, "Ex-Chesapeake Executives Fined," *Richmond (Va.) Times-Dispatch,* May 5, 2005, p. C1.

———, "Firm Picks New CEO, Reveals Cutbacks," *Richmond (Va.) Times-Dispatch,* November 11, 2005, p. C1.

———, "Packaging Firm Cuts Earnings: Chesapeake Found Accounting Problems," *Richmond (Va.) Times-Dispatch,* November 21, 2000, p. C1.

———, "What and Where Is Chesapeake? CEO Tom Johnson Has Transformed Former Paper Company," *Richmond (Va.) Times-Dispatch,* June 18, 2001, p. D16.

Brown, John Murray, "Boxmore Agrees £191m U.S. Takeover," *Financial Times,* December 16, 1999, p. 32.

Buxton, Mary Wakefield, *Bringing in the Wood: The Way It Was at Chesapeake Corporation,* Urbanna, Va.: Rappahannock Press, 1999, 187 p.

Chesapeake World, special 80th anniversary edition, Richmond, Va.: Chesapeake Corp., 1998.

Clark, Barry, "Chesapeake Modernizes Mill with Computerized Roll Handling System," *Pulp and Paper,* March 1984, pp. 62–65.

Cramer, Kelly, "Packaging Firm Buys Company: Chesapeake Unit Gets Product Display Firm," *Richmond (Va.) Times-Dispatch,* August 18, 1999, p. C1.

Dill, Alonzo Thomas, *Chesapeake, Pioneer Papermaker: A History of the Company and Its Communities,* 2nd ed., West Point, Va.: Chesapeake Corp., 1987, 424 p.

Glowacki, Jeremy J., "Chesapeake Corp.: Committed to Specialty Markets," *Pulp and Paper,* September 1995, pp. 38–39.

"G-P, Chesapeake Form Tissue Partnership," *Pulp and Paper,* August 1999, p. 17.

Jereski, Laura, "Recovering," *Forbes,* February 15, 1993, pp. 240–41.

Johnson, Jim, "Paper Giants Launch Joint Venture," *Waste News,* July 5, 1999, p. 1.

Johnson, Stephen S., "Packaging Profits," *Forbes,* January 2, 1995, p. 178.

Jones, Chip, "Top Chesapeake Officer Resigns," *Richmond (Va.) Times-Dispatch,* March 8, 1996.

Kim, Queena Sook, "Chesapeake Plans to Sell Off Four Units to Focus on Specialty Packaging Line," *Wall Street Journal,* January 15, 2001, p. B4.

Koncel, Jerome, "First Quarter Results Disguise a Bright Future," *Paper Trade Journal,* June 1986, p. 52.

"Long-Log, Tree-Length Requirements Increase," *Forest Industries,* August 1982, pp. 22–23.

Marsh, Virginia, "Chesapeake in Agreed £194m Bid for Field," *Financial Times,* January 21, 1999, p. 22.

Powell, Robert, "Global Path Transformed Chesapeake," *Richmond (Va.) Times-Dispatch,* June 2, 2003, p. D13.

Rayner, Bob, "Warlike Ideas Served Ex-CEO: Change Was Hallmark of J. Carter Fox's Leadership at Chesapeake Corp.," *Richmond (Va.) Times-Dispatch,* August 19, 1997.

Slack, Charles, and Lawrence Latane III, "Mill, Factory Being Sold: Chesapeake Corp. Shifting Focus," *Richmond (Va.) Times-Dispatch,* April 3, 1997.

Smith, Kenneth, "Chesapeake Producing Multi-Ply Liner on New Management at West Point," *Pulp and Paper,* April 1986, p. 108.

———, "P&P Interview: Chesapeake Looking for Recovery, Record Sales in 1984," *Pulp and Paper,* April 1984, pp. 130–34.

Starkman, Dean, "Chesapeake to Buy Shorewood Stake, Bolstering Its Bid," *Wall Street Journal,* November 30, 1999, p. C17.

———, "Chesapeake to Cut 5% of Its Payroll, Take a Charge," *Wall Street Journal,* December 30, 1999, p. C18.

———, "Georgia-Pacific, Chesapeake Corp. in Joint Venture," *Wall Street Journal,* June 28, 1999, p. B8.

———, "Shorewood Agrees to International Paper Acquisition," *Wall Street Journal,* February 17, 2000, p. C15.

Stipp, David, "Recycling Waste Paper with a Pressure Cooker," *Wall Street Journal,* January 7, 1991, p. B1.

Taylor, Robert, "Redesigned Waste Oil Reclamation System Cuts Chesapeake Fuel Costs," *Pulp and Paper,* December 1983, p. 94.

Wagner, Barbara Hetzer, "Companies with Star Potential," *Business Month,* December 1989, p. 45.

Wuerl, Peter, "Chesapeake Starts Up $73 Million Tri-Kraft Machine at West Point Mill," *Paper Trade Journal,* April 1986, pp. 44–45.

The Clemens Family Corporation

2700 Funks Road
Hatfield, Pennsylvania 19440
U.S.A.
Telephone: (215) 368-2500
Fax: (215) 362-1750
Web site: http://www.clemensfamilycorp.com

Private Company
Incorporated: 2000
Employees: 2,075
NAIC: 424470 Meat and Meat Product Merchant Wholesalers; 112210 Hog and Pig Farming; 311611 Animal (Except Poultry) Slaughtering

∎ ∎ ∎

The Clemens Family Corporation is a privately held, family-run umbrella corporation consisting of several businesses: the company's legacy business, Hatfield Inc., doing business as Hatfield Quality Meats, whose pork products are distributed along the East Coast and as far west as Ohio; Country View Family Farms, a hog production company that supplies Hatfield Quality Meats; Wild Bill's Foods, a beef jerky company; CFC Logistics, a refrigerated warehouse business; PV Transport, a public trucking company; and CFC properties, a real estate development company. The Clemens Family Corporation employs 24 family members and has more than 200 family shareholders.

ESTABLISHING A FAMILY TRADITION: 1879–1946

John C. Clemens began his business at about age 16 in 1879 when his father gave him a hog to butcher on the family farm. Clemens began processing meats, which soon included chicken, duck, and turkey, and taking his products to Philadelphia to sell. He eventually added produce and dairy to his retail business and founded a meatpacking operation in Mainland, Pennsylvania, in 1895. Within a few years, Clemens had narrowed his business to pork processing and retail sales. In 1923, he named his pork business Pleasant Valley Packing Company.

Clemens married in 1900 and had 14 children, ten of whom lived beyond infancy and all of whom worked for the business. The young Clemenses were given the choice of "more chores, or work in the business." Clemens eventually sold his retail operation to two of his sons; this venture split from the family business to become Clemens Family Markets. He continued to operate Pleasant Valley until his retirement in 1941, when he sold the meat business to sons John S. and Abram.

BECOMING AND GROWING AS HATFIELD: 1946–95

On August 1, 1946, disaster hit the Pleasant Valley Packing Company in the form of a fire that caused losses in excess of $100,000. The Clemens brothers began cleanup operations immediately. However, World War II rationing made steel for rebuilding almost impossible to obtain. Consequently, the Clemenses approached Ellis Delp, David Cassel, and Ella Finn, who owned Hatfield Packing Company, a neighboring competitor, which, at the time, was experiencing its own financial difficulties because of the war rationing. Hatfield Packing Company agreed to be acquired by John S. and Abram, who were joined by two other Clemens brothers, Ezra and Lester. The two businesses merged in 1946 under the Hatfield name, and within days of the sale, war rationing ended. Each brother oversaw a portion of the business with John S. Clemens serving as the president.

During the 1950s and the 1960s demand grew for Hatfield products and Hatfield Packing Company grew steadily over the decades under several changes of command. In 1949 and again in 1958, the company expanded its facilities. By 1964, Hatfield had a total of 108 employees and $6 million in sales. By 1998, sales were at $350 million and the company had 1,500 employees. In 1973, Lester Clemens, a member of the second generation, became president and his brother, John, chairman of the board. From 1981 to 1990, John W. Clemens, the oldest son of John S. Clemens, assumed the company presidency, marking the transition to the third generation of the Clemens family at Hatfield Packing Company.

From the 1960s through the 1980s, the business continued to grow. In the late 1980s, the renamed Hatfield Quality Meats undertook its largest expansion with the addition of more than 275,000 square feet of operating space. In 1990, Clair "Butch" Clemens, the second oldest son of John S. Clemens, was named the new president of Hatfield. He served as president until 1995 when Philip Clemens replaced him. During his tenure, Hatfield went from the 51st largest meat and/or poultry processor in the United States to the 28th largest in 1994.

PHILIP CLEMENS, REFORMING THE FAMILY BUSINESS: 1995–97

Philip Clemens, son of Lester Clemens, had started working at Hatfield in about 1971, after earning an associate's degree in accounting from Peirce College. He started Hatfield's human resources department in 1971 and then went on to become executive vice-president of the company in 1992 and eventually chairman and chief executive in 1994. Although the 1990s were a decade of significant advances for the company, the company's financial future began to look grim.

Clemens took on the task of getting Hatfield back on track. However, this was no small task in a company where 12 members of the family's third generation were actively involved in the business, and where any family member who joined the company could expect to eventually become a top-level manager and then a chairman of the board based on tenure alone.

In 1996, Philip Clemens persuaded the family to establish four "voting trusts" of approximately equal size, one for each of Lester, Ezra, John S., and Abram's descendants. Each Clemens family shareholder submitted his shares to a trust, whose trustee voted their shares. Any major decision required 75 percent of shareholders' approval. In 1997, he created a Family Advisory Council to deal with shareholder, managerial, or family issues.

At the same time, Clemens also made investments in technological improvements and continued to expand capacity. The company began a hog farming operation called Smiling Porker Farms. It purchased the Luger Meat Company of Beaver Falls, Pennsylvania; the meat business of Hershey Meats and Commissary of Hershey, Pennsylvania; and Medford's Foods of Chester, Pennsylvania. Under Philip Clemens, The Clemens Family Corporation grew into a more diversified enterprise. In 1997, it purchased Wild Bill's Foods, maker of beef jerky. Wild Bill's dated back to about 1974 when Ted Cundiff, who remained president of the new Clemens subsidiary, began to make jerky using the venison hunted by family and friends.

FROM A FAMILY BUSINESS TO A MODERN CORPORATION: 1997–2000

Despite these changes, company sales leveled off from 1997 to 1998. Faced with the prospect of creating family discord if he instituted the needed changes in family leadership and company planning, Philip Clemens submitted his resignation to the board in 1998. However, the board urged him to stay on. Thus in 1999, he recruited an outside consultant to come up with a succession planning process.

KEY DATES

1895: John C. Clemens founds a meatpacking operation, in Mainland, Pennsylvania.

1923: Clemens names his pork business Pleasant Valley Packing Company.

1941: Clemens retires and sells his business to two of his sons, John S. and Abe.

1946: Pleasant Valley Packing Company purchases the Hatfield Packing Company and assumes the Hatfield name.

1973: Lester Clemens becomes president and his brother, John Clemens, chairman of the board.

1981: John W. Clemens assumes the company presidency.

1990: Clair "Butch" Clemens, the second oldest son of John S. Clemens, is named the new president of Hatfield Quality Meats.

1995: Philip Clemens, son of Lester Clemens, becomes company president.

1997: Company purchases Wild Bill's Foods.

2000: Corporation reorganizes itself into a holding company called The Clemens Family Corporation; Philip Clemens is chairman and chief executive and Doug Clemens is president of Hatfield.

2004: CFC Logistics opens its irradiation facility.

2005: Company shuts down CFC's irradiation facilities.

2007: Company acquires Maryland-based Nick's Sausage; it also enters into a joint venture with Creta Farms.

Clemens and the consultant formed a succession-planning committee that formulated the following recommendations. The board of directors would be disbanded and reconstituted with more independent as opposed to family members. Two high-level family employees would be asked to leave the business and two middle managers would be encouraged to gain experience outside the company. An Owners' Advisory Council, consisting of some of those asked to leave the board and management and responsible for representing shareholder interests and promoting solidarity, would replace the Family Advisory Council. Most significantly, the corporation would reorganize itself into a holding company, renamed The Clemens Family Corporation, with Philip Clemens as chairman and chief executive.

Doug Clemens, a fourth-generation Clemens, would become president of Hatfield.

These changes took place in 1999 and 2000, shocking many family members used to Hatfield's family-first way of doing business. However, the results were undeniable; in 2001, Hatfield Quality Meats and Wild Bill's Foods achieved record revenues. By 2002, Wild Bill's had doubled in size, and in 2004, it employed 110 people and sold more than one million pounds of jerky in the United States, Canada, and Japan for revenues of $12 million. While the family got used to being a "business-first family," Clemens took additional steps to further the growth of The Clemens Family Corporation and the connection between his company's conservative Christian values and the ways in which it did business.

CREATING AN ETHICAL BUSINESS: 2000–02

One area of reform involved the treatment of the animals that the company relied on for its existence. During the 1990s, Philip Clemens had worked with Dr. Temple Grandin, a renowned animal advocate who helped slaughterhouses to establish humane ways of raising, transporting, and slaughtering its livestock. In 2002, at the Animal Handling Conference, Clemens delivered a speech in which he stressed the importance of "[p]roper handling by our receiving staff and the pen personnel. … Once the process of harvesting is begun, it must be done in a very stress free and humane way."

Clemens also placed emphasis in his speech on the ways in which his company shared through charitable giving and participation in the community. The company made donations to local food banks and the Salvation Army; it provided local scholarships, worked closely with 4-H clubs, and had a matching gift program for its employees' charitable donations. Treating its employees well was also important to The Clemens Family Corporation. Clemens cited his company's long-standing profit-sharing plan as one of the chief ways in which his family's corporation communicated a sense of direct worth to its employees. Hatfield had an onsite day-care facility, an infirmary with nurses and doctors, a fitness center, a subsidized cafeteria, and an employee store.

RADIATION, COMMUNITY RESISTANCE, AND THE FUTURE: 2003–07

However, the community expressed its dissatisfaction with the Clemens family in 2003 when its CFC Logistics, the cold storage arm that Hatfield founded in

2002, chose to employ a technology piloted in the 1960s: irradiating foods with cobalt 60. Although the U.S. Department of Agriculture, the Centers for Disease Control and Prevention, the U.S. Environmental Protection Agency, and the U.S. Food and Drug Administration had approved irradiation for controlling disease-causing microorganisms, Bucks County, Pennsylvania, residents opposed the company's plans to make its irradiation operation available to businesses for food, cosmetic, and pharmaceutical products nationally.

The proposed 1,600-square-foot irradiator was to be located inside an existing 150,000-square-foot cold storage facility and would feature an underground tank with a rack of cobalt 60 at the bottom. After Concerned Citizens of Milford Township spoke out publicly about the public dangers of the irradiator at a Nuclear Regulatory Commission (NRC) hearing in September 2003, CFC Logistics President Jim Wood said in a 2003 *Philadelphia Inquirer* article, "We've been pretty viciously attacked over the last four months by a small group ... slandering us on safety issues. The irony is that the whole point of this technology is to improve public health and safety."

The issue went to the Atomic Safety and Licensing Board, which refused to block the license from the NRC. While the Milford Board of Supervisors made haste to rewrite its zoning ordinance and citizens petitioned Bucks County Court to halt delivery of the cobalt, CFC Logistics forged ahead and began full production in 2004, irradiating ground beef and poultry for two customers, making it only one of two companies in the United States irradiating beef. In the end, public opinion won out on the issue. CFC closed down its irradiation facility the next year and began to use it as a cold storage warehouse.

Beyond its brief experience with irradiation, the company continued to grow in the early years of the 21st century and to revisit the issues that were central to its own identity. In 2007, it acquired a Maryland firm called Nick's Sausage. It also entered into a joint venture with Creta Farms, a Greek producer of healthful deli meats made with extra virgin olive oil. Meanwhile, Philip Clemens continued to talk publicly about the challenges of running a family business in the modern world. In 2006, he gave a presentation at a Pennsylvania college, addressing the question "Are You a Family Business or a Business Family?"

Carrie Rothburd

PRINCIPAL SUBSIDIARIES

Hatfield Quality Meats; Country View Family Farms; Wild Bill's Foods; CFC Logistics.

PRINCIPAL COMPETITORS

ConAgra Foods, Inc.; Smithfield Foods, Inc.; Tyson Foods, Inc.

FURTHER READING

Clemens, Philip, "Creating an Animal Welfare Mindset in Your Company," presented at Animal Handling Conference, 2002.

Graef, Christine, "Milford, Pennsylvania–Area Residents Object to Proposed Meat Irradiation Facility," *Indian Country Today,* January 13, 2004.

Marsh, Jim, "Location Is Business Key for Cold Storage Company," *Eastern Pennsylvania Business Journal,* March 29, 2004, p. 6.

Naedele, Walter F., "Group Presses U.S. to Halt Irradiation of Food in Bucks," *Philadelphia Inquirer,* September 11, 2003, p. B1.

———, "Plan to Irradiate Food Generates Heat in Milford: A Company Hopes to Open the Facility at an Existing Warehouse by Labor Day," *Philadelphia Inquirer,* June 18, 2003, p. B1.

Reilly, P. J., "Made in Lancaster County; Boy Meats World; Lancaster County Native Is Brains Behind Worldwide Beef Jerky Enterprise," *Intelligencer Journal,* June 1, 2004, p. A1.

Rizzo, Melinda, "Then and Now: Hatfield Family Retains Meat Business but Diversifies," *Eastern Pennsylvania Business Journal,* February 25, 2002, p. 6.

Compañia de Minas Buenaventura S.A.A.

Carlos Villaron 790
Lima, 13
Peru
Telephone: (51 1) 419-2538
Fax: (51 1) 471-7349
Web site: http://www.buenaventura.com

Public Company
Incorporated: 1953 as Compañia de Minas Buenaventura
   S.A.
Employees: 2,946
Sales: $684.7 million (2006)
Stock Exchanges: Bolsa de Valores de Lima New York
Ticker Symbols: BUENAVC1; BVN
NAIC: 212111 Hydroelectric Power Generation;
   212112 Electric Power Distribution; 212221 Gold
   Ore Mining; 212222 Silver Ore Mining; 212231
   Lead Ore and Zinc Ore Mining; 212234 Copper
   Ore and Nickel Ore Mining; 541330 Engineering
   Services

■ ■ ■

Compañia de Minas Buenaventura S.A.A., the leading Peruvian producer of precious metals, is sitting on a gold mine: Yanacocha, the largest one in Latin America. It shares ownership of this mine with U.S.-based Newmont Mining Company. Besides being Peru's chief gold producer, Buenaventura ranks second in the extraction of silver, of which Peru ranks second in the world only to Mexico. The company, which directly owns six mining units, mines ores containing lead and zinc as well as gold and silver. Its treatment plants, after removing rock and earth, yield concentrates that are smelted and refined by other firms. Buenaventura also holds controlling interests in two other mining companies and smaller stakes in a number of others. In addition, it owns a distributor of electric power and a consulting company offering mining engineering services.

BUENAVENTURA'S FIRST MINING OPERATIONS: 1953–75

Descended from a distinguished Peruvian family, Alberto Benavides de la Quintana was a mining engineer working for Cerro de Pasco Corporation, the U.S.-based company that dominated mining in Peru. In the early 1950s Benavides had his eye on Julcani, a mine in central Peru, dating from the 18th century, that Cerro de Pasco was no longer interested in renting from the owner, which had failed to make it a going concern.

In 1953 Benavides established Buenaventura (Good Fortune) to successfully exploit this mine. According to one account, he and his Peruvian backers put up the initial money and took 60 percent of the stock. Cerro de Pasco subscribed 20 percent, and Sociedad Minera Suizo-Peruana Julcani S.A., which had formerly owned the mine, took the rest. According to other accounts, however, Cerro de Pasco took a one-third share. Cerro de Pasco also lent Buenaventura $200,000 in return for the right to buy the mineral concentrates extracted from the mine. A plant with capacity to handle several hundred metric tons of ore a day was installed next to the mine, with the yield consisting of silver, zinc, and bismuth concentrates.

COMPANY PERSPECTIVES

Mission: To form and maintain a multidisciplinary team of quality people for corporate excellence. To execute mining-metallurgical operations safely and efficiently, applying the highest standards in the industry. To promote growth and organizational development, primarily through explorations and metallurgical research. To seek joint businesses with similar world-class companies overseas. To acquire and develop mining assets in Latin America. To diversify into the production of other metals or industrial minerals and energy. To maintain contact with and transmit an attitude of transparency with our shareholders, authorities, and other stakeholders. To apply the best practices of Corporate Governance. To achieve environmental excellence with respect to operations and explorations. To develop and promote strategic alliances with the communities in which we operate, participating actively toward their sustainable development. To seek to attain a work environment that promotes human and professional development in the company's areas of work. To explore hydrological resources and promote its rational use.

Buenaventura opened another mine, Recuperada, in 1956, about 25 miles west of Julcani at Huachocolpa, where, four years later it inaugurated the Corralpampa concentrate plant, which processed the mine's lead, zinc, and cadmium ores. Also in 1960, it began mining operations at Orcopampa, a deposit in southern Peru where, in 1967, it opened a concentration plant for ore containing gold, silver, and copper. Also in 1960, Buenaventura began assessing the commercial potential of two gold and silver mines in the Uchucchacua zone, about 265 miles northeast of Lima, where a concentration plant was installed in 1975. By 1985 this plant had the capacity to process 1,000 metric tons of ore per day.

These various company operations were employing over 1,000 workers in the mid-1960s, mining ore and converting it to concentrates of lead, copper, silver, and zinc. Buenaventura's revenues came to about $4 million in 1965. The company was first listed on the Bolsa de Valores de Lima in 1971. In 1972 Buenaventura acquired a majority stake in Compañia Minera Colquirrumi S.A., which had mines in northern Peru, and Compañía Minera Condesa S.A. in central Peru.

A GOLDEN GLOW: 1974–88

Cerro de Pasco ceased to exist at the beginning of 1974, when the Peruvian government bought its properties and established an agency, Centromín Perú, to administer them. Centromín thus became Buenaventura's minority partner, but only for its properties already in existence, not future ones. Over time it divested some of the shares, and its participation fell to one-sixth. Benavides retained excellent connections among both the civil authorities and the military figures that ruled Peru. By 1979 Buenaventura was the most important private Peruvian-owned mining company, with gross sales (including Colquirrumi's sales) of $56.5 million that year. The company was about to begin construction of a hydroelectric plant at Uchucchacua. It was offering management services to smaller family firms in this field and was acting as a consultant for mining projects in Bolivia, Ecuador, and Venezuela.

World silver prices, which had sharply increased in the late 1970s, declined over the next decade from the 1980 peak, and consequently Buenaventura began investigating, and subsequently exploiting, Orcopampa's gold potential, while continuing to extract silver as a byproduct. In 1983 it established a subsidiary named Compañía de Minas Orcopampa S.A. for the mine and plant, which constituted Buenaventura's main source of revenue. Orcopampa was the largest private-sector gold producer in Peru by 1985. The combination of Buenaventura's other mines and Orcopampa also ranked second in Peru's silver production.

During the year Buenaventura completed a major project: the Gandolini Tunnel, almost three miles long, for the drainage of water from Julcani. This allowed Buenaventura to expand the partly exhausted mine. The hydroelectric power plant at Orcopampa, partly financed by the International Finance Corp., a unit of the World Bank, was completed in 1988. Electrical, infrastructural, and mine capacity expansion by Buenaventura at Orcopampa was mainly financed by reinvesting company profits.

President and, from 1980, chairman of the board of Buenaventura, Benavides was described by David G. Becker as one of Peru's most progressive business leaders and a pioneer in regional development. Becker credited him for the development of an entire city, Santiago de Cocha Ccasa, at company expense around one of its mines. Buenaventura provided not only homes and municipal facilities but also worked to attract other businesses to the area. The residential area near the Uchucchacua mine was intended to be attractive as well as functional, and economic ties were fostered to the neighboring town of Oyón.

KEY DATES

■

1953: Compañía Minas de Buenaventura is incorporated by Alberto Benavides de la Quintana.

1965: Buenaventura's annual revenues have reached about $4 million.

1974: A government agency, Centromín Perú, becomes Buenaventura's partner for existing mines.

1979: Buenaventura has become the largest private Peruvian-owned mining company.

1984: Buenaventura receives a one-fifth stake in the exploitation of the Yanacocha gold mine.

1985: The company's Orcopampa facility has become the largest private-sector gold mine in Peru.

1993: Production begins at Yanacocha, which develops into Latin America's largest gold mine.

1996: Buenaventura is listed on the New York Stock Exchange.

1997: The company has become Peru's chief producer of silver.

2005: Gold production at Yanacocha reaches its peak.

THE YANACOCHA GOLD BONANZA: 1984–96

Buenaventura's most important venture was still to come. Since 1982 geologists working for Newmont Mining had been exploring gold deposits at Yanacocha, above the Andes Mountains treeline near Cajamarca in northern Peru, that were unusually free of impurities such as copper, arsenic, and lead. "With my 45 years in mining," Newmont's general manager in Peru later told Sally Bowen for an article in *AméricaEconomía,* "I'd never seen a vein like this." Yet there was no commercial way to exploit the deposits until the development of a technique called dump-leaching.

Newmont was not ready to invest further until 1992, when the government routed the terrorist insurgent movement Shining Path. Then it founded Minera Yanacocha S.A., with the French government agency Bureau de Recherches Geologiques et Minieres (BRGM), Buenaventura, and the International Finance Corp. as minority partners. Buenaventura, which had been invited into the joint-venture project in 1984 because of its reputation and excellent government con-

nections, received a 20 percent share in Minera Yanacocha.

Production began in 1993 at the 62,000-acre site. Dump-leaching required sprinkling the gold bearing material with salts of prussic acid. The solution was then drained off and deposited in pools from which the gold-silver mixture was separated and then smelted in small furnaces. The deadly cyanide-bearing prussic acid solution was transported in extra-resistant double lined plastic for safety. Heavily armed guards patrolled the nearby hills to protect the facilities from Shining Path remnants or other malefactors. They were said to be capable of repelling an attack of up to 400 well armed combatants. By 1996 Yanacocha was the leading gold mine in Latin America, producing 625,000 ounces a year, and doing so at a production cost of only $121 an ounce, about a third of the market price, making Yanacocha the lowest-cost gold mine in the world.

ON SOUNDER FINANCIAL FOOTING: 1996–2001

Buenaventura had been offering its shares on the Lima exchange for many years and had well over 1,000 small shareholders. In 1996 it was listed on the New York Stock Exchange for the first time and collected $175 million from the sale of American Depositary Receipts, the equivalent of shares. By this time its stake in the Minera Yanacocha consortium had increased to 32.3 percent. Its share rose again, to 43.65 percent, in 1996, after the French government tried to include BRGM's 24.7 percent stake in a privatization sale to an Australian corporation, Normandy Mining Ltd. Newmont and Buenaventura exercised what they described as their right of first refusal concerning the creation of new shareholders. The dispute, which was taken to court, ended in 2000, when BRGM and Normandy accepted an additional payment of $80 million, beyond the court-ordered $109 million from Newmont and Buenaventura, with the latter providing $40.6 million of this sum.

Financial management of Buenaventura had fallen to Benavides's son Roque by this time. "In geology and project vision, Alberto Benavides is extraordinary," a stockbroker told Peter Hudson for an article in *AméricaEconomía.* "But he isn't a financier; if he had had to manage alone the ADR business and the negotiations with BRGM, he would have been eaten alive." Roque Benavides Ganoza became president and chief executive officer of Buenaventura in 2001.

FURTHER EXPANSION: 1997–2006

Yanacocha's gold output passed a million ounces a year for the first time in 1997. The mine actually consisted of three separate mines to be combined eventually into one open pit. In addition to this mine and gold bearing Orcopampa, the company had five mainly silver producing mines and was Peru's chief silver producer, accounting for about 15 percent of production. More than half of this output was from Uchucchacua. Besides Yanacocha and Buenaventura's wholly owned units, its facilities included Shila, a gold-silver mine, where production began in 1989, about 15 miles south of Orcopampa. Shila was owned by a subsidiary which Buenaventura had formed in 1979 and in which it held two-thirds of the stock. Another such facility was Ishihuinca, a gold mine in southern Peru which Buenaventura acquired in 1985 by purchasing majority control of its owner, Inversiones Minera del Sur S.A. (Inminsur).

Production began at another Inminsur mine, Antopite, in 2000. This gold-silver mine was about 260 miles southeast of Lima. In addition, Buenaventura held appreciable, but minority, stakes in such mining companies as Sociedad El Brocal S.A.A., which was operating the silver-lead-zinc Coalquijirca mine near the settlement of Cerro de Pasco, and Compañía Minera Caudalosa S.A., plus a small stake in Sociedad Minera Cerro Verde S.R.L., a company that held the Cerro Verde copper mine in southern Peru. In 2005 it doubled its participation in this company to 18.5 percent.

Also in 2005, Buenaventura reopened its Recuperada mine, which it had shut down four years earlier because of low silver prices. A year earlier, Buenaventura had purchased the half-interest in the Paula gold-silver mine it did not already own and had merged it with Shila (although Paula was about 70 miles south of Shila). In 2006, Buenaventura purchased the remaining share of Inminsura that it did not already own and merged it into the parent company.

Gold production at Yanacocha fell from 3.33 million ounces in 2005 to 2.61 million ounces in 2006 (when production costs had passed $200 an ounce), indicating that the mine's bounty would slowly be coming to an end. Meanwhile, however, Buenaventura was enjoying the rise in world gold prices, its net sales reaching $548.07 million and its consolidated revenues, $648.87 million. Of the sales total, gold accounted for 63 percent; zinc, 12 percent; silver, 10 percent; and copper and lead, 6 percent each. Buenaventura accounted for about half of Peru's gold production. Alberto Benavides, now 86, was chairman of the board and the largest stockholder, with 14.61 percent of the shares; the combined Benavides family owned 27.2 percent.

Robert Halasz

PRINCIPAL SUBSIDIARIES

Buenaventura Ingenieros S.A.; Compañía de Exploraciones, Desarrollo e Inversiones Mineras S.A.C.–CEDEMIN; Compañía Minera Colquirrumi S.A. (90%).; Compañía Minera Condesa S.A (90%); Consorcio Energético de Huancavelica S.A.; Contacto Corredores de Seguros S.A.; Inversiones Colquijirca S.A (61%).; Minas Conga S.R.L. (60%); Minas Poracota S.A.; Minera La Zanja S.R.L. (53%); Minera Minasnioc S.A.C. (60%); S.M.R.L. Chaupiloma Dos de Cajamarca (60%).

PRINCIPAL OPERATING UNITS

Antopite; Colquijirca; Ishihuinca; Julcani/Recuperada; Orcopampa; Shila; Uchucchacua.

PRINCIPAL COMPETITORS

Compañia Minera Ares S.A.C.; Minera Aurífica Retomas S.A.; Minera Barrick Misquichilca S.A.

FURTHER READING

Becker, David G., *The New Bourgeoisie and the Limits of Dependence: Mines, Class and Power in "Revolutionary" Peru*, Princeton, N.J.: Princeton University Press, 1983, esp. pp. 179–81.

Bowen, Sally, "El Dorado en los Andes," *AméricaEconomía*, December 1993/January 1994, pp. 25–26.

Gooding, Kenneth, "Peruvian Company to Join Gold Index," *Financial Times*, July 1, 1998, p. 43.

Hudson, Peter, "El factor Alberto," *AméricaEconomía*, September 1996, pp. 74–75.

Lazaroff, Leon, "Staking a Claim," *LatinFinance*, March 1998, pp. 125–26.

Malpica Silva Santiestaban, Carlos, *El poder económico en el Perú*, Lima: Perugraph Editores, 1989, Vol. 1, pp. 340–47.

Purser, W. F. C., *Metal-Mining in Peru*, New York: Praeger, 1971, 339 p.

Tait, Nikki, "Newmont Settles Yanacocha Dispute," *Financial Times*, October 23, 2000, p. 34.

Copa Holdings, S.A.

P.O. Box 0816-06819
Complejo Business Park, Torre Norte
Urbanización Costa del Este
Panama City,
Panama
Telephone: (507) 304-2677
Toll Free: (800) 359-2672
Fax: (507) 304-2535
Web site: http://www.copaair.com

Public Company
Incorporated: 1944 as Compañía Panameña de Aviación, S.A.
Employees: 3,096
Sales: $851.2 million (2006)
Stock Exchanges: New York
Ticker Symbol: CPA
NAIC: 481111 Scheduled Passenger Air Transportation; 481112 Scheduled Freight Air Transportation; 488119 Other Airport Operations

∎∎∎

Copa Holdings, S.A., is the parent company for Copa Airlines of Panama and AeroRepública of Colombia. Copa's niche lies in flying midsized aircraft to medium-sized cities in Latin America and the United States. Flying from the "Hub of the Americas" at Tucumen International Airport in Panama City, it operates no domestic flights within Panama. Copa has been described as a legacy carrier with a low-cost work ethic.

AeroRepública, Colombia's second largest carrier, was added in 2005.

Partnerships have proved vital at various times in Copa's history. Originally an affiliate of Pan American World Airways, it was acquired by local investors in 1971 and flew more or less independently for a couple of decades until 1998, when Continental Airlines of the United States took a strategic interest in it. Copa joined the SkyTeam global alliance in 2007 and signed additional codeshare agreements with KLM and AeroMéxico.

Copa flies to about three dozen destinations in 21 countries from its Panama City hub; however, it offers no domestic service within tiny Panama. The 2005 acquisition of AeroRepública added a dozen destinations in Colombia. Copa has about three dozen planes in one of the youngest fleets in the Western Hemisphere. AeroRepública operates another dozen aircraft.

EARLY ORIGINS

Compañía Panameña de Aviación, S.A., the precursor to Copa Holdings, S.A., was formed by the government of Panama in June 1944. Pan American World Airways acquired a 40 percent holding in the airline a couple of months later and added another 33 percent two years after that. (The remainder of shares were acquired by Pan Am in 1968.)

Copa did not begin flight operations for another three years. As was the case with many other postwar airline launches, the original fleet of three planes was comprised of war surplus C-47 transports. It was

COMPANY PERSPECTIVES

Copa Holdings, through its Copa Airlines and AeroRepública operating subsidiaries, is a leading Latin American provider of passenger and cargo service. Copa Airlines currently offers approximately 126 daily scheduled flights to 40 destinations in 21 countries in North, Central and South America and the Caribbean. In addition, Copa Airlines provides passengers with access to flights to more than 120 other international destinations through codeshare agreements with Continental Airlines and other airlines. AeroRepública, the second-largest domestic carrier in Colombia, provides service to 12 cities in Colombia as well as international connectivity with Copa Airlines' Hub of the Americas through flights from Bogota, Bucaramanga, Cartagena, Cali and Medellin.

originally limited to domestic feeder services but soon shifted its emphasis to international routes.

Copa was not Panama's first airline. Pan Am had previously operated another subsidiary there called Panama Airways, Inc., from 1936 to 1941. In subsequent years several other carriers also flourished and in some cases eclipsed Copa before fading into oblivion.

Airline historian R. E. G. Davies notes that Copa was slow to embrace jets. Its Hawker Siddeley turboprops, first acquired in 1966, and Lockheed Electras added five years later allowed it to provide reliable and very economical service on short hops within the region. It began flying outside of Panama in the 1960s, with routes as far as the Caribbean and Colombia.

LOCAL OWNERSHIP

A group of local investors acquired Copa from Pan Am in March 1971. In 1986 Copa became a part of CIASA (Corp. de Inversiones Aereas SA), a Panamanian holding company.

By this time, the company was focused on international routes exclusively. The company had begun to operate the midsize Boeing 737, variants of which would be its workhorse for decades.

POST-INVASION COMMOTION

Copa launched its service to Miami in December 1, 1989. Less than three weeks later, the United States

invaded Panama to depose Manuel Noriega. Air Panama, Copa's state-owned rival, went bankrupt in the commotion that followed.

Air Panama dated back to 1966 and had been an affiliate of the Spanish airline Iberia. Its international network grew throughout the 1970s, and at the end of the decade it came under private ownership and took on British Airways as its new strategic partner. By the time of the invasion it had been reduced to a single plane, albeit a big one, a Boeing 747.

Copa and other airlines attempted to acquire Air Panama's routes but lost out to a private consortium called Panama Air International (PAI), which named Southwest Airlines cofounder Roland King as the relaunched airline's CEO. However, it lasted just a couple of years. The Air Panama name was carried a decade later by a small, tourist-oriented airline.

Copa's revenues were estimated at $35 million in 1991, and it was said to be profitable. It carried 220,000 passengers and eight million pounds of cargo during the year, its general manager told the *Journal of Commerce and Commercial.* Panama's large free trade zone made it a freight hub connecting the Caribbean, Central America, and Colombia, one of the country's largest trading partners.

The company then had three Boeing 737s and sometimes leased DC-8s. The fleet grew quickly, numbering 11 Boeing 737s by 1994. By this time, Copa had 650 employees.

Copa was participating in a loose alliance of Central American airlines, but it withdrew as its expansion plans brought it into conflict with the leader, El Salvador Grupo TACA.

1998 CONTINENTAL LINK

Seeking another strategic partner as its link with Grupo TACA unraveled, in 1997 Copa signed up to cooperate with American Airlines. However, the arrangement was short-lived.

Copa soon entered a more enduring relationship with another Texas-based carrier, Continental Airlines. In May 1998 Continental bought a 49 percent share of Copa for $53 million. It would prove to be a shrewd investment.

Business boomed for Copa on the strength of its alliance with Continental. At the same time, it was able to share in bulk purchasing savings on parts, fuel, and other items.

Los Angeles service increased to a daily schedule in June 2000. Copa also added three weekly nonstop

KEY DATES

1947: Copa begins flight operations as affiliate of Pan American World Airways.
1971: Pan Am sells its shares to local investors.
1986: Copa becomes a part of Panama holding company CIASA.
1998: Continental acquires stake in Copa.
2004: Fleet renewal program is launched.
2005: Copa buys Colombia's AeroRepública; completes initial public offering.
2007: Copa joins SkyTeam global alliance as associate of Continental Airlines.

flights to São Paulo, Brazil. Copa was increasingly profitable in the coming years, a rarity among airlines immediately after the September 11, 2001, terrorist attacks on the United States.

2005 AEROREPÚBLICA PURCHASE AND INITIAL PUBLIC OFFERING

Copa bought a controlling interest in AeroRepública, the second leading airline in Colombia, in March 2005. Like Copa, AeroRepública eschewed the hub system for a point-to-point network of secondary markets. Its fleet was different, though: 12 MD-80s. A subsequent bid to buy Colombia's bankrupt Avianca SA in collaboration with Continental was unsuccessful, however; ultimately Avianca chose to partner with Delta Air Lines.

Copa had an initial public offering (IPO) on the New York Stock Exchange in December 2005. The IPO was described as one of the most successful to ever come out of Latin America. In addition to Copa's string of increasing profits, Copa had fewer expensive social obligations than U.S. legacy carriers, an analyst explained to Reuters.

In the process, Continental sold a large chunk of its shares for $172 million, a handsome profit on its original investment. This reduced its holdings to 32 percent of Copa's equity; CIASA held all the voting shares. A secondary offering in June 2006 further trimmed Continental's share to 10 percent. By this time, noted the *Wall Street Journal*, the Continental alliance had helped Copa nearly double its passenger count to three million a year.

After a comprehensive fleet renewal program, the airline ended the year with two dozen Boeing 737s and a half-dozen smaller regional jets made by Brazil's

Embraer. The new planes helped keep maintenance and fuel costs down. A few more planes arrived in 2007, allowing Copa to end the year boasting three-dozen aircraft in one of the youngest fleets in the Western Hemisphere.

Copa posted more excellent results for 2006, but experienced a slump in its stock price on concerns it was running out of room to grow. The airline was looking for new traffic from new codeshare agreements with AeroMéxico and KLM Royal Dutch Airlines. The latter link had truly global implications, connecting the "Hub of the Americas" with the European market via Amerstam. Copa joined the SkyTeam global alliance in September 2007 as an associate member sponsored by Continental Airlines.

Frederick C. Ingram

PRINCIPAL SUBSIDIARIES

Compañía Panameña de Aviación, S.A.; AeroRepública S.A. (Colombia; 99.8%); Oval Financial Leasing, Ltd. (British Virgin Islands); OPAC, S.A.

PRINCIPAL OPERATING UNITS

Copa; AeroRepública.

PRINCIPAL COMPETITORS

Grupo TACA (Transportes Aereos del Continente Americano); AMR Corp.; Avianca SA; Mexicana de Aviación; DHL; GOL Linhas Aereas Inteligentes.

FURTHER READING

Assis, Claudia, "Panama Airline Copa Captures Wall Street Trio Imagination," *Dow Jones International News,* January 24, 2006.

Bocanegra, Nelson, "Continental Affiliate Copa Buys AeroRepública," *Reuters News,* March 7, 2005.

Cordle, Ina Paiva, "Copa Airlines' CEO Reflects on Company's Smooth Climb to Success," *Miami Herald,* November 13, 2006.

Cowan, Lynn, "Copa Holdings Opens Up 13% Post-IPO," *Dow Jones News Service,* December 15, 2005.

Davies, R. E. G., *Airlines of Latin America Since 1919,* Washington, D.C.: Smithsonian Institution Press, 1984.

Deagon, Brian, "Copa Doubles Profit, Clears Forecasts, but Weak Outlook Keeps Shares Falling," *Investor's Business Daily,* March 8, 2007, p. A1.

Hensel, Bill, Jr., "'A Dominant Player': Continental Alliance Gives It a Big Reach into Latin America; Panamanian Affiliate Helps Houston Airline Find Success in Region," *Houston Chronicle,* March 12, 2005, p. 1.

Higgs, Richard, "Panama Pickings," *Airline Business,* November 1991, p. 30.

"Interview—Copa to Aim for 50 Pct Hedge in 2007—CEO," *Reuters News,* December 22, 2005.

Kraul, Chris, "Latin Airline Finding Its Niche; Catering to Business Travelers, Copa Takes Off with Flights to Underserved Destinations via Its Hub in Panama City," *Los Angeles Times,* July 8, 2006, p. C1.

Lennane, Alex, "The Legacy Low Cost Carrier," *Airfinance Journal,* April 2006, pp. 34–37.

Lima, Evaldo Pereira, "Copa's Continental Aspirations," *Air Transport World,* November 1999, pp. 53–55.

Luxner, Larry, "A Tale of 2 Panamanian Airlines: 1 Profitable, 1 Looking for an Out," *Journal of Commerce and Commercial,* February 11, 1991, p. 5B.

Malone, Scott, "Copa Shares Take Off in Active U.S. IPO Market," *Reuters News,* December 15, 2005.

Millman, Joel, "As Rivals Crowd Copa Air, Continental Sells," *Wall Street Journal,* January 17, 2006, p. C1.

Shaw, Kirsten L., "COPA Gains from Panama's Economy," *Air Cargo World,* December 1991, p. 35.

CRA International, Inc.

John Hancock Tower
200 Clarendon Street, T-33
Boston, Massachusetts 02116-5092
U.S.A.
Telephone: (617) 425-3000
Fax: (617) 425-3132
Web site: http://www.crai.com

Public Company
Incorporated: 1965 as Charles River Associates
    Incorporated
Employees: 733
Sales: $349.9 million (2006)
Stock Exchanges: NASDAQ
Ticker Symbol: CRAI
NAIC: 541611 Administrative Management and
    General Management Consulting Services; 541618
    Other Management Consulting Services; 541690
    Other Scientific and Technical Consulting Services

∎∎∎

CRA International, Inc., provides a wide range of consulting services. It is one of the oldest and most respected firms in its field. Its varied practices fall into three platforms: Finance; Litigation and Applied Economics; Strategy and Business Consulting. After going public in 1998, the company has grown rapidly through acquisitions. Based in Boston, it operates from a network of more than 20 offices around the world. Its clients include larger corporations, government agencies, and law and accounting firms.

ORIGINS

The company was established in Massachusetts as Charles River Associates Incorporated (CRA) in February 1965. Within a few years, the firm's services were tapped by IBM to successfully defend itself in a very high profile antitrust case. The procedures dragged on for more than a dozen years before they were dropped by the government in 1982.

CRA typically hired experts with Ph.D.s. Such work could prove a quite lucrative sideline for professors, some of whom were making six figures testifying in antitrust cases. By 1995, the firm had revenues of $31.8 million and income of $2.4 million.

The firm underwent a management buyout during the year. Alan R. Willens stepped down as president and was replaced by James C. Burrows. Burrows had joined the company in 1967, serving as vice-president since 1971.

In 1997 longtime director Franklin M. Fisher was named chairman of the board. Along with other Charles River Associates economists, he was among the consultants who had testified for the defense in an IBM antitrust case. Fisher was a key government witness in a later case involving Microsoft Corporation.

Rowland T. Moriarty joined CRA's board in 1986 as a director and six years later became vice-chairman. He was appointed chairman in 2002. Fisher took the vice-chairman role for a few years before announcing his retirement.

PUBLIC IN 1998

In 1998 Charles River Associates listed its shares on the NASDAQ. The initial public offering of 27 percent of shares raised $40.5 million. The company was buoyed by robust mergers and acquisitions activity, an area of practice that accounted for more than a third of revenues. There was also demand from industries undergoing deregulation. These conditions prompted several other consulting firms to go public around the same time.

Revenues had risen to nearly $45 million in 1997, and income was more than $3 million. There were 120 consultants on the roster. CRA by then had added offices in Washington, D.C., and Palo Alto, California. In 1998 the company added offices in Toronto and Los Angeles. It also bought the Tilden Group of Oakland, California, for about $10 million in cash and stock.

NEUCO VENTURE

In 1997 CRA formed the NeuCo joint venture. NeuCo Inc. (originally a limited liability company) developed PC-based software to help power plants burn fuel more cleanly and efficiently. Other investors included Boston electric and gas company Nstar and Germany's Babcock-Borsig Power GmbH.

The new company soon won federal grant money to fund its research. Within a few years the software was installed at 50 power plants in the United States. NeuCo's revenues reached $5 million in 2001.

In 2006 NeuCo bought Pegasus Technologies Inc., a unit of Rio Tinto Energy America Services Co. Pegasus, which had been in business for 20 years, had sued NeuCo for alleged patent infringement. The acquisition ended that suit. The deal reduced CRA's share in NeuCo to 36 percent, resulting in it being unbundled from CRA's consolidated financial results.

2000 AND BEYOND

CRA's revenues were $82.5 million in 2000. A London office opened in the last half of the year. The company then launched units in Melbourne, Australia, and Wellington, New Zealand, with a focus on its energy consulting. Another acquisition added offices in Utah and Texas.

Some parts of CRA's business were vulnerable to a lackluster economy after 2000, as industrial clients cut back on consulting services. Litigation-related business was up, however. "More people are suing companies or accounting firms for not making money," quipped CRA's chief financial officer in the *Boston Business Journal.*

CRA maintained a full roster of professionals through the lean years. This gave it the capacity to handle the wave of mergers that accompanied an improving economy in 2004, CEO Jim Burrows told the *Boston Globe.*

Annual revenues were nearly $300 million by 2005. Net income was about $25 million, up 51 percent for the year. The company's rapid development was recognized by a number of business magazines. *Smart-Money* and others followed its shares as a "growth stock." Much of the increase came from acquisitions.

STRATEGIC ACQUISITIONS

CRA bought a dozen companies between 1998 and 2006. It looked to add complementary services while expanding its geographic range. Parts of the energy practice of PA Consulting were acquired in 2001. CRA was among the firms to buy parts of failed accounting giant Arthur D. Little Inc. in 2002. It picked up the $20 million-a-year chemical and energy unit for about $7 million plus performance incentives. This bolstered the international aspect of CRA's core consulting areas.

InteCap Inc. was added in March 2004 at a cost of $81.7 million. It was attractive to CRA because its specialty, intellectual property issues, was a growing field. InteCap had five U.S. offices and one in London and employed 180 consultants.

In November 2004, the company spent about $10 million (AUD 13 million) on Australia's Network Economics Consulting Group Pty Ltd. (NECG), a specialist in regulatory and economic consulting. Based in Canberra, Australia, NECG also had offices in Sydney and Melbourne. In the same month, CRA acquired parts of Tabors Caramanis & Associates for about $6 million. Based in Cambridge, Massachusetts, Tabors

KEY DATES

1965: Company is established as Charles River Associates Incorporated.

1997: CRA forms NeuCo joint venture to produce optimization software for power plants.

1998: CRA has initial public offering on the NASDAQ.

2005: Company changes name to CRA International, Inc.

2006: NeuCo acquires older rival Pegasus Technologies, diluting CRA's stake.

130,000 square feet of free space in a tightening commercial real estate market.

Frederick C. Ingram

Caramanis provided advice related to energy transmission to utility companies.

Lee & Allen Consulting Limited, a London firm with a Hong Kong branch, was acquired in April 2005 for about $16 million. Its 40 professionals billed about $14 million a year. Financial dispute resolution was its specialty. A couple of months later, CRA added London-based Economics of Competition and Litigation Limited, formerly known as Lexecon Ltd. The cost was about $17 million.

Parts of The Ballentine Barbera Group, LLC, of Washington, D.C., were bought in May 2006. The mostly cash deal was worth $23 million. Ballentine Barbera specialized in transfer pricing valuation. It had revenues of about $12 million a year.

NEW NAME

Charles River Associates adopted a new name in its 40th anniversary year. The new name, CRA International, Inc., was meant to reflect its growing global influence. There was cause for celebration, including a 25 percent growth rate over the previous several years. By this time, there were about 550 consultants in the company's 23 offices. Revenues were about $350 million in 2006 and expected to grow at least 10 percent the next year. Net income was growing at a double digit rate. In 2007 the company celebrated opening a new office in Hamburg, Germany, in 2007.

CRA's world headquarters took up four middle floors of the John Hancock Tower in Boston's Back Bay area. Spiraling rents there prompted the company to consider a move to less expensive offices, reported the *Boston Business Journal*. To do so, it would need to find

PRINCIPAL SUBSIDIARIES

CRA Security Corporation; CRA International Limited (Canada); CRA International (UK) Limited; InteCap Risk Solutions Limited (U.K.); CRA International Limited (New Zealand); CRA International Pty Ltd. (Australia); Network Economics Consulting Group Pty Ltd. (Australia); Lee & Allen Consulting Limited (U.K.); Lee & Allen Consulting, Inc.; Economics of Competition and Litigation Limited (U.K.).

PRINCIPAL DIVISIONS

Finance; Litigation and Applied Economics; Strategy and Business Consulting.

PRINCIPAL COMPETITORS

McKinsey & Company; Accenture; ERS Group, Inc.; BearingPoint; Abt Associates Inc.; Analysis Group.

FURTHER READING

Abelson, Jenn, "Big Deals Boost Growth Among Services Firms," *Boston Globe*, May 17, 2005, p. 1.

"American Firm Takes Tower Lease," *Dominion* (New Zealand), March 15, 2001, p. 28.

Arends, Brett, "It's Elementary: Hub's Moriarty a Boardroom Napoleon," *Boston Herald*, Bus. Sec., June 2, 2006, p. 25.

Bielen, Mike, "NeuCo Venture Formed," *Chemical Market Reporter*, October 13, 1997, p. 16.

"Burrows Elevated to CRA President," *Boston Globe*, Econ. Sec., March 16, 1995, p. 43.

Butterfield, Fox, "The Professor As Paid Expert," *New York Times*, Sec. 2, June 12, 1982, p. 43.

"Charles River Associates," *IPO Reporter*, May 25, 1998.

"Charles River Associates Acquires Forensic Firm," *International Accounting Bulletin*, May 9, 2005, p. 7.

"Charles River Associates Completes Acquisition of the Tilden Group," *Boston Business Journal*, December 16, 1998.

"Charles River Associates Expands IP Arm with Buy of InteCap," *Mass High Tech: The Journal of New England Technology*, March 15, 2004.

"Charles River Associates Incorporated Acquires Line of Business from PA Consulting," *Reuters Significant Developments*, August 22, 2001.

"Charles River Associates May Rise in First Day of Trading," *Boston Business Journal*, April 24, 1998.

"Charles River Associates Short Term Buy," *Emerging & Special Situations,* March 13, 1998, p. 19.

"Consulting Business Is Booming—But Not on Wall Street," *Public Utilities Fortnightly,* April 15, 1999, p. 62.

"CRA Expands to LA," *Chemical Market Reporter,* August 3, 1998, p. 33.

Fisher, Franklin M., John J. McGowan, and Joen E. Greenwood, *Folded, Spindled and Mutilated,* Cambridge, Mass.: MIT Press, 1983.

Grimaldi, James V., "Government's Adviser Has Conflict of Interest, Microsoft Lawyers Say," *Knight-Ridder/Tribune Business News: Seattle Times,* June 2, 1999.

Hillman, Michelle, "CRA the Latest to Weigh Leaving Hancock Tower," *Boston Business Journal,* November 19, 2007.

"Judge Ends Probe of Alleged Misconduct by Attorneys and Consultants in Enron Case," *Power Markets Week,* May 28, 2007, p. 22.

Laise, Eleanor, "Update on Russell Pearlman, Growth Stocks Are Back," *SmartMoney,* October 2004, p. 38.

Lane, Bill, "Five Firms Raise $170M in 2nd Quarter IPOs," *Boston Business Journal,* July 10, 1998.

"Law Judge Recommends That FERC Suspend Individuals from Practicing Before the Agency Due to Their Deceptive Behavior," *Foster Natural Gas Report,* March 23, 2007, p. 3.

Miller, Jeff, "NeuCo Gets Energized by Grant from DOE for $8M," *Mass High Tech: Journal of New England Technology,* February 7, 2003.

"Moriarty Appointed Chairman of Charles River Board," *Boston Business Journal,* July 19, 2002.

"Navigant, Charles River Snap Up ADL Units," *Energy Daily,* April 9, 2002, p. 3.

"NeuCo Inc. Settles Patent Suit, Acquires Pegasus Technologies," *Boston Business Journal,* May 16, 2006.

"NeuCo Reports Record Revenue Figures," *Boston Business Journal,* April 4, 2002.

Pearlman, Russell, "Growth Stocks Are Back," *SmartMoney,* March 2004, pp. 90–95.

Petersen, Melody, "Consultants Sing the Siren Song of Wall Street," *New York Times Abstracts,* May 26, 1998, p. D1.

"Polarisation Report Authors Quit London Economics," *Money Marketing,* October 19, 2000, p. 2.

Qualters, Sheri, "Charles River Associates Raises Cash for Acquisitions," *Boston Business Journal,* September 5, 2003.

Rulison, Larry, "Lawsuit Claims Hale Owes Boston Firm Money," *Baltimore Business Journal,* September 29, 2000, p. 6.

Syre, Steven, "Fighting over Talent," *Boston Globe,* July 10, 2007, p. C1.

Thurmond, Matt, "Like CRA? Be Patient," *Motley Fool,* June 10, 2005.

Walsh, Kerri, and Peck Hwee Sim, "Consultants: Chemical Firms Wrestle Down Costs," *Chemical Week,* August 6, 2003, pp. 18–21.

Warner, Judy, "Wealth of Assets Prompts Interest in IP Valuation," *Boston Business Journal,* September 24, 2004.

Wasserman, Elizabeth, "Microsoft Lawyer Accuses Witness of Conflict of Interest," *InfoWorld Daily News,* June 2, 1999.

Westheimer, Julius, "MoneyWi$e—Investors Go with the Flow," *Baltimore Daily Record,* February 20, 2004.

Wood, Lisa, "Charles River Associates Sets Up London Office," *Financial Times* (London), People Sec., July 31, 2000, p. 13.

"Working Together in Asia Pacific," *Management Consultant International,* March 2005.

Crown Equipment Corporation

40 South Washington Street
New Bremen, Ohio 45869
U.S.A.
Telephone: (419) 629-2311
Fax: (419) 629-2900
Web site: http://www.crown.com

Private Company
Incorporated: 1945 as Crown Controls Corporation
Employees: 8,300
Sales: $1.67 billion (2006 est.)
NAIC: 333924 Industrial Truck, Tractor, Trailer, and Stacker Machinery Manufacturing

■■■

Crown Equipment Company is an Ohio-based manufacturing firm that has had many popular products in its century of business, from coal-burning furnace thermostats and television antenna rotators to hand-pumped truck lifts and a work-assist vehicle known as "the Wave," yet few have heard of the firm outside its industrial marketplace. Despite its seeming anonymity in the American mainstream, Crown is an award-winning manufacturer of materials-handling forklifts. Owned and operated by the Dicke family, Crown is the number one name in electric lift trucks in the United States and the fifth largest lift truck manufacturer in the world.

ROOTS IN THE TWENTIES

Crown was formally organized in 1945, but its roots stretch back to the 1920s when Carl Dicke (pronounced Dickee) founded Pioneer Heat Regulator Company with his brothers, Oscar and Allen. The three Dicke siblings made quite a team: Oscar invented a thermostat for coal-fired home furnaces; Allen, an attorney, patented the concept; and Carl marketed it. When new home construction went bust during the Great Depression, the brothers sold Pioneer to Master Electric, a manufacturer in nearby Dayton. Carl Dicke continued to work as the Pioneer subsidiary's general manager through World War II.

Following a two-year health-related hiatus, Carl, his son Jim, and Allen founded Crown Controls Company to market thermostats manufactured by Master Electric Company in 1945. In 1947 Master Electric sold the manufacturing operation back to the family team for $85,000. Unfortunately for the Dickes, however, coal was quickly losing favor as a home heating fuel, giving way to electric heaters and natural gas furnaces.

With their core business slipping away, the Dickes sought a new business interest on which to build Crown's future. On a suggestion from a business associate, they began producing and marketing television antenna rotators in 1949. These devices, also known as directional antennas, turned antennas so they would get the best possible reception. In 1950 Allen Dicke traded his stake in Crown to Carl in exchange for Carl's share of a local farm.

COMPANY PERSPECTIVES

Crown Equipment Corporation designs, manufactures, distributes, services and supports material handling products that provide customers with superior value. Since its entry into the material handling equipment industry in 1956, Crown has distinguished itself from competitors with exceptional product designs and a unique business approach based on vertical integration. When it says Crown on the outside, it's a Crown on the inside.

A NEW ERA

Crown Controls reached a tragic turning point in 1952 when 50-year-old founder Carl Dicke died, leaving his 31-year-old son to manage the business on his own. Jim Dicke's company continued to manufacture television antennas throughout the 1950s (and into the 1990s, in fact), turning marketing responsibilities over to the world's largest manufacturer of television antennas, New York's Channel Master Corporation, in 1957. Channel Master's superior distribution generated increased sales of Crown's TV antennas, but left a void in the Ohio company's marketing program. Crown cast about for new ideas, dabbling in a variety of novelty products including "ice stoppers to keep the ice in your glass from bumping you in the nose," "fishing arrowheads," and a combination saw/drill. None of these products, however, had the staying power to sustain a growing business.

Jim Dicke's father-in-law, Warren Webster, suggested Crown develop a "hydraulic lift table" that would make lifting and moving heavy objects easier and safer. Webster was not the first to come up with this concept; the lift truck was initially invented in 1918 by Lester Sears of Cleveland, Ohio. His "Towmotor" launched an industry crowded with competitors by the time Crown entered the fray in the 1950s.

However, Webster and Dicke thought they had discovered an underexploited and potentially profitable segment of the forklift market. They would build small, walk-behind hand trucks for light industry. Crown had manufactured a hydraulic auto jack called a "bumper upper" for the Joyce-Cridland company in the postwar era, but had not found a market for the device. Tom Bidwell, an engineer at Crown, adapted the concept to the LT-500 (500-pound capacity lift truck), a "walkie lifter" he designed in 1957. This initial entry featured a hand-pumped hydraulic lift and was pushed like a cart.

Crown's line of "E-Z Lift" trucks entered a market choked with well-entrenched competitors, including Hyster, Clark, Yale, and Caterpillar. Thus the company needed to differentiate its products and win over both distributors and customers. In the early 1960s Crown hired two young industrial designers, David Smith and Deane Richardson, in the hopes of gaining market leverage through superior design. In 1963 the Industrial Designers Institute awarded the resulting hand-controlled pallet truck with Crown's first national Design Excellence Award.

It was the beginning of a relationship that would last for three decades. Although the design firm remained a separate business entity, it would continue to participate in the development of virtually every materials handler in Crown's continuously expanding line. Eventually, these products accumulated dozens of major design awards. These honors, and the features and benefits they recognized, helped Crown garner a growing roster of customers. The company's own distribution and service network grew to include more than 20 locations in the United States and over 100 independent dealerships.

MORE PRODUCTS, MORE RECOGNITION: 1960–89

Throughout the 1960s and 1970s, Crown continuously expanded the power, capacity, and capabilities of its materials handlers. Although internal combustion engines dominated the lift truck industry from its inception, Crown concentrated exclusively on production of electric vehicles. The company added rider trucks, including the industry's first side-stance model, during the 1970s, and earned its first national account with the development of a stockpicking truck.

During the 1980s Crown introduced narrow-aisle reach trucks designed by Richardson and Smith that reduced the distance these handlers needed to maneuver between shelves in warehouses by at least one-third. The company extended this line with the launch of the TSP series of turret stockpickers, combining narrow-aisle capabilities with reaches as high as 45 feet. Narrower aisles meant more rows of shelves in storage facilities, and higher reaches meant those shelves could tower ever higher, effecting more efficient use of space and cost savings for Crown clients. The innovation won a Design Excellence Award from the Industrial Designers Society of America in 1981 and was selected as the Design of the Decade by that group in 1989.

Like so many other industries, from autos to electronics, the lift truck market was assaulted by competition from Japanese companies in the 1980s.

KEY DATES

1920s: The Pioneer Heat Regulator Company is founded by Carl, Oscar, and Allen Dicke.

1930s: Pioneer is sold to Master Electric Company, located in Dayton, Ohio.

1945: Crown Controls Company is founded by Carl, Allen, and Jim Dicke.

1947: Master Electric sells Pioneer's manufacturing operations back to the Dickes.

1949: The Dickes gamble on a new product introduction: television antennas.

1950: Allen Dicke leaves the business and Carl Dicke dies suddenly, leaving Jim in charge of the company.

1957: Crown begins selling a hand-pumped lift truck called the "walkie lifter."

1963: Crown's hand-controlled pallet truck is awarded the company's first national Design Excellence Award from the Industrial Designers Institute.

1966: Crown opens a manufacturing plant in Sydney, Australia.

1968: The company bets on its European expansion by purchasing a manufacturing plant in

Ireland and opening a sales/service office in London.

1973: A new manufacturing facility is opened in Querétaro, Mexico.

1989: Crown's line of turret stockpickers earn the Design of the Decade award by the Industrial Designers Society of America (IDSA).

1998: Crown's "Work Assist Vehicle," known as the Wave, wins numerous awards, including one from the Chicago Athenaeum, a museum honoring design and architecture.

2000: The WP 2000 series Walkie Pallet truck is awarded a "Gold" Industrial Design Excellence Award from the IDSA.

2001: The company ceases production of its television rotator antennas after more than 50 years.

2002: Crown opens a new sales and service facility in San Antonio, Texas.

2006: Crown establishes a manufacturing plant in Suzhou, China.

American firms' controlling stake in the domestic market began to melt away under the onslaught. From 1980 to 1983 alone, Japanese imports priced up to 25 percent less than domestic trucks seized one-third of the U.S. market. By mid-decade, the United States was a net importer of forklifts. Although the U.S. government later determined many of these foreign rivals were guilty of dumping (selling goods below fair market value in order to capture market share) the damage was already done.

While domestic manufacturers met the competition by moving production capacity (and with it thousands of U.S. jobs) overseas, Crown continued to manufacture about 85 percent of its components domestically. More than national pride was behind this policy. According to a 1992 *Design News* article, Crown considered vertical integration vital to maintain fidelity to its designs and manufacturing quality. Instead of outsourcing, the company accomplished virtually everything, from forming sheet metal and plastic parts to designing and manufacturing circuit boards for electronic controls, in its own plants. Crown even built a factory in New

Knoxville, Ohio, to produce electric motors. The company also avoided the merger and acquisition trend that swept the forklift industry in the late 1980s and early 1990s.

Just as it had in decades past, Crown's design prowess helped it break into another segment of the intensely competitive lift truck industry, counterbalanced lift trucks. Launched in 1990, Crown's FC line of vehicles offered advanced ergonomics that improved comfort and efficiency, including tilt steering, adjustable seating, fingertip controls, onboard diagnostics, and more. Considered the company's most ambitious development in three decades, the FC series won three major design awards and, more importantly, captured market share.

ELECTRIC SUCCESS

Crown's concentration on development and production of electrically powered lift trucks also proved providential. Electric forklifts overtook internal combustion engined models and held a slight lead through the early 1990s. Advantages such as quieter operation, less expensive maintenance and repair, and longer working life helped draw customers from the internal combustion segment. Increasingly stringent emission regulations and general environmental concerns also helped drive the shift toward electric-powered lift trucks.

To offset the notoriously cyclical—one analyst even characterized it as "rollercoaster-like"—nature of the lift truck market, Crown established overseas manufacturing, distribution, and sales operations in Australia, England, Ireland, Germany, and Mexico. Increased housing starts, low interest rates, and demand were cited as the impetus behind rising sales in 1992, 1993, and 1994, when the industry recovered from downturns in 1990 and 1991.

In the middle and later years of the decade, Crown continued to create better-engineered products with increasingly sophisticated features. As industry analysts forecast that the U.S. lift truck industry's rally would continue, growing to $1.8 billion by 1997, Crown was determined to capture a bigger slice of the market. One product in particular helped them immensely: "the Wave." Designed by Crown's dynamic duo of Richardson and Smith, the "Work Assist Vehicle" (subsequently known as the Wave) was capable of elevating both its operator and its load up to seven feet and proved a singular achievement in the materials handling industry in 1997.

By 1998 the Wave was heralded by industrial designers and customers alike for its maneuverability and versatility, and garnered a slew of awards including one from the Chicago Athenaeum, a museum of architecture and design. While the Athenaeum was known for honoring items it deemed capable of creating "awareness about contemporary design excellence," its usual fare did not include industrial forklifts. The Wave, however, expanded the museum's thinking as well as its many members.

As the century came to a close, Crown was still on a roll: the Wave was selling well, several new products were in development (such as three-wheel, pivoting, and higher-reach lift trucks), and sales for the fiscal year had hit a phenomenal $968 million. In addition, the company had bought an 850,000-square-foot manufacturing plant in Celina, Ohio, for a total of four facilities in its home state (including its New Bremen headquarters, as well as plants in Fort Laramie and New Knoxville). Crown also had two other U.S. manufacturing plants (in Indiana and North Carolina), three international facilities (in Australia, Germany, and Mexico), as well as dozens of sales/service offices throughout the United States, Europe, and Asia (including Australia, Belgium, England, Germany, Korea, Malaysia, the Netherlands, New Zealand, and Singapore).

A NEW CENTURY

In the new millennium, very little had changed about Crown and the way it did business. Despite overtures from rivals and international conglomerates, Crown remained a private and closely held company. Jim Dicke's son and grandson (Jim II and Jim III, respectively) had joined the family enterprise and risen through the ranks to management. The emphasis on forward-thinking designs, vertical integration, and globalization still held, including the company's requirement that all sales and dealer personnel be factory-trained (either in New Bremen or its European headquarters near Munich) on all equipment. While some considered Crown old-fashioned, with quality and safety coming first, there was no disputing its bottom line: sales for fiscal 2000 broke the billion-dollar mark ($1.01 billion) for the first time.

Over the next few years Crown's award-winning walkie pallets, stockpickers, and Waves continued to dominate the lift truck industry. New models of each thrilled customers large and small who found the products' maneuverability hard to beat. The Wave even found itself adorning the pages of *Fast Company*'s July 2002 issue, when Craig Vogel and Jonathan Cagen, authors of *Creating Breakthrough Products,* waxed enthusiastically about its superior design and other merits. Cagen declared: "It's small and fun to use. It empowers people. Although it's more expensive than a rolling ladder, workers become more efficient, and they stay in their jobs longer because they're happier."

By 2004, despite some dips in the forklift industry, Crown's sales were a solid $1.1 billion with a worldwide workforce of 6,900. New sales offices had opened in both the United States and Asia, with the latter accounting for more than 10 percent of the company's business. The following year saw a surge in sales and Crown's international presence, as revenues hit $1.5 billion and employees climbed to over 7,600. The company also announced its intention to open a manufacturing facility in Suzhou, China, in 2006 to service the burgeoning Asia-Pacific market.

Crown remained the nation's top brand of electric lift trucks and the fifth largest lift truck manufacturer in the world. While there were serious questions about the economy and a possible recession in 2008, few would bet against Crown's three generations of Dickes (Jim Dicke, as chairman emeritus; Jim II as chairman and chief executive, and Jim III as president). Quality and ingenuity were a well-established Dicke trait, as Jim III told *Forbes Global* (December 10, 2007), "We've always aimed to be the BMW of the lift truck industry."

April Dougal Gasbarre
Updated, Nelson Rhodes

PRINCIPAL SUBSIDIARIES

Crown Equipment Pty Ltd. (Australia); Crown Gabel-stapler GmbH & Company AG (Germany).

PRINCIPAL COMPETITORS

Caterpillar Inc.; NACCO Materials Handling Group; Toyota Material Handling USA, Inc.

FURTHER READING

Aldridge, James, "Forklift Maker Opening 40,000-Square-Foot Center Here," *San Antonio Business Journal,* May 17, 2002, p. 5.

Avery, Susan, "Design Updates Lift Trucks to New Heights," *Purchasing,* August 19, 1993, p. 85.

———, "Lift Trucks: The Competition Heats Up," *Purchasing,* February 7, 1991, p. 58.

"Basic Handlers: Pallet Trucks, Walkie Stacker and Reach Trucks," *Modern Materials Handling,* February 1994, p. 54.

"Bigger, Better, Faster, More!" *Beverage World,* August 1993, p. 85.

"Crown Equipment Corporation," *Material Handling Product News,* September 15, 2000, p. 13.

"Crown Receives Design Recognition," *Modern Materials Handling,* July 31, 1999, p. 25.

Dicke, James F., II, *Crown Equipment Corporation: A Story of People and Growth,* New York: Newcomen Society, 1995.

"Doing the Wave," *Beverage World,* July 15, 1999, p. 38.

Hammonds, Keith H., "How to Design the Perfect Product," *Fast Company,* July 2002, pp. 122+.

"Lift Truck Market Picks Up Speed," *Purchasing,* September 8, 1994, pp. 34–39.

Maloney, Lawrence D., "Crown Puts Design on a Pedestal," *Design News,* July 20, 1992, p. 46.

Martin, James D., "One-Stop Shopping," *Chilton's Distribution,* March 1988, p. 90.

McGaffigan, James, "What Narrow Aisle Lift Trucks Can Do for You," *Handling & Shipping Management,* March 1984, p. 50.

"New Warehouse, New WMS Streamline Inventory Management," *Modern Materials Handling,* June 1998, pp. 30+.

Petreycik, Richard M., "Forklift Report: Changing Gears," *U.S. Distribution Journal,* September 15, 1993, p. 47.

Rohan, M. Thomas, "Making 'Em Overseas," *Industry Week,* December 12, 1983, p. 28.

Schmall, Emily, "The BMW of Forklifts," *Forbes Global,* December 10, 2007, p. 62.

Sears, Warren, "Our Friend the Forklift," *Beverage World,* April 1995, p. S24.

"Spotlight: Narrow-Aisle Lift Trucks," *Transportation & Distribution,* June 2002, pp. 43+.

"Stackers for Tight Spaces," *Manufacturers' Monthly,* September 1, 2005, p. 58.

Webb, Bailey, "Industrial News," *National Real Estate Investor,* August 1999, p. 20.

Weiss, Barbara, "Crown Controls to Build New $6M Forklift Plant," *American Metal Market,* June 9, 1986, p. 12.

Yengst, Charles R., "Where Have We Seen This Before?" *Diesel Progress Engines & Drives,* January 1991, p. 4.

Cystic Fibrosis
Foundation

6931 Arlington Road
Bethesda, Maryland 20814
U.S.A.
Telephone: (301) 951-4422
Toll Free: (800) 344-4823
Fax: (301) 951-6378
Web site: http://www.cff.org

Nonprofit Company
Incorporated: 1955 as National Cystic Fibrosis Research
     Foundation
Employees: 550
Operating Revenues: $226.4 million (2006)
NAIC: 813212 Voluntary Health Organizations

■ ■ ■

Cystic Fibrosis Foundation, based in Bethesda, Maryland, has been dedicated since the mid-1950s to finding a cure for cystic fibrosis (CF), an inherited disease affecting the lungs and digestive tracts, so named because of the "fibrosis" (tissue scarring) of the biliary tract (with "cystic" an adjective referring to the urinary bladder or gallbladder). While not yet completely successful in its mission, the organization has spearheaded significant advances in the treatment of CF. Once the scourge of childhood, CF had caused death before a victim reached school age; a half-century later the median survival age is approaching 37. The foundation boasts 80 chapters across the United States and more than 250,000 volunteers who host fund-raising programs and events. It provides funding to 115 CF

care centers, 94 of which are adult care programs. Another 54 affiliate programs also receive foundation support. In addition to treatment centers, the foundation supports more than ten research centers in its Research Development Program, provides grants to encourage independent research, and spurs drug development through grants to private companies. All told, it provides support for some 30 potential new treatments for the disease. The foundation is well respected for its efficiency, spending about 90 percent of the money it raises on care, education, and research programs. Profits made from investments in private companies are also used to fund further research.

CF RECOGNIZED AS SEPARATE DISEASE: 1938

While aspects of CF were recognized for many years, it was not until 1938, when Dr. Dorothy Andersen published "Cystic Fibrosis of the Pancreas and Its Relation to Celiac Disease: A Clinical and Pathological Study" in the *American Journal of Diseases of Children*, that CF was recognized as a separate disease. Dr. Andersen was also the first to posit that CF was a hereditary disease transmitted by a recessive gene possessed by both parents. As a result of her pioneering efforts, physicians began to specialize in the care of children with CF. One of their number was a young doctor at Columbia Presbyterian Medical Center in New York City, Dr. Paul di Sant'Agnese, who developed a key diagnostic tool that would remain in use more than half a century later, the sweat test.

During a severe heat wave in 1948 di Sant'Agnese and his colleagues first noticed that most of the people

COMPANY PERSPECTIVES

The mission of the Cystic Fibrosis Foundation, a nonprofit donor-supported organization, is to assure the development of the means to cure and control cystic fibrosis and to improve the quality of life for those with the disease.

admitted to the hospital for heat prostration were CF patients. This observation was reinforced four years later by another heat wave, during which di Sant'Agnese recognized that CF children were losing electrolytes at an abnormally high rate, leading to extremely salty perspiration. Believing that this phenomenon distinguished those with CF from the general population, in 1953 he and a colleague developed a simple and painless test to detect high levels of chloride to help in the diagnosis of CF. The child's hand or foot was placed on a culture medium, a sheet of agar laced with silver nitrate and potassium chromate, laid in a flat glass dish. Normal children left only faint impressions, while CF children, whose perspiration contained ten times as much salt, left a prominent imprint on the agar. The test was about 99 percent certain and the diagnosis could be later confirmed by more advanced tests.

FOUNDATION FORMED: 1955

In 1954 di Sant'Agnese and some parents of children suffering from CF formed the Cystic Fibrosis Association in New York City. Other chapters were soon formed in Connecticut and California. Some of those concerned parents included New York mother Doris Tulcin, trucking executive Robert L. Natal of Bayside Queens, New York, and Boston physician Dr. Wynne Sharples (who had two children with CF and whose husband, Dr. Robert Denton, developed a breathing apparatus to alleviate the suffering of CF victims), all of whom, as well as other concerned parents, would play lead roles in the organization. In 1955 they and other volunteers brought the association chapters together into a new nonprofit organization, the National Cystic Fibrosis Research Foundation. "We had to do something. Children were dying and physicians didn't know what the disease was. They had no prognosis for it. There was no research. There was nothing," Tulcin recalled in an interview with the Cystic Fibrosis News Bureau years later.

At first, the organization established its headquarters in Philadelphia, Pennsylvania. In 1955 the foundation

issued its first research grants to Dr. Andersen and di Sant'Agnese and Dr. Harry Shwachman. The first grant was $10,000. Fund-raising was conducted solely on the local level until September 1960 when the first national campaign was launched. A year later the foundation began its accredited care center program, opening a pair of centers. In 1962 the number of centers would increase to 30. By this time, the efforts of the foundation and CF researchers had succeeded in lengthening the median survival age of CF patients to approximately ten years.

In 1965 the trademarked term "65 Roses," the way CF is commonly referred to by children, was coined. One foundation volunteer, Mary G. Weiss, whose three young boys suffered from CF, was overheard by one of the children, four-year-old Richard, making a series of fund-raising telephone calls for the organization. He surprised her when he claimed to know what she was working for: "65 roses." What Richard misheard was easier for children to pronounce than cystic fibrosis and quickly caught on within the CF community.

A clinical fellowship program was sponsored by the foundation in 1965 as a way to bring basic scientists into CF research. It was also late in 1965 that the foundation laid plans for a five-year $1.5 million coordinated research program, intended to speed up the discovery of CF's cause and a way to control the disease. In order to help in this effort, a year later the foundation created a data registry to track the histories for all patients at its accredited care centers. Five years would not be enough time to complete the research mission, however. While this important work was carried on, the foundation also made progress in its educational effort. In 1968 it hosted its first National-International Medical Conference. The first national seminar held by the foundation to address the needs of young adults with CF was held in 1972.

MOVE TO WASHINGTON, D.C., IN 1978

The foundation in 1978 moved its headquarters from Philadelphia to the Washington, D.C., area, a more advantageous location given that it was the seat of federal power as well as the home of the National Institutes of Health, a major provider of research funding. It was also in 1978 that the foundation conducted its first national fund-raising event, Bowl for Breath, a bowling tournament. It was highly successful and became a fund-raising staple for local chapters of the organization. Some of that money would be put to use in increasing the number of foundation accredited care centers to 125 by the end of the year.

KEY DATES

1954: Cystic Fibrosis Association is formed.
1955: Association chapters combine to form National Cystic Fibrosis Research Foundation.
1965: The phrase "65 Roses" is trademarked.
1978: Headquarters are moved to Washington, D.C., area.
1989: CF gene is discovered.
1993: First CF drug is approved.
1997: Second CF drug is approved.
2000: Cystic Fibrosis Foundation Therapeutics is formed.
2005: Median survival age approaches 37.

The early 1980s brought a number of changes to the foundation. In 1981 the first satellite care centers were established for adults, needed because the life expectancy for CF sufferers had reached 20 years. At the start of the decade the Research Development Program was established, creating a network of university research centers. To support the program Doris Tulcin launched the first capital program ever conducted by a voluntary health organization, the goal to raise $15 million. Private enterprise was encouraged to become involved as well, provided with financial incentives to develop drugs for CF and other less common diseases from the Orphan Drug Act signed into law in 1983. Scientists were also making progress in their research during this period. In 1983 they were able to demonstrate that cells lining the lungs of CF patients did not properly move chloride into the airways. Moreover, CF was receiving more national attention due to well-known sportswriter and novelist Frank Deford, who wrote a book about his daughter, who died of CF at the age of eight. Deford was named chairman of the foundation's board of trustees and used his celebrity status to raise the profile of CF.

Working closely with Deford was the foundation's first chief executive officer, Robert K. Dresing, a successful businessman who owned three Ethan Allen furniture stores in Ohio and Florida. The father of a son with CF, Dresing became the volunteer president in 1982 and two years later became CEO, applying his business experience to the running of the organization. "I brought a bottom-line mentality to an organization that had never been run like a for-profit group." Among the changes he made were incentive-based pay and centralized management.

CF SERVICES ESTABLISHED: 1988

By the start of the second-half of the 1980s, the life expectancy of CF reached 25 years. The foundation enjoyed improved success in its fund-raising efforts, building donations to the $20 million mark in 1986, due in part to a made-for-television movie based on Deford's book that ran that year on the ABC network, *Alex: The Life of a Child.* The extra funds allowed the foundation in 1988 to establish CF Services, Inc., a national pharmacy that made CF drugs and treatments available across the country. The most significant event of this period, and arguably the turning point in the history of the foundation, was the 1989 discovery of the cystic fibrosis gene, along with its protein product, by scientists supported by the foundation: Francis Collins, John Riordan, and Lap-Chee Tsui. For the first time, rather than merely treat the symptoms of CF, researchers could replicate a healthy version of the gene to seek out the root cause of the disease in order to speed the creation of drugs and gene therapies.

In 1990 researchers achieved "proof of concept" in a lab dish, showing that gene therapy for CF was possible. Three years later a gene therapy trial began in CF patients and demonstrated correction in CF cells for treating nasal passages. Also in 1993 the Food and Drug Administration (FDA) approved the first biotech drug for CF, Pulmozyme, which breaks down the thick mucus deposited in lungs caused by CF.

The foundation underwent a major reorganization in 1993 that transferred some of its assets to a private company headed by Dresing, who would resign as the foundation's CEO and take about half of the foundation's employees to run the offshoot. Included were the foundation's healthcare service, direct-mail fund-raising operation, and mail-order pharmacy business. Dresing agreed to run these operations on an audited, no-profit basis for the benefit of the foundation, but was free to make a profit from other health-related ventures. Some trustees and outside observers questioned whether Dresing was receiving a sweetheart deal, or whether the foundation would be better served by considering other third-party companies to run the units. Deford, however, dismissed these criticisms, telling the *Washington Post,* "If you are happy with the people you have, then I don't think you should go through the motions of going outside." He added, "Do you really think we could get anybody to do this for free or at cost? He's not making any money out of this." By making the switch, the foundation also hoped it would be able to better focus its resources to finding a cure for CF.

APPROVAL OF SECOND CF DRUG: 1997

A second CF drug, TOBI, an inhaled antibiotic, received FDA approval in 1997. In that same year, the foundation established the Therapeutics Development Program in order to shepherd potential CF drugs through the development and regulatory approval process. Seven specialized clinical research centers were opened to form the Therapeutics Development Network. On another front, the foundation created the Adult Task Force to address issues faced by an increasing number of adults with CF due to the increasing age of survival.

Although a decade passed since the identification of the CF gene, progress on the development of drug treatments was not as great as the foundation had hoped. Rather than awarding small grants to academic researchers, by the start of the new century a greater emphasis was placed on encouraging private companies to become involved. Because the market for CF drugs was small, financial incentives were necessary.

In the 1990s the foundation had enjoyed a successful partnership with the development of TOBI. After funding the early FDA trials, it was able to sell the rights for $17 million in cash to PathoGenesis, which benefited because TOBI soon became its top-selling product. This experience led to the foundation adopting a new business model and the 2000 creation of Cystic Fibrosis Foundation Therapeutics to oversee drug discovery and development funding. In addition, Cystic Fibrosis National Bioinformatics Center was established to further spur drug and treatment development. While it was legal for it to invest in private companies, the foundation preferred to provide funding for development and trials and then take royalties. (Later investments would ask for multiples on the investment in lieu of royalties.)

By the spring of 2001 the foundation gave money to 11 companies, both established and start-ups, including Genzyme, MoliChem Medicines, Inologic, Altus Biologics, Structural GenomiX, Copernicus Gene System, and Genaera Corp. It also provided seed money to PathoGenesis, Inspire Pharmaceutics, and SciClone Pharmaceuticals. Another $46.9 million was pledged to Aurora Biosciences in May 2000, contingent on the discovery of three drug candidates and meeting certain milestones over a five-year period.

Basic science was not neglected, however. In 2000 researchers funded by the foundation completed the genetic map of *Pseudomonas aeruginosa* bacterium, the most common cause of CF lung infections. The private companies backed by the foundation would soon enjoy

successes as well. In 2003 Structural GenomiX scientists were able to determine the three-dimensional structure of a portion of the CF protein product, thus clearing the way for many more drug discovery possibilities. A year later there were about two dozen CF therapies in various stages of development. Some of the more promising ones proved to be disappointments: Boehringer Ingelheim's anti-inflammatory drug was pulled during Phase II trials in July 2004; Amelubant failed in trials later in the year; and in 2005 Targeted Genetics' aerosol gene treatment was terminated during Phase II trials. Others took their place in the pipeline, though.

The median age for survival for CF patients approached 37 years in 2005, a tribute to the efforts of the foundation over the course of 50 years. More drugs entering advanced clinical trials for FDA approval and new investments in companies to introduce more drug candidates into the pipeline promised to increase the survival age. Better diagnostic tools also offered hope, because early intervention could prevent lung deterioration and add decades to a patient's life. The day was likely approaching that the Cystic Fibrosis Foundation would reach its ultimate goal: putting itself out of business. On that day, with a cure found, another scourge of childhood, like polio, would begin to become a mere memory.

Ed Dinger

PRINCIPAL SUBSIDIARIES

CF Services Pharmacy; Cystic Fibrosis Foundation Therapeutics; Cystic Fibrosis National Bioinformatics Center.

FURTHER READING

Angier, Natalie, "New Advances Offer Cystic Fibrosis Victims Heartening Prospects," *New York Times,* August 28, 1990, p. C3.

"Breath of Fresh Air for Cystic Fibrosis Drug Pipeline," *Pharmaceutical Approvals Monthly,* December 1, 2007.

"Cystic Fibrosis Foundation Marks 50 Years in the Fight Against Cystic Fibrosis," *Medical News Today,* January 26, 2005.

"Cystic Fibrosis Unit Sets 5-Year Research Study," *New York Times,* December 5, 1965.

Madden, Stephen, "Sweet Charity," *Fortune,* February 13, 1989, p. 113.

Moukheiber, Zina, "Drug Money," *Forbes,* April 2, 2001, p. 80.

"Robert L. Natal, 57, Trucking Executive," *New York Times,* April 26, 1967.

Spayd, Liz, "Charity's Reorganization Questioned," *Washington Post,* October 23, 1993, p. A1.

"Warning Sweat," *Time,* August 5, 1957.

ditech.com

3200 Park Center Drive, Suite 150
Costa Mesa, California 92626
U.S.A.
Telephone: (714) 800-5800
Toll Free: (800) 803-7656
Fax: (714) 800-5801
Web site: http://www.ditech.com

Wholly Owned Subsidiary of Residential Capital LLC
Incorporated: 1995 as DiTech Funding Corporation
Employees: 400
Sales: $150 million (2006 est.)
NAIC: 522292 Real Estate Credit

■ ■ ■

Ditech.com provides mortgage loans to consumers through its web site and via telephone, operating as a direct-to-consumer lender on a national basis. The company offers first mortgages, fixed-rate second mortgages, and home equity lines of credit, conducting the bulk of its business with borrowers who are charged the prime interest rate. The company is organized as a business unit of Residential Capital, LLC, which controls the mortgage-related subsidiaries owned by General Motors Corporation. Cerberus Capital Management, L.P., a New York-based private equity firm, holds a 51 percent stake in Residential Capital, which is often referred to as "ResCap."

REDDAM STRIKES GOLD

Ditech.com enjoyed nationwide exposure early in its development, joining the elite tier of companies whose brands were household names. The widespread recognition of the company could be credited to its founder, John Paul Reddam, a professor of philosophy, Thoroughbred owner, and, after his achievements with ditech.com, one of North America's most successful consumer loan experts.

Born in 1955 in Windsor, Ontario, Canada, Reddam left his hometown with a bachelor's degree and a passion for horse racing. He earned his degree in psychology from the University of Windsor and cultivated his love for horse racing at the Windsor Raceway, where he frequently could be found watching harness races. Reddam attended graduate school at the University of Toronto, where he earned a master's degree in philosophy before earning his doctorate from the University of Southern California. He remained in California after completing his education, eventually joining the faculty at California State University, Los Angeles, where he taught philosophy. Reddam also actively joined the sport of horse racing after moving to California, purchasing his first Thoroughbred in 1988, the first of more than 60 racing and breeding horses he would acquire through the years.

Reddam began creating a name for himself in the residential loan sector in January 1995, the month he formed DiTech Funding Corporation, the name of his company at its inception. DiTech, a portmanteau of "direct" and "technology," was created to participate in the retail mortgage market, but unlike nearly all other

COMPANY PERSPECTIVES

People are smart. It's our mind that kept us from becoming dinner for prehistoric carnivores. It's our intellect that enabled us to place a robot on a planet a couple hundred million miles away. And it's our ability to apply knowledge that tells us it's not a good idea to stick a fork in a light socket. Or fry bacon in the nude for that matter. When you stop to think about it, proof of our smart is everywhere. We prove theorems. We build skyscrapers. We buy low and sell high. We cure diseases. We split atoms. And if we're really smart, we split aces and eights. It's true—people are smart. And it's the customer's smart that we respect and strive to live up to; because people know what they want in life. They know what's best for them and their family. And they know that if we offer competitive home mortgages and smart financial solutions, together, we can make the most of our smart. That is, if we're smart about it.

competitors in the market, Reddam's company conducted its business without traditional retail offices. DiTech became one of the first companies to offer mortgages online, which, along with a toll-free number, served as its means of conducting business with the public. The approach could work, but only if his marketing efforts convinced borrowers to switch from using traditional brokers and enter the more ephemeral realm of online mortgage banking.

MARKETING LEADS TO EARLY GROWTH

To succeed, Reddam's business plan needed to broadcast its message to a large audience. Initially, his efforts to market DiTech's services were limited to Southern California. He began in April 1995, when he started originating, selling, and servicing mortgage loans tied to the prime interest rate. The ambitious nature of Reddam and his business model soon spread DiTech's presence beyond the confines of California, extending the company's operating territory to seven states by the end of the year, an abbreviated one in which the company originated $302 million in loans. Quickly, the geography of the company's area of influence broadened, spilling out to include customers in 46 states by the end of 1996, when the company originated $621 million in loans. By the end of the following year,

DiTech originated $1.2 billion in loans secured by properties in 49 states. Within two years, the company had become a rising force, a new competitor in the field that owed its prominence to the power of marketing.

During the first three months of 1998, DiTech originated more than half the total amount of loans it originated in the previous year. The company was growing, and it was growing at a rapid pace. Reddam delved into other business areas of his chosen field, offering subprime rates to borrowers in 1996, but the reasons for his success went beyond which types of loans he was offering. Marketing propelled DiTech forward, giving it the volume of customers required to fuel its geographic march. Reddam advertised on radio, on billboards, and, most extensively, on television, airing commercials on several national cable channels. The commercials featured an exasperated loan officer continually frustrated by losing business to DiTech, prompting him to utter the marketing campaign's tagline, "lost another loan to DiTech." The advertisements turned DiTech into a household name, generating a wealth of business for the young company.

As his business grew, Reddam began servicing other types of loans, diversifying beyond DiTech's first product, prime first mortgage loans. He dabbled in subprime lending, but spent most of his energy marketing prime high-loan-to-value (HLTV) second mortgages. To convince consumers to replace their adjustable-rate real estate loans with fixed-rate loans, Reddam introduced a $395 flat-fee program, touting loans that enabled consumers to borrow up to 125 percent of their home's value, 125 LTV loans, with no restrictions on how the money was spent.

NEW OWNERS IN 1999

DiTech attracted customers in droves. In 1999, the company originated nearly $4 billion in loans, a volume of business that attracted the attention of GMAC Mortgage, part of the financing arm of automaker General Motors Corporation. One of the largest residential lenders in the United States, GMAC Mortgage acquired DiTech in 1999, a deal that reportedly netted Reddam $80 million. Reddam stayed with DiTech until the following year, leaving to pursue business interests that eventually led to his formation of another California-based finance company, CashCall, Inc.

Under the control of GMAC Mortgage, DiTech turned into ditech.com, but the slight change in name did not weaken the awareness of the company's brand. The widespread recognition of the name represented one of the primary reasons GMAC Mortgage completed

KEY DATES

1995: J. Paul Reddam establishes DiTech Funding Corporation.

1999: Reddam sells his company to GMAC Mortgage.

2005: Control of the company, operating as ditech.com, becomes the purview of Residential Capital Corporation.

2006: Richard D. Powers is named ditech.com's leader.

2007: A new marketing campaign, aimed at distancing the company from the subprime lending sector, is launched.

the purchase, giving its already stalwart position in the residential mortgage market the added boost of a well-known brand name, not to mention a nearly $4 billion addition to its loan portfolio. For its part, ditech.com enjoyed the vast resources possessed by the General Motors Corporation family of companies. It was able to invest in the development of new loan products, new technology, and in its customer-service infrastructure.

Within the folds of General Motors Corporation, ditech.com became a difficult company to track financially. It reported its loan production figures through GMAC Mortgage, making assessments of its progress during the first years of the decade more speculation than calculation. The company was profitable, however, at least according to Michael McCarthy, ditech.com's leader. Although no longer heavily involved in providing 125 LTV loans, ditech.com maintained its appeal among consumers, particularly those looking to refinance their mortgages.

ORGANIZATIONAL CHANGES IN 2005

After a lull in notable events, significant developments occurred as ditech.com celebrated its tenth anniversary. In 2005, General Motors Corporation reorganized its mortgage subsidiaries, putting the companies under the control of Residential Capital Corporation, a holding company that converted into a limited-liability company the following year. In November 2006, one month after Residential Capital Corporation became Residential Capital, LLC, General Motors Corporation announced it was selling a 51 percent interest in its finance arm to New York-based Cerberus Capital Management, L. P., a private equity firm.

POWERS TAKES COMMAND IN 2006

Amid the restructuring efforts, ditech.com gained a new leader. In mid-2006, McCarthy resigned as the company's general manager, which led to the appointment of Richard D. Powers to the company's top office. Under Powers' control, ditech.com would undergo the most substantial changes in its identity since the early days of Reddam's leadership. Powers joined ditech.com from Metrociti Mortgage Corp., where he served as president of the company's western division. Before working for Metrociti, Powers served as president of homebuilder KB Home's mortgage unit, a post he accepted after serving as a senior executive at Charter One Mortgage, an affiliate of Charter One Financial.

Shortly after joining ditech.com, Powers altered the message the company broadcasted over the airwaves. The biggest news in the mortgage industry at the time was the developing crisis in the subprime lending sector, a debacle of profound proportions that threatened to inflict heavy damage on the rest of the mortgage industry and the national economy as well. Subprime lenders, their fortunes tied to borrowers with suspect credit histories, were foundering in bunches, creating a maelstrom of negative publicity that stained the mortgage industry's image. Powers, who took the helm of ditech.com as the subprime sector began to reel, moved quickly to mitigate the damage incurred by his new company.

A NEW MARKETING MESSAGE

For roughly a decade, ditech.com had relied on a frustrated loan officer to convey the company's message to the public. The commercials were ingrained in the minds' of consumers, but Powers realized the company was delivering the wrong message. By surveying focus groups, Powers discovered consumers believed ditech.com was a subprime lender, precisely the last message the company wanted to send. Despite public perception of its involvement in the beleaguered sector, ditech.com only flirted with subprime lending, generating just 13 percent of its business from loans made to those with shaky credit histories, a percentage that was 7 points below the national average for mortgage lenders.

Powers sought to change public perception of ditech.com and distance his company from the troubled subprime sector by ordering a new advertising campaign. "We are doing a full-blown review of the various channels we utilize for getting our message out," Powers said in a November 26, 2006, interview with the *Orange County Register.* "We are making some changes." The company launched its "People Are Smart" campaign, which stressed making prudent decisions based on expert advice given by the company's loan consultants. Also, for the first time, ditech.com mentioned it was a "GMAC company" in its commercials, both onscreen and in a voice-over, thereby tapping into GMAC's reputation as a disciplined lender.

PRODUCT OFFERINGS

As ditech.com pressed forward, the company continued to retool its loan offerings to attract customers. Among its products was its "Real Life Plan," a three-in-one finance tool launched in 2007. The plan combined a fixed-rate, 30-year mortgage, a no-fee home equity line, and a no-fee MasterCard, enabling customers to pay down their loan principal at an accelerated pace. "We had all three products independently in the past," Powers explained in a June 2007 interview with *Origination News*. "GMAC introduced a credit card that pays back a mortgage. Following that a few competitors launched a couple of products, which tells me that there's something there, that we're on to something."

Ditech.com also enjoyed success with two other types of loan packages, which along with its Real Life Plan, ranked as the company's three most popular products as it prepared for the future. The company's "Sleep EZ Loan" was a 30-year loan structured to allow customers to pay only the interest for the first ten years of the loan. Ditech.com also offered "Equity Builder," which it claimed could save $68,000 in interest payments on a $250,000 loan over a 23-year period. Along with its stable of new products, the company also offered the $395 flat-fee home loan that had made it famous during the 1990s. The loan offerings, coupled with 24-hour, seven-days-a-week sales support and a strong Internet presence, were the tools Powers hoped

would lead to a successful future for ditech.com. The company had demonstrated a direct-to-consumer lender could succeed. In the years ahead, ditech.com intended to solidify its position in the mortgage industry and entice more consumers to take the direct approach to securing a home loan.

Jeffrey L. Covell

PRINCIPAL COMPETITORS

Countrywide Financial Corporation; E-LOAN, Inc.; Quicken Loans Inc.

FURTHER READING

Bergquist, Erick, "Joking Aside, Ditech Goes with New Tack in Its Ads," *American Banker*, November 14, 2006, p. 15.

"Ditech.com and Digital Convergence Introduce Redesigned Web Site," *PR Newswire*, December 1, 2000.

"Ditech.com Chief Out, Replacement Named," *National Mortgage News*, July 31, 2006, p. 21.

Dymi, Amilda, "Ditech's Combination Loan Evolves," *Origination News*, June 2007, p. 10.

Harrop, Froma, "Bankruptcy Is Now Just One Click Away," *Austin American-Statesman*, February 10, 2000, p. A19.

Muolo, Paul, "Three at Ditech Indicted, Founder Reddam Resigns," *National Mortgage News*, May 8, 2000, p. 1.

Padilla, Mathew, "Ditech.com Dreams of Big Growth in Home-Loan Business Despite Softening Market," *Orange County Register*, November 26, 2006.

Sinnock, Bonnie, "New Ditech Executive Vows to Retool Marketing," *National Mortgage News*, November 27, 2006, p. 12.

Taylor, Dennis, "DA Charges Firm's Claims Don't Add Up," *Business Journal*, January 5, 1998, p. 1.

Dot Hill Systems Corp.

2200 Faraday Avenue, Suite 100
Carlsbad, California 92008
U.S.A.
Telephone: (760) 931-5500
Toll Free: (800) 872-2783
Fax: (760) 931-5527
Web site: http://www.dothill.com

Public Company
Incorporated: 1999
Employees: 269
Sales: $239.2 million (2006)
Stock Exchanges: NASDAQ
Ticker Symbol: HILL
NAIC: 334112 Computer Storage Device
Manufacturing

■ ■ ■

Dot Hill Systems Corp. makes redundant array independent disks (RAID) storage products, such as storage area networks (SANs), primarily for businesses in the data-intensive industries of financial services, telecommunications, and government agencies. It outsources manufacturing and sells through channel partners, such as Sun Microsystems and Hewlett-Packard. Its products are certified to meet industry standards and military specifications, as well as RoHS and WEEE international environmental standards. The company has offices and manufacturing facilities in China, Germany, Israel, Japan, the Netherlands, and the United Kingdom, as well as the United States.

THE MERGER OF TWO STORAGE SYSTEM COMPANIES: 1999

Throughout the 1990s, the boom in e-commerce, Y2K upgrades, and business-to-business initiatives generated a heavy demand for data storage products. According to Mark Schlack, editor of *Storage* magazine in a 2003 article, faced with the new age of information, companies had to choose between throwing out data, making their existing storage systems more efficient, or buying new storage capacity. "Throwing it out is not really an option ... and making systems more efficient requires—at least in the short term—an increase in the number of employees, and that takes money. So most people just end up buying more storage." Other factors contributing to the increased demand for "data independence" included the falling cost of disk drive devices for storing data, the enormous storage requirements of email and software applications, and an increasing demand for data warehousing and analysis capabilities.

In 1999, banking on the growth of the data storage market, Box Hill Systems Corp. of New York acquired Artecon, Inc., of Carlsbad, California, and the two companies merged to form Dot Hill Systems. Both Box Hill, which had formed in 1988, and Artecon, which began in 1984, had turned a steady profit during the 1990s. The new Dot Hill specialized in the development of storage area networks or SANs, which relied on fiber channel technology and protocols to move information from data storage systems to servers at very high speed. The merger occurred just as the bottom dropped out of the tech industry. Dot Hill Systems immediately began trading on the New York Stock Exchange (NYSE). It employed 60 workers in Carlsbad and 160 in New York as well as 60 others in its offices worldwide.

Dot Hill initially focused all of its attention on data storage systems for the telecommunications market, specifically on developing a new storage product it called SANnet. About the size of two stacked pizza boxes, this storage solution debuted with ten disks backed up by two power supplies, two fans, two controllers, and two of every other necessary component. The SANnet box could store any sort of digital information, including voice-mail messages and online photos. It could survive a direct lightning hit, a prolonged dust storm, and temperature fluctuations from 23 to 150 degrees Fahrenheit. Network servers used SANnet boxes to store email, and the U.S. Army installed them in tanks to store maps and information from Global Positioning Systems.

FACING A SLOWING MARKET AND BROADENING ITS PRODUCT LINE: 1999–2002

Philip Black, former chief executive officer of Box Hill, and James Lambert, former chief executive officer of Artecon, together served as the joint heads of the new company, with Black focusing on international operations and Lambert on domestic concerns. Lambert had founded Artecon, Inc., with Dana Kammersgard, who eventually succeeded Lambert. In 1998, sales for the two companies combined had reached $33.2 million, and although in 1999 Dot Hill's revenue dipped to $30.1 million, the company continued to roll out new products that were readily accepted as the Internet demanded ever larger and faster storage capacity. In 2000, the company opened an office in Beijing called Dot Hill China to sell and maintain Dot Hill systems as well as to orchestrate efforts to find business partners in China.

By the first quarter of 2000, the company was back on track financially and was competing successfully with its larger, more powerful rivals, such as EMC, IBM, and Compaq. However, by the time that Lambert became sole chief executive in late 2000, Dot Hill had fallen into what would become a three-year slump that depleted most of its cash supply. From September to October 2000, the company's stock price was halved. In 2001, revenues dropped from $121 million the previous year to $56 million, and the company lost $42.7 million. From 2001 to 2002, the company lost $78 million.

In response to the decrease in sales, which Dot Hill attributed to the economic downturn overall, particularly in the telecommunications and commercial sectors, the company shuttered its manufacturing plant in Carlsbad and cut its workforce of 440 by 30 percent. More significantly for its future, Dot Hill broadened its product line to reach new industries and shifted its marketing efforts from direct to indirect sales. It began selling its products through resellers, systems integrators, and original equipment manufacturers (OEMs).

SIGNING WITH SUN, RECOVERING FROM A SLUMP: 2002–03

In 2002, the company signed a three-year contract to supply Sun Microsystems with low-end storage systems that could handle data ranging from 100 gigabytes to five terabytes. The contract with Sun specified that Dot Hill would make private-label products for Sun in return for which Sun would buy the outstanding shares, or up to 5 percent, of Dot Hill stock. The idea was that Sun would get its customers to buy storage when they bought Sun's servers.

The arrangement worked. The magnitude of the contract with Sun was such that, in the year following its inception, Dot Hill's revenues tripled, and the company returned to profitability. Sun's short-term loan and purchase orders, however, could not afford Dot Hill the market capitalization or shareholder equity it needed to remain on the NYSE, and in 2002, the company moved its listing to the American Stock Exchange.

In 2003, the company's share price began once again to rise from $3 to $15 and Dot Hill began to trade on the NASDAQ. By late December 2003, the recovery in the technology industry and the stock market turnaround spelled good news for Dot Hill. The industry's two biggest trends—demand for storage and the shift to Linux—worked in Dot Hill's favor, especially as Dot Hill worked on Linux open-source software. Revenues for 2003 reached $187.4 million, up from $46.9 million in 2002. During the period from

KEY DATES

1984: James Lambert and Dana Kammersgard found Artecon, Inc., of Carlsbad, California.

1988: Box Hill Systems Corp. of New York is founded.

1999: Box Hill acquires Artecon and Dot Hill Systems forms of the merger of the two; company begins trading on the New York Stock Exchange.

2000: Company opens an office in Beijing called Dot Hill China; Philip Black resigns as co-chief executive officer of Dot Hill, leaving James Lambert as the company's sole chief.

2001: Company shutters its manufacturing plant in Carlsbad and cuts its workforce of 440 by 30 percent.

2002: Company signs a three-year contract with Sun Microsystems; moves its listing to the American Stock Exchange.

2003: Dot Hill moves to the NASDAQ.

2004: Dot Hill acquires Chapparal Network Storage.

2006: Dana Kammersgard becomes chief executive officer.

December through March, the company, still in the red, raised $24 million of additional capital in a private placement that it put toward product development.

EXPANDING EARNINGS, CUSTOMERS, AND PRODUCTS: 2003–06

Dot Hill's revenues continued to increase at an exponential rate for the next several years, earning it a recurrent place on Deloitte's Technology Fast 50 Program for San Diego beginning in 2003. From 2000 to 2004, company revenues increased by 97.5 percent. From 2001 to 2005, they climbed about 315 percent. By 2006, Dot Hill was earning $239.2 million, up from $233.8 million the year before.

However, Dot Hill still needed to broaden its customer base in order to thrive. In 2004, the Sun contract accounted for 83 percent of Dot Hill's revenues, leading investors to see Dot Hill as overly dependent on Sun Microsystems and causing its stock price once again to drop to $5 a share. Thus, from 2005 to 2007, Dot Hill expanded and extended its product

purchase and development agreement with business partners. In 2005, it signed a new agreement with Sun stipulating that it would continue to develop storage solutions for Sun through January 2011. The company also entered into agreements with a number of companies, including Alliance Systems, Newtech, Fujitsu Siemens Computers, Stratus Technologies, On-Stor, Reldata, MiTAC International, SYNNEX, Promark Technology, Viglen, Hewlett-Packard, and SEPATON.

The company also developed its products in an aim to reach more customers. In mid-2004, after acquiring Chapparal Network Storage, a company that made subsystems that delivered data across storage networks and served primarily midrange companies, Dot Hill introduced a new high-end storage server made with low-cost parts. The Chapparal purchase enlarged Dot Hill to about 200 employees worldwide and allowed it to compete more effectively in the midrange. The following year, it created a new storage architecture and designed a highly modular system architecture as the foundation for a new generation of storage products. In 2006, it was awarded its 17th patent for improving the web browser interface that enabled system administrators to manage storage subsystems by accessing any browser around the globe.

NEW LEADERSHIP, NEW HEADQUARTERS, NEW FOCUS: 2006–07

During this period, too, Dot Hill also went through a changing of the guard. In August 2004, Lambert became vice-chairman of the company and Kammersgard was promoted to president. In his new position, Lambert focused more on corporate strategies while Kammersgard ran the company's day-to-day operations. In March 2006, Lambert retired as Dot Hill's chief executive after 22 years and Dana Kammersgard became the new chief executive officer and also joined the board of directors.

Dot Hill also expanded its physical base in 2006, nearly doubling the capacity of its headquarters when it moved into a new 58,000-square-foot facility with 12,000 square feet of climate-controlled lab space. The lab included more than 32 terabytes worth of Dot Hill storage products, supported by ten servers as well as a broad spectrum of competitive products for comparison.

The opening of an onsite technical training center followed one month later to offer comprehensive experiential learning in all technical aspects of Dot Hill products to both current and prospective OEM customers. The center was also used to train Dot Hill sales and support personnel. According to Kammersgard in a 2006 company press release, the new headquarters rendered Dot Hill "fully prepared for our next wave of growth." A year later, the Technology Council of Southern California named Dot Hill a finalist for "Hardware and Storage Company of the Year," and Kammersgard announced that Dot Hill would focus on transitioning its supply chain to new partners, reducing the cost of goods, adding more OEM customers to further diversify revenues, aggressively managing operating expenses, and launching new, higher margin products.

Carrie Rothburd

PRINCIPAL COMPETITORS

EMC Corporation; Hitachi Data Systems; International Business Machines Corporation.

FURTHER READING

Bigelow, Bruce V., "Data Storage Business Booms," *San Diego Union-Tribune,* September 17, 2000, p. H1.

Dougherty, Conor, "Carlsbad's Dot Hill Corp. Now Basks in Sunshine; Revenues Triple, Three-Year Slide Ends After Firm Signs Lucrative Contract," *San Diego Union-Tribune,* July 11, 2003, p. C1.

Freeman, Mike, "Dot Hill Trips over Job Cuts, Lower Revenues," *San Diego Union-Tribune,* March 22, 2001, p. C1.

Linecker, Adelia Cellini, "Dot Hill Systems Corp. Carlsbad, California; A Lucrative New Deal Gives Tech Firm a Lift," *Investor's Business Daily,* September 10, 2003, p. A6.

Stutzman, Erika, "Longmont, Colorado, Data Storage Firm Bought by Dot Hill Systems of California," *Boulder (Colo.) Daily Camera,* February 25, 2004.

Egmont Group

Vognmagergade 11
Copenhagen K, DK-1148
Denmark
Telephone: (+45 33) 30 55 50
Fax: (+45 33) 32 19 02
Web site: http://www.egmont.com

Private Company
Incorporated: 1878 as P. Petersen, Printers
Employees: 3,782
Sales: EUR 1.24 billion ($1.9 billion) (2006)
NAIC: 511120 Periodical Publishers; 511130 Book
Publishers; 512110 Motion Picture and Video
Production; 512120 Motion Picture and Video
Distribution; 512191 Teleproduction and Other
Postproduction Services

■ ■ ■

Egmont Group is a leading media group in the
Scandinavian market and one of the largest in Europe.
The Copenhagen-based company publishes magazines,
books, and comic books; produces and distributes motion pictures and television programming; is active in
broadcast television and movie theater operation;
develops advertising; and manages book clubs, among
other activities. Egmont's operations are grouped into
seven primary divisions. Egmont Magazines' flagships
are family-oriented *Hjemmet* (Home), the women's
magazine *ALT for damerne* (Everything for Women),
and celebrity gossip weekly *Her & Nu* (Here & Now).
Egmont produces local editions of these titles for most

of the Scandinavian markets. The company also
produces men's magazines and more than 80 special
interest magazine titles. This division represented more
than 15 percent of Egmont's EUR 1.24 billion ($1.9
billion) in 2006 revenues.

Egmont Kids & Teens is the Scandinavian regions's
leading publisher of youth-oriented magazines, comics,
games, and other products, including mobile services.
The largest part of this division is its comic books
production, led by longtime flagship *Donald Duck*,
under license from Disney. This division produced over
14 percent of the group's sales. Egmont Books, accounting for 16 percent of sales, includes Danish publishers
Aschehoug, Alinea, Forlag Malling Beck, as well as
Damm, present in both Norway and Sweden. The
company's publishing operations focus on fiction and
on the youth market. This division operates book clubs
and, since 2006, the chain of Tanum bookstores in
Norway. Egmont has been a prominent film producer
and distributor since its merger with Nordisk Film in
1992. That division produces and distributes motion
pictures and television programming; operates its own
chain of movie theaters; produces games for the PlayStation; and since 2006 owns 50 percent of record
company The Music Business Organisation. Egmont
also owns 50 percent of TV2 Group, which operates six
channels in Norway. The company's Egmont
International division includes the company's operations
in central and Eastern Europe, the United Kingdom,
China, and elsewhere. This division, focused on youth-
oriented book and magazine publishing, generated 22
percent of group sales. In all, Egmont is present in more
than 23 countries. The remaining division oversees the

COMPANY PERSPECTIVES

Storytelling is the cornerstone of all Egmont's activities. Egmont's mission is to create and tell stories in every medium imaginable. From paper to the plasma screen. From entertainment to education. From high to popular culture. From manga to music.

Egmont is visible in the daily lives of millions of people. Our Nordic media universe embraces weeklies, magazines, comics, youth magazines, games, activity products, books and educational materials. Egmont also encompasses films, TV programs and music, cinemas and TV stations, interactive games and game consoles.

Outside the Nordic region, we focus on books and magazines for children and young people. Since its inception in 1878, Egmont has been a solid company that makes a positive contribution to society—through donations to charitable causes, as a cultural broker and as a workplace for 3,800 dedicated and professional staff.—Steffen Kragh, president and CEO

company's Charitable Activities, which include the Nordisk Film Foundation and Egmont Højskolen adult schooling project. Egmont is controlled by a privately held family foundation. The company is led by CEO Steffen Kragh.

FLYSWATTER START IN 1878

Egmont H. Petersen was just 17 years old when he launched his own printing business in Copenhagen in 1878. Petersen had just finished a four-year apprenticeship. With few employment opportunities at the time, Petersen had little choice but to attempt to create his own business. In this, he was aided by his mother, Petrine, a seamstress, who put up all of her belongings, including her pots and pans and especially her sewing machine, as collateral against Egmont's purchase of a printing press. Because Petersen was underage, his business was placed under his mother's name. The company remained known as P. Petersen up until Egmont's death in 1914.

Petersen's first press was of the so-called flyswatter type. This type of press was operated by hand and capable of producing only one sheet, with just one color, at a time. Petersen launched his business in the

kitchen of his mother's boarding house. By day, he went about Copenhagen drumming up business, and printed at night for delivery the next morning.

Petersen's skill at highly decorative typography and borders, and his insistence on high quality, helped his business prosper. Within a year Petersen had completed the purchase of the press. He then moved into a dedicated print shop, adding new machines and hiring his first employees in 1880. The company's continued expansion led to several more moves. By 1895, P. Petersen employed 25 people. Petersen himself had earned the nickname of "Kunst" (Art) Petersen, for the quality of his work.

Part of the company's growth came from its commitment to adopting new technologies. In 1892, the company became the first in Denmark to print in color. This commitment continued into the next century. In 1919, for example, the company later became the first in the country to install offset printing machinery.

By that time, the company had moved to still larger quarters, in a building dubbed Gutenberghus after the inventor of the printing press. The first phase of construction was completed shortly after Egmont Petersen's death in 1914. By then, the company, which had been placed under the ownership of the Egmont H. Petersen Foundation, had changed its name to Gutenberghus.

HOME MAGAZINE SUCCESS IN 1904

Part of the reason behind the name change was that the company was no longer simply a printer. One of the company's major clients at the dawn of the 20th century had been the magazine *Damernes Blad*. The women's weekly was quite small, with a circulation of only 2,000. In 1902, the magazine's publisher went out of business, and Petersen, as its primary creditor, took over control of the magazine. By 1904, the company had transformed the magazine from a women-oriented title to a new family-oriented format called *Hjemmet* (Home). The new formula was an instant success and by the end of the year had seen its circulation rise to 24,000.

Hjemmet quickly became the cornerstone of a fast-growing magazine division within the company. By the time of Petersen's death, its circulation had topped 100,000 in Denmark. The title remained the company's flagship throughout the century and into the next. It also provided the company with its first international expansion. The company added a Norwegian edition in 1911, and by 1921 had introduced a Swedish version as well.

KEY DATES

1878: Egmont H. Petersen sets up a printing business with a single hand-operated press in his mother's kitchen.

1904: Company launches first successful magazine title *Hjemmet.*

1911: First international operations begin with launch of *Hjemmet* edition in Norway.

1914: Company changes name to Gutenberghus, after its new corporate headquarters.

1948: Company acquires license to produce Donald Duck comics in Scandinavian region.

1963: Company enters book publishing through acquisition of Aschehoug.

1976: Subsidiary is established in London.

1992: Company merges with Nordisk film group, is renamed Egmont Group, and becomes founding partner of TV2 television broadcasting group.

1998: Egmont acquires Reed Publishing's Children's Books division in the United Kingdom.

2007: Egmont acquires Bonnier's Denmark operations; announces plans to enter U.S. children's books publishing market.

The next phase of Gutenberghus's growth was led by Jens Christian Petersen (no relation to Egmont). I. C. Petersen, as he was known, introduced a more business-like orientation to the company, targeting greater efficiency. As part of that effort, the company launched several new areas of operation, including its own advertising agency, as well as a paper warehousing business. I. C. Petersen also changed the company's focus from a small number of large-scale customers, to a larger number of smaller customers.

Under I. C. Petersen, Gutenberghus grew into Denmark's leading printer and publisher. The company had also moved into a larger, purpose-built site in the heart of Copenhagen. By the time of his death, the company had expanded to include more than 200 printing presses and more than 1,000 employees.

IF IT QUACKS LIKE A DUCK: 1948

Axel Egmont Petersen, the founder's oldest son, took over as head of the company following I. C. Petersen's death in 1944. The company by then had been joined by Dan Folke, who had established an earlier career as a highly popular singer and songwriter. Folke provided the inspiration behind some of Gutenberghus's greatest successes as a magazine publisher. Folke had spent time traveling the United States in the 1920s, and in 1948 he went back to the United States, this time to secure the publishing license for the highly successful *Reader's Digest* magazine. By 1945, the company had launched a Norwegian edition, shortly followed by a Danish edition. Both became bestsellers for the company.

Folke also led Gutenberghus in the development of its own successful magazine format. In 1946, the company launched the women's format *ALT for damerne* (Everything for Women), which became the most successful magazine of its type in the Scandinavian region.

Yet Folke's and Gutenberghus' greatest success came with the company's launch into the comic book sector. In 1948, Folke, on his travels to the United States, met with Walt and Roy Disney, and secured the Scandinavian rights to the Donald Duck comic. The new comic was a huge success, and established Gutenberghus as a major force in the youth-oriented publishing market. By 1951, the company had secured the rights to launch Donald Duck comics in Germany and the Netherlands. For this purpose, the company established its German subsidiary that year.

By the end of the 1950s, Donald Duck had a circulation of 140,000 in Denmark alone. The company converted the magazine from a monthly to a weekly. Previously, the company had reprinted storylines developed by the American edition, which remained a monthly. In order to fill the pages of its new weekly edition, Gutenberghus began developing its own storylines. The company formed a new subsidiary for this operation, Gutenberghus Publishing Service. This permitted the company to expand further into the comics market, launching a new series of popular titles through the 1960s and 1970s. The company also launched the highly successful series of pocket books based on Donald Duck and other Disney characters.

BOOK PUBLISHER FROM THE SIXTIES

Gutenberghus had by then entered the mainstream book publishing market as well. For this, the company had taken over one of its major print customers, Aschehoug, which neared bankruptcy in 1963. This purchase gave the company a number of new titles, including *Flittige Hænder* and *Dansk Familieblad.* By the end of the 1960s, the company had combined its comic book expertise with its book publishing operations, publishing the highly popular Asterix series in both Denmark and Germany.

Further acquisitions boosted the company's publishing operations through the 1970s. These included Wangels Forlag and the Danske Bogsamleres Klub book club. The company also expanded its operations into the United Kingdom, founding a subsidiary to publish comic books for that market in 1976.

Further expansion through the 1980s helped boost the company's international operations. In 1984, for example, the company acquired Norway's Damm publishing group. The following year, Gutenberghus bought Franz Schneider Verlag, a children's book publisher based in Munich, as well as Forlaget Litas, which published children's books and operated a chain of retail toy stores.

A major expansion of the group's publishing arm was completed in 1988, when it acquired the Lademann group, which included the Komma, Holkenfeldt, and Sesam imprints. These companies were then regrouped under Gutenberghus's Aschehoug operations in 1991.

MEDIA GROUP IN THE NEW CENTURY

The collapse of the Soviet empire provided the company with new expansion opportunities. Starting from 1990, Gutenberghus established subsidiaries in Poland, Russia, and the Czech Republic. Through that decade and into the next, the company added operations in most of the Eastern European markets.

By then, the company had taken on a new name, Egmont Group. Part of the impetus toward this was its merger in 1992 with Nordisk Film Foundation. That company, which claimed the title of the world's oldest film production company, had been founded in 1906. The company had also established itself as a major producer of television programming. Egmont and Nordisk had previously collaborated on a television broadcasting project, WeekendTV, which had failed to launch in the early 1980s. Instead, in 1992, the newly merged company became founding partners of Norway's TV2 television group. TV2 quickly grew into the country's leading commercial broadcasting company.

By the year 2000, Egmont had parlayed its publishing and broadcasting operations into an extension into the fast-growing new media markets. The company launched its first interactive video game titles, for the Sony PlayStation, at the beginning of the 2000s. By the middle of that decade, the company claimed to be the leading Scandinavian producer of electronic entertainment products.

The company had also continued to expand its international publishing wing. In 1998, the company moved toward the lead in the British children's books publishing sector when it acquired the Children's Books division from Reed Publishing. In 2003, the company merged its Aschehoug and Lademann subsidiaries into a single unit, renamed as Aschehoug. The new company then became Denmark's second largest publisher. By October 2007, however, Egmont moved closer to the lead, following its acquisition of Bonnier's Danish publishing division.

From a single printing press, Egmont had grown into a major European media corporation. With sales of nearly EUR 1.24 billion ($1.9 billion), the company had expanded into an internationally operating company, with a presence in nearly 25 markets. The company continued to set its sights on a new horizon: in November 2007, the company announced plans to establish a U.S.-based children's books publishing division. The company expected to launch its first titles in that market by 2009.

M. L. Cohen

PRINCIPAL SUBSIDIARIES

Aktsiaselts Egmont Estonia; Aschehoug Dansk Forlag A/S; Dagmar Teatret A/S; Damm Förlag AB (Sweden); Denmark Ejendomsselskabet Gothersgade 55 ApS; Egmont AS; Egmont Bulgaria EAD; Egmont CR s.r.o. (Czech Republic); Egmont Creative A/S; Egmont d.o.o. (Croatia); Egmont Holding GmbH (Germany); Egmont Holding Ltd. (U.K.); Egmont Holding Oy (Finland); Egmont Hong Kong Ltd.; Egmont Hungary Kft. Budapest; Egmont International Holding A/S; Egmont Latvija SIA; Egmont Magasiner A/S; Egmont Polska sp. z o.o.; Egmont Romania S.R.L.; Egmont Serieforlaget A/S; Egmont Specialblade A/S; Egmont Tidskrifter AB (Sweden); Forlag Malling Beck A/S; Mailbox Media A/S; Mailbox Media MBM AB; N.W. Damm & Søn AS (Norway); Nordisk Film A/S; Ny Tid AS (Norway); Skandinaviske Skoledagbøker AS 85% (Norway); Tanum AS (Norway); The Music Business Organisation A/S (50.1%); UAB Egmont Lietuva (Lithuania); UnionPak A/S; Vagabond Media AB (Sweden).

PRINCIPAL COMPETITORS

Bertelsmann AG; VNU Business Media Europe Ltd.; Quebecor Inc.; Orkla ASA; Reed Elsevier PLC; SanomaWSOY Group; Axel Springer Verlag AG.

FURTHER READING

De Laine, Michael, "Egmont Makes Danish Merger," *Bookseller*, July 4, 2003, p. 9.

Eccleshare, Julia, "Egmont Buys Reed Children's Books," *Publishers Weekly*, May 11, 1998, p. 15.

"Egmont Acquires Student Calendars Publisher," *Nordic Business Report,* October 4, 2005.

"Egmont Plans US Unit," *Publishers Weekly,* November 19, 2007, p. 4.

Holman, Tom, "Egmont Bounces Back with Record Profit," *Bookseller,* April 5, 2002, p. 7.

Petersen, Jes Dorph, and Soren Kaster, *EGMONT 1878–2003,* Copenhagen: Aschehoug Dansk Forlag A/S, 2003.

EnPro Industries, Inc.

5605 Carnegie Boulevard, Suite 500
Charlotte, North Carolina 28209
U.S.A.
Telephone: (704) 731-1500
Fax: (704) 731-1511
Web site: http://www.enproindustries.com

Public Company
Incorporated: 2002
Employees: 4,700
Sales: $928.4 million (2006)
Stock Exchanges: New York
Ticker Symbol: NPO
NAIC: 339991 Gasket, Packing, and Sealing Device
　Manufacturing

■ ■ ■

EnPro Industries, Inc., is a leading manufacturer of engineered industrial products. EnPro serves dozens of industries, including chemical and petrochemical processing, pulp and paper manufacturing, food processing, pharmaceutical manufacturing, petroleum refining, and U.S. defense and shipbuilding. The company's subsidiaries include Garlock Sealing Technologies, a manufacturer of industrial gaskets and sealing systems; GGB, a manufacturer of bearings; Stemco, a developer of wheel-end component parts and systems for the truck and trailer market; Quincy Compressor, a manufacturer of air compressors; and Fairbank Morse Engine, a manufacturer of diesel engines and dual-fuel engines. EnPro divides its business into three segments: sealing

products, engineered products, and engine products and services. Sealing products account for nearly half of EnPro's annual sales. The company operates 32 manufacturing facilities in the United States and in eight other countries.

ORIGINS

When EnPro was formed in 2002, two companies were involved in its creation. EnPro was new in name, but its assets enjoyed a legacy stretching back to the 19th century, bearing the fingerprints of two American icons in the manufacturing industry. Goodrich Corporation, more well known as the tire-making pioneer BFGoodrich, and Coltec Industries, the former firearm pioneer Colt Industries, were the architects of EnPro's creation, each contributing the stories of their development to the formation of the $700-million-in sales entity that debuted in 2002.

COLTEC INDUSTRIES' BACKGROUND

In parsing the business EnPro called its own in 2002, Coltec figured as the dominant contributor to the industrial materials operations that began trading on the New York Stock Exchange in June. Coltec Industries' roots were embedded in the achievements of several luminaries, originating from the pioneering work of Samuel Colt, the inventor and industrialist who patented the first revolving cartridge firearm in 1836. His invention, which was a precursor to his legendary Colt.45 revolver, led to the establishment of the Colt's

COMPANY PERSPECTIVES

We've succeeded by executing clear strategies, designed to provide our businesses with the tools they need to prosper. We've improved operational efficiency through Total Customer Value, our lean manufacturing program, and with investments in our facilities and equipment. We've invigorated product development and marketing programs to create a new generation of products and to grow in new industrial and geographic markets. We've improved the mix of our businesses with a number of acquisitions, and we're poised to find more acquisition opportunities. We've managed our subsidiaries' asbestos claims to reduce their effect on our cash flows. The result is growing sales, improving segment profits, increasing cash flows we can use to expand the value of our company and a commitment to continue the effective execution of the strategies that have led to our success.

Patent Fire-Arms Manufacturing Company in 1847, the year Coltec could claim as its founding date. Coltec also was indebted to several other individuals whose manufacturing and engineering feats gave it a rich history. O. J Garlock patented his first industrial sealing systems in 1887, marking the beginning of a business fundamentally important to EnPro. Charles Morse, in 1893, manufactured the first internal combustion engine to be commercially successful in the United States. The Holley brothers, through Holley Motor Car Company, manufactured their first automobile at the dawn of the 20th century.

The entity that brought the companies together under one corporate banner was a coal company named Pennsylvania Coal and Coke Corporation. Founded in 1911, the company embarked on an acquisition campaign in the early 1950s, acquiring the successor to Colt's business, O. J. Garlock's business, and the Holley brothers' business. The arrival of the companies transformed Pennsylvania Coal and Coke from a miner into a manufacturer, a change in business focus that necessitated a name change. In 1954, the company became known as Penn-Texas Corporation, the first of three name changes that would be made in the next decade. After merging with the successor to Charles Morse's business, Fairbanks Morse and Co., in 1959, the company changed its name to Fairbanks Whitney Corporation. In 1964, the company settled on a lasting

corporate title, honoring the achievements of its earliest predecessor by adopting the name Colt Industries, Inc.

Over the course of the next several decades, Colt Industries continued to diversify. Under the leadership of David Margolis, who served as chairman and chief executive officer, the company built a presence in a number of industries, particularly businesses that operated in the automotive, aerospace, and industrial materials markets. By the mid-1980s, Margolis had built Colt Industries into a $1.6-billion-in-sales company with roughly 50 manufacturing facilities in operation throughout the world.

GUFFEY TAKES CHARGE OF COLTEC INDUSTRIES IN 1995

Arguably the most profound changes in Colt Industries' history occurred after Margolis' tenure and after the company shed its namesake business. In 1990, Colt Industries sold its firearms business, a divestiture that led it to change its name to Coltec Industries. A few years later, another leader took charge who would usher in the period of transformation that led to the formation of EnPro.

John W. Guffey embraced change. When he was promoted from president and chief operating officer to the post of chief executive officer in the summer of 1995, he wasted little time before implementing sweeping changes. Partly for logistical reasons and partly to jar Coltec Industries' corporate culture, he moved the company's headquarters from Park Avenue in New York City to Charlotte, North Carolina, within his first year in charge. He also ordered the disposal of the company's automotive original-equipment business, orchestrating the sale of a $400 million business that left Coltec Industries one-third smaller and focused on industrial equipment and aerospace equipment such as aircraft landing gear. The moves sent a shockwave throughout the organization, but they would pale in comparison to what happened to Coltec Industries after Guffey sat down to dinner with David L. Burner, the head of BFGoodrich Corporation.

BFGOODRICH ENTERS THE PICTURE

Burner headed a company that was no stranger to change. His company had been founded in 1870 by Dr. Benjamin Franklin Goodrich, who claimed the distinction of establishing the first rubber company located west of the Allegheny Mountains. A list of pioneering achievements in the design and manufacture of tires were credited to the company in subsequent decades,

KEY DATES

1995: John Guffey, Jr., is appointed chief executive officer of Coltec Industries.

1996: Guffey moves Coltec Industries' headquarters from New York City to Charlotte, North Carolina.

1999: Coltec Industries merges into BFGoodrich Corporation.

2002: Coltec Industries' industrial materials business is spun off as EnPro Industries.

2003: EnPro Industries' stock value increases by 250 percent.

2006: EnPro Industries acquires Amicon Plastics Inc.

2008: EnPro Industries acquires Sinflex Sealing Technologies.

including its invention of the tubeless tire in 1946. Like Guffey's company, however, BFGoodrich evolved into different business areas. In the early 1960s, the U.S. government turned to the Ohio-based company for its help in designing the space suits astronauts would wear at the end of the decade in the first manned space flights, marking the company's first involvement in the aerospace market. Shifting priorities led BFGoodrich to abandon the tire business entirely in 1988 as it focused its resources on developing aerospace and performance materials.

The year Guffey was promoted to chief executive officer of Coltec Industries, BFGoodrich celebrated its 125th anniversary as a company wholly devoted to aerospace and performance materials. In 1997, two years later, BFGoodrich completed the acquisition of a $1-billion-in-sales supplier of complex, integrated aircraft systems. Burner spearheaded the deal, and the following year, intent on strengthening BFGoodrich's aerospace business, he made a dinner appointment with Guffey.

The two chief executives met at Quail Hollow Country Club in Charlotte in November 1998. Guffey thought he would be discussing a business deal, but after Burner informed him that his management team had been scrutinizing Coltec Industries for three or four months and was interested in buying the company, the dinner conversation turned into an all-night affair. Guffey and Burner discussed details late into the night and resumed their meeting the following morning, when they sat across from each other over breakfast at the Park Hotel in Charlotte. After hours of discussion,

the two-day meeting resulted in an acceptable plan. Guffey and Burner had hatched out the particulars of an all-stock merger of Coltec Industries and BFGoodrich valued at $2.2 billion.

The proposed business combination promised to create a nearly $6-billion-in-sales aerospace and performance materials giant. It was a corporate marriage that numerous parties found unacceptable, triggering "what Wall Street observers say was one of the longest and most bitter acquisitions in U.S. industrial history—the deal from hell," according to the December 1999 issue of *Business North Carolina.* Partly because the merger would create a dominant competitor in the market for aircraft landing gear and partly because the merger called for BFGoodrich to move its corporate headquarters from Richfield, Ohio, to Charlotte, the announcement of the deal unleashed a storm of protest. The merger butted against two antitrust investigations, the intervention of three members of the U.S. Congress and the attorneys general of three states, and lawsuits filed by two competitors before it was completed in mid-1999.

1999 MERGER OF COLTEC INDUSTRIES AND BFGOODRICH

The merger greatly strengthened BFGoodrich's aerospace and performance materials businesses and gave it a third stream of revenue: Coltec Industries' industrial materials business. Burner anticipated the addition of the third business segment in a statement published in the November 30, 1998, issue of *Chemical Market Reporter.* "This merger," he said, "significantly enhances BFGoodrich's aerospace business, and with Coltec's high-margin, engineered industrial products business, we are adding an important third leg that balances our aerospace and performance materials portfolio and enhances our excellent prospects for continued growth." Following the merger, BFGoodrich derived 60 percent of its revenue from aerospace products, 25 percent from performance materials, and 15 percent from industrial materials.

BFGOODRICH PREPARES TO SPIN OFF ENPRO

Shortly after the merger was completed, Guffey left the BFGoodrich-Coltec organization, but Burner was not done orchestrating major deals. In 2001, he sold the company's performance materials business, a divestiture that left the company reliant on aerospace products and industrial materials. It also led to a name change, turning BFGoodrich Corporation into Goodrich Corporation. The sale was the first step of a two-step plan to leave Goodrich wholly focused on the aerospace market. Burner next set his sights on what he had referred to as the company's "third leg," Goodrich's Engineered Industrial Products division, a business that was about to gain independence and emerge as EnPro.

In January 2002, EnPro was incorporated as a subsidiary of Goodrich in anticipation of the spinoff of the Engineered Industrial Products division to Goodrich shareholders. Selected to lead the company was Ernest F. Schaub, a 30-year Goodrich veteran. Schaub, who was appointed as EnPro's president and chief executive officer in May 2002, had spent the previous three years serving as Goodrich's executive vice-president and president and chief operating officer of the company's Engineered Industrial Products division, the former Coltec Industries assets slated to debut as EnPro.

DEBUT OF ENPRO: 2002

EnPro began trading on the New York Stock Exchange in June 2002, an occasion heralded by Schaub in a statement published in the June 3, 2002, issue of *Business Wire*. "Today is a banner day for EnPro," Schaub announced. "We are truly excited to join a respected list of publicly traded industrial products companies, and to have the opportunity to succeed as a more tightly focused and flexible company that is prepared to respond to the changing demands of our markets."

Schaub took charge of a company that at its birth had revenues of roughly $700 million and employed 4,400 workers at 33 manufacturing facilities in nine countries. EnPro's operations included names well known to its clientele, including Garlock Sealing Technologies, Glacier Garlock Bearings, Fairbanks Morse Engines, Quincy Compressor, and Stemco. Its products—gaskets, metal polymer bearings, compressor systems, engines, and other engineered products—played a vital role in industrial applications. The one glaring weakness of the newly independent company was its exposure to asbestos lawsuits stemming from Garlock Sealing Technologies' use of asbestos in its products until 2001. The company was confident it could avoid any major repercussions, however. It noted that the gaskets containing asbestos were encapsulated and were primarily purchased by the U.S. Navy and large petrochemical companies, customers who understood the risks involved.

PROMISING FIRST YEARS

EnPro's first years in business produced encouraging results. After a shaky start (the company lost $3 million in 2002) Schaub could greet shareholders with positive news. EnPro posted $33.2 million in net income in 2003, recorded five victories in six asbestos lawsuits, and, most heartening to shareholders, registered a massive 250 percent increase in its stock value. Financial growth during the next two years was impressive as well, lifting net income to $58.6 million and revenues to $838 million by the end of 2005.

As EnPro prepared for the future, it relished its newfound independence. With Schaub at the helm, the company was looking to expand its business in the three operating segments composing its operations: engineered products, sealing products, and engine products and services. Part of the company's expansion plans hinged on completing acquisitions. In 2006, EnPro purchased Amicon Plastics Inc., a Houston, Texas-based producer of fluoropolymer and engineered plastic components for semiconductor, pump and valve, and oilfield customers. In 2008, the company completed another purchase, acquiring the assets of Sinflex Sealing Technologies, a distributor and manufacturer of industrial sealing products located in Shanghai, China. In the years ahead, further deals were expected as EnPro searched worldwide for opportunities to expand its business.

Jeffrey L. Covell

PRINCIPAL SUBSIDIARIES

EnPro Industries Int'l Trading (Shanghai) Co. Ltd. (China); Kunshan Q-Tech Air System Technologies Ltd. (China); Coltec Industries Inc.; Coltec do Brasil Productos Industriais Ltda. (Brazil; 89%); Coltec Finance Company Limited (U.K.); Coltec Industrial Products LLC; Coltec Industries France SAS (25%); Coltec Industries Pacific Pte. Ltd. (Singapore); Coltec International Services Co.; Coltec Productos y Servicios S.A. (Mexico; 25%); Stempro de Mexico S. de R.L. de C.V. (25%); Compressor Products Holdings, Inc.; Corrosion Control Corporation; GGB LLC; Garlock (Great Britain) Limited (U.K.); Garlock Korea, Inc. (89%); Garlock Sealing Technologies LLC; Garrison Litigation Management Group, Ltd. (92.3%); GGB Brasil Industria de Mancaia E Componentes Ltda. (Brazil); GGB, Inc.; HTCI Inc.; Holley Automotive Systems GmbH (Germany); QFM Sales and Services, Inc.; Stemco Holdings, Inc.

PRINCIPAL DIVISIONS

Engineered Products; Sealing Products; Engine Products and Services.

PRINCIPAL COMPETITORS

SKF USA Inc.; Federal-Mogul Corporation; Caterpillar Inc.

FURTHER READING

Antosiewicz, Frank, "EnPro Industries Buys Amicon," *Plastics News,* July 10, 2006, p. 5.

Cariaga, Vance, "Coltec's Guffey: Goodrich Merger Is Going to Happen," *Business Journal Serving Charlotte and the Metropolitan Area,* May 14, 1999, p. 4.

"EnPro Industries Acquires Chinese Sealing Products Distributor and Manufacturer," *PR Newswire,* January 24, 2008.

"EnPro Industries, Inc. Begins NYSE Trading As Fully Independent Company," *Business Wire,* June 3, 2002, p. 2061.

"Goodrich-Coltec Merger Complete," *Chemical Week,* July 21, 1999, p. 5.

Martin, Edward, "Good Rich Deal," *Business North Carolina,* December 1999, p. 20.

Mecia, Tony, "New Charlotte, N.C., Goodrich Spinoff Takes Off," *Charlotte Observer,* June 4, 2002.

Scheraga, Dan, "BFGoodrich, Coltec Merge into Engineered Materials and Aerospace Powerhouse," *Chemical Market Reporter,* November 30, 1998, p. 3.

Smith, Geoffrey, "How to Restructure," *Forbes,* April 21, 1986, p. 141.

Speizer, Irwin, "Goodrich Spinoff Needs Sales in Scale with Price," *Business North Carolina,* May 2004, p. 22.

ESTĒE LAUDER
COMPANIES

The Estée Lauder
Companies Inc.

767 Fifth Avenue
New York, New York 10153-0023
U.S.A.
Telephone: (212) 572-4200
Fax: (212) 572-6633
Web site: http://www.elcompanies.com

Public Company
Incorporated: 1946 as Estée Lauder Inc.
Employees: 28,500
Sales: $7.04 billion (2007)
Stock Exchanges: New York
Ticker Symbol: EL
NAIC: 325620 Toilet Preparation Manufacturing; 446120 Cosmetics, Beauty Supplies, and Perfume Stores; 454111 Electronic Shopping

■ ■ ■

Founded in 1946 by Estée Lauder and her husband, Joseph, The Estée Lauder Companies Inc. is one of the leading makers and marketers of upscale cosmetics, fragrances, and hair care and skin care products in the world. Estée Lauder products are sold in more than 135 countries, with around 51 percent of net sales originating in the Americas; 35 percent in Europe, the Middle East, and Africa; and 14 percent in the Asia-Pacific region. The company uses a variety of channels to distribute its products, concentrating primarily on upscale department stores, specialty retailers, upscale perfumeries and pharmacies, and prestige salons and spas. In addition, Estée Lauder products are available for purchase online at the firm's own web sites and those of certain retailers, and the company operates around 600 single-brand and multibrand, freestanding retail stores worldwide, with the majority situated in the United States. The Lauder family controls around 89 percent of the company's voting stock.

The company's main brands, in order of their introduction or acquisition, include the original Estée Lauder line, including skin treatment, makeup, and fragrances; Aramis, a group of men's toiletries (1964); Clinique, a hypoallergenic line (1968); Prescriptives, an upscale line aimed at the urban, multiethnic crowd (1979); Lab Series, a men's skin care line (1987); Origins, a botanical treatment line designed to appeal to the environmentally conscious consumer (1990); M•A•C, a professional makeup artist line of cosmetics and makeup products (1994); Bobbi Brown, a professional beauty line (1995); the La Mer skin care line (1995); Aveda, a "new age" cosmetics and hair and skin care line (1997); Jo Malone, a prestige skin care, fragrance, and hair care line originating in London (1999); Bumble and bumble, a salon-based line of quality hair care products (2000); and Darphin, a prestige skin care and makeup line originating in Paris (2003). In addition, Estée Lauder sells several brands, including American Beauty, Flirt!, and Good Skin, exclusively at the discount department stores and web site of Kohl's Corporation, and it also holds global licenses to sell fragrances and cosmetics under the Tommy Hilfiger, Donna Karan, Michael Kors, Sean John, Missoni, Daisy Fuentes, and Tom Ford brand names.

COMPANY PERSPECTIVES

The guiding vision of The Estée Lauder Companies is "Bringing the best to everyone we touch." By "The best," we mean the best *products*, the best *people* and the best *ideas*. These three pillars have been the hallmarks of our Company since it was founded by Mrs. Estée Lauder in 1946. They remain the foundation upon which we continue to build our success today.

THE DEVELOPMENT OF AN ENTREPRENEUR

Estée Lauder was born Josephine Esther Mentzer in Corona, Queens, New York, in 1908, the ninth child of Rose and Max Mentzer, who had immigrated from Hungary to the United States. Regarding her interest in cosmetics, which originated in childhood, Lauder reportedly recalled: "I loved to make everyone up. ... I was always interested in people being beautiful ... [people] who look like they have a cared-for face."

Lauder was first inspired to enter the business of cosmetics when her uncle, John Schotz, a chemist from Hungary, established New Way Laboratories in Brooklyn in 1924. Her uncle's products included a Six-in-One Cold Cream, Dr. Schotz Viennese Cream, and several perfumes. Lauder got her start by selling these products in New York City and then, from 1939 to 1942, in Miami Beach as well.

In 1944 Lauder began working in various New York salons and smaller department stores, selling her own product line from behind a counter. Of that original line, three skin creams were her uncle's creations. Lauder also sold a face powder, an eye shadow, and a lipstick called Just Red. Soon the entrepreneur was spending Saturdays selling her products on the floor in Bonwit Teller department store on Fifth Avenue. Lauder's next goal was to get her items into Saks Fifth Avenue. She convinced the Saks buyer that there was a demand for her products after a successful lecture and demonstration at the Waldorf Astoria that prompted customers to line up outside for more product information. One unique aspect of Lauder's products would remain a classic Estée Lauder approach over the years; the fledgling cosmetics dynamo was selling lipsticks in upscale metal cases at a time, just after World War II, when most lipsticks were packaged in plastic.

In 1946, the year Lauder's company officially got started, women's cosmetics was a $7 million business in the United States. The Saks connection helped Lauder achieve a reputation that would allow her to sell her products nationally. Beginning in the late 1940s, Estée Lauder traveled the country, making personal appearances in specialty and department stores and training staff in proper sales techniques. She made impressions on influential people early on, securing a spot in I. Magnin's of San Francisco, a store well-respected in the retail trade. I. Magnin's carried Lauder's products exclusively in the San Francisco area until the late 1970s. During these early years, Lauder met buyers all over the country and others in the business who would later help her achieve success.

Against the advice of their lawyer, Lauder and her husband entered full-scale into an industry known for extreme market swings and short-lived endeavors. Joseph Lauder worked every day at the small space they had rented, while their oldest son, Leonard, made deliveries to Saks and other stores on his bicycle.

One technique that Estée Lauder pioneered—now a standard in the cosmetics industry—was the gift-with-purchase offer. Lauder first began offering free sample items with any purchase to bring the customer back for more. Later, free products were made available to customers who made purchases of a specified minimum dollar amount. Lauder's gift-with-purchase offer gained her a loyal following and helped establish her business. Over the years, however, this practice would lead to markedly low profit margins in the cosmetic industry as a whole and at Lauder's company in particular.

THE 1953 DEBUT OF YOUTH DEW

Early in the 1950s, with $50,000 saved from business profits, Lauder began looking for an advertising representative. After learning that the amount was hardly enough to finance a full-scale campaign, she chose to begin advertising with the help of Saks Fifth Avenue's direct-mail program. The company's advertising budget would soon grow considerably, with the introduction of a new product.

Lauder reunited in the early 1950s with a fragrance executive she had met a decade earlier in order to develop a perfume. Following the examples of Helena Rubenstein and Elizabeth Arden, who had both made their starts in skin care and then moved on to fragrances, Lauder developed a bath oil with a fragrance that lasted for 24 hours. She called the bath oil Youth Dew and introduced it in 1953 at $8.50 a bottle.

With Youth Dew Estée Lauder became an overnight success. "Middle America went bananas for it," stated

KEY DATES

1946: Estée Lauder and her husband, Joseph, found Estée Lauder Inc.

1953: Company introduces the immensely successful bath oil, Youth Dew.

1964: The male fragrance Aramis makes its debut.

1968: Estée Lauder introduces Clinique, a hypoallergenic line.

1972: Leonard Lauder, son of the founders, is named company president.

1979: Prescriptives brand debuts.

1990: The botanical treatment line Origins is introduced.

1993: In its first licensing venture, Estée Lauder signs an exclusive deal with fashion designer Tommy Hilfiger.

1995: The Estée Lauder Companies Inc. goes public.

1997: Company makes a major move into the hair care segment with the purchase of Aveda Corporation.

2003: Estée Lauder enters into a strategic alliance with Kohl's Corporation to build and manage new cosmetic departments stocked with exclusive brands at Kohl's discount department stores.

2008: Fabrizio Freda is appointed president and COO and named heir apparent to the CEO slot.

former employee Andy Lucarelli, as quoted in *Estée Lauder: Beyond the Magic*. Youth Dew sales reached an unprecedented volume of 5,000 units a week in the mid-1950s. Furthermore, sales of skin care products increased because of the popularity of Youth Dew. Thirty years later, the fragrance still had sales of $30 million worldwide.

In 1958, 24-year-old Leonard Lauder joined the company. That year he married Evelyn Hausner, a Vienna-born schoolteacher who would later rise in the company and eventually take over for Estée Lauder herself, making appearances as company spokesperson.

In the early 1960s, Estée Lauder joined Rubenstein, Arden, Revlon, and Cosmetiques in the race to develop a skin care cream like the European products that were becoming popular during this time. Estée Lauder's Re-Nutriv, a careful blend of 25 ingredients, was introduced

in a well-orchestrated marketing program typical of most Estée Lauder ventures. Advertisers were careful not to make specific claims regarding the product's ability to revitalize skin or eliminate wrinkles, as such claims could get a cosmetics company into regulatory trouble. A full-page *Harper's Bazaar* ad simply read: "What makes a cream worth $115.00?" The expensive product generated lots of free press for the company.

Estée Lauder Inc. developed an identifiable image in the 1960s. Because the company could not afford color ads, they used black-and-white photos instead. Moreover, in 1971, model Karen Graham began portraying the serene, elegant "Estée Lauder look," a role she would fulfill for 15 years. Graham's identification with Estée Lauder was so successful, many people thought she was Estée Lauder herself.

Through the early 1960s, company sales climbed to $14 million. Lauder had by then gathered a small, talented staff that included Ida Steward, from Bristol-Myers; June Leaman, from Bergdorf Goodman; and Ira Levy, a graduate of the University of California, Los Angeles, all of whom would remain with the company for decades.

DEBUTS OF ARAMIS (1964) AND CLINIQUE (1968)

In 1964 the company introduced Aramis, a trendsetting male fragrance blended from citrus, herbs, and spice to evoke a woodsy scent. Estée Lauder soon met with increased competition, particularly from Revlon, which began to market its own fragrance for men, known as Braggi. Following the deaths of cosmetic leaders Helena Rubenstein and Elizabeth Arden (in 1965 and 1966, respectively), competition heated up between Revlon and Estée Lauder.

The introduction of the Clinique line in 1968 firmly established Estée Lauder's success in the cosmetics industry. Clinique's first national exposure had come via an interview between *Vogue* veteran Carol Phillips and dermatologist Norman Orentreich titled "Can Great Skin Be Created?" The article, published in the August 15, 1967, edition of *Vogue,* elicited outstanding reader response. Soon thereafter Phillips accepted an offer from Leonard Lauder to join the company and lead the development of the new Clinique line. From the development stage to full-scale introduction, Clinique was designed to be more than just an allergy-tested line of products. Rather, it cultivated an image as a well-researched and medically sound line of products produced in laboratories. The first 20 salespeople were given the title of "consultants"; they were rigorously trained and outfitted with white lab coats. Sales counters were brightly lit, products were packaged in clinical light green boxes, and a chart allowed customers to determine which Clinique products fit their particular skin type. As stated in the September 26, 1983, *Business Week,* "Clinique helped fuel a tenfold expansion of the big cosmetics company."

By 1968, sales for privately owned Estée Lauder, at $40 million, financed a move to new corporate headquarters in the General Motors building in 1969. The company was also able to support the Clinique venture, which lost approximately $3 million over the first seven years. Such patient financing became a trademark of Estée Lauder launches. By 1975 the Clinique line had become profitable, prompting competition from Revlon. Through a hasty and ultimately unsuccessful introduction of a product line designed to compete with Clinique, Revlon's Charles Revson made an important discovery. Estée Lauder held a significant influence over department store buyers, who generated customer loyalty through the exclusive sale of her products. Revlon products, on the other hand, were available at lower price discount centers and inspired no such loyalty.

After 12 years with the company, the founders' oldest son Leonard was named president of Estée Lauder Inc. in 1972. Leonard Lauder focused on maintaining good relations with store buyers. His methods ensured a systematic, goal-oriented method of selling company merchandise, coordinating the advertising levels for various product lines and the quality and quantity of store space to be devoted to those Lauder products. Estée Lauder, board chairman, spent mornings working at home and afternoons at the office in the General Motors building. Joseph Lauder oversaw production at the Melville, Long Island, plant.

NEW APPROACHES AND SCENTS

The challenge faced by Estée Lauder in the 1970s was to increase its overall presence while building on its respectable reputation. The company's private, family-controlled ownership gave it the flexibility to respond rapidly, when necessary, to industry trends and competition. Through the 1970s, such quick maneuvering was necessary as the company faced increased competition in the fragrance industry. Revlon scored a huge success with the mass-marketed fragrance "Charlie" in 1973, as did Yves Saint Laurent's "Opium," launched in Paris in 1977 and brought to the United States the following year.

During this time, Lauder had been working on a subtler version of its original Youth Dew fragrance. Noting the success of Opium, Lauder launched both Soft

Youth Dew and a spicier oriental version called Cinnabar in the fall of 1978. Because of the simultaneous introduction of the closely related products, some questions concerning the company's marketing plans were raised. Both retail buyers and consumers were confused over whether Cinnabar was a version of Youth Dew or a new product. Ronald Lauder commented, as quoted in the September 15, 1978, *Women's Wear Daily,* that the company would continue to market both fragrances and would "probably decide after Christmas which way to go." While the marketing approach was muddled, the privately owned company proved that it could react quickly in an aggressive market.

A new skin care line in the style of an upscale Clinique was introduced in 1979. The Prescriptives line was promoted as even more high-tech, with one-hour makeup and fashion consultations included as part of the program. When Prescriptives met with a lukewarm reception, the company regrouped to revise the approach. Estée Lauder's other divisions were challenged as well, as competition extended to the relatively slow market for men's fragrances.

In 1978, sales of the Estée Lauder line were approximately $170 million. Clinique sales stood at $80 million, and the Aramis line, which had developed into over 40 products, had estimated sales of $40 million. Men's products, although the lowest in revenue, were growing at a rate of 18 percent a year. Several men's fragrances were launched in lower-priced markets. With the widely successful 1978 debut of Ralph Lauren's Polo, Estée Lauder was prompted to consider launching a new men's product. JHL, named after Joseph Lauder, was introduced in 1982 and, like other Lauder products, was marketed as a more expensive and upscale fragrance. Sales clerks requested business cards from customers in order to send them free samples, and an elegant counter display was developed for promotional items.

In executive changes in 1982 Leonard Lauder, president of the company, was also named CEO. Ronald Lauder, another son of the founders and executive vice-president, became chairman of international operations; the division comprised half the company's sales volume, although less of its profits. The changes did not affect Estée Lauder's active chairmanship or Joseph Lauder's management of the company plants.

A BILLION DOLLARS AND
BEYOND

By 1983, Estée Lauder had reached a billion dollars in sales and was recognized as the premier cosmetics company. The company underwent several more executive changes. Ronald Lauder left active management to join the Reagan administration as deputy assistant defense secretary. Joseph Lauder died in January 1983. The family bought Mr. Lauder's stock for $28 million, at a price the IRS would later charge was undervalued, leaving the company liable for $42.7 million in taxes. The Lauders' lawyer countered that shareholder agreements from 1974 and 1976 controlled the price of the shares, because the stock of the family-owned company could not be sold.

Just as Estée Lauder reached a billion dollars in sales, its closest rival, Revlon—which had watched the Lauder empire grow from infancy—experienced a first drop in sales, to $1.2 billion. While still formidable, Revlon no longer had the guidance of its leader, Charles Revson, who died in 1975.

Unlike Revlon, which touted its large number of product introductions, Estée Lauder took a more careful approach. Clinique added only 12 new products since its inception, most of which were still being sold after 15 years. Estée Lauder's sole product launch in 1983, Night Repair, reportedly had years of research and development invested in it. Night Repair advertising copy claimed that the product was "a biological breakthrough" that "uses the night, the time your body is resting, to help speed up the natural repair of cells damaged during the day." Dr. Norman Orentreich, the dermatologist consulted in the groundbreaking 1967 *Vogue* interview preceding the introduction of Clinique, offered a different view. As quoted in the September 1984 issue of *Drug and Cosmetic,* Orentreich stated, "there is no topical preparation affecting the outermost layer of the stratum corneum that the FDA will allow [one] to call a cosmetic that will work." Such objections did not impair sales; in fact, Night Repair went on to become a top seller in the Estée Lauder line.

The company's increasing investment in laboratory research and development proved successful, as indicated by the sales of the Clinique line and Night Repair. As reported in the September 26, 1983, *Business Week,* Leonard Lauder stated that "growth in 1983 R & D expenditures will be twice the company's sales increase."

IMAGE REVIVAL UNDER NEW LEADER

In 1990, in a widely reported company change, Robin Burns was brought in to replace Robert J. Barnes as chief executive of the domestic division. Barnes, who had held the position for 26 years, remained with the company as a consultant for the international division. Burns started her career as a fabric buyer for Bloomingdale's at age 21 in 1974, joining the staff at Calvin Klein Cosmetics Corporation in 1983. Burns was instrumental to the introduction of the fragrances Obsession and Eternity during her seven-year tenure, turning the $6 million company into a $200 million success story. Leonard Lauder was quoted in the January 12, 1990, *Women's Wear Daily* as commenting that "Calvin told me, 'No matter what you've heard about her, she's ten times better.'"

Officially taking over the domestic division in May 1990, Burns revived the image of several Estée Lauder fragrances by the end of the year. Hoping to make the company's flagship Estée Lauder line more accessible by implementing changes in its advertising, Burns oversaw production of ads that featured Paulina Porizkova (the model representing the company's entire line starting in 1988), suggesting that a friendlier, less remote countenance would have a wider appeal for consumers. Furthermore, Burns opted to give the company's White Linen scent its own representative, model Paul Devicq.

Similarly, the Aramis line was reinvigorated with a campaign designed to reach a younger male audience. Ad spending was increased by 40 percent, and print ads, traditionally placed in the magazines *Fortune* and *Esquire,* were moved instead to *Rolling Stone, Cosmopolitan,* and *Gentlemen's Quarterly.* Television spots were switched from news programs such as *60 Minutes* to comedy programs such as *In Living Color,* which attracted young people.

The Prescriptives line was expanded in the 1990s with the introduction of All Skins, makeup formulated for working women of different ethnic backgrounds. Nearly all cosmetics companies at the time had been criticized for ignoring large segments of the population for too long. By mid-1992 All Skins was attracting 3,800 new customers a month.

LAUNCH OF ORIGINS IN 1990

In 1990 the company formed a new corporate division, Origins Natural Resources Inc., which catered to public concern for the environment. Recycled paper was used for product packaging and company correspondence, makeup shades emphasized natural skin tones, and animal products such as lanolin and petroleum-based active ingredients were not used in the makeup formulations. Origins was also offered via freestanding boutiques in Cambridge, Massachusetts, and Soho, Manhattan, which proved to be the new division's top-selling locations.

William Lauder, grandson of the founders, headed the Origins division. In a July 13, 1990, article in *Women's Wear Daily,* he summarized the contemporary Estée Lauder mission: "We are trying to rewrite the book on how a cosmetics company operates and thinks in the 21st century." The company's new approach included gearing more merchandise toward consumers of all economic backgrounds and a commitment to communicating with a growing international audience in addition to a wider variety of American consumers.

In January 1992 Daniel J. Brestle, the president of Prescriptives who had brought that division from a shaky start to $70 million in sales, was named president of Clinique Laboratories USA. The founders' two sons, Leonard and Ronald, continued to play active roles in the executive lineup. Leonard remained president and CEO of Estée Lauder Inc., while Ronald continued as chairperson of both the international and Clinique divisions. Evelyn Lauder, Leonard's wife, oversaw new product development as senior corporate vice-president. By 1992 Evelyn Lauder had gradually taken on Estée's role as company spokesperson as the founder made fewer appearances. Commenting on Estée Lauder's success in the industry in the July 13, 1990, *Women's Wear Daily*, Leonard Lauder summarized the Estée Lauder philosophy: "We think in decades. Our competitors think in quarters."

FIRST LICENSING VENTURE AND ACQUISITIONS

In 1993 the company entered into its first licensing venture, signing an exclusive global licensing deal with fashion designer Tommy Hilfiger. Two years later, Estée Lauder's Aramis subsidiary launched the Tommy fragrance for men, which it followed up with Tommy Girl, for women, and Hilfiger Athletics, for men.

In February 1995 Estée Lauder acquired a majority interest in Make-up Art Cosmetics Ltd. (M•A•C), maker of designer cosmetics aimed at professional makeup artists and fashion-conscious consumers; by 1998 the company had gained full control. Estée Lauder also acquired Bobbi Brown *essentials,* a professional beauty line developed by famous makeup artist Bobbi Brown. During this time Estée Lauder also hired a new spokesmodel, actress Elizabeth Hurley, who helped make Pleasures a top-selling fragrance after its debut in 1995.

By late 1995 Estée Lauder herself had stepped aside as chairperson, taking the honorary title of founding chair. Leonard Lauder assumed the chairmanship in addition to his duties as CEO, while COO Fred H. Langhammer added the title of president. Ronald Lauder continued as chairman of Clinique and the international operations.

1995 INITIAL PUBLIC OFFERING

In part as an estate planning measure and a method for some Lauder family members to cash out portions of their company stakes, The Estée Lauder Companies Inc. went public in November 1995, raising more than $450 million through the initial public offering (IPO). Secondary offerings over the next few years lowered the Lauder family's stake in the company to about 65 percent of the common stock and 93 percent of the voting stock. Some of the maneuvers by members of the Lauder family in connection with these offerings proved controversial, particularly a capital gains tax-deferral method used in the 1995 IPO that lawmakers outlawed in 1997.

For the fiscal year ending in June 1996 Estée Lauder posted profits of $160.4 million on sales of $3.19 billion, healthy increases over the previous year's figures of $121.2 million and $2.9 billion. Profits and sales increased again in fiscal 1997, reaching $197.6 million and $3.38 billion, respectively. In late 1997 the company returned to the acquisition arena, snapping up Sassaby Inc. and Aveda Corporation. The purchase of Sassaby brought to Estée Lauder the *jane* brand of color cosmetics, a trendy brand aimed at young consumers 13 to 18 years old. Unlike Estée Lauder's typically high-priced products sold primarily in department stores, the *jane* line consisted of mass-market items sold in drugstores, supermarkets, and discounters, such as Wal-Mart Stores, Inc., and thereby represented a new marketing channel for the company.

Aveda, purchased for $300 million, was a "new age" brand, consisting of a line of shampoos, cosmetics, and other beauty products positioned within the trendy aromatherapy area. This acquisition marked a major move by Estée Lauder into the hair care segment, where it had only a minor presence through its Origins line. It also represented another new distribution channel, as 85 percent of Aveda's sales came from hair salons. In November 1997 Estée Lauder struck another licensing deal, this time signing an exclusive worldwide agreement with Donna Karan International Inc. to develop a line of fragrances and cosmetic products under the Donna Karan New York and DKNY trademarks.

Prior to the 1997 acquisitions, it had appeared that Estée Lauder was in danger of losing market share because of its near exclusive focus on the department store channel, a channel that was seeing increasing numbers of customers defect to mass marketers and other outlets. Yet as with its acquisition of such popular brands as M•A•C and Bobbi Brown *essentials,* the company appeared to be shedding its conservative ways in gaining entrée into the mass market and hair salon channels. To support its brands, Estée Lauder continued to spend massive sums on advertising and promotion, $1.03 billion in fiscal 1998 alone, a figure representing more than 28 percent of sales.

The company also continued to seek strategic acquisition targets, such as Stila Cosmetics, Inc., a fast-growing upscale cosmetics company acquired in August 1999. Stila was Estée Lauder's third makeup-artist-brand acquisition, following the deals for M•A•C and Bobbi Brown. Later in 1999 the company expanded its stable of brands once more with the acquisition of the British firm Jo Malone Limited. Founded in 1983 by the company namesake, the firm showcased its prestige skin care, fragrance, and hair care products at a flagship store in London while also selling its products through a company catalog and a select group of specialty stores in the United States and Canada. In November 1999 Estée Lauder entered into another licensing deal with a hot fashion designer, this time gaining the worldwide rights for beauty products under the Kate Spade name.

TOUGHER TIMES AT START OF THE NEW CENTURY

At the beginning of 2000, Langhammer was promoted to president and CEO, as Leonard Lauder remained chairman and began concentrating more on identifying acquisitions and nurturing new companies brought into the fold. Only half a year later, Estée Lauder continued its acquisitions spree and followed up its Aveda purchase with that of another salon-based business. The company in June 2000 acquired majority control of Bumble and Bumble, LLC, which operated a premier hair salon in New York City and also distributed a line of hair care products to more than 1,400 upscale salons around the world as well as select specialty stores.

Acquisitions were placed on the back burner over the next few years as the company contended with a rougher economic stretch and carried out a number of operational makeovers. In early 2001 the firm announced plans to shift 10 to 20 percent of its business away from department stores, a sector that was seeing its share of the overall retail market gradually shrink, to other channels, including its own stores and the Internet. Additional freestanding M•A•C, Aveda, and Origins stores were subsequently opened. Also in 2001 Estée Lauder implemented a major reorganization of its top brand management, creating new group presidents responsible for the worldwide management of certain brand groupings, replacing the previous demarcation between domestic and international operations. One group centered on the flagship Estée Lauder brand and also included M•A•C and the firm's fragrance brands. A second group comprised principally the Clinique and Origins lines. The third encompassed Estée Lauder's "high-growth specialty" brands, including Aveda, Bobbi Brown, Bumble and bumble, *jane,* Jo Malone, Kate Spade, and Stila.

As a result of the tough economic climate, and more specifically a slowdown in department store and shopping mall traffic and a decline in international travel that undercut the travel retail market, Estée Lauder saw its net earnings fall 17 percent in fiscal 2002, to $289.4 million. This marked the first decline in profits in a decade, but the company enjoyed its 51st consecutive year of sales growth, eking out an increase of 2 percent, to $4.74 billion. At the beginning of 2003, William Lauder, grandson of the founders, was named chief operating officer, with Langhammer retaining the CEO post.

2003–06: GROWTH, RESTRUCTURING, AND REVITALIZATION EFFORTS

Acquisitions returned to the fore in April 2003 with the purchase of Laboratories Darphin, a producer of aromatherapy-based skin care products operating out of Paris and distributing its products in more than 50 countries around the world. A month later Estée Lauder signed another licensing deal with a famed fashion designer, Michael Kors, to develop a new line of fragrances and body and bath products. In perhaps the most important development of 2003, however, Estée Lauder entered into a strategic alliance with rapidly growing discount department store operator Kohl's Corporation to build and manage new cosmetic departments at the hundreds of Kohl's stores located around the country. Estée Lauder created a new division called BeautyBank to develop brands for sale exclusively at Kohl's outlets. The first three brands debuted in 2004: American Beauty, a luxurious makeup and advanced skin care line; Flirt!, a makeup line encouraging customers to experiment with its array of more than 250 shades; and Good Skin, a skin care line developed with expert input from a dermatologist. These lines were also made available for sale at Kohl's e-commerce web site.

As this move into the discount department store sector was beginning, Estée Lauder closed the book on its experiment with the mass market. In February 2004 it sold the *jane* cosmetics brand, whose sales had been hurt by a flood of competitors into the teen cosmetics market. In July 2004 the CEO position returned to the Lauder family when William Lauder assumed that post, succeeding Langhammer, who retired. This move was implemented three months after the death of Estée Lauder at age 97.

In 2005 the company aimed to revitalize its stagnating flagship Estée Lauder brand by reaching an agreement with superstar designer Tom Ford to develop both Estée Lauder brand products and products under the Tom Ford brand. Late that year, the company launched a restructuring designed to streamline operations after the addition of various brands over the years had created a variety of inefficiencies. The workforce was reduced by roughly 500 employees, mainly through a voluntary buyout program, as Estée Lauder took a restructuring charge of $92.1 million for fiscal 2006. An additional charge of $80.3 million was incurred in connection with the divestment of Stila, which was sold to a private equity firm in April 2006. William Lauder was determined to concentrate more of the company's resources on its larger brands, and Stila had been much less successful than the firm's other makeup artist brands, M•A•C and Bobbi Brown. Because of these special charges, net earnings fell 40 percent in fiscal 2006, to $161.9 million, while revenues maintained their steady climb, reaching $6.46 billion, up 3 percent over the results for 2005.

2007 AND BEYOND: OVERSEAS GROWTH AND NEW LEADERSHIP

By 2007 Estée Lauder Companies was enjoying tremendous growth and expansion of its brands outside North America and was making particular inroads into such key emerging markets as China and Russia. Back home the company was feeling pressure from consolidation in the department store sector, which remained its main sales channel, as it continued to seek opportunities to further penetrate other channels. During fiscal 2007, while sales in the Americas increased only 3 percent, overall sales jumped 9 percent, to $7.04 billion, thanks to much more robust revenue increases in other parts of the world.

In November 2007 Estée Lauder surprised many observers by announcing the appointment of Fabrizio Freda to the position of president and COO, effective in March 2008. Freda came to the company from one of its main rivals, the Procter & Gamble Company (P&G), where he had headed the global snacks division. The plan was for Freda to succeed William Lauder as CEO within 24 months. Via this appointment, Estée Lauder sought to tap into Freda's brand-building expertise, particularly on a global scale, and the operational discipline that was a hallmark of the P&G culture. The move also rekindled longstanding rumors of P&G's interest in acquiring Estée Lauder, but the Lauder family quickly quashed such speculation, emphasizing their desire to maintain the family ownership position.

Frances E. Norton
Updated, David E. Salamie

PRINCIPAL SUBSIDIARIES

Aramis Inc.; Aveda Corporation; Clinique Laboratories, LLC; ELCA Cosmeticos LDA (Portugal); Estée Lauder Cosmetics Limited (U.K.); Estée Lauder Europe, Inc.; Estée Lauder Inc.; Estée Lauder International, Inc.; Estée Lauder Nova Scotia Co. (Canada).

PRINCIPAL DIVISIONS

Aramis and Designer Fragrances; BeautyBank; Origins Natural Resources Inc.

PRINCIPAL COMPETITORS

L'Oréal S.A.; Coty Inc.; Revlon, Inc.; The Procter & Gamble Company; LVMH Moët Hennessy Louis Vuitton SA; Alticor Inc.; Avon Products Inc.; Elizabeth Arden, Inc.; Chanel S.A.; Shiseido Company, Limited; Kao Corporation; Limited Brands, Inc.; Bare Escentuals, Inc.; Beiersdorf AG; Clarins; Johnson & Johnson; PPR SA; Starwood Hotels & Resorts Worldwide, Inc.; Unilever.

FURTHER READING

Appelbaum, Cara, "Just Who Is an Aramis Man?" *Brandweek,* September 30, 1991, p. 26.

Beatty, Sally, "The CEO-in-Waiting at Estée Lauder Envisions Big Deals," *Wall Street Journal,* April 23, 2004, p. B1.

———, "Estée Lauder Courts Tom Ford to Revive Brand," *Wall Street Journal,* April 6, 2005, p. B1.

Belkin, Lisa, "The Make-Over at Estée Lauder," *New York Times Magazine,* November 29, 1987, pp. 32+.

Bender, Marylin, "The Beautiful World of Estée Lauder," *New York Times,* January 14, 1973.

———, "Estée Lauder: A Family Affair," in *At the Top,* Garden City, N.Y.: Doubleday, 1975.

Bird, Laura, and Laura Jereski, "To Offer Shares, Lauder Lifts Veil of Secrecy," *Wall Street Journal,* September 22, 1995, p. B1.

Born, Pete, "Estée Lauder Names New Chief Executive: Fred H. Langhammer," *Women's Wear Daily,* October 8, 1999, p. 1.

———, "In Surprise Move, Lauder Taps P&G Executive As Future CEO," *Women's Wear Daily,* November 9, 2007, p. 1.

———, "Lauder Readies Origins Brand, First in Decade," *Women's Wear Daily,* July 13, 1990, p. 1.

———, "Lauder Restructures Brand Management to Build Global Impact," *Women's Wear Daily,* May 18, 2001, p. 1.

Born, Pete, and Julie Naughton, "Lauder Banking on Beauty with Kohl's," *Women's Wear Daily,* June 25, 2004, p. 6.

Byron, Ellen, "Beauty, Prestige, and Worry Lines: CEO of Estée Lauder Faces Trying Times at Company Started by His Grandmother," *Wall Street Journal,* August 20, 2007, p. B1.

———, "Who Needs Soy Lecithin? 'S.T. Lawder,' Naturally," *Wall Street Journal,* December 28, 2007, pp. B1, B5.

Byron, Ellen, and Joann S. Lublin, "Lauder Scion on Way Out, P&G Executive on Way In," *Wall Street Journal,* November 9, 2007, pp. B1, B5.

Canedy, Dana, "Estée Lauder Is Acquiring Maker of Natural Cosmetics," *New York Times,* November 20, 1997, p. D4.

Clark, Evan, and Julie Naughton, "Following Profitable 2002, Estée Lauder Investing for Growth," *Women's Wear Daily,* August 19, 2002, pp. 1+.

Deveny, Kathleen, "How Leonard Lauder Is Making His Mom Proud," *Business Week,* September 4, 1989, pp. 68+.

———, "In a More Than Cosmetic Move, Burns Walks Softly to Lauder," *Wall Street Journal,* January 12, 1990, p. B1.

Doherty, Jacqueline, "Glamour Stock," *Barron's,* August 30, 1999, pp. 25–26, 28.

Duffy, Martha, "Take This Job and Love It," *Time,* August 6, 1990.

Edelson, Sharon, "Lauder's Populist Message," *Women's Wear Daily,* February 7, 1992, p. 12.

Ellison, Sarah, "Top Job to Return to Lauder Family at Estée Lauder," *Wall Street Journal,* January 7, 2004, p. B4.

"Estée Lauder Dies: Era Ends," *Women's Wear Daily,* April 26, 2004, p. 4.

Fallon, James, "Estée Lauder Goes to Oxford," *Women's Wear Daily,* September 6, 1991, p. F24.

Fallon, James, and Alev Aktar, "Lauder Buys Jo Malone Beauty Firm," *Women's Wear Daily,* October 25, 1999, p. 2.

Fine, Jenny B., "Secret Weapon: Evelyn Lauder Has Played a Vital—But Often Overlooked—Role in the Storied Success of Estée Lauder," *Women's Wear Daily,* October 5, 2002, pp. 34+.

Harting, Joan, "Lauder's Cinnabar Exudes Oriental Mystique," *Women's Wear Daily,* September 15, 1978.

Horyn, Cathy, "Estée's Heirs," *Harper's Bazaar,* September 1998, pp. 486–91, 550.

Israel, Lee, *Estée Lauder: Beyond the Magic,* New York: Macmillan, 1985, 186 p.

Jereski, Laura, "Estée Lauder Family Will Pay Taxes of $40 Million on Controversial Tactic," *Wall Street Journal,* November 26, 1997, p. A4.

Jereski, Laura, and Laura Bird, "Beauty Secrets: Ronald Lauder's Debts and Estée's Old Age Force a Firm Makeover," *Wall Street Journal,* November 8, 1995, pp. A1+.

Klepacki, Laura, "Estée Lauder Sells Jane Cosmetics Line," *Women's Wear Daily,* February 10, 2004, p. 2.

Kogan, Julie, "What Smell Success?" *Working Woman,* November 1982.

Langway, Lynn, "Common Scents," *Newsweek,* February 6, 1978.

Lauder, Estée, *Estée: A Success Story,* New York: Random House, 1985, 222 p.

"Lauder's Success Formula," *Business Week,* September 26, 1983, pp. 122+.

"Launch Fever," *Women's Wear Daily,* August 9, 1991.

Lloyd, Kate, "How to Be Estée Lauder," *Vogue,* January 1973.

"Looking for Deep Pockets," *Forbes,* January 21, 1991, p. 14.

Luppi, Elizabeth Jane, "Changing the Face of the American Cosmetics Industry: Avon and Estée Lauder, 1948–1968," master's thesis, University of California, Irvine, 2006.

Merrick, Amy, and Sally Beatty, "Kohl's Plans Estée Lauder Counters," *Wall Street Journal,* October 28, 2003, p. A6.

Mirabella, Grace, "Estée Lauder," *Time,* December 7, 1998, pp. 183–84.

Munk, Nina, "Why Women Find Lauder Mesmerizing," *Fortune,* May 25, 1998, pp. 96–98+.

Naughton, Julie, "Lauder Sells Stila Cosmetics," *Women's Wear Daily,* April 12, 2006, p. 2.

Naughton, Julie, and Alev Aktar, "Lauder Takes Stake in Bumble and Bumble," *Women's Wear Daily,* June 5, 2000, p. 2.

Naughton, Julie, and Kristin Finn, "Keeping It in the Family: Estée Lauder Cos. Taps William Lauder As CEO," *Women's Wear Daily,* January 7, 2004, p. 1.

Naughton, Julie, and Molly Prior, "Lauder Growth Strategy: Protect the Core Brands While Adding Even More," *Women's Wear Daily,* March 7, 2007, p. 1.

Parker-Pope, Tara, "Estée Lauder Buys Jane Brand's Owner for Its First Venture into Mass Market," *Wall Street Journal,* September 26, 1997, p. B19.

———, "Estée Lauder Sets Deal to Buy Aveda for $300 Million," *Wall Street Journal,* November 20, 1997, p. A10.

Prior, Molly, "Lauder Profit Falls, Firm Eyes International Growth," *Women's Wear Daily,* October 26, 2007, p. 12.

———, "Lauder's New Persona: The 'Humble Brand Keeper,'" *Women's Wear Daily,* May 26, 2006, p. 8.

Roth, Daniel, "Sweet Smell of Succession," *Fortune,* September 19, 2005, pp. 122–24+.

Rudnitsky, Howard, and Julie Androshick, "Leonard Lauder Goes Scalloping," *Forbes,* December 16, 1996, pp. 96+.

Salmans, Sandra, "Estée Lauder: The Scents of Success," *New York Times,* April 18, 1982, pp. F1, F27.

Severo, Richard, "Estée Lauder, Pursuer of Beauty and Cosmetics Titan, Dies at 97," *New York Times,* April 26, 2004, pp. A1, B6.

Sloan, Pat, "Burns Reshaping Lauder," *Advertising Age,* November 26, 1990.

Strom, Stephanie, "The Lipstick Wars," *New York Times,* June 28, 1992, pp. V1, V8.

Warren, Catherine, "Estée and Joe," *Women's Wear Daily,* January 7, 1983.

Watters, Susan, "Lauders Fight IRS Ruling over Father's Inheritance," *Women's Wear Daily,* June 14, 1991, p. 2.

Zinn, Laura, "Estée Lauder, the Sweet Smell of Survival," *Business Week,* September 14, 1992, p. 52.

Federal Deposit Insurance Corporation

———■———

550 17th Street NW
Washington, D.C. 20429-9990
U.S.A.
Telephone: (202) 898-7021
Toll Free: (800) 688-3342
Fax: (202) 942-3427
Web site: http://www.fdic.gov

Government Agency
Incorporated: 1933
Employees: 4,500
Total Assets: $50.76 billion (2006)
NAIC: 921130 Public Finance Activities

■ ■ ■

Federal Deposit Insurance Corporation (FDIC) is a Washington, D.C.-based government agency that insures deposits in banks and thrift institutions (savings and loans, and savings banks) for at least $100,000. Not only are depositors protected, confidence in the U.S. banking system is maintained should a bank or thrift fail, and the impact on the economy is mitigated. An outgrowth of the Great Depression of the 1930s, FDIC also examines and supervises approximately 5,250 banks and thrifts, including state-chartered banks that opt not to join the Federal Reserve System. FDIC is funded by premiums paid by banks and thrifts. It is managed by a five-person board of directors appointed by the president and confirmed by the U.S. Senate. By law, no more than three members may belong to the same political party. Business is mostly conducted through six regional

offices and field offices strategically located across the country.

19TH-CENTURY ROOTS: DEPOSIT INSURANCE

Bank insurance to protect depositors was far from a new concept when the FDIC was formed in the heart of the Great Depression. The seeds of the idea were planted following the United States' first bank failure in 1809, the Farmers Bank of Gloucester, Rhode Island. Others soon followed, prompting the state of New York in 1829 to adopt bank insurance that covered deposits as well as the circulating notes issued by banks that at the time served as legal tender. Other states soon followed suit with similar insurance programs, which included supervision to forestall bank failures. State insurance programs faded away after the national bank system was established in 1863 and many state banks adopted national charters. Because the notes issued by national banks were backed by the United States' Treasury, there was no need for bank insurance until the amount of deposits eclipsed bank notes in importance. By the start of the 20th century, deposits outweighed circulating notes seven to one, leading to several states adopting deposit insurance programs by 1930, but none of them explicitly guaranteed deposits. Rather, these deposit guaranty programs simply created a fund drawn from the participating banks. Even periods of economic turmoil in the generally prosperous 1920s proved the inadequacy of state insurance funds.

The federal government also made periodic attempts to create a deposit insurance program. In the

COMPANY PERSPECTIVES

The Federal Deposit Insurance Corporation (FDIC) is an independent agency created by the Congress that maintains the stability and public confidence in the nation's financial system by insuring deposits, examining and supervising financial institutions, and managing receiverships.

half-century before the creation of FDIC, in fact, 150 proposals were floated in Congress, usually in the wake of one of the country's periodic economic "panics." However, no legislation ever emerged. In the 1920s more than 600 banks, mostly small and rural, failed each year, yet neither the banking industry nor lawmakers expressed much concern because it was assumed that the failures were the result of mismanagement or inadequate capital. The country would be disabused of this notion a year after the stock market crash of 1929, an event that ushered in the Great Depression. In late 1930 the banking industry found itself in a death spiral that appeared inescapable. A number of bank failures prompted depositors to cash in their deposits, spurring healthy banks to liquidate assets while contracting credit, thus creating a cash crunch and leading to more assets being liquidated at depressed prices. Banks were soon unable to meet withdrawals and forced to closed, making depositors panicky and leading to regular "bank runs." In 1930, 1,350 banks closed their doors, including one of the largest in the country, New York City's Bank of United States, putting the lie to the notion that the problem was limited to poorly run, undercapitalized rural institutions.

PRESIDENT ROOSEVELT DECLARES BANK HOLIDAYS

Additional waves of bank closures were to follow. After 2,293 failures in 1931, conditions appeared to improve and only 1,453 failures occurred in 1932, but late in the year matters grew dire and a banking panic overwhelmed the country in the early months of 1933, leading every state in the country to declare a "bank holiday" by the time President Franklin Roosevelt took office on March 4, 1933. The new president wasted little time in declaring a four-day nationwide bank holiday and formulating a plan to meet the crisis.

Once the administration had stabilized the country's financial system through the passage of the Emergency Banking Act and the issuance of Federal

Reserve Notes to ease the liquidity problem, the idea of federal deposit insurance legislation was pursued. In fact, a deposit insurance bill had been passed by the House of Representatives the year before only to have the Senate fail to move on the matter. Even with the banking crisis making daily headlines, there remained a large number of people opposed to the idea of deposit insurance, even within the Roosevelt administration, who feared that it would reward bad management and impoverish the government. Moreover, it smacked of socialism, giving the government too much control over free enterprise.

GLASS-STEAGALL ACT OF 1933 GIVES BIRTH TO FDIC

The voters, on the other hand, demanded the security of deposit insurance and some of their elected officials championed the cause, in particular the chairman of the House Banking and Currency Committee, Alabama's Henry B. Steagall. Both the House and Senate were working on a comprehensive new banking law, and Steagall's counterpart in the Senate, Carter Glass of Virginia, although personally opposed to deposit insurance, realized that public opinion was such that it would have to be included if he were to achieve some of the reforms he desired. Thus, the Banking Act of 1933, the so-called Glass-Steagall Act, included a provision for deposit insurance that called for the creation of the Federal Deposit Insurance Corporation to administer the plan, funded initially by $140 million from the Federal Reserve System and $150 million from the U.S. Treasury. This money would be repaid in 1947 and 1948, drawn from assessments to FDIC-member banks, and the interest on the advanced money, $81 million, would also be repaid in 1950 and 1951.

In a matter of months about 8,000 non-Federal Reserve banks applied for admission into the FDIC and had to be examined. It was a tall task and hastily conducted, but it was completed in time for a temporary plan to be put into effect starting January 1, 1934. A polished version would emerge from the Banking Act of 1935, which provided $5,000 in protection for each depositor rather than the initial $2,500. FDIC was under the temporary auspices of Special Assistant to the Treasury Walter J. Cummings until February 1934, when Leo T. Crowley became FDIC's new chairman. He was a man uniquely qualified to lead the fledgling agency. He had run both a paper company and a public utility corporation, owned several Wisconsin banks, and headed the Wisconsin Banking Review Board. He had come to Washington in late 1933 in an effort to secure financial aid for several hundred Wisconsin banks hoping to meet FDIC standards and soon found himself

KEY DATES

1933: Federal Deposit Insurance Corporation (FDIC) is formed by act of Congress.

1947: FDIC begins paying back start-up funds to the Federal Reserve System and U.S. Treasury.

1951: Annual bank examinations resume.

1974: Deposit insurance coverage is doubled.

1989: Overseeing thrifts is added to FDIC responsibilities.

1991: Federal Deposit Insurance Corporation Improvement Act is signed.

1999: Comprehensive review of FDIC structure is launched.

2006: Deposit insurance reform bill is signed.

entrusted by the Roosevelt administration to run the new organization.

Crowley spent the next 12 years at the head of FDIC, the longest tenure of any chairman in the agency's history. He was also the agency's most influential head. After taking charge Crowley revisited the cursory admission bank exams and made sure that all member banks were adequately capitalized. In 1934 only nine insured banks failed, as well as 52 uninsured institutions, leading to increased consumer confidence and a 22 percent rise in total deposits for commercial banks. Opposition to deposit insurance within the banking industry also began to diminish.

As a result of FDIC and other monetary policy changes, bank runs became rare, but failures were not completely eliminated. During the first nine years of FDIC's existence, the United States experienced 390 failures of insured banks. They were all small institutions, however. Over the ensuing three decades there were relatively few failures, and in 1962 there were no failures at all. Moreover, in six years between 1943 and 1974 there were no insurance losses incurred from failures. It was no accident, of course, that the improving health of the banking industry coincided with the United States roaring back to fiscal health because of increased government spending during World War II in the first half of the 1940s. The war years forced FDIC to give up some Washington office space and move many employees to Chicago, and because of a lack of personnel the agency was unable to conduct an annual examination of each member bank.

Even after the war it took time for FDIC to build up its roster of qualified examiners and not until 1951

was it able to again fulfill its policy of annual bank examinations. In addition, the short-staffed agency had to supervise and examine some 4,000 federal credit unions during the war, and not until 1948 was the task transferred to the Federal Security Agency. As for Crowley, he had proven to be so valuable an administrator that during the war he held nine government posts in addition to his responsibilities with FDIC, including serving as head of the Foreign Economic Administration, in charge of the highly important lend-lease program.

Part of the reason for few bank failures during the postwar years was an aversion for risk-taking by bankers who were scarred by their experience during the Great Depression. In the 1960s, however, that attitude would begin to change, due in part to liberalized branching laws in many states that led to large bank holding companies, which looked to enter new product markets. The 1970s brought a period of interest rate volatility that became even more uncertain following the oil embargos of 1973 and 1978, which also resulted in severe inflation. To complicate the situation further, competition increased dramatically in the financial marketplace, forcing banks to look for new sources of income and the assumption of greater levels of risk.

INCREASING COVERAGE: 1974

Although the number of banks that failed in the 1970s were not historically high the amount of assets and insurance losses were. In fact, from 1973 to 1978 the 11 largest bank failures since FDIC was founded took place, including New York City's Franklin National Bank, which had deposits of nearly $1.5 billion. In 1973 insurance losses totaled $67.5 million. During the previous four decades the FDIC had lost only half that amount. To keep pace with changing realities, in 1974 deposit insurance coverage was doubled to $40,000, and four years later coverage for IRA and Keogh accounts was increased to $100,000. FDIC also adjusted the investment strategy of the funds it held. Instead of allowing the Treasury to determine whatever long-term issues it deemed appropriate, in the mid-1970s the FDIC took a more active role and shortened the maturity of its portfolio in order to have more funds available to deal with the increasing size of payouts.

The 1973 payout would pale in comparison to what was to follow in the 1980s and early 1990s, when the United States was rocked by a savings-and-loan (S&L) crisis. More than 1,400 FDIC-insured banks failed from 1982 through 1991, but the situation was far worse in the savings and loan industry. S&Ls had found it increasingly difficult to compete in the 1970s and felt compelled to take greater chances. Riskier investments also became more available when in the early 1980s the government eased regulations, allowing S&Ls to issue credit cards, make commercial loans, and offer higher market rates for deposits. Bad real estate loans proved to be the undoing of many S&Ls, and FDIC's counterpart, the Federal Savings and Loan Insurance Corporation, was unable to cope with the crisis, became insolvent, and was abolished in 1989. S&L deposits became the responsibility of FDIC.

PASSAGE OF IMPROVEMENT ACT: 1991

All told, the S&L crisis cost taxpayers about $125 billion. The FDIC during this turbulent period also had to absorb considerable losses. The agency exhausted its insurance fund, which despite growing to $18.3 billion by the end of 1987 was unable to keep up with payouts and by 1991 was $7 billion in arrears. To address this problem, in late December 1991 Congress passed the Federal Deposit Insurance Corporation Improvement Act, which made a number of changes to the way the FDIC operated. The flat rate for insurance was replaced with risk-based premiums, based on a financial assessment of individual banks, and the FDIC was able to borrow as much as $30 billion from the Treasury to cover insurance losses. At the same time, limitations were placed on how FDIC handled failing institutions, forcing the agency to adopt the resolution alternative that was least costly to the insurance fund. The agency also lost its authority to determine that a bank was simply too large to fail, believing that its closure would have a dire impact on the overall banking system. That authority had been used in 1980 and 1984, but in 1992 such a decision would have to be made in concert with the Federal Reserve, the Treasury, and the president.

Although 127 banks failed in 1992, costing the insurance fund $3.6 billion, the commercial banking industry began to rebound strongly in 1992. From 1980 to 1994 the FDIC managed the failure of more than 1,600 banks. From the ones that failed the agency took over $317 billion in assets, almost all of which were liquidated by the end of 1996. In that same year Congress capitalized the Savings Association Insurance Fund to cover thrifts while the Bank Insurance Fund continued to cover commercial banks. The FDIC was able to turn its attention from the cleanup of the S&L and banking crisis to better supervise banks and thrifts in order to keep them healthy and able to serve their customers and communities. To assist examiners in this mission, the FDIC launched an automated system called ALERT to allow an offsite review of a bank's databases. A year later, in response to the rising importance of electronic banking, the agency published its first electronic banking guidelines. In addition, FDIC took notice of increasing consolidation in the banking industry by reorganizing the way regional offices conducted risk-assessment programs.

In the final years of the 1990s, FDIC made special efforts to make sure that computer systems of member banks were ready for the year 2000 date change. At the same time, the Bank Insurance Fund grew to $30 billion and the Savings Association Insurance Fund reached $10 billion by the end of the decade, so that both entered the new century fully capitalized.

ENACTING CHANGES: 2006

To ensure that the agency remained current, in 1999 a comprehensive review of FDIC was launched and recommendations offered in 2000. In order to achieve greater financial flexibility during times of crisis, FDIC sought to charge premiums over the business cycle rather than on a pay-as-you-go method. Under the current system, because the insurance funds had reached a statutorily designated reserve ratio, more than 90 percent of institutions did not have to pay any premiums because they met certain financial thresholds. Should the fund dip below the designated reserve ratio, premiums could increase sharply if the fund did not return to the proper level within a year. As a result, the system was fraught with a certain amount of uncertainty that a revised method of charging premiums could remedy. It would also eliminate the subsidization of riskier institutions by strong members. FDIC also sought to combine the two insurance funds under its control to provide even greater flexibility during times of need. The proposed changes took time to wend their way through the legislative process and did not become law until President George W. Bush signed a deposit insurance reform bill in February 2006. In addition, coverage for certain retirement plan deposits was increased from $100,000 to $250,000, representing the first major change in deposit insurance coverage in a quarter-century.

In June 2006 Sheila C. Bair, a former executive for government relations of the New York Stock Exchange and assistant secretary for financial institutions for the U.S. Department of the Treasury, took over as FDIC's new chairman. She soon became concerned about the lax standards the banking industry had assumed in making "subprime" loans for mortgages and the reluctance to steer consumers toward safer, fixed-rate mortgages. As mortgage rates increased beyond people's means, leading to a large number of foreclosures, Bair led the charge to reset loans to fixed rates to stem the flow of foreclosures. While the crisis led to the closing of many mortgage companies, few FDIC-member banks failed because of the subprime crisis. The most glaring exception was an online bank, NetBank Inc., which had $2.5 billion in assets and held $2.3 billion in deposits. When federal regulators shut it down in September 2007 and appointed FDIC as the receiver, it represented the largest thrift failure in the 14 years since the end of the S&L crisis.

Ed Dinger

PRINCIPAL SUBSIDIARIES

Bank Insurance Fund; Savings Association Insurance Fund.

FURTHER READING

"Bank Reform Bill Swiftly Approved," *New York Times,* June 14, 1933.

"A Brief History of Deposit Insurance in the United States," Washington, D.C.: Federal Deposit Insurance Corporation, 1998.

"In FDIC We Trust?" *Economist* (U.S.), April 1, 1989.

Martin, Pamela, "She's Back. We're Glad: An Interview with FDIC Chairman Sheila Bair," *RMA Journal,* December 2006, p. 8.

"6,748 Banks Seek Deposit Insurance," *New York Times,* December 5, 1933.

Skillern, Frank L., Jr., "Federal Deposit Insurance Corporation and the Failed Bank: The Past Decade," *Banking Law Journal,* March 1982, p. 233.

Waddell, Harry, "The FDIC's First 50 Years," *ABA Banking Journal,* October 1982, p. 38.

Finarte Casa d'Aste S.p.A.

P.tta M Bossi 4
Milan, I-20121
Italy
Telephone: (+39 02) 863561
Fax: (+39 02) 89010475
Web site: http://www.finarte-semenzato.com

Public Company
Incorporated: 2002 as Finarte-Semenzato
Employees: 81
Sales: EUR 19.4 million ($28 million) (2006)
Stock Exchanges: Milan
Ticker Symbol: FCD
NAIC: 424990 Other Miscellaneous Nondurable Goods
    Merchant Wholesalers

■■■

Finarte Casa d'Aste S.p.A. is the leading auction house in Italy, and one of the world's leading auctioneers of modern and antique art, as well as a wide range of other collectible items, such as coins, ceramics, archaeological objects, furniture, carpets, and other home furnishings. The Milan-based company operates from two showrooms in Milan, as well as showrooms in Venice and Rome. The company also has joint-venture auction operations in Spain and Switzerland, and is part of the Italian National Association of Auction Houses. The company also participates on an international scale through International Auctioneers. In addition to conducting auctions, Finarte also provides a range of art- and auction-related financial services, including art

investing consulting services. Finarte is a publicly listed company, listed on the Milan Stock Exchange. The company is led by Chairman and prominent shareholder Giorgio Corbelli. Finarte posted revenues of EUR 19.4 million ($28 million) in 2006.

FOUNDED IN THE FIFTIES

Finarte, as its name implies, started out focused on the financial side of the art market. The company was founded by Gian Marco Manusardi, a banker in Milan, in 1959. The company initially provided banking and financial services to auction houses and art collectors. At that time, the art sector remained underserved by Italy's traditional banking sector. As such, Finarte became a pioneer in the provision of financial services and products including sales advances, loans using art as collateral, and hire-purchase financing. The company also provided direct financial support services to the country's auction houses.

It was not long, however, before Finarte itself entered the auction market. The company conducted its first auction in 1961. That auction focused on a selection of modern art held by London's Estorick Collection and included paintings from Picasso, Morandi, and Kandinsky, among others. The company's next art auction came the following year, this time featuring Old Master paintings.

From the start, Finarte's auctions were characterized by a high degree of specialization, with each auction focused on a specific segment of the art and auction field. This permitted the company to explore a wide range of auctions. By the end of the decade, the

KEY DATES

1956: Judicial sales business is formed in Venice by Franco Semenzato, which then holds first antiques auction the following year.

1959: Finarte is founded in Milan as financial services provider to art market.

1961: Finarte conducts first art auction.

1970s: Semenzato establishes showroom in Florence.

1981: Finarte acquires Manzoni Casa d'Aste in Milan.

1990: Finarte lists shares on Milan Stock Exchange.

2002: Finarte merges with Semenzato, creating Finarte-Semenzato.

2006: Company changes name to Finarte Casa d'Aste.

company had also held auctions focused on archaeological objects, fine furniture, majolicas, decorative art objects, jewelry, vintage cars, coins, and even the furnishings of a Venetian palazzo.

EVERYTHING COLLECTIBLE IN THE SEVENTIES

Through the 1970s, Finarte continued to expand its range of auctions. The company added antique furnishings, silverware, porcelain, Art Deco objects, African sculpture, carpets, and other items. In this way, the company covered virtually the entire sphere of everything collectible. At the same time, the company remained at the forefront of the core art market. In 1970, for example, the company completed an auction of Postimpressionist painting from the Geneva-based Oscar Ghez Collection.

Finarte's auctions also appeared more and more regularly. By the end of the 1960s, the company boasted about 15 auctions per year. That number doubled by the end of the 1970s. In keeping with the surge in trade, the company added a second showroom in Rome before the end of the decade.

At the start of the 1980s, Finarte sought new growth. In 1981, the company acquired Milanese rival Manzoni Casa d'Aste, adding its Via Manzoni, Milan showroom. The purchase of Manzoni, later merged into Finarte itself, added that company's expertise in the applied art auction segment.

While Finarte continued to develop its auction operations, it also expanded its financial services during the 1980s. In 1983, for example, the company joined with Lloyd Adriatico Insurance Company to form a joint venture, Lloyd Arte. That company provided art investment services and medium- and long-term investment products for the art collector's market. The company sought out other partnerships during this period. In 1984, for example, the company joined with rival auction house Semenzato to conduct the auction of the Achille Lauro Collection.

PUBLIC IN THE EIGHTIES

Finarte went public in 1986. The following year, the company took on its first major shareholder, Geneva-based Habsburg Feldman. The association with that company enabled Finarte to expand its operations beyond Italy. After conducting its first auctions in Geneva, the company established a subsidiary for that market, Finarte SA.

Finarte also took steps to expand its focus beyond the northern Italian market. In 1988, the company acquired Florence's Pitti auction group, giving it operations in central Italy. The following year, the company bought majority control of Rerum, an auction house that focused on the watch market, as well as other minor collectible items, such as toys, stock certificates, and cameras.

Fast-growing Finarte moved its stock listing to the main Milan Stock Exchange in the 1990s. The international art market was then undergoing a time of massive expansion, as prices began to soar. Finarte had earlier set a record in 1984, becoming the first in Italy to auction a painting for more than ITL 1 billion. Before the end of the decade, Finarte had topped that sale, selling a painting by Umberto Boccioni for more than ITL 2 billion. In 1990, the company set another record, negotiating the ITL 3.4 billion sale of Agostino Busti's *Il Bambaia* sculptures to the city of Milan. Finarte's own sales grew accordingly, and by 1990 the company posted revenues topping ITL 150 billion.

In 1992, Finarte hosted one of the world's most prominent auctions of the Riccardo and Magda Jucker Collection. That collection contained 40 works by such modern painters as Braque, Mondrian, Picasso, Matisse, Léger, and Kandinsky, as well as an important collection of Italian Futurist paintings. The sale, which went to the city of Milan, topped ITL 48 billion.

Finarte shut down its Rerum watch auction operation in 1992. In 1995, the company once again looked beyond Italy, this time targeting the Spanish market. For this, the company set up a joint venture with Spanish financial group Afinsa. The new operation held its first auction that same year.

JOINING FORCES AMID THE MARKET DOWNTURN

Finarte had grown into a leader in the Italian market. Nonetheless, the company remained a midsized concern when compared to such global leaders as Sotheby's and Christie's. In order to increase its weight in the art auction sector, the company sought out new partnerships. In 1995, for example, the company became a founding member of the Italian National Association of Auction Houses. On a more global level, the company joined International Auctioneers (IA) in 1997. That partnership among ten of the world's leading midsized auction houses provided Finarte with a global stage. As part of the IA partnership Finarte joined in the first simultaneous audio- and Internet-based auction in 2000.

Having celebrated its 1,000th auction since its founding, Finarte looked for new growth opportunities at the turn of the millennium. Yet the company's immediate ambitions were cut short as the terrorist attacks against the United States on September 11, 2001, cast a pall across the global art collecting sector. Adding to the market's pressures was the collapse of the dot-com bubble amid an overall crash of the high-technology sector. Much of the expansion of the art market over the decade had been driven by the surge in the numbers of new technology millionaires. With the sector in disarray, the art market collapsed.

The difficult market conditions led Finarte to approach its Venetian rival Semenzato. By September of that year, the two auction houses had agreed to a merger. As part of that merger, Finarte absorbed Semenzato's operations. Semenzato's management, including Giorgio Corbelli, nonetheless gained strategic positions in the newly renamed Finarte-Semenzato Casa d'Aste.

FOUNDING A VENICE AUCTION HOUSE

Semenzato was the slightly older company, having been founded by Franco Semenzato in 1956. Semenzato at first operated as a judicial sales company, but by 1957 had begun conducting its first auctions. Antiques, especially Venetian antiques, played a major role in the company's operations.

By the 1970s, Semenzato had set up a subsidiary, San Marco, which traded from a showroom in Florence. The company then expanded its focus beyond antiques, to include contemporary art, 19th-century art and furniture, and jewelry and watches.

Semenzato entered the Milanese market in 1983 through the acquisition of the Geri Gallery in that city.

By the end of the decade, Semenzato had opened its own showroom in Florence. The company also added a showroom in Rome. In 1989, the company restructured its operations under a single holding company, Franco Semenzato S.p.A. At that time, Semenzato added outside investors, selling a 25 percent stake, split between two Italian banks. By 1994, more than 51 percent of Semenzato had come under the control of Giorgio Corbelli.

This new financial backing enabled Semenzato itself to enter the financial services sector. In 1989, the company acquired a 20 percent stake in Lesarte S.p.A., which specialized in providing art-based financial services and products. Semenzato also completed a new acquisition, buying 96 percent of Brerarte. This allowed the company to expand its presence in the market for modern and contemporary art. In 1990, the company bought 30 percent of Milan auction house Orion. Through the next decade, Semenzato added several new offices, giving it a presence in most of Italy's major cities. Ten years later, Semenzato had grown into one of Italy's top auction houses, posting annual revenues of more than ITL 90 billion.

Semenzato struggled with the downturn of the international art market at the beginning of the decade. New troubles came to the company in May 2002, when Chairman Giorgio Corbelli was placed under arrest. Corbelli was accused of selling fake lithographs through another of his holdings, the Italian shopping channel Telemarket. Yet Corbelli found support in high places. As *Art Business News* reported, the then Italian culture undersecretary declared that a "fake lithograph is conceptually impossible because it already is a fake in that it is not an original but a duplicate."

ITALIAN AUCTION LEADER IN THE NEW CENTURY

Nonetheless, Corbelli's judicial problems led to his agreement to merge Semenzato with Finarte in October of that year. The newly renamed Finarte-Semenzato then became the clear leader in the Italian auction market. As the art industry began to show signs of a recovery, however, Finarte-Semenzato faced new troubles. The eruption of boardroom battle for control of the company, between Corbelli and the company's other major shareholder, Ruggiero Jannuzzelli, placed the company under new pressures. In the end, the Jannuzzelli side won out, if only temporarily. By March 2003, Finarte-Semenzato had restructured its operations, and put into place a new management structure.

Finarte-Semenzato struggled with declining sales and dwindling profits through the middle of the decade.

The company's effort to counter its shrinking revenues included the opening of a new showroom in Naples in 2003. In 2004, the company shut down its Via Manzoni showroom in an attempt to gain new efficiency. At the same time, the company added a dedicated furniture and antiques showroom, on Milan's Via Piranesi.

The company's ongoing troubles sparked a new management shuffle in 2004. By 2005, Giorgio Corbelli had regained control of the company. Corbelli was named chairman in that year. By 2006, the company had changed its name, to Finarte Casa d'Aste.

Finarte's continuing difficulties led to rumors that the company had become a takeover target in 2006. The company declared, however, that it had received no formal acquisition approaches. By the end of that year, the company's fortunes appeared to brighten, as it announced a gain in revenues to EUR 19.4 million ($28 million). Finarte remained a focal point for the Italian art market in the new century.

M. L. Cohen

PRINCIPAL SUBSIDIARIES

Davide Halevim Unique Auctions S.R.L. (51%); Eunomia S.R.L.; Finarte S.A.

PRINCIPAL COMPETITORS

Christie's International PLC; Sotheby's Inc.; Farsetti Arte; Phillips, de Pury & Company LLC; Porro & C; Pandolfini.

FURTHER READING

"Excellent Results at Auctions of Contemporary & Modern Art in Rome and Milan," *PR Newswire,* December 1, 2004.

"Finarte Casa D'aste: Chiusi Primi 9 Mesi Con Perdita Netta Di 2,41 Mln," *Borsa.it,* November 14, 2007.

Meyers, Laura, "Global Auctions Find International Success," *Art Business News,* February 2001.

Passino, Carla, "Where Passion Drives the Market," *Apollo,* July 2005.

Flotek Industries Inc.

———■———

7030 Empire Central Drive
Houston, Texas 77040
U.S.A.
Telephone: (713) 849-9911
Fax: (713) 896-4511
Web site: http://www.flotekind.com

Public Company
Incorporated: 1985
Employees: 157
Sales: $100.6 million (2006)
Stock Exchanges: American
Ticker Symbol: FTK
NAIC: 213112 Support Activities for Oil and Gas
Operations

■ ■ ■

Flotek Industries Inc. is an American Stock Exchange–listed company based in Houston, Texas, primarily serving the oilfield and mining industries. The company is organized around three business segments: downhole production equipment and tools, specialty chemicals, and transload and facility management services. Flotek's downhole (inside an oil or gas well) business is split between two main product lines, the Petrovalve line of pump valves and the Spidle Turbeco line of drilling tools and casing accessories. Flotek's flagship product, Petrovalve, is a proprietary product that was developed to replace the ball-and-seat valves that had been a standard component in downhole sucker-rod pumps for more than 80 years. The superior design of Petrovalve results

in better pump performance and extended service life as well as lower operating costs. The Spidle Turbeco subsidiary designs, manufactures, and maintains downhole drilling tools used in the oilfield, mining, and waterwell industries. Drilling tools include bits, hammers, keyseat wipers, mills, reamers, and stabilizers. Casing accessories include slip-on centralizers, integral joint centralizers, external casing packers, and shaker screen. Flotek's specialty chemical business is conducted through Oklahoma subsidiary Chemical & Equipment Specialties, Inc., doing business as CESI Chemicals. The company offers well stimulation additives and chemicals, and a line of cementing products to control well loss and other concerns. CESI also provides oilfield blending services for both dry and liquid products. Another Flotek subsidiary, Material Translogistics, Inc. (MTI), provides the company's transload and facility management services. Based in Louisiana, MTI provides consulting to oilfield service companies as well as management services for automated bulk handling and loading facilities, which transfer products from rail cars to trucks to oilfield ports for shipping.

CANADIAN INCORPORATION: 1985

While Flotek did not begin to hit its stride until the late 1990s, the foundation for the company was laid a dozen years earlier in Canada. On May 17, 1985, Flotek was incorporated under the laws of the Province of British Columbia. Based in Vancouver the oilfield services acquired Houston's Petrovalve International Inc. in December 1992 for about CAD 720,000. Petrovalve then began a 30-month CAD 1.2 million joint research project with the Alberta Research Council to improve what was then called the Petrovalve Plus Bottom Hole Pump Valve System. Improvements were made to the design as well as the valve's metallurgical characteristics.

The traditional valve was fraught with problems, providing an opening for a new system. According to *Oil & Gas Investor,* standard ball-and-seat valves "allow fluid to flow through when the ball is energized in a direction opposite to the seat, and seal when the ball is energized against the seat. Because the ball careens wildly in the pump chamber when fluid passes it, the ball is subjected to extensive wear caused by metal-on-metal contact." As a result, these valves had short life spans, leading to expensive pump repairs. Moreover, the ball cost producers in other ways, restricting flow in high-volume wells and hindering production. The Petrovalve device, according to *Oil & Gas Investor,* featured "a plunger shaped like a hemisphere, penetrated by a stem which projects vertically above and below. The movement of the plunger is constrained so that it seats itself center on center." Limited movement resulted in less wear and tear, thus extending the life of a pump and lowering production costs. In addition, because the plunger was much smaller than the ball, it did not restrict flow as much, again to the benefit of producers.

ACQUISITION OF TURBECO: 1994

In addition to oilfield industries, Flotek looked for other applications for the product. In late 1993 a stake was taken in Canadian Agtechnology Partners Incorporated (CAP), which also received an exclusive license to use Petrovalve technology for water well pumping applications. A few months later, in February 1994, Flotek acquired the rest of CAP. The company then

looked to diversify further in 1994 by acquiring Turbeco Inc., a seven-year-old Houston oilfield services company founded by William G. Jayroe, the addition of which established Flotek's slate of drilling products. The unit drew its name from its primary product at the time, the Cementing Turbulator. The Turbulator was a sleeve placed over a drill pipe before cementation was done in a newly drilled well, its main purpose to prevent mud from hindering the work.

While the Petrovalve system was being refined, Flotek began doing spadework in marketing the product in Canada and the United States. Jayroe was named president of USA Petrovalve, Inc., responsible for introducing Petrovalve to U.S. oilfields. Flotek also targeted Venezuela, establishing a small test program on some of the country's wells. The company's marketing efforts were helped a great deal when Flotek made a splash with the Petrovalve product at the annual Offshore Technology Conference held in Houston in early May 1994. Entered in the annual Technology of the Year competition sponsored by the International Petroleum Association, Petrovalve was ranked among the top 20. Given that the product was competing for the first time, this performance caught the attention of oilfield companies around the world. Less than a month later Flotek announced the opening of offices in Venezuela, where Petrovalves were being ordered in an advanced testing phase for 127 pumping wells in 14 oilfields in the Orinocco Belt, which contained more than 9,000 pumping wells. Early results revealed production increases that ranged from 35 percent to 200 percent. Given that the 14 oilfields represented just half of Venezuela's total capacity, the sales potential for Petrovalve was promising. In addition, the system was being tested elsewhere, including South Texas' Austin Chalk area, Alabama's Black Warrior Basin, New Mexico's San Juan Basin, and California's Kern County.

The obvious advantages offered by Petrovalve began winning over producers. In April 1995 three of the company's customers adopted the technology as the standard for their U.S. operations after testing the new valve under a number of field conditions. The independent companies included WRT Energy Corporation, Equinox Oil Company, and J.M. Huber Corp. Although generating sales of CAD 3.2 million from operations in Canada, the United States, and Venezuela in fiscal 1995 (the fiscal year ending February 28), Flotek was not on a solid financial footing, saddled with excessive debt taken on during the development of Petrovalve and in need of a change in direction. The company's chairman and chief executive officer, William R. McKay, was replaced by Jayroe and the company's headquarters was moved to Houston while the Vancouver office was closed. The company's incorporation was

KEY DATES

1985: Company is incorporated in Canada.
1992: Petrovalve International Inc. is acquired.
1995: Headquarters shifts to Houston.
2001: Flotek merges with Chemical & Equipment Specialties, Inc.
2005: Spidle Sales and Services, Inc., is acquired.
2007: Flotek seeks listing on New York Stock Exchange.

also transferred to the Province of Alberta. A bid to gain a listing on the NASDAQ failed, however, and the company's shares continued to trade on the less prestigious Vancouver Stock Exchange.

Jayroe brought some improvements to Flotek, selling CAP and taking other steps to trim debt. He also restructured the company's capital and sought to improve the company's marketing efforts. Sales grew to CAD 4.4 million in fiscal 1996 but improved only modestly to CAD 4.6 million in fiscal 1997, as the company continued to post net losses: CAD 4.5 million in fiscal 1996 and another CAD 4 million in fiscal 1997. The company's accumulated deficit ballooned to CAD 19 million.

NEW CHAIRMAN AND CEO: 1998

A new chairman and CEO, Jerry D. Dumas, Sr., was installed in September 1998, marking the turning point for the fortunes of Flotek. A graduate of Louisiana State University, Dumas brought a wide variety of experience to the job. He was a seasoned energy executive, having served as a group division president of Baker Hughes Tool, and president of HydroTech International, involved in the offshore pipeline construction business. In addition, Dumas, prior to joining Flotek, worked for Merrill Lynch, acting as vice-president of corporate and executive services for the firm's private client group.

Dumas shored up Flotek's finances, arranging new financing and voluntarily delisting from the Vancouver Stock Exchange, a move that saved on filing fees and regulatory expenses. The company was poised for expansion. In July 1999 Flotek acquired Trinity Tool, Inc., to beef up its Turbeco business. Two years later, in June 2001, Material Translogistics, Inc., (MTI) was added, providing another revenue stream. Six months later MTI won an important contract to provide a major oilfield service company with a transload facility in Raceland, Louisiana, a facility that could also be used to service other stimulation and drilling material companies.

COMPLETION OF CESI MERGER: 2001

An even more important transaction was completed in October 2001 when Flotek and Duncan, Oklahoma-based Chemical & Equipment Specialties, Inc., (CESI) were merged. Prior to the completion of that deal, Flotek was reincorporated in Delaware and shareholders approved a 120-to-1 reverse stock split, a move that reduced the number of shares available for trading and increased the price, thus giving it more prominence to potential investors. Not only did CESI cater to the oilfield industry with chemicals for cementing and stimulation, it also manufactured such specialized equipment as nitrogen pumpers, cement mixing units, and fracturing pumpers and blenders. Moreover, CESI complemented MTI, offering engineering services to oil service companies for the design and construction of bulk material handling and loading facilities.

Following the CESI merger, Dumas and his management team decided to focus their efforts on three oilfield industry segments: downhole production tools, downhole drilling tools, and specialty chemicals. Within the specialty chemical area, Flotek elected further to concentrate on more profitable value-added niches, primarily cementing, stimulation, acidizing, and fracturing. Later the company branched into production chemicals, such as capillary foam additives. CESI's capabilities were supplemented in 2002 with the acquisition of Denver-based IBS 2000, Inc., maker of environmentally neutral chemicals for the oil industry.

Flotek began growing revenues in the early 2000s. Sales increased from $11.34 million in 2002 (the fiscal year coincided with the calendar year) to $18.4 million in 2003, but the company continued to post net losses: $5.4 million in 2002 and another $7.4 million in 2003. The corner had been turned, however. In 2004 revenues approached $22 million and the company netted $2.2 million. Business was even stronger in 2005, as Flotek more than doubled sales to $52.9 million and net income jumped to $7.7 million. Much of that growth was the result of a deal made in late 2004 and completed in February 2005, the $8 million acquisition of Spidle Sales & Services Inc., that greatly enhanced Flotek's Drilling Products Group. Based in the Rocky Mountain region, the company was founded by its president, Agee Spidle. It was a downhole tool company serving energy, mining, water, and industrial drilling clients in North and South America, Europe, Asia, and Africa. The addition of Spidle benefited Flotek on several fronts: It added new products, increased market penetration, expanding the company's geographic footprint, and opened up new cross-selling opportunities between Flotek's specialty chemicals and downhole production equipment business. Also in 2005, Flotek acquired assets related to oilfield shale shaker screen from Phoenix E&P Technology, LLC, and the assets of Harmons Machine Works, Inc., a downhole oilfield and mining tool company based in Midland, Texas. In August 2005, Flotek added another Texas company, Precision-LOR, Ltd., a drilling tool rental and inspection service company.

AMERICAN STOCK EXCHANGE LISTING: 2005

Flotek's increasing revenues paved the way for Flotek's stock to jettison its over-the-counter status. In July 2005 Flotek shares began trading on the American Stock Exchange. Revenues topped the $100 million mark in 2006 and net income grew to $11.35 million. The company's aggressive growth continued in 2007 with the $31 million acquisition of Triumph Drilling Tools, a downhole equipment rental company; the $18.5 million purchase of Houston-based Cavo Drilling Motors, which offered a line of mud motors used by drillers; and the $7.1 million purchase of Sooner Energy Services Inc., a Norman, Oklahoma-based specialty chemical company.

Flotek's revenues and profits were on a record pace in 2007, leading the company to declare a 2-for-1 stock split in the summer. At the end of the year the company filed to be listed on the New York Stock Exchange. The company had barely scratched the surface of its potential, especially on the international scene. Given that energy prices were not likely to fall in the near term, Flotek's prospects looked promising for years to come.

Ed Dinger

PRINCIPAL SUBSIDIARIES

Chemical & Equipment Specialties, Inc.; Materials Translogistics, Inc.; Petrovalve International, Inc.; Turbeco, Inc.

PRINCIPAL COMPETITORS

Baker Hughes Incorporated; The Lubrizol Corporation; Omni Energy Services Corp.

FURTHER READING

"Flotek Industries Inc.," *Oil & Gas Investor,* August 2005, p. 54.

"Flotek Industries Inc.," *Oil & Gas Investor,* August 2006, p. 50.

"Flotek to Buy Spidle for $8 Million," *Houston Business Journal,* December 21, 2004.

Goldsmith, Jill, "Flotek Seeks Nasdaq Listing; New Valve Helps Pump Oil Faster," *Dow Jones News Service,* October 18, 1995.

Leach, W. H., Jr., "Nuts, Bolts and a Better Valve," *Oil & Gas Investor,* May 1995, p. 31.

Page, David, "Chemical & Equip. Specialties to Merge into Flotek," *Oklahoma City (Okla.) Journal Record,* August 17, 2001.

Gale International Llc

712 Fifth Avenue, 44th Floor
New York, New York 10019
U.S.A.
Telephone: (212) 586-1870
Fax: (212) 586-2591
Web site: http://www.galeintl.com

Private Company
Incorporated: 1988 as Gale & Wentworth L.L.C.
NAIC: 531190 Lessors of Other Real Estate Property

■ ■ ■

Gale International Llc is a New York City-based real estate development and investment company involved in both domestic and international projects. In the United States, Gale is heavily involved in downtown Boston, working with Morgan Stanley Real Estate to engineer the city's largest commercial real estate transaction, the $705 million sale of the One Lincoln Street office tower. In addition, the company is developing Seaport Square on 23 acres of land, the largest undeveloped site adjacent to Boston's central business district, and redeveloping the city's historic Filene's building. In addition to New York and Boston, Gale maintains an office in Irvine, California.

The company's most celebrated project, and one that prompted the 2006 sale of its multibillion-dollar portfolio of class A northeast office space to Mack-Cali Realty Corporation, is the development of Songdo (meaning "pine tree") International City, a $25 billion master planned city conceived by the South Korean government to be built on 1,500 acres of reclaimed land located close to the Incheon International Airport and one hour from the nation's capital, Seoul. Moreover, it is 50 miles from the North Korean capital of Pyongyang and within two hours by air of 50 cities in China with populations of more than one million each. Designated as a free economic zone and a bilingual city, where both Korean and English will be accepted, Songdo is intended to serve as a northeast Asia economic hub and a gateway to the vast China market. The ambitious project, to be developed piecemeal, has no timetable. Gale maintains international offices in Seoul and New Songdo, South Korea.

LINEAGE DATES TO 1922

Although not in a direct line, Gale International traces its history to the 1922 creation of the Daniel Gale Agency, founded by the grandfather of Gale International's chairman and managing partner, Stanley C. Gale. A young New Yorker who fell in love with the beauty of Long Island's North Shore and its less hectic pace of life, Daniel Gale believed that other city residents would be of a similar mind, and in 1922 he moved his family to Huntington Village to set up a real estate office. The business was able to survive the stock market crash of 1929 and the Great Depression that ensued. His son, H. Kent Gale, Stanley Gale's father, joined the agency in 1937. Six years later he married one of the sales associates, Jean, and after a stint in the military during World War II began to raise a family.

Following World War II, Long Island enjoyed explosive growth and the Daniel Gale Agency was well positioned to take advantage of it. In 1952 the company opened a second office in the former whaling village of Cold Spring Harbor and adopted a sperm whale as its logo, an image that over the years became ubiquitous on much of Long Island. In 1964 Daniel Gale died and Kent Gale took over a business that at the time consisted of two offices and a handful of sales associates. Under his leadership, the business added offices and extended its reach across the Island. In 1976 Daniel Gale became the exclusive real estate agent, with the exception of the Hamptons, for the real estate arm of the Sotheby's auction house.

In 1974 Kent Gale hired a sales associate named Patricia Petersen, who would be mentored by Kent and Jean Gale. Petersen became manager of the Cold Spring Harbor office, and then became a vice-president and the company's general manager in 1985. Petersen bought out Kent and Jean Gale in 1991 and became president and chief executive officer, and continued to run and grow the business under the Daniel Gale name. By 2005 Daniel Gale, Long Island's largest independent real estate firm, employed more than 400 agents, maintained 16 offices, and did an annual business in excess of $2 billion.

STAN GALE LEADS FAMILY FIRM
AFTER ONE YEAR

Stanley Gale worked only briefly with the family firm. In the late 1960s he enrolled at Rollins College in Florida, primarily to play soccer. He became a top scorer, and toyed with the idea of becoming a professional player, even trying out for an English league. In the end, however, he decided to follow in the footsteps of his grandfather and father. After graduating in 1972 he continued his studies at Rollins' Roy E. Crummer School of Business and Finance, earning an M.B.A. He then joined his father at Daniel Gale in 1974 but after a year in residential real estate he decided he wanted to become involved in commercial real estate and left for California, taking a position with Grubb & Ellis, an expanding San Francisco–area firm. Over the next decade Gale was able to gain a broad range of experi-

ence as Grubb & Ellis grew its business to include property and asset management and real estate development. He also learned the financial and investment aspects of the business.

In 1985 Gale decided to return to the East Coast. Rather than rejoin the family firm where Petersen was being groomed to take control, Gale opted to continue his career in commercial real estate, establishing a Northeast Region office of The Sammis Company, an Irvine, California-based investment and development company. A year later he was joined by his future partner, Finn Wentworth, a northern New Jersey native. After graduating with a degree in marketing from Lehigh University in 1980, Wentworth turned down an entry level job with AT&T, accepting less money with the commercial real estate firm of Cushman & Wakefield, Inc. After three years he took a position with Dallas-based Lincoln Property Company's Northeast Corridor operation, and then joined Gale to assume the same function.

FORMATION OF GALE &
WENTWORTH: 1988

In the late 1980s the savings and loan debacle led to a real estate recession that devastated the commercial real estate market in New York and New Jersey. Gale and Wentworth took advantage of the situation, buying out Sammis' New Jersey interests in 1988 to form their own real estate development and management firm, Gale & Wentworth, L.L.C., based in Floral Park, New Jersey. The next few years were difficult but the partners hung on and in the early 1990s began to team up with Wall Street firms such as Morgan Stanley and PaineWebber to acquire commercial real estate at depressed prices. As the economy recovered, the firm prospered, growing into one of the area's top commercial real estate firms, known as a fee developer. It would craft office building deals with corporations and then bring in Wall Street firms to supply the money to construct the building and office parks. Gale & Wentworth retained a small ownership stake in each project while also collecting generous management fees. The firm's Wall Street partners were pleased with the relationship as well, enjoying fat profits while the area's real estate market boomed until finally slumping in the early 2000s.

In 1997 Morgan Stanley acquired an 80 to 85 percent stake in Gale & Wentworth, leading to even greater investments from the Wall Street giant. The subsequent acquisition of the 8.2 million-square-foot office portfolio of Bellmead Development Corp. made Gale & Wentworth the largest private office-operating company in New Jersey. All told, in the five years after Morgan Stanley bought a controlling interest, Gale &

KEY DATES

1922: Daniel Gale Agency is founded.
1974: Stanley C. Gale joins family firm.
1988: Stanley Gale and Finn Wentworth form Gale & Wentworth L.L.C.
1999: Wentworth leaves firm for YankeesNets.
2001: Songdo, South Korea, project is launched.
2002: Gale & Wentworth is renamed The Gale Company.
2006: Gale Company assets are sold, leaving Gale International.

Wentworth grew its assets to $1.7 billion. The company also opened an office in southern California to become involved in commercial real estate in that market as well.

In 1998 Wentworth began to turn his attention away from real estate, becoming part owner of the New Jersey Nets National Basketball Association franchise. Gale would also invest in the Nets, which along with the New Jersey Devils hockey team would merge with the New York Yankees baseball team to form YankeesNets. In 1999 Wentworth became president and chief operating officer of YankeesNets, and his participation with Gale & Wentworth was limited to an advisory capacity. For the most part, Gale now looked after Wentworth's real estate investments, while Wentworth looked after Gale's sports' interests.

OPENING OF BOSTON OFFICE: 1999

Another man would emerge to essentially take Wentworth's place as Gale's partner, John Hynes III, who established a Boston office for Gale & Wentworth in 1999 after two decades of brokering leases. According to the *Boston Globe,* Hynes, whose grandfather had been Boston's mayor from 1950 to 1960, "had a desk and a two-word job description: Find Deals." Already in the works was a project financed by Morgan Stanley Real Estate Funds and State Teachers Retirement System of Ohio, a $350 million luxury office building with more than one million square feet of space, built purely on speculation. In 2001 it would be leased to State Street Financial for 20 years, representing the largest lease in Boston history. The deal established Gale & Wentworth's reputation beyond the New York City market, even overseas, leading to a mega-deal that found Hynes rather than the other way around.

In March 2001, while wrapping up the State Street deal, Hynes was contacted by a Korean American consultant, Jay Kim, who had pulled his name off the Internet because of State Street. Kim was representing a Korean real estate project but was having a difficult time finding a U.S. developer willing to take it on. When Hynes said during a quick coffee meeting that he was tied up with a big deal and could not consider the project at the moment, he became intrigued by the consultant's rejoinder that Hynes really had no idea what big was. Hynes flew to South Korea and soon telephoned Gale, telling him, as reported by *Forbes,* "Stan, you've got to get over here. These guys are serious. This is for real." The project in mind was the $25 billion Songdo development in South Korea. According to the *Boston Globe,* Hynes and Gale "liked the challenge of a new culture, a huge project, and a clean slate: there was nothing on the site. In fact, there wasn't even a real site; the city would be built on a landfill. 'It's like a big jigsaw puzzle,' says Hynes. 'You design the pieces and install them. It's the ultimate developer's dream.'"

The Songdo project grew out of the Asian financial crisis of the late 1990s. Following a $58 billion bailout from the International Monetary Fund, South Korea was pressured to seek outside investments and increase foreign reserves. Thus, the South Korean government agreed to bring in a foreign developer for the ambitious Songdo project. Jay Kim, a former Westinghouse nuclear power plant designer who came to the United States during the Korean War, was then recruited to seek out U.S. partners. However, the project appeared to be too risky to developers who were enjoying success in the United States. These rejections ultimately led Kim to the more receptive Hynes in Boston.

CREATION OF GALE INTERNATIONAL: 2001

Hynes was dispatched to South Korea later in 2001 to begin negotiations with the government as well as with Korean steelmaker Posco to finance the project. By the end of 2001 a deal was hammered out giving Gale & Wentworth's new subsidiary, Gale International Llc, a 70 percent stake and Posco 30 percent in a joint-venture company called New Songdo City Development Corporation. It was a landmark arrangement, according to the *Boston Globe,* representing the world's first Korean-U.S. real estate project and making Gale & Wentworth "the first foreign owner of Korean soil," but only after South Korea in 2003 overturned a law forbidding non-nationals from land ownership. Hynes was then charged with putting together a team of lawyers, consultants, and architects to create a wide-ranging master plan for Songdo that included financing and marketing as well as a design and budget.

While the first phase of the Songdo project was launched, a $2 billion effort that would include a pair of hotels, one million square feet of office space, 5,000 housing units, a trade and convention center, a golf course, and one private and four public schools, Gale & Wentworth remained active on other fronts. In 2001 the California offshoot entered the northern California market for the first time. A few months later, in February 2002, Stan Gale bought out Morgan Stanley's interest, and renamed the company The Gale Company. Although Wentworth would return to real estate after leaving YankeesNet, he would do so with a new business partner.

While The Gale Company continued to pursue its traditional business, Songdo was clearly becoming the firm's pet project. The company's Irvine, California, office, in fact would be converted into a sales office for New Songdo City residential units, catering to the area's large Korean population. Close to two years and $10 million would be spent simply assessing the viability of the project. By the time a master plan was submitted, Morgan Stanley was brought on board as a minority partner at a cost of $350 million, an investment that opened the door to $4 billion in Korean bank loans, the first of what would likely become $20 billion in loans before the project's completion. The project was not without controversy, however. Gale Company had squabbles with both the Korean government and Posco, and it had to contend with harsh criticism from the Korean press, which portrayed the firm as an opportunistic Western company. Nevertheless, the project continued to proceed.

In order to recapitalize Gale International, Stan Gale decided in 2006 to sell almost all of his commercial real estate holdings to rival New Jersey firm Mack-Cali Realty Corp. for a reported price of $545 million. Of that amount, $40 million was to be paid for Gale Real Estate Services Co., the management, construction, and maintenance arm, while $505 million was paid for 20 office buildings in New Jersey, Illinois, and Michigan, altogether containing 2.75 million square feet.

Although Gale International was very much devoted to the Songdo project, it pursued new develop-

ment projects in the United States as well. In the fall of 2006 Gale and Morgan Stanley acquired a 23-acre parcel of land in Boston for the Seaport Square project, a massive mixed-use project near the city's central business district. Late in 2006 the company and its partner acquired the former ExxonMobil site in Floral Park, New Jersey, in order to build the new headquarters for the New York Jets football team, part of a major planned development in Morris County. Early in 2007 the company and an investment partner bought the Filene's building in Boston for development. Clearly Gale had plenty of irons in the fire, enough to keep the firm occupied for many years to come.

Ed Dinger

PRINCIPAL COMPETITORS

Jones Lang LaSalle Incorporated; CB Richard Ellis Group, Inc.; Cushman & Wakefield, Inc.

FURTHER READING

Beranek, Suzanne, "Stan Gale '72 '73," *Crummer Connection,* Fall 2003.

Cortese, Amy, "An Asian Hub in the Making," *New York Times,* December 30, 2007, p. BU20.

Drake, Diana Lasseter, "Building a Bigger Sandbox," *NJBiz,* February 11, 2002.

English, Bella, "He'll Build This City," *Boston Globe,* December 13, 2004.

Hinderer, Katie, "Constructing a Metropolis: New Songdo City Breaks Ground," *Commercial Property News,* March 1, 2006, p. 27.

Houlusha, John, "Commercial Property/New Jersey; From Suburban Office Parks to Korean Mega-Project," *New York Times,* November 2, 2003.

Jordan, George E., "Gale Drops 'Wentworth,'" *Newark (N.J.) Star Ledger,* February 15, 2002, p. 39.

"1922: Daniel Gale Real Estate Launches in Huntington," *Long Island Business News,* January 9, 2004.

O'Reilly, Tim, "Gale Co. Selling Office Parks to Rival for $545 M," *Morristown (N.J.) Daily Record,* February 17, 2006.

Shankar, P., "The Return of Finn Wentworth," *NJBix,* November 1, 2004.

Steiner, Christopher, "Scratch Builders," *Forbes.com,* January 7, 2008.

Gaming Partners
International Corporation

1700 Industrial Road
Las Vegas, Nevada 89102
U.S.A.
Telephone: (702) 384-2425
Toll Free: (800) 728-5766
Fax: (702) 384-1965
Web site: http://www.gpigaming.com

Public Company
Incorporated: 2004
Employees: 760
Sales: $73.95 million (2006)
Stock Exchanges: NASDAQ
Ticker Symbol: GPIC
NAIC: 339932 Game, Toy, and Children's Vehicle Manufacturing; 551112 Offices of Other Holding Companies

∎∎∎

Gaming Partners International Corporation (GPI) is a leading manufacturer and supplier of casino table equipment, serving casinos throughout the world. GPI makes dice, playing cards, gaming chips, table layouts, gaming furniture, roulette wheels, chip trays, drop boxes, and dealing shoes. The company operates manufacturing facilities in Las Vegas, Nevada; San Luis, Mexico; and Beaune, France. Through its Las Vegas-based subsidiary, Gaming Partners International USA, GPI sells its products directly to casinos in the United States and Canada. The company's Beaune-based subsidiary, Gaming Partners International SAS, sells its European-manufactured products to casinos in countries outside North America.

A TALE OF THREE COMPANIES

GPI, the name, first appeared in 2004, but the assets controlled under the new corporate banner had a history dating back to the 1920s. GPI was the sum of its parts, an enterprise comprised of three companies: Etablissements Bourgogne et Grasset S.A. (B&G), The Bud Jones Company, and Paul-Son Gaming Corporation. Each of the companies figured as a pioneer in the gaming supply industry and each company possessed a unique identity. GPI had roots in Nevada and in France, where the chronological story of the company's formation began 80 years before its name first appeared.

B&G: A FOCUS ON SECURITY

In the city of Beaune, in the Burgundy region of France, two inventors were making pioneering discoveries in the use of plastics during the early 1920s. Étienne Bourgogne, a lithographer, and Claudius Grasset, an engineer, became the first to master the art of plastic film printing. Soon, their work turned to developing other uses for plastics. The partners were working on incorporating plastics into hair slides, brooches, and playing cards, when Grasset read an article in *Le Figaro* in 1925 that focused their work in a single direction. The newspaper article revealed that a counterfeiter had broken the bank at the Monte Carlo casino, using fake chips to bilk the casino of 600,000 francs.

Bourgogne and Grasset immediately began work on applying their knowledge of plastics to the manufacture

COMPANY PERSPECTIVES

The group concentrates on products that are very sensitive to casinos, particularly chips but also dice, wheels, cards, and associated products such as layouts and gaming tables. GPI is the developer and the manufacturer of these products and generally does direct sales to legal casinos all over the world. GPI is the casinos partner and advises its client on the best choices to make to ensure security, reliability and quality.

of casino chips, searching for a way to address the security problem. They produced a batch of chips using a process in which the impression of the chip was protected by a thin plastic film, making it exceedingly hard to copy, and sent their samples to the general manager of the Monte Carlo casino, Monsieur Blanc. When a response came back from Monsieur Blanc, the two partners were in business. Their company, B&G, received its first order for casino chips, marking the birth of a brand recognized for its ability to thwart counterfeiters.

Security was the focus of B&G's second owner, Daniel Senard, who purchased the company in 1945 after spending five years as a prisoner in a Nazi detention camp. Under Senard's leadership, numerous security features were added to B&G's chips, including color stripes, *lunettes* (see-through windows), white and golden lace, lamé, and invisible prints. The innovations made the company's chips, and their more international counterparts, *plaques* and *jetons,* renowned for their uncompromisable authenticity, which fueled B&G's growth. Casinos across Europe turned to B&G for supplies, beginning a period of steady geographic expansion that would see the company's products in use in Macao, the Philippines, Malaysia, Australia, Chile, Argentina, and South Africa. The company expanded its product line as well, launching a line of injection-molded plastic chips in 1990 before diversifying into the manufacture of roulette wheels, gaming tables, and other supplies several years later.

After a half-century of leading the company, Senard decided to sell B&G in 1994. He sold the company to a group of investors led by his son-in-law, Gerard P. Charlier, the executive in charge of GPI when it was formed. Charlier earned graduate degrees in business from IN-SEAD in Fontainebleau, France, and in electrical engineering from Stanford University in Palo Alto,

California, before primarily working as a consultant during the two decades leading up to his purchase of B&G. Under Charlier's charge, the drive to make B&G a more comprehensive competitor in the global gaming industry continued, exemplified by the company's decision in 2000 to acquire a U.S.-based dice, playing card, and gaming supply company named The Bud Jones Company.

BUD JONES, THE KING OF DICE

Like B&G, The Bud Jones Company drew its impetus from a glance at a newspaper. In 1934, a decade after Grasset read about fraud in *Le Figaro,* Bernard "Bud" Jones scoured through the help-wanted section in a Kansas City, Missouri, newspaper. He was 19 years old when he saw an advertisement for work as a dice maker, a chance introduction that became a lifelong obsession for the young Kansas City native. For the next two decades, Jones learned every aspect of the dice-making business, starting as an employee before becoming a manager and eventually part owner of several casino supply enterprises based in his hometown.

If not for a calamitous event, Jones probably would have remained in Kansas City for the rest of his life. The nation's largest, casino-grade dice manufacturer would never have been formed. During the mid-1950s, a fire destroyed Jones's gaming supply company, prompting him to move his family to Nevada. After settling in Las Vegas, he spent several years adjusting to his new surroundings before taking the risk of starting his own business. In 1965, the 40-year-old Jones established his company, forming a dice manufacturer named The Bud Jones Company.

Jones's business flourished in Las Vegas. The company became the largest producer of casino-quality dice in the United States. It diversified into the production of gaming tables and introduced coin-inlay gaming chips manufactured by surrounding an actual silver coin with molded plastic, a security feature that would have impressed Senard at B&G. The most important of Jones's diversifying moves was his launch of a line of injection-molded plastic gaming chips, the type of "American-style" casino chips that inspired B&G's entry into the niche in 1990. For Bud Jones Co., the success of its injection-molded chips served as its passport to markets throughout the world. By the 1980s, the company's chips ranked as one of the most popular brands of American-style chips in European, Far East Asian, and South African casinos. By the 1990s, Bud Jones Co. counted more than 500 casinos as customers, a roster of clients that operated in 50 countries.

Jones worked every day at the Las Vegas office of his company for 34 years, serving as its guiding figure

KEY DATES

1925: Etablissements Bourgogne et Grasset S.A. (B&G) is formed to produce casino chips with anti-counterfeiting features.

1945: B&G is sold to Daniel Senard, who develops numerous security features for the company's products.

1963: Paul-Son Gaming Supply is formed.

1965: The Bud Jones Company is formed.

2000: B&G acquires Bud Jones.

2002: B&G, Bud Jones, and Paul-Son Gaming merge, creating a company that operates as Paul-Son Gaming Corp.

2004: Paul-Son Gaming changes its name to Gaming Partners International Corporation.

2006: In the years after the merger, the company's sales nearly double to $73.9 million.

until he was forced to stop working because of illness at age 84 in 1999. Unwilling to name a successor, he sold the business in October 2000 to B&G, presenting the French company with an ideal opportunity to expand its product line and extend its presence into the United States. Jones passed away a year after the sale, by which time the new owners of his business had their sights set on a company very familiar to Jones, his crosstown rival, Paul-Son Gaming Corp.

PAUL-SON GAMING, BECOMING A LAS VEGAS GIANT

Paul S. Endy, Jr., was the fourth seminal figure in GPI's history. Born in Monterey Park, California, in 1929, Endy attended college at Long Beach City College and worked as an electrician for Bethlehem Steel before joining his family's business. His father, Paul S. Endy, Sr., owned T.R. King & Company, a gaming supply distributor and dice manufacturer. Paul, Jr., joined the company in the early 1950s and became his father's top salesman, spending his days on the road selling gaming supplies for the legal card rooms prevalent along California's coast. When his father retired in 1963, Paul, Jr., balked at the opportunity to take control of the family business. "I didn't get along with his partner," Paul, Jr., remarked in a December 5, 1994, interview with *Forbes.*

Endy decided to move to Utah and work on a ranch. While his wife tied up loose ends in California, Endy and his children headed off to Utah, but their journey ended in Las Vegas. For the third time in the history of GPI, the perusal of a newspaper led to the formation of a gaming supply company. While in Las Vegas, Endy saw an advertisement in a local newspaper for a bankruptcy sale. Regulators had seized the assets of a corrupt dice manufacturer and were liquidating the property. Endy leaped at the opportunity, borrowing $40,000 from his father to buy the business. In tribute to his father's financial help, as well as to the contributions of his three sons who joined the business, Endy named the company Paul-Son Gaming Supply.

Bud Jones enjoyed immediate success with his venture, but Endy struggled during his first years. He and his family lived behind the factory in a 16-foot trailer. The trappings were austere, and the company was lucky to get a weekly order for 500 dice. "I showered with a garden hose," Endy recalled in his December 5, 1994, interview with *Forbes.* Business improved after Endy brought in a partner, Curley Ashworth, to run operations, which gave him time to do what he did best: sales. He loaded all his supplies in a customized two-ton van and hit the road, driving a warehouse on wheels. He spent ten days a month in California, where he converted his father's former customers into Paul-Son Gaming customers.

Once Endy's business found its footing, orders and sales shot upward. The company opened an office in Reno, Nevada, in 1974 and an office in Atlantic City, New Jersey, in 1978. It diversified beyond cards and dice into gaming chips, gaming tables, and felt layouts. Paul-Son Gaming introduced new technologies, such as chips designed with encoded microfilm, and a proprietary molding system that enabled highly detailed graphics to be applied to chips. Moving manufacturing operations, aside from felt layouts and cards, to San Luis, Mexico, in 1982 proved to be a boon to business, as did the passage of the Indian Gaming Regulatory Act of 1988, which granted Native American tribes the right to regulate gaming on their land. In response to the growing stature of his company, Endy decided to convert to public ownership, taking the first step in December 1993 by forming Paul-Son Gaming Corporation to control all his gaming supply assets. The following March the company completed its initial public offering (IPO) of stock, netting $36 million from the sale.

Paul-Son Gaming entered the 1990s expecting market conditions to remain as they had during the 1980s. Dynamics in the casino industry changed, however, delivering a blow to the company's stalwart position. Gambling was as popular as ever, but casinos were generating the majority of their revenue from slot machines, video poker, and other electronic gaming machines, forms of gambling that left Paul-Son

Gaming's sales offices sitting idle. As it entered the late 1990s, the company began to struggle, its lackluster performance exacerbated by the loss of its leader. In October 1998, Endy suffered a stroke while on a fishing trip in Mexico. He passed away the following year at age 70, replaced as Paul-Son Gaming's chief executive officer by his son, Eric P. Endy, who joined the company permanently in 1983 after earning a master's degree in audiology.

THREE COMPANIES COMING TOGETHER IN 2002

While Paul-Son Gaming explored strategic alternatives, hinting at a possible sale of some or all of its assets, B&G watched from the wings, ready to take center stage. A deal was struck between the two companies in 2001, which, after some bickering between the two parties, resulted in a merger between B&G, its subsidiary, The Bud Jones Co., and Paul-Son Gaming. The transaction was completed in September 2002, combining all three businesses under the Paul-Son Gaming corporate banner. Although the resulting entity bore the Paul-Son Gaming name, B&G was the driving force behind the merger. Gerard Charlier, president and chief executive officer of B&G, became president and chief executive officer of the newly constituted Paul-Son Gaming. B&G's chairman, François G. Carette, became Paul-Son Gaming's chairman. In September 2004, the company changed its name to Gaming Partners International, Inc., a company based in Las Vegas that controlled two primary subsidiaries, Gaming Partners International USA, which comprised the operations of Paul-Son Gaming and The Bud Jones Co., and Gaming Partners International SAS, a Beaune-based subsidiary that inherited B&G's operations.

GPI stood as a formidable force in the gaming supply industry during the first decade of the 21st century. Its three parts gave it decades of experience in a broad range of products that belied the novelty of its name. With business relationships in more than 60 countries, the company maintained a preeminent position in the global gaming industry, a position secured thanks to the contributions of Étienne Bourgogne, Claudius Grasset, Bernard Jones, and Paul S. Endy, Jr. Financially, the

company performed impressively after the merger, increasing its revenues from $36.1 million in 2003 to $73.9 million in 2006. Its net income during the period swelled from $1.2 million to $5.1 million. In the years ahead, Charlier intended to honor the company's past by using the business relationships cultivated by his predecessors to build a lasting future.

Jeffrey L. Covell

PRINCIPAL SUBSIDIARIES

Gaming Partners International USA; Gaming Partners International SAS (France).

PRINCIPAL COMPETITORS

JOM Inc.; The United States Playing Card Company; Midwest Game Supply Co.; Gemaco Playing Card Co.

FURTHER READING

Fitch, Stephanie, "The Chips Are Down," *Forbes,* April 9, 2007, p. 106.

"Gaming Consolidation May Place Paul-Son on Hold," *Mergers & Acquisitions Report,* December 22, 1997.

"Gaming Partners International Corporation Announces Name and Trading Symbol Change," *Business Wire,* September 1, 2004.

Meeks, Fleming, "Let the Big Guys Come," *Forbes,* December 5, 1994, p. 72.

"Paul S. Endy, Founder of Paul-Son Gaming, Dies," *Business Wire,* April 12, 1999, p. 1541.

"Paul-Son Gaming Appoints Eric P. Endy Chairman, CEO," *Business Wire,* November 25, 1998, p. 1244.

"Paul-Son Gaming Corp. Announces Demand for Termination Fee from Bourgogne et Grasset and The Bud Jones Co.," *Business Wire,* April 30, 2001, p. 0640.

"Paul-Son Gaming Corporation, Bourgogne et Grasset and The Bud Jones Company to Combine," *Business Wire,* April 1, 2002, p. 0359.

"Paul-Son Set to Merge with French Company," *Las Vegas Review-Journal,* April 19, 2002, p. 2D.

"Paul-Son to Review Strategic Alternatives," *Business Wire,* October 6, 1997, p. 10061047.

Gordon Biersch Brewery Restaurant Group, Inc.

2001 Riverside Drive, Suite 3100
Chattanooga, Tennessee 37402
U.S.A.
Telephone: (423) 424-2000
Fax: (423) 752-1973
Web site: http://www.gordonbiersch.com

Private Company
Incorporated: 1992 as Trolley Barn Breweries, Inc.
Employees: 2,116
Sales: $100 million (2007 est.)
NAIC: 722110 Full-Service Restaurants

■■■

Gordon Biersch Brewery Restaurant Group, Inc., is a Chattanooga, Tennessee-based restaurant company that shares the Gordon Biersch name with Gordon Biersch Brewing Company but not their ownership. The company's casual dining restaurants serve the brewery's hand-crafted German lager-style beers but they set themselves apart from other "brew-and-chew" establishments by offering higher-end cuisine. All told there are 17 Gordon Biersch eateries located in 13 mostly western states and Washington, D.C. In addition, the company extends its reach to another three states by operating another 17 brewery restaurants under several other brands: Big River Grille and Brewery, with four units in Tennessee and Florida; Rock Bottom Restaurant Brewery, located in Atlanta and Charlotte, North Carolina; Seven Bridges Grille and Brewery in Jacksonville, Florida; A1A Ale Works in St. Augustine, Florida; Ragtime Tavern and Seafood Grill in Atlantic Beach, Florida; and Bluewater Grille in Chattanooga.

DAN GORDON GRADUATES FROM RENOWNED BREWING PROGRAM: 1987

The two men behind the creation of the Gordon Biersch brand were Dan Gordon and Dean Biersch. The man possessing the technical expertise in brewing was Gordon, born in San Jose in 1960 and raised in the northern California community of Los Altos. While studying economics at the University of California, Berkeley, he developed an interest in the engineering of food processing. Gordon spent a year as an exchange student at the Georg August University in Gottingen, Germany, and it was during this time he learned it was possible to study brewing. Gordon told the *Business Journal* in a 1993 profile, "I thought, how ideal. I could combine my personal interests of the mechanics of production and drinking beer." Gordon worked for a year at the Anheuser-Busch plant in Fairfield, California, gaining enough brewing experience to apply for admission to the prestigious five-year brewing program at the Technical University of Munich after he graduated from Berkeley in 1982. Becoming the first American to graduate from the program in a half a century, Gordon was offered jobs at Anheuser-Busch Co. and Adolph Coors Co. Instead, he decided to join forces with a young restaurateur, Dean Biersch, and open a combination microbrewery and restaurant.

DEAN BIERSCH, ASPIRING RESTAURATEUR

Biersch was also a northern California native, born in San Francisco and living in the area until high school took him to Los Angeles. He returned to the Bay Area for college, earning a degree in international relations from San Francisco State University. Along the way he earned money in the restaurant field, starting out as a fryer cleaner at the age of 15. After graduating from San Francisco State, he decided to pursue restaurant management and completed the management program at the Beverly Hilton hotel in Beverly Hills, California. He then became a catering manager for San Francisco's Hornblower Day Yachts Inc. While visiting a girlfriend in Mendocino in 1983 he also checked out California's first brewpub, the Mendocino Brewing Co., makers of Red Tail Ale. Impressed with the operation Biersch began developing his own variation on the brewpub concept: Instead of the usual fare of finger foods, he wanted to offer a regular dinner menu. Moreover, the microbrewery would eschew mild English ales in favor of the German lagers he had come to appreciate during visits to Central America, brews that would complement the type of cuisine he had in mind.

Gordon was thinking along the same lines as Biersch and began telling friends and colleagues about his vision of a microbrewery and restaurant. Eventually mutual acquaintances suggested that the two men meet, leading to Biersch cold-calling Gordon. "We spent a week around my parent's swimming pool getting to know each other," Gordon recalled to the *Business Journal*. Deciding a corporate job would always be available as a safety net, Gordon threw in with Biersch in 1987. Biersch's godfather, Robert W. Carrau, became their initial investor, paving the way for other investments and the securing of a line of bank credit.

FIRST GORDON BIERSCH BREWERY RESTAURANT: 1988

With more than $1 million in funds at their disposal, Gordon and Biersch restored an old theater in downtown Palo Alto which opened in 1988 under the Gordon Biersch Brewery Restaurant name. Gordon relied on secondhand equipment procured from Germany, and the brewing operations were separated from the 185-seat dining area by glass partitions. Initially Gordon brewed three lagers: Export, Marzen, and Dunkles. As for dishes, executive chef Jaime Carpenter offered such fare as chicken skewers with a Thai dipping sauce, lemon marinated chicken breast with smoked pepper butter and cumin Texmati rice, and oven-baked seabass. Moderately priced to attract repeat business, the Palo Alto establishment was an instant hit. Not only did it generate more than $2 million in sales in its first year, the restaurant enjoyed high margins because it supplied its own beer.

With a major success under its belt, Gordon and Biersch looked for a site to open a second unit, choosing downtown San Jose for a new location, taking advantage of a failed brewery restaurant, Biers Brasserie. Gordon and Biersch were able to pick up the operation's assets for a song and then apply their winning formula. The brewery-restaurant opened in April 1990 and once again became a sensation on the local scene. In its first full year of operation, 1991, at a time when other downtown eateries were fortunate to survive the effects of a recession, Gordon Biersch thrived, posting revenues of more than $3 million. The partners also turned their attention to the highly competitive San Francisco market. In the spring of 1991 they opened a Gordon Biersch unit in the city's Hills Plaza, a multiuse facility built on the site of the landmark Hills Brothers Coffee plant. Offering a first floor bar that could handle 170 people and a second floor dining room that could seat another 190, the 15,000-square-foot establishment, about three times the size of the Palo Alto unit, cost more than $3 million to open, the funding divided equally between Gordon Biersch and the Hills Plaza developer. As was the case with the previous establishment, the San Francisco operation was highly successful, taking in nearly $4 million in its first year.

Although interested in opening more brewery-restaurants, the partners began making plans to expand into retail sales. The goal was to one day bottle Gordon Biersch beer and to drive sales by opening restaurants in new markets. A Pasadena unit was added in December 1992, followed a year later by a fifth operation in Honolulu. Not only was it Hawaii's first microbrewery, it quickly became the top grossing restaurant there. During this time the company took some steps to become involved in the retail business, initially selling kegs of its brew from the restaurant operations at the San Jose Arena and San Francisco's Candlestick Park, where it would be served at both baseball and football games. In order to increase production to serve wholesale channels with Gordon Biersch beer, the company leased space in Emeryville, California, in 1994

KEY DATES

1988: Dan Gordon and Dean Biersch open first brewery-restaurant in Palo Alto, California.
1991: San Francisco unit opens.
1995: Majority ownership is acquired by Export Limited Partnership.
1999: Restaurant operations are sold to Big River Brewing Inc., which changes its name to Gordon Biersch Brewery Restaurant Group, Inc.
2004: New financing is provided by Hancock Park Associates.
2006: Plans for public offering are canceled.

to open a new brewery and kegging facility.

With annual sales around $20 million by 1995, the growing brewery-restaurant and wholesale brewery operation had outgrown its original decentralized organization. As part of the effort to impose more managerial structure to support the company's ambitious expansion plans, a new president and chief executive officer was hired in April 1995, Robert S. Burke, a well-seasoned restaurant executive. Under his direction, the plan was to open new brewery-restaurants in new markets in California, Arizona, Nevada, Oregon, and Washington, as well as to push forward the company's efforts to open a bottling plant.

ACQUISITION BY FERTITTA FAMILY: 1995

Burke's tenure with Gordon Biersch would be short-lived, however. Several months later a controlling interest in the company would be sold to the Fertitta family of Las Vegas, owners of Station Casinos, three gambling operations that catered to the local trade. Gordon had provided consulting services for them on a brewery-restaurant project they were developing in Las Vegas. During this time, Gordon Biersch was fielding offers from banks and investor groups to provide funding to support the company's expansion plans. The Fertittas asked to review the pitch and were impressed enough that they made a winning offer of $17 million to purchase 51 percent of Gordon Biersch's stock through one of their subsidiaries, Export Limited Partnership, a deal that closed in late 1995. Because the Fertittas wanted to have control over who was running their new commitment, Burke was eased out. Gordon and Biersch retained about 30 percent of the company between

them, and Gordon remained director of brewing and Biersch continued to head restaurant operations.

Burke was replaced in April 1996 by Thomas B. Allin, a 23-year McDonald's executive who invested $3 million in the company. He would only head the company for less than two years, during which time a pair of brewery restaurants as well as a brewery and bottling plant were opened, and plans were made to take the company public. He left in October 1997 in acrimonious fashion and several months later filed suit against Gordon Biersch and Export Limited, as well as Lorenzo Fertitta, claiming that he was fired without cause and charging that Gordon Biersch board members took steps to deflate his investment and stock options, potentially costing him millions if the company proceeded with its initial public offering of stock.

BIG RIVER ACQUIRING RESTAURANT OPERATION: 1999

Lorenzo Fertitta took over as CEO and moved Gordon Biersch's headquarters to Las Vegas. The company was selling six-packs of its Marzen and Pilsner, produced at its new 114,000-square-foot San Jose brewery. By early 1999 there were Gordon Biersch brewery-restaurants in 12 cities, six new units added in 1998, serving as a spearhead in new markets: the eateries brought name recognition, leading to draft beer sales at area bars, and eventually resulting in six-pack sales at grocery stores. It was a winning formula that grew revenues to $70 million. Although the restaurants were a key element in expanding the brand across the United States, the company did not feel the need to shoulder the burden of growing a brewpub chain. Thus, in the fall of 1999 it agreed to sell the restaurant side of the business to Chattanooga, Tennessee-based Big River Brewing Inc., a successful multibrand operator of restaurant-breweries.

Big River was founded by a group of investors in 1992 as Trolley Barn Breweries, Inc. A year later the company opened the Big River Grille & Brewing Works in Chattanooga, and over the next five years opened three more Big River units and another five restaurant-breweries in the southeast under a variety of names. In 1996 Colorado-based Rock Bottom Restaurants Inc. acquired a 50 percent interest in Trolley Barn, which changed its name to Big River Breweries and opened Rock Bottom brewery-restaurants in the Southeast. This direct relationship lasted until November 1998, when Big River bought back its stock from Rock Bottom, although the two companies continued to share a number of shareholders.

While Big River was not interested in giving up the brand it had cultivated, it recognized that Gordon Biersch was a hot brand and decided to devote its attention to it. Moreover, Big River changed its name to Gordon Biersch Brewery Restaurant Group, Inc. Led by CEO Allen Corey, the company elected to put a hold on growing its stable of brands, including Ragtime Seafood Tavern & Grille, A1A Aleworks, and Big River, and focus on growing the Gordon Biersch operation in the west while introducing it in the southeast and other parts of the country. The first step was to open a Gordon Biersch unit in Atlanta just before the close of 1999, the location originally slated to house a Big River operation.

Over the next year, the company opened another five Gordon Biersch units, entering such new markets as Miami and Columbus, Ohio. As a result, Gordon Biersch took on debt, forcing it to put a halt to expansion from 2002 to 2004. During this time, management took steps to improve operations on a number of fronts, from upgrading operating systems to establishing guest loyalty and communication programs. In October 2004 the company was able to arrange new financing through the Los Angeles-based private equity firm of Hancock Park Associates. The infusion of funds reduced the company's debt load and allowed it to proceed with expansion plans. New Gordon Biersch units opened in New Orleans in the fall of 2004, followed by Tysons Corner, Virginia, in September 2005, Chattanooga in June 2006, and a half a dozen more locations over the next year.

To fuel further growth, Gordon Biersch took steps to make an initial public offering of stock in 2006, hoping to raise around $50 million. Poor market conditions, however, prompted management to pull the offering in July 2006. Nevertheless, Gordon Biersch continued to nurture expansion plans. Like its namesake brewery cousin, Gordon Biersch Brewery Restaurant Group introduced its own brand of beer, Big River, in September 2007, followed by Big River Vienna Lager and Big River Red Ale. Plans were also in the works to open new brewery-restaurants in Dallas, Kansas City, Phoenix, and Myrtle Beach, South Carolina. In addition, the company signed a licensing deal to take the Gordon Biersch restaurant brand to Taiwan and China, the first unit to open in Taiwan in the spring of 2008. The hope was to open up to ten restaurants in the region over the next five years and as many as 20 within a decade.

Ed Dinger

PRINCIPAL COMPETITORS

BJ Restaurants, Inc.; Metromedia Restaurant Group; Rock Bottom Restaurants, Inc.

FURTHER READING

Aronovich, Hanna, "Brewed Success," *Food and Drink,* August 2005, p. 42.

Battaglia, Andy, "Big River Taps Plan to Expand Gordon Biersch Brewery Brand," *Nation's Restaurant News,* November 1, 1999, p. 4.

Hayes, Mary, "Entrepreneurs Brewing Plans for Expansion," *Business Journal,* September 21, 1992, p. 1.

———, "Gordon Biersch Brewing Big Future," *Business Journal,* September 20, 1993, p. 1.

LaVecchia, Gina, "Something's Brewing," *Restaurant Hospitality,* March 2000, p. 60.

Liddle, Alan, "Biersch Brewery Makes a Splash with Bay Area Diners," *Nation's Restaurant News,* May 18, 1992, p. 1.

———, "Biersch Proves Foam Is Where the Heart Is," *Nation's Restaurant News,* July 17, 1989, p. 3.

———, "Gordon Biersch Sells Control to Las Vegas Investor Group," *Nation's Restaurant News,* December 18, 1995, p. 3.

Liedtke, Mike, "On a Roll, Biersch Likely to Spill into Stock Market," *Contra Costa Times,* December 10, 1995, p. C1.

Pare, Mike, "Gordon Biersch Takes Its Brand to Asia," *Chattanooga Times/Free Press,* August 25, 2007.

DANONE

Groupe Danone

17, Boulevard Haussman
Paris, 75009
France
Telephone: (+33 1) 44 35 20 20
Fax: (+33 1) 44 35 25 00
Web site: http://www.danone.com

Public Company
Incorporated: 1966 as Boussois Souchon-Neuvesel
Employees: 88,124
Sales: EUR 13.95 billion ($18.41 billion) (2006)
Stock Exchanges: Euronext Paris Swiss New York
Ticker Symbols: BN (Euronext Paris); DA (New York)
NAIC: 311421 Fruit and Vegetable Canning; 311422
Specialty Canning; 311511 Fluid Milk Manufacturing; 311514 Dry, Condensed, and Evaporated
Dairy Product Manufacturing; 311999 All Other
Miscellaneous Food Manufacturing; 312111 Soft
Drink Manufacturing; 312112 Bottled Water
Manufacturing

■ ■ ■

Groupe Danone is one of the largest food companies in the world, placing particular emphasis on "healthy" food products. The operations of Danone (which is pronounced dah-KNOWN) revolve around four core businesses: fresh dairy products, principally yogurts; beverages, mainly bottled water; baby food; and clinical nutrition products. The company holds the number one position worldwide in dairy products, with Danone (Dannon in the United States) the world's top dairy product brand; the number two position worldwide in bottled waters, including two of the top five brands in the world, Evian and Volvic; and the number two position worldwide in baby foods with such brands as Blédina, Nutricia, Milupa, Mellin, Dumex, and Cow & Gate. Known until 1994 as BSN Groupe S.A., Groupe Danone sells its products in more than 150 countries; around two-thirds of revenues are generated in Europe, 16 percent in Asia, and 18 elsewhere in the world.

BOTTLEMAKING BEGINNINGS

In 1958, 39-year-old Antoine Riboud inherited the glassmaking company founded by his great uncle nearly a century before in Lyons. Riboud had begun his career working in its factory during World War II. Souchon-Neuvesel produced hollow glass, bottles, jars, flasks, and glass tableware. A small company, it recorded only about $10 million in sales that year.

Riboud concentrated on hollow glassmaking until 1966, when La Verrerie Souchon-Neuvesel merged with Glaces de Boussois, a maker of flat glass for automobiles and housing. The new company was named Boussois Souchon-Neuvesel, and Riboud was named president.

In 1967 the company boasted FRF 1.1 billion in sales and was renamed BSN. It had become a major European maker of glass containers, but was still dwarfed by its competitor and France's largest glassmaker, Compagnie de Saint-Gobain, founded in 1665 by Louis XIV. The next year Riboud made one of the largest French takeover bids ever for this company, with more than ten times as many employees as BSN, using tactics considered radical in France at the time: he proposed to swap BSN convertible bonds for Saint-Gobain stock. Saint-Gobain's board members fended off the offer by claiming that it violated French laws and European Economic Community rules on monopolies. Saint-Gobain also launched a major publicity campaign to rally support from stockholders against BSN's "cheap" bid. The *Wall Street Journal* called it "the David-vs.-Goliath campaign," and Riboud's tactics brought him the admiration of younger businessmen ready for fresh air in the French business establishment. Sadly, in the midst of such publicity, Riboud's apartment in Paris was bombed by a terrorist gang. In the end, shareholders came to Saint-Gobain's rescue, acquiring a 40 percent holding to BSN's 10 percent, and BSN dropped the bid.

DIVERSIFICATION INTO FILLING THE BOTTLES

BSN's defeat led Riboud to diversify into the food industry. "I saw it would be better to fill the bottles rather than just make them," he explained to *Forbes* in 1980. In 1970 BSN acquired Société Anonyme des Eaux Minérales d'Evian, Société Européenne de Brasserie, and Brasseries Kronenbourg, becoming a leader in natural spring water and baby food, as well as the largest brewer in France. The next year, in an effort to tap the consumer taste for premium beers, BSN introduced its Kanterbräu beer.

In the meantime, BSN established its first flat-glass manufacturing subsidiary, Flachglass A.G., in West Germany in 1970, and two years later it acquired a controlling interest in Glaverbel, a Belgian flat-glass producer. Together with earlier expansion programs in West Germany, Austria, and the Benelux countries, these acquisitions gave BSN almost half the European market for flat glass.

The establishment of the Common Market at the end of the 1950s forced French companies to be more competitive, and between the early 1960s and 1973 France became the fastest-growing industrialized country after Japan. BSN also experienced rapid growth, culminating in 1973 with a merger between BSN and Gervais Danone, France's largest food company and the leader in yogurt, natural cheese, desserts, and pasta. That year sales for the new BSN-Gervais Danone topped FRF 9 billion.

By 1973, however, BSN began to suffer from the impact of the energy crisis, which had severe consequences for the two main markets for flat glass, the construction and automotive industries. For the next five years the profits of many major French companies declined sharply, mainly because of higher costs for energy and raw materials. After a period of growth, the French foreign trade balance fell into deficit. Fortunately BSN had made most of its acquisitions with stock rather than cash, so the company's finances were able to weather the crisis. Riboud tried to help the flat-glass sector recover by building three new glass units in northern France and adding more efficient float-glass equipment to BSN plants all over Europe. Nonetheless, beginning in 1974, the company shut down 22 furnaces and reduced its workforce by 30 percent. In five years of restructuring the company spent FRF 2.5 billion. The crisis was a turning point for the company; from that point on glass would be primarily a complement to its food and beverage businesses.

BSN acquired a minority interest in Ebamsa (later known as Font Vella S.A.), the leading Spanish bottler of natural spring water in 1973, and between 1974 and 1977 introduced several new products, including Lacmil and Gervillage. In an effort to dominate the European beer market, in 1978 BSN acquired a minority interest in Alken, a large Belgian brewery. A year later it acquired one-third interests in the breweries Mahou in

KEY DATES

1958: Antoine Riboud inherits a glassmaking company called La Verrerie Souchon-Neuvesel.

1966: La Verrerie Souchon-Neuvesel merges with Glaces de Boussois, to form Boussois Souchon-Neuvesel.

1967: Company is renamed BSN.

1970: Company diversifies, acquiring Société Anonyme des Eaux Minérales d'Evian, Société Européenne de Brasserie, and Brasseries Kronenbourg.

1973: BSN merges with Gervais Danone, France's largest food company, to form BSN-Gervais Danone.

1981: Dannon, the largest American yogurt-maker, is acquired.

1982: Company sells the last of its flat-glass operations.

1983: Company name is changed back to BSN.

1986: Générale Biscuit S.A., the top producer of biscuits and toasted bread in continental Europe, is acquired.

1989: The European operations of RJR Nabisco are purchased.

1992: Acquisition of Volvic brand vaults company into the top spot worldwide in mineral water.

1994: BSN becomes Groupe Danone, incorporating its top international brand into its name.

1996: Franck Riboud succeeds his father as chairman and CEO.

1997: Company adopts new strategy focusing on dairy products, beverages, and biscuits.

2000: Most of the firm's beer operations are divested.

2003: Company sells its last remaining glass holding.

2006: Sale of last sauces business completes shift to three core businesses.

2007: Danone sells its biscuits operations to Kraft Foods and acquires Royal Numico N.V., a Dutch maker of baby foods and clinical nutrition products.

interests with Générale Occidentale, a move encouraged by the French government, which was eager to invigorate the food industry and actually drew up a special incentive agreement for investments in food processing and food exports. In 1980 the company entered Japan's dairy market through a joint venture with Japan's Ajinomoto Co., Inc. BSN also bought two French producers of frozen foods and ice cream and two breweries in Nigeria. As it moved into these new fields, BSN nearly doubled its annual sales in grocery products.

EXIT FROM FLAT GLASS

At the same time, BSN was finally leaving the flat-glass industry, prompted in part by the fear that another oil crisis was imminent. In 1980 BSN sold its West German flat-glass ventures to the British company Pilkington Brothers, and by 1981, BSN had sold its flat-glass subsidiaries in Germany, Austria, Belgium, and the Netherlands. The following year, it sold the French Boussois subsidiary, the last of its flat-glass operations, leaving it with only nine glass container factories. Also in 1981 BSN acquired Dannon, the largest U.S. yogurt-maker, from Beatrice for $84.3 million.

In 1983 BSN-Gervais Danone changed its name back to BSN. In an effort to increase efficiency, Riboud installed computerized production lines, which meant that the company had to lay off 1,000 of its 40,000 employees, a move opposed by the unions but encouraged by French President François Mitterrand, who praised BSN for its contribution toward modernizing French industry. By 1984, BSN had acquired all shares of the champagne makers Pommery et Greno and Lanson Pere et Fils, and had introduced a number of new yogurt products, as well as the Plastishield plastic-coated bottle. Since 1981, the company's sales had risen sharply, and that year it made a record capital investment totaling FRF 2.4 billion. However in July, the European Economic Community imposed fines of about $3.2 million on BSN and Saint-Gobain for price-fixing in the Benelux glass market.

BSN continued to grow in the latter half of the 1980s. In 1985 BSN sold its glass-jar and glass-tableware operations to Verreries Champenoises and acquired a minority interest in that company. BSN also bought the pharmaceuticals-maker Bottu, which specialized in pain relievers and artificial sweeteners.

1986–89: SNAPPING UP THE COOKIE MARKET

In 1986, the company's 20th anniversary year, sales were 35 times higher than the FRF 1.1 billion of its first year.

Spain and Wührer in Italy, and a majority interest in Anglo-Belge in Belgium. BSN next bought four French food manufacturing firms through an exchange of stock

That year, BSN acquired Générale Biscuit S.A., the top producer of biscuits and toasted bread in continental Europe and owner of the prominent European brand LU. BSN also merged its Kronenbourg and Société de Brasserie breweries under the Kronenbourg name. The company acquired Sonnen Basserman in West Germany, and became the world's largest bottler of natural spring water. It also bought a majority interest in Angelo Ghigi, an Italian pasta maker.

In August 1988 BSN acquired the Belgian Maes Group Breweries, the British H.P. Foods, and the American Lea & Perrins as part of Riboud's strategy to gain a more substantial market in Britain and the United States for BSN products (64 percent of BSN's total sales still came from France). Concentrating on growth, Riboud also built several new yogurt plants and bottling facilities in strategic locations, and he spent more than $100 million on European television advertisements for BSN brands.

In 1989 BSN bought the European operations of RJR Nabisco for $2.5 billion, making it the world's second largest producer of biscuits. Also in 1989 BSN made several Italian acquisitions and became the leader in food production in that country.

1990–96: GLOBAL EXPANSION

The early 1990s were marked by BSN's aggressive expansion into the newly opened markets of Eastern Europe, as well as into Asia, Latin America, and South Africa. In Eastern Europe, BSN began by extending the marketing and manufacturing of its existing brands into the region. It later started acquiring or taking controlling stakes in companies, such as cookie makers Cokoládovny of the Czech Republic and Bolshevik of Russia. In Asia, BSN entered into a joint venture, called Britannia Brands, with an Indian partner in 1990 to acquire RJR Nabisco's Asia-Pacific businesses, which included the leading biscuit maker in India and units in New Zealand, Singapore, Malaysia, and Hong Kong manufacturing and marketing biscuits, snacks, nuts, and other products. Three years later, BSN bought out its Asian partner, taking full control of the Britannia companies. China was another target of BSN growth; by the mid-1990s the company had established several joint ventures there producing biscuits, dairy products, Asian-style sauces, and other products. In Latin America, the company in 1994 took a 49 percent stake in Campineira de Alimentos, the number two producer of biscuits in Brazil.

In western Europe, BSN was active consolidating its position by taking control of several companies, including cookie makers Papadopoulos of Greece and W&R

Jacob of Ireland, French mineral water manufacturer Mont Dore, and Spanish dairy product producer Danone SA. The company also made selective divestments in areas in which it was unable to gain the number one or two position; an example of this was the champagne sector, which saw BSN sell its Lanson and Pommery brands to LVMH Moët Hennessy Louis Vuitton SA for about FRF 3.1 billion ($613.7 million) in 1990.

BSN also received much press in 1992 for its intervention in a takeover battle between the Agnelli family of Italy and Nestlé S.A. for control of the French mineral water company Source Perrier. BSN made a bid itself for the company that controlled Perrier, but only to signal that it sided with Nestlé, from which it hoped to buy Perrier's Volvic mineral water brand. In the end, Nestlé prevailed and agreed to sell Volvic to BSN for about $500 million. The addition of Volvic vaulted BSN into the top spot worldwide in noncarbonated mineral water.

In mid-1994 the company jettisoned its BSN name, which, according to the company "seemed to reflect the company's past rather than looking ahead to the future." In fact, glass containers, the founding business, were by this time responsible for less than 10 percent of overall revenues. In addition, the BSN name was not well known outside of France. The company settled on the name Groupe Danone, because the Danone brand was its number one international brand, accounting for about a quarter of revenues, and Danone products were produced in 30 countries and sold internationally. At the same time, the company adopted a new logo picturing a young boy looking up at a star. Soon thereafter, the company began expanding its use of the Danone brand beyond dairy products into biscuits, mineral water, and baby foods.

By 1995 Danone's sales had reached $16.18 billion, nearly double the 1989 figure of $8.43 billion. This growth was largely the result of Antoine Riboud's aggressive global expansion program in the 1990s, which included $5 billion spent on acquisitions. Riboud chose this juncture of Danone's history to retire, and named his 40-year-old son, Franck Riboud, to succeed him as chairman and CEO in mid-1996. A few months later, Danone entered into a joint venture with the Coca-Cola Company through which the companies agreed to sell refrigerated juice in Europe and Latin America under the joint Minute Maid and Danone brand names. Also in 1996, Danone entered into a joint venture with the Wahaha Group to help that Chinese dairy company expand into bottled water. This venture eventually made the Wahaha brand the leading bottled water brand in China.

LATE-CENTURY SHIFT TO FOCUS ON THREE CORE AREAS

In May 1997 Franck Riboud announced the adoption of a new company strategy focusing on three core business areas—dairy products, biscuits, and beverages (specifically water and beer)—in which the company had global leadership. These areas also represented 85 percent of group sales. In the second half of 1997 and in 1998, Danone sold more than half of its grocery product holdings and its entire confectionery business. These disposals included the Panzani, La Familia, Maille, Amora, William Saurin, Agnesi, Liebig, Carambar, and La Pie qui Chante brands. During 1999 Danone sold off additional grocery businesses, including Spanish frozen food maker Pycasa (sold to Nestlé), frozen and chilled ready-to-serve meal units Marie Surgelés and Générale Traiteur (sold to Unigate plc), and its 50 percent stake in Star S.p.A., an Italian maker of a wide range of food products. As a result of these divestments, in late 1999 Danone retained in its grocery sector only HP Foods Ltd., a U.K.-based maker of brown sauces and Asian specialties under the HP, Lea & Perrins, and other brands.

Also during 1999, Danone substantially reduced its holdings in the glass container sector, moving closer to its complete exit from the founding business. The company's container activities were first merged with the food and beverage glass packaging operations in Germany owned by Gerresheimer AG. This enlarged glass container operation adopted the BSN Glasspack name, with the U.K. management buyout firm CVC Capital Partners purchasing a 56 percent stake in the entity and Danone retaining a 44 percent interest.

A series of additional significant deals in 2000 further altered Danone's profile. The company bolstered its position in bottled water in the United States, and entered that nation's home and office water delivery sector, by spending $1.1 billion for McKesson Water Products Company, the third largest producer of packaged water in the United States with such brands as Sparkletts, Alhambra, and Crystal. In a separate deal, Danone acquired the Canadian water brand Naya. The company also sold most of its European beer operations to the U.K. brewer Scottish & Newcastle plc in a deal valued at roughly $2.6 billion. As a result, Danone's beverages activities were centered predominantly in bottled water.

On the biscuits side, Danone engineered a deal whereby a financial consortium took the U.K.-based biscuit maker United Biscuits (UB) private. Following this transaction, UB sold a number of operations to Danone, including savory biscuit operations in the United Kingdom, as well as biscuit businesses in Poland,

Hungary, Scandinavia, Italy, and Malaysia. Also in 2000 Danone attempted to further beef up its biscuits business by joining with Cadbury Schweppes PLC on a joint bid for Nabisco Holdings Corp., but the two companies' joint bid was topped by an offer from Philip Morris Companies Inc., which subsequently merged Nabisco into Kraft Foods Inc. Late in 2000 Danone backed away from making a bid for Quaker Oats Company, coveted for its Gatorade sports drink juggernaut, and Quaker ended up in the hands of another Danone rival, PepsiCo, Inc.

2001–03: RESTRUCTURING, DIVESTMENTS, PARTNERSHIPS

In 2001, while not completing any deals of the magnitude of the previous year, Danone continued its international expansion, making further inroads into developing countries in the dairy, water, and biscuit sectors. Also noteworthy was the firm's purchase of a 39 percent stake in Londonderry, New Hampshire-based Stonyfield Farm, Inc., a leading producer of organic fresh dairy products and the fourth largest yogurt maker in the United States; at the end of 2003, Danone increased its stake in Stonyfield to 80 percent. In March 2001, meanwhile, Danone launched a restructuring of its biscuit operations to deal with overcapacity in Europe. Six factories in Europe, including two in France, were earmarked for closure, eliminating about 2,000 jobs. Workers reacted to rumors about these cutbacks and to the announcement itself with street demonstrations, factory unrest, and strikes.

Danone continued to narrow its focus in 2002 and 2003. In the former year the company divested Galbani, its Italian meat and cheese business, and additional beer assets. In 2003 Danone sold its last remaining glass holding, the 44 percent stake in BSN Glasspack. Following these transactions, the company's only remaining operations outside dairy products, water, and biscuits were its sauce businesses (the HP, Lea & Perrins, and Amoy brands) and a 33 percent stake in the Spanish beer company Mahou.

Also in 2002, Danone and the Coca-Cola Company formed a joint venture through which Coca-Cola began marketing and distributing Danone's lower-end water brands in North America, including Dannon and Sparkletts. In a separate deal, Coke launched the importation and distribution of the high-end Evian brand within North America. Danone entered into two further water partnerships in 2003, in Europe with Eden Springs Ltd. and in the United States with Suntory Limited. Both of these centered on the home and office delivery sectors within the packaged water industry.

2004–06: COMPLETING SHIFT TO THREE CORE AREAS

In 2004 Danone further restructured its biscuits side by selling its Jacob's biscuits business in the United Kingdom and its Irish Biscuits business in Ireland. In the meantime, the firm's home and office water delivery operations were suffering from growing competition, particularly in the United States, leading Danone in late 2004 to write down the value of its U.S. and European operations within this sector by EUR 600 million ($810 million). As a result, net income for 2004 was shaved to EUR 317 million ($429 million), down 62 percent from the previous year. Revenues for the year totaled EUR 13.7 billion ($18.55 billion), an advance of just 4 percent over the 2003 total.

Danone's troubled position in the U.S. water sector led to the 2005 dissolution of its joint venture with Coca-Cola, with the latter buying out Danone's stake for roughly $100 million. Coca-Cola nevertheless continued to distribute the Evian brand in North America. Danone also jettisoned its home and office water delivery businesses in both the United States and Canada, with the U.S. business sold at a net loss of EUR 313 million ($370 million). Additional divestments in 2005 included the stake in Mahou, Danone's last beer asset, and the HP and Lea & Perrins sauce brands, with the latter sold to H.J. Heinz Company for around $855 million. When Danone sold its Amoy sauces business in Asia to Ajinomoto in January 2006, the shift to three core businesses—fresh dairy products, water, and biscuits—that Franck Riboud had launched in 1997 was essentially complete.

Danone was a frequent subject of takeover rumors because of its relatively small size in relation to such food and beverage giants as Nestlé, Kraft, Unilever, and Coca-Cola and because it had no controlling shareholder. The healthful products in its portfolio, led by Evian water, low-cholesterol yogurt Danacol, and the probiotic Activia yogurt, were increasingly attractive both because of the trend for healthier eating and because they were enjoying above-average rates of growth. Furthermore, Danone was also well positioned in another growth area for the global food industry: emerging markets. In July 2005 the company's stock soared on rumors that PepsiCo was preparing a bid for Danone. Numerous French politicians, including Dominique de Villepin, the prime minister, stepped forward vowing to fight to keep the company in French hands. Villepin, in fact, called Danone a "crown jewel," promising to defend it in the national interest of France. Riboud was also determined to maintain his company's independence. In the end, a PepsiCo bid never materialized.

2007 FORWARD: GOODBYE COOKIES, HELLO NUMICO

By 2006 the Wahaha brand was one of Danone's top four global brands, along with Danone, LU, and Evian. The Wahaha joint venture was responsible for between 5 and 6 percent of the group's operating profits, and its sales in 2006 totaled EUR 1 billion ($1.35 billion). This venture was thus the centerpiece of Danone's successful penetration of the Chinese market, but a protracted battle between Danone and its partner broke out in 2007 over who controlled the venture. After months of legal wrangling, name-calling, and allegations of double-dealing and mismanagement, the two sides called a truce late in the year and agreed to enter into talks to resolve their differences.

As this dispute played out, Groupe Danone significantly altered its portfolio via a major divestment and an even larger acquisition. In early July 2007 Danone reached an agreement to sell its biscuit operations to Kraft Foods for EUR 5.3 billion ($7.8 billion). Less than a week later Danone agreed to acquire Royal Numico N.V., a Dutch maker of baby foods and nutritional bars and shakes, for EUR 12.3 billion ($18.2 billion). After these deals gained regulatory approval, the only conditions being the sale of certain baby food product lines in France, Belgium, and the Netherlands, and were completed in the fall of 2007, Danone could boost an even more healthful line of products having ditched cookies and significantly bolstered its position in baby food. The company had been the market leader in France for baby food with its Blédina brand, which had been housed within its dairy business, but with the purchase of Numico, Danone became the number two maker of baby food worldwide. Numico marketed its products in more than 100 countries under such brands as Nutricia, Milupa, Mellin, Dumex, and Cow & Gate. Going forward, Danone envisioned a brighter future for itself with its nearly complete focus on high-growth health-oriented products.

Updated, David E. Salamie

PRINCIPAL SUBSIDIARIES

FRESH DAIRY PRODUCTS: Danone Ges.mbH (Austria); N.V. Danone S.A. (Belgium); Danone Serdika (Bulgaria); Danone a.s. (Czech Republic; 98.3%); Danone A/S (Denmark); Danone Finlande Oy; Blédina; Danone; Danone GmbH (Germany); Danone Grèce (Greece); Danone Kft (Hungary); Danone Ltd (Ireland); Danone SpA (Italy); Danone Sp zoo (Poland); Danone Portugal S.A. (55.17%); Danone SRL (Romania); Danone Industria (Russia; 70%); Danone Volga (Russia; 63.54%); Danone Spol s.r.o. (Slovakia); Danone (Slovenia); Danone S.A. (Spain; 57.15%); Danone AB (Sweden); Danone Nederland B.V. (Netherlands);

Danone Tikvesli (Turkey); Danone (Ukraine); Rodich (Ukraine); Danone Ltd (U.K.); Danone Argentina S.A. (99.45%); Danone Ltda. (Brazil); Danone Canada Delisle Inc.; Danone de Mexico; The Dannon Co. (U.S. A.); Stonyfield Farm (U.S.A.; 83.99%); Danone Djurdjura (Algeria); Danone Dairy Egypt; Al Safi Danone Company (Saudi Arabia; 50.1%); Danone Clover (South Africa; 55%); PT Danone Dairy Indonesia (70. 3%); Danone Japan. BEVERAGES: Danone Waters Beverage Benelux (Belgium); Evian (SAEME); Mont Roucous; Seat (99.86%); Smda; Volvic (SEV); Drinkco; Danone Waters Deutschland (Germany); Zywiec Zdroj (Poland); Aguas Font Vella y Lanjarón (Spain; 78.46%); Evian Volvic Suisse (Switzerland); Danone Hayat (Turkey); Danone Waters UK & Ireland; Aguas Danone de Argentina; Danone Naya (Canada); Bonafont (Mexico); Great Brands of Europe (U.S.A.); Salus (Uruguay; 58.46%); Tessala (Algeria); Frucor Beverages (Australia); Wahaha Group (China; 51%); Robust Group (China; 92%); Shenzhen Health Drinks (China); Aqua (Indonesia; 74%); Frucor (New Zealand). NUMICO: Royal Numico N.V. (Netherlands); Numico Research Australia Pty Ltd.; EAC Nutrition Ltd. A/S (Denmark); International Nutrition Co. Ltd. A/S (Denmark); Central Laboratories Friedrichsdorf GmbH (Germany); Numico Trading B.V. (Netherlands); Numico Beheer B.V. (Netherlands); Numico Research B.V. (Netherlands); Numico Nederland B.V. (Netherlands); Nutricia International B.V. (Netherlands); Nutricia Export B.V. (Netherlands).

PRINCIPAL COMPETITORS

Nestlé S.A.; Kraft Foods Inc.; General Mills, Inc.; Pepsi-Co, Inc.; The Coca-Cola Company.

FURTHER READING

Ball, Deborah, "Danone Toes Independent Line," *Wall Street Journal,* January 27, 2004, p. B4.

Ball, Deborah, and Jason Singer, "Danone's Deal for Numico Is Bid for Independence and Expansion," *Wall Street Journal,* July 10, 2007, p. A3.

Barrett, Amy, "Danone Is Selling Its Beer Assets to S&N," *Wall Street Journal Europe,* March 21, 2000, p. 5.

Bickerton, Ian, and Adam Jones, "Danone Makes EUR 12bn Move for Numico," *Financial Times,* July 10, 2007, p. 26.

Browning, E. S., "BSN Agrees to Sell Two Champagnes to Moet Vuitton," *Wall Street Journal,* December 10, 1990, p. A8.

————, "BSN Finds Eastern Europe Expansion Hard to Swallow," *Wall Street Journal,* January 5, 1993, p. B4.

"BSWho?" *Economist,* May 14, 1994, p. 70.

Clevstrom, Jenny, "France's Danone Hungers to Acquire, but Its Portfolio May Make It a Target," *Wall Street Journal,* August 17, 2006, pp. C1, C4.

La construction du Groupe: 30 ans de passion, Paris: Groupe Danone, 1996, 55 p.

"Danone Group: Feeding the Pacific Century Consumer," *Institutional Investor,* November 1995, p. C5.

Dawkins, William, "BSN in Takeover of Asian Nabisco," *Financial Times,* March 9, 1990, p. 28.

De Jonquieres, Guy, "Dynastic Hopes Fall Flat in France," *Financial Times,* March 25, 1992, p. 18.

Delaney, Kevin J., "Danone Plans to Restructure Biscuit Business," *Wall Street Journal Europe,* January 11, 2001, p. 4.

Deogun, Nikhil, and Shelly Branch, "Danone to Buy 40% Stake in Stonyfield Farm of U.S.," *Wall Street Journal Europe,* October 4, 2001, p. 5.

Edmondson, Gail, Ian Katz, and Elisabeth Malkin, "Danone Hits Its Stride: Franck Riboud Is Turning the French Food Titan into a World-Beater," *Business Week,* February 1, 1999, pp. 52+.

Foster, Lauren, and Adam Jones, "Danone Chief Plays a 'Beautiful' Game," *Financial Times,* July 31, 2006, p. 21.

"Franck Riboud Tries to Keep Danone Independent," *Economist,* November 19, 2005, p. 70.

"Friend or Foe?" *Economist,* February 29, 1992, p. 77.

Gleason, Mark, "Dannon Water Springs into U.S.," *Advertising Age,* January 15, 1996, p. 6.

Goad, G. Pierre, "Groupe BSN's Buyout of Joint Venture Simplifies Food Maker's Recipe in Asia," *Wall Street Journal,* August 9, 1993, p. B5A.

Housego, David, "BSN Finds Its Gateway to the East," *Financial Times,* February 22, 1990, p. 38.

Jack, Andrew, "Danone to Book FRF 1bn Gain on Disposals," *Financial Times,* October 10, 1997, p. 28.

Kamm, Thomas, "French Danone Agrees to Buy Water Unit of McKesson," *Wall Street Journal,* January 12, 2000, p. A16.

Koselka, Rita, "A Tight Ship," *Forbes,* July 20, 1992, p. 141.

Lubove, Seth, "Perched Between Perrier and Tap," *Forbes,* May 14, 1990, p. 120.

McGrane, Sally, "Danone Cuts Out the Cookies," *Time,* October 18, 2007.

McKay, Betsy, and Robert Frank, "Coca-Cola, Danone to Form Venture for Bottled Water," *Wall Street Journal Europe,* June 18, 2002, p. A4.

"The MT Interview: Franck Riboud," *Management Today,* August 1, 2006, p. 38.

Owen, David, "Son to Succeed Chairman at Danone," *Financial Times,* May 3, 1996, p. 22.

Racanelli, Vito J., "L'eau Valuation?" *Barron's,* November 18, 2002, pp. 23–24, 26.

Rawsthorn, Alice, "Gloves Come Off in Fight for Exor," *Financial Times,* February 24, 1992, p. 17.

Ridding, John, "BSN Puts New Name on the Table: Danone Wants to Expand Across the Globe," *Financial Times,* May 11, 1994, p. 31.

Rosenbaum, Andrew, "BSN Challenging Nestlé, Unilever," *Advertising Age,* June 25, 1990, p. 37.

Spencer, Mimosa, "Danone May Sell Cookie Division for $7.22 Billion," *Wall Street Journal Europe,* July 4, 2007, p. 5.

Tagliabue, John, "A Corporate Son Remakes Danone: By Focusing on Best-Selling Brands, French Food Maker Grows Globally," *New York Times,* April 1, 1998, p. D1.

Terhune, Chad, "Coke to Buy Danone's Stake in Bottled-Water Joint Venture," *Wall Street Journal,* April 25, 2005, p. B4.

Torres, Félix, and Pierre Labasse, *Mémoire de Danone: Barcelone, Paris, New York,* Paris: Le Cherche midi, 2003, 119 p.

Toy, Stewart, "The Son Also Rises at Danone: As Chairman, Franck Riboud Will Keep Up the Push Overseas," *Business Week,* May 20, 1996, p. 21.

Willman, John, and Samer Iskander, "Ahead of the Crowd: Profile of Franck Riboud, Chairman and Chief Executive of Danone," *Financial Times,* January 4, 1999, p. 14.

Woodruff, David, "France's Danone Advances at Full Speed," *Wall Street Journal,* June 23, 2000, p. A15.

Wrighton, Jo, "Paris Leaps to Defense of Danone Against Pepsi," *Wall Street Journal,* July 21, 2005, p. A9.

Hay House, Inc.

P.O. Box 5100
Carlsbad, California 92018-5100
U.S.A.
Telephone: (760) 431-7695
Toll Free: (800) 654-5126
Fax: (800) 650-5115
Web site: http://www.hayhouse.com

Private Company
Incorporated: 1987
Employees: 150
Sales: $70 million (2006 est.)
NAIC: 511130 Book Publishers

■ ■ ■

Hay House, Inc., is one of the leading publishers in the self-help, personal transformation movement. The company is known primarily for its titles dealing with the body-mind connection, the power of positive thought, meditation, and other topics in spiritual psychology. Hay House publishes books on holistic health modalities, such as aromatherapy, homeopathy, nutrition, and herbal medicine. Topics in esoteric spirituality include clairvoyance, angels, astrology, and numerology. Books on commonplace topics cover personal finance, pet care, parenting, and social commentary. In addition to publication of more than 300 books in print, Hay House has produced 350 sound recordings, including audiobooks and meditation guidance. Hay House offers several products complementary to self-reflection and mediation, such as card sets which feature positive affirmations over artistic illustrations, blank journals, aromatherapy candles, and magnet bracelets designed to heal specific emotions.

Company founder Louise L. Hay is a prominent leader of the personal growth movement. She has written more than 25 books and developed numerous meditations and tools for healing and positive affirmation of life. Her first two books, *Heal Your Body* and *You Can Heal Your Life,* are international bestsellers that continue to sell in bookstores worldwide. Hay House has sold more than 35 million copies of *You Can Heal Your Life* since its publication in 1984, and *Heal Your Body* has been translated into 35 languages.

LOUISE HAY'S SPIRITUAL JOURNEY TO THE FOUNDING OF HAY HOUSE

The story of the founding of Hay House begins with the personal journey Louise Hay embarked upon to heal her body from a life of hardship and abuse. Growing up in an impoverished household, she suffered physical abuse by both parents, and sexual abuse by her stepfather. At the age of 15, Hay quit school, left home, and began to work as a waitress. A year later, she found herself pregnant and gave the baby up for adoption. Eventually, Hay moved to New York City, where she found success as a fashion model. However, she suffered from low self-esteem, and she tended to enter into relationships with abusive men. She thought she found happiness when she met and married a well-to-do businessman. Then, when her 14-year marriage ended, Hay was again left searching, this time seeking to resolve her grief through a more spiritual approach to life.

In 1970, Hay joined the Church of Religious Science, which taught a belief in the God within each individual and in the power of positive thought to transform one's life. After three years of study, she entered a six-month meditation program at Maharishi International University, in Fairfield, Iowa. When Hay returned to New York City, she began taking classes to become a minister and teacher at the Church of Religious Science. From the start, her work as a teacher involved ideas about the mind-body connection, and Hay developed a philosophy of health that correlated emotions with specific ailments or areas of the body. She began writing affirmations that sought to transform thought patterns that create ill health into an interior language of positive well-being. When Hay herself was diagnosed with cancer, she correlated the illness to deep-seated pain and anger that originated in childhood trauma.

Rather than subject her body to the conventional medical model, the surgical removal of cancer from the body, Hay chose to view her disease as a spiritual problem. Otherwise, the cancer could return, even after surgery. Hence, physical healing entailed the use of holistic health modalities and an examination of her interior state of being. For physical wellness, Hay turned to nutrition, reflexology, and colon cleansing therapy, the last believed to rid the body of toxins that can overload the cells in the form of cancer. Emotional well-being involved psychotherapy, prayer, and meditation.

In one meditation, Hay visualized a stream of pure water cleansing her body and mind of the hatred she felt toward her parents for their abusive treatment. Also, Hay applied her knowledge of positive thought patterns to transform her self-concept through affirmations of self-love. For instance, she correlated cancer to feelings of hurt, grief, resentment, hatred, and resignation; her affirmation stated, "I lovingly forgive and release all of the past. I choose to fill my world with joy. I love and approve of myself" (Louise L. Hay, *Heal Your Body,* 2007). Hay gave herself six months to apply alternative methods of healing, and at the end of that time the doctor declared her cured of cancer.

INSPIRING SELF-HELP, PERSONAL TRANSFORMATION MOVEMENT

From her experience in natural healing, Hay emerged with a clear perspective on the workings of the mind-body connection, and she carried this perspective into teaching and writing. Hay developed a 12-page booklet of mind-body affirmations. Self-published in 1976 under the title *What Hurts,* this booklet provided the basis for the 1978 publication of *Heal Your Body.* Repeated reprinting of *Heal Your Body* led Hay to write more extensively, and she used funds from her divorce settlement to found Hay House in 1984. That year, Hay published an expanded version of *Heal Your Body* and a more extensive explanation of how to create personal health and well-being in *You Can Heal Your Life;* this book provided general affirmations for a spiritually aware life, as well as the mind-body affirmations. An audiotape of meditations, "What I Believe: Deep Relaxation Guided Meditations," followed in 1985.

After Hay's relocation to California and Hay House's incorporation in 1987, Hay became one of the inspirational leaders of the self-help, holistic health movement. In 1988 Hay House issued a revised and expanded version of *Heal Your Body* and reissued *You Can Heal Your Life.* Hay promoted the books through appearances on national television, and *You Can Heal Your Life* became a national bestseller. It spent 14 weeks on the *New York Times* bestseller list and held the number two spot for eight weeks. That year, Hay House generated sales that garnered a profit of slightly over $1 million.

Reid Tracy's leadership in business management at Hay House enabled Hay to continue writing books and to develop meditation tapes. In 1990 Hay wrote and published *Love Yourself, Heal Your Life Workbook* and released new audio meditation titles including "Self-Esteem" and "Self-Healing." Hay wrote *The Power Is Within You* (1991), *Life!* (1996), *Gratitude* (1998), and *Empowering Women: Every Woman's Guide to Successful Living* (1999). Hay House released these works in both print and audio formats.

ESTABLISHING LEADERSHIP THROUGH TOOLS FOR HEALING

Hay House expanded on a small scale by providing products and services to known authors. The company published audio recordings of books published elsewhere. Hay House provided this service to a number of well-known authors, including Harvey Diamond and Deepak Chopra. A notable audiobook, "Meditations for Enhancing Your Immune System: Strengthen Your Body's Ability to Heal," by Bernie S. Siegel, was released

KEY DATES

1976: Louise L. Hay self-publishes her first book, *Heal Your Body.*

1984: Hay House is founded in conjunction with publication of *You Can Heal Your Life.*

1988: *You Can Heal Your Life* reissue becomes a national bestseller.

1999: Hay House pioneers card sets with daily affirmations and colorful designs.

2003: Hay House opens an office in the United Kingdom.

2005: Hay House opens offices in South Africa and India.

2006: Four Hay House books reach the *New York Times* bestseller list in March.

in 1992. In 1995 Hay House issued "Staying on the Path," and "Meditations for Manifesting," by popular motivational speaker Dr. Wayne W. Dyer, as well as "101 Power Thoughts," by Hay. Another development involved an exclusive book distribution contract for Nataraji Publishing. Nataraji books included popular new age works by founder Shakti Gawain, such as *The Path of Transformation* and *Living in the Light.*

Hay House helped its authors to succeed by organizing author lectures around the country. Not only did these workshops stimulate book sales and raise the public profile of personal growth teachers, they provided a source of revenue. Hay House charged as much as $60 per person for a one-day event, with average attendance at 3,000 people. Hay House held about 25 events per year.

In 1999 Hay House developed a new tool for personal growth, which also stimulated book sales: the deck of self-help cards. Each card displayed an inspirational affirmation on an artful background. Hay House based these 50-card sets on the books and ideas of best-selling authors of the personal growth movement. Louise Hay led with "Power Thought Cards" (1999) and "Healthy Body Cards" (2002). Other decks involved the ideas of Wayne Dyer and *Course in Miracles* teacher Marianne Williamson. In addition to providing an easy-to-use self-help tool, the cards helped to sell books by offering potential readers with an easy way to begin to understand the ideas and to apply them daily.

EXPANDING SUBJECT RANGE WITH BOOKS BY KNOWN EXPERTS

During the late 1990s, Hay House began to publish more books in print, covering a wider range of topics. In 1998, under the new Hay House Lifestyles imprint, the company began to publish several comprehensive reference works on healing by experts in each area of wellness. Hay House started with book and compact disc gift combinations, including *Aromatherapy A–Z,* by Connie and Alan Higley, *101 Ways to Health and Healing,* by Louise Hay, and *101 Ways to Romance,* by Barbara De Angelis. Each book was accompanied by an appropriate music compilation. Later reference books included *Homeopathy A–Z,* by Dana Ulman, and *Healing with Herbs and Home Remedies,* by Hanna Kroeger.

Beginning in 1998, Hay House entered a phase of growth that involved first publication of a number of best-selling books. That year, Hay House also published a reprint of the 1991 book *Adventures with a Psychic,* by popular clairvoyant Sylvia Browne. The book became a *New York Times* bestseller due to Hay House's innovative distribution and promotional efforts. Hay House published new books written by Browne, which became national bestsellers also. These included *Book of Angels* (2003) and *Secrets and Mysteries of the World* (2005). Wayne Dyer began to publish with Hay House, as well; he wrote two best-selling books at this time: *10 Secrets for Success and Inner Peace* (2002) and *The Power of Intention* (2004). Hay House continued to issue audio recordings, and an inspirational card set accompanied *10 Secrets.*

One method Hay House used to attract prominent writers involved an innovative imprint partnership. The company offered authors the opportunity to create a publishing imprint, like a book brand that would become known to regular readers. Instead of receiving royalties, authors split profits by paying for editorial and distribution services. John Edward formed the Princess Imprint with Hay House in 2003. Edward was known for his television show, in which he contacted deceased relatives of members of a live audience. Hay House published *Crossing Over* and *Developing Your Own Psychic Powers* in 2003. In 2004, radio and television personality Tavis Smiley founded the Smiley Books imprint, which published works aimed to empower black youth.

MAXIMIZING EXPOSURE

With the growing popularity of alternative spirituality and healing, Hay sought to maximize its ability to bring the ideas of personal transformation to the public. To optimize its international appeal, Hay House opened several offices overseas. The company opened publishing and distribution offices in Australia in 1999, England in 2003, and South Africa and India in 2005. In addition to distributing primary titles from the United States, international offices published works by local authors. For instance, Hay House United Kingdom published *Spirit Messenger,* by Scottish clairvoyant Gordon Smith.

Hay House harnessed new technology to increase author exposure and cultivate author readership. In early 2005, Hay House initiated live programming over the Internet, on HayHouseRadio.com. Broadcasting 15 hours per week, HayHouseRadio offered authors, including Wayne Dyer, an opportunity to inspire listeners as well as to sell books. An agreement with Sirius Radio expanded the program's reach to two million satellite radio subscribers, primarily women, on the LIME network. An agreement with MediaBay provided customers with the option to download audiobooks onto their computers.

Hay House further facilitated communication between authors and their fans by providing tools for email marketing. A software license from Lyris Technologies dramatically improved effectiveness of newsletter distribution, as fewer newsletter emails were flagged as spam. For authors who took advantage of the service, such as Sylvia Browne and Louise Hay, sales from newsletters increased 20 percent.

SUCCESS CULMINATES IN SEVERAL NATIONAL BESTSELLERS

Hay House began to publish more books by the leading lights of spiritual self-help, rather than producing only the sound recordings. In 2006, the company established Hay House Classics division to reissue out-of-print but well-known books. These included *Divine Magic* by Doreen Virtue, known for her books on angels. The new imprint published a series of six books by Dr. Joseph Murphy, a leader in the Church of Religious Science during the 1960s. These works included *Believe in Yourself* and *Maximize Your Potential Through the Power of Your Subconscious Mind to Develop Self-Confidence and Self-Esteem,* originally published in 1963.

Hay House reached a new level of success when four newly published works became national bestsellers in March 2006. The books on the *New York Times* list for Advice, How-to, and Miscellaneous Paperback were: *Incredible You! 10 Ways to Let Your Greatness Shine Through* and *Inspiration: Your Ultimate Calling,* both by Dr. Wayne Dyer; *Left to Tell: Discovering God Amidst the Rwandan Holocaust,* by Immaculée Ilibagiza; and *If You Could See What I See: The Tenets of Novus Spiritus,* by Sylvia Browne. Browne's *Exploring the Levels of Creation* made the bestseller list in 2006 as well.

Several Hay House books became *New York Times* bestsellers in 2007. These included *Change Your Thoughts, Change Your Life: Living the Wisdom of the Tao,* by Dyer, and *Spiritual Connections,* by Browne. *The Law of Attraction,* which spent several months on the bestseller list, was one of several popular metaphysical books by Esther and Jerry Hicks, published by Hay House since 2003. The Hickses claimed to channel several otherworldly spirits under the name Abraham. In late 2007, Hay House published *New York Times* best-selling author Marianne Williamson's newest book, *The Age of Miracles: Embracing the New Midlife.* Given Williamson's previous success, this publication promised to become a bestseller in 2008.

As Hay House celebrated its 20th anniversary in 2007, Louise Hay continued to contribute her wisdom to the self-help personal growth movement. That year the company issued a special edition of *You Can Heal Your Life,* which included a new foreword by Hay. A DVD by the same title featured talks between Hay and leading health and spiritual psychology writers. Hay published an anthology of stories about the lives of personal growth authors, titled *The Times of Our Lives: Extraordinary True Stories of Synchronicity, Destiny, Meaning, and Purpose.* At 82 years old, Hay maintained daily communication with company President Reid Tracy from her home in San Diego.

Mary Tradii

PRINCIPAL SUBSIDIARIES

Hay House Audio; Hay House Australia Pty Ltd.; Hay House Publishers (U.K.); Hay House Publishers India; Hay House SA (Pty), Ltd. (South Africa).

PRINCIPAL OPERATING UNITS

Hay House Classics; Hay House Lifestyles; New Beginnings Press; Princess Books; Smiley Books.

PRINCIPAL COMPETITORS

Crown Publishing, Inc.; Inner Traditions International Ltd.; New Harbinger Publications, Inc.; Nightingale-Conant Corporation; The Penguin Group; Random House Audio; Rodale Press, Inc.; Sounds True, Inc.; Sourcebooks, Inc.; The Three Rivers Press, Inc.; Whatever Publishing, Inc.

FURTHER READING

Blake, John, "Need a Quick Word of Wisdom? Inspiration Is in the Cards," *Atlanta-Constitution,* May 4, 2002, p. B1.

Bone, Alison, "Affirming Life: Louise Hay Reveals How to Make the World a Better Place, and Prosper, Too," *Bookseller,* April 20, 2007, p. 21.

"DIY Origins of Self-Help," *Canberra Times,* August 7, 2005, p. 22A.

Farmanfarmaian, Roxane, "Hay House Tries Pay-Per-View," *Publishers Weekly,* March 22, 1990, p. 31.

———, "New Gift Imprint at Hay House," *Publishers Weekly,* June 8, 1998, p. 19.

"Hay House," *Publishers Weekly,* May 21, 2001, p. 62.

Hay, Louise L., *Heal Your Body: The Mental Causes for Physical Illness and the Metaphysical Way to Overcome Them,* Carlsbad, Calif.: Hay House, Inc., 2007.

———, *You Can Heal Your Life,* Carlsbad, Calif.: Hay House, Inc., 2004.

Holman, Tom, "Hay House Seeks Room in UK," *Bookseller,* February 28, 2003, p. 8.

Holt, Karen, "Hay House and Wiley Release English/Spanish Title," *Publishers Weekly,* November 1, 2003, p. 7.

———, "Princess Imprint Gives Hay House Bestseller," *Publishers Weekly,* October 20, 2003, p. 8.

Jones, Margaret, "The Blossoming of Natural Medicine," *Publishers Weekly,* May 11, 1992, p. 38.

Kinsman, Michael, "Reid Tracy, President, Hay House, Inc.," *San Diego Union-Tribune,* December 4, 2005, p. N4.

Mattarella, Joyce, "The Times of Our Lives, Brief Article; Book Review," *Subconsciously Speaking,* March 1, 2007, p. 4.

"New New Age Distributor," *Publishers Weekly,* September 19, 1994, p. 19.

Rackman, Anne, "Self-Help for Kids, Coloring Books for Adults," *Los Angeles Business Journal,* May 27, 1991, p. 25.

Reid, Calvin, "Hay House Gets Sirius," *Publishers Weekly,* November 14, 2005, p. 7.

Woods, Judith, "How Positive Thinking Helped Me Beat Cancer; Judith Woods Is Skeptical of Self-Help Guru Louise Hay's Claim That Mind Power Healed Her Body—But Could It Help Her Own Back Pain?" *Daily Telegraph,* April 23, 2007, p. 24.

Illumina, Inc.

9885 Towne Centre Drive
San Diego, California 92121-1975
U.S.A.
Telephone: (858) 202-4500
Toll Free: (800) 809-4566
Fax: (858) 202-4545
Web site: http://www.illumina.com

Public Company
Incorporated: 1998
Employees: 596
Sales: $184.6 million (2006)
Stock Exchanges: NASDAQ
Ticker Symbol: ILMN
NAIC: 334516 Analytical Laboratory Instrument Manufacturing

■■■

Illumina, Inc., is a NASDAQ-listed company based in San Diego, California, that provides academic institutions and life sciences and pharmaceutical companies with tools and systems to test and analyze genes. Illumina's flagship system is based on its proprietary BeadArray technology, which uses fiber-optic bundles and specially prepared beads containing a different molecule or DNA sequence. By dipping the bundle into a test sample, a laser is able to detect which beads react to the sample. Thus, the beads self-assemble into arrays, providing researchers with the ability to do large-scale testing of genetic variations, providing clues to researchers seeking to better understand human genetics in order to develop drugs and methods to diagnose diseases. Illumina's complementary Oligator technology synthesizes oligonucleotides, single-stranded DNA fragments that are able to connect to the end of human DNA and provide further insights to researchers. Not only does Illumina technology assist in the development of treatments, it has the potential to help physicians determine whether a patient is likely to respond to a certain treatment or not.

INCORPORATION IN 1998

Illumina was incorporated in April 1998; its founders included David R. Walt, John R. Stuelpnagel, Lawrence A. Bock, Anthony W. Czarnik, and Mark S. Chee. A chemistry professor at Tufts University, Walt developed the BeadArray technology in his laboratory. His work then came to the attention of venture capitalist Stuelpnagel, a man with a varied background. After receiving a degree in biochemistry and a doctorate in veterinary medicine from the University of California, Davis, he earned an M.B.A. from the University of California, Los Angeles. He then went to work for venture capital firm Catalyst Partners before joining Bock at another venture capital firm, CW Group. Bock was one of the pioneer investors in the biotechnology field, founding a dozen start-up companies in the industry. Stuelpnagel was attracted to Walt's technology because of an interest in the work of Affymetrix, Inc., a Santa Clara, California, company that had developed gene chip technology, which applied semiconductor manufacturing techniques to combinatorial chemistry in order to build large amounts of biological information on a quartz wafer. However, it was a painstaking process, and Stuelpnagel

COMPANY PERSPECTIVES

Illumina's mission is to develop next-generation tools for the large-scale analysis of genetic variation and function, the results of which will pave the way for personalized medicine, a key goal of genomics and proteomics.

recognized that Walt's BeadArray was an alternative process that had the potential of eclipsing the work of Affymetrix.

Stuelpnagel and Bock negotiated an exclusive license with Walt and Tufts University and began bringing in others to found a new company that took the name Illumina. Chee, the former head of Affymetrix's genetics research unit, was brought in to help develop the BeadArray technology as vice-president of genomics. The last founder was Czarnik, the former vice-president of chemistry at Irori Quantum Microchemistry, who served as Illumina's chief scientific officer. Stuelpnagel, in the meantime, became acting president and CEO, and Walt became the chairman of the company's Scientific Advisory Board.

With seed money from CW Group and ARCH Venture Partners, the fledgling company acquired the rights to 13 necessary patents. It then set up shop in a 10,000-square-foot facility in San Diego with seven employees in the autumn of 1998 and began developing Illumina's core technology. Hired as vice-president of product development was Richard J. Pytelewski. Later in the year the company raised $8.5 million in its first major round of financing, with CW Group and ARCH being joined by Venrock Associates and Tredegar Investments.

RECRUITING A NEW CEO: 1999

Stuelpnagel led Illumina until October 1999, when he successfully recruited Jay T. Flatley to fill the president and CEO positions on a permanent basis. With industrial engineering degrees from Stanford University and a B.A. in economics from Claremont McKenna College, Flatley was a seasoned life sciences executive. He cofounded Molecular Dynamics in the late 1980s and served as CEO from 1994 until September 1999, when the company was bought out. Flatley told *Fortune,* "The deal hadn't made me rich enough to stop working." Hence, after paying a visit to Illumina's operations and falling "in love" with the technology, Flatley was quick to accept Stuelpnagel's job offer.

According to *Fortune,* "Flatley knew that speed was the name of the game." He wasted no time moving on a number of fronts. A month after he took over, Illumina forged its first major collaboration arrangement with Applied Biosystems to develop, produce, and market certain array-based systems. As part of the deal, Applied Biosystems' parent company, PE Biosystems, bought a $5 million stake in Illumina. Another $28 million was raised through a private placement of stock in December 1999. Flatley prepared to take Illumina public.

COMPLETION OF STOCK OFFERING: 2000

Flatley's decision to act quickly proved decisive. The stock markets, especially the tech-heavy NASDAQ, were beginning to falter in 2000, prompting some biotech start-ups to postpone their offerings, but undeterred, Illumina filed for its initial public offering (IPO). With Goldman Sachs & Co. acting as lead underwriter, Illumina completed its IPO in July 2000, raising more than $100 million. The company had started the year with $33 million in cash, and with this infusion of new capital Illumina possessed an ample nest egg not only to see it through the developmental stages of its technology but also to shelter it from the harsh equity market for the biotech sector that prevailed following its IPO. Illumina's stock price enjoyed an immediate bump, increasing from the offering price of $16 per share to as high as $38 on the first day. The price would grow even higher before trending downward. Yet by the start of 2002 the price dipped to $12 and by the autumn of that year it traded around the $4 mark, eventually bottoming out below $2. Because Illumina still had $80 million in cash, it did not need to raise more capital and the disappointing price of its stock had little impact.

With funding no concern, Illumina tripled its workforce to more than 100 in 2000 and exercised a lease to acquire a pair of buildings to provide the expanding company with 105,000 square feet of space. In addition to the amount of cash on hand, Illumina began generating revenue in 2001 after launching its FastTrack Genotyping Services. The first customer, signed in May of that year, was GlaxoSmithKline. Over the ensuing months, another half-dozen genotyping services agreements were signed. Illumina also moved into its new facility located on an eight-acre property that provided ample space for future growth. By the end of the year Illumina's headcount numbered 180. Although Illumina posted a $24.8 million net loss on revenues of $2.5 million in 2001, the vast majority of that amount, $20.7 million, was due to increased spend-

```
┌─────────────────────────────────────────┐
│                                         │
│           KEY DATES                     │
│             ──■──                       │
│                                         │
│  1998:  Company is founded.             │
│  2000:  Initial public offering of stock is completed. │
│  2001:  First product is launched.      │
│  2004:  BeadStation Benchtop System is introduced. │
│  2005:  CyVera Corporation is acquired. │
│  2006:  Solexa, Inc., is acquired.      │
│                                         │
└─────────────────────────────────────────┘
```

ing on research and development, an investment that would reap future dividends.

HAPMAP PROJECT LENDING CREDIBILITY: 2002

Illumina gained market credibility in 2002 when the International HapMap Project was launched to create a detailed map of genetic variations in hopes of speeding up the discovery of genes associated with common illnesses, such as diabetes and heart disease. Illumina was chosen to participate in HapMap and became one of five U.S. participants to receive funding, awarded a $9 million grant from the National Institutes of Health in October 2002. Earlier, in May, Illumina launched its BeadLab system, a fully integrated turn-key production SNP (single nucleotide polymorphism) genotyping system geared toward major genotyping facilities. The first sale was to The Wellcome Trust Sanger Institute, which would be responsible for one-quarter of the HapMap. In all, BeadLab would be used to complete more than 60 percent of the project's genotyping, its system used by several other participants as well. As a result, Illumina technology was able to prove itself in the marketplace, leading to increasing sales for the company.

The year 2002 was also marked by some controversy, when late in the year Applied Biosystems sued Illumina for breach of contract because the efforts of their collaboration were not included in the BeadLab system. Because Applied Biosystems' assay did not perform as well as expected, Illumina had opted to use its independently developed GoldenGate assay. The matter made its way through the courts and a year later a judge directed the matter to arbitration. A settlement was finally reached in August 2004, calling for Illumina to pay back $8.5 million of the $10 million invested by Applied Biosystems in research and development.

Revenues increased 300 percent to $10 million in 2002, and grew at a similar pace a year later, topping $28 million. Some of those sales in 2003 came from the introduction of a second microarray platform, Sentrix BeadChip, unveiled in the middle of the year. This format catered to smaller-scale projects. The year also saw the installation of six BeadLab systems around the world and the signing of 26 genotyping service agreements. To keep pace with the growing business, Illumina beefed up its Sales, Marketing, and Customer Solutions units, nearly doubling them in size.

Illumina's impressive growth pattern continued in 2004. Early in the year it introduced its new BeadStation Benchtop System, a small unit that could run both DNA and RNA analysis applications. Hoping to ink 20 genotyping service contracts during the year, the company booked 52. The goal of selling 20 systems was also greatly exceeded: By the end of 2004, Illumina shipped three BeadLabs and 42 benchtop BeadStations. For the year, revenues increased to $50.6 million and the company trimmed its net loss to $6.2 million.

FIRST ACQUISITION: 2005

Illumina made its first acquisition in April 2005, paying $17.5 million in cash and stock for Connecticut-based CyVera Corporation, a developer of digital microbead technology that complemented Illumina's systems. CyVera offered lower-multiplex technology that could provide target validation and facilitate molecular test development. Illumina also launched several new products in 2005: the DASL Assay, used to generate gene expression profiles from degraded RNA samples; multi-sample, whole genome expression microarrays; the Infinium Assay, a new genotyping assay offering intelligent SNP selection and unlimited access to the genome; and the world's first whole-genome expression arrays for laboratory mice.

With revenues of $73.5 million, 2005 was a successful year for Illumina but would pale in comparison to 2006 when the company turned its first yearly profit, $40 million on sales of $184.6 million. During the year, the company launched 15 new products and increased the installed base of BeadArray Readers to 246. It also completed a secondary stock offering, raising another $97 million and in mid-November completed another acquisition, adding Solexa Inc. for about $512 million in stock. Based in Hayward, California, Solexa was a developer of cost-effective DNA sequencing machines that complemented what Illumina had to offer. According to the *San Diego Union-Tribune,* the merged company "will have all three pillars of modern genetic research; namely, tools used by academic and commercial researchers for gene sequencing, gene expression, and genotyping. Until now, Illumina's product line lacked tools for gene sequencing, while Solexa didn't offer instruments for genotyping." As a result, Illumina hoped to provide instruments that would not only increase the speed of genetic research but could also do so less expensively than rival systems. With revenues through the first three quarters of 2007 increasing by more than 80 percent over the same period the previous year, Illumina was ready to post another record year, and appeared poised to enjoy continued success for years to come.

Ed Dinger

PRINCIPAL SUBSIDIARIES

Illumina UK, Limited; Illumina GmbH; Illumina K.K.; Illumina Singapore Pte. Ltd.

PRINCIPAL COMPETITORS

Affymetrix, Inc.; Beckman Coulter, Inc.; Luminex Corporation.

FURTHER READING

Brown, Stuart F., "Soul of the New Gene Machines," *Fortune,* May 2, 2005, p. 113.

Crabtree, Penni, "Illumina's Stock Skyrockets After Hefty Earnings Report," *San Diego Union-Tribune,* July 20, 2006.

"The Illumina Story," *Lab-on-a-Chip.com,* August 31, 2005.

Pollack, Andrew, "A DNA Chip Maker Acquires Gene-Sequencing Company," *New York Times,* November 14, 2006, p. C3.

Rose, Craig D., "Illumina Buys Solexa in $650 Million Deal," *San Diego Union-Tribune,* November 14, 2006.

Shook, David, "Waiting for the Genomics Payoff," *Business Week Online,* October 15, 2002.

Somers, Terri, "Judge Says San Diego Biotech's Contract Dispute Should Go to Arbitration," *San Diego Union-Tribune,* December 20, 2003.

Welch, Mary, "Illumina Seeks $100M in IPO to Fund Work in Genetics," *Bioworld,* April 6, 2000.

Willett, Matthew, "Illumina Cashes In on Hot IPO Market with $96M Offering," *Bioworld,* August 1, 2000.

Intersil Corporation

1001 Murphy Ranch Road
Milpitas, California 95035
U.S.A.
Telephone: (408) 432-8888
Toll Free: (888) 468-3774
Fax: (408) 432-0640
Web site: http://www.intersil.com

Public Company
Incorporated: 1999
Employees: 1,423
Sales: $740.6 million (2006)
Stock Exchanges: NASDAQ
Ticker Symbol: ISIL
NAIC: 334413 Semiconductor and Related Device Manufacturing

■ ■ ■

Intersil Corporation is a leading designer and manufacturer of high-performance, analog semiconductors. The company's products are used in flat-panel displays, optical storage devices, and in power management applications. Intersil sells its products to original equipment manufacturers (OEMs), contract manufacturers, distributors, and value-added resellers. The company generates 36 percent of its sales from China, 22 percent from the United States, and 11 percent from South Korea. Intersil's manufacturing facility is located in Palm Bay, Florida.

ORIGINS

Intersil emerged as an independent company in 1999, but the history of its assets stretches back decades earlier, to its days as a component of Harris Corporation. Harris was formed in 1895 as the Harris Automatic Press Company, the entrepreneurial effort of brothers Alfred and Charles Harris. From its inception as the developer of an innovative automatic sheet feeder for printing presses, the company gradually diversified into the communications sector, becoming a pioneer of sophisticated technology developed by forward-thinking engineers. Harris's products and expertise were used in the first manned space flight, in weather satellites, and in advanced military applications for the Minuteman, Atlas, and Polaris missile systems.

Much of Harris's technological expertise stemmed from an acquisition the company made, one that greatly influenced Intersil's development. In 1967, Harris acquired Radiation Incorporated, a manufacturer of space and military electronics based south of Cape Canaveral in Melbourne, Florida. (A decade later, Harris acknowledged the importance of the Radiation acquisition by moving its headquarters from Cleveland, Ohio, to Melbourne.) Radiation meant much to Harris, supplying technology that, among other applications, was instrumental to the Apollo mission to the moon. For the legacy of Intersil, Radiation meant much as well: The Melbourne company entered the microelectronics business early, developing its first working semiconductor for use in digital communications equipment four years before it was acquired by Harris.

COMPANY PERSPECTIVES

Intersil has a unique strategy that is clearly working. Our balance of application specific standard products and general purpose proprietary products drives excellent revenue growth and expands gross margins. We understand our customers' needs and work to exceed their expectations at every turn. Our fab-lite manufacturing strategy provides us access to a broad range of process technologies with very low capital investments, creating significant free cash flow. And our constant focus on expenses drives better operating and net income leverage.

Radiation's involvement in the nascent semiconductor sector formed the foundation of Harris's semiconductor business, which became known as Harris Semiconductor. Harris Semiconductor, the predecessor to Intersil, gained a substantial boost to its stature from another acquisition, the purchase of General Electric Co.'s semiconductor operations in 1988. The acquisition more than doubled the size of Harris Semiconductor's operations, making Intersil indebted to the contributions of General Electric for much of what it inherited in 1999.

INDEPENDENCE IN 1999

By the mid-1990s, Harris was in the midst of its centennial celebrations. The company, with 27,000 employees stationed throughout the world, was generating $3.5 billion in sales from four major businesses: electronic systems, semiconductors, communications, and office systems marketed under the name "Lanier." Profound changes were soon afoot, however. Harris would begin its second century with a much narrower focus. The company decided to concentrate its energies on the global communications equipment market, specifically on the digital communications equipment used in digital television broadcast. The change in strategy became apparent to the public in 1999. Lanier Worldwide, Harris's office systems subsidiary, was spun off as a tax-free dividend to Harris shareholders. Also included in the divestitures made during the year was Harris Semiconductor, which the company announced in June 1999 it intended to sell to Sterling Holding Co. LLC for approximately $700 million.

As Harris prepared for a new era to begin, the company made several significant changes to its semiconductor operations. Much like its parent company, the division became leaner, concentrating its energies in two directions: analog products and wireless networking products. Harris Semiconductor's logic business was pared away, sold to Texas Instruments Inc. The division's operating costs were trimmed by $40 million as it consolidated its fabrication facilities by closing three plants and moving some manufacturing offshore. The division's product catalog was overhauled entirely, reduced from 25,000 separate items to 4,500 separate items.

A WIRELESS NETWORKING LEADER TAKING SHAPE

In the years preceding the sale of Harris Semiconductor, divestments and streamlining efforts were coupled with investments. The division's parent company spent heavily on building up Harris Semiconductor's capabilities in the wireless networking market, a market generating considerable interest at the close of the 20th century. For four years, the years immediately preceding the sale of Harris Semiconductor, Harris directed considerable resources toward developing the type of wireless semiconductors that enabled laptop computers and other mobile electronic devices to connect to the Internet without a telephone line. As a result, by the time Sterling Holding agreed to acquire the division, Harris Semiconductor held sway as a leader in the emerging market for wireless, local area networking, or WLAN, chips.

For Sterling Holding, the combination of Harris Semiconductor's WLAN and analog businesses represented an attractive package, one well worth the $700 million price tag. Sterling Holding was a Citicorp Venture Capital investment-portfolio company intent on recouping its investment by selling Harris Semiconductor on Wall Street. To lead the company and navigate it toward its initial public offering (IPO) of stock, Sterling Holding picked Harris Semiconductor's leader at the time of the sale, 46-year-old Gregory L. Williams. Williams was appointed Harris Semiconductor's president in October 1998, joining the division after a stint as a senior executive at Phoenix-based Motorola Semiconductor.

IPO IN 2000

Harris Semiconductor officially began operating as Intersil Corporation in August 1999. "We're ecstatic," Williams said in an August 23, 1999, interview with *Electronic News.* "Out of the chute, revenues are around $530 million." The company's IPO, which Williams told *Electronic News* was "years away," occurred six

KEY DATES

1967: Harris Corporation acquires Radiation Inc., which forms the basis of the semiconductor operations that will become Intersil.

1988: The size of Harris Corporation's semiconductor operations more than doubles with the purchase of General Electric Co.'s semiconductor assets.

1999: Harris Semiconductor, a division of Harris Corporation, is sold and renamed Intersil Corporation.

2000: Intersil completes its initial public offering of stock.

2002: Intersil strengthens its analog business by purchasing Elantec Semiconductor Inc.

2003: Intersil exits the wireless networking business.

2004: Intersil acquires Xicor Corp. and BitBlitz Communications Inc.

2007: Revenues reach $740.6 million.

months later, when the investing public was given the chance to evaluate Intersil's potential. Investors were presented with a company reliant on analog and mixed-signal products for the power and wireless data networking markets.

INTERSIL LEADS THE WLAN MARKET

Although Intersil derived half of its revenues from power semiconductor sales, the company's dominant position in the WLAN sector garnered much of the business press's attention. The industry was abuzz with excitement about the potential of wireless products. Intersil ranked as the market leader in wireless chip sales, enjoying a commanding lead thanks largely to Harris's investments in the sector during the second half of the 1990s. In 2002, Intersil's wireless chip sales jumped 125 percent to $239 million, which accounted for 51 percent of all wireless chip sales. Looking ahead, there were predictions of robust growth in the market, which put Intersil in the enviable position of capturing the lion's share of escalating demand for so-called Wi-Fi chips. "It's a hot market," an analyst remarked in an April 7, 2003, interview with *Investor's Business Daily.* "We forecast 49 percent revenue growth at a compound annual rate through 2006." According to the analyst's estimate, the wireless chip market was on a path to

eclipse $1 billion in sales, a volume that would more than double Intersil's revenues from the WLAN market.

As Intersil entered 2003, the company faced a critical period in its existence. In the technological race for dominance in the WLAN market, the company enjoyed a commanding lead, but there were ample reasons for concern. Competition was intense, ratcheted up by a host of new entrants in the sector and by the redoubled efforts of Intersil's closest rivals, namely Broadcom Corp. and the world's largest chipmaker, Intel Corp. Intel had been slow to enter the wireless segment of the market, but the March 2003 release of its Centrino line for mobile devices signaled its intent to launch a full-scale attack on the WLAN market. The arrival of Intel, a company with annual sales exceeding $25 billion, represented a formidable threat to Intersil's leadership position, but mounting competition was not the only challenge the company faced.

"Plain and simple," an analyst said in a June 2, 2003, interview with *EBN*, "prices are falling faster than units are growing." The menacing presence of Intel and other competitors was exacerbated by declining prices for wireless chips, crimping profit margins severely. The price of 802.11b chipsets, which composed much of the WLAN market, plunged from an average of $16.06 in early 2002 to $6.61 in early 2003. Intersil's sales from its wireless networking business reflected the drop in prices, falling from a high of nearly $75 million in the third quarter of 2002 to $51 million in the first quarter of 2003.

INTERSIL CASHES OUT IN 2003

Falling prices and increased competition forced Intersil's management to make a difficult decision. In July 2003, the company revealed it was exiting the business entirely, bowing out while it still ranked as the largest wireless chipmaker. Midway through the month, Intersil agreed to sell its Wireless Networking Product Group to GlobespanVirata Inc., a Red Bank, New Jersey-based manufacturer of semiconductors for digital-subscriber-line (DSL) modems and other broadband equipment. The deal, a cash-and-stock transaction, was valued at $365 million.

The news of Intersil's departure from the wireless market came as a shock to some industry observers, but within a short time the decision drew applause from nearly every pundit. "From a business strategy standpoint, it was a good move for Intersil to get out even though it was the market leader in Wi-Fi," an analyst explained in the July 17, 2003, edition of the *Orange County Register,* typifying the reaction to the deal brokered with GlobespanVirata. "It (Intersil) was a smaller company, especially compared to companies like Broadcom, Texas Instruments, and Agere. With Intel looming to join the fray, it was a strategic move to get out while they could."

The divestiture, by itself, would not have elicited praise if Intersil did not maintain a solid position in the analog semiconductor market. The sale of the Wireless Networking Product Group earned nods of approval because it was perceived to be a drag on the company's financial performance in a much larger, more robust market. Analog chips represented a $30-billion-per-year business comprising fast-growing markets, particularly the market for power management chips. The chips helped regulate the amount of electricity a device used, which became more important as designers put more advanced capabilities on chips. Increased capabilities meant more power, and more power meant more heat, causing a host of problems, including system failure, system malfunction, and the shortened life span of batteries.

A FUTURE IN ANALOG

When industry observers looked at Intersil stripped of its wireless business, they liked what they saw. Since its inception, the company had possessed a strong analog business (its inheritance from Harris) but Intersil had expanded greatly on the operations it took from its former parent company. In 2002, Intersil paid $1.4 billion for Elantec Semiconductor Inc., a specialist in the analog arena. The acquisition was defining, making analog-related sales greater than wireless-related sales and giving the company a new leader. Rich Beyer, president and chief executive officer of Elantec, became president and chief executive officer of Intersil following the acquisition. It was Beyer who presided over the sale of the Wireless Networking Product Group and steered the company toward its focused assault on analog chip sales.

INTERSIL'S RICH BEYER

Beyer was an industry veteran. A former officer in the U.S. Marine Corps, Beyer earned undergraduate and graduate degrees in Russian from Georgetown University and graduate degrees in marketing and international business from Columbia University before beginning his career in the telecommunications and computer industries. Beyer held a number of senior executive positions with telecommunications and computer companies before joining National Semiconductor Corporation in 1993. At National Semiconductor, Beyer rose to the posts of executive vice-president and chief operating officer, leaving in 1996 to serve as president and chief operating officer of VLSI

Technology, Inc. He joined Elantec in 2000, leading the company for the two years preceding its purchase by Intersil. Once at the helm of Intersil, his plans for shaping the company into an analog specialist took form.

ACQUISITIONS IN 2004

Once Beyer had shed Intersil's wireless business, he focused on three areas of growth: power management, optical storage drivers, and flat-panel-display drivers. He strengthened the company's position through internal means—one-third of Intersil's payroll was comprised of engineers, providing a steady supply of new products—and by completing acquisitions. Beyer orchestrated two acquisitions in the wake of the wireless divestiture, targeting two companies that bolstered Intersil's analog business. In March 2004, Intersil announced it had agreed to buy a smaller rival, Xicor Corp., in a cash and stock deal valued at $529 million. The purchase strengthened Intersil's capabilities to make chips for cellular telephones, laptop batteries, and high-end, liquid-crystal-display (LCD) screens. Next, in May 2004, Beyer announced plans to buy BitBlitz Communications Inc., a developer of high-speed serializer-deserializers, retimers, and transponders that expanded Intersil's presence in the market for high-performance analog communications.

By 2007, eight years of independence had seen significant changes in the assets spun off by Harris. Intersil transformed itself during its first decade of business, setting its sights exclusively on the analog chip business. Financially, the decision to shed its wireless business and to focus on analog sales proved to be successful in the years immediately following the restructuring. Revenues increased from $535.8 million in 2004 to $740.6 million in 2006. Perhaps more impressive, the company's profits increased substantially during the period, jumping from $40.7 million in 2004 to $151.9 million in 2006. Beyer and his management team needed no further validation that their strategy was working, ensuring that Intersil would continue to expand its presence in the analog sector in the years ahead.

Jeffrey L. Covell

PRINCIPAL SUBSIDIARIES

Intersil Communications, Inc.; Elantec Semiconductor, Inc.; Intersil Americas Inc.; Intersil Investment Company; Xicor LLC; Poweready, Inc.; Analog Integration Partners, LLC; Xicor, Inc. Integration Holding Company; Sapphire Worldwide Investments Inc. (British Virgin Islands); Elantec Semiconductor Malaysia Sdn. Bhd.; Intersil China Limited; Intersil K.K. (Japan); Intersil YH (Korea); Intersil Advanced Technology (Labuan) Ltd.; Intersil Services Company Sdn. Bhd. (Malaysia); Intersil Pte. Ltd. (Singapore); Intersil Ltd. (Taiwan); Xicor Hong Kong Limited; Intersil Analog Services Pvt. Ltd.; Intersil S.A. (Belgium); Intersil Sarl (France); Intersil GmbH (Germany); Intersil Srl (Italy); Intersil Holding GmbH (Switzerland); Intersil Europe Sarl (Switzerland); Intersil Wireless B.V. (Netherlands); Intersil Limited (U.K.); Xicor, GmbH (Germany); Xicor Limited (U.K.); Intersil Luxembourg Participations Sarl; Elantec Semiconductor U.K. Limited; Intersil Swiss Holding Sarl (Switzerland).

PRINCIPAL COMPETITORS

Analog Devices, Inc.; Texas Instruments Incorporated; Maxim Integrated Products, Inc.

FURTHER READING

Chuang, Tamara, "Milpitas, Calif.-based Firm Exits Wireless Networking Business," *Orange County Register,* July 17, 2003.

Detar, James, "Firms Look to Juice Up Devices," *Investor's Business Daily,* August 18, 2003, p. A6.

———, "Intersil's Obstacles: Intel and Broadcom," *Investor's Business Daily,* April 7, 2003, p. A5.

Dunn, Darrell, "Big Promise, Big Risks Define WLAN Market," *EBN,* June 2, 2003, p. 1.

———, "Harris Semiconductor to Become Intersil Corp.," *Electronic Buyers' News,* July 19, 1999, p. 8.

"DVDINSIDER: Intersil Corporation Acquires BitBlitz Communications," *DVD News,* May 25, 2004.

"Everything Old Is New Again," *Electronic News (1991),* July 19, 1999, p. 4.

"Harris Semi Becomes Intersil," *Electronic News (1991),* August 23, 1999, p. 10.

"Harris Semiconductor Breaks," *Semiconductor Industry & Business Survey,* August 2, 1999.

"Intersil Cashes in Wireless Chips," *Daily Deal,* July 17, 2003.

Shinkle, Kirk, "Intersil's Xicor Acquisition Intended to Accelerate Its Analog Push," *Investor's Business Daily,* March 18, 2004, p. A6.

Souza, Crista, "Intersil Demanding Place at Analog Table," *EBN,* May 19, 2003, p. 8.

———, "Intersil Shakes Up WLAN Community with Divestiture," *EBN,* July 21, 2003, p. 3.

Jarden Corporation

555 Theodore Fremd Avenue, Suite B-302
Rye, New York 10580
U.S.A.
Telephone: (914) 967-9400
Fax: (914) 967-9405
Web site: http://www.jarden.com

Public Company
Incorporated: 1993 as Alltrista Corporation
Employees: 25,000
Sales: $3.84 billion (2006)
Stock Exchanges: New York
Ticker Symbol: JAH
NAIC: 335211 Electric Housewares and Household Fan
Manufacturing; 326113 Unsupported Plastics Film
and Sheet Manufacturing; 326199 All Other
Plastics Product Manufacturing; 327213 Glass
Container Manufacturing; 331491 Nonferrous
Metal Rolling, Drawing, and Extruding; 332115
Crown and Closure Manufacturing; 339920 Sport-
ing and Athletic Goods Manufacturing

∎ ∎ ∎

Jarden Corporation is primarily a supplier of consumer products and recreational equipment. The company makes a diverse range of consumer products, including Ball home canning products, Oster appliances, K2 skis and snowboards, Coleman outdoor equipment, and Bicycle playing cards. Jarden also makes plastic and zinc products, including zinc penny blanks, a facet of its business that dates from its existence as part of Ball Corporation. The company was spun off from Ball Corporation in 1993 as Alltrista Corporation and changed its name to Jarden in 2002.

THE BALL HERITAGE: 1880–1993

Although Jarden's existence as a separate corporate entity began 1993 with the formation of Alltrista, its roots stretch to the late 1800s and the inception of the Wooden Jacket Can Company. The Wooden Jacket Can Company was founded in 1880 by five brothers in Buffalo, New York, to produce and sell wood-jacketed tin containers to hold paint, varnishes, and kerosene. Eventually, however, their product evolved into tin-jacketed glass containers, and the brothers—whose surname was Ball—rechristened the company Ball Brothers Glass Manufacturing Company. In 1884 the Ball brothers learned that the patent for sealed glass home canning jars, which had been held by John Mason, had expired. They began producing their own version of the jars, imprinted with the Ball name.

In 1887 the brothers moved their jar business to Muncie, Indiana. In the late 1880s, Indiana was in the middle of a natural gas boom, which made it an excellent location for Ball, whose glassmaking operation required great quantities of gas. Soon after the move, Ball began expanding its business by acquiring other small companies, including a zinc mill, a rubber manufacturing plant, and a paper packaging operation. The company continued to expand into the 1900s, further diversifying by acquiring a metal beverage container company, an aerospace research firm, a petroleum equipment maker, and a telecommunications

COMPANY PERSPECTIVES

Our objective is to build a world-class consumer products company that enjoys leading positions in markets for branded consumer products. We will seek to achieve this objective by continuing our tradition of product innovation, new product introductions and providing the consumer with the experience and value they associate with our brands. We plan to leverage and expand our domestic and international distribution channels, increase brand awareness through co-branding and cross selling initiatives and pursue strategic acquisitions, all while driving margin improvement.

division. By the mid-1980s, Ball Corporation had annual sales of more than $1 billion.

A NEW OLD COMPANY: BIRTH OF ALLTRISTA IN 1993

In the early 1990s, Ball's management began assessing its large and extremely diverse portfolio of businesses to determine what direction the company should take. Its decision was to focus on its larger businesses and to shed smaller subsidiaries. The company established Alltrista Corporation, containing the assets of seven of these smaller subsidiaries. Alltrista was spun off in early April 1993, giving Ball shareholders one share of Alltrista stock for every four shares of Ball stock. The company began trading on the NASDAQ under the ticker symbol JARS.

Headquartered in Muncie, the newly formed Alltrista consisted of seven diverse businesses, some of which were more than 100 years old. The oldest was the Consumer Products Company, which consisted of the original Ball jar business along with a line of other canning-related products. Despite the corporate name change, Alltrista continued to use the well-known Ball script trademark on its canning products. Another of Alltrista's century-old businesses was the Zinc Products Company, which first produced zinc caps for Ball's canning jars in the 1880s. At the time of the Alltrista spinoff, Zinc Products was a major manufacturer of the zinc penny blanks used to make U.S. pennies. In addition, the company made battery cans, automotive trim, electrical fuse strip, and architectural materials.

Alltrista also held three plastics businesses: Industrial Plastics Company, Unimark Plastics

Company, and Plastic Packaging Company. Industrial Plastics manufactured heavy-gauge thermoplastic sheet and thermoformed products, such as molded inner door liners for refrigerators. Unimark Plastics Company, which Ball had purchased in 1978, was a custom injection molder that sold mainly to the medical and consumer products markets. Plastic Packaging Company produced plastic sheet and containers for use in the food processing industry. Its plastic products featured barrier layers that reduced the oxygen and moisture that could pass through them, making them ideal for shelf-stable, aseptic food packaging applications.

The last two companies in Alltrista's portfolio were its Metal Services Company and The LumenX Company. Metal Services Company was a metal decorating operation that manufactured thin-gauge metal containers for various consumer products, such as canned goods. Alltrista's LumenX Company, which Ball had acquired in the late 1980s, built customized industrial inspection systems that used x-ray and machine vision technologies. LumenX products were used primarily by the automotive and automotive component industries.

Alltrista's president and CEO was William Peterson, who had for 27 years worked in various administrative capacities for Ball. Its senior vice-president and CFO was Thomas Clark, who had previously been Ball's vice-president for corporate planning and development. All seven of the spun-off subsidiaries retained the same management they had had while still under the Ball umbrella.

DIVESTITURES AND ACQUISITIONS: 1994–99

When Alltrista was spun off, it was essentially a collection of companies that Ball no longer wanted. Some were profitable, some were not, and there was little coherence among the businesses or the markets they served. Alltrista's management was faced with the task of analyzing the businesses and deciding how to shape the unwieldy, patchwork-quilt company into a whole and profitable business. Because tax laws prohibited any significant divestitures for two years after the spinoff, the company first determined which areas it wanted to grow.

Its first step was to expand the home canning line. In 1994 Alltrista purchased Toronto, Canada-based Bernardin Ltd. Like Ball Corporation, Bernardin had a rich history in the canning products market; since 1881, the company had been producing metal lids for commercial and home canning containers. Alltrista also acquired the Fruit-Fresh brand product line in 1994. Fruit-Fresh, an

KEY DATES

1880: Wooden Jacket Can Company, the earliest predecessor to Jarden Corporation, is founded.

1887: After changing its name to Ball Brothers Glass Manufacturing Co., the company moves from New York to Indiana.

1993: Now known as Ball Corporation, the company sheds some of its smaller businesses and spins them off as Alltrista Corporation.

1996: Alltrista acquires Kerr Group, Inc., one of its main rivals in the home canning market.

1999: Alltrista acquires Triangle Plastics Inc., which makes it the largest industrial thermoform manufacturer in North America.

2001: Martin Franklin, through Marlin Partners, acquires Alltrista and becomes its new chief executive officer.

2002: After acquiring Tilia International, the company changes its name to Jarden Corporation.

2003: Jarden acquires Diamond Brands, Lehigh Consumer Products, and VillaWare.

2004: The purchase of United States Playing Card Co. and Sunbeam Products Inc. more than triples annual sales.

2005: Jarden acquires The Holmes Group.

2007: K2 Sports is acquired for $1.2 billion.

agent used in canning and preserving to prevent browning and protect flavor, was marketed through Alltrista's Consumer Products division.

The company further grew its Consumer Products division with the March 1996 acquisition of Kerr Group, Inc., one of Alltrista's main competitors in the home canning products market. After completing the $14.6 million acquisition, Alltrista closed Kerr's manufacturing plant in Jackson, Tennessee, and consolidated its operations into Alltrista's plant in Muncie, Indiana.

The year 1996 also marked the end of the IRS-imposed divestiture moratorium, and Alltrista was ready to prune the weak areas of its portfolio. In April, the company made its first move in this direction with the sale of its Metal Services division. Although Metal Services was Alltrista's largest company in terms of sales, it earned little or no profit. Moreover, it had just lost its

largest customer in 1995, which was bound to depress its top line.

In 1997 Alltrista's management turned their attention to expanding the Industrial Plastics division. On May 19, the company purchased the Arkansas-based Viking Industries, a producer of large thermoformed plastic products, such as tubs, showers, surrounds, and whirlpools. Viking's primary markets were the manufactured housing and recreational vehicle industries, new markets for Alltrista. The company believed that both industries, and manufactured housing especially, showed great growth potential. The Viking purchase also dovetailed well with Alltrista's existing plastics operation, creating operational synergies. For example, prior to its acquisition, Viking had relied on outside suppliers for the large plastic sheet it used in its thermoforming operations. Alltrista, however, produced the necessary sheet through its Industrial Plastics division, thereby reducing overall cost and improving efficiency.

According to Thomas Clark, who had become Alltrista's CEO in 1995, the sort of operational integration achieved with the Viking purchase was likely to be a hallmark of future acquisitions. "In the past we have looked at the three plastics businesses as separate organizations and separate activities," he said in a December 1997 interview with the *Wall Street Corporate Reporter*. "We will tend to take a more integrated view in the future."

The year 1997 also marked Alltrista's second divestiture, when the company sold the line of machine vision inspection equipment produced by its LumenX subsidiary. The following year, the company exited the LumenX business altogether, when it sold the subsidiary's remaining product line: x-ray inspection equipment. Alltrista also initiated plans to close down an unprofitable plastics plant located in Puerto Rico.

Alltrista ended 1997 with net sales of $255.2 million, a 10.8 percent increase over the previous year, and a net profit of $14.8 million. The increase in total sales was primarily attributable to the Kerr and Viking acquisitions within Alltrista's food containers and Industrial Plastics businesses: sales of food containers grew 39 percent, while Industrial Plastics' sales showed a 62 percent gain. As the year's final milestone, Alltrista moved from the NASDAQ to the New York Stock Exchange on December 31, trading under the ticker symbol ALC.

NEW VISION: 1998

Alltrista marked its fifth anniversary as an independent company in 1998 by redefining its vision, strategy, and growth goals. The company set its sights high, aiming for $500 million in sales and $50 million in operating earnings by the year 2002. To meet this ambitious goal, Alltrista, which had grown an average of 7 percent yearly since the spinoff, would have to double its growth rate in the ensuing years. The new company vision brought with it various other changes. Alltrista reorganized its business into two distinct segments: metal products and plastic products. The metals segment included the zinc operation and the consumer products division, including the home canning products business. Group vice-presidents were named to oversee the two segments.

To help drive growth, Alltrista began seeking new opportunities for its metals division. Already the primary supplier of one-cent zinc blanks to both the U.S. and Royal Canadian mints, the company tapped European markets in 1998. One of its earliest wins was a three-year contract to supply the Birmingham Mint in Britain with 55 metric tons of zinc blanks for the new unified euro coins. Alltrista also initiated negotiations with mints in Poland and South Korea to supply blanks for their coins.

The company looked to overseas markets to boost sales of its home canning lines as well. It began preparing to test market its canning jars in Hungary, with the plan to expand into Poland and the Czech Republic if Hungarian sales were promising. Because home canning was far more prevalent in Eastern Europe than in the United States, Alltrista believed that the targeted markets had tremendous growth potential. The home canning products business also expanded its U.S. and Canadian product lines in 1998, introducing a decorative "elite" line of canning jars and closures. In addition, the company added a new housewares line, called Golden Harvest, which included tumblers and other glassware products.

In September 1998, Alltrista moved its corporate headquarters from Muncie to Indianapolis, Indiana. According to Clark, the main impetus behind the relocation was the need to be near a major airport as the company grew more geographically far-flung. Alltrista did not bring its manufacturing business with it to Indianapolis; both the consumer products and plastics packaging operations remained in Muncie.

TRIANGLE PLASTICS
ACQUISITION: 1999

In March 1999, the company proved itself serious about achieving its growth goal when it announced plans to purchase Triangle Plastics Inc. for $148 million. Triangle was an Iowa-based thermoforming company with 1998

sales of $114 million, a growth rate of around 15 percent, five production facilities, and 1,100 employees. It produced heavy-gauge components for a whole slew of industries, several of which were new to Alltrista. Through its subsidiary, TriEnda Corp., Triangle also manufactured thermoformed materials-handling products, such as plastic pallets. TriEnda, which contributed around 40 percent of Triangle's total sales, had a customer base that included the U.S. Postal Service, and grocery, printing, textile, chemical, and pharmaceutical companies. Alltrista planned to consolidate Triangle's five production facilities with its own plastics group.

The Triangle acquisition, which was completed in late April 1999, made Alltrista the largest industrial thermoformer in North America. It also stood the company in good stead as it worked to quicken its growth rate. "Triangle Plastics is a key step in achieving our goal to grow our company to $500 million in sales with $50 million in operating earnings by the year 2002," Clark said in a March 15, 1999, press release. "To meet this goal we must grow by 15 percent annually, and the Triangle Plastics business fits this criteria." The scope of the Triangle acquisition made investors edgy, however; the company's stock dropped 16 percent in the two weeks after Alltrista announced the purchase.

In May, Alltrista stated that it planned to sell its plastics packaging business to a Missouri-based maker of sheet plastic. As Alltrista positioned its plastics segment to grow in the areas of thermoforming and injection molding, the packaging division, which used different manufacturing processes and served a different market, was no longer a good fit. The division, which had 1998 sales of $28 million, was sold for approximately $30 million.

A FOCUS ON PLASTICS FOR THE
21ST CENTURY

As the 1990s wound down, Alltrista geared up for substantial growth in the new century. The company's main area of focus was expected to be its plastics division, where it planned to add capabilities and new markets to its portfolio by way of both acquisition and internal growth. One potential area of growth in the plastics segment was an expanded geographic coverage, which would allow Alltrista to serve a wider customer base. Another likely rapid growth area was the company's newly acquired Triangle Plastics subsidiary, TriEnda. Alltrista's management believed that there was a growing and largely untapped market for TriEnda's main product: thermoformed plastic pallets for materials handling. In a March 15, 1999, press release, Clark said that only in recent years have plastics begun to displace wood and corrugated packaging and pallets. Noting that plastic pallets account for only 4 to 6 percent of the U.S. market, he said, "We are at an early point of plastics penetrating this market, therefore growth opportunities should be significant."

Alltrista also anticipated increased sales in its zinc products division. Part of that growth was likely to be driven by a higher demand for U.S. penny blanks, as well as a continued demand for blanks used to produce the euro one-cent and five-cent coins. Another avenue of growth in the zinc business was the increasing substitution of zinc for other materials in various industrial applications. The company's sales of battery cans, however, was likely to decline greatly in the coming years, as two of its main buyers of the cans decided to relocate their operations to foreign companies.

BEGINNING OF THE FRANKLIN ERA: 2001

Few individuals could have anticipated the dramatic transformation Alltrista would experience in the first decade of the new century. Nearly every expectation about what the future held in store—growth from plastics, growth from Triangle, growth from zinc products—was rendered moot by the intervention of a young British dealmaker named Martin Franklin. The effect of Franklin's influence on Alltrista was profound. Within roughly five years, a company generating nearly $250 million in annual sales was collecting nearly $4 billion in annual sales. A company with 2,000 employees saw its payroll swell exponentially, eclipsing 25,000 employees. Alltrista, a company struggling to find its identity, became Jarden, a company that controlled a bevy of well-known consumer brands.

Born in London, England, in 1964, Franklin was the son of Roland Franklin, who spent 25 years working alongside famed British corporate raider Sir James Goldsmith. The duo specialized in hostile takeovers, accumulating fortunes by buying and breaking apart massive conglomerates such as Crown Zellerbach and Diamond International. Martin Franklin followed in his father's footsteps. After earning an undergraduate degree in political science at the University of Pennsylvania, he served a stint at the New York office of investment banker Rothschild Inc. before joining his father in the $1.3 billion leveraged buyout of British paper and packaging conglomerate DRG. Franklin, 24 years old when the deal was completed, spent two years selling DRG's assets piecemeal. "I did more deals in two years than most investment bankers will probably do in a lifetime," Franklin remarked in an October 27, 2003, interview with *Forbes*.

After dissecting DRG, Franklin began building his own conglomerate. He teamed up with an executive named Ian Ashken and purchased a small chain of eye care stores owned by General Electric's pension fund. He and Ashken paid $2.3 million for the chain and merged it with a shell company trading on the American Stock Exchange. They christened the public company Benson Eyecare and used it as a vehicle to acquire a slew of optical products businesses. Once they had patched together a mini-empire in vision wear, the pair turned to the auction block. They sold Benson Eyecare in 1996 for $300 million. In 1998, a spinoff of their acquisitive efforts, Lumen Technologies, a manufacturer of specialized short-arc lamps, was sold for $250 million. Another spinoff, branded eyewear marketer Bolle, was sold for $96 million in 2000.

By the time Franklin's involvement in the eye-care business was winding down, he had set his sights on Alltrista. The company was struggling mightily at the time, facing declining sales of canning jars and plastic parts to the truck industry. Its stock value was declining as well, triggering unrest from shareholders, one of whom was Franklin. Franklin, through his Rye, New York-based company, Marlin Partners, had taken a 9.9 percent stake in Alltrista, which he used to make an offer for the company in March 2000, submitting a $30-per-share bid for all of its assets. Alltrista's board of directors rejected his offer and a second offer in early 2001. After being denied for a second time, Franklin took another approach, demanding two seats on the company's board. Alltrista's board members, convinced Franklin would win the seats if he launched a proxy fight, agreed to give him the two seats. "We assumed that with only two seats on the board he would be reasonably manageable," a board member said in an October 27, 2003, interview with *Forbes*. "We miscalculated." By September 2001, Marlin Partners had acquired Alltrista, which was led by its new chairman and chief executive officer, Martin Franklin, and his colleague, Ian Ashken, who became Alltrista's chief financial officer. Franklin soon relocated Alltrista's headquarters to Rye, New York, where Marlin Partners was based.

ACQUISITION SPREE: 2002–07

"I frankly don't know what previous management's strategy was," Franklin said in a September 6, 2002, interview with *Investor's Business Daily*. "Whatever it was, it didn't work." His strategy with Alltrista was clear: shed assets such as the thermoformed plastics division and focus on branded businesses such as the company's home canning operations. Franklin's strategy hinged on acquisitions, the first of which was the May

2002 purchase of Tilia International, the manufacturer of the FoodSaver vacuum-packaging food system. He paid $160 million for Tilia and aimed to make a series of similar acquisitions. "We're looking for other branded domestic consumables with similar distribution requirements—a brand either No. 1 or No. 2 in a niche market," Franklin explained in his September 6, 2002, interview with *Investor's Business Daily*.

Shortly after purchasing Tilia, Franklin decided it was time to change the name of his company. Franklin combined "jar," reflective of the company's leading market position in the home canning market, with "den," reflective of the company's focus on products used in the home, and came up with "Jarden," a name that also had the connotation of the French word for garden, *jardin*.

Franklin's acquisition campaign proceeded at a brisk pace under the Jarden banner. In early 2003, he purchased Diamond Brands, a maker of toothpicks, kitchen matches, and plastic cutlery. Before the end of the year, he brokered deals for VillaWare, a high-end kitchen products manufacturer, and Lehigh Consumer Products, a seller of rope, cord, and twine. Sales increased 60 percent in 2003, reaching $587 million. In July 2004, he paid $232 million for United States Playing Card Co., a leading manufacturer of playing cards, children's card games, collectible tins, puzzles, and card accessories. Several months later, Franklin made his boldest move, paying $746 million for Sunbeam Products Inc., a company that had declared bankruptcy three years earlier and had reorganized as American Household Inc. The acquisition, expected to triple Jarden's annual sales, gave the company a stable of well-known brands such as Mr. Coffee, Coleman outdoor gear, and Oster appliances.

ADDITION OF K2 SPORTS: 2007

Franklin and his management team continued to look for acquisition candidates after the Sunbeam acquisition. In 2005, Jarden paid $420 million plus stock for The Holmes Group, a deal that gave the company ownership of brands such as Bionaire, Crock-Pot, Rival, and White Mountain. Next, in early 2007, the company acquired Pure Fishing Inc., a maker of fishing lures and tackle, for roughly $400 million, securing brands such as Berkley, Abu Garcia, Mitchell, Stren, Trilene, and Gulp. The biggest acquisition in Franklin's first six years as chief executive officer followed, the August 2007 purchase of K2 Sports, a designer, manufacturer, and marketer of 16 brands of snowboards, skis, and related footwear. Franklin paid a staggering $1.2 billion for K2 Sports. In the years ahead, further acquisitions were expected as Franklin looked to build a powerhouse of consumer branded products. His efforts in the previous five years had led to a 443 percent increase in Jarden's share price, a record of performance that would be difficult to improve upon in the coming five years.

Shawna Brynildssen
Updated, Jeffrey L. Covell

PRINCIPAL SUBSIDIARIES

Alltrista Limited (Canada); Alltrista Newco Corporation; Alltrista Plastics Corporation; American Household, Inc.; Application des Gaz, S.A.S. (France); Australian Coleman, Inc.; Bafiges, S.A.S. (France); Beacon Exports, Inc.; Bernardin, Limited (Canada); Bicycle Holding, Inc.; BRK Brands, Inc.; BRK Brands Europe Limited (U.K.); BRK Brands Pty. Ltd. (Australia); Camping Gaz CD Spol S.R.O. (Czech Republic); Camping-Gaz International (Deutschland) GmbH (Germany); Camping Gaz International Portugal Lda. (Portugal); Camping Gaz Italia S.r.l. (Italy); Camping Gaz Suisse A.G. (Switzerland); Canadian Playing Card Company, Ltd. (Canada); CC Outlet, Inc.; Coleman Benelux B.V. (Netherlands); Coleman Brands Pty. Limited (Australia); Coleman Country, Ltd.; Coleman (Deutschland) GmbH (Germany); Coleman EMEA, S.A.S. (France); Coleman International Holdings, LLC; Coleman Japan Company Ltd.; Coleman Latin America, LLC; Coleman UK Holdings Limited (U.K.); Coleman UK Limited (U.K.); Coleman Venture Capital, Inc.; Coleman Worldwide Corporation; Desarrollo Industrial Fitec, S. de RL. De C.V. (Mexico); Dicon Global, Inc. (Canada); Dicon Safety Products (Europe) Limited (U.K.); Dongguan Holmes Electrical Products Co., Ltd. (China); Dongguan Huixun Electrical Products Co., Ltd. (China); Dongguan Raider Motor Corporation, Ltd. (China); Electronica BRK de Mexico, S.A. de C.V.; Esteem Industries Limited (Hong Kong); First Alert, Inc.; First Alert Holdings Inc.; Hearthmark, LLC; Holmes Motor Corporation; Holmes Products (Europe) Limited (U.K.); Holmes Products (Far East) Limited (Bahamas); International Playing Card Company, Ltd. (Canada); Jarden Acquisition ETVE, S.L. (Spain); Jarden Acquisition I, Inc.; Jarden Plastic Solutions Limited (U.K.); Jarden Receivables, LLC; Jarden Zinc Products, Inc.; Jarden Products Corporation; Kansas Acquisition Corp.; L.A. Services, Inc.; Laser Acquisition Corporation; Lehigh Consumer Products Corporation; Loew-Cornell, Inc.; Naipes Heraclio Fournier, S.A. (Spain); Nippon Coleman, Inc.; Oster GmbH (Germany); Oster de Chile Comercializadora Ltda. (Chile); Oster de Colombia, Ltda. (Colombia); Oster de Venezuela, S.A.; Pine Mountain Corporation; Productos Coleman, S.A.U. (Spain); Quoin, LLC; Raider Motor

Corporation (Bahamas); Rival Consumer Sales Corporation; Rival de Mexico, S.A. de C.V.; Servicios Sunbeam-Coleman de Mexico, S.A. de C.V.; SI II, Inc.; Sunbeam Americas Holdings, LLC; Sunbeam Corporation (Canada) Limited; Sunbeam Holdings, S.A. de C.V. (Mexico); Sunbeam International (Asia) Limited (Hong Kong); Sunbeam Latin America, LLC; Sunbeam Mexicana, S.A. de C.V. (Mexico); Sunbeam-Oster de Acuna, S.A. de C.V. (Mexico); Sunbeam Products, Inc.; SunCan Holding Corp. (Canada); The Coleman Company, Inc.; The United States Playing Card Company; THL-FAIP Corp.; USPC Holding, Inc.

PRINCIPAL DIVISIONS

Branded Consumables; Consumer Solutions; Outdoor Solutions; Process Solutions.

PRINCIPAL COMPETITORS

Universal Security Instruments Inc.; Applica Incorporated; Igloo Corporation; Kellwood Company; NACCO Industries, Inc.; VF Corporation.

FURTHER READING

Allen, Mike, "Jarden Acquires K2," *San Diego Business Journal,* August 27, 2007, p. 16.

Brady, Diane, "Household Name?" *Business Week,* November 29, 2004, p. 106.

Cariaga, Vance, "Jarden Corp. Rye, New York, CEO Gives His Company a Needed Face Lift," *Investor's Business Daily,* September 6, 2002, p. A7.

DeWitte, Dave, "N.Y. Company Buys Pure Fishing," *Cedar Rapids (Iowa) Gazette,* April 11, 2007.

Elstein, Aaron, "Acquisitive Jarden Faces a Tougher Road Ahead," *Crain's New York Business,* April 23, 2007, p. 4.

Gallagher, Leigh, "Master of the Mundane," *Forbes,* October 27, 2003, p. 158.

Heikens, Norm, "Indianapolis-Based Alltrista to Move Headquarters to New York," *Indianapolis Star,* October 17, 2001.

Jefferson, Greg, "Alltrista Gets Legs," *Indiana Business Journal,* March 29–April 4, 1999.

Koenig, Bill, "Plastic, Metal Products Maker Alltrista Opens Indianapolis Headquarters," *Indianapolis Star and News,* September 15, 1998.

Lauzon, Michael, "Alltrista Corp. Acquiring Triangle," *Plastics News,* March 22, 1999, p. 1.

Lieber, Tammy, "First a Move, Now a Name Change for Alltrista," *Indianapolis Business Journal,* May 6, 2002, p. 4.

Linecker, Adella Cellini, "Jarden Corp. Rye, New York; Home Canning Supplier Plays Its Cards Right," *Investor's Business Daily,* March 1, 2004, p. A8.

"President & CEO of Alltrista," *Wall Street Corporate Reporter,* December 2, 1997.

Swiatek, Jeff, "Diverse Indianapolis Manufacturer Alltrista Puts Itself Up for Sale," *Indianapolis Star,* October 11, 2000.

White, Jennifer, "Jarden Shopping for More Ways to Keep Growing," *HFN: The Weekly Newspaper for the Home Furnishing Network,* August 8, 2005, p. 60.

———, "Jarden's Growth Spurt," *HFN: The Weekly Newspaper for the Home Furnishing Network,* September 25, 2006, p. 24.

———, "Sunbeam Products Transitions into Jarden Division," *HFN: The Weekly Newspaper for the Home Furnishing Network,* April 4, 2005, p. 44.

Jardine Matheson Holdings Limited

Jardine House
33–35 Reid Street
Hamilton, HM EX
Bermuda
Telephone: (441) 292-0515
Fax: (441) 292-4072
Web site: http://www.jardines.com

Public Company
Founded: 1832 as Jardine, Matheson & Company
Incorporated: 1984
Employees: 240,000
Sales: $27.14 billion (2006)
Stock Exchanges: London Bermuda Singapore
Ticker Symbols: JAR (London); JARD (Singapore)
NAIC: 551112 Offices of Other Holding Companies; 235110 Plumbing, Heating, and Air-Conditioning Contractors; 235950 Building Equipment and Other Machinery Installation Contractors; 236116 New Multi-Family Housing Construction (Except Operative Builders); 236210 Industrial Building Construction; 236220 Commercial and Institutional Building Construction; 237110 Water and Sewer Line and Related Structures Construction; 237210 Land Subdivision; 237310 Highway, Street, and Bridge Construction; 237990 Other Heavy and Civil Engineering Construction; 336111 Automobile Manufacturing; 336300 Motor Vehicle Parts Manufacturing; 421110 Automobile and Other Motor Vehicle Wholesalers; 421120 Motor Vehicle Supplies and New Parts Wholesalers; 441110 New Car Dealers; 441120 Used Car Deal-

ers; 442110 Furniture Stores; 445110 Supermarkets and Other Grocery (Except Convenience) Stores; 445120 Convenience Stores; 446110 Pharmacies and Drug Stores; 488119 Other Airport Operations; 488310 Port and Harbor Operations; 488510 Freight Transportation Arrangement; 524126 Direct Property and Casualty Insurance Carriers; 524130 Reinsurance Carriers; 524210 Insurance Agencies and Brokerages; 524292 Third Party Administration of Insurance and Pension Funds; 531110 Lessors of Residential Buildings and Dwellings; 531120 Lessors of Nonresidential Buildings (Except Miniwarehouses); 531130 Lessors of Miniwarehouses and Self-Storage Units; 541330 Engineering Services; 561510 Travel Agencies; 721110 Hotels (Except Casino Hotels) and Motels; 722110 Full-Service Restaurants

■ ■ ■

Jardine Matheson is one of the oldest names in East Asia, and Jardine Matheson Holdings Limited is the parent company for the Jardine Matheson Group, an international array of diverse companies with operations mainly in Asia, centered around Hong Kong and China. Of British origin, Jardine Matheson played a key, and rather dubious, role in the founding of Hong Kong, where the group was headquartered until 1984, when it relocated to Bermuda in anticipation of the July 1997 transfer of control of Hong Kong to China. Controlled through a complicated set of minority holdings by the

COMPANY PERSPECTIVES

The Group's strategy is to build its operations into market leaders across Asia, each with the support of Jardine Matheson's extensive knowledge of the Region and its long-standing relationships. Through a balance of cash producing activities and investment in new businesses, the Group aims to produce sustained growth in shareholder value.

Keswick family (descendants of cofounder William Jardine), the group is headed by Jardine Matheson Holdings, owner of an 80 percent stake in the publicly traded, Bermuda-incorporated Jardine Strategic Holdings Limited. The latter, in turn, owns 53 percent of Jardine Matheson Holdings. This cross-shareholding structure was adopted in 1986 to thwart hostile takeovers.

In addition to its stake in Jardine Strategic, Jardine Matheson Holdings has two principal wholly owned subsidiaries: Jardine Pacific Holdings Ltd., which controls a wide-ranging portfolio of Asian businesses, mainly in transport services, engineering and construction, restaurants, and information technology services; and Jardine Motors Group Holdings Ltd., which concentrates on the distribution, sales, and service of motor vehicles in Hong Kong, China, Macau, and the United Kingdom. Jardine Matheson Holdings also holds a 31 percent stake in the London-based, publicly traded Jardine Lloyd Thompson Group plc, an insurance broker, adviser on risk management, and provider of employee benefits services.

Jardine Strategic holds stakes in a number of publicly traded companies, including majority stakes in Dairy Farm International Holdings Ltd. and Mandarin Oriental International Ltd. The former is a pan-Asian retail group whose more than 3,500 outlets include supermarkets, hypermarkets, convenience stores, health and beauty stores, home furnishings stores, and restaurants. The latter develops and manages the more than 20 Mandarin Oriental luxury hotels and resorts worldwide. Jardine Strategic also owns a 47 percent interest in Hongkong Land Holdings Ltd., which owns and manages roughly five million square feet of prime office and retail property in central Hong Kong, as well as additional commercial and residential developments elsewhere in Asia. Another Jardine Strategic holding is a 64 percent stake in Jardine Cycle & Carriage Ltd., which in turn owns just over 50 percent of the

Indonesian conglomerate PT Astra International. Most prominently, Astra is the largest independent motor group in Southeast Asia, involved in manufacturing, assembling, and distributing motor vehicles and components in Indonesia, Malaysia, and Singapore. Other Astra activities center on the areas of agribusiness, heavy equipment, financial services, information technology, and infrastructure.

BIRTH OF TRADING COMPANY IN CANTON, CHINA: 1832

William Jardine was born in 1784 in Dumfriesshire, Scotland. After studying medicine, Jardine went to work for the British East India Company as a ship's surgeon, but left the East India Company in 1832 to establish a trading company in Canton, China, with James Matheson, who was born in 1796, the son of a Scottish baronet, and served for several years as Danish consul in China.

Trading with the Chinese was made extremely difficult by a xenophobic Manchu government, which believed that as the center of the universe, China already possessed everything in abundance and had no need for the products of "foreign barbarians." Among other things, Jardine, Matheson & Company (Jardine Matheson) was restricted to a small plot of land on the banks of the Pearl River, near Canton, and was prevented from "keeping women" or dealing with Chinese merchants who were not officially sanctioned *cohongs*. On one occasion, Jardine was struck a blow to the head as he attempted to petition local authorities. Entirely unaffected by the attack, he earned the nickname "Iron-Headed Old Rat" among the Chinese.

Unable to make money selling manufactured goods to the Chinese, Jardine Matheson began smuggling opium into China aboard ships chartered from Calcutta in British India. Opium clippers sailed under cover of darkness to forbidden ports, while company agents bribed harbormasters and watchmen to prevent being discovered by the authorities. The Chinese government declared the opium trade to be illegal, but was virtually powerless to stop it. Finally, Chinese authorities seized and destroyed 20,000 chests of opium worth $9 million.

OPIUM WAR LEADS TO FOUNDING OF HONG KONG IN 1842

Jardine persuaded the British Foreign Secretary Lord Palmerston to send warships to China to enforce a judgment for reparations and to preserve free trade. The

KEY DATES

1832: William Jardine and James Matheson establish a trading company in Canton, China, called Jardine, Matheson & Company (Jardine Matheson).

1844: Following the First Opium War and the ceding of Hong Kong to Britain, Jardine Matheson moves its main office to Hong Kong.

1889: Hongkong Land, a property development company, is formed in association with Jardine Matheson.

1906: Company is incorporated in Hong Kong as Jardine, Matheson & Company Limited.

1923: Jardine Engineering Company is formed.

1954: Jardine Matheson is forced out of China.

1961: Company goes public with a listing on the Hong Kong Stock Exchange.

1970: Jardine Matheson and Robert Fleming & Co. form a Hong Kong-based investment banking joint venture called Jardine Fleming & Co. Ltd.

1979: Company returns to China with the opening of a representative office in Beijing.

1980: Jardine Matheson cements its relationship with Hongkong Land when the two firms increase their interests in each other.

1984: Jardine Matheson Holdings Limited is established as a Bermuda-incorporated holding company.

1986: Hongkong Land is broken apart, with Dairy Farm and Mandarin Oriental becoming independent, publicly traded firms; Jardine Strategic Holdings Limited is formed to hold stakes in Hongkong Land, Dairy Farm, and Mandarin Oriental.

1988: Jardine Pacific Ltd. is formed as the trading and services arm of the group.

1992: The group has a 25 percent stake in Cycle & Carriage Ltd., a publicly listed Singaporean firm with interests in motor vehicles and property.

1999: Company swaps its half-interest in Jardine Fleming for an 18 percent stake in Robert Fleming.

2000: Jardine Matheson nets $1.2 billion from Chase Manhattan Corporation's acquisition of Robert Fleming; Cycle & Carriage acquires a 31 percent stake in Indonesian conglomerate PT Astra International.

2002: The group increases its interest in Cycle & Carriage to more than 50 percent.

2005: Jardine Cycle & Carriage pushes its stake in Astra over the 50 percent mark.

---

hostilities that ensued became known as the First Opium War. The Chinese lost and were forced to sign a treaty on August 29, 1842, that awarded the British $6 million in reparations, opened the ports of Canton, Amoy, Foochow, Ningpo, and Shanghai, and ceded the island of Hong Kong to Britain.

Jardine Matheson purchased the first plot of land to be sold in Hong Kong and moved its main office there in 1844. The colony's first governor, Sir Henry Pottinger, endorsed the opium trade (in defiance of Queen Victoria) and later won the support of Parliament, which viewed the opium trade as a method to reduce the British trade deficit with China. When the company's opium boats sailed into Hong Kong they were greeted by a cannon salute. Jardine Matheson profited greatly from its privileged position in Hong

Kong, and, through the strength of its opium trade, began to develop commercial interests throughout the region. Jardine Matheson became known among the local Chinese as a *hong* (the word implies "big company" but has no relation to the name Hong Kong), and its chairman became known as a *taipan,* literally a "big boss."

During this period Thomas Keswick (pronounced KEZ-ick), also from Dumfriesshire, married Jardine's niece and was subsequently taken into the Jardine family business. Their son William Keswick established a Jardine Matheson office in Yokohama, Japan, in 1859 and later became a leading figure in company management. The Keswick family grew in influence within the company, largely displacing the Matheson interests.

EXPANDING BEYOND TRADING IN LATTER HALF OF 19TH CENTURY

Jardine Matheson established trading offices in major Chinese ports and helped to set up enterprises as diverse as brewing and milling cotton, in addition to trading tea and silk. The company introduced steamboats to China and, in 1876, constructed the first railroad in China, linking Shanghai with Jardine Matheson docks downriver at Woosung. In 1889 William Keswick's brother James Johnstone Keswick established Hongkong Land, a development company closely associated with Jardine Matheson ever since.

Continued hostilities between China and Britain resulted in a Second Opium War in 1860 and a war to protect colonial interests in 1898. As victors in both these wars, the British gained trade concessions and colonies throughout China and won virtually unrestricted commercial rights to conduct business in China. The opium trade, which China had been forced to recognize as legal, had become an extremely sensitive subject. Thousands of addicts (known as "hippies" because they would lie on their hips while smoking opium) had created a serious social problem. Elements in Parliament called for an end to commercial activities that perpetuated the pain and suffering of these addicts. The issue was seized by nationalists who argued for an end to the domination of colonial powers in China, and it eventually led to uprisings such as the Boxer Rebellion (1900) and the Republican Revolution (1911). For its own protection and business interests, Jardine Matheson was forced to curtail trading opium.

By 1906, the year it incorporated in Hong Kong as a limited company (Jardine, Matheson & Company Limited), Jardine Matheson had expanded into a wider range of operations, but experienced strong competition from another British trading house called Butterfield & Swire, which was also based in Shanghai and Hong Kong. The competition between Jardine Matheson and the Swires began in earnest in 1884 when Butterfield & Swire set up a rival sugar refinery in Hong Kong in an attempt to break Jardine Matheson's monopoly. The competition spread into shipping and trading, but remained on the whole civilized and constructive. In 1923 the Jardine Engineering Company was formed as a firm specializing in infrastructure-related machinery, equipment, and services in Hong Kong and China.

Jardine Matheson continued to operate in China relatively unobstructed by the Nationalist government, which had grown increasingly corrupt. The company continued to expand its interests in China and, with other foreign interests such as Swire and Mitsui, became one of the largest companies in the country.

SUFFERING SEVERELY DURING WORLD WAR II

In the summer of 1937 Japanese forces attacked China in an attempt to expand Japanese commercial and strategic interests on the Asian mainland. Jardine Matheson officials stationed in areas overrun by the Japanese were branded as agents of European imperialism and imprisoned. The company's compradores (Chinese intermediaries) were scattered, and its factories were looted; approximately 168,000 spindles were stripped from Jardine Matheson textile mills. Japanese military adventurism in China led to the occupation of several more Chinese ports, including Shanghai and Canton, where Jardine Matheson conducted a substantial portion of its business. Tony Keswick, a grandson of William Keswick, managed the company's affairs in Shanghai until 1941, when he moved to Hong Kong after having been shot by a Japanese. He was replaced by his brother John, who himself was forced to flee when the city came under siege. Jardine Matheson had been effectively prevented from doing any further business in China, but continued to operate in Hong Kong, which, as British territory, the Japanese were unwilling to invade.

As a member of the anti-Comintern pact, Japan was unofficially allied with Nazi Germany and Fascist Italy in the war in Europe. The increasingly belligerent military leaders in Japan pledged to evict European imperialists from Asia and to establish a trans-Asian "Co-Prosperity Sphere." On December 1, 1941, Japanese forces invaded British colonies in Asia, including Hong Kong. Jardine Matheson officials in the colony were imprisoned with other Europeans at Stanley Prison. John Keswick, however, managed to escape to Ceylon (Sri Lanka), where he served with Admiral Earl Mountbatten's staff.

FATE OF CHINA FOLLOWING POSTWAR COMMUNIST TAKEOVER

When the war ended in 1945, the British resumed control of Hong Kong and John Keswick returned to oversee the rebuilding of Jardine Matheson facilities damaged during the war. The company owned a small airline, textile mills, real estate, a brewery, wharves, godowns (warehouses), and cold-storage facilities. In 1949, however, after four years of civil war, Communist forces seized control of the Chinese mainland.

In Shanghai, John Keswick attempted to work with the Communists (who had invited capitalists to help rebuild the economy), in the belief that they would be more orderly and less corrupt than the Nationalists.

Keswick argued for British recognition of the new government, and even attempted to run his company's ships past Nationalist blockades. By 1950, however, new government policies were enacted that increased taxes, restricted currency exchanges, and banned layoffs. Ewo Breweries, a Jardine Matheson subsidiary in Shanghai, was ordered to reduce its prices by 17 percent, despite heavy increases in the cost of raw materials. The government forced Ewo to remain open, despite a $4 million annual loss.

Companies based in Hong Kong were bound to observe a British trade embargo placed against China as a result of the Korean War. Conditions had deteriorated to a point where it was impossible to continue operating in China (on one occasion Keswick was arrested as he attempted to leave Shanghai). Compelled to close its operations in China, Jardine Matheson entered into negotiations with the government and, in 1954, settled the nationalization of its assets in China by writing off $20 million in losses. The company continued to trade with the seven official Chinese state trading corporations and attended the biannual Canton Trade Fair, where Chinese companies negotiated approximately half their nation's foreign trade.

Many of Jardine Matheson's management traditions changed after the war. Although managers continued to be recruited primarily from Oxford and Cambridge, the company started placing younger men in higher positions. John Keswick, whose nephews Henry and Simon were too young to run the company, returned to Britain in 1956 to direct the family estate and appointed Michael Young-Herries to manage the operations in Hong Kong.

PUBLIC COMPANY IN 1961

In the late 1950s John and Tony Keswick enlisted support from three banks in London and purchased the last Jardine family interests in the company. Jardine Matheson became a publicly traded company in 1961 with a listing on the Hong Kong Stock Exchange and, with additional capital provided by shareholders, acquired controlling interests in the Indo-China Steam Navigation Company and Henry Waugh Ltd. and established the Australian-based Dominion Far East Line shipping company. Hongkong Land, meanwhile, opened the Mandarin Hotel in Hong Kong in 1963.

In 1966 China embarked on its second campaign to form a nation of communes. During this campaign, called the "Cultural Revolution," China ceased virtually all trade with Hong Kong. Although Jardine Matheson lost a significant amount of trade with the Chinese, its association of textile companies in Hong Kong

continued to generate large profits from exports to the United States. The company's greatest achievement during this period was the sale of six Vickers Viscount aircraft to the Chinese. By 1969 the Cultural Revolution had lost its momentum and Jardine Matheson was once again doing business with the Chinese.

In 1970 Jardine Matheson and the British investment banking firm Robert Fleming & Co. formed a Hong Kong-based joint venture called Jardine Fleming & Co. Ltd., Asia's first homegrown investment bank. Three years later Hongkong Land acquired the Oriental Hotel in Bangkok, a move that eventually led to the formation of the Mandarin Oriental Hotel Group.

In the meantime, the Keswick family in 1972 attempted to install Henry as the new *taipan,* but met considerable resistance from supporters of Managing Director David Newbigging, the son of a former director of Jardine Matheson. The Keswicks prevailed after winning the support of institutional shareholders in London, and Henry Keswick was named senior managing director, while his father John resumed the chairmanship to ensure that the Keswicks did not lose control of the company.

Three years later Henry stepped down and returned to London and was replaced by Newbigging. Henry, remarked *Fortune,* lacked the "panache" of the elder Keswicks and made "more than a few enemies" through his bold financial maneuvers. Henry did, however, complete a buyout in 1973 of Reunion Properties, a large real estate firm based in London. Keswick financed the takeover by creating an additional 7 percent of Jardine Matheson equity, but through the acquisition nearly doubled the company's assets. Henry Keswick also oversaw the acquisition of Theo H. Davies & Company that same year. Davies, a large trading company active in the Philippines and Hawaii, controlled 36,000 acres of sugar plantations. A few months after it was purchased by Jardine Matheson, world sugar prices rose dramatically.

DOWNTURN IN PROFITS

At the time Newbigging assumed the senior directorship of Jardine Matheson, a disturbing trend began to arise in Hong Kong. Throughout its history, Jardine Matheson had operated as a trading agent, or "middleman," arranging sales between producers in one location and consumers in another. Manufacturers in Hong Kong, however, discovered ways to sell their products directly to customers, bypassing agents such as Jardine Matheson. Even Hawker-Siddeley, a British company, managed to arrange the sale of six Trident jetliners to the Chinese without the negotiating expertise of Jardine Matheson.

Between 1975 and 1979, Jardine Matheson's profits grew at an annual rate of only 10 percent (a poor record for Hong Kong). Newbigging responded by disposing of underperforming Jardine Matheson subsidiaries outside Hong Kong. He redoubled efforts to increase trade with China (which invited the company in 1979, when it opened a representative office in Beijing) and resumed investments in Hong Kong-based enterprises. Jardine Matheson, however, had little expertise in these enterprises and lost money in almost every venture.

CEMENTING THE RELATIONSHIP WITH HONGKONG LAND IN 1980

During the 1970s British companies in Hong Kong such as Jardine Matheson, Swire, Hutchison, and Wheelock Marden were consistently outperformed by local, ethnically Chinese *hongs*. Most of these *hongs* became public companies in the early 1970s and invested heavily in Hong Kong industries, which experienced strong growth during a decade-long bull market. These companies became serious competitors of the British establishment by the end of the decade.

Cheung Kong (Holdings) Limited, a local *hong* run by an influential figure named Li Ka-shing, achieved a dominant position in the Hong Kong property market by 1980, threatening the business of Hongkong Land, the development company that was still closely associated with Jardine Matheson. In addition, when the shipping magnate Sir Yue-Kong Pao decided to diversify from ships into property a year earlier, his first move was to outbid Jardine Matheson for the Hongkong & Kowloon Wharf & Godown Company, over which the two groups had previously shared control.

When it was discovered that a secret partner had begun acquiring shares of Jardine Matheson stock in late 1980, many observers suspected that either Li or Pao (or worse, both) were attempting to purchase a large enough share in Jardine Matheson to win control over Hongkong Land. Newbigging announced in early November that Jardine Matheson and Hongkong Land had agreed to increase their interests in each other, to make it impossible for any party to gain control of either company. The cross-ownership scheme, however, placed both companies deeply into debt.

The defensive actions required during 1980 forced Jardine Matheson to sell its interest in Reunion Properties to raise cash. Newbigging was criticized for being too conservative and placing too much emphasis on local and regional operations. Although members of the Keswick family attempted to have Newbigging removed, perhaps no one worked as tirelessly as John Keswick. Newbigging finally stepped down as senior managing

director in June 1983, but retained the titular position of chairman. He was replaced as *taipan* by 40-year-old Simon Keswick, brother of Henry Keswick.

The election of Simon Keswick, who had not yet proved his business acumen, initially worried many investors of Jardine Matheson. Upon taking control, however, Simon moved decisively to reduce the company's debts and to place Hongkong Land on firmer financial ground. To raise cash, he authorized the sale of Jardine Matheson's majority stake in Rennies Consolidated Holdings, a South African hotel, travel, and industries group based in Johannesburg, for $180.1 million. Keswick also established a new decentralized system of managerial control, which split operations into a Hong Kong and China division and an international division.

UNDER NEW BERMUDA-BASED HOLDING COMPANY IN 1984

In early 1984 Newbigging was replaced as chairman by Simon Keswick. With the company thoroughly under Keswick family control, Simon announced on March 28 that Jardine Matheson & Company would establish a new holding company called Jardine Matheson Holdings Limited, incorporated in Bermuda. The announcement came at an extremely sensitive point in negotiations between the British and Chinese governments on the future of Hong Kong. Many observers regarded Keswick's plan as an attempt to remove Jardine Matheson from the uncertain business environment in Hong Kong, and as a solid display of no confidence in the Sino-British arrangement under which China would resume sovereignty over Hong Kong on July 1, 1997.

In defense of his actions, Simon Keswick admitted that Bermuda provided Jardine Matheson with a more stable operating environment than Hong Kong, but noted that the company was not abandoning its interests in Hong Kong, merely reducing its exposure there from 72 percent of total assets to a planned 50 percent. In addition, he pointed out that Bermuda (a British colony since 1612) permitted companies to purchase their own shares, a practice not allowed in Hong Kong.

In 1984 Jardine Matheson disposed of its sugar interests in Hawaii. The company also expanded into motor vehicles by investing in Mercedes-Benz distributorships, which led to the eventual formation of Jardine International Motors Management Ltd. in 1990. In 1985 Keswick announced that, after 153 years, Jardine Matheson would leave the shipping business and that the company's fleet of 21 ships would be sold. By the end of the year many of the assets Jardine Matheson acquired during the 1970s had been sold, reducing holdings by 28 percent.

FURTHER SERIES OF RESTRUCTURING MOVES: 1986

In 1986 Keswick dismantled much of Hongkong Land, selling the company's residential real estate portfolio and demerging two of its key units into the independent Dairy Farm International Holdings Ltd. and Mandarin Oriental International Ltd., both of which were listed on the Hong Kong Stock Exchange. Dairy Farm was a pan-Asian producer, wholesaler, and retailer of dairy and other foods products that had been founded in 1886 and acquired by Hongkong Land in 1972. Keswick's plan to reduce Hongkong Land to real estate alone caused its managing director, David J. Davies, to resign in protest.

Renewed fears of a takeover attempt led to additional 1986 restructuring moves. Jardine Strategic Holdings Limited, placed on the Hong Kong Stock Exchange, was formed to hold stakes in Jardine Matheson Ltd. (the Hong Kong-based arm responsible for managing the activities of the group), Dairy Farm, Hongkong Land, and Mandarin Oriental. In 1988 Jardine Pacific Ltd. was formed as the trading and services arm of the group.

Simon Keswick announced in June 1987 that he would relinquish the position of senior managing director to a 37-year-old American named Brian M. Powers. The nomination of Powers to become *taipan* caused great concern among members of the company's more traditional Scottish establishment. Keswick, who had reversed the company's decline with drastic and unpopular measures, and who had yet to demonstrate their success, defended his choice of Powers. He explained that Jardine Matheson was an international company with Hong Kong interests (rather than the other way around) and that, as such, Powers was best qualified to manage its affairs.

MODERATELY SUCCESSFUL INTERNATIONAL EXPANSION

In any case, Powers's reign proved to be short-lived and into the 21st century Simon and Henry Keswick essentially managed the group from London. Continuing to be wary of the fast-approaching return of Hong Kong to Chinese control Jardine Matheson during the late 1980s and early 1990s was determined to become more geographically diversified, subsequently meeting with middling success in its ventures in North America, Europe, and areas of Asia outside Hong Kong and China. In 1987 Jardine Matheson announced that it planned to buy a 20 percent stake in Bear Stearns but pulled out following that year's October stock market crash; following resulting shareholder lawsuits, it settled

with shareholders of Bear Stearns four years later by agreeing to pay $60 million in compensation.

In 1993 Jardine Matheson spent £300 million to acquire a 26 percent stake in Trafalgar House, a construction, engineering, and shipping conglomerate based in the United Kingdom. Trafalgar, a group more troubled than it was believed to be, became an albatross around Jardine's neck. After supporting its investment and attempting to turn it around for several years, Jardine Matheson decided to cut its losses in 1996, that year selling its stake to Kvaerner A/S, a Norwegian-based shipbuilder, at a loss of about £100 million.

By 1992 Jardine Matheson had also acquired a 25 percent stake in Cycle & Carriage Ltd., a Singapore-based publicly traded company with motor vehicle operations in Singapore, Malaysia, Australia, and New Zealand and property investment and development activities in Singapore and Malaysia. India was another area of Jardine Matheson growth, most significantly with the 1996 purchase of a 20 percent stake in Tata Industries of India for INR 1.25 billion ($25 million). The privately held Tata boasted of numerous alliances with foreign companies, including AT&T, IBM, Singapore Airlines, and Mercedes-Benz, the last of which had connections with Jardine Matheson, but Jardine Matheson was the first outsider granted a stake in the group. Tata had several areas of interest in common with Jardine, including motor vehicle distribution, retailing, and property development. Jardine Matheson's Tata stake built on the group's previous investments in India, which included a number of joint ventures and a 5 percent stake in Housing Development Finance Corporation of Mumbai, a leading Indian financial institution. Overall, India had the potential to provide Jardine Matheson with the second beachhead it had sought, unsuccessfully, for so long.

ROCKY RELATIONSHIP WITH CHINA IN ADVANCE OF 1997 HONG KONG HANDOVER

Meanwhile, the group's rocky relationship with China continued in the early 1990s. Still concerned about possible takeover attempts, Jardine Matheson sought an exemption from Hong Kong's takeover code, which conflicted with takeover legislation enacted in Bermuda, but was refused. In response, the group in 1991 moved its primary stock exchange listing from Hong Kong to London, thereby enabling Jardine Matheson to remain under the British legal system. Chinese authorities were angered, feeling that the move reflected a lack of confidence in the post-transfer-of-control legal system. The following year, perhaps in retaliation, China blocked a consortium led by Jardine Matheson that had gained development rights to Hong Kong's ninth container terminal. Then, in late 1994, Jardine Matheson moved its Asian stock listing from Hong Kong to Singapore, provoking further consternation among the Chinese.

Relations seemed to improve somewhat during 1995. Jardine Matheson's new managing director in Hong Kong, Alasdair Morrison, another Scot, issued a general apology to China in January 1995 over the group's actions in previous years. Morrison emphasized that Jardine Matheson intended to continue to do business in Hong Kong and China and to invest additional money there. By 1996 Jardine Matheson had about 70 joint ventures in China, a number that had been growing rapidly. That year, Jardine formed a consortium with Li Ka-shing's Hutchison Whampoa Limited and Cosco Pacific Limited, which was owned by China's largest shipping group, to develop and run a river trade terminal.

In early 1997, Jardine Matheson's insurance broking subsidiary, JIB Group plc, of which Jardine Matheson held 60 percent, merged with the insurance broking group Lloyd Thompson Group plc to form Jardine Lloyd Thompson Group plc. Jardine Matheson held an initial 34 percent interest in the new firm. In June 1997 takeover speculation arose once again when two companies owned by Li Ka-shing bought 3.03 percent of Jardine Matheson Holdings and 3.06 percent of Hongkong Land.

When control over Hong Kong passed to China on July 1, 1997, Jardine Matheson remained closely tied to the former British colony, where more than half of its profits were generated, but had developed increasing interests elsewhere in China and outside the region, most notably in India. At the time, Dairy Farm was an increasingly international retailer, operating supermarkets, convenience stores, drugstores, and restaurants across Asia and in Australia, New Zealand, Spain, and the United Kingdom. Mandarin Oriental was in the midst of its own international expansion, having opened a hotel in Hawaii and purchased the five-star Hyde Park hotel in London, both in 1996. Hongkong Land, meantime, continued to dominate the property market in Hong Kong, controlling 70 percent of the real estate in the city center.

POST-HANDOFF ECONOMIC CRISIS

In the immediate post-handoff period, Jardine Matheson, still led by Morrison, saw its profits tumble from the impact of the Asian economic crisis, including an 84 percent net profit plunge in 1998. The company and its affiliates reacted by jettisoning a number of underperforming businesses. Among these were Dairy Farm's retailing activities in Spain and the United Kingdom. In 1998, during this same period, Dairy Farm acquired a 32 percent stake in Hero, Indonesia's largest supermarket chain. The following year Dairy Farm acquired Giant, operator of seven hypermarkets/supermarkets in Malaysia. Despite the downturn, Hongkong Land initiated a number of property developments in Hong Kong, Singapore, the Philippines, and Vietnam. Mandarin Oriental, meantime, began a concerted push into the U.S. market in 1998 with the beginning of the development of a new hotel in Miami, Florida, which opened in 2000.

By the late 1990s the globalization of the investment banking business had undermined the position of the Asia-focused Jardine Fleming, whose operations were further hampered by the economic crisis. Thus, in early 1999 Jardine Matheson elected to turn over its half-interest in the venture to its partner, Robert Fleming, in a transaction valued at about $300 million that left Jardine Matheson with an 18 percent stake in the Scottish investment bank. When Chase Manhattan subsequently acquired Robert Fleming for $7.7 billion in August 2000, Jardine Matheson's share of the proceeds amounted to $1.2 billion.

In both 2000 and 2001 the Keswicks fended off dissident shareholders' attempts to dismantle the cross-shareholding structure between Jardine Matheson Holdings and Jardine Strategic that had been erected in 1986 to thwart takeovers. In an attempt to pacify minority shareholders, the group used a substantial portion of its proceeds from the sale of Robert Fleming on stock buybacks, so that by the end of 2002 Jardine Matheson Holdings held a 79 percent stake in Jardine Strategic, and Jardine Strategic held a 51 percent stake in Jardine Matheson Holdings.

CHANGING PORTFOLIO OF BUSINESSES IN EARLY 21ST CENTURY

The Keswick family thus retained control of Jardine Matheson into the 21st century, as the group was one of two British-controlled *hongs* that remained, the other being Swire Pacific. Taking over as managing director in February 2000 was Percy Weatherall, who had most recently headed Hongkong Land. Numerous changes to the group's array of businesses subsequently occurred in the early years of the new century.

Dairy Farm, whose Hong Kong supermarket chain, Wellcome, had been battered by a price war with Hutchison Whampoa's Park 'N Shop chain, made a further retreat from the international scene by exiting from the Australian market in 2001 and from New Zealand a year later. In 2000 Cycle & Carriage acquired a 31 percent stake in PT Astra International, a large Indonesian conglomerate best known for its automotive operations. Two years later, Jardine Matheson spent roughly $240 million to increase its stake in Cycle & Carriage to more than 50 percent, making it a group subsidiary. By 2003 this unit, renamed Jardine Cycle & Carriage Ltd., was contributing 22 percent of the group's overall profits. Then in 2005 Jardine Cycle increased its interest in Astra to more than 50 percent, enabling Jardine Matheson to consolidate Astra as a subsidiary as well.

During this same period, Mandarin Oriental continued its international expansion, most prominently via the 2000 acquisition of the Rafael Group, which included six luxury hotels located in New York City; Aventura, Florida; Bermuda; Geneva, Switzerland; Fuschl, Austria; and Munich, Germany. By the end of 2004, a year in which it opened hotels in New York City and Washington, D.C., Mandarin Oriental was managing a network of 21 luxury hotels with a total of nearly 8,000 rooms and also had five additional hotels in development.

2004 FORWARD: BOOMING PROFITS, GROWTH ORIENTATION

Buoyed by a strong recovery in its core Asian markets and a sharp increase in the value of investment properties held by Hongkong Land, Jardine Matheson recorded soaring profits of $947 million in 2004 on revenues of $8.97 billion. These strong results continued through 2006, when net profits hit $1.35 billion on revenues of $16.28 billion. The cash-rich group continued to buy back its own shares and those of its affiliates during this period and also in 2005 spent $186 million to take a 20 percent stake in Rothschild Continuation Holdings, a holding company of the venerable Rothschild banking group that included among its interests the investment bank's London-based arm, N M Rothschild & Sons Limited. This purchase rekindled a relationship between the two British family firms dating back to 1838, when Rothschild appointed Jardine, Matheson & Co. to act as its agent in China.

In the spring of 2006 Weatherall retired as managing director and was succeeded by Anthony Nightingale, holder of numerous positions at the group, including the managing directorships of Dairy Farm, Hongkong Land, Jardine Strategic, and Mandarin Oriental. By 2007, its 175th anniversary year, Jardine Matheson was clearly in growth mode. For instance, Hongkong Land

was in the midst of an aggressive development of commercial properties in Singapore, while Mandarin Oriental had set a goal of increasing its total room count to more than 10,000. Already operating more than 20 luxury hotels around the world, Mandarin Oriental had another 19 properties under development and slated to open between 2008 and 2010. Included among these were to be the first Mandarin Orientals in mainland China, in Sanya, Beijing, and Guangzhou. The Beijing hotel was expected to open in time for that city's hosting of the 2008 Summer Olympics.

Although often criticized for the complex web of cross-shareholdings that kept the group in Keswick family control despite their direct ownership stake of little more than 10 percent, Jardine Matheson had seen its share price increase at a compound annual rate of 21.3 percent between 1997 and 2007. As the group continued to deploy excess cash flow into stock buybacks and was poised to increase its stake in Jardine Strategic to 85 percent, speculation arose late in 2007 that the Keswick family might move to unwind the cross-holdings and buy back enough shares to acquire more than 50 percent of Jardine Matheson's stock, cementing the family's control in a more direct manner. Whether or not such an eventuality came to pass, Jardine Matheson appeared to be in a strong position thanks to its well-timed acquisition of Astra, its newest moves into the Chinese market in a variety of sectors, its strong investments in numerous rapidly growing Asian markets, and the international expansion of the Mandarin Oriental group.

Updated, David E. Salamie

PRINCIPAL SUBSIDIARIES

Dairy Farm International Holdings Ltd. (62%); Hongkong Land Holdings Ltd. (37%); Jardine Cycle & Carriage Ltd. (Singapore; 51%); Jardine Lloyd Thompson Group plc (U.K.; 31%); Jardine Matheson Ltd.; Jardine Motors Group Holdings Ltd.; Jardine Pacific Holdings Ltd.; Jardine Strategic Holdings Limited (80%); Mandarin Oriental International Ltd. (59%); Matheson & Co., Ltd. (U.K.); PT Astra International Tbk (Indonesia; 25%); Rothschilds Continuation Holdings AG (Switzerland; 17%); Jardine Matheson International Services Ltd.; Jardine Matheson Ltd. (Hong Kong); Jardine Matheson Ltd. (Indonesia); Jardine Matheson (China) Ltd.; Jardine Matheson (Malaysia) Sdn. Bhd.; Jardine Matheson Europe B.V. (Netherlands); Jardine Matheson Ltd. (Philippines); Jardine Matheson (Singapore) Ltd.; Jardine, Matheson & Co., Ltd. (Taiwan); Jardine Matheson (Thailand) Ltd.; Jardine Matheson Ltd. (Vietnam).

PRINCIPAL COMPETITORS

Swire Pacific Limited; Hutchison Whampoa Limited; China Resources Enterprise, Limited; New World Development Company Limited; The Wharf (Holdings) Limited.

FURTHER READING

Appleyard, Bryan, "How the 'Princely Hong' Fought Off the Chinese," *Times* (London), November 4, 1980, p. 19.

Blake, Robert, *Jardine Matheson: Traders of the Far East,* London: Weidenfeld and Nicolson, 1999, 280 p.

Cheong, W. E., *Mandarins and Merchants: Jardine, Matheson, & Co., a China Agency of the Early Nineteenth Century,* London: Curzon Press, 1979, 298 p.

Chua, Jean, "A Restructuring Could Liven Things at Jardine," *Business Times* (Singapore), June 19, 2004.

Clifford, Mark L., "The Taipan's Last Chance: Can Alasdair Morrison Fix Jardine Matheson, One of British Hong Kong's Remaining Crown Jewels?" *Business Week* (international ed.), May 10, 1999, p. 122E4.

Connell, Carol Matheson, *A Business in Risk: Jardine Matheson and the Hong Kong Trading Industry,* Westport, Conn.: Praeger, 2004, 188 p.

Crisswell, Colin N., *The Taipans: Hong Kong's Merchant Princes,* Hong Kong: Oxford University Press, 1981, 249 p.

Davies, Simon, and John Ridding, "Taipans Who Missed the Boat," *Financial Times,* March 2/March 3, 1996, p. 7.

Edelstein, Michael, *Overseas Investment in the Age of High Imperialism: The United Kingdom, 1850–1914,* New York: Columbia University Press, 1982, 367 p.

Gargan, Edward A., "The Humbling of a Heavyweight," *New York Times,* November 30, 1995, pp. D1, D6.

Guyot, Erik, "Jardine Companies' Shares Likely to See Lower Volume of Trading in Singapore," *Wall Street Journal,* September 19, 1994, p. A9D.

———, "Tycoon Buys into Two Firms Within Jardine," *Asian Wall Street Journal,* August 6, 1997, p. 1.

Hill, R., "Venerable Trading House with Youth at the Helm," *International Management,* August 1975, p. 30.

Holberton, Simon, "The End of a Chapter at Jardine Matheson," *Financial Times,* December 21, 1994, p. 23.

Jardine, Matheson & Company, an Historical Sketch: An Outline of a China House for a Hundred Years, 1832–1932, London: Jardine, Matheson & Co., 1934.

"Jardine Matheson Group: 175 Years of the Right People," *Thistle: The Magazine of Jardine Matheson,* vol. 3, 2007, pp. 12–19.

"Jardine's Battle with Hong Kong's New Businessmen," *New York Times,* November 25, 1980, p. D4.

"Jardine's Bolt Hole," *Economist,* April 6, 1996, p. 68.

Kay, William, "The China House," *Independent* (London), June 20, 2001.

Kennedy, Carol, "Can Two Hongs Get It Right?" *Director,* February 1996, pp. 34–40.

Keswick, Maggie, ed., *The Thistle and the Jade: A Celebration of 150 Years of Jardine, Matheson & Co.,* London: Octopus, 1982, 272 p.

Kristof, Nicholas D., "An Asian Trading Empire Picks an American 'Tai-Pan,'" *New York Times,* June 21, 1987, p. F8.

———, "A Hong Kong Dynasty Weathers the Storm," *New York Times,* December 1, 1986, p. D1.

Le Pichon, Alain, ed., *China Trade and Empire: Jardine, Matheson & Co. and the Origins of British Rule in Hong Kong, 1827–1843,* Oxford: Published for the British Academy by Oxford University Press, 2006, 626 p.

Lelyveld, Joseph, "Jardine's—Where the Hong Kong Action Is," *New York Times,* January 13, 1974, p. 145.

Mackay, Angela, "Jardine Looks to Indonesia to Drive Growth," *Financial Times,* February 26, 2004, p. 31.

Mitchell, Mark, "Living in the Past," *Far Eastern Economic Review,* August 24, 2000, pp. 46–47, 50–51.

Morris, Kathleen, "There's No Place Like Home," *Financial World,* August 2, 1994, pp. 36–38.

Mortished, Carl, "Jardine's Dynasty Under Threat After Retreat from Hong Kong," *Times* (London), May 11, 2000, p. 31.

Mungan, Christina, "Jardine Matheson Responds to Recession: Company to Merge Its Half of Jardine Fleming into U.K.'s Robert Fleming," *Asian Wall Street Journal,* December 4, 1998, p. 1.

"The Noble Houses Look Forward," *Economist,* October 1, 1994, p. 77.

Ridding, John, "Li Ka-shing Plants a Seed," *Financial Times,* August 6, 1997, p. 19.

Ringshaw, Grant, "The Noble House Under Siege," *Sunday Telegraph* (London), April 22, 2001, p. 7.

Saigol, Lina, and Peter Thal Larsen, "Rothschild's New Partnership with Jardine Matheson Is a Family Affair," *Financial Times,* June 23, 2005, p. 23.

Sender, Henny, "Fixed Assets: British Hongs Still Tied to the Colony," *Far Eastern Economic Review,* July 8, 1993, p. 22.

Shameen, Assif, "Can Jardine Matheson Remake Itself into a Growth Story?" *Edge* (Singapore), October 8, 2007.

Silverman, Gary, "Bruising Battle on the Beach," *Financial Times,* June 3, 2000, p. 9.

———, "Haunted House: Jardines Looks to Regain Its Old Agility," *Far Eastern Economic Review,* May 15, 1997, p. 84.

Smith, Craig S., "Jardine Lies Low in Colony's Handover: Firm That Helped Launch Hong Kong Can't Quite Escape It," *Wall Street Journal,* June 4, 1997, p. A15.

"A Tale of Two Hongs," *Economist,* June 30, 2007, p. 13.

Vines, Stephen, "Secrets of Survival in the Noble House," *Spectator,* January 27, 2007.

Whitmore, John, "How Jardine Matheson Takes Expansion in Its Stride," *Times* (London), February 23, 1976, p. 17.

Wong, Jesse, "Jardine's Chairman Faces Daunting Task of Reviving Hong Kong Trading House," *Wall Street Journal,* November 8, 1985, p. 36.

Wren, Christopher S., "Jardine Moving Plan Is Jolt to Hong Kong," *New York Times,* April 2, 1984, p. D1.

KeyCorp

127 Public Square
Cleveland, Ohio 44114-1306
U.S.A.
Telephone: (216) 689-6300
Toll Free: (800) 539-6070
Fax: (216) 689-0519
Web site: http://www.key.com

Public Company
Founded: 1825 as Commercial Bank of Albany
Incorporated: 1958 as Society Corporation
Employees: 18,500
Total Assets: $99.98 billion (2007)
Stock Exchanges: New York
Ticker Symbol: KEY
NAIC: 551111 Offices of Bank Holding Companies; 522110 Commercial Banking; 522292 Real Estate Credit; 523110 Investment Banking and Securities Dealing; 523920 Portfolio Management; 523930 Investment Advice; 524210 Insurance Agencies and Brokerages; 525910 Open-End Investment Funds; 532420 Office Machinery and Equipment Rental and Leasing

■ ■ ■

One of the 15 largest banks in the United States, Key-Corp is involved in retail and commercial banking as well as a number of other sectors within the financial services industry. Its community banking operations encompass more than 950 full-service branches and more than 1,400 ATMs in 13 northern-tier states:

Oregon, Washington, and Alaska in the Northwest; Colorado, Idaho, and Utah in the Rocky Mountain region; Ohio, Michigan, Indiana, and Kentucky in the Great Lakes region; and New York, Vermont, and Maine in the Northeast. Via this network, KeyCorp offers individuals and small businesses a variety of deposit, lending, investment, and wealth management products and services.

KeyCorp also operates a number of other business units that reach a broader swath of the country, 29 states in all. These include operations focusing on real estate capital, equipment financing, global treasury management, asset management, investment banking, capital markets services, insurance, and financial planning. The KeyCorp of the early 21st century is a product of the 1994 merger of "old" KeyCorp, whose ultimate predecessor was the Commercial Bank of Albany, founded in Albany, New York, in 1825, and Society Corporation, a Cleveland-based institution dating back to its establishment in 1849 as Society for Savings.

THE ROAD TO KEYCORP

KeyCorp's history dates back to 1825 when New York Governor DeWitt Clinton signed a bill chartering the Commercial Bank of Albany, KeyCorp's direct ancestor. In 1865 Commercial Bank was reorganized under the National Banking Act of 1864, and its name was changed to National Commercial Bank of Albany. Also during this time, another bank that would eventually become part of KeyCorp opened, the Trust and Deposit Company of Onondaga in Syracuse, established in

1869. In 1919 this bank merged with First National Bank of Syracuse to become First Trust and Deposit Company. Around the same time, the National Commercial Bank of Albany went through another reorganization, consolidating with Union Trust Company to become National Commercial Bank and Trust Company.

These two banking concerns operated independently over the next several decades, growing via a number of acquisitions. In 1967 First Trust and Deposit Company adopted a "key" symbol, the foundation for the KeyCorp name and its signature logo. Four years later, First Trust and Deposit merged into National Commercial Bank and Trust, creating First Commercial Banks, Inc. With that transaction, First Commercial had 89 offices in New York State. The name was changed to Key Banks Inc. in 1979, and then six years later, with its expansion beyond branch banking and into other financial services, the institution's holding company adopted the name KeyCorp.

Victor J. Riley, Jr., became president and CEO of the bank in 1973. He continued to serve in this capacity into the early 1990s, when he was one of the longest-tenured bank CEOs in the country. Riley led the bank from its days as a strictly upstate New York bank to its position as the country's 29th largest financial institution in 1991 with $23 billion in assets, up from $2.4 billion ten years earlier. Between 1981 and 1991, the bank's stock produced an impressive 810 percent total return including dividends, third among the 50 largest banks, according to the company's annual report.

During the 1970s and early 1980s, KeyCorp bought banks throughout the upstate area as well as 25 offices from the Bank of New York. Initially, Riley's plan was for KeyCorp to become a regional concern by acquiring banks in New England as well, starting with its purchase of a bank in Maine: Augusta-based Depositors Corporation, acquired in early 1984. However, at the same time, to keep the large New York banking establishments from dominating the New England banking system, a move was made to exclude New York banks from purchasing banks in Massachusetts and Connecticut.

LOOKING WEST

Riley looked to the West when his New England strategy was thwarted. He anticipated that when U.S. trade with Asia increased, the economies of western states would also improve. KeyCorp bought a string of banks, and in the four years between 1985 and 1990 quintupled its assets from $3 billion to $15 billion. While other banks were focusing on large cities, especially in the Northeast, KeyCorp was focusing on areas of low population in which banking services were scarce. Furthermore, KeyCorp avoided the pricing wars that often occurred in highly competitive markets.

While eastern banks were buying other eastern banks at premium prices, KeyCorp continued its westward expansion, acquiring inexpensive and promising banks in Wyoming, Idaho, and Utah. In 1985 Riley bought two banks in Alaska and Alaska Pacific Bancorporation; he used Alaska's interstate banking laws to purchase a bank in Oregon, which became known as Key Bank of Oregon. The next year, KeyCorp acquired Northwest Bancorp of Albany, Oregon, and Pacwest Bancorp of Portland, Oregon, which also became part of Key Bank of Oregon.

Many leaders in the banking industry thought Riley was making a mistake when he started buying banks in Alaska and the Northwest in 1984. Critics doubted his ability to manage such banks from a home office in Albany, New York. The purchase certainly seemed like a mistake when oil prices dropped dramatically, and Alaska plunged into a recession. KeyCorp moved quickly to restructure loans for borrowers hit by recession and foreclosed on loans when necessary.

KeyCorp also continued to buy banks in small towns and cities in New York State. In 1986 it acquired four savings banks in the mid-Hudson Valley. In the same year, it increased its western holdings by purchasing Beaver State Bank in Beaver, Oregon.

Although KeyCorp had been shut out of acquisitions in much of New England a few years before, in 1987 Riley bought eight branch offices in Maine from Fleet/Norstar Financial for $14 million. They became part of Key Bank of Maine. KeyCorp also opened a unique subsidiary based in Albany, Key Bank USA N.A., which provided banking services by mail to customers nationwide who were not within a Key Bank region.

REGIONAL DIVERSITY WITH A SMALL-TOWN APPROACH

Regional diversity had advantages and disadvantages for KeyCorp. On the positive side, KeyCorp was not so

KEY DATES

■

1825: Commercial Bank of Albany is chartered in Albany, New York.

1849: The Society for Savings is founded in Cleveland, Ohio.

1865: Commercial Bank of Albany is reorganized as National Commercial Bank of Albany.

1869: Syracuse-based Trust and Deposit Company of Onondaga is established.

c. 1919: Trust and Deposit merges with First National Bank of Syracuse to become First Trust and Deposit Company; National Commercial Bank of Albany merges with Union Trust Company to become National Commercial Bank and Trust Company.

1958: Society for Savings is reorganized as Society Corporation.

1967: First Trust and Deposit adopts a "key" symbol.

1971: First Trust and Deposit and National Commercial Bank merge to form First Commercial Banks, Inc.

1979: First Commercial changes its name to Key Banks Inc.; Society Corp. acquires Harter BanCorp.

1984: Key Banks ventures outside New York with the purchase of a bank in Maine; Society Corp. purchases Interstate Financial Corporation.

1985: Key Bank is renamed KeyCorp and also expands to the west, acquiring its first banks in Alaska; Society Corp. acquires Centran Corp.

1990: Society Corp. acquires Trustcorp, Inc.

1991: Society Corp. purchases Ameritrust Corporation.

1994: KeyCorp and Society Corp. merge to form a "new" KeyCorp, which is based in Cleveland.

1999: Major restructuring is launched.

vulnerable to economic slumps in one region. Director H. Douglas Barclay told the *Wall Street Journal,* "Problems in one or two states can be contained. Over time it all balances out." While the Northwest was in a slump, the Northeast was booming. Then, the tables were turned and the Northwest picked up while the Northeast was in recession. Nevertheless, geographic

diversity also made KeyCorp expensive to run, with operating costs as a percentage of assets high. Top executives also spent a lot of time on the road, visiting branches far from the Albany headquarters.

Consistent with the small-town approach, Riley rarely replaced personnel in the banks KeyCorp purchased, choosing instead to stay with management familiar to the local population. He told *Business Week,* "You cannot go into a new state and start shuffling people around and maintain yourself as a retail bank."

The small-town philosophy, which had led Wall Street to commonly refer to it as the "Wal-Mart of banking," also helped the bank avoid costly bad loans. KeyCorp's policy was to lend to people and businesses in the areas it served. It avoided the pitfall of many other banks, lending outside the states in which it had branches. In 1990 bad loans made up only 4 percent of its $9.9 billion load portfolio; most of those bad debts were at its Alaska banks, hard hit by a decline in oil exploration. Furthermore KeyCorp's lending practices were financially conservative. The company did not make any loans greater than $20 million and its average commercial loan was only about $2 million. Furthermore, no single industry group represented more than 24 percent of KeyCorp's commercial loans.

After more than ten years of acquisitions that had brought KeyCorp into the top 50 list, KeyCorp shifted its focus to reducing its high overhead costs. In 1990 its efficiency ratio was about 66 percent, meaning that about 66 cents worth of every dollar in revenue was spent on overhead. By the end of 1992, its efficiency ratio had improved to 61.9 percent and was more in line with the efficiency ratios of comparable banks. KeyCorp merged its operations into two computer centers and brought its four mortgage companies together as one. The banking company also sold a car-leasing business and a finance company that were unprofitable. Still KeyCorp lacked a standardized reporting system for its hundreds of branches. This became a priority for William Dougherty, the company's chief financial officer, who set to work linking KeyCorp's branches by computer and consolidating its back-office operations. By the end of 1992, all of KeyCorp's banks were linked electronically, with primary processing centers in Albany and in Tigard, Oregon. Six secondary sites handled business more suited to regional processing.

CONSOLIDATION AND FURTHER ACQUISITIONS

In line with the trend in banking toward consolidation of holdings, KeyCorp consolidated several New York State operations into one financial institution. Key Bank of Eastern New York, Key Bank of Central New York, and Key Bank of Western New York became a single nationally chartered bank, Key Bank of New York State, N.A., with its offices in Albany.

KeyCorp benefited from the country's thrift crisis in the early 1990s by buying from the government assets of two large failed New York thrifts: Empire Federal Savings and Loan and Goldome Savings Bank. With the Goldome purchase, KeyCorp moved from its status as an unknown in the mortgage industry to become the 19th largest mortgage banker in the nation. Furthermore, the Goldome purchase turned out to be profitable as the market for new and refinanced mortgage loans boomed, with interest rates the lowest they had been in decades.

In 1992 KeyCorp acquired Valley Bancorporation of Valley Falls, Idaho, which became part of Key Bank of Idaho. KeyCorp also bought the 48 branches of Security Pacific Bank in Washington, which became part of Key Bank of Washington. The company negotiated several other deals as well that were completed in early 1993; Puget Sound Bancorp, with assets of $4.7 billion, merged with Key Bank of Washington; 40 branches of New York's First American Bankshares and nine branch offices of National Savings Bank of Albany were acquired; and KeyCorp also bought its first holding in Colorado, Home Federal Savings Bank of Fort Collins.

By the end of 1992, KeyCorp had its operations and its expenses under control, using a computer system to keep track of its coast-to-coast snowbelt holdings. Its earnings were also looking better. For a long time earnings stood at 90 cents for every $100 in assets, but in 1992, they pulled past the industry standard of one dollar per $100 in assets.

While other banks in the Northeast had been saddled with bad real estate loans, KeyCorp's net earnings were increasing because its Northwest holdings, which in 1990 made up more than 39 percent of its holdings, were booming. Although it owned banks in some larger western cities, the majority of its banks were located in small towns such as Troy, Idaho, with a population of 820 and Gig Harbor, Washington, with a population of 2,429.

Riley and Dougherty were credited with taking KeyCorp into the ranks of the top 50 U.S. financial institutions, with total assets of more than $30 billion by early 1993. According to the *Economist,* KeyCorp's "loan book and profitability are the envy of other banks." That article explained that KeyCorp avoided the "easy money" made from big development loans for commercial property and corporate loans for highly leveraged transactions. This kept KeyCorp out of some of the deep troubles that other banks encountered. Key-

Corp also refrained from making loans to third world nations. In 1992 the bank held only 25 loans that were worth more than $12.5 million and only one worth more than $30 million, a loan to the owner of the bank's headquarters in Albany. From this prudent position, KeyCorp next pursued a merger with Society Corporation.

FROM SOCIETY FOR SAVINGS TO SOCIETY CORPORATION

The Society for Savings was founded by Samuel H. Mather as a mutual savings bank in Cleveland, Ohio, in 1849. Within three years, Mather's part-time business had collected deposits of $150,000; by 1857, Society had become Mather's full-time job. Ten years later, the bank built its first headquarters, a three-story building on Cleveland's Public Square. Society outgrew that building by 1890, when the bank erected Cleveland's first "skyscraper," a ten-story stone structure that featured two massive murals depicting the story of "the goose that laid the golden egg." At the time, the Society for Savings was the tallest structure between New York and Chicago.

The bank earned a reputation for security and conservatism during its first half-century in business by surviving four depressions and financial panics. It emerged from the Great Depression's federally mandated bank holiday as one of Cleveland's four largest banks, with deposits of over $100 million. By the time Society celebrated its centenary in 1949, it was the largest mutual savings bank west of the Allegheny Mountains. Although it still had only one office, Society had garnered 200,000 depositors and over $200 million in deposits.

Society National Bank was formed in 1955 as a commercial bank of the National Banking Association. Society National acquired the assets and liabilities of the Society for Savings mutual bank in 1958. The terms of the merger also made Society a public company. Voting certificates were issued to depositors of record at the end of 1958 at $500 each. Society Corporation was then created and became the first entity in Ohio formed under the 1956 federal Bank Holding Company Act. Before 1960, Society National became the first commercial bank in the United States to use online teller terminals, one of the decade's newest electronic data systems.

Society Corp.'s adoption of the holding company structure enabled it to grow rapidly between 1958 and 1978, when it acquired 12 community banks, including: Fremont Savings Bank, Western Reserve Bank of Lake County, Springfield Bank, Xenia National Bank, Erie

County Bank, Farmers National Bank & Trust Co., Tri-County National Bank, Second National Bank of Ravenna, Peoples Bank of Youngstown, 1st State Bank & Trust, American Bank, and First National Bank of Clermont County. The subsidiary banks had combined assets of over $500 million in 1972.

Society Corp.'s history as a mutual savings bank was often derided by analysts, but by the mid-1970s, the heritage was recognized as an advantage. Savings accounts, a source of strength and stability, represented 65 percent of the bank's $1.5 billion in total deposits. In 1979, when Ohio's banking laws were revised to permit banks to establish branches in counties contiguous to the home office's county, Society Corp. was poised for its second growth spurt. The expansion was accomplished through dozens of small acquisitions and three billion-dollar mergers between 1979 and 1989.

1979 ACQUISITION OF HARTER BANCORP.

Society Corp.'s opening salvo in its acquisitions spree occurred in 1979 with the acquisition of Canton, Ohio's largest bank, Harter BanCorp. Harter entered Society Corp.'s 12-bank stable second only to Society Corp.'s flagship Society National Bank, adding $400 million in assets to the holding company's $1.8 billion. Society Corp. acquired five smaller banks over the next three years. Second National Bank of Bucyrus, with assets of $34.6 million, was purchased in 1980 for $5.2 million. Second National helped fill a gap between Society Corp.'s northern Ohio banks and its Dayton and Columbus affiliates, thereby giving the corporation access to counties that it had not been able to reach in the past. Later that year, Society Corp. acquired Community National Bank (Mount Gilead, Ohio) and merged its $15 million assets and customers with Second National of Bucyrus. The new entity was renamed Society National Bank of Mid-Ohio. In 1981, Society Corp. purchased First National Bank of Carrollton and merged it with Harter BanCorp.'s flagship Harter Bank & Trust. Lancaster National Bank's $30 million in assets and three branch offices were added to Society Corp.'s roster at a cost of $2.78 million later that year. The acquisition of Citizens Bank of Hamilton for $10.7 million in cash and notes closed Society Corp.'s first round of relatively small acquisitions.

The corporation regrouped over the next two years by reorganizing its top management structure and consolidating its bank holdings. Early in 1982, a tripartite management team was formed, with J. Maurice Struchen, chairman and CEO of Society Corp., Robert W. Gillespie, vice-chairman of Society Corp. and COO of Society National Bank, and Gordon E. Hef-

fern, president and COO of Society Corp., sharing the corporation's top responsibilities. The team concept helped coordinate policymaking, planning, and operating between the holding company and its largest subsidiary. It also helped Society Corp.'s management prepare for interstate banking and inter-industry acquisitions.

Later in 1982, Society Corp. merged three of its northwest Ohio banks—Society National Bank of Northwest Ohio, Fremont Savings Bank, and American Bank in Port Clinton—to form a $250 million, 15-office, five-county bank. Society Corp. also joined with three other banks, National City Corporation (Cleveland), Fifth Third Bancorp (Cincinnati), and Third National Bank of Dayton, to form an ATM network of 400 machines. The virtually statewide network gave over one million customers access to accounts in most major Ohio cities.

1984 ACQUISITION OF INTERSTATE FINANCIAL

By the end of 1983, Society Corp. had net earnings of $8.01 million on total assets of $4.3 billion, and was poised for another major acquisition. In the spring of 1984, Society Corp. merged with Interstate Financial Corporation, parent of Third National Bank in Dayton. The acquisition increased Society Corp.'s assets to $5.1 billion and gave the corporation a stronger foothold in Dayton metropolitan area banking, where Interstate was the second largest bank. Interstate's subsidiary, North Central Financial Corp., had offices in Ohio, Indiana, Virginia, Maryland, and Florida, and held $1.1 billion in mortgage loans.

Within a little over a year, Society Corp. would make an even larger acquisition, but in the meantime, the corporation contented itself with the purchase of BancSystems Association, a regional bank card processor headquartered in suburban Cleveland. BancSystems provided MasterCard and Visa credit and debit card processing for 140 banks and savings and loan associations, and employed over 300 people. The acquisition helped Society Corp. diversify its income base into more non-interest sources, giving it over 1.4 million credit card accounts and annual volume of $2.3 billion in processed transactions. Later in 1984, Society Corp. set up barriers to a takeover by prohibiting two-tier pricing and establishing a two-thirds majority in case a takeover vote was called.

1985 ACQUISITION OF CENTRAN

The corporation further shored up its takeover defenses with the purchase of Centran Corp., a holding company of Cleveland's fourth largest bank, Central National, in 1985. Society Corp. offered Centran's stockholders a choice of cash or stock totaling $220 million for its assets of $3.1 billion and 82 offices in northern and central Ohio. The acquisition made Society Corp. one of the state's top five banks. The merger had some drawbacks, however. Centran carried with it the vestiges of ill-advised bond investments made in 1980, an unsuccessful attempt to expand into consumer finance that lost another $20 million, and problems with international loans. Centran lost $70 million on the bad bonds and had to be bailed out by Marine Midland Banks, Inc., which held influential stock in the company. Society Corp. offered Marine Midland $26 million in cash and $50 million in non-voting adjustable-rate perpetual preferred stock, thereby limiting this bank's voice in the merged company. Following the takeover of Centran, Heffern continued as chair and CEO of Society Corp., while Wilson M. Brown, Jr., chairman, president, and CEO of Centran, became president and chief administrative officer of Society Corp. Gillespie was named deputy chairman and chief operating officer. All three combined to maintain the tripartite "office of the chairman."

The merger was deemed a success when the positive results started pouring in as early as 1985: both Society Corp. and Centran chalked up record earnings for the year, and once their two primary banks were integrated, Society National Bank ranked second in Cleveland. Society Corp.'s assets reached $9 billion, up from $6.1 billion before the acquisition, while the company saved $28 million in annual operations in the process of the merger. Society Corp. became Ohio's third largest bank holding company, next to National City Corporation (Cleveland), with $12 billion in assets, and Banc One Corporation (Columbus), with $9.6 billion in assets. Society Corp. had 250 bank branches statewide and about 6,500 employees. One of the reasons for the bank's continuing success was its tradition of conservatism. The company's executives were proud of the fact that it had avoided most of the decade's banking pitfalls: agricultural, energy, and foreign loans, and the financing of leveraged buyouts.

In 1987 Heffern retired and was succeeded as CEO by Gillespie, who, at 42, became the youngest chief executive to head one of Ohio's top-ten bank holding companies. The promotion gave Gillespie a total of four titles: CEO and president of Society Corp. and CEO and president of Society National Bank. Gillespie had spent his entire career at Society Corp., starting out as a part-time teller while in graduate school at Case Western Reserve University. Also in 1987, Society Corp. was able to set earnings records by repurchasing some of its stock after the October 1987 stock market crash. Profits rose

to $89 million, and the stock appreciated almost $10 per share within less than a year.

Ohio's interstate banking legislation opened the state to banks from virtually any other state with similar legislation in October 1988. By 1990, new state laws enacted around the country had made old federal laws against interstate banking irrelevant, and in the summer of 1989, a federal thrift reform law that permitted the purchase of savings and loans was passed.

The country had entered an era of "superregional banks," such as NBD Bancorp of Detroit, PNC Financial Corporation of Pittsburgh, and Banc One of Columbus. To prepare for the increased competition that would come from these powerful banks, Society Corp. began to consolidate its holdings. Society Bank of Eastern Ohio was merged into Society National Bank, creating a bank with assets of $7.5 billion and 132 offices. Society National was then reorganized into nine districts to take advantage of the growing bank's economies of scale. Late in the year, Society Corp. increased its impact in central Ohio with the purchase of 13 branches of Citizens Federal Savings and Loan Association. The acquisition increased Society Corp.'s number of offices in the Columbus area by 50 percent, and raised the assets of the newly merged bank to $2.75 billion. Society Corp. sold BancSystems Association Inc. to Electronic Data Systems Corp. of Dallas to garner an estimated $6 million profit late in 1989.

ACQUISITIONS OF TRUSTCORP (1990) AND AMERITRUST (1991)

Society Corp. began the 1990s with two major acquisitions that placed it among the area's superregional banks. In 1990 the purchase of Toledo's Trustcorp, Inc., through an exchange of $430 million in stock gave Society Corp. operations in Ohio, Michigan, and Indiana and raised its total assets to almost $16 billion, thereby ranking the company among the United States' 40 largest banks. Trustcorp's BB credit rating pulled Society Corp.'s A-plus down to an A because of several loan losses on downtown Toledo real estate projects. Society Corp. was also obliged to settle a $5.6 million shareholder lawsuit against Trustcorp and assign extra funds to reserves that would cover any defaulted loans. By the fall of 1991, Society Corp. had turned its newest subsidiary around and renamed its affiliates Society Bank & Trust; Society Bank, Indiana; and Society Bank, Michigan.

Society Corp. worked to pare down its non-interest expenses during the recession of the early 1990s that slowed loan demand and cut into profits. In March

1990 it repurchased Marine Midland's interest in the corporation for $49.25 million, thereby saving the preferred dividends paid on the stock. That spring, Society Corp. vowed to cut about 10 percent, or $40 million, from its $390 million in annual non-interest expenses.

In September 1991 Society Corp. announced the largest bank acquisition in Ohio history. It merged with Cleveland's Ameritrust Corporation. The tax-free agreement called for an exchange of $1.2 billion in Society Corp. stock, and created a new corporation with combined assets of $26 billion. The addition of Ameritrust's retail and trust locations throughout Ohio, Indiana, Michigan, Texas, Florida, Missouri, Colorado, New York, and Connecticut made Society Corp. the largest bank in Cleveland and the 29th largest in the country. The two banks' trust departments together became the 15th largest in the country in terms of revenues. Merging Ameritrust and Society Corp. required the elimination of about 2,000 positions and closing or selling 90 branches. Society Corp. also had to divert about $46 million to Ameritrust's reserve against problem loans.

Society Corp.'s acquisitions in 1992 and 1993 were modest, compared to the purchases made in the first two years of the decade, but they expanded the Great Lakes corporation geographically. In 1992, the corporation purchased First of America Bank-Monroe (Michigan), a $149 million bank, from First of America Bank Corporation. Early in 1993, Society Corp. completed its purchase of First Federal Savings and Loan Association of Fort Myers, a $1.1 billion thrift with 24 branch offices in central and southwestern Florida.

1994 MERGER OF KEYCORP AND SOCIETY CORP.

In October 1993 Society Corporation and KeyCorp agreed on a so-called merger of equals valued at $3.9 billion. In this deal, completed in March 1994, Key-Corp was merged into Society Corporation, which was the surviving entity but took the KeyCorp name. The new KeyCorp, which adopted Society's headquarters in Cleveland as its base, was led by Victor Riley as chairman and CEO and Society's Robert Gillespie as president and COO. With $58 billion in assets, Key-Corp ranked as the 11th largest bank in the country.

The merger created a branch network ranging across 13 states, all in the northern tier, save Society's Florida branches. Society's other branches in Ohio, Michigan, and Indiana filled in a gap in KeyCorp's operations, which encompassed Alaska, Washington, Oregon, Idaho, Utah, Wyoming, Colorado, New York, and Maine. The combination was designed to mesh KeyCorp's strength in community banking with Society's more robustly developed array of financial products, which included strong investment management, specialty finance, and large corporate banking operations.

The actual implementation of the merger ended up being a protracted one hampered by culture clashes and in the short run failing to deliver on the initial synergistic promises. A number of restructuring moves were needed, including divesting certain peripheral operations, such as its residential mortgage servicing unit, which was sold to NationsBank Corporation in March 1995. On the addition side, KeyCorp expanded into the booming market for subprime lending, the sector of the lending market serving higher-risk individuals with lower credit ratings. The company acquired Chicago-based AutoFinance Group, Inc., a subprime auto lender, in September 1995 for $325 million in stock and Champion Mortgage Co., Inc., a subprime home-equity lender based in Parsippany, New Jersey, for $200 million in stock in August 1997. KeyCorp in July 1997 also acquired Leasetec Corporation, a concern based in Boulder, Colorado, specializing in the leasing of information-technology and telecommunications equipment.

The branch network was overhauled as well. In March 1995 KeyCorp gained its first branches in Vermont and also became the number one bank in Maine by purchasing the Maine and Vermont operations of Bank of Boston for nearly $200 million. In mid-1996 the company sold its Florida banking operation having determined that it would be unable to become a major player in that market. Late that same year, KeyCorp launched a major restructuring. Seeking further efficiencies in its operations, the company announced plans to close or shut down 280 branches across the country and eliminate about 3,000 jobs. Among the subsequent cuts was the sale of all of the branches in Wyoming. In addition, in 1997 KeyCorp dismantled its regional-bank structure by consolidating its various state-chartered banks into a single national bank, KeyBank National Association. To raise its profile among consumers around the country, KeyCorp in 1996 launched a highly successful and long-running television ad campaign featuring actor Anthony Edwards. In the midst of all these developments, a transition in leadership occurred as well. Riley turned over the CEO position to Gillespie in September 1995 and then the chairmanship one year later.

MOVE INTO INVESTMENT BANKING AND FURTHER RESTRUCTURING

As the barriers between commercial and investment banking continued to crumble, KeyCorp late in 1998 made its own move into investment banking, purchasing McDonald & Company Investments, Inc., for around $581 million in stock. The deal enabled KeyCorp to add the stock and bond underwriting capabilities of Cleveland-based McDonald and thereby broaden its offerings to corporate clients in small and medium-sized markets.

Still dealing with a higher cost structure than many of its peers, KeyCorp ended the decade with further restructuring moves. In October 1999 the company sold its 28 branches on Long Island after concluding that this was another market where it was destined to remain a minor player. The move freed up resources to invest in markets with higher growth potential, such as Salt Lake City, Denver, Seattle, and Portland, Oregon. Just a month later, the company launched a major restructuring that eventually yielded annual cost savings of roughly $300 million. KeyCorp reduced its workforce by nearly 4,100 mainly through management cuts and the consolidation and outsourcing of various "back-office" functions, including processing and customer-service operations. As this overhaul began, KeyCorp unloaded another peripheral business, selling its relatively small, $1.3 billion credit card portfolio to Associates First Capital Corporation and recording a $332 million pretax gain in the process. KeyCorp aimed to concentrate its lending in such areas as commercial and small-business loans and home-equity lines of credit.

In the early months of 2001, Gillespie retired from both the CEO position and the chairmanship. His handpicked successor was Henry L. Meyer III, who had been president and COO and who had come from the company's Society side, having joined that concern in 1972. Meyer continued to oversee the restructuring launched in late 1999 and spearheaded the jettisoning of another troubled unit. In May 2001 KeyCorp announced plans to exit from the automobile leasing business and also to cut back on its indirect auto lending. In connection with these pullbacks, the company recorded more than $400 million in charges, cutting net income for 2001 to just $132 million, down from the previous year's total of just over $1 billion.

RETURN TO GROWTH

By 2002 KeyCorp was confident enough in its restructuring and turnaround efforts to enter into another period of acquisitions that lasted through 2006.

During this period, the company made its first bank acquisition in seven years, the $66 million, December 2002 purchase of Union Bankshares, Ltd., a Denver-based seven-branch banking operation with assets of $475 million. In July 2004 KeyCorp bolstered its Michigan branch network by purchasing Sterling Bank & Trust FSB, a privately held thrift based in Southfield with ten branches and approximately $380 million in deposits. Later in 2004, KeyCorp spent $195 million for EverTrust Financial Group Inc. of Everett, Washington, which operated 12 bank branches and two commercial loan offices and had assets of $770 million.

KeyCorp was also busy beefing up its operations in three areas in which it was ranked among the nation's leaders: commercial real estate, equipment leasing, and asset management. Purchases in the commercial real estate field included Conning Asset Management (Hartford, Connecticut; June 2002), Malone Mortgage Company (Dallas; July 2005), and ORIX Capital Markets, LLC (Dallas; December 2005). In December 2004 KeyCorp acquired the equipment leasing unit of American Express Company's small business division. Then in April 2006 the company bought Austin Capital Management, Ltd., an asset management firm based in Austin, Texas, that specialized in selecting and managing hedge fund investments mainly for institutional investors.

Toward the end of this array of acquisitions, KeyCorp began focusing more intently on its 13-state branch banking business and on other "relationship-based" businesses that best meshed with its retail banking operations. A number of businesses unrelated to its retail banking network were thus jettisoned. KeyCorp sold its indirect auto lending business in the spring of 2006 and then sold Champion Mortgage to a unit of HSBC Holdings plc in November 2006 for $2.5 billion. In February 2007 KeyCorp pulled back on its foray into investment banking by selling the branch network of McDonald Investments to a subsidiary of UBS AG for $219 million.

In 2007, as the deteriorating housing market and credit crisis began sending ripples through the U.S. banking industry, KeyCorp announced its largest acquisition since 1998. In a deal completed in early 2008, the company bought U.S.B. Holding Co., Inc., parent of Union State Bank, for $547 million. Adding U.S.B. and its $3 billion in assets and 31 branches doubled KeyCorp's branch network in New York's Hudson Valley and pushed its total assets close to the $100 billion mark. Soon thereafter, however, KeyCorp announced its results for 2007, reporting that its fourth-quarter earnings had plummeted 83 percent after it had been forced to set aside $363 million during the quarter to cover rising loan delinquencies and defaults. Full-year earnings dropped 13 percent to $919 million. The credit crisis that precipitated these results also sparked speculation about a possible merger between KeyCorp and crosstown rival National City Corporation, which had been hit even harder by the crunch. Such a merger of equals, the second for KeyCorp, had the potential to create the sixth largest bank in the United States as well as a much more competitive institution than the two predecessors.

April S. Dougal
Updated, Wendy J. Stein; David E. Salamie

PRINCIPAL SUBSIDIARIES

KeyBank National Association.

PRINCIPAL OPERATING UNITS

KeyBank Regional Banking; KeyBank Commercial Banking; KeyBank Real Estate Capital; Key Equipment Finance; Global Treasury Management Group; Media and Telecommunications Group; Victory Capital Management; KeyBanc Capital Markets.

PRINCIPAL COMPETITORS

National City Corporation; Fifth Third Bancorp; U.S. Bancorp; Citizens Financial Group, Inc.; JPMorgan Chase & Co.; Wells Fargo & Company; Bank of America Corporation; Huntington Bancshares Incorporated; Sovereign Bancorp, Inc.; M&T Bank Corporation; Washington Mutual, Inc.

FURTHER READING

Benoit, Ellen, "The Hunger," *Financial World*, December 11, 1990, pp. 62+.

———, "KeyCorp's Northern Lights," *Financial World*, October 31, 1989, pp. 20+.

Boraks, David, "Key, Meyer Look Past Turnaround," *American Banker*, October 2, 2002, p. 1.

Brannigan, Martha, "NationsBank to Buy Assets from Key-Corp," *Wall Street Journal*, February 24, 1995, p. A4.

Cahill, Joseph B., "KeyCorp Plans to Cut 3,000 Jobs in Bid to Increase Efficiency, Spur Growth," *Wall Street Journal*, November 24, 1999, p. C18.

Chakravarty, Subrata N., "Two Strong Partners," *Forbes*, November 8, 1993, p. 44.

Chase, Brett, "2,700 Jobs, 280 Branches Due for Axe at Key-Corp," *American Banker*, November 26, 1996, pp. 1+.

Cocheo, Steve, "Unlocking KeyCorp's Acquisition Strategy," *ABA Banking Journal*, July 1986, pp. 29+.

Fraust, Bart, "Society to Buy Centran, Creating Ohio's 2nd Largest Holding Company," *American Banker*, September 25, 1984, pp. 2+.

Fuller, John, "Society Seeks Centran Merger," *Cleveland Plain Dealer*, September 25, 1984, p. 1A.

———, "A Tale of Two Bankers," *Cleveland Plain Dealer*, September 30, 1984, p. 1E.

Herzog, Lester W., Jr., *150 Years of Service and Leadership: The Story of National Commercial Bank and Trust Company*, New York: Newcomen Society in North America, 1975, 25 p.

Hill, Miriam, "Society to Take Over Ameritrust," *Cleveland Plain Dealer*, September 14, 1991, pp. 1A, 4A.

Hill, Miriam, and Diane Solov, "Biggest Ohio Bank Merger to Create a $58 Billion Company," *Cleveland Plain Dealer*, October 5, 1993, p. 1A.

Jereski, Laura, "Small Towns Add Up to Big Banking for Key-Corp," *Business Week*, April 30, 1990, p. 104.

Klucina, John L., "KeyCorp Growth Linked to Strategy of Acquisitions," *Albany (N.Y.) Times Union*, April 13, 1986, p. D1.

Lipin, Steven, "KeyCorp and Society Hope Differences Become Asset," *Wall Street Journal*, October 5, 1993, p. B4.

Lubinger, Bill, "Key Will Sell Its Credit Cards to Texas-Based Operation," *Cleveland Plain Dealer*, December 29, 1999, p. 1C.

———, "KeyCorp to Fire 3,000," *Cleveland Plain Dealer*, November 24, 1999, p. 1A.

Mahoney, Mike, "Merger Looks Bright for Banks," *Cleveland Plain Dealer*, July 14, 1985, pp. 1D, 2D.

Maturi, Richard J., "Frost Belt Bank," *Barron's*, August 11, 1986, p. 75.

Mazzucca, Tim, "Execution Time at Key's Retail Lines," *American Banker*, December 20, 2006, p. 1.

———, "Key Sets Exit from Another Noncore Line," *American Banker*, September 7, 2006, p. 1.

———, "KeyCorp Puts a Subprime Unit on the Selling Block," *American Banker*, August 2, 2006, p. 1.

Miller, Jay, "Nat City Ills Revive Talk of Key Combo," *Crain's Cleveland Business*, January 7, 2008, p. 1.

Murray, Matt, "KeyCorp Agrees to Buy McDonald & Co. to Add Investment-Banking Capability," *Wall Street Journal*, June 16, 1998, p. A4.

———, "KeyCorp Remains at a Crossroads After Bank Merger," *Wall Street Journal*, November 23, 1994, p. B4.

———, "KeyCorp Slashing Work Force, Branches," *Wall Street Journal*, November 26, 1996, p. A3.

———, "Missed Opening: KeyCorp Fails to Prove It Can Unlock Promise of a Merger of Equals," *Wall Street Journal*, August 25, 1998, p. A1.

Murray, Teresa Dixon, "KeyCorp Selling McDonald," *Cleveland Plain Dealer*, September 7, 2006, p. C1.

———, "KeyCorp to Buy Bank in New York," *Cleveland Plain Dealer*, July 28, 2007, p. C1.

———, "Mortgage Crisis Hits KeyCorp Profit," *Cleveland Plain Dealer*, October 17, 2007, p. C3.

Novack, Janet, "Behavior Modification," *Forbes,* June 17, 1996, p. 54.

"'Old Stone Bank' Is 88 This Week," *Cleveland Plain Dealer,* June 13, 1937, p. 29A.

Papiernik, Richard L., "The Honeymooners," *Financial World,* March 29, 1994, pp. 90–91.

Phillips, Stephen, "KeyCorp to Shut up to 560 Branches," *Cleveland Plain Dealer,* October 12, 1995, p. 1C.

Rehak, Judith, "Banking on Change," *Chief Executive* (U.S.), June 1997, p. 25.

Reilly, Patrick, "KeyCorp Junking Car Leasing Biz," *American Banker,* May 18, 2001, p. 1.

———, "KeyCorp Putting Retail Banking, Specialty Units Under One Roof," *American Banker,* December 18, 2000, p. 1.

Ringer, Richard, "Society Corp. Wins Trustcorp with Bid of $455 Million," *American Banker,* June 20, 1989, pp. 1+.

Schiller, Zach, "KeyCorp Set to Acquire McDonald Brokerage," *Cleveland Plain Dealer,* June 16, 1998, p. 1A.

Sherman, Henry Stoddard, *Myron T. Herrick (1854–1929): Cleveland Banker, Governor of Ohio, Ambassador to France— And the Society for Savings, 1849–1949,* New York: Newcomen Society in North America, 1949, 28 p.

"A Small Success," *Economist,* November 10, 1990, p. 101.

Stern, Gabriella, and Joseph Pereira, "KeyCorp to Buy Maine, Vermont Banks," *Wall Street Journal,* June 27, 1994, p. A4.

Strozniak, Peter, "Agent of Change," *Inside Business,* October 2002, pp. B32+.

Svare, J. Christopher, "Society Launches Bid for Great Lakes' Supremacy," *Bank Management,* April 1992, pp. 22+.

Vanac, Mary, "KeyCorp Chief to Retire," *Cleveland Plain Dealer,* January 19, 2001, p. 1C.

———, "KeyCorp Stands at Crossroads," *Cleveland Plain Dealer,* January 25, 2002, p. C1.

———, "Tough Calls," *Cleveland Plain Dealer,* February 9, 2003, p. G1.

Wilke, John R., "The Inter-Regional: Nationwide Banking Is Getting a Preview at Growing KeyCorp Offices from Alaska to Maine," *Wall Street Journal,* May 31, 1991, p. A1.

Wiseman, Paul, "Life of Riley—A Wild and Woolly Banker," *USA Today,* September 14, 1992, p. 2B.

———, "'Wal-Mart of Banking' Built on Discipline," *USA Today,* September 14, 1992, p. 1B.

Laing O'Rourke PLC

Bridge Place - Anchor Boulevard
Admirals Park, Crossways
Dartford, DA2 6SN
United Kingdom
Telephone: (+44 01322) 296200
Fax: (+44 01375) 392089
Web site: http://www.laingorourke.com

Private Company
Incorporated: 2001
Employees: 27,300
Sales: £3.49 billion ($6.8 billion) (2006)
NAIC: 237990 Other Heavy and Civil Engineering Construction; 236210 Industrial Building Construction; 236220 Commercial and Institutional Building Construction; 237310 Highway, Street, and Bridge Construction

■ ■ ■

Laing O'Rourke PLC is one of the world's largest, globally operating construction companies. Based in the United Kingdom, Laing O'Rourke is also a highly vertically integrated company, with operations ranging from the manufacture of precast concrete building components to engineering to construction to property development and sales. In the United Kingdom the company operates through a number of divisions. These include Construction North, covering the north Midlands to Scotland, and Construction South, ranging from the south Midlands to London and the Southeast. The Infrastructure division includes the company's operations in civil engineering and utilities construction. Among this division's most high-profile projects are the St. Pancras Channel Tunnel Rail Link and Terminal 5 at Heathrow Airport, Europe's largest construction project in the middle of the first decade of the 2000s. The company also operates two specialist civil engineering divisions, Laing O'Rourke Energy and Laing O'Rourke Utilities.

The company's specialist contracting operations are conducted under Expanded Limited. These include Expanded Structures, a leading provider of reinforced concrete basements, foundations, and sub- and superstructures; Expanded Demolition; and Expanded Piling. This division also includes the company's Strongforce prestressing and posttensioning forms division, and stonemasonry specialist Vetter UK. The company is a leading building services provider through Crown House Technologies, and the leading plant hire group through Select Plant Hire. At the midpoint of the first decade of the 2000s, Laing O'Rourke extended its operations to include residential development through its Explore Living subsidiary. The company's international business includes its 2006 acquisition of Australia's Barclay Mowlem, a partnership in India with Delhi Land & Financial; Germany's Naturstein Vetter; and the Al Naboodah Laing O'Rourke joint venture in Dubai. Laing O'Rourke remains a privately held company controlled by founder Ray O'Rourke. The company's sales neared £3.5 billion ($6.8 billion) in 2006, up from just £340 million in 2001.

CONCRETE CONTRACTOR IN 1978

Ray O'Rourke was born in County Mayo, Ireland. In 1967, when he was 20 years old, O'Rourke immigrated to England, where he took work as a construction laborer. Yet O'Rourke's ambitions soon led him to enroll in the University of East London, where he earned a civil engineering degree. O'Rourke then joined the Kier construction group, then later took a position at the Murphy construction company. In 1978, however, O'Rourke decided to go into business for himself. Joined by brother Des, O'Rourke established R. O'Rourke & Son, a subcontracting company based in the family's garage. The pair were joined by Bernard Dempsey, who later became the company's chairman.

O'Rourke launched its business with work orders totaling just £11,000. The company started out by providing contract concrete services. O'Rourke completed its first £2,300 contract, a precast frame at a site in Bracknell for Foundation House, that same year. While concrete remained the mainstay of O'Rourke's business, the company quickly showed itself as an industry innovator. At the time, building subcontractors tended to focus their operations on a single area of construction. O'Rourke, however, saw potential in expanding the range of the company's services. By the early 1980s, the company offered flooring and installation services, as well as precast concrete. As part of its expansion, the company began building up its own design and engineering staff.

By the middle of the 1980s, O'Rourke's firm had grown into a major operation in the London area. A major milestone for the company came with a contract to work on the Broadgate office complex in London. There, O'Rourke came in contact with Peter Rogers, part of the Stanhope development group behind the Broadgate project. Rogers was impressed by O'Rourke's work, and became one of the company's major clients.

Encouraged, the company continued to build out its range of operations through the 1990s. O'Rourke expanded into Europe in that decade, starting with a contract for the 1992 Olympic Games in Barcelona. By the end of the decade, the company had become one of the most vertically integrated contractors in the United Kingdom. The company's operations by then spanned a wide range of activities, including purchasing, planning, and surveying. By the turn of the millennium, O'Rourke's revenues had reached £200 million.

Yet O'Rourke by then felt limited by the group's focus on the subcontracting sector. As Ray O'Rourke told *Building* magazine, "there was no more we could achieve as a specialist." The company set its sights on further growth and began seeking the vehicle to achieve this. The company's chance came in 2001, amid the troubles afflicting Laing Plc, the country's most-well known construction and property group.

FOUNDING A BRITISH CONSTRUCTION LEADER IN 1848

Laing traced its origins back to 1848, when James Laing inherited the Sebergham, Cumberland-based stonemasonry and building company owned by his father. Laing's first project was to build three houses on a plot of land acquired for £30. Laing sold two of the houses for profit, keeping the third for himself and his family.

Laing's son John joined him in the business, which later became known as Laing & Son. By 1867, the company's growth had led it to establish new headquarters in Carlisle. John Laing took over as head of the company following his father's death in 1882. The company then began shifting its focus to completing larger construction projects in the region. The next generation, under John William Laing, joined the business in 1895, taking over the leadership in 1910. The company expanded strongly under John William Laing and in the post–World War I period extended its operations into London. By 1921, the company had opened a dedicated office in London. This then became the company's headquarters in 1926.

By then, Laing had become a major construction company in England. In addition to carrying out home construction, the company tackled larger projects. These included the building of factories, and a large number of projects, including military camps, housing projects, and others for the British government and local and regional councils. A major company milestone came with the launch of the Easiform wall system, based on the use of concrete blocks. This made it possible to build housing more quickly and more economically, and was rapidly adopted by the country's local housing councils. Before long, Laing had built thousands of buildings based on the Easiform system, emerging as one of the country's leading construction groups.

As such, Laing contributed greatly to the British war effort, helping to build and repair many of the

KEY DATES

1848: James Laing takes over his father's stonemasonry business and builds his first homes.

1924: Laing introduces Easiform building system, becoming Britain's leading construction and property group.

1952: Laing goes public on London Stock Exchange.

1959: Laing wins contract to build M1 Motorway.

1975: Laing creates Laing International to encompass growing operations in Europe, the Middle East, and the United States.

1978: Ray O'Rourke founds concrete subcontracting business.

1992: O'Rourke wins contract for Barcelona Olympic Games.

1999: Laing completes construction of Millennium Dome at a loss.

2001: O'Rourke acquires Laing's construction division for £1.

2002: Laing O'Rourke launches construction of Heathrow Airport's Terminal 5.

2007: Laing O'Rourke's revenues top £3.5 billion.

country's military facilities, including equipment depots, training camps, and various defense projects. In the postwar period, Laing remained highly active, building a wide range of factories, housing, public buildings and offices, wharves, and opencast coal sites. The company's property development wing also grew strongly. By the early 1950s, the company counted more than 150 houses, 250 apartments, 136 shops, and 92 factories, as well as three office blocks. Mostly located in the London area, these generated significant rental revenues for the company.

HIGH PROFILE IN THE SIXTIES

Laing added a number of other activities during the time. The company took over Triad Floors Ltd., which manufactured precast concrete flooring. The company also controlled Thermalite Ltd., which produced lightweight concrete panels. The company also owned Manor Properties (Elstree) Ltd., a property group founded in 1951.

Laing went public in 1952. The company entered a new era of high-profile contracts. In 1959, for example,

the company was selected to build Britain's first freeway, the M1 Motorway. The company completed the 53-mile roadway, linking London with Rugby, in just 19 months. At the time, the M1 contract was the largest ever awarded to a British company. Other major projects completed over the next decades included the Coventry Cathedral in 1962, and the Barbican Centre in 1976.

Laing also expanded beyond the United Kingdom during this period. The Middle East formed a major market for the group from the 1970s. Laing had also made strong roads in Europe, particularly in Spain. By the middle of the 1970s, the company's Spanish unit was one of the country's leading contractors. In 1975, Laing formed a dedicated subsidiary for its growing international business. This was extended again into the United States at the start of the 1980s. California, where the company began developing retirement homes and communities, became a major market for the group during this time.

Laing continued to rack up high-profile projects through the 1990s. The company was part of the joint venture building the Second Severn Crossing bridge, a cable-stayed structure stretching for five miles. The company also served as project manager for the Hong Kong Convention and Exhibition Centre, completed in 1997. The company also managed the construction of the Millennium Dome in London starting from 1999.

SOLD FOR JUST £1 IN 2001

Yet by then Laing was in trouble. By the late 1990s, the company had booked massive losses on 13 of its largest construction contracts, including the Millennium Dome project. The company attempted to broaden its operations, launching a new Investment division. Through this division, the company took part in the privatization of British Rail, acquiring a controlling stake in the Chiltern Rail operations. While losses in its construction division continued, the company's property arm also stumbled.

By the beginning of the 2000s, Laing's minority shareholders led a revolt against the Laing family. By then, the family held just 23 percent of the group's stock, yet, through the company's antiquated two-tier stock structure, controlled more than 53 percent of voting rights. In the end, the Laing family backed down, and new management took over the company. Laing then began a restructuring, which included the sale of both its construction and property arms.

O'Rourke quickly emerged as the leading candidate to acquire Laing's construction group. Initially, O'Rourke had been prepared to offer as much as £30 million to acquire what was then one of the United

Kingdom's most iconic construction groups. Yet, after examining Laing's books, O'Rourke returned with a new offer, for just one British pound. Laing, saddled with losses, finally accepted O'Rourke's offer in September 2001. The combined company then changed its name to Laing O'Rourke.

BUILDING A GLOBAL BUILDER

Under Ray O'Rourke's leadership, the Laing operations were reorganized and rapidly returned to profitability. The company's growth then became nothing short of spectacular. From revenues of just £340 million in 2001, the company's fortunes soared, nearing £3.5 billion by 2006.

The early 2000s were marked by several new high-profile contracts. The first of these came in 2001, when Laing O'Rourke launched construction of the transformation of St. Pancras into a 13-platform terminal for the Channel Tunnel Rail Link. The following year, the company started work on what was to be Europe's single largest construction project, the building of Heathrow Airport's Terminal 5. By 2003, Laing O'Rourke, through its Al-Naboodah Laing O'Rourke joint venture in the United Arab Emirates, had broken ground on Dubai Airport's Terminal 3 substructure.

Laing O'Rourke continued to seek new horizons at mid-decade. The company entered the Australian market, setting up a property development subsidiary there in 2004. The company soon jump-started its Australian presence, buying Barclay Mowlem, one of that market's leading construction and engineering groups in 2006. In the meantime, in England, Laing O'Rourke achieved still greater vertical integration, setting up its own homebuilding subsidiary, Explore Living.

By this time one of the world's largest construction groups, Laing O'Rourke remained committed to its status as a privately owned, family-run group. Founder Ray O'Rourke remained firmly in command of the company's growing empire, joined by son Cathal. O'Rourke had grown from simple laborer to one of the world's most powerful construction leaders in the new century.

M. L. Cohen

PRINCIPAL SUBSIDIARIES

Explore Capital Limited; Explore Living Plc; Explore Living South East Limited; Laing O'Rourke (Ireland) Limited; Laing O'Rourke Construction North Limited; Laing O'Rourke Construction South Limited; Laing O'Rourke Holdings Limited; Laing O'Rourke Infrastructure Limited; Laing O'Rourke NA Limited; Malling Products Limited; Naturstein Vetter GmbH; R O'Rourke & Son Limited; Select Plant Hire Company Limited; Vetter UK Limited.

PRINCIPAL DIVISIONS

Construction North; Construction South; Laing O'Rourke Energy; Laing O'Rourke Utilities.

PRINCIPAL COMPETITORS

Sumitomo Corp.; China Chang Jiang Energy Corp.; Siemens Power Generation Inc.; North China Grid Company Ltd.; Bouygues S.A.; VINCI S.A.; Nippon Steel Corp.; JFE Holdings Inc.; Mitsubishi Heavy Industries Ltd.; Halliburton Co.; Eiffage; RSEA Engineering Corp.

FURTHER READING

Barrick, Adrian, "What Makes Ray Run?" *Building,* July 2004.

Batchelor, Charles, "Condemned to Making the Best of the Wreckage," *Financial Times,* September 28, 2001, p. 25.

Bradshaw, Della, "Concrete Giant Adds People Development to Mix," *Financial Times,* May 14, 2007, p. 3.

Clark, Phil, "If Anybody Can Turn Laing Round, Ray Can," *Building,* March 2001.

Cole, Cheryl, "Construction Disposal Loss to Laing at £1," *Birmingham Post,* September 28, 2001, p. 23.

"Exceptional Growth for Laing O'Rourke," *Contract Journal,* August 15, 2007.

Griggs, Tom, "Laing O'Rourke Targets Margins," *Financial Times,* August 8, 2007, p. 19.

McGoran, Fiona, "O'Rourke Is Given Building Firm for Free," *Sunday Times,* July 29, 2001, p. 1.

McGreevy, Ronan, "Things Looking up for Laing O'Rourke," *Sunday Times,* July 4, 2004, p. 1.

Neild, Larry, "Irish Skill Turns Firm into Global Force," *Daily Post,* February 14, 2007, p. 8.

Smy, Lucy, "Contractors Move into Housebuilding," *Financial Times,* April 6, 2005, p. 24.

LECG Corporation

2000 Powell Street, Suite 600
Emeryville, California 94608
U.S.A.
Telephone: (510) 985-6700
Toll Free: (888) 858-LECG
Fax: (510) 653-9898
Web site: http://www.lecg.com

Public Company
Incorporated: 1988 as The Law and Economics Consulting Group, Inc.
Employees: 1,300
Sales: $353.85 million (2006)
Stock Exchanges: NASDAQ
Ticker Symbol: XPRT
NAIC: 541110 Offices of Lawyers; 541211 Offices of Certified Public Accountants; 541611 Administrative Management and General Management Consulting Services; 541618 Other Management Consulting Services

∎ ∎ ∎

LECG Corporation is a leading economic consulting firm, offering expert witnesses and analytical services in a variety of fields. LECG is known for a decentralized, entrepreneurial culture that amply rewards its consultants, most of whom hold Ph.D.s. Formed by professors from the University of California at Berkeley, it has been based in Emeryville, California, since its founding in 1988. LECG has three dozen offices in ten countries.

BERKELEY ORIGINS

The original incarnation of LECG was formed in 1988 as an S corporation by professors at the University of California at Berkeley. Based in Emeryville, California, the firm was known as The Law and Economics Consulting Group, Inc. It would be renamed LECG, Inc., in October 1997, a couple of months before its initial public offering (IPO).

Founders included economics professor David Teece and Tom Jorde, a professor of law. Teece became chairman. A native of New Zealand, Teece had immigrated to the United States after earning a master of commerce degree from Canterbury University. According to a 2007 profile of Teece in the *Wall Street Journal,* he began his consulting career early, helping Exxon Corp. defend against price-fixing allegations while studying for his Ph.D. at the University of Pennsylvania. After graduating, he joined the faculty of the University of California at Berkeley, where he received tenure at the age of 33.

Teece remained involved with the business community in New Zealand. He bought a house there and in 1999 his CHL New Zealand investment group acquired LWR Industries, which made the country's Canterbury brand of clothing.

According to the *Wall Street Journal* story, the concept of free market justice thrived during the Reagan era. By the time the original LECG was launched in 1988, an entire industry had sprung up around the expert witness business. In a kind of arms race, prosecutors and defense vied for parity by obtaining the most credible economic analyses. Teece boasted experience

COMPANY PERSPECTIVES

LECG, a global expert services firm, provides independent expert testimony and analysis, original authoritative studies, and strategic consulting services to clients including *Fortune* Global 500 corporations, major law firms, and local, state, and federal governments and agencies around the world. LECG's highly credentialed experts and professional staff conduct economic and financial analyses to provide objective opinions and advice that help resolve complex disputes and inform legislative, judicial, regulatory, and business decision makers. LECG's experts are renowned academics, former senior government officials, experienced industry leaders, and seasoned consultants.

testifying in some of the biggest precedent-setting cases of the day.

LECG's economic analysis proved applicable to many different industries, keeping the firm in demand and allowing the senior partners to supplement their professors' salaries with six-figure incomes. As one of the leading witnesses, Teece himself could rake in more than a half-million dollars in a year. In a structure similar to the law profession, new Ph.D.s handled some of the grub work and were billed at lower rates.

LECG's revenues reached $20 million in 1993, resulting in net income of $3 million. By 1995 revenues were up to about $25 million; they were still growing at a double-digit rate.

FIRST INITIAL PUBLIC OFFERING

Though LECG did not invent the business model of professor-turned-consultant, it was one of the first of the "research boutiques" to go public. LECG, Inc., floated its shares on the New York Stock Exchange in December 1997 (ticker symbol "XPT").

The company was soon acquired by Navigant Consulting, Inc. (then called The Metzler Group, Inc.), another publicly traded consulting firm, in a deal worth $214 million. LECG continued to operate independently for a time as a wholly owned subsidiary. However, Navigant had felt the need to scale back after a multiyear buying spree, allowing for the spinoff of the unit in a couple of years.

Meanwhile, there was significant international expansion in the late 1990s. LECG opened offices in

New Zealand, Belgium, and the United Kingdom in 1997. At the time of the Metzler buy, LECG had ten U.S. and four international offices. It employed 160 people. Revenues rose more than 40 percent for the year to $44 million. It expanded its Argentina operations in 1998 with the purchase of Cordoba-based Expectativa—Economic Consulting, a specialist in regulatory issues for utilities.

SPIN OFF FROM NAVIGANT

The company averaged 25 percent growth throughout most of the 1990s, reaching revenues of $74 million in 2000. There were then 96 experts and 168 professional staffers on board. In September 2000 LECG Corporation was spun off from Navigant in a $43 million management buyout. Thirty-five consultants participated, with backing from Chicago's Thoma Cressey Equity Partners. David Teece returned to his former role of chairman. Revenues exceeded $100 million in 2001 and rose by a third the next year. However, the company was beginning to post losses.

LECG was among the many firms to pick over the assets and staff of accounting giant Arthur Andersen after its sensational collapse in 2002. It paid about $3 million to add 35 of Andersen's insurance-related employees (including ten consultants).

PUBLIC AGAIN

LECG went public again in November 2003, this time on the NASDAQ (under the ticker symbol "XPRT"). The successful initial offering raised $127.5 million. By this time, LECG had nearly two dozen offices located in seven countries.

The company returned to profitability with a $19 million operating profit in 2003 as revenues reached $166 million. Some observers grumbled that the surplus would have been greater if the experts were not so amply compensated, but generosity was part of the company's formula for loyalty in a field keenly competitive for talent. The company's top two consultants, Teece and David Kaplan, were drawing in the neighborhood of $2 million a year, information the *East Bay Business Times* gleaned from a company's proxy statement.

ACQUISITIONS AFTER 2003

With fresh capital in hand from the IPO, the company then went on a buying spree, acquiring about a dozen companies in the next few years. In March 2004 it acquired Los Angeles-based Economic Analysis LLC for

KEY DATES

1988: Professors at the University of California at Berkeley form The Law and Economics Consulting Group, Inc. (LECG).

1995: Revenues are about $25 million.

1997: LECG goes public but is soon acquired by Navigant Consulting (then called Metzler Group).

1998: Argentina's Expectativa—Economic Consulting is acquired.

2000: LECG is spun off from Navigant in a management buyout.

2003: LECG becomes a public company again, sparking multiyear acquisition spree.

2004: Company buys Economic Analysis LLC, Silicon Valley Expert Witness Group, and Washington Advisory Group.

2005: Lancaster Consulting and Beach & Company International are added as total revenues approach $300 million.

2006: California's BMB Mack Barclay is acquired.

2007: LECG buys Vienna, Virginia-based Secura Group LLC.

$16 million. This added 50 employees. The purchase of Toronto's Low Rosen Taylor Soriano occurred about the same time.

The company bought Silicon Valley Expert Witness Group, Inc., in August 2004. The deal was worth about $9 million. Washington Advisory Group, LLC, was acquired in October 2004. Revenues were $217 million in 2004, producing operating income of $28.9 million.

By 2005 revenues were up to $287 million and the company was reporting operating profits of $37.5 million. The buying had continued with the December 2005 acquisition of Beach & Company International LP for $500,000. In the same month, Lancaster Consulting LLC was purchased for $1.5 million.

LECG added California's BMB Mack Barclay, Inc., in May 2006. The price was about $13 million plus a potential $8.8 million in performance incentives. LECG retained the staff of the acquired company, though, as was the case with most of its acquisitions, it restyled the unit under its own brand. LECG ended 2006 with rapidly rising revenues of $353.9 million and a growing workforce of about 1,200 employees.

Continuing the acquisitions, LECG picked up The Secura Group LLC in 2007. Secura had been formed in 1986 by former Federal Deposit Insurance Corporation Chairman Bill Isaac and specialized in advising financial institutions. It had a staff of ten professionals based in Vienna, Virginia, and a Los Angeles branch office.

Frederick C. Ingram

PRINCIPAL SUBSIDIARIES

LECG, LLC; LECG Limited New Zealand; LECG Limited UK; LECG Canada Holding, Inc.; LECG Canada Ltd.; LECG Holding Company (UK) Ltd.; LECG Consulting France, SAS; LECG Consulting Spain, SL; LECG Consulting Belgium, NC; LECG Consulting Italy, SrL; Silicon Valley Expert Witness Group, Inc.

PRINCIPAL DIVISIONS

Antitrust & Competition; Bankruptcy; Claims Services; Electronic Discovery; Energy; Entertainment, Sports & Media; Environment & Insurance Claims; Finance & Damages; Financial Services; Forensic Accounting; Healthcare; Intellectual Property; International Arbitration; Labor & Employment; Life Sciences; Mergers & Acquisitions; Petroleum & Chemicals; Property Insurance Claims; Public Policy; Securities; Stock Options Backdating; Strategy & Performance Improvement; Telecommunications; Transfer Pricing; Transportation.

PRINCIPAL COMPETITORS

CRA International Inc.; Huron Consulting Group Inc.; FTI Consulting, Inc.; Navigant Consulting, Inc.; National Economic Research Associates, Inc.

FURTHER READING

Adler, Neil, "Secura Agrees to Sell to Calif. Advisory Firm," *Washington Business Journal,* March 15, 2007.

Anders, George, "An Economist's Courtroom Bonanza; Whether It's Motley Crue or Antitrust Law, Berkeley's David Teece Is Ready to Testify," *Wall Street Journal Online,* Page One Sec., March 19, 2007.

Bergh, Roeland Van den, "LWR Bidder an Academic Heavyweight," *Dominion* (New Zealand), June 10, 1999, p. 17.

"BIL Ready to Take Low Bid for LWR," *Christchurch Press,* June 9, 1999, p. 30.

Cole, Jim, "Emeryville's LECG Files for IPO," *East Bay Business Times,* August 25, 2003.

————, "LECG's IPO Riches," *East Bay Business Times,* June 25, 2004.

Fanelli, Christa, "Thoma Cressey Breaks Off LECG," *Buyouts,* November 6, 2000.

Gallagher, Dan, "LECG Jumps 23 Percent in IPO," *East Bay Business Times,* November 14, 2003.

Kraeuter, Chris, "Gaming the System," *Forbes.com,* May 31, 2006.

"LECG Buys Competitor for $4M," *San Francisco Business Times,* October 12, 2005.

"LECG Buys Firm for $13.2m," *East Bay Business Times,* May 8, 2006.

"LECG Corp.—XPRT: Complete Acq. of Economic Analysis LLC for $16.3 Million," *Knobias,* April 1, 2004.

"LECG Inc.," *Going Public: The IPO Reporter,* December 8, 1997.

"LECG Inc. Short Term Buy," *Emerging & Special Situations,* December 15, 1997, p. 19.

Marshall, Jonathan, "Group of UC Economists Hope to Cash in on IPO," *San Francisco Chronicle,* October 30, 1997, p. C1.

————, "Signing Up Laura Tyson; LECG Latest to Enlist Former Clinton Chief Economic Adviser," *San Francisco Chronicle,* April 26, 1997, p. D1.

McMorris, Frances A., "New Set of Companies Test IPOs This Week," *Daily Deal,* IPO Sec., November 11, 2003.

McMorris, Frances A., and David Carey, "Ashford Prices; LECG, Sirva File for Offerings," *Daily Deal,* IPO Sec., August 26, 2003.

"Metzler Group Closes Acquisition of LECG Inc.," *Dow Jones News Service,* August 20, 1998.

"Metzler to Buy LECG for $214 Mln," *Reuters News,* July 1, 1998.

Moreira, Peter, and Frances A. McMorris, "LECG Jumps in Debut," *Daily Deal,* IPO Sec., November 17, 2003.

Pfeffer, Jeffrey, "How to Hold on to Star Talent; Law Firms and Other Professional Services Outfits Are Often Victims of the Talent Drain. The Solution? Generosity," *Business 2.0,* July 12, 2006.

Rosenberg, Alec, "LECG's IPO Raises $127.5 Million," *Oakland (Calif.) Tribune,* November 15, 2003.

Leidy's, Inc.

266 Cherry Lane
Souderton, Pennsylvania 18964-0257
U.S.A.
Telephone: (215) 723-4606
Toll Free: (800) 222-2319
Fax: (215) 721-2003
Web site: http://www.leidys.com

Private Company
Incorporated: 1972
Employees: 270
Sales: $75.2 million (2007 est.)
NAIC: 311611 Animal (Except Poultry) Slaughtering, 311612 Meat Processed from Carcasses, 424470 Meat and Meat Product Merchant Wholesaling

■ ■ ■

Leidy's, Inc., partners with small family farms that are committed to raising hogs in a stress-free, humane environment with an all-natural diet. Its Nature's Tradition line of 100 percent natural pork products has no antibiotics or other additives and has been recognized by the American Humane Society with its Free-Farmed Certification. The company also makes and sells deli meats, as well as prepackaged pork products under the Cerico and Pennsylvania Farm Fresh labels. It distributes its items to small retail grocers in the northeastern and midwestern states. Processed products include bacon, boxed pork, cured sausage, fresh pork, fresh sausage, and ham, as well as other cured meats. The Leidy farm still stands on its original site, a Pennsylvania land grant awarded in 1753.

ENTERING THE AGRICULTURAL MARKETPLACE: THE EARLY YEARS

In 1893, Milton Leidy and his son, Olin, started butchering hogs and selling pork products to their neighbors in Montgomery County, Pennsylvania. Like many in the North Penn and Indian Valley areas of the Keystone state, Milton Leidy was a German immigrant. His family had arrived in the area in 1727, part of the wave of German families who settled in Pennsylvania beginning in the early 1700s. Theirs was a tight-knit community, bound together by its German farm heritage, Mennonite faith, and ties of business and marriage. After a railroad came through the state in the 1860s, many in the community began to transport their goods to Philadelphia to sell at the Philadelphia Farmers' Market in addition to door to door. The Leidys began selling vegetables from the family farm as well as meat at the market in Philadelphia during the summer.

Milton Leidy's early business was entirely a manual operation that he ran from the farmhouse his father, Thomas G. Leidy, had built in 1856 on land given the family as a land grant in 1753. The Leidys even scraped the hair off their hogs by hand. Yet "[Olin] didn't like the retail business much," Harold Leidy, Olin's son, told the *National Provisioner* in 1994. "The women customers did more picking over stuff than buying it. So Dad went on the road and picked up quite a few stores that started selling our products." Olin succeeded Milton

COMPANY PERSPECTIVES

Leidy's pork is *special.* Our ongoing dedication and uncompromising standards of quality from the hogs we breed and raise, to the traditional processing methods, ensure that our customers receive only the most tender and juicy natural pork.

Leidy as sole owner of Leidy's in 1925. Soon thereafter, he purchased a truck and began to sell the family's pork products, including sausage, scrapple, and bacon, wholesale to storeowners during the winter months.

MODERNIZING A FAMILY
BUSINESS: 1948–96

Harold Leidy joined the business during the 1940s as his father's partner at age 22, and, in 1948, Olin and Harold formed a partnership called O. M. Leidy & Son. Harold became sole proprietor of the business when Olin retired around 1960. At about the same time, Harold Leidy's sons, Tom and Terry Leidy, joined the family business; Tom Leidy came aboard in 1957 and Terry Leidy in 1962.

The company focused exclusively on meat processing and packing and abandoned the vegetable business. The Leidys bought better processing equipment and refrigerated trucks and renovated the family farmhouse. The 250-pound hogs that Leidy's slaughtered and processed were raised by local hog farmers with whom the company developed an ongoing supply relationship. In 1972, Leidy's renovated the family's old barn, transforming it into a modern kill floor. It added new curing, smoking, processing, and shipping facilities in 1975. The next year, Tom and Terry took the reins of the company when Harold retired.

During the 1980s, modernization continued as Leidy's improved its cut floor and finished its product area, smokehouse, and packaging area. Plant improvements continued into the mid-1990s. In 1990, the old barn was renovated to serve as company headquarters. In 1994, the company invested $50,000 to drill a new well so that it did not have to rely on expensive and chlorinated municipal water. In 1995, it began a series of improvements that would last for more than the next decade; it enhanced its hog pens, hog coolers, warehouse, and smoked meat areas. By 1996, it had doubled its square footage.

PRESERVATION AND GROWTH:
1994–2003

These renovations enabled Leidy's to expand its business. By 1994, the company's 180 employees were processing 775 hogs per day and selling a line of more than 30 fresh and processed pork products. Leidy's products were distributed daily to within 100 miles of the plant to small supermarkets in suburban Philadelphia, Washington, D.C., and New York City. The company had annual sales of $31 million and an annual growth rate of 4 percent.

After the plant improvements of the early 1990s, business soared. Between 1996 and 2003, Leidy's almost doubled its annual sales, reaching revenues of slightly upwards of $50 million. The company employed about 275 workers during this time and distributed its products to small, independent supermarket chains in Pennsylvania, New Jersey, New York, Delaware, Connecticut, and Maryland. When Andrew Leidy, son of Tom Leidy, became president of the company in the summer of 2003, the business was slaughtering 1,000 to 1,200 hogs daily.

Andrew Leidy had started working for the company making boxes when he was still in high school. Subsequently he worked in many other capacities. After high school, he earned a bachelor's degree in marketing from Philadelphia University, but did not decide to leave Leidy's. Rather, he felt called, he confided to the *Philadelphia Inquirer* in 2003, to take on the responsibility of carrying the family business and traditions forward. "You have that sense of history, sense of family, sense of roots."

NEW CHALLENGES IN THE
MODERN MARKETPLACE: 2001–06

Part of that commitment was to remain a meatpacker and not become a hog farmer. As a small business, Leidy's was challenged by such meat-packing giants as Smithfield Foods and IBP Inc. with their ability to integrate vertically. In the face of their competition, Leidy's had to ensure its steady supply of pork. Andrew Leidy's strategy was to develop closer relationships with hog farmers.

In so doing, Leidy faced the decision to invest more heavily in the family business. "You used to talk about spending for projects in hundreds of dollars, but now you have to spend in the millions," he explained in a 2001 *Philadelphia Inquirer* article. Part of this need arose as a result of increased regulation. Whereas once meatpackers had to deal with the U.S. Department of Agriculture, they now had to deal regularly with the Environmental Protection Agency, the Immigration and

KEY DATES

1727: Jacob Leidy arrives in Philadelphia from Germany.

1753: The Leidy farm is founded on a land grant from William Penn.

1856: Thomas G. Leidy builds a farmhouse, which still serves as Leidy's corporate headquarters.

1893: Milton Leidy and his young son, Olin, begin a retail farming operation.

1925: Olin succeeds Milton as sole owner of Leidy's operation.

1948: Olin forms a partnership with his son, Harold, called O.M. Leidy & Son.

1957: Tom Leidy joins the family business.

1962: Terry Leidy joins Leidy's.

1975: New curing, smoking, processing, and shipping areas are built.

1976: Harold Leidy retires; Tom and Terry Leidy assume control.

1990: The old farmhouse is renovated to serve as Leidy's corporate offices.

2003: Andrew Leidy, son of Tom Leidy, becomes president of the company.

2005: James B. Styer becomes president of Leidy's.

live in groups, as they would naturally, while preventing the dominant sows from eating more than their share and keeping those less dominant from getting enough to deliver a healthy litter. It was precisely this problem that had earlier led hog farmers to keep pregnant sows confined in crates, an arrangement that had come to be viewed as less than humane.

The new feeding systems cost about 10 percent more than the old industry standard, leading to an accompanying challenge: Leidy's needed to command a higher price for meat from animals that had more room in which to move around. Leidy's offered to pay some of the first farmers to adopt the more humane methods, and, by 2007, about 14 percent of the 5,800 hogs Leidy's processed each week came from sows that were allowed to wander during their pregnancy. The meat from the offspring of these free-ranging hogs was sold under the company's Nature's Tradition label and cost about $2 dollars per pound more than its comparable non-free-ranging pork.

As the first decade of the new century came to a close, Leidy's could be said to be reinventing itself once again. No longer strictly a family-managed business, Leidy's, which processed in the vicinity of 5,800 hogs each week, hoped to create a niche for itself in the growing "organic" meats market while continuing to produce its processed products.

Carrie Rothburd

Naturalization Service, and the Occupational Safety and Health Administration. This made it more difficult for small to midsized slaughterers to stay independent.

A mere two years after Andrew Leidy took the helm at Leidy's, James B. Styer succeeded him as president. Under Styer's leadership, Leidy's continued to prosper, although its annual revenues were a little uneven: $70 million in 2005, followed by $65 million in 2006.

REINVENTING LEIDY'S FOR THE ORGANIC MARKETPLACE: 2007

Then, in 2007, Leidy's joined with other pork producers in improving the living conditions for hogs in their care. The company worked with a professor at the University of Pennsylvania's New Bolton Center to install feeding systems that allowed their brood sows to

PRINCIPAL COMPETITORS

Hormel Foods Corporation; Smithfield Foods, Inc.; Tyson Fresh Meats, Inc.

FURTHER READING

"All in the Family: Trading on Tradition," *National Provisioner,* November 1994, p. 24.

Brady, Thomas J., and Harold Brubaker, "The Philadelphia Inquirer Business People Column," *Philadelphia Inquirer,* September 29, 2003.

Brubaker, Harold, "Farmyard Freedom; Food Producers Are Finding That Animals Allowed to Roam Can Bring Higher Prices," *Philadelphia Inquirer,* March 21, 2007, p. C1.

———, "Meatpacker Adapts Through Buyout," *Philadelphia Inquirer,* May 13, 2001, p. C 1.

LendingTree, LLC

———■———

11115 Rushmore Drive
Charlotte, North Carolina 28277
U.S.A.
Telephone: (704) 541-5351
Toll Free: (800) 555-8733
Fax: (704) 541-1824
Web site: http://www.lendingtree.com

Wholly Owned Subsidiary of IAC/InterActiveCorp
Incorporated: 1996 as Credit Source USA
Employees: 850
Sales: $428.8 million (2006)
NAIC: 812990 All Other Personal Services

■ ■ ■

LendingTree, LLC, is a Charlotte, North Carolina-based online lending and realty service exchange company. Users are able to complete a single online application for a mortgage, credit card, car loan, home equity loan, refinancing loan, personal loan, as well as access student loans and other commercial lending products. The company's services can also be accessed via a toll-free telephone number. Users then receive, at no cost, competing offers from a pool of about 200 lenders, including Bank of America, Chase, Citibank, PNC Bank, and Wachovia Mortgage Corporation, the company's true customers. LendingTree makes its money from fees related to the business that its sites generate for lenders. The company's family of brands also includes HomeLoanCenter.com, GetSmart.com,

LendingTree Loans, and LendingTree Settlement Services, LLC.

FOUNDER: AN ASPIRING ENTREPRENEUR AT AN EARLY AGE

LendingTree was the intellectual offspring of Douglas Robert Lebda. He was the son of Walter Robert Lebda, owner and president of Townecraft of Central Pennsylvania, marketer of cookware and china, as well as a real estate investor. The younger Lebda demonstrated an interest in business at a young age, retrieving golf balls with friends at night from a water hazard at Bucknell Golf Club, where he also caddied; during the daytime he would sell the balls at a discount to players, who in many cases promptly deposited them back in the water, where they waited once again to be fished out by the enterprising young man. As a high school student he also worked for his father during summers, hawking pots and pans over the telephone. Like his father, Lebda enrolled at Bucknell University in Lewisburg, graduating in 1992 with a degree in business administration. He then went to work for PricewaterhouseCoopers in Pittsburgh.

FRUSTRATION LEADS TO INSPIRATION FOR LENDINGTREE

After being joined by his girlfriend, Tara Garrity, a 1994 Bucknell graduate, Lebda attempted in 1995 to arrange a mortgage for a $60,000 condominium, a task that he assumed he could easily accomplish given his financial acumen. "Back when I was with Pricewaterhouse," Lebda recalled in a 2000 interview with *Business North Carolina,* "I was one of the first experts on derivatives. There I was, 24 years old, sought after to speak at industry conferences all over the country." Finding the best loan terms on a mortgage, however, proved more difficult than he had assumed, involving countless phone calls and taking three months to complete. Adding insult to it all, his lender, who had been delaying the process for weeks, at the 11th hour demanded that Lebda buy flood insurance. The condominium was located on Pittsburgh's Mount Washington, several hundred feet above the three rivers that intersected the city, making a nuclear holocaust a more likely problem than flood damage to the property.

If he was having problems arranging a mortgage, Lebda realized that the average person must have viewed the process as an utter nightmare. This insight inspired him to take advantage of the Internet to create a loan marketplace where instead of borrowers being at the mercy of lenders, the tables would be turned and the lenders would be forced to bid for borrowers. The service would operate like the trading market: "Essentially put out a request that says 'Here's what I'm looking to buy' and multiple players bid on that and I can use the best product that works for me," Lebda explained to *Mortgage Banking* in 2000.

In early 1996 Lebda contacted a Bucknell fraternity brother, James Bennett, Jr., about going into business together. Bennett had enjoyed success with a start-up Internet venture: In 1994 he launched BookWire, a business-to-business book publishing portal he had just sold to Cahners Publishing Co. In March 1996 Lebda and Bennett wrote checks for $1,500 and established their Internet-based loan referral service under the name Credit Source USA. The operation was little more than Lebda's apartment and a Mail Boxes Etc. address.

By this point, Lebda had been accepted to the M.B.A. program at the University of Virginia Darden School of Business. He resigned from Pricewaterhouse and during the three-month period before entering graduate school he tried to sign up banks to participate

with Credit Source USA. That fall, he and Garrity married and moved to Charlottesville, Virginia, where he attended classes in the morning while she researched potential customers in the business library, and in the afternoons he worked on Credit Source as well. He also ironed out the business model at school, pitching the concept to classmates in a competition for new business ideas. Lebda lost out to a student who wanted to open a new nightclub in Charlottesville.

After a year of effort, Lebda was starting to field interest from investors and potential customers, in particular National City Bank of Cleveland, and decided to forgo his second year of business school. He and Garrity looked for a city to serve as the company's home office, determined to avoid Silicon Valley. A weekend trip to Charlotte, North Carolina, was enough to convince them to move there. Not only did the area offer a pool of well-educated white-collar workers, it was home to Bank of America and First Union Bank, and in nearby Winston-Salem, Wachovia Bank maintained its headquarters.

LENDINGTREE GOES LIVE: 1998

By the fall of 1997 Lebda was able to raise $1 million in seed money and launched the Credit Source USA web site. In November 1997 he hired the company's fifth employee, Chief Technology Officer Rick Stiegler, a former Morgan Stanley vice-president, who revamped the architecture of the site and led to Credit Source USA being rebranded and incorporated as LendingTree in 1998. On July 1, 1998, LendingTree.com went online. Serving as CEO and chairman was chief financial backer Robert G. Wilson, a former Goldman Sachs partner who would hold these posts for the next year. By this time Bennett also joined the company full-time, serving as senior vice-president of strategy and corporate development, as did Tara Garrity Lebda, who headed lender relations until leaving to raise a family in June 2000 (also citing burnout as a reason for her departure).

LendingTree began operations in 1998 with only a handful of lenders and offered just five loan products. At the end of the year the company posted revenues of $409,000. The online lending field was already crowded by this point but LendingTree was able to gain credibility in the marketplace by selling its Lend-X application service provider technology developed by Stiegler. The company realized that banks were a natural customer for LendingTree's technology infrastructure and Wachovia became the first customer, going live in March 1999. By the end of 2000 Lend-X would be private-labeled to more than 20 financial institutions, but it was the addition of Freddie Mac (Federal Home

KEY DATES

1996: Company is founded as Credit Source USA.
1998: LendingTree.com is launched.
2000: Company goes public.
2002: Company turns first profit.
2003: IAC/InterActiveCorp acquires LendingTree.
2005: Founder Douglas Lebda leaves to become IAC president.
2007: IAC announces plan to spin off LendingTree.

Loan and Mortgage Corporation) as a Lend-X user that solidified LendingTree's reputation as a player to be taken seriously.

Revenues increased to $7 million in 1999 and by the end of the year LendingTree's roster of lenders numbered 94 and included many leading regional and national banks. The company was also winning over investors. After raising $15 million in two previous financing rounds, in September 1999 the company completed a third round, raising $50 million from Capital Z Financial Services Fund II L.P.; G.E. Capital; the Goldman Sachs Group Inc.; Marsh & McLennan Capital; and Priceline.com. Lebda was soon on a fourth round of funding, setting his sights on another $15 million, but was asked what would it actually take to establish LendingTree as the dominant player in the market and to accelerate growth. After some consideration, he returned to investors, this time asking for $50 million while presenting a plan to take the company public. The company filed for its initial public offering (IPO) of stock on December 1, 1999, with Merrill Lynch serving as lead underwriter.

TAKEN PUBLIC: 2000

As LendingTree prepared for its IPO, it gained greater visibility by launching a new advertising campaign in January 2000, featuring the highly successful tagline, "When banks compete, you win!" Management then began its roadshow to convince investors that the company's marketplace business model differentiated it from competitors who were either lenders or referral sites. Given that the mortgage industry was in flux at the time, with the Commerce Department reporting a two-year low in new home sales, and companies generally lumped together with LendingTree, like E-Loan Inc. and Mortgage.com Inc., were seeing their stocks hammered, differentiation was clearly in order. LendingTree bolstered its case further when two weeks before the

IPO was to be conducted it invested in LoanTrader Inc., a wholesale lending company that connected lenders and brokers. As a result, brokers were for the first time brought into the equation for LendingTree, a move that demonstrated to potential investors that LendingTree was not content to remain idle in a competitive landscape. When the IPO was completed in mid-February 2000, LendingTree netted $43.8 million.

LendingTree shares had been priced at $12 and quickly rose above $20 but in a matter of weeks dipped below $4 and settled around $6 as the stock market suffered through a difficult stretch and Internet-related stocks were hit especially hard. LendingTree had more than its share of critics, who maintained that it was on the verge of joining a multitude of other dot-com companies in the dustbin. Nevertheless, LendingTree hung on and continued to grow. In August 2000, with backing from Capital Z. Financial Services Fund, the company was able to make its first acquisition, buying the assets of HomeSpace Services Inc., an online real estate e-commerce company, for $12 million. The deal included a national network of 7,000 real estate agents as well as alliances with Delta Airlines and Costco Wholesale club, representing significant new lines of revenue.

LendingTree posted sales of $30.8 million in 2000. That amount more than doubled in 2001 to $64 million. Moreover, the number of loans closed increased by 160 percent to $12.1 billion, making LendingTree the top site for consumers seeking competitive loans. Over the course of the year 31 lenders were brought into the fold, increasing the number of participants to 145. Taking advantage of low interest rates and a refinancing boom, LendingTree saw revenues improve another 74 percent in 2002 to more than $111 million and for the first time in its history LendingTree recorded a profit on the year, netting $5 million, after losing $32 million the previous year. The company also laid the ground for even greater growth as it expanded LendingTree Realty Services Exchange, adding 2,500 new real estate agents during the year, leading to $1 billion worth of closed real estate transactions in 2002.

ACQUISITION BY IAC: 2003

With its stock price soaring in 2003, LendingTree was rumored to be a highly attractive takeover target. Eager to be on a more secure financial footing, Lebda decided in 2003 to sell the company to USA Interactive (later renamed IAC/InterActiveCorp), headed by media baron Barry Diller who was assembling a collection of Internet-based businesses. The stock swap was valued as high as $734 million. Lebda and his management team stayed on and soon dipped into Diller's deep pockets to make acquisitions to expand LendingTree further. In 2003 RealEstate.com was acquired along with GetSmart. com. The latter had a similar business model and brought with it new customers and technology that LendingTree was able to incorporate into its own system.

More acquisitions followed in 2004. LendingTree picked up Domania.com, provider of customer acquisition and retention services to the banking, real estate, and mortgage industries. Online mortgage lender HomeLoanCenter.com was purchased, representing LendingTree's first venture in the direct lending business. In November 2004 LendingTree acquired iNest, a new-home builder referral network that was folded into RealEstate.com. The year 2004 was also marked by tragedy. In March, Rick Stiegler had died suddenly at the age of 47.

In 2005 Lebda left the company that he founded, tapped by Diller to become president of the parent company, IAC. Replacing him as LendingTree's CEO was the head of RealEstate.com, Tom Reddin. In Lebda's new role, he would also oversee other ventures, including Home Shopping Network, Ticketmaster, and Match.com. He left LendingTree as it was on its way to growing revenues 131 percent to $367.8 million in 2005. Revenues continued to grow in 2006, albeit at a slower rate, improving 17 percent to $428.8 million. LendingTree's services were used by 20 million customers, resulting in $152 billion in closed loan transactions.

The year 2007 was a time of flux for LendingTree, as it was indeed for the mortgage industry, hard hit by a slump in the housing market, high interest rates, and a deterioration in the number of mortgages issued. On the one hand, the company launched its High Yield Savings Account marketplace, on the other it had to contend with the departure of Reddin, who elected to leave the company for personal reasons in April 2007. A month later, LendingTree laid off one-fifth of its workforce, about 440 jobs, due to poor market conditions. LendingTree was soon able to fill the vacancy at the top post, naming C. D. Davies, a former Wachovia Corp. mortgage head, as its new CEO. More turmoil was in store for the company, however. A second round of layoffs ensued, and in mid-December a third round eliminated another 220 positions. Moreover, a month

earlier IAC announced that it planned to spin off four companies to focus on its core web businesses. One of those businesses to be set free as a public company was LendingTree.

Ed Dinger

PRINCIPAL SUBSIDIARIES

LendingTree Loans; HomeLoanCenter.com; GetSmart. com; LendingTree Settlement Services, LLC.

PRINCIPAL COMPETITORS

Countrywide Financial Corporation; ditech.com; Wells Fargo Home Mortgage.

FURTHER READING

Bergquist, Erick, "LendingTree Has Survived—But Now Will It Prosper?" *American Banker,* May 10, 2001, p. 1.

Birger, Jon, "New Executive: Jamey Bennett," *Crain's New York Business,* June 29, 1998, p. 15.

Choe, Stan, "LendingTree to Be Sold," *Charlotte Observer,* May 6, 2003, p. 1A.

"Doug Lebda," *Triangle Business Journal,* June 23, 2000, p. 6A.

Downey, John, "Lending Tree Prepares to Branch Out," *Business Journal Serving Charlotte and the Metropolitan Area,* February 4, 2000, p. 3.

"Marketing Strategies: Web Loan Marketer to Launch Ad Campaign," *Financial Net News,* December 8, 1997.

Martin, Edward, "Nursery Stock," *Business North Carolina,* November 2000, p. 26.

Milligan, Jack, "A House-Hold Name," *Mortgage Banking,* May 2004, p. 22.

Rothacker, Rick, "Lending Site Lays Off 20% of Its Staff," *Charlotte Observer,* May 12, 2007, p. 1D.

———, "LendingTree Grafts First New Limb," *Charlotte Observer,* August 3, 2000, p. 1D.

———, "Spin Off Ahead for Loan Web Site," *Charlotte Observer,* November 6, 2007, p. 1D.

Sacirbey, Omar, "LendingTree's IPO Mantra: Stick to the Map," *IPO Reporter,* February 28, 2000.

Schiavone, Louis L., "LendingTree.com," *Mortgage Banking,* December 2000, p. 24.

Loews Corporation

667 Madison Avenue
New York, New York 10021-8087
U.S.A.
Telephone: (212) 521-2000
Fax: (212) 521-2525
Web site: http://www.loews.com

Public Company
Incorporated: 1969
Employees: 21,600
Sales: $17.91 billion (2006)
Total Assets: $76.88 billion (2006)
Stock Exchanges: New York
Ticker Symbol: LTR
NAIC: 551112 Offices of Other Holding Companies;
524126 Direct Property and Casualty Insurance
Carriers; 312221 Cigarette Manufacturing; 213111
Drilling Oil and Gas Wells; 486210 Pipeline
Transportation of Natural Gas; 211111 Crude
Petroleum and Natural Gas Extraction; 721110
Hotels (Except Casino Hotels) and Motels

∎ ∎ ∎

Loews Corporation is a holding company with diversified interests in insurance, tobacco, the energy industry,
hotels, and watches. Run from the post–World War
II era to the late 1990s by brothers Preston Robert
(Bob) and Laurence (Larry) Tisch, the company was
amassed through "value investing." The Tisches earned a
reputation for purchasing troubled firms, making them
profitable, and selling them at a premium. Bob
was known for his operational savvy, while elder brother
Larry was considered the financial genius. In the
early 21st century, Loews remained in the control of
the Tisch families, who held more than 20 percent
of the firm's publicly traded stock. Two sons of
Larry, James and Andrew Tisch, and a son of Bob,
Jonathan Tisch, began running the company in the late
1990s.

Among Loews' major holdings is an 89 percent
stake in the publicly traded CNA Financial Corporation, one of the largest property and casualty insurance
companies in the United States; CNA contributes
roughly 58 percent of Loews' revenues. Another 22
percent of revenues is derived from the wholly owned
Lorillard, Inc., the oldest and third largest U.S. cigarette
maker and the producer of such brands as Newport,
Kent, and True; late in 2007, however, Loews announced plans to spin off Lorillard. Loews derives
around 12 percent of its revenues from its 51 percent
stake in the publicly traded Diamond Offshore Drilling,
Inc., one of the world's leading contract drillers of
offshore oil and gas wells. Other energy holdings include
a 70 percent interest in the publicly traded Boardwalk
Pipeline Partners, LP, operator of interstate natural gas
pipeline systems, and full ownership of HighMount
Exploration & Production LLC, a firm engaged in the
exploration and production of natural gas in the United
States. Another wholly owned subsidiary is Loews
Hotels Holding Corporation, operator of 18 hotels and
resorts in the United States and Canada.

EARLY INVOLVEMENT IN HOTELS

The Tisch brothers received an early business education from their father, Al, who owned a manufacturing plant in Manhattan. Bob and Larry were given the task of making phone sales to retail stores and wholesale distributors. The two brothers also helped operate a few summer camps their parents owned in New Jersey. This "hands-on" experience was coupled with formal training. After a brief hiatus spent in the army, Bob graduated with a degree in economics from the University of Michigan in 1948. Larry graduated cum laude from New York University's School of Commerce at the age of 18, went on to earn an M.B.A. from the Wharton School in Philadelphia, and later enrolled in Harvard University's law school.

In 1946 Al and Sadye Tisch sold their summer camps and purchased the Laurel-in-the-Pines Hotel in Lakewood, New Jersey. The hotel business went well, and soon became more than the parents could handle alone. Larry dropped out of Harvard in order to help run the business and Bob soon followed. It was not long before the older couple decided to sign over their share of the hotel (worth about $75,000 at the time) to their sons and give them control of the operation.

The brothers soon began leasing two other small New Jersey hotels and managed to turn a profit. Then, in 1952, they acquired two grand but old hotels in Atlantic City called the Brighton and the Ambassador. They demolished one to build a motel in its place, and quickly resold the other at a profit. Later, the Tisches liquidated some of their New Jersey investments to purchase their first two hotels in New York City. These early transactions established the pattern that would

characterize their later business dealings, which grew increasingly diverse and valuable.

In 1956, with only eight years' experience in the business, Bob and Larry erected the $17 million Americana Hotel in Bal Harbour, Florida, and paid for it in cash. Although it was subsequently sold to Sheraton in the 1970s, it represented an important step in the brothers' careers. With the Americana, they firmly established themselves among the major hotel operators, and later acquired such prominent hotels in the United States as the Mark Hopkins, the Drake, the Belmont Plaza, and the Regency.

ADDING THEATERS (1960) AND TOBACCO (1968)

In 1959 a major antitrust ruling forced Metro-Goldwyn-Mayer (MGM) to relinquish ownership of Loew's Theaters. This decision created an opportunity for the Tisch brothers, allowing them to move into a new business area. Six months before MGM was to divest Loew's, Bob and Larry purchased a large stake in the theater chain; by May 1960 they had gained control of the company.

The brothers did not enter into the theater business because they knew about the motion picture industry, nor did they purchase Loew's because it was already a profitable operation on its own. On the contrary, Loew's theaters were losing money. They were large, multitiered movie houses with high ceilings and interiors reminiscent of the industry's "golden age," by this time long past. They played only one motion picture at a time and were rarely filled to capacity. Television and the proliferation of films coming out of Hollywood meant that theaters would have to cater to various tastes simultaneously in order to secure larger audiences. The old Loew's theaters were not designed for this purpose.

The reason Bob and Larry Tisch purchased Loew's had to do with real estate. The Loew's theaters, although antiquated, were located on valuable city property. It was the opportunity to acquire this valuable property that prompted the brothers to purchase the company. Almost immediately they began liquidating the theaters, demolishing 50 of them in a matter of months and then selling the vacant lots to developers. This, of course, hastened the demise of the palatial movie house, but it was nonetheless a necessary business tactic. Loew's remained a prominent participant in the movie industry into the early 1980s.

The long-established and well-recognized Loews name became the corporate title under which all Tisch operations (including hotels) were placed. Loews Corporation, a holding company formed in 1969, ran

KEY DATES

1956: Tisch brothers erect the Americana Hotel in Bal Harbour, Florida, establishing themselves as major hotel operators.

1960: Tisch brothers gain control of Loew's Theaters (the apostrophe is later dropped from the corporate name).

1968: Tisch brothers acquire Lorillard, the oldest U.S. tobacco manufacturer.

1969: Tisch brothers create a holding company, Loews Corporation, for their diversified interests.

1974: Loews acquires CNA Financial Corporation.

1979: Company purchases a majority stake in Bulova Watch Co.

1985: Movie theaters are divested and a 25 percent stake in CBS is purchased, with Larry Tisch becoming president.

1990: Company acquires Houston drilling firm Diamond M Offshore.

1992: Odeco Drilling is acquired.

1993: Diamond M and Odeco are merged to form Diamond Offshore Drilling, Inc.

1994: CNA acquires Continental Corporation.

1995: Loews engineers the sale of CBS to Westinghouse, with Loews gaining nearly $900 million from the sale; Loews takes Diamond Offshore public.

1998: Tisch brothers step down as co-CEOs; James Tisch is promoted to president and CEO. Lorillard and other tobacco firms reach $206 billion settlement with 46 states over tobacco-related health costs.

2002: New management team at CNA begins an overhaul that eventually repositions the firm as primarily a commercial property and casualty insurer.

2003: Loews enters the natural gas pipeline business via the acquisition of Texas Gas Transmission, LLC.

2005: Company takes its pipeline subsidiary, Boardwalk Pipeline Partners, LP, public.

2007: Loews spends $4 billion for an array of U.S. natural gas exploration and production assets that form the basis for the new subsidiary HighMount Exploration & Production LLC; company announces its intention to spin Lorillard off as a separate, publicly traded company.

2008: Loews sells Bulova to Citizen Watch Co., Ltd.

smoothly and efficiently, turning substantial profits every year. By 1968 the brothers again had the capital and the inclination to diversify and invest in a new business sector. This time they acquired Lorillard Industries, the nation's oldest tobacco manufacturer.

Lorillard, the maker of Kent and Newport cigarettes, had once been a major company with a large share of the tobacco market. Managerial incompetence and discord, however, had paralyzed the company, bringing it near collapse. Upon assuming control of Lorillard, the first thing Larry Tisch did was examine the firm's subsidiaries, particularly its candy and cat food divisions, which were consuming a disproportionate amount of resources. The brothers discovered that the top executives spent 75 percent of their time on candy and cat food, which together made up only 5 percent of Lorillard's total business. Lorillard divested itself of these interests and of the executives who were so fond of them, then redirected the company toward its tobacco operations. Market share slippage was reversed, and Lo-

rillard climbed back to the top ranks of the U.S. tobacco market.

ACQUISITIONS OF CNA (1974) AND BULOVA (1979)

A similar scenario took place in 1974, when Loews acquired CNA Financial Corporation, a large insurance firm. The Chicago-based conglomerate had reported a $208 million deficit that year and was expected to lose more. Like Lorillard, its subsidiaries were draining the financial resources of the company. CNA's tangential interests were poorly managed and veritable "money pits." Moreover, there was considerable waste at the top of CNA's corporate structure.

When Loews took charge it divested unprofitable or distractive subsidiaries to concentrate on the worthwhile core businesses. The Tisch brothers then took aim at the wastefulness that plagued CNA's headquarters. Many executives were fired as Tisch austerity measures prevailed over past CNA lavishness. The 3,000-square-foot suite of the former chairman was rented out, as was the corporate dining room. The streamlining had a dramatic and positive effect. In 1975 CNA earned a $110 million profit, and remained financially sound over the next decade, achieving annual revenues of over $3 billion by the late 1980s.

Loews' next major turnaround target was the Bulova Watch Co. In 1979 the Tisch brothers bought 93 percent of the then-troubled firm for $38 million. At the time, Bulova's quality-control problems had contributed to its slip from the top of the watch market to the number two spot. Not only had longtime rival Seiko Corporation won the market share battle, but Bulova was also threatened by Timex Enterprises Inc.'s introduction of competitively priced entries. It looked to some observers as if Bulova had squandered its brand cachet; the name was simply not recognized by a new generation of consumers.

The Tisch brothers applied their proven method of managerial restructuring, but without total success. Bulova's problems went beyond personnel and corporate networks: the product itself needed to be revised. James Tisch, Larry's son, headed the operation and immediately introduced 600 new watch styles, complete with extended warranties. To deal with the image problem, an extensive advertising campaign was launched. The company recovered, albeit slowly. By 1984 it had cut its losses to $8 million (roughly half of its 1980 total), yet it was still not paying for itself. The company did not turn a profit until 1986. That year, Bob Tisch accepted an appointment as U.S. Postmaster General. Despite the concerns of those who felt his absence would weaken the company's performance, most analysts contended that Bob Tisch's move to Washington, D.C., would help Loews, citing the advantages of both political and financial connections.

INVESTMENT IN CBS

Late in 1985 Larry Tisch sold the company's namesake movie theaters and purchased a significant amount of CBS Inc. stock to help the company fight a takeover attempt by Ted Turner. Throughout 1986 Tisch increased Loews' holdings in CBS to 24.8 percent and obtained a seat on the board of directors. He was elected president of CBS that September, much to the relief of stockholders and employees, who had grown frustrated and uneasy during the Turner takeover attempt.

Tisch's popularity was short-lived, however. Intending to operate CBS as if it were any other business, he took measures to alleviate waste and make CBS more cost-effective. Wage cuts and spending reductions, along with wholesale firings, caused a serious rift in the huge

broadcasting firm. The news division, traditionally given considerable leeway in regard to fiscal accountability, was especially hard hit. Some wondered if Tisch would be able to mend CBS without sacrificing the people and principles that once made it the most respected of the three major American broadcasting networks. Eventually, Loews reduced its investment in CBS to 18 percent through sale of stock back to the company.

Bob Tisch's activities and interests outside Loews garnered attention as well. He was one of New York City's most vocal supporters and had been elected over 15 times to the chairmanship of New York's Convention and Visitors Bureau. In fact it was Bob Tisch and the bureau's president, Charles Grillett, who came up with the idea of using an old jazz expression, the "big apple," to signify New York City. Later, Bob would represent the metropolis as its "official ambassador" (read lobbyist) in Washington, D.C. In 1990 he accepted the chairmanship of that city's chamber of commerce. In 1991 Bob Tisch paid over $75 million to acquire half of the New York Giants professional football team.

ENTRANCE INTO OFFSHORE DRILLING

Over the course of the 1980s, the Tisches had reduced their stake in Loews from 45 percent to 24 percent, prompting some analysts to speculate that they were preparing to dismantle their conglomerate. Instead, the company, which had amassed a $1.75 billion "war chest," started investing in new ventures, most notably oil. By 1990 Loews had spent $75 million on oil rigs and acquired Diamond M Offshore Inc., a Houston, Texas, drilling company. Loews amassed the world's largest fleet of offshore drilling rigs with the 1992 purchase of Odeco Drilling, Inc., which was merged with Diamond M in 1993 to form Diamond Offshore Drilling, Inc. In spite of that status, Loews' drilling segment lost over $103 million in 1992, 1993, and 1994. The company's annual report for the latter year blamed regional overcapacity and reduced demand for the negative results.

While other large hotel companies struggled in the early 1990s, Loews Hotels thrived under the direction of Jonathan Mark Tisch, son of Bob Tisch. Jonathan Tisch was praised for creative, ambitious, and often philanthropic promotions. His annual "Monopoly Power Breakfasts" featured celebrity contestants who played the famous Parker Brothers game competing on a customized board. Proceeds of the event went to charities. The upscale hotel chain's "Good Neighbor Policy" and its recycling programs earned it industry accolades as well. Following an industry-wide trend, Loews

Hotels lost $1.79 million in 1993, then reported a net profit of $17.02 million in 1994.

The Tisches continued to apply their turnaround strategies to Bulova in the early 1990s. In 1995 they completed the divestment of that subsidiary's defense interests in order to concentrate on the core timepiece business. Although sales and profits declined as a result, Bulova was able to stay in the black in the early 1990s.

Loews' two largest investment areas, cigarettes and insurance, were very vulnerable in the early 1990s. Price wars prompted Lorillard to launch a bargain cigarette brand, Style, in 1992, then cut the retail price of its flagship Newport brand 25 percent in 1994. In the decidedly antismoking climate that predominated, cigarette manufacturers already faced with legislation that banned smoking from virtually all public places also encountered many lawsuits. As of fiscal year 1994, Lorillard was a named defendant in 17 individual and class-action suits brought by cigarette smokers, their estates and heirs, and even flight attendants who claimed to be victims of secondhand smoke.

When Loews subsidiary CNA Financial acquired Continental Corporation in December 1994 for $1.1 billion, it became the third largest property and casualty insurer in the United States. It also took on Continental's liabilities regarding Fibreboard Corporation, a company that manufactured asbestos insulation products from 1928 to 1971. In 1993 Continental and its codefendants reached a $2 billion settlement (of which Continental was responsible for $1.44 billion) to cover past and potential liabilities.

EXIT FROM CBS

Another key divestment came in 1995, when Loews engineered the sale of CBS to Westinghouse Electric Corporation for $5.4 billion. This ended Larry Tisch's controversial reign at CBS, and Loews' share of the proceeds amounted to nearly $900 million, swelling the company's coffers. In late 1995, Loews took Diamond Offshore public, selling about 30 percent of the company in an offering that raised $300 million.

Titular changes in the early 1990s seemed to indicate preparations for a changing of the guard at Loews. In the late 1980s, Bob had occupied the positions of president and chief operating officer, while Larry acted as chairman and CEO. Yet as the two brothers became septuagenarians, they consolidated their responsibilities, becoming cochairmen and co-CEOs. James S. Tisch, son of Larry and a likely successor, advanced to president and chief operating officer, while Andrew H. Tisch, another son of Larry, led Lorillard.

In late 1995 Lorillard agreed to buy six discount cigarette brands from B.A.T. Industries PLC for about $33 million, but in April 1996 the Federal Trade Commission rejected the deal on antitrust grounds. Loews Hotel, meantime, entered into a joint venture with MCA Inc. in 1996 to develop three themed luxury hotels in Orlando, Florida, as part of MCA's expansion of its Universal Studios Florida theme park. The first, the Portofino Bay Hotel, opened in the fall of 1999 with 750 rooms. This property aimed to replicate the famous Italian seaside village of Portofino. The Hard Rock Hotel opened in January 2001 and the Royal Pacific in June 2002. After helping to develop the hotels, Loews Hotels managed the properties under a contract arrangement. With the travel industry enjoying a resurgence in the economic boom time of the late 1990s, Loews Hotels moved ahead with other expansion plans as well. The company returned to Miami in 1998 with the opening of the Loews Miami Beach Hotel, an 800-room property in the Art Deco district of Miami Beach. In early 2000 the 590-room Loews Philadelphia Hotel was opened near the downtown convention center, and Loews Hotels also purchased the Coronado Bay Resort hotel in San Diego, California.

SUCCESSION TO NEW TISCH GENERATION

In 1997 Loews lost more than $900 million on a pretax basis from its $70 billion securities portfolio as a result of the bearish Larry Tisch's short-selling strategies against the long-running bull market. Net income as a result fell to $793.6 million from the $1.38 billion figure of the previous year. Late in 1998 the succession from one Tisch generation to another came to fruition. The Tisch brothers stepped down from their co-CEO positions but remained cochairmen. James Tisch was promoted to president and CEO. In addition, an office of the president was formed consisting of James Tisch, Andrew Tisch, who also held the title of chairman of the executive committee, and Jonathan, who also continued to serve as president and CEO of Loews Hotels.

The new leadership at Loews faced many challenges, not the least of which was the increasing level of litigation and regulation facing Lorillard. The settlement costs from tobacco-related suits began to reach significant levels in 1997, when Lorillard paid out $122 million. Payments then escalated to $346.5 million the following year. Late in 1998 Lorillard and the other major tobacco companies reached a $206 billion settlement with 46 states for the reimbursement of public healthcare costs associated with smoking. Settlements with other states totaled another $48 billion. Lorillard took pretax charges of $579 million and $1.07 billion in 1998 and 1999, respectively, in connection with the settlements, the payments for which were to continue into the 2020s. In September 1999 the U.S. Justice Department filed a massive lawsuit against the major tobacco makers, modeled after the state lawsuits, with a potential industry liability well in excess of the state settlement.

Individual and class-action lawsuits continued as well, with Lorillard a defendant in no fewer than 825 cases as of the end of 1999. The most important of these was a class-action lawsuit filed in Florida, *Engle v. R.J. Reynolds Tobacco Co., et al.* The *Engle* trial began in October 1998, with a jury returning a verdict against the defendants in July 1999, finding that cigarette smoking is addictive and causes lung cancer, and that the tobacco companies had engaged in "extreme and outrageous conduct" in concealing the dangers of smoking from the public. The penalty phase of the trial then commenced. In April 2000 the jury awarded $12.7 million in compensatory damages to three sample plaintiffs, but then three months later delivered a potentially huge blow to the industry when it awarded $144.9 billion in punitive damages, by far the largest punitive damage award in U.S. history, dwarfing the $5 billion awarded in a suit against Exxon Corporation in connection with the *Exxon Valdez* oil spill. Lorillard's share was $16.25 billion. The tobacco companies immediately vowed to appeal, a process destined to last years. In the meantime, Lorillard and the other tobacco firms had been able to manage the increasing litigation payments simply by raising cigarette prices.

TURNAROUND EFFORTS AT CNA

Meanwhile, with the insurance market slumping and earnings down, CNA was undergoing a restructuring. In 1998 the company cut its workforce by 2,400, consolidated some processing centers, and exited from certain areas, such as entertainment and agriculture insurance. In October 1999 CNA sold its personal lines insurance business, which included automobile and homeowners insurance, to the Allstate Corporation. In early 2000 CNA put its life insurance and life reinsurance units on the block but in August of that year announced that it would keep them.

CNA's struggles continued. In 2001 the company was forced to boost its claims reserves by $2 billion, in part to cover asbestos-related claims as well as to cover shortfalls in the amounts set aside for various liability policies, including commercial auto and medical malpractice. In addition, CNA was responsible for around $470 million in claims related to the destruction of the World Trade Center during the September 11, 2001, terrorist attacks on the United States. Late in

2001 CNA launched a restructuring to streamline its property-casualty and life insurance operations that involved the elimination of 1,850 jobs, while at the same time moving to discontinue its variable life and annuity business. A charge of $125 million was booked in connection with this restructuring. CNA consequently posted a net loss of more than $1.6 billion for 2001, which pushed Loews into the red as well, to the extent of a $589.1 million loss.

To further prop up CNA, Loews pumped an additional $1.75 billion into the company. In 2002 Loews installed a new management team led by CEO Stephen W. Lilienthal to completely overhaul CNA. By 2004 CNA had repositioned itself as primarily a commercial property and casualty insurer having jettisoned its life, group, reinsurance, and trust businesses. The effort to clean up the aftermath of poor underwriting practices in the 1990s continued as CNA had to increase its reserves by an additional $1.8 billion in 2003. Once again, the red ink at CNA spilled over to Loews, as the latter suffered a net loss of $610.7 million that year. By 2006, however, CNA appeared to have turned a corner, posting its strongest results ever, including record net income of $1.11 billion.

END OF TOBACCO ROAD,
FURTHER ENERGY VENTURES

In the meantime, on the tobacco front, Loews in early 2002 created a tracking stock called Carolina Group that was intended to reflect the performance of its Lorillard subsidiary. An initial public offering (IPO) of Carolina Group stock raised $1.1 billion, but Loews nonetheless retained full ownership of Lorillard. The litigation picture for U.S. tobacco brightened the following year when a Florida appeals court vacated the $144.9 billion *Engle* judgment and ordered the decertification of the class involved in the case. This ruling was upheld by the Florida Supreme Court in 2006. Rulings had also come down on the side of the tobacco companies in regard to the Justice Department's lawsuit, which appeared to negate another major threat. By 2007 Lorillard remained a defendant in roughly 2,900 cigarette-related product-liability lawsuits. Loews, however, had plans to extricate itself from the tobacco field. In December 2007 the company announced its intention to spin off Lorillard as a separate, publicly traded company in mid-2008.

When Larry Tisch died in November 2003, Bob Tisch became sole chairman, a position he held until his own death almost two years later. At that point, Andrew and Jonathan Tisch were named cochairmen, with James Tisch remaining president and CEO. This leadership troika pushed Loews further into the energy field, building on the Diamond Offshore business that the previous Tisch generation had created.

In May 2003 Loews acquired Texas Gas Transmission, LLC (TGT), from the Williams Companies, Inc., for $795 million in cash plus the assumption of $250 million in debt. TGT owned and operated a 5,800-mile natural gas pipeline and storage system originating in Louisiana and Texas and extending to markets in the South and the Midwest. Then in December 2004 Loews more than doubled its natural gas pipeline assets by acquiring Gulf South Pipeline, LP from Entergy-Koch, LP for $1.14 billion. Gulf South's assets included 8,000 miles of natural gas pipeline in the U.S. Gulf Coast region, making for a complementary fit with the TGT system. Loews created a new subsidiary called Boardwalk Pipeline Partners, LP for its pipeline operations, and it took this subsidiary public in November 2005 through an IPO of 14.5 percent of Boardwalk's shares. Most of the $271.4 million in net proceeds was used to pay down Boardwalk's debt.

Loews plunged even deeper into energy in July 2007 with its acquisition of an array of natural gas exploration and production assets from Dominion Resources, Inc., for $4 billion. The assets included properties in the Permian Basin in Texas, the Antrim Shale in Michigan, and the Black Warrior Basin in Alabama with proven reserves of natural gas and natural gas liquids of approximately 2.5 trillion cubic feet of gas equivalent. These assets formed the basis for a new Loews subsidiary called HighMount Exploration & Production LLC. Several months later, in January 2008, Loews offloaded the smallest of its subsidiaries, Bulova, selling it to the Japanese watchmaker Citizen Watch Co., Ltd., for $250 million. With one divestment complete and another (Lorillard) pending, Loews was posed to narrow its holdings to the property and casualty insurance operations of CNA, its various energy interests, and Loews Hotels.

April Dougal Gasbarre
Updated, David E. Salamie

PRINCIPAL SUBSIDIARIES

CNA Financial Corporation (89%); Lorillard, Inc.; Boardwalk Pipeline Partners, LP (70%); Diamond Offshore Drilling, Inc. (51%); HighMount Exploration & Production LLC; Loews Hotels Holding Corporation.

PRINCIPAL COMPETITORS

American International Group, Inc.; American Financial Group, Inc.; The Travelers Companies, Inc.; Berkshire Hathaway, Inc.; The Allstate Corporation; Prudential Financial, Inc.; MetLife, Inc.

FURTHER READING

Ahlberg, Erik, "Loews to Buy Gulf South Pipeline from Entergy-Koch for $1.14 Billion," *Wall Street Journal*, November 23, 2004, p. B3.

Bary, Andrew, "A New Leaf?: Loews' Neglected Stock Could Jump if Tobacco Unit Is Spun Off," *Barron's*, November 30, 1998, pp. 23–24.

———, "Smoking Out Value at Loews," *Barron's*, December 31, 2007, p. 16.

———, "Sweet 'n' Loews," *Barron's*, December 30, 2002, pp. 22–23.

Bender, Marylin, "Loews and Its 'Mutual Fund,'" *New York Times*, February 18, 1973, p. 205.

Brooker, Katrina, "Like Father, Like Son," *Fortune*, June 28, 2004, p. 110–12+

Browning, E. S., "Tisches Got Stampeded by Bull Run," *Wall Street Journal*, August 15, 1997, p. C1.

Campoy, Ana, "Loews Ventures Deeper into Oil and Gas Territory," *Wall Street Journal*, June 5, 2007, p. A10.

Carrns, Ann, "Loews Hotels: The Road Less Traveled," *Wall Street Journal*, May 21, 1997, p. B14.

"Citizen Will Buy Bulova for $250 Million," *Jewelers Circular Keystone*, November 1, 2007, p. 34.

Cochran, Thomas N., "Something for Everyone," *Barron's*, April 17, 1989, p. 40.

Cole, Robert J., "Loews Wants All of Bulova," *New York Times*, January 20, 1979, p. 27.

Dodds, Lynn Strongin, "Nothing to Fear," *Financial World*, September 30, 1986, p. 100.

Fabrikant, Geraldine, "CBS Accepts Bid by Westinghouse," *New York Times*, August 2, 1995, p. A1.

———, "Loews Executives Facing Some Difficult Choices," *New York Times*, November 18, 2003, pp. C1, C11.

Fairclough, Gordon, and Milo Geyelin, "Tobacco Companies Rail Against Verdict, Plan to Appeal $144.87 Billion Award," *Wall Street Journal*, July 17, 2000, pp. A3, A6.

Geyelin, Milo, and Gordon Fairclough, "Taking a Hit: Yes, $145 Billion Deals Tobacco a Huge Blow, but Not a Killing One," *Wall Street Journal*, July 17, 2000, pp. A1, A8.

Hager, Bruce, "Loews Sees the Future, and It's Oil," *Business Week*, March 19, 1990, pp. 126–27.

———, "Tisch the Younger Takes His Turn," *Business Week*, July 8, 1991, pp. 88–89.

Hamilton, Martha M., "Loews Corp. Hits a Gusher: Firm's Investment in Drilling Rigs Pays Off Big in Newly Thriving Gulf of Mexico," *Washington Post*, November 21, 1996, p. D1.

Jensen, Elizabeth, "Sharp Contrast: Why Did ABC Prosper While CBS Blinked?" *Wall Street Journal*, August 2, 1995, p. A1.

Kadlec, Daniel, "Tisch's Bad Bet," *Time,* November 30, 1998, p. 130.

Lesly, Elizabeth, "Loews Could Be Worth More Dead Than Alive," *Business Week,* December 13, 1993, pp. 104–7.

Lohse, Deborah, "Loews Announces Succession in Tisch Family," *Wall Street Journal,* November 5, 1998, p. A4.

Louviere, Vernon, "Running a Conglomerate Like a Candy Store," *Nation's Business,* August 1981, pp. 46+.

O'Connell, Vanessa, "Florida Appeals Court Overturns $145 Billion Tobacco Judgment," *Wall Street Journal,* May 22, 2003, p. A3.

O'Connell, Vanessa, Donna Kardos, and Anjali Cordeiro, "Loews Plans to Spin Off Lorillard," *Wall Street Journal,* December 18, 2007, p. A15.

Ozanian, Michael, "America's Most Undervalued Stock," *Financial World,* May 29, 1990, pp. 22–24.

Pesmen, Sandra, "Jonathan Tisch's Road Show," *Business Marketing,* February 1991, pp. 68–70.

Rosenberg, Hilary, "Like Fathers, Like Sons: As the Generations Shift, the Loews Style Remains," *New York Times,* May 30, 1999, p. BU1.

Rudolph, Barbara, "All in the Family Fortune: The Loews Chairman Made Billions As a Savvy Manager and Investor," *Time,* September 22, 1986, pp. 74+.

Sheridan, Mike, "Rather Than REIT, Tisch Sets Loews Hotels on New-Development Track," *Hotel Strategies,* June 1999, pp. 8–9.

Smith, Randall, "For Tisch Empire, It Looks Like It's Back to the Basics," *Wall Street Journal,* August 2, 1995, p. C1.

Sparks, Debra, "Tisch: The Ultimate Bear," *Business Week,* June 8, 1998, p. 112.

Winans, Christopher, *The King of Cash: The Inside Story of Laurence Tisch,* New York: Wiley, 1995, 288 p.

Lush Ltd.

Unit 3, 19 Willis Way
Poole, BH15 3SS
United Kingdom
Telephone: (+44 01202) 668545
Fax: (+44 01202) 493785
Web site: http://www.lush.co.uk

Private Company
Incorporated: 1995
Employees: 1,450
Sales: £145 million ($275 million) (2007 est.)
NAIC: 325620 Toilet Preparation Manufacturing; 325611 Soap and Other Detergent Manufacturing; 453998 All Other Miscellaneous Store Retailers (Except Tobacco Stores); 454113 Mail-Order Houses

■ ■ ■

Lush Ltd. is a Poole, England-based producer and distributor of soaps, shampoos, cosmetics, and related items. Lush calls itself a "vegetarian" company; the company refuses to use animal byproducts in its formulations. Some 70 percent of the group's products are even labeled as "vegan," containing no milk, honey, beeswax, lanolin, or related ingredients. Much of the company's range of products feature fresh fruits and vegetables and other fresh ingredients, limiting their shelf life. While some products do contain synthetic ingredients, primarily preservatives, the company has long been a leader in the campaign against animal testing. As such, Lush tests its products only on human volunteers. The company also limits the amount of packaging it uses by producing its soaps and shampoos in solid form. All of Lush's products are manufactured in its five production facilities, based in Poole. The company also distributes its own products, through a chain of more than 450 stores across 46 countries. While the company oversees its U.K. network, its international operations are generally conducted in partnership with a local franchise holder. In addition, Lush operates a second, more upscale retail format, B Never Too Busy To Be Beautiful. That chain of three U.K.-based stores features more traditional cosmetics and skin care and beauty care items. Lush is led by husband-and-wife team and cofounders Mark and Mo Constantine.

BACKING THE BODY SHOP IN 1978

Born in Sutton, Surrey, in 1952, Mark Constantine developed an interest in cosmetics at an early age. By the time he was 14, he had begun doing the makeup for local theater groups "to get girls," as he told the *Daily Telegraph*. Constantine went on to train at the Institute of Trichology, where he learned how to create his own haircare formulations. Constantine started work at a local hairdresser. Before long he was hired to work at the Elizabeth Arden salon in London.

Constantine met his wife and future business partner, Mo, when they were both 17 years old. Over the next several years, Constantine began experimenting with his own soap and shampoo formulations. For this, Constantine, a self-described "hippy," turned to the

COMPANY PERSPECTIVES

A Lush Life. We believe ... in making effective products from fresh organic fruit and vegetables, the finest essential oils and safe synthetics. We believe in buying ingredients only from companies that do not commission tests on animals and in testing our products on humans. We invent our own products and fragrances. We make them fresh by hand using little or no preservative or packaging, using only vegetarian ingredients and tell you when they were made. We believe in happy people making happy soap, putting our faces on our products and making our mums proud. We believe in long candlelit baths, sharing showers, massage, filling the world with perfume and in the right to make mistakes, lose everything and start again. We believe our products are good value, that we should make a profit and that the customer is always right.

natural and fresh ingredients that were to become the foundation of his later success. In 1976, the couple joined with a friend, Elizabeth Weir, to form their own company, called Constantine & Weir.

The company's big break came just one year later. The Constantines had come across an article about a new and highly unusual shop called The Body Shop. In the article, the store's creator, Anita Roddick, announced that she was seeking suppliers for the store's bath care, hair and skin care, and cosmetics products. Constantine drove over to Roddick's shop with samples of his own formulations. Roddick promptly placed an order with Constantine & Weir for more than £1,600 of products.

The Body Shop garnered headlines and a strong customer following over the next several years, becoming one of Great Britain's retail success stories, and Constantine & Weir's part in that success was considerable. Indeed, by the mid-1980s, the company was responsible for creating and producing more than 70 percent of The Body Shop's product line. As Constantine told the *Observer:* "We made pretty much all their products. Peppermint foot lotion, that was me." Other "iconic" Body Shop products created by Constantine & Weir included a strawberry body shampoo and henna hair colorings. If The Body Shop sold the products, the rights to the formulations nonetheless remained held by Constantine & Weir.

MAIL-ORDER FLOP IN THE NINETIES

Constantine & Weir remained the quiet force behind The Body Shop's product development through that company's public offering in 1984. The listing changed the relationship between the two companies. As Constantine acknowledged: "When they went public nobody fully appreciated that they did not own the rights, we did. So they had to stop us in a way."

With The Body Shop beginning to develop more of its own products, Constantine & Weir recognized that the company would soon require a new outlet for its formulations. In 1988, the company launched a new enterprise, a mail-order business called Cosmetics To Go.

Cosmetics To Go grew strongly from the start and by the early 1990s boasted a customer list of more than one million. When The Body Shop at last insisted on buying the rights to Constantine & Weir's formulations, the company agreed. The deal was for £9 million, payable in three installments. The Constantines also agreed to a non-compete clause that barred them from opening their own retail shops for the next three years.

Yet Constantine quickly discovered that there was a great difference between running a manufacturing business and operating as a direct distributor. Constantine's biggest error was to price the company's products too low, in part because he had not figured in the backroom costs of operating the mail-order end of the business. As a result, the company lost money on every item it sold. At the same time, the company was confronted with the notoriously poor service of the British Post Office of the time. Meantime, the non-compete clause crippled the company. As Constantine told *New Business Magazine:* "[A]greeing not to open shops was a mistake we should never have made. We'd have been better off with no money and opening shops."

The breaking point came in 1993. The company ran a special promotion and found itself swamped with more than 130,000 orders, just when a water leak destroyed its computer system. By then, the company had gone through the first two installments of The Body Shop's payments. The company was forced to declare bankruptcy. To add insult to injury, the company's creditors claimed the final installment from The Body Shop.

LUSH START IN 1994

The collapse of his business haunted Constantine. As he admitted to *New Business Magazine:* "It was horrific. I felt ashamed and that I had let a lot of people down.

KEY DATES

1976: Mark and Mo Constantine and Elizabeth Weir found wholesale soaps and cosmetics company Constantine & Weir.

1977: Company begins supplying The Body Shop, growing into that company's main supplier of soaps and cosmetic products.

1988: Company founds Cosmetics-to-Go mail-order firm.

1991: Company agrees to buyout of intellectual property rights by The Body Shop.

1993: Cosmetics-to-Go goes bankrupt.

1994: Cosmetics House store opens in Poole; the business is renamed Lush.

1996: First international Lush store opens in Vancouver.

1999: Retail network tops 70 stores worldwide, including stores in Australia, Japan, Croatia, Sweden, and Singapore.

2001: Lush launches takeover offer for The Body Shop.

2003: Company creates second retail format, B Never Too Busy To Be Beautiful.

2007: Lush announces plans to double worldwide retail network to 1,000 stores.

My confidence took a huge hit." Yet Constantine's family, friends, and even customers encouraged him to try again. Backed by most of his original creative team, Constantine agreed. For the new business, Constantine decided to focus on developing a line of preservative-free soaps and lotions using fresh ingredients. In 1994, he launched a new company, called Cosmetics House, based from a single store in the town of Poole.

Cosmetics House at first struggled for survival. With no production equipment, the company was forced to mix its formulations using household appliances and plastic tubs. Ingredients were purchased at the local supermarket. However, Constantine had learned an important lesson from the debacle, that he needed a proper financial team to back up his creative efforts. As Constantine told *Forbes:* "I never wanted to be in the dark again without the proper finance guys. You have to have a little muscle behind you."

Constantine soon found not only a business angel, but a financial partner. Constantine's new company had come to the attention of Peter Blacker and his finance director, Andrew Gerrie. Blacker, the highly successful founder of British Ensign Estates, was seeking a vehicle that would allow him to take advantage of a generous capital gains tax break offered by the then-Conservative government. Gerrie was sent to meet with Constantine, and stayed on as the company's finance director. Together with Blacker, Gerrie invested more than £125,000, acquiring a 23 percent stake in the company.

LAUNCHING LUSH IN 1995

The company recognized that it needed a more evocative name. One of the company's customers suggested the name "Lush," and a new high street phenomenon was born. Lush developed a highly distinctive retail format, creating an interior that resembled as much a delicatessen as a traditional retail shop. In keeping with the company's ethics, packaging was kept to a minimum. Most of the products sold in the store were displayed with no packaging at all. Customers served themselves, and their purchases were wrapped in ordinary butcher paper by the cashiers. The lack of packaging provided an unexpected side effect: the store was highly fragrant. Indeed, the store's mix of fragrances could be smelled all along Poole's High Street.

Blacker in the meantime had been scouting for new locations for the Lush retail format. Blacker encouraged the company to aim high for its first expansion. Instead of choosing to build the company slowly in less expensive markets, the company went straight to the heart of London. In October 1995, the company opened stores in Covent Garden and on King's Road, Chelsea.

The new stores were immediate successes, and by the end of that year the company's sales topped £1 million ($1.5 million). The company quickly announced plans for further expansion, including the opening of another four London locations. The company also set up a new mail-order business. In order to fund further expansion, the company brought in new shareholders. For this, Gerrie established a separate retail subsidiary, rather than in the parent company itself. In this way, Lush raised an additional £500 million in funding while keeping its debt to a minimum.

BUILDING A GLOBAL FOOTPRINT

Lush quickly attracted the attention of the British press. Before long, the company found itself flooded with requests to open Lush franchises. The company initially refused these requests, preferring to focus on their own operations. In 1996, however, the company was approached by Mark Wolverton, part of Wolverton Securities in Canada, to open a Lush shop in Vancouver.

Wolverton had put together an investment team, complete with business plan, and won the company over. The Canadian group quickly opened its first two shops.

The company set up a dedicated office to review those requests in order to choose candidates most likely to fit with the company's highly ethical, vegetarian focus. At the same time, Gerrie's financial expertise allowed the company to maintain control of its growing network of stores by creating and selling minority stakes in regional subsidiaries. In Canada, for example, Lush's stake remained at 53 percent.

By 1998, the company had expanded into Sweden, Australia, and even Croatia, joining with local partners for each new market. The company's growth was remarkable. From 20 stores at the beginning of 1998, the company's network jumped to 70 by the end of 1999. By then, the company had added Japan, Italy, Brazil, and Singapore to its list of markets.

Lush also remained highly profitable. This was in large part due to the fact that in the cosmetics industry, the largest part of a company's expense typically went into its product packaging and marketing operations. Yet Lush did not use packaging for the most part. At the same time, the company avoided advertising. Instead, the company relied on word-of-mouth, including the growing number of celebrities using its products.

By 2001, Lush's success led Constantine to launch a buyout offer for The Body Shop, which struggled as it entered the new century. The Roddicks refused Constantine's offer, however, and in 2006 instead sold to L'Oréal.

Undaunted, Lush continued to build its own global operations. By 2003, the company had nearly 250 stores, including 46 in the United Kingdom and its first stores in the United States. In that year, also, the company launched a new retail format, called B Never Too Busy To Be Beautiful. The first B Never store opened that year, followed by two others by mid-decade. The new format featured a more upscale range of cosmetics especially perfumes and other fragrances developed by Constantine.

Yet Lush remained the company main focus as it shifted into high gear at the middle of the decade. By the end of 2007, the company's retail network approached 500 stores. By then the company was present in more than 45 countries, posting total revenues of £145 million. Backed by a solid organization, the latest Constantine venture was also his greatest. Lush appeared only at the beginning of its growth, announcing plans to expand its global network to 1,000 stores or more in the new century.

M. L. Cohen

PRINCIPAL SUBSIDIARIES

Lush North America Inc.

PRINCIPAL COMPETITORS

The Procter & Gamble Company; Cit Group Inc.; Johnson & Johnson; L'Oréal SA; Colgate-Palmolive Co.; Alliance Boots plc; Unilever; Rhodia S.A.

FURTHER READING

Donald, Caroline, "You're Not Supposed to Eat the Pineapple Grunt: You're Supposed to Wear It," *Independent,* March 23, 1996, p. 6.

Eade, Christine, "Scents of Direction," *Property Week,* October 1, 2004, p. 80.

Fallon, James, and Tsukasa Furukawa, "A Fresh Approach: Preservative Free," *WWD,* December 1, 1995, p. 8.

Lacey, Hester, "From Bath Bombs to Birdsong," *Independent on Sunday,* February 11, 2007, p. 22.

Matthews, Imogen, "The Dish on Lush: How Sweet It Is!" *Household & Personal Products Industry,* October 2003, p. 47.

Murray-West, Rosie, "Bouncing Bath Bombs Incoming!" *Daily Telegraph,* May 6, 2006, p. 35.

Nagel, Andrea, "Lush Said Eyeing The Body Shop," *WWD,* February 28, 2006, p. 16.

Ryle, Sarah, "Mammon: Cosmetic Surgeon on the High Street," *Observer,* December 5, 2004, p. 16.

Tether, David, "Lush Couple with a Shed Load of Ideas," *Guardian,* April 13, 2007, p. 27.

Metro International S.A.

11, Boulevard Royal L-2449
Luxembourg
Web site: http://www.metro.lu

Public Company
Incorporated: 1995
Employees: 1,500
Sales: $416.5 million (2006)
Stock Exchanges: Stockholm Bourse de Luxembourg
Ticker Symbol: MTROSDBB.ST
NAIC: 511110 Newspaper Publishers

■ ■ ■

Metro International S.A. is one of the world's leading newspaper publishers. The Luxembourg-based company controls the *Metro* chain of free dailies, producing more than 70 editions in 23 countries worldwide. The company distributes more than eight million copies each day, and claims a daily global readership of over 23 million. Its distribution model, primarily through mass transit systems, assures it one of the youngest readerships in the world. Nearly 75 percent of the company's readers are under the age of 50, and more than 40 percent fall within the elusive and advertiser-coveted 18- to 35-year-old segment. *Metro* also claims a female readership of more than 50 percent, as opposed to just 15 percent for mainstream "paid" newspapers. As a publisher of free dailies, Metro generates all of its revenues through sales of advertisements. These typically account for 40 percent of the content of an average *Metro*. In 2006, the company's sales topped $416.5

million. In that year, the company posted its first annual profit since its founding in 1995. Major stockholders include former parent Modern Times Group, and its parent, the Swedish industrial and investment giant AB Kinnevik. Per Mikael Jensen was named CEO of Metro International in 2007.

NEWSPAPER REVOLUTIONARY IN 1995

Metro was the brainchild of three Maoist-oriented Swedes, Pers Anders Anderson, Robert Braunerhielm, and Monica Anderson. In the early 1990s, the trio had developed an idea to launch a free daily newspaper and went in search of financial backers for the project. The search proved difficult, however.

Their fortunes changed when the idea of a free daily attracted the attention of Pelle Tornberg, then in charge of AB Kinnevik's growing television operations. Tornberg had been studying the idea of extending the group's media operations into the newspaper publisher market. Yet Tornberg was discouraged by the Swedish newspaper market's poor climate. As he told *Business Week:* "Newspaper readership had been declining for many years, and the typical reader was more than 50 years old. The advertising demographics were terrible."

Tornberg quickly recognized the potential of giving away the newspaper, and attracting a younger, more active readership. The restructuring of AB Kinnevik provided the opportunity to pursue the idea. In 1995, Kinnevik spun off its media operations into a new company, the Modern Times Group. Led by Jan Sten-

COMPANY PERSPECTIVES

Metropolitans lead the way. Every morning, in over 100 major cities across the world, millions of industrious metropolitans take to the streets, buses and trains on their way to work. They are young, well networked trend-setters, cash-rich but time-poor, with healthy media appetites and perpetually shifting tastes. With its unbiased views, engaging features and simple design, Metro has been the preferred source of morning news for metropolitans since its launch in early 1995; and it comes for free!

beck, the Modern Times Group agreed to back the launch of the free daily, called *Metro.* The name captured the company's targeted distribution channel—Stockholm's mass transit system.

The first edition of *Metro* appeared in 1995. The launch of the new newspaper was greeted by a great deal of criticism and skepticism from the outset. Media critics complained about the newspaper's digest format, which featured condensed articles, generally drawn from wire services. *Metro* also avoided taking up any political position, and adopted a no-editorial policy. While many in the industry remained skeptical that a free newspaper would be able to operate at a profit, the traditional newspaper sector greeted the new title with alarm.

The Stockholm edition soon proved the skeptics wrong. By the end of its first year, *Metro* had become profitable. The new daily was able to attract a strong advertiser base. This was particularly true among smaller local firms eager to tap into the newspaper's relatively young and affluent readership. In this way, *Metro* provided advertisers with access to a market that typically eschewed traditional paid newspapers. Indeed, far from draining readership from Stockholm's other newspapers, *Metro* claimed to have the effect of increasing interest in newspaper readership on a general level.

BUILDING A CHAIN

Tornberg, who became CEO of the Metro operations, also recognized the possibility of developing a full-fledged chain of *Metro*-formatted newspapers. The company's first extension came overseas, with the launch of a *Metro* edition in Prague in 1997. The success of that launch encouraged the company to begin preparations for a wider rollout of the *Metro* title, starting with Budapest and Göteborg in 1998. The following year, the

company added a new *Metro* for the Malmo market, as well as editions for Helsinki and for the metropolitan region of the Netherlands. Metro's operations outside of the Nordic region were placed into a dedicated subsidiary, MTG Publishing AB, created in 1996.

The Modern Times Group had, in the meantime, begun acquiring other publishing interests. These included a major stake in Sweden's *Finanstidningen* business daily and the monthly business magazine *Kapital.* Yet Modern Times Group's expansion targeted especially its media holdings, including television stations. As such, the company began preparations for the spinoff of its free daily operations. The first step toward this came in 1999 with the incorporation of a new holding company, Metro International. That company was registered in Luxembourg and took over all of the Metro operations. The following year, the Modern Times Group spun off Metro International as an independent, publicly listed company.

Metro launched a number of new editions in 2000, including in Milan, Rome, Warsaw, Athens, and Poland. In that year, the company added its first editions outside of Europe, targeting Santiago, Chile, and Toronto. The year 2000 also marked the company's entry into the United States, with the launch of its Philadelphia edition.

The company's expansion efforts were not without their difficulties. Its entry into the United States faced opposition from a number of major newspapers, including *USA Today,* the *Philadelphia Inquirer,* and the *New York Times.* Metro's rivals countered the company's entry plans with lawsuits challenging the right to distribute newspapers at mass transit locations. Metro's slow start in New York City in the meantime allowed others, and notably the Tribune Company, to beat the company to the punch with their own free dailies.

Metro's high-speed expansion drive also brought its own financial burdens. The company remained unprofitable, in part because of the high debt load required to fuel its expansion. At the same time, not all of the group's international editions proved viable. Such was the case with its Zürich edition, launched in 2000. That edition failed to achieve the group's requirement that each edition achieve profitability within three years of its launch. By 2002, the Zürich edition was shut down.

COMPETING AGAINST ITS IMITATORS

Metro also lost the race to enter some of Europe's most important newspaper markets. In the United Kingdom, for example, Associated Newspapers, publisher of the *Evening Standard,* rushed its own free daily to the market. Worse for Metro International, the new London newspaper was called *Metro.* The latter's strong success with British commuters presented Metro International with a major obstacle for its plans to enter the United Kingdom.

Metro also failed to find a formula for an entry into Germany. In France, the company faced widely held protests by that country's newspaper unions for its planned entry. The company pushed ahead with its Paris edition, only to suffer a new setback when members of the French unions broke into its distribution center. The Paris edition finally debuted in 2002.

Yet the company was faced with stiffening competition as a number of new rivals appeared. Chief among these was Norway's Schibsted and its free daily, *20 Minutes.* The success of *20 Minutes* in Zürich was largely responsible for Metro's pullout from that market. The more elaborate *20 Minutes* format also proved highly popular with French and Spanish commuters, forcing Metro to adapt its own format for these markets.

While doing battle with its imitators, Metro also continued adding new markets. In 2001, the company added editions in Boston, Copenhagen, Barcelona, and Madrid. The following year, the company added editions in Marseille and Lyon in France, as well as in Aarhus, Sweden, and moved into the Far East with Hong Kong and Seoul editions.

MOVING TOWARD PROFITABILITY

The year 2003 saw the continued rollout of the *Metro* "chain," with editions in La Coruña, Pusan, Zaragoza, and Seville. The following year, Metro added new editions in Bordeaux, Lille, and Toulouse in France, as well as in Valencia, Lisbon, and Alicante. By the end of that year, Metro had added its New York City edition as well. By then, *Metro* had grown into the world's fourth largest newspaper, by circulation.

The company continued to face financial troubles, however. Metro was forced to turn to major shareholder Kinnevik for a capital injection of $16 million in 2003. In 2005, the company raised an additional $16.5 million through the sale of 49 percent of its Boston edition to the *New York Times.* The added capital served only to fuel the company's continued expansion, as it neared its goal of 70 editions, for a total of 100 cities, across 20 countries. New locations for the company in 2005 included editions for three new French cities, Rennes, Strasbourg, and Nantes. The company also teamed up with CanWest and Torstar to fill out its Canadian presence, adding editions for Vancouver and Ottawa. Metro and Torstar later bought out CanWest in 2007.

By the middle of the first decade of the 2000s, Metro had made progress toward becoming profitable as well. At the end of 2006, the company celebrated its first full year of profits, posting $13 million on sales of $416 million. Metro was forced to remain on its guard, however, as the financial health of a number of its editions remained quite fragile. Indeed, by 2007 the company had been forced to shut down its Polish edition. Despite the launch of its first Brazilian edition, in São Paulo, that year, Metro's financial picture once again appeared bleak. In November 2007, the company announced a third-quarter loss of nearly $33 million.

Part of Metro's difficulties were linked to the poor economic climate. In the United States, for example, the credit crisis resulted in a significant drop in advertising spending. At the same time, Metro continued to lose out to rivals in a number of key markets, particularly in France. The company continued to be hurt by its absence from the U.K. and German markets, as well.

Nonetheless, the company remained optimistic. New CEO Per Mikael Jensen, formerly Metro's global editor-in-chief, took over from Pelle Tornberg in November 2007. Jensen promised to revisit the format of a number of *Metro* editions, seeking better to tailor the daily to specific local markets. The company also appeared to be making headway in its ability to attract advertisers seeking to develop pan-regional marketing campaigns. Among its major clients the company included Nokia, Microsoft, Canon, and British Airways. With a readership of more than 23 million each day,

Metro had revolutionized the global newspaper market in the new century.

M. L. Cohen

PRINCIPAL SUBSIDIARIES

Clarita B.V. (Netherlands); Edizione Metro Sarl (Italy); Everyday Distribution AB (Sweden); Metro Ceska Republika a.s. (Czech Republic); Metro Holdings Inc. (U.S.A.); Metro Holland B.V. (Netherlands); Metro International Luxembourg Holdings S.A.; Metro International UK Ltd.; Metro International AB (Sweden); Metro Nordic Sweden AB; Metro Publication (Schweiz) AG (Switzerland); Metro Sweden Holding AB; Metro Xpress Denmark A.S. (Denmark); Metronews S.L. (Spain); Metrorama Publishing Ltd. (Greece); MTG Metro Gratis Kft (Hungary); OY Metro Lehti Ab (Finland); Publication Metro France S.A.S.; Rally Television AB (Sweden); TidningsAB Metro (Sweden); Tiempos Modernos S.A. (Chile); TPP Sp.zo. o. (Poland); Transjornal Edição de Publicações SA (Portugal).

FURTHER READING

"CEO of Global Free-Paper Publisher Metro International Stepping Down," *Editor & Publisher,* February 13, 2007.

Fishbein, Jennifer, "Free Dailies King Dethroned?" *Business Week Online,* October 25, 2007.

———, "Free Papers, Costly Competition," *Business Week,* November 19, 2007, p. 94.

Hjelt, Paola, "What's Black, Green and Read All Over," *Fortune International,* June 28, 2004, p. 16.

Johnson, Branwell, "Free Press Empire Goes on Offensive," *Marketing Week,* November 27, 2003, p. 14.

Levine, Joshua, "Paper Tiger," *Forbes,* April 29, 2002, p. 64.

"Media Lifeline: Metro International," *Campaign,* November 2, 2007, p. 15.

"Metro International Edges Towards the Black," *Campaign,* August 19, 2005, p. 13.

Orr, Deborah, "Business Biscotti," *Forbes Global,* February 17, 2003, p. 20.

"Pelle Tornberg, President and Chief Executive, Metro International, Sweden," *Business Week,* June 7, 2004.

Smith, Adam, Ulla Plon, Jonathan Shenfield, and Jane Walker, "The Rise of the Free Press," *Time International,* May 23, 2005, p. 44.

"Will Afternoon Freesheet Work?" *Campaign,* April 2006, p. 8.

Motorola, Inc.

———■———

1303 East Algonquin Road
Schaumburg, Illinois 60196
U.S.A.
Telephone: (847) 576-5000
Toll Free: (800) 262-8509
Fax: (847) 576-5372
Web site: http://www.motorola.com

Public Company
Incorporated: 1928 as Galvin Manufacturing Corporation
Employees: 66,000
Sales: $42.88 billion (2006)
Stock Exchanges: New York
Ticker Symbol: MOT
NAIC: 517212 Cellular and Other Wireless Telecommunications; 334210 Telephone Apparatus Manufacturing; 541519 Other Computer Related Services; 517910 Other Telecommunications; 334119 Other Computer Peripheral Equipment Manufacturing

■ ■ ■

Electronic communications pioneer Motorola, Inc., is the world's number two maker of mobile phones (trailing Nokia Corporation), with a market share of about 17 percent. The company also is a leading supplier of such wireless infrastructure equipment as cellular transmission base stations, amplifiers, and servers. Its remaining operations focus on three business segments: enterprise mobility solutions; mobile devices; and home and networks mobility. These produce cordless phones, two-way radios, pagers, cable modems, broadband set-top boxes, and other communications products and systems for the automotive, computer, industrial, transportation, navigation, energy, consumer, and lighting markets.

ORIGINS IN RADIO TECHNOLOGY

The story of Motorola is that of a U.S. classic. It begins during the 1920s, when a small-town Illinois boy, Paul Galvin, went to Chicago to seek his fortune. Galvin had returned from World War I with an interest in the technological changes of the time. In 1920 he worked for a Chicago storage-battery company, and one year later he opened his own storage-battery company with a hometown friend, Edward Stewart. After two years of rocky operations, the government closed the business for nonpayment of excise taxes.

The former partners, undaunted by this setback, joined forces again three years later when Galvin bought an interest in Stewart's new storage-battery company. Yet with the rise of electric power, batteries lost popularity with the public. To keep their business afloat, Stewart created a device that allowed a radio to be plugged into an ordinary wall outlet, aptly named the "battery eliminator." Once again, the storage-battery company failed, although Galvin was able to buy back the eliminators at the company's public auction. Joe Galvin joined his brother Paul at this time to peddle the eliminators to various retail distributors, such as Sears, Roebuck and Company. In 1928 Paul formed the

Galvin Manufacturing Corporation with five employees and $565, and continued making battery eliminators.

During the Great Depression, Galvin Manufacturing Corporation found itself burdened by inventory that it could not sell because of restricted market conditions and underselling by other manufacturers. To rectify this situation, Galvin began experimenting with the virtually untouched automobile-radio market. Before this time, automobile radios had been deemed impractical because they had very poor reception. The first commercially successful car radio came out of Galvin Manufacturing in 1930 under the brand name Motorola. The name, coined by Galvin, was a hybrid of "motor" and "victrola." The units sold for about $120 including accessories and installation, which compared favorably with the $200 to $300 custom-designed units then available.

During the 1930s the company also established its first chain of distributorships (Authorized Motorola Installation Stations), began advertising its products in newspapers and on highway billboards, and started to research radios to receive only police broadcasts. The market for police radios appeared so promising that the company formed a police radio department. In 1937 Galvin Manufacturing entered the home-radio market, introducing the first push-button tuning features.

In 1936, after a tour of Europe with his family, Galvin returned home convinced that war was imminent. Knowing that war could provide new opportunities, he directed the company's research into areas he felt could be useful to the military. The Handie-Talkie two-way radio and its offspring, the Walkie-Talkie, resulted. Used by the U.S. Army Signal Corps, these were among the most important pieces of communications equipment used in World War II.

Galvin was always concerned with the welfare of his employees, and in 1947 he instituted a very liberal profit-sharing program that was used as a model by other companies. By this time, the company employed around 5,000 people and had formed an early human relations department. The company's good labor relations enabled it to remain nonunion throughout its history. After Galvin's son Robert and Daniel Noble, an engineer who would eventually have a tremendous impact on the future of the company, joined the company in 1947, its name was officially changed to Motorola, Inc.

The first Motorola television was introduced that same year. It was more compact and less expensive than any competing models: Motorola charged $180, while its nearest competitor charged more than $300. The Motorola "Golden View" set became so popular that within months of its introduction the company was the fourth largest seller of televisions in the nation.

Later in 1947, Motorola bought Detrola, a failing automobile-radio company that had manufactured car radios for the Ford Motor Company. The purchase was made on the condition that Motorola retain Detrola's contract with Ford. This deal greatly strengthened the company's automobile-radio business. Motorola subsequently supplied 50 percent of the car radios for Ford and Chrysler as well as all of the radios for American Motors.

POSTWAR SHIFT OF EMPHASIS TO ELECTRONICS

The creation of the transistor in 1948 by Bell Laboratories marked a major turning point for Motorola. The company had concentrated on the manufacture of consumer products, and Paul Galvin felt that the company was unequipped to enter the transistor and diode field. With Galvin's son Robert and Dan Noble advocating the company's expansion into this new market, however, Motorola formed a semiconductor development group. The first product to result from this effort was a three-amp power transistor, and later a semiconductor plant was constructed in Arizona. Following this expansion, Motorola supplied transistors to other companies for use in products that Motorola also manufactured. In effect, Motorola found itself in the awkward position of supplying its competitors with parts.

During the 1950s, Motorola became involved in the Columbia Broadcasting System's failed entry into the color television industry. Motorola used the CBS-designed and produced color tubes in its color television sets. After a convoluted struggle for approval from the Federal Communications Commission (FCC), the CBS system was rejected in favor of a system developed by the Radio Corporation of America (RCA). Despite this setback, Motorola pioneered many new features in television technology, including a technique for reducing

KEY DATES

1928: Paul Galvin forms Galvin Manufacturing Corporation, initially making "battery eliminators."

1930: Company introduces the first commercially successful car radio under the brand name Motorola.

1947: Company institutes a profit-sharing program, introduces its first television, and changes its name to Motorola, Inc.

1956: Robert Galvin, son of Paul, takes over company leadership upon the death of his father.

1974: Motorola sells its consumer products division, including Quasar television; unveils its first microprocessor, the 6800; and launches an innovative employee training and involvement program.

1977: Codex Corporation, a data communications company, is acquired.

1978: Universal Data Systems is acquired.

1982: Company acquires Four-Phase Systems, Inc., a maker of computers and terminals and a software designer.

1983: Company makes its last car radio; Motorola's first cellular telephone network begins commercial operation.

1988: Motorola is awarded the first annual Malcolm Baldrige National Quality Award; George Fisher succeeds Galvin as CEO.

1993: Gary L. Tooker takes over as CEO.

1997: Christopher Galvin, son of Robert, is named CEO.

1998: Motorola undergoes major restructurings, creating a new divisional organization, consolidating operations, cutting the workforce by about 10 percent, and taking a $1.95 billion charge.

1999: The $5 billion Iridium satellite phone venture enters bankruptcy protection; a portion of the Semiconductor Components Group spins off as ON Semiconductor.

2000: Company completes acquisition of General Instrument Corporation, the leading maker of broadband set-top boxes, in a $17 billion stock swap; Mike S. Zafirovski becomes head of the wireless phone division.

2001: Edward D. Breen becomes president and COO.

2002: Zafirovski replaces Breen as president and COO.

2003: Motorola spins off the remainder of its semiconductor business as publicly traded SPS Spinco Inc.

2004: Ed Zander replaces Galvin as CEO.

2007: Motorola acquires Leapstone Systems and Symbol Technology.

---

the number of tubes in black-and-white sets from 41 to 19.

DECENTRALIZED MANAGEMENT AND INTERNATIONAL EXPANSION

By the middle of the decade, Paul Galvin realized that the company had become too large for one man to continue making all the decisions. He granted divisional status to various businesses, giving each its own engineering, purchasing, manufacturing, and marketing departments and regarding each as an individual profit center. This was the beginning of Motorola's famous decentralized management scheme. As part of this reorganization, Robert Galvin became president and each divisional manager, an executive vice-president.

Paul Galvin became chairman of the board and CEO, posts he retained until his death in 1956, whereupon Robert Galvin took over the company leadership. Beginning in 1958, Motorola became involved in the U.S. space program. Virtually every manned and unmanned space flight since that time utilized some piece of Motorola equipment.

Motorola made several acquisitions during the 1960s that left observers baffled. It purchased, and sold almost immediately, Lear Inc.'s Lear Cal Division, which manufactured aircraft radios. This was followed by the purchase and subsequent divestment of the Dalberg Company, a manufacturer of hearing aids. Acquisitions were also considered in the fields of recreation, chemicals, broadcasting, and even funeral homes. This trend continued into the 1970s and constituted a period of real adjustment for Motorola. Nevertheless, three very important corporate strategies grew out of this floundering.

First, the company began to expand operations outside the United States, building a plant in Mexico and marketing Motorola products in eight countries, including Japan. An office in Japan was opened in 1961, and in 1968 Motorola Semiconductors Japan began to design, market, and sell integrated circuits. Second, Robert Galvin instituted several progressive management policies. In 1974 the company launched an employee training and involvement program that emphasized teamwork and empowered workers at all levels to make decisions. Such policies laid the groundwork for Motorola's much touted quality and efficiency gains of the 1980s. Third, in the late 1970s, Motorola gradually began to discontinue its consumer-product lines in favor of high-tech electronic components.

Motorola's radio and television interests were the first to go. In 1974 Motorola sold its consumer products division, which included Quasar television, to the Matsushita Electric Industrial Company of Japan. That year Motorola also unveiled its first microprocessor, the 6800. Three years later the company acquired Codex Corporation, a data-communications company based in Massachusetts. In 1978 Universal Data Systems was added. Motorola began phasing out its car-radio business at the end of the decade, and made its last car radio in 1983. These maneuvers were intended to concentrate Motorola's activities in high technology.

1980S: FOUR-PHASE, CELLULAR PHONES, AND TQM

Motorola's largest acquisition theretofore, and one of the most important in company history, came in 1982 with its purchase of Four-Phase Systems, Inc., for $253 million. A California-based manufacturer of computers and terminals, Four-Phase also wrote software for its own machines. The purchase puzzled observers because Four-Phase was in serious trouble at the time. Although Four-Phase did quite well in the 1970s, by the end of that decade its product line was aging, its computer-leasing base had grown too large, and its debt was tied to the rising prime rate. These problems had their origin in the company's insistence upon manufacturing its own semiconductors instead of purchasing commercially available components, an insistence that consumed time and money, and also meant that new product developments at Four-Phase were slow in coming. Motorola, however, was looking for a custom-computer manufacturer and was impressed with the sales force at Four-Phase: Motorola's strategy was to branch

into the new fields of office automation and distributed data processing.

Distributed data processing involved the processing of data through computers that were geographically distributed. The purchases of both Four-Phase and Codex made perfect sense when viewed in light of Motorola's intent to enter this field. The plan was simple: data processing provided by Four-Phase computers would be linked by data-communications equipment provided by Codex, and Motorola proper would provide the semiconductors and much of the communications equipment for the operation. The goal was to create a fully mobile data-processing system that would allow access to mainframe computers from a pocket unit. Motorola also figured that its experience in portable two-way radios and cellular remote telephone systems would prove valuable in this endeavor. Although Motorola was able to turn Four-Phase around temporarily, Four-Phase lost more than $200 million between 1985 and 1989.

The cellular remote telephone system was developed by American Telephone and Telegraph's Bell Laboratories in the early 1970s. The system functioned by dividing an area into units, or cells, each with a low-level transmitter that had 666 channels. As a driver using a phone moved from cell to cell, his call was carried on the transmitter in each successive cell. After he left a cell, the channel he was using became available for another call in that cell. (Earlier remote systems relied on a powerful transmitter covering a large area, which meant that only a few channels were available for the whole area.) Motorola aided in the design and testing of the phones and supplied much of the transmission-switching equipment. In 1983 the company's first cellular telephone network began commercial operation, following 20 years and $200 million in development.

Motorola's early estimates of the cellular phone market seemed astronomical—one million users by the early 1990s—though in fact there were more than four million users by 1989. However, the system developed major problems. There were massive licensing and construction problems and delays. Added to this were complaints about the quality and reliability of Motorola's phones compared to Japanese-manufactured remote phones. A surplus of phones, coupled with the desire to capture a large market share, soon prompted Japanese companies to cut their prices radically, some by as much as half. Motorola went straight to the U.S. government to request sanctions against the Japanese companies. In 1986 the Commerce Department declared that eight Japanese companies were in fact "dumping" their products (selling at a below-cost price) and were liable to pay special duties. This gave Motorola a new edge in the cellular-phone market; it soon became the world's top supplier of cellular phones, although the competition remained intense.

Motorola's relations with Japanese companies has been checkered. In 1980 it formed a joint venture with Aizu-Toko K.K. to manufacture integrated circuits in Japan. Two years later Motorola acquired the remaining 50 percent interest in the company from Aizu-Toko and created Nippon Motorola Manufacturing Company, a successful operation run along Japanese lines mostly by Japanese. Also in 1982, Motorola received a $9 million order for paging devices from Nippon Telegraph and Telephone. These ventures were followed by vigorous pleas from Robert Galvin for the U.S. government to respond in kind to Japan's trade tactics. In fact, Galvin was a founder of the Coalition for International Trade Equity. This organization lobbied Congress for legislation that would impose tariffs on foreign companies subsidized by their governments. Motorola further called for a surcharge on all imports to reduce the U.S. trade deficit. Other major companies in the United States (Boeing and Exxon among them) rejected these measures on the grounds that they would spark trade wars that would damage the position of U.S. companies doing business with Japan.

In 1986, Motorola made a groundbreaking deal with Japan's Toshiba to share its microprocessor designs in return for Toshiba's expertise in manufacturing dynamic random access memories (DRAMs). Prior to this arrangement, the Japanese had driven Motorola, along with nearly every other U.S. semiconductor company, out of the DRAM market.

In 1988, Motorola took on the Japanese in another way: that year its Boynton Beach, Florida, plant began producing the company's Bravo model pocket pager in a fully automated factory. The prototypical facility used 27 small robots directed by computers and overseen by 12 human attendants. The robots could build a Bravo within two hours of the time an order was received at corporate headquarters in Schaumburg, Illinois; the process normally would take three weeks.

Motorola's adoption of "Total Quality Management" (TQM) principles during the 1980s furthered its push for quality and earned it the admiration of analysts and competitors alike. Building on the foundation laid by his employee empowerment programs of the 1970s, Robert Galvin was able to instill a drive for continuous quality improvement in his teams of workers. From 1981 to 1986, Motorola reduced its defect rate by 90 percent. By 1992, the company had achieved "six sigma quality": less than 3.4 mistakes per million. The corporation did not sacrifice productivity for these quality improvements, either: from 1986 to 1994, sales per employee increased 126 percent, in spite of a net increase in the workforce. Some divisions had achieved such high-quality rates that they were striving to reduce error rates to defects per *billion* in the 1990s. The corporation's ongoing goals were to reduce error rates tenfold every two years and simultaneously reduce production time tenfold every five years. Motorola's campaign for quality was highlighted by its 1988 receipt of the first annual Malcolm Baldrige National Quality Award. That year, George Fisher succeeded Robert Galvin as CEO, becoming the first non-Galvin to head the company.

In 1989 Motorola introduced the world's smallest portable telephone, but soon found that its new product was excluded from the Tokyo and Nagoya markets, two cities that together represented more than 60 percent of the $750 million Japanese cellular phone market. When Motorola cried foul, the Japanese government agreed to allow adapted Motorola phones in Tokyo, but only for use in automobiles. This excluded the 90 percent of portable phones used on trains. In response to these restrictions, Motorola led the push to impose trade sanctions on certain Japanese imports. Then-President George H. W. Bush publicly accused Japan of being an unfair trading partner and threatened to take punitive action if the Japanese did not remove barriers to free trade.

The growth of the computer industry provided both opportunities and challenges for Motorola. Throughout the 1980s, the company's most popular 68000 family of microchips powered personal computers (PCs) and workstations built by Apple Computer, Inc., Hewlett-Packard Company, Digital Equipment Corporation, and Sun Microsystems, Inc., among others. Upstart competitor Intel Corporation, whose chips were the cornerstone of International Business Machines Corporation (IBM) and IBM-compatible PCs, launched a successful campaign to capture the microchip market. Intel combined ever increasing power and speed with aggressive marketing to win the semiconductor market from Motorola. Undaunted, Motorola teamed up with industry giants Apple and IBM to develop the PowerPC in the 1990s. Throughout most of the 1990s, Motorola maintained the number three ranking among the world's semiconductor manufacturers, behind Intel and Japan's NEC Corporation.

1990S: COMMUNICATIONS COME TO THE FORE

In many respects, however, Motorola's computer chip operations were eclipsed by its communications interests during the 1990s. The company's 45 percent leading share of the global cellular phone market and staggering 85 percent of the world's pager sales forced it to place an increased emphasis on consumer marketing in the early 1990s. Accordingly, Motorola recruited market specialists from General Electric, Black & Decker, Apple, and (as *Fortune* put it in a 1994 article) "even Mattel." The company began selling its pagers at mass merchandisers and offering them in a variety of colors. Evidence of its re-entry into the consumer market after nearly 20 years came in the form of a 1993 television and print campaign targeted at women, especially mothers.

Over the course of the 1980s, Motorola's sales and profits tripled to $9.6 billion and $498 million, respectively, in 1989. By 1993, sales vaulted more than 56 percent to $16.96 billion and earnings more than doubled to over $1 billion. The company underwent its third transfer of power that year, when Robert Galvin "retired" to the office of chairman of the board's executive committee at the age of 71, at the same time that Fisher left to take the top spot at Eastman Kodak. Gary L. Tooker, former president and chief operating officer, advanced to the chief executive office, and Galvin's son, Christopher, assumed Tooker's responsibilities.

Although some analysts worried that Motorola, like many other large successful corporations, would fall into complacency, the company was determined to stay in the vanguard of the wireless communication revolution with such innovations as the Motorola Integrated Radio Service (MIRS) that combined features of cellular phones, pagers, and two-way radios in a system that could rival all three. Motorola hoped to undermine the cellular "duopolies" organized by the FCC by operating the system over Specialized Mobile Radio (SMR) frequencies that had been limited to use by taxis and tow trucks. Motorola also continued work on its multibillion-dollar "Iridium" project (launched in 1990 then spun off as a limited partnership), a plan to wirelessly interconnect the entire globe through a system of low-earth-orbiting satellites, with a projected completion date of 1998.

Continuing globalization at Motorola focused on Asian, Eastern European, and Latin American markets in the early 1990s. In 1993, the company announced "Corporate America's biggest manufacturing venture in China": two plants for the manufacture of simple integrated circuits, pagers, and cellular phones. By 1995 sales in China and Hong Kong had almost doubled, reaching $3.2 billion, nearly 12 percent of overall Motorola revenues.

The good times at Motorola lasted through 1995, a year in which the company posted profits of $1.78 billion on sales of $27.04 billion. The latter figure was nearly triple the company's 1989 revenue figure. Then, seemingly, Motorola took a sudden downturn. Revenue growth slowed dramatically and profits fell. In 1997 the company reported net income of $1.18 billion on sales of $29.79 billion. There were numerous reasons for the downturn, including price wars and declining sales of cellular phones, slumps in the semiconductor and paging industries, troubles at Apple Computer which impacted sales of the PowerPC chip, and the Asian economic crisis which began in 1997. Perhaps most importantly, however, Motorola seemed to have lost its ability to stay on the cutting edge of technology, particularly in the wireless telephone field. Motorola had dominated the wireless world in the analog era, but it was not fully prepared when the switch to digital technologies began in the mid-1990s. Because it hung onto its analog cellular technology for too long, its share of the U.S. wireless phone market plunged from 60 percent in 1994 to 34 percent in early 1998.

In the midst of these travails came another leadership change. In January 1997 Tooker moved into the chairmanship, while Christopher Galvin took over as CEO. The appointment of Galvin, whose background was in marketing and management rather than in engineering, seemed well-timed; a number of observers had concluded that Motorola's troubles stemmed at least in part from its inability to listen to its customers. The company's autonomous divisions were creating products, many of them innovative, without first determining if the market desired them. The company's flat, decentralized organizational structure created further problems. Motorola's paging, cellular, two-way radio, and satellite communications units operated as separate divisions, which did not collaborate with each other despite the increasing amount of overlap in these technologies. Galvin attempted to address these problems through a 1998 restructuring that merged all of the company's communications operations into a new entity called the Communications Enterprise. Within this organization were several customer-focused sectors, with the three main ones being: personal communications, which served the consumer market and included wireless phones, pagers, and some two-way radios; network solutions, which served telecommunications providers and concentrated on wireless-telephone infrastructure and satellite communications; and a commercial, government, and industrial solutions group that was created to design and build communications systems for large organizations.

Motorola's semiconductor and integrated circuit operations were also restructured in the late 1990s; these units were reorganized into two areas: the Semiconductor Products Sector, which adopted a concentration on embedded semiconductors, and the Integrated Electronic Systems Sector, which focused on embedded electronic systems for various industrial markets. Motorola began winding down its involvement in the general-purpose semiconductor sector, a process that culminated in 1999 with a management buyout, led by Texas Pacific Group, of a portion of the Semiconductor Components Group. As part of the transaction, Motorola received $1.6 billion in cash and a 10 percent stake in the new company, renamed ON Semiconductor. Galvin's restructuring efforts also included the launch in mid-1998 of a 12-month program of factory consolidation, divestments of underperforming units, and asset write-downs; as well as the elimination of 15,000 workers from the company payroll, a 10 percent workforce reduction. Motorola took a $1.95 billion charge related to the restructuring, leading to a net loss for 1998 of $962 million; sales fell 1 percent from the previous year, to $29.4 billion, as a result of the divestments.

It appeared that 1999 might be considered a turnaround year for Motorola, as revenues surpassed the $30 billion mark for the first time; the company also returned to profitability. Motorola finally began selling substantial numbers of digital cellular telephones during the year, although sales were hampered by shortages of components. The company was also returning to the cutting edge through its attempt to develop a new technology to deliver voice, data, and video from the Internet to wireless devices. This endeavor was telling in that Motorola, a go-it-alone company historically, was partnering with Cisco Systems Inc. and Sun Microsystems Inc. In addition to forging alliances, Motorola was also working to shift from being strictly a maker of hardware to being a software designer as well. For example, the company was working to equip all of its cellular telephones with an Internet browser.

ACQUIRING GENERAL INSTRUMENT

Motorola also turned to acquisitions in 1999, in a very big way, with the announcement of a $17 billion stock swap for General Instrument Corporation, the leading maker of broadband set-top boxes. Completed in early 2000, this was the largest acquisition in Motorola history, and it gave the company a significant presence in the emerging broadband telecommunications sector. Broadband visionaries spoke of a dramatic convergence whereby all the main telecom services—telephony, cable television, video, e-mail, high-speed Internet access, and interactive gaming—would be delivered to a television via a single set-top box. Following the completion of the acquisition, General Instrument became the new broadband communications sector within the Communications Enterprise. This new sector also included Motorola's existing cable modem operations. General

Instrument also brought to Motorola its 67 percent stake in Next Level Communications, a supplier of the emerging digital subscriber line (DSL) technology. With DSL, basic copper telephone wires were able to be used for high-speed Internet access.

However, there was a dark cloud hanging over Motorola as the 21st century began; the Iridium satellite phone system, which began operation in late 1998 following $5 billion in development costs, immediately began having technological glitches and, even though it allowed its users to use their cellular phones anywhere on the planet, suffered from low demand because of its extremely high rates (e.g., $3 per minute calls). In August 1999 Iridium LLC, in which Motorola held an 18 percent stake, began operating under bankruptcy protection. Motorola subsequently took a $740 million charge related to Iridium in late 1999, leaving it with a $460 million cash exposure to the venture. In early 2000 Motorola also faced a possible $3.5 billion lawsuit from a group of Iridium bondholders. Despite these setbacks, Motorola moved forward with another, even larger satellite venture, Teledesic L.L.C., in which it was the chief contractor and held a 26 percent stake. A $10 billion project, Teledesic aimed to create, by 2004, a low-orbit satellite system for the delivery of voice, data, and high-speed Internet access to handheld devices. Motorola's prominent involvement in the satellite and broadband ventures, however risky they might be, provided ample evidence that the company was back on the technological cutting edge.

NEW LEADERSHIP, LEADING EDGE DESIGNS, AND CUSTOMER RELATIONS

Meanwhile, back on earth, the $37.6 billion Motorola, once the leader in cellphones, was being bested by Nokia. When Motorola missed the switch to digital phones in the mid-1990s, it had lost ground to both Nokia and Ericsson. Among consumers, it had gained a reputation for shoddy products and models that were too complex and too expensive. As a result, its market share in cellphone handsets fell from 17 percent to 13 percent by 2000. Its Shark phone bombed in Europe in 2000.

Galvin responded by attempting drastic organizational changes within the company from 1999 to 2000. He combined all 30 Motorola units that made cellphones, wireless equipment, satellite, and cable modem products into two communications business units, one responsible for getting all communications businesses working together to meet customers' needs, the new Communications Enterprise. The other, the

Personal Networks Group, was charged with coordinating Net strategies, mostly software being developed by the company as a whole. He also aimed at changing the company's corporate culture, leaving behind Motorola's tradition of warring divisions in favor of becoming a more cooperative place, one that fostered collaboration among managers and customer service on the part of employees. The company would also shift from being engineer-driven to customer-driven.

In this regard, there was pressure on Galvin to move fast. By February 2001, the company's stock had crashed more than 60 percent (although its revenues were still higher than Cisco's, Intel's, and Microsoft's). In April 2001, it reported its first quarterly loss in 15 years, and by year's end, it posted its first annual loss in 46 years. To put this drop in better perspective, after the dot-com and telecom busts of 2001, industry sales as a whole fell 30 percent. Still the general economic malaise was translating into slower demand in its semiconductor business and cutbacks by telecom companies that bought Motorola's wireless equipment. All in all, Motorola lost $5.8 billion in 2001.

Galvin's critics pointed out that he was indecisive and his management style was too hands-off to handle these hard times. Brought up on his father's management style of delegating, he focused on vision and strategy. Executives began to lobby for Galvin to give up the CEO post to become a visionary chairman, but he refused. By July 2001, however, it was clear that his reorganization had failed, and the beleaguered CEO restructured again to remove one layer of management and have the heads of Motorola's six main businesses (cellphones, semiconductors, wireless networks, broadband communications, government and industrial systems, and smart electronics) report to him directly. He began to meet with the head of each sector weekly and to meet monthly with top managers about key corporate initiatives. From mid-2000 to mid-2001, he replaced 11 of the 19 managers in the wireless group and appointed Mike S. Zafirovski head of the wireless phone division in 2000.

Zafirovski had arrived at Motorola in 2000 from General Electric, where he had turned around the lighting business. He was a man with a reputation for drive and ambition. At Motorola's ailing cellphone division, he reduced phone models from more than 100 to about 20 and slashed operating expenses. Zafirovski endorsed Galvin's plan to weed out the lowest performing 10 percent of managers and supported employee bonuses based on profitability.

Galvin also brought in Edward D. Breen as president and COO in 2001 to assist with improving the performance of the floundering company. Breen had been CEO of General Instrument Corp. in the late 1990s and had built that company into the nation's premier maker of cable set-top boxes. Less than a year later, however, Breen left Motorola to head Tyco International Ltd. and Zafirovski replaced Breen as COO.

Yet while Motorola struggled at home, its China market grew. Sales volume in China, the world's largest cellular market, reached $5 billion by 2002, 13 percent of Motorola's worldwide total. Motorola had been in China since 1986, where it had invested in manufacturing and research and development facilities; by 2002, it sold more cellphones in China than any other company.

By mid-2003, Motorola's share of the cellphone market had improved, although the company lagged far behind Nokia, which had 38 percent. It returned to profitability in the third quarter of 2003 after six straight quarters of losses. Still having lost the lead in communications chips to Texas Instruments and with its wireless networks business having finished 2002 in the red, management trimmed the workforce to 93,000, 38 percent of its 2000 figure.

When Christopher Galvin resigned as chair and CEO in September 2003, Motorola spun off the remainder of its semiconductor business as a separate, publicly traded company called SPS Spinco Inc. Ed Zander, who replaced Galvin in 2004, continued the effort to dismantle Motorola's disabling bureaucracy and to end its culture of internal competition. In place of this competition, he instituted a bonus plan based on customer satisfaction, product reliability, and collaboration across the company. Before joining Motorola, Zander had been a managing director of Silver Lake Partners, a leading private equity fund focused on investments in technology industries. Until June 2002, he was president and chief operating officer of Sun Microsystems. Zander also took steps to reorganize operations around customer markets rather than products, to continue to move the company away from engineering innovations and toward responding to consumer demand. His strategy was one of "seamless mobility," enabling consumers to easily transport digital information from home to car to the workplace.

By the end of 2004, Motorola was doing a better job of estimating customer orders and delivering products on time. It had also at last created a common chassis and parts for its different phone models. This enabled it to introduce 20 new models of phones at the end of the year, which bumped up its market share of cellphones from 13.5 to 16.6 percent, upstaging Samsung for the number two spot.

One of the phones introduced in 2004, the Razr, almost instantly became the handset of the moment and played a large part in boosting earnings to $1.5 billion on revenues of $31.3 billion, making 2004 the company's most profitable year ever. The sleek, stylish Razr set a new design standard for cellphones as well as driving a remarkable turnaround for Motorola. The company began to position itself to carve out a lead in the music-phone business. By mid-2005, its cellphone share was up to 18 percent; by year's end it was at 19 percent, and the Razr was the best-selling mobile phone in the United States. The company decided to use the Razr as a new platform for a suite of cellphones.

UNCERTAIN FUTURE

Unfortunately, the Rokr music phone, made in conjunction with Apple, proved a disappointment and Motorola once again fell behind the curve. Also failing to capture the imaginations of consumers were the pebl, a clamshell phone with rounded edges, and the Krzr. Still, Motorola's share of the worldwide mobile phone market continued to improve from 13 to 22 percent, just behind Nokia, in 2006.

Then suddenly in the fourth quarter of 2006, earnings plummeted. In early 2007, Motorola faced its first sales decline in four years as activist hedge fund manager Carl C. Icahn, who had acquired a sizable percent of Motorola's shares, lobbied for a seat on its board. Icahn wanted to see Motorola spend its stockpiled $11.2 billion on a massive stock repurchase. He was voted down for the board seat, but the company did eventually acquiesce to $5 billion in buybacks as Samsung assumed the number two spot in cellphone sales.

At the same time Zander focused on cutting business costs and eliminated 3,500 jobs with another 4,000 layoffs to follow in 2008. While seeking to create another hit product, it struggled to improve production efficiency, to better forecast how many phones to build, and to sell some of its noncore businesses. It also continued to make strategic acquisitions. Leapstone Systems, Inc., a communications software developer that provided a unified platform for converged video, voice, and data service bundles across multiple networks and devices, and Symbol Technologies, Inc., manufacturer of products and systems for mobile computing, advanced data capture, and radio frequency identification, were both acquired in 2007. Then, at the beginning of February 2008, only a month after Zander had stepped down as CEO, replaced by Greg Brown, the company stated that it was considering a spinoff or sale of its rapidly declining cellphone business. Clearly, Motorola was at an existential crossroads.

April Dougal Gasbarre
Updated, David E. Salamie; Carrie Rothburd

PRINCIPAL SUBSIDIARIES

Tut Systems, Inc.; Symbol Technologies; Motorola, Inc.; Motorola Good Technology Group; General Instrument Corporation; Motorola Ventures Motorola A/S (Denmark); Motorola AB (Sweden); Motorola Argentina, S.A.; Motorola Asia Pacific Limited; Motorola Asia Treasury Pte. Ltd. (Singapore); Motorola Australia Pty., Ltd.; Motorola New Zealand Limited; Motorola B.V. (Netherlands); Motorola Canada Limited; Motorola Chile S.A.; Motorola (China) Investment Ltd.; Motorola Cellular Equipment Co., Ltd.; Motorola (China) Electronics Ltd.; Motorola de Costa Rica S.A.; Motorola de Mexico, S.A.; Motorola Electronics Pte. Limited; Motorola Electronics Sdn. Bhd. (Malaysia); Motorola Technology Sdn. Bhd. (Malaysia); Motorola Electronics Taiwan Limited; Motorola Espana S.A.; Motorola Finance B.V. (Netherlands); Motorola Ges.m.b.H. (Austria); Motorola GmbH (Germany); Motorola Electronics GmbH (Germany); Motorola India Private Limited; Motorola Industrial Ltda. (Brazil); Motorola Israel Limited; Beeper Communications Israel Ltd.; MIRS Communications Limited (Israel); Motorola South Israel Limited; Motorola Japan Limited; Motorola Korea Inc.; Motorola Limited (U.K.); Motorola Finance EMEA Limited (U.K.); Motorola Ireland Ltd.; Motorola N.V. (Belgium); Motorola Portugal Comunicacoes, Lda.; Motorola S.A.S. (France); Motorola S.p.A. (Italy); Motorola S.R.O. (Czech Republic); Motorola (Thailand) Limited; Motorola Trading Center Pte. Ltd. (Singapore); Motorola Venezuela.

PRINCIPAL OPERATING UNITS

Enterprise Mobility Solutions; Home and Networks Mobility; Mobile Devices.

PRINCIPAL COMPETITORS

Telefonaktiebolaget LM Ericsson; Nokia Corporation; Sony Ericsson Mobile Communications AB; Samsung Electronics Co., Ltd.; LG Group; AT&T Mobility; Sprint Nextel; T-Mobile USA.

FURTHER READING

Alster, Norm, "A Third-Generation Galvin Moves Up," *Forbes*, April 30, 1990, pp. 57+.

Barboza, David, "Motorola Rolls Itself Over: After a Bad Year, Almost Everything Is Coming Up Rosy, and Wireless," *New York Times,* July 14, 1999, p. C1.

Bettner, Jill, "'Underpromise, Overperform,'" *Forbes,* January 30, 1984, pp. 88+.

Brown, Kathi, *A Critical Connection: The Motorola Service Station Story,* Rolling Meadows, Ill.: Motorola University Press, 1992, 253 p.

Carpenter, Dave, "Motorola Mulls Breakup, Phone Unit Sale," *Associated Press,* February 1, 2008.

Cauley, Leslie, "Motorola Corp. Unveils Deal for $11 Billion," *Wall Street Journal,* September 16, 1999, p. B10.

————, "Motorola Profit Meets Estimates, Despite Iridium Woes, Shortages," *Wall Street Journal,* January 18, 2000, p. B6.

Coy, Peter, and Ron Stodghill II, "Is Motorola a Bit Too Patient?" *BusinessWeek,* February 5, 1996, pp. 150–51.

Crockett, Roger O., "All This and Icahn Too; As Ed Zander Battles Falling Earnings, Motorola Attracts a Demanding Investor," *BusinessWeek,* February 12, 2007, p. 34.

————, "Can Mike Z Work More Magic at Motorola?" *BusinessWeek,* April 14, 2003, p. 58.

————, "Has Motorola Found Its Cable Guy?" *BusinessWeek,* September 27, 1999, p. 50.

————, "How Motorola Got Its Groove Back," *BusinessWeek,* August 8, 2005, p. 68.

————, "Memo To: Ed Zander. Subject: Motorola; Words of Advice for the 'Operations Guy' As He Prepares to Take the Helm," *BusinessWeek,* December 29, 2003, p. 44.

————, "Motorola: Can Chris Galvin Save His Family's Legacy?" *BusinessWeek,* July 16, 2000, p. 72.

————, "Motorola Can't Seem to Get Out of Its Own Way," *BusinessWeek,* January 22, 2001, p. 71.

————, "Motorola Girds for a Shakeup," *BusinessWeek,* April 13, 1998, p. 33.

————, "Motorola Needs a Revolutionary: The New CEO Will Have to Slash and Innovate—Fast," *BusinessWeek,* October 6, 2003, p. 52.

————, "Motorola: Slow and Steady Isn't Winning Any Races," *BusinessWeek,* August 10, 1998, p. 62.

————, "A New Company Called Motorola," *BusinessWeek,* April 17, 2000, p. 86.

————, "Reinventing Motorola," *BusinessWeek,* August 2, 2004, p. 82.

————, "Zander May Be Running Out of Minutes," *BusinessWeek,* July 30, 2007, p. 31.

Crockett, Roger O., and Catherine Yang, "Why Motorola Should Hang Up on Iridium," *BusinessWeek,* August 30, 1999, p. 46.

Crockett, Roger O., and Peter Elstrom, "How Motorola Lost Its Way," *BusinessWeek,* May 4, 1998, pp. 140+.

Dreyfack, Kenneth, "It's Now or Never for Motorola Computers," *BusinessWeek,* September 15, 1986, pp. 184J+.

Einhorn, Bruce, "Winning in China: Can Motorola Hang On to Its Top Spot As Local Rivals Come On Strong?" *Business-*

Week, January 27, 2003, p. 98.

Elstrom, Peter, "Did Motorola Make the Wrong Call?" *Business Week,* July 29, 1996, p. 66.

Elstrom, Peter, Gail Edmondson, and Eric Schine, "Does This Galvin Have the Right Stuff?" *Business Week,* March 17, 1997, pp. 102+.

Feder, Barnaby J., "Some Humbling Times for a High-Tech Giant," *New York Times,* October 13, 1996, sec. 3, p. 1.

Galarza, Pablo, "Keep the Faith," *Financial World,* January 30, 1996, pp. 30–32.

Galvin, Robert W., *The Idea of Ideas,* Rolling Meadows, Ill.: Motorola University Press, 1993.

Hardy, Quentin, "Galvin's Task: Make Motorola Scary Again," *Wall Street Journal,* March 7, 1997, p. B8.

————, "Higher Calling: How a Wife's Question Led Motorola to Chase Global Cell-Phone Plan," *Wall Street Journal,* December 16, 1996, pp. A1+.

————, "Motorola Prepares Major Restructuring," *Wall Street Journal,* March 31, 1998, p. A3.

————, "Motorola Selects Christopher Galvin, Grandson of Firm's Founder, As CEO," *Wall Street Journal,* November 15, 1996, p. A3.

————, "Motorola Unveils a Major Reorganization," *Wall Street Journal,* July 10, 1998, p. B5.

————, "Next Leader in the Motorola Dynasty Faces Task of Reshaping Corporation," *Wall Street Journal,* November 18, 1996, p. B10.

————, "Unsolid State: Motorola, Broadsided by the Digital Era, Struggles for a Footing," *Wall Street Journal,* April 22, 1998, pp. A1+.

Harris, Nicole, "Motorola Sees Strong Growth This Year," *Wall Street Journal,* January 19, 2000, p. B6.

Henkoff, Ronald, "Keeping Motorola on a Roll," *Fortune,* April 18, 1994, pp. 67–68+.

————, "What Motorola Learns from Japan," *Fortune,* April 24, 1989, pp. 157+.

Hill, G. Christian, and Don Clark, "Motorola to Slash Staff, Take Big Charge," *Wall Street Journal,* June 5, 1998, p. A3.

McWilliams, Gary, "Microprocessors Are for Wimps," *Business Week,* December 15, 1997, p. 134.

"Motorola's New Strategy," *Business Week,* March 29, 1982, pp. 128+.

Naik, Gautam, "Motorola Still Is Struggling in Europe," *Wall Street Journal,* February 11, 2000, p. A12.

————, "Nokia Widens Lead in Wireless Market While Motorola, Ericsson Fall Back," *Wall Street Journal,* February 8, 2000, p. B8.

Petrakis, Harry Mark, *The Founder's Touch: The Life of Paul Galvin of Motorola,* New York: McGraw-Hill, 1965; 3rd ed., Chicago: Motorola University Press/J.G. Ferguson, 1991, 242 p.

Roth, Daniel, "Burying Motorola: From Poster Boy to Whipping Boy," *Fortune,* July 6, 1998, pp. 28–29.

————, "Motorola Lives!" *Fortune,* September 27, 1999, pp. 305–06.

Schoenberger, Karl, "Motorola Bets Big on China," *Fortune,* May 27, 1996, pp. 116–18+.

Schonfeld, Erick, "Hold the Phone: Motorola Is Going Nowhere Fast," *Fortune,* March 30, 1998, p. 184.

Slutsker, Gary, "The Company That Likes to Obsolete Itself," *Forbes,* September 13, 1993, pp. 139+.

Tetzeli, Rick, "And Now for Motorola's Next Trick," *Fortune,* April 28, 1997, pp. 122–24+.

Therrien, Lois, "Motorola Sends Its Work Force Back to School," *Business Week,* June 6, 1988, pp. 80+.

———, "The Rage to Page Has Motorola's Mouth Watering," *Business Week,* August 30, 1993, pp. 72+.

———, "The Rival Japan Respects," *Business Week,* November 13, 1989, pp. 108+.

Thurm, Scott, Joann S. Lublin, and Leslie Scism, "Galvin Must Show a Motorola Recovery Before Dismissal Pressure Grows Intense," *Wall Street Journal,* June 8, 1998, p. A3.

Upbin, Bruce, "Motorola Inside," *Forbes,* May 31, 1999, pp. 51–52.

Upbin, Bruce, and Michael Ozanian, "Analytic Myopia," *Forbes,* June 1, 1998, pp. 42–43.

Yee, David, "Motorola: More Than Chips," *Financial World,* Fall 1994, p. 14.

Zajac, Andrew, "Technical 'Convergence' at Heart of Motorola Merger," *Chicago Tribune,* September 15, 1999.

Navigant Consulting, Inc.

---

615 North Wabash Avenue
Chicago, Illinois 60611
U.S.A.
Telephone: (312) 573-5600
Toll Free: (800) 621-8390
Fax: (312) 573-5678
Web site: http://www.navigantconsulting.com

Public Company
Incorporated: 1983 as Metzler & Associates, Inc.
Employees: 2,300
Sales: $681.75 million (2006)
Stock Exchanges: New York
Ticker Symbol: NCI
NAIC: 541611 Administrative Management and General Management Consulting Services; 541618 Other Management Consulting Services

■ ■ ■

Navigant Consulting, Inc., is an international consulting firm specializing in regulated industries. It also provides policy advice to government agencies and has supplied experts to testify in forensic accounting cases. From its origins as an adviser to the energy industry, the firm has expanded its range of services through acquisitions. It has also developed an international reach, with offices in London, Toronto, and Hong Kong. The company's 1996 initial public offering was the impetus for one of its shopping sprees, and after a round of divestments in 2000 it started another round of buying. The name sug-

gests the assistance it provides clients in navigating changing business conditions.

ORIGINS

Navigant Consulting, Inc., traces its origins to The Metzler Group Inc., which went public in 1996. Metzler Group had evolved from Metzler & Associates, a consulting practice formed in 1983 by Richard Metzler.

Based in the Chicago suburbs, Metzler Group specialized in the energy industry. It was particularly focused on how gas and electric utilities utilized information technology. Revenues had reached $14 million by 1995 and were growing at a double-digit pace. It was time to capitalize on this momentum by taking its shares to the market.

PUBLIC IN 1996

Metzler Group became a public company in October 1996 in an initial public offering (IPO) that raised $37 million. Metzler & Associates continued to exist after the IPO as a subsidiary. Richard Metzler had resigned as the firm's CEO the year before its IPO, and left the firm altogether two years after that.

Flush with fresh capital, the company hit the acquisition trail, buying 14 companies in the next three years. First was Burgess Consultants, Inc., a Chicago-area utilities consultant with strengths in regulatory and litigation support. Another early purchase was Barrington Consulting Group, bought in a deal worth up to $28.5 million, based on performance targets.

Metzler made a particularly ambitious acquisition in 1997, buying Sacramento's Resource Management International Inc. (RMI). RMI had annual revenues of about $36 million to Metzler's $21 million. It had been formed in 1980 by Lloyd Harvego and also specialized in the energy industry. Other firms purchased during the year included the much smaller Reed Consulting Group.

As it prepared for the utilities industry to undergo a round of consolidation, Metzler was looking to add mergers and acquisitions professionals, noted the *Mergers & Acquisitions Report*. It was also following its energy clients into other fields, such as telecommunications.

The 1998 acquisition of LECG Inc., a specialist in economic consulting, added to Metzler's range of offerings. The stock swap was worth $274 million. Based in Emeryville, California, LECG had 14 offices around the world. Metzler did not hold on to LECG very long, however.

Other 1998 acquisitions included London-based financial services consultant Troika. Peterson Consulting, also of Chicago, was purchased in a $191 million stock trade. Peterson had annual revenues of about $80 million.

In 1999 Metzler added Strategic Decision Group Inc. of Menlo Park, California, in a $125 million stock swap. The acquired firm had annual revenues in excess of $50 million and served clients in a variety of industries. This was another unit that would be sold within a couple of years.

NEW NAME, NEW LEADERSHIP

In July 1999 Metzler Group was renamed Navigant Consulting, Inc. Its stock listing moved from the NAS-DAQ to the Big Board (NYSE) shortly afterward. The new name was meant to suggest the company's role in helping clients navigate change.

There were more big changes coming at home. In May 2000 the board dismissed CEO Robert Maher and a couple of other officers after reviewing some loans to them, as well as subsequent stock purchases that drew

unwelcome scrutiny from the Securities and Exchange Commission.

After a short time with three executives sharing the CEO desk, the company hired William M. Goodyear as its new leader. He had previously been CEO of Bank of America, Illinois. It was a difficult year: the company's share price had fallen from $54 to less than $3, noted *Crain's Chicago Business*. The company hired advisers to explore strategic options, possibly including the sale of the firm.

Rather than sell itself, the company decided to unload some of its recent acquisitions. In October 2000 LECG was sold to a group of its professionals for $50 million. The next month, Navigant closed the deal on the spinoff of Strategic Decisions Group. This was worth $22 million. Navigant had owned the unit for only a year and a half.

In all, about 20 businesses were divested in 2000. The streamlined firm emerged with two business units: Energy & Water and Financial & Claims. Revenues were $235 million in 2001. Navigant then employed 1,100 consultants. The company soon set out on another multiyear shopping spree; this time it would be a buyer's market.

ANOTHER ACQUISITION DRIVE

The company began its new acquisition drive in 2001. Herndon, Virginia's Tim D. Martin & Associates, Inc., was obtained in June in a deal worth up to $1 million. Formed in 1986, Martin & Associates specialized in benchmarking databases for the electric industry. The acquisition complemented Navigant's existing product, Generation Knowledge Service.

Navigant then bought Chambers Associates, Inc. This was a Washington, D.C., consultant on public policy matters and class-action suits, both areas in which Navigant was already involved. Chambers Associates had been formed in 1981.

The Hunter Group of St. Petersburg, Florida, was acquired in September 2002 for $25.4 million. Formed in 1988, it specialized in fixing deeply troubled hospitals, sometimes through headline-generating mass layoffs, and had revenues of more than $27 million a year. David Hunter had formed the firm in 1988.

Also in 2002, Navigant bought the Advanced Energy Systems of A.D. Little, a Cambridge, Massachusetts, consulting firm that had gone bankrupt. Navigant paid $6.5 million for the unit.

Navigant spent nearly $50 million on acquisitions in 2002 alone. Consulting services were typically

KEY DATES

1983: Richard Metzler launches consulting firm to advise the utility industry.
1996: Metzler Group goes public.
1998: Acquisitions include London-based financial services consultant Troika.
1999: Metzler Group is renamed Navigant Consulting, Inc.
2000: Navigant divests a dozen business units.
2001: Another acquisition spree is launched.
2007: Acquisitions in Canada and the United Kingdom strengthen Navigant's international reach.

susceptible to downturns in the economy, prompting some firms to sell. Two divisions were bought from Arthur Andersen after its collapse. Sarbanes-Oxley prompted other accounting firms to unload their consulting units due to potential conflicts of interest. Revenues climbed 10 percent to $258 million in 2002. The next year, they were up another 23 percent at $318 million.

Navigant had more checks to write, focusing its purchases on firms in healthcare, forensic accounting, and financial services. In 2004 it acquired Tucker Alan Inc. for $90 million in cash and stock. Tucker Alan focused on litigation consulting and forensic accounting. It had revenues of $60 million a year and more than a dozen offices. Another 2004 acquisition was Virginia's Capital Advisory Services LLC, which concentrated on the financial services industry. Navigant paid $11 million for it. Also acquired during the year was Invalesco Group, a healthcare industry specialist.

In February 2005 Navigant bought Casas Benjamin & White LLC, a healthcare-oriented practice with offices in Chicago and Atlanta. This cost $47.5 million. Another healthcare consultancy, the Tiber Group, was purchased a couple of months later for $8.4 million.

Later in 2005 Navigant added Kroll Lindquist Avey Co., a Canadian subsidiary of Kroll Inc. that specialized in forensic accounting. Montreal forensic accounting specialist Leclerc Juricomptables was added in 2007.

Navigant had acquired more than a dozen firms over the previous few years. The buying continued in 2006 with the purchase of the Inkster Group, a specialist in corporate investigations. London's Precept Programme Management was also added.

Revenues were up to $681.8 million in 2006. Stock options backdating probes and international construction projects kept its Dispute, Investigative & Regulatory Advisory Services unit busy, while the Business, Financial & Operations Advisory segment saw growth in merger integration and other advisory work.

Frederick C. Ingram

PRINCIPAL SUBSIDIARIES

Peterson Consulting, LLC d/b/a Navigant Consulting, Inc.

PRINCIPAL DIVISIONS

Dispute, Investigative & Regulatory Advisory Services; Business, Financial & Operations Advisory Services.

PRINCIPAL COMPETITORS

CRA International, Inc.; Huron Consulting Group Inc.; Accenture Ltd.; LECG, Inc.; McKinsey & Company; Kroll Inc.

FURTHER READING

"Bean-Counters and Rice Have People Talking: Kroll Said to Be in Play Following a Handful of Resignations," *National Post's Financial Post & FP Investing* (Canada), June 29, 2005, p. FP9.

Berke, Jonathan, "Sale of ADL Units Approved," *Daily Deal,* April 8, 2002.

"CEO Interview—Robert Maher," *Wall Street Transcript Digest,* December 15, 1997.

"Consultant Groups in Deal," *New York Times,* February 9, 1999, p. C2.

"Consultant Raises War Chest, Inks Big Buy," *Corporate Financing Week,* February 9, 2004, pp. 9+.

"Consulting Firm in Acquisition," *New York Times,* July 4, 1998, p. D4.

"Consulting's Role in Enabling Large Client Projects," *Management Consultant International,* June 2006, pp. 1+.

Daniels, Steve, "Short-Sellers Circle Navigant Consulting; Big Run-Up Leaves Shares Looking Pricey," *Crain's Chicago Business,* February 16, 2004, p. 3.

Delevett, Peter, "Navigant Guiding New Theme: The 'Smart' Organization," *Business Journal,* October 8, 1999, p. 10.

Edelstein, Michael, "Deal Flow Alert: Navigant Seeks Help," *Mergers & Acquisitions Report,* June 5, 2000.

"Energy Consultants Announce $65 Million Merger Deal," *New York Times,* June 3, 1997, p. D4.

Evans, Melanie, and Michael Romano, "Consultant Consolidation: Accenture, Navigant in Acquisition Mode," *Modern Healthcare,* April 25, 2005, p. 22.

Fanelli, Christa, "Thoma Cressey Breaks Off LECG," *BuyOuts,* November 6, 2000.

Gaines, Sallie L., "Consultancy Trend to Turn Explosive: Hired Guns Range from Low Jobs to Top-Level Strategy Analyst," *Ottawa Citizen,* March 20, 1999, p. J8.

Graebner, Lynn, "RMI Sells to Illinois Firm for $82 Million," *Sacramento Business Journal,* August 15, 1997, p. 1.

Hundley, Kris, "Health Care Consultancy Bought," *St. Petersburg (Fla.) Times,* September 25, 2002, p. 1E.

"Inkster Group to Join Navigant Consulting," *Toronto Star,* February 8, 2006, p. E3.

Kulatilaka, Nalin, and Jim Lang, "Using Real Options to Develop Winning Strategies," *Petroleum Economist,* April 2000, p. 22.

Leger, Kathryn, "Gomery Inquiry Was Bonanza for Lawyers: Corruption Probe Used Forensic Services of Fraud Specialist Leclerc Juricomptables," *Gazette* (Montreal), February 23, 2007, p. B2.

Levine, Daniel Rome, "In Post-Enron Era, Navigant Gets the Call," *Crain's Chicago Business,* Markets Sec., August 14, 2006, p. 4.

Maremont, Mark, "Options Sleuth's Own Slip; In Backdating Probes, Navigant Consulting's Work Is Close to Home," *Wall Street Journal,* Eastern ed., March 30, 2007, p. C1.

"Metzler Group Inc.," *Going Public: The IPO Reporter,* September 9, 1996.

"Metzler Promises Further Deals As It Buys Local Rival," *Management Consultant International,* April 1, 1997.

Moore, Heidi, "Five Buyers Bail Out Arthur D. Little," *Daily Deal,* April 7, 2002.

———, "Navigant Acquires CBW," *Daily Deal,* February 15, 2005.

Murphy, H. Lee, "Industry Disarray Spells Opportunity for Navigant," *Crain's Chicago Business,* May 5, 2003, p. 31.

———, "Riding the Market Recovery; Rising Tide Lifts Most Boats—It's Just a Matter of Degree," *Crain's Chicago Business,* March 21, 2005, p. 4.

Nakashian, David, "Stock Highlight: Navigant Consult.," *Value Line Investment Survey (Part 2—Selection & Opinion),* October 26, 2001, p. 2677.

"Navigant Buys Kroll Lindquist," *Toronto Star,* August 11, 2005, p. D2.

"Navigant Buys Troika in a Bid to Be 'Top Player,'" *Financial Adviser,* August 2, 2007.

"Navigant Consulting Gets Tucker," *Daily Deal,* February 3, 2004.

"Navigant Offers Rx for Ailing Hospitals; Health Care Practice Grows, but Consultant Draws Criticism in L.A.," *Crain's Chicago Business,* Markets Sec., June 6, 2005, p. 4.

"Navigant Rejects Mergers and Will Remain Independent," *New York Times,* October 15, 1999, p. C4.

Poole, Claire, "Navigant Consulting Sheds Assets," *Daily Deal,* January 6, 2005.

Romano, Michael, "Turnaround Expert Hunter Exits," *Modern Healthcare,* May 31, 2004, p. 42.

Ronnow, Karin, "US Metzler Group Consolidates with Purchase of New Firms," *Management Consultant International,* September 1997, p. 4.

"Same Name, New Firm," *Chicago Tribune,* November 25, 1999.

Seewald, Nancy, "A.D. Little Sold to Five Buyers," *Chemical Week,* April 17, 2002, p. 10.

Sikora, Martin, "Navigant Heeds Deal Advice of Its Own Pros: The Business Services Heavyweight Is Cued by Its Practice Chiefs in Bulking Up and Adding Skills," *Mergers & Acquisitions: The Dealmaker's Journal,* March 1, 2005.

Singh, Shruti Date, "Aiming to Ensure Navigant Moves 'In the Right Direction,'" *Crain's Chicago Business,* People Sec., May 1, 2006, p. 6.

———, "Navigant Expects Quieter Deal Pace; Growth Has Surged on 13 Acquisitions Since 2001," *Crain's Chicago Business,* December 13, 2004, p. 13.

———, "Navigant in Demand on Coast; Hurricane-Hit Areas Clamor for Insurance Consultants," *Crain's Chicago Business,* News Sec., October 10, 2005, p. 16.

Strahler, Steven R., "Snoops in the Cubicles; HP Scandal Doesn't Dampen Demand for Corporate Gumshoes," *Crain's Chicago Business,* News Sec., October 30, 2006, p. 3.

Stuart, Scott, "Anticipating Hot Energy M&A, Metzler Looks to Add Pros," *Mergers & Acquisitions Report,* January 19, 1998.

"US Consultant Raises Share Cash Before Accounting Rules Bite," *Accountant,* January 1999, p. 4.

"Utility Consulting Company Ousts Chief," *New York Times,* November 23, 1999, p. C27.

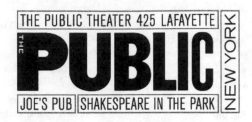

New York Shakespeare
Festival Management

The Public Theater
425 Lafayette Street
New York, New York 10003
U.S.A.
Telephone: (212) 539-8500
Web site: http://www.publictheater.org

Nonprofit Company
Founded: 1954
Employees: 82
Operating Revenues: $18 million (2007 est.)
NAIC: 711110 Theater Companies and Dinner Theaters

■ ■ ■

New York Shakespeare Festival Management, generally known as The Public Theater, is a nonprofit, New York City-based arts organization. It administers the Shakespeare in the Park program of Shakespeare plays performed in the Delacorte Theater in New York's Central Park each summer. The Shakespeare Lab is also offered each summer to train actors in classical performance. In addition, The Public Theater produces new plays, musicals, Shakespeare, and other classics in its six theaters at its downtown headquarters, the "Public Theater," the former Astor Library. The Public Theater is responsible for the development of such works as *Hair, A Chorus Line, That Championship Season,* and *Bring in 'Da Noise, Bring in 'Da Funk.* All told, Public Theater productions have garnered 4 Pulitzer Prizes, nearly 40 Tony Awards and 40 Drama Desk Awards, and 135 Obies (awarded to Off-Broadway productions).

More than 250,000 people attend Public Theater–related shows each year.

FOUNDER, A PRODUCT OF THE GREAT DEPRESSION

Until the early 1990s the history of The Public Theater was essentially the biography of its charismatic founder, Joseph Papp. He was born Josef Yosi Papirofsky in 1921 in the working class Williamsburg neighborhood of Brooklyn. The second of four children, he was the son of Jewish immigrants, his father a trunk maker from Poland, his mother a seamstress from Lithuania. Even during the prosperous 1920s the family was poor, and matters did not improve with the advent of the Great Depression of the 1930s, during which the family moved regularly, sometimes in the middle of the night. As a child he learned to sing and play the harmonica and as a high school student alternated as president of the Dramatic Society. He also developed an interest in Shakespeare after a teacher forced his class to memorize passages from *Julius Caesar.* Due to the beneficence of Mrs. August Belmont, Papp and his classmates were able to attend a pair of Broadway productions of *Hamlet* in 1936, one starring John Gielgud, the other Leslie Howard. Shakespeare embodied the theater to the young man, who mounted a picture of Gielgud on his bedroom wall. The Great Depression was also to influence his later decision to create a Shakespeare festival that charged no admission; the difficulties of that period led him to become a staunch Communist from the age of 15 until his early 30s.

Papp graduated from high school in 1938 but was unable to attend college. Instead he enrolled in a night

COMPANY PERSPECTIVES

∎

As the nation's foremost theatrical producer of Shakespeare and new work, The Public Theater is dedicated to achieving artistic excellence while developing an American theater that is accessible and relevant to all people through productions of challenging new plays, musicals and innovative stagings of the classics.

course for playwriting and took a job at a Manhattan laundry service, followed by a stint as a shipping clerk for a jewelry company before becoming the office manager. Although a part of management he helped unionize the business and was fired in early 1942, a short time after the United States had entered World War II. Unable to find a job, he joined the U.S. Navy, despite not knowing how to swim. It was a major turning point, as it turned out, for his career in the theater. Essentially for his own amusement, Papp began putting on skits in the barracks during basic training. He was then recruited by some officers to make use of a theater on the base to provide entertainment for the men, and he began cobbling together variety shows. For the duration of the war he continued to mount shows around the world, wherever there was suitable space. In 1945 he was assigned to a newly formed Special Services entertainment unit to help entertain the troops. His efforts culminated in a 1946 show, starring Bob Fosse, performed at the Brooklyn Naval Yard, across the river from the church where years later the New York Shakespeare Festival would be born.

PAPP ENTERS ACTOR'S LABORATORY: 1946

Soon after the Naval Yard show, the 25-year-old Papp was discharged. He made his way to California where by sheer chance he was able to take advantage of the G.I. Bill to attend the Actor's Laboratory in Los Angeles. Most of the class had already been chosen when he arrived, and only a handful of auditions remained and no more were to be scheduled. Because one of the applicants needed an audition partner, Papp was brought in to give a cold reading of a scene from Eugene O'Neill's *Desire Under the Elms*. While the applicant was thanked and dismissed, Papp was asked to remain and explain why he wanted to be in the theater. Unlike most of the applicants he expressed no desire to become a

star. Rather, he spoke from the heart about his love for Shakespeare, his time in the navy, and his politics. To his surprise, he was awarded a coveted slot in the Lab.

The Lab included many leftists, a large number of whom participated in the Federal Theater Project of the 1930s, and Papp eagerly embraced both their acting technique and socialist theater ideology. A popular student, he was made managing director of the school, but would be put out of a job in 1950 due to the ongoing Communist witch hunt, spurred on by the House Un-American Activities Committee (HUAC), which led to many notable writers, actors, and directors being blacklisted by the entertainment industry, and the exertion of enough pressure to force the closure of the Lab.

ELIZABETHAN WORKSHOP
FORMED: 1953

Papp was able to secure a job as assistant stage manager for the National Company touring production of Arthur Miller's *Death of a Salesman,* and when it came to an end in 1952 he returned to New York City, taking a day job as a stage manager for live CBS television programming, the *Studio One* drama anthology as well as the celebrity game show *I've Got a Secret.* It was because of television that he also changed his last name to Papp because, as he explained, Papirofsky was too long to fit on the screen during the post-show credits. In his spare time he served as director of the Equity Library Theater, and in 1953 organized the Elizabethan Workshop, working with actors in a Lower East Side church, the Emmanuel Presbyterian Church, across the river from the Naval Yard. The program would soon change its name to the Shakespeare Workshop. Papp envisioned building a theater modeled after an Elizabethan playhouse, like the Globe where Shakespeare's greatest works were staged, and in 1954 he received a provisional charter for a nonprofit theater that would pursue this dream as well as the mission of encouraging interest in Shakespeare and other Elizabethans.

Papp's first Shakespeare productions, five of them, were performed for free in Emmanuel Presbyterian Church in 1955. The following year he took Shakespeare outdoors, with backing from the New York City Parks Department, performing *Julius Caesar* and *The Taming of the Shrew* in the Lower East Side's 2,000-seat East River Park Amphitheater. The cast and crew worked without pay. In 1957 Papp took Shakespeare throughout the five boroughs using a mobile stage that would then be placed in Central Park close to the Belvedere Castle off West 81st Street, the future home of the Delacorte Theater. A year later The New York Shakes-

KEY DATES

1954: Joseph Papp founds New York Shakespeare Festival.
1956: First outdoor performances are presented free of charge.
1962: Delacorte Theater opens in Central Park.
1967: Public Theater is established in former Astor Library.
1975: *A Chorus Line* debuts.
1991: Papp dies.
1993: George C. Wolfe is named artistic director.
2002: Mara Manus is named executive director.
2005: Oskar Eustis succeeds Wolfe as artistic director.

peare Festival won its first Tony Award, given for distinguished service to the theater community.

Papp also received less-welcome attention in 1958, called to testify before HUAC for alleged Communist activities. Asked if his plays contained propaganda intended to advance the Communist agenda, he replied, "Sir, the plays we do are Shakespeare's plays. ... I cannot control the writings of Shakespeare. He wrote plays 500 years ago." While Papp denied that he had been a member of the Communist Party after June 1955, he refused to testify about his activities prior to that date, citing the Fifth Amendment. As a result, Papp was fired from his CBS job but was subsequently reinstated following an arbitration hearing. Two years later he would leave CBS in order to devote all of his attention to his nonprofit theater.

Papp's HUAC testimony also jeopardized the existence of the Festival. One of the assistants to the autocratic head of the Parks Department, Robert Moses, was appalled at the idea of a Communist sympathizer like Papp producing Shakespeare for the masses and while his boss was on vacation issued an ultimatum: Either Papp charged admission, supposedly to support a "grass erosion fund," or the Festival would be forced out of Central Park. Papp refused, and upon his return Moses backed his lieutenant, thus making the battle between Papp and Moses. The matter went to court and Papp prevailed on appeal in 1959, allowing Shakespeare in the park free of charge. Moses requested $250,000 from the city to build a permanent home for the Festival that would at least be more presentable than the makeshift stage Papp employed.

DELACORTE THEATER OPENS: 1962

The new theater was budgeted at $400,000. Making up the $150,000 shortfall would be publishing executive George T. Delacorte, president of the Dell Publishing Company. Because of his donation, the amphitheater would eventually take his name. The theater was scheduled to be ready in the spring of 1961, but was not, forcing shows that summer to be performed in the Wolfman Memorial Skating Rink. The first performance in the Delacorte Theater, given in June 1962, would be *Merchant of Venice,* starring James Earl Jones and George C. Scott.

By the time the Delacorte opened, the city of New York had become enthusiastic backers of the New York Shakespeare Festival, but having achieved his dream Papp was far from satisfied. In 1965 he took an interest in the old Astor Library on Lafayette Street, New York's first major public library. No longer needed by its owner, it had been sold and was slated to be demolished and replaced by an apartment house, although the landmarks commission had the right to seek an alternative to demolition. Papp paid a visit to the building, recognized that it could house several theaters, and he successfully negotiated with the developers of the apartment house to acquire the property in January 1966. Thus, the Astor Library became the first building to be spared the wrecking ball under the city's landmarks preservation law.

The Astor Library building was renamed the New York Shakespeare Public Theater. It was large enough to accommodate the office needs of the company as well as provide ample rehearsal space and six theaters. The first of the theaters to open was the Anspacher in 1967, the first production the groundbreaking rock musical *Hair,* which would lead to a Broadway production, the first of many Public Theater shows to follow that commercial path. For the most part, however, Papp was not interested in commercial success, preferring to develop new playwrights and to produce plays of social significance. If the shows were good enough they would simply find a wider audience, and sometimes honors. In 1969 The Public Theater produced Charles Gordone's *No Place to Be Somebody,* which was awarded the Pulitzer Prize for drama in 1970, and in 1972 Jason Miller's *That Championship Season* was performed and won the Pulitzer the following year. Also in the early 1970s a production of *Two Gentlemen of Verona* and David Rabe's *Sticks and Bones* won Tony Awards, as did Miller for most promising playwright. In the fall of 1972 four Public Theater–produced plays were playing on Broadway.

A CHORUS LINE: 1975

In 1973 Papp took over the management of Lincoln Center Theater as the New York Shakespeare Festival joined the Lincoln Center for the Performing Arts, but he did not fare as well uptown and after five years resigned to devote his full attention to The Public Theater. Despite his artistic successes Papp and The Public Theater were regularly strapped for cash. Then in 1975 the company would be presented with a cash cow that would cover its deficits for the next dozen years, the landmark musical *A Chorus Line,* winner of nine Tony Awards and the Pulitzer Prize. It would become the longest running Broadway musical of its era.

The Public Theater began the 1980s with another triumph, a revival of *The Pirates of Penzance,* which would be transferred to Broadway and win three Tony Awards. Other Broadway transfers included *Plenty* in 1983, and *The Mystery of Edwin Drood* in 1985, a musical that garnered five Tony Awards. The decade would also bring an exchange with London's Royal Court Theater, the introduction of the Festival Latino de Nueva York, and Festival Latino, celebrating the work of Latino playwrights.

In 1990 Papp once again demonstrated his independent spirit, turning down a $323,000 grant from the National Endowment for the Arts because he was unwilling to sign an obscenity clause initiated by Senator Jesse Helms in the wake of a controversial National Endowment for the Arts (NEA)-funded Robert Mapplethorpe exhibition. It was to be Papp's last hurrah. His health failing, Papp retired in the summer of 1991, leaving his handpicked successor, JoAnne Akalaitis, with an organization that was once again in serious financial straits. Two months later the 70-year-old Papp died of prostate cancer.

Akalaitis served as the artistic director of The Public Theater for 19 months. She reopened contacts with the NEA and launched a number of initiatives, such as making the company's facilities more accessible to Off- and Off-Off Broadway companies, but made enemies with the press and clashed with her board of trustees. In March 1993 she was ousted in favor of 38-year-old writer-director George C. Wolfe, whose play *The Colored Museum* had premiered at The Public Theater in 1987. In 1993 he directed *Twilight: Los Angeles, 1992* to critical success and a Broadway transfer.

Wolfe placed his own stamp on The Public Theater as it sought out a new identity in the post-Papp years. During Wolfe's tenure, 11 productions would make their way to Broadway, resulting in one Pulitzer and eight Tony Awards. He directed one of the most successful of these productions, *Bring in 'Da Noise, Bring in 'Da Funk,* winner of four Tony Awards. The show would also become The Public Theater's first production to tour nationally, on the road for two years, starting in 1997. In 1998 The Public Theater opened Joe's Pub, a music and performance venue named for Papp.

More successful productions followed in the new century for Wolfe, including *Lackawanna Blues,* a television production of which would be directed for HBO by Wolfe; *Topdog/Underdog,* a Suzan-Lori Parks play directed by Wolfe that would receive the Pulitzer for drama; and *Elaine Stritch at Liberty,* which would move to Broadway and win a Tony Award. While successful artistically, Wolfe did not prove to be an especially adept business manager. Following the terrorist attacks in New York and Washington, D.C., on September 11, 2001, the organization struggled to raise money. The board sought to bring in someone to shoulder some of the business responsibilities, and in 2002 Mara Manus, a former program officer at the Ford Foundation, joined Wolfe as executive director. The combination worked, as Wolfe retained his artistic autonomy while Manus helped to improve the company's fiscal health. The relationship lasted until February 2004 when Wolfe announced he would be leaving The Public Theater.

In 2005, Oskar Eustis, the artistic director of Trinity Repertory Theater in Providence, Rhode Island, and a respected director and producer, was selected to replace Wolfe, taking over in June of that year. At the same time, The Public Theater was able to erase the deficit that had accumulated since 2001 and had grown its endowment to $18.5 million. Many of the playwrights whose work would be seen on The Public Theater stages had been groomed by Wolfe, but Eustis had developed relationships with a number of other noted playwrights, such as David Henry Hwang, Tony Award–winning author of *M. Butterfly,* and began to make his own mark as well. He also made changes to the organization in 2007, creating a new position, associate artistic director, to focus on new play development.

Ed Dinger

PRINCIPAL COMPETITORS

Performance Space 122; Nederlander Producing Company of America, Inc.; Dodger Theatricals; Jujamcyn Theaters; The Shubert Organization, Inc.

FURTHER READING

Atkinson, Brooks, "New Shakespeare Theatre in Central Park," *New York Times,* March 30, 1962.

Barnes, Clive, "Papp's Enterprises: Sound Art and Shaky Finances," *New York Times,* December 7, 1968.

Calta, Louis, "Park Troupe Told to End Free Plays," *New York Times,* April 16, 1959.

Epstein, Helen, *Joe Papp: An American Life,* Boston: Little, Brown and Company, 1994, 554 p.

Fowle, Farnsworth, "Park Play Talks Break Up in Huff," *New York Times,* May 15, 1959.

"How Papp Got It Right," *American Theatre,* January 2007, p. 74.

Kandel, Myron, "The Bard's New Home in the Park," *New York Times,* May 27, 1962.

"My Kingdom for a Check," *Forbes,* April 4, 1988, p. 128.

O'Quinn, Jim, "Change of Will (Dismissal of Joanne Akalaitis As New York Shakespeare Festival's Artistic Director)," *American Theatre,* May–June 1993, p. 43.

Pogrebin, Robin, "3 Leaders Wanted: Art Lovers/Math Skills/ Charisma. Thick Skin Reqd.," *New York Times,* February 19, 2004.

Rothstein, Mervyn, "Joseph Papp, Theater's Champion, Dies," *New York Times,* November 1, 1991.

Shepard, Richard F., "Papp Digging Theater Below Festival Building," *New York Times,* July 9, 1969.

Sullivan, Dan, "'Papp Is a Love Person,'" *New York Times,* October 15, 1967.

Walsh, Thomas, "Joseph Papp: 1921–1991," *Back Stage,* November 8, 1991, p. 1.

———, "NYSF Changes the Guard," *Back Stage,* March 19, 1993, p. 1.

PepsiCo, Inc.

—■—

700 Anderson Hill Road
Purchase, New York 10577-1444
U.S.A.
Telephone: (914) 253-2000
Fax: (914) 253-2070
Web site: http://www.pepsico.com

Public Company
Incorporated: 1965
Employees: 168,000
Sales: $35.14 billion (2006)
Stock Exchanges: New York Chicago Amsterdam Swiss
Ticker Symbol: PEP
NAIC: 311211 Flour Milling; 311212 Rice Milling; 311230 Breakfast Cereal Manufacturing; 311411 Frozen Fruit, Juice, and Vegetable Manufacturing; 311421 Fruit and Vegetable Canning; 311423 Dried and Dehydrated Food Manufacturing; 311821 Cookie and Cracker Manufacturing; 311822 Flour Mixes and Dough Manufacturing from Purchased Flour; 311823 Dry Pasta Manufacturing; 311919 Other Snack Food Manufacturing; 311920 Coffee and Tea Manufacturing; 311930 Flavoring Syrup and Concentrate Manufacturing; 311999 All Other Miscellaneous Food Manufacturing; 312111 Soft Drink Manufacturing; 312112 Bottled Water Manufacturing

■ ■ ■

One of the world's top consumer product companies, PepsiCo, Inc., is a world leader in both convenient foods and beverages. The company is the second largest producer of soft drinks in the world, trailing only The Coca-Cola Company, and is by far the world leader in salty snacks. PepsiCo's global operations are divided into three divisions: PepsiCo Americas Beverages, PepsiCo Americas Foods, and PepsiCo International.

PepsiCo Americas Beverages, which generates about 30 percent of total revenues, includes the firm's carbonated and noncarbonated beverage operations in North America and Latin America. PepsiCo holds a 31 percent share of the carbonated soft drink market in the United States, with four of its brands—Pepsi-Cola, Mountain Dew, Diet Pepsi, and Diet Mountain Dew—ranking among the top ten soft drinks in the U.S. market. In addition, the company is the U.S. leader in several other beverage categories, including sports drinks (Gatorade), bottled water (Aquafina), chilled juice (Tropicana), enhanced water (Propel), bottled tea (Lipton, via a joint venture with Unilever), and ready-to-drink coffee (Starbucks, via a joint venture with Starbucks Corporation).

PepsiCo Americas Foods, contributor of 45 percent of revenues, includes Frito-Lay North America, Quaker Foods North America, and food and snack businesses in Latin America. Frito-Lay controls a staggering 65 percent of the U.S. salty snack market and produces nearly all of the top snack chip brands sold in the United States, including Lay's, Doritos, Tostitos, Ruffles, Fritos, and Cheetos. Quaker produces a variety of food products, including Quaker oatmeal, Quaker grits, Cap'n Crunch and Life cereals, Aunt Jemima syrups and pancake mixes, and the Rice-A-Roni, Pasta Roni, and Near East side dish brands. Among the Latin American snack brands are Gamesa and Sabritas in Mexico.

PepsiCo International, generator of 25 percent of revenues, encompasses all of PepsiCo's food and beverage businesses outside North America and Latin America. Overall, PepsiCo garners about 41 percent of its revenues outside the United States, with its brands marketed in more than 170 countries around the world. On a worldwide basis, PepsiCo's product portfolio includes 17 brands that generate more than $1 billion in sales each year.

When Caleb D. Bradham concocted a new cola drink in the 1890s, his friends' enthusiastic response convinced him that he had created a commercially viable product. For 20 years, "Doc" Bradham prospered from his Pepsi-Cola sales. Eventually, he was faced with a dilemma; the crucial decision he made turned out to be the wrong one and he was forced to sell. His successors fared no better and it was not until the end of the 1930s that Pepsi-Cola again became profitable. Seventy years later, PepsiCo, Inc., was a mammoth multinational supplier of carbonated and noncarbonated beverages and convenient foods. PepsiCo's advance to that level was almost entirely the result of its management style and the phenomenal success of its television advertising.

UP-AND-DOWN EARLY YEARS UNDER THE FOUNDER

Doc Bradham, like countless other entrepreneurs across the United States, was trying to create a cola drink similar in taste to Coca-Cola, which by 1895 was selling well in every state of the union. On August 28, 1898, at his pharmacy in New Bern, North Carolina, Bradham gave the name Pepsi-Cola to his most popular flavored soda. Formerly known as Brad's Drink, the new cola beverage was a syrup of sugar, vanilla, oils, cola nuts, and other flavorings diluted in carbonated water. The enterprising pharmacist followed Coca-Cola's method of selling the concentrate to soda fountains; he mixed the syrup in his drugstore, then shipped it in barrels to the contracted fountain operators who added the soda water. He also bottled and sold the drink himself.

In 1902 Doc Bradham closed his drugstore to devote his attention to the thriving new business. The next year, he patented the Pepsi-Cola trademark, ran his first advertisement in a local paper, and moved the bottling and syrup-making operations to a custom-built factory. Almost 20,000 gallons of Pepsi-Cola syrup were produced in 1904.

Again following the successful methods of The Coca-Cola Company, Bradham began to establish a network of bottling franchises. Entrepreneurs anxious to enter the increasingly popular soft drink business set themselves up as bottlers and contracted with Bradham to buy his syrup and sell nothing but Pepsi. With little cash outlay, Pepsi-Cola reached a much wider market. Bradham's first two bottling franchises, both in North Carolina, commenced operation in 1905. By 1907, Pepsi-Cola had signed agreements with 40 bottlers; over the next three years, the number grew to 250 and annual production of the syrup exceeded one million gallons.

Pepsi-Cola's growth continued until World War I, when sugar, then the main ingredient of all flavored sodas, was rationed. Soft drink producers were forced to cut back until sugar rationing ended. The wartime set price of sugar, 5.5 cents per pound, rocketed after controls were lifted to as much as 26.5 cents per pound in 1920. Bradham, like his rivals, had to decide whether to halt production and sit tight in the hope that prices would soon drop, or stockpile the precious commodity as a precaution against even higher prices; he chose the latter course. Unfortunately for him, the market was saturated by the end of 1920 and sugar prices plunged to a low of two cents per pound.

Bradham never recovered. After several abortive attempts to reorganize, only two of the bottling plants remained open. In a last ditch effort, he enlisted the help of Roy C. Megargel, a Wall Street investment banker. Very few people, however, were willing to invest in the business and it went bankrupt in 1923. The assets were sold and Megargel purchased the company trademark, giving him the rights to the Pepsi-Cola formula. Doc Bradham went back to his drug dispensary and died 11 years later.

REORGANIZATION AND EVENTUAL SUCCESS

Megargel reorganized the firm as the National Pepsi-Cola Company in 1928, but after three years of continuous losses he had to declare bankruptcy. That same year, 1931, Megargel met Charles G. Guth, a somewhat autocratic businessman who had taken over as

KEY DATES

1898:	Pharmacist Caleb D. Bradham begins selling a cola beverage called Pepsi-Cola.
1905:	Bradham begins establishing a network of bottling franchises.
1923:	Bradham's company goes bankrupt.
1928:	Roy C. Megargel reorganizes the firm as the National Pepsi-Cola Company.
1931:	Company again goes bankrupt and is resurrected by the president of Loft Inc., Charles G. Guth.
1933:	The size of Pepsi bottles is doubled, increasing sales dramatically.
1936:	Pepsi-Cola Company becomes a subsidiary of Loft.
1939:	First national radio ads for Pepsi begin to air.
1941:	Loft and Pepsi-Cola merge, the new firm using the name Pepsi-Cola Company; company's stock begins trading on the New York Stock Exchange.
1964:	Diet Pepsi debuts; Mountain Dew is acquired from Tip Corporation.
1965:	Pepsi-Cola merges with Frito-Lay to form PepsiCo, Inc., with the two predecessors becoming divisions.
1967:	Frito-Lay introduces Doritos tortilla chips to the national U.S. market.
1977:	PepsiCo acquires Taco Bell.
1978:	PepsiCo acquires Pizza Hut.
1981:	Frito-Lay introduces Tostitos tortilla chips.
1986:	The Kentucky Fried Chicken (KFC) chain is acquired.
1997:	Taco Bell, Pizza Hut, and KFC are spun off into a new company called Tricon Global Restaurants.
1998:	PepsiCo acquires Tropicana Products for $3.3 billion.
1999:	Pepsi Bottling Group is spun off to the public, with PepsiCo retaining a 35 percent stake.
2001:	PepsiCo acquires the Quaker Oats Company for $14 billion.
2005:	Revenues surpass $30 billion; market capitalization exceeds that of The Coca-Cola Company for the first time.

president of Loft Inc., a New York-based candy and fountain store concern. Guth had fallen out with Coca-Cola for refusing the company a wholesaler discount and he was on the lookout for a new soft drink. He signed an agreement with Megargel to resurrect the Pepsi-Cola company, and acquired 80 percent of the new shares, ostensibly for himself. Then, having modified the syrup formula, he canceled Loft's contract with Coca-Cola and introduced Pepsi-Cola, whose name was often shortened to Pepsi.

Loft's customers were wary of the brand switch and in the first year of Pepsi sales the company's soft drink turnover was down a third. By the end of 1933, Guth bought out Megargel and owned 91 percent of the insolvent company. Resistance to Pepsi in the Loft stores tailed off in 1934, and Guth decided to further improve sales by offering 12-ounce bottles of Pepsi for a nickel, the same price as six ounces of Coke. The Depression-weary people of Baltimore, where the 12-ounce bottles were first introduced, were ready for a bargain, and Pepsi-Cola sales increased dramatically.

Guth soon took steps to internationalize Pepsi-Cola, establishing the Pepsi-Cola Company of Canada in 1934 and in the following year forming Compania Pepsi-Cola de Cuba. He also moved the entire U.S. operation to Long Island City, New York, and set up national territorial boundaries for the bottling franchises. In 1936 Pepsi-Cola Ltd. of London commenced business.

Guth's ownership of the Pepsi-Cola Company was challenged that same year by Loft Inc. In a complex arrangement, Guth had organized Pepsi-Cola as an independent corporation, but he had run it with Loft's employees and money. After three years of litigation, the court upheld Loft's contention and Guth had to step down, although he was retained as an adviser. James W. Carkner was elected president of the company, by this time a subsidiary of Loft Inc., but Carkner was soon replaced by Walter S. Mack, Jr., an executive from the Phoenix Securities Corporation.

Mack established a board of directors with real voting powers to ensure that no one person would be able to wield control as Guth had done. From the start, Mack's aim was to promote Pepsi to the hilt so that it might replace Coca-Cola as the world's best-selling soft drink. The advertising agency Mack hired worked wonders. In 1939, a Pepsi radio jingle, the first one to be aired nationally, caught the public's attention: "Pepsi-Cola hits the spot. Twelve full ounces, that's a lot. Twice as much for a nickel, too. Pepsi-Cola is the drink for you." The jingle, sung to the tune of the old British hunting song "D'Ye Ken John Peel," became an advertising hallmark; no one was more impressed, or concerned, than the executives at Coca-Cola.

In 1940, with foreign expansion continuing strongly, Loft Inc. made plans to merge with its Pepsi-Cola subsidiary. The new firm, formed in 1941, used the name Pepsi-Cola Company because it was so well-known. Pepsi's stock was listed on the New York Stock Exchange for the first time.

Sugar rationing was even more severe during World War II, but this time the company fared better; indeed, the sugar plantation Pepsi-Cola acquired in Cuba became a most successful investment. As inflation spiraled in the postwar U.S. economy, sales of soft drinks fell. The public needed time to get used to paying six or seven cents for a bottle of Pepsi which, as they remembered from the jingle, had always been a nickel. Profits in 1948 were down $3.6 million from the year before.

In other respects, 1948 was a notable year. Pepsi moved its corporate headquarters across the East River to midtown Manhattan, and for the first time the drink was sold in cans. The decision to start canning, while absolutely right for Pepsi-Cola and other soft drink companies, upset the franchised bottlers, who had invested heavily in equipment. However, another decision at Pepsi-Cola, to ignore the burgeoning vending machine market because of the necessarily large capital outlay, proved to be a costly mistake. The company had to learn the hard way that as canned drinks gained a larger share of the market, vending machine sales would become increasingly important.

THE POSTWAR STEELE AND CRAWFORD ERA

Walter Mack was appointed company chairman in 1950, and a former Coca-Cola vice-president of sales, Alfred N. Steele, took over as president and chief executive officer, bringing 15 other Coke executives with him. Steele continued the policy of management decentralization by giving broader powers to regional vice-presidents, and he placed Herbert Barnet in charge of Pepsi's financial operations. Steele's outstanding

contribution, however, was in marketing. He launched an extensive advertising campaign with the slogan "Be Sociable, Have a Pepsi." The new television medium provided a perfect forum; Pepsi advertisements presented young Americans drinking "The Light Refreshment" and having fun.

By the time Steele married movie star Joan Crawford in 1954, a transformation of the company was well underway. Crawford's adopted daughter, Christina, noted in her bestseller *Mommie Dearest*: "[Steele had] driven Pepsi into national prominence and distribution, second only to his former employer, Coca-Cola. Pepsi was giving Coke a run for its money in every nook and hamlet of America. Al Steele welded a national network of bottlers together, standardized the syrup formula ..., brought the distinctive logo into mass consciousness, and was on the brink of going international." In fact, Pepsi-Cola International Ltd. was formed shortly after Steele's marriage.

Crawford became the personification of Pepsi's new and glamorous image. She invariably kept a bottle of Pepsi at hand during press conferences and mentioned the product at interviews and on talk shows; on occasion she even arranged for Pepsi trucks and vending machines to feature in background shots of her movies. The actress also worked hard to spread the Pepsi word overseas and accompanied her husband, now chairman of the board, on his 1957 tour of Europe and Africa, where bottling plants were being established.

Steele died suddenly of a heart attack in the spring of 1959. Herbert Barnet succeeded him as chairman and Crawford was elected a board member. Pepsi-Cola profits had fallen to a postwar low of $1.3 million in 1950 when Steele joined the company, but with the proliferation of supermarkets during the decade and the developments in overseas business, profits reached $14.2 million in 1960. By that time, young adults had become a major target of soft drink manufacturers and Pepsi's advertisements were aimed at "Those who think young."

Steele and Crawford had been superb cheerleaders, but a stunt pulled in 1959 by Donald M. Kendall, head of Pepsi-Cola International, is still regarded as one of the great coups in the annals of advertising. Kendall attended the Moscow Trade Fair that year and persuaded U.S. Vice President Richard Nixon to stop by the Pepsi booth with Nikita Khrushchev, the Soviet premier. As the cameras flashed, Khrushchev quenched his thirst with Pepsi and the grinning Nixon stood in attendance. The next day, newspapers around the world featured photographs of the happy couple, complete with Pepsi bottle.

THE PEPSI GENERATION

By 1963, Kendall was presiding over the Pepsi empire. His rise to the top of the company was legendary. He had been an amateur boxing champion in his youth and joined the company as a production line worker in 1947 after a stint in the U.S. Navy. He was later promoted to syrup sales where it quickly became apparent that he was destined for higher office. Ever pugnacious, Kendall has been described as abrasive and ruthlessly ambitious; beleaguered Pepsi executives secretly referred to him as White Fang. Under his long reign, the company's fortunes skyrocketed.

Pepsi-Cola's remarkable successes in the 1960s and 1970s were the result of five distinct policies, all of which Kendall and his crew pursued diligently: advertising on a massive, unprecedented scale; introducing new brands of soft drinks; leading the industry in packaging innovations; expanding overseas; and, through acquisitions, diversifying their product line.

The postwar baby boomers were in their mid- to late teens by the time Kendall came to power. A company flyer from the late 20th century stated, "Pepsi was there to claim these kids for our own." These "kids" became the "Pepsi Generation." In the late 1960s Pepsi was the "Taste that beats the others cold." Viewers were advised "You've got a lot to live. Pepsi's got a lot to give." By the early 1970s, the appeal was to "Join the Pepsi people, feelin' free." In mid-decade an American catchphrase was given a company twist with "Have a Pepsi Day," and the 1970s ended on the note "Catch the Pepsi Spirit!"

The Pepsi Generation wanted variety and Pepsi was happy to oblige. Company brands introduced in the 1960s included Patio soft drinks, Teem, Tropic Surf, Diet Pepsi—the first nationally distributed diet soda, introduced in 1964—and Mountain Dew, acquired from the Tip Corporation, also in 1964. Pepsi Light, a diet cola with a hint of lemon, made its debut in 1975, and a few years later Pepsi tested the market with Aspen apple soda and On-Tap root beer. The company also introduced greater variety into the packaging of its products. Soon after Kendall's accession, the 12-ounce bottle was phased out in favor of the 16-ounce size, and in the 1970s Pepsi-Cola became the first U.S. company to introduce one-and-a-half and two-liter bottles; it also began to package its sodas in sturdy, lightweight plastic bottles. By the end of the decade, Pepsi had added 12-pack cans to its growing array of packaging options.

1965 MERGER WITH FRITO-LAY TO CREATE PEPSICO, INC.

The company's expansion beyond the soft drink market began in 1965 when Kendall met Herman Lay, the owner of Frito-Lay, at a grocer's convention. Kendall arranged a merger with this Dallas-based snack food manufacturer and formed PepsiCo, Inc. Herman Lay retired soon thereafter but retained his substantial PepsiCo shareholding. The value of this stock increased dramatically as Frito-Lay products were introduced to Pepsi's nationwide market. At the time of the merger, key Frito-Lay brands included Fritos corn chips (created in 1932), Lay's potato chips (1938), Chee-tos cheese-flavored snacks (1948), Ruffles potato chips (1958), and Rold Gold pretzels (acquired by Frito-Lay in 1961). Doritos tortilla chips were introduced nationally in 1967. The addition of Frito-Lay helped PepsiCo achieve $1 billion in sales for the first time in 1970. That same year, the corporation moved into its new world headquarters in Purchase, New York.

During the 1970s, Kendall acquired two well-known fast-food restaurant chains, Taco Bell, in 1977, and Pizza Hut, in 1978; naturally, these new subsidiaries became major outlets for Pepsi products. Kendall also diversified outside the food and drink industry, bringing North American Van Lines (acquired in 1968), Lee Way Motor Freight, and Wilson Sporting Goods into the PepsiCo empire.

Overseas developments continued throughout Kendall's tenure. Building on his famous Soviet achievement, he negotiated a trade agreement with the U.S.S.R. in 1972; the first Pepsi plant opened there two years later. Gains were also made in the Middle East and Latin America, but Coca-Cola, the major rival, retained its dominant position in Europe and throughout much of Asia.

By the time PepsiCo greeted the 1980s with the slogan "Pepsi's got your taste for life!" Kendall was busy arranging for China to get that taste too; production began there in 1983. Kendall put his seal of approval on several other major developments in the early 1980s, including the introduction of Pepsi Free, a non-caffeine cola, and Slice, the first widely distributed soft drink to contain real fruit juice (lemon and lime). The latter drink was aimed at the growing 7-Up and Sprite market. Additionally, Diet Pepsi was reformulated using a blend of saccharin and aspartame (NutraSweet). "Pepsi Now!" was the cry of company commercials, and this was interspersed with "Taste, Improved by Diet Pepsi." On the Frito-Lay side, meantime, the Tostitos brand of crispy round tortilla chips was introduced in 1981.

In 1983 the company claimed a significant share of the fast-food soft drink market when Burger King began selling Pepsi products. A year later, mindful of the industry axiom that there is virtually no limit to the amount a consumer will buy once the decision to buy has been made, PepsiCo introduced the three-liter container.

By the mid-1980s, the Pepsi Generation was over the hill. Kendall's ad agency spared no expense in heralding Pepsi as "The Choice of a New Generation," using the talents of superstar Michael Jackson, singer Lionel Richie, and the Puerto Rican teenage group Menudo. Michael Jackson's ads were smash hits and enjoyed record high exposure. The company's high profile and powerful presence in all of the soft drink markets, direct results of Kendall's strategies, helped it to weather the somewhat uncertain economic situation of the time.

On only one front had Kendall's efforts failed to produce satisfactory results. Experience showed that for all its expertise, PepsiCo simply did not have the managerial experience required to run its subsidiaries outside the food and drink industries. A van line, a motor freight concern, and a sporting goods firm were indeed odd companies for a soft drink enterprise; and Kendall auctioned off these strange and ailing bedfellows, vowing never again to go courting in unfamiliar territories.

THE COLA WARS

With his house in excellent order, the PepsiCo mogul began to prepare for his retirement. He had bullied and cajoled a generation of Pepsi executives and guided them ever upward on the steep slopes of Pepsi profits. However, he had one last task: to lead PepsiCo to victory in the Cola Wars.

Hostilities commenced soon after The Coca-Cola Company changed its syrup recipe in the summer of 1985 and with much fanfare introduced New Coke. Pepsi, caught napping, claimed that Coca-Cola's reformulated drink failed to meet with consumer approval and pointed to their own flourishing sales. Serious fans of the original Coke were not about to switch to Pepsi and demanded that their favorite refreshment be restored. When blindfolded, however, it became manifestly apparent that these diehards could rarely tell the difference between Old Coke, New Coke, and Pepsi; indeed, more often than not, they got it wrong. In any event, The Coca-Cola Company acceded to the public clamor for the original Coke and remarketed it as Coca-Cola Classic alongside its new cola.

Some advertising analysts believed that the entire "conflict" was a clever publicity ploy on the part of Coca-Cola to demonstrate the pre-eminence of its original concoction ("It's the Real Thing!"), while introducing a new cola, allegedly a Pepsi taste-alike, to win the hearts of waverers. More interesting perhaps than the possible differences between the colas were the very real differences in people's reactions. Four discrete fields were identified by Roger Enrico and Jesse Kornbluth in their book, *The Other Guy Blinked: How Pepsi Won the Cola Wars:* the totally wowed (possibly caffeine-induced); the rather amused; the slightly irritated; and the distinctly bored.

The latter group must have nodded off in front of their television sets when Pepsi took the Cola Wars beyond the firmament. "One Giant Sip for Mankind," proclaimed the ads as a Pepsi "space can" was opened up aboard the U.S. space shuttle *Challenger* in 1985. Presumably, had a regular can been used, Pepsi-Cola would have sloshed aimlessly around the gravity-free cabin. This scientific breakthrough, together with the almost obligatory hype and hoopla, and more mundane factors such as the continued expansion in PepsiCo's outlets, boosted sales to new heights, and Pepsi's ad agency glittered with accolades. The debate persisted, at least within Coke and Pepsi corporate offices, as to who won the Cola Wars. The answer appeared to be that there were no losers, only winners; but skirmishes would inevitably continue.

NEW WAVE OF INTERNATIONAL GROWTH AND DIVERSIFICATION

D. Wayne Calloway replaced Donald M. Kendall as chairman and chief executive officer in 1986. Calloway had been instrumental in the success of Frito-Lay, helping it to become PepsiCo's most profitable division. The new chairman realized that his flagship Pepsi brand was not likely to win additional market share from Coca-Cola, and focused his efforts on international growth and diversification.

Calloway hoped to build on the phenomenal success of the Slice line of fruit juice beverages, which achieved $1 billion in sales and created a new beverage category within just two years of its 1984 introduction. From 1985 to 1993, PepsiCo introduced, acquired, or formed joint ventures to distribute nine beverages, including Lipton Original Iced Teas, Ocean Spray juices, All Sport drink, H2Oh! sparkling water, Avalon bottled water, and Mug root beer. Many of these products had a "New Age" light and healthy positioning, in line with consumer tastes, and higher net prices. In 1992 PepsiCo introduced Crystal Pepsi, a clear cola that, while still a traditional soda, also tried to capture the momentum of the "New Age" beverage trend.

In the restaurant segment, PepsiCo's 1986 purchase of Kentucky Fried Chicken (KFC) and 1990 acquisition of the Hot 'n Now hamburger chain continued its emphasis on value-priced fast foods. The company strayed slightly from that formula with the 1992 and 1993 purchases of such full-service restaurants as California Pizza Kitchen, which specialized in creative wood-fired pizzas; Chevys, a Mexican-style chain; East Side Mario's Italian-style offerings; and D'Angelo Sandwich Shops.

Pepsi lost a powerful marketing tool in 1992, when Michael Jackson was accused of child molestation. Although the case was settled out of court, Pepsi dropped its contract with the entertainer. The firm launched its largest promotion ever in May 1992 with the "Gotta Have It" card, which offered discounts on the products of marketing partners Reebok sporting goods, Continental Airlines, and the MCI long distance company telephone. The company also launched a new marketing (or, as the company phrased it, "product quality") initiative early in 1994, when it announced that packaged carbonated soft drink products sold in the United States would voluntarily be marked with a "Best if Consumed By" date.

Although Pepsi had commenced international expansion during the 1950s, it had long trailed Coca-Cola's dramatic and overwhelming conquest of international markets. In 1990 CEO Calloway pledged up to $1 billion for overseas development, with the goal of increasing international volume 150 percent by 1995. At that time, Coke held 50 percent of the European soft drink market, while Pepsi claimed a meager 10 percent. Pepsi's advantage was that it could compete in other, less saturated segments. The company's biggest challenge to expanding its restaurant division was affordability. PepsiCo noted that, while it took the average U.S. worker just 15 minutes to earn enough to enjoy a meal in one of the firm's restaurants, it would take an Australian 25 minutes to achieve a similar goal. Pepsi still had other options, however. In 1992, for example, the company forged a joint venture with General Mills called Snack Ventures Europe that emerged as the largest firm in the $17 billion market. By 1993, PepsiCo had invested over $5 billion in international businesses, and its international sales comprised 27 percent, or $6.71 billion, of total annual sales.

In January 1992 Calloway was credited by *Business Week* magazine with emerging from the long shadow cast by his predecessor "to put together five impressive years of 20 percent compound earnings growth, doubling sales and nearly tripling the company's value on the stock market." Calloway also worked to reshape PepsiCo's corporate culture by fostering personal responsibility and a decentralized, flexible management style.

THE ENRICO RESTRUCTURING

Calloway, who was battling prostate cancer, retired as CEO in April 1996 and was replaced by Roger A. Enrico, who became chairman as well later in the year (Calloway died in July 1998). Since joining Frito-Lay's marketing department in 1971, Enrico had stints heading both Pepsi-Cola and Frito-Lay before becoming head of the restaurants division in 1994. He engineered a quick turnaround of the struggling chains by changing the overall strategy, for example adopting more franchising of units rather than company ownership. Under Enrico, the marketing of new concepts was also emphasized, with one notable success being the introduction of stuffed-crust pizza at Pizza Hut.

After taking over leadership of PepsiCo, Enrico quickly faced major problems in the overseas beverages operations, including big losses that were posted by its large Latin American bottler and the defection of its Venezuelan partner to Coca-Cola. PepsiCo ended up taking $576 million in special charges related to international writeoffs and restructuring, and its international arm posted a huge operating loss of $846 million, depressing 1996 profits. Among the moves initiated to turn around the international beverage operations, which faced brutal competition from the entrenched and better organized Coca-Cola, was to increase emphasis on emerging markets, such as India, China, Eastern Europe, and Russia, where Coke had a less formidable presence, and to rely less on bottling joint ventures and more on Pepsi- or franchise-owned bottling operations.

Another area of concern was the restaurant division, which had consistently been the PepsiCo laggard in terms of performance. Enrico concluded that in order to revitalize the beverage division and to take advantage of the surging Frito-Lay, which accounted for 43 percent of PepsiCo's operating profits, the restaurants had to go. Hot 'n Now and the casual dining chains were soon sold, and in January 1997 PepsiCo announced that it would spin off its three fast-food chains into a separate publicly traded company. The spinoff was completed in October 1997 with the formation of Tricon Global Restaurants, Inc., consisting of the Taco Bell, Pizza Hut, and KFC chains. The exit from restaurants removed one obstacle facing Pepsi in its battle with Coke: that most large fast-food chains had been reluctant to carry Pepsi beverages, not wanting to support the parent of a major competitor. Consequently, Coke held a huge market share advantage over Pepsi in the fast-food channel. Pepsi subsequently made some inroads, for example, in 1999 sealing a ten-year deal with the 11,500-plus-outlet Subway chain.

Enrico placed more emphasis, however, on building sales of Pepsi in its core supermarket channel. In this regard, he launched an initiative called "Power of One" that aimed to take advantage of the synergies between Frito-Lay's salty snacks and the beverages of Pepsi-Cola. This strategy involved persuading grocery retailers to move soft drinks next to snacks, the pitch being that such a placement would increase supermarket sales. In the process, PepsiCo would gain sales of both snacks and beverages while Coca-Cola could benefit only in the latter area. Power of One harkened back to the original rationale for the merger of Pepsi-Cola and Frito-Lay. At the time, the head of Pepsi, Kendall, had told Frito-Lay's leader, Herman W. Lay: "You make them thirsty, and I'll give them something to drink." The promise of this seemingly ideal marriage had never really been achieved, however, until the Power of One campaign, which in 1999 helped increase Frito-Lay's market share by 2 percent and boosted Pepsi's volume by 0.6 percent.

LATE-CENTURY ACQUISITIONS AND NEW PRODUCTS

In the meantime, Enrico was active on a number of other fronts. The company in 1997 nationally launched the Aquafina bottled water brand, which quickly gained the number one position in a fast-growing sector. In a move into the nonsalty snack category, Frito-Lay acquired the venerable Cracker Jack brand that year, and subsequently bolstered the brand through renewed advertising, a new four-ounce-bag package, the addition of more peanuts, the inclusion of better prizes, and the strength of Frito-Lay's vast distribution network. In August 1998 PepsiCo opened up another front in its ongoing war with Coca-Cola by acquiring juice-maker Tropicana Products, Inc., from the Seagram Company, Ltd., for $3.3 billion in cash, PepsiCo's largest acquisition to that point. Coca-Cola had been the owner of Tropicana's archrival, Minute Maid, since 1960, but Tropicana was the clear world juice leader, led by the flagship Tropicana Pure Premium brand. Tropicana had a dominating 41 percent share of the fast-growing chilled orange juice market in the United States. The brand was also attractive for its growth potential; not only were sales of juice growing at a much faster rate than the stagnating carbonated beverage sector, there was also great potential for brand growth overseas. Psychologically, the acquisition also provided PepsiCo with something it very much needed: it could boast of holding at least a dominant position over Coca-Cola.

In 1999 PepsiCo divested itself of another low-margin, capital-intensive business when it spun off Pepsi Bottling Group, the largest Pepsi bottler in the world, to the public in a $2.3 billion initial public offering (IPO).

PepsiCo retained a 35 percent stake. PepsiCo was focused exclusively on the less capital-intensive businesses of beverages and snack foods.

On the beverage side, Enrico, who had gained a reputation as a master marketer, spearheaded a bolder advertising strategy for the flagship Pepsi brand. In 1999 Pepsi-Cola was the exclusive global beverage partner for the movie blockbuster *Star Wars, Episode 1: The Phantom Menace.* The company also revived the old "Pepsi Challenge" campaign of the 1970s with the new Pepsi One diet drink facing off against Diet Coke. Pepsi's "Joy of Cola" advertising campaign gained accolades and in 2000 captured renewed attention following the signing of a string of celebrities to endorsement deals, including singer Faith Hill and baseball stars Sammy Sosa and Ken Griffey, Jr. Pepsi also greatly increased the number of vending machines it had around the United States, making a renewed push to gain on Coke in another area where the archenemy had long dominated.

By the end of 1999, after three and one-half years at the helm, Enrico had clearly turned PepsiCo into a stronger, much more focused, and better performing firm. Although revenues were more than one-third lower because of the divestments, earnings were higher by more than $100 million. Operating margins had increased from 10 percent to 15 percent, while return on invested capital grew from 15 percent to 20 percent. Net debt had been slashed from $8 billion to $2 billion. During 1999, Steve Reinemund was named president and COO of PepsiCo. Reinemund had headed Pizza Hut from 1986 to 1992 then was placed in charge of Frito-Lay. In the latter position, he oversaw a division whose sales increased 10 percent per year on average and whose profits doubled. During his tenure, Frito-Lay's share of the U.S. salty snack sector jumped from 40 to 60 percent.

EARLY 21ST-CENTURY ACQUISITION OF QUAKER OATS

In October 2000 Enrico announced that he intended to vacate his position as CEO by the end of 2001 and his position as chairman by year-end 2002. Reinemund was named the heir apparent. Also that month, PepsiCo reached an agreement to acquire a majority stake in South Beach Beverage Company, maker of the SoBe brand. Popular with young consumers, the SoBe drink line featured herbal ingredients and was the fastest-growing brand in the burgeoning noncarbonated alternative beverage sector. PepsiCo completed this deal in January 2001 at a cost of $337 million.

An even more tempting target soon attracted PepsiCo's attention: the powerhouse Gatorade brand owned by the Quaker Oats Company. Gatorade held an astounding 83.6 percent of the U.S. retail market for sports drinks and was the world leader in that segment with annual sales of about $2 billion. PepsiCo entered into talks with Quaker about acquiring the company for about $14.8 billion in stock, but by early November the two sides had failed to reach an agreement. Coca-Cola and Groupe Danone quickly came forward to discuss acquiring Quaker. Coke came exceedingly close to signing a $15.75 billion takeover agreement, but the company's board pulled the plug on the deal at the last minute. Danone soon bowed out as well. At that point, PepsiCo reentered the picture and sealed a deal in early December. The terms were essentially the same as Pepsi-Co's earlier offer: 2.3 shares of its stock for each share of Quaker. When the deal was completed on August 2, 2001, this translated into a final purchase price of $14 billion.

This coup for PepsiCo not only brought onboard the valuable Gatorade brand and made PepsiCo the clear leader in the fast-growing noncarbonated beverage category, it also added Quaker's small but growing snack business, which included granola and other bars as well as rice cakes. Quaker's non-snack food brands, including the flagship Quaker oatmeal, Life and Cap'n Crunch cereals, Rice-A-Roni, and Aunt Jemima syrup, did not fit as neatly into the PepsiCo portfolio but were highly profitable. Upon completion of the merger, Enrico and the head of Quaker, Robert S. Morrison, became vice-chairmen of PepsiCo, Morrison remained chairman, president, and CEO of Quaker, and Reinemund became chairman and CEO of PepsiCo, thereby accelerating a management transition. At that same time, PepsiCo's CFO, Indra Nooyi, who was the highest ranking Indian-born woman in corporate America, became president and CFO.

To gain regulatory approval for the Quaker Oats takeover, PepsiCo had to divest All Sport, its competing energy drink, which was sold to the Atlanta-based Monarch Company, Inc. Concerned that the company was gaining unfair market control with the addition of Gatorade, the Federal Trade Commission placed additional conditions on the deal. PepsiCo was barred from distributing Gatorade through its existing bottling system in the United States for a ten-year period, and it could not include both Gatorade and Pepsi-Cola products in certain marketing and promotional arrangements. Thanks to the Quaker Oats acquisition, as well as the introduction of successful new products, such as the cherry-flavored, caffeine-packed Mountain Dew Code Red, PepsiCo saw its revenues surge 5.7 percent in 2001, to $26.94 billion.

RESTRUCTURING AND FURTHER INNOVATION

In a major reorganization launched in 2003, PepsiCo divided its global operations into four divisions, most notably by creating a PepsiCo International unit that united all of the company's beverage, snack, and food businesses outside of North America. PepsiCo Beverages North America encompassed the firm's core domestic carbonated beverages business along with its growing noncarbonated lines, which included Gatorade, Tropicana, Aquafina, and other brands. Frito-Lay North America, the most profitable of the four divisions, had subsumed Quaker's snack brands, including Quaker Chewy granola bars, Quaker Fruit and Oatmeal bars, and Quaker Quakes rice cakes. By far the smallest of the four units was Quaker Foods North America, which had been left with a predominantly breakfast-oriented product lineup consisting primarily of Quaker oatmeal, Quaker grits, Cap'n Crunch and Life cereals, Aunt Jemima syrups and pancake mixes, and the Rice-A-Roni, Pasta Roni, and Near East side dish brands.

Also occurring in 2003 was the national rollout of Sierra Mist, a lemon-lime carbonated beverage aimed at a younger demographic that immediately became one of PepsiCo's $1 billion brands. In the meantime, over at Frito-Lay various new product developments centered around Americans' growing concerns about the healthfulness of the foods they were consuming. Reduced-fat versions of Lay's and Cheetos debuted in 2002, while Frito-Lay's nonfried "Baked" line was further expanded. In addition Frito-Lay began eliminating artery-clogging trans fats from its products, a process completed in 2004.

Pushing further in this same direction, Frito-Lay in 2003 branched into the natural and organic snacks category for the first time. Under the overall umbrella name "Natural," the company launched a slew of new products made with certified organic ingredients. In 2004 a number of Frito-Lay products as well as those of other PepsiCo units began sporting "Smart Spot" symbols as a further way of alerting consumers to their status as a more healthful choice. To include the symbol, a PepsiCo product had to meet certain criteria, including limits on the amount of fat, both saturated and trans, cholesterol, sodium, and added sugar. By the end of 2005, more than 250 company products featured the Smart Spot symbol, and these products were generating more than 40 percent of PepsiCo's overall North American sales. Consumer interest in these more healthful products was quite evident in that during 2005 they achieved sales growth two-and-a-half times the rate of the rest of the PepsiCo portfolio.

Efforts were also undertaken to improve the company's operational efficiency. Late in 2003 a $147 million restructuring charge was taken in connection with a streamlining of both North American and international operations involving the closure of several plants and a workforce reduction of approximately 850. About a year later, Frito-Lay North America closed four plants and cut nearly 800 more jobs in a restructuring that entailed an additional charge of $150 million.

On the acquisitions front, PepsiCo paid $750 million to General Mills in February 2005 to gain full control of Snack Ventures Europe. This business, with annual sales in excess of $1 billion, was the largest snack food company in continental Europe, with operations in Belgium, France, the Netherlands, Spain, Portugal, Greece, the Baltics, Hungary, and Russia. Later in the year, PepsiCo significantly bolstered its juice business in continental Europe by acquiring Punica Getränke GmbH, a leading German maker of fruit juices and juice-based drinks. Midyear, rumors flew back and forth across the Atlantic that PepsiCo was preparing a bid for Groupe Danone. This prospect provoked a nationalistic furor in France, a furor that quickly died away when no such takeover materialized.

THE PEPSICO JUGGERNAUT

In 2005 PepsiCo reached a milestone, as sales surpassed $30 billion for the first time, amounting to $32.56 billion. Also noteworthy was that PepsiCo was clearly outperforming archrival Coca-Cola in the early 21st century, with stronger growth in both revenues and profits and a stock price that had risen by more than a third since the beginning of 2001, a period during which Coke's stock fell 30 percent. Perhaps the most dramatic evidence for PepsiCo's surge came in December 2005 when the company's market capitalization exceeded that of Coca-Cola for the first time in their 108-year rivalry.

Such accomplishments were attained despite Coke's continued lead in carbonated beverages, a position that in reality had become less valuable because of that sector's flattening sales. PepsiCo had consistently outflanked its rival in the rapidly growing noncarbonated field, attaining ownership outright or via joint venture of the leading brand in nearly every noncarbonated beverage category in the U.S. market, including sports drinks (Gatorade), bottled water (Aquafina), chilled juice (Tropicana), enhanced water (Propel), bottled tea (Lipton), and ready-to-drink coffee (Starbucks). In addition, PepsiCo's strong position in snack and other foods through Frito-Lay and Quaker had positioned the company more as a branded food and beverage company than strictly a beverage company.

In fact, by 2005 the company was highlighting its ranking as the number three branded food and beverage company in the world, trailing only Nestlé S.A. and Kraft Foods Inc.

In 2006 and early 2007 PepsiCo completed a series of smaller acquisitions both at home and abroad. In the international arena, the company expanded its snacks side by picking up Sara Lee Corporation's nut business in the Netherlands, Belgium, and France; Star Foods, the number one seller of potato chips in Poland; and the New Zealand snack company Bluebird Foods. PepsiCo extended its position in all-natural snacks by purchasing Stacy's Pita Chip Company of Randolph, Massachusetts. The company also added more depth to its array of non-cola beverages by acquiring IZZE Beverage Company, a producer of all-natural sparkling fruit juices based in Boulder, Colorado, and Naked Juice Company, a maker of super-premium juices based in Azusa, California.

In July 2006 PepsiCo entered into a 25-year strategic alliance with Ocean Spray Cranberries, Inc., through which it agreed to market, bottle, and distribute single-serve cranberry juice products in the United States and Canada under the Ocean Spray name. The two companies also agreed to jointly develop new juice-based products. Amid growing concerns about childhood obesity in the United States, PepsiCo in 2006 joined with the Alliance for a Healthier Generation and other beverage and food producers on two initiatives: an end to the sale of all sodas in elementary and middle schools and to all non-diet sodas in high schools and the setting of voluntary guidelines for snacks and side items sold in U.S. schools. In perhaps the biggest development of 2006, Nooyi succeeded Reinemund as PepsiCo CEO that October. Nooyi, who had been instrumental in such key actions of the previous decade as the spinning off of the firm's restaurants and the acquisitions and integrations of Tropicana and Quaker Oats, gained the chairmanship as well in May 2007.

Under Nooyi, PepsiCo's strategy continued largely unchanged although the firm faced an increasingly challenging environment at home where weak demand for carbonated soft drinks coupled with rising raw materials costs to put pressure on margins. PepsiCo continued to look overseas for growth prospects, and during 2007 much of the $500 million the company earmarked for acquisitions went toward non-U.S. purchases, including Sandora, LLC, the leading juice company in Ukraine. In early 2008 the company announced an agreement to acquire Penelopa, the leading producer and seller of branded nuts and seeds in Bulgaria. Apparently bigger deals were not out of the question either, as news reports revealed that PepsiCo had approached Nestlé in late spring 2007 about a possible megamerger but was rebuffed.

In November 2007 PepsiCo restructured its global operations in part to broaden the management experience of potential successors to Nooyi. The company's food businesses in North America and Latin America were combined into the largest of the three units, PepsiCo Americas Foods, which was headed by John Compton. PepsiCo Americas Beverages included the beverage businesses in those same regions and was headed by Massimo d'Amore. The existing international chief, Michael White, headed the third unit, PepsiCo International, which included the company's food and beverage businesses throughout the rest of the world.

April Dougal Gasbarre
Updated, David E. Salamie

PRINCIPAL DIVISIONS

PepsiCo Americas Foods; PepsiCo Americas Beverages; PepsiCo International.

PRINCIPAL COMPETITORS

The Coca-Cola Company; Nestlé S.A.; Cadbury Schweppes plc; Groupe Danone; Kraft Foods Inc.; Kellogg Company; General Mills, Inc.; Campbell Soup Company; The Procter & Gamble Company; Mars, Incorporated; Snyder's of Hanover, Inc.; The Hain Celestial Group, Inc.; ConAgra Foods, Inc.; Ocean Spray Cranberries, Inc.

FURTHER READING

Adamy, Janet, and Chad Terhune, "PepsiCo Buys General Mills' Stake in Europe Venture for $750 Million," *Wall Street Journal*, December 14, 2004, p. B6.

Barris, Mike, "Pepsi Beats Coke in Bidding for Ukraine Juice Maker," *Wall Street Journal*, June 8, 2007, p. B3.

Bary, Andrew, "Fat Chance," *Barron's*, January 19, 2004, pp. 15–16.

———, "Pepsi's Still in the Chips," *Barron's*, June 6, 2005, p. 16.

Berman, Dennis K., Deborah Ball, and Betsy McKay, "How Junk Food Spoiled Megadeal: Nestlé's Wellness Drive Scotched PepsiCo Talks," *Wall Street Journal*, July 19, 2007, p. C1.

"Boards of Pepsi-Cola and Frito-Lay Approve Merging As PepsiCo," *Wall Street Journal*, February 26, 1965, p. 8.

Bongiorno, Lori, "The Pepsi Regeneration," *Business Week*, March 11, 1996, pp. 70+.

Brady, Diane, "A Thousand and One Noshes: How Pepsi Deftly Adapts Products to Changing Consumer Tastes," *Business Week*, June 14, 2004, pp. 54, 56.

Brooker, Katrina, "The Pepsi Machine," *Fortune*, February 6, 2006, pp. 68–70, 72.

Bruss, Jill, "A Winning Hand: A Gangbuster Year Leaves PepsiCo Holding All the Right Cards," *Beverage Industry*, January 2002, pp. 30–32, 34–36.

Bush, Jason, "Wooing the Next Pepski Generation," *Business Week*, October 29, 2007, p. 74.

Byrne, John A., "PepsiCo's New Formula," *Business Week*, April 10, 2000, pp. 172–76+.

Byrnes, Nanette, and Julie Forster, "A Touch of Indigestion," *Business Week*, March 4, 2002, pp. 66–67.

Capparell, Stephanie, *The Real Pepsi Challenge: The Inspirational Story of Breaking the Color Barrier in American Business*, New York: Free Press, 2007, 349 p.

Cappelli, Peter, and Harbir Singh, "Do Pepsi and Oatmeal Mix?" *Wall Street Journal*, December 5, 2000, p. A26.

Collins, Glenn, "PepsiCo Pushes a Star Performer," *New York Times*, November 3, 1994, pp. D1, D8.

———, "PepsiCo to Spin Off Its Fast-Food Business," *New York Times*, January 24, 1997, p. D1.

Collins, Glenn, and Stephanie Strom, "Can Pepsi Become the Coke of Snacks?" *New York Times*, November 3, 1996.

Day, Sherri, "PepsiCo Plans to Cut 750 Jobs and Close Several Plants," *New York Times*, December 3, 2003, p. C2.

De Lisser, Eleena, "Pepsi Has Lost Its Midas Touch in Restaurants," *Wall Street Journal*, July 18, 1994, p. B1.

Deogun, Nikhil, "Pepsi Challenge: Can Company's Brass Mute Flashy Culture and Make Profits Fizz?" *Wall Street Journal*, August 8, 1997, pp. A1+.

———, "PepsiCo to Buy Quaker for $13.4 Billion," *Wall Street Journal*, December 4, 2000, pp. A3, A8.

———, "PepsiCo to Reorganize U.S. Operations," *Wall Street Journal*, June 2, 1997, p. A3.

———, "Revamped PepsiCo Still Needs to Conquer Wall Street," *Wall Street Journal*, July 27, 1998, p. B4.

Deogun, Nikhil, Betsy McKay, and Jonathan Eig, "PepsiCo Aborts a Play for Quaker Oats," *Wall Street Journal*, November 3, 2000, p. A3.

Deutsch, Claudia H., "A Woman to Be Chief at PepsiCo," *New York Times*, August 15, 2006, p. C1.

Dietz, Lawrence, *Soda Pop: The History, Advertising, Art, and Memorabilia of Soft Drinks in America*, New York: Simon and Schuster, 1973, 184 p.

Duncan, Amy, "Pepsi's Marketing Market: Why Nobody Does It Better," *Business Week*, February 10, 1986.

Enrico, Roger, and Jesse Kornbluth, *The Other Guy Blinked: How Pepsi Won the Cola Wars*, New York: Bantam, 1986, 280 p.

Fisher, Anne B., "Peering Past PepsiCo's Bad News," *Fortune*, November 14, 1983, pp. 124+.

Frank, Robert, "PepsiCo's Critics Worry the Glass Is Still Half Empty," *Wall Street Journal*, September 30, 1996, p. B4.

Gibney, Frank, Jr., "Pepsi Gets Back in the Game," *Time*, April 26, 1999.

"Gulp, Munch, and Merge," *Forbes*, July 15, 1968, pp. 20–21.

"Herman W. Lay of PepsiCo," *Nation's Business,* September 1969, pp. 88–89, 92–95.

"Holders of Pepsi-Cola and Frito-Lay Approve Proposal for Merger," *Wall Street Journal,* June 9, 1965, p. 8.

Kraar, Louis, "Pepsi's Pitch to Quench Chinese Thirsts," *Fortune,* March 17, 1986.

Lousi, J. C., and Harvey Z. Yazijian, *The Cola Wars,* New York: Everest House, 1980, 386 p.

Mack, Walter, and Peter Buckley, *No Time Lost,* New York: Atheneum, 1982, 211 p.

Martin, Milward W., *Twelve Full Ounces,* New York: Holt Rinehart, 1962, 136 p.

McCarthy, Michael J., "Added Fizz: Pepsi Is Going Better with Its Fast Foods and Frito-Lay Snacks," *Wall Street Journal,* June 13, 1991, pp. A1+.

McKay, Betsy, "Fit to Eat?: PepsiCo Challenges Itself to Concoct Healthier Snacks," *Wall Street Journal,* September 23, 2002, p. A1.

———, "Juices Up: Pepsi Edges Past Coke and It Has Nothing to Do with Cola," *Wall Street Journal,* November 6, 2000, pp. A1+.

———, "PepsiCo Reorganizes Some Business Units," *Wall Street Journal,* August 9, 2001, p. B4.

———, "Pepsi Net Rises but Tests Lie Ahead," *Wall Street Journal,* October 12, 2007, p. B4.

———, "Pepsi Revamps, with Eye on Succession," *Wall Street Journal,* November 6, 2007, p. A15.

———, "Pepsi to Pump Up Water Brands," *Wall Street Journal,* July 25, 2007, p. B2.

McKay, Betsy, and Jonathan Eig, "PepsiCo Hopes to Feast on Profits from Quaker Snacks," *Wall Street Journal,* December 4, 2000, p. B4.

McKay, Betsy, and Nikhil Deogun, "PepsiCo's Enrico to Pass CEO Baton to His Number Two by End of Next Year," *Wall Street Journal,* October 4, 2000, p. B1.

"PepsiCo—More Than Just 'Pepsi,'" *Financial World,* November 4, 1970, pp. 5, 26.

"Pepsi's Sitting on Trop of the World After Making Juicy Deal with Seagram," *Beverage World,* August 15, 1998, p. 14.

Prokesch, Steven E., "PepsiCo Poised for Growth," *New York Times,* July 16, 1985, p. D1.

Reeves, Scott, "The Pepsi Challenge," *Barron's,* August 11, 1997, pp. 17–18.

Rothman, Andrea, "Can Wayne Calloway Handle the Pepsi Challenge?" *Business Week,* January 27, 1992.

Santoli, Michael, "How Coke Is Kicking Pepsi's Can," *Fortune,* October 28, 1996, pp. 70–73+.

Sellers, Patricia, "If It Ain't Broke, Fix It Anyway," *Fortune,* December 28, 1992, pp. 49+.

———, "PepsiCo's New Generation," *Fortune,* April 1, 1996, pp. 110–13+.

———, "Pepsi Opens a Second Front," *Fortune,* August 8, 1994, pp. 70–76.

———, "Why Pepsi Needs to Become More Like Coke," *Fortune,* March 3, 1997, pp. 26–27.

Sparks, Debra, "Will Pepsi Take the Wall Street Challenge?" *Financial World,* April 8, 1996, pp. 26–29.

"Steady Gains for PepsiCo," *Financial World,* March 1, 1972, pp. 7, 19.

Stevenson, Richard W., "Keeping the Party Going at Fast-Paced PepsiCo," *New York Times,* May 25, 1986, p. F1.

Stoddard, Bob, *Pepsi: 100 Years,* Los Angeles: General Publishing Group, 1997, 207 p.

Terhune, Chad, "In Switch, Pepsi Makes Diet Cola Its New Flagship," *Wall Street Journal,* March 16, 2005, p. B1.

Terhune, Chad, and Joann S. Lublin, "Pepsi's New CEO Doesn't Keep Her Opinions Bottled Up," *Wall Street Journal,* August 15, 2006, p. B1.

"Wayne Calloway's Nonstop Cash Machine," *Forbes,* September 7, 1987.

"Who Acquired Who?" *Forbes,* April 1, 1967, p. 69.

Williams, Christopher C., "New Boss Should Keep Fizz in Pepsi," *Barron's,* August 21, 2006, p. 13.

Winter, Greg, "PepsiCo Sets a New Course with Deal for Quaker Oats," *New York Times,* December 5, 2000, p. C8.

Zellner, Wendy, "Frito-Lay Is Munching on the Competition," *Business Week,* August 24, 1992, pp. 52–53.

Polaroid Corporation

1265 Main Street
Building W3
Waltham, Massachusetts 02451-1743
U.S.A.
Telephone: (781) 386-2000
Toll Free: (800) 343-5000
Fax: (781) 386-8588
Web site: http://www.polaroid.com

*Wholly Owned Subsidiary of Petters Group Worldwide,
LLC*
Founded: 1937
Employees: 3,000
Sales: $1 billion (2007 est.)
NAIC: 325992 Photographic Film, Paper, Plate, and
Chemical Manufacturing; 333315 Photographic
and Photocopying Equipment Manufacturing;
334119 Other Computer Peripheral Equipment
Manufacturing; 334310 Audio and Video Equip-
ment Manufacturing; 334419 Other Electronic
Component Manufacturing; 511210 Software
Publishers

■ ■ ■

Best known for its pioneering line of instant cameras,
which were first produced under the guidance of
company founder Edwin H. Land in 1948, Polaroid
Corporation has been reincarnated as a producer of a
variety of consumer electronics products. The original
Polaroid Corporation had sunk into bankruptcy in 2001
as digital cameras steadily eroded the market for instant

photography. A new Polaroid soon emerged and was
acquired in 2005 by Petters Group Worldwide, LLC, a
privately held conglomerate whose portfolio includes a
variety of consumer product companies. Under Petters'
stewardship, Polaroid continues to churn out instant
film, but its core business has evolved into a line of
Polaroid-branded consumer electronics, including digital
cameras, LCD televisions, and portable DVD players.
Through a partnership with ZINK Imaging, Inc., the
company is also pursuing a new wave of instant
photography in the form of a line of digital instant
printers and cameras that output full-color digital
photos without using any ink. Among other Polaroid
products are security ID-card systems designed for various commercial applications.

BEGINNINGS IN POLARIZATION RESEARCH

In 1926 Edwin Land's desire to create useful products
based on scientific invention prompted him to pursue
independent research on polarization rather than to
return to Harvard University after his freshman year.
After creating a prototype synthetic polarizer in New
York, Land returned to Harvard in 1929. A polarizing
material selectively screens light waves. It could, for
example, block waves of light that create glare while allowing other waves through. With the help of George
Wheelwright III, a young Harvard physics instructor,
Land obtained access to a laboratory and began producing small sheets of polarizing material. Land applied to
patent this process in 1929, and a patent was granted in
1934. In June 1932, eager to explore the invention's
practical applications, Land and Wheelwright

abandoned their academic careers and founded Land-Wheelwright Laboratories, backed with Wheelwright's capital.

In 1933 the men incorporated their laboratory. Land-Wheelwright's staff—Land, Wheelwright, their wives, and a handful of other researchers—concentrated on developing polarizing material for no-glare car headlights and windshields. Enthusiasm for their work ran high, but commercial success eluded the Land-Wheelwright crew. Rebuffed by carmakers in Detroit, the company had no customers during the height of the Great Depression.

Photography giant Eastman Kodak Company provided the company's first financial break when it made a $10,000 order for photographic polarizing filters, later dubbed Polafilters. These plates, which consisted of a sheet of polarizing material sealed between two glass discs, increased contrast and decreased glare in photographs taken in bright light. Land-Wheelwright accepted the order and delivered the filters to Kodak. By this time, a friend, Professor Clarence Kennedy of Smith College, had dubbed the material "Polaroid," and the name was adopted in 1935. That same year, Land negotiated with American Optical Company to produce polarized sunglasses. Such glasses could screen out glare rather than simply darken the landscape, and Land-Wheelwright contracted to begin production of Polaroid Day Glasses, a longtime source of revenue for Polaroid.

In 1937 Land formed Polaroid Corporation to acquire the operations that he and Wheelwright had begun. Eight original shareholders fronted $375,000 to back Land and his projects. They invested in Land and his ideas, allotting him a voting trust of stock that gave him control of the company for the next decade. Wheelwright left the company in 1940 to become a navy lieutenant and never rejoined the firm. Researchers had devised a number of commercial applications for Polaroid polarizing sheets (such as desk lamps, variable-density windows, lenses, and three-dimensional photographs called Vectographs) but most of these products never became significantly profitable.

Polaroid continued to court the major automakers, attempting to induce one of them to demonstrate its headlight system at the 1939 New York World's Fair. The carmakers all refused the project, but Chrysler Corporation agreed to run a Polaroid three-dimensional (3-D) movie at its display. Audiences dodged water that seemed to spray out of a garden hose into the crowd and gawked through Polaroid-made glasses of oppositely polarized lenses as an automobile appeared to dance itself together in the air above them. The public loved 3-D, but filmmakers were content with the magic of color and sound, and passed over the new technology.

In another unsuccessful marketing project, variable-density windows were installed on the observation car of the *City of Los Angeles*. Two polarized discs were mounted in the train wall; by means of a knob, passengers could turn the inner disk so that the window gradually became grayer until it was completely dark. As with the 3-D process, the novelty of polarized windows was not hugely successful.

CONTRIBUTIONS TO WORLD WAR II EFFORT

In 1939 Day Glasses were the source of most of Polaroid's $35,000 profit. Although sales rose to $1 million in 1941, the company's 1940 losses had reached $100,000, and it was only World War II military contracts that saved Land and his 240 employees. By 1942 the wartime economy had tripled Polaroid's size. A $7 million navy contract to work on the Dove heat-seeking missile project was the largest contract Polaroid had ever had, although the bomb was not used during World War II. Polaroid produced a number of other products for the armed forces, including a device that determined an aircraft's elevation above the horizon, an infrared night viewing device, goggles, lenses, color filters for periscopes, and range finders.

Also during the war, the 3-D technology was employed in a machine-gunner training unit. Polaroid designed a trainer in which the student operated a life-size antiaircraft gun against the 3-D simulation of an attacking plane. Reconnaissance planes were equipped to take 3-D Vectographs, which provided relief maps of enemy territory. When viewed with polarized glasses, the 3-D pictures exposed contours of guns, planes, and buildings that camouflage obscured in conventional photographs. Vectographs were used in planning almost all Allied invasions, including that of Normandy. By the

KEY DATES

1932: Edwin H. Land and George Wheelwright III found Land-Wheelwright Laboratories.

1935: Polaroid is adopted as the brand name for Land-Wheelwright's polarizers.

1937: Land forms Polaroid Corporation to acquire the operations of Land-Wheelwright.

1948: The first Polaroid Land camera, the Model 95, is introduced and is the first instant camera.

1957: Polaroid stock is listed on the New York Stock Exchange.

1963: Polaroid introduces its first color film.

1972: Company introduces the revolutionary SX-70 camera.

1976: After Eastman Kodak Company introduces its own line of instant cameras, Polaroid sues for patent infringement.

1977: Top-selling OneStep Land camera makes its debut.

1991: Polaroid's suit against Kodak is settled, with the latter paying the former $925 million.

1995: New CEO Gary T. DiCamillo initiates the first of several restructurings/workforce reductions.

2001: Its sales sliding and debt growing, Polaroid files for Chapter 11 bankruptcy protection.

2002: The assets of Polaroid are sold for $255 million; a new Polaroid Corporation is formed, majority owned by a private-equity unit of Bank One Corporation.

2003: Petters Group Worldwide, LLC, licenses the Polaroid brand for a line of consumer electronics products, including portable DVD players and plasma televisions.

2005: Petters acquires Polaroid for $426 million.

instant photography was Polaroid's only research line with potential to save the company. Land had first considered developing instant photography technology in 1943, when, on Christmas Day, his three-year-old daughter asked to see the photographs her parents had taken earlier that day. Prompted by his daughter's query, Land conceived, in a flash, an instant self-developing film and a camera that would process it. By 1946, however, the research on the film was far from complete. Nonetheless, Land announced early that year that the instant camera system would be demonstrated at the February 21, 1947, winter meeting of the Optical Society of America. Working around the clock, Polaroid scientists developed a working model of the system, which allowed Land to take an instant picture of himself at the Optical Society meeting. The photograph developed itself within a minute. The image of Land peeling back the negative paper from an instantly produced picture of himself made front page news in the *New York Times,* was given a full page in *Life* magazine, and was splashed across the international press.

It was not until November 26, 1948, that the camera was offered to the public by Jordan Marsh, Boston's oldest department store. The original camera, the Land Model 95, which weighed five pounds when loaded, sold for $89.75; film cost $1.75 for eight sepia-toned exposures. On the first day the camera was offered, demonstrators sold all 56 of the available units, and the cameras kept selling as fast as the factory could produce them. First-year photographic sales exceeded $5 million. By 1950 more than 4,000 dealers sold Polaroid cameras, when only a year earlier Kodak had virtually monopolized the U.S. photography market.

The 1950s were a decade of rapid expansion. Sales mounted, spurred on by an aggressive television advertising campaign. Instant photography could be demonstrated graphically on television. Black-and-white film was introduced in 1950 to an enthusiastic public. Enthusiasm quickly turned to ire, however, as the black-and-white images began to fade and disappear. Unable to develop a nonfading black-and-white film, Polaroid provided sponge-tipped tubes of a liquid polymer, which the consumers hand applied to each picture to set the image. This awkward process was not eliminated until 1963.

Despite the inconvenience, demand for instant photography held. To accommodate growing sales, Polaroid built a plant in Waltham, Massachusetts. The company's common stock was listed on the New York Stock Exchange in 1957. Polaroid formed its first international subsidiaries in 1959, in Frankfurt and Toronto. In 1960 it established Nippon Polaroid

end of the war, in 1945, Polaroid's sales had reached $16 million. As military contracts declined, though, so did staff, and Polaroid was down to about 900 employees, from a wartime high of 1,250. Sales fell to just $4 million in 1946 and were less than $2 million in 1947.

1948 DEBUT OF INSTANT PHOTOGRAPHY

By 1946 Land had realized that Polaroid Corporation was in deep trouble. Land also had come to believe that

Kabushiki Kaisha in Japan and licensed a Japanese firm to produce two cameras for overseas sale.

During the 1960s Polaroid continued to offer improvements and variations on the original instant film and camera, although other products were also introduced. Polaroid's first color film was introduced in 1963, along with a pack-loading black-and-white film. In 1965 the inexpensive Swinger was pitched to teens. Selling for less than $20, the camera took only black-and-white pictures, sustaining the market for Polaroid black-and-white film. In 1966 the ID-2 Land Identification system was introduced. It produced full-color laminated cards in two minutes, allowing the company to provide instant driver's licenses and other photo identification cards. In 1967 Polaroid began construction on several new factories to boost production of cameras, film, color negatives, and chemicals. The company's stock split two for one in 1968. During the late 1960s Polaroid was outpacing other top stock market performers. In 1970 sales reached $500 million.

In October 1970 two black workers at Polaroid called upon other black employees to leave their jobs until Polaroid ceased all business in South Africa. Polaroid had no subsidiaries or investments in the country, but its products were distributed through Frank & Hirsch and some items were sold directly to the government. South African commerce accounted for less than 0.1 percent of the company's annual profits. Polaroid sent two black and two white employees to South Africa to assess the situation, and in 1971 the company decided to stop selling its products to the South African government. In addition, black workers at Frank & Hirsch would receive equal pay for equal work and be educated for promotion. Polaroid established a foundation to subsidize black education in South Africa, and made $25,000 in contributions to black cultural associations. Polaroid ended its association with Frank & Hirsch in 1977.

DEBUT OF THE SX-70 IN 1972

In 1972 the October cover of *Life* magazine featured a cluster of children grasping after a photograph whizzing out of the new SX-70 wielded by inventor Land. The revolutionary SX-70 was the first integrated camera and film system, and the pictures developed outside the camera by themselves. The public eagerly purchased the camera. Despite the fact that sales in the early 1970s continued to grow at a rate of 20 percent per year, the tremendous expense of research, manufacturing, and marketing for the SX-70 caused earnings to fall. Financial analysts began to question Polaroid's stability. In 1974 Polaroid executives admitted that the company did not expect to make more than $3 a share that year.

Actually, earnings were only 86 cents per share. Polaroid stock plummeted. By July 1974, just 26 months after the SX-70 was introduced, the stock had fallen from $149 to $14.

In 1975 Land turned the presidency of Polaroid over to Bill McCune, a senior vice-president who had been with the company since 1939 and had worked closely with Land on the development of the first instant camera and film. Manufacture of the SX-70 remained very costly, and numerous design features required modification. Yet Land was satisfied with the camera and wished to pursue research on Polavision, an instant motion picture system. McCune and others, however, favored improving the SX-70. Highly skeptical of Polavision, McCune wanted to base new product lines on market research, rather than following Land's method of creating a consumer demand for Polaroid's latest invention. Land introduced Polavision at the 1977 annual meeting, and a limited introduction followed. Although a scientific marvel, the instant films lasted only two-and-a-half minutes and were silent. Videotaping was just hitting the market, and so Polavision was never a consumer success.

Land received his 500th patent and was inducted into the National Inventors Hall of Fame in 1977. Polaroid's corporate culture began to shift when McCune was voted CEO in 1980. While Land's entrepreneurial drive had created the company, a more diversified, market-oriented management was needed to continue to propel it. In 1982 Land retired fully, devoting his attention to research at the Rowland Institute for Science, which he had founded in 1965. The company founder died in 1991 at age 81.

In the meantime, Polaroid in 1977 introduced the OneStep Land camera, an inexpensive fixed-focus camera backed by a television advertising campaign featuring the actors Mariette Hartley and James Garner. The OneStep reigned for four years as the best-selling camera, instant or conventional, in the United States.

In 1976 Polaroid entered a costly and lengthy patent-infringement battle with Eastman Kodak Company. Kodak had been producing the negative component of Polaroid's black-and-white film since 1944, and its color negative since 1957. With the introduction of the Polaroid SX-70, though, Kodak terminated its partnership with Polaroid, and began its own instant-photography research. In 1976 Kodak introduced the EK-4 and EK-6 instant cameras and PR-10 instant film. Polaroid filed suit within a week, charging 12 patent infringements in camera film and design.

Legal preparations dragged on for five years, until the trial began in October 1981. Ten of the 12 original counts were pressed. After 75 days of testimony and three years of deliberation, U.S. District Court Judge Rya Zobel ruled that seven of the ten Polaroid patents were valid and had been infringed upon. As a result, Kodak's line of instant-photography products was terminated in 1986. When settlement talks began, Polaroid claimed about $6.1 billion in damages, lost sales, and interest. The case was not settled until 1991 and resulted in a payment by Eastman Kodak of $925 million.

FENDING OFF A HOSTILE TAKEOVER, 1988–89

In August 1988 Shamrock Holdings, Inc., offered to buy Polaroid at $40 a share plus 40 percent of the award from the Kodak settlement. Polaroid's board of directors rejected the offer, and soon after, the company sold 14 percent of its outstanding shares to an employee stock ownership program (ESOP). Shamrock charged that the ESOP was a form of management entrenchment, and sued. Delaware courts upheld Polaroid's position, and Shamrock raised its offer to $45 a share. Polaroid's board again rejected the offer and subsequently announced a $1.1 billion common stock buyback. Shamrock again sued Polaroid in February 1989 for management entrenchment, but Polaroid's tactics were again upheld. The fight against Shamrock was led by Chairman McCune and I. MacAllister Booth, who had become president in 1983 and CEO in 1985. The pair pruned Polaroid staff in the early 1980s and reorganized the company into three divisions: consumer photography, industrial photography, and magnetic media.

The first success reaped from this new marketing strategy was the Spectra, introduced in 1986. The upscale Spectra came out of market research indicating that instant camera users wanted better picture quality. Again responding to this desire, Polaroid introduced Hybrid IV, an instant film of near 35-millimeter quality, during the early 1990s. Polaroid also introduced a line of conventional film and videotapes starting in 1989. Marketing strategies also continued to become more sophisticated. In 1990 a $60 million advertising campaign emphasized new uses for instant cameras. Suggested uses included recording household items for insurance purposes or keeping a visual record of properties when house hunting. In addition, the company cultivated its nonconsumer markets, which contributed at least 40 percent of photographic sales.

While Polaroid's product lines became more fully guided by market demand, Polaroid continued to be a research-and-development-driven company. By the early 1990s, the company had become the world market leader in instant photography and electronic imaging, and a major world manufacturer and marketer of conventional films, videotapes, and light polarizing filters and lenses. In addition to its instant photography products, Polaroid had by the early 1990s developed a presence in the medical imaging field, with such products as the 1993-released Helios medical laser imaging system, which produced a medical diagnostic image without chemical processing, and the Polaroid EMS Photo Kit, a camera specifically designed for the 35,000 emergency medical team (EMT) squads in the United States. A series of electronic imaging products were also developed for the business segment, including desktop computer film recorders, the Polaroid CI-5000 and CI-3000, and the CS-500i Digital Photo Scanner. In addition, Polaroid developed the ProCam, an instant camera earmarked for the business customer.

For the nonprofessional or amateur consumer, the long-awaited "Joshua" instant camera was introduced first in Europe in 1992, and then in the United States as "Captiva" in the summer of 1993. Captiva, indistinguishable in appearance from a 35-millimeter camera, took high-quality instant photos that were not ejected in the usual manner, but stored in the rear of the camera, which in turn contained a viewing window enabling the user to see the development of the last exposed frame. Because the photos were smaller than regular-sized 35-millimeter pictures, the camera appealed to those whose lifestyles favored a more compact and instant camera. "HighDefinition" instant film for the amateur photographer came on the market in 1992, further closing the gap in quality between 35-millimeter and instant film.

MOUNTING LATE-CENTURY TROUBLES

In the mid- to late 1990s Polaroid faced an increasingly uncertain future. Overall sales were stagnant, the $2.15 billion figure of 1992 being repeated in 1997, before a more dismal result was announced for 1998: $1.89 billion. Demand for instant film was on the decline, in part because of the rapid growth of one-hour photo shops for conventional film and as well as the ascendance of digital cameras, and the company's other forays were less than total successes. The Captiva had a very strong debut, but then sales dropped off and Polaroid cut back production.

Booth retired in late 1995 and was replaced as chairman and CEO by Gary T. DiCamillo, who had been an executive at the Black & Decker Corporation, where he earned a reputation for cost-cutting, improving productivity, and rapidly developing new products. Soon after taking over, DiCamillo initiated a restructuring at

Polaroid, which included a workforce cut of about 15 percent, or 1,570 jobs, and a charge of $247 million for 1995, leading to a net loss of $140.2 million for the year. DiCamillo also overhauled the company's management team, bringing in additional marketing and product development-oriented leaders from such firms as RJR Nabisco and Kraft Foods.

Further changes came in 1996. Polaroid largely abandoned its venture into medical imaging, an area in which it had invested about $800 million, selling the bulk of its loss-making Helios unit to Sterling Diagnostic Imaging Inc. This sale led in part to a $33 million charge recorded in 1996, a year in which the company reported a net loss of $41.1 million.

The new management team at Polaroid concentrated on rolling out 30 to 40 new products each year, aiming to diversify the company's offerings. These included a disposable flashlight, alkaline batteries, a new line of polarized sunglasses, and the firm's first digital camera, the PDC 2000, which debuted in 1996. Polaroid in December 1997 announced an additional workforce reduction of 15 percent, or about 1,500 jobs. The company took another restructuring charge of $323.5 million, resulting in a 1997 net loss of $126.7 million. During 1998 Polaroid announced additional job cuts of 600 to 700 employees, took a restructuring charge of $50 million, and posted a net loss of $51 million. The worldwide economic difficulties that began in 1997 proved particularly troublesome for Polaroid, which had long generated a significant portion of its revenue outside the United States. The hardest hit market for Polaroid was Russia, which had been the company's second largest market in 1995, accounting for $200 million in revenues; for 1998 Polaroid sold only about $25 million worth of goods in that economically troubled nation.

As Polaroid's red ink continued to flow, speculation about a possible takeover was rife. In addition, while DiCamillo had initially emphasized broadening the company's product mix when he came on board, he announced in early 1999 that he was considering selling four business units—sunglasses, graphic arts, glare-reducing polarizers, and holography—that had been key components of his diversification efforts. DiCamillo said that he wanted to focus the company on its core instant photography business. The emphasis would also be on the consumer market, with particular attention given to developing youth-oriented instant cameras, such as the I-Zone Instant Pocket Camera, which was a slender camera that produced miniature instant prints. The Pocket Camera had been a great success following its May 1998 debut in the Osaka region of Japan, and was released in the United States in the summer of 1999.

Also introduced by the company in 1999 were Pop-Shots, the first instant one-time-use camera, and the JoyCam, a smaller, economically priced version of Polaroid's standard instant camera.

INTO BANKRUPTCY

Strong sales of the new youth-oriented items enabled Polaroid in 1999 to post its first annual profit, $9 million, since 1994. Revenues increased for the first time since 1996, rising 7 percent to $1.98 billion. On a historical scale, this turnaround in the making ended almost instantly. Sales dropped off in the second half of 2000 as the economy worsened and the initial lure of the new products began to fade. By the fourth quarter of that year, Polaroid was back in the red, and in early 2001 the company announced it would suspend payment of a dividend after having continuously paid dividends since 1952.

Polaroid was teetering on the brink of bankruptcy as its massive debt load had grown to more than $930 million. The firm had been deeply in debt ever since its late 1980s financial maneuvering to fend off the Shamrock hostile takeover. In February 2001 Polaroid announced another restructuring involving a workforce reduction of 11 percent, or 950 employees. Just four months later, the company unveiled plans to slash 2,000 more jobs, or a quarter of its remaining workers, and then a month after that began exploring a total or partial sale of the company assets. During the first six months of 2001, Polaroid suffered an operating loss of $170 million on sales of $664 million. Finally, on October 12, 2001, Polaroid was forced to file for Chapter 11 bankruptcy protection.

Controversy surrounded the bankruptcy from the start. Especially contentious was the treatment of Polaroid's rank-and-file workers and company retirees, particularly in comparison to that of the firm's executives and directors, who were the recipients of large payments and bonuses. In addition to the massive layoffs, the company terminated the healthcare and retirement benefits of retirees to save money, and eventually Polaroid's underfunded pension fund was taken over by a government agency, which slashed the retirees' monthly retirement checks. Since the implementation of the ESOP, Polaroid workers had been required to take part of their pay in the form of company stock, but were largely barred from selling the stock while still employed. The stock price had steadily fallen to little more than a quarter per share by the time of the filing. Ultimately, the employee shareholders received next to nothing for their stock. On July 31, 2002, the assets of Polaroid were sold for $255 million, what *Business Week* termed "a song." Via this deal, a private-equity unit of Bank One Corporation secured a 65 percent stake in a newly organized Polaroid Corporation, while unsecured creditors got the other 35 percent. In a further blow to Polaroid's Massachusetts workers, the firm closed its Waltham plant around this same time, shifting film assembly to plants in Mexico and the Netherlands.

DEVELOPMENT OF A NEW POLAROID MODEL

DiCamillo had resigned from Polaroid in May 2002, leaving the firm in the hands of its finance chief and a top lawyer. That November, Jacques Nasser, the former CEO of Ford Motor Company, was named nonexecutive chairman. Finally, in March 2003, a new CEO was brought onboard, J. Michael Pocock, a former executive of Compaq Computer Corporation. That year, Polaroid introduced a sleeker and more contemporary successor to its OneStep camera, the Polaroid One, and also sold its commercial optics division to Precision Optical Systems, Inc.

By the end of 2003 the workforce had been trimmed to just 3,400 employees, a far cry from the firm's peak employment level of nearly 21,000, which occurred in 1978 when Polaroid was still an esteemed technology leader. Financially, the new Polaroid had virtually no debt and was able to post a profit of $71.3 million on sales of $752.7 million in 2003. Its principal products remained instant cameras and film, with additional lines in sunglasses and security ID-card systems for commercial applications.

Perhaps most importantly for the long term, however, the company began a concerted push to extend the still well-respected Polaroid brand into new market segments through licensing deals. Most notably, Petters Group Worldwide, LLC, obtained a license to affix the Polaroid brand to the previously generic consumer electronics products it had been selling, including portable DVD players and plasma televisions. This Polaroid line was launched in 2003. In addition, the Hong Kong-based World Wide Licenses Limited, a subsidiary of Character Group plc of the United Kingdom, was granted a worldwide license to produce and sell Polaroid brand digital cameras.

In May 2004 shares in Polaroid again began trading publicly, albeit over the counter. By that year, the licensing strategy was clearly bearing fruit. Petters Group, a Minnetonka, Minnesota, concern that had previously acquired and reinvigorated the Fingerhut catalog company, generated around $300 million in revenues in 2004 from Polaroid-branded televisions and DVD players produced mainly by Chinese contract manufacturers

and sold in the United States through the discount outlets of Wal-Mart Stores, Inc., and Target Corporation. Encouraged by this successful start, Petters soon reached a deal to acquire Polaroid outright.

2005 FORWARD: THE PETTERS ERA

Petters Group Worldwide completed its acquisition of Polaroid in April 2005 for $426 million. Polaroid thus became a wholly owned subsidiary of Petters. One of Petters' immediate goals was to begin introducing Polaroid-branded consumer electronics products in overseas markets. Initially led by the parent company's founder, chairman, and CEO, Tom Petters, Polaroid in August 2007 gained a new CEO, Michael London. The new leader was a 35-year veteran of the retail industry, most recently serving for a decade as an executive at consumer electronics giant Best Buy Co., Inc. Around this same time, Polaroid was in the process of shifting its headquarters from Waltham to an office building at 300 Baker Avenue in Concord, Massachusetts, with the move slated to be consummated sometime in 2008. Also in 2007, the company sold its eyewear division to Ormond Beach, Florida-based StyleMark Inc., which gained the right to produce and distribute Polaroid brand sunglasses.

In January 2008 Polaroid unveiled its latest product lineup at the annual International Consumer Electronics Show (CES) in Las Vegas. By this time, Polaroid had quickly become the leading consumer brand of portable DVD players in the United States and also held the top spot in mass-market digital cameras. In addition, Polaroid was among the top five brands of LCD televisions in North America. Beyond these products and its continued production of instant film, Polaroid was venturing even wider into consumer electronics, including its Freescape line of digital media-sharing products, which were designed to enable consumers to "unlock" the digital content they had stored in their various electronics devices (e.g., computers, digital cameras, portable music players) and channel them into a central home entertainment center.

One other product unveiled at the 2008 CES show pointed to a potential new era for Polaroid instant photography. A promising area of research at the time of the company's bankruptcy filing involved instant digital printing. In its troubled state, Polaroid was unable to fund further development of this innovation and eventually, in 2005, sold the technologies behind it to a group of investors. They called their startup ZINK Imaging, Inc., the ZINK standing for "zero ink." ZINK collaborated with Polaroid on the development of a line of printing products using this ink-free printing technology. The printers used heat to activate and colorize dye crystals that had been embedded in paper specially designed for the devices. At CES, Polaroid announced plans to begin selling later in 2008 a pocket-sized mobile ZINK printer able to quickly produce small color photos from digital cameras and camera phones. Although Polaroid was clearly no longer the technological juggernaut of its heyday, the ZINK devices provided a promising, and highly fitting, avenue for leveraging what remained a powerful brand.

Elaine Belsito
Updated, David E. Salamie

PRINCIPAL SUBSIDIARIES

Polaroid Latin America Corporation; Polaroid (France) S.A.; Polaroid GmbH (Germany); Polaroid Asia Pacific Services Ltd. (Hong Kong); Polaroid Far East Limited (Hong Kong); Polaroid India Pvt. Ltd.; Polaroid (Italia) S.p.A. (Italy); Nippon Polaroid Kabushiki Kaisha (Japan); Polaroid de Mexico S.A. de C.V.; Polaroid (Europa) B.V. (Netherlands); Polaroid Trading B.V. (Russia); Polaroid España, S.A. (Spain); Polaroid AG (Switzerland); Polaroid (U.K.) Limited.

PRINCIPAL COMPETITORS

Eastman Kodak Company; FUJIFILM Holdings Corporation; Matsushita Electric Industrial Co., Ltd.; Sony Corporation; Samsung Electronics Co., Ltd.; SANYO Electric Co., Ltd.; Canon Inc.; Olympus Corporation; Seiko Epson Corporation; Toshiba Corporation; Royal Philips Electronics N.V.; Nikon Corporation; Hewlett-Packard Company; Lexmark International, Inc.

FURTHER READING

Alster, Norm, "Double Exposure," *Forbes*, September 14, 1992, pp. 408+.

Bailey, Steve, and Steven Syre, "In Hindsight, Perhaps Polaroid Should Have Sold," *Boston Globe*, October 22, 1998.

Bandler, James, "Polaroid Hopes Its New Inventions Develop into Profits," *Wall Street Journal*, August 22, 2001, p. B4.

———, "Polaroid Plans to Sell Assets for $265 Million," *Wall Street Journal*, April 19, 2002, p. A17.

Beam, Alex, "A Troubled Polaroid Is Tearing Down 'The House That Land Built,'" *Business Week*, April 29, 1985, pp. 51+.

Bernstein, Peter W., "Polaroid Struggles to Get Back into Focus," *Fortune*, April 7, 1980, pp. 66+.

Blout, Elkan, "Polaroid: Dreams to Reality," *Daedalus*, Spring 1996, pp. 39+.

Brouillard, Sarah, "Petters Group Pulls Ahead with Polaroid Purchase," *Minneapolis/St. Paul Business Journal*, May 5, 2006.

Bulkeley, William M., "Polaroid, Emphasizing Marketing Push, Says Cheese: Instant-Camera Maker Hires Kraft's Posa to Rejuvenate Its Stagnant Brand," *Wall Street Journal*, November 5, 1996, p. B4.

———, "Polaroid to Slash Work Force by 2,000, to 5,500," *Wall Street Journal*, June 14, 2001, p. A3.

Byrnes, Nanette, and Adrienne Hardman, "Cold Shower: Why Polaroid Shareholders Can Thank Roy Disney for His Aborted Takeover," *Financial World*, September 28, 1993, pp. 38–39.

Deutsch, Claudia H., "Deep in Debt Since 1988, Polaroid Files for Bankruptcy," *New York Times*, October 13, 2001, p. C1.

———, "Through a Lens, Digitally: Polaroid Girds for the New Era in Instant Photography," *New York Times*, March 27, 2000, p. C1.

———, "Touching Up a Faded Polaroid," *New York Times*, January 3, 1998, pp. D1, D2.

Dumaine, Brian, "How Polaroid Flashed Back," *Fortune*, February 16, 1987, pp. 72+.

"Edwin Land: Inventor of Polaroid Camera," *Los Angeles Times*, March 2, 1991.

Elliott, Stuart, "Polaroid Hopes the Flash of a New Campaign Wins Back Its Image of Being on the Cutting Edge," *New York Times*, October 6, 2003, p. C5.

Gretzner, Bonnie, "Polaroid's Instant Response," *Photo Marketing*, February 2003, pp. 18, 20.

Hakim, Danny, "Ford's Ex-Chief Hired to Rebuild Polaroid," *New York Times*, November 12, 2002, p. C4.

Hammonds, Keith H., "Why Polaroid Must Remake Itself—Instantly," *Business Week*, September 19, 1988, pp. 66+.

Hillman, Michelle, "Polaroid to Exit Iconic Waltham HQ for Concord Space," *Boston Business Journal*, June 29, 2007.

Klein, Alec, "On a Roll: The Techies Grumbled, but Polaroid's Pocket Turned into a Huge Hit," *Wall Street Journal*, May 2, 2000, p. A1.

———, "Polaroid Hopes New Cameras Click with Young Users," *Wall Street Journal*, February 4, 1999, p. B10.

———, "Polaroid May Sell Four Businesses Once Viewed As Key," *Wall Street Journal*, March 1, 1999, p. B10.

Krasner, Jeffrey, "Bank One Completes Polaroid Deal," *Boston Globe*, August 1, 2002, p. C1.

———, "A Developing Story: Polaroid Aims to Make Name for Itself by Licensing Brand to Others," *Boston Globe*, May 10, 2003, p. C1.

———, "DiCamillo Quits Polaroid: Embattled CEO Ends 6-Year Run," *Boston Globe*, May 9, 2002, p. C1.

———, "Minnesota Firm to Acquire Polaroid," *Boston Globe*, January 8, 2005, p. E1.

———, "Once-Ailing Polaroid Pays Off for New Owners," *Boston Globe*, September 18, 2003, p. A1.

———, "Polaroid Agrees to $265M Sale to Bank One Unit," *Boston Globe*, April 19, 2002, p. A1.

————, "Polaroid Cuts R&D, Digital Plans," *Boston Globe*, August 2, 2005, p. C1.

Lattman, Peter, "Rebound," *Forbes*, March 28, 2005, p. 58.

McElheny, Victor K., *Insisting on the Impossible: The Life of Edwin Land*, Reading, Mass.: Perseus Books, 1998, 510 p.

McWilliams, Gary, "Larry, We Hardly Knew Ye," *Business Week*, December 27, 1993, p. 40.

————, "A Radical Shift in Focus for Polaroid," *Business Week*, July 26, 1993, pp. 66–67.

Morgello, Clem, "Booth: Creating a New Polaroid," *Dun's Business Month*, August 1985, pp. 51+.

Nossiter, Daniel D., "No Instant Success: But New Focus Brightens the Picture at Polaroid," *Barron's*, July 5, 1982, pp. 11+.

Nulty, Peter, "The New Look of Photography: The Transition from Film to Electronic Imaging," *Fortune*, July 1, 1991.

Ozanian, Michael K., "Darkness Before Dawn," *Financial World*, June 6, 1995, pp. 42–45.

————, "Out of Focus," *Forbes*, January 22, 2001, p. 69.

Palmer, Jay, "Spending Kodak's Money: Polaroid Uses Its Settlement Bounty to Sow Seeds of Future Growth," *Barron's*, October 7, 1991, pp. 16+.

Pereira, Joseph, "Wall Street Sees a Turnaround Developing at Polaroid: Strong Reception for New Small Camera and Medical Devices Lifts Stock," *Wall Street Journal*, July 13, 1993, p. B4.

Polaroid Corporation: A Chronology, Cambridge, Mass.: Polaroid Corporation, 1983.

"Polaroid Sharpens Its Focus on the Marketplace," *Business Week*, February 13, 1984, pp. 132+.

"Polaroid: Turning Away from Land's One Product Strategy," *Business Week*, March 2, 1981, pp. 108+.

Rosenberg, Ronald, "Snapping Back," *Boston Globe*, April 4, 1999, p. F1.

Sharpe, Rochelle, and Geoffrey Smith, "Hazy Picture at Polaroid," *Business Week*, December 4, 2000, pp. 95–96.

"Sharper Focus," *Economist*, April 24, 1993, pp. 72–73.

Smith, Geoffrey, "Polaroid: A Sweet Deal," *Business Week*, August 5, 2002, p. 90.

Solomon, Steven, "Polaroid: Instant Turnaround?" *Financial World*, December 1, 1979, pp. 17+.

Syre, Steven, "Polaroid Slowly Fades Away," *Boston Globe*, October 14, 2001, p. E1.

Wensberg, Peter C., *Land's Polaroid: A Company and the Man Who Invented It*, Boston: Houghton Mifflin, 1987, 258 p.

Wurman, Richard Saul, *Polaroid Access: Fifty Years*, n.p.: Access Press, 1989.

PT Indosat Tbk

Wisma Antara 1st Fl.
Jl. Medan Merdeka Selatan No. 17
Jakarta, 10110
Indonesia
Telephone: (+62 21) 3000 7001
Fax: (+62 21) 3000 5702
Web site: http://www.indosat.com

Public Company
Incorporated: 1967
Employees: 7,786
Sales: IDR 12.23 trillion ($1.36 billion) (2006)
Stock Exchanges: New York
Ticker Symbol: IIT
NAIC: 513390 Other Telecommunications; 513220 Cable and Other Program Distribution; 513310 Wired Telecommunications Carriers; 541512 Computer Systems Design Services

■ ■ ■

PT Indosat Tbk is Indonesia's second largest telecommunications provider. The company provides per- and postpaid cellular telephone services and fixed-line and fixed-line-wireless international calling services. The company operates in the corporate and commercial markets, providing data transmission and other services. Indosat's cellular business is its largest and fastest-growing business. These operations include both GSM 800 and GSM 1800 standards. IM3 is the company's primary brand for its cellular phone operations. With nearly 17 million subscribers in 2007, Indosat claims a

27 percent market share. Cellular telephone services account for more than 75 percent of its revenues. Nearly all of the group's cellular telephone revenues come from its prepaid calling cards. These accounted for more than 95 percent of Indosat's total cellular telephone customer base. Indosat was historically the monopoly provider of fixed-line international services in Indonesia. Despite losing its monopoly amid the deregulation of the telecommunications sector, Indosat remains the dominant provider in this segment. Nonetheless, fixed-line services in heavily impoverished Indonesia remain its smallest area of business, generating just 9 percent of revenues. The company MIDI data and network services division offers leased line, satellite transponder leading and broadcasting, and a range of Internet-based services to Indonesia's corporate and commercial sectors. This division generated 15.5 percent of the group's revenues. In 2006, Indosat's revenues topped IDR 12 trillion ($1.36 billion). The company is listed on the New York Stock Exchange and is led by President Johny Swandi Sjam. The company's largest shareholder has been Singapore's ST Telemedia, itself controlled by Singapore government investment arm Temasek. In late 2007, ST Telemedia indicated it planned to sell its more than 40 percent stake in Indosat. The Indonesian government remains Indosat's second largest shareholder, with more than 14 percent.

ITT SUBSIDIARY IN 1967

One of the world's most populated countries, Indonesia was also one of its most impoverished in the mid-1960s. At the beginning of the Suharto regime, which lasted into the late 1990s, the vast majority of the country's

COMPANY PERSPECTIVES

Vision: To become the leading cellular/wireless focused, fully integrated telecommunication network and services provider in Indonesia. Mission: To provide and develop innovative and quality products, services, and solutions, which offer the best value to our customers.

population subsisted on as little as $100 per year. Even into the 2000s, as many as 14 percent of the population, by then more than 220 million, lived on less than $1 per day.

Seeking foreign investment, Indonesia's government recognized that its rudimentary telecommunications infrastructure, especially its international dialing facilities, required drastic upgrades. The country's own geography, composed of thousands of islands, further hampered the rollout of an efficient telecommunications network in Indonesia. The lack of submarine telecommunication cables connecting the islands, and Indonesia itself, with its Southeast Asian neighbors represented a major obstacle to building a national telecommunications network.

The creation of the International Telecommunications Satellite Organization, or Intelsat, provided the opportunity for Indonesia to make a leap forward into the modern telecommunications era. The government already operated a domestic communication satellite, Palapa, launched in 1967 under telecommunications monopoly Perumtel (later PT Telkom). Yet the government sorely lacked funds to carry out further upgrades to its international telecommunications infrastructure.

Instead, the Suharto government turned to a foreign partner to provide the necessary investment. In 1967, the government signed a 20-year agreement with ITT of the United States. The agreement called for ITT to build and operate an Intelsat earth station, which would be owned by the Indonesian government. The terms of the agreement provided highly lucrative terms for ITT; indeed, the original agreement was later contested as exploitative and possibly illegal. Nonetheless, the decision to extend the Intelsat franchise to a foreign company proved a milestone in the development of Indonesia's modern telecommunications infrastructure.

By 1969, ITT had launched its Indosat international communications service from an earth station built at Jatiluhur. That station connected to Intelsat's satellites serving the Indian Ocean Region. Under the agreement, Indosat generated strong profits for ITT throughout the 1970s. In 1979, the company added a second earth station, gaining access to the Pacific Ocean Region satellites of the Intelsat consortium. Indosat not only encouraged the arrival of foreign investment into Indonesia, it also provided significant training opportunities for a new generation of telecommunications-savvy Indonesians.

GOVERNMENT CONTROL IN 1980

The beginning of the 1980s marked a new era in Indonesia's telecommunications sector, however, as the country finally became linked to the international market through submarine cables. These were built and controlled by Perumtel, however. In the meantime, the unbalanced nature of the agreement with ITT had increasingly come under fire. Many accused the agreement of unfairly favoring the U.S. company, while others suggested that certain clauses of the agreement represented an affront to Indonesia's sovereignty.

In the end, the government pushed through a buyout of the Indosat operations. Indosat then became a state-owned company in charge of the country's international telecommunications. Perumtel retained the monopoly over the country's domestic telephone sector. The amicable termination of the ITT contract cost the Indonesian government nearly $44 million at the time.

Two years later, the government carried out a restructuring of the sector, transferring all of Indosat's domestic assets into Perumtel. Indosat then took over Perumtel's international telecommunications assets, including its control of the country's international submarine cable network. The restructuring instituted a highly complex cross-shareholding relationship between the two companies.

Originally established as a satellite-based company, Indosat's operations shifted toward a focus on the country's growing submarine cable infrastructure. By the end of the 1980s, these represented the majority of Indonesia's international telecommunications traffic. By then, too, Indosat had achieved significant growth, with revenues building to more than $500 million.

PARTIAL PRIVATIZATION IN 1989

At the end of the 1980s, Indonesian's telecommunications penetration rate continued to lag behind even the average for the world's emerging markets. Part of the reason behind this lay in the government's inability to provide the financial resources for building out the country's infrastructure. Funding for this investment had all but ended in 1985, despite steady increases in demand for telecommunications services.

KEY DATES

1967: Indonesian government signs contract with ITT to build and operate Intelsat earth station in Indonesia.

1969: Indosat launches commercial operations as international telecommunications provider.

1980: Indonesian government takes control of Indosat, which becomes a state-owned company with a monopoly on the international telecom sector.

1989: Privatization and deregulation of Indonesian telecommunications sector begins.

2002: Company acquires Satelindo, which is then merged into its IM3 business.

2006: Indosat wins bid for wireless fixed-line license.

2007: Subscriber base nears 17 million.

In 1989, the government recognized that the only solution for the country's telecommunications problems was to open the market to private investors. In 1989, the government passed Telecommunications Act No. 3, which allowed Perumtel and Indosat to seek funding from the private sector. While the new legislation did not lead to deregulation (the government maintained monopoly control over the sector), both Indosat and Perumtel became partially privatized over the next decade. Both companies were later listed on the Jakarta and New York Stock Exchanges, although the government maintained majority control through the decade.

Initially, private sector investments were limited to a series of build-to-transfer agreements. This meant that private-sector companies extended the country's telecommunications infrastructure, then turned over ownership in these projects to Perumtel/Telkom and Indosat. In exchange, the investing companies received revenues from two government-owned companies.

With market penetration continuing to lag, however, the government at last opened the sector to direct foreign investment. This began in 1993, when the first foreign companies were allowed to enter the market, establishing services such as paging and email. Both Telkom and Indosat became partners in these efforts, further complicating the two companies' cross-shareholding structure. A new milestone in the sector came in 1994, when the government established a joint-operations program called Bahasa Kerja Sama Operasi, or KSO. Under this initiative, the government auctioned off a number of regional build-operate-transfer (BOT) agreements, which were eagerly picked up by the global telecommunications sector. The goal of the KSO program was to establish a regional operating structure, similar to the "baby Bells" in the United States. Over the next three years, the KSO program generated more than $10 billion in investment into the country's telecom sector.

CELLULAR FOCUS IN THE NEW CENTURY

In the end, the KSO scheme failed, however, in part because of resistance from Telkom and Indosat to relinquish their monopoly positions. The sector was doubly hit in the late 1990s, as the economic collapse of much of the Southeast Asian region caught up with Indonesia.

The end of the Suharto regime, however, spelled new opportunities. A review of the telecommunications sector led to the institution of a new deregulation effort in 2000. As a lead-up to deregulation, the "Byzantine" cross-shareholding arrangement between Telkom and Indosat was unraveled. Indosat took over the 22.5 percent held by Telkom in cellular phone operator Satelindo, the country's second largest operator in that sector. Satelindo had been set up as a partnership with two other companies, Bima Graha and Deutsche Telekom, which held a combined 70 percent.

The deregulation of Indonesia's telecommunications sector came into law in 2000, with full implementation to be carried out by the middle of the decade. Indosat began preparing to develop domestic fixed-line and other operations. Yet the mobile telephone market clearly represented the most dynamic market in Indonesia. By 2001, Indosat had taken over Bimagraha Telekomindo, boosting its stake in Satelindo by an additional 45 percent. By the following year, the company had bought out Deutsche Telekom as well, becoming the sole owner of Satelindo. By then, too, Indosat had acquired another major mobile telephone group, PT Satelit Palapa Indonesia. That acquisition formed the basis for the rollout of Indosat's new mobile brand, Indosat Multi Media Mobile (IM3), based on the GSM 1800 standard.

The Indonesian government continued its privatization effort, selling more than 50 percent of its holding in Indosat in 2002. The largest part of that, more than 40 percent, went to ST Telemedia, owned by Temasek, the state-owned investment arm of neighboring Singapore. By then, Indosat had successfully obtained a fixed-line license, and began rolling out its service in the Jakarta and Surabaya regions.

Indosat merged all of its cellular telephone communications into a single brand, IM3, in 2003. The company then positioned itself as a full-service provider, featuring both GSM 800 and GSM 1800 standards. Indosat then began building up its customer base and market share. The launch of a new series of prepaid telephone cards helped stimulate the company's growth. By the beginning of 2004, the company counted more than eight million customers. By the end of that year, that figure topped 9.5 million. Prepaid customers remained the company's dominant market, and through the middle of the decade continued to represent more than 95 percent of the group's cellular phone revenues.

In an effort to woo a greater share of the postpaid market, the company launched its new "Matrix" service in 2005. The new service, available as a basic program and as three optional packages, provided premium services for lower rates. Indosat also remained at the forefront of telecommunications technology, rolling out 3.5G services—including video transmission, Internet access, and other high-speed data services—in November 2006. The company also became the first in Indonesia to receive a license to deploy a local wireless fixed telecommunications network, starting in the Jabotabek region.

In the meantime, the position of Temasek and the Singapore government as major shareholders, either directly or indirectly, in Indonesia's two major telecommunications groups had raised a red flag in the Indonesian government. Temasek was told to sell its holding in either Indosat or Telkom. At the end of 2007, it appeared likely that Temasek would sell its Indosat stake, with potential buyers rumored to include Qatar Telecom. That company, which already owned a 25 percent stake in ST Telemedia, appeared the most likely candidate.

In the meantime, Indosat continued to build its market share. By the end of 2007, the company's subscriber base neared 17 million, for a 27 percent share of the market. With the lowest penetration rate in the Southeast Asian region, and the world's fourth largest population, the Indonesian market promised further growth for Indosat in the new century.

M. L. Cohen

PRINCIPAL SUBSIDIARIES

Indosat International Finance Company B.V. (Netherlands); Indosat Singapore Pte Ltd.; PT Aplikanusa Lintasarta; PT Indosat Mega Media; PT Multi Media Asia Indonesia; PT Satelindo Multi Media.

PRINCIPAL COMPETITORS

Elnusa Tbk, PT; Astra International Tbk, PT; Telkomunikasi Selular, PT; Excelcomindo Pratama Tbk, PT; Bakrie and Brothers Tbk, PT; Global Mediacom, PT; Bakrie Telecom Tbk, PT; Humpuss, PT; Infoasia Teknologi Global Tbk, PT.

FURTHER READING

"Bidders Waiting in the Wings for Sell-off Decision," *Financial Times,* November 22, 2007, p. 17.

"Cellular Phone Operators Undercut Each Other in Prices; Indosat Cuts IM3 Local Tariff to 40%," *Indonesian Commercial Newsletter,* October 12, 2004, p. 38.

Donnan, Shawn, "Indosat Suffers Despite Rise in Users," *Financial Times,* March 31, 2005, p. 20.

"Full Steam Ahead," *Asiamoney,* February 2004, p. 47.

Hidayat, Taufan, and Shawn Donnan, "Price of Doing Business in Indonesia Still High," *Financial Times,* April 9, 2003, p. 31.

"Indonesian GSM Licence," *Privatisation International,* September 1995, p. 18.

"Indosat, Nokia Expand Pact," *Total Telecom,* November 29, 2006.

"Indosat's Triumph Could Breathe Life into Asian High Yield," *Euroweek,* June 17, 2005, p. 19.

Leahy, Joe, and Tom McCawley, "'Landmark' Deal Set to Unlock Telecoms Growth Potential," *Financial Times,* May 25, 2001, p. 30.

"PT IndoSat Launches the Country's First Carrier Ethernet Service," *Telecom Asia,* February 2007, p. 12.

Qdoba Restaurant Corporation

———— ■ ————

4865 Ward Road, Suite 500
Wheat Ridge, Colorado 80033-1902
U.S.A.
Telephone: (720) 898-2300
Toll Free: (888) 497-3622
Fax: (720) 898-2396
Web site: http://www.qdoba.com

Wholly Owned Subsidiary of Jack in the Box Inc.
Founded: 1995
Employees: 900
Sales: $330 million (2007 est.)
NAIC: 722211 Limited-Service Restaurants; 533110 Lessors of Nonfinancial Intangible Assets (Except Copyrighted Works)

■ ■ ■

Qdoba Restaurant Corporation is the second largest fast-casual Mexican restaurant chain in the United States, trailing only Chipotle Mexican Grill, Inc. The company manages the Qdoba Mexican Grill system, which includes more than 400 outlets in 39 states and the District of Columbia. Positioned as purveyors of "nouveau" Mexican cuisine, Qdoba restaurants feature a menu centering on large signature burritos offering unique flavors, such as ancho chile barbecue, fajita ranchero, and poblano pesto. Other menu offerings include tacos, taco salads, grilled quesadillas, nachos, soups, and breakfast items. Qdoba workers prepare items in front of the customer, topping them with personally selected ingredients, including a number of distinctive salsas. The prices for main courses run from

$5 to $7, while sides go for roughly $2.50 to $4. The typical Qdoba, which offers dine-in, takeout, and catering (Q-to-Go) options, has a seating capacity ranging from 60 to 80 persons, including outdoor patio seating.

From a single location that opened in Denver, Colorado, in 1995 under the name Zuma, Qdoba (pronounced cue-doe-buh) had developed into a chain of 85 outlets in 16 states by early 2003. At that time, San Diego-based fast-food hamburger chain operator Jack in the Box Inc. acquired Qdoba for $45 million. The deep pockets of its parent enabled Qdoba to expand at a faster pace, with the chain reaching the 400-unit mark in November 2007 and plans to open more than 75 additional outlets over the succeeding year. Approximately 80 percent of Qdoba restaurants are owned and operated by franchisees, with the remainder owned and operated by the corporation.

1995–97: FROM ZUMA TO Z-TECA

Qdoba was founded in September 1995 by Anthony Miller and Robert Hauser, two Generation Xers who opened their Zuma restaurant at Grant Street and Sixth Avenue in Denver. Miller, an investment banker from New York, concentrated on the operations side and was the firm's first CEO, while Hauser, a graduate of the Culinary Institute of America and formerly chef at the five-star La Cirque restaurant in New York City, supervised the food side. Company lore held that the restaurant had been named after a cat that had belonged to Miller's college roommate.

The 1,300-square-foot restaurant, built at a cost of $200,000, offered big burritos weighing more than a pound each, filled with fresh ingredients, and assembled along a production line in front of the customer. Zuma was clearly a fast-casual restaurant, an emerging category of chains that were a bit fancier than typical fast-food restaurants such as Taco Bell while offering faster service than casual-dining chains such as Chevys. Positioned as a "fresh Mexican grill," Zuma offered its customers a number of options for burrito fillings: *carnitas* (pork), chicken, or beef; cilantro-lime rice; pinto or black beans; optional cheese and sour cream; and several salsas that varied in their level of heat. From the beginning, Hauser developed unique flavors for the menu, including poblano pesto, made from poblano peppers, green chiles, garlic, almonds, and pine nuts; and a molé sauce made from a base of dark semisweet chocolate, chili pepper, garlic, and other spices. Most of the burritos on the menu initially sold for less than $5.

Positive reviews from local restaurant critics and strong word of mouth helped Zuma generate $1.5 million in revenue during its first year. The first snag for the nascent operation arose in late 1996. In order to use the Zuma name, the company had had to license it from its owner in Boston. The lawyer for Miller and Hauser's business advised that owning a name outright was a necessity before carrying out plans to franchise the concept in other states. Therefore in early 1997, Zuma was renamed Z-Teca Mexican Grill. Around this same time, two more Z-Teca outlets were opened in Denver. Several more opened in Colorado by the end of the year, including units in the Denver metro area, Boulder, and Golden. By early 1998 there were 12 Z-Tecas open in Colorado, Texas, Maryland, Arizona, and Kansas, among which were the first franchise outlets.

NEW INVESTORS AND MANAGERS, ACCELERATING EXPANSION

In February 1998 fast-food giant McDonald's Corporation purchased a minority stake in Z-Teca competitor and fellow Denver-based chain Chipotle Mexican Grill, which had been founded in 1993. This investment by McDonald's, which acquired majority control of Chipotle in 1999, spurred interest in the fast-casual Mexican sector from investors as well as a great deal of publicity. To at least a certain extent, Z-Teca was able to ride Chipotle's coattails to an important capital infusion. In March 1998 the company announced that Western Growth Capital LLC, a Denver-based investment group, had made a significant investment in Z-Teca, becoming its largest shareholder. At the same time, additional investments were made by three industry veterans—Dan Carney, the founder of Pizza Hut; Jack Laughery, former CEO of Hardee's; and Martin Hart, a board member of Papa John's America. The new funding enabled the chain to begin franchising in earnest.

While the company founders had succeeded in creating a viable model in terms of the menu and the customer service approach, they realized that professional management was needed to expand Z-Teca into a national chain with hundreds of outlets. Thus in 1998 Gary J. Beisler was hired as COO. He brought two decades of quick-service restaurant experience to Z-Teca, including his most recent stint as senior vice-president of operations for Rally's Hamburgers, Inc. Beisler had played a key role in expanding Rally's from a small chain into a major player in the fast-food hamburger sector with nearly 500 outlets.

Beisler further strengthened Z-Teca's management team with several additional hires, including Richard Pugh, a colleague of Beisler's from Rally's who was named vice-president of operations; Karen Guido, named vice-president of marketing on the basis of previous marketing experience at Vicorp Restaurants, Inc.'s Village Inn chain and at Domino's, Inc.; and Eric Grundmeier, formerly with Einstein/Noah Bagel Corporation, who was hired as director of purchasing and distribution. The new management team led Z-Teca into a faster rate of expansion, particularly on the franchise side. More than a dozen agreements were soon in place with area developers around the country

---

KEY DATES

■

1995: Anthony Miller and Robert Hauser open Zuma, a "fresh Mexican grill" centering on big burritos, located in Denver, Colorado.

1997: Zuma changes its name to Z-Teca Mexican Grill; several more Z-Tecas are opened.

1998: Additional capital investments enable franchising of the Z-Teca concept to begin in earnest; Gary J. Beisler is brought onboard as COO; expansion of menu beyond big burritos commences.

2000: Chain changes its name to Qdoba Mexican Grill, while the corporate parent becomes Qdoba Restaurant Corporation.

2003: The 85-unit Qdoba is sold to Jack in the Box Inc. for $45 million.

2007: Restaurant count hits 400.

---

experienced in multiunit franchising. Between mid-1998 and mid-1999 the number of units doubled to 42 in 14 states, with 29 of the restaurants being franchises.

During this same period, Z-Teca introduced a new store design and image created by outside designers. Design elements included new packaging; new poster boards; warmer interior decor featuring earth colors, stainless steel, and copper; and such decorative touches as ancient Mexican hieroglyphics and a mural depicting women making tortillas by hand on a Mexican farm. As Miller told the *Denver Rocky Mountain News* in July 1998, "This is the evolution of our overall branding efforts from simple logo to something more sophisticated that has more design elements."

Another important development in 1998 was the beginning of Z-Teca's transformation from a big burrito concept to more of a full-fledged Mexican grill offering "nouveau Mexican" cuisine. The restaurant menu expanded to include tacos, taco salads, nachos, and seasonal soups. This augmentation was designed in part to strengthen the chain's appeal to female customers as customer user studies had shown that the original focus on burritos had appealed primarily to men. Having spearheaded many of the significant changes that Z-Teca was undergoing, Beisler was promoted to CEO in December 1999 with Miller remaining chairman.

NEW NAME IN 2000

As Z-Teca began its steady expansion around the country, its name once again became an issue. In a

number of markets, the similar name "Azteca" was already being used by a restaurant, and the company also faced federal trademark infringement lawsuits from Seattle-based Azteca Restaurant Enterprises and Z'Tejas Grills of Scottsdale, Arizona. Although Z-Teca had filed a federal copyright name registration, the other two restaurant chains had registered their names earlier. On this basis, Z-Teca eventually had to pay Azteca a $27,500 court settlement and also reached an out-of-court settlement with Z'Tejas for an undisclosed amount. It also elected to change its name once again, this time using professional help to avoid future nomenclature disputes. In the early months of 2000, a transition to the name Qdoba Mexican Grill was carried out, with the corporate parent changing its name as well from Z-Teca Restaurant Corporation to Qdoba Restaurant Corporation. Beisler asserted to *Chain Leader* in November 2000 that the Qdoba name "means absolutely nothing, and thus was something we could use for any idea and any geographic area in our gradual plan to go national."

By the end of 2000, the Qdoba chain had grown to encompass 55 units, 41 franchised, in 17 states, including California, Illinois, Georgia, and North Carolina. Systemwide sales totaled approximately $38 million, with the average company-owned restaurant pulling in $825,000 in revenues that year while the franchise average amounted to $750,000. The average customer check totaled $7.

Qdoba continued its steady growth over the next two years. While continuing to open new company-owned outlets, the company on the franchise side entered into a number of substantial territorial expansion deals. In late 2002, for example, Qdoba announced a deal with a sister company of RMD Corp., the largest Hooters franchisee, for the opening of 25 Qdoba outlets in southern Florida. By this time, Qdoba had commitments in place for more than 200 new units that were in various stages of development. Most of the new stores were sited in higher-end shopping centers catering to the chain's target customers, busy adults heading dual-income families. Qdoba ended 2002 with 85 restaurants, 57 of which were franchises, and systemwide sales of $65 million. The chain continued to post strong same-store sales growth, with this key figure for 2002 standing at 12 percent.

2003 ACQUISITION BY JACK IN THE BOX

By the end of 2002 Chipotle Mexican Grill had become the clear leader of the fast-casual Mexican restaurant sector, as the financial backing and operational expertise of its McDonald's parent helped push the store count of

Qdoba's crosstown rival up to 230. Qdoba, seeking to grow at a faster clip, gained its own deep-pocketed fast-food parent in January 2003 when the company was sold to San Diego-based Jack in the Box Inc. for $45 million in cash. At the time of the purchase, Jack in the Box was operating around 1,850 hamburger outlets in 17 mainly western and southern states. For its part, Jack in the Box was seeking to diversify its operations while the entire fast-food hamburger sector was suffering from stagnating sales. It was also in the midst of a refranchising program through which it was converting some of its company-owned outlets into franchises, and by acquiring Qdoba it hoped to tap into the pool of franchisees that the Mexican chain had developed.

Under its new parent, Qdoba operated as a wholly owned subsidiary and kept its headquarters in Denver and retained its existing team of executives. The same month of the acquisition, Qdoba added grilled quesadillas to its menu and a new signature burrito called the Queso that featured a three-cheese sauce—an innovative mixture of Swiss, white cheddar, and Monterey Jack cheeses—and could include either adobe-marinated grilled chicken or steak. Over the next two years, as planned, Qdoba parlayed the capital funds of its parent into a more rapid rate of growth, opening up 66 new restaurants in fiscal 2004 and 73 the following year. By early October 2005, the Qdoba chain consisted of 250 outlets in 37 states: 57 company-owned and 193 franchises. Systemwide sales reached approximately $220 million.

By this time, the menu was showcasing another signature burrito, the grilled vegetable. This item featured sautéed and grilled red peppers, zucchini, and yellow squash, tossed in a garlic herb seasoning. Qdoba also had begun offering a catering service called Q-to-Go consisting of a hot taco, Naked Burrito, or nacho buffet suitable for groups of 20 or more people. Interestingly, since the chain's beginnings as Zuma, the menu at Qdoba had featured the Naked Burrito: the contents of a big burrito served in a container or on a plate without the tortilla, and eaten with utensils. The original concept, according to Hauser, as quoted in the *Denver Post* in December 1996, was designed to "appeal to business professionals who don't want to risk spilling sauce on their suits." Much later, the low-carbohydrate diet craze breathed new life into this concept, and one of Qdoba's competitors, Moe's Southwest Grill, LLC, began selling "Buck Naked" burritos. Qdoba had trademarked the term "Naked Burrito," and so it sued Moe's for trademark infringement. As part of a settlement the two sides reached in March 2005, Moe's agreed to stop using the term "Buck Naked."

Also in 2005, Qdoba replaced its marketing tagline "Not just big burritos, big flavor" with the new tagline "What are you going to love at Qdoba?" The accompanying advertising campaign emphasized the various choices the chain offered and the unique flavor profiles available at the restaurants. The accompanying marketing campaign included television and radio spots, print ads, in-store material, and direct mail. At this time, Qdoba's annual advertising budget amounted to around $2.5 million. Same-store sales remained strong at Qdoba, including an 11.8 percent increase during fiscal 2005.

MAINTAINING AN AGGRESSIVE GROWTH RATE

In 2006 and 2007 Qdoba maintained its aggressive rate of growth, opening its 300th unit in the summer of 2006 and its 400th outlet in November 2007. Although same-store sales growth slowed in these years to 5.9 percent and 4.6 percent, respectively, these figures were nevertheless more than respectable. By 2007 systemwide revenues had reached an estimated $330 million.

Qdoba's menu continued to evolve during this period. In the fall of 2006 the chain had one of its most successful new product introductions with the launch of Mexican Gumbo soup, which was simply Qdoba's tortilla soup poured over the fillings of a burrito. In 2007 a chicken mango salad was offered on the menu as a limited-edition summer item. That fall, Qdoba also added seasoned shredded pork to its menu along with a new signature burrito, the Ancho Chile Barbecue Burrito. At the same time, the slow-selling Chicken Molé Burrito was pulled from the menu. In July 2007 Qdoba announced that it had launched an initiative to remove artery-clogging trans fats from all of its menu items by the end of the year. Future growth plans called for Qdoba Mexican Grill to expand by between 75 and 100 new restaurants per year, with around 80 percent of these slated to be franchise outlets.

David E. Salamie

PRINCIPAL COMPETITORS

Chipotle Mexican Grill, Inc.; Baja Fresh Mexican Grill; Moe's Southwest Grill, LLC; Rubio's Restaurants, Inc.; El Pollo Loco Holdings, Inc.

FURTHER READING

Aronovich, Hanna, "New Flavors: New Menu Items and Expansion Ensure That Customers Nationwide Can Sample

Qdoba's Nouveau-Mex Flavor, the Company Says," *Food and Drink*, May/June 2005, pp. 46, 48, 50.

Basquez, Anna Maria, "Z-Teca Restaurant Takes Big Burrito Concept National," *Denver Rocky Mountain News*, July 4, 1997, p. 1B.

Bernstein, Charles, "What's in a Name?" *Chain Leader*, November 2000, pp. 25–26.

Bertagnoli, Lisa, "Industrial Lite: A Soft Yet Modern Interior Helps Consumers Differentiate Qdoba Mexican Grill from Its Competitors," *Chain Leader*, November 2003, pp. 28–30, 32.

Brand, Rachel, "Burger Chain Makes a Run for the Border with Qdoba Buyout," *Denver Rocky Mountain News*, January 23, 2003, p. 2B.

Brandau, Mark, "Gary J. Beisler," *Nation's Restaurant News*, October 16, 2006, pp. 68, 70.

Breuhaus, Brian, "Burrito Blow-out?" *Restaurant Business*, April 1, 1998, p. 20.

Bunn, Dina, "Z-Teca Chain Plans Design Make-over," *Denver Rocky Mountain News*, July 28, 1998, p. 4B.

Cavanaugh, Bonnie Brewer, "Qdoba Mexican Grill," *Nation's Restaurant News*, January 28, 2002, pp. 168–69.

Cebrzynski, Gregg, "'Emotional' Qdoba Campaign to Reinforce Positioning," *Nation's Restaurant News*, May 2, 2005, p. 15.

Cox, Jack, "Expansion Excites Restaurant Owners," *Denver Post*, December 31, 1996, p. E2.

Dunn, Julie, "Q the Spotlight: Qdoba Mexican Grill, Hot on the Expansion Trail, Hopes to Stand Out in Unwrapping at Least 80 More of Its Fast-Casual Restaurants This Year," *Denver Post*, April 16, 2007, p. C1.

Farkas, David, "Fresh Competition: Qdoba Plays Up Food Quality, Options, and Speed of Service to Set Itself Apart from Rival Burrito Chains," *Chain Leader*, August 2004, pp. 58–59, 65–66, 68.

Forgrieve, Janet, "Qdoba Looking to Spice Up Growth," *Denver Rocky Mountain News*, September 22, 2005, p. 5B.

French, Liz, "Fresh Ideas," *American Executive*, April 2007, pp. 61–63.

Littman, Margaret, "Mex It Up: Chipotle Targets a Niche Audience, While Qdoba Goes After the Mass Market," *Chain Leader*, July 2005, pp. 22–23.

Parker, Penny, "Investors Are Pumping Big Bucks into Big Burritos," *Denver Post*, March 2, 1998, p. C1.

———, "Z-Teca to Franchise Restaurants," *Denver Post*, June 11, 1997, p. C2.

Pate, Kelly, "Qdoba Chain Sells for $45 Mil," *Denver Post*, January 22, 2003, p. C1.

———, "Z-Teca Changing Its Name," *Denver Post*, December 15, 1999, p. C1.

Petersen, Chris, "'Nouveau' Food: Qdoba Mexican Grill Says It Brings New Flavor Profiles to the Mexican Fast-Casual Segment, As Well As a Healthier Approach to Its Food Preparation," *Food and Drink*, May/June 2007, pp. 94–95.

Rogers, Monica, "Outside the Box: Qdoba Chef Ed Wilroy Sidesteps Cliches and Defines Fresh, 'Nuevo-Mex' Fare," *Chain Leader*, March 2003, pp. 46–50, 52.

Ruggless, Ron, "Z-Teca Plans Expansion of Fresh-Made Burrito Concept," *Nation's Restaurant News*, July 27, 1998, p. 76.

Spector, Amy, "Jack in the Box Buys Qdoba," *Nation's Restaurant News*, February 3, 2003, pp. 1, 77.

Spielberg, Susan, "Qdoba Mexican Grill: Jack in the Box Brings Upscale Burrito Brand into the Fold, Prepares for Rapid Growth," *Nation's Restaurant News*, January 31, 2005, pp. 172, 174.

Thorn, Bret, "Ted Stoner," *Nation's Restaurant News*, September 20, 2007, p. 42.

Walkup, Carolyn, "Expansion Has Become Name of the Game for Qdoba Mexican Grill," *Nation's Restaurant News*, November 6, 2000, p. 26.

America's Home Loan Experts®

Quicken Loans, Inc.

20555 Victor Parkway
Livonia, Michigan 48152
U.S.A.
Telephone: (734) 805-5000
Toll Free: (800) 226-6308
Fax: (734) 805-8400
Web site: http://www.quickenloans.com

Wholly Owned Subsidiary of Rock Holdings, Inc.
Incorporated: 1985 as Rock Financial Corp.
Employees: 4,100
Operating Revenues: $750 million (2006 est.)
NAIC: 522292 Real Estate Credit; 522298 All Other Nondepository Credit Intermediation; 524127 Direct Title Insurance Carriers

∎∎∎

Quicken Loans, Inc., is the top online mortgage lender in the United States. The company offers a variety of different loan options that it bundles for sale to larger financial institutions after closing, although it eschews the riskier subprime type. Rock Holdings, the parent company of Quicken Loans Inc., also owns Title Source, Inc., which offers title insurance and settlement services. The privately owned company's billionaire founder Daniel Gilbert serves as its chairman and continues to hold a sizable stake.

BEGINNINGS

Quicken Loans was founded in 1985 as Rock Financial by Detroit-area native Daniel Gilbert, a 22-year-old Wayne State University first-year law student and part-time real estate broker. Gilbert, who had shown an entrepreneurial bent from childhood when he sold candy and pizzas to neighbors, saw an opportunity to increase his earnings by writing mortgage loans, which required no license in Michigan. Investing $5,000 to form the small company, he soon added the services of his brother and a friend. The business grew so quickly, however, that Gilbert never took up the practice of law after his 1987 graduation.

During the late 1980s and early 1990s Rock Financial opened a half-dozen branch offices in southeast Michigan and developed relationships with real estate professionals, home builders, lawyers, and financial planners to bring it referrals. Like many similar firms, after its loans were closed Rock sold them in bulk on the wholesale market to larger banking companies.

In 1992 the firm was organized as an S corporation, and Gilbert added the title of board chairman to his duties as president and CEO. By 1993 revenues had grown to $18.2 million, and net income to $1.1 million.

CREATION OF FRESH START DIVISION: 1994

In 1994 the firm founded a new division called Fresh Start that targeted the so-called subprime loan market, serving individuals with poor credit records or other financial problems. Over the next several years nearly 20 Fresh Start loan centers were opened in strip malls and office buildings in Michigan, Ohio, Illinois, Indiana, Texas, Nevada, and Missouri. Their services were typically marketed through direct mail and other advertisements.

In March 1997 Rock created a Specialty Lending division that offered "high loan-to-value" second mortgages for borrowers with little or no equity in their homes. The program was operated out of a call center at the firm's headquarters in the northern Detroit suburb of Bingham Farms, and marketed in nearly 20 states.

For 1997 the firm's revenues jumped to $52.1 million from the 1996 total of $29.6 million, with net income of $7.3 million recorded. Rock closed on 12,950 loans, which were worth $1.2 billion. About two-thirds of this dollar amount was made up of conventional home loans, with slightly more than a fifth being subprime loans and the rest consisting of second mortgage loans. Some 92 percent were made on property located in Michigan.

In May 1998 Rock Financial went public on the NASDAQ, selling 3.3 million shares for $10 each. After the offering, founder Daniel Gilbert held 52.9 percent of the firm's common stock and 75 percent of its shareholder votes. The firm was also shifted from an S to a C corporation. During 1998 the company signed loan agreements worth $2.35 billion, up 93 percent from the year before. It had nearly 30 branch offices.

DEBUT OF WEB-BASED LOANS: 1999

With the surging growth of the Internet Gilbert saw a new way to reach customers and increase the company's reach outside of Michigan. In January 1999 the firm closed nine branch offices that dealt primarily in subprime loans, and launched RockLoans.com, to which the managers of the closed offices were transferred. One of the first direct mortgage lenders on the Internet, it offered low rates and fast service, giving it an edge over many online competitors that served as middlemen.

After successfully test-marketing the new online loan program in several areas, the firm began working to get approval to write mortgages in all 50 states and preparing a national ad campaign. In July plans to close 12 of the remaining 15 Rock Financial offices were announced as online mortgage business surged. Although much of the loan process could be done via the Internet, the firm still needed trained mortgage bankers to finalize deals over the phone, with signed documents faxed or mailed to complete the agreement.

In the fall a deal for the firm to be acquired by Quicken/QuickBooks financial software maker Intuit, Inc. was announced. The stock-based deal was initially worth $370 million, but by the time it closed at year's end Intuit's booming share price had increased its value to $532 million. Rock subsidiary Title Source, Inc., was also purchased for $6 million in cash.

Intuit subsequently folded the company into its QuickenMortgage online loan service, which had been launched two years earlier to offer loan quotes from partners including HomeSide Lending, Chase Manhattan Mortgage Corp., and Countrywide Home Loans. QuickenMortgage typically made $400 to $600 per successful referral, but could earn $2,500 to $3,500 when loans were made directly through the former Rock Financial (whose name was retained in Michigan).

Rock CEO Dan Gilbert would head the unit, which was soon renamed Quicken Loans, Inc. Based at the firm's headquarters in Livonia, Michigan, it would offer conventional mortgages, jumbo loans, Federal Housing Administration (FHA) loans, home equity loans/credit, refinancing, and subprime loans. As it had always done, the firm closed loans but sold them in bulk to wholesale lending firms around the United States. At this time the number of mortgages that originated online was estimated at just 1.5 percent of the industry total.

LAUNCH OF QUICKENLOANS.COM: 2000

The QuickenLoans.com web site was soon launched with a multimillion-dollar media campaign. It had been carefully designed after examining records of visits to predecessor sites and interviewing users. Quicken Loans would also be promoted via such Intuit products as the popular TurboTax and Quickbooks accounting software, and through ads on other web sites.

QuickenLoans.com initially continued to offer leads to outside lenders, but a problem immediately cropped up when Countrywide decided to exit. Because FHA rules required that lenders have a physical presence in the area where loans were made, Quicken had used its

and decided to divest a portfolio of e-commerce businesses that also included insurance and bill management units. In July 2002 control of Quicken Loans was bought by a group led by Dan Gilbert for an estimated $64 million, far less than the price of three years earlier. Gilbert took a 62 percent ownership stake.

The company became a unit of newly formed Rock Holdings, Inc., and remained headquartered in Livonia, Michigan. It struck a deal to license the Quicken Loans trademark in perpetuity, while its mortgage offerings would continue to be promoted at Quicken.com and through Intuit's Quicken and Turbo Tax software offerings. Title insurance and settlement subsidiary Title Source, Inc., was also a part of the deal, and the firm would continue to operate Rock Financial's three loan centers. The company employed 1,100.

In December 2002 Quicken Loans settled Federal Trade Commission charges that it had violated the Fair Credit Reporting Act by failing to notify rejected applicants that their loans had been denied because of bad credit scores. The company agreed to provide such information in the future, and avoided other sanctions.

In the summer of 2003 the firm announced plans to create the federally chartered Rock Bank, which would operate in all 50 states and offer savings and checking accounts online and at several retail locations in southeastern Michigan. It would also give Quicken Loans blanket federal exemption from the increasingly complex array of local laws restricting mortgage loans that were starting to appear. The plan was abandoned late the next year, however, as the company decided to sharpen its focus on the mortgage business. With interest rates rising, the firm also began working on new ways to win business including introducing adjustable-rate and interest-only loans and instant-approval online home equity loans.

During 2003 Quicken Loans signed a $1 million-plus deal to become a presenting sponsor of the Detroit Pistons basketball team, using the Rock Financial brand name, and became a sponsor of Roger Penske's Indy Racing Team. At year's end the firm was ranked 13th on *Fortune* magazine's list of the "100 Best Companies to Work For," where it would reappear consistently in future years. The company encouraged its employees with a variety of performance-based bonuses and awards, discounted home loans, paid educational opportunities, concert and sports tickets, and free slushie drinks from the in-house "Soft Rock Café." During 2003 the value of loans closed surged 75 percent to $12 billion, and its employee headcount to 1,700.

In 2004 Quicken Loans announced its Livonia headquarters would be expanded and a new $29.1 million facility would be added in nearby Troy, which

association with Countrywide to fulfill this requirement. The FHA problem was eventually resolved, while Countrywide and other "bricks-and-mortar" lenders subsequently founded their own online units, which became strong competitors of the firm.

Falling interest rates and a jump in refinancings helped business grow rapidly, and Quicken Loans soon announced plans to more than double the size of its call center. During 2001 the firm closed on $4.6 billion in loans and generated $172 million in revenue for Intuit.

In early 2002 the company promoted veteran executives Bill Emerson and Pat McInnis to the jobs of CEO and president, respectively, with Dan Gilbert continuing to serve as chairman. At this time the firm also announced it had resolved the issue of transmitting legally binding signatures electronically, which remained the one part of the mortgage process that could not be done electronically. Seeking to reach new users, Quicken Loans was partnering with a variety of other online firms to generate visits to its site including Yahoo! Real Estate, for which it provided content.

GILBERT LEADS BUYBACK IN 2002

In the aftermath of the dot-com shakeout of the early 2000s, Intuit began to reevaluate its corporate strategy

would create 1,200 new jobs. The latter was helped by city and state tax credits nearly equal to the project cost. During the year *National Mortgage News* reported that Quicken Loans had become the nation's number one online mortgage firm.

Ever the entrepreneur, Chairman Dan Gilbert had invested his own money in other businesses and as a partner in private investment firm Camelot Ventures, which took stakes in contact lens and software development companies and catalog retailer Red Envelope. After failing in a bid to acquire baseball's Milwaukee Brewers, in March 2005 he bought controlling interest in the National Basketball Association's Cleveland Cavaliers for $375 million, after which the Cavaliers' home was renamed the Quicken Loans Arena. The firm celebrated its 20th anniversary there with a concert by the Black-Eyed Peas and Kid Rock, with Gilbert busing his entire staff and their families to Cleveland for the weekend.

OPENING OF NEW BRANCH IN CLEVELAND: 2006

In April 2006 the company opened a new Internet loan office in Cleveland that would employ more than 300, bringing Quicken Loans' total payroll to about 3,500.

In May a U.S. appeals court in California ordered the firm to pay refunds to customers in that state who had been charged interest from the day of their mortgage signing, rather than from the date the loan was recorded in county offices, which often occurred weeks later. The firm vowed to appeal the decision.

In October 2006 the Rock Financial Junior Achievement Finance Park opened in downtown Detroit, with $1 million in funding from the company. It was expected to give 10,000 middle school students exposure to the world of business each year. A short time later Dan Gilbert also announced he was investing $10 million to found Bizdom U., a free two-year business training program based at Wayne State University. The program would teach young people how to become entrepreneurs, and would invest $25,000 to $500,000 in their new businesses upon graduation. The first 13 students were enrolled in January 2007.

For 2006 Quicken Loans closed $18 billion in mortgages, up from $16 billion the year before. Revenue jumped to an estimated $750 million from $554 million. Despite a downturn in the industry brought on by the subprime lending crisis, the firm was continuing to grow, hiring an average of 200 new employees per month, and its headcount increased to 3,900 by year's end.

The company continued to rely heavily on advertising to bring in new customers, and spent more than $50 million during the year on a variety of promotional efforts. On the technological front, it was operating in a completely paperless environment, processing 175,000 phone calls and 2.4 million internal emails each day.

In the summer of 2007 Gilbert helped found a new company called RockBridge Equity Partners, LLC, which was headquartered in the Quicken Loans offices, but set up as a separate financial entity. RockBridge would seek growing companies to fund, particularly those in Michigan. Gilbert's other side ventures included stakes in sports wall graphics firm Fathead LLC, ticket broker Flash Seats LLC, and ePrize, Inc., an online promotions company.

As the subprime crisis deepened, in the fall of 2007 the firm froze hiring of loan writers in Michigan and stopped writing "nonconforming" mortgages to less-qualified borrowers that it could no longer be sold on the wholesale market. Nonconforming loans accounted for less than a third of the total and were phased out within a few weeks' time.

MOVE TO DOWNTOWN DETROIT

In November 2007 Quicken Loans announced its suburban Detroit offices would be consolidated in the city's struggling downtown after their leases expired in 2010. City and state incentives of $200 million over 20 years had helped sweeten the pot, with Detroit banking on the creation of thousands of ancillary jobs in the area and many millions of dollars spent over time by the firm's well-paid workers. Gilbert was also working to convince other suburban business owners to move downtown in a bid to support the city's long hoped-for comeback.

During 2007 the company also opened another Internet Home Lending Center in North Scottsdale, Arizona, which would employ less than 100 to start. For the year mortgage volume topped $19 billion.

Nearing the end of its first quarter-century, Quicken Loans, Inc., had become the top Internet-only mortgage firm in the United States. The firm was weathering the subprime lending crisis by eschewing loans that it could not sell on the secondary market, and continued working to streamline the process of lending money online so it could grab a bigger piece of the overall mortgage pie.

In January 2008, *Fortune* announced that Quicken Loans had risen to number two on its list of the "100 Best Companies to Work for in America." It was the fifth year the company had appeared within the list's "Top 20" best companies.

In January 2008, Rock Holdings Inc., the parent company of Quicken Loans Inc. and Title Source Inc., made two acquisitions. Quicken Loans Inc. and Rock-Bridge Equity Partners joined to acquire One Reverse Mortgage, a fast-growing provider of FHA-backed reverse mortgage programs headquartered in San Diego. Title Source Inc. acquired TransUnion Title and Escrow of California, enabling Title Source to expand its business in one of the country's largest real estate markets.

Frank Uhle

PRINCIPAL SUBSIDIARIES

Title Source, Inc.

PRINCIPAL COMPETITORS

CitiMortgage, Inc.; Wachovia Corporation; Bank of America Corporation; Lending Tree, LLC; E-Loan, Inc.; JPMorgan Chase & Co.; Washington Mutual, Inc.; Wells Fargo & Company; HSBC Finance Corp.; Countrywide Financial Corp.

FURTHER READING

Bergquist, Erick, "Quicken Loans' Many Motives for Seeking OTS Charter," *American Banker*, August 6, 2003, p. 9.

"Betting on the 'Net to Rock-et to the Top," *Bank Advertising News*, May 17, 1999, p. 1.

Burke, Monte, "Net Game: Dan Gilbert, the New Owner of the Cleveland Cavaliers, Likes to Play Rough," *Forbes*, October 10, 2005, p. 82.

Garritano, Anthony, "Quicken Loans to Embrace Electronic Closings," *National Mortgage News*, October 30, 2006, p. 12.

Grant, Rick, "Quicken Set to Sell Unit," *National Mortgage News*, July 8, 2002, p. 1.

Henderson, Tom, and Sheena Harrison, "Detroit Needs Entrepreneurs, and He's Put Serious Money into Getting Them Started," *Crain's Detroit Business*, January 1, 2007, p. 1.

Howell, Donna, "Quicken Loans Speeds Up the Mortgage Application Process Enabling Online Signatures," *Investor's Business Daily*, February 19, 2002, p. A8.

Howes, Daniel, "Inside the Go-Go World of Quicken Loans," *Detroit News*, September 14, 2006, p. 1.

——, "Quicken Sold on Detroit; Move to Bring 4,000 Suburban Jobs to Downtown Technology Park," *Detroit News*, November 13, 2007, p. 1.

Klayman, Ben, "Rock Closes $22 Mln in Internet Mortgage Loans in March," *Reuters News*, April 8, 1999.

Merx, Katie, "Quicken Ready to Rock: New Lenders Set $10 Billion Goal," *Crain's Detroit Business*, March 4, 2002, p. 3.

——, "A Quickened Pace," *Crain's Detroit Business*, October 20, 2003, p. 1.

Morath, Eric, "Housing Slump Hits Quicken," *Detroit News*, October 15, 2007, p. 1.

Murray, Michael, "Quicken Makes It Simple," *Real Estate Finance Today*, September 3, 2001.

Murray, Teresa Dixon, "Cavs Owner to Bring 350 Jobs to City," *Cleveland Plain Dealer*, September 9, 2005, p. A1.

"Quicken Agrees to Change Online Loan Disclosures," *Associated Press Newswires*, December 30, 2002.

"Quicken Loans Still No. 1," *Mortgage Technology*, November 1, 2007, p. 21.

"Quicken Moves Ahead to Become No. 1 Online Retail Lender," *National Mortgage News*, December 20, 2004, p. 16.

Ridgway, Nicole, "Intuit Unit to Offer Govt-Backed Home Loans Online," *Dow Jones News Service*, January 19, 2000.

Schiavone, Louise L., "Quickening the Pace," *Mortgage Banking*, December 1, 2005, p. 44.

——, "The Reincarnation of Quicken Mortgage," *Mortgage Banking*, March 1, 2000, pp. 24–31.

Schiffmann, William, "Intuit Buys Online Mortgage Provider Rock Financial," *Associated Press Newswires*, October 7, 1999.

Schwartz, Mathew, "Tweak This!" *ComputerWorld*, January 31, 2000, p. 64.

Stempel, Jonathan, "Quicken Loans May Face Mortgage Interest Refunds," *Reuters News*, May 24, 2006.

Story, Louise, and Vikas Bajaj, "Even As Industry's Troubles Grow, Mortgage Ads Keep Up the Pitch," *New York Times*, August 25, 2007, p. 9A.

Valade, Jodie, "Average Doesn't Cut It for Cavs' Next Owner," *Cleveland Plain Dealer*, February 20, 2005, p. A1.

Rich Products Corporation

One Robert Rich Way
Buffalo, New York 14213-1714
U.S.A.
Telephone: (716) 878-8000
Toll Free: (800) 828-2021
Fax: (716) 878-8765
Web site: http://www.richs.com

Private Company
Founded: 1945
Incorporated: 1965
Employees: 6,000
Sales: $2.4 billion (2006 est.)
NAIC: 311411 Frozen Fruit, Juice, and Vegetable Manufacturing; 311412 Frozen Specialty Food Manufacturing; 311514 Dry, Condensed, and Evaporated Dairy Product Manufacturing; 311612 Meat Processed from Carcasses; 311712 Fresh and Frozen Seafood Processing; 311812 Commercial Bakeries; 311813 Frozen Cakes, Pies, and Other Pastries Manufacturing; 311822 Flour Mixes and Dough Manufacturing from Purchased Flour; 311999 All Other Miscellaneous Food Manufacturing; 711211 Sports Teams and Clubs; 722110 Full-Service Restaurants; 722320 Caterers

∎ ∎ ∎

Rich Products Corporation is one of the leading frozen food manufacturers in the United States. Selling its more than 2,000 products largely to the foodservice and in-store bakery sectors, but also to the retail marketplace, the company specializes in toppings, icings, desserts, breads, rolls, sweet goods, Italian specialties, pizza products, appetizers, fruit concentrates and drink mixes, shrimp and seafood, and barbecue meats. Rich Products pioneered the nondairy industry with a soybean-based whipping cream, and later became known for Coffee Rich, a cream substitute used in coffee. The rights to these products have been licensed to Dean Foods Company. Another alliance is with Sara Lee Corporation, whereby Rich provides sales, marketing, and distribution for all Sara Lee in-store bakery goods. Rich Products operates around 28 production facilities, 11 of which are located outside the United States, specifically in Canada, Mexico, Brazil, the United Kingdom, South Africa, China, India, and Thailand. The company markets its products in more than 80 countries around the world. Privately owned by the Rich family since its founding, Rich Products also owns a number of other businesses, including three minor league baseball teams—the Buffalo Bisons, Northwest Arkansas Naturals, and Jamestown Jammers; the Palm Beach National Golf and Country Club located in West Palm Beach, Florida; Rich Renaissance Catering, Inc.; several restaurants; and intermodal transportation specialist ROAR Logistics, Inc.

ROOTS IN NONDAIRY INNOVATION

Robert E. Rich, Sr., first learned about product substitution during World War II through the War Food Administration. After the war, he put that knowledge to use and directed a laboratory team to search for a vegetable-based replacement for whipped cream. His

COMPANY PERSPECTIVES

At Rich's, we believe that it's not just "what we do" that is important, but also "how we do it." Rich's carries on a tradition of doing business that has endured for more than 60 years.

Founded on the vision of a food industry pioneer, fortified by three generations of the Rich family, and maintained by a committed leadership team and more than 6,000 associates, the company lives by The Rich Promise. "We will treat our customers, associates and communities the same way. Like family."

product was to be based on soybeans. In 1945 Rich was on his way to visit a distributor on Long Island and packed some of his soybean-based whipping cream in dry ice for the long train ride from Buffalo, New York. He had intended just to keep the cream cool, but it was frozen solid when he arrived in Long Island. When Rich mashed the frozen mass, he found that it still whipped up beautifully. The discovery launched the beginning of a frozen nondairy products industry.

Rich's innovation, named Rich's Whip Topping, was lauded as "the miracle cream from the soya bean." This was 1945, when the frozen food industry was burgeoning. Rather than marketing to supermarkets, Rich targeted his product to the foodservice sector, reasoning that restaurants, schools, hospitals, and other cost-conscious operators seemed a likely audience for the product. Rich quietly built solid markets, carving a niche that remains unchallenged.

During its early years, Rich continued to create variations on its Whip Topping. In the 1950s the company came out with the first commercial line of frozen cream puffs and eclairs. Its next innovation came in 1961 with the development of Coffee Rich, the nation's first frozen nondairy creamer. Since its introduction, Coffee Rich dominated the market, claiming a 90 percent share into the 1980s. The product was also ahead of its time in health considerations: along with Whip Topping, Coffee Rich was the only 100 percent cholesterol-free, low-fat cream product distributed nationally.

In the 1960s Rich Products began marketing frozen dough. While supermarkets wanted the aroma of fresh baked goods tempting shoppers, it was too much trouble for them to set up expensive bakeries on their facilities, and frozen dough met their needs perfectly. In

the early 1960s, Rich began construction on a nondairy plant in Fort Erie, Ontario, just across the Niagara River from Rich's Buffalo headquarters. This plant is still in operation, producing both frozen dough and nondairy products. By the mid-1980s, Rich was operating what was the world's largest frozen dough plant in Murfreesboro, Tennessee. The dough, for breads, rolls, and pastries, was sold to supermarket chains throughout the country. Rich Products Corporation was incorporated in 1965. In 1969 Rich acquired Elm Tree Baking Company in Appleton, Wisconsin, adding frozen baked goods to its product line.

AGGRESSIVE EXPANSION

The 1970s were marked by spurts of growth for Rich. To keep up with product demand, Rich had to expand its production capabilities rapidly. During this time, Rich acquired nine plants, including Federal Bakers Supply in Garfield, New Jersey, and L.K. Baker Company in Columbus, Ohio. Other operations were purchased in Winchester, Virginia, and Claremont and Fresno, California. Rich also purchased Palmer Frozen Foods, a regional frozen bakery goods producer and distributor in eastern Pennsylvania.

Rich also expanded its product line to seafood specialties, soup bases, and gravy mixes. As late as 1975, however, about 71 percent of Rich's revenues were still coming from nondairy replacement products. The expansion into seafood began in 1976 with the acquisition of SeaPak Corporation, which had plants in Brunswick, Georgia, and Brownsville, Texas.

Rich launched an aggressive campaign of growth through acquisition that saw its sales quadruple over the next eight years. Acquisitions included the H.J. Heinz Company's frozen dessert plant in Lake City, Pennsylvania, contributing cream pies and cakes to Rich's line, and PREAM, a nondairy coffee powder, from Early California Foods of Los Angeles. By 1982 company sales were at $400 million, and sales of nondairy replacement products accounted for about half of those revenues.

Succeeded by his son, Robert Rich, Jr., as president of the company, Rich, Sr., remained chairman. Together they developed an unusual acquisition strategy, giving preference to other father-and-son companies. Rich, Sr., contended that all the company's takeovers were friendly and that most of their acquisitions' owners stayed on afterward. Other acquisitions in the 1980s included the former Lloyd J. Harris plant, a Saugatuck, Michigan-based pie producer, and Casa Di Bertacchi Corporation of Vineland, New Jersey, a producer of frozen Italian pasta and meat specialties purchased in 1982.

KEY DATES

1945: Robert E. Rich, Sr., makes the discovery that leads to the introduction of Rich's Whip Topping.

1961: Coffee Rich nondairy creamer is introduced.

1965: Rich Products Corporation is incorporated.

1969: Frozen baked goods are added to the product line.

1976: Company expands into frozen seafood with the acquisition of SeaPak Corporation.

1980: Company introduces Freeze Flo, a process that allows products to remain soft while frozen.

1982: Casa Di Bertacchi, producer of frozen Italian specialties, is acquired.

1983: Company expands outside food with the purchase of the Buffalo Bisons minor league baseball team.

1988: Company expands into barbecue and specialty meats through the purchase of Byron's, Inc.

1995: Revenues reach $1 billion.

1998: Rich swaps the rights to its retail nondairy product line for the Jon Donaire specialty dessert business of Suiza Foods Corporation (later Dean Foods Company).

1999: J.W. Allen, maker of frozen cakes, bakery mixes, and icings, is acquired.

2000: New line of specialty drinks and drink mixes is launched.

2003: Rich Products purchases cheesecake specialist Mother's Kitchen Inc.

2006: Robert E. Rich, Sr., dies at age 92; his son, Robert E. Rich, Jr., is named company chairman; William G. Gisel, Jr., is promoted to president and CEO, becoming the first non-family member to hold that position.

INTRODUCTION OF FREEZE FLO, 1980

In 1980 the company introduced a process called Freeze Flo that allowed products to remain soft while frozen, spurring the development of products such as frozen pie fillings that could be eaten right out of the freezer. The process took seven years and nearly $5 million to develop. By 1983 the company held 39 patents and was bringing in $2.5 million a year in licensing to 50 companies, mostly overseas. Rich incorporated Freeze Flo into many of its own new products, such as Rich's Grand America Ice Cream, the only ice cream on the market that could be shipped and stored at zero degrees Fahrenheit.

In 1983 Rich acquired Nashville's Tennessee Doughnut Company and Antoinetta's Frozen Italian Specialties of Harleysville, Pennsylvania. The company also purchased the Class AAA Buffalo Bisons baseball franchise, based in Rich's headquarters city. The team went on to set new minor league attendance records into the 1990s, becoming the best-drawing minor league baseball team in the nation. In 1984 Rich acquired a second baseball franchise, the Class AA Wichita (Kansas) Wranglers.

In 1986 Rich entered into a joint venture with J.R. Wood Inc., of Atwater, California. Together they launched Rich Fruit Pak, a frozen fruit processing plant in Escalon, California. The company formed Rich Communications Corporation in 1987. This served as the parent company to a pair of Western New York radio stations: WGR-AM Newsradio 550 and WGR-FM "97 Rock." These stations supplied the area with broadcasts of the NFL Buffalo Bills, the NHL Buffalo Sabres, and the Bisons. In 1988 Rich's frozen food line added barbeque and specialty meats with the acquisition of Byron's, Inc., of Gallatin, Tennessee.

These additions notwithstanding, the company's plan to expand via acquisition of family-owned food companies was slowed when the numerous leveraged buyouts of the 1980s pushed prices too high. Rich avoided the large debts that were often necessary to complete such transactions. Instead, the company concentrated on in-house development of a technology to make cholesterol-free frozen foods.

INTERNATIONAL EXPANSION

In 1990, in its 32nd acquisition since 1969, Rich acquired the Blue Bird Baking Company, a major producer of pies and cakes. Having virtually reached its operating capacity, Rich planned to increase the capacity in six of its nine bakery manufacturing plants by 35 percent in order to make room for new products. Rich launched a multimillion-dollar capital expenditure plan that included plant expansions and renovations in California, Ohio, Wisconsin, Pennsylvania, Tennessee, and Virginia. In the spring of 1990, Rich built a $17 million research and development center.

In 1992 Rich acquired the Seneau Baking Company of Marlborough, Massachusetts, which became Rich Marlborough, a state-of-the-art bakery products manufacturing plant. The company also acknowledged the strength of its Mexican market that year by opening a broker's office in Guadalajara, joining the Rich offices in Monterrey and Mexico City. Whipped toppings, fruit fillings, glazes, and Better Creme icings were some of the company's bestsellers in Mexico. By that time, Rich also had offices in Japan, Singapore, Australia, and the United Kingdom.

International expansion continued in 1993 with the establishment of Rich Products of South Africa, which began making and distributing frozen dough products. The following year the company purchased a manufacturing plant in Toluca, Mexico, in order to begin making frozen dough in that nation. Also in 1994 Rich Products formed a third baseball franchise in Jamestown, New York, the Jamestown Jammers, which became a Class A affiliate of the Detroit Tigers playing in the New York-Penn League.

Growth outside the United States was key to meeting a new company goal of increasing revenues by 25 percent per year. By 1995, the year the company celebrated its 50th year in business, sales had reached $1 billion. That year, Rich expanded its manufacturing capacity in the United States through the opening of a nondairy products plant in Niles, Illinois. The company also expanded into the Indian market that year through a joint venture with Kwality Foods, the largest maker of ice cream in India. Called Rich Kwality Products Ltd., the venture was established to make nondairy products for distribution in India. Rich Products also established a joint venture with UFM of Thailand called Rich Products Manufacturing (Thailand) Co., Ltd., for the manufacture of frozen dough products. Back home, Rich entered into an alliance with Sara Lee Corporation in 1997, whereby Rich began marketing Sara Lee frozen cake and dessert products to in-store bakeries.

During 1998 Rich expanded in China through the establishment of a wholly owned subsidiary that opened a new state-of-the-art nondairy facility in Suzhou, China. This plant was particularly important for increasing production, and distribution throughout Asia, of the newly introduced Rich's Gold Label Whip Topping, which quickly became the leading nondairy topping in the region.

ASSET SWAP WITH SUIZA FOODS, 1998

In mid-1998 Rich Products entered into an asset swap with Suiza Foods Corporation, a leading fresh milk and dairy food company based in Dallas. Rich granted Suiza the world rights (except India and Israel) to market and sell its retail refrigerated and frozen creamer lines, which included the Coffee Rich, Farm Rich, Poly Rich, and Rich Whip brands. Rich retained ownership of both the brands and the plants where the products were made. In return, Rich received from Suiza control of the Jon Donaire line of fully prepared frozen desserts. The Jon Donaire line was marketed to the foodservice and in-store bakery sectors, which fit in with Rich's strategic direction involving a de-emphasis of retail sales. Owing to the firm's product line expansion over the decades, less than 5 percent of Rich's sales were generated by its line of nondairy whipped toppings and creamers by the time of the asset swap. (Suiza Foods later acquired Dean Foods Company and then adopted the latter's name.)

William G. Gisel, Jr., was named to the new position of chief operating officer of Rich Products in 1999. Gisel had joined the company in 1982 with a position in the legal department, then eventually became a key player in Rich's international expansion. In 1996 he was named president of Rich Products Food Group. As COO, Gisel became the highest ranking nonfamily member in company history. Remaining chairman and president of the company were Robert Rich, Sr., and Robert Rich, Jr., respectively. Meanwhile, a third generation of Rich family members were reaching management positions at the family-controlled firm, including three children of Rich, Jr.

There were a number of additional developments in 1999 that also helped set the stage for the company at the dawn of the 21st century. The pie plant located in Saugatuck, Michigan, was sold. Major improvements were made to two company plants: the nondairy plant in Buffalo and a bakery facility in Hilliard, Ohio, where the industry's highest capacity donut production line was installed through a multimillion-dollar project. Then, in late 1999, Rich Products acquired J.W. Allen & Co., a family-owned firm based in Wheeling, Illinois. J.W. Allen produced about 400 products at its plants in Wheeling and in Morristown, Tennessee, including frozen cakes, bakery mixes, and icings. The products were primarily marketed to in-store bakeries. The addition of J.W. Allen's $110 million in annual sales increased Rich Products' revenues to more than $1.5 billion.

EARLY 21ST-CENTURY GROWTH INITIATIVES

Entering the new century with no intention of being acquired itself or of going public, Rich Products Corporation sought additional overseas expansion opportunities, ventured into e-commerce through an initiative where clients could purchase such products as Byron's barbecue sauce, and continued to pursue the development of new products, most notably a new line of specialty drinks, including fruit smoothies, nutritional drinks, and coffee-based concoctions. The latter, launched in January 2000, included both ready-to-drink and ready-to-mix items for the foodservice sector, and these drinks and mixes, unlike most of Rich's products, did not require refrigeration. On the international front, the company expanded in Asia again with the opening of an office in Ho Chi Minh City, Vietnam, in 2000.

In 2001, as part of a major overhaul of its bakery manufacturing network aiming at improving efficiency, Rich Products contracted with AmeriCold Logistics, LLC, to build a 150,000-square-foot distribution center adjacent to Rich's bakery products plant in Murfreesboro, Tennessee. The plan also involved the closure of plants in Appleton, Wisconsin, and Marlborough, Massachusetts. Also launched in 2001 was a $35 million expansion of its operations in Buffalo that included the installation of new computer systems for manufacturing and order fulfillment, staff increases for both the information technology and research and development departments, and a renovation of its 56-year-old factory in its home base.

Further growth initiatives were launched outside the United States in 2002. Through a $9.5 million expansion, Rich's Fort Erie, Ontario, plant began making a new line of partially baked breads and rolls for such chain restaurant customers as Pizza Hut and Subway. The company also opened a new 20,000-square-foot plant in Kidderminster, England, which began producing cookies for supermarket, foodservice, and bakery customers in the United Kingdom.

Acquisitions returned to the agenda in 2003. Building on its California-based Jon Donaire dessert business, Rich Products gained a dessert operation on the East Coast by purchasing Mother's Kitchen Inc. of Burlington, New Jersey. Mother's Kitchen was one of the largest cheesecake makers in the industry and produced 26 varieties of cheesecake and 12 varieties of premium cakes and pies, selling them to the foodservice and retail bakery markets. Also in 2003, Rich Products reentered the whipped toppings business in the United States by acquiring the private-label frozen nondairy whipped topping and creamer lines of Morningstar Foods Inc., a subsidiary of Dean Foods. Included in the deal was a 144,000-square-foot plant in Arlington, Tennessee. Late in 2003 the company formed a new Buffalo-based associated company called ROAR Logistics, Inc. ROAR, whose name was an acronym for rail, ocean, air, and road, was set up as an intermodal company specializing in arranging shipping of container freight via trains and trucks.

AIMING FOR SALES OF $3 BILLION BY 2010

By 2004 revenues had surpassed the $2 billion mark, and the company set an ambitious goal of reaching $3 billion in sales by 2010. At this time Rich Products was feeling increased competitive pressure because of consolidation in the food industry and therefore continued to seek ways of boosting the efficiency of its operations. Early in 2004, then, the company launched another restructuring, one that included the elimination of around 170 jobs from its Buffalo factory. That plant's production of frozen nondairy products was shifted to the newly acquired plant in Arlington, Tennessee, and to plants in Illinois and California, leaving the Buffalo plant to focus on the newer unrefrigerated beverage and dessert product lines. Later in 2004 Rich Products launched an expansion of its Arlington facility to increase nondairy production capacity and add a 120,000-square-foot frozen warehouse.

In June 2004 Rich entered into a joint venture with Mexican bakery giant Grupo Bimbo S.A. de C.V. to make a variety of frozen and fresh-baked specialty bakery products and sell them to foodservice and in-store bakery customers throughout Mexico and the United States and in other countries as well. The venture was named Fripan S.A. de C.V. and included a 125,000-square-foot facility in Lerma, located about 25 miles west of Mexico City. Early in 2005, the firm's 60th anniversary year, Rich Products acquired Rolling Pin Manufacturing Corporation, producer of ready-to-finish and fully-finished yeast-raised and cake donuts for supermarkets. The deal included plants in South San Francisco and Pine Bluff, Arkansas, but the Arkansas facility was shut down later in 2005 as part of a manufacturing consolidation program. The manufacturing overhaul also included the closure of a plant in Winchester, Virginia.

Also in 2005, Rich Products extended its line of meat products through the purchase of Battistoni Italian Specialty Meats, a Buffalo-based maker of Italian sausage and deli meats. Its U.K. unit, in the meantime, bolstered its position by acquiring leading independent baker David Powell Bakeries. This company produced premium muffins, shortbreads, cinnamon buns, specialty breads, and other sweet and savory baked goods, mainly for the foodservice sector, from its facilities in Fareham, Hampshire, where Rich Products subsequently relocated its U.K. headquarters.

In February 2006 company founder Robert E. Rich, Sr., died at age 92. His son, Robert, Jr., was subsequently named chairman of the company, which continued to be owned by the Rich family. In August 2006 Gisel was promoted to president and CEO, becoming the first nonfamily member to hold that position. Revenues that year reached $2.4 billion.

In response to growing consumer demand for more healthful food products, Rich Products announced in 2006 that it had reformulated more than 500 of its products to remove artery-clogging trans fats from their formulas. The company continued to build its healthy products portfolio in early 2007, when GLP Free Manufacturing was acquired. Based in Grand Island, New York, GLP produced a variety of items free of gluten, lactose, and nuts, including brownies, bread, cookies, and pizza dough. Such items were particularly tailored for people with celiac disease, and gluten-free foods were a fast-growing niche in the industry, with sales predicted to reach $1.7 billion by 2010. As Rich Products continued to seek out growth opportunities toward its $3 billion revenue goal, it also maintained its vigilant approach to costs. As part of a spending reallocation program that placed greater emphasis on Rich's operations in nondairy products, seafood, bakery items, and desserts, the company announced a trimming of 100 jobs, which translated into a 1.7 percent cut in the global workforce of 6,000.

Carol Keeley
Updated, David E. Salamie

PRINCIPAL SUBSIDIARIES

B.R. Guest, Ltd.; Rich Products of Canada, Ltd.; Productos Rich S.A. de C.V. (Mexico); Rich de Argentina SA; Rich's do Brasil Ltda. (Brazil); Rich Products Limited (U.K.); Rich Products (C.I.S.) LLC (Russia); Rich Products Australia Pty Ltd.; Rich Products Korea Co., Ltd.; Rich Products Manufacturing Co., Ltd. (Thailand).

PRINCIPAL DIVISIONS

Food Service Division; In-Store Bakery Division; Consumer Brands Division.

PRINCIPAL COMPETITORS

ConAgra Foods, Inc.; Kraft Foods Inc.; Nestlé S.A.; Sara Lee Corporation; Dean Foods Company; The Schwan Food Company.

FURTHER READING

Anzalone, Charles, "Robert Rich Sr. and His Non-Dairy Dynasty," *Buffalo News,* Buffalo Magazine, April 30, 1995, p. M6.

Billoni, Michael J., *Robert E. Rich: Memoirs of an Innovator,* Buffalo, N.Y.: Canisius College Press, 2000, 442 p.

Bridger, Chet, "Rich Products Launches $35 Million Expansion, Cuts 32 Workers," *Buffalo News,* December 4, 2001, p. E3.

Chamberlain, Ross, "Rich's Success Story: Always in When Opportunity Calls," *Quick Frozen Foods,* August 1982, pp. 20+.

Cone, Edward, "The Best-Laid Plans," *Forbes,* July 24, 1989, p. 10.

Cooke, James Aaron, "How Rich Products Went Global," *Logistics Management and Distribution Report,* September 1998, pp. 48–53.

Crispens, Jonna, "New Products Priority in Rich Project," *Supermarket News,* February 25, 1991, p. 31.

Epstein, Jonathan D., "Rich Products to Lay Off 100 Workers, 12 Locally," *Buffalo News,* November 8, 2007, p. B8.

Fink, James, "Gisel Thrives in Expanded Role at Rich Products," *Business First of Buffalo,* February 7, 2000, p. 4.

Frumkin, Paul, "Food Pioneer Rich Dies at 92," *Nation's Restaurant News,* February 27, 2006, pp. 3, 6.

Garrison, Bob, "Rich Tradition," *Refrigerated and Frozen Foods,* December 1999, pp. 16–18+.

Greenberg, Jonathan, "All in the Family," *Forbes,* April 25, 1983, p. 147.

Howard, Theresa, "Robert Rich Sr.," *Nation's Restaurant News,* January 1995, p. 166.

Lahvie, Ray, "Rich Products Acquires Seneau Baking Company," *Bakery Production and Marketing,* July 24, 1992, p. 20.

Linstedt, Sharon, "Hiding Behind the Bakery Door: Rich Products Supplies Thousands of Items to Food Service Industry," *Buffalo News,* October 24, 1999, p. B20.

———, "Rich Licenses Rights to Three Products," *Buffalo News,* July 17, 1998, p. A1.

Malchoff, Kevin, "Frozen Food and Foodservice: The Perfect Match," *Frozen Food Digest,* July 1991.

McCarthy, Robert J., "Robert E. Rich Sr., 92, Dies in Florida," *Buffalo News,* February 16, 2006, p. B1.

"Rich Products in Venture with Mexican-Based Bakery Firm," *Nation's Restaurant News,* June 28, 2004, p. 180.

"Rich Products to Acquire Mother's Kitchen Desserts," *Nation's Restaurant News,* August 11, 2003, p. 72.

"Rich Products Unveils Trans-Fat-Free Items," *Nation's Restaurant News,* March 6, 2006, p. 58.

"Rich's Acquires Rolling Pin," *Modern Baking,* February 2005, p. 13.

Riddle, Judith, "Rich Products Expanding Non-Dairy to Guadalajara," *Supermarket News,* February 17, 1992, p. 62.

"Robert E. Rich Sr.: Father of Non-Dairy FF," *Quick Frozen Foods,* August 1983, pp. 61+.

Robinson, David, "Rich Products Buys GLP Free Mfg.," *Buffalo News,* February 6, 2007, p. B8.

Rosenbaum, Rob, "Freeze Flo Success Grounded in Skills of Rich Researchers," *Business First of Buffalo,* October 28, 1985.

Schroeder, Richard, "How Rich Forsook the Cow for the Soybean," *Buffalo News,* March 26, 1995, p. B14.

———, "1,700 Products, $1 Billion in Sales: That's the Profile of Rich Products in Its 50th Year," *Buffalo News,* March 26, 1995, p. B13.

"Son of Rich Products Founder Named Chairman," *Nation's Restaurant News,* August 14, 2006, p. 82.

Thayer, Warren, "Bob Rich on His Father, ECR, and Frozens' Future," *Frozen Food Age,* June 1995, p. 1.

Williams, Fred O., "Battistoni Meat Firm Bought by Rich Products," *Buffalo News,* March 17, 2005, p. B7.

———, "Rich Products Acquires Competitor in Midwest," *Buffalo News,* November 9, 1999, p. E5.

———, "Rich Products Has Big Plans for Growth," *Buffalo News,* May 2, 2004, p. C13.

———, "Rich's Moving Non-Dairy Work," *Buffalo News,* February 6, 2004, p. B4.

Rosetta Stone Inc.

1101 Wilson Boulevard, Suite 1130
Arlington, Virginia 22209
U.S.A.
Telephone: (540) 432-6166
Toll Free: (800) 788-0822
Fax: (540) 432-0953
Web site: http://www.rosettastone.com

Private Company
Founded: 1991 as Fairfield Language Technologies
Employees: 658
Sales: $91.3 million (2006 est.)
NAIC: 511210 Software Publishers

■ ■ ■

Rosetta Stone Inc. is one of the leading providers of language-learning tools worldwide, with product users in more than 150 countries. Rosetta Stone utilizes the visual, audio, and interactive capabilities of computer software technology to create a unique system of foreign language instruction. By providing the language learner with an interactive immersion through word-image correlations and word pronunciation and listening practice, Rosetta Stone replicates intuitive language acquisition as experienced by toddlers. The software begins with basic words, phrases, and sentences, it then advances student progress with pronunciation refinement, grammar development, listening comprehension, conversation simulation, and writing exercises. Testing and tracking tools assist the student in reinforcing language skills. Ro-

setta Stone offers specialized packages for institutional education and homeschooling situations.

Language instruction can be purchased as CD-ROM software or through online subscriptions for 3, 6, or 12 months. Rosetta Stone Language Learning Library includes: Arabic, Chinese (Mandarin), Danish, Dutch, English (American), English (British), Farsi (Iran), French, German, Greek, Hebrew, Hindi, Indonesian, Italian, Japanese, Korean, Latin, Pashto (Afghanistan), Polish, Portuguese (Brazil), Russian, Spanish (Latin America), Spanish (Spain), Swahili, Swedish, Tagalog (Filipino), Thai, Turkish, Vietnamese, and Welsh. Software is available in up to three levels, with each level teaching more complex language skills.

FRUSTRATION MOTIVATES LANGUAGE SOFTWARE DEVELOPMENT

Brothers-in-law Allen Stoltzfus and John Fairfield developed Rosetta Stone language-learning software out of frustration in attempting to learn Russian. The language instruction applied the usual method of rote learning through memorized translations of words and grammar. After the experience of total immersion in a foreign language as students at a German university, Stoltzfus and Fairfield found the conventional approach to language acquisition to be unnecessarily difficult. A scholar who loved travel, Stoltzfus determined the best way to learn a language would be organic and intuitive, like the process of learning one's first language as a toddler. Children learn their native language through the visual association of nouns and verbs with the pronunciation of identifying words. Hence, Stoltzfus conceived the idea of creating a language immersion tool that imitated this process, and he perceived that computer software could be used as a platform for this method of language instruction. Fairfield, who held a Ph.D. in computer science, provided the technological skills for software development. Together Fairfield and Stoltzfus formed Fairfield Language Technologies (FLT) to further develop the concept. Eventually, Stoltzfus's brother Eugene joined the organization to create the visual elements and learning structure.

FLT software provided images and the associated foreign language words without translation so a student would learn to think in the foreign language. For instance, in the Spanish-language software, a closeup image of red fabric, accompanied by "rojo," the Spanish word for red, provided direct experience of the word's meaning. The program then took the student to the next step, phrase development, showing a picture of a red tomato with the word "rojo"; then, the phrase "un tomate rojo" appeared. Hence, the language learner intuitively absorbed the word meanings, as well as the fact that the descriptor, "rojo," was correctly stated after the noun, "tomate." Repetition reinforced the instruction, such as with images of a red blouse and a red pepper. Software tests utilized the same method of instruction, such as showing four sets of images from which the student chose the identifying phrase-image association that was incorrect. At higher levels of language acquisition, students expanded their vocabulary and learned to build sentences.

Software capabilities included audio listening and recording devices for pronunciation practice and testing. A sound recording of word pronunciation accompanied each image, encouraging proficiency in pronunciation and listening comprehension. Students could match their verbal skills against a digital voice print. The software included auto-correct writing exercises and progress tracking tools as well.

CD-ROM AND ONLINE TECHNOLOGY PROVIDES FORMAT FOR LANGUAGE ACQUISITION TOOL

Fairfield and Stoltzfus solidified the basic software concept during the 1980s, but consumer technology capable of supporting the concept did not develop until the early 1990s. By 1992, the invention of CD-ROM technology provided a usable, accessible format. The company introduced its software under the Rosetta Stone brand name in 1993, offering software packages in English, Spanish, French, and German. FLT gradually added languages, and by the end of 2000, the Rosetta Stone Language Library comprised 24 languages, including Russian, Latin, Polish, Welsh, Thai, Hindi, Korean, Chinese, Japanese, and Swahili.

FLT operated successfully and profitably from the beginning. The company sold its software to NASA, the U.S. State Department, the Peace Corps, and several *Fortune* 500 companies. Shortened versions of the software package made Rosetta Stone widely available to consumers at a low cost. Moreover, the exclusion of word translation facilitated transference of the software to any country, regardless of native language. As such, the software quickly developed a worldwide user-base of more than four million people in 55 countries. The company opened an office in Windsor, England, to distribute software internationally. Ease of use and teaching effectiveness earned Rosetta Stone software numerous awards from computer magazines, trade associations, and educational curriculum developers.

For educational purposes, FLT offered additional software capabilities and supplemental materials. The Student Management System provided adaptability to teacher-specified curriculum, learning exercises, testing options, and a mechanism for tracking student progress. Packages included a student workbook, language book, and teacher's manual with quizzes and study guide. Beginning in 2001, FLT improved teacher monitoring with online tracking of student progress and test scores.

The development of the Internet provided new opportunities for the distribution of Rosetta Stone language-learning software. FLT offered Rosetta Stone products through Travlang, Inc., the leading provider of language-learning tools for travelers. At travlang.com, subscribers could purchase software for home use or subscribe to monthly access to the language library through an Internet connection. In the summer of 2002

KEY DATES

1991: John Fairfield and Allen Stoltzfus form Fairfield Language Technologies.
1993: Fairfield Language Technologies launches CD-ROM software in four languages.
2001: Online presence of Rosetta Stone products expands distribution to libraries, travelers, and corporate executives.
2002: Retail kiosks open in 22 locations.
2006: Death of Allen Stoltzfus in 2002 leads to management buyout and name change.
2007: Spunky marketing campaign promotes Version 3 software.

LanguageExpress, LLC, became the exclusive distributor of Rosetta Stone for online public library usage. LanguageExpress offered the Rosetta Stone Language Library through its web site, providing access to more than 80 million people through 3,000 local libraries.

Through a partnership with GlobalAutoIndustry.com, FLT offered access to the language-learning technology at that company's web site. The site provided automotive industry executives access to the language skills they needed to conduct business globally. Also, GlobalAutoIndustry.com featured Rosetta Stone software in the company's eJournals and quarterly paper version of the journal.

Another means to expand FLT's potential customers involved the establishment of retail kiosks at shopping malls and airports. In 2002, FLT opened kiosks in six cities along the East Coast; the company added an additional 16 kiosks by the end of the year. The company expanded further, with 64 kiosks, for a total of 86 kiosks in 23 states, including multiple locations at one airport, by the end of 2007.

NEW LEADERSHIP OVERSEES RAPID GROWTH

The death of Allen Stoltzfus in October 2002 impelled management changes at FLT. Eugene Stoltzfus took the positions of president and chairman of the board, while Fairfield continued as vice-president of research and development. In 2003, the company hired Tom Adams as chief executive officer. Adams brought international experience involving language learning through immersion to FLT. Swedish by birth, Adams had spent his childhood in France and England.

Significant developments at this time included a January 2004 agreement with Berlitz International to offer Rosetta Stone's 27 online language-learning programs as an additional option to Berlitz customers. Berlitz had a long-standing reputation for the language and cross-cultural education it provided to corporate executives and government leaders at 450 locations worldwide. The Rosetta Stone method of dynamic immersion complemented the Berlitz method of live conversational classroom instruction. Berlitz agreed to provide access to Rosetta Stone instruction anytime, not just in the classroom.

In September 2005, FLT signed a $4.2 million contract with the U.S. Army to provide language-learning products to all active personnel in the Army and the National Guard, as well as reservists and Department of Army civilian personnel. The Army distributed 29 languages online through its e-Learning platform, and more than 60,000 used the software in the first year.

Supported by increased advertising exposure, the company grew rapidly at this time. The company raised its marketing investment from $3 million in 2003 to as much as $10 million in 2004 and $20 million in 2005. For 2005, year over year revenues increased 400 percent, making FLT ripe for a management buyout, particularly after the loss of Stoltzfus, the company's primary architect. In January 2006, private equity firms ABS Capital Partners and Norwest Equity Partners purchased FLT. The company's name was changed to Rosetta Stone Inc.

ENDANGERED LANGUAGES PRESERVED

Rosetta Stone's immersion method of instruction proved to be an excellent tool for preserving dying tribal languages. In particular, the use of images and visual cues from native cultures, rather than direct translation, provided native tribes with a natural way of learning their indigenous language without significant loss of meaning. In 2004, the company developed software on the Miceosukee language for the Seminole tribe in Florida. Collaboration between Rosetta Stone and Kanien'keha Onkwawen:na Raotitiohkwa, the community language and cultural center of the Mohawk tribe, resulted in the release of Mohawk Language Software for the Kahnawa:ke language, in early 2006. In February 2007 the company released software for the Inupiaq language of the Inupiat people, who live in 11 villages along the coast and rivers of northwestern Alaska, north of the Arctic Circle. The NANA Regional Corporation, an organization of the Native Alaskans, distributed 1,000 copies to members of the tribe.

Success with these projects led Rosetta Stone to establish the Endangered Languages Program, for which the company would provide 90 percent subsidy to create software on dying languages. In 2006 Rosetta Stone began a search for two endangered languages to support. Of 20 responses, the company chose the Navajo and Chitimacha tribal languages. The Sitimaxa language of the Chitimacha tribe, in Charneton, Louisiana, was considered a dead language until the U.S. Library of Congress mailed tapes of recordings to the tribe in 1986. Originating from wax cylinders, the 200 hours of recordings were produced by linguist Morris Swadesh during the 1930s. Along with field notes on pronunciation and word definitions, the tribe used the recordings to revive Sitimaxa. Several years later the tribe encountered Julian Granberry, a friend of Swadesh who used the materials to teach himself the Sitimaxa language. Granberry visited the Chitimachas in 1997, and he began teaching the language in the tribe's schools. Having attained significant advancement in language revival, Rosetta Stone chose to subsidize the software for the Chitimacha tribe. The software was released in late 2007.

VERSION 3 CAPABILITIES MERIT CREATIVE MARKETING

Rosetta Stone introduced several improvements to its software in 2007. These included a proprietary speech-recognition technology that provided more effective pronunciation practice and analysis. The Contextual Formation and Milestone features provided simulations of real-life situations for conversational development. Adaptive Recall tracked the language learner's development, to determine weak areas that indicated a need for additional practice. The company refined its sequential learning process as well. Initially, Rosetta Stone Version 3 was available in a limited number of languages: French, German, Italian, Russian, Portuguese (Brazil), Arabic, Spanish (Latin America), Spanish (Spain), English (American), and English (British).

A new brand identity accompanied the product release. To reflect the international nature of the programs and their users, Rosetta Stone adapted a "global tapestry" with images of the worldwide diversity of peoples and customs, displayed in an array of vivid colors.

Rosetta Stone implemented its first major promotional campaign for Version 3. Designed by Red Peg Marketing, the campaign used creative, lighthearted techniques of selling. In one advertisement, a farm boy visibly yearned to impress an Italian supermodel as he held a box of Rosetta Stone Italian-language software. For three days in the fall of 2007, models traversed the streets of New York City and flirted with strangers in French, Arabic, and a variety of other languages. The models presented targets of their faux-romantic affection with cards that offered a one-week free trial of Rosetta Stone's Version 3 software.

Rosetta Stone created a contest that sought stories about how learning a foreign language made a difference to the writer's life. The "Rosetta Stories" contest offered a free trip for two valued at $5,000 for the most interesting real-life tale. Entrants submitted 300-word original essays that fit under one of three categories: love, work, or family. The Grand Prize was a free trip for two to any destination where a Version 3 language was spoken.

CONTINUED SUCCESS

In 2007 Rosetta Stone continued to leverage its unique instructional method into global expansion. The company increased its presence in the Japanese market with the formation of Rosetta Stone Japan, Inc. In July 2007, the new subsidiary introduced Version 2 software in 20 languages. The Rosetta World Version 3 Personal Edition followed in November 2007, with availability in ten languages. The company launched a special web site for the Japanese market, at www.rosettaworld.co.jp. The site quickly drew potential customers, with many sampling the free product demonstration.

The easy-to-use interface of Rosetta Stone software continued to attract agencies of the federal government, whose personnel frequently required a rapid language-acquisition option. After sampling Rosetta Stone software, the Immigration and Customs Enforcement Agency (ICE) signed a three-year contract with the company. Language-learning tools, particularly in Spanish and Arabic, were made available to 15,000 ICE employees. In December 2007, Rosetta Stone introduced its Arabic-Military Edition program. Custom designed to meet the immediate needs of the U.S. Army, which renewed its contract with the company annually, the new software included content specific to the needs of soldiers in the field and other military situations. Moreover, the program provided a quicker language-acquisition process for newly deployed troops.

Mary Tradii

PRINCIPAL SUBSIDIARIES

Rosetta Stone Japan, Inc.

PRINCIPAL OPERATING UNITS

Personal; Organizations; Schools; Home School.

PRINCIPAL COMPETITORS

Auralog, Inc.; Syracuse Language Systems, Inc.; Transparent Language, Inc.

FURTHER READING

"Allen G. Stoltzfus, 59, Software Developer," *Sunday News* (Lancaster, Pa.), October 6, 2002, p. B4.

"Army News Service: U.S. Army to Provide Rosetta Stone Foreign Language Training," *Defense AT&L,* January–February 2006, p. 60.

Baar, Aaron, "Carmichael Lynch Wins Language Software Job," *ADWEEK Midwest Edition,* September 2, 2004.

"Berlitz Signs Agreement to Provide Online Language Courses," *AsiaPulseNews,* January 6, 2004.

Bradshaw, Vic, "Kiosk Business Expanding Nationally," *Daily News Record,* August 19, 2002.

Fried, John J., "The Philadelphia Inquirer Technology Testdrive Column," *Philadelphia Inquirer,* August 28, 2005.

Huggins, Paul, "Free Way to Learn Language: Decatur Public Library Offering Online Access to Rosetta Stone Program," *Decatur Daily,* September 20, 2007.

Jacobs, Jan G., "Rosetta Stone Aids Language Study," *MacWEEK,* May 17, 1993, p. 16.

Kang, Cecilia, "Customs Enlists Rosetta to Train Officers' Tongues," *Washington Post,* October 22, 2007, p. D2.

"The Language of Love," *PR Week,* October 22, 2007, p. 32.

Morris, George, "Saving a Language: Chitimachas Working to Revive Their Lost Tribe," *Advocate,* November 25, 2007, p. D1.

Munson, Kristen, "New Computer Program Helps Students Learn English," *Dispatch,* July 19, 2005.

Pack, Thomas, "A Digital Rosetta Stone," *Link-Up,* November 2000, p. 32.

Paine-Carter, Emily, "Library Helps with Languages and Computers," *Roanoke Times,* April 20, 2007, p. NW2.

Pearlstein, Joanna, "The Rosetta Stone," *Macworld,* January 1994, p. 81.

Perenson, Melissa J., "Language Fest," *PC Magazine,* March 12, 1996, p. 78.

"Rosetta Stone in Talks with DDB on Creative," *ADWEEK Western Edition,* April 20, 2006.

"Rosetta Stone Japan Launches New Language-Learning Software," *AsiaPulseNews,* November 12, 2007.

"Rosetta Stone Language Library," *T H E Journal (Technological Horizons in Education),* August 2002, p. 37.

"Rosetta Stone Releases Interactive Mohawk Language Software; A Mohawk Community and Rosetta Stone Have Developed First-Ever Mohawk Immersion Software Through Rosetta Stone's Endangered Language Program," *CNW Group,* April 20, 2006.

"Travlang, Inc. Partners with Fairfield Language Technologies to Present Rosetta Stone Language Courses," *Market News Publishing,* May 10, 2001.

Tsubata, Kate, "Program Immerses in Foreign Language," *Washington Times,* January 23, 2006, p. B04.

Wright, Dan, "Company Selected for Export Program," *Daily News-Record,* January 29, 2005.

Russian Railways Joint Stock Co.

Novaya Basmannaya Ul. 2
Moscow, 107144
Russia
Telephone: (+7 495) 262 99 01
Fax: (+7 495) 262 34 22
Web site: http://www.rzd.ru

Government-Owned Company
Incorporated: 2001
Employees: 1.2 million
Sales: RUB 650 billion ($25.91 billion) (2006)
NAIC: 482111 Line-Haul Railroads; 488210 Support
   Activities for Rail Transportation

■ ■ ■

Russian Railways Joint Stock Co. (RZD) is one of the world's largest railway system operators. The government-owned company oversees a network of 85,500 kilometers of railroad spanning 11 time zones, the second largest in the world behind that of the United States. RZD, one of the largest companies in Russia, plays a central role in that country's economy. In particular, RZD is responsible for transporting more than 83 percent of all freight (by volume) across the country, and 41 percent of all passengers. The company employs more than 1.2 million people, and generates revenues of RUB 650 billion ($26 billion) per year, equivalent to 3.6 percent of Russia's gross domestic product. The company's railway operations are organized into 17 territorial branches, while its total operations include nearly 1,000 enterprises and 165

subsidiaries. Once known as the Ministry of Railways, RZD represents a crucial step in the restructuring of the country's economy. The separation of RZD from the Russian government was carried out in 2003, as part of a massive three-step reform program put into place in 2001 and expected to be completed by 2010. As part of that process, RZD is expected to eliminate the cross-subsidy arrangement by which its highly profitable freight operations were required to bail out its perennially money-losing passenger transport wing. The company has also been streamlining its operations, as part of a privatization process that may eventually include RZD itself. RZD is led by Vladimir Yakunin, a close associate of Russian President Vladimir Putin.

PRE-SOVIET BEGINNINGS

The first Russian-built locomotives appeared in Czarist Russia in the early 1830s. The country's first railway line was completed in 1837, linking Saint Petersburg with Tsarskoye Selo. Construction of a national railway system began in earnest at the beginning of the next decade. In 1842, the imperial government established a dedicated Department of Railways. The country's first major railroad, linking Moscow and Saint Petersburg, was completed by 1851.

Railroads played an essential role in transport in Russia, as well as in the future Soviet Union. The vast distances of an empire that at its height spanned 11 time zones made road travel impractical, even with the arrival of the internal combustion engine. At the same time, the harsh climatic conditions of much of the empire made road construction all but impossible. The importance of the country's growing railway system was underscored by the creation of the new Ministry of Communications in 1865. The ministry then took over direction of the railways department.

Further work on the railroad had by then connected Saint Petersburg with Warsaw and with Nizhniy Novgorod. Moscow quickly emerged as the country's major railroad hub, adding lines reaching Nizhniy Novgorod, Sergiyev Posad, and elsewhere. The Moscow-based railway network topped 2,000 kilometers. The Moscow railway system also developed a strong suburban network in order to serve the city's rapidly growing population. The first phase of this effort was completed near 1900, with the construction of the 54-kilometer Inner Circle Line. The larger Outer Circle Line, covering nearly 560 kilometers, was launched in 1943 and completed in 1960.

The Ministry of Communications became one of the country's most important and most powerful government bureaus at the end of the 19th century. The national rail network grew rapidly, particularly in Russia's European regions, from the mid-1870s. By the beginning of the 20th century, the railway network had been extending to include the regions of central Asia, the Urals, and beyond. Much of the construction of the country's rail network was carried out by a number of independent companies. These included South-Eastern Railways, a company founded in 1866, which built and operated a line linking Ryazan and Kozlovsky (later Michurinsk). Another company, Privolzhsk Railways, operated in the Lower Volga region, and throughout the southwestern region of European Russia. That company's first operations connected Umet and Atkarsk in 1871, and later expanded its network to include nearly 4,200 kilometers of railroad.

The construction of the Trans-Siberian Railway represented a major event in the history of the Russian railway system. Completed in 1905, the new line was an important step in the completion of the rail system's East-West expansion, providing a link to the vast mineral resources of the Siberian region. Further expansion of the network boosted the total reach from under 45,000 kilometers of track by 1900 to more than 58,500 kilometers by the outbreak of World War I. Total freight transports by then reached 132,000 tons per year.

DESTRUCTION AND RECONSTRUCTION

The country's railway system played a major role in the swift spread of the Russian Revolution and the new Soviet government's victory during the country's Civil War. Yet the railway system also suffered greatly during this period. By the end of the Civil War, more than 90 percent of the country's locomotives, 80 percent of its rolling stock, and 60 percent of its railways had been destroyed.

Reconstruction of the network became a priority of the Soviet government. Under the People's Commisariat of Communications, the railway system had been restored to pre–Civil War levels by 1928. By the end of the 1930s, the system had been nearly doubled, topping 106,000 kilometers. The vast importance of the rail system to the Soviet government's industrialization policies could be seen in the dramatic rise in freight levels made in the pre–World War II era. By 1940, the country's rail network handled more than 600 million tons of freight per year.

The Nazi invasion of the Soviet Union during World War II brought new disaster to the rail network, particularly in the European regions of the country. Nonetheless, the rail system enabled the Soviet government to rapidly dismantle the region's industrial installations. These were then shipped to safety in the country's Asian regions, particularly to the Urals and Siberia, where they could continue to support the country's war effort. The rail system also provided a swift means of troop transport, allowing the Soviets to rapidly replenish the fronts. Indeed, a major factor of Germany's failure in its effort to conquer the Soviet Union was its reliance on the country's underdeveloped road network.

The move into the Cold War era provided new impetus for the expansion of the Soviet Union's railway system. A new era of succeeding five-year plans and intensified industrialization activities placed new burdens on the country's railroad network. This was rapidly expanded over the next 40 years, topping 115,000 kilometers in the early 1950s. By the end of the Soviet era, the country's rail network was the largest in the world, at nearly 145,000 kilometers.

Major projects carried out during this period included the construction of a second Trans-Siberian

KEY DATES

1837: Construction of first railway line in Russia links Saint Petersburg with Tsarskoye Selo.

1842: Department of Railways is created to oversee further development of Russia's rail network.

1865: Ministry of Communications supersedes Department of Railways.

1913: Russian rail network reaches 48,500 kilometers carrying 132,000 tons of freight per year.

1940: Massive expansion of rail network during early Soviet era increases network to 106,000 kilometers and 600 million tons of freight per year.

1975: Total freight tonnage tops 3.6 billion per year.

1989: Company completes 3,200-kilometer Baikal-Amur Magistral line, half of which crosses permafrost.

2001: Phase I of Russian Railway reform system is launched.

2003: Phase I of reform is completed with creation of Russian Railways Joint Stock Co.

2007: Russian Railways announces plans to invest RUB 1.3 trillion in infrastructure upgrades and expansion through 2010.

railway. The impressive Baikal-Amur Magistral, or BAM, represented a triumph of Soviet engineering. Nearly half of the 3,200 kilometer line, which extended from Us-Kut to Komsomolsk, was constructed on permafrost. In this way, the railway system permitted transport from mineral-rich regions impossible to serve by other transport methods. Started in the late 1970s, construction on the BAM was finally completed in 1989.

The era also saw the conversion of large parts of the railroad system from diesel locomotives to more efficient and more powerful electric locomotives. Launching in the 1970s, the system ultimately grew to nearly 39,000 kilometers of electrified track. The new power source and the continued extension of the system enabled further expansion of the network's freight capacity. By the mid-1970s, the network handled more than 3.6 billion tons per year. This figure topped 4.1 billion tons by the late 1980s. The system had also become the major method of passenger transport as well, accommodating more than 4.3 billion passengers per year.

STRUGGLING IN THE POST-SOVIET ERA

The collapse of the Soviet Union, however, brought significant changes to what was then known as Soviet Union Railways. The breakup of the union into many independent states also led to the dismantling of the railway system into independent, national entities. The immediate result for what became known as Russian Railways was a reduction in the length of mainline track covered by its network, to just 127,000 kilometers.

Yet the collapse of the Soviet Empire also exposed the fragility of the railroad system. The country's increasing economic difficulties during the 1980s had resulted in steady declines in investment in its railroad infrastructure. At the same time, the railways were operating at high losses, particularly in passenger rail operations. Into the 1990s, they operated at high deficits. Ticket revenues made up just 47 percent of the cost of long-distance transport, and just 27 percent of local transport. Yet the low income level of the Russian population and the country's dependence on its rail network made it impossible to raise ticket prices to profitable levels.

At the same time, the railroad system remained burdened by the Soviet collective economic system. In this way, Russian Railways remained responsible for a vast range of auxiliary operations, including medical care, schooling, and other social services for its more than two million employees. Into the 1990s, these costs represented 11 percent of the company's operating expenses. Another leftover from the Soviet era was the system of cross-subsidies, in which Russian Railways' profitable freight operations were required to make up the losses of its passenger side.

As a result, Russian Railways limped into the 1990s with a rapidly aging rail network, outmoded locomotives, and rolling stock sorely in need of replacement. The collapse of Russia's economy in the early 1990s only exacerbated the difficulties at Russian Railways. Into the middle of the decade, the network continued to lose more than $2.1 billion per year. This prompted the International Monetary Fund to step in with a $10 billion loan, with the condition that the railway ministry adopt "commercial and efficient management" practices.

Yet the system's management, led by Railway Minister Gennady Fadeev, remained dominated by people who had risen through its ranks during the Soviet era. Fadeev nonetheless put up a successful resistance to calls for the privatization of the railway system. Instead, the government focused on modernizing the rail system. Part of this effort included plans to build a 650-kilometer rail project linking Moscow and Saint Petersburg, a project that failed to materialize, however. At the same time, the government began trimming back its network, shedding its least viable lines. In the early 2000s, the country's total railway system had been reduced to less than 86,000 kilometers.

REFORM IN THE NEW CENTURY

Efforts to reform Russia's railway system became serious with the new millennium. By 2001 the government had put into place a three-phase system. As part of the first phase, the Ministry of Railways was disbanded, replaced by an independently operating, yet government-controlled, Russian Railways. Part of this process included further streamlining to the new organization's operations. The company spun off a number of its non-core operations, including its manufacturing subsidiaries, into privately held companies. This helped reduce its payroll as well, with its total employees dropping to 1.2 million by the middle of the decade.

The first phase of the reform was completed in 2003, just one year behind schedule, under the presidency of Vladimir Putin. The company turned its attention toward carrying out the second and more delicate phase of Russian Railways' reform program. This involved ending the cross-subsidy arrangement that had long crippled the company's ability to use its freight profits for its infrastructure investments. However transferring the high cost of operating the country's perennially loss-making, yet vital, passenger rail transport remained a thorny issue. A new era for the company began when Putin replaced Fadeev with close associate Vladimir Yakunin.

Yakunin led the company in stepping up its infrastructure investment. In 2007, for example, the company announced plans to spend RUB 1.3 trillion through 2010 on modernizing its infrastructure and expanding its railway. New projects included a 240-kilometer high-speed network reaching into Finland and a 300-kilometer line in Siberia. The company also relaunched its plans to complete the high-speed rail link between Saint Petersburg and Moscow as early as 2012.

By then, Russian Railways expected to have completed the final phase of its reform program. This included the possibility of the company's privatization. In the meantime, Russian Railways appeared to have emerged from the difficult period following the collapse of the Soviet Union. Indeed, the company boasted being one of the world's largest and most efficient rail freight networks in the world. Russian Railways at the same time remained a vital component for the future of the Russian economy.

M. L. Cohen

PRINCIPAL SUBSIDIARIES

Kaliningrad Railways; Oktober Railways; Moscow Railways; SouthEastern Railways; North Caucasus Railways; Northern Railways; Gorky Railways; Kuibishev Railways; Privolzhsk Railways; Sverdlovsk Railways; South Urals Railways; West Siberian Railways; Krasnoyarsk Railways; Eastern Siberian Railways; Zabaikal Railways; Far Eastern Railways; Sakhalin Railways.

PRINCIPAL COMPETITORS

Siemens AG; Société Nationale des Chemins de Fer Français; SNCF International; Vivendi S.A.; Cia Vale do Rio Doce; East Japan Railway Co.; Compania Nationala de Cai Ferate; Deutsche Bahn AG; HZ-Hrvatske Zeleznice doo.

FURTHER READING

Belova, Anna G., and Louis S. Thompson, "RZD Reform Makes Good Progress," *Railway Gazette International,* October 2005, p. 633.

Bringinshaw, David, "Russian Rail Revolution Enters Final Phase," *International Railway Journal,* October 2006, p. 17.

———, "RZD Faces a Bright Future," *International Railway Journal,* October 2006, p. 13.

———, "RZD Plans Huge Investment Programme," *International Railway Journal,* June 2007, p. 21.

"Finnish-Russian Link to Get Tilting Trains," *International Railway Journal,* October 2007, p. 5.

"Freight Reforms Make Progress," *Railway Gazette International,* November 2006, p. 720.

Lukov, Boris E., "RZD Faces Funding Challenge," *Railway Gazette International,* August 2004, p. 483.

Ostrovsky, Arkady, "Life Rolls On in 'A Country Within a Country,'" *Financial Times,* October 19, 2004, p. 6.

"Russian Railways Gains Its Independence," *International Railway Journal,* April 2003, p. 4.

"Russian Railways Plans to Sell 49% of Transcontainer, the Country's Largest Operator of Intermodal Wagons," *International Railway Journal,* April 2007, p. 10.

"Russian Railways: Side Tracked," *Economist,* July 20, 1996, p. 57.

"Russians Lead Bidding on North-South Rail," *MEED Middle East Economic Digest,* November 9, 2007, p. 26.

Wagstyle, Stefan, "Russian Railways Chief to Sell Off Stakes in Subsidiaries," *Financial Times,* April 25, 2006, p. 8.

Salix Pharmaceuticals, Ltd.

1700 Perimeter Park Drive
Morrisville, North Carolina 27560-8404
U.S.A.
Telephone: (919) 862-1000
Fax: (919) 228-4265
Web site: http://www.salix.com

Public Company
Incorporated: 1993 as Salix Holdings, Ltd.
Employees: 215
Sales: $208.5 million (2006)
Stock Exchanges: NASDAQ
Ticker Symbol: SLXP
NAIC: 325412 Pharmaceutical Preparation Manufacturing

■ ■ ■

North Carolina-based Salix Pharmaceuticals, Ltd., is a NASDAQ-listed company that focuses on drugs that treat gastrointestinal (digestive tract) diseases. Rather than incurring the expense of developing products from scratch, the company acquires late-stage or already marketed proprietary drugs, and then relies on its in-house sales force to maximize market potential in the United States by targeting gastroenterologists. The company also plans to forge international alliances to market its products overseas, eliminating the expense of establishing an international sales force. To further reduce overhead, Salix outsources manufacturing. Products already on the market include Colazal, for the treatment of ulcerative colitis; Azasan, an immune system suppressant; Proctocort and Anusol-HC, hemorrhoid treatments; Xifaxan, used to treat traveler's diarrhea; Pepcid OS, a short-term treatment of gastroesophageal reflux disease; and several preparatory colonoscopy products: Visicol, and MoviPrep, and OsmoPrep. In addition, Salix has a pipeline of drug candidates for which it is seeking approval from the Food and Drug Administration (FDA).

LAUNCH OF SALIX: 1989

Salix was founded in November 1989 in Palo Alto, California, as Salix Pharmaceuticals, Inc., by Randy W. Hamilton and Dr. Lorin K. Johnson. Hamilton, a sociology graduate of California State University, Long Beach, had been director of strategic planning and business development for SmithKline Diagnostics, where he gained considerable marketing experience. He had headed Asian business development for California Biotechnology Inc. Hamilton became Salix's chief executive officer. Serving as chief scientific liaison was Johnson, a former assistant professor of pathology at Stanford University Medical Center. He then went on to head anti-inflammatory therapeutics for California Biotechnology Inc. before teaming up with Hamilton to start Salix. For seed money the partners relied on their own savings as well as investments from friends, consultants, and others, eschewing traditional venture capitalists.

REORGANIZING OVERSEAS: 1993

From the start, Salix pursued late-stage gastrointestinal drugs. The early years were dedicated to acquiring drug

COMPANY PERSPECTIVES

Salix Pharmaceuticals is dedicated to being the leading specialty pharmaceutical company providing products to gastroenterologists and their patients.

candidates and raising additional funds to keep the company afloat until it was able to bring products to market. In December 1993 the operation was reorganized with the incorporation of Salix Holdings, Ltd., in the British Virgin Islands to serve as the holding company for Salix Pharmaceuticals as well as an international subsidiary, Glycyx Pharmaceuticals, Ltd., which itself was incorporated in Bermuda. Salix encountered some difficulty in securing further capital. Having bypassed the stage where venture capitalists were typically involved, the company sought funds from investment banks in the United States only to find that the minimum amount, about $30 million, was more than it sought. If Salix had accepted a deal in this range it would have given up a larger stake in the business than its founders believed was warranted. Moreover, the banks placed a value on the company that the founders thought was more appropriate for a company with drugs in the early stages of development, not the final stages, as was the case with Salix.

STOCK LISTING IN TORONTO: 1996

In 1995 Salix turned to Canada for money, hiring Canaccord Capital Corp. to sell some debt securities. In 1996 the company was able to sell about $4.5 million in these securities. Because Canada's pharmaceutical sector was far less crowded than the United States, Salix decided to conduct an initial public offering (IPO) of stock in the country, underwritten by Haywood Securities Inc., Dlouhy Investments Inc., and Moss, Lawson & Co., Ltd. Completed in May 1996, the IPO raised $14 million. To satisfy investors, Salix then sought a listing on the Toronto Stock Exchange, Canada's premiere equity market. Once the company was better established, it hoped to be listed on a U.S. stock market, preferably the tech-oriented NASDAQ.

Salix's connection to North Carolina was also established in the mid-1990s. In 1995 the company recruited Robert P. Ruscher to serve as director of corporate affairs. Ruscher had been an associate of a Palo Alto law firm and then moved to Raleigh, North Carolina, joining an area law firm, Wyrick Robbins Yates & Ponton. He continued to work for the law firm while running a one-person corporate development operation for Salix out of Raleigh.

FIRST PRODUCT TO MARKET

Salix brought its first product, Colazide (balsalazide disodium), to market in 1997. It had been licensed from Biorex Laboratories Limited, and in July 1997 gained approval from the United Kingdom Medicines Control Agency for the treatment of mildly to moderately active ulcerative colitis. A new drug application to the FDA in the United States was also in the works when the product became available in the United Kingdom in October 1997, accounting for the company's first product revenues. For the year, Colazide generated sales of $245,000. Combined with revenues from collaborative agreements and other sources, Salix recorded sales of more than $2 million in 1997 and a net loss of nearly $5 million. In October 1997 the company was able to complete a secondary stock offering in Canada and an IPO of stock in the United States.

Product sales more than doubled to $559,000 in 1998, as Colazide received approval in several other countries, including Austria, Belgium, Denmark, Italy, Luxembourg, and Sweden. It was also in 1998 that Salix Holdings changed its name to Salix Pharmaceuticals, Ltd. Sales of Colazide dipped slightly to $491,000 in 1999 but on the strength of $2.6 million in milestone and other payments, the company increased total revenues to more than $3 million while trimming its net loss to $4.6 million.

The final weeks of 1999 also brought a changing of the guard at Salix, with Hamilton stepping down as CEO in favor of Ruscher. "I thought it was time for new blood," Hamilton explained to Raleigh's *News & Observer*. Salix moved its headquarters to Raleigh to accommodate Ruscher, but continued to maintain a nine-person Palo Alto clinical development operation. Hamilton also stayed on to serve as Salix's chairman.

Salix entered the new century with some financial concerns, finding itself with little cash on hand and its stock relegated to penny stock status. By mid-December 1999 shares of Salix were trading as low as CAD 0.18. However, the company was able to benefit from the merger of a pair of major European pharmaceutical companies, Astra and Zeneca. A few years earlier Astra had licensed a treatment for inflammatory bowel disease from Salix and had since invested nearly $20 million to develop the drug and began selling it in a handful of European countries under various names. The merged company, AstraZeneca, did not consider the product large enough to keep and returned the license to Salix.

KEY DATES

1989: Company is founded in Palo Alto, California, as Salix Pharmaceuticals, Inc.
1993: Salix Holdings, Ltd., is formed in British Virgin Islands.
1996: Company gains listing on Toronto Stock Exchange.
1997: First product sales are recorded.
1998: Name is changed to Salix Pharmaceuticals, Ltd.
1999: Headquarters are moved to Raleigh, North Carolina.
2001: Company is reincorporated in Delaware.
2005: InKine Pharmaceutical, Inc., is acquired.

RAISING MUCH NEEDED CASH: 2000

In May 2000 Ruscher was able to sell the European rights to the drug, which the company would rename Colazal, to Shire Pharmaceuticals. The $24 million deal included stock but more importantly an upfront cash payment of $9.6 million that kept the company afloat at a time when it had just two months of cash remaining. Moreover, the money allowed Salix to take Colazal through the final stage of gaining FDA approval and to launch the product in the U.S. market. After the FDA approved the drug for sale in July 2000, Salix began to assemble a 30-person, direct sales force. The company ended 2000 with a net loss of nearly $3 million, but was able to increase product revenues to $6.3 million and total revenues to more than $14.5 million. Investors took note of the company's improving fortunes, bidding up the price of Salix stock to nearly CAD 4 a share in the early months of the year, and after an analyst for Boston's Leerink Swann & Co. touted the company in August the price soared to CAD 10.25. Salix was then able to complete a private placement of stock in November 2000, raising more than $14 million, in an offering placed by Leerink Swann. Subsequently, the company delisted its stock from the Toronto Stock Exchange and began trading exclusively on the NASDAQ. A year later the company changed its place of incorporation from the British Virgin Islands to the state of Delaware.

After a dozen years in business, Salix had begun to turn the corner. With the launch of its first U.S. product, the company increased product revenues to $14.1 million in 2001, and $8 million in other pay-

ments brought total revenues to $22.35 million. Salix also raised $28.1 million in another private placement of stock. A public offering in March 2002 raised an additional $57.4 million. In 2002 Salix had no ancillary income but increased total revenues to $33.5 million solely on the strength of improving product sales. Moreover, Salix was on the verge of launching its second U.S. product, Xifaxan.

Because Salix had reached a stage in its development where marketing would play an ever more important role, Ruscher turned over daily control to a new CEO, Carolyn Logan, head of sales and marketing who had assembled the sales force, which had grown to 60 people. Staying on as chairman, Ruscher focused on further drug acquisitions and corporate strategy. A year later, he would resign entirely but not before fending off a hostile takeover bid.

For many months Salix had been rumored to be an acquisition target for larger firms, another indication that the company was coming of age. In 2003 a Canadian drug company, Axcan Pharma Inc., made an unsolicited tender offer of $8.85 per share. Although the suitor would improve the offer to $10.50 per share, it was soundly rejected by Salix shareholders, winning less than 6 percent of the vote in a proxy fight completed in June 2003. Nevertheless, the fight cost Salix $1.7 million in legal fees. Three months later Ruscher announced that he would be leaving the company by the end of the year. He was replaced as chairman by John Chappell, a former SmithKline Beecham senior executive and Salix board member since 1993.

In May 2004 Salix received marketing approval for Xifaxan from the FDA and subsequently launched the product in the United States. Colazal, in the meantime, was continuing to expand its market share, with sales increasing to $85.4 million in 2004, a marked improvement over the $55.8 million posted a year before. As a result, Salix was able to top the $100 million mark in total revenues in 2004 and achieve profitability for the first time in its history, netting $6.8 million.

INKINE PHARMACEUTICAL: 2005

Sales increased to $155 million in 2005 and the company posted a net loss of $60.6 million, but that loss was the result of a $74 million write-off connected to a major acquisition. In September 2005 Salix completed the $190 million stock acquisition of InKine Pharmaceutical, a Pennsylvania drug company with complementary gastrointestinal products. Its flagship product was Visicol, a tablet used to cleanse the bowel prior to colonoscopy. The Salix sales force was already calling on doctors who might prescribe InKine products, so the acquisition made sense from that reason alone. It also allowed Salix to beef up its sales force and grow its pipeline of future products.

Having new products to sell was important because it lessened Salix's dependence on Colazal, which saw a dip in sales in 2006. Moreover, the drug was expected to soon face competition from generic versions. The company's bid to achieve diversity was strengthened in 2006 with the approval of two bowel cleansing products, OsmoPrep and MoviPrep, the former a tablet and the later a liquid agent. In addition, in September 2006, Salix acquired the U.S. marketing rights to Sanvar, a treatment for acute esophageal variceal bleeding, a complication of late-stage liver cirrhosis. Contributions from these new products helped Salix grow revenues 35 percent to $208.5 million in 2006.

Salix sought diversification in a different vein in 2007. As part of an effort to establish a hospital-based source of revenues, the company acquired the U.S. rights to Pepcid OS (oral suspension) and Diuril OS from Merck & Co. Inc. in a deal that included a $55 million upfront payment. A $100 million credit facility with Bank of America N.A. helped to finance the deal. At the end of 2007 Salix gained some protection for its Colazal franchise, authorizing a generic version of the drug with Watson Pharmaceuticals, Inc. Salix also appeared to be well positioned for the near-term. Revenues through three-quarters of the year enjoyed a 33 percent increase, the company had licensed some of its colonoscopy products to European countries, and several products were on the verge of FDA approval to drive revenues even higher in the years to come.

Ed Dinger

PRINCIPAL SUBSIDIARIES

Salix Pharmaceuticals, Inc.; Glcyx Pharmaceuticals Ltd.

PRINCIPAL COMPETITORS

GlaxoSmithKline plc; Pfizer Inc.; The Procter & Gamble Company.

FURTHER READING

Critchley, Barry, "TSE A Greener Pasture for Salix," *Financial Post,* July 13, 1996, p. 45.

Ranii, David, "Acquisition to Boost Salix Pharmaceuticals' Product Portfolio, Sales, Force," *Raleigh (N.C.) News & Observer,* June 24, 2005.

———, "CEO of Raleigh, N.C.-based Pharmaceutical Sees Good Times Ahead," *Raleigh (N.C.) News & Observer,* July 18, 2000.

———, "President, CEO of Research Triangle Park, N.C., Drug Company," *Raleigh (N.C.) News & Observer,* July 17, 2002.

———, "Raleigh, N.C.-based Drug Company Reports Success in Selling First Product," *Raleigh (N.C.) News & Observer,* May 2, 2001.

———, "Raleigh, N.C.-based Pharmaceutical Company Raises Profile," *Raleigh (N.C.) News & Observer,* September 8, 2000.

Vollmer, Sabine, "Chairman to Leave Post at Raleigh, N.C.-based Salix Pharmaceuticals," *Raleigh (N.C.) News & Observer,* September 3, 2003.

———, "2 Drugs Part of Salix's Strategy: Sales Expected to Rise This Year," *Raleigh (N.C.) News & Observer,* March 1, 2007.

Seyfarth Shaw LLP

131 South Dearborn Street, Suite 2400
Chicago, Illinois 60603-5577
U.S.A.
Telephone: (312) 460-5000
Fax: (312) 460-7000
Web site: http://www.seyfarth.com

Limited Liability Partnership
Founded: 1945 as Seyfarth, Shaw & Fairweather
Employees: 1,608
Sales: $385.6 million (2006)
NAIC: 541110 Offices of Lawyers

■ ■ ■

Seyfarth Shaw LLP is a Chicago, Illinois-based law firm that made its mark as a management-oriented labor specialist, gaining a reputation as a "union buster" in the 1970s and 1980s. Since then Seyfarth has expanded to become more of a full-service law firm with greater geographic scope. Seyfarth primarily serves *Fortune* 500 companies in such industries as financial services; healthcare; hospitality; insurance; life sciences, pharmaceuticals, biotechnology, and medical devices; media; professional services; retail; technology; and telecommunications. All told, the firm employs more than 750 attorneys. In addition to its main office in Chicago, Seyfarth maintains domestic operations in Atlanta, Boston, Houston, Los Angeles, New York, Sacramento, San Francisco, and Washington, D.C. The

firm also has an office in Brussels to provide international labor and employment services.

WORLD WAR II–ERA ROOTS

Seyfarth Shaw was founded in Chicago in 1945 by attorneys Henry Edward Seyfarth, Lee Charles Shaw, and Owen Fairweather. Seyfarth was born in 1908 in Blue Island, Illinois. He graduated from the University of Illinois in 1928 and two years later received his law degree from the University of Chicago Law School. Seyfarth then went to work for the state, serving as an assistant Cook County state's attorney until 1935, when he joined the Chicago law firm of Pope and Ballard and became a partner. Three years after taking a position with Pope & Ballard, he was joined by Shaw, five years his junior.

Lee Shaw was born in 1913 in Red Wing, Minnesota. He enrolled at the University of Michigan, where he played football as an offensive and defensive lineman alongside future President Gerald Ford. He completed his undergraduate degree at the University of Chicago in 1936 and two years later earned his law degree at the university's law school. Shaw then joined his fellow alumnus, Seyfarth, at Pope & Ballard, where he was an associate until making partner in 1944.

The third founding partner, Owen Fairweather, was born in 1913 in Chicago, the son of the comptroller at the University of Chicago. He earned his undergraduate degree from Dartmouth College and then graduated cum laude from the University of Chicago Law School in 1938. He also went to work for Pope & Ballard. During World War II he and Shaw would leave the firm

COMPANY PERSPECTIVES

We recognize that the measure of our worth to our clients and to each other is based on a set of core values that define our purpose: teamwork, client service, innovation, excellence and commitment.

to serve on the National War Labor Board in Washington, D.C., charged with monitoring labor issues during the war.

Fairweather and Shaw, by the time they left for Washington, were well versed in labor law, as was Seyfarth, because at Pope & Ballard they specialized in labor law, a new practice established by the firm in the wake of the 1935 passage of the National Labor Relations Act. Commonly known as the Wagner Act, it established the rights of workers to unionize, bargain collectively, and take part in strikes.

The right of workers to unionize and bargain collectively had been a contentious, and sometimes violent, struggle in the United States for many years. The advent of the Great Depression in the 1930s brought it even further to the forefront. Soon after President Franklin Roosevelt took office in 1933 the Congress passed the National Industrial Recovery Act, intended to help the economy rebound from the difficult times. The act also gave employees the right to organize and to negotiate employment contracts as a group. The act was subsequently deemed to be unconstitutional by the Supreme Court, however.

With a wave of strikes crippling the nation in 1933 and 1934, Congress acted once again on behalf of labor unions, passing the Wagner Act in 1935, named for its leading champion, New York Senator Robert R. Wagner. Not only were workers' rights guaranteed, the act provided for the creation of the National Labor Relations Board to guarantee union elections, arbitrate deadlocked contract negotiations, and to penalize employers for unfair labor practices. At first, many employers simply ignored the new law, assuming that it would be struck down by the courts. Yet two years after its passage, the constitutionality of the Wagner Act was upheld, and employers had no choice but to abide by the new regulations. As a result, there was a major surge in union membership and a need for lawyers to represent the interests of both sides. Pope & Ballard chose to represent management in contract negotiations and other matters.

SEYFARTH, SHAW ESTABLISHED: 1945

After World War II ended in August 1945, Shaw and Fairweather returned to Chicago from their stint with the National War Labor Board, and together with their senior colleague, Seyfarth, broke away from Pope & Ballard to set up a boutique law firm specializing in the new labor law. They were soon joined by a fourth partner, Raymond I. Geraldson. Born in Racine, Wisconsin, he had earned his law degree from the University of Wisconsin in 1935 and a year later received an LL.M. (master of laws) from Columbia University. He then practiced in his hometown from 1937 until 1945.

The fledgling Chicago law firm took the name Seyfarth, Shaw, Fairweather & Geraldson. The most influential of the partners were Fairweather and Shaw. Not only was Fairweather a highly regarded labor lawyer, he also became a prolific writer on the subject, authoring many law journal articles and six books, including the seminal text *Practice and Procedure in Labor Arbitration*, along with *Labor Relations and the Law in West Germany and the United States, Labor Relations and the Law in Italy and the United States,* and *Labor Relations and the Law in Belgium and the United States.*

Lee Shaw, on the other hand, had a direct influence on the law itself. His time with the National War Labor Board led to his being named to the drafting panel for the Labor Management Relations Act of 1947, often referred to as the Taft-Hartley Act, which was a major revision of the Wagner Act. It was meant to correct such shortcomings as the delineation of unfair union activities and the ability of the government to curtail a strike that threatened the national interest. The impetus to amending the Wagner Act was the Republican Party takeover of the House and Senate in the 1946 elections, and the drive to dismantle as much of Roosevelt's New Deal legislation as possible. Democratic President Harry Truman vetoed the Taft-Hartley Act, but the Republican-controlled Congress was able to override his veto and it became law. Labor leaders called it a "slave labor" bill and for the next dozen years there was a clamoring for the act to be repealed, but efforts to have it amended failed.

Seyfarth wasted little time in making use of Taft-Hartley. In July 1947 the firm filed the first strike damage suit in U.S. District Court in Chicago against the United Steelworkers of America on behalf of its client, the Globe company, manufacturer of meat processing, packing house, and other heavy equipment. Geraldson prepared the bill, which called for $75,000 in damages and an additional $30,000 for each week the

KEY DATES

1945: Firm is established in Chicago.
1971: Washington, D.C., office opens.
1973: Los Angeles office opens.
1984: San Francisco office is established.
1991: First overseas expansion occurs in Brussels.
1996: Company enters Atlanta market.
1999: Boston office opens.
2003: Company completes merger with D'Ancona & Pflaum LLC.

Steelworker walkout continued. The suit contended that the union violated Taft-Hartley by going on strike in order to obtain a wage increase despite having a collectively bargained contract that was to run until April 1948.

Seyfarth would make its mark with other Chicago area companies as well, including International Harvester and the Dryden Company. With a growing reputation the firm took on work across the country. In the 1960s Shaw represented the Las Vegas casinos during their labor negotiations. He would plant the firm's flag further westward in the early 1970s, taking on Cesar Chavez and his United Farm Workers on behalf of growers. Although a tough negotiator, he was respected by his adversaries, and a number of unions attempted to hire him.

WASHINGTON, D.C., OFFICE OPENED: 1971

After Seyfarth established an office in Washington, D.C., in 1971, a third office was added in Los Angeles in 1973. It was here in its fight with the United Farm Workers that Seyfarth fashioned a reputation as a union buster, an image that would be burnished later in the decade in Illinois when the firm squared off against unionizing firefighters.

For several years the Associated Fire Fighters of Illinois fought for better contracts, employing public relations strikes in which they picketed yet responded to emergencies. In the mid-1970s Seyfarth entered the fray when the firefighters of Danville walked off the job and the firm introduced a new tactic: a willingness to negotiate a contract with firefighters only, insisting that all officers be left out of the union in the name of maintaining management control. Matters would come to a head in Normal, Illinois, where Seyfarth represented the city against a young fire department, which had been profes-

sional for less than a decade and part of the union for only two years. Normal was also considered an ideal place to draw the line against the union because it was predominantly white-collar and Republican and had no public employee unions. Contract negotiations were again held up over the issue of keeping officers out of the bargaining unit, which Seyfarth critics contended was just a ploy to precipitate a strike, turn public opinion against the strikers, and ultimately crush the union.

After weeks of fruitless negotiations, the Normal firefighters went on strike, but returned in answer to a court injunction under the assumption that meaningful negotiations would ensue. Within a day negotiations broke off, the firefighters resumed their strike, and this time 24 of them were sentenced to jail for 42 days each. While the leaders spent the entire time in jail, the other firefighters alternated days in jail with days on duty in the firehouse. The situation received national press attention, the firefighters received unexpected community support, and on the day the firefighters were to be fired a tentative contract was reached to bring the 56-day strike to an end.

Seyfarth was more successful in the late 1970s in its work to break the walkout of United Steelworkers at Newport News Shipbuilding and the pressmen's strike at the *Washington Post.* As a result, the firm garnered the antipathy of organized labor. Labor organizer Vinnie O'Brien expressed a typical opinion of Seyfarth in a 1997 interview with the *Champaign-Urbana News-Gazette:* "They'll stall, delay, whatever they can to cut the heart out of an organizing movement. Labor management is an oxymoron to them."

The 1980s was a time of transition for Seyfarth, as the founders grew elderly and the old guard gave way to a new. (Fairweather died in 1987, followed by Seyfarth in 1991, and Shaw in 1999.) The largest labor law firm in the country, Seyfarth looked to add a corporate practice. In early 1982 the firm jumpstarted the process by raiding the ranks of Marshall, Bratter, Green, Allison & Tucker to establish an office in New York City. The following year Seyfarth found itself being the one raided. Four of the Marshall, Bratter attorneys who had joined the Los Angeles office and represented the entire securities department left to establish an outpost for Skadden, Arps, Slate, Meagher & Flom. A month later, three partners from the Washington office defected to Jones, Day, Reavis & Pogue, and 14 lawyers in the main Chicago office left for other firms as well. Despite these losses the firm continued to grow in the 1980s, opening an office in San Francisco in 1984 and growing the Los Angeles office in 1988 through the merger with the Beverly Hills firm of Pollard, Bauman, Slome, and McIntosh.

Seyfarth also maintained something of a notorious image in the 1980s, fanned by its work in 1984 with Yale University and the attempt to break a new clerical union. Labor struck back when the AFL-CIO began urging law students to decline interviews with Seyfarth and a number of other "union-busting" law firms. In 1986 the *New York Times* reported that more than 200 students at Harvard Law School, about 20 percent of the school's second- and third-year classes, pledged not to seek jobs with Seyfarth and four other firms because of their anti-union activities. Protests against Seyfarth law school recruiting would continue through the rest of the decade and into the 1990s.

FULL-SERVICE ASPIRATIONS

Seyfarth's bid to become a full-service law firm, and expand geographically, began to take shape in the early 1990s. A Sacramento office was opened in 1990, where work was conducted for clients in California and other western states. In that same year, the San Francisco office, which five years earlier had but one attorney, added six new partners and 15 associates from Adams, Duque & Hazeltine to bring the total to 26. The six partners were insurance litigators who brought with them a considerable client base. In 1991 Seyfarth expanded overseas, establishing a presence in Brussels to practice labor and employment and international law.

More offices were added in the second half of the 1990s. A Houston office was opened in 1995 and concentrated on labor and employment, commercial litigation, and intellectual property law. A year later an office was opened in Atlanta that enjoyed exceptional growth. Finally, in 1999 an office was opened in Boston with a pair of partners and five associates.

COMPLETION OF LARGEST MERGER: 2000

Seyfarth enjoyed steady growth in the new century, as the firm continued to diversify its services and beef up its presence in key markets. In the summer of 2000 the Atlanta office added 40 attorneys from McCullough Sherrill. The Boston office also expanded at a fast pace through mergers, adding the corporate firm of Chappell White in 2001. A year later the immigration and labor and employment practices of Palmer & Dodge were brought into the fold as well as a group of lawyers from Schnader Harrison Segal & Lewis LLP.

In 2003 Seyfarth completed the largest merger in its history, adding another Chicago firm, the 100-year-old D'Ancona & Pflaum LLC. Seyfarth added 60 attorneys and strengthened such practice areas as corporate, securities, mutual funds, pension fund investments, venture capital, litigation, real estate, and estate planning. A slate of national and international clients were brought in as well. Seyfarth's Chicago office numbered 270 lawyers, making it one of the city's top ten largest law firms.

Seyfarth continued to increase its ranks piecemeal, strengthening particular practices through strategic hirings, while making occasional larger additions. In the fall of 2005 the New York office added 15 attorneys from Mandel Resnik Kaiser Moskowitz & Greenstein specializing in real estate, corporate law, and litigation. Early in 2007 four attorneys from Pryor Cashman Sherman & Flynn LLP fortified the corporate and finance group in the New York office. In just two years, in fact, the New York office doubled in size. To accommodate the 185 employees the office moved to a larger midtown Manhattan location. A year earlier the Chicago office had also moved into new offices to house its growing headcount.

Ed Dinger

PRINCIPAL COMPETITORS

Littler Mendelson, PC; Paul, Hastings, Janofsky, & Walker LLP; Proskauer Rose LLP.

FURTHER READING

Bloomer, J. Philip, "Seyfarth, Shaw: Necessary or Notorious," *Champaign-Urbana (Ill.) News-Gazette*, November 23, 1997.

Flint, Jerry, "A New Breed—Professional Union Breakers," *Forbes*, June 25, 1979, p. 29.

"Henry E. Seyfarth, Founding Partner of Top Labor Law Firm," *Chicago Sun-Times*, August 18, 1991, p. 67.

Hoekstra, Dave, "Lee Shaw, 86, Helped Found Labor Law Firm," *Chicago Sun-Times*, November 23, 1999, p. 70.

Lewin, Tamar, "Business and the Law; Hiring Away Legal Talent," *New York Times*, July 12, 1983.

Margolick, David, "Departures a Key Issue for Law Firm," *New York Times*, January 10, 1982, p. 30.

Martin, Douglas, "Lee Shaw, 86, Lawyer, Dies," *New York Times*, November 25, 1999, p. C17.

"Owen Fairweather, 73, Prolific Author and Labor Attorney," *Chicago Sun-Times*, February 28, 1987, p. 37.

"Sue CIO in 1st Plea Strike Damage Here," *Chicago Daily Tribune*, July 31, 1947, p. 1.

◐ Shermag

Shermag, Inc.

2171 rue King Ouest
Sherbrooke, Quebec J1J 2G1
Canada
Telephone: (819) 566-1515
Fax: (819) 566-7323
Web site: http://www.shermag.com

Public Company
Incorporated: 1977
Employees: 750
Sales: CAD 155.92 million (2007)
Stock Exchanges: Toronto
Ticker Symbol: SMG
NAIC: 337122 Nonupholstered Wood Household
    Furniture Manufacturing; 337121 Upholstered
    Household Furniture Manufacturing

■ ■ ■

Shermag, Inc., is one of Quebec's leading designers, manufacturers, and distributors of residential furniture. Shermag products include both mass production home furnishings and custom, made-to-order furniture. Shermag offers bedroom furniture in 20 styles, including the Shaker-style Atlantic Collection, the elegant Bourbon Street Collection, the classical Chateauneuf Collection, the sleek Loft Collection, and the Asian-influenced Yao Collection. Youth and infant bedroom furniture in seven styles include bunk beds, cribs, changing tables, and related case goods. Also, Shermag is a leading worldwide producer of glider rockers. Shermag's 16 collections of dining room sets are produced in modern and

traditional styles. Shermag offers customized sofas and chairs in fabric and leather upholstery. Accessories include accent side tables, office furniture, and home entertainment centers. Shermag furniture is manufactured with solid woods, such as birch, maple, and oak, and accented with wood veneer, such as cherrywood. Nearly 40 percent of Shermag's production is outsourced to China. Production in Canada is vertically integrated, as Shermag handles every aspect of production, from logging and processing wood solids and wood veneer, to assembling and distributing products to major department stores, mass market chain stores, and independent retailers of high-end furniture throughout the United States and Canada. Exports to the United States comprise approximately 65 percent of revenues.

ECONOMICS PROFESSOR
TURNS ENTREPRENEUR

Shermag founder Serge Racine had two foundational careers before becoming an entrepreneur in the furniture business. As a professor of economics, Racine taught at Georgetown University in Washington, D.C., and then at the University of Sherbrooke in Quebec. In 1972 Racine left teaching and took the position of city manager of Sherbrooke. While in that position, Racine encountered an opportunity in furniture production in 1977, when a group of businesspeople sought assistance from the city of Sherbrooke to establish a furniture factory. Although the city did not support the project, Racine saw its merits and left his job, with an annual salary of $65,000, to become an entrepreneur in furniture production.

COMPANY PERSPECTIVES

■

Shermag's corporate mission is to be the home furnishing company of CHOICE. This mission means that not only will the Company offer choice to its retailers and their customers, but that its employees, shareholders, business partners, customers and the communities in which it operates will desire to be associated with the Company.

Racine raised $50,000 to start Shermag, along with silent partner Gilles Sirois. Racine acquired a small furniture company producing glider rockers and garnered first-year sales of CAD 2.5 million. With Racine earning a first-year salary of $22,000, Shermag struggled as he sought investors and gathered funds to acquire small, regional furniture-makers. Racine's goal was to develop the company into a full-line, home furniture manufacturer. Acquisitions included a bedroom furniture manufacturer in Disraeli and a dining room furniture manufacturer in St-Étienne-de-Lauzon, both in Quebec. With the addition of three factory acquisitions, Shermag produced a complete line of furniture under the brand names Marius Ouelette, Open Home, as well as Shermag. By 1986 Shermag's customers included 1,200 retail furniture and department stores throughout Canada.

After years of absorbing the losses of acquired companies, Shermag became profitable. For 1986, Shermag posted sales of CAD 23.2 million and earned a profit of CAD 2.2 million. The company solidified its position with a public offering of stock in July 1986. At CAD 5.35 per share, Shermag raised CAD 14.2 million, well above the original CAD 10 million, due to strong demand from investors. Shermag applied the funds to reduce long-term and short-term debt, to modernize its manufacturing facilities, and to fund working capital for further expansion. Shermag acquired a controlling interest in Conant Ball Company, of Massachusetts, and began distribution to retailers in the United States.

ACQUISITIONS AND VERTICAL INTEGRATION FOSTERS GROWTH AND PROFITABILITY

Expansion at Shermag involved developing a vertically integrated structure for efficient sourcing and processing of raw materials, as well as to continue developing its product line. High lumber prices prompted Shermag to invest in hardwood production. Toward that end, in October 1986, Shermag purchased a 33.33 percent interest in Les Produits Forestiers Andre Poulin, Inc., a sawmill and wood-drying operation that processed oak, ash, cherrywood, and other fine hardwoods for furniture production. Shermag increased its interest in the CAD 10 million operation to 50 percent in early 1988, then acquired the remaining 50 percent interest the following December. Shermag sold one of two sawmills but retained the facility at Notre-Dame-de Montauban, which carried rights to hardwood logging on Canadian public lands.

Other acquisitions supported product and market expansion. In February 1987 Shermag acquired the Scanway Corporation for CAD 3.2 million. A Scandinavian manufacturer of ready-to-assemble, white melamine furniture, Scanway brought significant new customers to Shermag, including retailer IKEA Svenska AB of Sweden, and KIT A TOUT, a chain distribution company. The acquisition included manufacturing operations in St-Jean, Quebec.

Shermag entered the upholstered furniture market through two acquisitions. In August 1987 Shermag applied CAD 1.5 million in working capital to purchase Creations Mobilieres Chanderic Inc., based in Vercheres, Quebec. Shermag expanded the work crew from 50 to 65 employees with the expectation of increased sales through the company's customer network. A year later Shermag acquired another upholstered furniture manufacturer, Meubles Dema, Inc., a subsidiary of Domicil, Inc., of Montreal. Shermag doubled the staff to 20.

Other acquisitions in 1988 expanded production capacity and created new distribution outlets in the United States. The purchase of Nadeau & Nadeau included a manufacturing facility in St-François-de-Madawaska, New Brunswick. In September 1988 Shermag purchased a 30 percent interest in Grange Furniture, Inc., which handled France's Grange SA operations in the United States. Shermag already supplied 20 percent of the furniture inventory to Grange's 29 retail stores, located in major U.S. cities.

Operating profitably on approximately CAD 44 million in revenues during the late 1990s, Shermag began to modernize operations for productivity and efficiency. The Canadian government contributed CAD 1.1 million to the CAD 4.3 million manufacturing improvement project. Changes involved implementation of new technology and the upgrade of production equipment.

KEY DATES

■

1977: Serge Racine quits his job and starts Shermag with $50,000.

1986: Revenues reach CAD 24 million; first public issue of stock raises CAD 14 million for expansion.

1988: Shermag becomes vertically integrated with acquisition of sawmill and wood-processing company.

1990: Revenues decline due to new competition after U.S.-Canada free trade agreement.

1995: Currency exchange rates favor Canada; exports to United States exceed 50 percent of revenues.

1997: Shermag builds a new sawmill, expands timber rights to meet demand for hardwoods.

2003: Shermag enters infant and youth furniture markets.

2005: Decline in U.S. currency hinders exports; Shermag outsources mass-produced goods manufacturing to Asia.

2007: Chinese outsourcing continues as Shermag closes four of eight remaining plants.

U.S.-CANADA FREE TRADE AGREEMENT IMPACTS OPERATIONS

Though Racine actively supported the free trade agreement between the United States and Canada, signed in 1988, the pact affected Shermag in a variety of ways. Initially, free trade hurt Shermag's business. Reduced restrictions on trade increased competition from furniture manufacturers in the United States. Moreover, in conjunction with an economic recession, Shermag's exports to the United States declined significantly. These conditions resulted in financial problems, first at Scanway, which accounted for 10 percent of Shermag sales. Shermag ceased operations at the subsidiary, which underwent federal bankruptcy reorganization. Accompanied by multiyear losses, revenues at Shermag declined to a low of CAD 27.7 million by 1992.

To deal with its overall financial problems, Shermag initiated a restructuring program in 1991. Reorganization of debt resulted in a merger of Shermag with its major shareholder, Corp. de Gestion Shermag, owned by Racine and Sirois. The move allowed new investment through a CAD 1 million debenture, convertible to stock, as well as the private placement of nearly three

million shares for CAD 2 million by Quebec Federation of Labour Solidarity Fund. Negotiations resulted in a three-way ownership split, with Racine's Corp. de Gestion Shermag owning 32.63 percent, QFL Solidarity Fund owning 30 percent, and the public, 37.37 percent.

By the mid-1990s, Shermag's economic fortunes turned with the currency exchange of a weakened Canadian dollar against a stronger U.S. dollar. With free trade, the exchange rate made Canadian goods more attractive to retailers in the United States. Shermag began to serve that market with bedroom and dining room sets for department stores. Shermag offered new furniture in casual contemporary designs that appealed to the tastes of baby-boomers in the United States. These involved simpler lines and lighter wood stains than those used in the European-style furniture offered by the company. Also, Shermag began producing more furniture from solid wood, rather than the veneered composites popular during the 1980s.

Shermag's focus on the U.S. furniture market led the company to shift distribution from 900 stores of varying sizes in Canada to major retailers in the United States. Shermag became a major supplier to 18 of the 25 largest retailers in the United States. These included J. C. Penney, Bloomingdale's, Burdines, Jordan Marsh, Macy's, Dayton-Hudson, and Sears and involved 2,000 stores. Exports rose from 20 percent of production in 1991 to approximately 50 percent in 1995.

EXPANDING TO MEET DEMAND IN U.S. MARKET

Shermag reorganized and upgraded its facilities to meet the new demand for Canadian-made goods. In December 1994 Shermag began a CAD 1.5 million facilities upgrade and expansion at St-François-de-Madawaska. The following August Shermag invested CAD 1 million to transform a warehouse in Eaton, Quebec, into a 20,000-square-foot wood veneer plant. At the nearby Chanderic plant in Lennoxville, Shermag increased production by 50 percent to meet demand for glider rockers in the United States.

In late 1995 Shermag purchased Rosaire Bedard, Ltee, known for its solid wood dining room tables and chairs. Shermag planned to increase production at the St-Étienne-de-Lauzon, facility with the goal of doubling dining room furniture sales to CAD 10 million. A year later Shermag acquired Sofas International, Inc., expanding its capacity for the manufacture of upholstered furniture. The two-year-old Saint-Léonard, Quebec, company reported CAD 1 million in revenue for 1995. Shermag aimed to increase revenues to CAD 5 million in two years based on the natural extension of sales of upholstered furniture complementary to its wood furniture for family rooms and living rooms.

As business grew, Shermag experienced a shortage in the supply of hardwoods which, in turn, led to higher overhead prices. The company required 20 million board-feet per year to meet production. Hence, Shermag sought control over supply and cost by expanding its sawmill operations. In 1997 Shermag acquired Megabois, Inc., which operated a sawmill in Lac-Megantic. Then Shermag entered a 50-50 partnership agreement with Gerard Crete el fils, Inc., to build and operate a second sawmill in Notre-Dame-de-Montauban under the newly formed Scierie Montauban, Inc. Shermag obtained full ownership of that company in 1999. To supply its sawmills, Shermag found hardwood sources in the United States and obtained a 25-year extension on its timber-cutting rights on Canadian public lands.

As Shermag organized for efficiency and growth, the company applied CAD 7 million to expansion of its operating facilities. Shermag acquired a 120,000-square-foot distribution center in Sherbrooke, Quebec. The facility provided enough space to consolidate the inventory produced at Shermag's 11 manufacturing plants. The company converted its warehouse in Victoriaville, where furniture destined for North American retailers was stored, to a manufacturing facility. In 2000 Shermag tripled its veneer manufacturing capacity by adding 25,000 square feet to its Placages Lennox factory.

Success in upholstered furniture after the acquisition of Sofas International, led Shermag to expand that area of business. The company began producing leather furniture and introduced six styles of leather sofas at the trade shows in the fall of 2000. In May 2003 Shermag acquired Jaymar Furniture, a special-order upholstered furniture company, with leather and fabric options. The acquisition included a 150,000-square-foot manufacturing facility near Montreal.

In 2002 Shermag entered the youth market in bedroom furniture, initially as a private-label manufacturer for Drexel Heritage. Shermag produced bed frames in a sleigh style with accompanying dressers specifically for Drexel Heritage Home Stores. Upon closer look at its production, Shermag found that it already produced many items appropriate to the youth market, such as desks and hutches, as well as appropriate wood stains, in light colors. Hence, in early 2003, Shermag introduced a complete line of juvenile furniture, including bunk beds in maple wood. Later, Shermag developed a TV armoire compatible with video game equipment.

Success with youth furniture prompted Shermag to develop a full line of infant furniture. The line included cribs, changing tables, and twin and full beds, available in six styles and a variety of light wood stains and veneers. Shermag organized the infant and youth furniture under Chanderic, its glider-rocker division.

While comparable competitors experienced lower sales and profits, Shermag thrived on excellent product quality and customer service. Shermag obtained 75 percent of sales from exports to 50 accounts in the United States.

BUSINESS CONDITIONS LEAD TO RESTRUCTURING AND LAYOFFS

After nearly a decade of steady growth, bolstered by free trade and a favorable exchange rate, the weakening of the U.S. dollar in 2003 eroded the competitive edge of Canadian exporters to the United States. Furthermore, Shermag faced increasing competition from Asian furniture manufacturers.

In order to address the new business conditions, in February 2005 Shermag announced it would restructure operations. The company had begun to transfer manufacturing of high-volume goods to China in 2001. As factory workers resisted the changes, labor strikes quickened the pace of outsourcing in 2004 and 2005. For instance, a prolonged strike at the Disraeli plant prompted Shermag to outsource production of glider rockers to Asia; Shermag used Russian sources of birch to produce the rockers. This move fit with the company's strategy of exporting the manufacture of mass-produced goods to Asia.

Other restructuring involved layoffs due to excess inventory of home furnishings. In March 2005 the company laid off half of the 160 employees at Victoriaville; Shermag closed the plant completely by the end of the year. In August, Shermag laid off 83 workers at its St-Étienne plant in Quebec. Shermag consolidated its upholstery operations at the Jaymar facility in Terrebonne, Quebec. This involved closure of the Saint-Léonard, Quebec facility, and the layoff of 70 employees.

Shermag consolidated support operations as well. In December 2005 the company announced the consolidation of sawmill operations at Notre-Dame-de-Montauban. Shermag halted operations at Lac-Megantic and placed the facility up for sale as the company began sourcing raw materials overseas. Committed to maintaining a vertically integrated structure, Shermag rebuilt the Montauban facility after a fire in March 2006 destroyed it. Shermag consolidated all warehousing and distribution under one 350,000-square-foot facility in LaSalle, near Montreal. Shermag closed and put up for sale its Sherbrooke and Victoriaville distribution centers and closed the leased Jean-sur-Richelieu facility.

Shermag expected the changes to reduce material handling costs, to simplify supply chain management, and to improve customer service.

In order to align production with demand, Shermag initiated a made-to-order production protocol, a move that also provided consumers with customized furniture options. Shermag opened a development center in Sherbrooke to speed the shift toward the high-end furniture market. New products included the new Land line of home entertainment centers, which offered flexibility to a customer's particular electronics setup. To increase its visibility in high-quality furniture, in April 2006 the company signed an agreement to develop, market, and manufacture a new collection of furniture in partnership with the prominent *Metropolitan Home* magazine. World-renowned interior designer Benjamin Noriega-Ortiz was chosen to design the fashion-forward Metropolitan Home Furniture Collection. Another strategy involved an exclusive agreement with The Rug Studio to distribute custom-made area rugs throughout North America.

Shermag's strategies failed to produce the desired results. The value of the U.S. dollar continued to decline against the Canadian dollar, eliminating economic gains from restructuring. A downturn in the U.S. housing market in late 2006 and an increase in competition from the improved quality of Chinese furniture both negatively impacted furniture sales. Further, sales of custom furniture did not meet expectations. As such, in September 2006, Shermag cut production at its bedroom furniture manufacturing facility in Disraeli, Quebec, and then closed the facility in early 2007. Also, Shermag halted operations at the St-Étienne-de-Lauzon dining room production facility. By June 2007 8 of 16 factories had closed, and the number of employees was reduced by half, from 2,400 to 1,200. Production output in Asia accounted for 35 percent of all production by the end of fiscal 2007.

Net revenues at Shermag decreased to CAD 188.71 million for fiscal 2006 and CAD 155.92 for fiscal 2007. Shermag reported a net loss of CAD 30.62 million in 2006 and CAD 17.29 million in 2007. Losses included more than CAD 30 million in extraordinary costs, such as employee severance pay and impairment of long-lived assets.

NEW LEADERSHIP ACCELERATES CHANGE

Dissatisfied with the pace and quality of change at Shermag, investor activist George Armoyan raised his ownership interest in the company from 12 percent in the summer of 2006 to 20 percent in the fall of 2007.

As a result, Armoyan qualified for a board seat, leading CEO Jeffrey Casselman to relinquish his seat to Armoyan's Clarke, Inc. After Casselman left the company in November, Armoyan increased the pace of outsourcing to Asia. Shermag closed four of eight remaining plants, two in Quebec and two in New Brunswick, including its state-of-the-art Edmundston facility. Layoffs of 320 people reduced employee count to 750 people. Armoyan expected to rejuvenate Shermag by focusing on the strong Canadian market for home furniture.

Mary Tradii

PRINCIPAL SUBSIDIARIES

Jaymar Furniture Co. Inc.; Scierie Montauban, Inc.; Shermag Corporation (U.S.A.).

PRINCIPAL COMPETITORS

American Leather; Basset Industries; Broyhill Furniture Industries, Inc.; Décor-Rest Furniture, Inc.; Durham Furniture, Inc; Dutailer, Inc.; Ethan Allen Interiors, Inc.; LADD Furniture Inc.; McCreary Modern, Inc.; Meubles Canadel, Inc.; Palliser Furniture Ltd.; Precendent, Inc.; Sklar Peppler Furniture Corporation; Stanley Furniture Company, Inc.; Superstyle Furniture Ltd.; Trend Leather Inc.

FURTHER READING

"Acquisition Costs Hit Earnings," *Financial Post,* February 16, 1988, p. 26.

Blackwell, Richard, "Shermag to Close Half Its Plants," *Globe & Mail,* December 11, 2007, p. B3.

DeCloet, Derek, "Armoyan Outlines Plans to Shake Up Shermag," *Globe & Mail,* October 10, 2007.

Dunn, Brian, "Shermag Gets into Leather," *HFN: The Weekly Newspaper for the Home Furnishing Network,* September 4, 2000, p. 24.

"Furniture Makers Find Profitable Niche in U.S.; Strong Rebound in Industry That Had Been Hard Hit by Bankruptcies," *Globe & Mail,* February 22, 1996, p. B29.

Gibbens, Robert, "Shermag Gets $65M to Restructure: Furniture Firm Transforming Itself to Make-to-Order," *Montreal Gazette,* June 13, 2006, p. B3.

———, "Shermag Must 'Stop the Hemorrhage'; Activist Investor Named Director," *Montreal Gazette,* October 11, 2007, p. B1.

Horsman, Matthew, "On Their Own: Furniture Maker Finally Finds His Niche: Ex-Teacher Turns Valuable Lessons into Profits," *Financial Post,* September 27, 1986, p. 20.

"Issue Brings $14.2 Million to Shermag," *Globe & Mail,* July 19, 1986, p. B6.

Jones, Robert, "Furniture Maker to Buy Failing Rival Nadeau," *Globe & Mail,* January 9, 1988.

Karleff, Ian, "Shermag Looks Within for Key to Market Expansion," *Financial Post,* July 18, 1998, p. 21.

Kitchen, Jane, "Chanderic Shift Focuses onto Youth, Infant Market," *Home Textiles Today,* October 20, 2003, p. S27.

Knell, Michael J., "Shermag Sets Sights on Youth Market," *Home Textiles Today,* April 7, 2003, p. S18.

Lamey, Mary, "Shermag Knocking on Wood; Furniture Maker Looks to Increase U.S.," *Montreal Gazette,* August 19, 1994, p. D1.

Marotte, Bertrand, "Shakeup at Shermag Sees Sudden Departure of CEO," *Globe & Mail,* November 21, 2007, p. B9.

———, "Shermag Facing More Layoffs, Plant Closings," *Globe & Mail,* June 15, 2007, p. B4.

Marowits, Ross, "Ailing Shermag Shipping Quebec Work to Asia," *Toronto Star,* February 13, 2007, p. D04.

"Metropolitan Home Magazine to Partner with Shermag for Signature Branded Collection," *CNW Group,* April 24, 2006.

"News Bulletins: Shermag in Talks," *Globe & Mail,* September 4, 1991, p. B2.

O'Mara, Sheila Long, "Drexel Heritage Enters Youth Bedroom Market," *Home Textiles Today,* November 18, 2002, p. S18.

"Serge Racine: CEO of Shermag Inc.," *Report on Business 1000,* July 1998, p. 56.

"Shermag," *Globe & Mail,* August 16, 1988, p. B2.

"Shermag Announces Consolidation of Upholstery Operations; Long Term Contract Signed at Jaymar Facility," *CNW Group,* December 1, 2005.

"Shermag Closing 4 Plants in Quebec and N.B.," *Canadian Broadcasting Corporation,* December 10, 2007.

"Shermag Enters into New Credit Facility Agreements," *CNW Group,* June 12, 2006.

"Shermag, Inc. to Purchase Jaymar Furniture," *HFN: The Weekly Newspaper for the Home Furnishing Network,* May 12, 2003, p. 3.

"Shermag Loss Falls As Cost Cuts Take Hold," *Globe & Mail,* November 14, 2006, p. B5.

"Shermag Must Repay Loan After Plant Closures: Minister," *Canadian Broadcasting Corporation,* December 11, 2007.

"Shermag Plans Two Shutdowns, 300 More Layoffs," *Globe & Mail,* February 13, 2007, p. B5.

"Shermag Reports Fiscal 2005/2006 Results," *CNW Group,* June 15, 2006.

"Shermag Signs Distribution Agreement with The Rug Studio," *CNW Group,* March 13, 2007.

"Shermag to Establish New Distribution Centre in Montreal," *CNW Group,* April 10, 2006.

Swift, Allan, "Shermag Strike a Drag on Revenues," *Montreal Gazette,* November 12, 2004, p. B3.

Sigma-Aldrich
Corporation

3050 Spruce Street
St. Louis, Missouri 63103-2530
U.S.A.
Telephone: (314) 771-5765
Toll Free: (800) 521-8956
Fax: (314) 286-7874
Web site: http://www.sigma-aldrich.com

Public Company
Incorporated: 1975
Employees: 7,600
Sales: $1.8 billion (2006)
Stock Exchanges: NASDAQ
Ticker Symbol: SIAL
NAIC: 325188 All Other Inorganic Chemical Manufacturing; 325199 All Other Basic Organic Chemical Manufacturing; 325413 In-Vitro Diagnostic Substance Manufacturing; 325414 Biological Product (Except Diagnostic) Manufacturing; 325998 All Other Miscellaneous Chemical Product and Preparation Manufacturing; 422210 Drugs and Druggist Sundries Wholesalers; 422690 Other Chemical and Allied Products Wholesalers; 454111 Electronic Shopping; 454113 Mail-Order Houses; 541710 Research and Development in the Physical, Engineering, and Life Sciences

∎ ∎ ∎

Sigma-Aldrich Corporation is a developer, manufacturer, and distributor of a wide range of biochemicals, organic chemicals, chromatography products, diagnostic reagents, and laboratory equipment and kits. The company is the world's leading seller of chemicals to research laboratories, pharmaceutical companies, and hospitals, with a product line that includes approximately 100,000 substances and 30,000 equipment products sold principally under five well-known chemical brands: Sigma, Aldrich, Fluka, Riedel-de Haën, and Supelco. Of these 100,000 substances, roughly 46,000 of them are manufactured by the company, and the company-manufactured products account for around 60 percent of overall sales. Sigma-Aldrich has more than 70,000 customers in more than 165 countries; more than 70 percent of its sales to these customers are on the small side, averaging about $400. About 60 percent of sales are generated outside the United States. The company maintains manufacturing facilities in Missouri, California, Connecticut, Florida, Illinois, Kansas, Massachusetts, New Jersey, Ohio, Pennsylvania, Texas, Wisconsin, Australia, Canada, France, Germany, India, Ireland, Israel, Japan, Singapore, Switzerland, and the United Kingdom.

BORN THROUGH A 1975 MERGER

Sigma-Aldrich Corporation is the result of a 1975 merger between two specialty chemical companies, one that manufactured biochemicals (Sigma Chemical Company) and another that manufactured organic chemicals (Aldrich Chemical Company, Inc.). While offering divergent products, both companies regarded high-quality products and customer service a priority. The merger, therefore, represented a convergence of business strategy as well as the creation of a diversified product line that ranked Sigma-Aldrich at the top of the specialty chemical industry. In particular, because of the scientific community's involvement in the growing field of biomedical research, Sigma-Aldrich's product catalog became standard issue in pharmaceutical laboratories around the world.

Sigma Chemical Company was started in 1945 in St. Louis. At a time when sugar was scarce, Dan Broida, a biochemist, began a storefront business to manufacture saccharin. The company later went on to produce biochemicals and diagnostic products. Sigma's customers ranged from hospitals to university laboratories. Scientific fields concerned with the study of life sciences, as well as disease diagnostics, use biochemicals as the basic substances to develop pharmaceuticals and diagnostic tests.

Aldrich Chemical Company, founded by the Harvard-educated chemist Dr. Alfred R. Bader, began manufacturing organic chemicals in a Milwaukee garage six years after Broida established Sigma. Aldrich's first products were those chemicals not offered by Eastman Kodak Company, a leader in the chemical industry. Bader soon decided that his company could engage in direct competition with larger companies, and he began offering a broad line of organics sold to research laboratories of pharmaceutical companies. The company did exceedingly well and its customer list soon included Abbott Laboratories and Ciba-Geigy Ltd., among others.

The 1975 merger between the two companies matched skill for skill and talent for talent. Broida assumed the role of chairman and Bader took the position of company president. While the combined company interests still remained small compared to those of the larger industry firms, the business acumen of Sigma-Aldrich's management went a long way in securing an impressive percentage of the specialty chemical research market. By 1979 the company laid claim to between 30 and 40 percent of the $100 million research market. Sales climbed to $68 million, representing an annual increase of 15 percent. Earnings jumped 24 percent to $9.2 million, causing Wall Street analysts to predict continued growth of 20 percent a year.

Sigma-Aldrich's marketing success, achieved by neither a large sales force nor expensive advertising outlays, relied on the distribution of catalogs. In addition to advertising products available on a phone-order basis, the catalog offered detailed information about the physical properties of the marketed chemicals. The value of the catalog as a reference source as well as an advertising tool was evident, and it soon became a company trademark. Initially compiled by Bader in the early 1950s as a one-page, one-chemical listing, the catalog grew to include 40,000 chemicals by the late 1970s. Sigma-Aldrich's small sales force distributed 300,000 free copies of the catalog in 1979.

The company's reputation among chemists as a manufacturer of quality products matched a distribution network that ensured most orders would be filled in 24 hours. Interestingly enough, in the early years of Sigma-Aldrich's business an average order amounted to less than $100. This indicated a customer profile of academicians or laboratory researchers experimenting with relatively small quantities of chemicals. Although this profile was altered somewhat in the ensuing years because of the increasing pressure to supply bulk commercial chemicals, Sigma-Aldrich fiercely defended its business as first and foremost a service to the research community.

Overseas expansion in the late 1970s found 125 countries purchasing Sigma-Aldrich's products with company subsidiaries operating in Canada, the United Kingdom, Japan, Germany, and Israel. Nearly 40 percent of sales in 1979 resulted from overseas business.

EXPLOSIVE GROWTH

In the 1980s the company's growth matched the explosion in the U.S. biomedical research market. Despite such gains Sigma-Aldrich's management, much to the chagrin of some industry analysts, refused to alter the strategy that laid the framework for previous company growth. Rather than set long-term goals or exploit the bulk chemical market as some observers suggested, Broida defended his company's straightforward "opportunistic" policy of keeping pace with state-of-the-art developments in the scientific fields of immunology, microbiology, and endocrinology. By supplying chemicals in small quantities to research centers, Sigma-Aldrich's growth and profits corresponded to breakthrough research in the development of pharmaceuticals from recombinant DNA.

Wall Street analysts also criticized the company's B-Line Systems, Inc., subsidiary, which had been inherited from the Sigma side of the company lineage. Manufacturing metal frameworks for industrial plants, the subsidiary was criticized for competing in the business of specialty chemicals on the one hand, and for

KEY DATES

1945: Sigma Chemical Company is founded in St. Louis by Dan Broida to manufacture saccharin.

1951: Alfred R. Bader launches Aldrich Chemical Company, Inc., as a Milwaukee-based manufacturer of organic chemicals.

1975: Sigma Chemical and Aldrich Chemical merge to form Sigma-Aldrich Corporation, which is based in St. Louis.

1981: Broida dies; Tom Cori takes over as company president.

1989: Fluka Chemie AG is acquired.

1991: Company establishes its fine chemicals division to handle bulk sales.

1993: Supelco, Inc., is acquired.

1997: Company purchases 75 percent interest in Riedel-de Haën.

1998: Genosys Biotechnologies, Inc., is acquired.

1999: The remaining 25 percent of Riedel-de Haën is acquired; major restructuring is launched.

2000: Company divests B-Line Systems and focuses fully on chemicals for the life sciences and high-technology markets.

2004: Fine chemicals unit is rebranded SAFC.

2005: In the largest acquisition in company history, Sigma-Aldrich acquires JRH Biosciences; company is reorganized into four units: Research Essentials, Research Specialties, Research Biotech, and SAFC.

contributing small profit margins on the other. Despite such criticism, however, the company's lack of long-term debt, its sparkling earnings record, and its annual profit increase of 20 to 25 percent mitigated the seriousness of such complaints.

Upon Dan Broida's death in 1981 several changes in policy and management affected the company structure. Tom Cori, a nine-year Sigma veteran, became company president. Common stock, formerly controlled by a 50 percent insiders interest, became more widely held. In 1985, 2.2 million of the 8.68 million outstanding shares were sold for $129.5 million. Most of this stock had been held by relatives of Broida, and the sale reduced their holdings to 1.3 million shares. This figure represented approximately the same interest held by the Bader family.

Of the 2.2 million shares sold the company purchased 500,000. Apparently Bader had been opposed to the company purchase partially on the grounds that $13 million was borrowed to finance the transaction. Company debts totaled $32.4 million in short-term loans due in part to a $16 million expansion program started in 1980. Some five million shares, on the other hand, were estimated to be available for trade in the over-the-counter market. Price per share between July and September 1985 ranged from $60.50 to $71, well over the company's $14 per share book value. A three-for-one stock split was soon in order.

ACQUISITION OF FLUKA AND CREATION OF FINE CHEMICALS DIVISION

By 1986 some 1.5 million company catalogs circulated yearly. Sigma-Aldrich's orders continued to average less than $150 each; on the other hand company profits totaled $29 million on volume of $215 million. Although president of a company with such impressive achievements, Cori did not rest on his laurels. Limited governmental funds for scientific research as well as the effect of the strong dollar on overseas sales offered some cause for concern. To facilitate expansion by broadening Sigma-Aldrich's product line, the company purchased Pathfinder Laboratories. The new subsidiary, costing $1.5 million in stock during 1984, manufactured radioactive chemicals. A much larger acquisition came in 1989 when Sigma-Aldrich purchased one of its main European competitors, Switzerland-based Fluka Chemie AG, from Ciba-Geigy and F. Hoffmann-La Roche Ltd. Fluka, maker of biochemicals and organic chemicals for the laboratory market, had annual sales of about $55 million.

In 1991 Sigma-Aldrich took a significant step toward filling more bulk orders through the establishment of a fine chemicals division, which was charged with large-scale manufacturing of chemicals for the pharmaceutical and biopharmaceutical industries. That same year, Bader retired from his position as chairman and was named chairman emeritus. Cori took on the additional title of chairman.

Bader's new role was short-lived, however, as in early 1992 he was voted off the board of directors and stripped of his chairman emeritus title. The reason for the board's action was never made public, although it was speculated to involve either an allegation that Bader had made a bet against the company's stock through a call option, a charge Bader denied, or the fact that Bader had failed to report his exercising of the option to the Securities and Exchange Commission in a timely manner, an action that Bader said had been "an honest mistake." In any event, Bader, who was held in high esteem by numerous Sigma-Aldrich customers on six continents, continued to be one of the largest holders of the company's stock into the early 21st century, when he held about 6 percent.

ACQUISITIONS OF SUPELCO (1993) AND RIEDEL-DE HAËN (1997)

While sales and earnings growth slowed in the early and mid-1990s to 15 percent or less per year, Sigma-Aldrich continued to expand aggressively through such internal growth initiatives as the adding of manufacturing and distribution capacity as well as through acquisitions. In May 1993 the company acquired Supelco, Inc., from Rohm and Haas Company for $54.7 million. Based in Bellefonte, Pennsylvania, Supelco was a worldwide supplier of chromatography products used to analyze and purify drugs and had annual sales of $48 million. In 1994 David R. Harvey was named president and chief operating officer, with Cori remaining chairman and CEO.

In the area of plant expansion, Sigma-Aldrich by 1997 had three new manufacturing facilities up and running: the first in St. Louis specializing in industrial tissue culture products, the second in the United Kingdom for pharmaceutical intermediates, and the third in Israel for immunochemicals. Meantime, in 1996, the company was fined $480,000 by the federal government for illegally exporting toxic substances that could be used to make chemical weapons; Sigma-Aldrich said that it had "inadvertently violated" U.S. export laws and that there was no evidence that the substances had actually been used to make such weapons.

Acquisitions returned to the fore in the late 1990s. In June 1997 the company purchased a 75 percent interest in Riedel-de Haën, a German maker of laboratory chemicals. In March 1999 Sigma-Aldrich purchased the remaining 25 percent. In December 1998 the company stepped up its presence in the biotechnology sector with the $39.5 million purchase of Texas-based Genosys Biotechnologies, Inc., one of the world's leading suppliers of custom synthetic DNA products, essential components of gene research.

RESTRUCTURING AND DIVESTMENT OF B-LINE

In spite of the company's acquisition drive, growth slowed to a trickle by 1998, when sales increased by just 6 percent and net income barely edged ahead, increasing by only 0.1 percent. During 1999, a year in which the company was proceeding in a similar direction, significant changes took place at Sigma-Aldrich. In October, Harvey was promoted to president and CEO, with Cori remaining chairman. One month later, Harvey announced that the company would launch a major restructuring and would sell its noncore B-Line Systems subsidiary.

Through the restructuring, Sigma-Aldrich was reorganized into four main business units: laboratory products, which focused on chemicals used for research conducted in academia and industry and which accounted for about 55 percent of the company's revenues; life sciences, which concentrated on specific areas of research, including molecular biology, immunochemistry, cell biology, and chromatography (20 percent of sales); fine chemicals, which was retooled to include both large-scale manufacturing of chemicals and custom manufacturing (15 percent of sales); and diagnostics, which focused on products used to help diagnose and treat diseases, with a particular emphasis on tests in the areas of coagulation and immunoassay (10 percent). Sigma-Aldrich also planned to drive growth through e-commerce, having successfully launched an award-winning web site in September 1998 through which 5 percent of U.S. orders were being placed by the end of 1999. With the completion in May 2000 of the sale of B-Line Systems to Cooper Industries, Inc., for $425 million, Sigma-Aldrich could, for the first time in its history, plan for the future as a company with a single focus, supplying chemicals for the life sciences and high-technology markets.

In the wake of the B-Line Systems divestiture, Sigma-Aldrich pursued sales gains in part by pursuing modest acquisitions. In 2000, for example, the company purchased ARK Scientific GmbH Biosystems, a German oligonucleotide producer; First Medical, Inc., a diagnostic immunoassay developer based in Mountain View, California; and Amelung GmbH, a German maker of coagulation instrumentation. In February 2001 Sigma-Aldrich spent $37.2 million for Isotec, Inc., of Miamisburg, Ohio, a producer of stable isotopes and isotopically labeled compounds used in life science research, medical diagnostics, and PET imaging applications. In a major investment in the future, Sigma-Aldrich in late 2001 opened a new $55 million research and development facility in St. Louis for its biotechnology unit (formerly the life sciences unit). In the meantime, Cori retired at the end of 2000 and Harvey added the chairmanship to his duties.

In the most significant development of 2002, Sigma-Aldrich announced plans to divest its poorly performing diagnostics division, which was generating only a little more than 6 percent of overall revenues. Completed by April 2003, the divestment left the company with three strong business units: scientific research, biotechnology, and fine chemicals. Each of these units had their own R&D, manufacturing, and sales operations. Late in 2002 Sigma-Aldrich agreed to pay a $1.76 million fine to the federal government for exporting without a license a biological chemical with weapons potential. The case involved Research Biochemicals, Inc., a firm Sigma-Aldrich had acquired in 1997.

INCREASING EMPHASIS ON FINE CHEMICALS

Since the restructuring launched in 1999, the fine chemicals unit had gained greater prominence. Seeking to change its image as simply a supplier of laboratory chemicals, Sigma-Aldrich moved aggressively to raise its profile in custom manufacturing. Toward this end, the company in 2004 completed two key acquisitions: Ultrafine, a leading supplier of contract chemical manufacturing services for drug development based in Manchester, England; and Madison, Wisconsin-based Tetrionics, a producer of high-potency cytotoxic (cell-killing) active pharmaceutical ingredients. To further heighten the profile of its fine chemicals unit, Sigma-Aldrich late in 2004 rebranded the business SAFC (standing for Sigma-Aldrich Fine Chemicals).

SAFC was boosted from a top-25 global position in fine chemicals into the top ten via the $366.8 million, February 2005 purchase of the JRH Biosciences division of the Australian firm CSL Limited, the largest acquisition in Sigma-Aldrich's history. Based in the Kansas City suburb of Lenexa, Kansas, JRH specialized in the production of cell cultures and serums used in the development and manufacturing of biopharmaceuticals. JRH's sales for 2004 totaled $150 million. The acquisition of JRH pushed SAFC's 2005 sales to $437 million, or approximately 26 percent of Sigma-Aldrich's total revenues of $1.67 billion.

The year 2005 was significant for several other developments. The acquisition of Proligo Group in April bolstered Sigma-Aldrich's position in research tools for the rapidly growing field of genomics. Boulder, Colorado-based Proligo, a firm with 2004 sales of $40 million that was acquired from Degussa AG, supplied custom DNA, custom RNA, and certain raw materials used in DNA and RNA synthesis. In another reorganization announced in July 2005, Sigma-Aldrich split its scientific research and biotechnology units into three units, each serving a distinct market segment: Research Essentials, responsible for high-volume sales of chemicals to pharmaceutical, academic, and research

clients; Research Specialties, offering thousands of products via print and online catalogs, primarily to individual scientists; and Research Biotech, developer of innovative products for life-science research. SAFC was unaffected by this reorganization into an overarching four-unit structure. Finally, at the end of the year, Harvey retired as CEO while remaining chairman. Taking over the management reins was Jai Nagarkatti, a 29-year company veteran who had worked his way up from chemist to president and COO, the latter position attained in August 2004.

LAUNCH OF NEW STRATEGIC PLAN IN 2006

Revenues grew steadily throughout the initial years of the 21st century, reaching a record $1.8 billion by 2006. The net income of $276.8 million for that year was another best-ever figure. During the year a new strategic plan was launched that, in addition to completing the reorganization announced the previous July, involved four other initiatives: expanding in the faster-growing markets of Canada, Latin America, and the Asia-Pacific region; strengthening the firm's e-commerce channels; implementing process improvement actions to increase profitability; and propelling future growth via strategic and bolt-on acquisitions.

Among the moves made into markets outside the United States and Europe, Sigma-Aldrich in July 2006 opened a state-of-the-art pharmaceutical chemical laboratory in Bangalore, India. Earlier that year, the company bought its largest distributor in China, Beijing Superior Chemicals and Instruments Company, Ltd., and also established a wholly foreign owned enterprise in that nation, Sigma-Aldrich (Shanghai) Trading Co. Ltd. Sigma-Aldrich completed three other strategic acquisitions in 2006: the Iropharm unit of Honeywell International Inc., which operated a plant in Arklow, Ireland, where active pharmaceutical ingredients were produced; Pharmorphix Limited of Cambridge, England, a provider of research services to pharmaceutical and biotech customers; and Advanced Separation Technologies, Inc. (Astec), a Whippany, New Jersey, concern specializing in the development of chemicals used in separating and/or analyzing complex mixtures.

This acquisition spree continued in 2007 with the February purchase for $60 million of Epichem Group Limited, a British maker of chemicals for the semiconductor and solar panel industries that was integrated into SAFC. In line with its strategic plan, Sigma-Aldrich increasingly focused on markets outside the United States and Europe to help reach its goal of annual sales growth of 10 percent. In September 2007 the company announced plans to build a new multipurpose manufacturing and warehousing campus in Wuxi, China. On the Internet front, meantime, Sigma-Aldrich by the third quarter of 2007 had met another goal: increasing web-based ordering for its three research-based units to more than 40 percent of overall sales.

Updated, David E. Salamie

PRINCIPAL SUBSIDIARIES

Sigma-Aldrich Co.; Aldrich Chemical Company, Inc.; Sigma-Aldrich B.V. (Netherlands); Sigma-Aldrich Chemie GmbH (Germany); Proligo International GmbH (Germany); Sigma-Aldrich Chemie Verwaltungs GmbH (Germany); Sigma-Aldrich Grundsteucks Verwaltungs GmbH & Co. KG (Germany); Sigma-Aldrich Chimie S.N.C. (France); Supelco, Inc.; Advanced Separation Technologies, Inc.; Sigma-Aldrich Biotechnology Holding Co., Inc.; Sigma-Aldrich Research Biochemicals, Inc.; Sigma-Aldrich, Inc.; Sigma-Aldrich Finance Co.; Sigma-Aldrich Chemie GmbH (Switzerland); Sigma-Aldrich Production GmbH (Switzerland); Sigma-Aldrich N.V./S.A. (Belgium); Sigma-Aldrich Chemie B.V. (Netherlands); Sigma-Aldrich Italia S.r.l. (Italy); Sigma-Aldrich (Shanghai) Trading Co. Ltd. (China); Sigma-Aldrich Denmark A/S; Sigma-Aldrich Finland Oy; Sigma-Aldrich Norway AS; Sigma-Aldrich Sweden AB; Sigma-Aldrich Company, Ltd. (U.K.); SAFC Biosciences Limited (U.K.); Pharmorphix Limited (U.K.); Sigma-Aldrich Handels GmbH (Austria); Sigma-Aldrich spol.s.r.o. (Czech Republic); Sigma-Aldrich (O M) Ltd. (Greece); Sigma-Aldrich Kft (Hungary); Sigma-Aldrich Financial Services Limited (Ireland); Sigma-Aldrich Ireland Ltd.; Sigma-Aldrich Sp. z.o.o. (Poland); Sigma-Aldrich Quimica S.A. (Spain); Sigma-Aldrich de Argentina S.A.; Sigma-Aldrich Pty., Limited (Australia); Sigma-Aldrich Oceania Pty. Limited (Australia); Sigma-Aldrich New Zealand Ltd.; SAFC Biosciences Pty. Ltd. (Australia); Sigma-Aldrich Quimica Brasil Ltda. (Brazil); Sigma-Aldrich Canada Ltd.; Sigma-Aldrich Chemicals Private Ltd. (India); Sigma-Aldrich Japan KK; Sigma-Aldrich Korea Ltd.; Sigma-Aldrich Quimica S.A. de C.V. (Mexico); Sigma-Aldrich Pte. Ltd. (Singapore); Sigma-Aldrich (M) Sdn. Bhd. (Malaysia); Sigma-Aldrich Pty. Ltd. (South Africa); Silverberry Limited (Ireland); Shrawdine Limited (Ireland); Sigma-Aldrich Ireland Ltd.; SAFC, Inc.; SAFC Biosciences, Inc.

PRINCIPAL DIVISIONS

Research Essentials; Research Specialties; Research Biotech; SAFC.

PRINCIPAL COMPETITORS

Merck KGaA; General Electric Company; Evonik Degussa GmbH; BASF Aktiengesellschaft; Royal DSM N.V.; Applied Biosystems Group; Thermo Fisher Scientific, Inc.; Roche Holding Ltd.; Invitrogen Corporation; Tyco International Ltd.; Lonza Group Ltd.; Wako Chemicals USA, Inc.; VWR International Inc.; Millipore Corporation; Qiagen N.V.

FURTHER READING

Bader, Alfred, *Adventures of a Chemist Collector,* London: Weidenfeld and Nicolson, 1995, 288 p.

Boswell, Clay, "Sigma-Aldrich Expands SAFC," *Chemical Market Reporter,* January 24, 2005, pp. 2, 27.

————, "Sigma-Aldrich Set for Global Growth in Pharmaceuticals and Fine Chemicals," *Chemical Market Reporter,* August 3, 1998, p. 17.

————, "Sigma-Aldrich's New SAFC Aims for Top 10," *Chemical Market Reporter,* November 1, 2004, pp. 6, 8.

Byrne, Harlan S., "Sigma-Aldrich: The Right Chemistry for Strong Performance," *Barron's,* May 17, 1993, pp. 47–48.

Corey, Andrea, "Sigma-Aldrich Restructuring, Selling Metals Division," *St. Louis Business Journal,* February 21, 2000, p. 8.

————, "Web Site Eases Ordering for Sigma-Aldrich Clients," *St. Louis Business Journal,* February 14, 2000, p. 40.

Desloge, Rick, "Sigma-Aldrich Goes on Acquisition Spree," *St. Louis Business Journal,* October 13, 2006, pp. 1+.

Dwyer, Joe, III, "Sigma-Aldrich Using Catalog Blitz to Further Market Share," *St. Louis Business Journal,* March 12, 1990, p. 7A.

Flannery, William, "Sigma-Aldrich Meeting Erupts over Dispute," *St. Louis Post-Dispatch,* May 6, 1992, p. 1B.

Jarvis, Lisa, "SAFC Forges Ahead," *Chemical Market Reporter,* November 21/December 4, 2005, pp. 34–35.

————, "Sigma-Aldrich Division Plans $55 Million Research Facility," *Chemical Market Reporter,* July 10, 2000, p. 5.

Lerner, Matthew, "Sigma-Aldrich Strengthens Role As Pharma Supplier," *Chemical Market Reporter,* July 7, 1997, p. 14.

Manor, Robert, "Bad Bet?: Sigma-Aldrich Founder Bader Decries Dismissal," *St. Louis Post-Dispatch,* April 16, 1992, p. 1B.

McCoy, Michael, "Image Improvement at Sigma-Aldrich: Firm's Purchase of Ultrafine Is Part of Profile Raising in Custom Manufacturing," *Chemical and Engineering News,* May 31, 2004, p. 17.

Melcher, Rachel, "Sigma-Aldrich Buys British Chemical Maker," *St. Louis Post-Dispatch,* February 13, 2007, p. C2.

————, "Sigma-Aldrich Invests in Biotech," *St. Louis Post-Dispatch,* September 28, 2007, p. B4.

————, "Sigma-Aldrich Looks to Evolve with Plan," *St. Louis Post-Dispatch,* November 2, 2005, p. B1.

————, "Sigma-Aldrich Mixes Theory, Magic for Another Reconstruction," *St. Louis Post-Dispatch,* January 12, 2003, p. E1.

————, "Sigma-Aldrich Tries to Bolster Branding of Fine Chemicals," *St. Louis Post-Dispatch,* October 26, 2004, p. B1.

Mirasol, Feliza, "SAFC Speeds into New Year," *ICIS Chemical Business Americas,* January 29/February 4, 2007, pp. 32–34.

————, "Sigma-Aldrich Upgrades Fine Chemicals Operations," *Chemical Market Reporter,* May 17, 1999, p. 9.

Montgomery, Leland, "Betting on Biotech with Sigma-Aldrich," *Financial World,* June 11, 1991, pp. 21–22.

Moore, Samuel K., "Sigma-Aldrich Reorganizes Chemicals, Sells Metals Operation," *Chemical Week,* December 1, 1999, p. 16.

Mullin, Rick, "Sigma-Aldrich: Building a High-Tech Platform," *Chemical Week,* May 8, 2002, pp. 21–24.

————, "Sigma-Aldrich's New Five-Year Plan," *Chemical and Engineering News,* February 20, 2006, pp. 20–21.

Ouellette, Jennifer, "CFO Forum: Reorganization Key to Sigma-Aldrich Growth Strategy," *Chemical Market Reporter,* September 29, 2003, pp. 17–18.

Papanikolaw, Jim, "Sigma-Aldrich Sells Its B-Line Systems to Cooper Industries," *Chemical Market Reporter,* April 3, 2000, p. 3.

Rothenberg, Eric, "Consistent Chemistry," *Financial World,* August 9, 1988, p. 42.

Scott, Alex, "Sigma-Aldrich Acquires Custom Manufacturer," *Chemical Week,* June 30/July 7, 2004, p. 37.

"Sigma-Aldrich: A Little Company Carves a Big Niche," *Dun's Review,* September 1979, pp. 34+.

"Sigma-Aldrich Buys Proligo for RNA Technology," *Chemical Market Reporter,* February 21, 2005, p. 2.

Simon, Ruth, "Mail-Order Enzymes," *Forbes,* May 19, 1986, p. 46.

Stamborski, Al, "Sigma Announces It Will Sell Its Only Non-Life Sciences Business," *St. Louis Post-Dispatch,* March 28, 2000, p. C7.

Steyer, Robert, "Sigma Sees Sales Doubling in Five Years," *St. Louis Post-Dispatch,* May 2, 1990, p. 7B.

Thayer, Ann M., "Sigma-Aldrich: Back on Track," *Chemical and Engineering News,* October 8, 2001, pp. 17–19.

Van Arnum, Patricia, "Sigma-Aldrich Builds Its Position in the Life Sciences Arena," *Chemical Market Reporter,* June 19, 2000, p. 15.

Sole Technology Inc.

20161 Windrow Drive
Lake Forest, California 92630
U.S.A.
Telephone: (949) 460-2020
Toll Free: (877) 438-6437
Fax: (949) 460-2010
Web site: http://www.soletechnology.com

Private Company
Incorporated: 1996
Employees: 140
Sales: $200 million (2007 est.)
NAIC: 424340 Footwear Merchant Wholesalers;
315999 Other Apparel Accessories and Other Apparel Manufacturing

■■■

Sole Technology Inc. is a designer and marketer of footwear and apparel for skateboarding and snowboarding. The company primarily operates as a developer of footwear for the skateboarding market, selling its merchandise through a stable of brands: etnies, etnies Girl, etnies Plus, éS, and Emerica. For snowboarders, the company sells footwear under the brand name ThirtyTwo. Sole Technology's apparel is sold under the brand name Altamont Apparel. The company also operates the Sole Technology Institute Lab, the first skateboarding-oriented, biomechanical research facility in the world. Sole Technology's brands are sold in more than 70 countries. The company maintains regional offices in New York, China, the Netherlands, Switzerland, and the United Kingdom. Its footwear is manufactured in Asia.

ORIGINS

Growing up in the Paris suburb L'Hay-les-Roses, Pierre André Senizergues tried a variety of sports before discovering the activity that would lead to two successful careers. He tried judo, running, sailing, and windsurfing before, at age 15 in 1978, he tried skateboarding for the first time. "Skateboarding, wow," Senizergues remembered in a May 2006 interview with *Sole Collector,* "it captured my passion more than any other sport I've done before because I could do it anywhere I wanted. I didn't need a teacher. I could hang around with my friends and we could talk about it day and night."

Senizergues devoted nearly all his free time to his newfound passion. After school and on weekends, Senizergues could be found at a location near the Eiffel Tower honing his skateboarding skills with his peers. He excelled at the sport, growing more adept with each passing day, but eventually he was forced to change his priorities. Unemployment was soaring in France, convincing Senizergues that he needed to concentrate on finding a stable job. He attended Paris' Universitaire de Technology and earned a degree in industrial software in 1984, which he used to secure a job at IBM France. Senizergues began programming laser printers. His attempt at pursuing a conventional career lasted three months.

"I realized there was something going wrong because I was wearing a suit," Senizergues recalled in his

May 2006 interview with *Sole Collector*. "I was just thinking about skateboarding all the time." In 1985, once he had enough money for airfare, he headed to California, skateboarding's Mecca, and began riding in Venice Beach. Unlike in Paris, crowds gathered to watch Senizergues and other elite skateboarders showcase their talents. In the crowd one day was Steve Rocco, team manager for Sims Skateboards, who offered to sponsor Senizergues. The French phenomenon entered his first professional contest and won the event, beginning a professional career that would see him capture 12 French championships, five European championships, two World Cup events, and one World Championship.

Despite his obvious talent, Senizergues realized his career as a professional skateboarder could not extend too far into his 30s. A back injury in 1989 made manifest Senizergues' fears, hastening his exit from the professional ranks. His retirement as a professional skateboarder did not mark the end of involvement in the sport, however. Senizergues continued to make money from skateboarding, making the transition from athlete to businessman as the 1980s ended.

SENIZERGUES AND RAUTUREAU APPLE JOIN FORCES IN 1988

The path that led Senizergues to become a skateboard executive began in his home country. In 1986, a 200-year-old French shoe manufacturer, Rautureau Apple, partnered with a French skateboarder, Alain "Platoon" Montagnet, to launch a line of high-top, durable shoes for the European skate and surf markets. They christened the line "etnics," but they were unable to register the name because of its similarity to an existing shoe brand named "Etonics." To resolve the matter, the name of the shoes was changed to "etnies."

Senizergues was approached by Rautureau Apple in 1988, when he was offered a sponsorship deal to skateboard for the new brand of shoes. "I thought about

it for a little bit," Senizergues recalled in his interview with *Sole Collector*. "But then I got pretty interested because I knew they really wanted to make skate shoes … so I started riding for them and started designing shoes." Senizergues' first shoe was dubbed Senix, a name inspired by his surname. "I had no idea how important fashion was to a shoe," he said. "I only dealt with function, so the first one I designed was like a tank."

Senizergues' back injury and subsequent retirement as a professional followed one year after he signed with etnies, but his involvement with the brand continued. In 1989, he convinced Rautureau Apple's management that he could shepherd etnies' entry into the lucrative U.S. market, an offer he later characterized as an audacious boast. "I had no experience and knew nothing about how to run a business," he said in an August 2006 interview with the *Financial Times*. Senizergues signed a licensing agreement with Rautureau Apple—marking the beginnings of etnies U.S.A., the first skateboarding shoe distribution company owned and directed by a professional skateboarder—and set up shop in California. He used his savings and $250,000 in vendor financing to establish the distribution company, and quickly realized how brash his promise to Rautureau Apple had been.

YEARS OF STRUGGLE

When Senizergues took on the responsibilities of a distributor, he accepted a bigger challenge than he anticipated. The U.S. economy was slipping into a recession, exacerbating conditions in an already anemic skateboard market. Skate shops were closing and those retail locations that remained open generally were unwilling to take on new brands, particularly a little-known European brand. To make a difficult situation worse, Senizergues received his first shipment of shoes from Korea three months late, which led to 80 percent of the orders being canceled.

It was an inauspicious start for the etnies brand in the United States, but, surprisingly, Senizergues deepened his commitment to the brand's success after his first stumbling steps. In 1991, he hired a professional skateboarder he knew, Don Brown, to help with marketing, sales, and shipping and began advertising in U.S. magazines such as *TransWorld Skateboarding*. The following year, he signed a licensing deal with Rautureau Apple that gave him worldwide distribution rights to the etnies brand and the authorization to begin designing etnies shoes in the United States.

When Senizergues began to design shoes, his passion for skateboarding found full expression. Rather than merely distributing a product, Senizergues could

KEY DATES

1985: After moving to California, Pierre André Senizergues' professional skateboarding career begins.

1988: Senizergues begins riding professionally for the etnies brand, a line of footwear made by France-based Rautureau Apple.

1989: Senizergues signs a licensing agreement with Rautureau Apple, marking the beginning of etnies U.S.A.

1992: Senizergues acquires the worldwide distribution rights to the etnies brand, a deal that touches off vibrant growth for his company.

1995: Senizergues introduces new footwear lines, éS and ThirtyTwo.

1996: Sole Technology is formed to manage Senizergues' brands.

2003: Sole Technology opens Sole Technology Institute, a biomechanical research facility.

2006: Altamont Apparel is introduced as a new line of clothing.

create a product, tapping into his experience and knowledge about skateboarding to create shoes his peers desired. When he visited skate parks, he talked to skateboarders, asked for their input, and determined that his target audience wanted ankle-high, low-top shoe styles. He, along with Don Brown, bucked the industry trend of making high-top shoes and began designing what became the etnies Lo-Cut, part of a new line that also included Lo-Down, Senix Lo-Top, Rap, Intercity, and Mid-Top Screw.

COMMERCIAL SUCCESS

When the new line debuted in 1993, Senizergues' company began to flourish for the first time. The economy had improved, the retail market for skateboard equipment had improved, and the sport itself was experiencing a resurgence in popularity, all of which occurred at roughly the same time etnies unveiled its new line of shoes. After five years of posting lackluster financial results, the company began to grow robustly. Revenues reached $1 million in 1993 and proceeded to rise exponentially in the succeeding years, hitting $6 million in 1994 and climbing to $10 million in 1995.

As his business gathered momentum, Senizergues became more aggressive and more ambitious, making a

flurry of moves that led to the creation of Sole Technology. etnies U.S.A. restructured and changed its name to etnies America in 1994, one year before a European sales office was opened in Basel, Switzerland. The most notable event of 1995 occurred elsewhere, however, taking place at the company's headquarters in Lake Forest, California, where Senizergues launched new footwear brands. The éS line debuted, a brand geared for advanced skateboarders who demanded more technically sophisticated shoes than the etnies line. Senizergues, who formed a professional bicycle motocross, or BMX, team in 1995, added a third sport to his company's purview during the year by launching a line of snowboard footwear under the brand name ThirtyTwo.

FORMATION OF SOLE TECHNOLOGY: 1996

Diversification, in part, led to the creation of Sole Technology as the umbrella organization for Senizergues' brands, but the formation of the parent company also drew its impetus from events overseas. In 1995, Rautureau Apple was purchased by a European shoe conglomerate before being sold to a U.S. company. Senizergues, unsure about how his licensing agreement would be affected by the new ownership arrangement, formed Emerica in 1996 as a precautionary measure. Later in the year, Rautureau Apple put the etnies brand up for sale, which drew interest from several sporting goods companies, including industry behemoth Nike, Inc., but Senizergues swooped in and purchased the brand that represented his company's lifeblood, paying $1 million for the full rights to the etnies brand. Before the end of 1996, Senizergues formed Sole Technology to function as the parent company for the etnies, éS, Emerica, and ThirtyTwo brands, giving him the corporate entity to organize his existing holdings and to house his future creations.

Once Senizergues transformed his distribution agreement into a diversified, action-sport company, he never looked back. The decision to begin designing his own footwear proved to be the turning point in his business endeavors, touching off double-digit sales growth that continued into the 21st century. Senizergues delegated design responsibilities to professional shoes designers in 1997, freeing him to focus on brand growth. New product introductions during the late 1990s included failures and successes. The introduction of a low-price brand of footwear named Sheep was quickly discontinued; the addition of etnies Girl became a permanent addition to Sole Technology's family of brands. In 1999, when the company moved into a new headquarters facility in Lake Forest, production of its footwear was relocated from Korea to China.

As Sole Technology entered the 21st century, one of its greatest challenges was dealing with its own success. Commercial appeal was a dangerous attribute to exude for a company that catered to the desires of skateboarders, who preferred to think of themselves as iconoclastic individuals distinctly separate from the mainstream. By becoming successful, Sole Technology risked alienating the type of customer it depended upon heavily. "As soon as the core customer sees anyone on the street wearing the shoes, they stop wearing them," a skateshop owner remarked in a June 9, 1998, interview with *Footwear News*. "These kids want to be unique in appearance." Senizergues was confronted with the Catch-22 inherent in his market niche: The more successful a brand became, the greater the chances the brand's popularity would fade.

A FOCUS ON RESEARCH AND DEVELOPMENT

Senizergues faced a dilemma. He was able to sustain the appeal of Sole Technology's brands by remaining true to the ideals first expressed when he began designing shoes. Senizergues placed a premium on research and development, he became a sponsor of the sport at the local level, and he presented himself and his company as part of the grassroots development of skateboarding and its action-sport cousins: BMX, snowboarding, and surfing.

The promotion of skateboarding played a vital role in sustaining Sole Technology's esteem among its core customer base. The company sponsored numerous events and competitions, going as far as designing and partly financing the etnies Skatepark of Lake Forest in 2003, but its most distinctive efforts were demonstrated on the research and development front. Senizergues brought in a group of new product managers in 2000, adding a new upper tier of research and development executives. In 2003, the company's product development efforts became the focal point of its operations when Senizergues opened the Sole Technology Institute, the world's first research facility dedicated to studying the biomechanics of skateboarding. A 10,000-square-foot facility located in Lake Forest, the Sole Technology Institute was used as a proving ground for new technologies aimed at developing the most advanced, technical skateboarding footwear possible.

20TH ANNIVERSARY OF ETNIES BRAND

As the 20th anniversary of the etnies brand approached, Senizergues could look back on a gratifying record of progress. The brand's success had spawned éS, Emerica, ThirtyTwo, and etnies Girl, necessitating the creation of Sole Technology to oversee the growth of each brand. Sole Technology, in turn, had become one of the largest action-sport companies in the United States, its size and commercial success a testament to Senizergues' achievements. As the company expanded, Senizergues began to relinquish control and give his company the support a genuine corporation required. In 2004, he hired his first chief operating officer and he hired brand-marketing managers for each of Sole Technology's five major brands.

By the time the etnies brand turned 20 years old in 2006, there was much to celebrate. Sole Technology was selling its merchandise in more than 70 countries, collecting nearly $200 million in annual revenue. A line of clothing under the Altamont Apparel line was launched, and a massive, 315,000-square-foot distribution center was acquired.

Further progress was expected in the years ahead, as Senizergues paused to note his accomplishments and looked to the years ahead. "In the beginning, when I was designing the shoes, the only thing I was thinking was: How can I design a better skate shoe?" Senizergues explained in his May 2006 interview with *Sole Collector*. "When I got into this," he continued, "I was passionate about designing and I could only see as far as the shoes I was making. What we're trying to do here is not so much about the 20 years of etnies, but celebrating skateboarding for the last 20 years and making sure to realize that we're here to support skateboarding, period. And we're going to keep on supporting it for years to come."

Jeffrey L. Covell

PRINCIPAL SUBSIDIARIES

Sole Technology Institute.

PRINCIPAL COMPETITORS

Skechers U.S.A., Inc.; Nike, Inc.; DC Shoes, Inc.; Vans, Inc.

FURTHER READING

Adams, Melissa, "The Soleman," *OC Metro*, January 2006, p. 30.

Bellantonio, Jennifer, "French Skater Putting Sole in Lake Forest Shoe Maker," *Los Angeles Business Journal*, June 3, 2002, p. 9.

Foster, Lauren, "Sole Man Wins Board Approval," *Financial Times*, August 2006.

Herrera, Paul, "Sole Technology Buys Building in Fontana for Distribution Center," *Press-Enterprise*, May 10, 2006.

"Industry Insider: Etnies," *Sole Collector*, May 2006.

Melville, Greg, "Crossover Artists: While Aiming to Hit the Big Time, How Does a Skate-Shoe Company Keep Its Edge," *Footwear News*, June 8, 1998, p. 22.

Nguyen, Hang, "Sole Technology Steps into Europe," *Orange County Register*, January 12, 2007.

Tschorn, Adam, "Sole Tech Unveils Apparel Brand," *Daily News Record*, July 24, 2006, p. 56.

Special Olympics, Inc.

1133 19th Street, NW
Washington, D.C. 20036-3604
U.S.A.
Telephone: (202) 628-3630
Toll Free: (800) 700-8585
Fax: (202) 824-0200
Web site: http://www.specialolympics.org

Nonprofit Company
Incorporated: 1968
Employees: 160
Operating Revenues: $84.76 million (2006)
NAIC: 713990 All Other Amusement and Recreation Industries; 813990 Other Similar Organizations (Except Business, Professional, Labor, and Political Organizations)

■ ■ ■

Special Olympics, Inc., is an international organization dedicated to empowering individuals with intellectual disabilities to become physically fit, productive, and respected members of society through sports training and competition. It offers more than 1.4 million children and adults with intellectual disabilities year-round training and participation in a program of competitive sports events fashioned after the Olympic Games free of charge. Special Olympics is affiliated with the United States Olympic Committee and has been authorized to use the name "Olympics" since 1971 in recognition of the fact that the philosophy of Special Olympics is aligned with the Olympic ideal of sportsmanship and love of participation for its own sake. Special Olympics also runs programs that provide health screenings and healthcare to participants and that promote equality, skill building, and meaningful inclusion in their communities for people with intellectual challenges.

FOUNDING THE GAMES: 1955–68

On July 20, 1968, the First International Special Olympics Games took place at Soldier Field in Chicago, Illinois. Approximately 1,000 athletes with intellectual disabilities from throughout the United States and Canada competed in track and field events, swimming, and floor hockey. The games were the culmination of the work of Eunice Kennedy Shriver, the Chicago Park District, and the Kennedy Foundation to promote the social and emotional benefits of physical activity and competition for people with intellectual disabilities.

Shriver had been the director of the Joseph F. Kennedy, Jr., Foundation since 1957, the first charitable foundation devoted to the benefit of people with intellectual disabilities, and a firm believer that the "best investment for social good is in people and the unlimited possibilities of the human mind and spirit." In 1955, she had traveled around the United States talking to experts and visiting the institutions that then housed people with intellectual disabilities. She recalled of this experience in *Special Olympics: The First 25 Years,* "There was a complete lack of knowledge about their capacities. They were isolated because their families were embarrassed and the public was prejudiced."

In 1961, Shriver organized a summer day camp, Camp Shriver, for 35 children with intellectual disabilities in the Washington, D.C., area. Using the camp as a model, she recruited public and private organizations to create similar recreational programs in other communities. The camp became a yearly event for the Shrivers. By 1963, the Kennedy Foundation supported 11 similar camps, and more than 300 similar programs began between 1963 and 1968.

In 1965, the Chicago Park District piloted a program of activities and sports for people with intellectual disabilities with a grant from the Kennedy Foundation. The district later came up with the idea of expanding the pilot into a citywide competition. A second grant from the Kennedy Foundation and the American Alliance for Health, Physical Education and Recreation in 1968 funded the first Special Olympics in Chicago. "The Chicago Special Olympics prove a very fundamental fact," Shriver said at the opening ceremonies while an athlete ran down the track with the Special Olympics torch, "that exceptional children—children with mental retardation—can be exceptional athletes, the fact that through sports they can realize their potential for growth."

INCORPORATION, GROWTH, AND TRAINING: 1968–83

In December 1968, Senator Ted Kennedy announced the establishment of Special Olympics Inc. and presented checks for $10,000 to each of six cities that had plans to hold regional athletic competitions for people with intellectual disabilities. Rafer Johnson, a former Olympic gold medalist and longtime friend of the Kennedys, joined Shriver in raising funds for Special Olympics. With Johnson's help, the First Annual Western Regional Special Olympics took place in July 1969 in Los Angeles with athletes from Arizona,

California, Colorado, Hawaii, New Mexico, Nevada, and Utah. The Second International Olympic Summer Games took place the following year in Chicago with 2,000 athletes from all 50 states, the District of Columbia, Puerto Rico, and France. In France that same year, 500 special athletes also participated in the First French Special Olympics Games.

During the early 1970s, research began to show the positive effects for people with intellectual disabilities of exercise and physical skill building as well as the benefits of having something to strive for and excel in. The Kennedy Foundation sponsored "Choices on Our Conscience: The First International Symposium on Human Rights, Retardation and Research," where the scientific community pooled ideas and findings on programs for people with intellectual disabilities in 1971. As the decade wore on, Special Olympics gained momentum, adding competitive games worldwide. The games had corporate sponsors and the athletes wore uniforms. In 1977, Special Olympics Inc. introduced the First International Special Olympics Winter Games in Colorado. By 1979, the International Special Olympics Summer Games had become an every-four-year summer event and had grown to feature 3,500 athletes from 20 countries and to involve almost one million athletes worldwide through 17,000 local, area, chapter, and national events.

Starting in the 1980s, Special Olympics focused on upgrading the quality of its training methods for athletes and coaches. For the first games in 1968, instructions for a basic ten-minute warm-up workout for participants were handed out. After 1980, Special Olympics launched a training and certification program for coaches and published its first Sports Skills Guide. In 1983, Special Olympics International announced its official training program for athletes, a program that in 2001 would be the first to receive accredited status from the National Council for Accreditation of Coaching Education.

GAINING WORLDWIDE RECOGNITION: 1981–91

The Second, Third, and Fourth International Special Olympics Winter Games took place in 1981, 1985, and 1989 while the Sixth and Seventh International Special Olympics Summer Games were held in 1983 and 1987. The 1987 games drew 4,700 athletes from 73 countries. The Special Olympics name was growing in notoriety and recognition. The following year, 1988, the International Olympic Committee signed an agreement in which it officially recognized Special Olympics. Earlier, the United Nations had named 1986 the International Year of Special Olympics.

KEY DATES

1968: The First International Special Olympics Games takes place at Soldier Field in Chicago, Illinois; Senator Ted Kennedy announces the establishment of Special Olympics Inc.

1969: The First Annual Western Regional Special Olympics takes place in Los Angeles.

1970: The Second International Special Olympics Games takes place at Soldier Field in Chicago, Illinois.

1980: Special Olympics forms its Directorate of International Development.

1984: Sargent Shriver is elected president of Special Olympics by the board of directors.

1990: Sargent Shriver is appointed chairman of the board of Special Olympics.

1991: Special Olympics International Games changes its name to Special Olympics World Games.

1996: Timothy P. Shriver replaces his father as president of Special Olympics.

2004: President George W. Bush signs the Special Olympics Sport and Empowerment Act into law.

Organizational advances to spread the reach of Special Olympics as a movement also took place in the 1980s. In 1980, the Directorate of International Development formed; it helped set up programs in 90 nations in Europe, Africa, Latin America, and the Far East by the end of the decade. Special Olympics Unified Sports debuted in 1988 to provide another level of challenge for higher-ability athletes and to promote equality, skill building, and meaningful inclusion in their communities and outside of Special Olympics for people with intellectual challenges. Teams of approximately equal numbers of Special Olympics athletes and athletes without intellectual disabilities trained and competed together on sports teams. Unified Sports programs were often initiated by community partners, including parks and recreation departments, schools, Boys and Girls Clubs of America, and community sports organizations.

Special Olympics International Games became Special Olympics World Games in 1991, a year after Sargent Shriver, Eunice Kennedy Shriver's husband, took the helm as president of the organization. Shriver was the former director of the Peace Corps and the Of-

fice for Economic Development. A record 5,700 athletes from 104 countries competed at the Eighth Summer Games in 1991. Several new and expanded events were added, and for the first time, special athletes competed alongside regular athletes in the Unified Sports events of basketball, bowling, soccer, softball, team handball, and volleyball.

REACHING MILESTONES: 1992–99

By mid-decade, Special Olympics was the largest amateur sports organization in the world. It had programs operating in 120 countries and in all 50 states. About half a million children and adults with intellectual disabilities took part in its 23 sports. There were more than 25,000 trained and certified Special Olympics coaches in the United States. Each sport had its own Sports Skills Guide that demonstrated learning progressions for teaching that sport by skill and by subtask to aid mastery by people with intellectual disabilities.

Special Olympics gained much media exposure during the 1990s as it celebrated three important milestones. The decade opened in 1992 with a celebration to kick off the 25th anniversary of Special Olympics at the United Nations in New York City. Throughout the next 14 months, a tour van containing a multimedia exhibit about Special Olympics made stops in 70 cities around the United States. In 1993, the fifth Special Olympics World Summer Games took place for the first time outside the United States as 60 nations sent 1,550 athletes to compete in 22 sports in Austria. The decade came to a close in 1999 with a celebration of the 30th anniversary of Special Olympics at the White House.

NEW DIRECTIONS FOR A NEW CENTURY: 1999–2000

Under the leadership of Timothy P. Shriver, Eunice and Sargent Shriver's son, Special Olympics launched its most ambitious growth agenda ever. Tim Shriver had assumed the presidency of the organization in 1996 and later became its chairman in 2003 when Sargent Shriver retired from this position. Tim Shriver's goal was to build Special Olympics into an international movement. Shriver had a background as a leading educator and had worked in substance abuse, violence, dropout, and teen pregnancy prevention. He created the New Haven Public Schools' Social Development Project and cofounded the Collaborative for Academic, Social, and Emotional Learning (CASEL), the leading research organization in the United States in the field of social and emotional learning.

Shriver helped initiate the Healthy Athletes program, providing health screenings for athletes worldwide and educating professionals about the health needs of persons with intellectual disabilities. He sought corporate sponsorship for Special Olympics World Summer Games in 1999 and was successful in recruiting corporations, individuals, and local, state, and federal governments to donate approximately $38 million. For only the second time in its history, the games made a profit; this time, the profit totaled $2.5 million. The games hosted a record 7,000 athletes from 150 countries, joined by about 57,000 volunteers, coaches, and family members. About 400,000 people were in attendance. As the organization grew, so did its revenue. Special Olympics' gross revenue increased almost 500 percent from 1991 to 2001, while its fund-raising income increased by almost 800 percent. The 2001 World Winter Games in Anchorage, Alaska, drew about 2,500 athletes and raised $17 million.

Recognizing that the games had reached their feasible upper limit in size, Special Olympics leadership began in 2000 to focus on growing Special Olympics regional games set in six locations around the world, thereby giving the one million athletes who participated in these a higher profile. As part of this goal, Special Olympics joined the General Association of International Sports Federations to expand its reach globally and to work cooperatively with other sports organizations. The move was part of an internal reorganization aimed at doubling the number of athletes participating worldwide by 2005; increasing the capabilities of regional staff (including moving athletes into positions of responsibility); creating Special Olympics University for dissemination of training and technical assistance; and increasing the organization's commitment to professional development.

GLOBAL OUTREACH: 2000–01

The first year of the 21st century also marked Special Olympics China Millennium March, with Arnold Schwarzenegger and Special Olympics athletes lighting the Special Olympics torch, called the Flame of Hope, at the Great Wall, followed by gala events in Beijing, Shanghai, and Shenzhen. Also during 2000, the first Global Athlete Congress took place in The Hague with 60 athletes from throughout the world discussing the future of the Special Olympics movement.

Worldwide, Special Olympics staff and volunteers kept spreading the organization's message of inclusion and possibility for people with intellectual disabilities. In 2001, Special Olympics presented a *Special Report on the Health Status and Needs of Individuals with Mental Retardation* to the Senate Committee on Appropriation.

It also commissioned a two-year study about how people around the world viewed the roles and capabilities of people with intellectual disabilities in the workplace, the classroom, and in daily social life; the *Multinational Study of Attitudes Toward Individuals with Intellectual Disabilities* was completed in 2003. In addition, Special Olympics began a major African campaign to reach 100,000 special athletes in Africa by 2005. In 2002, it partnered with Universal Studios and with the Nelson Mandela Children's Fund to host special events to promote its message. In 2003, the World Summer Games took place for the first time outside the United States in Dublin, Ireland.

The inaugural Global Youth Summit, held during the World Winter Games in Anchorage in 2001, was another of the organization's initiatives to increase community involvement in Special Olympics and to spread the word about the capabilities of people with intellectual disabilities. Thirty-four students with and without intellectual disabilities worked in pairs to report on the games. By 2007, 60 Summit participants, ranging in age from 12 to 18, worked with their peers around the world to share the Special Olympics message of inclusion and acceptance through televised forums, webinars, blogs, podcasts, and stories published on web sites and in hometown newspapers. Also in 2001, Unified Reading Teams read and discussed Maria Shriver's book *What's Wrong with Timmy?* in an effort to educate elementary school students about what it means to have a disability.

CONTINUING THE DRIVE FOR ACCEPTANCE: 2002–07

A major step forward toward acceptance occurred in 2004 when President George W. Bush signed the Special Olympics Sport and Empowerment Act into law after it passed both the House of Representatives and the Senate unanimously. This act provided ongoing financial support for Special Olympics. Meanwhile, global growth continued through 2006 and 2007 with a series of groundbreaking regional competitions in places such as El Salvador, Italy, India, and the United Arab Emirates.

Timothy Shriver joined Eunice Kennedy Shriver in receiving the Surgeon General's Medallion, for "exemplary service above and beyond the call of duty for making a difference in the lives of our fellow citizens" in 2006. Eunice Shriver had received the medallion in 2001 for "being a leader in the worldwide struggle to enhance the life of individuals with intellectual disabilities." Surgeon General Richard H. Carmona noted the strides that Special Olympics had made in leveling the playing field for people with intellectual disabilities, saying in 2006, "The accomplishments speak for themselves as far as all the good Special Olympics has done in the United States and around the world."

A year later, 7,500 special athletes attended the 2007 Special Olympics World Summer Games in Shanghai, China, comprising the most accomplished of the 2.5 million athletes who competed in 165 countries to get to the games. They were living proof of the fact that Special Olympics is about people who are challenged and who overcome their disabilities.

Carrie Rothburd

FURTHER READING

Bueno, Ana, *Special Olympics: The First 25 Years,* San Francisco: Foghorn Press, 1994.

Hatch, Adam, "Special Olympics Helps Backers Sell Their Brands," *Herald-Sun,* April 20, 1999, p. A1.

Spee-Dee Delivery Service, Inc.

———————————————— ■ ————————————————

P.O. Box 1417
St. Cloud, Minnesota 56302-1417
U.S.A.
Telephone: (320) 251-6697
Toll Free: (800) 862-5578
Fax: (320) 251-1846
Web site: http://www.speedeedelivery.com

Private Company
Founded: 1978
Employees: 1,400
Sales: $67.4 million (2006 est.)
NAIC: 484121 General Freight Trucking, Long-Distance, Truckload

■ ■ ■

Established as a small, family-operated business in the late 1970s, Spee-Dee Delivery Service, Inc., has gradually radiated outward from its central Minnesota home base of St. Cloud. Still headed by founder Donald Weeres, Spee-Dee wins over customers from larger delivery companies by offering a combination of dependable service and low prices. Spee-Dee walk-in counter locations are situated in Minnesota, Wisconsin, Iowa, North and South Dakota, Nebraska, and Illinois. The company also offers on-call pickup service in the upper Midwest.

EVERYONE CHIPS IN DURING EARLY YEARS: 1978–87

In 1978 husband and wife team Don and Sylvia Weeres established an on-call courier service. Don, in his Chevy truck, carried his first package to Hutchinson, Minnesota, roughly 50 miles away, charging 88 cents for the trip, the *St. Cloud Times* recounted. As with many start-ups, life was less than glamorous. The couple operated out of a garage. Sylvia handled the administrative side of the business and also held down a job at Anderson Trucking Inc. The couple's three young daughters would start chipping in as well, sorting packages and washing trucks.

"The girls would walk over to the business from school because they were too young to stay home alone," Don Weeres recalled in the *St. Cloud Times*. Raised on a farm in Richmond, Minnesota, he most likely had also become acquainted with the ins and outs of a family business venture early in life.

By finding a niche, carrying packages deemed too heavy by the United States Postal Service or other private companies, the small enterprise began turning a profit in the third year. The overnight delivery service accepted packages weighing up to 100 pounds. The company's cause was further aided by a group of loyal employees.

TWO MILLION PACKAGES AND COUNTING IN SECOND DECADE

In 1988, Spee-Dee Delivery's 166 employees and 107 vehicles handled nearly two million packages a year. Sales had reached $4.6 million. The company also moved to a new location during its tenth anniversary year.

The kickoff of a state lottery in 1990 yielded a new source of revenue for Minnesota and for Spee-Dee

Delivery. Located roughly 80 miles northwest of the capital city of St. Paul, the company won the lottery's courier-service contract valued at about $500,000 a year. Spee-Dee's drivers would deliver instant tickets and game related materials throughout the state to participating vendors, the *Star Tribune* reported.

The growing company doubled the size of its facility in 1992. By the approach of the mid-decade, Spee-Dee was well established as a $20 million regional carrier. The Minnesota-based company served all of neighboring Wisconsin as well as parts of North Dakota and South Dakota. "Most of our expansion over the years has been customer-driven," Spee-Dee Sales Manager Craig Heurung noted in a March 1994 *Catalog Age* article.

Pricing was a draw for a big in-state customer. Re-uel Nygaard, vice-president of operations for Fingerhut, told *Catalog Age,* "We ship virtually all our Minnesota-destined packages through Spee-Dee; it really fulfills the same way UPS will—only at a lower rate."

Another, albeit smaller, cataloger, called on the carrier for other reasons. "When you talk to people at Spee-Dee to get a trace, they take immediate responsibility and get back to you. You're talking to real people instead of a corporation," Patterson Dental's customer service manager, John Schilling, told *Catalog Age.*

Depending solely on land delivery and funneling all packages through its St. Cloud hub, the company charged up to 33 percent less for comparable UPS residential delivery and up to 17 percent less for commercial delivery. *Catalog Age* also found customers lauded Spee-Dee's overnight delivery as having "fewer restrictions and fewer extra charges than UPS ground service imposes."

Spee-Dee Delivery's rate structure, though, differed from that of UPS. The regional carrier's commercial and residential customers paid the same price, but prices varied among its three designated rate zones. The commercial sector constituted 85 to 90 percent of business.

Keeping an eye on its competition, Spee-Dee tracked UPS rate hikes and typically raised its own fees in response. However, the smaller player always maintained its price edge. Price increases in 1994 were as much as 4.5 percent for UPS, while Spee-Dee's bumped up 2.2 percent, according to *Catalog Age.*

OPPORTUNITY KNOCKS AS DECADE WINDS DOWN

A 15-day UPS strike in 1997 produced dilemmas for U.S. businesses. Yet the absence of the ubiquitous brown trucks created corresponding opportunities for smaller operations, such as Spee-Dee Delivery.

Joyce Evans wrote for the *Milwaukee Journal Sentinel* in August: "An entrepreneur could buy a company truck and designate an employee to do the job, or he could hire a private, cross-country hauler. These thoughts ran through my mind the other day when I saw a white van marked 'Spee-Dee Delivery' blocking our driveway. I had never seen that service before. I noticed that the van was crammed full of packages, and I watched the driver jump out to drop off several in our buildings."

Spee-Dee Delivery also benefited from an industrial development boom in St. Cloud. Manufacturing had risen nearly 30 percent in central Minnesota during the 1990s, versus a fall of 9 percent on a national basis.

The city's central location, favorable land prices, a willing workforce, as well as governmental financial incentives, added up to a winning combination for snagging expanding businesses, according to the *St. Cloud Times.* Spee-Dee Delivery itself occupied space in one of the industrial parks in the greater St. Cloud area. Growing with the region, the company topped its office section with a third floor during 1999.

SERIOUS TIMES IN THE NEW MILLENNIUM

Life turned upside down on September 11, 2001, with the terrorist attacks on the United States and acute concerns regarding national safety. Routine deliveries faced inspection, as the nation operated under "high alert."

"At the Duluth International Airport, a sentry stopped vehicles entering the base of the 148th Fighter Wing. A sign near his post indicated a '100% ID check in progress.' Trucks from United Parcel Service and Spee-Dee Delivery Service were allowed through. Later,

KEY DATES

1978: Donald Weeres establishes a central Minnesota package delivery business.
1990: Spee-Dee earns Minnesota state lottery delivery contract.
1992: Company doubles its facility size.
1997: United Parcel Service (UPS) strike raises profile of smaller carriers, including Spee-Dee Delivery.
2001: Sales approach $60 million mark.
2003: Drivers deliver nearly 70,000 packages per day.
2007: Weeres sets financial goal of $100 million in sales.

concrete barricades were put up to block traffic on the road leading to the base," the *Duluth News Tribune* reported. The Coast Guard at the port of Duluth on Lake Superior and the border patrol in Grand Forks, North Dakota, also heightened security measures.

Fear was pervasive in the days and months following the attacks, infiltrating every aspect of life. Citizen soldiers would be called on to fight the "war on terror." In addition, for the next few years, the $59 million delivery operation, and businesses across the nation, would face homeland economic concerns, as well as those of security.

Some normalcy emerged over time. In 2003, Don Weeres received the St. Cloud Area Entrepreneurial Success Award. Each year the St. Cloud Area Chamber of Commerce recognized a major local business "grown out of a small enterprise," the *St. Cloud Times* explained. Spee-Dee delivered almost 70,000 packages per day. Employees numbered 1,100. Its 886 vehicles logged 38.5 million miles a year.

Sylvia Weeres, meanwhile, had broadened her reach as well. She sat on the board of the Minnesota Trucking Association and engaged in the philanthropic efforts of the organization.

Other issues loomed for the trucking industry, however. Spee-Dee had eliminated its index-based fuel surcharge in early January 2004. The hiatus was short-lived. Driven by diesel fuel prices, the company had to again ask customers to share the pain and added back the surcharge in November.

The delivery operation also faced problems inherent to traffic gridlock, as more than 100 Spee-Dee trucks

navigated the Twin Cities metropolitan area each day. "Congestion is worse and safety has gone down in the metro area," Don Weeres told the *St. Cloud Times.* "We can keep adding lanes to the freeway, but we'll always be behind." A funding stalemate among state lawmakers, and a federal treasury strained by the wars in Iraq and Afghanistan, exacerbated Minnesota's transportation infrastructure woes.

In 2007, the metro area traffic situation worsened when a major bridge collapsed into the Mississippi River. The disaster, which claimed 13 lives and also left more than 100 motorists injured, brought national and international attention to the problem of overburdened, if not crumbling, infrastructure.

MEASURING SUCCESS: 2005–07

On the employee front, the Teamsters Union endeavored in 2005 to organize about 150 Spee-Dee Delivery drivers, according to the *St. Cloud Times.* Organizing efforts over the prior decade had been defeated. Delivery truck drivers in central Minnesota earned a median hourly wage nearly $2.50 an hour lower than their counterparts in the Twin Cities. Yet at close to $12 per hour, they brought home more than some drivers in North Dakota, Wisconsin, and other parts of Minnesota.

Don and Sylvia Weeres' co-creation provided jobs for 1,400 people and served six states by 2007. The couple, no longer saddled with working seven days a week, 12 to 16 hours a day, could step back and recognize their accomplishment.

"The business wouldn't have existed if it wasn't both of us doing it," Don Weeres told the *St. Cloud Times* in February 2007. Sylvia Weeres concurred, with a caveat explained by *Times* writer Amy Trang, "She also jokes that the sliding door between her office and Don's is there for the times when they disagree."

The operation they built included the 160,000-square-foot St. Cloud facility along with 30 additional sites in the Upper Midwest. The number of packages processed each day had climbed to 75,000.

Self described as "not an IT person," according to the *St. Cloud Times,* Don Weeres stopped delivering packages himself when the company moved to computer-assisted delivery. However, Weeres clearly recognized IT's importance to the business: technology was Spee-Dee's largest investment at mid-decade.

Weeres told Dawn Peake, "Customers use it all the time. It's almost to the point that the proof of delivery is as important as the package itself, and the competition has all the technology so we don't have as much of a choice." A Global Positioning System (GPS) was also on the horizon for Spee-Dee Delivery, allowing customers real-time tracking of trucks.

One thing Weeres said was not yet part of the picture was a change of ownership. Despite opportunities to sell, Weeres declined offers, citing his commitment to employees as one reason. As part of an effort to retain employees, the company maintained a combination 401(k) plan and stock ownership plan allowing for purchase of shares. Spee-Dee Delivery also endeavored to promote from within.

As for the future, Weeres told the *St. Cloud Times:* "Spee-Dee is not a $100 million company, and that is a goal I have. That's probably the only financial one we've had. The rest have been service on the map."

Kathleen Peippo

PRINCIPAL COMPETITORS

United Parcel Service, Inc.

FURTHER READING

Bakst, Brian, "Competing Bridge Collapse Inquiries Feed Political Tensions," *Duluth News Tribune,* December 22, 2007, p. D8.

"Chamber Rewards Owner of Spee-Dee Delivery," *St. Cloud Times,* April 5, 2003, p. 6A.

Evans, Joyce, "Difficult Times Call for Creativity," *Milwaukee Journal Sentinel,* August 23, 1997, p. 1.

Halena, Sue, "St. Cloud Ripe for Industrial Development," *St. Cloud Times,* October 24, 1999, pp. 1A, 6A–7A.

———, "Teamsters Try to Organize Spee-Dee Drivers," *St. Cloud Times,* January 20, 2005, p. 4A.

Peake, Dawn, "A Delivery Domain," *St. Cloud Times,* April 1, 2007, pp. 18F–21F.

Schumacher, Lawrence, "Business Groups Shift Support to Tax for Roads," *St. Cloud Times,* December 20, 2004, pp. 1A, 5A.

"Security Tightened Throughout Twin Ports," *Duluth News Tribune,* September 12, 2001, p. 2A.

"Spee-Dee Delivery in Midwest," *Catalog Age,* March 1994, p. 10.

Trang, Amy, "'Co-preneurs' Are Teams in Work, Life," *St. Cloud Times,* February 13, 2007, p. 1A.

Whereatt, Robert, "Some Retailers Won't Bet on Lottery," *Star Tribune: Newspaper of the Twin Cities,* March 10, 1990, p. 3B.

The Standard Register Company

600 Albany Street
Dayton, Ohio 45401
U.S.A.
Telephone: (937) 221-1000
Toll Free: (800) 755-6405
Fax: (937) 221-1855
Web site: http://www.standardregister.com

Public Company
Incorporated: 1912
Employees: 3,500
Sales: $894.9 million (2006)
Stock Exchanges: New York
Ticker Symbol: SR
NAIC: 323116 Manifold Business Forms Printing; 541990 All Other Professional, Scientific, and Technical Services; 561431 Other Business Service Centers (Including Copy Shops)

■ ■ ■

The Standard Register Company is one of the leading providers of customized business forms for print and electronic formats, serving more than 14,000 middle- to large-sized manufacturing, financial, and healthcare corporations. Standard Register's primary business involves document design, printing, and warehousing and distribution. Services include document migration from print to digital formats, and conversion of documents at newly acquired companies or newly opened branch locations. Document-related products include papers and inks for document security and fraud prevention. Standard Register offers consultations on the development of efficient workflow processes that determine document design.

Standard Register's Print-on-Demand (POD) Services involve traditional document printing services, but employ new technologies for flexibility and efficiency. These services are provided through four regional facilities, where offset, long-run orders are handled, and at 21 STANFAST Print Centers, for digital, short-run document printing and everyday photocopying. All 25 POD locations provide warehousing, fulfillment, and distribution services, and the company's proprietary Smartworks enterprise document services platform provides customers with online access to inventory information for document supply management. POD Services include a variety of marketing solutions, such as software for marketing collateral materials development and flexible printing options for customized communications materials.

Standard Register's labeling operations involve identification and bar-code labels for document management, inventory control, hospital patient wristbands, equipment registration, and other materials tracking requirements. Instructional, product warning, and vehicle stickers are just a few of the labels produced with special environmental conditions in mind. Standard Register's label manufacturing operations are located at seven regional facilities, all located east of the Mississippi River, and one facility in Monterrey, Mexico.

FOUNDER'S INNOVATIVE DEVICE

Standard Register was founded upon an invention of Theodore Schirmer. It was a fairly simple, yet revolutionary adaptation of the autographic register, which had been devised in 1883 by James C. Shoup. Shoup's machine featured two separate rolls of paper—one printed with lines, the other blank—interlayered with carbon paper. When a user wrote on the top document, for example, a sales receipt, the machine made a copy for record-keeping. The user turned a crank, thereby propelling the finished set of handwritten records out of the machine and advancing a fresh set to the frame. Although a significant advance over the alternative, writing out copies in longhand, the autographic register's primary drawback was that the layers of carbon and forms often slipped, becoming misaligned.

Schirmer applied the concept of the chain and sprocket to the autographic register. His "standard register" featured a wooden cylinder with sprocket wheels at either end. The pins corresponded to holes punched down the margins of a continuous roll of paper. His idea earned a patent, but Schirmer could not attract enough start-up capital to begin production. In a last-ditch effort to get his idea off the ground, he contacted John Q. Sherman's real estate brokerage in the hope that Sherman would lend him the necessary funds.

After initially rejecting the idea, Sherman asked Schirmer to build a prototype. Together they refined the machine so that it would produce up to eight copies of a document at a single writing. Keeping the multiple documents aligned allowed all the layers of paper to be preprinted with lines, check blocks, and other organizational formats, thereby vastly increasing their utility.

Convinced that the idea was feasible, John Sherman liquidated his real estate firm and called on business associates, including his brother William C. (W. C.) Sherman, to contribute the necessary start-up capital. Standard Register was incorporated in 1912 with Thomas Schirmer as president and John Sherman as a director. They founded the business in rented space with some machining equipment and two printing presses bought on credit. Sherman traveled to the West Coast to set up sales operations there.

EARLY STRUGGLES AND SUCCESS

Although the fledgling company's second floor office saved it from the Great Dayton Flood of 1913, the firm nearly went under in a flood of debt and backlogged orders. With Standard Register slipping into receivership, W. C. Sherman began to take an active role in its management. He summoned John back from California, and together they devised a plan to save the business. They borrowed against their own life insurance policies in order to raise enough money to buy out Standard Register's primary investors, including Thomas Schirmer. John assumed the duties of the office of president, and William became vice-president and treasurer. In order to fill past-due orders and revive cash flow, the brothers borrowed to create their own power source, doubled production, and freed the company from receivership within seven months.

Standard Register had entered a market dominated by Moore Corporation, the Canadian company that had founded the business forms industry in the 1880s. Moore and other well-entrenched competitors derided Standard Register's documents as "mutilated," "ventilated," and even "smallpox" forms. Nevertheless, Standard Register's innovative machines and documents gained a following. By 1916, the company had generated enough capital to erect a purpose-built factory.

In the early 1930s, it occurred to John Sherman to apply the pin-feed concept to machine-written documents in order to speed up the process with continuous forms. He designed a cylindrical rubber platen equipped with sprockets at either end that could replace the friction feeder in virtually any business machine. Called a "registrator platen," the invention helped broaden the potential market for Standard Register's specialized forms.

In spite of the Great Depression, Standard Register's annual sales reached about $1 million in 1933 and quintupled to over $5 million by 1938. This rapid growth was fueled in part by international licensing agreements. The company authorized R. L. Crain Limited, a Canadian firm, to produce its patented forms in 1934, and affiliated with W.H. Smith & Son (Alacra) Ltd. in England a year later. William Sherman succeeded his brother John as president upon the latter's death in 1939.

KEY DATES

1912: Founder Theodore Schirmer finds an investor to produce autographic registers with Schirmer's innovations.

1916: Standard Register builds its first factory dedicated to the manufacture of autographic registers.

1932: The invention of the register platen expands the company's product offering to specialized forms.

1940: Standard Register launches the Paperwork Simplification program, initiating custom-designed forms for more efficient record-keeping.

1956: Rapid domestic and international growth leads the company to go public.

1972: As widespread computerization increases demand for business forms, sales reach $1.4 billion.

1983: The first STANFAST Print-on-Demand service center opens.

1995: Standard Register launches Smartworks software for transferring document management to the local computer environment.

1997: Standard Register acquires UARCO, a chief documents management competitor, for $245 million.

2000: SMARTworks.com facilitates Standard Register's shift to online business forms processing.

2001: Standard Register initiates a major restructuring that dramatically streamlines operations as print documents migrate to electronic format.

EXPANSION OF CUSTOMIZED BUSINESS FORMS, POSTWAR GROWTH

At the outset of the United States' entry into World War II, Standard Register was stunned to learn that it had been pronounced "nonessential" by the federal government and was slated to be shut down for the duration of the war. However, the government and the military soon discovered that the business forms that Standard Register provided were vital to many operations. In fact, an arsenal actually shut down because of a lack of forms and documents. Standard Register wound up winning awards for its efforts on the home front.

Standard Register's Paperwork Simplification program intended to save paper by producing customized business forms. Launched in 1940, the program facilitated the creation of more efficient record-keeping systems, and it comprised an industry innovation that furthered the company's growth. Moreover, Paperwork Simplification was a harbinger of the evolution of the business forms industry from strictly manufacturing and marketing forms to selling custom-made information gathering and retrieval systems. It became vital to Standard Register's continued success in the postwar era, particularly at the advent of the computer age, when threats to paper business forms compelled the transformation of the industry.

William Sherman served as Standard Register's president until his death in 1944. At that time Milferd A. Spayd, who had joined the company in 1933, advanced to Standard Register's presidency. His ascension coincided with a period of rapid growth for the business forms industry overall and Standard Register in particular.

During the 1950s, Standard Register added factories in Pennsylvania, California, and Arkansas; licensed new overseas affiliates in Cuba, Venezuela, and Sweden; and created distributorships in Peru, Nicaragua, Guatemala, and Haiti. Sales volume nearly quadrupled, from $11.4 million in 1946 to over $43 million in 1956. The company went public in 1956, but the Sherman family (and by marriage, the Clarks) continued to hold a controlling stake in the company through the early 1990s.

Automation drove the business forms industry's growth in the 1960s. The boom in computers and optical scanners helped make business forms one of the fastest-growing industries in the United States, expanding at twice the rate of the gross national product, from $530 million in 1962 to $1.4 billion in 1972. Standard Register's sales more than quadrupled, from $24.4 million to $107.9 million, during that same period. By 1966, the company had added international affiliates in Australia, Brazil, Finland, France, Ireland, Japan, and South Africa. On the domestic front, new factories in Pennsylvania and Vermont added production capacity and increased distribution flexibility. Under the direction of President Kenneth P. Morse beginning in 1966, the Paperwork Simplification Program evolved into a forms management program that not only helped clients slim their record-keeping systems, but also helped manage clients' inventory of forms. David Henwood of Prescott, Ball & Turben (Cleveland) would later call Standard Register's forms management program "the Cadillac of the industry."

ADAPTING TO MATURING BUSINESS FORMS INDUSTRY

The business forms business started to show signs of maturity in the 1970s, when its annual growth rate slowed from double-digit percentages to 9 percent and down to 4 percent by the early 1980s. After having solidly held the number two spot in the industry for decades, Standard Register slipped to number three in 1973, when rival UARCO Inc. slid past it. Under the leadership of D. F. Whitehead during the 1970s, Standard Register refocused its customer base from the large, but cyclical companies it had traditionally targeted (automotive, steel, and tire companies) to more stable markets, including the financial, healthcare, direct-mail, and service industries. Revenues from healthcare clients increased from $5 million in 1970 to more than $60 million by 1982. Printing personalized letters and contest forms for the rapidly growing direct-mail segment multiplied from $1 million in 1970 to $32 million by 1982. Serving these new target markets helped Standard Register regain the number two standing in the business forms industry, as its annual sales nearly tripled from $107 million in 1972 to $319.6 million in 1981.

Standard Register adjusted to changes in its industry by diversifying into compatible businesses. In 1975, Standard Register acquired Universal Tape and Label. This entry into the labels business coincided with increasing adaptation of bar-code labeling, and the company took advantage of those opportunities by offering bar-code technology. The company opened its first STANFAST Print-on-Demand center in Dayton, providing customers with a variety of printing services using the new, relatively compact, computerized copying and printing machines for short-run printing. The entry into on-demand, short-run printing services anticipated changes wrought by digital imaging technology, particularly as many companies implemented flexible, just-in-time inventory controls to reduce warehousing expense.

ADAPTIVE STRATEGY DURING RECESSIONARY TIMES

Its emphasis on service enabled Standard Register to maintain profit margins in spite of an early 1980s recession that shaved competitors' profits. In fact, from 1981 to 1985, the company's profits doubled from $15.4 million to $31.8 million, while revenues only increased by about 27.5 percent, from $319.6 million to $441.05 million. That trend reversed in the latter years of the decade, however, as Standard Register's sales increased by over 60 percent to $708.9 million, while its net income grew at less than half that rate to $40.4 million

by 1989. The recessionary period of the late 1980s and early 1990s took its toll on the forms industry, which found itself burdened with overcapacity, rising paper prices, weakening demand, and intensifying competition. When its profits were nearly halved from 1989 to $21.8 million in 1990, Standard Register was forced to close plants and furlough 5 percent of its workforce.

Notwithstanding the economic slowdown, the company continued to adapt to new technologies, both within its own operations and in its customer-oriented services and products. Internally, Standard Register adopted automated manufacturing resource planning (MRP) software that helped it decrease waste, manage its inventory of over 13,000 items, and generally become more productive. Externally, Standard Register surprised some analysts by adopting electronic data interchange (EDI), an electronic ordering system that was proclaimed an important factor in the long heralded "paperless office." The company subscribed to an outside EDI network in addition to its own proprietary service, AccuServ. It was a classic example of the firm's adoptive strategy: Brent Rawlins, a specialist at Standard Register, pointed out that the EDI terminals installed at client sites served as a "constant reminder to do business with Standard Register." Instead of allowing the new technology to reduce its markets, the company used innovation to its advantage.

Standard Register furthered its efforts in this area through strategic alliances with electronic forms imaging and software firms, combining their longstanding customer relationships with the software companies' document management applications. Partners included Computer Sciences Corp., Saros Corp., and F3 Software Corp. in systems that coordinated ordering, pricing, and design of business forms.

In addition to initiating the transition to digital document management, Standard Register entered areas of business that closely augmented existing business operations. In 1986, Standard Register entered the document security forms market with the acquisition of the business forms division of Burroughs Corporation. In 1992, the company introduced the Positive Patient Identification System to hospitals. The device utilized a bar-code system to identify patients and to track the care they received. For its direct-mail business, Standard Register introduced the Image Seal machine, which folded and sealed a document as it passed through the equipment, thus preparing the document for mailing.

The company also boosted its direct-mail operations through the 1994 acquisition of rival UARCO Inc.'s 22-year-old direct-mail division, Promotional Graphics. Combined with Standard Register's own

COMMUNICOLOR Division, the Kansas-based entity expanded the firm's geographic reach westward, added $20 million in annual revenue, and broadened its product offerings.

These various activities helped increase Standard Register's revenues by an aggregate of about 7 percent from $716.4 million in 1990 to $767.4 million in 1994. Net income more than doubled from its recession-battered low of $21.8 million to $43.9 million during that same period. While this result established a new record for earnings, it was only 8 percent more than 1987's net, when annual revenues stood at only $666.7 million. Nevertheless, forms management services generated more than one-third of Standard Register's annual revenues, nearly as much as its traditional lines, including custom continuous forms, unit sets (multicopy sets of individual forms with or without carbon), and stock forms. The segment upon which the company was founded, document processing equipment, chipped in just over 11 percent.

John Darragh retired as president and chief executive officer after just over a decade of leading Standard Register and was succeeded by Peter S. Redding. Paul H. Granzow, who had served as chairman since 1984, continued in that capacity through the mid-1990s.

TRANSFERRING FROM PRINT TO ELECTRONIC FORMAT

Standard Register continued to parlay its expertise in custom business forms to the digital environment by offering new products and services to existing customers. Through its earlier alliance with software developers, Standard Register developed the Smartworks suite of document management software. Launched in 1995, Smartworks allowed customers to create new business documents for paper or online usage, to reorder printed documents, to request documents from stock, and to distribute electronic documents through the Internet. Another innovation, Teller-Select, worked with Windows 95 to produce custom documents onsite, on-demand.

In 1997, Standard Register expanded its customer base and digital imaging and document management capacities through the $245 million acquisition of UARCO, a major competitor. The consolidation of printing and warehouse facilities would provide revenue growth with the advantages of economies of scale.

Standard Register capitalized on its nationwide customer base to support the expansion of its network of on-demand, digital print centers. Standard Register planned to open STANFAST centers in every major metropolitan city, relying on the referrals from its sales

network to provide a base of business. During the late 1990s, the company opened several new STANFAST locations, including Memphis, Charlotte, Portland, and Indianapolis, for a total of 35 stores by the end of 1997. The STANFAST network provided the company with a mechanism for efficient customer service, as Smartworks allowed documents to be printed near customers' local offices through Internet distribution of image files to various STANFAST locations.

DRAMATIC CHANGE IN BUSINESS STRUCTURE

By 2000, automated documentation resulted in a steep decline in the demand for paper business forms. To maintain profitability and viability in the face of change and new competition in digital printing, Standard Register reorganized and reduced its operations. Under new CEO Dennis Rediker, the company divested low profit businesses while it leveraged new growth opportunities in new technologies. The flexibility of local printing through STANFAST print centers allowed the company to close 21 production facilities and 21 warehouses. The company also reduced overhead by closing 110 of its 200 sales offices as customers increasingly relied on online inventory management of print documents through Smartworks or required no business forms inventory due to paperless workflow processes. The changes resulted in a workforce reduction of 1,600 employees.

Standard Register intended the introduction of new technologies to offset loss of paper-based business. In June 2004 the company introduced Design on Demand, an Internet-based technology for custom development of marketing communications, such as brochures. The company's new ExpeData Digital Solutions introduced a digital pen for filling out digital forms. The company expected the technology to be particularly useful in hospitals. Technology in development at Standard Register's labeling services involved usage of radio frequency identification labels to locate a pallet, container, or box of goods from a distance; the radio chip would include information about the contents of the shipment as well.

The difficult transition to profitability took longer than expected, prompting further organizational restructuring. Standard Register divested its equipment services business in early 2005. Several STANFAST locations closed, reducing the number to 21 print centers by the end of 2006. Workforce reduction of another 1,400 employees involved administrative positions, including several high-level executives. Standard Register consolidated domestic labeling operations and opened a new facility near manufacturing customers in

Monterrey, Mexico. With investment in short-run label production equipment and computerized manufacturing, Standard Register sought to create quality label products with fast, flexible, efficient systems.

During this time profitability fluctuated wildly as the revenue stream shifted with the transition from analog to digital products and services. Nevertheless, the extent of Standard Register's success in a decades-long adaptation to electronic processes promised a brighter future. The year 2006 marked the fourth year in a row in which *InformationWeek* listed Standard Register among its top 100 technology innovators and the sixth year among the top 500. In 2007, Standard Register signed two high-profile partnership agreements with Hewlett-Packard (HP). In the first agreement, Standard Register provided management for HP's outsourced print marketing materials. In accordance with the second agreement, HP offered Smartworks through its Managed Print Services division, giving Standard Register access to HP's primary customers. The partnership was expected to contribute significantly to Standard Register's profitability for years to come.

April Dougal Gasbarre
Updated, Mary Tradii

PRINCIPAL SUBSIDIARIES

SMARTworks.com.

PRINCIPAL OPERATING UNITS

Digital Solutions; Document and Label Solutions; Print on Demand Services.

PRINCIPAL COMPETITORS

FedexKinkos Office and Print Services, Inc.; R.R. Donnelley & Sons Company; WorkflowOne; Xerox Corporation.

FURTHER READING

"AccessPlus Joins Forces with Standard Register," *Print Week,* March 16, 2006, p. 28.

Breakey, James, "New Directions for the Forms Industry," *Office,* January 1979, p. 169.

"Business-Form Makers Return to Form," *Financial World,* November 12, 1975, p. 14.

"Business Forms: Riding Computer Boom," *Financial World,* November 26, 1969, p. 20.

Degnan, Christa, "Standard Register Widens Services with Procurement," *PC Week,* August 23, 1999, p. 36.

"Electronics: Threat to Paper?" *Pulp & Paper,* August 1976, p. 17.

Flax, Steven, "Win on Price, Lose on Price," *Forbes,* November 8, 1982, p. 108.

"Forms Meeting Functions," *InformationWeek,* August 7, 1995, p. 28.

"Forms Printer Reports Restructuring Progress," *Graphic Arts Monthly,* August 2001, p. 24.

Gubser, Jay, "Paper Will Not Be the Way of the Future," *Office,* January 1979, p. 162.

"In Brief: Standard Register to Offer Payment Software," *American Banker,* August 6, 1998, p. 14.

King, Julia, "Printer Turns Service Apps into New Business," *Computerworld,* July 31, 2000, p. 30.

Montgomery, Christopher, "Dayton, Ohio, Digital Information Company Rewriting Future," *Dayton Daily News,* February 21, 2004.

"Mounting Demand Puts Operations of Standard Register in Top Form," *Barron's,* November 7, 1966, p. 28.

"Ohio Concern Acquires Select PlanetPrint Operations," *Finance and Commerce Daily,* July 16, 2002.

Olson, Thomas, "Families Fight While Standard Hopes," *Cincinnati Business Courier,* February 25, 1991, p. 1.

"Patient Wristbands to Carry More Data Than Ever, As Vendors Push Bar-Code Use," *Hospital Materials Management,* June 2004, p. 11.

Robbins, Susan, "Business Form Makers Grow at Record Pace," *Commercial and Financial Chronicle,* March 10, 1975, p. 1.

Robertson, Jason, "Will a Digital Pen Write the Next Chapter for Standard Register?" *Dayton Daily News,* February 6, 2005.

Schied, John P., "A Brief History of the Forms Industry," *Office,* May 1973, p. 57.

Skolnik, Rayna, "Standard Register Sells in Top Form," *Sales & Marketing Management,* October 11, 1982, p. 49.

Spayd, M. A., "A Business Built on Holes in Paper," *Industrial Development and Manufacturing Record,* April 1960, p. 12.

———, *A Business Built on Holes! The Standard Register Company,* New York: Newcomen Society in North America, 1957.

"Standard Register Acquires UARCO Direct Mail Division," *Printing-Impressions,* August 1994, p. 5.

"Standard Register Closes Indiana Plant, Plans Mexico Opening," *Label & Narrow Web,* May–June 2006, p. 8.

"Standard Register Has Sold Its Equipment Services Business to Pitney Bowes," *Purchasing,* February 17, 2005, p. 52.

"Standard Register Offers Web Marketing Service, New Solution Allows Clients to Design and Order Jobs for Delivery Within 24 Hours," *Graphic Arts Monthly,* October 2002, p. 24.

"Standard Register Signs Accord to Buy Uarco for $245 Million," *Wall Street Journal,* December 2, 1997, p. 1.

"Standard Register to Shrink in Renewal Plan," *Graphic Arts Monthly,* February 2001, p. 26.

Tanzillo, Kevin, "EDI Becomes Standard," *Communications News,* November 1990, p. 22.

Trembly, Ara C., "Standard Register Agrees to Acquire In-Systems Technologies," *National Underwriter Property & Casualty-Risk & Benefits Management,* July 8, 2002, p. 21.

"Two Printers Form Alliance," *Graphic Arts Monthly,* June 2000, p. 34.

"Watch Out for Big Brother," *Forbes,* May 1, 1967, p. 44.

Williams, Geoff, "The Paper Chase: Standard Register Company Evolves in the Digital Age," *Inside Business,* November 2004, p. OB40.

Sun World International, LLC

16350 Driver Road
Bakersfield, California 93308
U.S.A.
Telephone: (661) 392-5000
Fax: (661) 392-5092
Web site: http://www.sun-world.com

Private Company
Incorporated: 1976
Employees: 500
Sales: $110 million (2006 est.)
NAIC: 111410 Food Crops Grown Under Cover;
111219 Other Vegetable (Except Potato) and
Melon Farming; 111320 Citrus (Except Orange)
Groves; 111336 Fruit and Tree Nut Combination
Farming

■ ■ ■

Sun World International, LLC, develops, grows, and
markets fruits and vegetables, operating one of the
world's largest fruit-breeding programs. Sun World
specializes in developing unique produce, using roughly
16,000 acres of agricultural land in California and
agreements with other growers in California, Mexico,
and Chile to produce table grapes, seedless watermelons,
and red and yellow sweet peppers, among other types of
produce. Sun World maintains administrative, research,
farming, packing, and marketing facilities in Coachella,
California, and Bakersfield, California. The company is
owned by Black Diamond Capital Management LLC.

PRODUCE PACKER AND
MARKETER TAKES SHAPE

Sun World pursued two different business strategies during its first 30 years of business, starting out in 1976 as
a packer and marketer of fresh fruits and vegetables in
California. The company scored its first success by making a move into Flame Seedless table grapes, an early-
season variety that enjoyed a rapid increase in demand
largely thanks to Sun World's marketing efforts. Commercial success enabled the company to grow and to
diversify into a range of produce commodities, expansion that was fueled by forging numerous marketing alliances with major fruit and vegetable growers and packers in the state. Sun World had its hand in marketing
and packing a bevy of items such as carrots, leaf lettuce,
asparagus, green onions, sweet corn, cherries,
cantaloupes, citrus, dates, and strawberries.

Sun World flourished during its first years in
business. The company staked a physical presence in
locations such as Thermal, Coachella, Indio, Irvine,
Vista, Santa Barbara, Reedley, Orange Cove, and Lodi
by building, acquiring, or agreeing to manage packing
facilities. The company's initial phase of development
also included a joint venture with United Brands in the
early 1980s. Sun World acquired an interest in and assumed management of Interharvest, a major, Salinas
Valley-based lettuce company that was renamed Sun
Harvest after the two joint-venture partners took
control. The joint venture proved to be a misstep,
however, its success derailed by a year of labor problems
and difficult conditions in the lettuce market. Sun
World and United Brands shut down the lettuce operation, conceding failure at roughly the same time Sun

COMPANY PERSPECTIVES

We're putting flavor back into fresh produce. Just look for the Sun World label to experience our quality difference! Sun World's product mix has been carefully assembled to respond to its customers' needs. Wherever possible, Sun World provides year-round continuity of its value-added, specially-bred products from a variety of locations.

World's management saw more profound problems on the horizon.

A NEW DIRECTION

Sun World enjoyed an encouraging start to its business life. The company's involvement in the commodity produce business had met with success. It was physically expanding with each passing year, and it was broadening its reach, increasing the number and variety of the fruits and vegetables it packed and marketed. The investment in Interharvest had not panned out, but the loss incurred represented only a minor blemish on an otherwise impressive record of performance. Despite the success of the first few years, there was cause for concern at the company's headquarters as Sun World entered the 1980s. Management noted that many crops in California were overplanted, a consequence, executives believed, of favorable tax treatment given to agricultural developments. Executives foresaw a bleak picture once the surfeit of produce hit the market, a nightmarish scenario of excess supply and cascading prices that would gravely injure their vibrant enterprise.

Sun World management resolved to reduce the company's exposure to a saturated market by exiting the commodity produce business and forging a new identity in the realm of "designer" produce. The company acquired the worldwide rights to Le Rouge Royale pepper, a hybrid, sweet red pepper that had been genetically engineered in Israel. Sun World introduced Le Rouge Royale in 1983, a product offering that helped establish the company's reputation as a premium marketer of branded produce. Once the company secured a foothold in proprietary, branded produce, it pushed headlong into the business, devoting the 1980s to transforming itself into a developer, grower, and marketer of designer fruit and vegetables.

Although Sun World allocated considerable time and money for research and development, the company made its most significant progress during the 1980s by acquisitions. After introducing the Divine Ripe tomato in 1986, Sun World acquired the exclusive marketing rights to a seedless watermelon in 1988, striking a deal with Oklahoma City, Oklahoma-based American Sun Melon that gave the company a product it renamed Sun World Seedless. The biggest acquisition of the period occurred at the end of the decade, when the company bought Superior Farming Company, a purchase that gave Sun World more than 40,000 acres of prime central California farmland. For a company looking to distinguish itself as a supplier of branded produce, the acquisition proved ideal. Sun World gained a plant-breeding laboratory near Bakersfield and a fruit-breeding program that gave the company ownership of a wealth of proprietary fruits such as the Superior Seedless table grape, the Amber Crest peach, and the Black Diamond plum, as well as several dozen promising plum, peach, and apricot varieties.

By the beginning of the 1990s, Sun World held sway in the branded produce market, having thoroughly transformed itself from the packer and marketer formed 15 years earlier. The company ranked as the nation's largest producer and marketer of tangerines, mandarins, seedless watermelons, as the largest U.S. grower of colored sweet peppers, and as one of the world's largest independent marketers of oranges, grapefruit, and lemons. At the heart of the company were its proprietary lines of genetically engineered produce that offered value-added features such as enhanced flavor, longer shelf life, and seedlessness, qualities that enabled retailers to glean higher profit margins than they earned from conventional, commodity produce. Sun World sold Le Rouge and Le Jaune Royale sweet peppers, Divine Ripe tomatoes, Sun World Seedless watermelons, Superior Seedless table grapes, as well as roughly 90 additional fruit and vegetable brands owned or exclusively marketed by the company. Sun World grew its own produce and, through alliances with other growers, sourced its fruits and vegetables from suppliers in California, Mexico, and South America. The company also served as a marketing agent for more than 500 growers.

Sun World could look forward to the 1990s with anticipation. Increasingly, produce items were being sold under brand names, creating ideal market conditions for a company with Sun World's talents. The company's research and development center had created more than 30 patented fruit varieties since it had been established, proving to be a vital contributor to extending Sun World's reach in the designer produce sector. Howard Marguleas, one of Sun World's founders and its chairman and chief executive officer, was joined by his son, David Marguleas, who served as senior vice-president of

KEY DATES

1976: Sun World is formed as a produce packer and marketer.

1983: The introduction of Le Rouge Royale, a sweet red pepper, brings Sun World into the market for designer produce.

1989: Sun World acquires Superior Farming Company.

1994: Sun World declares bankruptcy.

1996: Cadiz Land Company acquires Sun World.

2003: Sun World again declares bankruptcy.

2005: Sun World is acquired by Black Diamond Management LLC.

2006: Sun World generates $110 million in sales in its 30th year of business.

marketing, and together they looked to increase Sun World's already stalwart market position. The pair began to focus on consumer advertising efforts for essentially the first time, seeking to develop a connection directly with consumers that would strengthen the company's bargaining power with retailers. "We are beginning now to formulate a consumer advertising campaign," David Marguleas informed *Supermarket News* in an April 26, 1993, interview. "Clearly, over the long-term, that is one of our goals."

SUN WORLD FALTERS IN 1994

As it turned out, the father-and-son team was forced to deal with issues far less appealing than cultivating awareness of their company's brands. Sun World declared bankruptcy roughly 18 months after David Marguleas gave his interview with *Supermarket News,* touching off a two-year period during which the fate of the company hung in the balance. By September 1995, 11 months after the company filed for Chapter 11, the U.S. Department of Agriculture was threatening to strip Sun World of its license, alleging the company had fallen more than $1 million behind in payments to growers. As the situation worsened, Sun World struggled to secure a restructuring plan, at last finding salvation in late 1995 when Cadiz Land Company agreed to acquire the troubled firm.

Based in Rancho Cucamonga, California, Cadiz Land dabbled in farming, but primarily operated as a water management company. The company owned 42,000 acres of land and water holdings in the Mojave Desert, which it hoped to combine with Sun World's

nearly 20,000 acres of agricultural land and packing facilities. Sun World's unsecured creditors agreed to support the acquisition in December 1995. In June 1996, the U.S. Bankruptcy Court in San Bernardino approved the deal, which paved the way for the completion of the acquisition in September 1996, when Sun World began operating as a division of Cadiz Land.

Having survived its first, great crucible, Sun World entered the late 1990s ready to put its troubles behind it and focus on more positive developments. In 1999, the company's expertise in agriculture was acknowledged when it was selected to become the exclusive manager of the development of the Egyptian Tushka Project, an integral component of the Egyptian government's multibillion-dollar South Valley Project, a mammoth infrastructure project that aimed to irrigate more than 500,000 acres of desert. The relationships formed in overseeing the Egyptian Tushka Project soon led to what promised to be a transforming event for Sun World. In January 2002, Cadiz Land announced it had reached a tentative agreement with Kingdom Agricultural Development Co., a private Egyptian company controlled by Saudi Arabian Prince Alwaleed Bin Talal Bin AbdulAziz Alsaud. The agreement called for the merger of Sun World and Kingdom Agricultural to create a new company that would turn nearly 100,000 acres in southern Egypt into agricultural land. The proposed combination of the two companies fizzled six months later, however, with both parties citing technical reasons for the deal's collapse.

A SECOND COLLAPSE IN 2003

Not long after Sun World entertained the prospect of uniting with an Egyptian partner, the company again was beset by financial turmoil. At the start of 2003, for the second time in its history, Sun World declared bankruptcy. "The filing was necessary to protect our employees, customers, growers, and to allow Sun World to meet seasonal working capital requirements," the company's chief executive officer said in a January 31, 2003, interview with the *Sacramento Bee*. Sun World maintained it was financially healthy, casting blame for the crisis on its parent company. Cadiz Land, which was suffering from the failure of a major water-management project, had decided not to provide seasonal operating cash to Sun World, withholding the roughly $15 million it provided annually to Sun World. Unexpectedly strapped for cash, Sun World searched for a loan and found one, but the new loan was conditioned on Sun World reaching an agreement with holders of its first-mortgage notes. When Sun World was unable to gain their approval, the company was forced to declare bankruptcy.

The search for a solution to Sun World's financial woes commenced. One month after the company sought protection from creditors under Chapter 11 of the U.S. Bankruptcy Code, it received $15 million in debtor in possession (DIP) financing, which allowed the lender to be placed ahead of other creditors owed money. Ableco Finance LLC had emerged as Sun World's savior, but when the two parties appeared in court to gain approval for the deal, a requirement for DIP financing, events took an unexpected turn. Black Diamond Management LLC, a Lake Forest, Illinois-based firm that managed $3 billion in institutional capital, surprised everyone involved in the matter by showing up in court and presenting a $40 million DIP offer with lower loan fees than the Ableco offer. The bankruptcy judge, in an unusual move, allowed bidding between Ableco and Black Diamond to commence in the courtroom. Sun World representatives sat and watched the proceedings, with the future of their company being determined before their eyes.

NEW OWNERS FOR THE FUTURE

Black Diamond emerged as the victor in the bidding war over Sun World. The offer of DIP financing proved to be only the first step in a plan with larger ambitions. When Sun World emerged from bankruptcy in early 2005, its new owner was its creditor, Black Diamond, which paid $127.75 million for Sun World in a court auction. The transaction was concluded in February 2005. Sun World had settled into its new arrangement by the time the company celebrated its 30th anniversary in 2006, enabling it to enjoy the festivities without the specter of financial collapse. The company generated roughly $110 million in sales during its anniversary, a total collected from distributing 12 million cartons of fresh produce. In the years ahead, Sun World hoped to increase its volume by promoting unique produce varieties with improved flavor, size, color, and seasonality.

Jeffrey L. Covell

PRINCIPAL COMPETITORS

Chiquita Brands International, Inc.; Dole Food Company, Inc.; Fresh Del Monte Produce Inc.

FURTHER READING

Burrows, Kate, "Sunny Success," *Food and Drink,* January–February 2005, p. 182.

"Cadiz Land Co. Unveils Plan to Acquire Sun World," *Knight-Ridder/Tribune Business News,* June 4, 1996, p. 6040270.

Carnal, Jim, "California Agribusiness Giants Make Bids on Sun World International," *Knight-Ridder/Tribunes Business News,* January 16, 1996, p. 1160028.

Crider, Jeff, "Some Creditors Back Plan to Buy Bankrupt Fruit and Vegetable Grower Sun World," *Knight-Ridder/Tribune Business News,* December 16, 1995, p. 12160013.

De Lollis, Barbara, "Agriculture Department May Revoke Sun World International's License," *Knight-Ridder/Tribune Business News,* September 7, 1995, p. 9070026.

Drum, David, "Sun World International: Meeting the Demand for Proprietary Produce," *California Business,* July 1990, p. 13.

Mejia, John, "Sun World Has Designs on the Perfect Tomato," *Supermarket News,* June 11, 1990, p. 28.

Rodriguez, Robert, "Ag Firm Caught in a Bind," *Fresno Bee,* January 31, 2003, p. C1.

"Sun World Gets Bankruptcy Financing," *Fresno Bee,* February 4, 2003, p. C5.

Waters, John, Jr., "Ontario, Calif.–Area Farming Know-How Makes Gains in Mid-East," *Business Press,* February 4, 2002.

Weston, Cael, "Brands Make Their Mark," *Supermarket News,* April 26, 1993, p. 78.

Sveaskog AB

—■—

Pipers väg 2A, Solna
Stockholm, S-105 22
Sweden
Telephone: (+46 08) 655 90 00
Fax: (+46 08) 655 94 14
Web site: http://www.sveaskog.se

State-Owned Company
Incorporated: 2001
Employees: 1,027
Sales: SEK 6.03 billion ($862 million) (2006)
NAIC: 113210 Forest Nurseries and Gathering of Forest
    Products; 113110 Timber Tract Operations

■ ■ ■

Sveaskog AB is the largest owner of forests in Sweden.
The Stockholm-based company owns nearly 4.5 million
hectares of land, including 3.35 million hectares of
productive forest. Sveaskog owns land throughout
Sweden, with special concentrations in Norrbotten and
Västerbotten. Other major regions for the company
include Bergslagen, Svealand, and Götaland. Approximately 80 percent of the company's forest holdings
are in the country's northern region. In terms of
production, however, the faster growing conditions of
the group's smaller southern holdings account for
almost 60 percent of its productive value. Altogether,
Sveaskog owns 15 percent of Sweden's forests. Owned
by the Swedish government, Sveaskog was formed in
2001 in order to nationalize the forest holdings of Assi-
Domän AB. The company has been steadily shedding its

wood products and other operations to refocus
exclusively as a forest owner. The company has also been
developing a network of ecoparks, which are set aside
for nature conservation and tourism purposes. In 2007,
the company operated 15 ecoparks for a total surface of
175,000 hectares. The company has set aside 34 ecoparks in all. Sveaskog is led by Chairman Bo Dockered
and CEO Gunnar Olofsson. Sveaskog posted total
revenues of SEK 6.03 billion ($862 million) in 2006.

FOREST OWNERSHIP CHANGES FROM 1545

The history of Swedish state intervention in the ownership and management of the nation's forests reaches
back to the 16th century. In 1545, under the reign of
King Gustaf Vasa, the government decreed that all "land
without settlements belongs to the State." Asserting its
ownership over the country's forests was also a means by
the royal and newly Protestant government to counter
the influence and power of the Catholic Church. As
part of the decree, the Swedish government reclaimed all
of the forest lands held by the Church.

For the next several centuries, the king's forests
were primarily reserved as hunting grounds. Forests also
provided the supply of timber for the construction of
ships and buildings, as well as firewood. The country's
forests remained an important source of game, as well as
berries and mushrooms until well into the 19th century.
Sweden's forests were also used to encourage settlement
beyond the country's more populated urban regions.
Starting in the 17th century, the government began
distributing forest lands to individuals for settling.

The first industrial uses of the country's forests came toward the beginning of the 18th century. The development of new production methods and materials, especially iron, stimulated the demand for new fuel sources. The government in turn gave away large areas of the country's forests, where the timber was used for the production of charcoal. The growing iron industry continued to claim and clear large amounts of the country's forests into the early 19th century. In 1810, for example, nearly 340,000 hectares had been sold to the country's iron producers.

The government's policies of supporting the country's population growth and industrial expansion through the giving away of land had a significant impact on its own forest holdings. By 1850, the Swedish government's own landholding had reached their lowest levels.

The advent of the Industrial Revolution and the development of steam-driven machinery represented a turning point for Sweden's forests. Through the 19th century and into the 20th century, forestry products, including timber, as well as pulp and paper, grew to become the most important economic resource for the country.

At the same time, Sweden's strong population growth during this period put additional pressures on the nation's forests. Into the 20th century, vast areas of former forest were cleared to provide room for new settlements and fields for grazing. The rising demand for new homes and other construction, on the one hand, and firewood on the other, added to the destruction of the country's forest reserves.

PROTECTING SWEDEN'S NATIONAL RESOURCE IN 1859

As a result, the country began to experience its first wood shortages as early as the middle of the 19th century. This prompted the government to begin taking its first steps toward regaining control of what was soon to become the country's most important national resource.

In 1859, the Swedish government established a new forest-owning body, Domänverket. This forestry service became responsible for buying back and otherwise reacquiring land for the State. In particular, Domänverket began reacquiring land that had been cleared and overgrazed. Similarly, as the country's iron mills began to close, these lands reverted back to state control. Domänverket also began developing the nation's expertise in silviculture, and established schools and training facilities for a new generation of forestry engineers.

Domänverket was not only charged with managing the forests held by the Swedish government. It was also given responsibility for monitoring the condition of the forests under public and church ownership. Domänverket also took over the regulation of hunting and conservation. At the same time, however, Domänverket sought to develop new means to exploit the country's virgin forests. This helped give rise to a new era for the country's timber and pulp and paper industries.

Between the 1870s and the 1970s, Domänverket's forest land purchases added nearly 750,000 hectares to the nation's vast holdings. By the middle of the 1970s, the Swedish government's holdings of productive forest lands had grown to more than 4.1 million hectares. This figure, which included more than 1.4 million hectares of mountain land, accounted for about 20 percent of all productive forests in Sweden.

DEVELOPING A COMMERCIAL SIDE

For much of that century, Domänverket remained exempt from legislation put into place to govern the private sector. This effort began with the passage of the Forestry Act of 1903. This legislation put into place requirements specifying that clear felled forest land be replanted. The legislation also created the first supervisory authorities, including the first Regional Forestry Boards, established in 1905. These took over parts of Domänverket's former oversight and development mandates, as Domänverket itself began developing commercial uses for the lands under its control.

This effort received a new boost in 1911, when Domänverket achieved a greater independence in its operations. Over the next decade, the government-owned body began to develop a range of commercial operations, including timber and other forestry products. This led to the creation of a new subsidiary, ASSI, in 1941. ASSI's strong growth continued through the 1950s. In 1957, ASSI was separated from Domänverket, which functioned under the Ministry of Agriculture. Instead, ASSI was placed under the Ministry of Industry.

KEY DATES

1859: Domänverket is created by Swedish government to manage its forest landholdings.
1911: Domänverket begins developing independent commercial operations.
1941: ASSI is formed as a subsidiary for forest products operations.
1957: ASSI is transferred to Ministry of Industry.
1968: Domänverket is placed under similar regulations as private sector and is transferred to Ministry of Industry.
1993: AssiDomän AB is spun off by Swedish government as public company.
1999: Sveaskog is created as a subsidiary for its landholdings, which becomes majority controlled by Swedish government.
2001: Sveaskog acquires full control of AssiDomän, then begins selling off its industrial operations.
2007: Sveaskog largely completes restructuring as pure forest landholding company owned by the Swedish government.

The growth of Domänverket's commercial operations fit in with the overall objectives of Sweden's forestry policies throughout the middle decades of the 20th century. The forest industry provided an important source of government-created employment during the Depression years of the 1930s; the country's impressive forest road network was built during this time. In the post–World War II era, forestry products industries emerged as the motor for the country's economic prosperity. As such, the country's forestry policies targeted high production, and not conservation, in order to ensure supply to its fast-growing pulp and paper and wood products sectors.

Domänverket's growing commercial operations inevitably led to suggestions that the company be privatized in the early 1960s. This proposition was rejected by the government, however. Nonetheless, in 1968, Domänverket was subject to a new set of regulations that placed it on a similar level with the country's privately owned forestry companies. The new regulations also transferred Domänverket from the Ministry of Agriculture to the Ministry of Industry.

Under its new mandate, Domänverket focused on developing its long-term profit picture, in part by the investment into a wider range of operations. Through

the next decades, Domänverket added a number of new business areas, including sawmill operations, commercial tourism businesses, consulting services, and concrete and gravel production.

ASSIDOMÄN IN 1993

Decades of focus on high production had left the country's forests in a fragile condition, with new shortfalls in the country's wood supply looming by the year 2000. Only limited efforts had been made to preserve the forests' ecological balance as the country's emphasis remained on maximum productivity. Regeneration of the country's forests in particular had taken a back seat to the supply of the country's all-important forestry products needs.

Recognition of a looming environmental crisis, coupled with the country's dwindling supply of productive forests, brought about a series of changes in Sweden's forest management initiatives starting from the 1980s. New research efforts were launched that began to view the forest as an ecosystem, rather than merely as a source of wood. These efforts led to the drafting of the Forest Policy of 1993, which for the first time sought to balance environmental concerns with productivity.

As part of this process, the Swedish government moved to privatize its main forest holding. Domänverket was incorporated in 1991, then in 1992 spun off as Domän AB. While still 100 percent controlled by the Swedish government, the new body was expected to operate on a commercial basis. The restructuring of the state's forestry holdings continued into 1993, when ASSI and Domän were recombined into a single company, AssiDomän. That company was then listed on the Stockholm Stock Exchange, and became a major force in the forest products industry.

PURE FOREST OWNER IN THE NEW CENTURY

The conflicts stemming from Swedish government control of AssiDomän ultimately led to the decision to streamline the government's holding. Priority was given especially to the separation of the company's forestry products operations, including sawmills and other manufacturing facilities, on the one hand, and its forest landholdings on the other.

A major facet of AssiDomän's restructuring was the creation of a new subsidiary, Sveaskog, in 1999. Over the next two years, Sveaskog took control of Assi-Domän's forest holdings. At the same time, the Swedish government acquired control of Sveaskog. By 2001, the government had taken over full control of AssiDomän as well, which became a subsidiary of Sveaskog.

As part of its mandate, however, Sveaskog was required to restructure its focus wholly around its control of the state's forest holdings. The company began to divest the manufacturing and other industrial operations formerly held by AssiDomän. In March 2001, for example, the company sold its corrugated and container board production operation to Kappa Alpha Holdings in a deal worth SEK 10.4 billion. The company also spun off its paper mill operations into a new company, Billerud. In 2003, the company spun off its sawmilling and timber processing operations into a new company combining these operations with those of Mellanskog Industri AB. The new company became known as Setra Group AB.

Sveaskog divested its logistics wing, ScandFibre Logistics, to a consortium of five Swedish forest products groups in 2005. In that year, the company also agreed to the $443 million sale of AssiDomän Carton-board Holding, also known as Frovi, to Korsnas AB. This sale, finalized in 2006, largely completed Sveaskog's conversion to a pure-play forest owning group.

Sveaskog continued to develop its forest portfolio through the decade. In 2002, the company acquired 200,000 hectares of productive forest land from Körsnas. By 2007, the company's total land holdings had risen to 4.45 million hectares, including 3.35 million hectares of productive forest. In this way, Sveaskog became the single largest forest land holder in Sweden, accounting for fully 15 percent of the country's productive forest land.

Yet conservation remained an important element of Sveaskog's mandate. The company launched development of a national network of "ecoparks," setting aside land for nature conservation and ecotourism purposes. By 2007, the company operated 15 of a projected 34 parks, with a total area of more than 175,000 hectares.

The company also became responsible for intensified silviculture development, including seed production and planting operations. In 2006 alone, the company planted more than 36 million seedlings in the ongoing effort to regenerate Sweden's forests and ensure their long-term productivity.

At the same time, Sveaskog played a leading role in developing forest-based biofuel products. In 2006, for example, the company's delivery of felling residues reached an equivalent of 1.6 TWh. Sveaskog also joined with Smurfit Kappa in a research project seeking to develop a synthetic gas from black liquor, a pulp mill byproduct.

The company's operations remained highly profitable as well. In 2006, the company posted operating profits, following the revaluation of its forest holdings, of more than SEK 1.6 billion, on total revenues of SEK 6.03 billion. Sveaskog appeared prepared to lead Sweden into a new era of forestry management.

M. L. Cohen

PRINCIPAL SUBSIDIARIES

Sveaskog Naturupplevelser AB; Setra Group AB; Svenska Skogsplantor AB.

PRINCIPAL COMPETITORS

SCA Skog AB; Bergvik Skog AB; Holmen Skog AB; Statens fastighetsverk; Fortifikationsverket; Persson Invest Skog AB.

FURTHER READING

"Acquire and Invest," *TTJ—The Timber Industry Magazine,* October 4, 2003, p. 17.

"Export Volumes of Sawn Timber Rise but Prices Fall," *TTJ—The Timber Industry Magazine,* November 13, 2004, p. 8.

Hunt, Martin, "Changing Times," *TTJ—The Timber Industry Magazine,* November 23, 2002, p. 22.

———, "Sawn Timber Output Rises As Companies Join Forces," *TTJ—The Timber Industry Magazine,* July 12, 2003, p. 14.

"Korsnas Buys AssiDomän," *Official Board Markets,* November 19, 2005, p. 18.

"Sveaskog Completes Acquisition of Sawmill and Forest," *Nordic Business Report,* September 2, 2002.

"Sweden Buys Back Its Forests," *Daily Deal,* September 28. 2001.

"Swedish Government to Buy AssiDomän," *Paperboard Packaging,* December 2001, p. 13.

"Swedish State Forestry Company Sveaskog Made a SKr 12m Loss on Its Wood Product Operations During the Third Quarter," *TTJ—The Timber Industry Magazine,* November 13, 2004, p. 8.

Synthes, Inc.

Glutz Blotzheim-Strasse 1-3
Solothurn,
Switzerland
Telephone: (+41 032) 720 40 60
Fax: (+41 032) 720 40 61
Web site: http://www.synthes.com

Public Company
Incorporated: 2004
Employees: 8,451
Sales: $2.39 billion (2006)
Stock Exchanges: Swiss
Ticker Symbol: SYST
NAIC: 339113 Surgical Appliance and Supplies
    Manufacturing; 551112 Offices of Other Holding
    Companies

∎ ∎ ∎

Synthes, Inc., is one of the world's leading osteosynthesis specialists, developing implants, instruments, biomaterials, and systems for the treatment and/or regeneration of the human skeleton and related soft tissues. The Solothurn, Switzerland-based company is the world leader in the traumatology sector, and has long played a prominent role in the treatment of bone fractures. Synthes is also a top producer of implants, including plats, screws, rods, and hooks used to treat spinal column injuries and conditions. Among the company's products in this area is its Prodisc system, which allows for the complete replacement of intervertebral discs. The company's cranio-maxillofacial division is a leading

developer of treatments specifically for facial, jaw, and skull conditions. Synthes has also been developing new technologies, such as resorbable implants and bone graft substitutes.

Synthes's product development is conducted in partnership with the AO Foundation, founded in order to pioneer the research and development of treatments for bone fractures and conditions. The company operates on a worldwide scale, with subsidiaries in 35 countries. The North American market is the company's largest, accounting for nearly 64 percent of its turnover of $2.4 billion in 2006. Europe is the group's next largest market, at nearly 22 percent. Synthes is listed on the Swiss stock exchange. The company is led by CEO Hansjoerg Wyss.

PIONEERING OSTEOSYNTHESIS

Synthes, Inc., represented the culmination of nearly 60 years of cooperation between members of Switzerland's medical and industrial sectors, and played a pioneering role in the creation and development of osteosynthesis techniques. Bone fractures had long been an area of interest for the medical community; since the advent of modern medicine in the 19th century, various efforts had been made to improve on bone setting and healing techniques. Yet these efforts remained largely mechanical, involved the use of casts and other devices to immobilize the broken bone, and indicated a general lack of understanding of the process involved in the healing of fractures. The result was that the setting of fractures continued to be at best a cumbersome process, and at worse, potentially crippling.

COMPANY PERSPECTIVES

Quality, innovation and consistent customer orientation. By continuously developing better solutions, Synthes lays the foundations for its excellent market position. Our goal is to provide the safest and most advanced implants, instruments and technologies that ensure reliable operating procedures, rapid recovery and a painfree life after surgery. We guarantee high quality, constant innovation and consistent customer orientation. Working closely together with surgeons in hospitals all over the world, our product development teams of scientists, engineers and product managers identify real clinical needs. This provides the basis for developing products with increased benefits for patients, surgeons and OR personnel.

In the 1940s, a number of surgeons had begun investigating the use of various types of fixation devices to aid recovery. These efforts also included the use of implants, as well as various rehabilitation techniques. Toward the end of that decade, the medical community began to make progress toward understanding the mechanisms involved in fracture healing and functional recovery. A major proponent in this effort was Belgian surgeon Robert Danis, who published his *Théorie et Pratique de l'Osteosynthèse* in 1949.

The book caught the attention of Maurice Müller, a surgeon in Switzerland, who met with Danis, then brought his theories back to Switzerland. There, Müller formed an association with three other surgeons, Robert Schneider, Martin Allgöwer, and Hans Willenegger, in order to explore and develop the techniques described by Danis's work. In 1950, the four partners created the Arbeitsgemeinschaft für Osteosynthese (Association for the Study of Osteosynthesis), or AO.

Over the next several years, AO emerged as a pioneering force in the development of new osteosynthesis techniques and treatments. By the late 1950s, the association began seeking out industrial partners to help develop its technologies into marketable products. For this, the association turned to Bettlach-based Mathys AG, founded as a manufacturer of machines and machine components in 1946 by Robert Mathys. Through the 1950s, Mathys had developed expertise in working with special non-corrosive and acid-resistant stainless steels. This expertise made Mathys an attractive partner for AO, and in 1958, Mathys agreed to manufacture the implants and other instruments designed by AO.

With Mathys providing the funding, the partnership quickly resulted in a new range of bone fixation products. Mathys soon grew into an internationally operating company, developing a wide range of medical products, including surgical tools and equipment, as well as implants and other devices and materials produced under license from AO.

AO interests also turned toward developing internal fixation products. The company founded a research laboratory for the creation of new surgical techniques in 1959. At the same time, the success of the partnership with Mathys encouraged AO to seek additional partnerships to assist it in manufacturing products using its technologies. In particular, the company sought out a partner capable of producing a new range of internal fixation devices under its development.

This led AO to the Straumann Institute in 1960. That company had been founded in 1920 by Reinhard Straumann, a metallurgical engineer who developed a range of specialty alloys for use by the Swiss watchmaking industry, particularly by the Rolex and IWC watch companies. In 1954, Straumann founded a new company, Dr. Ing. R. Straumann Research Institute, focused on the creation of specialized metal alloys. In the late 1950s, then under the direction of Straumann's son Fritz Straumann, the company began seeking a means to put its alloy expertise to practical use. In 1960, Straumann contacted AO, forming a partnership that led to the production of the first Synthes-branded internal fixation products.

NORTH AMERICAN ENTRY IN 1974

By the end of the 1960s, Straumann and AO had successfully developed a new generation of non-corroding alloy that could be used for internal implants. This breakthrough enabled the company to emerge as a global leader in the fast-growing osteosynthesis field. Through the 1970s, Straumann put into place an international sales and marketing network. For the U.S. market, an entirely new company was created, called Synthes USA, Inc., located in West Chester, Pennsylvania. Synthes became the third licensee for AO's technologies, operating as an independent company. Over the next decade, Synthes USA, which also expanded in Canada, became the largest of the three AO licensees.

At the end of the 1970s, Mathys extended its materials expertise to include ceramics, launching its

KEY DATES

1946: Robert Mathys founds company producing machines and machine components in Bettlach, Switzerland.

1950: Arbeitsgemeinschaft für Osteosynthese (AO) is founded by four Swiss surgeons.

1954: Dr. Ing. R. Straumann Research Institute is established to develop specialized metal alloys.

1958: AO and Mathys reach product development agreement, with Mathys becoming licensee for AO-developed osteosynthesis technologies.

1960: AO and Straumann launch partnership to develop internal fixation devices.

1974: Synthes USA is created to produce and market AO technology for North American market.

1984: AO is restructured as AO Foundation with headquarters in Davos, Switzerland.

1990: Stratec Medical is created as spinoff of Straumann's osteosynthesis and joint-replacement operations.

1996: Stratec goes public with listing on Swiss stock exchange.

1999: Stratec merges with Synthes USA, creating Stratec-Synthes.

2004: Stratec-Synthes merges with Mathys, creating Synthes, Inc., as global licensee for AO Foundation technologies.

2006: Synthes creates new Latin American subsidiary in Costa Rica.

first ceramics-based implants in 1978. That company then added a new range of granulates at the beginning of the 1980s. AO had also been growing as well, and by the early 1980s had expanded far beyond Switzerland to represent a worldwide organization of surgeons, researchers, and other operating room personnel. This led AO to restructure itself as the AO Foundation in 1984, setting up a global headquarters in Davos, Switzerland, that year.

Straumann, meantime, became the first to develop dental implants, which represented a major breakthrough in dental care. The company introduced its first implant in 1974, backed by a one-step surgical procedure. The rapid growth of the dental implant market through the 1980s led Straumann, then under the leadership of Thomas Straumann, to refocus itself

on this division at the beginning of the 1990s. The company then spun off its osteosynthesis and joint-replacement operations to a management buyout group led by Rudolf Maag. These operations, which retained the company's AO licenses, were then renamed Stratec Medical. The reformed Straumann then refocused its operation on its dental implant business. That company went public in 1998 as Straumann Holding.

Stratec Medical set out to expand its range of operations. The company had been developing its implant technologies, traditionally focused on the long bone in the arms and legs, to respond to other skeletal areas. The company had launched its first maxillo-facial implants in the 1970s, and by the 1980s had begun developing spine reconstruction, regeneration, and replacement products. Into the early 1990s, Stratec complemented its implant and fixation portfolio with a range of surgical power tools. In 1991, the company also launched a dedicated U.S. subsidiary, Stratec Spine, to develop spinal reconstruction products for the North American market. Toward the middle of the decade, the company's interests in computer-assisted surgical techniques led it to form a dedicated subsidiary for that market, Medivision Ltd., in 1995.

SINGLE AO LICENSE HOLDER FOR THE NEW CENTURY

Stratec went public in 1996, listing its stock on the Swiss stock exchange. The company continued to develop new surgical procedures, resulting in the launch of the Integra 360 technique, combining several of the company's spinal reconstruction products into a single, standardized surgical platform.

Despite its strong product development during the 1990s, particularly its focus on the maxillo-facial and spinal segments, Stratec's growth nonetheless faced the geographic limitations under its AO license agreement. The company took the first step toward overcoming that limitation when it reached a merger agreement with Synthes USA in 1999. The new company, which retained Stratec's public listing, then took on the name of Stratec-Synthes.

Stratec-Synthes next moved to boost its range of technologies. In 1999, the company acquired Norian Corp., based in the United States, which had been developing artificial bone substances. By 2001, Stratec-Synthes had decided to specialize its operations wholly on the osteosynthesis market, selling its joint-replacement business. This divestment was followed in 2003 by the sell-off of its Medivision unit, to Praxim SA.

In that year, Stratec-Synthes reached a new merger agreement with Mathys, the last of the three AO license holders, to combine their osteosynthesis operations into a single company, renamed Synthes, Inc. That merger was completed in 2004, boosting Synthes into the top three of the global osteosynthesis market.

The unified Synthes sought new growth opportunities as it turned toward the mid-decade. The company boosted its U.S. position with the acquisition of Spine Solutions Inc., which focused on the total spine disc replacement segment. The following year, the company bought another U.S. company, Gelifex, adding its expertise in spinal disc nucleus replacement. These acquisitions helped boost Synthes's revenues past $2 billion by the end of 2005. With more than 60 percent of its sales generated in the United States, Synthes built a new and larger North American headquarters in West Chester that year. In that year, also, Synthes launched a new division, Synthes Vet, to adapt its technologies for the small but growing veterinary market.

Synthes continued to develop both its product lines and its geographic reach in the second half of the first decade of the 2000s. In 2006, the company received U.S. Food and Drug Administration approval for its new Prodisc-L artificial lumbar disc. In that year, also, the company, already present in approximately 35 countries worldwide, boosted its Latin American presence with the creation of a new subsidiary in Costa Rica. As a global leader in the osteosynthesis market, Synthes appeared to have found the right formula for its own growth in the new century.

M. L. Cohen

PRINCIPAL SUBSIDIARIES

HFSC Company (U.S.A.); Norian Corporation (U.S.A.); SMGT, Inc. (U.S.A.); Spine Solutions, Inc. (U.S.A.); Synthes Asia Pacific (Australia); Synthes GmbH; Synthes LAT, Inc. (U.S.A.); Synthes, Inc. (U.S.A.); Synthes Spine, Inc. (U.S.A.).

PRINCIPAL COMPETITORS

Stryker Corp.; Biomet Inc.; Zimmer Holdings Inc.; ENCO spol S.R.O.; Smith and Nephew United Inc.; Getinge AB; STERIS Corp.; Centerpulse Orthopedics AG; William Demant Holding A/S; Bacou-Dalloz S.A.; DePuy Inc.

FURTHER READING

Loyd, Linda, "Spine Product Rivals Now Battle in Court," *Philadelphia Inquirer,* July 26, 2007.

"Synthes, Globus Settle Suit on Secrets," *Philadelphia Inquirer,* August 21, 2007.

"Synthes-Stratec Buys Mathys," *Swiss News,* September 2003, p. 18.

"Synthes-Stratec Most Dynamic," *Swiss News,* July 2003, p. 2.

TransCanada Corporation

TransCanada Tower
450 First Street Southwest
Calgary, Alberta T2P 5H1
Canada
Telephone: (403) 920-2000
Toll Free: (800) 661-3805
Fax: (403) 920-2200
Web site: http://www.transcanada.com

Public Company
Founded: 1951 as TransCanada PipeLines Limited
Incorporated: 2003
Employees: 3,550
Sales: CAD 8.83 billion ($8.94 billion) (2007)
Stock Exchanges: Toronto New York
Ticker Symbol: TRP
NAIC: 486210 Pipeline Transportation of Natural Gas;
   493190 Other Warehousing and Storage; 221111
   Hydroelectric Power Generation; 221112 Fossil
   Fuel Electric Power Generation; 221113 Nuclear
   Electric Power Generation; 221119 Other Electric
   Power Generation; 221121 Electric Bulk Power
   Transmission and Control; 325182 Carbon Black
   Manufacturing

■ ■ ■

Calgary-based TransCanada Corporation is one of North
America's leading owners of natural gas pipeline and is
also involved in a growing array of power generation
projects. The company's network of natural gas pipelines
extends more than 59,000 kilometers (36,500 miles).

Much of this network is comprised of the trans-
Canadian pipeline upon which the firm was founded,
and after which it was named. This pipeline connects
the rich natural gas fields of Alberta with customers
across Canada and in the United States as well. Another
major portion of this network, acquired in 2007,
encompasses 17,000 kilometers (10,500 miles) of
pipeline linking fields in Louisiana, Oklahoma, Texas,
and the Gulf of Mexico to the U.S. Midwest.

In addition to its pipelines, TransCanada is one of
the continent's largest providers of gas storage facilities
with the capacity to store approximately 360 billion
cubic feet of gas. The company is also a growing
independent power producer, with outright ownership
or interests in a variety of projects in Canada and the
United States with a collective power generation capacity of around 7,700 megawatts. TransCanada's power
plants encompass a diverse mix of nuclear, natural gas,
coal, hydro, and wind generation facilities. Among other
company interests, TransCanada's Cancarb Limited
subsidiary is a leading international manufacturer of
high-quality, thermal carbon black.

OVERCOMING THE HURDLES TO
A TRANS-CANADIAN PIPELINE

TransCanada overcame engineering and financial hurdles
in its early years. Building a gas pipeline across Canada
was a project equal in scale to the building of the cross-
country railway and was the subject of one of the most
contentious chapters in Canada's economic and political
history.

Although a trans-Canadian natural gas pipeline had been proposed as early as 1931, its actual establishment was linked to political, social, and economic events that took place in an atmosphere peculiar to Canada in the 1950s. For one, the country's population was booming, especially in the cities. The population of metropolitan Montreal alone grew from 1.83 million in 1956 to 2.57 million in 1966. The 1950s also witnessed the greatest economic boom in Canada's history, and the energy shortage was real. At no period of history was this more apparent than during the World War II era, when Canadians learned that they could not depend on energy from the United States, as the United States put its own energy needs first. The young generation of the 1950s was self-consciously Canadian and deeply suspicious of its neighbor to the south. Although economic prosperity increased, so did U.S. ownership of most of Canada's wealth: approximately 70 percent of Canada's oil industry, 56 percent of its manufacturing industry, and 52 percent of Canadian mines were owned by U.S. businesses, and these percentages would grow. Growing national sentiment called for railways and a trans-Canadian pipeline to be built completely within Canada, regardless of cost.

Economic boom times, the looming energy shortage, and the election of a new government in 1957, which brought renowned nationalist John Diefenbaker to the helm as prime minister, all set the stage for the adoption of a plan to harvest Alberta's rich deposits of natural gas. At the same time, the St. Lawrence Seaway, which would enable Canadian agricultural and industrial products to be shipped worldwide, was under construction.

As it turned out, it took an almost epic struggle to build the trans-Canadian pipeline. L. D. M. Baxter, a Canadian financier, was the first to advocate a trans-Canadian pipeline to bring Alberta natural gas to eastern Canada, although even he had doubts about the plan's feasibility. The obstacle, as he saw it, was the Laurentian Shield of northern Ontario, a vast rocky area that is the chief geographical barrier separating eastern

from western Canada. Canadians were not alone, however, in perceiving the value of a pipeline. On the U.S. side, the prospect of natural gas from Canada also tempted some businessmen to invest in such a venture. Clint Murchison, a Texan and head of Canadian Delhi Oil Company, believed the pipeline could be run through the Laurentian Shield.

By 1954 both Canadian and U.S. interests had agreed on the usefulness of a pipeline through Canada that also would export gas to the United States. The difficulty, however, was in reaching agreement on the financing of the scheme. Because it was to be an all-Canadian route, the U.S. participants, who had formed a company called TransCanada PipeLines, insisted that financing should be split evenly, while the Canadian interest group, Western Pipe Lines Limited, opposed this 50-50 proposal because the United States had far greater financial resources at its disposal than did Canada. The Canadian group wanted the United States to take on 90 percent of the cost. In the end the Canadian investors agreed to the 50-50 split and sought to persuade their government to finance the pipeline. The person sponsoring the pipeline bill in Parliament was C. D. Howe, the minister of transport. An engineer by training, he would come to view the pipeline as the crowning achievement of his career.

FINANCING, APPROVAL, AND CONSTRUCTION OF THE PIPELINE

TransCanada PipeLines Limited (TCPL) was incorporated in 1951 to undertake the pipeline project. The first president of the new company was Nathan Eldon Tanner, who remained at the helm until the pipeline was completed. While other members of the board of directors had greater influence and experience, Tanner was a mediator. The major problem to be negotiated in 1955 was convincing the government of the financial viability of the company. After prolonged negotiations, the Royal Bank of Canada lent TCPL CAD 25.5 million, and a Montreal financier successfully negotiated large loans from the Canada Bank of Commerce as well as from the Royal Bank, thus enabling the company to win crucial government backing.

The pipeline bill reached the floor of Parliament in 1956, and engendered months of rancorous debate and fears of a tighter U.S. hold, despite the strenuous effort of Transport Minister Howe to convince doubters of the wholly Canadian nature of the enterprise. By then, Canadian interests lobbying against the pipeline bill regarded it as a sellout to U.S. interests. Opponents felt that the pipeline would only provide the United States with cheap Canadian gas. Even in the United States op-

KEY DATES

1951: TransCanada PipeLines Limited (TCPL) is incorporated to undertake the construction a trans-Canadian natural gas pipeline.

1956: Canada's Parliament approves construction of the pipeline.

1958: TCPL completes construction of the 2,200-mile-long pipeline, at the time, the longest in the world.

1967: Company extends its pipeline along the Great Lakes in the United States.

1992: The Iroquois extension of the mainline TCPL pipeline is completed.

1998: In a CAD 15.6 billion deal, TCPL merges with NOVA Corporation.

1999: Major restructuring is launched to refocus the firm on its natural gas pipeline and power generation businesses.

2003: TransCanada Corporation is set up as a holding company for TransCanada PipeLines and other subsidiaries; company acquires a minority stake in the Bruce Power nuclear facility in Ontario.

2007: TransCanada significantly expands its natural gas pipeline and storage assets by purchasing American Natural Resources Company and ANR Storage Company for $3.4 billion.

position was beginning to mount. In the coal industry in particular fears were voiced that Canadian natural gas would displace coal and lead to layoffs, while only Canadians would benefit. Howe was not a smooth negotiator, but his expertise and influence ultimately combined to steer the bill successfully through Parliament. The pipeline was finally approved in June 1956.

Building commenced on a monumental scale in 1957. By December 1, the Toronto-to-Montreal segment had been completed. The entire project was finished in October 1958, as originally scheduled. More than 2,200 miles long, it was the longest pipeline in the world, and was expanded almost continuously.

In 1958 Tanner resigned as CEO and president; his replacement was James Kerr. Kerr was new to the pipeline business. He had worked for Canadian Westinghouse since 1937, becoming a divisional vice-president of Westinghouse in 1956; like others on the board of directors of TCPL, Kerr was a Canadian nationalist, who accepted the offer to become head of TCPL out of a sense of patriotism. At this time, TCPL's deficit was the company's biggest problem, one that it would not overcome until 1961.

In the 1960s the company entered the computer age, developing a highly sophisticated computer system that could measure and control the flow of gas precisely, the first such system devised for pipelines. The company diversified into the chemical industry during this decade, establishing the first of numerous gas-extraction plants in Empress, Alberta. In 1967 TCPL was permitted to extend its pipeline along the Great Lakes in the United States, an extension that was completed that same year. One year later, TCPL celebrated the tenth anniversary of its pipeline operations. Between 1958 and 1968, operating revenue had multiplied nearly sevenfold, from CAD 30 million to CAD 200 million, and net income had risen from a deficit of CAD 8.5 million to a surplus of CAD 17.5 million, while the proportion of Canadian shareholders had grown to 94 percent.

By the 1970s TCPL was a world leader in pipeline technology. Vast subterranean natural gas pockets lay untouched in northern and western Canada, and exploiting this natural wealth was the goal of the company in the 1970s. The publicly traded company was majority owned by Dome Petroleum Limited from 1979 to 1983, when Canada's largest and most profitable conglomerate, Bell Canada Enterprises Inc. (BCE), purchased a 44 percent interest in TCPL. The new shareholder gave TCPL the extra financial support it needed to focus on geographic expansion, rather than diversification, as annual growth in Canadian demand for natural gas slowed to about 2 percent in the late 1980s. Beginning in late 1985, deregulation of the Canadian natural gas industry led to price competition. By 1988, prices for TransCanada's gas, which had previously been locked in with long-term contracts, ran about 80 percent higher than many competitors' prices. At the same time, growing demand in the United States that was unmet by U.S. energy companies helped draw TransCanada into that market.

EXPANSIONS AND NEW PROJECTS

In 1990 TCPL proposed the biggest pipeline construction project in Canadian history: a CAD 2.4 billion expansion of its system. The expansion called for the erection of about 1,600 kilometers of pipeline, a 15 percent increase in TransCanada's total system capacity. Unlike the vast majority of its previous growth, about 75 percent of the gas transported by this pipeline was designed for the Iroquois Gas Transmission System (of which TCPL would own a 29 percent interest), and eventual use in U.S. residences and businesses in coastal New England.

Not surprisingly, the primary stumbling block to this international expansion was the question of who would pay for it. TCPL's Canadian customers (especially industrial gas users) resisted footing the bill, saying that the U.S. customers who would benefit from the "megaproject" should pick up the accompanying "megacheck." In spite of this opposition, TCPL won approval from the U.S. Federal Energy Regulatory Commission (FERC) to deliver western Canadian gas to the northeastern United States. Other FERC and Canadian National Energy Board rulings gave TCPL permission to expand its Great Lakes gas transmission system and mainline systems, respectively, which allowed Canadian natural gas to be carried through TCPL's mainline system to Iroquois, Ontario, across the St. Lawrence River to New York, Connecticut, and New Jersey in the United States. The Iroquois extension was completed in late 1992.

The company also obtained a contract to sell to the California market and received a license to export natural gas to Michigan in 1990. These authorizations not only gave TransCanada one of the world's largest pipeline construction projects and entrée into the competitive U.S. natural gas market, but also helped siphon off a glut of gas in Alberta and thereby boost gas prices deflated by post-deregulation competition. In April 1992 TCPL sought approval of another construction project, a CAD 500 million expansion of domestic services in Saskatchewan, Manitoba, and Ontario.

The company appeared to have been unaffected by the recession of the early 1990s, with the president and CEO, Gerald Maier, expecting an annual earnings growth rate of from 10 percent to 15 percent in the 1990s. Like most established utilities, TCPL was accustomed to making slow but steady increases in profits. Net income in 1990 rose a surprising 14.9 percent from 1989, while the company pursued streamlining, divesting itself of unprofitable businesses, such as its interests in Les Mines Selbaie and the Montreal Pipeline Ltd. in Quebec province. Then, in the first half of 1992, the company's overall profit jumped 30 percent, making TransCanada one of Canada's "10 most popular stocks." The company took advantage of its popularity with new stock and debenture issues. In the spring of 1993, BCE divested the last of its TCPL holdings, "selling high."

VENTURING INTO POWER GENERATION AND OVERSEAS

By the early 1990s, TCPL had also developed interests in electric power generation projects. The company had full ownership of the 36-megawatt Nipigon Power Plant in Nipigon, Ontario, which used waste heat from an adjacent compressor station on TransCanada's mainline pipeline. The company also held a 40 percent stake in the 500-megawatt Ocean State Power Plant in Rhode Island. In June 1997 TCPL transferred its three Ontario power plants—the Nipigon facility along with two 40-megawatt plants in Kapuskasing and North Bay that had been completed in 1996—to a limited partnership called TransCanada Power, L.P. The company sold 50 percent of the shares in this entity to the public and retained the other half.

In the fall of 1994, meantime, TCPL bought into its first major venture outside North America with an investment in a $2.5 billion Colombian pipeline project. TCPL was a primary participant in the undertaking, sharing about 40 percent of the investment and responsibility with fellow Canadian company IPL Energy Inc. Other partners included British Petroleum Co. PLC; Total S.A. of France; Triton Energy Corp. of Dallas, Texas; and Ecopetrol, a state-owned Colombian oil company. The project proposed to develop one of the world's largest oil discoveries, the Cusiana oilfield. It was estimated that the area contained 1.5 billion barrels of oil. Completed in 1997, the $2.3 billion venture was considered TransCanada's shot at "international credibility." At this same time, TransCanada was also participating in a $320 million gas-to-electricity power plant project in Tanzania. Maier, who had advanced to chairman and was succeeded as CEO by George Watson in 1994, hoped that these international efforts would serve as a launchpad to accelerated earnings growth and elevation into the ranks of "world-class" pipeline companies.

In March 1996 TransCanada ventured further into the midstream portion of the natural gas industry by acquiring the 50.5 percent of Alberta Natural Gas Company Ltd. (ANG) it did not already own. Among its Alberta-centered assets, ANG gathered, marketed, and distributed natural gas and also processed it into natural gas liquids, ethane, and carbon dioxide. ANG also owned a key pipeline that transmitted natural gas from the Alberta border through British Columbia to connect with the Pacific Gas Transmission System, which served markets in the U.S. Pacific Northwest, California, and Nevada. Another ANG unit was ANGUS Chemical Company, a leading producer of specialty chemicals derived from nitroparaffins with plants in Louisiana and Germany.

TCPL in 1997 announced plans for a new pipeline to carry natural gas from Emerson, Manitoba, to the Chicago region. The CAD 1.7 billion joint project with Minneapolis-based utility Northern States Power Company was abandoned a year later after the partners failed to garner enough support from natural gas producers. Competition from the nascent Alliance Pipeline L.P., a consortium led by Enbridge Inc., played a key role in this project's demise. By late 2000 Alliance Pipeline had succeeded in beginning operation of a 3,000-kilometer (1,860-mile) pipeline transmitting natural gas from northeastern British Columbia to the outskirts of Chicago.

1998 MERGER WITH NOVA

In an environment featuring increasing competition from Alliance, Enbridge, and other players as well as a drive for consolidation fueled by deregulatory initiatives in both the United States and Canada, TransCanada engineered a dramatic merger. In July 1998 TCPL merged with NOVA Corporation, also based in Calgary, in a CAD 15.6 billion deal that at the time ranked as the largest merger in Canadian corporate history. The marriage brought together TransCanada's primary pipelines carrying natural gas out of Alberta to central Canada and the United States with NOVA's Alberta System, a network of 22,400 kilometers (13,900 miles) of pipeline used to gather natural gas within the province and deliver it to provincial boundary points for connection with other pipelines, including the TCPL mainline. The merger was thus highly complementary: the Alberta System supplied roughly 90 percent of the gas volume carried by TransCanada's primary lines.

The merged entity, which ranked as one of the largest energy-services companies in North America, retained the TransCanada PipeLines name. Upon completion of the merger, NOVA's commodity chemicals business was split off into an independent public company, NOVA Chemicals Corporation. Via the merger, TCPL also gained NOVA's interests in various international energy projects, mainly natural gas pipelines and related operations in South America. TCPL further bolstered its international profile in July 1998 by purchasing the Netherlands division of Occidental Petroleum Corporation for $275 million. This division held stakes in offshore natural-gas production operations in the Dutch North Sea and in the natural gas pipeline system servicing the area.

MAJOR RESTRUCTURING

The TransCanada-NOVA merger quickly turned sour and eventually prompted a major overhaul that created a company highly focused on a couple of key areas. The amalgamation required hundreds of employee layoffs as duplications in various company functions were eliminated. Merger-related charges of CAD 390 million cut net income for 1998 to CAD 361 million, almost half the total for the previous year. As the company's difficulties mounted in 1999, Watson resigned abruptly midyear and was replaced as CEO by Douglas Baldwin, a 40-year-plus veteran of Imperial Oil Limited, who had retired from that firm at the end of 1998.

By the time Baldwin took over, TCPL was contending with a CAD 11.6 billion debt load bloated by the merger with NOVA. Flirting with bankruptcy because of this debt, the company was also in danger of being taken over because of a dramatic drop in the price of its stock. Late in 1999 Baldwin and the company board slashed the annual dividend to conserve cash, prompting investors to further pummel its stock, and also embarked on a major divestment program that ultimately jettisoned CAD 3.5 billion worth of noncore businesses. The restructuring refocused TransCanada on two main businesses (natural gas transmission and related gas marketing operations and power generation) with a geographic footprint restricted to Canada and the northern tier of the United States. Because the pipeline industry was highly regulated in Canada, and therefore offered few opportunities for growth, TCPL placed its hopes for future expansion on its power generation business.

After selling ANGUS Chemical to the Dow Chemical Company late in 1999, the larger of the divestments included a sale of the company's natural gas liquids and extraction facilities in Alberta and British Columbia, which were sold to the Williams Companies, Inc. By 2001 TransCanada's various international businesses and interests had been sold through a number of piecemeal transactions. The company was able to wrap up the planned divestments in 2001, although a sale of Cancarb announced in September 2000 later fell through. By the end of 2001, TCPL had reduced its debt to a more manageable CAD 9.35 billion, while cash flow was growing significantly and shareholder return was improving as well.

A GROWING POWER GENERATION BUSINESS

As this overhaul progressed, TCPL moved boldly to significantly expand its position in its chosen growth arena, power generation. In 2000 the company purchased full ownership of the Ocean State Power Plant in Rhode Island, the capacity of which had been bumped up to 560 megawatts. TransCanada also built several cogeneration facilities, power plants that capture the heat generated by conventional natural gas-fueled electricity generation to create a second energy source. In 2001 construction was completed on two cogeneration facilities in Alberta, an 80-megawatt plant near Carseland and a 40-megawatt plant near Redwater. Construction began that same year on two more Alberta cogeneration facilities, an 80-megawatt plant near Grande Prairie and a 165-megawatt near Fort McMurray, both of which began operation in 2003.

Baldwin, initially appointed CEO on an interim basis, remained in the post longer than expected but finally retired in mid-2001 when the restructuring had largely been completed. Promoted to CEO was Harold "Hal" Kvisle (pronounced QUIZ-lee), who had joined TransCanada in 1999 after ten years of executive leadership at international subsidiaries of the New Zealand firm Fletcher Challenge Ltd. Kvisle had played a key role in TransCanada's turnaround efforts and in the buildup of its power generation business.

In 2003 the firm changed to a holding company structure, setting up TransCanada Corporation as the parent for TransCanada PipeLines and other subsidiaries. That February, TransCanada took another big step into power generation by spending CAD 451 million for a minority stake in the Bruce Power nuclear facility, located near Port Elgin, Ontario, on Lake Huron. The Bruce facility included eight nuclear reactors, six of which were operating by early 2004 with an aggregate capacity of 4,660 megawatts. Bruce Power also operated a small, nine-megawatt adjacent wind farm, the first commercial wind farm in the province.

Also in 2003 TransCanada began construction of two more power plants, both located in eastern Canada. A 550-megawatt natural gas-fired cogeneration power plant located near Trois-Rivières, Quebec, went into operation in September 2006, with its entire output going to Hydro-Québec. In 2005 TransCanada began operating a 90-megawatt natural gas-fired cogeneration facility on the site of the Irving Oil Limited refinery in Saint John, New Brunswick. In April 2005 the company purchased from USGen New England, Inc., a series of hydroelectric facilities on the Connecticut and Deerfield Rivers in New Hampshire, Vermont, and Massachusetts. These operations had a total generating capacity of 567 megawatts. The purchase price was roughly $503 million.

TransCanada also ventured further into wind power. It held an initial 50 percent stake (later raised to 62 percent) in Cartier Wind Energy Inc., which began constructing a 740-megawatt wind project in the Gaspé region of Quebec. The first portion of this project, with a capacity of 110 megawatts, began generating energy for Hydro-Québec in November 2006. In September

2005 TransCanada sold its minority stake in Trans-Canada Power, L.P., to EPCOR Utilities Inc. for CAD 529 million. At the time, TransCanada Power was operating 11 plants in the United States and Canada with a total capacity of 774 megawatts. TransCanada Corporation elected to divest this interest in order to concentrate on its larger, directly owned power businesses in Canada and the United States.

Two more such projects were soon under construction: a 550-megawatt natural gas-fired plant located in downtown Toronto, slated for start-up in mid-2008, and a 683-megawatt natural gas-fired plant sited near Halton Hills, Ontario, slated for completion in 2010. By 2007 revenues from TransCanada's power generation approached that of the flagship pipeline operations. With the company's diverse and growing array of power plants reaching a collective total of 7,700 megawatts, net income from this business had skyrocketed from just CAD 40 million in 1999 to CAD 514 million in 2007.

PIPELINE ACQUISITIONS AND NEW ENDEAVORS

TransCanada was quite active on the pipeline front as well during this same period. In November 2004 TransCanada acquired the Gas Transmission Northwest System (formerly the Pacific Gas Transmission System) for $1.7 billion. This 2,174-kilometer (1,348-mile) pipeline essentially served to expand the company's pipeline system in British Columbia and Alberta, enabling TransCanada to ship natural gas from Alberta to the U.S. Pacific Northwest and down to California and Nevada. In February 2007 the company significantly bolstered its natural gas pipeline and storage assets by purchasing American Natural Resources Company and ANR Storage Company from El Paso Corporation. The total purchase price of $3.4 billion included $457 million of assumed debt. TransCanada gained 17,000 kilometers (10,500 miles) of pipeline linking natural gas production fields in Louisiana, Oklahoma, Texas, and the Gulf of Mexico to the midwestern states of Wisconsin, Illinois, Indiana, Ohio, and Michigan. The deal also nearly tripled the company's gas storage capacity with the addition of underground gas storage facilities in Michigan with an aggregate capacity of around 230 billion cubic feet.

In addition to growing through acquisition, Trans-Canada was pursuing no fewer than three major pipeline projects. With oil prices skyrocketing, and discoveries of new fields dwindling, the Albertan oil sands had become an increasingly vital source of crude oil. TransCanada proposed a new crude oil pipeline designed to transport heavy oil-sands crude from Hardisty, Alberta, to refineries in southern Illinois and Cushing, Oklahoma. This project, dubbed Keystone, involved the conversion of 1,240 kilometers (770 miles) of existing Canadian pipeline from natural gas to crude oil transmission plus the construction of 2,200 kilometers (1,360 miles) of new pipeline and pump stations in the United States. By late in 2007 the estimated cost of Keystone had grown to $5.2 billion. By that time, ConocoPhillips had committed to shipping crude oil on the pipeline, and in early 2008 the U.S. oil giant acquired a 50 percent stake in the project. Designed to carry 590,000 barrels of oil a day, Keystone needed U.S. and Canadian regulatory approval before moving forward, but TransCanada hoped to have the pipeline in operation by late 2009.

TransCanada was also part of a consortium working to develop the Mackenzie Gas Project, a proposal for a 1,220-kilometer (755-mile) natural gas pipeline along the Mackenzie Valley of Canada's Northwest Territories. The pipeline would run from onshore gas fields in the northern Northwest Territories to the border with Alberta, where it would interconnect with TransCanada's Alberta System. The consortium, led by ExxonMobil Canada Ltd., hoped to have this CAD 16.2 billion project up and running by 2010.

Most ambitious of all was TransCanada's Alaska Pipeline Project, a 2,700-kilometer (1,670-mile) pipeline designed to carry natural gas from Prudhoe Bay in Alaska to northwestern Alberta. The company's proposal called for the pipeline to follow the route of the existing trans-Alaska oil pipeline and the Alaska Highway, continue through northern British Columbia, and finally connect with the Alberta System. TransCanada faced numerous hurdles before construction could even begin on this massive project, projected to cost $26.5 billion. In addition to regulatory approval, the company had to secure a license from the state of Alaska and gain long-term commitments from potential shippers, particularly BP p.l.c., ConocoPhillips, and Exxon Mobil Corporation. By early 2008 the projected completion date was 2017.

Sina Dubovoj
Updated, David E. Salamie

PRINCIPAL SUBSIDIARIES

TransCanada PipeLines Limited; NOVA Gas Transmission Ltd.; TransCanada PipeLine USA Ltd.; TransCanada Energy Ltd; Cancarb Limited.

PRINCIPAL COMPETITORS

Enbridge Inc.; Fortis Inc.; U.S. Gas Transmission; The Williams Companies, Inc.; Dynegy Inc.; Petro-Canada.

FURTHER READING

Brethour, Patrick, "TransCanada Pipeline Proposal Fires Up Tension with Enbridge," *Globe and Mail*, February 10, 2005, p. B2.

Byfield, Mike, "Birth of an Oil-Patch Titan: TransCanada's Gerry Maier Wrestles U.S. Giants in a Billion-Dollar Pipeline Duel," *Alberta Report*, October 28, 1991, pp. 42–46.

Carlisle, Tamsin, "TransCanada, Nova Agree to Merge Their Operations," *Wall Street Journal*, January 27, 1998, p. B4.

Chase, Steven, "TCPL: Penny Wise, Pound Foolish?" *Globe and Mail*, December 10, 1999, p. B12.

———, "TCPL Sells Chemical Arm," *Globe and Mail*, August 3, 1999, p. B1.

———, "TCPL's George Watson Resigns," *Globe and Mail*, July 17, 1999, p. B1.

Chu, Showwei, "TransCanada Plugs into Power," *Globe and Mail*, August 7, 2003, p. B12.

Cook, James, "Back from the Dead," *Forbes*, April 3, 1989, pp. 90+.

Ebner, Dave, "Conoco Signs On to Oil Sands Pipeline," *Globe and Mail*, November 4, 2005, p. B1.

———, "TransCanada Alone in Bid for Alaska Contract," *Globe and Mail*, January 5, 2008, p. B6.

———, "TransCanada Bulks Up for Winter: Buys Pipelines, Storage Facilities from El Paso in $3.4-Billion Deal," *Globe and Mail*, December 23, 2006, p. B5.

———, "TransCanada Set to Boost Keystone Pipeline," *Globe and Mail*, January 31, 2007, p. B7.

———, "TransCanada's Keystone Line to Ship Oil Sands Crude," *Globe and Mail*, February 1, 2006, p. B5.

Fagan, Drew, and Christopher Donville, "$2.4-Billion TCPL Project Approved," *Globe and Mail*, May 10, 1991, p. B1.

Fleming, James, "Bell Pursues a Startled Quarry," *Maclean's*, December 19, 1983, pp. 28+.

Goad, G. Pierre, "BCE Agrees to Sell Stake in TransCanada," *Wall Street Journal*, September 11, 1990, p. A3.

Ip, Greg, "TransCanada Launches Bid for ANG," *Globe and Mail*, January 20, 1996, p. B1.

Jang, Brent, "Nova, TCPL Tying the Knot," *Globe and Mail*, January 26, 1998, p. B1.

Kilbourn, William, *Pipeline: TransCanada and the Great Debate, a History of Business and Politics*, Toronto: Clarke, Irwin, 1970, 222 p.

McGee, Suzanne, and Gary Lamphier, "Recession-Resistant TransCanada PipeLines Is Poised to Realize Strong Growth Potential," *Wall Street Journal*, November 6, 1990, p. C2.

McGee, Suzanne, and Sonia L. Nazario, "TransCanada Pipe-Lines Plans to Buy Canada-to-California Link from PG&E," *Wall Street Journal*, September 6, 1991, p. A4.

Newman, Peter C., *Promise of the Pipeline*, Calgary: TransCanada PipeLines, 1993, 70 p.

———, "Tending Canada's Only Megaproject," *Maclean's*, March 2, 1992, p. 32.

Nguyen, Lily, "TCPL Head Injects Some Balance to Balance Sheet," *Globe and Mail*, October 9, 2000, p. B10.

———, "TCPL Investors Cheer $1.15-Billion Asset Sale," *Globe and Mail*, August 4, 2000, p. B1.

———, "TCPL Picks CEO from Own Ranks," *Globe and Mail*, March 22, 2001, p. B1.

———, "TCPL Sells Netherlands Assets," *Globe and Mail*, August 24, 2000, p. B3.

Share, Jeff, "After Successful Turnaround TransCanada CEO Ready for Bright Future in Natural Gas, Power," *Pipeline and Gas Journal*, January 2003, pp. 18–24, 26–27.

Sheppard, Robert, "Pressured TransCanada Starting to Cut New Deals," *Globe and Mail*, June 20, 1988, p. B1.

———, "TCPL Plans to Sell $200 Million in Energy Assets to Lighten Debt," *Globe and Mail*, September 17, 1988, p. B3.

"Tall Order," *Oilweek*, May 4, 1998, pp. 24+.

"TransCanada Buying ANR Pipeline, Storage from El Paso," *Pipeline and Gas Journal*, January 2007, p. 4.

CJSC Transmash Holding

Ozerkovskaya Nab 54/1
Moscow, 115054
Russia
Telephone: (+7 495) 744 70 93
Fax: (+7 495) 744 70 94
Web site: http://www.tmholding.ru

Public Company
Incorporated: 2002
Employees: 53,000
Sales: $2.1 billion (2007)
Stock Exchanges: Moscow
Ticker Symbol: BBD.BT
NAIC: 336510 Railroad Rolling Stock Manufacturing;
551112 Offices of Other Holding Companies

■ ■ ■

CJSC Transmash Holding has emerged from the reform of the Russian railway system as the country's largest producer of locomotives, rolling stock, and other railroad infrastructure equipment. Created in 2001, Transmash has benefited from the privatization of most of the Russian railroad industry under President Vladimir Putin. Among Transmash's holdings are Demikhovsky Engineering Plant, which manufactures 80 percent of all electric trains in Russia, and is also the largest manufacturer of electric rail rolling stock in Europe; Bryansk Engineering Plant, the top producer of diesel locomotives and freight rolling stock in Russia; Novocherkassk Electric Locomotive Plant (Novocherkasskij Elektrovozostroitelnyj Zavod, or NEVZ),

in Rostov, a major producer of electric-powered passenger, freight, and traction locomotives; a 25 percent stake in Tver Carriage Works, which is the leading manufacturer of passenger railcars in Russia; Bezhitsk Steel Foundry, based in Bryansk, the country's top producer of car castings, such as bolsters, bogies, couplers, axle boxes, and other products, including check valves; Tsentrovarmash, in Tver, also a major producer of rail components; and Moscow-region-based Kolomensky Zavod, which manufactures medium-speed diesel locomotives, as well as diesel-powered marine and rail engines and generators. The company's Metrowagonmash, in Mytishchi, produces rolling stock and components for subway systems and other railways; Penzadieselmash manufactures diesel engines and turbochargers; while Oktyabrsky Electric Railway Car Repair Plant, based in Saint Petersburg, is one of the leaders in the repair and maintenance sector.

In addition to these companies, Transmash oversees Saint Petersburg-based KMT Industrial Group, which designs and manufactures passenger railcar equipment. In 2005, the company formed Transconverter, a joint venture with Siemens AG, which produces high-voltage static converters for the Transmash's locomotive and railcars. In order to gain access to new high-speed technologies, the company also acquired Dessau, Germany's FTD Fahrzeugtechnik Dessau AG. Altogether, Transmashholding employs more than 53,000 people and generates annual revenues of more than $2.1 billion. The company is led by Dmitry Komissarov, chairman, and Petr Sinshinov, general director, both of whom are close associates of Vladimir Putin. The company is listed on the Moscow Stock Exchange.

Major shareholders include OJSC HC Kuzbassrazrezugol and TransGroup AC. Russian Railways remains the company's single largest customer, accounting for 55 percent of its sales in 2006.

POST-SOVIET RAILWAYS COLLAPSE

The collapse of the Soviet Union inaugurated a bleak period for Russia's railroad industries. Investment in the railroads, already low in the 1980s, all but ended in the early 1990s. The difficult transition to a market economy, which plunged the country into an extended economic crisis through much of the decade and into the next, had far-reaching consequences for the country's railroads.

This was especially true for the dense network of engineering and manufacturing factories set up during the Soviet era. Even into the end of the 1980s, Soviet Union Railways continued to place orders for as many as 1,000 new locomotives each year. Yet, with the collapse of that government, new orders for locomotives shrank drastically. As *Railway Gazette International* reported, during the 1990s, Russian Railways, which inherited the country's rail system, bought just 100 locomotives.

As a result, the country's railroad engineering and manufacturing sector experienced a deep crisis, with many of the largest companies, such as Novocherkasskij Elektrovozostroitelnyj Zavod (Novocherkassk Electric Locomotive Plant, or NEVZ), going bankrupt during this time. The reform of the Russian railroad industry was an imperative part of the country's overall economic restructuring. Yet throughout the decade, the Railways Ministry remained dominated by people who had built their careers during the Soviet era. As a result, the reform process proceeded only sluggishly, with little positive result.

PRIVATIZING THE INDUSTRY IN 2001

Vladimir Putin's election signaled the start of the long-delayed reform process. Putin quickly solidified his policies by placing his own allies into top ministry and industrial positions. In particular, Putin installed close associate Vladimir Yakunin as the head of the sprawling and deeply troubled Russian Railways, helping to push through a massive streamlining of that company.

By 2001, the government had begun the privatization of its railroad industry in earnest. New companies appeared to take advantage of the new opportunities available as waves of Russia's largest factories came up for sale. Among these new companies was Transmash, which appeared to have been formed as part of a company called Galls Group, which acquired the assets of Bryansk Engineering Plant (BMZ) in 2001.

Founded in 1873, the Bryansk factory had grown into Russia's leading producer of main line diesel locomotives, as well as engines, and a major manufacturer of freight railcars. Like other factories in its sector, BMZ's fortunes collapsed with the end of the Soviet Empire, and by the beginning of the new century the company had gone bankrupt.

As part of its restructuring of BMZ's assets, Transmash itself sought out new shareholders. In 2002, the company brought in two major investors, TransGroup, a leading rail operator in the country, and OJSC HC Kuzbassrazrezugol, part of Urals Mining and Metallurgical Company. The company itself dated its formation from this time.

With its new shareholders came a new chairman, in the form of Dmitry Komissarov, former head of Soyuz Integratsiya. His appointment to this position came as something of a surprise, given his lack of experience in the railroad sector. Yet Komissarov brought other features to Transmash, notably his close friendship with Vladimir Putin.

GROWTH THROUGH ACQUISITIONS

Transmash held a front-row seat in the ongoing privatization of Russia's manufacturing and engineering sectors. By 2002, the company had added two more major holdings in the railway sector. The first consisted of control, through a 25 percent stake, in Tverskoi vagonostroitelny zavod (Tver Railway Car Works, or TVZ). That company, founded in 1898 as Tver Carriage Works, had grown into Russia's leading manufacturer of passenger railcars. Transmash also

KEY DATES

KEY DATES

2001: Transmash is created in order to acquire Bryansk Engineering Plant (BMZ) and other privatized rail industry manufacturers in Russia.
2005: Company forms Transconverter joint venture with Siemens AG.
2006: Company launches restructuring and consolidation of assets.
2007: Company forms partnerships with Bombardier and Alsthom.

acquired a controlling stake in Muromsky strelochny zavod (Muromsky Switch Factory), which helped form the basis of the company's later components manufacturing business.

From the start, Transmash worked closely with the Ministry of Railways and Russian Railways as they carried out the continued reform of the railway sector. This enabled the company to snap up more companies slated for privatization. The next major addition to Transmash's holdings was Novocherkassky elektrovozostroitelny zavod (Novocherkassk Electric Locomotive Plant) in Rostov. That operation, established by the Soviets in 1936, was the country's leading producer of electric-powered locomotives.

Also acquired by Transmash in 2003 was Kuvshinsky zavod transportnogo oborudovaniya (Kuvshinsky Transport Equipment Factory). That purchase helped broaden Transmash's operations, as it developed a full-range of railroad-oriented manufacturing and engineering expertise.

PARTNERSHIP WITH RUSSIAN RAILWAYS

The company's first round of acquisitions had enabled it to build, in the space of just two years, a collection of businesses posting total revenues of more than $500 million. By then, the reform of the Russian rail system had taken a major step forward with the creation of the Russian Railways Joint Stock Co. in 2003.

Transmashholding became the major supplier to Russian Railways as it embarked on a massive upgrade of the aging Russian railways system. Into 2006, Russian Railways accounted for 55 percent of the company's total revenues. In 2007, the two companies' relationship deepened, when Russian Railways announced its intention to buy a "blocking stake" in Transmashholding (25 percent plus one share).

At the same time, Transmash continued picking off many of the country's leading manufacturers in the sector as the privatization process continued into the middle of the decade. By 2006, the company boasted nearly a dozen major production facilities. These included diesel locomotive and engine producer Kolomensky Zavod. Located in Kolomna, near Moscow, that company also became the oldest member of Transmashholding, dating its origins back to 1863.

The addition of Demikhovsky Engineering Plant (DMZ) in Orekhovo-Zuyevo, Moscow, gave the company a boost in the electric railroad segment. That factory had been formed in 1935, and had emerged as the single largest producer of electric trains, accounting for 80 percent of Russia's total market. DMZ also claimed to be the largest manufacturer of railcars for electric trains in Europe. The company's rolling stock operations were further boosted with the addition of Metrowagonmash, based in Mytishchi, which produced rolling stock for subway systems and commuter railroads.

GOING FORWARD WITH INTERNATIONAL PARTNERSHIPS

Transmash began seeking further partnerships at mid-decade. Among the first of these was an agreement with Siemens AG to create a joint venture, Transconverter, in 2005. That company began producing high-voltage static converters to be included in Transmash's electric locomotives, trains, and passenger railcars. Transmash also moved to position itself as a major player in the coming market for high-speed trains in Russia. To this end, the company acquired control of Dessau, Germany-based FTD Fahrzeugtechnik Dessau AG.

With its initial acquisition phase completed by 2006, Transmash was faced with the task of restructuring its newly vast holdings. A major part of this restructuring was the consolidation of the company's assets, particularly in gaining full control of all of its operations. In order to carry out this phase, the company brought in a new "strongman" Petr Sinshinov, as general director. Sinshinov had worked with Russian billionaire Oleg Deripaska before joining Kuzbassrazrezugol. Sinshinov was also closely associated with Vladimir Putin. The restructuring and consolidation of the company's assets was seen as a necessary step for the company as it sought further international partnerships. The company also hoped to attract a major foreign investor as well.

With the restructuring completed in 2007, Transmash turned its attention to forming new partnerships.

In July 2007, the company signed an agreement with Swiss-Canadian Bombardier to form two Russia-based joint ventures. The first of these involved a project to develop advanced propulsion technologies. The second established a manufacturing platform at Novocherkassk using Bombardier's MITRAC technology to manufacture traction converters for the next generation of locomotives on order from Russian Railways.

Transmash continued to seek foreign partners through 2007. In December of that year, the company announced that it had reached a cooperation agreement with France's Alsthom, one of the world's preeminent high-speed train specialists. The agreement called for the creation of a number of joint ventures ranging from producing components to full-scale rolling stock. At the same time, Alsthom appeared to have gained the edge in becoming the foreign partner backing Russian Railways' proposed purchase of the blocking stake in Transmash. In that event, Transmash appeared to be firmly on the rails toward leading the modernization of the Russian rail system.

M. L. Cohen

PRINCIPAL SUBSIDIARIES

Bezhitsk Steel Foundry; Bryansk Engineering Plant; Demikhovsky Engineering Plant; FTD Fahrzeugtechnik Dessau AG (Germany); Kolomensky Zavod; Metrowagonmash; Novocherkassk Electric Locomotive Plant; Penzadieselmash; Transconverter; Tsentrosvarmash; Tver Carriage Works; KMT Industrial Group.

PRINCIPAL COMPETITORS

Indian Railways Board; General Motors Corp.; Siemens AG; Alstom S.A.; MAN AG; Titran Joint Stock Co.; Kawasaki Heavy Industries Ltd.; Hyundai Mobis Company Ltd.; Union Tank Car Co.; Bombardier Transportation (Schweiz) AG; Voith AG; Bombardier Inc.; Knorr-Bremse AG; Qiqihar Vehicle Group Jinche Industrial Co.; Changchun Railway Vehicles Company Ltd.; Tangshan Locomotive and Rolling Stock Works.

FURTHER READING

"Novocherkassk Electric Locomotive Plant Almost Doubled Production," *Inzhenernaia Gazeta,* October 14, 2003, p. 2.

"Russian Market to Boom, but High Speed Plans Slow Down," *Railway Gazette International,* October 2005, p. 598.

"RZD Acquires Blocking Stake in Transmashholding," *Russia & CIS Business and Financial Newswire,* December 26, 2007.

"RZD Planning to Acquire Transmashholding Stake with Foreign Investor," *Russia & CIS Business and Financial Newswire,* September 21, 2007.

Schmouker, Olivier, "Qui Est Transmashholding?" *Lesaffaires. com,* December 3, 2007.

"Transmash and Bombardier Sign Partnership," *Railway Gazette International,* July 2007, p. 450.

"Transmash Consolidation," *Railway Gazette International,* October 2007, p. 661.

"Transmashholding, Alstom to Form Joint Ventures in Russia," *Russia & CIS Business and Financial Newswire,* December 17, 2007.

"Transmashholding Buys Fahrzeugtechnik Dessau AG," *Russia & CIS Business and Financial Newswire,* June 20, 2006.

"Transmashholding Completes Consolidation of Assets," *Russia & CIS Business and Financial Newswire,* August 31, 2007.

Oil Transporting Joint Stock Company Transneft

Ul. Bolshaya Polyanka 57
Moscow, 119180
Russia
Telephone: (+7 495) 950 81 78
Fax: (+7 495) 950 89 00
Web site: http://www.transneft.ru

Public Company
Incorporated: 1993
Employees: 12,000
Sales: RUB 202.42 billion ($7.13 billion) (2006)
Stock Exchanges: Moscow
Ticker Symbol: TRNFP
NAIC: 486910 Pipeline Transportation of Refined Petroleum Products; 486110 Pipeline Transportation of Crude Oil

∎ ∎ ∎

Oil Transporting Joint Stock Company Transneft is Russia's primary crude oil pipeline operator. The publicly traded company, controlled by the Russian government, operates the world's largest unified pipeline network. At the beginning of 2007, Transneft's network covered nearly 48,000 kilometers of pipeline, and transported nearly 460 million tons of oil. This figure represented 93 percent of Russia's total oil production capacity (the country is the world's second largest oil producer). As part of the pipeline network, the company also operated 386 refilling stations and 833 reservoirs, with a total capacity of 14 million cubic meters. Since much of the company's pipeline was constructed during the Soviet era, Transneft is also responsible for carrying out maintenance, upgrades, and replacement of the rapidly aging network.

The company also oversees the continued extension of its pipeline. The company expects to commission the first 2,700-kilometer leg of the new East Siberian oil pipeline in 2008. That pipeline, which will total 4,700 kilometers upon completion, will ultimately provide direct oil transmission from the Eastern Siberia oilfields to Japan, South Korea, and China. In 2007, also, Transneft became part of a trilateral agreement to construct and operate a 285-kilometer pipeline transporting Russian oil from Burgas, in Bulgaria, and Alexandroupolos, in Greece. That pipeline is expected to be completed in 2011. Transneft is listed on the Moscow Stock Exchange.

BAKU OILFIELDS IN THE MID-19TH CENTURY

The Baku oilfields, discovered in the early 1860s, became something of a Russian Wild West, as fortune seekers arrived to stake a claim to what was then one of the world's largest known oil deposits. By the end of the decade there were 120 wells in operation, more than 100 oil companies, and more than two dozen factories, including the first refineries. Many of these facilities were built within the town, and quite a number of them were even operated from residential sites. The fields also attracted a number of major companies of the time, especially the Nobel group.

From the start, transporting the crude oil from the Baku fields to the growing number of refineries, and

KEY DATES

1879: First pipeline in Tsarist Russia links Baku oilfields to Cherny Gorod.
1906: The 835-kilometer Transcaucasian pipeline is completed.
1918: Pipeline operations are nationalized by Soviet government.
1993: Oil Transporting Joint Stock Company Transneft is formed to replace former Soviet-era Glavtransneft.
1999: Company launches first phase of construction of Baltic Pipeline System.
2008: Transneft expects to complete first phase of 4,700-kilometer East Siberian Pipeline.

then from the refineries elsewhere in Russia, had created a major obstacle. At the time, the development of pipelines remained in their infancy, with the first being developed in the United States. While suggestions were made to construct a pipeline connecting the Baku fields to their refineries as early as 1863, the proposal was rejected. Instead, oil was transported in wooden barrels, and later in wineskins. The cost of such transportation methods was high: if a "pood" (the old Russian measurement, equivalent to approximately 400 kilograms) cost three kopecks at the oil well, by the time it had arrived in Baku, it cost as much as 23 kopecks.

Before long transporting oil became even more difficult. Within a few years, the city of Baku had seen a proliferation of fires, while the presence of a more or less unregulated oil industry had seen the development of alarming levels of pollution. By the end of the 1860s, the city's authorities addressed these issues by shifting the focus of the oil industry outside of the city proper. For this, the city created a new industrial zone, called Cherny Gorod, or the Black City.

FIRST PIPELINE IN 1879

The difficulties of transporting oil to Cherny Gorod remained a major impediment to the growth of the Russian oil industry. Yet calls to construct a pipeline continued to meet resistance, in part from groups, including the region's coopers and transport companies, that benefited from the difficult transport conditions. The impetus toward the construction of the country's first pipeline came from the Nobel company, which in 1877 contracted for the construction of a pipeline connecting its refinery in Cherny Gorod to its wells in the

Baku fields. Construction of the pipeline, just 10 kilometers in length, was hampered by repeated acts of sabotage. By 1879, however, the pipeline had been completed and became the first in Russia to become operational.

The Nobel company soon expanded use of the pipeline beyond its own uses. The company agreed to transport the oil production of its rivals through the pipeline, charging five kopecks per pood for the services. As a result, the company quickly recovered the construction costs of the pipeline. That success inspired others to build their own pipelines, and by the end of 1879, a second pipeline was under construction.

The major figure behind the early technical development of Russia's pipelines was Vladimir Shukhov, an engineer working for the Bari company. Shukhov helped solve many of the technical problems of moving oil, and his work "Pipelines and Their Use in Oil Industry," published in 1881, helped set the standard for pipeline design during this period. Shukhov's theories helped launch the development of new oil hydraulics technologies, capable of transporting crude oil over longer distances.

By the mid-1880s, the Baku fields boasted a total of 96 kilometers of pipeline, and were transporting as much as 200,000 poods per day. At the beginning, oil was largely refined into kerosene, used for lighting lamps and heaters. The invention of the first internal combustion engines, however, set the stage for a new surge in demand for oil.

HOOKING UP THE GROZNY FIELDS IN 1895

The demand for oil was met by the discovery of the vast oil deposits in Grozny. At first, these fields too faced difficult transport conditions. Into the early 1890s, transport of the Grozny oil remained the province of horse-drawn carts. This spawned an entire industry, with more than 300 carts hauling as much as 15,000 poods of oil each day. The first pipeline in Grozny appeared only in 1895, built by the Bari company and based on five-inch pipes and stretched approximately 13 kilometers.

The construction of three large-scale refineries in Grozny in 1896 led to the construction of new pipelines. By 1898, the region boasted five pipelines, each operated by different oil companies, with a total throughput capacity of 190 million poods per year. The availability of this capacity stimulated the extraction of oil, and by 1900 the Grozny fields had boosted production past 25 million poods of oil.

Oil by then represented a significant export product for the Russian Empire. As early as 1882, talks had been held discussing the construction of a Transcaucasian pipeline in order to bring oil from the Baku fields to the Black Sea ports in Batumi. Yet, as these plans included proposals to construct a new series of refineries at the ports themselves, the Baku refinery companies helped to quash early plans for the pipeline, favoring the use of rail transport.

The rapid increases in oil output toward the end of the century soon outpaced the railroad's capacity. Proposals for the construction of the Transcaucasian pipeline were developed in the mid-1880s, yet met with continued resistance almost to the end of the 1890s. Construction at last began in 1896, but was only completed in 1906. The total length of the pipeline, which included 16 pumping stations, was 835 kilometers.

NATIONALIZATION IN 1918

The Russian oil industry remained dominated by chaos and indecisiveness through the years of World War I. As a result, the country's pipeline construction lagged far behind its chief rival, the United States. Whereas the United States had successfully completed more than 14,000 kilometers of pipeline, including a well-developed system of trunk pipelines, Russia's own network barely reached 1,300 kilometers.

The outbreak of World War I placed further pressures on the Russian oil industry in general, as total production levels slipped strongly by the height of the conflict. Yet the oil industry's blackest period came during the Civil War, which saw the destruction of much of its pipeline capability and a deep slump in its oil extraction rates.

The nationalization of the country's oil industry came in 1918. The Bolsheviks, and later the Soviet government, recognized the strategic importance of the country's oil reserves and the need to ensure their transport. New pipelines were under construction during the Civil War, with calls to build a pipeline from oilfields in Emba to the city of Saratov. Another pipeline, linking the Baku-Batumi pipeline to Triflis, was launched in 1921.

Yet the early years of Soviet pipeline development were hampered by a lack of materials, especially pipe, and other construction equipment. Most of the country's pipeline plans remained stalled in their early development stages. The situation remained hampered by ongoing drops in budget allocations to the oil industry through the 1920s. As a result, no pipelines were completed in the Soviet Union between 1917 and 1927.

FILLING OUT THE FIRST FIVE-YEAR PLAN

The launch of the first of the Soviet Union's many five-year plans provided a new boost to its pipeline construction. By 1928, the country had launched construction of a 618-kilometer span linking Grozny with Tuapse. A second Batu-Batumi pipeline, totaling 834 kilometers, was also constructed during this time. By 1931, the country had begun building a 455-kilometer pipeline connecting Armavir and Trudovaja.

By the end of the first five-year plan, the Soviet Union had put into place nearly 2,000 kilometers of trunk pipelines. Construction continued through the 1930s, and by the outbreak of World War II, the country had nearly doubled its total network. Further construction of the permanent network was deeply disrupted during the war, however, as the Nazi invasion destroyed much of the country's oil industry installations. Pipeline construction carried out during the period largely served to support the country's military effort. Of note was the construction of a 28-kilometer benzene pipeline, built on the bottom of Ladoga Lake, which was credited with helping the city of Leningrad (Saint Petersburg) survive the long Nazi blockade of the city.

INTENSIFIED GROWTH DURING THE COLD WAR

Work on the country's pipeline system intensified during the Cold War. The Soviet domination of Eastern Europe gave the country new and captive export markets. At the same time, the intensification of the country's oil industry operations demanded further expansion of its pipeline capacity. Overseeing construction of the Soviet pipeline network was a new body, U.S.S.R. Ministry of Oil Industry Main Production Department for Oil Transportation and Supplies, or Glavtransneft. A number of pipeline projects were launched in the immediate postwar period, including a 183-kilometer link built to accommodate as much as three million tons per year.

Increases in the country's pipeline network were dramatic. By 1950, the Soviet Union counted more than 5,000 kilometers of pipeline; just five years later, that total had doubled. At the end of that decade, the country had launched construction of its first international pipeline, extending into Poland, Czechoslovakia, Hungary, and East Germany, for a total length of more than 6,000 kilometers.

The development of the vast oil reserves in the Siberian region brought the country's pipeline network there in the 1960s. Siberia became the site of much of the country's pipeline construction through the 1970s, with the launch of a number of large-scale projects. Among these was the Druzhba pipeline, which was extended to more than 10,000 kilometers by the time of its completion. During the 1980s, Glavtransneft's operations focused especially on filling out the Siberian region's trunk pipeline network. By the end of that decade, the Soviet Union's total pipeline network topped 94,000 kilometers.

BREAKUP AND REINCORPORATION IN THE NINETIES

The breakup of the Soviet Union had immediate consequences for Russia's pipeline operations, as much of the network installed by the Soviets rested beyond its borders. As a result, the country's pipeline network covered only 49,000 kilometers. Much of that network was rapidly aging and in desperate need of maintenance, and even replacement. Complicating matters was the highly heterogeneous nature of the network, a legacy of its more than 40 years of construction. As an example, the network included a wide variety of pipe diameters, ranging from 40 centimeters to as much as 122 centimeters.

The first step toward developing the pipeline system was taken in 1993, with the completion of the restructuring of the former Glavtransneft. A new company was formed, Oil Transporting Joint Stock Company Transneft, which in turn oversaw 11 companies formed to operate the country's trunk pipelines. Transneft remained fully controlled by the Russian government.

Transneft initially served the role as intermediary between Russia's oil companies and refiners. Following further reforms of the market, this position was taken away from Transneft. Instead, the company was forced to reorient itself from being a former bureaucracy to becoming a commercially viable corporation. Nonetheless, the company continued to enjoy its position as a natural monopoly.

NEW PIPELINES FOR THE NEW CENTURY

Transneft carried out extensive maintenance of the network through the 1990s, helping to reduce the number of corrosion failures and leaks. The company also carried out a decommissioning of parts of the pipeline, reducing its total network to 45,000 kilometers by 1999. The pipeline system still retained the stigma of its Soviet-era construction, however. In 2006, for

example, the reliability of its pipelines were once again called into question after a leak at the Druzhba pipeline spilled 50 tons of oil in one day.

The surging demand for oil, particularly from the developing world, in the meantime put new pressure on Transneft to expand the network. This became all the more important as Russia's oil and gas reserves began to form an increasingly central role in the rebuilding of the highly fragile Russian economy. In the late 1990s, Transneft launched construction of the Baltic Pipeline System, linking the western Siberian field to the Primorsk terminal on the Baltic Sea. The first phase of that project was completed in 2001; in 2003, Transneft launched an extension of that pipeline, more than tripling its capacity to 42 million tons per year.

Transneft launched two other high-profile projects into the middle of the first decade of the 2000s. The first was the construction of a new East Siberian pipeline. That project, expected to reach 4,700 kilometers upon completion, provided new transportation potential for Russian oil to the Asian markets, especially Japan, South Korea, and China. The first leg of that project was expected to be completed in 2008.

In 2007, Russia, Greece, and Bulgaria reached a trilateral agreement to construct and operate a pipeline transporting Russian oil from Burgas, in Bulgaria, to Alexandroúpolis, in Greece. Transneft became a major partner in the consortium for the 285-kilometer project, slated for completion by 2011. The new pipeline was expected to help relieve the bottleneck caused by the increasingly restrictive oil transportation policies in the Bosporus straits, controlled by Turkey.

By the end of 2007, Transneft's pipeline network once again neared 48,000 kilometers. The company was responsible for transporting more than 460 million tons of oil per year, generating revenues of RUB 202.42 billion ($7.13 billion). Transneft continued to enjoy its status as a government-held, pipeline monopoly. Many of Russia's privately held oil companies had begun lobbying to be allowed to build and operate their own pipelines. With its expanding network, Transneft appeared to be well-prepared to meet any future competition.

M. L. Cohen

PRINCIPAL SUBSIDIARIES

Baltnefteprovod Ltd.; CJSC Transneft; JSC Center for Metrology Maintenance; Non-Governmental Pension Fund Transneft; OJSC Chernomortransneft (CHMT); OJSC Diascan Center for Technical Diagnosis; OJSC

Druzhba MN; OJSC Privolzhsknefteprovod; OJSC Severny MN; OJSC Severo-Zapadny MN; OJSC Sibnefteprovod; OJSC Svyaztransneft; OJSC Transsibneft; OJSC Tsentrsibnefteprovod (CSN); OJSC Uralsibnefteprovod; OJSC Verkhnevolzhsknefteprovod; OJSC Volzhsky Podvodnik; OOO Transneft Finance; OOO Vostoknefteprovod; Transpress Ltd.; VSTO TSUP Ltd.; JSC Giprotruboprovod.

PRINCIPAL COMPETITORS

Saudi Arabian Oil Co.; PetroChina Company Ltd.; Brega Marketing Co.; SONATRACH; Qatar Petroleum; TransMontaigne Inc.; Alfa S.A. de C.V.; AB Mazeikiu Nafta; Roggio S.A.; Botas Boru Hatlari Ile Petrol Tasima A.S.; LINZ AG; KazTransOil; PETROMSERVICE S.A.; Technische Werke Ludwigshafen-am-Rhein AG.

FURTHER READING

"Construction of 15% of East Siberian Pipeline Complete," *Pipeline & Gas Journal*, April 2007, p. 14.

"Decision Looms for Siberian Pipeline," *Pipeline & Gas Journal*, December 2004, p. 10.

Gorst, Isabel, "State Pipeline Company Rethinks Transport Strategy," *Petroleum Economist*, February 1999, p. 30.

"No Way Out: Oil Pipelines," *Economist*, May 28, 1994, p. 64.

"Russia, Bulgaria, Greece Sign Pipeline Agreement," *Pipeline & Gas Journal*, April 2007, p. 14.

"Russian Oil Leak Stirs Debate over Safety of Transneft Pipelines," *Pipeline & Gas Journal*, September 2006, p. 14.

Samoilov, B., and P. Truskov, "Transneft Holds onto Key Transportation Role, Tries to Ensure Reliability," *Oil and Gas Journal*, November 8, 1999, p. 41.

"Transneft Chief Foresees Pacific Pipeline," *Pipeline & Gas Journal*, December 2001, p. 12.

"Transneft Discloses More Pipeline Priorities," *Pipeline & Gas Journal*, September 2004, p. 10.

"Transneft Hanging onto Pipeline Monopoly," *Petroleum Economist*, May 2004, p. 38.

"Transneft Pipeline System to Grow 10 Percent by 2003," *Pipeline & Gas Journal*, April 2003, p. 12.

"Transneft: The Backbone of Russia's Oil Renaissance," *Euromoney*, June 2003, p. 71.

"Transneft Transforms," *Petroleum Economist*, November 1997, p. 25.

Trelleborg AB

■

Box 153
Trelleborg, SE-231 22
Sweden
Telephone: (+46 410) 670 00
Fax: (+46 410) 427 63
Web site: http://www.trelleborg.com

Public Company
Incorporated: 1905 as Trelleborgs Gummifabriks Aktie-
    bolag
Employees: 22,362
Sales: SEK 27.04 billion ($3.67 billion) (2006)
Stock Exchanges: Stockholm OMX Nordic
Ticker Symbol: TRELB
NAIC: 326211 Tire Manufacturing (Except Retreading);
    326220 Rubber and Plastics Hoses and Belting
    Manufacturing; 326299 All Other Rubber Product
    Manufacturing; 336399 All Other Motor Vehicle
    Parts Manufacturing; 336413 Other Aircraft Parts
    and Auxiliary Equipment Manufacturing; 339991
    Gasket, Packing, and Sealing Device Manufacturing

■ ■ ■

With more than 100 years behind it, Trelleborg AB
ranks as one of the world's top players in the so-called
industrial rubber sector—that is, the non-tire portion of
the rubber industry. Trelleborg, which takes its name
from the town in Sweden where it was founded in 1905
and is still headquartered, specializes particularly in sealing, protecting, and damping products and engineered
solutions based on advanced polymer technology and

plastics for a variety of industrial environments. The
Trelleborg Engineered Systems unit serves the process,
infrastructure, construction, oil and gas, and other
industries, offering such products as industrial hoses,
rubber sheetings, tunnel seals, chemical protection suits,
industrial vibration damping solutions, and rubber sealing membranes. Trelleborg Automotive is the world
leader in antivibration products for light vehicles and
also produces brake shims, vehicle boots, and engine
cooling hoses. Trelleborg Sealing Solutions is among the
global leaders in precision seals for the aerospace,
automotive, and industrial sectors. Trelleborg Wheel
Systems produces solid industrial tires for forklift trucks
and other material-handling equipment as well as tires
for agricultural and forestry machinery. About 70
percent of Trelleborg's sales are generated in Europe,
around 22 percent in North and South America, and
approximately 8 percent in the Asia-Pacific region and
other markets.

DUNKER-LED BEGINNINGS

Henry Dunker, the founder of Trelleborg, was born in
1870 in Esbjerg, Denmark. His mother, Henriette, was
Danish, while his father, Johan, was of German origin.
The family moved to Helsingborg, Sweden, in 1872
when Johan Dunker took on the job of expanding that
town's harbor. The elder Dunker eventually pursued his
long-simmering idea of setting up a Swedish rubber
production plant to produce rubber galoshes, a
potentially lucrative venture given the nation's
preponderance of rain and slush. In partnership with
some wealthy Helsingborg businessmen, Johan Dunker
formed Helsingborgs Gummifabriks Aktiebolag in 1890.

Before too long, production of rubber galoshes began, and Henry Dunker, then in his early 20s, was installed as president of the company. The death of his father in 1898 left Henry firmly in control.

In the meantime, Johan Kock, another young entrepreneur, had been one of the founders of AB Velox. Formed in Malmö, Sweden, in 1896, Velox moved a year later to Trelleborg, located on the Baltic Sea, where it stood as the southernmost Swedish town. With cycling growing rapidly in popularity at this time in Sweden, Velox was formed primarily to manufacture bicycle tires, although it also produced technical rubber products, such as industrial hoses, belts, gaskets, molded components, and roll coverings.

Poorly managed, the debt-ridden Velox faced liquidation by 1905. Henry Dunker, with ambitions of becoming the undisputed leader of the Swedish rubber industry, seized this opportunity. On October 30 of that year, he engineered the formation of a new company, Trelleborgs Gummifabriks Aktiebolag, which took over the assets of Velox. Dunker, who was named president, controlled 51.1 percent of the new firm's shares, with the other 48.9 percent held by Kock. Gustaf Lagergren, an associate of Dunker, was the first chairman, but Kock took over this position in 1909.

Dunker divided production between his two rubber enterprises: the Helsingborg business focusing on consumer products such as rubber galoshes and balls, and the Trelleborg company concentrating on tires and industrial rubber products. These firms remained separate, and Dunker was eventually dubbed "Galosh King" as he grew Helsingborgs Gummifabriks into Europe's leading producer of galoshes and rubber shoes.

Under Dunker's leadership, Trelleborgs Gummifabriks meanwhile quickly expanded and by 1911 was able to tout itself as the largest rubber producer in Scandinavia. In addition to continuing to produce bicycle tires and a wide variety of technical rubber products, the company established itself within two areas that remained central to the firm for decades to come: automobile tires, first produced in 1907, and rubber coats, which debuted in 1910. The first Trelleborg car tires were of the pneumatic rubber variety, a breakthrough product that helped spur the exploding growth of motoring. By the beginning of World War I, Trelleborgs Gummifabriks was generating more than half of its sales from tire production, although bicycle tires still accounted for the majority of tire revenues. The sales of rubber coats grew large enough by 1915 to justify the establishment of a separate unit, the coat department. Among the other new products introduced during this period were rubber heels and soles for shoes, mattresses and air cushions, football bladders, rubber gloves, and items made from hard rubber, often called ebonite, such as handles for pots and pans and handrails for trains and trams. In the meantime, the company in 1908 first used its logo consisting of the letter "T" inside a triangle standing on one of its points.

NAVIGATING THROUGH WORLD WARS AND THE GREAT DEPRESSION

A vital supplier of government orders during World War I, Trelleborgs Gummifabriks saw its sales double during the war years while profits hit record levels. Total sales during the four war years totaled SEK 18.6 million. Among the items produced by the company for the Swedish defense forces were gas protection suits, rubber raincoats, and tires. As the war dragged on, the company contended with the shortage of raw rubber by increasingly turning to the recycling of scrap rubber.

After an initial upswing immediately after the war, the Swedish economy fell into a deep and lengthy recession lasting from 1920 to 1922. Sales at Trelleborgs Gummifabriks fell by two-thirds, layoffs resulted in a workforce reduction of one-third, and wages were cut by 30 percent. In 1921 the company recorded the first full-year loss in its history. Despite the hard times, the firm's first subsidiary, a Stockholm-based sales company, was established. During the succeeding recovery, sales of hard-rubber products, pneumatic tires, and coats were particularly strong, and revenues reached SEK 5 million by 1925. Foreign sales doubled during this period, and products were being exported to ten countries, including Australia and the United States. In 1926 the firm established its first foreign subsidiary, the London-based Trelleborg Ebonite Works Ltd., a move designed to circumvent the high tax on direct imports from Sweden.

Although sales fell for three straight years during the Great Depression of the early 1930s, Trelleborgs Gummifabriks fared surprisingly well given the depths of the economic crisis mainly because of the rapidly increasing demand for automobiles and hence for automobile tires as well. Between 1931 and 1935 sales

KEY DATES

1905: Henry Dunker spearheads the founding of Trelleborgs Gummifabriks Aktiebolag, based in Trelleborg, Sweden, with an initial focus on bicycle tires and industrial rubber products.

1907: Production of automobile tires begins.

1926: First foreign subsidiary, the London-based Trelleborg Ebonite Works Ltd., is established.

1962: Dunker dies at age 92, leaving majority control of the company in the hands of several funds and foundations.

1964: Company stock begins trading on the Stockholm Stock Exchange.

1976: Phaseout of the production of passenger car and truck tires is completed; most bicycle tire production is soon discontinued as well.

1977: Trelleborgs Gummifabriks shortens its name to Trelleborg AB.

1986: Shift from rubber company to industrial conglomerate is confirmed with the purchase of 40 percent stake in Swedish mining, metals, and trading company Boliden AB, which is entirely taken over by 1988.

1995: A string of divestments reduces Trelleborg to three core business areas: mines and metals, rubber products, and distribution.

1996: Acquisitions to build up core rubber operations begin.

1997: Divestment of Boliden commences with the sale of 55 percent of Boliden's common shares on the Toronto Stock Exchange.

1999: A phaseout of the firm's distribution operations begins as Trelleborg embarks on a new era concentrating solely on industrial rubber and polymer products.

2000: Trelleborg acquires the BTR antivibration systems business of Invensys plc and the automotive components operations of the Laird Group PLC.

2003: The precision seals business of Smiths Group plc is acquired.

of automobile tires produced at the Trelleborg plant doubled, and by the late 1930s car tires were Trelleborgs Gummifabriks' largest product line. At mid-decade, overall sales were nearing SEK 8 million, while the

workforce, numbering more than 1,000, was producing four categories of rubber products: bicycle tires, car tires, industrial products, and clothing. The rapidly growing coat department had expanded into the production of protective clothing and diving suits while continuing to make its core rainwear. Two highly popular ebonite products of the mid-1930s were the yo-yo and the bowling ball.

On September 1, 1939, the same day that World War II broke out, Dunker loosened his reins on the company by appointing Hilding Ståhlbrandt president. Ståhlbrandt had been the sales manager at the sugar company Svenska Sockerfabriks AB and before that had served for a number of years as the plant manager at the Mazetti AB chocolate company. Also in 1939 Trelleborgs Gummifabriks aimed to push past its limitations as a small company on a global scale by entering into a long-term technical and commercial cooperation agreement with B. F. Goodrich Company, at the time the world's fourth largest producer of automobile tires. The outbreak of World War II, however, forced this agreement to be mothballed, and Trelleborgs Gummifabriks also had to postpone plans to build a new and larger tire plant in Trelleborg.

During the war, although the country remained neutral, Sweden launched a major rearmament program, and Trelleborgs Gummifabriks once again served as a major supplier to the nation's armed forces. Sales surged as the company produced tires for all of the army's vehicles and bicycles, huge numbers of raincoats, tent components, and gas protection gear, including overalls, gloves, and rubber boots. Other war-related production included bulletproof fuel tanks, aircraft engine components, and various rubber components for submarines. Civilian production continued on a much more limited scale, including raingear sold under the Akvarex brand name and bicycle tires, the latter remaining the firm's best-known consumer item. In keeping with the self-sufficiency required during a period of widespread rationing, demand for the company's rubber preserving-jar rings skyrocketed. On the raw material front, reclaimed scrap rubber once again came to the fore, while Trelleborgs Gummifabriks also gained access to supplies of synthetic rubber from Germany through a controversial agreement engineered by the Swedish government.

POSTWAR PROSPERITY

Kock died in 1945, at which point Dunker succeeded him as chairman. A widower without any children, Kock left his estate to three foundations. His 48.9 percent interest in the company he helped found remained in the possession of these foundations until late in the 20th century, when they gradually sold off most of their Trelleborg shares. In the meantime, the first few years following World War II were difficult ones for Trelleborgs Gummifabriks because of shortages of capital, raw materials, and labor. Business began to take off in 1948 when sales rose to SEK 49.6 million, the company generated gross profits of SEK 13.8 million, and the workforce increased to more than 2,200. Also in 1948, construction was completed on the war-delayed car tire plant in Trelleborg, an expansion that tripled capacity from 200 to 600 tires per day. Among other capital investments, a new warehouse and distribution building opened in Trelleborg, and part of the clothing production operation was shifted to a new plant in Skurup, Sweden. Also in the immediate postwar years, Trelleborgs Gummifabriks and B. F. Goodrich resumed their alliance. Among the alliance activities was a contract by which B. F. Goodrich started supplying vinyl resins to its Swedish partner as Trelleborgs Gummifabriks began producing products made from plastics for the first time. In July 1949 Ståhlbrandt died suddenly of a heart attack. At the urging of Dunker, Ståhlbrandt's son, Åke, succeeded his father as company president at age 35.

One of the major developments of the 1950s was a concerted internationalization drive. The company over the course of the decade established a network of agents and dealers in 65 countries, starting first with the Nordic countries, then moving on to the major industrialized nations of Europe, and finally to Turkey, Czechoslovakia, Poland, Israel, Egypt, India, the United States, South America, Africa, and the Far East. The major lines of products exported by Trelleborgs Gummifabriks during this period included bicycle tires, car tires, wheelbarrow tires, rubber flooring, rubber belts and tubes, and bowling balls. The company next took its global ambitions to the next level by establishing overseas sales companies, first in Denmark (1959) and then in Norway, Finland, the United States, and Germany. The first foreign production plant was established in the Netherlands in 1962 for the manufacture of battery cases. Eventually, these and other moves helped push the portion of sales generated outside of Sweden from just 4 percent in 1950 to nearly 40 percent in 1970.

The 1950s also saw a number of changes in the firm's array of products. The company introduced the world's first winter tire, the Wittmer, in 1953, the same year that the firm's partnership with B. F. Goodrich led to the introduction of Europe's first tubeless car tire, the Safe-T-Tire. In 1958 Trelleborgs Gummifabriks introduced a low-profile tire called the T Farmer, which was designed mainly for transport equipment for forestry and agricultural applications as well as for large

farming machinery, such as harvesters. The rise of plastics as an alternative base material to rubber led to the establishment of a subsidiary called AB Trelleborgplast. Starting in 1957, this subsidiary, based in Ljungby, Sweden, began manufacturing plastic sheeting, coated fabric, and refrigerator moldings made from polyvinyl chloride (PVC). Vinyl floor tiles produced by this unit used asbestos as a filler material. In the meantime, fierce competition, primarily from Japanese manufacturers, forced the company to discontinue production of a number of product lines, including air mattresses, inflatable rubber boats, and bowling balls. By 1960 sales exceeded SEK 200 million, while the number of employees neared 5,000.

Over the course of a number of months in late 1959 and much of 1960, Trelleborgs Gummifabriks and B. F. Goodrich were involved in negotiations concerning the U.S. firm's desire to gain a minority or even a majority interest in the Swedish concern. A deal appeared likely until the autumn of 1960 when the health of the 90-year-old Dunker deteriorated, and the company's board decided not to go forward with the founder's health in such a fragile state. Dunker died in May 1962, at age 92 and as the wealthiest person in Sweden. Like Kock, Dunker died a childless widower, and he left his fortune of around SEK 60 million (some SEK 35 million after imposition of Sweden's inheritance tax) to a number of funds and foundations, generally called the Dunker interests. The will of Sweden's "Rubber King" stipulated that these entities retain their majority control of the voting rights in Trelleborgs Gummifabriks. Part of the income from the Dunker interests pays for the operation of the Dunker Hospital in Helsingborg, while another portion goes to the City of Helsingborg to be used, in the words of the will, "for an independent purpose of benefit to the citizens of Helsingborg." The city has used money from the Dunker interests to fully or partially fund Helsingborg City Theater, Helsingborg Concert Hall, the Museum of Culture in Fredriksdal, a new stand at the Olympia football stadium, and the Dunker Cultural Center.

In 1963, following Dunker's death, a new share issue provided Trelleborgs Gummifabriks with about 500,000 new shareholders. The following year, the company's shares began trading on the Stockholm Stock Exchange. In the meantime, the company was also active on the acquisitions front, purchasing Stensholms Fabriks AB, a maker of specialized sealing rings (later renamed Stefa Industri AB), and AB Ekparkett, producer of parquet floors, both in 1962. Among new product areas pursued in the mid-1960s were wear-resistant rubber products for the mining industry and heat-resistant textile conveyor belts. On the tire front, Trelleborgs Gummifabriks produced its first radial tire, the T-Belt, in 1964.

In 1965 Trelleborgs Gummifabriks and the other company that Dunker had been instrumental in developing, by this time known as Helsingborgs Gummifabriks AB Tretorn, entered into a loose cooperative grouping. The two firms remained independent legal entities with different owners but had a common majority owner, the Dunker interests, and a common board, group management, and president (Åke Ståhlbrandt). This arrangement was intended to help the two companies compete in the rapidly changing European business landscape, which had seen the establishment of the European Economic Community and the European Free Trade Association. Among the cooperative activities were the combining of certain purchasing and sales operations. By 1969 what was known internally and externally as the Trelleborg-Tretorn Group ranked as the seventh largest rubber company in Europe, with combined sales of SEK 651 million. Trelleborgs Gummifabriks, with about 6,500 employees, generated SEK 501 million of these revenues, while Tretorn, a 2,800-employee concern concentrating on rubber and canvas shoes, boots, and balls, posted sales of roughly SEK 150 million. One development of particular note during the late 1960s was the discontinuation of Akvarex raincoats and trench coats because of brutal competition from textile imports from low-wage countries. The plant in Skurup shifted its focus to protective suits, including certified fire and chemical protection suits, bulletproof vests, and storm hats. Competition in the tire sector was fierce as well and prompted Trelleborgs Gummifabriks to limit its ambitions in this area to producing tires for the Scandinavian market.

1970–83: PROLONGED PERIOD OF DECLINE

By 1970, industrial rubber products accounted for 62 percent of Trelleborgs Gummifabriks' total sales, while the portion generated by tires had declined to 29 percent. A sharp economic downturn that began in 1971 and featured skyrocketing wage inflation further undermined the company's auto tire operations, which had been suffering from the expensive transition to radial tires, major worldwide overproduction, and abnormally low prices. Tire inventories mounted, the tire operations eventually began operating in the red, and finally the difficult decision was made to exit from one of the firm's historically most important businesses. The phasing out of passenger car and truck tires began in 1975 and was completed the following year. The company, however, retained its position in specialty tires, such as low-profile tires for agricultural and forestry equipment.

Also in 1975, the bicycle tire business recorded a loss for the first time in the company's history mainly because fierce competition had entirely undercut the United States as a viable market. Most bicycle tire production was therefore phased out, although limited production continued under a contract with the Swedish government for civil emergency planning purposes. This arrangement ended in 1996, at which point Trelleborg and its predecessor, AB Velox, had produced more than 100 million bicycle tires and tubes over a nearly 100-year period.

These historic closures precipitated a one-quarter reduction in the company workforce in Trelleborg, while the resulting financial hit contributed to three straight loss-making years, the first since the early 1920s, with the red ink for 1976 to 1978 adding up to about SEK 100 million. The downturn prompted Ståhlbrandt to resign from his position as president in 1976, although he remained chairman of the board. Brought onboard as the new president was Arne Lundqvist, who had previously been president of Svenska IBM AB.

Cost-cutting came to the fore under the new leader, who also launched a major restructuring that radically decentralized what had been a strictly hierarchical organization with the establishment of around 40 independent profit centers. Trelleborgs Gummifabriks also shortened its name to Trelleborg AB in 1977, and the following year the alliance arrangement with Helsingborgs Gummifabriks AB Tretorn was ended and along with it the shared presidency. Helsingborgs Gummifabriks later became known as simply Tretorn AB, and this firm by the end of the 20th century had positioned itself as a producer of outdoor lifestyle footwear and tennis balls. PUMA AG Rudolf Dassler Sport acquired Tretorn in 2001. Under Lundqvist, meanwhile, Trelleborg attempted to create a third leg to stand on in addition to the rubber and plastics operations, but the president's diversification attempts, most notably into the manufacture of precision mechanical parts, were neither successful nor lasting. Although Trelleborg returned to modest profitability in 1979, the decade had proven exceedingly difficult: whereas total sales more than doubled between 1970 and 1980, from SEK 517 million to SEK 1.34 billion, profits grew only from SEK 24 million to SEK 35 million. In the early 1980s the board of directors grew increasingly dissatisfied with the company's inability to produce more robust profits, and the search for a new leader was launched early in 1983.

1983–89: ASTOUNDING GROWTH AS AN INDUSTRIAL CONGLOMERATE

With a background that included management positions at appliance giant AB Electrolux, Rune Andersson became the fifth president of Trelleborg in May 1983. Andersson immediately made his mark by replacing the highly decentralized structure implemented by his predecessor with the creation of six independently operating business areas. In addition, unprofitable units were shut down, and noncore subsidiaries were sold. Profit growth was quickly reestablished (notably, a 130 percent increase in 1984), the Trelleborg share price began ascending, and capital was freed up for a huge expansion.

The initial acquisitions of the Andersson era served to bolster Trelleborg's international position in the industrial rubber sector. In 1984 the company acquired Atlas A/S Den Norske Remfabrik, the largest industrial rubber company in Norway, with annual sales of more than SEK 100 million. The following year, Trelleborg purchased Bakker Rubberfabriek B.V., one of the oldest and most respected rubber companies in the Netherlands, and Spondon Plastics, a U.K. manufacturer of battery cases. Also added in 1985 was Goodall Rubber Company, which generated revenues of SEK 550 million as a distributor of industrial rubber products throughout the United States and Canada. That year, Trelleborg's newfound health was clear from the profits of SEK 167.2 million that were generated from the total sales of SEK 2.13 billion. Also, Åke Ståhlbrandt stepped down from the board of directors after 42 years of company service. Ernst Herslow was named the new chairman.

Trelleborg's shift from rubber company to industrial conglomerate became clear in 1986 via the SEK 700 million ($107 million) purchase of a 40 percent stake in the much larger Boliden AB, a Swedish mining, chemicals, and trading company. At the time, Boliden itself was in the midst of taking over Swedish contracting and building materials company Ahlsell AB. By 1988 Trelleborg had acquired full control of Boliden, and with the 1987 purchase of a number of operations of the U.S. firm Allis-Chalmers Corporation that produced crushing and screening equipment for the mining and processing industries, mining and metals had become Trelleborg's largest business area, surpassing rubber and plastics.

Among numerous other deals completed in this period, in 1986 Trelleborg merged its specialty tire operations with Viskafors AB to form Swedish Tyre AB, which was 48 percent owned by Trelleborg. Also in 1986, the company acquired the Mataki Group, a producer of roofing materials and specialty chemicals, from the Danish firm Superfos A/S. In 1988 Trelleborg acquired Malmö-based Bröderna Edstrand AB, the largest independent steel wholesaler in Sweden with annual sales of SEK 2.2 billion, and Saab-Scania Enertech AB, a producer of heating systems with annual sales of SEK 1.3 billion. Andersson also made an aborted run at taking over Aktiebolaget SKF, the world's leading producer of roller bearings, in 1988; after being rebuffed by that company's major shareholders, he sold the 10 percent stake he had built in SKF at a tidy profit.

The deal making continued in 1989, highlighted by the purchase of a 50 percent stake in Canadian mining company Falconbridge Limited, with the Canadian firm Noranda Inc. taking the other 50 percent. Toronto-based Falconbridge, a concern with annual revenues of SEK 13.3 billion, was the world's second largest producer of nickel and had copper and zinc operations as well. Trelleborg also sold its chemicals unit, Boliden Kemi, to the Finnish firm Oy Kemira Ab in 1989. Fueled by the acquisitions spree and skyrocketing metal prices that bolstered the position of Boliden, revenues at Trelleborg reached a record SEK 26.49 billion ($4.25 billion) in 1989, nearly ten times the 1986 level of SEK 2.8 billion, while profits soared correspondingly from SEK 315 million to SEK 2.74 billion ($440 million) over the same period. Rubber and plastic products generated less than 13 percent of overall revenues by the end of the 1980s. The company's share price reached an all-time high of SEK 235 in October 1989, having increased an astounding 7,604 percent over the previous ten years.

1990–98: A NARROWED FOCUS

In May 1990 Kjell Nilsson succeeded Andersson as Trelleborg president and CEO. Nilsson, a close associate of Andersson whom the latter brought with him from Electrolux, had previously led a turnaround at Boliden. Andersson, meantime, replaced Herslow as company chairman. By the end of 1990 Trelleborg was organized into nine business areas: Boliden Mineral, Boliden International, Boliden Metal, Ahlsell (HVAC distribution), Bröderna Edstrand (steel distribution), Enertech (heating systems), Ventilation, Swegon (a publicly listed industrial group with operations in construction, climate control, and distribution acquired in 1990), and Trelleborg Industri (rubber and plastics). The company also continued to own a 50 percent stake in Falconbridge, while in July 1990 the mineral processing systems subsidiary Svedala Industri AB was taken public and became an associated company 49.5 percent owned by Trelleborg. In 1991 another business area was added via the takeover of the forest products group Munksjö AB, producer of corrugated-board packaging, specialty paper, tissue and household paper, and pulp. Not neglecting its rubber area, Trelleborg in 1991 also acquired the tire division of the U.S.-based Monarch Rubber Company to become the world's largest manufacturer of solid industrial tires. The following year the company purchased Rubore Materials Sweden AB, a manufacturer of brake shims featuring a thin rubber sheeting to prevent screeching in car brakes.

These acquisitions were a mere sideshow, however, to Trelleborg's dramatic fall from its late 1980s pinnacle. A host of negative economic developments pushed the company into a tailspin in the early 1990s. In addition to the general worldwide economic downturn that followed in the wake of the Persian Gulf War, Trelleborg was also forced to contend with plummeting metal prices, a collapse of the Swedish construction market, a decline in the dollar exchange rate, and sharp wage increases in Sweden. As a result, pretax profits for 1991 plunged 78 percent, and then the company suffered substantial pretax losses in 1992 and 1993: SEK 1.56 billion ($205 million) and SEK 1.52 billion ($190 million), respectively. Trelleborg embarked on an extensive streamlining program while also divesting large portions of its sprawling operations to reduce a heavy debt burden. Enertech was sold in the spring of 1993 to Wolseley plc for SEK 650 million. Late in the year Trelleborg sold its remaining shares in Svedala Industri and also sold 75 percent of the shares in Munksjö through a public offering. The company in 1994 sold its remaining shares in Swegon and reduced its stake in Falconbridge. The remaining shares in the latter were jettisoned the following year, with the Falconbridge divestments alone generating proceeds of more than SEK 7 billion and a capital gain of SEK 3 billion. Also in 1995, Trelleborg sold its remaining shares in Munksjö to Jefferson Smurfit PLC for SEK 805 million. This retrenchment enabled Trelleborg to become virtually debt-free, return to strong profitability, and concentrate on three core areas: mines and metals, rubber products, and distribution. The company posted pretax profits of SEK 3.51 billion ($493 million) in 1995 on revenues of SEK 21.3 billion ($ 2.99 billion).

Its financial position turned entirely around, Trelleborg returned to growth mode but this time the focus was squarely on the core founding business, rubber products. A new wave of internationalization was launched that concentrated in particular on emerging markets, including China, Singapore, Malaysia, the Philippines, Brazil, Poland, and the Czech Republic. In 1996 a number of rubber companies both inside and outside of Sweden were acquired, with the annual sales of the acquired operations totaling approximately SEK 1.6 billion. The most important of these were: CMPP, a

France-based producer of industrial hose and rubber sheeting with sales of SEK 600 million, purchased from the Michelin Group; Horda AB, a Swedish rubber company with sales of SEK 360 million that produced such items as automotive components, building profiles and other extruded profiles, composites and granulate for the cable industry, and retreading materials; and the Spanish firm Ibercaucho, a SEK 300 million concern specializing in rubber sheeting, fenders, and expansion joints.

Another watershed event occurred in June 1997 when Trelleborg began its exit from mines and metals by selling about 55 percent of the common shares of Boliden on the Toronto Stock Exchange. Proceeds from this sale totaled SEK 4.4 billion, and Trelleborg recorded a capital gain of SEK 1.5 billion. The proceeds enabled Trelleborg to make further acquisitions, including the 1997 purchase of Yale–South Haven Inc., a firm based in South Haven, Michigan, that generated annual sales of SEK 1 billion ($130 million) from the production of antivibration components for the automobile industry. That year Trelleborg also expanded its distribution side by the acquisition of Skoogs AB, one of Sweden's leading electrical appliance wholesalers, and the purchase of a majority stake in Starckjohann Oyj, a Finnish wholesaler specializing in the heating, water, and sanitation sectors.

1999 FORWARD: BECOMING ONE OF THE TOP NON-TIRE RUBBER COMPANIES IN THE WORLD

By early 1999 Nilsson had become a figure of controversy, in part because of reports of irregularities in the sale of Boliden shares. The board of directors elected to replace Nilsson as president and CEO with Fredrik Arp in February of that year. Arp was a former top executive of Trelleborg, including a stint as head of the tire division; he had left the firm in 1995 to become president and CEO of the Swedish packaging company PLM AB. The new leader moved swiftly to erase the final vestiges of Trelleborg's forays as a conglomerate. Later in 1999 the remaining shares of Boliden common stock were spun off to Trelleborg shareholders. Trelleborg continued to own Boliden preference shares, but these were eventually converted to common stock and were completely divested by 2003. A number of other businesses, including Skoogs, were either divested or liquidated in 1999. Then late in 1999 Trelleborg sold a 51 percent stake in its remaining distribution operations to the venture capital company Nordic Capital and reorganized as Trenor Holding AB. Included within Trenor were Ahlsell, Bröderna Edstrand, and Starckjohann. Trelleborg completed its exit from the distribution sector in 2004 by selling its 49 percent stake in Trenor to Nordic Capital.

The proceeds from this dramatic series of divestments were used to build up Trelleborg's core industrial rubber and polymer operations—in particular through three major acquisitions of U.K.-based companies, two of which occurred in 2000. In March of that year the company acquired the BTR antivibration systems (AVS) business of Invensys plc for SEK 2.1 billion ($250 million) to become the world's leading producer of antivibration devices for the automotive industry and the number two AVS supplier to the nonautomotive industrial sector. In the automotive sector, the addition of the BTR unit, which specialized in the engine and suspension mount business, complemented Trelleborg's existing strength in the body mount area. BTR operated 17 factories in seven countries and generated annual revenues of nearly SEK 4.2 billion ($500 million). In late December 2000 Trelleborg purchased the automotive components operations of the Laird Group PLC for SEK 1.5 billion ($156 million). The Laird operations had annual sales of SEK 2.8 billion ($270 million) with a manufacturing base of 16 plants in six countries, mainly in Europe. The deal strengthened Trelleborg's position in the AVS sector while also moving the company into the noise-reduction and fluid systems businesses.

In April 2002 Rune Andersson resigned after 19 years at the company, 11 as chairman. Taking over as chairman was Anders Narvinger, the president of the Association of Swedish Engineering Industries and Trelleborg board member since 1999. Pretax profits for 2002 totaled SEK 902 million ($93 million) on net sales of SEK 17.63 billion ($1.81 billion). More than half of the firm's sales were generated by the Trelleborg Automotive unit, which focused on automotive and industrial AVS, brake shims, thermoplastic boots, and gas springs. The company's three other units were Trelleborg Wheel Systems, specializing in agricultural tires and solid industrial tires; Trelleborg Engineered Systems, producer of industrial hoses, fender systems, rubber sheeting, dredging hose systems, tunnel seals, and chemical-resistant suits; and Trelleborg Building Systems, supplier of waterproofing and sealing products, primarily for the European construction sector.

In 2003 a new unit, Trelleborg Sealing Solutions, was created following the acquisition of the precision seals business of Smiths Group plc for SEK 6.28 billion ($810 million), the third of Trelleborg's transformational acquisitions and the largest in its history. The acquired business, which mainly operated under the name Busak+Shamban, specialized in polymer-based precision seals for the industrial, automotive, and aerospace

markets. It had annual sales of SEK 5.5 billion ($710 million). Its operations were located mainly in Europe and North America, but the business maintained production facilities in Brazil, Canada, Denmark, France, India, Italy, Japan, Malta, Mexico, Poland, Sweden, the United Kingdom, and the United States. By 2004 this acquisition, coupled with the two major deals completed in 2000 as well as a number of smaller fill-in-type purchases completed during this period, pushed Trelleborg's revenues back up to SEK 22.91 billion ($3.12 billion), nearing the level of conglomerate-era Trelleborg.

The sale of its 49 percent stake in Trenor Holding in 2004 enabled Trelleborg to circle back to a firm focus on industrial rubber and polymer products, a return to the roots that Henry Dunker had established a century earlier. In the wake of the acquisition of the Smiths unit, Trelleborg concentrated on improving its existing business units through efficiency efforts, smaller acquisitions, expansion into new markets, and new product development. In January 2004 the company bolstered its automotive hose business by the purchase of Metzeler Automotive Hose Systems from Metzeler Automotive Profile Systems S.A. for SEK 275 million ($37 million). In October 2005, the year of Trelleborg's centenary, Peter Nilsson was named president and CEO following Arp's departure to become president of Volvo Car Corporation. Nilsson had previously led Trelleborg Engineered Systems.

In January 2006 the company acquired the U.K.-based CRP Group for SEK 956 million ($123 million). CRP specialized in underwater polymer systems and solutions for offshore oil- and gas-extraction projects. In October of that same year, the Trelleborg Engineered Systems unit was further bolstered with the purchase of Spartanburg, South Carolina-based Reeves Brothers, Inc., for SEK 1.33 billion ($180 million). By acquiring Reeves, Trelleborg became the world leader in polymer-coated fabrics used in such areas as the graphics, personal protection equipment, aerospace, defense, and fluid solutions industries. At the end of 2006, the Trelleborg Building Systems unit was integrated into Trelleborg Engineered Systems. Also during the year, the Goodall Rubber hose distribution business was divested.

By this time, Trelleborg AB ranked as the world's third largest industrial (i.e., non-tire) rubber company, trailing only Continental AB and Hutchinson S.A. Revenues for 2006 reached a record SEK 27.04 billion ($3.67 billion), but pretax profits fell 24 percent to SEK 1.19 billion ($162 million). Rising prices for raw materials pushed profits down, while the Trelleborg Automotive unit was further hurt by production cuts by the U.S. Detroit-based automakers. Later in 2006 the company launched a restructuring of this unit that involved the closure of two plants in England, and in early 2007 Trelleborg was considering whether to jettison certain parts of its automotive business. Also in 2007, Trelleborg continued to pursue smaller acquisitions, while the Trelleborg Sealing Solutions unit began replacing the Busak+Shamban brand name with the Trelleborg moniker.

David E. Salamie

PRINCIPAL SUBSIDIARIES

AVS Brasil Getoflex Ltda (Brazil); Busak and Shamban Belgium SA; Trelleborg do Brasil Solucões em Vedacão Ltda (Brazil); Busak and Shamban Bulgaria EOOD; Busak and Shamban CZ spol s r.o. (Czech Republic); Busak and Shamban Hankuk Ltd. (South Korea; 75%); Busak and Shamban Japan KK; Trelleborg Sealing Solutions Polska Sp.zo.o (Poland); Busak and Shamban Suomi Oy (Finland); Busak and Shamban Suisse SA (Switzerland); Busak and Shamban Sverige AB; Trebolit AB; Busak and Shamban Österreich GmbH (Austria); Chemtrading Alpha Holding AG (Switzerland); Gromedi Oy (Finland); Mar-Con Polymers Ltd. Oy (Finland); Trelleborg Automotive Czech Republic S.r.o.; Trelleborg Automotive China Holding AB; Trelleborg Automotive Poland Sp.zo.o; Trelleborg Automotive S.R.L. (Romania); Trelleborg Automotive Slovakia s.r.o.; Trelleborg Engineered Systems Lithuania UAB; Trelleborg Corporation (U.S.A.); Trelleborg Sealing Solutions US, Inc.; Trelleborg CRP Inc. (U.S.A.); Trelleborg Wheel Systems Americas Inc. (U.S.A.); Trelleborg YSH Inc. (U.S.A.); Trelleborg YSH SA de CV (Mexico); Trelleborg Engineered Systems China Holding AB; Trelleborg Engineered Systems Group AB; Trelleborg Fluid Solutions Czech Republic s.r.o.; Trelleborg Gummi AG (Czech Republic); Trelleborg Holding AB; Trelleborg Building Systems AB; Trelleborg Industrial AVS AB; Trelleborg Holding Danmark A/S (Denmark); Trelleborg Phoenix A/S (Denmark); Trelleborg Sealing Solutions Denmark A/S; Trelleborg Holding France SA; Trelleborg Industrie SA (France); Trelleborg Holdings Italia S.r.l. (Italy); Trelleborg Holding Norge AS (Norway); Trelleborg Viking AS (Norway); Trelleborg Holdings (UK) Ltd.; Trelleborg Sealing Solutions UK Ltd.; Trelleborg Automotive (UK) Ltd.; Trelleborg Hong Kong Holdings Ltd. (China); Trelleborg Industri AB; Trelleborg Industrie S.p.A. (Italy); Trelleborg Insurance Ltd. (Bermuda); Trelleborg International BV (Netherlands); Trelleborg Automotive Germany GmbH; Trelleborg Fluid Solutions Germany GmbH; Trelleborg Wheel Systems GmbH (Germany); Trelleborg Lesina s.r.o. (Czech Republic); Trelleborg Protective Products AB; Trelleborg Treasury AB; Trelleborg Wheels AB; Trelleborg Wuxi Holding AB; Trelleborg Rubore AB; MHT Takentreprenören I Malmö AB; TSS China Holding AB; TSS Holdings Sweden AB; Trelleborg Forsheda Sweden AB; Velox AB.

PRINCIPAL DIVISIONS

Trelleborg Engineered Systems; Trelleborg Automotive; Trelleborg Sealing Solutions; Trelleborg Wheel Systems.

PRINCIPAL COMPETITORS

Continental AG; Hutchinson S.A.; Bridgestone Corporation; Freudenberg & Co. Kommanditgesellschaft; Tokai Rubber Industries, Ltd.; Tomkins plc; Cooper-Standard Automotive Inc.

FURTHER READING

Aspegren, Carl, and Agneta Ulfsäter-Troell, *The First 100 Years,* Trelleborg, Sweden: Trelleborg AB, 2005, 295 p.

Begin, Sherri, "Trelleborg to Buy Laird Auto Businesses," *Rubber and Plastics News,* November 20, 2000, p. 1.

Brown-Humes, Christopher, "Trelleborg to Buy PSS for SEK 6.5bn," *Financial Times,* July 22, 2003, p. 24.

Carnegy, Hugh, "Trelleborg Divestment Was 'Reluctant' Decision," *Financial Times,* July 28, 1995, p. 23.

Davis, Bruce, "Precision Deal: Trelleborg Acquires Smiths' Seals Unit," *Rubber and Plastics News,* July 28, 2003, p. 1.

———, "Trelleborg Buys Ibercaucho," *European Rubber Journal,* December 1996, p. 8.

———, "Trelleborg Names Arp, Caplea to Top Posts," *Rubber and Plastics News,* March 8, 1999, p. 28.

———, "Trelleborg Signals Acquisitions," *European Rubber Journal,* July/August 1997, pp. 10–11.

———, "Trelleborg to Acquire BTR AVS Unit for $250m," *European Rubber Journal,* February 2000, p. 2.

Davis, Bruce, and Marty Whitford, "Buy American: Trelleborg Industri to Purchase Auto Parts Firm Yale–South Haven," *Rubber and Plastics News,* March 3, 1997, p. 1.

Johansson, Carolina, "Trelleborg's Efforts to Cut Debt Are Starting to Pay Off," *Wall Street Journal Europe,* November 8, 1993, p. 12.

McIvor, Greg, "Trelleborg Mining Arm to List in Toronto," *Financial Times,* February 13, 1997, p. 29.

McNulty, Mike, "Trelleborg Plans $178 Million Purchase: Reeves Brothers Deal Will Expand Company's Manufacturing Base in U.S., China," *Rubber and Plastics News,* October 2, 2006, p. 1.

Meyer, Bruce, "Hungry for More: Trelleborg Plans to Edge Out Top Dogs in Sealing," *Rubber and Plastics News,* October 29, 2007, p. 1.

Moore, Miles, "Trelleborg Cooperating in Justice Probe," *Rubber and Plastics News,* July 23, 2007, p. 7.

Moore, Stephen D., "Trelleborg Thrives As Andersson Directs Swedish Firm Toward Basic Industries," *Wall Street Journal*, Western ed., October 23, 1989, p. B9D.

Shaw, David, "Trelleborg Enters Third Phase," *European Rubber Journal*, January 2004, p. 16.

———, "Trelleborg Set to Expand by Acquisitions," *European Rubber Journal*, January 2000, p. 14.

Taylor, Robert, and Kenneth Gooding, "Starring Role Born of Sense of Timing: The Rise of Sweden's Trelleborg," *Financial Times*, August 18, 1989, p. 17.

Ulfsäter-Troell, Agneta, and Carl Aspegren, *Despot och charmör: Henry Dunker—millenniets helsingsborgare*, Helsingborg, Sweden: Helsingborgs museer, 2002.

Webb, Sara, "Rubber King Looks to Expand Empire," *Financial Times*, July 13, 1988, p. 29.

White, Liz, "Trelleborg Aims to Be the Best in AVS," *European Rubber Journal*, June 2000, p. 41.

———, "Trelleborg Buys Smiths' Polymer Seals Operation," *European Rubber Journal*, September 2003, p. 6.

———, "Trelleborg Expands in South Korea, China," *European Rubber Journal*, June 2003, p. 4.

———, "Trelleborg to Acquire Metzeler Auto Hose Unit," *European Rubber Journal*, January 2004, p. 2.

White, Liz, and Bruce Davis, "Trelleborg to Focus on Rubber Operations," *Rubber and Plastics News*, May 31, 1999, p. 12.

Turtle Wax, Inc.

625 Willowbrook Center Parkway
Willowbrook, Illinois 60527-7969
U.S.A.
Telephone: (630) 455-3800
Fax: (630) 455-3890
Web site: http://www.turtlewax.com

Private Company
Incorporated: 1944 as Plastone Co.
Employees: 125
Sales: $200 million (2007 est.)
NAIC: 325612 Polish and Other Sanitation Good Manufacturing; 324191 Petroleum Lubricating Oil and Grease Manufacturing; 325611 Soap and Other Detergent Manufacturing; 325613 Surface Active Agent Manufacturing; 325998 All Other Miscellaneous Chemical Product and Preparation Manufacturing; 424690 Other Chemical and Allied Products Merchant Wholesalers; 811192 Car Washes

■ ■ ■

Turtle Wax, Inc., is the world's largest manufacturer of car-care products. A dominant force in exterior car-care products in the United States, family-owned Turtle Wax sells its products in 90 countries around the world. The company derives around 80 percent of its revenues from its more than 1,250 retail products, including car waxing and washing products, metal polishes, rubbing compounds, wheel and tire cleaners, vinyl and leather protectants, odor removers, and engine treatments and performance-enhancement products. Its industrial division, from which approximately 10 percent of revenues derive, supplies bulk wax, detergent, and other supplies to operators of car washes. The remaining 10 percent of sales come from Turtle Wax's own network of 20 automated car wash centers located in the Chicago and Kansas City metro areas.

FROM BATHTUB TO TURTLE WAX

Benjamin Hirsch, the founder of Turtle Wax, wanted to be a chemist, but had to drop out of college during the Great Depression. Instead, he became a magician, supporting his family with his silks and wand. He never lost his interest in chemistry, however, nor his fascination with cars. In the late 1930s he developed a car wax and mixed up batches at night in the bathtub. His wife, Marie, filled the bottles by hand. During the day, Hirsch traveled by streetcar to gas stations around Chicago, selling the wax he named Plastone. In 1944 he invested $500 and opened the Plastone Co., which operated out of a series of storefronts.

To promote his wax, Hirsch would go into a parking lot and shine one fender of each car. He then waited for the owners to arrive and hope to persuade them to buy his wax to finish the job. Plastone was a few years old when, according to company lore, Hirsch made a sales call in Turtle Creek, Wisconsin. The name of the town clicked in his mind with the hard shell of a turtle and the protection his wax offered. Thus in 1953, a new name was born for the company, Turtle Wax, Inc., and for the wax, Turtle Wax Super Hard Shell.

Our Mission is to innovate and market products and services that exceed consumer expectations and grow the Turtle Wax brand.

Turtle Wax will be the global leader in car care by: focusing on and thoroughly understanding our consumers; developing innovative products and services that delight consumers; recognizing that profitability is critical to our continued success.

In the early years, Hirsch nearly went bankrupt several times. "It was an arduous period," remembered Turtle Wax Chairman Sondra Hirsch Healy in a 1993 *Chicago Tribune* article. "We moved around a lot in the Chicago area. I can remember we, my brother and I, slept on the countertop of this storefront on Clark Street." Her father kept the company going by borrowing money from his employees and giving them stock in repayment. Some of those employees, or their children, relatives, and friends, still worked for Turtle Wax decades later.

As the popularity of the wax grew, Hirsch wanted to diversify. To appeal to a larger group of customers, he saw the need to sell products through grocery stores, not just to gas stations and hardware stores. In the mid-1950s Hirsch branched out, developing shoe polish, rug shampoo, and floor wax. The company even produced a line of dessert toppings called Party Day.

TRANSITION TO SECOND GENERATION

By 1966, the company boasted huge factory facilities. Its brand-name products, for auto care and household cleaning, had established a foothold in the market, and the firm had opened a 55,000-square-foot factory in Skelmersdale, England. Then Hirsch died. As was the case with many fledgling family companies, there was no plan for succession, and Hirsch's widow took over control of the firm. His daughter Sondra, a graduate of the Goodman School of Drama, left her job teaching drama in the Wilmette schools and joined the company as vice-president of public relations. "I felt I had to hold the company together," she told the *Chicago Tribune* in 1993.

Hirsch had been the developer and marketer of the company. With his death, the family followed the conservative advice of those who believed the company had to concentrate on the company's automotive products to survive. Products not related to car care were eliminated, and the company was 99 percent automotive by 1971, the year in which Mrs. Hirsch died. That year, Sondra Hirsch married Denis Healy, a chemist and product developer whom she had met at a trade show in Miami Beach in 1970. Healy joined Turtle Wax as general vice-president. In 1972 Sondra Healy was named chairman of the board, and, in 1977, Denis Healy became president of the company.

Denis Healy had spent most of his career developing new products. He started with Colgate-Palmolive Company, then moved to Mennen Company, and finally to W.M. Barr & Company, a packager of aerosol and liquid products. With this background, he began rebuilding Turtle Wax's marketing and development efforts, in both the automotive and broader consumer markets.

NEW PRODUCT PUSH

In 1982 the company introduced several new car-care products. Minute Wax, a silicone-based spray wax, was aimed at the increasing numbers of women who drove and maintained their own cars. For the growing number of older cars on the road, Color Back, a finish restorer, was developed to revive dull finishes. Another introduction, Clear Coat, was a nonabrasive wax and polish designed for new cars.

The Healys also reinstituted Ben Hirsch's efforts to move more strongly into supermarkets and consumer products. John Dellert, then vice-president of marketing, explained the company's strategy for moving into new markets in a 1985 *Advertising Age* article: "We had to come up with what we felt was a unique product that could command a much higher price and then could support advertising to educate the consumer on our presence in the category."

They began with shoe polish. In 1983 the company introduced a six-color line of Turtle Wax Shoe Polish. After success in test markets, the line went national, representing the first phase of the supermarket assault. At the time, the $125 million retail shoe polish and paste business was dominated by Kiwi. Marketed in the United States by Sara Lee Corporation's Kiwi Polish Company, Kiwi accounted for nearly 80 percent of the market. To persuade grocery store buyers to stock its polish, Turtle Wax priced its 3.5-ounce bottles at $2.49, with a built-in margin of $1.12 for retailers, compared to a 95-cent price and 50-cent margin for Kiwi.

Once the polish was on the shelves, Turtle Wax launched a $2 million television advertising campaign, larger than any previous introduction for a shoe polish.

unique, beaker-type bottle, in 5-, 10-, and 16-ounce sizes, all premium priced. The ad campaign compared the new product's clear spray with Armor All's cloudy spray, with the tagline, "Introducing new Clear Guard from Turtle Wax ... a clear new challenge to Armor All."

In 1985 Turtle Wax introduced a disposable wax-coated cloth and wax-filled sponge, which offered convenience and less mess. During this time, the company also undertook its first licensing agreement. Together with American Greetings Corporation, Turtle Wax introduced a line of air fresheners for children's bedrooms. Turtle Wax took the technology it had been using for years to make air fresheners in the shapes of playing cards and dice and packaged them to resemble the Strawberry Shortcake and Care Bears characters. "That's a sort of test for us," Denis Healy told *Advertising Age* at the time. "We're looking to license our name and we're looking to license other people's names."

CREATION OF AN INDUSTRIAL PRODUCTS DIVISION

Turtle also pushed into a new market with the creation of its industrial products division in 1977. The new division reflected the company's decision to place more emphasis on the potential business in the industrial market and not to focus only on the retail arena. "Because of our name, we've grown by osmosis into developing bulk chemicals [soaps and waxes] for the car wash business. It was treated as kind of a weak sister, but the business still grew a respectable 5 percent to 10 percent each year," Charles Abate, vice-president of operations and industrial products, told the *Chicago Tribune* in 1986. "The key is to remember that we are a surface treatment company," said Turtle Wax President Denis Healy in the same article.

The division first concentrated on the car wash industry, which in 1986 had an estimated 9,000 firms across the country, ranging from large chains to small neighborhood operations. Although the technology of the car wash business had changed dramatically in the previous decade, little attention had been given by most manufacturers to developing soaps and waxes appropriate for the new equipment and the lightweight plastics used in cars. Turtle Wax saw an opportunity, and had the financial resources, to develop a national distributor network for its industrial products.

By 1995, the company was the name brand marketer of chemicals for the commercial car wash industry. It marketed a full line of products to all types of car washes through Sam's Club stores and through distributors of car wash chemicals and equipment. The

---

KEY DATES

1944: Benjamin Hirsch founds Plastone Co. to sell a car wax he had invented of the same name.

1953: The wax is rebranded Turtle Wax Super Hard Shell, and the company takes the name Turtle Wax, Inc.

1966: Company opens a factory in Skelmersdale, England.

1972: Sondra Healy, daughter of the founder, is named chairman.

1977: Turtle Wax creates an industrial products division to begin supplying bulk chemicals to the car wash industry.

1989: Company creates its auto appearance division after launching a chain of full-service car washes in the Chicago area.

1997: Among several late 1990s acquisitions, Turtle Wax purchases the CD-2 line of automotive additives.

2004: The Platinum Series of premium car-care products is launched.

2005: Denis Healy, Jr., grandson of the founder, is named CEO; new leader shifts the firm away from manufacturing to become more of a consumer products marketer.

2006: ICE, a clear synthetic car wax, is introduced.

During 1984, the company spent $1.9 million (58 percent of all the advertising dollars for shoe care products for the year) advertising Turtle Wax Shoe Polish. Within a year, Turtle Wax ranked second, above American Home Products Corporation's Griffin and Knomark, Inc.'s Esquire polishes, with nearly 10 percent of the market. The campaign also gained the company valuable shelf space at many mass merchandiser and retail outlets.

TAKING ON ARMOR ALL

Turtle Wax used the same strategy to take on Armor All Products Corporation, which introduced the first vinyl protectant/beautifier in 1974, and, within 11 years, had 80 percent or more of the estimated $175 million vinyl protectant retail business. Turtle Wax developed Clear Guard and introduced it in 1985, pricing it higher to give retailers a larger margin and unleashing an advertising blitz and rebate offer to lure customers away from Armor All. Unlike other brands on the market, Clear Guard contained no water. A spray, it was packaged in a

industrial division manufactured six Turtle products: car wash pre-soak, two types of foaming detergent, sealer wax, foaming brush detergent, and high-pressure powder detergent. Users in 1995 included 12,000 self-service car wash operations, 9,000 exterior car washes, and 9,000 full-service operations, as well as pressure wash operators cleaning trucks, buses, and trains.

ONGOING NEW PRODUCT DEVELOPMENT

Throughout the last half of the 1980s and into the 1990s, Turtle Wax continued to develop new products. The year 1986 saw the introduction of household cleaning products. "Every bit of research we've done shows not only a high consumer awareness of our name but a perception that we've been selling household products for some time," Charles A. "Chuck" Tornabene, vice-president of marketing, explained in a May 5, 1986, *Chicago Tribune* article.

That year, six new products came on the market from the consumer products division. Rust Eater, designed to "convert rust to a primed surface that will never re-rust," was introduced with a big television ad campaign and customer rebate program. Three new aerosol products, under the Turtle Wax name, included a spot remover, an upholstery cleaner, and a carpet cleaner. Graphics of pets adorned the packages of the new cleaners, highlighting the special formulation of the products to get rid of pet stains and odors. Repel fabric protector and the Brillante brand of metal polishes were also marketed under the Turtle Wax umbrella.

The company also faced some challenges during this time. In 1986, for example, Turtle Wax agreed to pay nearly $100,000 in civil penalties and to discontinue its use of "potentially deceptive containers," which were not, according to allegations, filled to capacity. The payment settled a lawsuit filed by the district attorney's office in Los Angeles.

In the mid-1980s, Turtle Wax's automotive division responded to changing trends in the car care industry by adding new automotive products. The year 1987 saw the introduction of Zip Wax Hydro-System Spray Wash. A person needed only to attach a garden hose to the fitting on top of the plastic bottle and he or she could wash and wax a car. The product came in three formulations: wash, wax and wash, and wax. That same year the company also introduced a nonabrasive car wax, aimed at new cars, and a Clean Machine Car Detailer for cleaning all car surfaces, inside and out. At the time, Turtle Wax had an impressive 40 percent share of the $120 million-a-year car wax and polish market. Top-selling Super Hard Shell alone reached a 29 percent share of the overall market, a new high.

ENTERING PREMIUM SEGMENT IN 1988

In 1988 the company entered the premium segment of the car wax market with Turtle Wax Plus with Teflon. This put the company head to head with Rain Dance, which had been the dominant brand among premium car waxes. Premium waxes accounted for about 20 percent of retail car wax sales. The company worked on the new product for 16 months, during which time it had to convince Du Pont that its Teflon could be functionally used in a mass-market car wax. Until this product, the only Teflon car waxes available were for the professional market. The new wax sold for about $2 more than midpriced or premium-priced car waxes, including Turtle Wax Super Hard Shell, which had increased its market share to 30 percent.

Determined to reach into every segment of the market, the company introduced Liquid Crystal into the super-premium segment of the car wax market in 1989. For the first time in the company's history, the name Turtle Wax was not associated in any way with the product. Aimed at car buffs, the suggested retail price for Liquid Crystal was $15 to $16, while Super Hard Turtle Wax sold for $4 to $5.

Demographic and consumer research by Turtle Wax showed that about half of all automobile owners regularly washed and waxed their vehicles, and 90 percent would give their cars a basic cleaning "from time to time." The heaviest users were people, primarily 18- to 40-year-old males, who regarded their car as an extension of themselves. Nonetheless, women were a growing segment of the market, representing about 40 percent of the car-care product market in 1991, up from about 25 percent ten years earlier.

In 1993 Turtle Wax expanded its overseas operations, increasing its presence in Europe and entering into a deal with one of Japan's largest auto retail chains. New products during this period included Formula 2001, to protect new tires; Instant Foam 'n Shine, the first no-wait car wax; and Color Wax, a car wax that came in different colors to match a car's paint job. Phil Katcher, products editor at *Automotive Marketing*, a trade publication, told the *Chicago Tribune:* "That product breathed a lot of life into what was a pretty stagnant market. The car wax market had been hurt by automakers switching to no-wax car finishes."

Continuing to go after the top segments of the market, in 1995 Turtle Wax took aim at classic car owners. The company teamed up with Chuck Bennett, maker of Zymol Natural Liquid Auto Polish, to offer the pricey polish ($20 a bottle) to the mass market. The polish contained coconut and banana oils, almond paste and aloe, and a touch of vitamin E. Turtle Wax also announced it would use informercials to introduce two new products in 1996: Lubricator 2001, a new engine treatment, and Sudden Shine, an auto polish.

COMPANY CHAIN OF CAR WASHES

In addition to its three products divisions, Turtle Wax in the mid-1990s also owned and operated the largest chain of full-service car washes in the Chicago area through its auto appearance division, which had been formed in 1989. Turtle Wax's Car Wash and Auto Appearance Centers provided a wide-ranging menu of detailing services as well as car washes. The centers also served as a testing ground for industrial division products. The first ten centers were located in buildings converted from other uses. In 1990 Turtle Wax hired the Chicago architectural firm of Perkins & Will to design two state-of-the-art facilities, in Bloomingdale and Aurora, Illinois. To attract and keep customers, the centers offered yearly wash plans. For $199 (in 1994), a plan member received unlimited car washes on weekdays; for $259, the car could be washed on weekends as well. In 1996 Turtle Wax expanded its car wash chain to the Kansas City metropolitan area.

In the mid-1990s Turtle Wax car waxes had over a 60 percent share of the U.S. market, with a 95 percent brand awareness. Products from the automotive division were being marketed in Europe (the United Kingdom, Germany, Scandinavia), Central and South America (Mexico, Venezuela, Panama), Australia, and the Far East (Japan, South Korea). Through its industrial division, the company was the name brand marketer of chemicals for the commercial car wash industry. Items from the consumer products division including shoe polish, furniture polish, and other polishes and cleaners were sold through food, drug, and mass merchandise chains. Revenues were an estimated $145 million.

LATE-CENTURY NEW PRODUCTS AND ACQUISITIONS

In the late 1990s Turtle Wax continued to churn out new products. Among the 1998 additions to the company lineup was Express Shine Spray Car Wax, a no-rub liquid formula requiring users to just spray on and wipe dry. The following year an odor eliminator and deodorizer called Odor-X made its debut. Licensing opportunities were also being pursued. In 1996 the company entered into a deal with Wen Products, Inc., of Naperville, Illinois, to roll out a $60 Turtle Wax brand motorized waxer. This was the first major licensing deal for the company since the 1992 licensing of the Turtle Wax brand to Bloch New England for a line of polishing cloths and bonnets.

Acquisitions formed another important avenue for both growth and product line diversification during this period. In 1997 Turtle Wax acquired Alemite CD-2 Co., a firm founded in 1942 and based in Arlington Heights, Illinois, with annual sales of $20 million. In this deal, Turtle Wax gained the CD-2 line of automotive additives, including various fuel, oil, and transmission fluid additives. The CD-2 line was a big seller in various developing countries, where older cars were more common and needed special treatment. Turtle Wax ventured further into the under-the-hood segment with the 1999 purchase of Marvel Oil Company. This firm, founded in Chicago in 1923 but long based in Port Chester, New York, produced the Marvel Mystery Oil line of engine oils, fuel treatments, and lubricants. Turtle Wax augmented its European car-care product lineup in 1998 by purchasing Abel Bonnex SA of France and Valma B.V. of the Netherlands from Sara Lee Corporation. Later, the company acquired the ClearVue brand of automotive glass cleaner.

In 1999 Denis Healy, Jr., was named president of the company, and he helped his CEO father over the next few years boost sales and margins and cut bank debt by $21 million. After reaching a record of just over $200 million in 2002, sales lagged in 2003 at least in part because fewer consumers were washing and waxing their cars themselves. This setback prompted the Healy family to consider selling the business. Instead, they turned the CEO reins over to an outsider, Dennis S. Bookshester, former CEO of Fruit of the Loom, Inc., and the retail division of Carson Pirie Scott & Company. Bookshester took over in January 2004, and later that year Turtle Wax launched what become one of its fastest-selling lines in years, the Platinum Series of premium car-care products, which eventually included liquid and paste waxes, shine protectants, and a wheel cleaner and car wash.

EARLY 21ST-CENTURY MAKEOVER

Despite the success of the Platinum Series, overall sales failed to fully recover, and Bookshester was let go. Denis Healy, Jr., was named CEO in mid-2005 and led a major overhaul that most noticeably changed Turtle Wax from a manufacturing-based company to more of a consumer products marketer. The firm's plant in Chicago was shut down, with the production shifting to an outsourced network of manufacturers. Turtle Wax also moved its headquarters, which had been at the same location as the plant. In 2006 the company shifted to new quarters in the Chicago suburb of Willowbrook. Turtle Wax did not entirely abandon manufacturing as it kept its U.K. plant in Skelmersdale.

With its focus more on marketing and sales, Turtle Wax ramped up its R&D budget, spending more than $12 million in 2006 to inject new life into the product lineup. In May 2006 the firm launched its largest ad campaign ever, a $10 million push featuring what Turtle Wax felt was a breakthrough product. A departure from traditional waxes, ICE was a clear, synthetic car wax touted for not leaving a white residue, requiring no elaborate buffing, and being safe for the nonmetal portions of a car's surface. Strong ICE sales helped push company revenues up 15 percent in fiscal 2006 to approximately $200 million. In keeping with its brand marketing efforts, Turtle Wax reached another licensing deal late in 2007. Rancho Dominguez, California-based Carrand Companies Inc., a leading maker of car-care tools and accessories, began producing a Turtle Wax line that included brushes, mitts, sponges, and related tools and items. Through such licensing deals and the drive to develop new products, the Healy family sought to increase sales by 50 percent by 2011.

Ellen D. Wernick
Updated, David E. Salamie

PRINCIPAL SUBSIDIARIES

Abel Bonnex SA (France); Turtle Wax Europe B.V. (Netherlands); Valma B.V. (Netherlands); Turtle Wax Limited (U.K.).

PRINCIPAL COMPETITORS

The Clorox Company; The Procter & Gamble Company; Meguiar's, Inc.; Church & Dwight Co., Inc.; Ecolab Inc.

FURTHER READING

Bittar, Christine, "Turtle Wax Goes After Odors," *Brandweek,* November 16, 1998, p. 4.

Crown, Judith, "Car Wash Cleanup: Turtle Wax Bets Brand Name on Growing Full-Service Chain," *Crain's Chicago Business,* March 13, 1989, p. 3.

———, "Turtle Wax Speeds Up Push into Car Wash Biz," *Crain's Chicago Business,* March 18, 1996, p. 34.

Greenberg, Karl, "Turtle Wax Sees Ice As a Clear Winner," *Brandweek,* December 5, 2005, p. 10.

Greising, David, "Turtle Wax, Armor All Polish Their Speeches," *Chicago Sun-Times,* May 18, 1988, p. 54.

Gruber, William, "Car Wash a Stretch for High-Rise Firm," *Chicago Tribune,* May 4, 1990, sec. 3, p. 2.

Hodge, Sally Saville, "Turtle Wax Hoping Its Drive for Industrial Sales Will Wash," *Chicago Tribune,* February 14, 1986, Business sec., p. 1.

Howell, Debbie, "Turtle Wax Showcases Its Versatility," *DSN Retailing Today,* July 25, 2005, p. 24.

Jannot, Mark, "Waxing Creative," *Chicago,* August 1988, p. 63.

Lazarus, George, "Info Shine for Turtle Wax," *Chicago Tribune,* November 20, 1995, Business sec.

———, "Turtle Puts On High-Priced Shine," *Chicago Tribune,* August 29, 1989, Business sec., p. 4.

———, "Turtle Wax Back Out of Its Shell," *Chicago Tribune,* February 11, 1985, Business sec., p. 4.

———, "Turtle Wax Did It, but It Took a While," *Chicago Tribune,* August 24, 1987, Business sec., p. 4.

———, "Turtle Wax Hopes Consumers Take a Shine to Odor-X," *Chicago Tribune,* April 7, 1999, Business sec., p. 3.

———, "Turtle Wax Takes on a Teflon Shine," *Chicago Tribune,* October 10, 1988, Business sec., p. 4.

———, "Turtle Wax Ventures Out of Its Shell into Household Cleaning Products," *Chicago Tribune,* May 5, 1986, Business sec., p. 9.

Liesse, Julie, "Chuck Tornabene: Exec Gives New Polish to Turtle Wax," *Advertising Age,* January 14, 1991, p. 28.

Malham, Howell J., Jr., "Soap Opera," *Chicago Tribune,* April 14, 1994, sec. 5, pp. 1, 13.

McGeehan, Pat, "Turtle Wax Emerges from Car-Market Shell," *Advertising Age,* August 26, 1985, pp. 4, 51.

Millman, Nancy, "Turtle Wax Hopes Public Takes a Shine to Products," *Chicago Sun-Times,* August 23, 1985, p. 57.

———, "Turtle Wax Leaves Garage for House," *Chicago Sun-Times,* June 8, 1987, p. 48.

Nolan, Mike, "Turtle Wax Leaving Bedford Park," *Daily Southtown* (Chicago), September 2, 2005.

Pincus, Ted, "Turtle Wax Going Like 60 to Make Prospects Shine," *Chicago Sun-Times,* May 2, 2006, p. 49.

Randle, Wilma, "Strong Family Histories Help Turtle Wax Shine," *Chicago Tribune,* April 11, 1993, Sec. 7, p. 5.

Schmeltzer, John, "Turtle to Polish Marketing, Let Others Make Products," *Chicago Tribune,* November 2, 2005, Business sec., p. 1.

"Turtle Wax Agrees to Penalty," *Chicago Tribune,* August 22, 1986, Business sec., p. 2.

"Whipped Wax," *Home Mechanix,* October 1994.

Ulta Salon, Cosmetics & Fragrance, Inc.

1135 Arbor Drive
Romeoville, Illinois 60446
U.S.A.
Telephone: (630) 226-0020
Toll Free: (866) 340-3704
Fax: (630) 226-8367
Web site: http://www.ulta.com

Public Company
Founded: 1990
Employees: 7,100
Sales: $755.1 million (2007)
Stock Exchanges: NASDAQ
Ticker Symbol: ULTA
NAIC: 446120 Cosmetics, Beauty Supplies, and Perfume Stores

■ ■ ■

Before Ulta Salon, Cosmetics & Fragrance, Inc., entered the beauty retail scene, shoppers had to visit multiple stores to find cosmetics and fragrance items. They would make one stop at the department store to buy such prestige brands as Elizabeth Arden and Estée Lauder, another stop at a drugstore for mass products including Revlon and Neutrogena, and yet another stop at the hair salon to find specialty shampoos and other haircare products. According to consumer researcher Datamonitor, women use at least 12 personal care products every day; building a niche to simplify and enhance women's shopping experiences, then, was both a logical and potentially profitable idea. Ironically, after following retail trends in the 1990s, it was not a woman who came up with the idea for Ulta, but a man. Dick George had a plan to provide convenience for busy middle- to upper-income American women by creating the ultimate one-stop beauty shop.

PAMPERED BEGINNINGS

Ulta was established with a $12 million venture capital investment in the cosmetics industry, at a time when the market was valued at nearly $1 billion. The idea started in 1990 with Dick George, former president of Osco Drug, who had studied the shopping trends of moderate- to higher-income female shoppers. After realizing many of these women were looking for an escape from the worries of work, families, and busy lives, George persuaded 12 of his Osco executive colleagues to join him in a new retail venture. Their eventual prototype became "Ulta3." The "ulta" was an abbreviation for "ultimate beauty store" and the superscript number "3" represented the store's three main features: fragrances, cosmetics, and salon products.

The first store, built in 1990, indulged women with 6,000 square feet of all the products that made them look good and feel better. Ulta3 stocked over 25,000 beauty items and featured a 2,500-square-foot full-service hair and nail salon in the center of the store. Per George's instructions, interior designers paid close attention to such feminine details as elegant étagères for displaying products and widened aisles for unrestricted, comfortable browsing. For an added pleasure, the prices of most products were discounted 10 to 50 percent below suggested retail prices. To top it off, store management promised to match prices from competing

COMPANY PERSPECTIVES

Ulta is the largest beauty retailer that provides one-stop shopping for prestige, mass and salon products and salon services in the United States. Ulta provides affordable indulgence to its customers by combining the product breadth, value and convenience of a beauty superstore with the distinctive environment and experience of a specialty retailer. Ulta offers a unique combination of over 21,000 prestige and mass beauty products across the categories of cosmetics, fragrance, haircare, skincare, bath and body products and salon styling tools, as well as salon haircare products. Ulta also offers a full-service salon in all of its stores. The Company currently operates 248 retail stores across 31 states and also distributes its products through the Company's website: www.ulta.com.

stores, even such deep discounters as Kmart and Wal-Mart.

By 1995, five years after its inception, Ulta3 was growing rapidly and changes were underway. Terry Hanson, one of the initial Osco investors, took over as chief executive when Dick George left to become president and chief executive officer of Handy Andy, a discount home improvement store chain. By the end of 1995, there were 50 Ulta3 stores in Illinois, Minnesota, Georgia, Texas, Arizona, and Colorado, and the discount concept had caught on. The meaning of the raised 3 in the store's name had come to mean "selection, savings, and service." To keep up with the chain's expansion plans, new managers and marketing professionals were hired, and the company's workforce had mushroomed from 20 to 800.

Ulta3's success continued for the remainder of the decade. Although the store faced fierce competition from the Cosmetic Center, another discount cosmetics retailer, Ulta's sales volume doubled between 1994 and 1995 and was predicted to double again in 1996 according to an article in the December 10, 1995, issue of the *Chicago Tribune*. The *Tribune* followed Ulta's success closely, since the chain had its base in suburban Chicago, headquartered about 30 miles southwest of the city in Romeoville. Rival Cosmetic Center, however, had been in business for over 35 years and was based near Washington, D.C. Its Mid-Alantic location did not stop the chain from encroaching on the midwestern cosmetics and beauty care market with almost three dozen stores in the Chicago area (the first had opened in 1987).

Another competitor, Sephora, a European beauty retailer launched in France in 1969 and bought by luxury retail powerhouse LVMH (Moët Hennessy Louis Vuitton) in 1997, had also invaded the market with its first U.S. store in 1998 and plans for rapid growth. By the time the decade drew to a close, Sephora had proved itself as a major threat: it had the financial backing of a billion-dollar conglomerate and an aggressive expansion plan to open stores in the finest U.S. malls at a breakneck pace. Not only did Sephora carve itself a healthy slice of the cosmetics and beauty care market, but at the expense of former stalwart Cosmetic Center, which had fallen on hard times and dissolved. It was soon very clear Ulta3 needed a change to survive at the very least, let alone thrive in the coming years. In December 1999 came a welcome breath of fresh air: Lyn Kirby was hired as Ulta3's new president and chief executive.

A CORPORATE FACELIFT, 2000–04

Lyn Kirby's presence and foresight helped Ulta find its way in the increasingly crowded and often cutthroat cosmetics marketplace. In the late 1970s direct-sales beauty care company Avon had enticed Kirby to move to the United States from her native Australia. For nearly 20 years Kirby rose through the corporate ranks before ending her tenure at Avon in 1995 as a corporate vice-president with expertise in product development, marketing, and advertising. From Avon, Kirby moved to the vice-president and general manager position at Limited Brands, Inc., where she stayed for three years. In March 1998, she became president of Circle of Beauty, a subsidiary of Sears, until she was offered the top slot at Ulta in December 1999.

From the start, Kirby's vision was to move the company away from its discount position to a retailer that encompassed mass beauty products, prestige brands, and a full-service salon. One of the first steps in the company's transformation was to drop the "3" from its name to become simply "Ulta." Kirby told *MMR (Mass Market Retailers)* magazine in a July 23, 2001, article, "Ulta today is positioned as a retailer offering affordable indulgence rather than discount prices."

Kirby immediately got to work sprucing up the stores, the merchandise, the locations, the service, and targeting a specific market. Pursuing college-educated women in their mid-30s with an annual income of over $70,000, Ulta moved away from the drugstore image to create an experience more akin to a spa. Floor and ceiling designs were made to look more elegant and low-

KEY DATES

1990: Drugstore executives Dick George and Terry Hanson create discount retailer Ulta3.

1995: Hanson becomes chief executive of Ulta3 when George leaves the company.

1998: French beauty retailer Sephora opens its first store in the United States.

1999: Lyn Kirby is hired as president; Ulta3 drops discount structure and becomes Ulta.

2001: Ulta stores expand to 13 locations throughout the United States.

2002: Ulta merges salon services with retail products.

2004: Company sales reach $434 million for the year.

2007: Ulta raises $123.9 million in an initial public offering on the NASDAQ.

profile gondolas held prestige brands shoppers usually found in high-end department stores. The in-store salon provided any service an upscale department store would offer, and sales personnel were trained to provide knowledgeable assistance to their customers while allowing them to browse leisurely on their own. In contrast to Sephora stores, mostly located within shopping malls, the 10,000-square-foot Ulta stores were positioned in strip centers or what Kirby called "lifestyle centers."

The new Ulta experience apparently gave women what they wanted: sales for 2003 surpassed $360 million and a year later had increased nearly 20 percent to $434 million. By 2004, the company operated 150 stores in 19 states and had plans for consistent growth, projecting as many as 500 stores by 2012 and 1,000 by 2017.

PRIVATE TO PUBLIC, 2005–07

Ulta had wooed its customers, but attracting some prestige brands had presented a challenge. Many prestige companies needed to be convinced shoppers would abandon department stores for an off-mall retailer. After relentless pursuit, Ulta managed to gain access to a variety of prestige fragrances and upscale cosmetics by 2005 such as Elizabeth Arden, Estée Lauder, Lancôme, Clinique, and Bare Escentuals. As Kirby's vision for Ulta was finally becoming reality, the company experienced a steady rise in sales. For fiscal 2006 sales had climbed to $579.1 million, up from $491.2 million in 2005.

In a position of fiscal stability and with plans for continued growth, Ulta decided to go public. In

October 2007 Ulta shares began trading on the NAS-DAQ at $18. Share prices soared to a high of $35.43 within five days. The initial public offering sold about 8.54 million shares, raising $123.9 million, which the company allocated to reduce debt and pay dividends.

While the initial offering had provided Ulta's management with optimistic enthusiasm, the 2007 economy was at near-recession levels and competition had steadily increased. Ulta share prices dropped to nearly $15 by the end of 2007, and European competitor Sephora had become a top rival with more than 126 American (and 500-plus worldwide) stores. Additionally, other competitors such as Bare Escentuals and Bluemercury had plans of opening their own branded boutiques, cutting into Ulta's market.

Despite the soft economy and volatile marketplace, Kirby's outlook remained positive. She maintained the belief that women considered beauty a necessity, not a luxury, and would forgo expenditures on other items before giving up their favorite shampoo or lipstick. Ulta's goal was to increase its store base to 1,000 locations by 2017 in the nearly $8 billion cosmetics and beauty care industry. The company ended 2007 with $755.1 million in sales, a 30 percent increase from the previous year, and more than doubled its workforce from 3,000 in 2006 to 7,100 for 2007.

Jodi Essey-Stapleton

PRINCIPAL COMPETITORS

Bath & Body Works, Inc.; The Body Shop International Plc; Macy's, Inc.; Nordstrom, Inc.; Sephora USA, Inc.; Target Corporation.

FURTHER READING

"Beauty Experts Give Upscale Image," *Drug Store News,* May 2, 2005, p. 129.

Brookman, Faye, "Ulta Cracks Beauty's Class System," *WWD* (*Women's Wear Daily*), November 9, 2007.

Evans, Matthew W., "Ulta Profits Increase 16 Percent," *WWD,* December 12, 2007, p. 3.

Fields-White, Monee, "Extreme Makeover; Post IP Euphoria Fading, Cosmetics Retailer Ulta Tries to Catch Investor Eyes with Ambitious Expansion Plans," *Crain's Chicago Business,* November 19, 2007, p. 4.

Kukec, Anna Marie, "More Than Just Cosmetic Changes in 5 Years, Ulta3 Has Made Its Imprint on the Discount Market," *Chicago Tribune,* December 10, 1995, p. 1.

Nagel, Andrea, "Ulta Brightens Up Beauty Image," *WWD,* February 25, 2005, p. 12.

Pinto, David, "Kirby Has Found Ulta's Niche," *MMR* (*Mass Market Retailers*), July 23, 2001, p. 19.

Unified Grocers, Inc.

———————— ■ ————————

5200 Sheila Street
Commerce, California 90040
U.S.A.
Telephone: (323) 264-5200
Fax: (323) 265-4006
Web site: http://www.uwgrocers.com

Private Cooperative
Incorporated: 1925
Employees: 2,800
Sales: $4 billion (2007 est.)
NAIC: 424410 Grocery and Related Product Whole-
 salers

■ ■ ■

The largest wholesale grocery cooperative in the western
United States, Unified Grocers, Inc., serves independent
retailers in California, Oregon, Washington, Idaho,
Texas, Arizona, Nevada, Alaska, Hawaii, and the Pacific
Rim. The company has four divisions, Northern
California, Southern California, Oregon, and
Washington, that serve its members through nine
distribution centers, offering products in all food
categories. Unified also owns two manufacturing facilities for the co-op's private-label dairy and bakery. It
provides insurance and insurance-related services,
including workers' compensation and liability insurance
policies, to both members and customers.

ORIGINS OF AN INDEPENDENT
GROCERS COOPERATIVE

In 1922, a group of 15 independent Southern
California grocers met in the Green Hotel in Pasadena,
California, and formed a purchasing cooperative that
gave them buying power to compete with large grocery
chains. The company's first purchase was a carload of
soap, which its founding members divided among
themselves in a Southern California rail yard.

Three years later, in 1925, Certified Grocers of
California Ltd. incorporated and issued stock to 50
members. In 1928, the co-op merged with a small
retailer-owned wholesale company called Co-operative
Grocers, and, in 1929, in a move that nearly tripled its
revenues of a year earlier, it acquired Walker Brothers
Grocery. By 1938, Certified Grocers had 310 members,
380 stores, and revenues that exceeded $10 million.

Certified Grocers debuted a line of branded food
products under the Springfield label in 1947, adding
nonfood items and its own coffee and bean products in
the early 1950s. In 1956, Certified also added deli
items, and, in the 1960s and 1970s, a meat center,
frozen food and deli warehouse, produce distribution
center, creamery, central bakery, and specialty foods
warehouse, which operated as Grocers Specialty, Inc.

Membership grew dramatically beginning in the
1940s through the 1970s. By 1988, Certified and its
retailers controlled close to 19 percent of the Southern
California and Las Vegas, Nevada, area retail grocery
market, making it number one for wholesale market
share in all of these markets. In 1990, the co-op served
almost 3,000 stores in California, Arizona, Nevada,

COMPANY PERSPECTIVES

Unified Grocers is a retailer-owned wholesale grocery cooperative that provides grocery products and services to independent retailers throughout the Western United States. Unified and its subsidiaries offer independent retailers all the resources they need to compete in today's supermarket industry.

Hawaii, and along the Pacific Rim. Expansion efforts in California targeted the northern part of the state and the San Joaquin Valley, and there were plans to recruit members in the Marshall Islands and Indonesia. The company divided its clients into shareholders or "member-patrons" and non-members or "associate patrons." Both sets of clients were required to purchase a fixed amount of groceries each week, with company profits (with the exception of those generated by Grocers Specialty) distributed back to members.

EXPANSION AND MERGER IN THE FACE OF INCREASING COMPETITION

As it grew in numbers, the co-op also expanded to support its members. By the early 1990s, Certified had approximately ten distribution centers, three dry grocery warehouses, two frozen deli warehouses, a produce warehouse, and a fleet of delivery trucks driven by about 500 drivers. Among its items for distribution were dry grocery products, frozen foods, fresh produce, meat, dairy, ice cream, bakery, health and beauty aids, and general merchandise. The company marketed its own food products, including those produced by its bakery and dairy, under the Springfield, Gingham, Golden Creme, and Special Value private labels and supplied ethnic foods through its wholly owned subsidiary Grocers Specialty Co. It also helped retailers acquire real estate sites, designed stores, supplied advertising and inventory financing, and sold insurance to members.

Paralleling Certified's growth, however, a mounting number of grocery chains grew large enough to establish their own warehousing and distribution arms in the 1990s. In addition, a trend toward consolidation involving some of the midsize chains began to occur; upon being acquired by a larger self-distributing company, these chains were no longer a part of Certified. Certified Grocers lost about 30 percent of its business in the early 1990s as a result of this trend. In 1993 alone, revenues dropped to $2 billion from the 1992 total of $2.4 billion.

Al Plamann, who became chief executive in 1994, put a positive spin on these mergers, calling them "great opportunities for independents" in the *Progressive Grocer* in 1998. "Most independents are effective at competing with chains by creating an environment that attracts and holds shoppers," he told the magazine. As prices throughout the grocery sector dropped overall, however, the co-op took moves to preserve its niche by broadening its offerings, creating more incentives for retailers to join, facilitating the spinoff of stores from chains to its members, and investing in its Hispanic and specialty business. It also assisted some of its older California customers in joining its Apple Markets banner and ad group beginning in 1996. All Apple Markets had a common look and feel, but were still independently owned.

In a grander move to deal with its declining customer base, Certified Grocers merged with United Grocers of Oregon to form Unified Western Grocers in 1999. United Grocers had been founded in 1915 by a trio of men who sought collective purchasing power and economies of scale for small Portland-based grocers and, thus, pricing parity with the major grocery chains. In the 1950s, United grew rapidly, forming a trucking department and a general merchandise division and buying Northwest Grocery Company and Fridegar Grocery Company. In 1963, United purchased Raven Creamery, around which it built its frozen food department.

As a result of the merger, the new company increased its purchasing power and saved about $40 million during the next three-year period by eliminating redundant facilities and departments. The new cooperative had $3.2 billion in revenues, employed 3,500, and served 725 retail members in Washington, Oregon, California, Nevada, Arizona, Hawaii, Alaska, Idaho, and Montana. It operated ten corporate stores under the SaveMax, Thriftway, and Apple Markets names. It was the largest retailer-owned co-op in the western United States, capitalizing on United Grocers' strong produce presence and Certified Grocers' large selection of specialty foods.

Plamann became president and chief executive of Unified Western Grocers, which operated through three divisions (Southern California, Northern California, and the Pacific Northwest); each maintained its own marketing office, while distribution and business logistics were centralized. The company relied on Unified Grocers' distribution center in Milwaukie, Oregon, along with Certified Grocers' three warehouses, fluid milk plant, and bakery in California. Immediately following the merger, Certified purchased 32 supermarkets and set up a new satellite communication system to connect its truck drivers to its dispatchers. Also in 2000, Grocers Specialty Co. acquired Gourmet Specialties, Inc., a distributor of gourmet and ethnic food products, and Central Food Sales, exclusive distributor of several kosher products, and J. Sosnick & Son, wholesale distributor of candy, gourmet items, and kosher food.

Two years after the merger the West Coast was faced with both a deteriorating economy and volatile power supply problem. In addition, the move toward consolidation and self-distribution among grocers continued. However, Unified Western Grocers, then the tenth largest co-op in the United States with sales exceeding $3 billion, took steps to expand into new categories and businesses "in an efficient and effective manner that [allowed it] to compete on an equal footing with the integrated chains," according to Plamann in 2001 in *Supermarket News*. It launched a major effort to expand its customer base into Northern California, Hawaii, Arizona, Nevada, and the Pacific Northwest and to include convenience stores, liquor stores, specialty stores, and grocery stores throughout California and Oregon via its Neighborhood Markets program. These smaller stores could buy groceries from Unified Western Grocers at a rate slightly higher than the member rate. The possibility of growth in this new market sector was

extensive as Unified Western Grocers then served only about 800 neighborhood stores in an area that included 8,500 in Southern California, 7,000 in Northern California, and 1,700 in Oregon.

Another area of expansion for Unified Western Grocers' Pacific Northwest Division was in its new lines of organic and Hispanic produce. In 2001, it reorganized Grocers Specialty Company into three divisions—general merchandise/health and beauty care, Hispanic, and gourmet specialties, which included both natural and non-Hispanic ethnic foods—and added new products. Although not immediately profitable in 2001, the gourmet and health food sector by 2002 was delivering a profit to the co-op.

As one of only two co-op wholesalers able to consistently keep traditional wholesalers out of its primary operating areas, Unified Western Grocers also took steps to upgrade its warehouse and transportation system in 2001. After obtaining a grant from the California Air Resources board (the first transportation company in the state to do so) it equipped its fleet of more than 400 tractor-trailers with state-of-the-art pollution control equipment. Unified Western Grocers also partnered with two regional dairies, WestFarm Foods and Mallories Dairy, in 2001 to replicate its successful Southern California dairy program.

There were signs of a turnaround beginning in 2002 for Unified Western Grocers, which closed seven underperforming retail stores in Northern California and Oregon that year and converted its remaining supermarkets to its new Marketplace format. In 2003, it exited the retail business, selling or closing the last of the 12 stores it owned to invest more heavily in distribution, which then accounted for more than 95 percent of its sales volume and served more than 3,000 members. According to the *Los Angeles Business Journal,* the co-op was then one of the four largest private companies in Los Angeles County.

Unified Western Grocers continued its focus on higher-end specialty and gourmet foods and perishables in 2004 with the launch of its "Fresh Obsessed" vendor partnership program. The program helped members differentiate themselves from nontraditional competitors by emphasizing enhanced selection and lower cost on produce, service deli, service bakery, and meats. Additionally, specialty products offered the benefit of higher margins and distinction from big-box competitors. Complementing Fresh Obsessed was Gourmet Specialties' own line of natural foods, Natural Value, and a magazine called *Natural Solutions* provided information about health foods.

2005–07: LARGEST WHOLESALE DISTRIBUTOR IN THE WESTERN UNITED STATES

Although co-op membership had dropped to 2,500 by the middle of the decade, from 2002 to 2007, independents in Southern California had picked up a market share of 2 percent to 3 percent and, in Northern California and the Pacific Northwest, there was a resurgence of independent grocers. Sales for 2005 for Unified Western Grocers were up to $2.8 billion in 2003 and $3 billion in 2004 which ranked it as the fourth largest grocery co-op and the largest wholesale grocery distributor in the United States, according to *Supermarket News*. Although sales for 2005 were down slightly, they rose again in 2006 to $2.95 billion. The co-op did some internal reorganizing in 2006, changing the name of its specialty division to Market Centre.

With the purchase in 2007 of Associated Grocers, Inc. of Seattle, Washington, Unified Western Grocers became Unified Grocers, a $4 billion grocery wholesale company. Associated Grocers was a wholesale cooperative providing food, nonfood, general merchandise, and retail sales to stores in Washington, Oregon, Alaska, Hawaii, Guam, and the Pacific Rim. Founded in 1934, it had more than 320 customer locations. The name change for the co-op was part of a rebranding that involved rethinking the grocery market based on lifestyle "clusters" rather than geography. Unified's members served four such clusters: large, affluent urban and suburban households; mid- to downscale rural seniors; low-income urban households; and bicultural and unacculturated Hispanics.

As Unified's member grocers faced the ongoing threat of ever encroaching Wal-Mart Supercenters and other large grocery chains, Unified took steps to accommodate future growth. It gained control space in Commerce, California, for a produce warehouse and for trailers and expanded one of its buildings to bring all its buyers together in one location. It also expanded its Stockton distribution center and reracked facilities in Portland and in Santa Fe Springs. According to Plamann in a 2007 *Supermarket News* article, "The last few years have seen a renaissance among independents, with dramatic growth in the last three years. ... Given the dynamism of the retail marketplace, we as suppliers need to think about what happens to our members from a consumer perspective and satisfy those needs."

Carrie Rothburd

PRINCIPAL SUBSIDIARIES

Grocers & Merchants Insurance Service; Grocers & Merchants Management Co.; Grocers Capital Co.; Grocers General Merchandise Co.; Grocers Specialty Co.; Springfield Insurance Company.

PRINCIPAL COMPETITORS

C & S Wholesale Grocers, Inc.; SUPERVALU INC.; Associated Wholesale Grocers, Inc.; Costco Wholesale Corporation; The Kroger Company; Safeway Inc.; Wal-Mart Stores, Inc.

FURTHER READING

Angrisani, Carol, "Wellness Magazine Pushes Store Label," *Supermarket News*, October 24, 2005, p. 43.

Glover, Kara, "Certified Grocers Sees Market Share Slipping Away," *Los Angeles Business Journal*, November 7, 1994.

Tobenkin, David, "Certified Grocers of California: Grocery Co-op Supplies Soup to Sites," *Los Angeles Business Journal*, February 5, 1990.

Zwiebach, Elliot, "Co-ops Survive with Differing Approaches," *Supermarket News*, July 22, 2002, p. 56.

———, "Unified Sees Threat from Tesco," *Supermarket News*, February 19, 2007.

———, "Unified to Launch Effort to Expand Customer Base," *Supermarket News*, June 11, 2001, p. 4.

———, "Unifying Unified: Two Western Cooperatives Are Forging a Single, Solid Entity, Focusing on Savings, and Weighing Further Alliances," *Supermarket News*, March 6, 2000, p. 1.

The Vermont Country Store

5650 Main Street
Manchester Center, Vermont 05255-9711
U.S.A.
Telephone: (802) 362-8460
Fax: (802) 362-8288
Web site: http://www.vermontcountrystore.com

Private Company
Founded: 1945
Employees: 500
NAIC: 452990 All Other General Merchandise Stores;
     454113 Mail-Order Houses

■ ■ ■

The Vermont Country Store is a unique mail-order and retail operation that sells unusual goods of practical and nostalgic interest. The company's two stores, in Weston and Rockingham, Vermont, offer a hands-on experience of a general store from the late 19th century. Buttermilk red paint and long porches displaying antiques and oddities invite curiosity. Wood floors and walls, exposed wood ceiling beams with baskets hanging down, old-time pictures, solid oak counters, and other antique fixtures provide the interior atmosphere. In the Weston store, a checkerboard and checkers sit on a wooden barrel near the potbellied, wood-burning stove; in earlier times such a spot provided a cozy place to wait for the mail, tell stories, and keep up on local events. A stereopticon, circa 1890, provides patrons with an old-fashioned peep show of pinup girls. A big, hand-turned, two-wheeled coffee grinder contributes to the numerous aromas that permeate the air.

The Vermont Country Store presents goods in the manner of the old general stores. Aged Vermont cheddar cheese is cut from a 38-pound wheel and packaged in 19th-century style. Behind the sales counters, jars of local food specialties line the walls. Unusual condiments include fiddlehead ferns, watermelon pickles, and a variety of jams not found in chainstores, such as quince or wild elderberry; the cider jelly is made from a hundred-year-old recipe. The foods can be sampled with Vermont Common Crackers proffered from a wooden barrel. A colorful array of penny candy is displayed at child's-eye level in a glass-enclosed case, in clear glass apothecary jars, or wooden buckets. The Vermont Country Store sells its own line of fresh-milled whole-grain flours and cereals, such as fine yellow corn flour for making Johnnycakes, old-style pancakes that can be topped with Vermont maple syrup. Other goods are displayed in wood boxes and baskets, and on wood shelves.

As "Purveyors of the Practical and Hard-to-Find," The Vermont Country Store specializes in offering tried-and-true items that even high technology cannot improve, but which usually cannot be found in modern big-box stores. Simple household gadgets include a pants-stretcher, a wire-loop rug beater, and an apple parer that peels and cores an apple with one crank. Newspaper columnists responding to requests for information on hard-to-find items frequently refer their readers to The Vermont Country Store.

In its quest to offer the best products available, particularly those that stimulate customers' childhood memories, the company has revived many discontinued products. Oxydol laundry soap, Charles' Chips, Ship'n Shore blouses, Evening in Paris perfume, and Tangee Lipstick are just some of the name brand items. Other products are practical in their low-technology simplicity, such as the Olivetti portable manual typewriter and Timex watches.

The bulk of the company's revenue comes from its mail-order business and an online store. The company's original catalog, "Voice of the Mountains," promotes about 500 items with a down-home style. On simple newsprint, the catalog displays products in black-and-white photographs or illustrations that are accompanied by clever descriptions and sales pitches. Drawings of country scenes, as well as customer testimonials, fill the spaces between products. The color "Goods & Wares" catalog offers items of nostalgic and practical interest. The Vermont Country Store distributes more than 50 million catalogs annually.

FAMILY BUSINESS PROVIDES INSPIRATION FOR THE VERMONT COUNTRY STORE

Vrest Orton founded The Vermont Country Store in 1945 out of nostalgia for the general store opened by his parents in North Calais, Vermont, in 1897. When Orton was a teenager, the family moved to Massachusetts and opened a department store. As a young adult, Orton pursued diverse interests. After college and military service during World War I, he traveled west and walked through Mexico and Central America with a typewriter strapped to a burro. After a short time at the U.S. consulate in Guaymas, illness prompted him to return to the East Coast and pursue a writing career.

In New York City during the 1920s, he worked for prominent social critic H. L. Mencken at the *American Mercury*, and he wrote numerous literary books, such as *Dreiserana*, about U.S. novelist Theodore Dreiser. Also, he founded *Colophon*, a renowned bookseller's magazine. However, the sight of broken men during the Great Depression tainted Orton's view of modern city life. A Vermont vacation renewed his love for country values, and he felt at home for the first time in many years. On that trip, in 1934, Orton bought an 1860 brick house in Weston, a mountain town six miles down a dirt road from the nearest major thoroughfare. Orton expected to stay in New York City, but returned to his home state that winter with his new wife, Ellen, also a Vermont native.

The Ortons sought to create a simpler life, outside the currents of modernization. Orton continued his writing and publishing activities, and sold his books through the mail. A friendship with poet Robert Frost, who spent his summers in Vermont, led Orton to write *Vermont Afternoons with Robert Frost*. Orton contemplated the idea of opening a general store, but then World War II started, and the Ortons moved to Washington, D.C., where Orton worked at the Pentagon, writing speeches and publicity pieces. The decision to open a store upon returning to Weston coincided with local businessmen's desire to develop Weston as a tourist destination.

In 1945, on Weston's one street, Orton purchased an 1828 building that happily looked similar to his father's North Calais store. Orton restored it into an authentic replica of a late 19th-century store, using some fixtures from his father's store. While preparing the store for business, Orton compiled a mail-order catalog that offered 36 Vermont-made products, including Tubbs Snowshoes, a sewing chest, a desk box for stationery, a rocking horse, bowls, serving plates, trays, books, and grains. He printed the catalog in his garage, and in October he distributed copies to 1,000 people on the family's Christmas card list. After a successful first mail-order run, The Vermont Country Store opened in the spring of 1946.

PURVEYOR OF THE PRACTICAL AND TRADITIONAL

Orton stocked the store with items useful to Vermont farm families, but which could not be found elsewhere. These included calico aprons, mustache wax, garter belts, suspenders, balsam soap, and bag balm ointment. He revived products that had gone out of use due to modern technology. Long before gourmet became a household word, Orton sold peppercorn mills, wood steak mallets, nutmeg grinders, and other standard, old-style kitchen tools no longer available in chainstores. He offered fresh-roasted, whole-bean coffee that could be

KEY DATES

1945: Vrest and Ellen Orton mail a 12-page catalog to those on their Christmas card list.

1946: The Vermont Country Store opens for business.

1952: An article in the *Saturday Evening Post* attracts new customers nationwide.

1959: Company opens the Bryant Restaurant in a neighboring building.

1967: Overflowing business leads the company to open a store in Rockingham.

1984: Main office and warehousing and distribution are relocated to Manchester.

1993: State-of-the-art distribution center opens in North Clarendon.

1998: Online store debuts.

1999: "Goods & Wares" catalog emerges from experiments with various new catalogs.

2000: Expansion begins on new distribution, fulfillment, and call center in North Clarendon.

freshly ground at the store. He researched traditional New England foods that could be sold in jars, such as lobster spread, fiddlehead greens, Indian pudding, and yellow-eyed beans.

Orton offered five-pound bags of freshly milled whole-grain flours and cereals, processed at a nearby stone mill. The store also sold brown bread made from the whole grains, and Ellen Orton wrote *Cooking with Wholegrains* to sell in the store.

During the slow business days of the store's first years, Orton looked for unusual items to sell. He offered a custom-built, 1890s rubber-topped buggy for sale, priced at $150, and sold one to a Georgia man. Frequently, customers asked to buy fixtures in the store, such as the kerosene lamps and the chairs by the potbellied stove. In response Orton found craftsmen to make replicas he could sell. The catalog attracted people to the store, and the business grew slowly. By 1951, the company distributed a 500-item catalog to a mailing list of 35,000 people. That year, 75,000 people visited the store.

DEVELOPING AS A TOURIST DESTINATION

Orton used his New York connections to gain publicity for the store. The Vermont Country Store received its first major boost in business in 1952, after the *Saturday Evening Post* published an article entitled "The Happy Storekeeper of the Green Mountains." The article told Orton's personal story, and it featured large color photographs of the store's interior displays and outdoor surroundings. Due to the magazine's national distribution, the article attracted new customers from all over the country, for both the catalog and the store.

As The Vermont Country Store began to develop as a tourist destination, Orton expanded the store and added a lunch counter. In 1959, he purchased and renovated the Bryant family house, located at the end of a row of buildings adjacent to the store. Installation of a mahogany bar, circa 1885, a soda fountain, and other antique fixtures gave the restaurant a late 19th-century atmosphere. The Bryant House, as the restaurant was named, offered traditional New England fare for lunch and afternoon tea. Orton turned the upstairs rooms into a museum that displayed an ornately carved mahogany bedroom set, women's dresses, and other 19th-century artifacts.

As the tourist business prospered, Orton expanded the Weston store. The store served about 150,000 patrons per year, and during the peak summer season, the overflow of customers waited in line outside the store. Orton addressed this problem by opening a store in Rockingham, 18 miles east of Weston. Orton developed the property around the store as a tourist destination, with nature trails, a covered bridge dating to 1872, and an 1810 gristmill and waterwheel.

SECOND GENERATION TAKES THE LEAD

In the early 1970s, Lyman Orton became president of The Vermont Country Store. When he took the lead, business at the two stores was in decline, as high gasoline prices during the early 1970s dampened the tourist trade. However, the company's mail-order business exploded, especially after 1976, when Orton swapped catalog mailing lists with other companies. Thus Orton oversaw The Vermont Country Store's first major expansion of the mail-order business. In 1984 Orton relocated administration and operations to new facilities in Manchester. The office moved into a newly constructed building containing office space as well as space for the warehouse, distribution, and order fulfillment functions.

To maintain quality service, Orton computerized operations and organized the warehouse to accommodate growth. The company learned to pace growth with capabilities of space, stock, and staff, to control quality of service by controlling quantity of catalogs mailed. At a time when mail order was subject to scams and consumer distrust, Orton built trust and loyalty with a policy to ship product orders the day after they were received.

The Vermont Country Store maintained its loyal customers by offering products of unique nostalgic value. In 1979 the company rescued a Vermont food from extinction. Cross crackers, made by the Cross Baking Company since 1830, were sold at the store from the beginning. After that company closed in 1979, The Vermont Country Store acquired its equipment and added space to the Rockingham store for a bakery and renamed the product Vermont Common Crackers.

As the definition of nostalgia changed across generations, The Vermont Country Store offered appropriate products. For instance, as electric typewriters became more complex and desktop computers ubiquitous, the Olivetti portable manual typewriter became a low-tech alternative. Although more expensive than a new electric typewriter, the Olivetti sold well into the 21st century.

When Vrest Orton died in 1986, he left the state of Vermont with one of its premier country stores. Moreover, The Vermont Country Store provided the inspiration for thousands of imitation stores throughout the United States.

NEW OUTLETS FOR BUSINESS

During the late 1980s and early 1990s, business at The Vermont Country Store grew at approximately 10 percent of annual sales. The company expanded into a second warehouse in the late 1980s, then opened a new 72,000-square-foot state-of-the-art distribution facility in North Clarendon in 1993. A minor expansion of the Rockingham store involved building a barn from reclaimed wood adjacent to the existing store.

In 1994 a nonfamily member took the helm of The Vermont Country Store, when Bob Allen became president of the company. Allen had started with the company as an administrative assistant in 1971. By the time he assumed control, the company was mailing 15 million "Voice of the Mountains" catalogs and continuing to garner repeat business and a generally positive response.

Allen sought to build on the company's successes by developing niche markets with catalogs that focused on specialized categories of consumer goods. The first such catalog, "Green Mountain Mercantile," launched in the summer of 1994, presented women's clothing and accessories in simple watercolor pictures. The new catalog concept succeeded with a mailing to a list of 550,000 female customers.

A few years later, Allen experimented with other niche product markets. In 1997 The Vermont Country Store launched "Apothecary," a 64-page catalog of hundreds of personal care items. In 1998, the "Household" catalog offered products of interest to the company's older, established customer base, but with a wider array of merchandise than offered in the "Voice of the Mountains." A four-color catalog of home goods and gifts, titled "Goods & Wares," was designed to attract a younger consumer market. Together the catalogs added 6,000 stockkeeping units to the company's inventory. Only the "Goods & Wares" catalog survived these marketing experiments.

Internet technology presented The Vermont Country Store with the opportunity to expand its reach, and the company introduced an online store in 1998. Concerned that increased consumer interest would generate questions about specialized merchandise, the company tested a toll-free number in 1998 and 1999, but it did not result in a significant sales increase. Instead, the company added a chatline to answer customer questions when the web site relaunched in 2000.

In May 2000 construction began on a new call center and warehouse, distribution, and order fulfillment center in North Clarendon. The $5.7 million project accommodated a 160,000-square-foot distribution and fulfillment center capable of receiving and distributing 23,000 units of merchandise. The company's longtime truck supplier assisted with the design of the warehouse and added 20 percent efficiency through its suggestions for layout. The call center provided capacity for 175 customer service agents, although The Vermont Country Store planned to begin with 110 call stations.

FINDING AND PROMOTING "NEW" NOSTALGIC BRANDS

With a new staff member hired for the purpose of researching old products, The Vermont Country Store continued to generate nostalgic interest. The company gained exclusive rights to sell Tangee lipstick, popular during the 1940s and 1950s; when applied to the lips, Tangee lipstick adjusted to a woman's natural coloring. After Montgomery Ward closed, the founding family of Ship'n Shore blouses repurchased the business, and The Vermont Country Store gained exclusive rights to sell their products. Children's toys included the Bozo punching bag and Rock 'em Sock 'em Robots. Brand-name personal care items from the 1970s included Lifebuoy deodorant soap and "Gee, Your Hair Smells Terrific" shampoo.

The Vermont Country Store made some concessions to contemporary sensibilities when it added 500 square feet to its Rockingham store. The August 2006 project involved installation of a heating and air conditioning system. Previously, customers had to endure the discomfort of humid summers, and insufficient heat from the wood-burning stove during Vermont's cold winters.

Mary Tradii

PRINCIPAL COMPETITORS

Adam's Farm; Dan & Whit's General Store; Taftsville Country Store; Waits River General Store.

FURTHER READING

Beck, Jane C., "Selling Tradition," *Visit'n,* December 1995, p. 44.

Bracco, Edgar J., "The Country Store; This One's the Last Word in Nostalgia," *Worcester Telegram & Gazette,* July 10, 1994, p. F1.

Cyr, Diane, "Vermont's $50 Million Secret or Why They're Called the Green Mountains," *Catalog Age,* October 1994, p. 133.

De View, Lucille, "Nostalgia in a Vermont Catalog," *Press-Enterprise,* December 1, 2002, p. E02.

Dowling, Melissa, "Mailer Taps Trendy Niche," *Catalog Age,* October 1997, p. 7.

Dresnok, Cheryl, "Job Openings Going Unfilled in Manchester Area," *Vermont Business,* May 1986, p. 26.

Graff, Christopher, "Country Comforts—Vermont Country Store Thrives on the Nostalgic Charm of Yesteryear," *Commercial Appeal,* June 15, 2005, p. M3.

Hanes, Phyllis, "In the North, Vermont Country Stores Symbolize Era of Penny Candy and Overalls," *Christian Science Monitor,* April 18, 1988, p. 23.

Jensen, Brennen, "Preserving a Sense of Place," *Chronicle of Philanthropy,* September 16, 2004.

Kirkendall, Elizabeth, "Biodegradable Diapers, Hair Nets," *San Francisco Chronicle,* June 28, 1989, p. 10/Z1.

Kroll, Barb and Ron, "Vermont's Heritage for Sale, Bit by Bit," *Globe and Mail,* May 4, 1985.

Levey, Richard H., "Loose Cannon: Only Skin Deep," *Direct (Online Exclusive),* February 5, 2007.

"Major Expansion for VT Country Store," *Catalog Age,* July 2000, p. 5.

McDowell, Edwin, "Vrest Orton, 89, Founder of Store," *New York Times,* December 5, 1986, p. D20.

McKeen, Sid, "Oh, So Very Cunning, Those Vt. Catalog People," *Worcester Telegram & Gazette,* April 14, 1991, p. C3.

Negus, Beth, "Vt. Country Store Overhauls Site," *Direct,* November 15, 1999, p. 16.

Orton, Vrest, "It's So Old It's New," *Journal of Retailing,* April 1948.

"A Quirky Retailer Lives on 'Memories'; The Vermont Country Store President Bob Allen on Its Profitable Niche Selling Products That Were Favorites of Past Generations," *Business Week Online,* November 23, 2004.

Robinson, Sue, "Vt. Country Store Rolls Out Internet Center," *Burlington Free Press,* September 30, 2000, p. 5B.

Rosenfield, James R. "A Footnote to Sotheby's, and Two Contrasting Catalogs," *Direct Marketing,* July 1990, p. 21.

Shenton, Edward, "The Happy Storekeeper of the Green Mountains," *Saturday Evening Post,* March 15, 1952, p. 26.

Smith Monkman, Carol, "Catalog Offers a Fond Glance at Gadgets Gone By," *Seattle Post-Intelligencer,* November 14, 1998, p. B3.

Stern, Michael and Jane, "Chicken Pie, Like Country Store, Recalls Old Times," *Richmond (Va.) Times-Dispatch,* September 11, 1985, p. 33.

Stout, Marilyn, "Old-Time Crackers Bounce Back," *New York Times,* November 4, 1981, p. C13.

"VNA Trucks Help Fill Million Orders/Year," *Modern Materials Handling,* October 15, 2000, p. 9.

Wasserman, Ted, "Purgatory for Products? Vermont," *Brandweek.com,* January 23, 2006, p. 34.

Weisse-Tisman, Howard, "Vermont Country Store Celebrates New Addition to Rockingham Outlet," *Brattleboro Reformer,* August 12, 2006.

Washington Mutual, Inc.

1301 Second Avenue
Seattle, Washington 98101-3033
U.S.A.
Telephone: (206) 461-2000
Toll Free: (800) 788-7000
Fax: (206) 377-2495
Web site: http://www.wamu.com

Public Company
Incorporated: 1994
Employees: 49,403
Total Assets: $330.1 billion (2007)
Stock Exchanges: New York
Ticker Symbol: WM
NAIC: 551111 Offices of Bank Holding Companies;
   522120 Savings Institutions

■ ■ ■

Seattle-based Washington Mutual, Inc. (WaMu), one of the nation's leading financial services companies, is the outgrowth of a demand to rebuild its home city after a devastating late 19th-century fire. Since then the company has transitioned from a building loan to a mutual bank. Until the 1960s, the company operated solely in the Seattle area. Then, an acquisition drive during the 1990s propelled Washington Mutual to the top ranks of U.S. home mortgage makers. Faced with a steady downward pressure in the sector at the midpoint of the first decade of the 2000s, Washington Mutual has redirected its attention to its retail banking business.

19TH-CENTURY ORIGINS

The birth of the financial institution responsible for forming Washington Mutual, Inc., occurred shortly after the near-death of the city. In 1880, Seattle was a small town in Washington Territory just about to begin its rise toward becoming the Pacific Northwest's most influential commercial hub. With a population of 4,000 at the beginning of the decade, Seattle was little more than a settlement situated in the upper reaches of a sprawling territory that was yet to be incorporated into the United States. Before the decade was through, however, statehood arrived and Seattle, after nine years of growth, transformed itself into a burgeoning metropolis. The population of Seattle leaped from 4,000 in 1880 to 40,000 by 1889, the year Washington was admitted to the Union as the 42nd state and the year the city of Seattle was reduced to a pile of ashes.

On June 6, 1889, a glue pot in the basement of a downtown building boiled over and touched off the "Great Seattle Fire," engulfing the downtown district in flames. Before the raging blaze was extinguished, 25 city blocks were razed, 120 acres in total, destroying the heart of the city and erasing a decade of robust growth. Overnight, Seattle had been turned into a pile of smoking rubble. Just as the city was shedding the vestiges of its pioneer roots, it was time to rebuild, time to begin anew. It was also the time for the formation of the city's newest financial institution, an enterprise created specifically to help in rebuilding the city of Seattle.

In September 1889, 15 weeks after flames had turned to ashes, a group of Seattle's business leaders convened to discuss the prospects of forming a building loan company. In attendance were shipbuilders, lawyers, doctors, bankers, and politicians, some of whom had recently arrived in Seattle whereas others had been denizens of the city for years. The group of prominent citizens were intent on forming a financial institution that would answer the demand for the resources to build or rebuild houses, something commercial banks were reluctant to finance at the time. A general building loan business was officially established that evening, and was to be incorporated as Washington National Building Loan and Investment Association. Washington National began its business while the city of Seattle still remained visibly scarred by the early summer fire.

Initially led by Edward Oziel Graves, who was the former assistant treasurer for the U.S. Treasury's Bureau of Engraving and Printing, Washington National was supported by one employee during its inaugural year, Ira Hill Case, who occupied one desk in a second-floor office shared by a dozen other businessmen representing an equal number of divergent business interests. The beginnings were modest, to be sure, but not long after its creation, Washington National made banking history. The association's first loans were approved in February 1890, one of which was an amortized home loan, perhaps the first of its kind in the United States. Washington National went on to approve more than 2,000 amortized home loans during the ensuing 20 years, becoming a much-used source for home mortgage loans.

Washington National represented one of 3,500 building and loan associations in the United States at the time of its establishment, but when the company began to flounder after the turn of the century it chose to distance itself from the building society movement. In 1908, the enterprise changed its name to Washington Savings and Loan Association and embarked on a course that gradually steered the newly named financial institution toward the mutual banking field. Along with the name change came additional sweeping changes, as new leadership restructured Washington Savings and Loan to

invigorate business. Membership fees were eliminated, the terms of interest and loan repayment schedules were precisely established, an aggressive advertising program was launched, and customers were granted the freedom to withdraw deposits at any time, with any interest accrued up to the day of withdrawal.

The changes implemented spurred the institution's growth, igniting a five-year period of unprecedented expansion. Between 1908 and 1913, the number of loans granted by Washington Savings and Loan soared from 300 to 2,700. Assets increased elevenfold, jumping from $346,576 to more than $4 million, and the number of accounts operated by the association leaped from 400 to 2,700. Helped in large part by this growth spurt, Washington Savings and Loan ranked not only as the oldest savings institution in Washington, but also as the state's largest savings institution, providing the association with firm footing as it entered a new phase in its development.

WORLD WAR I CONVERSION INTO A MUTUAL BANK

In 1917, while the country's newspapers covered the progress of war overseas, Washington Savings and Loan converted into a mutual savings bank and once again changed its name. Rechristened Washington Mutual Savings Bank, the recast institution boasted more than 16,000 depositors at the time of the United States' entrance into World War I and benefitted substantially from the century's first epic military struggle. During World War I, Washington Mutual's assets rose 68 percent, recording a gain of more than $4 million, and real estate loans registered an even greater increase, of 250 percent.

After the conclusion of the war, recessionary economic conditions hobbled Seattle's economic growth, but despite the anemic financial situation Washington Mutual's deposits increased strongly, rising from $15 million in 1921 to more than $26 million two years later. Such encouraging growth came to a stop by the end of the decade, however, as the Wall Street stock market crash of 1929 gave way to a decade-long economic depression that wrought devastation for the U.S. banking industry. Although the years were difficult, Washington Mutual persevered, avoiding the financial ruin that swept away many of the country's financial institutions. It was during the first months of this unrivaled economic plunge that Washington Mutual completed the first acquisition in its history, acquiring Continental Mutual Savings Bank in July 1930.

By the end of the 1930s, Washington Mutual was just shy of 100,000 depositors and about to benefit once

KEY DATES

1889: Washington National Building Loan and Investment Association is established to help rebuild after Great Seattle Fire.

1908: Name change to Washington Savings and Loan Association marks shift away from building loan business.

1917: Company converts to mutual savings bank and is renamed Washington Mutual Savings Bank.

1930: First acquisition is completed on the heels of stock market crash.

1947: Home county branches open, following postwar legislative changes.

1964: Acquisitions extend outside greater Seattle area.

1982: Era of financial diversification begins.

1990: Regional expansion drive takes off.

1996: Purchase of 158-branch American Savings Bank, a $1.4 billion deal, nearly doubles size of company.

2000: Washington Mutual ranks as largest thrift in the nation in wake of series of purchases.

2003: Fortunes change as bottom drops out of mortgage market.

2006: Washington Mutual adds credit-card operation.

again from the economic growth engendered by the century's second great military struggle. During World War II, Washington Mutual, by then more than a half-century old, sold nearly $30 million in war bonds. In 1941, the bank merged with Coolidge Mutual Savings Bank, increasing its resources to more than $77 million and its deposits to more than $72 million, and gaining Washington Mutual its first branch office, the quarters formerly occupied by Coolidge Mutual, which became known as the Times Square Branch. After the war, when banking legislation permitted mutual banks to establish branches in their home county, Washington Mutual opened two banking offices, one in 1947 and another in 1948.

During the 1950s, the promulgation of additional banking legislation paved the way for mutual banks to establish statewide networks of service, but despite the opportunity to do so Washington Mutual did not move outside the greater Seattle area until 1964. Branches were established in the Seattle area during the interven-

ing years, however, with five Washington Mutual offices opening their doors between 1955 and 1961. When Washington Mutual finally did move outside the Seattle area, the stage was set for an era of geographic expansion that extended the bank's presence throughout Washington. From 1964 forward, the physical growth of Washington Mutual was driven by internal expansion and by external means, as the bank took on the role of an aggressive acquisitor. This chapter in the bank's history began with the acquisition of Citizens Mutual Savings Bank in 1964.

STATEWIDE EXPANSION BEGINNING IN 1964

Citizens Mutual Savings Bank's existence as a mutual bank was only hours old when Washington Mutual sealed the deal to purchase the eastern Washington-based financial institution. Founded in 1902 as Citizens Savings and Loan Society, the thrift operated as a savings and loan up until its acquisition by Washington Mutual, acquiring the Pullman Savings and Loan Association the year prior to the 1964 Washington Mutual acquisition. With its base in Spokane and the newly acquired Pullman Savings and Loan adding a presence in Pullman, Citizens Savings and Loan represented an opportunity for Washington Mutual to expand into eastern Washington, but banking legislation at the time did not permit a mutual bank to merge with a savings and loan. To clear this obstacle, Citizens Savings and Loan converted into a mutual bank in 1964, as Washington Mutual had done 47 years earlier, changing its name to Citizens Mutual Savings Bank just prior to its merger with Washington Mutual. Once completed, the transaction extended Washington Mutual's presence beyond the greater Seattle area for the first time, giving the bank branches in Pullman and Spokane and establishing a pattern the Seattle-based concern would follow in the years ahead.

The year after the Citizens Mutual Savings Bank acquisition, Washington Mutual completed a similar deal when Liberty Savings and Loan Association converted into a mutual bank to facilitate its acquisition by Washington Mutual. Established in 1919, Liberty Savings and Loan Association became Liberty Mutual Savings Bank in 1965, giving Washington Mutual branch offices in Yakima, Kennewick, and Grandview, Washington. The same scenario was played out in 1973 when the Grays Harbor Savings and Loan Association converted into Grays Harbor Mutual Savings Bank just before its acquisition by Washington Mutual, adding a branch office in Grays Harbor to the Seattle-based bank's growing empire.

Against the backdrop of these acquisitions, Washington Mutual expanded geographically through internal means by establishing branch offices on its own. Between 1965 and 1973, the bank opened 15 branch offices in the Seattle area and in regions across the state, building itself into a dominant force in Washington State. Swelled by acquisitions and internal expansion, Washington Mutual entered the 1980s as a venerable yet rising financial institution, its near-century of business in the Seattle area and two decades of statewide expansion generating considerable momentum for the decade ahead. During the 1980s, this momentum would not be checked, as the bank diversified quickly. Although industry observers would charge that the bank spread itself in too many directions during the decade, the far-flung expansion effected during the 1980s proved to be the catalyst for Washington Mutual's animated growth during the 1990s.

1982 ARRIVAL OF KILLINGER

During the 1980s, the subsidiary companies that would compose The Washington Mutual Financial Group came together. The proliferation of diversified financial subsidiaries grouped under the Washington Mutual corporate umbrella began in 1982 when the bank acquired Murphey Favre, Inc., and Composite Research & Management Co., and formed Washington Mutual Insurance Services. Murphey Favre was the Northwest's oldest securities brokerage firm, Composite Research & Management Co. operated as an investment adviser and portfolio management firm, and Washington Mutual Insurance Services was a full-service retail insurance agency. Beginning with these three subsidiaries, Washington Mutual formed or acquired a host of other operating companies that carried the bank into a variety of new business areas, including travel services, real estate partnerships, junk bonds, and commercial construction loans.

None of the subsidiary companies was more important to the future of Washington Mutual than the 1982 acquisition of Murphey Favre, a distinction entirely due to the arrival of a young Murphey Favre executive named Kerry K. Killinger. At the time of the 1982 acquisition, Killinger was 32 years old and had served as a securities analyst and investment broker for the company before being named executive vice-president. Once brought into the Washington Mutual fold, Killinger rose quickly through the bank's executive ranks, becoming president in 1988 and chief executive officer two years later. During Killinger's rise, Washington Mutual was moving in a different direction, as the bank began to decline and suffer from waning profitability. With earnings slipping late in the decade, a

new program aimed at restoring profitability and invigorating growth was launched that would dramatically amplify the magnitude of Washington Mutual's geographic scope.

UNPRECEDENTED GROWTH

During Washington Mutual's 100th anniversary year, the new strategy was adopted, a program of growth spearheaded by Killinger, who informed the *Puget Sound Business Journal* that in the coming years it was Washington Mutual's goal "to be the premier consumer bank in the Northwest." Toward this objective, Killinger turned to a "back-to-basics" approach by focusing on consumer loans and checking accounts. Once Killinger was named chairman of Washington Mutual in 1990, the bank's bid to become the dominant financial institution in the region began in earnest, as the newly named chairman, president, and chief executive officer orchestrated an acquisition campaign that swallowed up competitors at a rate of about two per year. For the first time in the bank's history, it extended its presence beyond Washington's borders, compensating for its belated entry into the regional banking arena by expanding aggressively at a time when the savings and loan industry in general was faring poorly.

In 1991, Washington Mutual ranked as Washington's largest independently owned financial institution, with $8 billion in assets and 84 financial centers and 17 home loan centers in its home state, Oregon, and Idaho. These impressive figures would be dwarfed by the magnitude of the bank four years later, as Washington Mutual's acquisition spree ignited its growth, carried the bank into Montana and Utah, and necessitated the formation of Washington Mutual, Inc., as a holding company in August 1994. Between 1991 and 1995, Washington Mutual's profits more than doubled, leaping from $80.6 million to $190.6 million, its deposits increased from $5.4 billion to $10.6 billion, and its assets swelled from $8 billion to $21.6 billion. Meanwhile, the number of branch offices operated by the bank had increased dramatically, reaching a total of 248 financial centers and 23 loan centers by the end of 1995. The first half of the 1990s represented a period of growth unrivaled in Washington Mutual's history. As the bank entered the late 1990s it did not slow its pace of growth.

In early 1996, Washington Mutual acquired Coos Bay, Oregon-based Western Bank, giving it 42 branch offices in 35 communities. Next, the bank acquired Ogden-based Utah Federal Savings Bank. The bank appeared to be continuing its aggressive campaign to dominate the Pacific Northwest, an objective Killinger touched on when he said, "Our strategy calls for continued growth through selective acquisitions of consumer banks, commercial banks, and other financial service businesses that offer long-term value to our shareholders." Killinger put his words into action in July 1996 when Washington Mutual completed the largest acquisition in its 107-year history. After searching for an entry into the lucrative California market for two years, Killinger found his target in Irvine, where the 158-branch American Savings Bank was headquartered. In a $1.4 billion deal completed at the end of July, Washington Mutual acquired American Savings Bank and nearly doubled its size, making it the third largest savings and loan in the United States. Buoyed enormously by the acquisition of American Savings Bank, Washington Mutual entered the late 1990s intent on continuing its ambitious expansion program. Further acquisitions in the California market were expected.

END OF CENTURY DRIVE FOR THE TOP

Killinger, speaking at a mergers and acquisitions conference in February 1997, confirmed those California dreams, according to an *American Banker* article. "We like this market because it's very fragmented and is the last market in the country that is still going through significant consolidation," Killinger said. "It's been delayed here simply because of the lingering recessionary factors—but that's about to change." Killinger planned to concentrate on northern California for its commercial banking growth but was "willing, able, and ready to execute expansion through acquisitions of consumer banks throughout the West," quoted *American Banker*. As Washington Mutual, Detroit-based Comerica Inc., and North Carolina's NationsBank Corp. looked longingly to California, takeover speculation spiked share prices among California area thrifts. If prices climbed too high, Washington Mutual planned to turn to internal methods of growth, and escalate its stock repurchase program, Christopher Rhoads reported.

Killinger did not wait long to make his move. Washington Mutual acquired Great Western Financial Corp. in 1997 and H.F. Ahmanson & Co. (Home Savings of America thrift) in 1998. The company then made headway into the subprime market with the 1999 purchase of Long Beach Financial Corp.

By 2000, Washington Mutual had climbed to the top of the ranks among the nation's thrifts, with 60 percent of its $188 billion in assets from California, according to the *San Francisco Business Times*. Washington Mutual's rapid advancement in the California market, however, took "a back seat to high-profile and often turbulent megamergers like Wells Fargo's marriage to Norwest and NationsBank's takeover of Bank of America," Ron Leuty observed. Despite a series of post-merger personnel cuts and computer system conversions, Washington Mutual had avoided major glitches and bad press.

After a brief period of digesting its new operations, Washington Mutual embarked on another series of purchases. In this round were PNC Financial Services Group Inc.'s residential mortgage operations, Bank United Corp., and FleetBoston Financial Corp. "WaMu's management has a history of which Alexander the Great would have been proud," Sanford Bernstein & Co. analyst Jonathan Gray said in a July 2001 *U.S. Banker* article. Its appetite for growth was yet to be satiated.

Washington Mutual had accomplished something not seen in more than a decade when it attained home loan origination leadership. Home Savings of America, part of Washington Mutual since 1998, had been the last thrift to top the leaderboard. Unfortunately, the period was also marked by a savings and loan meltdown. Scores of thrifts closed, during the late 1980s, in the wake of rising interest rates, industry deregulation, and mismanagement.

INTO THE 21ST CENTURY

Washington Mutual assets had grown tenfold in just a half decade. In addition to being the nation's largest thrift, WaMu was the seventh largest banking company and first in both mortgage servicing and origination. Acquiring compatible companies that could quickly contribute to earnings helped drive WaMu's success thus far, according to an August 2001 *ABA Banking Journal* article.

In addition to advancing in terms of sheer size, WaMu was shaking up its product mix. Prime single family mortgages constituted nearly three-quarters of its portfolio at the end of the first quarter of 2001, down from 82 percent at the end of 1998. WaMu planned further reduction, down to 60 percent, Steve Cocheo reported. In their place WaMu was endeavoring to increase the number of higher revenue nonresidential loans. A new consumer bank concept, conducive to cross-selling products, was introduced to help facilitate the process.

Washington Mutual's appetite got the best of it in 2002 when Dime Bancorp Inc. appeared to be too much for WaMu to swallow. Integration of the retail banking system got off to a rocky start in some East Coast branch locations, causing inconveniences and concerns for customers. Moreover, legal disputes had cropped up for the subprime mortgage lender acquired earlier, *American Banker* reported in June.

On the heels of internal operation challenges, Washington Mutual was confronted with external stress. The mortgage market dramatically dropped off in the last quarter of 2003. WaMu cut jobs and earnings predictions. A plan to pare back expenses by $1billion over the next 18 months was formulated.

"The news jolted investors, coming as it did from a company whose strong earnings gains during the mortgage boom allowed it to snap up smaller competitors and successfully export its Seattle-style coffeehouse branch model to such far-flung places as Chicago and New York," Robert Julavits wrote for *American Banker* in December 2003.

As Washington Mutual regrouped, a major competitor planned a surge into its home territory, the *Puget Sound Business Journal* reported. Countrywide Financial Corp., which had surpassed Wells Fargo & Co. as the top mortgage originator, was after even more market share.

Washington Mutual, meanwhile, continued to close lending and loan origination offices, eliminating jobs by the thousands. It also sold its consumer finance division to Citigroup Inc. for $1.5 billion to maintain retail banking growth, according to *American Banker*. Washington Mutual purchased Providian Financial in October 2005 for more than $6 billion, diversifying into the credit-card business. WaMu quickly began marketing its new service to its retail banking and mortgage customers.

In addition to providing a new business niche, Providian moved WaMu into job offshoring. From that start, WaMu began examining the entire company for areas in which offshoring would be viable, *American Banker* reported. A growing number of mortgage lenders had begun to engage in the cost-saving measure.

Washington Mutual divested a large portion of its mortgage servicing rights during 2006. Although the home loan business segment threatened profits, the retail-banking, credit-card services, and commercial-banking business buoyed up the company. The contribution of those groups, along with the sale of the asset management unit WM Advisors and continued cost-cutting, including the elimination of about 10,000 jobs, yielded a 4 percent rise in profits, totaling $3.56 billion, for the year. Chairman and CEO Kerry Killinger's total compensation was $14.2 million, the *Seattle Times* reported in March 2007.

The housing market slump deepened in 2007, eroding confidence in the U.S. economy abroad and creating fear at home. "For Sale" signs lingered on lawns in upscale neighborhoods. In addition, lower-income families faced foreclosure, dragged under by subprime loans. Financial service companies, predictably, came under fire.

The *Financial Times* reported in November 2007: "Washington Mutual slumped 17.3 percent to $20.04 [per share] after it warned that mortgage lending would decline to an eight-year low next year. The group's shares extended losses after Andrew Cuomo, New York's attorney-general, subpoenaed Fannie Mae and Freddie Mac, seeking information on loans they bought from banks, including Washington Mutual, and details of their due diligence." Killinger, meanwhile, emphasized the health of WaMu's retail banking business. The company concentrated on adding branches, bringing in more customers, and increasing the number of products each customer purchased, Barbara Rehm reported for *American Banker.*

In December 2007, the $330-billion-asset company announced a plan to counter the mortgage drain. Among its actions, WaMu would raise new capital through a preferred stock offering, exit the subprime loan business, and reduce the dividend.

For 2007, Washington Mutual recorded its first annual loss in at least a dozen years. Write-offs in its home loans group largely contributed to the $67 million shortfall. The news, coming in January 2008, further fueled speculation of a sale. Drew DeSilver wrote: "While declining to comment specifically on reports that WaMu has had preliminary talks with JPMorgan Chase, Killinger said he was 'working very hard to return the company to much higher levels of profitability, which I believe it is capable of doing.'" Earlier in the month Bank of America announced its intention to acquire the troubled Countrywide Financial.

Jeffrey L. Covell
Updated, Kathleen Peippo

PRINCIPAL OPERATING UNITS

Commercial Group; Home Loans Group; Retail Banking Group; Card Services Group.

PRINCIPAL COMPETITORS

Bank of America Corporation; Wells Fargo & Company; Wachovia Corporation.

FURTHER READING

Augstums, Ieva M., "Lender Gets a Life Ring," *Duluth News Tribune*, January 12, 2008, pp. 7B+.

Bryant, Chris, "GM Loss and Desperate Dollar Spark Heavy Falls," *Financial Times,* November 8, 2007, p. 42.

Chan, Gilbert, "Seattle Thrift Buys American Savings Bank of California," *Knight-Ridder/Tribune Business News,* July 23, 1996, p. 7.

Cocheo, Steve, "Kerry Killinger Builds His Dream Bank," *ABA Banking Journal,* August 2001, p. 22.

Cole, Jim, "Home-Loan Margins Tight, WaMu Touts Transformation," *American Banker,* October 24, 2005, p. 1.

———, "WaMu on Latest Alterations," *American Banker,* August 8, 2006, p. 1.

DeSilver, Drew, "Washington Mutual Posts First Quarterly Loss in a Decade," *Seattle Times,* January 17, 2008.

Dobbs, Kevin, "WaMu Cutting Jobs, Slashing Dividend," *American Banker,* December 11, 2007.

Engleman, Eric, "WaMu Foes Are Circling," *Puget Sound Business Journal,* August 6, 2004, p. 1.

Epes, James, "How WaMu Accounts for Enterprise Bank Buy," *Puget Sound Business Journal,* June 9, 1995, p. 13.

Fogarty, Mark, "WAMU THE CONQUERER: Washington Mutual Becomes the Superhero of the Industry," *US Banker,* July 2001, p. 50.

Julavits, Robert, "N.Y. Snafu Raises Fears WaMu's Getting Too Big," *American Banker,* June 12, 2002, p. 1.

———, "WaMu Will Cut $1B; Full-Timers on Hit List," *American Banker,* December 10, 2003, p. 1.

Kapiloff, Howard, "Wash. Mutual Faces Big-League Challenges in California," *American Banker,* July 25, 1996, p. 12.

Killinger, Kerry, "One-Stop Shopping at Washington Mutual," *Bottomline,* November 1987, p. 27.

Leuty, Ron, "WaMu Banks on California After Digesting Acquisitions," *San Francisco Business Times,* June 2, 2000, p. 8.

Martinez, Amy, "Struggling WaMu Gives CEO Bonus of $4.1 Million," *Seattle Times,* March 20, 2007, p. 1C.

Morgan, Murray, *The Friend of the Family,* Seattle: Washington Mutual Financial Group, 1989.

Neurath, Peter, "Good 'Bad News' for Bank," *Puget Sound Business Journal,* January 22, 1990, p. 18.

Prakash, Snigdha, "Wamu's Bench Strength Touted As Key to Its Merger Prowess," *American Banker,* March 19, 1998, p. 1.

Pulliam, Liz, "Expansion of Washington Mutual Took Off with New Chairman," *Knight-Ridder/Tribune Business News,* July 23, 1996, p. 72.

Rehm, Barbara A., "WaMu CEO: Branch Expansion Remains a High Priority," *American Banker,* November 15, 2007.

Rhoads, Christopher, "Washington Mutual's CEO Puts California on Edge," *American Banker,* February 4, 1997, p. 1.

"Seattle-Based Washington Mutual Inc. to Acquire Oregon's Western Bank," *Knight-Ridder/Tribune Business News,* October 12, 1995, p. 10.

Shenn, Jody, "… While Adding More Jobs Abroad," *American Banker,* February 17, 2006, p. 24.

Steverman, Ben, "Mortgage Gets Messier," *Business Week Online,* December 12, 2007.

Virgin, Bill, "SEC Inquiry of WaMu," *Seattle Post-Intelligencer,* December 21, 2007, p. D1.

Wolcott, John, "What Puts the Wham in WAMU?" *Puget Sound Business Journal,* September 2, 1991, p. 20.

Wilco Farm Stores

———————————————————————————— ■ ————————————————————————————

200 Industrial Way
P.O. Box 258
Mt. Angel, Oregon 97362
U.S.A.
Telephone: (503) 845-6122
Toll Free: (800) 382-5339
Fax: (503) 845-9310
Web site: http://www.wilco.coop

Cooperative
Incorporated: 1967
Employees: 450
Sales: $163 million (2007 est.)
NAIC: 424910 Farm Supplies Merchant Wholesalers;
    444130 Hardware Stores

■ ■ ■

Wilco Farm Stores is a grower-owned farm supply cooperative with ten retail farm stores throughout the mid–Willamette Valley in McMinnville, Newberg, Canby, Cornelius, Oregon City, Silverton, Stayton, and Springfield in Oregon, and Battle Ground in southwest Washington. It operates through three divisions: agronomy products and services, including seed processing and marketing; bulk petroleum products for farm and home, including six retail gas stations; and retail farm stores. Stores vary in size and product mix; however, all have the following departments: lawn and garden products, Western and work clothing and boots, pet foods and supplies, livestock equipment and supplies, bagged livestock feed, and farm hardware. Wilco also has eight agronomy centers that provide professional agronomist services and sell commercial quantities of fertilizers and agricultural chemicals in Whiteson, Donald, Harrisburg, Mt. Angel, Cornelius, and Stayton, Oregon, and in Chehalis and Sumner, Washington. The co-op's central office is in Mt. Angel, Oregon. Wilco has more than 3,000 members and several hundred thousand nonmember customers.

CREATING A CO-OP: 1967

In 1967, five mid-Willamette Valley-based farmer-owned cooperatives—Mt. Angel Farmers Union Warehouse, Santiam Farmers Cooperative, Donald Farmers co-op, Valley Farmers co-op of Silverton, and Canby Cooperative—merged to form Wilco. These cooperatives themselves were the product of ten mergers that had occurred during the prior 35 years. The new Wilco, whose name came from "Willamette Consolidated," set up headquarters in Mt. Angel, Oregon. Its products and services included farm, home, and ranch supplies. Lee McFarland, a graduate of Oregon State University who had been with Pacific Supply Cooperative in Portland since 1956, was named general manager of the co-op on a two-year contract.

As a cooperative, Wilco was dedicated to the co-op mission of serving its patron-members by offering competitive prices and assistance with livestock and crop-growing questions. Membership was limited to full- or part-time farmers and ranchers, who paid a membership fee and received annual patronage dividends (cooperative profits) in direct proportion to the amount of their purchases for each year. Members

COMPANY PERSPECTIVES

The mission of Wilco is to be a successful cooperative agribusiness with quality employees, profitably serving, with integrity, the needs of customers in the Willamette Valley and surrounding areas. Wilco has built its reputation on being an integrity based organization that stands behind its word and its quality products and services. Our team members ensure every customer, both internally and externally, is treated with courtesy and respect and that their interaction with Wilco is always hassle free and pleasant.

also had the right to vote on such issues as electing board members, establishing and/or changing bylaws, and other cooperative-related matters. Nonmember patrons could shop at Wilco locations, but did not receive the benefit of a year-end dividend or enjoy the privilege of voting.

EARLY SUCCESS, WEATHERING HARD TIMES, AND REORGANIZATION: 1968–89

The new co-op was immediately a successful venture, achieving the greater efficiencies it had forecast through consolidation. In 1968, its revenues were $6.3 million and it employed 90 full-time people. In 1969, according to plan, Lee McFarland resigned as general manager and was succeeded by Tom Gorman, who had been assistant manager. The co-op also purchased a ten-acre industrial site in Mt. Angel, Oregon, to prepare for future growth. However, the first half of the 1970s was a period of agricultural depression in the Northwest. In 1970, farm losses from the previous year depressed revenues to $5.9 million.

The years 1974 and 1975 represented boom years for the Wilco co-op and, despite the return of hard times throughout the remainder of the decade, the co-op was investing in growth again in the second half of the 1970s. In the late 1980s, it upgraded its facilities and equipment and updated its image. In 1987 alone, Wilco consolidated all petroleum activities, including transportation, into a single operating division, the Farmers' Petroleum Department. Purchasing activities were consolidated into a single department responsible for coordinating and negotiating all product needs. In addition, the Stayton, Mt. Angel, and Donald branches for seed processing underwent improvements and

enlargements and the Mt. Angel Farm Store was remodeled.

PREPARING FOR THE 21ST CENTURY

During the late 1990s and the start of the next century, Wilco again expanded through acquisition, both horizontally, by adding more stores, and vertically, by adding suppliers. In 1996, it merged with West Valley Farmers, expanding its business geographically eastward from the Willamette River. With the addition of West Valley, Wilco covered most of the four-county mid-Willamette area and revenues grew to $70 million by 1998.

In 2000, Wilco again expanded through acquisitions. It assumed operation of the Farm Store in Tangent, Oregon, and purchased the Eugene Farmers Cooperative, Cenex Harvest States (CHS) Supply and Marketing, and the CHS Harrisburg Ag Center. These purchases afforded the co-op the benefit of combining all its southern market agronomy activities in Harrisburg, Oregon. The following year, Wilco acquired Valley Lime, a local company with a long history of providing liming services to growers.

The opportunity to expand into Washington State arrived in 2002 when Cenex Harvest States Supply offered its 15,000-square-foot store in Battle Ground, Washington, for sale. The Battle Ground store dated back to the 1920s, when it had opened as a dairy cooperative with a bottling plant and cheese manufacturing facility; it was known over the years as the Washington Dairyman's Cooperative, Clark County Dairymen's Cooperative, and Agco. After Cenex purchased the store, it began to sell fuel, feed, and farm supplies.

EXPANDING GEOGRAPHICALLY AND DEMOGRAPHICALLY: 2002–07

Wilco first expressed interest in purchasing the Battle Ground store in 2002. At that time, Wilco operated seven stores in Oregon, having closed its Mt. Angel store following the remodel of another store in Silverton, only four miles away. Wilco also owned seven retail-commercial gas stations, two grass seed–processing plants, and a bulk fuel delivery service. However, talks around the store in Battle Ground fell apart, and it was not until 2004 that the purchase finally occurred.

The 15,000-square-foot Battle Ground store proved within its first year to be one of the company's best performers, rivaling sales at Wilco's top store in

KEY DATES

1967: Wilco forms from the merger of the Mt. Angel Farmers Union Warehouse, the Santiam Farmers Cooperative, the Donald Farmers co-op, Valley Farmers co-op, and the Canby Cooperative with Lee McFarland as manager.

1969: Farmers Oil Co. merges with Wilco; Lee McFarland resigns and is succeeded by Tom Gorman.

1996: West Valley Farmers merges with Wilco.

2000: Wilco purchases Eugene Farmers Cooperative, CHS Supply and Marketing, and Harrisburg Ag Center; the co-op combines all agronomy activities in Harrisburg, Oregon.

2001: Wilco acquires Valley Lime.

2004: Wilco purchases the Cenex Harvest States Supply store in Battle Ground, Washington.

2006: Wilco partners with Agriliance to add agronomy operations in Chehalis, Washington.

2007: Wilco purchases Dutch Country and Pacific Harvest in Washington County; the co-op purchases Canby Farm Garden and Pet Center; the co-op opens its first "Equine Destination Store."

2008: Wilco begins construction of a new liquid fertilizer plant at its Mt. Angel Agronomy Center; the co-op opens a farm store in the Springfield/Eugene communities.

McMinnville, Oregon. Less than six months after acquiring it, Wilco moved the store to a new 35,000-square-foot property and expanded the store's product mix to attract a wider base of customers.

The focus on a larger customer base was a response to a demographic shift then occurring in the mid-Willamette Valley. Large commercial farms were being split into smaller parcels, new hobby farms, and ranchettes. Jeff Duyck characterized the change in the following way in the *Forest Grove News-Times* in 2007: "The agricultural base is shrinking as more and more farms get cut up into smaller acreages where someone works in town and comes home to their small horse ranch." Duyck sold Pacific Harvest and Dutch Country Mercantile (and its previous incarnation, C.C. Ruth & Co.) in Washington County, Oregon, to Wilco in 2007. According to Duyck, the demand for small-farm sup-

plies was skyrocketing. "[T]here are more and more houses in the county and that plays right into Wilco's retail side." Pacific Harvest served larger agricultural operations with seed, fertilizer, and irrigation supplies, while Dutch Country sold livestock feeds, equipment, and supplies, and pet food and supplies.

THE RISE OF HOBBY FARMING

Susan Aldrich-Markham, an Oregon State University extension agent, attributed the trend toward hobby farming to Washington County's ample water supply, crop diversity, and easy access to metropolitan Portland for distribution and sales. "The more people who are coming out there, the more hobby farms you're going to have," she expressed in a 2007 *Forest Grove News-Times* article. According to data from the Oregon Department of Agriculture, farms earning $1,000 or less increased sharply from 1997 to 2002, including 2,851 new hobby farms, while there were overall declines or only modest increases in larger farms. In Washington County, where the number of total farms declined, 18 small new farms popped up during that five-year period.

Wilco CEO Doug Hoffman explained to the *Forest Grove News-Times,* in February 2007, that the co-op had wanted to move into Washington County for years to attract the region's burgeoning hobby farm community. The company's first store in Washington County followed the opening of a new location by Coastal Farm and Supply, the company's main regional competitor. Wilco, which had yearly sales of more than $140 million in 2007, broke ground on a 20,000-square-foot full-service retail outlet in Cornelius that summer. In addition to carrying a full line of implements, the new store also sold a large selection of clothing from Carhartts to Levi's. "As the land transitions from productive ag land to ranchettes, hobby farms or high density farming like nursery, we transition our businesses," Hoffman explained.

COMBINING NEW DIRECTIONS AND TRADITIONAL CUSTOMERS: 2007–08

Also in 2007, Wilco purchased Canby Farm Garden and Pet Center. That same year, it built and opened its first "Equine Destination Store," a 15,000-square-foot farm store that combined its purchase of FarmGro Supply in Newberg, Oregon, with an existing store. In addition to horse supplies, equipment, English and Western tack, saddles, and riding apparel, the store offered basic farm hardware, a covered garden nursery area, a store-within-a-store work wear and boot department, and a complete pet department with grooming services.

Yet while Wilco focused on growing "lifestyle stores" to meet the needs of the hobby farmer, it still made a point of serving its traditional base of large commercial farmers as it completed the second half of the decade and planned for its future. In 2006, Wilco partnered with Agriliance, the nation's largest supplier of products used by the agricultural industry to create Wilco Agriliance, adding agronomy operations in Chehalis, Washington. In September 2007, Agriliance LLC was repositioned with Land O'Lakes Inc. and CHS Inc. Land O'Lakes acquired the crop protection products business along with related training, technical, and support services. CHS acquired the wholesale crop nutrients business, which began to operate as part of its Ag Business segment.

The co-op also began constructing a new liquid fertilizer plant at its Mt. Angel Agronomy Center in 2008 and expanded its area, moving into the Springfield/Eugene communities and surrounding areas with a new store.

Carrie Rothburd

PRINCIPAL COMPETITORS

Coastal Farm & Ranch.

FURTHER READING

Fehrenbacher, Gretchen, "Westward Ho: Wilco Farm Stores Will Move Farther West from Old Town Battle Ground," *Columbian,* September 17, 2004, p. E1.

Nelson, Jonathan, "A New Home for Wilco; Farm Supply Store Moves West in Battle Ground," *Columbian,* March 25, 2005, p. E1.

World Vision International, Inc.

---

800 West Chestnut Avenue
Monrovia, California 91016
U.S.A.
Telephone: (626) 303-8811
Fax: (626) 301-7786
Web site: http://www.wvi.org

Private Partnership
Incorporated: 1950
Employees: 26,000
Operating Revenues: $2.6 billion (2007)
NAIC: 813110 Religious Organizations

■ ■ ■

World Vision International, Inc., is a Christian relief, development, and advocacy organization dedicated to helping individuals and communities combat hunger, poverty, and injustice. World Vision functions as a partnership of autonomous, interdependent national offices, setting fundamental policy but letting its national members determine matters related to staffing, budget, and strategy. Nearly 80 percent of World Vision's funding comes from private sources such as individuals, corporations, and foundations. The balance is collected from governments and multilateral agencies such as the United Nations. Roughly half of the organization's donations are made to its child sponsorship program, which supports more than 2.2 million children. World Vision maintains a presence in approximately 100 countries, operating through primary offices in Geneva, Switzerland; Bangkok, Thailand; Nairobi, Kenya; the

Republic of Cyprus; Los Angeles, California; and San Jose, Costa Rica.

BOB PIERCE'S INSPIRATION

The visionary behind World Vision was its founder, Reverend Robert (Bob) Pierce, a pastor and missionary whose personal crusade became a global movement of impressive proportions. The seminal event in Pierce's life occurred after he left his father-in-law's church, where he served as a youth pastor. Pierce, in his early 30s, joined Youth for Christ, a missionary organization. He embarked on his first international tour in 1947, bound for China, where four months of evangelical rallies were planned. The trip marked a turning point in his life, one observed by his daughter in a book she published about her father. "My father went to China a young man in search of adventure," Marilee Pierce Dunker wrote in a passage excerpted in the March 2005 issue of *Christianity Today.* "He came home a man with a mission."

When Pierce arrived in China, he began preaching at churches large and small, quickly attracting audiences in the thousands and earning a reputation as a fiery evangelist. One sermon proved to be the catalyst for a multibillion-dollar organization with a global reach. A missionary invited Pierce to preach to the children of a mission school. In attendance was a young girl named White Jade who was galvanized by Pierce's words. She rushed home to tell her father of her newfound belief in Jesus Christ and her father responded by beating her and throwing her out of the house, ordering her to never return. Disowned and battered, White Jade

COMPANY PERSPECTIVES

World Vision is an international partnership of Christians whose mission is to follow our Lord and Saviour Jesus Christ in working with the poor and oppressed to promote human transformation, seek justice and bear witness to the good news of the Kingdom of God.

returned to the mission school and told her principal, Tena Hoelkedoer, of her plight. Hoelkedoer, who already was caring for six orphans in her home, could not afford to house another, but Pierce intervened, offering Hoelkedoer $5, reportedly his last $5, to help pay for White Jade's food and clothing. He promised to send the same amount each month, an arrangement that served as the model for what became World Vision's child sponsorship program.

After China, Pierce traveled to South Korea and witnessed a nation on the brink of devastation. Men of fighting age were leaving home to prepare for war, putting a heavy financial burden on the wives and children they left behind. As the country geared for war, the instances of poverty were increasing before Pierce's eyes; once major hostilities commenced, the suffering, Pierce realized, would increase exponentially. He returned to the United States in 1950 and formed World Vision in September, using the deteriorating conditions on the Korean Peninsula to elicit support for the world's needy children. He filmed documentaries in Asia and showed the films to American audiences, urging those gathered to help care for the hungry and poor. In 1953, when the end of the war left hundreds of thousands of orphans in its wake, Pierce came up with the idea of providing sponsors with photographs of the children they were supporting, giving World Vision the signature element of its child sponsorship program.

Pierce dedicated himself and his organization to helping the world's children, a mission that demanded he live an itinerant lifestyle. He traveled as much as ten months a year pursuing the five primary objectives he established early in World Vision's history: Christian social welfare, emergency aid, evangelistic outreach, Christian leadership development, and missionary challenge. In 1957, Pierce gained a constant companion, his second-in-command, Larry Ward, who was appointed vice-president of World Vision in 1959 and executive vice-president and overseas director in 1967. Shortly after Ward joined the organization, he joined

Pierce in his travels, visiting nearly 24 countries during a two-year period. The pair gathered news and information about mission activities and the needs of children, enabling World Vision to widen its influence beyond Asia and become a truly global relief and development organization.

EARLY GROWTH PROMPTS OPERATIONAL CHANGES

The growth of the organization soon required changes to the way it operated. The scope and scale of its work shaped World Vision, forcing it to evolve to realize optimal results. Initially, Pierce funded evangelical Protestant missionaries, but within a short time he shifted World Vision's contributions to emerging Asian churches. A church in Korea, for example, would manage an orphanage whose funding was provided by World Vision. Before long, however, the arrangement proved to be impractical, a consequence of the growing resources at World Vision's disposal. Individual churches were overwhelmed by the demands placed on their administrative operations, finding it difficult to run multimillion-dollar programs effectively while pursuing their primary church mission. In response, World Vision began running its own programs, taking the burden away from the churches and putting itself in a position to develop into a comprehensive relief and empowerment organization.

Pierce succeeded in creating what would become one of the largest Christian relief organizations in the world, but success came at a price. Pierce's relationship with his family suffered profoundly from his years abroad. One of his daughters, Sharon, committed suicide after he ignored her pleas to return home. In 1963, worn out by his constant travels, he suffered a nervous breakdown. He also had a contentious relationship with World Vision's board of directors, displaying a temper as fiery as his sermons. The board frequently took exception to Pierce's habit of making financial commitments without prior consultation, an ongoing struggle that prompted World Vision leaders to propose organizational changes in 1967. The changes were intended to make Pierce more financially accountable, which infuriated the World Vision founder. Pierce, in perhaps what was meant to be a test of wills, submitted his letter of resignation. To the reported shock of Pierce's family, the World Vision board accepted his resignation the following day, ending Pierce's 17-year involvement with the organization.

Pierce left a relief and welfare ministry with offices in nine countries that supported more than 30,000 children behind him. He also left harboring bitter feelings, angry that the organization he had founded had

KEY DATES

1950: Reverend Robert Pierce forms World Vision.

1953: Pierce discovers an effective marketing tool for his child sponsorship program by using photographs of needy children.

1967: After quarreling with World Vision's board of directors, Pierce resigns from the organization.

1970s: World Vision's decentralized structure is established.

1979: World Vision operates offices in 40 countries.

1989: World Vision operates offices in 55 countries.

1996: Dean Hirsch is appointed president.

2004: After tripling during the previous eight years, World Vision's budget reaches $1.5 billion.

2007: World Vision ends its 57th year with 26,000 employees and a budget of $2.6 billion.

been appropriated by others. Not long after his resignation, Pierce collapsed in Switzerland, where he would spend a year in a hospital recovering from exhaustion. In 1970, he founded a small hunger-relief organization that became Samaritan's Purse, which he led until his death in 1978.

THE POST-PIERCE ERA

For World Vision, the years following Pierce's departure witnessed enormous growth. The organization expanded its operating territory throughout Asia and into Africa, Europe, the Middle East, and Latin America. It also broadened the scope of its work. Although child sponsorship programs continued to represent a major part of World Vision's work, the organization began to tackle the problems of insufficient housing, food, health-care, and education by creating development projects that aimed to establish or to improve the basic infrastructure of communities. The organization, too, developed its own infrastructure, becoming a federation of national chapters, each separately incorporated and each operating autonomously. As the decades progressed, the "World Council" was formed to set World Vision's fundamental policy, but each national chapter of World Vision operated under the control of its own national director and board of directors, who were responsible for the staffing, budget, and strategic direction of their particular group.

World Vision grew robustly in the post-Pierce era. During the 1970s, the organization began recruiting employees from the countries in which it operated, a

policy that sometimes meant hiring non-evangelical Christian staff. The number of countries from which World Vision hired indigenous employees rose sharply during the decade, jumping from a presence in nine countries when Pierce left the organization to offices in 40 countries by the end of the 1970s. The increase in World Vision's physical stature fueled an exponential rise in the number of children it aided. The organization sponsored roughly 32,000 children when Pierce resigned. By the end of the 1970s, World Vision's child sponsorship program included 214,000 children.

DEAN HIRSCH ERA

There were three critical periods during World Vision's first half-century of development. Clearly, the era of Pierce's control ranked as the most important period in the organization's history. Without Pierce, World Vision would not exist. The 1970s were years of tremendous importance, witnessing explosive growth and the establishment of a decentralized structure. The third defining period of the organization's development occurred during the years surrounding its 50th anniversary, an era that would take its name from the influential leader of the period, Dean R. Hirsch.

Hirsch joined World Vision in 1976, beginning his career as manager of the organization's computer operations. Promotions followed as the Westmont College graduate distinguished himself. Hirsch served as chief operating officer, vice-president for development, and vice-president for relief operations before being appointed international president of World Vision in 1996.

The years before Hirsch took control of the organization saw the continued expansion of World Vision. The 40 offices in operation by the end of the 1970s increased to 55 offices by the end of the 1980s, when the organization's child sponsorship program included more than 830,000 children. As World Vision entered the 1990s, its annual budget exceeded $200 million, making it one of the largest Christian relief organizations in the world, but the total would be dwarfed by the increases made during Hirsch's leadership. Between 1996 and 2004, World Vision's budget tripled, reaching $1.5 billion, a sum it distributed to children and communities in 100 countries.

WORLD VISION IN THE 21ST CENTURY

World Vision held sway as a powerful economic force under Hirsch's tutelage. As head of an organization with extensive geographic reach and financial resources, Hirsch held court with the largest political and economic institutions in the world, collaborating with the United Nations, the World Bank, the World Trade Organization, and numerous other agencies that relied on World Vision to provide medicine, education, emergency food, and shelter to suffering communities. The capabilities of the organization were put on display in late 2004 when a tsunami pummeled South Asian shorelines the day after Christmas. As it did in most parts of the world, World Vision maintained a solid presence in the region, employing 3,700 workers in Indonesia, Thailand, Sri Lanka, India, and Myanmar. In each of the countries, World Vision possessed warehouses stocked with emergency supplies, which were augmented by supplies stored in other World Vision warehouses in Europe, North America, and the Middle East. As the supplies were airlifted in, a team of 24 disaster specialists was flown in to spearhead recovery efforts.

As World Vision prepared for its second half-century of service, the organization continued to thrive under the control of Hirsch. By 2007, the organization's annual budget had increased to $2.6 billion, 80 percent of which was earmarked for disaster relief and development efforts. World Vision spent the balance on advocacy, fund-raising, and operational costs. In the years ahead, the organization planned to devote its considerable resources to pursuing a humanitarian mission it divided into six components: ongoing efforts to better the lives of children; emergency relief; promotion of justice; partnerships with local churches; generating public awareness of the causes of poverty; and adherence to the teachings of Jesus Christ.

Jeffrey L. Covell

PRINCIPAL SUBSIDIARIES

World Vision Australia; World Vision Austria; World Vision Brazil; World Vision Burundi; World Vision Canada; World Vision Chile; World Vision China; World Vision Colombia; World Vision Costa Rica; World Vision Finland; World Vision France; World Vision Germany; World Vision Guatemala; World Vision Haiti; World Vision Honduras; World Vision Hong Kong; World Vision India; World Vision Indonesia; World Vision Ireland; World Vision Japan; World Vision Korea; World Vision Liberia; World Vision Malawi; World Vision Malaysia; World Vision Mexico; World Vision Netherlands; World Vision New Zealand; World Vision Philippines; World Vision Singapore; World Vision South Africa; World Vision Spain; World Vision Swaziland; World Vision Switzerland; World Vision Taiwan; World Vision Tanzania; World Vision Thailand; World Vision United Kingdom; World Vision United States; World Vision Zambia.

PRINCIPAL COMPETITORS

Cooperative for Assistance and Relief Everywhere, Inc.; World Relief Corporation of National Association of Evangelicals; Samaritan's Purse; Canadian Food for the Hungry International.

FURTHER READING

Greene, Elizabeth, "Connecting with Generation Y," *Chronicle of Philanthropy,* July 24, 2003.

Holt, Shirleen, "Partners Find Real Ambitions Are to Do Good," *Seattle Times,* August 16, 2005.

Johnson, Larry, "World Vision's New Weapon," *Fund Raising Management,* June 1993, p. 22.

Le Pla, Ruth, "A Matter of Faith: Passion in the Boardroom," *New Zealand Management,* November 2006, p. S18.

Stafford, Tim, "The Colossus of Care," *Christianity Today,* March 2005.

———, "Imperfect Instrument," *Christianity Today,* March 2005.

Zed Group

C/ Rozabella, 4
Complejo Europa Empresarial
Edificio Bruselas, 1a Planta
Las Rozas, Madrid 28230
Spain
Telephone: (+34 91) 640 48 00
Fax: (+34 91) 640 48 77
Web site: http://www.lanetrozed.com

Private Company (Subsidiary of Wisdom Group)
Incorporated: 1996 as LaNetro
Employees: 1,400
Sales: EUR 320 million ($454 million) (2006 est.)
NAIC: 517212 Cellular and Other Wireless Telecommunications

■ ■ ■

Zed Group is one of the world's leading players in the fast-growing mobile value-added wervices (MVAS) market. Zed Group develops, produces, and distributes ringtones, graphics, video, games, positioning services, information, and other content for use in mobile telephone handsets. Based in Spain, Zed Group has built a global network through a string of major acquisitions. These include Monstermob, the U.K.-based MVAS leader, acquired in 2007, and Zed, purchased from TeliaSonera in 2004. Zed Group also includes founding business LaNetro, a leading mobile telephone Internet portal in Spain; Play Wireless, which develops games for mobile telephone platforms; Denver, Colorado-based 9 Square, a leading player in the U.S. market; and Alvento, which focuses on providing Zed Group content to the business-to-business sector. Altogether, Zed Group operates in 37 countries, including all of the major European cities, as well as the world's two largest mobile telephone markets, China and the United States. With partnerships with more than 100 mobile telephone providers, the company potentially reaches approximately 1.6 billion of the total 2.7 billion mobile telephone users in the world.

The ringtone segment drove much of the MVAS market in the early 2000s. Nonetheless, Zed has invested in adapting itself to the arrival of true broadband mobile telecommunications in the second half of the decade. As such, the company claims to be the first to offer a so-called web 2.0-based platform, integrating the mobile telephone and Internet markets and incorporating user-generated content, "community" tools, including blogs and networking and dating sites, and other communication services such as chat, messenger, and e-mail. The majority of Zed's sales are made directly to consumers, through the free subscription Club Zed Standard and the paid subscription service Club Zed Premium. Zed is led by CEO, Chairman, and cofounder Javier Pérez Dolset. The company is part of the Wisdom Group, which also consists of eight more of the Pérez Dolset family's multimedia-based companies, including video-game developer Pyro. The company claims annual revenues of more than EUR 320 million ($454 million).

SPANISH INTERNET PIONEERS IN THE EARLY NINETIES

Javier Pérez Dolset was born in 1969 and studied at Madrid's Autonoma University, where he earned a degree in economics. Pérez Dolset later received a degree in European business studies from the British University in Humberside. The nascent video market provided Pérez Dolset with his first move into running his own business. Joined by brother Ignacio Pérez Dolset and their father Juan Antonio Pérez Ramírez, he took over management of a video-game distribution business called Proein.

The Pérez Dolset brothers were quick to spot the potential offered by the Internet, then at its very beginnings in Spain. In 1993, the brothers began developing Teleline, which offered both Internet access and content. That business grew strongly over the next few years. By 1996, Teleline had hit the big time, when the Pérez Dolset brothers agreed to sell a 50 percent stake in the company to Spanish telephone company Telephonica. The Teleline service later changed its name to Terra.

The sale of the Teleline shares enabled the Pérez Dolset brothers to pursue new areas of interest in the rapidly developing multimedia market. Ignacio Pérez Dolset led the creation of highly successful video-game developer Pyro Studios. Javier Pérez Dolset targeted the less developed market for interactive leisure and entertainment content. This led to the creation of La-Netro in 1996.

From the start, LaNetro targeted the market beyond personal computers, with plans to offer content to any device capable of connecting to the Internet. The company developed a highly successful web portal, LaNetro.com, which provided a range of leisure and other locally based information services.

LaNetro's market began to broaden at the end of the decade, with the arrival of new generations of hand-held personal digital assistants and interactive web-

television services. Especially important in the company's future development was the appearance of the first WAP-enabled mobile telephones. The WAP protocol permitted mobile telephone users limited access to the Internet for the first time. LaNetro.com was quickly expanded to support the new protocol, and the company began developing new services and content specifically for the mobile telephone market.

RINGTONES DRIVE GROWTH

The enormous growth of the mobile telephone market in Spain and elsewhere provided vast new areas of growth for LaNetro and other players who rushed into what became known as the mobile value-added services (MVAS) market. A major stimulant to this market was the new capability for users to personalize their telephones, particularly the handset's distinctive "ringtone." An entire industry rapidly developed around the ringtone market.

LaNetro grew strongly as an early player in this new market, and in 2000 sought to capitalize on the market's growth with plans to go public. The company was forced to put these plans on hold, however, as the high-technology sector, and the telecommunications market in particular, experienced a sharp downturn at the beginning of the century. The failure to go public also cut short the group's expansion plans: the company had announced its intention to spend nearly EUR 60 million developing its operations throughout Europe as well as into Central and South America.

Instead, LaNetro focused on a new range of content and services for the MVAS market. In 2001, the company began offering geo-referencing services for the mobile and fixed markets. For this, the company incorporated positioning technologies in order to provide locally specific content to its customers. The company remained committed to supporting a broad range of platforms, providing its services across all major mobile and handheld platforms, including the GSM-WAP, GPRS, and UTMS mobile telephone standards.

By the end of 2001, the company had rolled out its Aqui Cerca service, providing content and services across both its web portal and through the WAP protocol based on the user's geographic location. An early success for this effort came that same year when Portugal telecom group Movensis agreed to incorporate LaNetro's geopositioning technologies for its own mobile telephone users.

The surge in mobile telephone use in the early 2000s convinced LaNetro to focus its operations entirely on the MVAS market in 2002. The company once again turned its attention toward international expansion,

KEY DATES

1996: Brothers Javier and Ignacio Pérez Dolset found LaNetro in order to develop Internet-based content and services.

2000: LaNetro pulls planned public offering.

2002: Company decides to focus its operations on mobile value-added services (MVAS) market.

2004: Company acquires Zed, a provider of MVAS content, from TeliaSonera, forming LaNetro Zed and becoming leader in European market.

2005: Company enters U.S. and Chinese markets and launches Club Zed subscription platform.

2006: LaNetro Zed acquires Spain b2b MVAS provider Alvento Soluciones.

2007: LaNetro Zed acquires control of Monstermob Plc and changes name to Zed Group.

Germany, and as far away as in the Philippines and Malaysia. Zed's growth (from 2002 to 2003 the company's revenues jumped by 73 percent) reflected the surge in the global MVAS market. Indeed, by 2004 the region covered by the newly expanded LaNetro Zed represented an estimated total market of nearly $8 billion. With a presence in 13 countries, LaNetro Zed claimed the European leadership in the MVAS market.

LaNetro Zed continued to build up its network in Europe, notably with the launch of services in France in 2005. Yet the company was eyeing expansion farther abroad. In that year, the company established its first operations in what had become the world's two largest mobile telephone markets, the United States and China. The latter country offered particular promise for growth, given its enormous population and the extremely low fixed-telephone penetration. The addition of operations in these two countries allowed LaNetro Zed to claim a presence in the world's top 15 mobile telephone markets.

MEETING MONSTERMOB IN 2007

The launch of Club Zed in 2005 represented a new milestone for the company. By introducing a subscription-based model, the company was able to generate a new degree of brand loyalty among its customer base. In addition, the new service was made available in two formats, the free Standard, and the paid Premium. The latter provided customers with access across the full range of the company's content, and represented a new source of revenue for the company. The company first launched Club Zed in Spain and Italy. Its success led to a wider rollout the following year.

By then, the company had set its sights on new acquisition targets. The company took out a major rival in 2006 when it acquired fellow Spaniard Alvento Soluciones. That company had focused its operations on the business-to-business sector; instead of providing content directly to consumers, it contracted with mobile telephone service providers. The addition of Alvento gave LaNetro Zed separate access to this important market.

The purchase of Alvento came just ahead of a new attempt to bring LaNetro Zed public. The company began preparing a new initial public offering (IPO) in May 2006, with the IPO slated for the middle of July. The company sought to sell a 23 percent stake, hoping to raise more than EUR 1 billion. In the end, however, the company was once again forced to postpone the public offering due to a lack of investor demand. Instead, the company sold a 25 percent share to Spanish publishing group Planeta.

targeting the acquisition of a fast-growing rival to provide it with a broader geographic base. In order to fund this effort, the Pérez Dolset brothers had founded a new holding company, Wisdom, for their various business interests. By then, these interests included Pyro; Play Wireless, a video-game developer dedicated to the mobile telephone market; and the Proein distribution business, as well as the LaNetro Internet and mobile operations, other content developers, and the group's own computer-animated film production company, later called Ilion Animation Studios.

The creation of Wisdom permitted the Pérez Dolset brothers to bring in outside investors, including Apax Partners Funds and iNova Capital. The family nonetheless maintained a 43 percent stake in the holding company, and management control of their fast-growing multimedia empire. The strong financial basis permitted LaNetro to target new foreign moves. Through 2003, the company added an office in Mexico, while also moving into the German and U.K. markets. By the end of that year, the company also claimed a spot among the top-three MVAS providers in Spain.

ACQUIRING SCALE IN 2004

With the backing of Wisdom, LaNetro made its first major acquisition, of European rival Zed, a subsidiary of TeliaSonera, in 2004. Zed had been created in 2000 as part of Finland's Sonera, and had grown into a major MVAS provider, with operations reaching much of northern Europe, including the United Kingdom and

The company's expansion drive reappeared at the end of 2006. In December of that year, LaNetro Zed began talks with U.K.-based Monstermob Plc. One of the leaders in the global ringtone and MVAS market, Monstermob had grown strongly with the British ringtone market, in particular through the surprising global success of its "Crazy Frog" product. After going public, Monstermob launched its own ambitious expansion in 2004, spending more than $200 million to acquire companies throughout Europe, Russia, Asia, the United States—where it acquired Colorado-based 9 Square—and China.

Monstermob's growth was abruptly cut short, however, after authorities in its two main markets, the United Kingdom and China, drafted new rules pertaining to ringtone and other MVAS content sales. With the market for ringtones starting to decline, as consumers began opting instead to download full-length songs and other content, Monstermob's fortunes plummeted. By the beginning of 2007, the company reported a loss of £105 million.

These difficulties provided LaNetro Zed with the opportunity to acquire majority control of Monstermob at the beginning of that year. In February 2007, the company completed the deal, paying $67 million for a 53 percent stake in Monstermob. The addition of Monstermob broadened LaNetro Zed's market reach to 31 countries.

PIONEERING THE WEB 2.0 MARKET FOR MOBILES

The rollout in 2007 of new generations of mobile telephones, and the deployment of new broadband, Internet-connected mobile telephone protocols in the meantime offered new perspectives for growth for the company, which changed its name to Zed Group. By the end of that year, the company had launched the first of its so-called web 2.0 products featuring user-generated and community-based content specifically developed for the mobile telephone market. In this way, the company expected to capture the success of such popular web-based community sites as YouTube, MySpace, and Facebook.

With sales of more than EUR 320 million ($454 million), Zed claimed a leading position in the global MVAS market, with operations spanning 37 countries, and agreements with more than 100 mobile telephone services providers for a potential market of more than 1.6 billion consumers. Zed Group had proven its ability to adapt to the rapid developments in the global content and MVAS market in the new century.

M. L. Cohen

PRINCIPAL SUBSIDIARIES

9 Squared Inc. (U.S.A.); Alvento Soluciones SA; Lanetro.com SA; Monstermob Group Plc (U.K.).

PRINCIPAL COMPETITORS

Infospace Inc.; Glu Mobile, Inc.; Marchex, Inc.; MIVA, Inc.; Openwave Systems Inc.

FURTHER READING

"A to Zed of Content," *Mobile Entertainment,* May 2006.

Bowers, Simon, "Zed to Acquire Majority Stake in MonsterMob," *Guardian,* December 28, 2006, p. 25.

Fitchard, Kevin, "Investor Caution Underscored As LaNetro Zed Pulls IPO," *Euroweek,* July 21, 2006, p. 18.

Gibbs, Colin, "Zed Pays $66.8M for MonsterMob," *RCR Wireless News,* February 26, 2007, p. 8.

Hopewell, John, "Zed in Bed with Monster," *Daily Variety,* December 29, 2006, p. 11.

Judge, Elizabeth, "Monstermob Slips As Mobiles Fashion Rings Changes," *Times,* May 26, 2007, p. 63.

"LaNetro Zed Buys Up Rival Mobile Content Provider Alvento," *Europe Intelligence Wire,* July 6, 2006.

"Zed Strengthens Focus on US Market," *PR Newswire,* October 22, 2007.

Zurich Financial Services

Mythenquai 2
Zürich, 8022
Switzerland
Telephone: (+41) 44 625 25 25
Fax: (+41) 44 625 35 35
Web site: http://www.zurich.com

Public Company
Founded: 1872 as Versicherungs-Verein
Incorporated: 2000
Employees: 58,000
Total Assets: $379.52 billion (2007)
Stock Exchanges: Swiss
Ticker Symbol: ZURN
NAIC: 524126 Direct Property and Casualty Insurance
  Carriers; 524113 Direct Life Insurance Carriers;
  551112 Offices of Other Holding Companies

∎∎∎

Zurich Financial Services is one of the biggest insurance firms based in Europe. One of the largest property and casualty insurers in the world, serving both individual and commercial customers, Zurich has strong positions in this sector in Switzerland, the United Kingdom, the United States, and several other markets. Overall, what the group calls its General Insurance business operates through a network encompassing more than 150 countries throughout the world. Zurich's Global Life business offers life insurance, annuities, and other investment products to individuals in Europe, the United States, and numerous emerging markets.

Although Zurich's history ultimately dates back to 1872, its incarnation as Zurich Financial Services stems from the 1998 merger of Swiss-based Zurich Insurance Company and the financial services operations of U.K.-based B.A.T. Industries PLC.

EARLY YEARS: FOCUSING ON REINSURANCE AND MARINE INSURANCE

The insurance business developed relatively late in Switzerland but has gone on to achieve great importance. Initially the basic concepts of the business were taken from neighboring countries and adapted to Swiss conditions. Swiss insurance practice, legislation, and expertise reached such a high level, however, that they spread abroad. The forerunners of Zurich Financial Services, including Zürich Versicherungs-Gesellschaft (Zurich Insurance Company), played a decisive part in the international activities of the Swiss insurance business from the start.

The original phase of growth in the Swiss insurance business took place in the middle of the 19th century. Its development was sustained by the beginning of industrialization, the building of the railway network, the creation of more efficient credit banks, and the enterprising spirit of the time. Switzerland was emerging then as a leading financial center and was set to become one of the most important countries in the insurance industry. Statesman and entrepreneur Alfred Escher made a considerable contribution to the insurance business, and with the founding in 1856 of the Schweizerische Kreditanstalt (known internationally as Credit

COMPANY PERSPECTIVES

At Zurich our mission is to recognize, understand and manage change on behalf of individuals and businesses around the world. As a global organization with 135 years of experience in providing insurance protection, we possess an excellent perspective on our complex environment and the trends that influence it, as well as specific local knowledge of particular markets.

Suisse) he paved the way for Zürich's international influence as a financial center.

Initially insurance business was carried out by specialist companies in the individual insurance classes. Two insurance companies in Basel and in St. Gall were already working in marine insurance. As exports were growing, it was felt by Swiss economists and other financial experts that it was necessary to create another marine insurance company in Zürich. Seventeen leading manufacturers and traders became members of the founding committee, formed in June 1869 on the initiative of the board of Credit Suisse. On October 9, 1869, the statutes of the Schweiz Transport-Versicherungs-Gesellschaft (Switzerland Transport Insurance Company) were approved by the ruling council of the canton of Zürich and on January 15, 1870, the company began trading. The first president of the board was John Syz-Landis and the first managing director was Wilhelm Berend Witt. It was intended from the outset that the company should be international in its activities.

It soon became apparent to the young company that it required the support of considerable reinsurance, which could not be covered by existing companies. Schweiz therefore took the decision to found its own reinsurance company. The shareholders in Schweiz were invited to take a share in the proposed company through a circular letter, dated October 23, 1872, from a ten-person founding committee under the leadership of Syz-Landis. The members of the committee had collaborated in the founding of Schweiz and belonged to the board of the company. The new company was to be run by the firm Versicherungs-Verein (Insurance Association) and was to take on a part of Schweiz's risks in the manner of a surplus reinsurance. By November 16, 1872, the statutes had been approved by the ruling council of the canton of Zürich. The licensing document carried the signature of the poet Gottfried Keller, who was first state clerk in Zürich from 1861 to 1876,

and in that capacity signed the documents for the ruling council.

Close ties existed between the two companies thanks to the unified personnel in all their divisions, operating from one office. Together with reinsurance, the Versicherungs-Verein from its inception also dealt with direct marine insurance both at home and abroad. Substantial damage claims and fierce competition in the insurance markets caused considerable problems for the young company. The direct marine and reinsurance businesses on their own proved insufficiently profitable to sustain the young company, which consequently looked toward new fields of activity.

LATE 19TH CENTURY: SWITCHING TO ACCIDENT AND LIABILITY INSURANCE

On a proposal put forward by the board, it was therefore decided at the Versicherungs-Verein general meeting in April 1874 to extend the company's activities to accident insurance. This class of insurance had grown rapidly in importance as industrialization spread. At first, however, this type of insurance had been limited, covering travel insurance and workers' insurance. Accident insurance first became available in England, where from 1849 the Railway Passengers Assurance Company was the first to provide insurance coverage against railway accidents. Later it was to extend coverage to other types of transportation. In Germany a law was first passed on June 7, 1871, that took into consideration the greater risks for employees caused by the increasing mechanization of factories. This law forced manufacturers to pay compensation for any personal injury to their workers. The increased liability made it necessary for companies to insure their workforce against accidents in the factory and the requirement brought about the creation of collective workers' insurance (*Arbeiterkollektivversicherung*).

In view of the high level of industrialization occurring in the Swiss economy, it was evident that similar developments would take place in the confederation. The board of Versicherungs-Verein recognized the sign of the times and broke ground in Switzerland with its introduction of accident insurance, which occurred in 1875. The significance of this step was underlined by the change in the company's name to the Transport-und Unfall-Versicherungs-Aktiengesellschaft Zürich (Zurich Transport and Accident Insurance Limited). The importance that Swiss industry attached to this branch of insurance is shown by the fact that another accident insurance company was also created in 1875, Winterthur, named after the city in which it was founded.

KEY DATES

1872: Versicherungs-Verein (Insurance Association) is formed to provide reinsurance for Switzerland Transport Insurance Company.

1875: Company expands into accident insurance and changes its name to Transport- und Unfall-Versicherungs-Aktiengesellschaft Zürich (Zurich Transport and Accident Insurance Limited); expansion outside of Switzerland begins as well.

1894: Expansion into liability insurance prompts another name change, to: Zürich Allgemeine Unfall- und Haftpflicht-Versicherungs-Aktiengesellschaft (Zurich General Accident and Liability Insurance Limited).

1912: U.S. expansion begins with the formation of an accident and liability insurance firm in New York.

1922: Zurich expands into life insurance with establishment of Vita Lebensversicherungs-Gesellschaft as a subsidiary.

1955: Company name is simplified to Zürich Versicherungs-Gesellschaft (Zurich Insurance Company).

1965: Alpina Versicherungs-Aktiengesellschaft of Switzerland is acquired.

1969: Agrippina Versicherung AG, based in Germany, is acquired.

1989: Baltimore-based Maryland Casualty Group is acquired.

1990: Company expands into asset management with the establishment of Zurich Investment Management.

1996: Zurich acquires an 80 percent interest in Kemper Corporation, a U.S. life insurance firm, and a 97 percent interest in Kemper Financial Services, which is renamed Zurich Kemper Investments.

1997: Zurich gains majority control of Scudder, Stevens & Clark, which is merged into Zurich Kemper to form Scudder Kemper Investments (later renamed Zurich Scudder Investments).

1998: Zurich merges with British American Financial Services (BAFS) to form Zurich Financial Services, which is set up with a dual Swiss-U.K. holding company structure.

2000: Group is unified under a single Swiss holding company, Zurich Financial Services.

2001: Zurich spins off its reinsurance division into a separate, independent firm, Converium Holding AG.

2002: Company sells the bulk of its asset management business, including Zurich Scudder, to Deutsche Bank AG; net loss of $3.43 billion is posted.

2005: Zurich launches a global brand campaign centering on the tagline "Because change happenz."

Zurich's growth as a separate company only began with the introduction of accident insurance. Transport insurance was discontinued "for the foreseeable future" at the end of 1880, and the company stopped taking on more reinsurance business. For a while the name of the company stayed as it had been, although from 1886 it added an explanatory sentence to clarify its activities, declaring that "the company deals exclusively in accident insurance." When liability insurance began to be developed in Germany as a new branch of insurance alongside accident insurance, with the two branches becoming independent of one another, Zurich also started offering liability insurance. The company was able from then on to offer insurance coverage not only against accidents but also against employers' liabilities for assessment of damages. The expansion of business

into these areas led to the company's change of name to the Zürich Allgemeine Unfall- und Haftpflicht-Versicherungs-Aktiengesellschaft (Zurich General Accident and Liability Insurance Limited) on December 14, 1894. The company kept this name until 1955. These changes finally brought about the complete separation of Zurich from Schweiz, although friendly relations and business contacts were preserved. Zurich began to develop into a worldwide company.

The company first had to build up its own independent workforce. Until 1875 Schweiz's staff had also taken care of Zurich's business. The development of accident insurance required a specialized staff, both for internal running of the company and for customer services, because this insurance sector catered to a different clientele and operated within a completely different structure. This was particularly the case for liability insurance, with its complex legal aspects. In 1880 the company had 27 employees. By 1900 the number had grown to 140. Business in this branch of insurance was stimulated in Switzerland by laws passed between 1875 and 1881 establishing liability for railway and steamer companies as well as for factories.

Together with its activities in Switzerland, company business was extended to other areas at an early stage. The first step was taken as early as 1875 in Germany, where agencies were opened in Berlin, Hamburg, Stuttgart, and Reutlingen. Further areas of business to be developed were the Rhineland, Westphalia, Saxony, and Alsace-Lorraine, the latter at that time part of the German empire. In the same year representative offices were opened in Austria-Hungary and in Denmark. Dealings in France followed in 1878. The Berlin branch that was opened in 1880 came to take on a particularly important role in the company's further development, because it was from here that business in Denmark, Norway, Sweden, Finland, and Russia was coordinated.

EARLY 20TH CENTURY:
ENTERING U.S. AND OTHER
MARKETS

At the end of 1880, with the resignation of Witt, Zurich was for the first time given its own chief executive, Heinrich Müller. He was devoted to the business and set the company on a firm footing without neglecting the continued development of its activities abroad. His successor, Fritz Meyer, came from the treasury for the town of Zürich and made sure he consolidated the company's technical reserves. During his time in office, from 1900 to 1918, the company erected its own administrative office building on the Mythenquai in Zürich, where the company headquarters are still to be found. Above all, it also developed its workers' accident insurance business in France and considerably expanded its business in offering insurance against liability in Germany, where the introduction of the Civil Code on January 1, 1900, extended the need for such insurance into numerous new areas. The company's premium income in 1900 was CHF 15.4 million. Business in Switzerland accounted for CHF 3.7 million of this total, while France represented the largest premium income with CHF 5.5 million, followed by Germany with CHF 5 million.

A decisive move for Zurich was engaging in new business in the United States, although Zurich ran its U.S. subsidiary in Chicago in collaboration with a German fire insurance company. Zurich received the authorization to trade in the state of New York in 1912. The New York insurance commissioner had great influence on other states in the union. The U.S. accident

and liability insurance company grew unexpectedly strong and brought in considerable premium income, but was also a heavy burden in terms of provisions and costs. To cover reserves, a large amount of capital was invested in U.S. dollars in the United States; after World War I this capital formed the basis for the further expansion of the U.S. company. Since then it had occupied a particularly important central role in the Zurich insurance group's activities. At the same time Zurich gained a foothold in England, Canada, Italy, and Spain. In 1925 an agreement was made with Ford Motor Company, the largest car manufacturer of that time, whereby preferential insurance terms were offered on Ford cars.

While establishing branches and founding subsidiaries under its own name in foreign countries according to national law, Zurich also acquired domestic insurance companies. This policy, like the starting of activities in the United States and the creation of a life insurance company for the group, dated from the time of August Leonhard Tobler, who first served as vice-director of the company and then was the head of Zurich from 1918 to 1927. It was under his leadership that the company developed into an internationally active insurance group, a status that continued to grow with the acquisition of substantial insurance companies. The continuity in the management of the company contributed to this achievement.

During the first 50 years of its existence, Zurich's activities were limited to damage and accident insurance. As a result of the decline of the German currency because of inflation after World War I, the German life insurance companies that held a strong position in the Swiss insurance markets were no longer able to fulfill their commitments in Swiss francs. They were therefore forced to withdraw from Switzerland. Swiss companies filled the gaps created in the market, with the result that numerous new life insurance companies were founded there. In 1922, in the course of these developments, the Vita Lebensversicherungs-Gesellschaft was created as a subsidiary of Zurich. It soon undertook business abroad, where it grew rapidly. It showed pioneering spirit when in 1926 it introduced a health service that offered regular checkups with a doctor and published medical leaflets giving advice on healthy living. Much later, in 1993, Vita was renamed Zurich Life.

NUMEROUS ACQUISITIONS IN
POSTWAR ERA

World War II caused the loss for Zurich of important areas of business in central and Eastern Europe. The rebuilding of Zurich in Germany began in Düsseldorf and Frankfurt. The Frankfurt tower block next to the old opera house became the administrative center for the German Zurich network in 1961. A string of further insurance companies was tied to the German branch of the company. The Deutsche Allgemeine Versicherungs-Aktiengesellschaft (German General Accident Insurance Ltd.), founded in 1923, concentrated particularly on offering motor insurance through direct sales. Zurich resumed its policy of international expansion, which had been halted by the war, in numerous other countries. The company opened many new offices as well as its own life insurance companies, in particular in the United States, Canada, the United Kingdom, and Australia.

The period after World War II was marked for Zurich by its development into a company dealing in all branches of insurance. Because of the systematic extension of the classes covered by the company, the branch-related balancing-out of risks was put alongside the international one. Until the beginning of the 1950s, the emphasis of activities had lain in the field of accident and liability insurance, whose dominant position was expressed in Zurich's slogan "The world's largest purely accident and liability insurer." The company was innovative in its introduction of these branches of insurance in major countries. The company's expansion into further sectors was reflected in its change of name to Zürich Versicherungs-Gesellschaft (Zurich Insurance Company) in 1955. In 1970 fire insurance was also offered by the company for the first time in Switzerland.

The acquisition of large insurance companies and groups in various foreign countries had a crucial bearing on the scope of the company's business and was a policy carried out under the management of Fritz Gerber, the chairman and for many years director general of the company. Three important examples illustrated this policy. In 1965 Zurich bought the Alpina Versicherungs-Aktiengesellschaft in Switzerland, which had established its own network abroad. In 1969 Agrippina Versicherung AG was acquired from a private bank. Agrippina had been created in Cologne in 1844 as a marine insurance company and was therefore well established in the German insurance market, with a number of subsidiaries of its own. The acquisition in 1989 of the Maryland Casualty Group, with its headquarters in Baltimore, Maryland, greatly strengthened Zurich's business with private customers as well as doubling premium income in the United States.

From 1972, Zurich's centenary year, to 1990, the parent company's gross premiums rose from CHF 2.3 billion to CHF 6.1 billion, and those of the Zurich insurance group from CHF 4 billion to CHF 17.1 billion. By 1990, Zurich did business worldwide in almost 80 countries, with a particularly strong presence

in its traditional markets in Switzerland, the United States, and Germany. Its successful international development could be attributed largely to the use the company had made of the respected name of the financial center of Zürich together with its historical role in the expansion of accident and personal liability insurance. With a view to future business in the European Common Market, Zurich International companies were established in Belgium, Germany, the United Kingdom, France, Italy, and the Netherlands and offered special Euro-policies for industrial insurance. This type of insurance was supported by computer system Zurinet, ensuring international communication of information.

TRANSFORMATIONAL DEVELOPMENTS UNDER HÜPPI

In 1991 Rolf Hüppi took over as president and CEO of Zurich, with Gerber remaining chairman. Under the leadership of Hüppi, a 28-year veteran of the firm, Zurich in the early 1990s placed an emphasis on targeting specific sectors of the insurance market within the countries in which it operated. Faced with the heightened, and increasingly globalized, competitive landscape of the 1990s, Hüppi believed that his company needed to rein in its sprawling international operations to successfully compete. Peripheral and underperforming businesses were jettisoned in favor of such core niches as the Swiss life insurance market. Hüppi bolstered the latter through the 1991 acquisition of Geneva Insurance and a 1992 deal with Swiss Bank Corporation (SBC), through which Zurich began selling life insurance at SBC branches. U.S. operations were expanded in 1993 with the establishment of Zurich Reinsurance Centre Holdings Inc., which quickly became one of the largest reinsurers in the United States.

In the mid- to late 1990s, with the global consolidation of the financial services sector progressing at a rapid clip, Hüppi (who became chairman in 1995) thoroughly transformed Zurich through a series of major transactions. In early 1996 Zurich, through a $2 billion transaction, acquired an 80 percent interest in Kemper Corporation, which was headquartered in Long Grove, Illinois, and a 97 percent interest in Kemper Financial Services, the latter being the asset management unit of the former. By gaining control of Kemper and its two life insurance subsidiaries, Zurich gained its first significant presence in the U.S. life insurance market and increased its overall presence in the life insurance sector, a company goal. The addition of Kemper Financial Services greatly advanced Zurich's position in asset management and gave it a foothold in the U.S.

money management business. The group had first entered this sector in 1990 with the establishment of Zurich Investment Management. Kemper, which was renamed Zurich Kemper Investments Inc., managed $42 billion in mutual fund assets at the time of the takeover.

Zurich Kemper was soon greatly expanded with the acquisition in 1997 of majority control of Scudder, Stevens & Clark Inc., a New York mutual fund firm with about $120 billion in assets under management. In a complicated transaction, Zurich paid about $2 billion to take control of Scudder and merge it into Zurich Kemper to form Scudder Kemper Investments, which initially was 69.5 percent owned by Zurich and 30.5 percent owned by Scudder's senior management. Scudder Kemper (which was later renamed Zurich Scudder Investments) was based in New York.

1998 MERGER WITH BAFS, FORMATION OF ZURICH FINANCIAL SERVICES

Further growth occurred in 1998 when Zurich merged with British American Financial Services (BAFS), the financial services unit of U.K.-based B.A.T. Industries PLC, in a $38 billion transaction. The merger created a "new" Zurich, which began operating under the name Zurich Financial Services. A dual holding company structure was set up whereby Zurich was 55 percent owned by Zurich Allied AG, which had a listing on the Swiss Exchange, and 45 percent owned by Allied Zurich p.l.c., which had a listing on the London Stock Exchange.

The addition of BAFS increased Zurich's gross premiums written from $23.7 billion to $40 billion and made Zurich the fifth largest insurance group in the world. Among the insurance holdings of BAFS was Los Angeles-based Farmers Group, Inc., one of the largest property-casualty insurance firms in the United States. BAFS also brought to Zurich substantial U.K. insurance operations, including Allied Dunbar Assurance, one of the largest life insurance and pension firms in the United Kingdom, and Eagle Star Holdings, a leading U.K. multiline insurer with strong commercial lines. The enlarged U.K. operations of Zurich led the group to begin speaking of having three "home" markets in the United States, the United Kingdom, and Switzerland. Zurich also gained an additional asset management business, London-based Threadneedle Asset Management, which increased the group's assets under management from $262 billion to $341.8 billion. This made Zurich one of the top ten asset managers in the world. Overall the newly formed Zurich intended to focus on four core businesses: non-life insurance, life insurance, reinsurance, and asset management.

In October 2000 the complicated structure of Zurich Financial was simplified with the unification of the group under a single Swiss holding company, also called Zurich Financial Services. The new Zurich had a primary stock listing on the Swiss Exchange and a secondary listing in London. Unfortunately, by this time, Zurich was being hurt by poor performance at the Zurich Scudder unit, which was suffering from difficulties integrating the varied corporate cultures that had existed at Scudder and Kemper, as well as from the volatile equity markets of 2000 and 2001.

DOWNTURN AND RETRENCHMENT

Disappointing groupwide earnings led to the announcement in early 2001 that Zurich planned to exit from the reinsurance market in order to focus on non-life insurance, life insurance, and asset management. The reinsurance division, Zurich Re, was subsequently spun off into an independent, separately traded public firm, Converium Holding AG, in December 2001. Other underperforming units were earmarked for divestment as well. Zurich also launched a restructuring of its head office with the aim of achieving annual savings of $200 million by 2002. In a further restructuring effort initiated in July 2001, the company consolidated its global operations into five divisions, four of which were geographically oriented: Continental Europe, North America Corporate, North America Consumer/Latin America, and United Kingdom, Ireland, Southern Africa, and Asia/Pacific. The other division, Global Asset, included Zurich Scudder and other asset management businesses, such as Zurich Capital Markets, Centre, and Capital Z Partners.

In the meantime, soon after the announcement of the spinoff of Zurich Re, Zurich revealed that it was exploring strategic options for its troubled asset management operations. Late in 2001 Zurich reached an agreement to sell the bulk of its Global Asset unit, including Zurich Scudder but not including Threadneedle Asset Management, to Deutsche Bank AG. As part of this deal, which was valued at $2.5 billion and concluded in the spring of 2002, Zurich received a majority stake in Deutscher Herold, Deutsche's German life insurance business, plus the German bank's insurance operations in Italy, Spain, and Portugal.

During 2001, the disastrous year that heralded this retrenchment, Zurich ended up posting a net loss of $387 million. The company's travails were compounded by the events of September 11, as it eventually had to pay out roughly $900 million in claims related to that day's terrorist attacks. By February 2002 Zurich's share price had fallen by more than 60 percent over the previous 12 months, and Hüppi finally bowed to months of pressure from shareholders and analysts and announced his intention to resign later in the year. In May 2002 James J. Schiro was appointed the new CEO. Schiro, a former CEO at the accounting firm PricewaterhouseCoopers, had joined Zurich just two months earlier as COO in charge of finance. The American became the first foreigner to head Zurich Financial.

SCHIRO-LED TURNAROUND

Schiro moved aggressively to turn around a company whose financial state was edging toward a collapse. Among other initiatives, Zurich raised $2.4 billion in new capital from shareholders through a rights offering, embarked on a program to slash the workforce by 4,500 employees, and sharply cut operating expenses in a push to increase annual earnings by $1 billion. The company also moved to refocus on its core insurance businesses, jettisoning additional non-insurance units plus some smaller insurance operations in peripheral markets. Among the more significant divestments carried out in 2003 were that of Threadneedle, the U.S. unit Zurich Life, and the Swiss private bank Rüd Blass & Cie AG.

In 2002, prior to completing these divestments, Zurich further strengthened its balance sheet by increasing its provisions against losses by $1.9 billion and writing down the value of the equities in its investment portfolio by nearly $1 billion. These special provisions, coupled with an additional charge of $746 million to write down the value of its asset management unit, led to a staggering net loss for 2002 of $3.43 billion. The turnaround strategy led by Schiro, however, paid off only a year later, when Zurich managed to post net earnings of $2.12 billion. In 2004 Zurich further bolstered its balance sheet and increased its earnings to $2.47 billion.

The strength of this turnaround was increasingly evident by 2005 when despite a record year for catastrophic natural disasters that included Hurricanes Katrina and Rita in the United States and major flooding and wildfires in Europe, Zurich Financial still managed to increase its net earnings by 30 percent to $3.21 billion. Claims for natural disasters that year amounted to $1.3 billion. Also during the year, Zurich reached a deal to sell Universal Underwriters Insurance Company, its U.S. subsidiary that specialized in providing insurance to auto dealers, to a private equity group, but the sale fell through in early 2006. Late in 2005 Zurich launched a global brand campaign centering on its new tagline "Because change happenz" and aiming to raise the profile of the Zurich brand around the world. The company followed up by incorporating the Zurich name into more of its various businesses.

In the first quarter of 2006 Zurich booked a $325 million charge to cover the cost of settling allegations of bid rigging and other broker compensation wrongdoing in the U.S. commercial insurance sector that had been brought by officials of 12 U.S. states. The company delisted its stock from the London Stock Exchange that year because of low trading volume, leaving its stock to be traded only on the Swiss Exchange. Seeking to gain further inroads into one of the fastest-growing insurance markets in the world, Zurich in May 2006 became the first foreign insurer to be granted a license to open a property and casualty insurance branch in Beijing. The new unit focused on corporate customers, including foreign companies active in China and large and medium-size Chinese companies, especially those operating overseas. For the year, Zurich enjoyed a further surge in net income of 41 percent, to $4.53 billion, while its return on equity of 19 percent represented a strong gain over the 15.5 percent figure for the previous year.

AN ACQUISITIVE TURN IN 2007

An increasingly confident Zurich Financial turned acquisitive once again in 2007, although this buying spree centered on smaller deals in the company's core businesses, mainly in emerging markets. In March 2007 the company acquired ACC Seguros y Reaseguros de Daños, S.A., a Spanish credit and surety insurer. A month later Zurich became the first foreign insurance company to gain control of a leading Russian property and casualty insurance firm when it bought a 66 percent stake in Nasta Insurance Company, subsequently renamed Zurich Retail Insurance Company Ltd. Zurich also purchased a minority stake and gained management control of a Chinese insurance-brokerage firm that was renamed Zurich Insurance Brokers (Beijing) Ltd. In December 2007 the company announced plans to create a new Hong Kong-based unit to expand its offerings to corporate customers in Japan, Greater China, Southeast Asia, and Australasia. That same month, Zurich sought to capture a larger share of the growing life insurance market in southern Europe by reaching a deal to purchase Italian life insurer DWA Vita SpA for approximately $140 million. Through deals such as these and other initiatives, Zurich Financial sought to spark a new period of growth following its recovery from the dark days of 2001 and 2002.

Peter Koch (translated from the German by Philippe A. Barbour)
Updated, David E. Salamie

PRINCIPAL SUBSIDIARIES

Assuricum Company Limited; Genevoise, Compagnie d'Assurances sur la Vie SA; Zurich Group Holding; Zurich Insurance Company; Zurich Life Insurance Company Ltd.; "Zurich" Investment Management AG; Zurich Australia Limited; Zurich Australian Insurance Limited; Zurich Financial Services Australia Limited; Zürich Versicherungs-Aktiengesellschaft (Austria; 99.98%); B G Investments Ltd. (Bermuda); Centre Group Holdings Limited (Bermuda); CMSH Limited (Bermuda); ZCM Holdings (Bermuda) Limited; ZG Investments Limited (Bermuda); ZG Investments II Ltd. (Bermuda); ZG Investments III Ltd. (Bermuda); ZG Investments IV Ltd. (Bermuda); Zurich International (Bermuda) Ltd.; Chilena Consolidada Seguros de Vida S.A. (Chile; 98.95%); BONNSECUR GmbH & Co. Liegenschaften Deutscher Herold KG (Germany; 84.35%); DA Deutsche Allgemeine Versicherung Aktiengesellschaft (Germany); DEUTSCHER HEROLD Aktiengesellschaft (Germany; 76.83%); Zürich Beteiligungs-Aktiengesellschaft (Germany); Zurich Deutscher Herold Lebensversicherung Aktiengesellschaft (Germany; 84.35%); Zurich Versicherung Aktiengesellschaft (Germany; 94.96%); Eagle Star Life Assurance Company of Ireland Limited; Orange Stone Holdings (Ireland); Orange Stone Reinsurance (Ireland); Zurich Financial Services EUB Holdings Limited (Ireland); Zurich Insurance Ireland Ltd.; Zurich Investments Life S.p.a. (Italy); Zurich Life Insurance Italia S.p.A. (Italy); Zurich - Companhia de Seguros S.A. (Portugal); Zurich Retail Insurance Company Ltd. (Russia; 66%); South African Eagle Insurance Company Limited (73.61%); Zurich España, Compañía de Seguros y Reaseguros, S.A. (Spain; 99.78%); Zurich Vida, Compañía de Seguros y Reaseguros, S.A.—Sociedad Unipersonal (Spain); Zurich Insurance (Taiwan) Ltd. (98.9%); Allied Dunbar Assurance p.l.c. (U.K.); Allied Zurich Limited (U.K.); Eagle Star Holdings Limited (U.K.); Eagle Star Insurance Company Limited (U.K.); ZPC (Construction) Company Limited (U.K.); Zurich Assurance Ltd. (U.K.); Zurich Employment Services Limited (U.K.); Zurich Financial Services (UKISA) Limited (U.K.); Zurich International (UK) Limited; Zurich International Life Limited (U.K.); Zurich Invest (Jersey) Ltd. (U.K.); Zurich Specialties London Limited (U.K.); Centre Reinsurance Holdings (Delaware) Limited (U.S.A.); Crown Management Services Limited (U.S.A.); Farmers Group, Inc. (U.S.A.); Farmers New World Life Insurance Company (U.S.A.); Farmers Reinsurance Company (U.S.A.); Farmers Services, LLC (U.S.A.); Kemper Corporation (U.S.A.); Kemper Investors Life Insurance Company (U.S.A.); Universal Underwriters Insurance Company (U.S.A.); Zurich American Insurance Company (U.S.A.); Zurich Finance (U.S.A.), Inc.; Zurich Holding Company of America, Inc. (U.S.A.).

PRINCIPAL DIVISIONS

General Insurance; Global Life; Farmers Management Services.

PRINCIPAL COMPETITORS

Allianz SE; AXA; ING Groep N.V.; American International Group, Inc.; Assicurazioni Generali S.p.A.; Aviva plc; The Travelers Companies, Inc.

FURTHER READING

Banks, Howard, "A Zurich in Your Future?" *Forbes,* April 20, 1998, pp. 85–86.

Carew, Rick, "Zurich Financial Buys into China," *Wall Street Journal Europe,* September 5, 2007, p. 23.

Deogun, Nikhil, and Tom Lauricella, "Zurich Financial Seeks a Merger to Reinvigorate Its Scudder Unit," *Wall Street Journal,* April 23, 2001, p. C1.

Evans, Richard, "Premium Insurer: Zurich Financial Stresses Service over Price, but Sells at a Discount," *Barron's,* January 31, 2000, pp. 22, 24.

Fleming, Charles, "Zurich Financial Swings to Profit," *Wall Street Journal Europe,* August 21, 2003, p. M3.

———, "Zurich Insurance Group Is Looking for a New Focus: Multinational Seeks to Distinguish Itself by Targeting Specific Markets," *Wall Street Journal,* June 26, 1992, p. B3.

Gelnar, Martin, and Goran Mijuk, "Zurich Financial Halts Sale of Insurer," *Wall Street Journal,* January 18, 2006, p. B3D.

Greil, Anita, "Converium Raises $1.1 Billion for Zurich Financial in IPO," *Wall Street Journal Europe,* December 12, 2001, p. 19.

———, "Zurich Financial Struggles," *Wall Street Journal Europe,* October 8, 2001, p. 14.

Howard, Lisa S., "Zurich Financial Services to Exit Reinsurance Market," *National Underwriter Property and Casualty-Risk and Benefits Management,* March 26, 2001, p. 2.

Hundert Jahre "Schweiz" Allgemeine Versicherungs-Aktien-Gesellschaft Zürich, 1869–1969, Zürich: Art Institut Orell Füssli Zürich AG, [1969].

Koch, Peter, "Der schweizerische Beitrag zur Entwicklung des Versicherungs-wesens," *Versicherungswirtschaft,* 1985.

———, "Versicherer aus aller Welt in Deutschland," *Versicherungskaufmann,* July 1987.

Lipin, Steven, "Kemper Agrees to Be Acquired by Group Headed by Zurich Insurance for $2 Billion," *Wall Street Journal,* April 11, 1995, p. A3.

Lucchetti, Aaron, and Marcus Walker, "Deutsche Bank to Buy Zurich Financial Assets," *Wall Street Journal,* September 24, 2001, p. C17.

Lüönd, Karl, *Inspired by Tomorrow: Zurich—125 Years; History and Vision of a Global Corporation,* Zürich: Neue Zürcher Zeitung, 1998, 269 p.

Markram, Bianca, "Zurich's New Approach to Life," *Reactions,* May 2004, p. 16.

Mijuk, Goran, "Zurich Financial, Baloise Set to Buy Smaller Rivals," *Wall Street Journal Europe,* December 27, 2006, p. 19.

Mijuk, Goran, and Anita Greil, "Zurich Financial Unit Sale Aids Restructuring," *Wall Street Journal Europe,* June 17, 2003, p. M6.

Mijuk, Goran, and Ian McDonald, "Zurich Financial Largely Averts Subprime Damage," *Wall Street Journal Europe,* August 17, 2007, p. 17.

Parekh, Rupal, "Zurich Settles Some Bid-Rigging Charges," *Business Insurance,* March 27, 2006, p. 1.

———, "Zurich Unit, States Finalize Settlements to Resolve Probes," *Business Insurance,* December 11, 2006, p. 3.

Sclafane, Susanne, "Zurich: $2 Billion Loss, 4,500 Staff Cuts," *National Underwriter Property and Casualty,* September 16, 2002, p. 26.

Silverman, Gary, and Friederike von Tiesenhausen, "Bank One Buys Half of Zurich Life for $500m," *Financial Times,* May 31, 2003, p. 8.

Simonian, Haig, "ZFS Emerges from Internal Strife to Find Uncertainty," *Financial Times,* June 12, 2007, p. 24.

———, "ZFS Makes Move into Russia," *Financial Times,* February 15, 2007, p. 23.

———, "ZFS Views the Future with New Confidence," *Financial Times,* August 16, 2005, p. 23.

———, "Zurich Makes a Virtue Out of Being Boring," *Financial Times,* August 18, 2006, p. 22.

Steinmetz, Greg, "Kemper Purchase to Make Zurich Insurance a Tougher Competitor in the U.S. Market," *Wall Street Journal Europe,* June 7, 1995, p. 9.

Steinmetz, Greg, and Margaret Studer, "B.A.T. Seals Its Union with Zurich Insurance," *Wall Street Journal,* October 17, 1997, p. B14.

Studer, Margaret, "Hüppi Isn't Done with Makeover of Swiss Insurance: Big Year Is on the Horizon for an Empire Builder Who's Eager to Please," *Wall Street Journal Europe,* December 29, 1998, p. 9.

———, "Weak Dollar Aids Zurich Insurance's Shopping Spree: Bidder for Kemper Seeks Stronger Life Operations and Global Expansion," *Wall Street Journal,* April 12, 1995, p. B4.

"Swiss Miss," *Economist,* March 30, 2002, p. 66.

Tuckey, Steve, and Daniel Hays, "Zurich Bid-Rigging Deals Hit $325 Million," *National Underwriter Property and Casualty,* April 3, 2006, pp. 8, 33.

25 Jahre "Vita," 1922–1947, Zürich: "Vita" Lebensversicherungs-Aktiengesellschaft, [1948].

Unsworth, Edwin, "Deal Strengthens Zurich: Merger with B.A.T. Unit to Create Financial Services Giant," *Business Insurance,* October 20, 1997, pp. 1+.

Walker, Marcus, and Martin Gelnar, "Zurich Names Schiro Its CEO," *Wall Street Journal Europe,* May 15, 2002, p. M1.

Woodruff, David, Richard A. Melcher, and Paula Dwyer, "Who Says Insurers Are Dull?: A Buying Binge by Rolf Hüppi Has Zurich Insurance Hopping," *Business Week,* June 23, 1997, p. 54.

Zürich Allgemeine Unfall- und Haftpflicht-Versicherungs-Aktiengesellschaft, *75 Jahre "Zürich": Werden und Wachsen der Gesellschaft, 1872–1947,* Zürich: Art Institut Orell Füssli AG, 1948.

"Zurich" Allgemeine Unfall- und Haftpflicht-Versicherungs-Aktiengesellschaft in Zürich: Die Gesellschaft in den ersten fünfzig Jahren ihres Bestehens, 1872–1922, Zürich: Zürich Allgemeine in Zürich, 1923.

"Zurich Financial Services: Re Structure," *Economist,* September 8, 2001, pp. 80–81.

Index to Companies

Listings in this index are arranged in alphabetical order under the company name. Company names beginning with a letter or proper name such as Eli Lilly & Co. will be found under the first letter of the company name. Definite articles (The, Le, La) are ignored for alphabetical purposes as are forms of incorporation that precede the company name (AB, NV). Company names printed in **bold** *type have full, historical essays on the page numbers appearing in bold. Updates to entries that appeared in earlier volumes are signified by the notation* **(upd.)**. *Company names in light type are references within an essay to that company, not full historical essays. This index is cumulative with volume numbers printed in bold type.*

A

A and A Limousine Renting, Inc., **26** 62
A & A Medical Supply, **61** 206
A&E Plastics, **12** 377
A&E Television Networks, 32 3–7
A&K Petroleum Company *see* Kerr-McGee Corp.
A&M Records, **23** 389
A&N Foods Co., *see* Nippon Suisan Kaisha, Ltd.
A&P *see* The Great Atlantic & Pacific Tea Company, Inc.
A & W Brands, Inc., 25 3–5 *see also* Cadbury Schweppes PLC.
A-dec, Inc., 53 3–5
á la Zing, **62** 259
A-Mark Financial Corporation, 71 3–6

A-1 Supply *see* International Game Technology.
A-R Technologies, **48** 275
A.A. Mathews *see* CRSS Inc.
A. Ahlström Oy *see* Ahlstrom Corp.
A.B. Chance Industries Co., Inc. *see* Hubbell Inc.
A.B.Dick Company, 28 6–8
A.B. Leasing Corp., *see* Bozzuto's, Inc.
A.B. Watley Group Inc., 45 3–5
A-BEC Mobility, **11** 487
A.C. Delco, **26** 347, 349
A.C. Moore Arts & Crafts, Inc., 30 3–5
A.C. Nielsen Company, 13 3–5 *see also* ACNielsen Corp.
A. Duda & Sons, Inc., 88 1–4
A/E/C/ Systems International, *see* Penton Media, Inc.
A.E. Fitkin & Company, **6** 592–93; **50** 37
A.E. Lottes, **29** 86
A. F. Blakemore & Son Ltd., 90 1–4
A.G. Becker, **20** 260
A.G. Edwards, Inc., 8 3–5; **32** 17–21 **(upd.)**
A.G. Industries, Inc., *see* American Greetings Corp.
A.G. Stanley Ltd. *see* The Boots Company PLC.
A.H. Belo Corporation, 10 3–5; **30** 13–17 **(upd.)**
A.H. Robins Co., *see* Wyeth.
A. Hirsh & Son, **30** 408
A. Hölscher GmbH, **53** 195
A. Johnson & Co. *see* Axel Johnson Group.
A.L. Pharma Inc., 12 3–5 *see also* Alpharma Inc.
A.L. Van Houtte Inc. *see* Van Houtte Inc.

A. Leon Capel and Sons, Inc. *see* Capel Inc.
A.M. Castle & Co., 25 6–8
A. Michel et Cie., **49** 84
A. Moksel AG, 59 3–6
A. Nelson & Co. Ltd., 75 3–6
A. O. Smith Corporation, 11 3–6; **40** 3–8 **(upd.); 93** 1–9 **(upd.)**
A.P. Møller - Maersk A/S, 57 3–6
A.P. Orleans, Inc., *see* Orleans Homebuilders, Inc.
A.S. Abell Co., **IV** 678
A.S. Watson & Company Ltd., 84 1–4
A.S. Yakovlev Design Bureau, 15 3–6
A. Schilling & Company *see* McCormick & Company, Inc.
A. Schulman, Inc., 8 6–8; **49** 3–7 **(upd.)**
A. Sulka & Co., **29** 457
A.T. Cross Company, 17 3–5; **49** 8–12 **(upd.)**
A.T. Massey Coal Company, Inc., **34** 164; **57** 236
A.T. Mays, **55** 90
A-T-O Inc. *see* Figgie International, Inc.
A.W. Baulderstone Holdings Pty. Ltd., **55** 62
A.W. Faber-Castell Unternehmensverwaltung GmbH & Co., 51 3–6
A. Wilhelmsen A/S, **74** 278
AA Energy Corp., *see* AMR Corp.
AADC Holding Company, Inc., **62** 347
AAF-McQuay Incorporated, 26 3–5
AAI Corporation, **37** 399
Aai.FosterGrant, Inc., **60** 131, 133
Aalborg Industries A/S, 90 5–8
AAON, Inc., 22 3–6
AAPT, **54** 355–57
AAR Corp., 28 3–5

Allison Engine Company, **21** 436

Allison Engineering Company *see* Rolls-Royce Allison.

Allison Gas Turbine Division, 9 16–19

Allmanna Svenska Elektriska Aktiebolaget *see* ABB Ltd.

Allmänna Telefonaktiebolaget L.M. Ericsson *see* Telefonaktiebolaget L.M. Ericsson.

Allmerica Financial Corporation, 63 29–31

Allou Health & Beauty Care, Inc., 28 12–14

Alloy, Inc., 55 13–15

Allparts, Inc., **51** 307

Allsport plc, **31** 216, 218

The Allstate Corporation, 10 50–52; **27** 30–33 (upd.)

ALLTEL Corporation, 6 299–301; **46** 15–19 (upd.)

Alltrista Corporation, 30 38–41 *see also* Jarden Corp.

Allwaste, Inc., 18 10–13

Allweiler, 58 67

Alma Media Group, **52** 51

Almac Electronics Corporation, *see* Arrow Electronics, Inc.

Almacenes de Baja y Media, **39** 201, 204

Almacenes Exito S.A., 89 47–50

Almaden Vineyards, *see* Canandaigua Brands, Inc.

Almanacksförlaget AB, **51** 328

Almanij NV, 44 15–18 *see also* Algemeene Maatschappij voor Nijverheidskrediet.

Almay, Inc. *see* Revlon Inc.

Almeida Banking House *see* Banco Bradesco S.A.

Almost Family, Inc., 93 41–44

ALNM *see* Ayres, Lewis, Norris & May.

Aloha Airlines, Incorporated, 24 20–22

ALP *see* Associated London Properties.

Alp Sport Sandals, **22** 173

Alpargatas S.A.I.C., 87 13–17

Alpex, S.A. de C.V., **19** 12

Alpha Airports Group PLC, 77 32–35

Alpha Beta Co., *see* American Stores Co.

Alpha Engineering Group, Inc., **16** 259–60

Alpha Healthcare Ltd., *see* Sun Healthcare Group Inc.

Alpha Networks Inc. *see* D-Link Corp.

Alpha Processor Inc., **41** 349

Alpha Technical Systems, **19** 279

Alphaform, **40** 214–15

AlphaGraphics Inc. *see* G A Pindar & Son Ltd.

Alphanumeric Publication Systems, Inc., **26** 518

Alpharma Inc., 35 22–26 (upd.)

Alphonse Allard Inc., *see* Provigo Inc.

Alpine Confections, Inc., 71 22–24

Alpine Electronics, Inc., 13 30–31

Alpine Gaming *see* Century Casinos, Inc.

Alpine Lace Brands, Inc., 18 14–16 *see also* Land O'Lakes, Inc.

Alpine Securities Corporation, **22** 5

Alpnet Inc. *see* SDL PLC.

Alpre, **19** 192

Alps Electric Co., Ltd., II 5–6; **44** 19–21 (upd.)

Alric Packing, *see* Associated British Foods plc.

Alrosa Company Ltd., 62 7–11

Alsco *see* Steiner Corp.

ALSO Holding AG, **29** 419, 422

Alsthom, *see* Alcatel S.A.

ALTA Health Strategies, Inc., **11** 113

Alta Vista Company, **50** 228

Altadis S.A., 72 6–13 (upd.)

ALTANA AG, 87 18–22

AltaSteel Ltd., **51** 352

AltaVista Company, 43 11–13

ALTEC International, **21** 107–09

Altera Corporation, 18 17–20; **43** 14–18 (upd.)

Alternative Living Services *see* Alterra Healthcare Corp.

Alternative Tentacles Records, 66 3–6

Alternative Youth Services, Inc., *see* Res-Care, Inc.

Alterra Healthcare Corporation, 42 3–5

Altex, **19** 192–93

Alticor Inc., 71 25–30 (upd.)

Altiris, Inc., 65 34–36

Altman Weil Pensa, **29** 237

Alton Towers, **55** 378

Altos Hornos de México, S.A. de C.V., 42 6–8

Altra Broadband Inc., **63** 34

Altran Technologies, 51 15–18

Altron Incorporated, 20 8–10

Altura Energy Ltd. *see* Occidental Petroleum Corp.

Aluar Aluminio Argentino S.A.I.C., 74 10–12

Aluma Systems Corp., *see* Tridel Enterprises Inc.

Alumalsa *see* Aluminoy y Aleaciones S.A.

Alumax Inc., **I** 508; **22** 286; **56** 11

Aluminoy y Aleaciones S.A., **63** 303

Aluminum and Stainless, Inc. *see* Reliance Steel & Aluminum Co.

Aluminum Company of America, IV 14–16; **20** 11–14 (upd.) *see also* Alcoa Inc.

Aluminum Forge Co., *see* Marmon Group, Inc.

Alupak, A.G., **12** 377

Alusuisse, **73** 212–13

Alvic Group, **20** 363

Alvin Ailey Dance Foundation, Inc., 52 14–17

Alvis Plc, 47 7–9

ALZA Corporation, 10 53–55; **36** 36–39 (upd.)

Alzouman Aviation, **56** 148

AM Cosmetics, Inc., **31** 89

Am-Safe, Inc., *see* The Marmon Group, Inc.

AM-TEX Corp., Inc., **12** 443

Amagasaki Spinners Ltd. *see* Unitika Ltd.

Amalgamated Bank, 60 20–22

Amalgamated Sugar Co., **14** 18; **19** 467–68

Amana Refrigeration Company, **38** 374; **42** 159

Amaray International Corporation, **12** 264

Amarillo Gas Company *see* Atmos Energy Corp.

Amarillo Railcar Services, **6** 580

Amati Communications Corporation, **57** 409

Amax Gold, **36** 316

AMAX Inc., IV 17–19 *see also* Cyprus Amex.

Amazon.com, Inc., 25 17–19; **56** 12–15 (upd.)

AMB Generali Holding AG, 51 19–23

AMB Property Corporation, 57 25–27

Ambac Financial Group, Inc., 65 37–39

Ambassadors International, Inc., 68 16–18 (upd.)

Amberg Hospach AG, **49** 436

AmBev *see* Companhia de Bebidas das Américas.

Amblin Entertainment, 21 23–27

AMBRA, Inc., **48** 209

AMC Entertainment Inc., 12 12–14; **35** 27–29 (upd.)

AMCA International Corporation, *see* United Dominion Industries Ltd.

AMCC *see* Applied Micro Circuits Corp.

Amcell *see* American Cellular Network.

AMCOL International Corporation, 59 29–33 (upd.)

Amcor Ltd., IV 248–50; **19** 13–16 (upd.); **78** 1–6 (upd.)

AMCORE Financial Inc., 44 22–26

Amcraft Building Products Co., Inc., **22** 15

AMD *see* Advanced Micro Devices, Inc.

Amdahl Corporation, III 109–11; **14** 13–16 (upd.); **40** 20–25 (upd.) *see also* Fujitsu Ltd.

Amdocs Ltd., 47 10–12

AME Finanziaria, **IV** 587; **19** 19; **54** 20

Amec Spie S.A., 57 28–31

Amedysis, Inc., 53 33–36

Amer Group plc, 41 14–16

Amer Sport, **68** 245

Amerace Corporation, **54** 373

Amerada Hess Corporation, IV 365–67; **21** 28–31 (upd.); **55** 16–20 (upd.)

Amerchol Corporation *see* Union Carbide Corp.

AMERCO, 6 351–52; **67** 11–14 (upd.)

Ameren Corporation, 60 23–27 (upd.)

AmerGen Energy LLC, **49** 65, 67

Ameri-Kart Corp., *see* Myers Industries, Inc.

America Online, Inc., 10 56–58; **26** 16–20 (upd.) *see also* CompuServe Interactive Services, Inc.; AOL Time Warner Inc.

America Today, *see* Koninklijke Vendex KBB N.V. (Royal Vendex KBB N.V.)

America West Holdings Corporation, 6 72–74; **34** 22–26 (upd.)

America's Car-Mart, Inc., 64 19–21

AngioDynamics, Inc., **81** 26–29
Anglian Water Plc, **38** 51
Anglo-Abrasives Ltd. *see* Carbo PLC.
Anglo American Industrial Corporation, **59** 224–25
Anglo American PLC, IV 20–23; **16** 25–30 (upd.); **50** 30–36 (upd.)
Anglo-Canadian Telephone Company of Montreal *see* British Columbia Telephone Co.
Anglo-Dutch Unilever group, **9** 317
Anglo Energy, Ltd., **9** 364
Anglo Industries, Inc., *see* Nabors Industries, Inc.
Anglovaal Industries Ltd., **20** 263
Anheuser-Busch Companies, Inc., I 217–19; **10** 99–101 (upd.); **34** 34–37 (upd.)
ANI America Inc., **62** 331
Anixter International Inc., 88 13–16
Anker BV, 53 45–47
ANMC *see* Amedisys, Inc.
Ann Street Group Ltd., **61** 44–46
Anne Klein & Co., **15** 145–46; **40** 277–78; **56** 90
Annecy Béon Carrières, **70** 343
Anneplas, **25** 464
Annie's Homegrown, Inc., 59 48–50
AnnTaylor Stores Corporation, 13 43–45; **37** 12–15 (upd.); **67** 33–37 (upd.)
Anocout Engineering Co., **23** 82
ANR Pipeline Co., 17 21–23
Anritsu Corporation, 68 28–30
The Anschutz Company, 12 18–20; **36** 43–47 (upd.); **73** 24–30 (upd.)
Ansco & Associates, LLC, **57** 119
Ansell Ltd., 60 35–38 (upd.)
Anselmo L. Morvillo S.A., **19** 336
Ansett Australia, *see* Air New Zealand Ltd.
Ansoft Corporation, 63 32–34
Answer Products, Inc., **76** 237
ANSYS Technologies Inc., **48** 410
Antalis, **34** 38, 40
AntarChile S.A., **69** 141, 143
Antares Capital Corp., **53** 213
Antares Electronics, Inc., *see* Control Data Systems, Inc.
Antenna Company, **32** 40
Anteon Corporation, 57 32–34
ANTEX *see* American National Life Insurance Company of Texas.
Anthem Electronics, Inc., 13 46–47
Anthem P&C Holdings, **15** 257
Anthony & Sylvan Pools Corporation, 56 16–18
Anthony Industries Inc. *see* K2 Inc.
Anthracite Industries, Inc. *see* Asbury Carbons, Inc.
Anthropologie, Inc. *see* Urban Outfitters, Inc.
Antinori *see* Marchesi Antinori SRL.
The Antioch Company, 40 42–45
Antique Street Lamps, **19** 212
ANTK Tupolev *see* Aviacionny Nauchno-Tehnicheskii Komplex im. A.N. Tupoleva.
Antofagasta plc, 65 46–49

Antonio Puig, S.A. *see* Puig Beauty and Fashion Group S.L.
Antonov Design Bureau, 53 48–51
ANZ *see* Australia and New Zealand Banking Group Ltd.
AO Sidanco, **45** 50
AO VimpelCom, **59** 300
Aohata Corporation, **57** 202, 204
AOK-Bundesverband (Federation of the AOK), 78 12–16
Aoki Corporation, **9** 547, 549; **29** 508
AOL Time Warner Inc., 57 35–44 (upd.)
Aon Corporation, III 203–05; **45** 25–28 (upd.)
AP *see* The Associated Press.
AP&L *see* American Power & Light Co.
Apache Corporation, 10 102–04; **32** 42–46 (upd.); **89** 58–65 (upd.)
APACHE Medical Systems, Inc., **16** 94
Apanage GmbH & Co. KG, **53** 195
Apartment Furniture Rental, **26** 102
Apartment Investment and Management Company, 49 24–26
Apasco S.A. de C.V., 51 27–29
Apax Partners Worldwide LLP, 89 66–69
APB *see* Atlantic Premium Brands, Ltd.
APCOA/Standard Parking *see* Holberg Industries, Inc.
Apex Digital, Inc., 63 35–37
Apex Oil, **37** 310–11
Apex One Inc., **31** 137
APH *see* American Printing House for the Blind.
APi Group, Inc., 64 29–32
APL Limited, 61 27–30 (upd.)
Aplex Industries, Inc., **26** 363
APLIX S.A. *see* Velcro Industries N.V.
APM Ltd. *see* Amcor Limited
APN *see* Affiliated Physicians Network, Inc.
Apogee Enterprises, Inc., 8 34–36
Apogee Sound International LLC, **62** 39
Apollo Advisors L.P., **16** 37; **26** 500, 502; **43** 438
Apollo Group, Inc., 24 40–42
Apollo Heating & Air Conditioning Inc., **15** 411
Apollo Investment Fund Ltd., **31** 211; **39** 174
Apollo Ski Partners LP of New York, *see* Vail Associates, Inc.
Apothekernes Laboratorium A.S., **12** 3–5
Appalachian Travel Services, Inc., *see* Habersham Bancorp.
Apparel Ventures, Inc. *see* The Jordan Company, LP.
Appetifrais S.A., **51** 54
Applause Inc., 24 43–46 *see also* Russ Berrie and Co., Inc.
Apple & Eve L.L.C., 92 5–8
Apple Bank for Savings, 59 51–53
Apple Computer, Inc., III 115–16; **6** 218–20 (upd.); **36** 48–51 (upd.); **77** 40–45 (upd.)
Apple Corps Ltd., 87 29–34
Apple Orthodontix, Inc., **35** 325

Apple South, Inc. *see* Avado Brands, Inc.
Applebee's International Inc., 14 29–31; **35** 38–41 (upd.)
Applera Corporation, **74** 71
Appliance Recycling Centers of America, Inc., 42 13–16
Applica Incorporated, 43 32–36 (upd.)
Applied Beverage Systems Ltd., **21** 339
Applied Biomedical Corp., **47** 4
Applied Bioscience International, Inc., 10 105–07
Applied Biosystems, **74** 72
Applied Communications, Inc., **6** 280; **29** 477–79
Applied Data Research, Inc., **18** 31–32
Applied Engineering Services, Inc. *see* The AES Corp.
Applied Films Corporation, 48 28–31
Applied Industrial Materials Corporation, *see* Walter Industries, Inc.
Applied Laser Systems, **31** 124
Applied Learning International, **IV** 680
Applied Materials, Inc., 10 108–09; **46** 31–34 (upd.)
Applied Micro Circuits Corporation, 38 53–55
Applied Network Technology, Inc., **25** 162
Applied Power Inc., 9 26–28; **32** 47–51 (upd.)
Applied Signal Technology, Inc., 87 35–38
Applied Technology Solutions *see* RWD Technologies, Inc.
Applied Thermal Technologies, Inc., **29** 5
Apria Healthcare Inc., **43** 266
Aprilia SpA, 17 24–26
Aprolis, **72** 159
APS *see* Arizona Public Service Co.
APSA, **63** 214
AptarGroup, Inc., 69 38–41
Aqua Alliance Inc., 32 52–54 (upd.)
Aqua Cool Pure Bottled Water, **52** 188
Aqua de Oro Venture, **58** 23
Aquafin N.V., **12** 443; **38** 427
aQuantive, Inc., 81 30–33
Aquarion Company, 84 12–16
Aquarius Group *see* Club Mediterranee SA.
Aquarius Platinum Ltd., 63 38–40
Aquatech, **53** 232
Aquila Energy Corp., **6** 593
Aquila, Inc., 50 37–40 (upd.)
Aquitaine *see* Société Nationale des Petroles d'Aquitaine.
AR Accessories Group, Inc., 23 20–22
ARA *see* Consorcio ARA, S.A. de C.V.
ARA Services, II 607–08 *see also* Aramark.
Arab-Israel Bank Ltd., **60** 50
Arab Japanese Insurance Co., *see* Mitsui Marine and Fire Insurance Co., Ltd.
Arab Leasing International Finance, **72** 85
Arab Potash Company, 85 10–13
Arab Radio & Television, **72** 85
Arabian American Oil Co. *see* Saudi Arabian Oil Co.

Australian and Overseas Telecommunications Corporation *see* Telecom Australia.

Australian Consolidated Press, **27** 42; **54** 299

Australian Mutual Provident Society, **IV** 61, 697

Australian Tankerships Pty. Ltd., **25** 471

Australian Telecommunications Corporation, **6** 342

Australian Wheat Board *see* AWB Ltd.

Austria Tabak, **55** 200

Austrian Airlines AG (Österreichische Luftverkehrs AG), 33 49–52

Austrian Star Gastronomie GmbH, **48** 63

Authentic Fitness Corp., 20 41–43; **51** 30–33 (upd.)

Auto Helloes Co. Ltd., **76** 37

Auto Parts Wholesale, **26** 348

Auto Shack *see* AutoZone, Inc.

Auto Value Associates, Inc., 25 26–28

Autobacs Seven Company Ltd., 76 36–38

Autobytel Inc., 47 32–34

Autocam Corporation, 51 34–36

Autodesk, Inc., 10 118–20; **89** 78–82 (upd.)

Autogrill SpA, 49 31–33

Autoliv, Inc., 65 53–55

Autologic Information International, Inc., 20 44–46

Automated Loss Prevention Systems, **11** 445

Automated Sciences Group, Inc. *see* CACI International Inc.

Automated Security (Holdings) PLC, *see* Sensormatic Electronics Corp.

Automatic Coil Corp., **33** 359, 361

Automatic Data Processing, Inc., III 117–19; **9** 48–51 (upd.); **47** 35–39 (upd.)

Automatic Liquid Packaging, **50** 122

Automatic Payrolls, Inc. *see* Automatic Data Processing, Inc.

Automatic Retailers of America, Inc., *see* Aramark Corporation

Automatic Sprinkler Corp. of America *see* Figgie International, Inc.

Automatic Toll Systems, **19** 111

Automatic Voting Machine Corporation *see* American Locker Group Inc.

AutoMed Technologies, Inc., **64** 27

Automobiles Citroën, 7 35–38

Automobili Lamborghini Holding S.p.A., 13 60–62; **34** 55–58 (upd.); **91** 25–30 (upd.)

Automotive Diagnostics, *see* SPX Corp.

Automotive Group *see* Lear Corp.

Automotive Industries Holding Inc., **16** 323

AutoNation, Inc., 50 61–64

Autonet, **6** 435

Autonom Computer, **47** 36

Autoroutes du Sud de la France SA, 55 38–40

Autosite.com, **47** 34

Autotote Corporation, 20 47–49 *see also* Scientific Games Corp.

AutoTrader.com, L.L.C., 91 31–34

Autoweb.com, **47** 34

AutoZone, Inc., 9 52–54; **31** 35–38 (upd.)

AVA AG (Allgemeine Handelsgesellschaft der Verbraucher AG), 33 53–56

Avado Brands, Inc., 31 39–42

Avalon Correctional Services, Inc., 75 40–43

Avalon Publishing Group *see* Publishers Group, Inc.

AvalonBay Communities, Inc., 58 11–13

Avantel, **27** 304

Avantium Technologies BV, 79 46–49

Avaya Inc., **41** 287, 289–90

Avco *see* Aviation Corp. of the Americas.

Avco Corp., **34** 433

Avco Financial Services Inc., 13 63–65 *see also* Citigroup Inc.

Avdel, **34** 433

Avecia Group PLC, 63 49–51

Avecor Cardiovascular Inc., **22** 360

Avecor, Inc. *see* M. A. Hanna Co.

Aveda Corporation, 24 55–57

Avedis Zildjian Co., 38 66–68

Avendt Group, Inc., *see* Marmon Group, Inc.

Aventine Renewable Energy Holdings, Inc., 89 83–86

Aventis Pharmaceuticals, **34** 280, 283–84; **38** 378, 380; **63** 232, 235

Avery Communications, Inc., **72** 39

Avery Dennison Corporation, IV 251–54; **17** 27–31 (upd.); **49** 34–40 (upd.)

AvestaPolarit, **49** 104

Avex Electronics Inc., **40** 68

Avgain Marine A/S, **7** 40; **41** 42

Avia Group International, Inc. *see* Reebok International Ltd.

Aviacionny Nauchno-Tehnicheskii Komplex im. A.N. Tupoleva, 24 58–60

Aviacsa *see* Consorcio Aviacsa, S.A. de C.V.

Aviall, Inc., 73 42–45

Avianca Aerovías Nacionales de Colombia SA, 36 52–55

Aviation Corp. of the Americas, **9** 497–99

Aviation Inventory Management Co., **28** 5

Aviation Sales Company, 41 37–39

Aviation Services West, Inc. *see* Scenic Airlines, Inc.

Avid Technology Inc., 38 69–73

Avimo, **47** 7–8

Avionics Specialties Inc. *see* Aerosonic Corp.

Avions Marcel Dassault-Breguet Aviation, I 44–46 *see also* Groupe Dassault Aviation SA.

Avis Group Holdings, Inc., 6 356–58; **22** 54–57 (upd.); **75** 44–49 (upd.)

Avista Corporation, 69 48–50 (upd.)

Aviva PLC, 50 65–68 (upd.)

Avnet Inc., 9 55–57

Avocent Corporation, **65** 56–58

Avon Products, Inc., III 15–16; **19** 26–29 (upd.); **46** 43–46 (upd.)

Avon Rubber plc, **23** 146

Avondale Industries, Inc., 7 39–41; **41** 40–43 (upd.)

Avonmore Foods Plc, **59** 205

Avril Alimentaire SNC, **51** 54

Avstar, **38** 72

Avtech Corp., **36** 159

AVTOVAZ Joint Stock Company, 65 59–62

AVX Corporation, 67 41–43

AW Bruna Uitgevers BV, **53** 273

AW North Carolina Inc., **48** 5

AWA *see* America West Holdings Corp.

AWA Defence Industries (AWADI) *see* British Aerospace plc.

AwardTrack, Inc., **49** 423

AWB Ltd., 56 25–27

Awesome Transportation, Inc., **22** 549

Awrey Bakeries, Inc., 56 28–30

AXA Colonia Konzern AG, III 210–12; **49** 41–45 (upd.)

AXA Financial, Inc., 63 26–27

AXA Private Equity *see* Camaïeu S.A.

AXA UK plc, **64** 173

Axcan Pharma Inc., 85 25–28

Axe-Houghton Associates Inc., **41** 208

Axel Johnson Group, I 553–55

Axel Springer Verlag AG, IV 589–91; **20** 50–53 (upd.)

Axsys Technologies, Inc., 93 65–68

Ayala Corporation, **70** 182

Ayala Plans, Inc., **58** 20

Aydin Corp., 19 30–32

Aynsley China Ltd. *see* Belleek Pottery Ltd.

Ayres, Lewis, Norris & May, Inc., **54** 184

AYS *see* Alternative Youth Services, Inc.

AZA Immobilien AG, **51** 196

Azcon Corporation, 23 34–36

Azerbaijan Airlines, 77 46–49

Azerty, **25** 13

Azienda Generale Italiana Petroli *see* ENI S.p.A.

AZL Resources, *see* Tosco Corp.

Azlan Group Limited, **74** 338

Aznar International, **14** 225

Azon Limited, *see* Illinois Tool Works Inc.

AZP Group Inc., **6** 546

Aztar Corporation, 13 66–68; **71** 41–45 (upd.)

AZZ Incorporated, 93 69–72

B

B&D *see* Barker & Dobson.

B&G Foods, Inc., 40 51–54

B&J Music Ltd. *see* Kaman Music Corp.

B & K Steel Fabrications, Inc., **26** 432

B & L Insurance, Ltd., **51** 38

B&M Baked Beans, **40** 53

B & O *see* Baltimore ;amp; Ohio Railroad.

B&Q plc *see* Kingfisher plc.

B&S *see* Binney & Smith Inc.

Beacon Roofing Supply, Inc., **75** 59–61
Bealls, *see* Stage Stores, Inc.
Beamach Group Ltd., **17** 182–83
Beaman Corporation, **16** 96
Bean Fiberglass Inc., **15** 247
Bear Automotive Service Equipment
  Company, *see* SPX Corp.
Bear Creek Corporation, 38 91–94
Bear Instruments Inc., **48** 410
Bear Stearns Companies, Inc., II
  400–01; 10 144–45 (upd.); **52** 41–44
  (upd.)
Bearings, Inc., 13 78–80
Beasley Broadcast Group, Inc., 51
  44–46
Beatrice Company, II 467–69 *see also*
  TLC Beatrice International Holdings,
  Inc.
Beatrice Foods, **21** 322–24, 507, 545; **38**
  169; **43** 355
Beatrix Mines Ltd., **62** 164
Beaulieu of America, **19** 276
Beauté Prestige International S.A. *see*
  Shiseido Company Ltd.
BeautiControl Cosmetics, Inc., 21
  49–52
Beauty Systems Group, Inc., **60** 260
Beaver Lake Concrete, Inc. *see* The
  Monarch Cement Co.
Beazer Homes USA, Inc., 17 38–41
Beazer Plc, *see* Hanson PLC.
bebe stores, inc., 31 50–52
BEC Group Inc., **22** 35; **60** 133
BEC Ventures, **57** 124–25
Bechstein, **56** 299
Bechtel Group, Inc., I 558–59; **24**
  64–67 (upd.)
Beck's North America, Inc. *see* Brauerei
  Beck & Co.
Becker Drill, Inc., **19** 247
Becker Group of Germany, **26** 231
Beckett Papers, 23 48–50
Beckley-Cardy Group *see* School Specialty,
  Inc.
Beckman Coulter, Inc., 22 74–77
Beckman Instruments, Inc., 14 52–54
BECOL *see* Belize Electric Company Ltd.
Becton, Dickinson & Company, I
  630–31; 11 34–36 (upd.); **36** 84–89
  (upd.)
Bed Bath & Beyond Inc., 13 81–83; **41**
  49–52 (upd.)
Bedcovers, Inc., **19** 304
Bee Chemicals, *see* Morton International.
Bee Discount, **26** 476
Beech Aircraft Corporation, 8 49–52 *see*
  also Raytheon Aircraft Holdings Inc.
Beech Holdings, Inc., **9** 94
Beech-Nut Nutrition Corporation, 21
  53–56; 51 47–51 (upd.)
Beecham Group PLC, *see*
  GlaxoSmithKline plc.
Beechcroft Developments Ltd., **51** 173
Beeck-Feinkost GmbH, **26** 59
ZAO BeeOnLine-Portal, **48** 419
Beer Nuts, Inc., 86 30–33
Beerman Stores, Inc., *see* Elder-Beerman
  Stores Corp.

Beers Construction Company, **38** 437
Befesa *see* Abengoa S.A.
Behr GmbH & Co. KG, 72 22–25
Behring Diagnostics *see* Dade Behring
  Holdings Inc.
Behringwerke AG, **14** 255; **50** 249
BEI Technologies, Inc., 65 74–76
Beiersdorf AG, 29 49–53
Beijing Contact Lens Ltd., **25** 56
Beijing Dentsu, **16** 168
Beijing-Landauer, Ltd., **51** 210
Beijing ZF North Drive Systems Technical
  Co. Ltd., **48** 450
Beirao, Pinto, Silva and Co. *see* Banco
  Espírito Santo e Comercial de Lisboa
  S.A.
Bejam Group PLC *see* The Big Food
  Group plc.
Bekaert S.A./N.V., 90 53–57
Bekins Company, 15 48–50
Bel *see* Fromageries Bel.
Bel Air Markets, *see* Raley's Inc.
Bel Fuse, Inc., 53 59–62
Bel/Kaukauna USA, 76 46–48
Belco Oil & Gas Corp., 40 63–65
Belcom Holding AG, **53** 323, 325
Belden CDT Inc., 19 43–45; **76** 49–52
  (upd.)
Beldis, **23** 219
Beldoch Industries Corp., *see* Donnkenny,
  Inc.
Belgacom, 6 302–04
Belgian Rapid Access to Information
  Network Services, **6** 304
Belgo Group plc, **31** 41
Belize Electric Company Limited, **47** 137
Belk, Inc., V 12–13; **19** 46–48 (upd.);
  72 26–29 (upd.)
Bell and Howell Company, 9 61–64; **29**
  54–58 (upd.)
Bell Atlantic Corporation, V 272–74; **25**
  58–62 (upd.) *see also* Verizon
  Communications.
Bell Canada Enterprises Inc. *see* BCE, Inc.
Bell Canada International, Inc., 6
  305–08
Bell Communications Research *see*
  Telcordia Technologies, Inc.
Bell Fibre Products, **12** 377
Bell Helicopter Textron Inc., 46 64–67
Bell Helmets Inc., **22** 458
Bell Industries, Inc., 47 40–43
Bell Laboratories *see* AT&T Bell
  Laboratories, Inc.
Bell Microproducts Inc., 69 63–65
Bell Mountain Partnership, Ltd., **15** 26
Bell-Northern Research, Ltd. *see* BCE Inc.
Bell Resources, *see* TPG NV.
Bell Sports Corporation, 16 51–53; **44**
  51–54 (upd.)
Bellcore *see* Telcordia Technologies, Inc.
Belleek Pottery Ltd., 71 50–53
Belleville Shoe Manufacturing
  Company, 92 17–20
BellSouth Corporation, V 276–78; **29**
  59–62 (upd.) *see also* AT&T Corp.
Bellway Plc, 45 37–39
Belmin Systems, *see* AT&T Istel Ltd.

Belo Corporation *see* A.H. Belo
  Corporation
Beloit Corporation, 14 55–57 *see also*
  Metso Corp.
Beloit Tool Company *see* Regal-Beloit
  Corp.
Belron International Ltd., 76 53–56
Belvedere S.A., 93 77–81
Bemis Company, Inc., 8 53–55; **91**
  53–60 (upd.)
Ben & Jerry's Homemade, Inc., 10
  146–48; **35** 58–62 (upd.); **80** 22–28
  (upd.)
Ben Bridge Jeweler, Inc., 60 52–54
Ben E. Keith Company, 76 57–59
Ben Franklin Retail Stores, Inc. *see*
  FoxMeyer Health Corp.
Ben Myerson Candy Co., Inc., **26** 468
Benair Freight International Limited *see*
  Gulf Agency Company
Benchmark Capital, 49 50–52
Benchmark Electronics, Inc., 40 66–69
Benchmark Tape Systems Ltd, **62** 293
Benckiser Group, **37** 269
Benckiser N.V. *see* Reckitt Benckiser plc.
Benderson Development Company, **69**
  120
Bendick's of Mayfair *see* August Storck
  KG.
Bendix Corporation, I 141–43
Beneficial Corporation, 8 56–58
Benefits Technologies, Inc., **52** 382
Benelli Arms S.p.A., **39** 151
Benesse Corporation, 76 60–62
Bénéteau SA, 55 54–56
Benetton Group S.p.A., 10 149–52; **67**
  47–51 (upd.)
Benfield Greig Group plc, 53 63–65
Benguet Corporation, 58 21–24
Benihana, Inc., 18 56–59; **76** 63–66
  (upd.)
Benjamin Moore and Co., 13 84–87; **38**
  95–99 (upd.)
Benjamin Sheridan Corporation, **62** 82
Benlee, Inc., **51** 237
Benn Bros. plc, **IV** 687
Bennett's Smokehouse and Saloon, **29**
  201
Bennigan's, *see* Metromedia Co.
Benpres Holdings, **56** 214
BenQ Corporation, 67 52–54
Bensdorp, **29** 47
Benson & Hedges, Ltd. *see* Gallaher Ltd.
Bentalls, **37** 6, 8
Bentex Holding S.A., **48** 209
Bentley Laboratories, **22** 360
Bentley Mills, Inc., *see* Interface, Inc.
Bentley Motor Ltd., **21** 435
Bentley's Luggage Corp., **58** 370
Bentoel, PT, **62** 97
Benton International, Inc., **29** 376
Benton Oil and Gas Company, 47
  44–46
Bentwood Ltd., **62** 342
Bercy Management *see* Elior SA.
Beresford International plc, **27** 159
Beretta *see* Fabbrica D' Armi Pietro
  Beretta S.p.A.

Big V Supermarkets, Inc., **25** 66–68
Big Y Foods, Inc., **53** 66–68
BigBen Interactive S.A., **72** 33–35
BigBurger Ltda., **74** 48
Bigelow-Sanford, Inc., **31** 199
BII *see* Banana Importers of Ireland.
Bike Athletics, **23** 449
BIL *see* Brierley Investments.
Bilfinger & Berger AG, **I** 560–61; **55** 60–63 (upd.)
Bill & Melinda Gates Foundation, **41** 53–55
Bill Acceptance Corporation Ltd., **48** 427
Bill Barrett Corporation, **71** 54–56
Bill Blass Ltd., **32** 78–80
Billabong International Ltd., **44** 55–58
Billing Concepts, Inc., **26** 35–38; **72** 36–39 (upd.)
Billiton International, **IV** 532; **22** 237
BillPoint Inc., **58** 266
Bilsom, **40** 96–97
Bilt-Rite Chase-Pitkin, Inc., **41** 416
Biltwell Company, *see* Hartmarx Corp.
Bimar Foods Inc., **19** 192
Bimbo, *see* Grupo Industrial Bimbo.
Bimbo Bakeries USA, **29** 341
Bimbo, S.A., **36** 162, 164
Bin Zayed Group, **55** 54, 56
Binderline Development, Inc., *see* Defiance, Inc.
Bindley Western Industries, Inc., **9** 67–69 *see also* Cardinal Health, Inc.
The Bing Group, **60** 55–58
Bingham Dana LLP, **43** 68–71
Bingo Express Co., Ltd., **64** 290
Bingo King *see* Stuart Entertainment Inc.
Binks Sames Corporation, **21** 63–66
Binney & Smith Inc., **25** 69–72
Binnie & Partners, **22** 89
Binter Canarias *see* Iberia.
Bio Balance Corporation *see* New York Health Care, Inc.
Bio-Clinic, **11** 486–87
Bio-Dental Technologies Corporation, **46** 466
Bio Foods Inc. *see* Balance Bar Co.
Bio-Rad Laboratories, Inc., **93** 82–86
Bio Synthetics, Inc., **21** 386
Biodevelopment Laboratories, Inc., **35** 47
Biogemma, **74** 139
Biogen Idec Inc., **14** 58–60; **36** 90–93 (upd.); **71** 57–59 (upd.)
Bioindustrias, *see* Valores Industriales S.A.
bioKinetics, **64** 18
Biokyowa, *see* Kyowa Hakko Kogyo Co., Ltd.
Biolase Technology, Inc., **87** 55–58
bioMérieux S.A., **75** 69–71
Biomet, Inc., **10** 156–58; **93** 87–94 (upd.)
Bionaire, Inc., **19** 360
BioScience Communications, **62** 115
Bioscot, Ltd., **63** 351
Biosite Incorporated, **73** 60–62
Biotage, Inc. *see* Dynax.
Biovail Corporation, **47** 54–56
BioWare Corporation, **81** 50–53
Biralo Pty Ltd., **48** 427

Bird Corporation, **19** 56–58
Birdair, Inc., **35** 99–100
Birds Eye Foods, Inc., **69** 66–72 (upd.)
Birdsall, Inc. *see* Nicor Inc.
Bireley's, **22** 515
Birkenstock Footprint Sandals, Inc., **12** 33–35; **42** 37–40 (upd.)
Birmingham & Midland Bank *see* Midland Bank plc.
Birmingham Steel Corporation, **13** 97–98; **40** 70–73 (upd.) *see also* Nucor Corporation
Birra Peroni S.p.A., **59** 357
Birse Group PLC, **77** 54–58
Birthdays, **70** 20–22
Biscayne Bank *see* Banco Espírito Santo e Comercial de Lisboa S.A.
Bishop & Co., *see* First Hawaiian, Inc.
BISSELL, Inc., **9** 70–72; **30** 75–78 (upd.)
Bisset Gold Mining Company, **63** 182–83
The BISYS Group, Inc., **73** 63–65
Bit LLC, **59** 303
Bit Software, Inc., **12** 62
Bitco Corporation, **58** 258
Bits & Pieces, **26** 439
Bitumen & Oil Refineries (Australia) Ltd. *see* Boral Ltd.
Bituminous Casualty Corporation, **58** 258–59
Bivac International, **55** 79
BIW *see* Bath Iron Works.
BIZ Enterprises, **23** 390
Bizarro e Milho, Lda., **64** 91
BizBuyer.com, **39** 25
Bizimgaz Ticaret Ve Sanayi A.S., **55** 346
BJ Services Company, **25** 73–75
BJ's Pizza & Grill, **44** 85
BJ's Restaurant & Brewhouse, **44** 85
BJ's Wholesale Club, *see* Waban Inc.
BJK&E *see* Bozell Worldwide Inc.
BK Tag, **28** 157
BK Vision AG, **52** 357
BL Systems *see* AT&T Istel Ltd.
BL Universal PLC, **47** 168
The Black & Decker Corporation, **III** 435–37; **20** 64–68 (upd.); **67** 65–70 (upd.)
Black & Veatch LLP, **22** 87–90
Black Box Corporation, **20** 69–71
Black Clawson Company, *see* Thermo Fibertek, Inc.
Black Diamond Equipment, Ltd., **62** 34–37
Black Entertainment Television *see* BET Holdings, Inc.
Black Hills Corporation, **20** 72–74
Black Horse Agencies, *see* Lloyds TSB Group plc.
Black Pearl Software, Inc., **39** 396
Blackbaud, Inc., **85** 34–37
BlackBerry *see* Research in Motion Ltd.
Blackboard Inc., **89** 105–10
Blackfoot Telecommunications Group, **60** 59–62
Blackhawk Holdings, Inc. *see* PW Eagle Inc.
BlackRock, Inc., **79** 66–69

Blacks Leisure Group plc, **39** 58–60
Blackstone Dredging Partners LP, **69** 197
The Blackstone Group, L.P., **IV** 718; **11** 177, 179; **22** 416; **26** 408; **37** 309, 311; **61** 208; **69** 101, 103; **75** 378
Blackwater USA, **76** 70–73
Blackwell Publishing (Holdings) Ltd., **78** 34–37
Blaine Construction Company *see* The Yates Companies, Inc.
Blair Corporation, **25** 76–78; **31** 53–55
Blakeman's Floor Care Parts & Equipment *see* Tacony Corp.
Blandburgh Ltd., **63** 77
Blanes, S.A. de C.V., **34** 197
BLD Europe, **16** 168
Blendax, *see* The Procter & Gamble Company
Blessings Corp., **19** 59–61
Blimpie International, Inc., **15** 55–57; **49** 60–64 (upd.)
Bliss Manufacturing Co., *see* HMI Industries, Inc.
Blizzard Entertainment, **78** 38–42
Bloch & Guggenheimer, Inc., **40** 51–52
Block Communications, Inc., **81** 54–58
Block Drug Company, Inc., **8** 62–64; **27** 67–70 (upd.) *see also* GlaxoSmithKline plc.
Block Management, **29** 226
Block Medical, Inc., *see* Hillenbrand Industries, Inc.
Blockbuster Inc., **9** 73–75; **31** 56–60 (upd.); **76** 74–78 (upd.)
Blodgett Holdings, Inc., **61** 34–37 (upd.)
Blohm Maschinenbau GmbH, **60** 193
Blokker Holding B.V., **84** 21–24
Blonder Tongue Laboratories, Inc., **48** 52–55
Bloomberg L.P., **21** 67–71
Bloomingdale's Inc., **12** 36–38
Blount International, Inc., **12** 39–41; **48** 56–60 (upd.)
Blow-ko Ltd., **60** 372
BLP Group Companies *see* Boron, LePore & Associates, Inc.
BLT Ventures, **25** 270
Blue, **62** 115
Blue Arrow PLC, **9** 327; **30** 300
Blue Bell Creameries L.P., **30** 79–81
Blue Bell Mattress Company, **58** 63
Blue Bird Corporation, **35** 63–66
Blue Bunny Ice Cream *see* Wells' Dairy, Inc.
Blue Byte, **41** 409
Blue Chip Stamps, **30** 412
Blue Circle Industries PLC, **III** 669–71 *see also* Lafarge Cement UK.
Blue Coat Systems, Inc., **83** 42–45
Blue Cross and Blue Shield Association, **10** 159–61
Blue Cross and Blue Shield Mutual of Northern Ohio, **12** 176
Blue Cross and Blue Shield of Greater New York, *see* Empire Blue Cross & Blue Shield.

Central Electric and Telephone Company, Inc. *see* Centel Corp.

Central Elevator Co., **19** 111

Central European Distribution Corporation, 75 90–92

Central European Media Enterprises Ltd., 61 56–59

Central Florida Investments, Inc., 93 137–40

Central Florida Press, **23** 101

Central Freight Lines, Inc., **53** 249

Central Garden & Pet Company, 23 108–10; **58** 57–60 (upd.)

Central Hudson Gas And Electricity Corporation, 6 458–60

Central Illinois Public Service Company *see* CIPSCO Inc.

Central Independent Television, 7 78–80; **23** 111–14 (upd.)

Central Indiana Power Company, **6** 556

Central Investment Corp., **12** 184

Central Japan Railway Company, 43 103–06

Central Maine Power, 6 461–64

Central Mining and Investment Corp., **IV** 79, 95–96, 524, 565

Central Newspapers, Inc., 10 207–09 *see also* Gannett Company, Inc.

Central Ohio Mobile Power Wash *see* MPW Industrial Services, Inc.

Central Parking Corporation, 18 103–05

Central Plains Steel Company *see* Reliance Steel & Aluminum Co.

Central Research Laboratories, **22** 194

Central Soya Company, Inc., 7 81–83

Central Sprinkler Corporation, 29 97–99

Central Supply Company *see* Granite Rock Co.

Central Telephone & Utilities Corporation *see* Centel Corp.

Central Trust Co., **11** 110

Central Vermont Public Service Corporation, 54 53–56

Central West Public Service Company *see* Centel Corp.

Centrale Verzorgingsdienst Cotrans N.V., **12** 443

Centre de Diffusion de l'Édition *see* Éditions Gallimard.

Centre Investissements et Loisirs, **48** 107

Centre Partners Management LLC, **70** 337

Centrepoint Properties Ltd., **54** 116–17

Centric Group, **69** 153

Centrica plc, 29 100–05 (upd.)

Centron DPL Company, Inc., **25** 171

Centros Commerciales Pryca, **23** 246, 248

Centrum Communications Inc., **11** 520

Centuri Corporation, 54 57–59

Centurion Brick, **14** 250

Century Aluminum Company, 52 71–74

Century Bakery *see* Dawn Food Products, Inc.

Century Brewing Company *see* Rainier Brewing Co.

Century Business Services, Inc., 52 75–78

Century Casinos, Inc., 53 90–93

Century Communications Corp., 10 210–12

Century Development *see* Camden Property Trust.

Century Manufacturing Company, **26** 363

Century Papers, Inc., *see* National Sanitary Supply Co.

Century Supply Corporation, **39** 346

Century Telephone Enterprises, Inc., 9 105–07; **54** 60–63 (upd.)

Century Theatres, Inc., 31 99–101

Century 21 Real Estate, **21** 97; **59** 345; **61** 267

Century Union (Shanghai) Foods Co., **75** 372

Century Wood Door Ltd., **63** 268

CenturyTel *see* Century Telephone Enterprises, Inc.

Cenveo Inc., 71 100–04 (upd.)

CEP Industrie, **55** 79

CEPA *see* Consolidated Electric Power Asia.

CEPAM, **21** 438

CEPCO *see* Chugoku Electric Power Company Inc.

Cephalon, Inc., 45 93–96

Cepheid, 77 93–96

CEPSA *see* Compañia Española de Petroleos S.A.

Cera Trading Co. *see* Toto Ltd.

Ceradyne, Inc., 65 100–02

Ceramconsult AG, **51** 196

Ceramesh, **11** 361

Ceramic Tile International, Inc., **53** 176

Cerberus Capital Management LP, **73** 289

Cerberus Group, **69** 261

Cerberus Limited *see* Elektrowatt AG.

Cerco S.A., **62** 51

Cereal and Fruit Products, **32** 519

Cereal Industries, *see* Associated British Foods plc.

Cereal Partners Worldwide, **10** 324; **36** 234, 237; **50** 295

Cereol SA, **36** 185; **62** 51

CERES, **55** 178

Cerestar, *see* Cargill, Inc.

Ceresucre, **36** 185

Ceridian Corporation, **38** 58; **71** 262 *see also* Control Data Systems, Inc.

Cerner Corporation, 16 92–94

Cerprobe Corporation *see* Kulicke and Soffa Industries, Inc.

Cerro de Pasco Corp., **40** 411

Cerro E.M.S. Limited *see* The Marmon Group, Inc.

CertainTeed Corporation, 35 86–89

Certegy, Inc., 63 100–03

Certified Grocers of Florida, Inc., **15** 139

Cerulean, **51** 249, 251

Cerus, **23** 492

Cerveceria Cuauhtémoc Moctezuma, **25** 281

Cerveceria Moctezuma, **23** 170

Cerveceria Polar, I 230–31 *see also* Empresas Polar SA.

Cerveceria y Malteria Quilmes S.A.I.C.A. y G., **70** 62

Ceska Nezavisla Televizni Spolecnost, **61** 56

Ceská Sporitelna a.s. *see* Erste Bank der Osterreichischen Sparkassen AG

Ceské aerolinie, a.s., 66 49–51

Cesky Telecom, a.s., 64 70–73

Cessna Aircraft Company, 8 90–93; **27** 97–101 (upd.)

CET *see* Compagnie Européenne de Télésecurité.

CET 21, **61** 56, 58

Cetelem S.A., 21 99–102

Cetus Corp., **41** 201; **50** 193

CeWe Color Holding AG, 76 85–88

CFC Investment Company, **16** 104

CFM *see* Compagnie Française du Méthane.

CFP *see* Compagnie Française des Pétroles.

CFR Corporation *see* Tacony Corp.

CG&E *see* Cincinnati Gas & Electric Co.

CGE *see* Alcatel Alsthom.

CGIP, **57** 380

CGM *see* Compagnie Générale Maritime.

CGR Management Corporation, **51** 85

CH Mortgage Company I Ltd., **58** 84

Chace Precision Metals, Inc., **29** 460–61

Chaco Energy Corporation *see* Texas Utilities Co.

Chadbourne & Parke, 36 109–12

Chadwick's of Boston, Ltd., 29 106–08

Chalk Line Productions, Inc., **58** 124

Chalk's Ocean Airways *see* Flying Boat, Inc.

Challenge Corp. Ltd. *see* Fletcher Challenge Ltd.

Challenger Minerals Inc., *see* Global Marine Inc.

Challenger Series, **55** 312

Challice, **71** 238

The Chalone Wine Group, Ltd., 36 113–16

Chamberlain Group, Ltd., **23** 82

Chambon Offshore International, **60** 149

Chambosse Brokerage Co., **29** 33

Champ Industries, Inc., **22** 15

Champalimaud, **36** 63

Champcork–Rolhas de Champanhe SA, **48** 118

Champion Enterprises, Inc., 17 81–84

Champion Forge Co., **41** 366

Champion Industries, Inc., 28 74–76

Champion International Corporation, IV 263–65; **20** 127–30 (upd.) *see also* International Paper Co.

Champion Modular Restaurant Company, Inc. *see* Checkers Drive-Up Restaurants Inc.

Champion Productions, **56** 74

Championship Auto Racing Teams, Inc., 37 73–75

Champps Americana, *see* Unique Casual Restaurants, Inc.

Champs Sports *see* Venator Group Inc.

Chancellor Beacon Academies, Inc., 53 94–97

Civil & Civic Contractors *see* Lend Lease
Corporation Ltd.
Civil Aviation Administration of China,
31 102; **33** 98
CJ Banks *see* Christopher & Banks Corp.
CJ Corporation, **62** 68–70
CJSC Transmash Holding, **93** 446–49
CKE Restaurants, Inc., **19** 89–93; **46**
94–99 (upd.)
CKS Group Inc. *see* marchFIRST, Inc.
CKS Inc., **23** 479
Clabir Corp., **12** 199
Claire's Stores, Inc., **17** 101–03
Clairol, *see* Procter & Gamble Co.
CLAM Petroleum, *see* Louisiana Land and
Exploration Co.
Clancy-Paul Inc., *see* InaCom Corp.
Clapp-Eastham Company *see* GenRad,
Inc.
Clara Candy, **15** 65
CLARCOR Inc., **17** 104–07; **61** 63–67
(upd.)
Clare Rose Inc., **68** 83–85
Claremont Technology Group Inc., **31**
131
Clariden Bank, **21** 146–47; **59** 142, 144
Clarify Corp., **38** 431
Clarion Company Ltd., **64** 77–79
Clark & McKenney Hardware Co. *see*
Clarcor Inc.
Clark Bar Candy Company, **53** 304
The Clark Construction Group, Inc., **8**
112–13
Clark, Dietz & Associates-Engineers *see*
CRSS Inc.
Clark Equipment Company, **8** 114–16
Clark Filter, Inc., *see* CLARCOR Inc.
Clark Retail Enterprises Inc., **37** 311
Clark-Schwebel, Inc., **28** 195
Clarkins, Inc., **16** 35–36
Clarksburg Casket Co., **56** 23
CLASSA *see* Compañia de Líneas Aéreas
Subvencionadas S.A.
Classic FM plc, **39** 198–200
Classic Vacation Group, Inc., **46** 100–03
Clause/Tézier, **70** 346; **74** 139
Claxson Interactive Group, **54** 74
Clayco Construction Company, **41**
225–26
Clayton Brown Holding Company, **15**
232
Clayton Dubilier & Rice Inc., **25** 501; **29**
408; **40** 370; **49** 22
Clayton Homes Incorporated, **13**
154–55; **54** 76–79 (upd.)
Clayton-Marcus Co., *see* LADD Furniture,
Inc.
Clayton/National Courier Systems, Inc.,
see Consolidated Delivery & Logistics,
Inc.
Clayton Williams Energy, Inc., **87**
113–116
CLE *see* Compagnie Laitière Européenne.
Clean Harbors, Inc., **73** 88–91
Cleancoal Terminal, *see* Westmoreland
Coal Co.
Clear Channel Communications, Inc.,
23 130–32 *see also* Live Nation, Inc.

Clear Shield National Inc., *see* Envirodyne
Industries, Inc.
Clearly Canadian Beverage Corporation,
48 94–97
Clearwire, Inc., **69** 95–97
Cleary, Gottlieb, Steen & Hamilton, **35**
106–09
Cleco Corporation, **37** 88–91
The Clemens Family Corporation, **93**
156–59
Clement Pappas & Company, Inc., **92**
52–55
Clemente Capital Inc., **25** 542
Cleo Inc., **35** 131 *see also* Gibson
Greetings, Inc.
Le Clerc, **21** 225–26
Clessidra SGR, **76** 326
Cleve-Co Jig Boring Co., **23** 82
Cleveland-Cliffs Inc., **13** 156–58; **62**
71–75 (upd.)
Cleveland Cotton Products Co., **37** 393
Cleveland Electric Illuminating Company
see Centerior Energy Theodor.
Cleveland Fabric Centers, Inc. *see*
Fabri-Centers of America Inc.
Cleveland Grinding Machine Co., **23** 82
**Cleveland Indians Baseball Company,
Inc.**, **37** 92–94
Cleveland Iron Mining Company *see*
Cleveland-Cliffs Inc.
Cleveland Precision Instruments, Inc., **23**
82
Cleveland Range Ltd. *see* Enodis plc.
Cleveland Twist Drill Company *see*
Acme-Cleveland Corp.
Click Messenger Service, Inc., *see*
Consolidated Delivery & Logistics, Inc.
Click Trips, Inc., **74** 169
Click Wine Group, **68** 86–88
ClickAgents.com, Inc., **49** 433
Clicks Stores *see* New Clicks Holdings
Ltd.
ClientLogic Corporation *see* Onex Corp.
Clif Bar Inc., **50** 141–43
Clifford & Wills, *see* J. Crew Group Inc.
Clifford Chance LLP, **38** 136–39
Cliffs Corporation, *see* Cleveland-Cliffs
Inc.
Climaveneta Deutschland GmbH *see*
De'Longhi S.p.A.
Clinical Partners, Inc., **26** 74
Clinical Pathology Facility, Inc., **26** 391
Clinique Laboratories, Inc., **30** 191
Clinton Cards plc, **39** 86–88
Clipper Group, **12** 439
Clipper, Inc., **IV** 597
La Cloche d'Or, **25** 85
Cloetta Fazer AB, **70** 58–60
Clopay Corp., **34** 195
The Clorox Company, **III** 20–22; **22**
145–48 (upd.); **81** 83–90 (upd.)
Close Brothers Group plc, **39** 89–92
Clothesline Corporation, **60** 65
The Clothestime, Inc., **20** 141–44
Clougherty Packing Company, **72**
72–74
Clover Club, **44** 348
Clovis Water Co., **6** 580

Clow Water Systems Co., **55** 266
CLRP *see* City of London Real Property
Company Ltd.
CLSI Inc., **15** 372; **43** 182
Club Corporation of America, **26** 27
Club de Hockey Canadien Inc., **26** 305
Club Méditerranée S.A., **6** 206–08; **21**
125–28 (upd.); **91** 121–27 (upd.)
Club Monaco Inc., **62** 284
ClubCorp, Inc., **33** 101–04
Cluett Corporation, *see* Celebrity, Inc.
Cluster Consulting, **51** 98
Clydesdale Group, **19** 390
CM&P *see* Cresap, McCormick and
Paget.
CMAC Investment Corporation *see*
Radian Group Inc.
CMC *see* Commercial Metals Co.
CME *see* Campbell-Mithun-Esty, Inc.;
Central European Media Enterprises
Ltd.; Chicago Mercantile Exchange Inc.
CMG Worldwide, Inc., **89** 157–60
CMGI, Inc., **76** 99–101
CMI International, Inc., *see* Hayes
Lemmerz International, Inc.
CMIH *see* China Merchants International
Holdings Co., Ltd.
CML Group, Inc., **10** 215–18
CMO *see* Chi Mei Optoelectronics Corp.
CMP Media Inc., **26** 76–80
CMP Properties Inc., **15** 122
CMS Energy Corporation, **V** 577–79;
14 114–16 (upd.)
CMS Healthcare, **29** 412
CN *see* Canadian National Railway Co.
CNA Financial Corporation, **III**
228–32; **38** 140–46 (upd.)
CNB Bancshares Inc., **31** 207
CNBC, Inc., **28** 298
CNC Holding Corp. *see* Cole National
Corp.
CNCA *see* Caisse National de Crédit
Agricole.
CNEP *see* Comptoir National d'Escompte
de Paris.
CNET Networks, Inc., **47** 77–80
CNF Transportation *see* Consolidated
Freightways, Inc.
CNG *see* Consolidated Natural Gas Co.
CNH Global N.V., **38** 147–56 (upd.)
CNI *see* Community Networks Inc.
CNN *see* Cable News Network.
CNP *see* Compagnie Nationale à
Portefeuille.
CNPC *see* China National Petroleum
Corp.
CNS, Inc., **20** 145–47 *see also*
GlaxoSmithKline plc.
CNTS *see* Ceska Nezavisla Televizni
Spolecnost.
Co-Counsel, Inc., **29** 364
Co-Op Blue Square Consumer
Cooperative Society, **41** 56–58
Co-operative Group (CWS) Ltd., **51**
86–89
Co-operative Insurance Society Ltd., **51**
89
Coach and Car Equipment Corp., **41** 369

Comtel Electronics, Inc., *see* Palomar Medical Technologies, Inc.

Comunicaciones Avanzados, S.A. de C.V., **39** 195

Comverse Technology, Inc., 15 124–26; 43 115–18 (upd.)

Comviq GSM AB, **26** 331–33

Con Ed *see* Consolidated Edison, Inc.

ConAgra Foods, Inc., II 493–95; 12 80–82 (upd.); 42 90–94 (upd.); 85 61–68 (upd.)

Conair Corporation, 17 108–10; 69 104–08 (upd.)

Conaprole *see* Cooperativa Nacional de Productores de Leche S.A. (Conaprole).

Concentra Inc., 71 117–19

Concept, Inc., **23** 154

Concepts Direct, Inc., 39 93–96

Concepts in Community Living, Inc., **43** 46

Concert Communications Company, **15** 69; **27** 304–05; **49** 72

Concesiones de Infraestructuras de Transportes, S.A., **40** 217

Concha y Toro *see* Viña Concha y Toro S.A.

Concord Camera Corporation, 41 104–07

Concord EFS, Inc., 52 86–88

Concord Fabrics, Inc., 16 124–26

Concord Leasing, Inc., **51** 108

Concord Watch Company, S.A., **28** 291

Concorde Acceptance Corporation, **64** 20–21

Concorde Hotels & Resorts, *see* Société du Louvre.

Concrete Enterprises, Inc., **72** 233

Concrete Safety Systems, Inc., **56** 332

Concretos Apasco, S.A. de C.V., **51** 28–29

Concurrent Computer Corporation, 75 106–08

Condé Nast Publications, Inc., 13 177–81; 59 131–34 (upd.)

CONDEA Vista Company, **61** 113

Condor Systems Inc., **15** 530

Cone Communications, **25** 258

Cone Mills LLC, 8 120–22; 67 123–27 (upd.)

Conexant Systems, Inc., 36 121–25

Confecciones Cuscatlecas, S.A. de C.V., **64** 142

Confederation Freezers, **21** 501

ConferencePlus, Inc., **57** 408–09

Confiseriefabrik Richterich & Co. Laufen *see* Ricola Ltd.

Confluence Holdings Corporation, 76 118–20

Congas Engineering Canada Ltd., **6** 478

Congoleum Corp., 18 116–19

Congress Financial Corp., **19** 108

Congressional Information Services *see* Reed Elsevier.

Conic, *see* Loral Corp.

Conifer Records Ltd., **52** 429

Coniston Partners, **6** 130

CONMED Corporation, 87 117–120

Conn-Selmer, Inc., 55 111–14

Conn's, Inc., 67 128–30

Connect Group Corporation, **28** 242

Connecticut General Corporation *see* CIGNA Corp.

Connecticut Health Enterprises Network, *see* PHP Healthcare Corp.

Connecticut Light and Power Co., 13 182–84

Connecticut Mutual Life Insurance Company, III 236–38

Connecticut Telephone Company *see* Southern New England Telecommunications Corp.

Connecticut Yankee Atomic Power Company, **21** 513

The Connection Group, Inc., **26** 257

Connective Therapeutics, Inc. *see* Connetics Corp.

Connectix Corporation, **28** 245

The Connell Company, 29 129–31

Conner Corp., **15** 327

Conner Peripherals, Inc., 6 230–32

Connetics Corporation, 70 64–66

Connie Lee *see* College Construction Loan Insurance Assoc.

Connoisseur Communications, **37** 104

Connolly Data Systems, **11** 66

Connolly Tool and Machine Company, **21** 215

Connors Bros. Income Fund, **64** 61 *see also* George Weston Ltd.

Connors Steel Co., **15** 116

ConocoPhillips, IV 399–402; 16 127–32 (upd.); 63 104–15 (upd.)

ConQuest Telecommunication Services Inc., **16** 319

Conquistador Films, **25** 270

Conrad Industries, Inc., 58 68–70

Conrad International Corporation, **62** 179

Conrail Inc. *see* Consolidated Rail Corp.

Conrock Co., *see* CalMat Co.

Conseco Inc., 10 246–48; 33 108–12 (upd.)

Conseo GmbH, **68** 289

Conshu Holdings, **24** 450

Conso International Corporation, 29 132–34

Consodata S.A., **47** 345, 347

CONSOL Energy Inc., 59 135–37

Consolidated Analysis Centers, Inc. *see* CACI International Inc.

Consolidated Asset Management Company, Inc., **25** 204

Consolidated-Bathurst Inc., **26** 445

Consolidated Cigar Holdings, Inc., **15** 137–38; **28** 247

Consolidated Citrus Limited Partnership, **60** 189

Consolidated Container Company L.L.C., **73** 106

Consolidated Conversion Co., *see* Cubic Corp.

Consolidated Delivery & Logistics, Inc., 24 125–28 *see also* Velocity Express Corp.

Consolidated Edison, Inc., V 586–89; 45 116–20 (upd.)

Consolidated Electric Power Asia, **38** 448

Consolidated Electric Supply Inc., **15** 385

Consolidated Foods Corp., **29** 132

Consolidated Freightways Corporation, V 432–34; 21 136–39 (upd.); 48 109–13 (upd.)

Consolidated Gas Company *see* Baltimore Gas and Electric Co.

Consolidated Graphics, Inc., 70 67–69

Consolidated International, **50** 98

Consolidated Natural Gas Company, V 590–91; 19 100–02 (upd.) *see also* Dominion Resources, Inc.

Consolidated Papers, Inc., 8 123–25; 36 126–30 (upd.)

Consolidated Plantations Berhad, **36** 434–35

Consolidated Power & Light Company, **6** 580

Consolidated Products, Inc., 14 130–32

Consolidated Rail Corporation, V 435–37

Consolidated Restaurant Cos. *see* Landry's Restaurants, Inc.

Consolidated Specialty Restaurants, Inc., *see* Consolidated Products Inc.

Consolidated Stores Corp., **29** 311; **35** 254; **50** 98

Consolidated Theaters, Inc., **14** 87

Consolidated Tire Company, **20** 258

Consolidated TVX Mining Corporation, **61** 290

Consolidation Services, **44** 10, 13

Consorcio ARA, S.A. de C.V., 79 113–16

Consorcio Aviacsa, S.A. de C.V., 85 69–72

Consorcio G Grupo Dina, S.A. de C.V., 36 131–33

Consorcio Siderurgica Amazonia Ltd. *see* Siderar S.A.I.C.

Consortium, **34** 373

Consortium de Realisation, **35** 329

Consortium De Realization SAS, **23** 392

Constar International Inc., 64 85–88

Constellation Brands, Inc., 68 95–100 (upd.)

Constellation Enterprises Inc., **25** 46

Constitution Insurance Company, **51** 143

Construcciones Aeronáuticas SA, **7** 9 *see also* European Aeronautic Defence and Space Company EADS N.V.

Construction Developers Inc., **68** 114

Construction DJL Inc., **23** 332–33

Constructora CAMSA, C.A., **56** 383

Constructora y Administradora Uno S.A., **72** 269

Construtora Norberto Odebrecht S.A. *see* Odebrecht S.A.

Consul GmbH, **51** 58

Consumer Products Company, **30** 39

Consumer Value Stores *see* CVS Corp.

ConsumerNet, **49** 422

Consumers Cooperative Association *see* Farmland Industries, Inc.

Consumers Distributing Co. Ltd., *see* Provigo Inc.

Consumers Electric Light and Power, **6** 582

Elior SA, 49 126–28

Elisra Defense Group, 68 222, 224

Elite Acquisitions, Inc., 65 150

Elizabeth Arden, Inc., 8 166–68; 40 169–72 (upd.)

Eljer Industries, Inc., 24 150–52

Elkay Manufacturing Company, 73 134–36

ElkCorp, 52 103–05

Elkjop ASA, 49 113

Ellanef Manufacturing Corp., 48 274

Ellen Tracy, Inc., 55 136–38

Ellerbe Becket, 41 142–45

Ellesse International S.p.A. *see* Reebok International Ltd.

Ellett Brothers, Inc., 17 154–56

Ellington Recycling Center, 12 377

Elliot Group Limited, 45 139–40

Elliott & Co. (Henley) Ltd. *see* Gibbs and Dandy plc.

Elliott Bay Design Group, 22 276

Ellipse Programmes, 48 164–65

Ellis & Everard, 41 341

Ellis-Don Ltd., 38 481

Ellis Park Race Course, 29 118

Ellisco Co., 35 130

Elma Electronic AG, 83 127-130

Elmer Candy Corporation, 88 79–82

Elmer's Products, Inc. *see* Borden, Inc.

Elmer's Restaurants, Inc., 42 128–30

Elmo Semiconductor Corp., 48 246

Elna USA *see* Tacony Corp.

Elphinstone, 21 501

Elpida Memory, Inc., 83 131-134

Elrick Industries, Inc., *see* Myers Industries, Inc.

Elron Industries, 75 304–05

Elscint Ltd., 20 202–05

Elsevier NV, IV 610–11 *see also* Reed Elsevier.

Elsinore Corporation, 48 148–51

Eltra Corporation, *see* AlliedSignal Inc.

Eltron International Inc., 53 374

Elvirasminde A/S *see* August Storck KG.

Elvis Presley Enterprises, Inc., 61 88–90

ELYO, 42 387–88

eMachines, Inc., 63 155

Email Ltd., 62 331

EMAP plc, 35 164–66

Embankment Trust Ltd., IV 659

EMBARQ Corporation, 83 135-138

Embassy Suites, *see* Promus Companies, Inc.

Embedded Support Tools Corporation, 37 419, 421

Embers America Restaurants, 30 180–82

Embotelladora Andina S.A., 71 139–41

Embotelladora Central, S.A., 47 291

Embraer *see* Empresa Brasileira de Aeronáutica S.A.

Embraer-Liebherr Equipamentos do Brasil S.A., 64 241

Embrex, Inc., 72 106–08

EMC Corporation, 12 147–49; 46 162–66 (upd.)

EMC Technology Services, Inc., 30 469

EMCOR Group Inc., 60 118–21

EMD Holding, Inc., 64 205

EMD Technologies, 27 21; 40 67

Emerson, 46 167–71 (upd.)

Emerson Electric Co., II 18–21

Emerson Radio Corp., 30 183–86

Emery Worldwide Airlines, Inc., 6 388–91; 25 146–50 (upd.)

Emge Packing Co., Inc., 11 92–93

Emhart Corp., *see* Black & Decker Corp.

EMI Group plc, 22 192–95 (upd.); 81 130–37 (upd.)

Emigrant Savings Bank, 59 174–76

Emil Moestue as, 51 328

Emil Schlemper GmbH *see* Acme United Corp.

The Emirates Group, 39 137–39; 81 138–42 (upd.)

Emmis Communications Corporation, 47 117–21

Empaques de Carton Titan, 19 10–11

Empi, Inc., 27 132–35

Empire Blue Cross and Blue Shield, III 245–46 *see also* WellChoice, Inc.

Empire-Cliffs Partnership, 62 74

The Empire District Electric Company, 77 138–41

Empire Family Restaurants Inc., 15 362

Empire Iron Mining Partnership, 62 74

Empire of America, 11 110

Empire of Carolina Inc., 66 370

Empire Resorts, Inc., 72 109–12

Empire Resources, Inc., 81 143–46

Empire State Pickling Company, 21 155

Empire Steel Castings, Inc., 39 31–32

Empire Stores, 19 309

Employee Solutions, Inc., 18 157–60

employeesavings.com, 39 25

Employers General Insurance Group, 58 259

Employers Insurance of Wausau, 59 264

Employers Reinsurance Corp., II 31; 12 197

Emporsil-Empresa Portuguesa de Silvicultura, Lda, 60 156

Empresa Brasileira de Aeronáutica S.A. (Embraer), 36 182–84

Empresa Colombiana de Petróleos, IV 415–18

Empresa Constructora SA, 55 182

Empresa de Distribucion Electrica de Lima Nortes SA, 73 142

Empresa de Obras y Montajes Ovalle Moore, S.A., 34 81

Empresa Eléctrica de Guatemala S.A., 49 211

Empresa Nacional de Telecomunicaciones, 63 375

Empresas Almacenes Paris S.A., 71 142–44

Empresas CMPC S.A., 70 84–87

Empresas Copec S.A., 69 141–44

Empresas Emel S.A., 41 316

Empresas Frisco, 21 259

Empresas ICA Sociedad Controladora, S.A. de C.V., 41 146–49

Empresas La Moderna, 21 413; 29 435

Empresas Penta S.A., 69 56

Empresas Polar SA, 55 139–41 (upd.)

Empresas Públicas de Medellín S.A.E.S.P., 91 174–77

Empresas Tolteca, 20 123

Emprise Corporation, *see* Delaware North Companies Inc.

EMS-Chemie Holding AG, 32 257

EMS Technologies, Inc., 21 199, 201

Enbridge Inc., 43 154–58

ENCAD, Incorporated, 25 151–53 *see also* Eastman Kodak Co.

Encompass Services Corporation, 33 141–44

Encon Safety Products, Inc., 45 424

Encor Inc., 47 396

Encore Acquisition Company, 73 137–39

Encore Computer Corporation, 13 201–02; 74 107–10 (upd.)

Encore Distributors Inc., 17 12–13

Encore Wire Corporation, 81 147–50

Encryption Technology Corporation, 23 102

Encyclopedia Britannica, Inc., 7 165–68; 39 140–44 (upd.)

Endeavor Pharmaceuticals Inc. *see* Barr Pharmaceuticals, Inc.

Endemol Entertainment Holding NV, 46 172–74; 53 154

ENDESA S.A., V 606–08; 46 175–79 (upd.)

Endevco Inc., 11 28

Endicott Trust Company, 11 110

Endo Pharmaceuticals Holdings Inc., 71 145–47

Endo Vascular Technologies, Inc., 11 460

ENDOlap, Inc., 50 122

Endovations, Inc., 21 47

Endurance Specialty Holdings Ltd., 85 116–19

ENECO *see* Empresa Nacional Electrica de Cordoba.

Enercon, Inc., 6 25

Energas Company, 43 56–57

Energen Corporation, 21 207–09

Energieversorgung Ostbayern AG, 23 47

Energis plc, 44 363; 47 122–25

Energizer Holdings, Inc., 32 171–74

Energy & Minerals, Inc., 42 354

Energy Absorption Systems, Inc., 15 378

Energy Africa Limited *see* Tullow Oil plc

Energy Atlantic, LLC *see* Maine & Maritimes Corp.

Energy Biosystems Corp., 15 352

Energy Brands Inc., 88 83–86

Energy Coatings Co., 14 325

Energy Conversion Devices, Inc., 75 133–36

Energy Electromechanical Projects S.A., 64 8

Energy Film Library, 31 216, 218

Energy Foundation, 34 386

The Energy Group, 26 359

Energy Resource Technology, Inc. *see* Helix Energy Solutions Group, Inc.

Energy Steel Corporation, *see* Valmont Industries, Inc.

Energy Systems Group, Inc., *see* Southern Indiana Gas and Electric Co.

Famous Atlantic Fish Company, **20** 5
Famous-Barr, **46** 288
Famous Brands Ltd., **86** 144–47
Famous Dave's of America, Inc., **40** 182–84
Famous Footwear *see* Brown Shoe Company, Inc.
Famous Restaurants Inc., **33** 139–40
Fanafel Ltda., **62** 348, 350
Fancom Holding B.V., **43** 130
Fannie Mae, **45** 156–59 (upd.)
Fannie May Confections Brands, Inc., **80** 114–18
Fansteel Inc., **19** 150–52
Fantastic Sam's, **26** 476
Fanthing Electrical Corp., **44** 132
Fanuc Ltd., **III** 482–83; **17** 172–74 (upd.); **75** 137–40 (upd.)
Fanzz, **29** 282
FAO Schwarz, **46** 187–90
Faprena, **25** 85
Far-Ben S.A. de C.V., **72** 128
Far Eastern Air Transport, Inc., **23** 380
Far Eastern Bank, **56** 363
Farah Incorporated, **24** 156–58
Farben *see* I.G. Farbenindustrie AG.
Farberware, Inc., *see* Lifetime Brands, Inc.
Farbro Corp., **45** 15
FAREC Fahrzeugrecycling GmbH, **58** 28
Faribault Foods, Inc., **89** 212–15
Farley Northwest Industries Inc., **I** 440–41
Farley's & Sathers Candy Company, Inc., **62** 137–39
Farm Electric Services Ltd., **6** 586
Farm Family Holdings, Inc., **39** 155–58
Farm Fresh Catfish Company, **54** 167
Farm Journal Corporation, **42** 131–34
Farm Power Laboratory, **6** 565; **50** 366
Farm Progress Group *see* Rural Press Ltd
Farmacias Ahumada S.A., **72** 126–28
Farmacias Ahumada S.A., **69** 312
Farmcare Ltd., **51** 89
Farmer Bros. Co., **52** 117–19
Farmer Jack Supermarkets, **78** 109–13
Farmer Mac *see* Federal Agricultural Mortgage Corp.
Farmers Insurance Group of Companies, **25** 154–56
Farmers Petroleum, Inc., **48** 175
Farmland Foods, Inc., **7** 174–75
Farmland Industries, Inc., **48** 172–75
Farmstock Pty Ltd., **62** 307
FARO Technologies, Inc., **87** 164–167
Farouk Systems, Inc., **78** 114–17
Farrar, Straus and Giroux Inc., **15** 158–60
FAS Acquisition Co., **53** 142
FASC *see* First Analysis Securities Corp.
Fasco Consumer Products, **19** 360
FASCO Motors *see* Tecumseh Products Co.
Fashion Bug, *see* Charming Shoppes, Inc.
Fashion Fair Cosmetics *see* Johnson Publishing Company, Inc.
Fashion Resource, Inc. *see* Tarrant Apparel Group.
Fasint Ltd., **72** 128

Fasson *see* Avery Dennison Corp.
Fast Air, **31** 305
Fast Fare, *see* Crown Central Petroleum Corp.
Fast Trak Inc. *see* Ultimate Electronics, Inc.
Fastenal Company, **14** 185–87; **42** 135–38 (upd.)
FASTWEB S.p.A., **83** 147-150
Fat Bastard Wine Co., **68** 86
Fat Face Ltd., **68** 147–49
FAT KAT, Inc., **51** 200, 203
Fatburger Corporation, **64** 122–24
Fate S.A., **74** 10
Fateco Förlag, **14** 556
FATS, Inc., *see* Firearms Training Systems, Inc.
Faultless Starch/Bon Ami Company, **55** 142–45
Fauquet, **25** 85
Faurecia S.A., **70** 91–93
FAvS *see* First Aviation Services Inc.
Fay's Inc., **17** 175–77
Faydler Company, **60** 160
Fayette Tubular Products, *see* Danaher Corp.
Faygo Beverages Inc., **55** 146–48
Fayva, *see* Morse Shoe Inc.
Fazoli's Management, Inc., **27** 145–47; **76** 144–47 (upd.)
FB&T Corporation, **14** 154
FBC *see* First Boston Corp.
FBO *see* Film Booking Office of America.
FBR *see* Friedman, Billings, Ramsey Group, Inc.
FBS Fuhrpark Business Service GmbH, **58** 28
FC Holdings, Inc., **26** 363
FCA Ltd. *see* Life Time Fitness, Inc.
FCC *see* Federal Communications Commission.
FCI *see* Framatome SA.
FDIC *see* Federal Deposit Insurance Corp.
Featherlite Inc., **28** 127–29
Feature Enterprises Inc., **19** 452
FECR *see* Florida East Coast Railway, L.L.C.
Fedders Corporation, **18** 172–75; **43** 162–67 (upd.)
Federal Agricultural Mortgage Corporation, **75** 141–43
Federal Cartridge, **26** 363
Federal Deposit Insurance Corporation, **93** 208–12
Federal Express Corporation, **V** 451–53 *see also* FedEx Corp.
Federal Home Life Insurance Co., **IV** 623
Federal Home Loan Mortgage Corp. *see* Freddie Mac.
Federal Insurance Co., *see* The Chubb Corp.
Federal Laboratories, **57** 230
Federal Light and Traction Company, **6** 561–62
Federal-Mogul Corporation, **I** 158–60; **10** 292–94 (upd.); **26** 139–43 (upd.)
Federal National Mortgage Association, **II** 410–11 *see also* Fannie Mae.

Federal Packaging Corp., **19** 78
Federal Paper Board Company, Inc., **8** 173–75
Federal Prison Industries, Inc., **34** 157–60
Federal Reserve Bank of New York, **21** 68
Federal Signal Corp., **10** 295–97
Federated Department Stores Inc., **9** 209–12; **31** 190–94 (upd.)
Federated Livestock Corporation, **64** 306
Fédération Internationale de Football Association, **27** 148–51
Federation Nationale d'Achats des Cadres *see* FNAC.
Federation of Migro Cooperatives *see* Migros-Genossenschafts-Bund.
Federico Paternina S.A., **69** 164–66
FedEx Corporation, **18** 176–79 (upd.); **42** 139–44 (upd.)
FEE Technology, **29** 461–62
Feed-Rite, Inc., *see* Hawkins Chemical, Inc.
Feed The Children, Inc., **68** 150–52
FEI Company, **79** 168–71
Feikes & Sohn KG, *see* PWA Group.
Felco *see* Farmers Regional Cooperative.
Feld Entertainment, Inc., **32** 186–89 (upd.)
Feldmühle Nobel AG, **III** 692–95 *see also* Metallgesellschaft.
Fellowes Manufacturing Company, **28** 130–32
Femsa *see* Formento Económico Mexicano, S.A. de C.V.
Fenaco, **86** 148–51
Fendall Company, **40** 96, 98
Fendel Schiffahrts-Aktiengesellschaft, **6** 426
Fender Musical Instruments Company, **16** 200–02; **43** 168–72 (upd.)
Fendi S.p.A., **45** 344
Fenicia Group, *see* Lojas Arapua S.A.
Fenn, Wright & Manson, **25** 121–22
Fenton Hill American Limited, **29** 510
Fenway Partners, **47** 361
Fenwick & West LLP, **34** 161–63
Ferembal S.A., *see* Viatech Continental Can Company, Inc.
Ferfin, **24** 341
Ferguson Enterprises, **64** 409, 411
Fermec Manufacturing Limited, **40** 432
Fernando Roqué, **6** 404; **26** 243
Ferolito, Vultaggio & Sons, **27** 152–55
Ferragamo, **63** 151
Ferranti Business Communications, **20** 75
Ferrara Fire Apparatus, Inc., **84** 115–118
Ferrara Pan Candy Company, **90** 188–91
Ferrari S.p.A., **13** 218–20; **36** 196–200 (upd.)
Ferrellgas Partners, L.P., **35** 173–75
Ferrero SpA, **54** 103–05
Ferretti Group SpA, **90** 192–96
Ferris Industries, **64** 355
Ferro Corporation, **8** 176–79; **56** 123–28 (upd.)

FosterGrant, Inc., **60** 131–34
Fougerolle, *see* Eiffage.
Foundation Fieldbus, **22** 373
Foundation Health Corporation, 12
175–77
Founders of American Investment Corp.,
15 247
Fountain Powerboats Industries, Inc.,
28 146–48
Four Leaf Technologies *see* Groupe Open.
Four Media Co., **33** 403
Four Paws Products, Ltd., **58** 60
Four Queens Hotel and Casino *see* The
Elsinore Corp.
Four Seasons Hotels Inc., 9 237–38; **29**
198–200 (upd.)
Four-Ten Corporation, **58** 378
Four Winds, 21 153
4Kids Entertainment Inc., 59 187–89
Fournier Furniture, Inc., **12** 301
4P, **30** 396–98
Fourth Financial Corporation, 11
144–46
Fowler, Roenau & Geary, LLC, **37** 224
Fox and Hound English Pub and Grille
see Total Entertainment Restaurant
Corp.
Fox & Jacobs, *see* Centex Corp.
Fox Broadcasting Company, **21** 25, 360
Fox Children's Network, **21** 26
Fox Entertainment Group, Inc., 43
173–76
Fox Family Worldwide, Inc., 24 170–72
see also ABC Family Worldwide, Inc.
Fox Film Corp. *see* Twentieth Century Fox
Film Corp.
Fox, Inc., *see* Twentieth Century Fox Film
Corp.
Fox Network, **29** 426
Fox Paine & Company L.L.C., **63** 410,
412
Fox Ridge Homes, **70** 208
Foxboro Company, 13 233–35
Foxconn International, Inc. *see* Hon Hai
Precision Industry Co., Ltd.
FoxHollow Technologies, Inc., 85
132–35
FoxMeyer Health Corporation, 16
212–14 see also McKesson Corp.
Foxmoor, **29** 163
Foxworth-Galbraith Lumber Company,
91 188–91
Foxx Hy-Reach, **28** 387
Foxy Products, Inc., **60** 287
FP&L *see* Florida Power & Light Co.
FPA Corporation *see* Orleans
Homebuilders, Inc.
FPK LLC, **26** 343
FPL Group, Inc., V 623–25; **49** 143–46
(upd.)
Fracmaster Ltd., **55** 294
Fragrance Corporation of America, Ltd.,
53 88
Fragrance Express Inc., **37** 271
Framatome SA, 19 164–67 *aee also*
Alcatel S.A.; AREVA.
Franc-Or Resources, **38** 231–32
France-Loisirs, **IV** 615–16, 619

France Quick, **12** 152; **26** 160–61
France Télécom Group, V 291–93; **21**
231–34 (upd.)
Franchise Finance Corp. of America, **37**
351
Franciscan Vineyards, Inc., **34** 89; **68** 99
Francisco Partners, **74** 260
Franco-American Food Company *see*
Campbell Soup Co.
Francodex Laboratories, Inc., **74** 381
Francotyp-Postalia Holding AG, 92
123–27
Frank & Pignard SA, **51** 35
Frank & Schulte GmbH, *see* Stinnes AG.
Frank H. Nott Inc., *see* The David J.
Joseph Co.
Frank Holton Company, **55** 149, 151
Frank J. Zamboni & Co., Inc., 34
173–76
Frank Russell Company, 46 198–200
Frank Schaffer Publications, **19** 405; **29**
470, 472
Frank W. Horner, Ltd., **38** 123
Frank's Nursery & Crafts, Inc., 12
178–79
Franke Holding AG, **76** 157–59
Frankel & Co., **39** 166–69
Frankfurter Allgemeine Zeitung GmbH,
66 121–24
Franklin Brass Manufacturing Company,
20 363
Franklin Coach, **56** 223
Franklin Corp., **41** 388
Franklin Covey Company, 11 147–49;
37 149–52 (upd.)
Franklin Electric Company, Inc., 43
177–80
Franklin Electronic Publishers, Inc., 23
209–13
The Franklin Mint, 69 181–84
Franklin Mutual Advisors LLC, **52** 119,
172
Franklin National Bank, **9** 536
Franklin Plastics *see* Spartech Corp.
Franklin Resources, Inc., 9 239–40
Frans Maas Beheer BV, **14** 568
Franz Inc., 80 122–25
Franzia *see* The Wine Group, Inc.
Frape Behr S.A. *see* Behr GmbH & Co.
KG.
Fraport AG Frankfurt Airport Services
Worldwide, 90 197–202
Fraser & Neave Ltd., 54 116–18
Fray Data International, **14** 319
Frazer & Jones, **48** 141
FRE Composites Inc., **69** 206
Fred Campbell Auto Supply, **26** 347
Fred Meyer Stores, Inc., V 54–56; **20**
222–25 (upd.); 64 135–39 (upd.)
Fred Sammons Company of Chicago, **30**
77
Fred Schmid Appliance & T.V. Co., Inc.,
see Fretter, Inc.
Fred Usinger Inc., 54 119–21
The Fred W. Albrecht Grocery Co., 13
236–38
Fred Weber, Inc., 61 100–02

Fred's, Inc., 23 214–16; **62** 144–47
(upd.)
Freddie Mac, 54 122–25
Frederick Atkins Inc., 16 215–17
Frederick Gas Company, **19** 487
Frederick Manufacturing Corporation, 26
119; **48** 59
Frederick's of Hollywood Inc., 16
218–20; 59 190–93 (upd.)
Fredrickson Motor Express, **57** 277
Free-lance Uitzendburo, **26** 240
Free People LLC *see* Urban Outfitters, Inc.
Freedom Airlines, Inc. *see* Mesa Air
Group, Inc.
Freedom Communications, Inc., 36
222–25
Freedom Group Inc., **42** 10–11
Freeman Chemical Corporation, 61
111–12
Freeman, Spogli & Co., **32** 12, 15; **35**
276; **36** 358–59; **47** 142–43; **57** 11,
242
Freemans *see* Sears plc.
FreeMark Communications, **38** 269
Freeport-McMoRan Copper & Gold,
Inc., IV 81–84; **7** 185–89 (upd.); **57**
145–50 (upd.)
Freeport Power, **38** 448
Freescale Semiconductor, Inc., 83
151–154
Freeze.com LLC, 77 156–59
Freezer Queen Foods, Inc., **21** 509
Freight Car Services, Inc., **23** 306
Freixenet S.A., 71 162–64
Fremont Canning Company, *see* Gerber
Products Co.
Fremont Group, **21** 97
Fremont Investors, **30** 268
French Connection Group plc, 41
167–69
French Fragrances, Inc., **22** 213–15 *see*
also Elizabeth Arden, Inc.
French Quarter Coffee Co., *see* Unique
Casual Restaurants, Inc.
Frequency Electronics, Inc., 61 103–05
Fresenius AG, 56 138–42
Fresh America Corporation, 20 226–28
Fresh Choice, Inc., 20 229–32
Fresh Enterprises, Inc., 66 125–27
Fresh Express Inc., 88 97–100
Fresh Foods, Inc., 29 201–03
Fresh Start Bakeries, **26** 58
Freshbake Foods Group PLC, *see*
Campbell Soup Co.
FreshDirect, LLC, 84 130–133
Freshlike, **76** 17
Fretter, Inc., 10 304–06
Freudenberg & Co., 41 170–73
Friction Products Co., **59** 222
Frictiontech Inc., **11** 84
Friday's Front Row Sports Grill, *see*
Carlson Restaurants Worldwide.
Friden, Inc., **30** 418; **53** 237
Fried, Frank, Harris, Shriver &
Jacobson, 35 183–86
Fried. Krupp GmbH, IV 85–89 *see also*
ThyssenKrupp AG.
Friede Goldman Halter, **61** 43

Galaxy Carpet Mills Inc., **19** 276; **63** 300

Galaxy Energies Inc., **11** 28

Galaxy Nutritional Foods, Inc., 58
135–37

Galbreath Escott, **16** 474

Gale International Llc, 93 221–24

Gale Research Co., *see* The Thomson
Corporation

Galen Health Care, **15** 112; **35** 215–16

Galenica AG, 84 139–142

Galerías Preciados, **26** 130

Galeries Lafayette S.A., V 57–59; **23**
220–23 **(upd.)**

Galey & Lord, Inc., 20 242–45; **66**
131–34 **(upd.)**

Gallaher Group Plc, 49 150–54 **(upd.)**

Gallaher Limited, V 398–400; **19**
168–71 **(upd.)**

Gallatin Steel Company, *see* Dofasco Inc.

Galleria Shooting Team, **62** 174

Gallo Winery *see* E. & J. Gallo Winery.

Gallop Johnson & Neuman, L.C., **26** 348

The Gallup Organization, 37 153–56

Galoob Toys *see* Lewis Galoob Toys Inc.

GALP, **48** 117, 119

GALVSTAR, L.P., **26** 530

Galway Irish Crystal Ltd. *see* Belleek
Pottery Ltd.

Galyan's Trading Company, Inc., 47
142–44

Gamax Holding, **65** 230, 232

The Gambrinus Company, 40 188–90

Gambro AB, 49 155–57

The GAME Group plc, 80 126–29

Gamebusters, **41** 409

Gamesa Corporacion Tecnologica S.A., **19**
192; **73** 374–75

GameStop Corp., 69 185–89 **(upd.)**

GameTime, Inc., *see* PlayCore, Inc.

GAMI *see* Great American Management
and Investment, Inc.

Gaming Partners
InternationalCorporation, 92 225–28

GammaLink, *see* Dialogic Corp.

Gander Mountain Company, 20
246–48; **90** 203–08 **(upd.)**

Gannett Company, Inc., IV 612–13; **7**
190–92 **(upd.); 30** 215–17 **(upd.); 66**
135–38 **(upd.)**

Gano Excel Enterprise Sdn. Bhd., 89
228–31

Gantos, Inc., 17 199–201

GAP, *see* Grupo Aeroportuario del
Pacífico, S.A. de C.V.

The Gap, Inc., V 60–62; **18** 191–94
(upd.); 55 153–57 **(upd.)**

GAR Holdings, **19** 78

Garamond Press, **23** 100

Garan, Inc., 16 231–33; **64** 140–43
(upd.)

Garanti Bank, **65** 69

Garantie Mutuelle des Fonctionnaires, **21**
225

Garden City Newspapers Inc., **38** 308

The Garden Company Ltd., 82 125–28

Garden Escape, **26** 441

Garden Fresh Restaurant Corporation,
31 213–15

Garden of Eatin' Inc., **27** 198; **43** 218–19

Garden Ridge Corporation, 27 163–65

Garden State Life Insurance Company, *see*
GEICO Corp.

Garden State Paper, **38** 307–08

Gardenburger, Inc., 33 169–71; **76**
160–63 **(upd.)**

Gardener's Eden, *see* Williams-Sonoma,
Inc.

Gardner Advertising *see* Wells Rich Green
BDDP.

Gardner Denver, Inc., 49 158–60

Gardner Merchant Ltd., **11** 325; **29**
442–44

Gardner Rubber Co. *see* Tillotson Corp.

Gardners Candies *see* Sarris Candies Inc.

Garelick Farms, Inc., **26** 449

Garena Malhas Ltda., **72** 68

Garfinckel, Brooks Brothers, Miller &
Rhodes, Inc., **15** 94

Garfinckels, **37** 12

Garland Commercial Industries, Inc. *see*
Enodis plc.

Garland-Compton, **42** 328

Garland Publishing, **44** 416

Garmin Ltd., 60 135–37

Garrido y Compania, Inc., **26** 448

Garst Seed Company, Inc., 86 156–59

Gart Sports Company, 24 173–75 *see*
also Sports Authority, Inc.

Gartner Group, Inc., 21 235–37

Garuda Indonesia, 6 90–91; **58** 138–41
(upd.)

Gary Fisher Mountain Bike Company, *see*
Trek Bicycle Corp.

Gary-Williams Energy Corporation, **19**
177

Gas Energy Inc., **6** 457

Gas Light and Coke Company *see* British
Gas plc.

Gas Light Company *see* Baltimore Gas
and Electric Co.

Gas Natural SDG S.A., 69 190–93

Gas Service Company, **6** 593; **50** 38

Gas Tech, Inc., *see* Thermo Instrument
Systems Inc.

Gas Utilities Company, **6** 471

GASS *see* Grupo Ángeles Servicios de
Salud, S.A. de C.V.

Gastar Co. Ltd., **55** 375

Gastronome, **70** 322

Gasunie *see* N.V. Nederlandse Gasunie.

GATC *see* General American Tank Car
Co.

Gate Gourmet International AG, 70
97–100

GateHouse Media, Inc., 91 196–99

The Gates Corporation, 9 241–43

Gates Rubber, **26** 349

Gates/FA Distributing Inc., **29** 413–14

Gateway Corporation Ltd., II 628–30
see also Somerfield plc.

Gateway Educational Products Ltd. *see*
HOP, LLC

Gateway, Inc., 10 307–09; **27** 166–69
(upd.); 63 153–58 **(upd.)**

Gateway International Motorsports
Corporation, Inc., **43** 139–40

Gateway State Bank, **39** 381–82

Gateway Technologies, Inc., **46** 387

Gatliff Coal Co., **6** 583

The Gatorade Company, 82 129–32

Gatti's Pizza, Inc. *see* Mr. Gatti's, LP.

Gattini, **40** 215

Gatwick Handling, **28** 157

GATX, 6 394–96; **25** 168–71 **(upd.)**

Gaultier *see* Groupe Jean-Paul Gaultier.

Gaumont S.A., 25 172–75; **91** 200–05
(upd.)

Gaya Motor, P.T. **23** 290

Gaylord Brothers', **60** 109

Gaylord Container Corporation, 8
203–05

Gaylord Entertainment Company, 11
152–54; **36** 226–29 **(upd.)**

Gaymer Group, **25** 82

Gaz de France, V 626–28; **40** 191–95
(upd.)

Gazelle Graphics Systems, **28** 244; **69** 243

Gazprom *see* OAO Gazprom.

GB Foods Inc., **19** 92

GB-Inno-BM *see* GIB Group.

GB s.a. *see* GIB Group.

GB Stores, Inc., *see* Schottenstein Stores
Corp.

gbav Gesellschaft für Boden- und
Abfallverwertung, **58** 28

GBC *see* General Binding Corp.

GC Companies, Inc., 25 176–78 *see also*
AMC Entertainment Inc.

GCFC *see* General Cinema Finance Co.

GD Express Worldwide, *see* TPG NV.

GDE Systems, Inc., *see* Tracor Inc.

GDF *see* Gaz de France.

GDI *see* GO/DAN Industries, Inc.

GDS, **29** 412

GE *see* General Electric Co.

GE Aircraft Engines, 9 244–46

GE Capital Aviation Services, 36
230–33

GE Capital Corporation, **29** 428, 430; **63**
165

GE Capital Services, **49** 240

GE Medical Systems, **71** 350

GE SeaCo SRL, **29** 428, 431

GEA AG, 27 170–74

GEAC Computer Corporation Ltd., 43
181–85

Gear Products, Inc., **48** 59

Geberit AG, 49 161–64

Gebrüder Hepp, **60** 364

Gebrüder Märklin & Cie *see* Märklin
Holding GmbH.

Gebrüder Sulzer Aktiengesellschaft *see*
Sulzer Brothers Ltd.

GEC *see* General Electric Co.

GECAS *see* GE Capital Aviation Services.

Gecina SA, 42 151–53

Geco Mines Ltd., **64** 297

Gedney *see* M.A. Gedney Co.

Geerlings & Wade, Inc., 45 166–68

Geest Plc, 38 200–02 *see also* Bakkavör
Group hf.

Gefco SA, 54 126–28

Geffen Records Inc., 26 150–52

GEHE AG, 27 175–78

Golden Belt Manufacturing Co., 16 241–43

Golden Books Family Entertainment, Inc., 28 158–61 *see also* Random House, Inc.

Golden Circle Financial Services, **15** 328

Golden Corral Corporation, 10 331–33; **66** 143–46 (upd.)

Golden Enterprises, Inc., 26 163–65

Golden Gates Disposal & Recycling Co., **60** 224

Golden Grain Macaroni Co., **II** 560; **12** 411; **30** 219; **34** 366

Golden Krust Caribbean Bakery, Inc., 68 177–79

Golden Moores Finance Company, **48** 286

Golden Nugget, Inc. *see* Mirage Resorts, Inc.

Golden Ocean Group, **45** 164

Golden Peanut Company, *see* Gold Kist Inc.

Golden Poultry Company, **26** 168

Golden Press, Inc., *see* Western Publishing Group, Inc.

Golden Road Motor Inn, Inc. *see* Monarch Casino & Resort, Inc.

Golden State Foods Corporation, 32 220–22

Golden State Vintners, Inc., 33 172–74

Golden Telecom, Inc., 59 208–11

Golden West Financial Corporation, 47 159–61

Golden West Homes, **15** 328

Golden West Publishing Corp., **38** 307–08

Goldenberg Group, Inc., *see* Ply Gem Industries Inc.

Goldline Laboratories Inc., **11** 208

The Goldman Sachs Group Inc., II 414–16; **20** 254–57 (upd.); **51** 144–48 (upd.)

Goldner Hawn Johnson & Morrison Inc., **48** 412

Goldome Savings Bank, **11** 110

Goldsmith's, *see* Federated Department Stores Inc.

Goldstar Co., Ltd., 12 211–13

Goldwin Golf, **45** 76

Goldwyn Films *see* Metro-Goldwyn-Mayer Inc.

Goleta National Bank, **33** 5

Golf Card International, **56** 5

Golin/Harris International, Inc., 88 126–30

The Golub Corporation, 26 169–71

GOME Electrical Appliances Holding Ltd., 87 187–191

Gomoljak, **14** 250

Gonnella Baking Company, 40 211–13

The Good Guys!, Inc., 10 334–35; **30** 224–27 (upd.)

The Good Humor-Breyers Ice Cream Company, 14 203–05 *see also* Unilever PLC.

Good Times, Inc., *see* L.A. Gear, Inc.

Good Vibrations, Inc., **28** 345

Goodby Silverstein & Partners, Inc., 75 167–69

Goodfriend *see* Goody's Family Clothing, Inc.

Goodman Fielder Ltd., 52 140–43

Goodman Holding Company, 42 157–60

GoodMark Foods, Inc., 26 172–74

Goodrich Corporation, 46 209–13 (upd.)

Goodson Newspaper Group, **29** 262

GoodTimes Entertainment Ltd., 48 193–95

Goodwill Industries International, Inc., 16 244–46; **66** 147–50 (upd.)

Goodwin, Dannenbaum, Littman & Wingfield, **16** 72

Goody Products, Inc., 12 214–16

Goody's Family Clothing, Inc., 20 265–67; **64** 158–61 (upd.)

Goody's S.A. *see* Vivartia S.A.

The Goodyear Tire & Rubber Company, V 244–48; **20** 259–64 (upd.); **75** 170–78 (upd.)

Google, Inc., 50 204–07

Gordmans, Inc., 74 125–27

Gordon & Gotch *see* PMP Ltd.

Gordon Biersch Brewery Restaurant Group,Inc., 92229–32

Gordon Food Service Inc., 8 225–27; **39** 179–82 (upd.)

Gordon Jewelry Corporation, *see* Zale Corp.

Gordon Manufacturing Co., **11** 256

Gordon Publications *see* Reed Elsevier.

Gordon S. Black Corporation, **41** 197–98

Gordy Company, **26** 314

Gorges Foodservice, Inc., **14** 516; **50** 493

Gorgonz Group, Inc., **64** 300

Gorilla Sports Club, **25** 42

The Gorman-Rupp Company, 18 201–03; **57** 158–61 (upd.)

Gorton's, 13 243–44

The Gosho Co. *see* Kanematsu Corp.

Gosling Brothers Ltd., 82 146–49

Goss Holdings, Inc., 43 194–97

Gothenburg Light & Power Company, **6** 580

Gott Corp., **21** 293

Gottlieb Group, **38** 437

Gottschalks, Inc., 18 204–06; **91** 211–15 (upd.)

Gould Electronics, Inc., 14 206–08

Gould Paper Corporation, 82 150–53

Goulds Pumps Inc., 24 188–91

Gourmet Award Foods, **29** 480–81

Government Employees Insurance Company *see* GEICO Corp.

Government Technology Services Inc., **45** 69

Governor and Company of Adventurers of England *see* Hudson's Bay Co.

The Governor and Company of the Bank of Scotland, 10 336–38

Goya Foods Inc., 22 245–47; **91** 216–21 (upd.)

GP Strategies Corporation, 64 162–66 (upd.)

GPAA *see* Gold Prospectors' Association of America.

GPE *see* General Precision Equipment Corp.

GPI *see* General Parts Inc.

GPI, **53** 46

GPM Gas Corporation, **40** 357–58

GPS Pool Supply, **29** 34

GPS Industries, Inc., 81 169–72

GPT, **15** 125

GPU *see* General Public Utilities Corp.

GPU, Inc., 27 182–85 (upd.)

Graber Industries, Inc. *see* Springs Industries, Inc.

Grace *see* W.R. Grace & Co.

Grace Drilling Company, **9** 365

Grace-Sierra Horticultural Products Co., *see* Scotts Co.

GraceKennedy Ltd., 92 143–47

Graco Inc., 19 178–80; **67** 191–95 (upd.)

Gradall Industries, Inc., **52** 196

Gradco Systems, Inc., **6** 290

Gradiaz, Annis & Co., **15** 138

Graeter's Manufacturing Company, 86 165–68

Graf, **23** 219

Graficas Monte Alban S.A., **47** 326

Graftek Press, Inc., **26** 44

Graham Corporation, 62 165–67

Graham-Field Health Products, Inc. *see* GF Health Products, Inc.

Graham Packaging Holdings Company, 87 192–196

Grampian Country Food Group, Ltd., 85 155–59

Grameen Bank, 31 219–22

GrameenPhone, **69** 344–46

Gramercy Pictures, **23** 391

Gran Central Corporation, *see* St. Joe Paper Co.

Gran Dorado, **48** 315

Granada Group PLC, II 138–40; **24** 192–95 (upd.)

Granaria Holdings B.V., 66 151–53

GranCare, Inc., 14 209–11

Grand Bazaar Innovations Bon Marché, **26** 159–60

Grand Casinos, Inc., 20 268–70

Grand Home Furnishings *see* Grand Piano & Furniture Co.

Grand Hotel Krasnapolsky N.V., 23 227–29

Grand Metropolitan plc, I 247–49; **14** 212–15 (upd.) *see also* Diageo plc.

Grand Ole Opry *see* Gaylord Entertainment Co.

Grand Piano & Furniture Company, 72 151–53

Grand Prix Association of Long Beach, Inc., **43** 139–40

Grand Rapids Gas Light Company *see* MCN Corp.

Grand Union Company, 7 202–04; **28** 162–65 (upd.)

Grand Valley Gas Company, **11** 28

Grand-Perret, **39** 152–53

Grandes Superficies S.A., **23** 247

Groupe Axime, **37** 232
Groupe Barrière SA, **48** 199
Groupe Bisset, **24** 510
Groupe Bolloré, 67 196–99
Groupe Bourbon S.A., 60 147–49
Groupe Bruxelles Lambert, **26** 368
Groupe Bull *see* Compagnie des Machines Bull.
Groupe Casino *see* Casino Guichard-Perrachon S.A.
Groupe Castorama-Dubois Investissements, 23 230–32 *see also* Kingfisher plc.
Groupe CECAB S.C.A., 88 131–34
Groupe Crit S.A., 74 134–36
Groupe Danone, 32 232–36 (upd.); 93 233–40 (upd.)
Le Groupe Darty, *see* Kingfisher plc.
Groupe Dassault Aviation SA, 26 179–82 (upd.)
Groupe de la Cité, IV 614–16
Groupe des Assurances Nationales, **76** 169
Groupe DMC (Dollfus Mieg & Cie), 27 186–88
Groupe Euralis, 86 169–72
Groupe Fournier SA, 44 187–89
Groupe Glon, 84 155–158
Groupe Go Sport S.A., 39 183–85
Groupe Guillin SA, 40 214–16
Groupe Herstal S.A., 58 145–48
Groupe Jean-Claude Darmon, 44 190–92
Groupe Jean Didier, **12** 413
Groupe Jean-Paul Gaultier, **34** 214
Groupe Lactalis, 78 128–32 (upd.)
Groupe Lagardère S.A., **15** 293; **21** 265, 267
Groupe Lapeyre S.A., 33 175–77
Groupe LDC *see* L.D.C. S.A.
Groupe Le Duff S.A., 84 159–162
Groupe Léa Nature, 88 135–38
Groupe Legris Industries, 23 233–35
Groupe Les Echos, 25 283–85
Groupe Limagrain, 74 137–40
Groupe Louis Dreyfus S.A., 60 150–53
Groupe Monnoyeur, 72 157–59
Groupe Open, 74 141–43
Groupe Partouche SA, 48 196–99
Groupe Pechiney, **33** 89
Groupe Pinault-Printemps-Redoute, *see* Pinault-Printemps-Redoute S.A.
Groupe Poliet, 66 363–64
Groupe Poron, **35** 206
Groupe Promodès S.A., 19 326–28
Groupe Rallye, **39** 183–85
Groupe Rothschild, **22** 365
Groupe Rougier SA, 21 438–40
Groupe Roussin, **34** 13
Groupe Salvat, **IV** 619
Groupe SEB, 35 201–03
Groupe Sidel S.A., 21 252–55
Groupe Soufflet SA, 55 176–78
Groupe Tetra Laval, **53** 327
Groupe Vidéotron Ltée., 20 271–73
Groupe Yves Saint Laurent, 23 236–39 *see also* Gucci Group N.V.
Groupe Zannier S.A., 35 204–07
Groupement d'Achat AVP SAS, **58** 221

Groupement des Mousquetaires *see* ITM Entreprises SA.
Groupement Français pour l'Investissement Immobilier, **42** 153
Groupement pour le Financement de la Construction *see* Gecina SA.
GroupMAC *see* Encompass Services Corp.
Groux Beverage Corporation, **11** 451
Grove Manufacturing Co., *see* OshKosh B'Gosh, Inc.
Grove Worldwide, Inc., **59** 274, 278
Grow Biz International, Inc., 18 207–10 *see also* Winmark Corp.
Grow Group Inc., 12 217–19
GROWMARK, Inc., 88 139–42
Groz-Beckert Group, 68 184–86
GRS Inns Ltd *see* Punch Taverns plc.
Grubb & Ellis Company, 21 256–58
Gruma, S.A. de C.V., 31 234–36
Grumman Corp., I 61–63; 11 164–67 (upd.) *see aslo* Northrop Grumman Corp.
Grunau Company Inc., 90 209–12
Grundfos Group, 83 171–174
Grundig AG, 27 189–92
Gruner + Jahr AG & Co., **22** 442; **23** 85
Gruntal & Co., L.L.C., 20 274–76
Grupo Aeroportuario del Pacífico, S.A. de C.V., 85 160–63
Grupo Acerero del Norte, S.A. de C.V., **22** 286; **42** 6
Grupo Aeropuerto del Sureste, S.A. de C.V., 48 200–02
Grupo Ángeles Servicios de Salud, S.A. de C.V., 84 163–166
Grupo Antarctica Paulista *see* Companhia de Bebidas das Américas.
Grupo Banco Bilbao Vizcaya Argentaria S.A., **54** 147
Grupo Bimbo, S.A. de C.V., **31** 236
Grupo Bufete *see* Bufete Industrial, S.A. de C.V.
Grupo Cabal S.A., **23** 166
Grupo Campi, S.A. de C.V., **39** 230
Grupo Carso, S.A. de C.V., 21 259–61
Grupo Casa Saba, S.A. de C.V., 39 186–89
Grupo Clarín S.A., 67 200–03
Grupo Comercial Chedraui S.A. de C.V., 86 173–76
Grupo Corvi S.A. de C.V., 86 177–80
Grupo Cruzcampo S.A., **34** 202
Grupo Cuervo, S.A. de C.V., **31** 91–92
Grupo Cydsa, S.A. de C.V., 39 190–93
Grupo de Ingeniería Ecológica, **16** 260
Grupo Dina *see* Consorcio G Grupo Dina, S.A. de C.V.
Grupo Dragados SA, 55 179–82
Grupo DST, **41** 405–06
Grupo Editorial Random House Mondadori S.L., **54** 22
Grupo Elektra, S.A. de C.V., 39 194–97
Grupo Empresarial Angeles, **50** 373
Grupo Eroski, 64 167–70
Grupo Eroski, 64 167–70
Grupo Ferrovial, S.A., 40 217–19
Grupo Ficosa International, 90 213–16
Grupo Financiero Asemex-Banpais S.A., **51** 150

Grupo Financiero Banamex S.A., 54 143–46
Grupo Financiero Banorte, S.A. de C.V., 51 149–51
Grupo Financiero BBVA Bancomer S.A., 54 147–50
Grupo Financiero Galicia S.A., 63 178–81
Grupo Financiero Inbursa, **21** 259
Grupo Financiero Inverlat, S.A., **39** 188; **59** 74
Grupo Financiero Serfín, S.A., 19 188–90
Grupo Gigante, S.A. de C.V., 34 197–99
Grupo Hecali, S.A., **39** 196
Grupo Herdez, S.A. de C.V., 35 208–10
Grupo ICA, **52** 394
Grupo IMSA, S.A. de C.V., 44 193–96
Grupo Industrial Alfa, S.A. de C.V. *see* Alfa, S.A. de C.V.
Grupo Industrial Atenquique, S.A. de C.V., **37** 176
Grupo Industrial Bimbo, 19 191–93
Grupo Industrial Durango, S.A. de C.V., 37 176–78
Grupo Industrial Herradura, S.A. de C.V., 83 175-178
Grupo Industrial Lala, S.A. de C.V., 82 154–57
Grupo Industrial Maseca S.A. de C.V. (Gimsa) *see* Gruma, S.A. de C.V.
Grupo Industrial Saltillo, S.A. de C.V., 54 151–54
Grupo Irsa, **23** 171
Grupo Leche Pascual S.A., 59 212–14
Grupo Lladró S.A., 52 147–49
Grupo Marsans, **69** 9, 11–12
Grupo Martins, **59** 361
Grupo Mexico, S.A. de C.V., 40 220–23
Grupo Modelo, S.A. de C.V., 29 218–20
Grupo Nacional de Chocolates S.A. *see* Inversiones Nacional de Chocolates S.A.
Grupo Omnilife S.A. de C.V., 88 143–46
Grupo Pipsamex S.A., **37** 178
Grupo Portucel Soporcel, 60 154–56
Grupo Posadas, S.A. de C.V., 57 168–70
Grupo Pulsar *see* Pulsar Internacional S.A.
Grupo Quan, **19** 192–93
Grupo Salinas, **39** 196
Grupo Sanborns S.A. de C.V., **35** 118
Grupo Servia, S.A. de C.V., **50** 209
Grupo TACA, 38 218–20
Grupo Televisa, S.A., 18 211–14; 54 155–58 (upd.)
Grupo TMM, S.A. de C.V., 50 208–11
Grupo Transportación Ferroviaria Mexicana, S.A. de C.V., 47 162–64
Grupo Tribasa, **34** 82
Grupo Tudor, **IV** 471
Grupo Viz, S.A. de C.V., 84 167–170
Grupo Xtra, **39** 186, 188
Gruppo Banco di Napoli, **50** 410
Gruppo Buffetti S.p.A., **47** 345–46
Gruppo Coin S.p.A., 41 185–87
Gruppo Editoriale L'Espresso S.p.A., **54** 19–21

H.P. Hood, **7** 17–18

H.S. Trask & Co. *see* Phoenix Footware Group, Inc.

H. Samuel Plc, **61** 326

H.W. Johns Manufacturing Co. *see* Manville Corp.

H.W.S. Solutions, **21** 37

The H.W. Wilson Company, 66 166–68

Ha-Lo Industries, Inc., 27 193–95

Häagen-Dazs, *see* Nestlé S.A.

Haan Crafts Corporation, **62** 18

Haarmann & Reimer *see* Symrise GmbH and Co. KG

Haas, Baruch & Co. *see* Smart & Final, Inc.

Haas Publishing Companies, Inc., **22** 442

Haas Wheat & Partners, **15** 357; **65** 258–59

Habersham Bancorp, 25 185–87

Habitat for Humanity International, 36 258–61

Habitat/Mothercare PLC *see* Mothercare plc.

Hach Co., 18 218–21

Hachette Filipacchi Medias S.A., 21 265–67

Hachette S.A., IV 617–19 *see also* Matra-Hachette S.A.

Haci Omer Sabanci Holdings A.S., 55 186–89 *see also* Akbank TAS

Hacker-Pschorr Brau, **35** 331

Hackman Oyj Adp, 44 212–15

Hadco Corporation, 24 201–03

Hadron, Inc. *see* Analex Corp.

Haeger Industries Inc., 88 159–62

Haemocell, **11** 476

Haemonetics Corporation, 20 277–79

Haftpflichtverband der Deutschen Industrie Versicherung auf Gegenseitigkeit V.a.G. *see* HDI (Haftpflichtverband der Deutschen Industrie Versicherung auf Gegenseitigkeit V.a.G.).

Hagemeyer N.V., 39 201–04

Hagemeyer North America, **63** 289

Haggar Corporation, 19 194–96; **78** 137–41 (upd.)

Haggen Inc., 38 221–23

Hägglunds Vehicle AB, **47** 7, 9

Hagoromo Foods Corporation, 84 175–178

Hahn Automotive Warehouse, Inc., 24 204–06

Hahn Department Stores *see* Allied Stores Corp.

Haier Group Corporation, 65 167–70

Haights Cross Communications, Inc., 84 179–182

The Hain Celestial Group, Inc., 27 196–98; **43** 217–20 (upd.)

Hair Club For Men Ltd., 90 222–25

Hair Cuttery *see* Ratner Companies.

Hake Group, Inc. *see* Matrix Service Co.

Hakone Tozan Railway Co., Ltd., **68** 281

Hakuhodo, Inc., 6 29–31; **42** 172–75 (upd.)

HAL Inc., 9 271–73 *see also* Hawaiian Airlines, Inc.

Hale and Dorr, **31** 75

Hale-Halsell Company, 60 157–60

Haleko Hanseatisches Lebensmittel Kontor GmbH, **29** 500

Halewood, **21** 246

Half Price Books, Records, Magazines Inc., 37 179–82

Halfords Ltd., *see* Alliance Boots plc.

Halkin Holdings plc, **49** 338–39

Hall Bros. Co. *see* Hallmark Cards, Inc.

Hall, Kinion & Associates, Inc., 52 150–52

Hall Laboratories, Inc., **45** 209

Hall-Mark Electronics, **23** 490

Hallhuber GmbH, **63** 361, 363

Halliburton Company, III 497–500; **25** 188–92 (upd.); **55** 190–95 (upd.)

Hallmark Cards, Inc., IV 620–21; **16** 255–57 (upd.); **40** 228–32 (upd.); **87** 205–212 (upd.)

Hallmark Chemical Corp., *see* NCH Corp.

Hallmark Holdings, Inc., **51** 190

Hallmark Investment Corp., **21** 92

Hallmark Residential Group, Inc., **45** 221

Halo Lighting, **30** 266

Haloid Company *see* Xerox Corp.

Halstead Industries, **26** 4; **52** 258

Halter Marine, **22** 276

Hambrecht & Quist Group, **26** 66; **31** 349

Hambro Countrywide Security, **32** 374

Hambros Bank, **16** 14; **43** 7

Hamburg-Amerikanische-Packetfahrt-Actien-Gesellschaft *see* Hapag-Lloyd AG.

Hamburgische Electricitaets-Werke AG, **57** 395, 397

Hamelin Group, Inc. *see* Spartech Corp.

Hamer Hammer Service, Inc., **11** 523

Hamersley Holdings, **IV** 59–61

Hamil Textiles Ltd. *see* Algo Group Inc.

Hamilton Beach/Proctor-Silex Inc., 17 213–15

Hamilton Group Limited, **15** 478

Hamilton/Hall-Mark, **19** 313

Hamilton Oil Corp., **IV** 47; **22** 107

Hamilton Sundstrand, **76** 319

Hammacher Schlemmer & Company Inc., 21 268–70; **72** 160–62 (upd.)

Hammermill Paper Co., **23** 48–49

Hammers Plastic Recycling, **6** 441

Hammerson plc, IV 696–98; **40** 233–35 (upd.)

Hammery Furniture Company, *see* La-Z-Boy Inc.

Hammes Co., **38** 482

Hammond Manufacturing Company Limited, 83 179–182

Hamot Health Foundation, 91 227–32

Hampton Affiliates, Inc., 77 175–79

Hampton Industries, Inc., 20 280–82

Hampton Inns, *see* Promus Companies, Inc.

Hampton Roads Food, Inc., *see* Rally's.

Hampshire Group Ltd., 82 170–73

Hamworthy Engineering Ltd., **31** 367, 369

Han Comm Inc., **62** 174

Han-Fa Electrification Co. Ltd., **76** 139

Hancock Fabrics, Inc., 18 222–24

Hancock Holding Company, 15 207–09

Hancock Jaffe Laboratories, **11** 460

Hancock Park Associates *see* Leslie's Poolmart, Inc.

Handleman Company, 15 210–12; **86** 185–89 (upd.)

Handspring Inc., 49 183–86

Handy & Harman, 23 249–52

Handy Andy Home Improvement Centers, Inc., **26** 160–61

Hanes Holding Company, **11** 256; **48** 267

Hang Seng Bank Ltd., 60 161–63

Hanger Orthopedic Group, Inc., 41 192–95

Haniel & Cie. GmbH, *see* GEHE AG.

Hanjin Group *see* Korean Ail Lines Co. Ltd.

Hanjin Shipping Co., Ltd., 50 217–21

Hankook Tyre Manufacturing Company, *see* The Yokohama Rubber Co., Ltd.

Hankyu Corporation, V 454–56; **23** 253–56 (upd.)

Hankyu Department Stores, Inc., V 70–71; **62** 168–71 (upd.)

Hanley Brick, **14** 250

Hanmi Financial Corporation, 66 169–71

Hanna Andersson Corp., 49 187–90

Hanna-Barbera Cartoons Inc., 23 257–59, 387

Hannaford Bros. Co., 12 220–22

Hannen Brauerei GmbH, *see* Carlsberg A/S

Hannifin Corporation *see* Parker Hannifin Corp.

HANNOVER International AG für Industrieversicherungen, **53** 162

Hannover Papier, **49** 353

Hanover Bank *see* Manufacturers Hanover Corp.

Hanover Compressor Company, 59 215–17

Hanover Direct, Inc., 36 262–65

Hanover Foods Corporation, 35 211–14

Hanover Insurance Company, **63** 29

Hansa Linie, **26** 279–80

Hansen Natural Corporation, 31 242–45; **76** 171–74 (upd.)

Hansgrohe AG, 56 149–52

Hansol Paper Co., **63** 315–16

Hanson Building Materials America Inc., 60 164–66

Hanson Industries, **44** 257

Hanson PLC, III 501–03; **7** 207–10 (upd.); **30** 228–32 (upd.)

Hansvedt Industries Inc., **25** 195

Hanwha Group, 62 172–75

Hapag-Lloyd AG, 6 397–99

Happy Air Exchangers Ltd., **21** 499

Happy Kids Inc., 30 233–35

Haralambos Beverage Corporation, **11** 451

Harbert Corporation, 14 222–23

HARBIN Samick Corp., **56** 300

Hub International Limited, 89 260–64

Hub Services, Inc., *see* Dynegy Inc.

Hubbard Broadcasting Inc., 24 226–28;
79 207–12 (upd.)

Hubbard Construction Co., 23 332

Hubbell Inc., 9 286–87; 31 257–59
(upd.); 76 183–86 (upd.)

Huck Manufacturing Company, *see*
Thiokol Corp.

**The Hudson Bay Mining and Smelting
Company, Limited**, 12 259–61

Hudson Foods Inc., 13 270–72 *see also*
Tyson Foods, Inc.

Hudson I.C.S., **58** 53

Hudson Pharmaceutical Corp., 31 347

Hudson River Bancorp, Inc., 41 210–13

Hudson's *see* Target Corp.

Hudson's Bay Company, V 79–81; 25
219–22 (upd.); 83 187-194 (upd.)

Huf-North America, 73 325

Huffman Manufacturing Company, *see*
Huffy Corp.

Huffy Corporation, 7 225–27; 30
239–42 (upd.)

Hughes Aircraft Company, *see* GM
Hughes Electronics Corp.

Hughes Electronics Corporation, 25
223–25

Hughes Helicopter, **26** 431; **46** 65

Hughes Hubbard & Reed LLP, 44
230–32

Hughes Markets, Inc., 22 271–73 *see
also* Kroger Co.

Hughes Network Systems Inc., **21** 239

Hughes Space and Communications
Company, 33 47–48

Hughes Supply, Inc., 14 246–47

Hughes Tool Co. *see* Baker Hughes Inc.

Hugo Boss AG, 48 206–09

Hugo Neu Corporation, **19** 381–82

Hugo Stinnes GmbH, *see* Stinnes AG.

Huhtamäki Oyj, 64 186–88

HUK-Coburg, 58 169–73

The Hull Group, L.L.C., **51** 148

Hulman & Company, 44 233–36

Hüls A.G., I 349–50 *see also*
Degussa-Hüls AG.

Hulsbeck and Furst GmbH, **73** 325

Hulton Getty, **31** 216–17

Human Services Computing, Inc. *see* Epic
Systems Corp.

Humana Inc., III 81–83; 24 229–32
(upd.)

**The Humane Society of the United
States**, 54 170–73

Humanetics Corporation, **29** 213

Humanities Software, **39** 341

Humberside Sea & Land Services, 31 367

Humble Oil & Refining Company *see*
Exxon.

Hummel International A/S, 68 199–201

Hummel Lanolin Corporation, **45** 126

Hummel-Reise, **44** 432

Hummer, Winblad Venture Partners, **36**
157; **69** 265; **74** 168

Humongous Entertainment, Inc., **31**
238–40

Humps' n Horns, **55** 312

Hunco Ltd., **IV** 640; **26** 273

Hungarian-Soviet Civil Air Transport Joint
Stock Company *see* Maláv Plc.

Hungarian Telephone and Cable Corp.,
75 193–95

Hungry Howie's Pizza and Subs, Inc.,
25 226–28

Hungry Minds, Inc. *see* John Wiley &
Sons, Inc.

Hunt Consolidated, Inc., 7 228–30; 27
215–18 (upd.)

Hunt Manufacturing Company, 12
262–64

Hunt-Wesson, Inc., 17 240–42 *see also*
ConAgra Foods, Inc.

Hunter Fan Company, 13 273–75

Hunting plc, 78 163–16

Huntingdon Life Sciences Group plc,
42 182–85

Huntington Bancshares Incorporated,
11 180–82; 87 232–238 (upd.)

Huntington Learning Centers, Inc., 55
212–14

Huntleigh Technology PLC, 77
199–202

Hunton & Williams, 35 223–26

Huntsman Chemical Corporation, 8
261–63

Huntstown Power Company Ltd., **64** 404

Hurd & Houghton, *see* Houghton Mifflin
Co.

Huron Consulting Group Inc., 87
239–243

Huron Steel Company, Inc., *see* The
Marmon Group, Inc.

Hurricane Hydrocarbons Ltd., 54
174–77

Husky Energy Inc., 47 179–82

Husky Oil Ltd., **IV** 695

Husqvarna AB, **53** 126–27

Husqvarna Forest & Garden Company, *see*
White Consolidated Industries Inc.

Hussmann Corporation, **67** 299

Hussmann Distributing Co., Inc. *see* IC
Industries Inc.

Hutcheson & Grundy, **29** 286

Hutchinson-Mapa, **IV** 560

Hutchinson Technology Incorporated,
18 248–51; 63 190–94 (upd.)

Hutchison Microtel, **11** 548

Hutchison Whampoa Limited, 18
252–55; 49 199–204 (upd.)

Huth Inc., **56** 230

Hüttenwerke Kayser AG, **62** 253

Huttepain, **61** 155

Huttig Building Products, Inc., 73
180–83

HVB Group, 59 237–44 (upd.)

Hvide Marine Incorporated, 22 274–76

HWI *see* Hardware Wholesalers, Inc.

Hy-Form Products, Inc., *see* Defiance, Inc.

Hy-Vee, Inc., 36 275–78

Hyatt-Clark Industries Inc., **45** 170

Hyatt Corporation, III 96–97; 16
273–75 (upd.) *see* Global Hyatt Corp.

Hyatt Legal Services, **20** 435; **29** 226

Hyco-Cascade Pty. Ltd. *see* Cascade Corp.

Hycor Biomedical Inc. *see* Stratagene
Corp.

Hyde Athletic Industries, Inc., 17
243–45 *see also* Saucony Inc.

Hyde Company, A.L., *see* Danaher Corp.

Hyder plc, 34 219–21

Hydrac GmbH, **38** 300

Hydril Company, 46 237–39

Hydro-Carbon Light Company, *see* The
Coleman Company, Inc.

Hydro Electric, **49** 363–64

Hydro-Electric Power Commission of
Ontario, **6** 541

Hydro-Quebec, 6 501–03; 32 266–69
(upd.)

Hydrocarbon Technologies, Inc., **56** 161

Hydrodynamic Cutting Services, **56** 134

Hygrade Operators Inc., **55** 20

Hylsa *see* Hojalata y Laminas S.A.

Hylsamex, S.A. de C.V., 39 225–27

Hynix Semiconductor Inc., **56** 173

Hypercom Corporation, 27 219–21

Hyperion Software Corporation, 22
277–79

Hyperion Solutions Corporation, 76
187–91

HyperRoll Israel Ltd., **76** 190

Hyplains Beef, L.C., *see* Farmland Foods,
Inc.

Hypo-Bank *see* Bayerische Hypotheken-
und Wechsel-Bank AG.

Hyponex Corp., *see* Scotts Co.

Hyster Company, 17 246–48

Hyundai Group, III 515–17; 7 231–34
(upd.); 56 169–73 (upd.)

I

I Can't Believe It's Yogurt, Inc., **35** 121

I Pellettieri d'Italia S.p.A., **45** 342

I. Appel, **30** 23

I.B. Kleinert Rubber Company, **37** 399

I.C. Isaacs & Company, 31 260–62

I.D. Systems, Inc., **11** 444

I-DIKA Milan SRL, **12** 182

I. Feldman Co., **31** 359

I.G. Farbenindustrie AG, *see* BASF A.G.;
Bayer A.G.; Hoechst A.G.

I.M. Pei & Associates *see* Pei Cobb Freed
& Partners Architects LLP.

I. Magnin Inc., *see* R. H. Macy & Co.,
Inc.

I.N. Kote, *see* Inland Steel Industries, Inc.

I.N. Tek, *see* Inland Steel Industries, Inc.

I-X Corp., **22** 416

IAC/InterActive Corporation *see*
Ticketmaster

Iacon, Inc., **49** 299, 301

IAL *see* International Aeradio Ltd.

Iams Company, 26 205–07

IAN S.A. *see* Viscofan S.A.

IAWS Group plc, 49 205–08

IBANCO, **26** 515

Ibanez *see* Hoshino Gakki Co. Ltd.

IBC Group plc, **58** 189, 191

IBC Holdings Corporation, **12** 276

IBCA *see* International Banking and
Credit Analysis.

Katabami Kogyo Co. Ltd., **51** 179

Kate Industries, **74** 202

kate spade LLC, 68 208–11

Katharine Gibbs Schools Inc., **22** 442

Katherine Beecher Candies, Inc. *see* Warrell Corp.

Katies, **V** 35

Kativo Chemical Industries Ltd., *see* H. B. Fuller Co.

Katokichi Company Ltd., 82 187–90

Katy Industries Inc., I 472–74; 51 187–90 (upd.)

Katz Communications, Inc., 6 32–34 *see also* Clear Channel Communications, Inc.

Katz Media Group, Inc., 35 245–48

Kaufhalle AG, **V** 104; **23** 311; **41** 186–87

Kaufhof Warenhaus AG, V 103–05; 23 311–14 (upd.)

Kaufman and Broad Home Corporation, 8 284–86 *see also* KB Home.

Kaufmann Department Stores, Inc. *see* The May Department Stores Co.

Kaufring AG, 35 249–52

Oy Kaukas Ab *see* UPM-Kymmene

Kaukauna Cheese Inc., **23** 217, 219

Kawai Musical Instruments Manufacturing Co.,Ltd., 78 189–92

Kawasaki Heavy Industries, Ltd., III 538–40; 63 220–23 (upd.)

Kawasaki Kisen Kaisha, Ltd., V 457–60; 56 177–81 (upd.)

Kawasaki Steel Corporation, IV 124–25

Kawsmouth Electric Light Company *see* Kansas City Power & Light Co.

Kay-Bee Toy Stores, 15 252–53 *see also* KB Toys.

Kay Jewelers Inc., **61** 327

Kaydon Corporation, 18 274–76

Kaye, Scholer, Fierman, Hays & Handler, **47** 436

Kayex, *see* General Signal Corp.

Kaytee Products Incorporated, **58** 60

KB Home, 45 218–22 (upd.)

AO KB Impuls, **48** 419

KB Investment Co., Ltd., **58** 208

KB Toys, Inc., 35 253–55 (upd.); 86 237–42 (upd.)

KBLCOM Incorporated, **V** 644

KC *see* Kenneth Cole Productions, Inc.

KC Holdings, Inc., *see* Kimco Realty Corp.

KCI Konecranes International, **27** 269

KCK Tissue S.A., **73** 205

KCPL *see* Kansas City Power & Light Co.

KCS Industries, **12** 25–26

KCSI *see* Kansas City Southern Industries, Inc.

KCSR *see* Kansas City Southern Railway.

KD Acquisition Corporation, **34** 103–04; **76** 239

KD Manitou, Inc. *see* Manitou BF S.A.

KDI Corporation, **56** 16–17

Keane, Inc., 56 182–86

Keck's *see* Decorator Industries Inc.

The Keds Corp., **37** 377, 379

Keebler Foods Company, 36 311–13

Keene Packaging Co., **28** 43

KEG Productions Ltd., **IV** 640; **26** 272

Keio Teito Electric Railway Company, V 461–62

The Keith Companies Inc., 54 181–84

Keithley Instruments Inc., 16 299–301

Kelco, **34** 281

Kelda Group plc, 45 223–26

Keliher Hardware Company, **57** 8

Kelkoo S.A. *see* Yahoo! Inc.

Kelley Blue Book Company, Inc., 84 218–221

Keller Builders, **43** 400

Keller-Dorian Graveurs, S.A., *see* Standex International Corp.

Kelley Drye & Warren LLP, 40 280–83

Kellock Holdings Ltd., *see* The Governor and Company of the Bank of Scotland.

Kellogg Brown & Root, Inc., 62 201–05 (upd.)

Kellogg Company, II 523–26; 13 291–94 (upd.); 50 291–96 (upd.)

Kellwood Company, 8 287–89; 85 203–08 (upd.)

Kelly-Moore Paint Company, Inc., 56 187–89

Kelly Services, Inc., 6 35–37; 26 237–40 (upd.)

The Kelly-Springfield Tire Company, 8 290–92

Kelsey-Hayes Group of Companies, 7 258–60; 27 249–52 (upd.)

Kelso & Co., **21** 490; **33** 92; **63** 237; **71** 145–46

Kelvinator of India, Ltd., **59** 417

KemaNobel, *see* Asko Nobel N.V.

Kemet Corp., 14 281–83

Kemira Oyj, 70 143–46

Kemper Corporation, III 269–71; 15 254–58 (upd.)

Kemper Financial Services, **26** 234

Ken's Foods, Inc., 88 223–26

Kencraft, Inc., **71** 22–23

Kendall International, Inc., 11 219–21 *see also* Tyco International Ltd.

Kendall-Jackson Winery, Ltd., 28 221–23

Kendle International Inc., **87** 276–279

Kenetech Corporation, **11** 222–24

Kenexa Corporation, **87** 280–284

Kenhar Corporation *see* Cascade Corp.

Kenmore Air Harbor Inc., 65 191–93

Kennametal, Inc., 13 295–97; 68 212–16 (upd.)

Kennecott Corporation, 7 261–64; 27 253–57 (upd.) *see also* Rio Tinto PLC.

Kennedy-Wilson, Inc., 60 183–85

Kenner Parker Toys, Inc., **25** 488–89

Kenneth Cole Productions, Inc., 25 256–58

Kenneth O. Lester, Inc., **21** 508

Kenny Rogers' Roasters, **29** 342, 344

Kenroy International, Inc., *see* Hunter Fan Co.

Kensey Nash Corporation, 71 185–87

Kensington Associates L.L.C., **60** 146

Kensington Publishing Corporation, 84 222–225

Kent Electronics Corporation, 17 273–76

Kentrox Industries, **30** 7

Kentucky Electric Steel, Inc., 31 286–88

Kentucky Fried Chicken *see* KFC Corp.

Kentucky Institution for the Education of the Blind *see* American Printing House for the Blind.

Kentucky Utilities Company, 6 513–15

Kenwood Corporation, 31 289–91

Kenwood Silver Company, Inc., **31** 352

Kenwood Winery, **68** 146

Kenya Airways Limited, 89 286–89

Kenyon Corp., 18 276

Kenzo, 25 122

Keolis SA, 51 191–93

Kepco *see* Korea Electric Power Corporation; Kyushu Electric Power Company Inc.

Keppel Corporation Ltd., 73 201–03

Keramik Holding AG Laufen, 51 194–96

Kerasotes ShowPlace Theaters LLC, 80 179–83

Kernite SA, *see* NCH Corp.

Kernkraftwerke Lippe-Ems, **V** 747

Kerr Concrete Pipe Company, **14** 250

Kerr Corporation, **14** 481

Kerr Drug Stores, **32** 170

Kerr Group Inc., 24 263–65

Kerr-McGee Corporation, IV 445–47; 22 301–04 (upd.); 68 217–21 (upd.)

Kerry Group plc, 27 258–60; 87 285–291 (upd.)

Kerry Properties Limited, 22 305–08

Kerzner International Limited, 69 222–24 (upd.)

Kesa Electricals plc, 91 285–90

Kesko Ltd (Kesko Oy), 8 293–94; 27 261–63 (upd.)

Kessler Rehabilitation Corporation *see* Select Medical Corp.

Ketchikan Paper Company, **31** 316

Ketchum Communications Inc., 6 38–40

Kettle Chip Company (Australia), **26** 58

Kettle Foods Inc., 48 240–42

Kettle Restaurants, Inc., **29** 149

Kewaunee Scientific Corporation, 25 259–62

Kewpie Kabushiki Kaisha, 57 202–05

Key Industries, Inc., **26** 342

Key Pharmaceuticals, Inc., **41** 419

Key Production Company, Inc. *see* Cimarex Energy Co.

Key Safety Systems, Inc., 63 224–26

Key Tronic Corporation, 14 284–86

KeyCorp, 8 295–97; 92272–81 (upd.)

Keyes Fibre Company, 9 303–05

KeyLabs, **65** 34–35

Keypage *see* Rural Cellular Corp.

Keypoint Technology Corporation *see* ViewSonic Corp.

Keys Fitness Products, LP, 83 231-234

KeySpan Energy Co., 27 264–66

Keystone Consolidated Industries, Inc., **19** 467

Knorr Co. *see* C.H. Knorr Co.
Knorr Foods Co., Ltd., **28** 10
The Knot, Inc., 74 168–71
Knott's Berry Farm, 18 288–90
Knowledge Learning Corporation, 51 197–99; 54 191
Knowledge Systems Concepts, **11** 469
Knowledge Universe, Inc., 54 191–94
KnowledgeWare Inc., 9 309–11; 31 296–98 (upd.)
Knox County Insurance, **41** 178
Knoxville Glove Co., **34** 159
KNP BT *see* Buhrmann NV.
KNP Leykam, **49** 352, 354
KNSM *see* Koninklijke Nederlandsche Stoomboot Maatschappij.
Knudsen & Sons, Inc., *see* The J.M. Smucker Co.
KOA *see* Kampgrounds of America, Inc.
Koala Corporation, 44 260–62
Kobe Hankyu Company Ltd., **62** 170
Kobe Steel, Ltd., IV 129–31; 19 238–41 (upd.)
Kobold *see* Vorwerk & Co.
Kobrand Corporation, 82 191–94
Koç Holding A.S., I 478–80; 54 195–98 (upd.)
Koch Enterprises, Inc., 29 215–17
Koch Industries, Inc., IV 448–49; 20 330–32 (upd.); 77 224–30 (upd.)
Kodak *see* Eastman Kodak Co.
Kodansha Ltd., IV 631–33; 38 273–76 (upd.)
Koehring Cranes & Excavators, *see* Terex Corp.
Koei Real Estate Ltd. *see* Takashimaya Co., Ltd.
Koenig & Bauer AG, 64 222–26
Kogaku Co., Ltd., **48** 295
Kohl's Corporation, 9 312–13; 30 273–75 (upd.); 77 231–35 (upd.)
Kohlberg Kravis Roberts & Co., 24 272–74; 56 190–94 (upd.)
Kohler Company, 7 269–71; 32 308–12 (upd.)
Kohler Mix Specialties, Inc. *see*Dean Foods.
Kohn Pedersen Fox Associates P.C., 57 213–16
Kokkola Chemicals Oy, *see* OM Group, Inc.
Kokomo Gas and Fuel Company, **6** 533
Kokudo Corporation, **74** 301
Kokusai Kigyo Co. Ltd., **60** 301
Kolb-Lena, **25** 85
The Koll Company, 8 300–02
Kollmorgen Corporation, 18 291–94
Kölnische Rückversicherungs- Gesellschaft AG, *see* General Re Corp.
Komag, Inc., 11 234–35
Komatsu Ltd., III 545–46; 16 309–11 (upd.); 52 213–17 (upd.)
Kompass Allgemeine Vermögensberatung, **51** 23
KONE Corporation, 27 267–70; 76 225–28 (upd.)
Kongl. Elektriska Telegraf-Verket *see* Swedish Telecom.

Konica Corporation, III 547–50; 30 276–81 (upd.)
König Brauerei GmbH & Co. KG, 35 256–58 (upd.)
Koninklijke Ahold N.V., II 641–42; 16 312–14 (upd.)
Koninklijke Bols Wessanen, N.V., **29** 480–81; **57** 105
Koninklijke Grolsch BV *see* Royal Grolsch NV.
Koninklijke Hoogovens NV *see* Koninklijke Nederlandsche Hoogovens en Staalfabrieken NV.
Koninklijke Java-China Paketvaart Lijnen *see* Royal Interocean Lines.
NV Koninklijke KNP BT *see* Buhrmann NV.
Koninklijke KPN N.V. *see* Royal KPN N.V.
Koninklijke Luchtvaart Maatschappij N.V., I 107–09; 28 224–27 (upd.)
Koninklijke Nederlandsche Hoogovens en Staalfabrieken NV, IV 132–34
Koninklijke Nederlandsche Stoomboot Maatschappij, **26** 241
N.V. Koninklijke Nederlandse Vliegtuigenfabriek Fokker, I 54–56; 28 327–30 (upd.)
Koninklijke Nedlloyd N.V., 6 403–05; 26 241–44 (upd.)
Koninklijke Numico N.V. *see* Royal Numico N.V.
Koninklijke Paketvaart Maatschappij, **26** 242
Koninklijke Philips Electronics N.V., 50 297–302 (upd.)
Koninklijke PTT Nederland NV, V 299–301 *see also* Royal KPN NV.
Koninklijke Vendex KBB N.V. (Royal Vendex KBB N.V.), 62 206–09 (upd.)
Koninklijke Wessanen nv, II 527–29; 54 199–204 (upd.)
Koninklijke West-Indische Maildienst, **26** 242
Konishiroku Honten Co., Ltd., *see* Konica Corp.
Konrad Hornschuch AG, **31** 161–62
Koo Koo Roo, Inc., 25 263–65
Kookmin Bank, 58 206–08
Koop Nautic Holland, **41** 412
Koor Industries Ltd., II 47–49; 25 266–68 (upd.); 68 222–25 (upd.)
Kopin Corporation, 80 189–92
Köpings Mekaniska Verkstad, **26** 10
Koppel Steel, **26** 407
Koppers Industries, Inc., I 354–56; 26 245–48 (upd.)
Koramic Roofing Products N.V., **70** 363
Korbel Champagne Cellers *see* F. Korbel & Bros. Inc.
Körber AG, 60 190–94
Korea Automotive Motor Corp., *see* Robert Bosch GmbH.
Korea Electric Power Corporation (Kepco), 56 195–98
Korea Ginseng Corporation *see* KT&G Corp.

Korea Independent Energy Corporation, **62** 175
Korea Tobacco & Ginseng Corporation *see* KT&G Corp.
Korean Air Lines Co. Ltd., 6 98–99; 27 271–73 (upd.)
Korean Life Insurance Company, Ltd., **62** 175
Koret of California, Inc., 62 210–13
Kori Kollo Corp., **23** 41
Korn/Ferry International, 34 247–49
Korrekt Gebäudereinigung, *see* Randstad Holding n.v.
Kortbetalning Servo A.B., *see* Skandinaviska Enskilda Banken AB.
Kos Pharmaceuticals, Inc., 63 232–35
Koss Corporation, 38 277–79
Kosset Carpets, Ltd., *see* Shaw Industries.
Koszegi Industries Inc. *see* Forward Industries, Inc.
Kotobukiya Co., Ltd., V 113–14; 56 199–202 (upd.)
Koyland Ltd., **64** 217
KP Corporation, **74** 163
KPM *see* Koninklijke Paketvaart Maatschappij.
KPMG International, 10 385–87; 33 234–38 (upd.)
KPN *see* Koninklijke PTT Nederland N.V.
KPR Holdings Inc., **23** 203
KPS Special Situations Fund, L.P., **69** 360–62
Kraft Foods Inc., II 530–34; 7 272–77 (upd.); 45 235–44 (upd.); 91 291–306 (upd.)
Kraft Foodservice, **26** 504; **31** 359–60
Kraft Jacobs Suchard AG, 26 249–52 (upd.)
KraftMaid Cabinetry, Inc., 72 208–10
Kragen Auto Supply Co. *see* CSK Auto Corp.
Kramer Guitar, **29** 222
Kramer Machine and Engineering Company, **26** 117
Krames Communications Co., **22** 441, 443
Kransco, **25** 314; **61** 392
Krasnapolsky Restaurant and Wintergarden Company Ltd., **23** 228
Kraus-Anderson Companies, Inc., 36 317–20; 83 243-248 (upd.)
Krause Publications, Inc., 35 259–61
Krause's Furniture, Inc., 27 274–77
Krauss-Maffei AG, *see* Mannesmann AG.
Kredietbank N.V., II 304–056
Kreditanstalt für Wiederaufbau, 29 268–72
Kreher Steel Co., **25** 8
Krelitz Industries, Inc., *see* D&K Wholesale Drug, Inc.
Kresge Foundation *see* Kmart Corp.
Kreymborg, *see*Koninklijke Vendex KBB N.V. (Royal Vendex KBB N.V.)
Krispy Kreme Doughnut Corporation, 21 322–24; 61 150–54 (upd.)
Kristall, **62** 10
Kroenke Sports Enterprises, **51** 97

Létang et Rémy, **44** 205
Lettuce Entertain You Enterprises, **38** 103
Leucadia National Corporation, 11
260–62; 71 196–200 (upd.)
Leumi & Company Investment Bankers
Ltd., **60** 50
Leuna-Werke AG, **7** 142
Leupold & Stevens, Inc., 52 224–26
Level Five Research, Inc., **22** 292
Level 13 Entertainment, Inc., **58** 124
Level 3 Communications, Inc., 67
233–35
Levenger Company, 63 242–45
Lever Brothers Company, 9 317–19 *see*
also Unilever.
Leverage Group, **51** 99
Levernz Shoe Co., **61** 22
Levi Strauss & Co., V 362–65; 16
324–28 (upd.)
Leviathan Gas Pipeline Company, **21** 171
Levin Furniture *see* Sam Levin Inc.
Levine, Huntley, Vick & Beaver, **6** 28
Leviton Manufacturing Co., Inc., **54** 372
Levitt Corp., **21** 471
Levitt Investment Company, **26** 102
Levitz Furniture Inc., 15 280–82
Levolor Hardware Group, **53** 37
Levtex Hotel Ventures, **21** 363
Levy *see* Chas. Levy Company LLC.
Levy Home Entertainment, LLC, **60** 83,
85
Levy Restaurants L.P., 26 263–65
The Lewin Group, Inc., **21** 425
Lewis and Marks, **16** 27; **50** 32
Lewis Batting Company, **11** 219
Lewis Galoob Toys Inc., 16 329–31
Lewis Group Ltd., **58** 54–55
Lewis Homes, **45** 221
Lewis Refrigeration Company, **21** 500
Lex Service plc, **50** 42
Lexecon, Inc., **26** 187
Lexington Ice Company, **6** 514
Lexington Utilities Company, **6** 514
LEXIS-NEXIS Group, 33 263–67
Lexmark International, Inc., 18 305–07;
79 237–42 (upd.)
Leybold GmbH, **IV** 71; **48** 30
LF International, Inc., **59** 259
LFC Holdings Corp. *see* Levitz Furniture
Inc.
LFE Corp., *see* Mark IV Industries, Inc.
LG&E Energy Corporation, 6 516–18;
51 214–17 (upd.)
LG Chemical Ltd., **26** 425
LG Electronics Inc., **43** 428
LG Group, **34** 514, 517–18
LG Semiconductor, **56** 173
LGT Asset Management *see* AMVESCAP
PLC.
Li & Fung Limited, 59 258–61
Liaison Agency, **31** 216–17
Lianozovo Dairy, **48** 438
Libbey Inc., 49 251–54
Libbey-Owens-Ford Company, *see*
TRINOVA Corp.
Liber, **14** 556
The Liberty Corporation, 22 312–14

Liberty Hardware Manufacturing
Corporation, **20** 363
Liberty Life, **IV** 97
Liberty Livewire Corporation, 42
224–27
Liberty Media Corporation, 50 317–19
Liberty Mutual Holding Company, 59
262–64
Liberty Mutual Insurance Group, **11** 379;
48 271
Liberty National Insurance Holding
Company *see* Torchmark Corp.
Liberty Orchards Co., Inc., 89 302–05
Liberty Property Trust, 57 221–23
Liberty Software, Inc., *see* Jack Henry and
Associates, Inc.
Liberty Surf UK, **48** 399
Liberty Tax Service, **48** 236
Liberty Travel, Inc., 56 203–06
Librairie Générale Francaise *see* Hachette.
Librairie Larousse *see* Groupe de la Cité.
Librairie Louis Hachette *see* Hachette.
Librizol India Pvt. Ltd., **48** 212
Libyan National Oil Corporation, IV
453–55 *see also* National Oil Corp.
Liebert Corp., *see* Emerson.
Liebherr Haushaltgerate GmbH, **65** 167
Liebherr-International AG, 64 238–42
Life Assurance Holding Corporation, **71**
324–26
Life Care Centers of America Inc., 76
246–48
Life Investors International Ltd., **12** 199
Life is good, Inc., 80 213–16
Life Partners Group, Inc., **33** 111
Life Retail Stores *see* Angelica Corp.
Life Savers Corp., *see* Nabisco Foods
Group.
Life Science Research, Inc., *see* Applied
Bioscience International, Inc.
Life Technologies, Inc., 17 287–89
Life Time Fitness, Inc., 66 208–10
Life Uniform Shops *see* Angelica Corp.
LifeCell Corporation, 77 236–39
Lifeline Systems, Inc., 32 374; 53
207–09
LifeLock, Inc., 91 314–17
Lifemark Corp., *see* American Medical
International, Inc.
LifePoint Hospitals, Inc., 69 234–36
LifeScan Inc., **63** 206
Lifestyle Fitness Clubs, **46** 432
Lifetime Brands, Inc., 27 286–89; 73
207–11 (upd.)
Lifetime Corp., **29** 363–64
Lifetime Entertainment Services, 51
218–22
Lifetouch Inc., 86 243–47
Lifeway Foods, Inc., 65 215–17
LifeWise Health Plan of Oregon, Inc.,
90 276–79
Ligand Pharmaceuticals Incorporated,
10 48; **47 221–23**
Liggett & Meyers, **29** 195
Liggett-Ducat, **49** 153
Liggett Group Inc. *see* Vector Group Inc.
Light Savers U.S.A., Inc. *see* Hospitality
Worldwide Services, Inc.

Lightel Inc., **6** 311
Lil' Champ Food Stores, Inc., **36** 359
LILCO *see* Long Island Lighting Co.
Lille Bonnières et Colombes, **37** 143–44
Lillian Vernon Corporation, 12 314–15;
35 274–77 (upd.); 92 207–12 (upd.)
Lillie Rubin, **30** 104–06
Lilliput Group plc, **11** 95; **15** 478
Lilly & Co *see* Eli Lilly & Co.
Lilly Endowment Inc., 70 157–59
Lilly Industries, **22** 437
Limagrain *see* Groupe Limagrain.
Limburgse Vinyl Maatschappij, **76**
346–47
Limhamns Golvindustri AB *see* Tarkett
Sommer AG.
The Limited, Inc., V 115–16; 20
340–43 (upd.)
LIN Broadcasting Corp., 9 320–22
Linamar Corporation, 18 308–10
Lincare Holdings Inc., 43 265–67
Lincoln Automotive, **26** 363
Lincoln Benefit Life Company, *see* The
Allstate Corp.
Lincoln Center for the Performing Arts,
Inc., 69 237–41
Lincoln Electric Co., 13 314–16
Lincoln Industrial Corporation, **70** 142
Lincoln Liberty Life Insurance Co., *see*
First Executive Corp.
Lincoln Marketing, Inc., *see* Total System
Services, Inc.
Lincoln National Corporation, III
274–77; 25 286–90 (upd.)
Lincoln Property Company, 8 326–28;
54 222–26 (upd.)
Lincoln Snacks Company, 24 286–88
Lincoln Telephone & Telegraph
Company, 14 311–13
Lindal Cedar Homes, Inc., 29 287–89
Linde AG, I 581–83; 67 236–39 (upd.)
Linde Refrigeration *see* Carrier Corp.
Lindemans *see* Southcorp Ltd.
Lindley *see* Corporación José R. Lindley
S.A.
Lindsay Manufacturing Co., 20 344–46
Lindt & Sprüngli *see* Chocoladefabriken
Lindt & Sprüngli AG.
Linear Corporation Bhd, **66** 28
Linear Technology, Inc., 16 332–34
Linens 'n Things, Inc., 24 289–92; 75
239–43 (upd.)
Linfood Holdings Ltd., *see* Gateway
Corporation Ltd.
Ling Products, *see* Banta Corp.
Ling-Temco-Vought *see* LTV Corp.
Lingerfelt Development Corporation, **57**
223
Lingerie Time, **20** 143
Linguaphone Group, **43** 204, 206
Linificio e Canapificio Nazionale S.p.A.,
67 210–11, 246–48
Link House Publications PLC, **IV** 687
Link Motor Supply Company, **26** 347
Linroz Manufacturing Company L.P., **25**
245
LINT Company, **64** 237
Lintas: Worldwide, 14 314–16

Long Island College Hospital *see*
Continuum Health Partners, Inc.
Long Island Lighting Company, V
652–54
Long Island Power Authority, *see* KeySpan
Energy Co.
The Long Island Rail Road Company,
68 238–40
Long John Silver's, 13 320–22; 57
224–29 (upd.)
Long-Term Credit Bank of Japan, Ltd.,
II 310–11 *Sumitomo Mitsui Banking*
Corp.
The Longaberger Company, 12 319–21;
44 267–70 (upd.)
Longchamps, Inc., **38** 385; **41** 388
LongHorn Steakhouse, *see* Rare
Hospitality International Inc.
Longman Group Ltd., **IV** 611, 658
Longs Drug Stores Corporation, V 120;
25 295–97 (upd.); 83 249-253 (upd.)
Longview Fibre Company, 8 335–37; 37
234–37 (upd.)
Lonmin plc, 66 211–16 (upd.)
Lonrho Plc, 21 351–55 *see also* Lonmin
plc.
Lonza Group Ltd., 73 212–14
Lookers plc, 71 204–06
Loomis Armored Car Service Limited, **45**
378
Loomis Fargo Group, **42** 338
Loomis Products, Inc., **64** 349
Loop One2, **53** 240
Lor-Al, Inc., *see* Ag-Chem Equipment
Company, Inc.
Loral Space & Communications Ltd., 8
338–40; 54 231–35 (upd.)
Lord & Taylor, **15** 86; **21** 302
L'Oréal, III 46–49; 8 341–44 (upd.); 46
274–79 (upd.)
Lorentzen & Wettre AB, **53** 85
Lorillard Industries, **V** 407, 417; **22** 73;
29 195
Lorimar Telepictures, *see* Time Warner Inc.
Los Angeles Lakers *see* California Sports,
Inc.
Lost Arrow Inc., 22 323–25
LOT Polish Airlines (Polskie Linie
Lotnicze S.A.), 33 268–71
LOT$OFF Corporation, 24 300–01
Lotte Confectionery Company Ltd., 76
249–51
Lotus Cars Ltd., 14 320–22
Lotus Development Corporation, 6
254–56; 25 298–302 (upd.)
Lotus Publishing Corporation, **7** 239; **25**
239
Louart Corporation, **29** 33–34
Loudcloud, Inc. *see* Opsware Inc.
Louis Allis, **15** 288
Louis Cruise Lines, **52** 298–99
Louis Dreyfus *see* Groupe Louis Dreyfus
S.A.
Louis Dreyfus Energy Corp., **28** 471
Louis Kemp Seafood Company, *see* Tyson
Foods, Inc.
Louis Vuitton, 10 397–99 *see also* LVMH
Moët Hennessy Louis Vuitton SA.

Louisiana Corporation, **19** 301
The Louisiana Land and Exploration
Company, 7 280–83
Louisiana-Pacific Corporation, IV
304–05; 31 314–17 (upd.)
Louisville Gas and Electric Company *see*
LG&E Energy Corp.
Loup River Public Power District, **29** 352
LoVaca Gathering Company *see* The
Coastal Corp.
Love's Travel Stops & Country Stores,
Inc., 71 207–09
Lowe Group, *see* Interpublic Group of
Companies, Inc.
Lowe's Companies, Inc., V 122–23; 21
356–58 (upd.); 81 240–44 (upd.)
Löwenbräu AG, 80 223–27
Lower Manhattan Development
Corporation, **47** 360
Lowes Food Stores *see* Alex Lee Inc.
Lowney/Moirs, *see* Hershey Foods Corp.
Lowrance Electronics, Inc., 18 311–14
Lowrey's Meat Specialties, Inc., **21** 156
LPA Holding Corporation, 81 245–48
LPL Investment Group, **40** 35–36
LRC International, **69** 303
LRV Corporation, **61** 173
LS Management, Inc., **51** 229
LSB Industries, Inc., 77 244–47
LSG Sky Chefs, Inc., **68** 109
LSI *see* Lear Siegler Inc.
LSI Logic Corporation, 13 323–25; 64
243–47
LTR Industries, **52** 301–03
LTU Group Holding GmbH, 37 238–41
LTV Aerospace *see* Vought Aircraft
Industries, Inc.
The LTV Corporation, I 489–91; 24
302–06 (upd.)
The Lubrizol Corporation, I 360–62; 30
292–95 (upd.); 83 254-259 (upd.)
Luby's, Inc., 17 290–93; 42 233–38
(upd.)
Lucas Industries Plc, III 554–57
Lucas Ingredients, *see* Kerry Group plc.
Lucas-Milhaupt, Inc., **23** 250
LucasArts Entertainment Company, **32** 9
Lucasfilm Ltd., 12 322–24; 50 320–23
(upd.)
LucasVarity plc, *see* Kelsey-Hayes Group
of Companies.
Lucent Technologies Inc., 34 257–60
Lucille Farms, Inc., 45 249–51
Lucky-Goldstar, II 53–54 *see also*
Goldstar Co., Ltd.
Lucky Stores Inc., 27 290–93
Ludendo S.A., 88 237–40
Ludi Wap S.A., **41** 409
Ludovico, **25** 85
Lufkin Industries, Inc., 78 198–202
Luftfahrzeug-Betriebs GmbH, **60** 253
Lufthansa *see* Deutsche Lufthansa AG.
Luigino's, Inc., 64 248–50
Luitpold-Werk GmbH & Co., **56** 303
Lukens Inc., 14 323–25 *see also*
Bethlehem Steel Corp.
LUKOIL *see* OAO LUKOIL.

Lumbermens Building Centers *see* Lanoga
Corp.
Lumbertown USA, **52** 232
Lumex, Inc., *see* Fuqua Enterprises, Inc.
Lumidor Safety Products, **52** 187
Luminar Plc, 40 296–98
Lummus Crest, **26** 496
Lunar Corporation, 29 297–99
Lund Boat Co. *see* Genmar Holdings, Inc.
Lund Food Holdings, Inc., 22 326–28
Lund International Holdings, Inc., 40
299–301
L'Unite Hermetique S.A., *see* Tecumseh
Products Co.
Lurgei, **6** 599
LURGI *see* Metallurgische Gesellschaft
Aktiengesellschaft.
Lush Ltd., 93 305–08
Lutèce, **20** 26
Lutheran Brotherhood, 31 318–21
Luxair, **49** 80
Luxor, *see* Nokia Corp.
Luxottica SpA, 17 294–96; 52 227–30
(upd.)
LuxSonor Semiconductor Inc., **48** 92
Luzianne Blue Plate Foods *see* Wm. B.
Reily & Company Inc.
LVMH Moët Hennessy Louis Vuitton
SA, 33 272–77 (upd.) *see also*
Christian Dior S.A.
LXE Inc., **21** 199–201
Lycos *see* Terra Lycos, Inc.
Lydall, Inc., 64 251–54
Lyfra-S.A./NV, 88 241–43
Lyn Knight Currency Auctions, Inc, **48**
100
Lynch Corporation, 43 273–76
The Lynde Company, *see* Hawkins
Chemical, Inc.
Lynden Incorporated, 91 322–25
Lynx Express Delivery *see* Exel plc.
Lyondell Chemical Company, IV
456–57; 45 252–55 (upd.)
Lyonnaise des Eaux-Dumez, V 655–57
see also Suez Lyonnaise des Eaux.
Lyons *see* J. Lyons & Co. Ltd.
Lytag Ltd., **31** 398–99

M

M & C Saatchi, **42** 330
M&C Systems Co Ltd., **62** 245
M&F Worldwide Corp., 38 293–95
M&G Group plc, **48** 328
M and H Valve Co., **55** 266
M&I Bank *see* Marshall & Ilsley Corp.
M&M Limited, *see* Mars, Inc.
M and M Manufacturing Company, **23**
143
M&M/Mars, **14** 48; **15** 63–64; **21** 219
M & S Computing *see* Intergraph Corp.
M&T Capital Corporation, *see* First
Empire State Corp.
M/A Com Inc., **14** 26–27
M-Cell Ltd., **31** 329
M-R Group plc, **31** 312–13
M-real Oyj, 56 252–55 (upd.)
M-Web Holdings Ltd., **31** 329–30
M.A. Bruder & Sons, Inc., 56 207–09

Mercantile Estate and Property Corp. Ltd. *see* MEPC PLC.

Mercantile Stores Company, Inc., V 139; 19 270–73 (upd.) *see also* Dillard's Inc.

Mercator & Noordstar N.V., **40** 61

Mercator Software, **59** 54, 56

Mercedes Benz *see* DaimlerChrysler AG

Mercer International Inc., 64 273–75

Merchant Distributors, Inc., **20** 306

Merchant Investors *see* Sanlam Ltd.

Merchants Bank & Trust Co., **21** 524

Merchants Distributors Inc. *see* Alex Lee Inc.

Merchants Home Delivery Service, **6** 414

Merchants National Bank, *see* Deposit Guaranty Corp.

Mercian Corporation, 77 261–64

Merck & Co., Inc., I 650–52; 11 289–91 (upd.); 34 280–85 (upd.)

Mercury Air Group, Inc., 20 371–73

Mercury Asset Management (MAM), **14** 420; **40** 313

Mercury Communications, Ltd., 7 332–34 *see also* Cable and Wireless plc.

Mercury Drug Corporation, 70 181–83

Mercury General Corporation, 25 323–25

Mercury Interactive Corporation, 59 293–95

Mercury International Ltd., **51** 130

Mercury Marine Group, 68 247–51

Mercury Records, **23** 389, 391

Mercury Telecommunications Limited, **15** 67, 69

Mercy Air Service, Inc., **53** 29

Meredith Corporation, 11 292–94; 29 316–19 (upd.); 74 189–93 (upd.)

Merfin International, **42** 53

Merge Healthcare, 85 264–68

Merial, **34** 284

Meriam Instrument *see* Scott Fetzer.

Merico, Inc., **36** 161–64

Merida, **50** 445, 447

Meridian Bancorp, Inc., 11 295–97

Meridian Emerging Markets Ltd., **25** 509

Meridian Gold, Incorporated, 47 238–40

Meridian Healthcare Ltd., *see* NeighborCare, Inc.

Meridian Industrial Trust Inc., **57** 301

Meridian Oil Inc., **10** 190–91

Meridian Publishing, Inc., **28** 254

Merillat Industries, LLC, 13 338–39; 69 253–55 (upd.)

Merisant Worldwide, Inc., 70 184–86

Merisel, Inc., 12 334–36

Merit Distribution Services, *see* McLane Company, Inc.

Merit Medical Systems, Inc., 29 320–22

Merit Tank Testing, Inc., **IV** 411

MeritCare Health System, 88 257–61

Merita/Cotton's Bakeries, **38** 251

Meritage Corporation, 26 289–92

MeritaNordbanken, **40** 336

Meritor Automotive Inc. *see* ArvinMeritor Inc.

Merix Corporation, 36 329–31; 75 257–60 (upd.)

Merkur Direktwerbegesellschaft, **29** 152

Merpati Nusantara Airlines *see* Garuda Indonesia.

Merriam-Webster Inc., 70 187–91

Merrill Corporation, 18 331–34; 47 241–44 (upd.)

Merrill Lynch & Co., Inc., II 424–26; 13 340–43 (upd.); 40 310–15 (upd.)

Merrill Lynch Capital Partners, **47** 363

Merrill Lynch Investment Managers *see* BlackRock, Inc.

Merrill, Pickard, Anderson & Eyre IV, **11** 490

Merrill Publishing, **29** 57

Merrimack Services Corp., **37** 303

Merry-Go-Round Enterprises, Inc., 8 362–64

Merry Group *see* Boral Ltd.

Merry Maids *see* ServiceMaster Inc.

Merryhill Schools, Inc., **37** 279

The Mersey Docks and Harbour Company, 30 318–20

Mervyn's California, 10 409–10; 39 269–71 (upd.) *see also* Target Corp.

Merz Group, 81 253–56

Mesa Air Group, Inc., 11 298–300; 32 334–37 (upd.); 77 265–70 (upd.)

Mesaba Holdings, Inc., 28 265–67

Messerschmitt-Bölkow-Blohm GmbH., I 73–75 *see also* European Aeronautic Defence and Space Company EADS N.V.

Mestek, Inc., 10 411–13

Met Food Corp. *see* White Rose Food Corp.

Met-Mex Penoles *see* Industrias Penoles, S.A. de C.V.

META Group, Inc., **37** 147

Metal Box plc, I 604–06 *see also* Novar plc.

Metal-Cal *see* Avery Dennison Corp.

Metal Casting Technology, Inc., **23** 267, 269

Metal Management, Inc., 92 247–50

AB Metal Pty Ltd, **62** 331

Metalcorp Ltd, **62** 331

Metales y Contactos, **29** 461–62

Metaleurop S.A., 21 368–71

MetalExchange, **26** 530

Metallgesellschaft AG, IV 139–42; 16 361–66 (upd.)

MetalOptics Inc., **19** 212

Metalúrgica Gerdau *see* Gerdau S.A.

Metalurgica Mexicana Penoles, S.A. *see* Industrias Penoles, S.A. de C.V.

Metaphase Technology, Inc., *see* Control Data Systems, Inc.

Metatec International, Inc., 47 245–48

Metcalf & Eddy Companies, Inc., **6** 441; **32** 52

Metcash Trading Ltd., 58 226–28

Meteor Film Productions, **23** 391

Meteor Industries Inc., 33 295–97

Methane Development Corporation, **6** 457

Methanex Corporation, 40 316–19

Methode Electronics, Inc., 13 344–46

MetLife *see* Metropolitan Life Insurance Co.

MetPath, Inc., *see* Corning Inc.

Metra Corporation *see* Wärtsilä Corp.

Metra Steel, **19** 381

Metragaz, **69** 191

Metrastock Ltd., **34** 5

Metric Constructors, Inc., **16** 286

Metric Systems Corporation, *see* Tech-Sym Corp.

Metris Companies Inc., 56 224–27

Metro AG, 50 335–39

Metro Distributors Inc., **14** 545

Metro-Goldwyn-Mayer Inc., 25 326–30 (upd.); 84 263–270 (upd.)

Metro Holding AG, **38** 266

Métro Inc., 77 271–75

Metro Information Services, Inc., 36 332–34

Metro International S.A., 93 309–12

Metro-Mark Integrated Systems Inc., **11** 469

Metro-North Commuter Railroad Company, **35** 292

Metro Pacific, *see* First Pacific Co. Ltd.

Metro Southwest Construction *see* CRSS Inc.

Metro Support Services, Inc., **48** 171

Metrocall, Inc., 41 265–68

Metrol Security Services, Inc., **32** 373

Metroland Printing, Publishing and Distributing Ltd., **29** 471

Metromail Corp., **IV** 661; **18** 170; **38** 370

Metromedia Company, 7 335–37; 14 298–300 (upd.); 61 210–14 (upd.)

Metronic AG, **64** 226

Metroplex, LLC, **51** 206

Métropole Télévision S.A., 76 272–74 (upd.)

Metropolis Intercom, **67** 137–38

Metropolitan Baseball Club Inc., 39 272–75

Metropolitan Clothing Co., **19** 362

Metropolitan Edison Company, *see* GPU, Inc.

Metropolitan Financial Corporation, 13 347–49

Metropolitan Life Insurance Company, III 290–94; 52 235–41 (upd.)

The Metropolitan Museum of Art, 55 267–70

Metropolitan Opera Association, Inc., 40 320–23

Metropolitan Reference Laboratories Inc., **26** 391

Metropolitan Tobacco Co., **15** 138

Metropolitan Transportation Authority, 35 290–92

MetroRed, **57** 67, 69

Metrostar Management, **59** 199

METSA, Inc., **15** 363

Metsä-Serla Oy, IV 314–16 *see also* M-real Oyj.

Metsec plc, **57** 402

Metso Corporation, 30 321–25 (upd.); 85 269–77 (upd.)

Miele & Cie. KG, **56** 232–35

MiG *see* Russian Aircraft Corporation (MiG).

MIG Realty Advisors, Inc., **25** 23, 25

Migros-Genossenschafts-Bund, 68 252–55

MIH Limited, 31 329–32

Mikasa, Inc., 28 268–70

Mike-Sell's Inc., 15 298–300

Mikohn Gaming Corporation, 39 276–79

Milacron, Inc., 53 226–30 (upd.)

Milan AC S.p.A., 79 255–58

Milbank, Tweed, Hadley & McCloy, 27 324–27

Milchem, Inc., **63** 306

Mile-Hi Distributing, **64** 180

Miles Inc., **22** 148

Miles Laboratories, I 653–55 *see also* Bayer A.G.

Milgram Food Stores Inc., *see* Wetterau Inc.

Milgray Electronics Inc., **47** 41

Milk Specialties Co., **12** 199

Millea Holdings Inc., 64 276–81 (upd.)

Millennium & Copthorne Hotels plc, 71 231–33

Millennium Chemicals Inc., **30** 231; **45** 252, 254; **71** 149–50

Millennium Materials Inc. *see* Dyson Group PLC.

Millennium Pharmaceuticals, Inc., 47 249–52

Miller Automotive Group, **52** 146

Miller Brewing Company, I 269–70; **12** 337–39 (upd.) *see also* SABMiller plc.

Miller Companies, **17** 182

Miller Exploration Company *see* Edge Petroleum Corp.

Miller Freeman, Inc., **IV** 687; **28** 501, 504

Miller Group Ltd., **22** 282

Miller Industries, Inc., 26 293–95

Miller-Meteor Company *see* Accubuilt, Inc.

Miller, Morris & Brooker (Holdings) Ltd. *see* Gibbs and Dandy plc.

Miller Plant Farms, Inc., **51** 61

Miller Publishing Group, LLC, 57 242–44

Miller, Tabak, Hirsch & Co., **28** 164

Millet, **39** 250

Millet's Leisure *see* Sears plc.

Milliken & Co., V 366–68; **17** 327–30 (upd.); **82** 235–39 (upd.)

Milliman USA, 66 223–26

Millipore Corporation, 25 339–43; **84** 271–276 (upd.)

Mills Clothing, Inc. *see* The Buckle, Inc.

The Mills Corporation, 77 280–83

Millway Foods, **25** 85

Milne & Craighead, **48** 113

Milne Fruit Products, Inc., **25** 366

Milnot Company, 46 289–91

Milpark Drilling Fluids, Inc., **63** 306

Milsco Manufacturing Co., **23** 299, 300

Milton Bradley Company, 21 372–75

Milton CAT, Inc., 86 268–71

Milupa S.A., **37** 341

Milwaukee Brewers Baseball Club, 37 247–49

Milwaukee Electric Railway and Light Company, **6** 601–02, 604–05

Milwaukee Electric Tool, **28** 40

MIM Holdings, **73** 392

Mimi's Cafés *see* SWH Corp.

Minatome, **IV** 560

Mindpearl, **48** 381

Mindport, **31** 329

Mindset Corp., **42** 424–25

Mindspring Enterprises, Inc., **36** 168

Mine Safety Appliances Company, 31 333–35

Minebea Co., Ltd., 90 298–302

The Miner Group International, 22 356–58

Minera Loma Blanca S.A., **56** 127

Mineral Point Public Service Company, **6** 604

Minerales y Metales, S.A. *see* Industrias Penoles, S.A. de C.V.

Minerals & Metals Trading Corporation of India Ltd., IV 143–44

Minerals and Resources Corporation Limited *see* Minorco.

Minerals Technologies Inc., 11 310–12; **52** 248–51 (upd.)

Minerva SA, **72** 289

Minerve, **6** 208

Minitel, **21** 233

Minneapolis Children's Medical Center, **54** 65

Minneapolis Steel and Machinery Company, **21** 502

Minnehoma Insurance Company, **58** 260

Minnesota Brewing Company *see* MBC Holding Co.

Minnesota Mining & Manufacturing Company, I 499–501; **8** 369–71 (upd.); **26** 296–99 (upd.) *see also* 3M Co.

Minnesota Power, Inc., 11 313–16; **34** 286–91 (upd.)

Minntech Corporation, 22 359–61

Minn-Dak Farmers Cooperative, **32** 29

Minolta Co., Ltd., III 574–76; **18** 339–42 (upd.); **43** 281–85 (upd.)

Minorco, **IV** 97; **16** 28, 293

Minstar Inc., **15** 49; **45** 174

Minton China, **38** 401

The Minute Maid Company, 28 271–74

Minuteman International Inc., 46 292–95

Minyard Food Stores, Inc., 33 304–07; **86** 272–77 (upd.)

Mippon Paper, **21** 546; **50** 58

Miquel y Costas Miquel S.A., 68 256–58

Miracle Food Mart, *see* The Great Atlantic & Pacific Tea Co., Inc.

Miracle-Gro Products, Inc., *see* Scotts Co.

Mirage Resorts, Incorporated, 6 209–12; **28** 275–79 (upd.)

Miraglia Inc., **57** 139

Miramax Film Corporation, 64 282–85

Mirant, **39** 54, 57

MIRAX Corporation *see* JSP Corp.

Mircor Inc., **12** 413

Miroglio SpA, 86 278–81

Mirror Group Newspapers plc, 7 341–43; **23** 348–51 (upd.)

Misonix, Inc., 80 248–51

Misr Airwork *see* EgyptAir.

Misrair *see* AirEgypt.

Miss Erika, Inc., *see* Norton McNaughton, Inc.

Miss Selfridge *see* Sears plc.

Misset Publishers, **IV** 611

Mission Group *see* SCEcorp.

Mission Jewelers, **30** 408

Mission Valley Fabrics, **57** 285

Mississippi Chemical Corporation, 39 280–83

Mississippi Gas Company, **6** 577

Mississippi Power Company, **38** 446–47

Mississippi River Recycling, **31** 47, 49

Mississippi Valley Title Insurance Company, **58** 259–60

Missoula Bancshares, Inc., **35** 198–99

Missouri Gaming Company, **21** 39

Missouri Gas & Electric Service Company, **6** 593

Missouri Public Service Company *see* UtiliCorp United Inc.

Missouri Utilities Company, **6** 580

Mist Assist, Inc. *see* Ballard Medical Products.

Misys PLC, 45 279–81; **46** 296–99

Mitchell Energy and Development Corporation, 7 344–46 *see also* Devon Energy Corp.

Mitchells & Butlers PLC, 59 296–99

MiTek Industries Inc., *see* Rexam PLC.

Mitel Corporation, 18 343–46

MITRE Corporation, 26 300–02

MITROPA AG, 37 250–53

Mitsubishi Bank, Ltd., II 321–22 *see also* Bank of Tokyo-Mitsubishi Ltd.

Mitsubishi Chemical Corporation, I 363–64; **56** 236–38 (upd.)

Mitsubishi Corporation, I 502–04; **12** 340–43 (upd.)

Mitsubishi Electric Corporation, II 57–59; **44** 283–87 (upd.)

Mitsubishi Estate Company, Limited, IV 713–14; **61** 215–18 (upd.)

Mitsubishi Group, **21** 390

Mitsubishi Heavy Industries, Ltd., III 577–79; **7** 347–50 (upd.); **40** 324–28 (upd.)

Mitsubishi Kasei Corp., **14** 535

Mitsubishi Kasei Vinyl Company, **49** 5

Mitsubishi Materials Corporation, III 712–13

Mitsubishi Motors Corporation, 9 349–51; **23** 352–55 (upd.); **57** 245–49 (upd.)

Mitsubishi Oil Co., Ltd., IV 460–62 *see also* Nippon Mitsubishi Oil Corp.

Mitsubishi Rayon Co. Ltd., V 369–71

Mitsubishi Trust & Banking Corporation, II 323–24

Mitsui & Co., Ltd., I 505–08; **28** 280–85 (upd.)

NBC/Computer Services Corporation, **15** 163

NBD Bancorp, Inc., **11** 339–41 *see also* Bank One Corp.

NBGS International, Inc., **73** 231–33

NBSC Corporation *see* National Bank of South Carolina.

NBTY, Inc., **31** 346–48

NCB *see* National City Bank of New York.

NCC Industries, Inc., **59** 267

NCC L.P., **15** 139

NCH Corporation, **8** 385–87

nChip, **38** 187–88

NCI Building Systems, Inc., **88** 276–79

NCL Corporation, **79** 274–77

NCL Holdings *see* Genting Bhd.

NCNB Corporation, **II** 336–37 *see also* Bank of America Corp.

NCO Group, Inc., **42** 258–60

NCR Corporation, **III** 150–53; **6** 264–68 (upd.); **30** 336–41 (upd.); **90** 303–12 (upd.)

NCS *see* Norstan, Inc.

NCS Healthcare Inc., **67** 262

nCube Corp., **14** 15; **22** 293

NDB *see* National Discount Brokers Group, Inc.

NDL *see* Norddeutscher Lloyd.

NE Chemcat Corporation, **72** 118

NEA *see* Newspaper Enterprise Association.

Neatherlin Homes Inc., **22** 547

Nebraska Book Company, Inc., **65** 257–59

Nebraska Furniture Mart, *see* Berkshire Hathaway Inc.

Nebraska Light & Power Company, **6** 580

Nebraska Public Power District, **29** 351–54

NEBS *see* New England Business Services, Inc.

NEC Corporation, **II** 66–68; **21** 388–91 (upd.); **57** 261–67 (upd.)

Neckermann Versand AG *see* Karstadt AG.

Nedcor, **61** 270–71

Nederland Line *see* Stoomvaart Maatschappij Nederland.

Nederlands Talen Institut, *see* Koninklijke Vendex KBB N.V. (Royal Vendex KBB N.V.)

Nederlandsche Electriciteits Maatschappij *see* N.E.M.

Nederlandsche Handel Maatschappij, **26** 242

Nederlandsche Heidenmaatschappij *see* Arcadis NV.

N.V. Nederlandse Gasunie, **V** 658–61

Nedlloyd Group *see* Koninklijke Nedlloyd N.V.

NedMark Transportation Services *see* Polar Air Cargo Inc.

Needham Harper Worldwide *see* Omnicom Group Inc.

Needleworks, Inc., **23** 66

Neenah Foundry Company, **68** 263–66

Neenah Printing, *see* Menasha Corp.

NEES *see* New England Electric System.

Neff Corp., **32** 352–53

Neff GmbH, **67** 81

NEG Micon A/S, **73** 375

Negromex, **23** 171–72

NEI *see* Northern Engineering Industries PLC.

Neico International, Inc., **67** 226

NeighborCare, Inc., **67** 259–63 (upd.)

Neilson/Cadbury, *see* George Weston Ltd.

The Neiman Marcus Group, Inc., **12** 355–57; **49** 283–87 (upd.)

Nektar Therapeutics, **91** 350–53

Nelson Entertainment Group, **47** 272

Nelson Publications, **22** 442

Nelsons *see* A. Nelson & Co. Ltd.

NEMF *see* New England Motor Freight, Inc.

Neo Products Co., **37** 401

Neopost S.A., **53** 237–40

Neos, **21** 438

Nepera, Inc., **16** 69

Neptun Maritime Oyj, **29** 431

Neptune Orient Lines Limited, **47** 267–70

NER Auction Group, **23** 148

NERCO, Inc., **7** 376–79 *see also* Rio Tinto PLC.

NES *see* National Equipment Services, Inc.

Nesco Inc., **28** 6, 8

Nespak SpA, **40** 214–15

Neste Oil Corporation, **IV** 469–71; **85** 295–302 (upd.)

Nestlé S.A., **II** 545–49; **7** 380–84 (upd.); **28** 308–13 (upd.); **71** 240–46 (upd.)

Nestlé Waters, **73** 234–37

Net Investment S.A., **63** 180

NetApp *see* Network Appliance, Inc.

NetCom Systems AB, **26** 331–33

NetCreations, **47** 345, 347

NetEffect Alliance, **58** 194

Netezza Corporation, **69** 276–78

Netflix, Inc., **58** 248–51

NETGEAR, Inc., **81** 261–64

Netherlands Trading Co *see* Nederlandse Handel Maatschappij.

NetHold B.V., **31** 330

NetIQ Corporation, **79** 278–81

NetMarket Company, **16** 146

NetPlane Systems, **36** 124

Netscape Communications Corporation, **15** 320–22; **35** 304–07 (upd.)

NetStar Communications Inc., **24** 49; **35** 69

Nettingsdorfer, **19** 227

Nettle Creek Corporation, *see* Pillowtex Corp.

Net2Phone Inc., **34** 224

NetWest Securities, **25** 450

Network Appliance, Inc., **58** 252–54

Network Associates, Inc., **25** 347–49

Network Communications Associates, Inc., **11** 409

Network Equipment Technologies Inc., **92** 265–68

Network Solutions, Inc., **47** 430

Network Ten, **35** 68–69

NetZero Inc. *see* United Online, Inc.

Netzip Inc., **53** 282

Neuberger Berman Inc., **57** 268–71

Neuer Markt, **59** 153

Neuro Navigational Corporation, **21** 47

NeuStar, Inc., **81** 265–68

Neutrogena Corporation, **17** 340–44

Nevada Bell Telephone Company, **14** 345–47 *see also* AT&T Corp.

Nevada Community Bank, **11** 119

Nevada Power Company, **11** 342–44

Nevada Savings and Loan Association, **19** 412

Nevada State Bank, **53** 378

Nevamar Company, **82** 255–58

Nevex Software Technologies, **42** 24, 26

New Access Communications, **43** 252

New Asahi Co., *see* Asahi Breweries, Ltd.

New Balance Athletic Shoe, Inc., **25** 350–52; **68** 267–70 (upd.)

New Bauhinia Limited, **53** 333

New Belgium Brewing Company, Inc., **68** 271–74

New Brunswick Scientific Co., Inc., **45** 285–87

New Century Energies, **73** 384

New Century Equity Holdings Corporation, **72** 39

New Century Network, **13** 180; **19** 204, 285

New Clicks Holdings Ltd., **86** 295–98

New CORT Holdings Corporation *see* CORT Business Services Corp.

New Daido Steel Co., Ltd., **IV** 62–63

New Dana Perfumes Company, **37** 269–71

New Dimension Software, Inc., **55** 67

New England Audio Company, Inc. *see* Tweeter Home Entertainment Group, Inc.

New England Business Service, Inc., **18** 361–64; **78** 237–42 (upd.)

New England Confectionery Co., **15** 323–25

New England CRInc, *see* Wellman Inc.

New England Electric System, **V** 662–64 *see also* National Grid USA.

New England Motor Freight, Inc., **53** 250

New England Mutual Life Insurance Co., **III** 312–14 *see also* Metropolitan Life Insurance Co.

New England Paper Tube Co., **54** 58

New England Power Association *see* National Grid USA.

New Flyer Industries Inc., **78** 243–46

New Galveston Company, Inc., **25** 116

New Hampton Goldfields Ltd., **63** 182, 184

New Hampton, Inc., *see* Spiegel, Inc.

New Haven District Telephone Company *see* Southern New England Telecommunications Corp.

New Haven Electric Co., **21** 512

New Holland N.V., **22** 379–81 *see also* CNH Global N.V.

New Hotel Showboat, Inc. *see* Showboat, Inc.

New Impriver NV *see* Punch International N.V.

Nicolet Instrument Company, *see* Thermo Instrument Systems Inc.
Nicolon N.V. *see* Royal Ten Cate N.V.
Nicor Inc., 6 529–31; 86 303–07 (upd.)
Nidec Corporation, 59 313–16
Nielsen Marketing Research *see* A.C. Nielsen Co.
Niesmann & Bischoff, 22 207
NIF Ventures Co. Ltd., 55 118
Nigerian National Petroleum Corporation, IV 472–74; 72 240–43 (upd.)
Nihon Keizai Shimbun, Inc., IV 654–56
Nihon Noyaku Co., 64 35
Nihon Styrene Paper Company *see* JSP Corp.
Nihon Synopsis, 11 491
Nihon Waters K.K., 43 456
Nihron Yupro Corp. *see* Toto Ltd.
NII *see* National Intergroup, Inc.
NIKE, Inc., V 372–74; 8 391–94 (upd.); 36 343–48 (upd.); 75 279–85 (upd.)
Nikkei *see* Nihon Keizai Shimbun, Inc.
Nikkelverk, 49 136
Nikken Global Inc., 32 364–67
The Nikko Securities Company Limited, II 433–35; 9 377–79 (upd.)
Nikko Trading Co., *see* Japan Airlines Company, Ltd.
Nikolaiev, 19 49, 51
Nikon Corporation, III 583–85; 48 292–95 (upd.)
Nilpeter, 26 540, 542
Niman Ranch, Inc., 67 267–69
Nimbus CD International, Inc., 20 386–90
Nine West Group Inc., 11 348–49; 39 301–03 (upd.)
98 Cents Clearance Centers, 62 104
99¢ Only Stores, 25 353–55
Ningbo General Bearing Co., Ltd., 45 170
Nintendo Co., Ltd., III 586–88; 7 394–96 (upd.); 28 317–21 (upd.); 67 270–76 (upd.)
NIOC *see* National Iranian Oil Co.
Nippon Breweries Ltd. *see* Sapporo Breweries Ltd.
Nippon Cable Company, 15 235
Nippon Credit Bank, II 338–39
Nippon Del Monte Corporation, 47 206
Nippon Densan Corporation *see* Nidec Corp.
Nippon Educational Television (NET) *see* Asahi National Broadcasting Company, Ltd.
Nippon Electric Company, Limited *see* NEC Corp.
Nippon Express Company, Ltd., V 477–80; 64 286–90 (upd.)
Nippon Foundation Engineering Co. Ltd., 51 179
Nippon Gakki Co., Ltd *see* Yamaha Corp.
Nippon Global Tanker Co. Ltd., 53 116
Nippon Gyomo Sengu Co. Ltd., IV 555
Nippon Hatsujo Kabushikikaisha *see* NHK Spring Co., Ltd.

Nippon Helicopter & Aeroplane Transport Co., Ltd. *see* All Nippon Airways Company Ltd.
Nippon Hoso Kyokai *see* Japan Broadcasting Corp.
Nippon Idou Tsushin, 7 119–20
Nippon K.K *see* Nikon Corp.
Nippon Kogaku K.K. *see* Nikon Corp.
Nippon Kogyo Co. Ltd *see* Nippon Mining Co. Ltd.
Nippon Kokan K.K. *see* NKK Corp.
Nippon Life Insurance Company, III 318–20; 60 218–21 (upd.)
Nippon Light Metal Company, Ltd., IV 153–55
Nippon Meat Packers, Inc., II 550–51; 78 255–57 (upd.)
Nippon Mining Co., Ltd., IV 475–77
Nippon Mitsubishi Oil Corporation, 49 216
Nippon Oil Corporation, IV 478–79; 63 308–13 (upd.)
Nippon Paper Industries Co., Ltd., 57 101
Nippon Phonogram, 23 390
Nippon Reizo Co. *see* Nichirei Corp.
Nippon Seiko K.K., III 589–90
Nippon Sekiyu Co *see* Nippon Oil Company, Ltd.
Nippon Sheet Glass Company, Limited, III 714–16
Nippon Shinpan Co., Ltd., II 436–37; 61 248–50 (upd.)
Nippon Soda Co., Ltd., 85 303–06
Nippon Steel Corporation, IV 156–58; 17 348–51 (upd.)
Nippon Suisan Kaisha, Limited, II 552–53; 92 269–72 (upd.)
Nippon Telegraph and Telephone Corporation, V 305–07; 51 271–75 (upd.)
Nippon Tire Co., Ltd. *see* Bridgestone Corp.
Nippon Unipac Holding, 57 101
Nippon Yusen Kabushiki Kaisha (NYK), V 481–83; 72 244–48 (upd.)
Nippondenso Co., Ltd., III 591–94 *see also* DENSO Corp.
NIPSCO Industries, Inc., 6 532–33
NiSource, Inc., 38 81
Nissan Motor Company Ltd., I 183–84; 11 350–52 (upd.); 34 303–07 (upd.); 92 273–79 (upd.)
Nissay Dowa General Insurance Company Ltd., 60 220
Nisshin Seifun Group Inc., II 554; 66 246–48 (upd.)
Nisshin Steel Co., Ltd., IV 159–60
Nissho Iwai K.K., I 509–11
Nissin Food Products Company Ltd., 75 286–88
Nisso *see* Nippon Soda Co., Ltd.
Nissui *see* Nippon Suisan Kaisha.
Nitches, Inc., 53 245–47
Nittsu *see* Nippon Express Co., Ltd.
Niugini Mining Ltd., 23 42
Nixdorf Computer AG, III 154–55 *see also* Wincor Nixdorf Holding GmbH.

Nixdorf-Krein Industries Inc. *see* Laclede Steel Co.
Nizhny Novgorod Dairy, 48 438
NKI B.V., 71 178–79
NKK Corporation, IV 161–63; 28 322–26 (upd.)
NL Industries, Inc., 10 434–36
NLG *see* National Leisure Group.
NLI Insurance Agency Inc., 60 220
NLM City-Hopper, *see* Koninklijke Luchtvaart Maatschappij N.V.
NM Acquisition Corp., 27 346
NMC Laboratories Inc., *see* Alpharma Inc.
NMT *see* Nordic Mobile Telephone.
NNG *see* Northern Natural Gas Co.
Noah's New York Bagels *see* Einstein/Noah Bagel Corp.
Nob Hill Foods, 58 291
Nobel Drilling Corporation, 26 243
Nobel Industries AB, 9 380–82 *see also* Akzo Nobel N.V.
Nobel Learning Communities, Inc., 37 276–79; 76 281–85 (upd.)
Noble Affiliates, Inc., 11 353–55
Noble Broadcast Group, Inc., 23 293
Noble Roman's Inc., 14 351–53
Nobleza Piccardo SAICF, 64 291–93
Noboa *see also* Exportadora Bananera Noboa, S.A.
Nobody Beats the Wiz *see* Cablevision Electronic Instruments, Inc.
Nocibé SA, 54 265–68
Nocona Belt Company, 31 435–36
Nocona Boot Co. *see* Justin Industries, Inc.
Noel Group, Inc., *see* Lincoln Snacks Co.
NOF Corporation, 72 249–51
NOK Corporation, 41 170–72
Nokia Corporation, II 69–71; 17 352–54 (upd.); 38 328–31 (upd.); 77 308–13 (upd.)
Nokian Tyres PLC, 59 91
NOL Group *see* Neptune Orient Lines Ltd.
Noland Company, 35 311–14
Nolo.com, Inc., 49 288–91
Nolte Mastenfabriek B.V., *see* Valmont Industries, Inc.
Nomura Securities Company, Limited, II 438–41; 9 383–86 (upd.)
Nomura Toys Ltd., *see* Hasbro, Inc.
Non-Stop Fashions, Inc., *see* The Leslie Fay Companies, Inc.
Noodle Kidoodle, 16 388–91
Noodles & Company, Inc., 55 277–79
Nooter Corporation, 61 251–53
NOP Research Group, 28 501, 504
Nopri *see* GIB Group.
Norampac, 71 95
Norand Corporation, 72 189
Noranda Inc., IV 164–66; 7 397–99 (upd.); 64 294–98 (upd.)
Norandex, *see* Fibreboard Corp.
Norbro Corporation *see* Stuart Entertainment Inc.
Norcal Pottery Products, Inc., 58 60
Norcal Waste Systems, Inc., 60 222–24

Norcon, Inc., *see* VECO International, Inc.

Norcore Plastics, Inc., **33** 361

Nordbanken, **9** 382

Norddeutsche Affinerie AG, 62 249–53

Norddeutscher-Lloyd *see* Hapag-Lloyd AG.

Nordea AB, 40 336–39

Nordic Baltic Holding *see* Nordea AB.

Nordica S.r.l., **15** 396–97; **53** 24

NordicTrack, 22 382–84 *see also* Icon Health & Fitness, Inc.

Nordisk Film A/S, 80 269–73

Nordson Corporation, 11 356–58; 48 296–99 (upd.)

Nordstrom, Inc., V 156–58; 18 371–74 (upd.); 67 277–81 (upd.)

Nordwestdeutsche Kraftwerke AG *see* PreussenElektra AG.

Norelco Consumer Products Co., 26 334–36

Norelec, *see* Eiffage.

Norex Leasing, Inc., **16** 397

Norfolk Shipbuilding & Drydock Corporation, **73** 47

Norfolk Southern Corporation, V 484–86; 29 358–61 (upd.); 75 289–93 (upd.)

Norge Co., *see* Fedders Corp.

Noric Corporation, **39** 332

Norinchukin Bank, II 340–41

Norlin Industries, **16** 238–39; **75** 262

Norm Thompson Outfitters, Inc., 47 275–77

Norma AS *see* Autoliv, Inc.

Norman BV, **9** 93; **33** 78

Normandy Mining Ltd., **23** 42

Normark Corporation *see* Rapala-Normark Group, Ltd.

Norment Security Group, Inc., **51** 81

Normond/CMS, *see* Danaher Corp.

Norrell Corporation, 25 356–59

Norris Cylinder Company, *see* TriMas Corp.

Norris Oil Company, **47** 52

Norshield Corp., **51** 81

Norsk Aller A/S, **72** 62

Norsk Helikopter AS *see* Bristow Helicopters Ltd.

Norsk Hydro ASA, 10 437–40; 35 315–19 (upd.)

Norsk Rengjorings Selskap a.s., **49** 221

Norske Skog do Brasil Ltda., **73** 205

Norske Skogindustrier ASA, 63 314–16

Norstan, Inc., 16 392–94

Nortek, Inc., 34 308–12

Nortel Inversora S.A., **63** 375–77

Nortel Networks Corporation, 36 349–54 (upd.)

Nortex International, **19** 338

North African Petroleum Ltd., **IV** 455

North American Aviation, *see* Rockwell Automation.

North American Carbon, **19** 499

North American Coal Corporation, *see* NACCO Industries, Inc.

North American Company, **6** 552–53, 601–02

North American Energy Conservation, Inc., **35** 480

North American InTeleCom, Inc., **IV** 411

North American Medical Management Company, Inc., **36** 366

North American Mogul Products Co. *see* Mogul Corp.

North American Nutrition Companies Inc. (NANCO) *see* Provimi

North American Philips Corporation, *see* Philips Electronics North America Corp.

North American Plastics, Inc., **61** 112

North American Site Developers, Inc., **69** 197

North American Training Corporation *see* Rollerblade, Inc.

North American Van Lines *see* Allied Worldwide, Inc.

North American Watch Company *see* Movado Group, Inc.

North Atlantic Energy Corporation, **21** 411

North Atlantic Laboratories, Inc., **62** 391

North Atlantic Trading Company Inc., 65 266–68

North British Rubber Company, **20** 258

North Broken Hill Peko, **IV** 61

North Carolina Motor Speedway, Inc., **19** 294

North Carolina National Bank Corporation *see* NCNB Corp.

North Carolina Natural Gas Corporation, **6** 578

North Central Utilities, Inc., *see* Otter Tail Power Co.

North East Insurance Company, **44** 356

The North Face, Inc., 18 375–77; 78 258–61 (upd.)

North Fork Bancorporation, Inc., 46 314–17

North Pacific Group, Inc., 61 254–57

North Ridge Securities Corporation, **72** 149–50

North Sea Ferries, **26** 241, 243

North Shore Gas Company, **6** 543–44

North Star Communications Group Inc., **73** 59

North Star Container, Inc., **59** 290

North Star Steel Company, 18 378–81

North Star Transport Inc., **49** 402

North Star Tubes, **54** 391, 393

North Star Universal, Inc., *see* Michael Foods, Inc.

North State Supply Company, **57** 9

The North West Company, Inc., 12 361–63

North-West Telecommunications *see* Pacific Telecom, Inc.

North West Water Group plc, 11 359–62 *see also* United Utilities PLC.

Northbridge Financial Corp., **57** 137

Northbrook Holdings, Inc., **22** 495

Northcliffe Newspapers, *see* Daily Mail and General Trust plc.

Northeast Utilities, V 668–69; 48 303–06 (upd.)

Northern and Shell Network plc, 87 341–344

Northern Animal Hospital Inc., **58** 355

Northern Arizona Light & Power Co., **6** 545

Northern Dairies, *see* Northern Foods PLC.

Northern Drug Company, **14** 147

Northern Electric Company *see* Northern Telecom Ltd.

Northern Energy Resources Company *see* NERCO, Inc.

Northern Engineering Industries Plc *see* Rolls-Royce Group PLC.

Northern Fibre Products Co., **I** 202

Northern Foods plc, 10 441–43; 61 258–62 (upd.)

Northern Illinois Gas Co., *see* Nicor Inc.

Northern Indiana Power Company, **6** 556

Northern Indiana Public Service Company, **6** 532–33

Northern Infrastructure Maintenance Company, **39** 238

Northern Leisure, **40** 296–98

Northern Natural Gas Co. *see* Enron Corp.

Northern Pacific Corp., **15** 274

Northern Pacific Railroad, **26** 451

Northern Rock plc, 33 318–21

Northern Star Co., *see* Michael Foods, Inc.

Northern States Power Company, V 670–72; 20 391–95 (upd.) *see also* Xcel Energy Inc.

Northern Telecom Limited, V 308–10 *see also* Nortel Networks Corp.

Northern Trust Company, 9 387–89

Northfield Metal Products, **11** 256

Northland *see* Scott Fetzer Co.

Northland Cranberries, Inc., 38 332–34

Northland Publishing, *see* Justin Industries, Inc.

NorthPrint International, *see* Miner Group Int.

Northrop Grumman Corporation, I 76–77; 11 363–65 (upd.); 45 304–12 (upd.)

Northwest Airlines Corporation, I 112–14; 6 103–05 (upd.); 26 337–40 (upd.); 74 204–08 (upd.)

Northwest Engineering Co. *see* Terex Corp.

Northwest Express *see* Bear Creek Corp.

Northwest Industries *see* Chicago and North Western Holdings Corp.

Northwest Natural Gas Company, 45 313–15

Northwest Telecommunications Inc., **6** 598

NorthWestern Corporation, 37 280–83

Northwestern Flavors LLC, **58** 379

Northwestern Manufacturing Company, *see* Crane Co.

Northwestern Mutual Life Insurance Company, III 321–24; 45 316–21 (upd.)

Northwestern Public Service Company, **6** 524

Plymouth Mills Inc., **23** 66

PM Management Incorporated, **74** 234

PM Resources, Inc., **74** 381

PMC Contract Research AB, **21** 425

PMI Corporation *see* Physical
Measurements Information

The PMI Group, Inc., 49 331–33

PMP Ltd., 72 282–84

PMR Corporation *see* Psychiatric
Solutions, Inc.

PMS Consolidated, *see* M. A. Hanna Co.

PMT Services, Inc., 24 393–95

PN Gaya Motor, **56** 284

**The PNC Financial Services Group Inc.,
II** 342–43; **13** 410–12 (upd.); **46**
350–53 (upd.)

Pneumo Abex Corp., **I** 456–58; **III** 512;
38 293–94

PNL *see* Pacific Northwest Laboratories.

PNM Resources Inc., 51 296–300
(upd.)

PNP *see* Pacific Northwest Power Co.

POAS *see* Türkiye Petrolleri Anonim
Ortakliği

POB Polyolefine Burghausen GmbH, **IV**
487

Pocahontas Foods USA, **31** 359, 361

Pochet SA, **55** 307–09

Poe & Associates, Inc., **41** 63–64

Pogo Producing Company, 39 330–32

**Pohang Iron and Steel Company Ltd.,
IV** 183–85 *see also* POSCO.

Poland Spring Natural Spring Water Co.,
31 229

Polar Air Cargo Inc., 60 237–39

Polar S.A., **59** 418

Polaris Industries Inc., 12 399–402; **35**
348–53 (upd.); **77** 330–37 (upd.)

Polaroid Corporation, III 607–09; **7**
436–39 (upd.); **28** 362–66 (upd.); **93**
345–53 (upd.)

Polbeth Packaging Limited, **12** 377

**Policy Management Systems
Corporation, 11** 394–95

Policy Studies, Inc., 62 277–80

Poliet S.A., 33 338–40

Polioles, S.A. de C.V., **19** 10, 12

Politos, S.A. de C.V., **23** 171

Polk Audio, Inc., 34 352–54

Pollenex Corp., **19** 360

Polo/Ralph Lauren Corporation, 12
403–05; **62** 281–85 (upd.)

Polser, **19** 49, 51

**Polski Koncern Naftowy ORLEN S.A.,
77 338–41**

Polskie Linie Lotnicze S.A. *see* LOT Polish
Airlines.

Poly-Glas Systems, Inc., **21** 65

Polydesign, *see* Randstad Holding n.v.

Polydor B.V., **23** 389

Polydor KK, **23** 390

Polygon Networks Inc., **41** 73

PolyGram N.V., 23 389–92

Polyken Technologies, *see* Kendall
International, Inc.

Polymer Technologies Corporation, **26**
287

PolyMedica Corporation, 77 342–45

PolyOne Corporation, 87 384–395
(upd.)

Polyphase Corporation *see* Overhill Corp.

Polysius AG, **IV** 89

Pomare Ltd., 88 304–07

Pomeroy Computer Resources, Inc., 33
341–44

Pomeroy's, **16** 61; **50** 107

Pommery et Greno, **II** 475

Pompes Guinard S.A., **62** 217

Ponderosa Steakhouse, 15 361–64

Ponderosa System Inc., **12** 199

Pont-à-Mousson S.A., *see* Compagnie de
Saint-Gobain.

Pont Royal SA, **48** 316

Ponto Frio Bonzao, **22** 321

Pontos GmbH, **56** 152

Poof-Slinky, Inc., 61 298–300

Poore Brothers, Inc., 44 348–50

Pop Warner Little Scholars, Inc., 86
335–38

Pop.com, **43** 144

Pope & Talbot, Inc., 12 406–08; **61**
301–05 (upd.)

Pope Cable and Wire B.V. *see* Belden
CDT Inc.

Pope Resources LP, 74 240–43

Popeyes Chicken & Biscuits *see* AFC
Enterprises, Inc.

Pophitt Cereals, Inc., **22** 337

Poppe Tyson Inc., **23** 479; **25** 91

Popsicle, *see* Unilever PLC.

Popular Club Plan, *see* J. Crew Group Inc.

Popular, Inc., 41 311–13

Popular Merchandise, Inc., *see* J. Crew
Group Inc.

**The Porcelain and Fine China
Companies Ltd., 69** 301–03

Poron, S.A., **42** 268–69

Porsche AG, 13 413–15; **31** 363–66
(upd.)

Port Arthur Finance Corp., **37** 309

**The Port Authority of New York and
New Jersey, 48** 317–20

Port Dickson Power Sdn. Bhd., **36**
435–36

Port Imperial Ferry Corporation, 70
226–29

Port of London Authority, **48** 317

Port Stockton Food Distributors, Inc., *see*
Smart & Final, Inc.

Portage Industries Corp. *see* Spartech
Corp.

El Portal Group, Inc., **58** 371

Portal Software, Inc., 47 300–03

Porter-Cable Corporation, **26** 361–63

Porter Chadburn plc, **28** 252

Portex, **25** 431

Portia Management Services Ltd., **30** 318

Portillo's Restaurant Group, Inc., 71
284–86

Portland General Corporation, 6
548–51

Portland General Electric, **45** 313; **50** 103

Portland Plastics, **25** 430–31

Portland Shipyard LLC *see* Cascade
General Inc.

Portland Trail Blazers, 50 356–60

Portland-Zementwerke Heidelberg A.G.,
23 326

Portmeirion Group plc, 88 308–11

Portnet, **6** 435

Portsmouth & Sunderland, **35** 242, 244

Portucel *see* Grupo Portucel Soporcel.

Portugal Telecom SGPS S.A., 69 304–07

Portugalia, **46** 398

Posadas *see* Grupo Posadas, S.A. de C.V.

POSCO, 57 287–91 (upd.)

Posful Corporation, **68** 9

Positive Response Television, Inc., *see*
National Media Corp.

Post Office Group, V 498–501

Post Properties, Inc., 26 377–79

Postabank és Takarékpénztár Rt., **69** 155,
157

La Poste, V 470–72

Posterscope Worldwide, 70 230–32

Posti- Ja Telelaitos, 6 329–31

PostScript, *see* Fay's Inc.

Potain SAS, **59** 274, 278

**Potash Corporation of Saskatchewan
Inc., 18** 431–33

Potbelly Sandwich Works, Inc., 83
307-310

Potelco, Inc. *see* Quanta Services, Inc.

Potlatch Corporation, 8 428–30; **34**
355–59 (upd.); **87** 396–403 (upd.)

Potomac Edison Company, **38** 39–40

Potomac Electric Power Company, 6
552–54

Potter & Brumfield Inc., 11 396–98

Pottery Barn, *see* Williams-Sonoma, Inc.

Pottsville Behavioral Counseling Group,
64 311

Pou Chen Corporation, 81 309–12

Poul Due Jensen Foundation *see* Grundfos
Group

Poulan/Weed Eater *see* White
Consolidated Industries Inc.

Powell Duffryn plc, 31 367–70

Powell Group, **33** 32

Powell's Books, Inc., 40 360–63

Power Applications & Manufacturing
Company, Inc., **6** 441

Power Corporation of Canada, 36
370–74 (upd.); **85** 332–39 (upd.)

Power-One, Inc., 79 334–37

Power Parts Co., **7** 358

Power Team, *see* SPX Corp.

PowerBar Inc., 44 351–53

Powercor *see* PacifiCorp.

POWEREDCOM Inc., **74** 348

Powergen PLC, 11 399–401; **50** 361–64
(upd.)

Powerhouse Technologies, Inc., 27
379–81

PowerSoft Corp., **15** 374

Powerteam Electrical Services Ltd., **64** 404

Powertel Inc., **48** 130

Powerware Corporation *see* Eaton Corp.

POZEN Inc., 81 313–16

PP&L *see* Pennsylvania Power & Light
Co.

PPB Group Berhad, 57 292–95

PPG Industries, Inc., III 731–33; **22**
434–37 (upd.); **81** 317–23 (upd.)

RPISA *see* Refinaria de Petróleo Ipiranga S.A.

RPM International Inc., 8 454–57; **36** 394–98 (upd.); **91** 417–25 (upd.)

RSA Security Inc., 46 365–68

RSC *see* Rental Service Corp.

RSO Records, **23** 390

RSV, **26** 496

RTI Group, **58** 366

RTL Group SA, 44 374–78

RTM Restaurant Group, 58 322–24

RTR Funding LLC, **70** 275

RTS Packaging, LLC, **59** 347, 350

RTW Air Service(s) Pte. Ltd., **51** 123

RTZ Corporation PLC, IV 189–92 *see also* Rio Tinto plc.

Rubbermaid Incorporated, III 613–15; **20** 454–57 (upd.) *see also* Newell Rubbermaid Inc.

Rubicon Group plc, **32** 50

Rubio's Restaurants, Inc., 35 379–81

Rubo Lederwaren, **14** 225

Ruby Tuesday, Inc., 18 464–66; **71** 317–20 (upd.)

Rubyco, Inc., **15** 386

La Ruche Meridionale, **12** 153

Ruddick Corporation, **23** 260; **72** 163, 165

Rudolf Wolff & Co. Ltd., **64** 297

Ruel Smith Transportation Services, Inc., **39** 66

Ruff Hewn, **25** 48

The Rugby Group plc, 31 398–400

Ruger Corporation, *see* Sturm, Ruger & Co., Inc.

Ruhrgas AG, V 704–06; **38** 405–09 (upd.)

Ruhrkohle AG, IV 193–95 *see also* RAG AG.

Ruiz Food Products, Inc., 53 287–89

Rumasa, **69** 165

Rural Cellular Corporation, 43 340–42

Rural/Metro Corporation, 28 396–98

Rural Press Ltd., 74 282–85

Rush Communications, 33 373–75 *see also* Phat Fashions LLC.

Rush Enterprises, Inc., 64 336–38

Russ Berrie and Company, Inc., 12 424–26; **82** 304–08 (upd.)

Russell Associates Inc. *see* Pall Corp.

Russell Corporation, 8 458–59; **30** 399–401 (upd.); **82** 309–13 (upd.)

Russell Kelly Office Services, Inc. *see* Kelly Services Inc.

Russell Reynolds Associates Inc., 38 410–12

Russell Stover Candies Inc., 12 427–29; **91** 426–32 (upd.)

Russian Aircraft Corporation (MiG), 86 343–46

Russian Avionics Design Bureau CJSC, **68** 204

Russian Railways Joint Stock Co., 93 380–83

Rust International Inc., 11 435–36

Rust-Oleum Corporation, **36** 396

Rütgers AG, **60** 250

Ruth's Chris Steak House, 28 399–401; **88** 338–42 (upd.)

Rutherford Hill Winery, **48** 392

RWD Technologies, Inc., 76 320–22

RWE Group, V 707–10; **50** 396–400 (upd.)

RxAmerica, **22** 40; **25** 297

Ryan Aeronautical, *see* Teledyne, Inc.

Ryan Beck & Co., Inc., 66 273–75

Ryan Homes, Inc. *see* NVR Inc.

Ryan Insurance Company, *see* Aon Corp.

Ryan Milk Company of Kentucky, *see* Dean Foods Co.

Ryan's Restaurant Group, Inc., 15 419–21; **68** 327–30 (upd.)

Ryanair Holdings plc, 35 382–85

Ryder System, Inc., V 504–06; **24** 408–11 (upd.)

Ryecroft Foods Limited, **61** 387–88

Ryerson Tull, Inc., 40 381–84 (upd.)

Ryko Corporation, 83 329-333

Rykoff-Sexton, Inc., **21** 497; **26** 503, 505; **74** 350

The Ryland Group, Inc., 8 460–61; **37** 343–45 (upd.)

Ryobi US, **73** 332

Ryohin Keikaku Co., Ltd., **36** 420

Ryoshoku Ltd., 72 300–02

Rysher Entertainment, **22** 162; **25** 329

The Ryvita Company Limited, *see* Associated British Foods plc.

RZB *see* Raiffeisen Zentralbank Österreich AG.

RZD *see* Russian Railways Joint Stock Co.

S

S&A Restaurant Corp., *see* Metromedia Companies.

S&C Electric Company, 15 422–24

S&D Coffee, Inc., 84 339–341

S&H *see* Sperry and Hutchinson Co.

S&H Diving Corporation, **6** 578

S&K Famous Brands, Inc., 23 421–23

S&P *see* Standard & Poor's Corp.

S&S/Superior of Ohio, Inc. *see* Accubuilt, Inc.

S+T Gesellschaft fur Reprotechnik mbH, **29** 306

S.A.C.I. Falabella, 69 311–13

S.A. Cockerill Sambre *see* Cockerill Sambre Group.

S.A. de C.V., **29** 461

S.A. des Ateliers d'Aviation Louis Breguet *see* Groupe Dassault Aviation SA.

s.a. GB-Inno-BM *see* GIB Group.

S.A. Greetings Corporation, Ltd., *see* American Greetings Corp.

S.A. Innovation—Bon Marché N.V., **26** 160

S.C. Johnson & Son, Inc., III 58–59; **28** 409–12 (upd.); **89** 382–89 (upd.)

S.E. Rykoff & Co., **26** 503

S.G. Warburg and Co. *see* SBC Warburg.

S.Gallardo, SL., **74** 185

S. Grumbacher & Son *see* The Bon-Ton Stores, Inc.

S.I.P., Co., *see* The Parsons Corp.

S-K-I Limited, 15 457–59

S.K. Wellman Ltd., **59** 222

S.P. Richards Co., **45** 177–79

S Pearson & Son Ltd. *see* Pearson plc

S.R. Dresser Manufacturing Co. *see* Dresser Industries, Inc.

S.S. Kresge Company *see* Kmart Corp.

S.S. Pierce Company, **60** 267

S.S.V. Inc., **36** 420

S.T. Cooper & Sons, *see* Jockey International, Inc.

S.T. Dupont Company, **23** 55

SA Alliance Air, **28** 404

SA Express, **28** 404

Sa SFC NV, *see* Essef Corp.

SAA *see* South African Airways.

SAA (Pty) Ltd., 28 402–04

SAAB *see* Svenska Aeroplan Aktiebolaget.

Saab Automobile AB, 32 386–89 (upd.); **83** 334-339 (upd.)

Saab-Scania A.B., I 197–98; **11** 437–39 (upd.)

Saarberg-Konzern, IV 196–99 *see also* RAG AG.

Saarstahl AG, *see* Usinor SA.

Saatchi & Saatchi plc, I 33–35; **33** 328–31 (upd.)

SAB *see* South African Breweries Ltd.

SAB WABCO International AB, **53** 85

Saban Entertainment, *see* Fox Family Worldwide, Inc.

Sabanci Group, **54** 197–98

Sabanci Holdings *see* Haci Omer Sabanci Holdings A.S.

Sabaté Diosos SA, 48 348–50 *see also* OENEO S.A.

Sabela Media, Inc., **49** 423

Sabena S.A./N.V., 33 376–79

Saber Software Corp., **25** 348

Sabian Ltd., **38** 68

SABIC *see* Saudi Basic Industries Corp.

Sabine Transportation Company *see* Kirby Corp.

SABMiller plc, 59 352–58 (upd.)

SABO Maschinenfabrik AG, **21** 175

Sabratek Corporation, 29 410–12

Sabre Holdings Corporation, 26 427–30; **74** 286–90 (upd.)

Sabre Interactive, **46** 434

Sacer, **31** 127–28

Sach Bicycle Components *see* SRAM Corp.

Sachs-Dolmer G.m.b.H., *see* Makita Corp.

Sacilor *see* Usinor S.A.

OY Saco AB, **23** 268

SACOR, **IV** 504–06

Saddlebag Lake Resorts, Inc., **63** 23

SADE Ingenieria y Construcciones S.A., **38** 435, 437

Sadia S.A., 59 359–62

Saf-T-Hammer Corporation *see* Smith & Wesson Corp.

Safe Flight Instrument Corporation, 71 321–23

SAFECO Corporation, III 352–54

Safeguard Scientifics, Inc., 10 473–75

Safelite Glass Corp., 19 371–73

Safer, Inc., **21** 385–86

Sandwich Chef, Inc. *see* Wall Street Deli, Inc.

Sandy's Pool Supply, Inc. *see* Leslie's Poolmart, Inc.

Sanford C. Bernstein Inc., **63** 27

Sanford L.P., 82 325–29

Sanford-Brown College, Inc., **41** 419–20

Sanitation Systems, Inc. *see* HMI Industries.

Sanitec Corporation, 51 322–24

Sanko Peterson Corporation, **55** 306

Sankyo Company, Ltd., I 674–75; **56 301–04 (upd.)**

Sanlam Ltd., 68 331–34

SANlight Inc., **62** 293

Sano Corporation, **63** 142

The Sanofi-Synthélabo Group, I 676–77; 49 349–51 (upd.)

SanomaWSOY Corporation, 51 325–28

Sanpaolo IMI S.p.A., 50 407–11

Sanrio Company, Ltd., 38 413–15

Sansone Group, **69** 120

Santa Barbara Restaurant Group, Inc., 37 349–52

The Santa Cruz Operation, Inc., 38 416–21

Santa Fe Gaming Corporation, 19 377–79 *see also* Archon Corp.

Santa Fe Gold Corporation, **38** 232

Santa Fe Industries, **12** 19; **28** 498

Santa Fe International Corporation, 38 422–24

Santa Fe Pacific Corporation, V 507–09 *see also* Burlington Northern Santa Fe Corp.

Santa Fe Snyder Corp., **61** 75

Santa Fe Southern Pacific Corp., **6** 150, 599; **22** 491

Santa Isabel S.A., **69** 94

Santa Margherita S.p.A. *see* Industrie Zignago Santa Margherita S.p.A.

Santal, **26** 160

Santiago Land Development Corporation, **58** 20

Santos Ltd., 81 360–63

Sanwa Bank, Ltd., II 347–48; 15 431–33 (upd.)

Sanwa USA Inc., **70** 213

Sanyo Electric Co., Ltd., II 91–92; 36 399–403 (upd.)

Sanyo-Kokusaku Pulp Co., Ltd., IV 327–28

Sanyo White Cement Co. Ltd., **60** 301

Sao Paulo Alpargatas S.A., 75 347–49

SAP AG, 16 441–44; 43 358–63 (upd.)

Sapa AB, 84 342–345

SAPAC *see* Société Parisienne d'Achats en Commun.

Sapeksa, **55** 189

Sapirstein Greeting Card Company *see* American Greetings Corp.

Sappi Limited, 49 352–55

Sapporo Breweries Limited, I 282–83; 13 454–56 (upd.); 36 404–07 (upd.);

SAPRA-Landauer Ltd., **51** 210

Saputo Inc., 59 363–65

Sara Lee Corporation, II 571–73; 15 434–37 (upd.); 54 322–27 (upd.)

Saracen's Head Brewery, **21** 245

Saratoga Partners, **24** 436

Sarawak Trading, *see* Sime Darby Berhad.

Sargent & Lundy, **6** 556

Sarma, **26** 159–61

Sarmag, **26** 161

Sarnoff Corporation, 57 309–12

Saros Corp., **15** 474; **62** 141

Sarotti GmbH, **53** 315

Sarpe, **IV** 591

Sarriò S.A., **41** 325–26

Sarris Candies Inc., 86 347–50

Sartek Industries Inc., **44** 441

The SAS Group, 34 396–99 (upd.)

SAS Institute Inc., 10 476–78; 78 328–32 (upd.)

Saskatchewan Oil and Gas Corporation, *see* Wascana Energy Inc.

Sasol Limited, IV 533–35; 47 340–44 (upd.)

Sasu Ldc Sable, **68** 234

SAT *see* Stockholms Allmänna Telefonaktiebolag.

Satcom Group of Companies, **32** 40

Satellite Business Systems, **21** 14; **23** 135; **27** 304

Satellite Software International, *see* WordPerfect Corp.

Satellite Television PLC, **23** 135

Saturn Corporation, 7 461–64; 21 449–53 (upd.); 80 332–38 (upd.)

Saturn Industries, Inc., **23** 489

SATV *see* Satellite Television PLC.

Satyam Computer Services Ltd., 85 370–73

Saucona Iron Co., *see* Bethlehem Steel Corp.

Saucony Inc., 35 386–89; 86 351–56 (upd.)

Sauder Woodworking Co., 12 433–34; 35 390–93 (upd.)

Saudi Arabian Airlines, 6 114–16; 27 395–98 (upd.)

Saudi Arabian Oil Company, IV 536–39; 17 411–15 (upd.); 50 412–17 (upd.) *see also* Arabian American Oil Co.

Saudi Arabian Parsons Limited, *see* The Parsons Co.

Saudi Basic Industries Corporation (SABIC), 58 325–28

Saudia *see* Saudi Arabian Airlines.

Sauer-Danfoss Inc., 61 320–22

Saul Ewing LLP, 74 291–94

Saunders, Karp, and Megrue, LP, **26** 190; **28** 258; **70** 121

Saupiquet SA *see* Bolton Group B.V.

Saur S.A.S., 92 327–30

Sauza, **31** 92

Sav-on Drug, *see* American Stores Co.

Sava Group, **20** 263

Savacentre Ltd., *see* J Sainsbury plc.

Savannah Electric & Power Company, **38** 448

Savannah Foods & Industries, Inc., 7 465–67 *see also* Imperial Sugar Co.

Savannah Gas Company, **6** 448; **23** 29

Save Mart, **27** 292

Save.com, **37** 409

Savia S.A. de C.V., **29** 435

Savio, **IV** 422

Savoy Pictures Entertainment Inc., **25** 214

Sawdust Pencil Company, **29** 372

Sawgrass Asset Management, LLC, **48** 18

Sawhill Tubular Products, **41** 3

Sawtek Inc., 43 364–66 (upd.)

Saxon Oil, *see* Enterprise Oil plc.

Saxonville USA, **61** 254, 256

Sayers & Scovill *see* Accubuilt, Inc.

SB Acquisitions, Inc., **46** 74

SBAR, Inc., **30** 4

Sbarro, Inc., 16 445–47; 64 339–42 (upd.)

SBC Communications Inc., 32 399–403 (upd.)

SBC Transportation, Inc. *see* Schwebel Baking Co.

SBC Warburg, 14 419–21 *see also* UBS AG.

Sberbank, 62 314–17

SBI *see* State Bank of India.

SBK Entertainment World, Inc., **22** 194; **26** 187

SBM Group, **71** 178–79

SBS Broadcasting, **61** 58

SBS Technologies, Inc., 25 405–07

SCA *see* Svenska Cellulosa AB.

SCAC *see* Société Commercial d'Affrètements et de Combustibles.

Scaldia Paper BV, **15** 229

Scali, McCabe & Sloves, **71** 158

Scan Screen, **IV** 600

SCANA Corporation, 6 574–76; 56 305–08 (upd.)

Scanair, **34** 397–98

Scancem, **38** 437

Scandic Hotels AB, **49** 193

Scandinavian Airlines System, I 119–20 *see also* The SAS Group.

Scandinavian Broadcasting System SA, **53** 325

Scania-Vabis *see* Saab-Scania AB.

ScanSource, Inc., 29 413–15; 74 295–98 (upd.)

Scantron Corporation, *see* John H. Harland Co.

Scarborough Public Utilities Commission, 9 461–62

SCB Computer Technology, Inc., 29 416–18

SCEcorp, V 715–17 *see also* Edison International.

Scenic Airlines, Inc., *see* SkyWest, Inc.

Scenographic Designs, **21** 277

SCG Corporation, **56** 323

Schäfer, **31** 158

Schauman Wood Oy, *see* UPM-Kymmene Corp.

Schawk, Inc., 24 424–26

SCHC, Inc. *see* Shoe Carnival Inc.

Scheels All Sports Inc., 63 348–50

Scheid Vineyards Inc., 66 276–78

Schein Pharmaceutical Inc., *see* Bayer A.G.

Schell Brewing *see* August Schell Brewing Company Inc.

Schenck Business Solutions, 88 349–53

Seaquist Manufacturing Corporation, *see* Pittway Corp.

Searle & Co *see* G.D. Searle & Co.

Sears plc, V 177–79

Sears, Roebuck and Co., V 180–83; 18 475–79 (upd.); 56 309–14 (upd.)

Sears Roebuck de México, S.A. de C.V., 20 470–72

SEAT *see* Sociedad Española de Automoviles de Turismo.

Seat Pagine Gialle S.p.A., 47 345–47

Seattle Brewing and Malting Company *see* Rainier Brewing Co.

Seattle City Light, 50 423–26

Seattle Coffee Company, 32 12, 15

Seattle Electric Company, 6 565; 50 365–66

Seattle FilmWorks, Inc., 20 473–75

Seattle First National Bank Inc., 8 469–71 *see also* Bank of America Corp.

Seattle Lighting Fixture Company, 92 331–34

Seattle Pacific Industries, Inc., 92 335–38

Seattle Seahawks, Inc., 92 339–43

Seattle Times Company, 15 445–47

Seaway Food Town, Inc., 15 448–50 *see also* Spartan Stores Inc.

SeaWest, 19 390

SEB Group *see* Skandinaviska Enskilda Banken AB.

SEB S.A. *see* Groupe SEB.

Sebastian International, 48 422

Sebastiani Vineyards, Inc., 28 413–15

Seco Products Corporation, 22 354

The Second City, Inc., 88 354–58

Second Harvest, 29 432–34

SecPac *see* Security Pacific Corp.

Secure Horizons, *see* PacifiCare Health Systems, Inc.

Secure Networks, Inc., 25 349

Securicor Plc, 45 376–79

Securitas AB, 42 336–39

Securities Management & Research, Inc., *see* American National Insurance Co.

Security Capital Corporation, 17 424–27

Security Capital Group, 56 58–59

Security Data Group, 32 373

Security Dynamics Technologies, Inc., 46 367

Security Pacific Corporation, II 349–50

Security State Bank, *see* Habersham Bancorp.

SED International Holdings, Inc., 43 367–69

Seddon Group Ltd., 67 343–45

Sedgwick Sales, Inc., 29 384

see's Candies, Inc., 30 411–13

Seeburg Corporation, 15 538

Seed Solutions, Inc., 11 491; 69 341

Seeman Brothers *see* White Rose, Inc.

SEEQ Technology, Inc., 13 47; 17 32, 34; 64 246

SEGA Corporation, 73 290–93

Sega Enterprises, Ltd., 28 320

Sega of America, Inc., 10 482–85

Seguros Comercial America, 21 413

Seguros Monterrey Aetna, 45 294

Seguros Serfin S.A., 25 290

Segway LLC, 48 355–57

Seibert-Oxidermo, Inc., 55 321

Seibu Department Stores, Ltd., V 184–86; 42 340–43 (upd.)

Seibu Group, 36 417–18; 47 408–09

Seibu Railway Company Ltd., V 510–11; 74 299–301 (upd.)

Seibu Saison, 6 207

Seifu Co. Ltd., 48 250

Seigle's Home and Building Centers, Inc., 41 353–55

Seihoku Packaging Company *see* JSP Corp.

Seiko Corporation, III 619–21; 17 428–31 (upd.); 72 314–18 (upd.)

Seiko Instruments USA Inc., 23 210

Seikosha Co., 64 261

Seimi Chemical Co. Ltd., 48 41

Seino Transportation Company, Ltd., 6 427–29

Seirt SAU, 76 326–27

Seismograph Service Limited, 11 413; 17 419

Seita, 23 424–27 *see also* Altadis S.A.

Seitel, Inc., 47 348–50

The Seiyu, Ltd., V 187–89; 36 417–21 (upd.)

Sekisui Chemical Co., Ltd., III 741–43; 72 319–22 (upd.)

Selat Marine Services, 22 276

Selby Shoe Company, 48 69

Select Comfort Corporation, 34 405–08

Select Energy, Inc., 48 305

Select Medical Corporation, 65 306–08

Select Theatres Corp. *see* Shubert Organization Inc.

Selection Trust, IV 565

Selectour SA, 53 299–301

Selectronics Inc., 23 210

Selectrons Ltd., 41 367

Selee Corporation, 88 359–62

Selena Coffee Inc., 39 409

Self Auto, 23 232

Self-Service Drive Thru, Inc., *see* Rally's.

Selfix, Inc. *see* Home Products International, Inc.

Selfridges Plc, 34 409–11

Selig Chemical Industries, 54 252, 254

Selkirk Communications Ltd., 26 273

Sells-Floto, 32 186

The Selmer Company, Inc., 19 392–94

Seltel International Inc., 35 246

Sema plc, 59 370

Semarca, 11 523

SembCorp Logistics Ltd., 53 199, 203

Sembler Company, 11 346

SEMCO Energy, Inc., 44 379–82

Semi-Tech Global, 30 419–20

Seminis, Inc., 29 435–37

Seminole Electric Cooperative, 6 583

Seminole Fertilizer, *see* Tosco Corp.

Seminole National Bank, 41 312

Semitic, Inc., 33 248

Semitool, Inc., 18 480–82; 79 379–82 (upd.)

Sempra Energy, 25 413–16 (upd.)

Semtech Corporation, 32 410–13

Seneca Foods Corporation, 17 432–34; 60 265–68 (upd.)

Senega, 63 365

Sengstacke Enterprises *see* Real Times LLC.

Sennheiser Electronic GmbH & Co. KG, 66 285–89

Senomyx, Inc., 83 351–354

Sensi, Inc., *see* Deckers Outdoor Corp.

Sensient Technologies Corporation, 52 303–08 (upd.)

Sensormatic Electronics Corp., 11 443–45

Sensory Science Corporation, 37 353–56

Sentry Insurance Company, 10 210

Sentry Markets, Inc., *see* Fleming Companies, Inc.

La Senza Corporation, 66 205–07

Sepal, Ltd., 39 152, 154

AB Separator *see* Alfa-Laval AB

Sephora Holdings S.A., 82 335–39

SEPI *see* Sociedad Estatal de Participaciones Industriales.

Sepracor Inc., 45 380–83

Sequa Corporation, 13 460–63; 54 328–32 (upd.)

Sequana Capital, 78 338–42 (upd.)

Sequel Corporation, 41 193

Sequent Computer Systems Inc., 10 363

Sequoia Athletic Company, 25 450

Sera-Tec Biologicals, Inc. *see* Rite Aid Corp.

Seragen Inc., 47 223

Serco Group plc, 47 351–53

Sereg Valves, S.A., *see* Duriron Co. Inc.

Serewatt AG, 6 491

Serologicals Corporation, 63 351–53

Serono S.A., 47 354–57

Serta, Inc., 28 416–18

Servam Corp., *see* Service America Corp.

Service and Systems Solutions Ltd., 64 404

Service America Corp., 7 471–73

Service Co., Ltd., 48 182

Service Control Corp. *see* Angelica Corp.

Service Corporation International, 6 293–95; 51 329–33 (upd.)

Service Master L.P., 34 153

Service Merchandise Company, Inc., V 190–92; 19 395–99 (upd.)

Service Products Buildings, Inc. *see* Turner Construction Co.

Service Q. General Service Co., *see* Koninklijke Luchtvaart Maatschappij N.V.

The ServiceMaster Company, 6 44–46; 23 428–31 (upd.); 68 338–42 (upd.)

Services Maritimes des Messageries Impériales *see* Compagnie des Messageries Maritimes.

ServiceWare, Inc., 25 118

Servicios de Corte y Confeccion, S.A. de C.V., 64 142

Servicios Financieros Quadrum S.A., 14 156; 76 129

Servisair Plc, 49 320

Smith and Bell Insurance, **41** 178, 180

Smith & Butterfield Co., Inc., **28** 74

Smith & Hawken, Ltd., 68 343–45

Smith & Nephew plc, 17 449–52; **41** 374–78 **(upd.)**

Smith & Wesson Corp., 30 424–27; **73** 306–11 **(upd.)**

Smith & Wollensky Operating Corp., **32** 362

Smith Barney Inc., 15 463–65 *see also* Citigroup Inc.

Smith Cattleguard *see* Smith-Midland Corp.

Smith Corona Corp., 13 477–80

Smith International, Inc., 15 466–68; **59** 376–80 **(upd.)**

Smith McDonell Stone and Co., **14** 97

Smith-Midland Corporation, 56 330–32

Smith New Court PLC, *see* Merrill Lynch & Co., Inc.

Smith Sport Optics Inc., **54** 319–20

Smith Wall Associates, **32** 145

Smith's Food & Drug Centers, Inc., 8 472–74; **57** 324–27 **(upd.)**

Smithfield Foods, Inc., 7 477–78; **43** 381–84 **(upd.)**

SmithKline Beckman Corporation, I 692–94 *see also* GlaxoSmithKline plc.

SmithKline Beecham plc, III 65–67; **32** 429–34 **(upd.)** *see also* GlaxoSmithKline plc.

SmithMart *see* N.F. Smith & Asociates LP.

Smiths Group plc, **56** 83

Smiths Industries PLC, 25 429–31

Smithsonian Institution, 27 410–13

Smithway Motor Xpress Corporation, 39 376–79

Smitty's Super Valu Inc., **12** 391

Smittybilt, Incorporated, **40** 299–300

Smoby International SA, 56 333–35

Smoothie Island, **49** 60

Smorgon Steel Group Ltd., 62 329–32

SMP Clothing, Inc., **22** 462

Smucker's *see* The J.M. Smucker Co.

Smurfit-Stone Container Corporation, 26 442–46 **(upd.)** ; **83** 360-368 **(upd.)**

SN Repal *see* Société Nationale de Recherche de Pétrole en Algérie.

Snack Ventures Europe, **10** 324; **36** 234, 237

Snake River Sugar Company, **19** 468

Snam *see* Società Nazionale Metanodotti.

Snam Montaggi, **IV** 420

Snam Progetti, **IV** 420, 422

Snap-On, Incorporated, 7 479–80; **27** 414–16 **(upd.)**

Snapfish, 83 369-372

Snapper Inc., **64** 355

Snapple Beverage Corporation, 11 449–51

Snappy Car Rental, Inc. *see* Republic Industries, Inc.

SnapTrack Inc., **63** 203

SNC-Lavalin Group Inc., 72 330–33

SNCF *see* Société Nationale des Chemins de Fer Français.

SNE Enterprises, Inc., *see* Ply Gem Industries Inc.

SNEA *see* Société Nationale Elf Aquitaine.

Snecma Group, 46 369–72

Snell & Wilmer L.L.P., 28 425–28

Snell Acoustics, *see* Boston Acoustics, Inc.

Snelling Personnel Services, **52** 150

SNET *see* Southern New England Telecommunications Corp.

Snoqualmie Falls Plant, **6** 565

Snow Brand Milk Products Company, Ltd., II 574–75; **48** 362–65 **(upd.)**

Snow White Dairies Inc. *see* Dairy Mart Convenience Stores, Inc.

Snyder Communications, **35** 462, 465

Snyder Group Company, **56** 294

Snyder Oil Company, **24** 379–81; **45** 354

Snyder's of Hanover, **35** 213

SnyderGeneral Corp. *see* AAF-McQuay Inc.

Soap Opera Magazine, *see* American Media, Inc.

Sobeys Inc., 80 348–51

Socal *see* Standard Oil Company (California).

Socamel-Rescaset, **40** 214, 216

Socar, Incorporated, **45** 370

Socata *see* EADS SOCATA.

Sociade Intercontinental de Compressores Hermeticos SICOM, S.A., *see* Tecumseh Products Co.

La Sociale di A. Mondadori & C. *see* Arnoldo Mondadori Editore S.P.A.

Sociedad Aeronáutica de Medellín, S.A., **36** 53

Sociedad Andina de Grandes Almeneces, **69** 312

Sociedad Anonima de Instalaciones de Control, **73** 4

Sociedad Anónima Viña Santa Rita, **67** 136–37

Sociedad Anonimo de Electricidad, **72** 278

Sociedad de Inversiones Internacionales Parque Arauco S.A., **72** 269

Sociedad Española Zig Zag, S.A., **68** 258

Sociedad Estatal de Participaciones Industriales, **69** 11

Sociedad Macri S.A., **67** 346

Sociedade Anónima Concessionária de Refinacao em Portugal *see* SACOR.

Sociedade de Vinhos da Herdade de Espirra-Produçao e Comercializaçao de Vinhos, S.A., **60** 156

Società Anonima Lombarda Fabbrica Automobili, *see* Alfa Romeo

Società Finanziaria Idrocarburi, **69** 148

Società Finanziaria Telefonica per Azioni, V 325–27

Societa Industria Meccanica Stampaggio S.p.A., **24** 500

Societa Italiana Gestione Sistemi Multi Accesso *see* Alitalia—Linee Aeree Italiana, S.P.A.

Società Italiana per L'Esercizio delle Telecommunicazioni p.A., **V** 325–27

Società Meridionale Finanziaria, **49** 31

Società Sportiva Lazio SpA, 44 386–88

Société Africaine de Déroulage des Ets Rougier, **21** 439

Société Air France, 27 417–20 **(upd.)** *see also* Groupe Air France.

Société Anonyme Automobiles Citroën *see* PSA Peugeot Citroen S.A.

Société Anonyme Belge des Magasins Prisunic-Uniprix, **26** 159

Société Anonyme des Assurances Générales *see* Assurances Générales de France.

Société Anonyme des Fermiers Reúnis, **23** 219

Société Anonyme Française du Ferodo *see* Valeo.

La Societe Anonyme Francaise Holophane, *see* Holophane Corp.

Société, Auxiliaire d'Entreprises SA, **13** 206

Société BIC S.A., 73 312–15

Société Centrale d'Investissement, **29** 48

Société Civil des Mousquetaires *see* ITM Entreprises SA.

Société Civile Valoptec, **21** 222

Société Commercial d'Affrètements et de Combustibles, **67** 198

Société Commerciale Citroën, *see* Automobiles Citroën

Société Congolaise des Grands Magasins Au Bon Marché, **26** 159

Société d'Emboutissage de Bourgogne *see* Groupe SEB.

Société d'Exploitation AOM Air Liberté SA (AirLib), 53 305–07

Société d'Investissement de Travaux Publics, **31** 128

Société de Développements et d'Innovations des Marchés Agricoles et Alimentaires *see* SODIMA.

Société de Diffusion de Marques *see* SODIMA.

Société de Diffusion Internationale Agro-Alimentaire *see* SODIAAL.

Société de Fiducie du Québec, **48** 289

Société des Caves et des Producteurs Reunis de Roquefort, *see* Besnier SA.

Société des Ciments Français, **33** 339

Société des Etablissements Gaumont *see* Gaumont SA.

Société des Fibres de Carbone S.A., **51** 379

Société des Grandes Entreprises de Distribution, Inno-France, **V** 58

Société des Immeubles de France, **37** 357, 359

Société des Magasins du Casino, **59** 109

Société des Moteurs Gnôme, **46** 369

Societe des Produits Marnier-Lapostolle S.A., 88 373–76

Société du Figaro S.A., 60 281–84

Société du Louvre, 27 421–23

Société Economique de Rennes, **19** 98

Société Européenne de Production de L'avion E.C.A.T. *see* SEPECAT.

Société Française de Casinos, **48** 198

Société Générale, II 354–56; **42** 347–51 **(upd.)**

Société Générale de Banque *see* Generale
Bank.
Société Générale de Belgique S.A. *see*
Generale Bank.
Société Générale des Entreprises *see* Vinci.
Société Générale du Telephones, **21** 231
Société Industrielle Belge des Pétroles, **IV**
498–99
**Société Industrielle Lesaffre, 84
356–359**
Société Internationale Pirelli S.A., **V** 250
Société Laitière Vendômoise, **23** 219
**Société Luxembourgeoise de Navigation
Aérienne S.A., 64** 357–59
Societe Mecanique Automobile de l'Est/du
Nord, *see* PSA Peugeot Citroen S.A.
Société Nationale de Programmes de
Télévision Française 1 *see* Télévision
Française 1.
**Société Nationale des Chemins de Fer
Français, V** 512–15; **57** 328–32
(upd.)
Société Nationale des Pétroles d'Aquitaine,
21 203–05
Société Nationale Elf Aquitaine, IV
544–47; **7** 481–85 **(upd.)**
Société Norbert Dentressangle S.A., 67
352–54
Société Nouvelle d'Achat de Bijouterie, *see*
Finlay Enterprises, Inc.
Société Nouvelle des Etablissements
Gaumont *see* Gaumont SA.
Société Parisienne Raveau-Cartier, **31** 128
Société pour l'Étude et la Realisation
d'Engins Balistiques *see* SEREB.
Société pour le Financement de l'Industrie
Laitière, **19** 51
Société Samos, **23** 219
Société Succursaliste S.A.
d'Approvisonnements Guyenne et
Gascogne *see* Guyenne et Gascogne.
Société Suisse de Microelectronique &
d'Horlogerie *see* The Swatch Group SA.
Société Tefal *see* Groupe SEB.
Société Tunisienne de l'Air-Tunisair, 49
371–73
Society Corporation, 9 474–77
Socma *see* Sociedad Macri S.A.
Socony *see* Standard Oil Co. (New York).
Socony-Vacuum Oil Company *see* Mobil
Corp.
Socpresse, **60** 281
Sodak Gaming, Inc., **41** 216
Sodexho SA, 29 442–44; **91** 433–36
(upd.)
Sodiaal S.A., 19 50; **36** 437–39 **(upd.)**
SODIMA, **II** 576–77 *see also* Sodiaal S.A.
Sodimac S.A., **69** 312
La Sodis *see* Éditions Gallimard.
Sodiso, **23** 247
Soeker Exploration & Production Pty,
Ltd., **59** 336–37
Soekor, **IV** 93
Sofamor Danek Group, Inc. *see*
Medtronic, Inc.
Soffo, **22** 365
Soficom, *see* Eiffage.

SOFIL *see* Société pour le Financement de
l'Industrie Laitière.
Sofimex *see* Sociedad Financiera Mexicana.
Sofitam, S.A., **21** 493, 495
Sofitels *see* Accor SA.
Sofora Telecomunicaciones S.A., **63** 377
Soft Sheen Products, Inc., 31 416–18
Soft*Switch, **25** 301
Softbank Corporation, 13 481–83; **38**
439–44 **(upd.);** **77** 387–95 **(upd.)**
Softimage Inc., **38** 71–72
SoftKat *see* Baker & Taylor, Inc.
Softsel Computer Products, *see* Merisel,
Inc.
Software Architects Inc., **74** 258
Software Development Pty., Ltd., **15** 107
Software Dimensions, Inc. *see* ASK Group,
Inc.
The Software Group Inc., **23** 489, 491
Software Plus, Inc., **10** 514
Software Publishing Corp., **14** 262
Softwood Holdings Ltd., *see* CSR Ltd.
Sogara S.A., **23** 246–48
Sogedis, **23** 219
Sogo Co., **42** 342
Soil Teq, Inc., *see* Ag-Chem Equipment
Company, Inc.
Soilserv, Inc. *see* Mycogen Corp.
Sol Meliá S.A., 71 337–39
Sola International Inc., 71 340–42
Solair Inc., **14** 43; **37** 30–31
La Solana Corp., **IV** 726
Solar Wide Industrial Ltd., **73** 332
Solaray, Inc., **37** 284–85
Sole Technology Inc., 93 405–09
Solect Technology Group, **47** 12
Solectron Corporation, 12 450–52; **48**
366–70 **(upd.)**
Solera Capital, **59** 50
Solid Beheer B.V., **10** 514
Solid Cement Corporation, **59** 115
Solite Corp., **23** 224–25
Söll, **40** 96, 98
Solley's Delicatessen and Bakery, *see* Jerry's
Famous Deli Inc.
Solo Serve Corporation, 28 429–31
SOLOCO Inc., **63** 305
Solomon Valley Milling Company, **6** 592;
50 37
Solutia Inc., 52 312–15
Solvay & Cie S.A., I 394–96; **21**
464–67 **(upd.)**
Solvay S.A., 61 329–34 **(upd.)**
Somali Bank, **31** 220
Somerfield plc, 47 365–69 **(upd.)**
Somerville Packaging Group, **28** 420
Sommer-Allibert S.A., 19 406–09 *see also*
Tarkett Sommer AG.
Sonat, Inc., 6 577–78 *see also* El Paso
Corp.
Sonatrach, 65 313–17 **(upd.)**
Sonecor Systems, **6** 340
Sonera Corporation, 50 441–44 *see also*
TeliaSonera AB.
Sonergy, Inc., **49** 280
**Sonesta International Hotels
Corporation, 44** 389–91
Sonet Media AB, **23** 390

SONI Ltd., **64** 404
Sonic Automotive, Inc., 77 396–99
Sonic Corp., 14 451–53; **37** 360–63
(upd.)
Sonic Duo, **48** 419
Sonic Innovations Inc., 56 336–38
Sonic Restaurants, **31** 279
Sonic Solutions, Inc., 81 375–79
SonicWALL, Inc., 87 421–424
Sonnen Basserman, **II** 475
Sonoco Products Company, 8 475–77;
89 415–22 **(upd.)**
Sonofon *see* Telenor ASA.
The Sonoma Group, **25** 246
Sonor GmbH, **53** 216
SonoSite, Inc., 56 339–41
Sony Corporation, II 101–03; **12**
453–56 **(upd.);** **40** 404–10 **(upd.)**
Sony Ericsson Mobile Communications
AB, **61** 137
Soo Line Corporation *see* Canadian Pacific
Ltd.
Soo Line Mills, *see* George Weston Ltd.
Sooner Trailer Manufacturing Co., **29** 367
Soparind, *see* Bongrain S.A.
Sope Creek, **30** 457
Sophus Berendsen A/S, 49 374–77
SOPORCEL, **34** 38–39
Soporcel-Sociedade Portuguesa de Papel,
S.A., **60** 156
Sorbee International Ltd., 74 309–11
Sorbents Products Co. Inc., **31** 20
Sorbus, **6** 242
Sorenson Research Company, **36** 496
Sorg Paper Company *see* Mosinee Paper
Corp.
Soriana *see* Organización Soriana, S.A. de
C.V.
Sorin S.p.A., **61** 70, 72
Soros Fund Management LLC, 28
432–34
Sorrento, Inc., 19 51; **24** 444–46
SOS Staffing Services, 25 432–35
Sosa, Bromley, Aguilar & Associates *see*
D'Arcy Masius Benton & Bowles, Inc.
Soterra, Inc., **15** 188
Sotetsu Rosen, **72** 301
Sotheby's Holdings, Inc., 11 452–54; **29**
445–48 **(upd.);** **84** 360–365 **(upd.)**
Soufflet SA *see* Groupe Soufflet SA.
Sound Advice, Inc., 41 379–82
Sound of Music Inc. *see* Best Buy Co.,
Inc.
Sound Video Unlimited, **16** 46; **43** 60
Souplantation Incorporated *see* Garden
Fresh Restaurant Corp.
The Source Enterprises, Inc., 65 318–21
Source Interlink Companies, Inc., 75
350–53
Source One Mortgage Services Corp., **12**
79
Source Perrier, *see* Nestlé S.A.
Sourdough Bread Factory *see* Matt
Prentice Restaurant Group.
Souriau, **19** 166
South African Airways Ltd., *see* Transnet
Ltd.

The South African Breweries Limited, I
287–89; 24 447–51 (upd.) *see also*
SABMiller plc.
South African Transport Services *see*
Transnet Ltd.
South Asia Tyres, 20 263
South Australian Brewing Company, 54
228, 341
South Beach Beverage Company, Inc.,
73 316–19
South Carolina Electric & Gas Company
see SCANA Corp.
South Carolina National Corporation, 16
523, 526
South Carolina Power Company, 38
446–47
South Central Bell Telephone Co. *see*
BellSouth Corp.
South Central Railroad Co., 14 325
South Coast Gas Compression Company,
Inc., 11 523
South Coast Terminals, Inc., 16 475
South Dakota Public Service Company, 6
524
South Florida Neonatology Associates, 61
284
South Fulton Light & Power Company, 6
514
South Jersey Industries, Inc., 42 352–55
South Overseas Fashion Ltd., 53 344
South Wales Electric Company, 34 219
South West Water Plc *see* Pennon Group
Plc.
South Western Electricity plc, 38 448; 41
316
South-Western Publishing Co., *see* The
Thomson Corp.
Southam Inc., 7 486–89 *see also*
CanWest Global Communications
Corp.
Southcorp Limited, 54 341–44
Southdown, Inc., 14 454–56 *see also*
CEMEX S.A. de C.V.
Southdown Press *see* PMP Ltd.
Southeast Public Service Company, *see*
Triarc Companies, Inc.
Southeastern Freight Lines, Inc., 53 249
Southeastern Personnel *see* Norrell Corp.
Southern and Phillips Gas Ltd., *see*
Southern Electric PLC.
Southern Blvd. Supermarkets, Inc., 22
549
Southern California Edison Co. *see* Edison
International.
Southern California Fruit Growers
Exchange *see* Sunkist Growers, Inc.
Southern California Gas Co., *see* Sempra
Energy.
The Southern Company, V 721–23; 38
445–49 (upd.)
Southern Connecticut Gas Company,
84 366–370
Southern Cooker Limited Partnership, 51
85
Southern Corrections Systems, Inc. *see*
Avalon Correctional Services, Inc.
Southern Cross Paints, 38 98

Southern Electric PLC, 13 484–86 *see
also* Scottish and Southern Energy plc.
Southern Electric Supply Co., 15 386
Southern Electronics Corp. *see* SED
International Holdings, Inc.
Southern Equipment & Supply Co., 19
344
Southern Financial Bancorp, Inc., 56
342–44
Southern Foods Group, L.P. *see* Dean
Foods Co.
Southern Forest Products, Inc., 6 577
Southern Gage, *see* Illinois Tool Works
Inc.
Southern Guaranty Cos., *see* Winterthur
Group.
Southern Indiana Gas and Electric
Company, 13 487–89
Southern Minnesota Beet Sugar
Cooperative, 32 29
Southern National Bankshares of Atlanta,
10 425
Southern National Corporation *see* BB&T
Corporation
Southern Natural Gas Co., 6 577
Southern New England
Telecommunications Corporation, 6
338–40
Southern Oregon Broadcasting Co., *see*
Affiliated Publications, Inc.
Southern Pacific Transportation
Company, V 516–18 *see also* Union
Pacific Corp.
Southern Peru Copper Corp.,
Southern Peru Copper Corporation, 40
411–13
Southern Phenix Textiles Inc., 15 247–48
Southern Poverty Law Center, Inc., 74
312–15
Southern Power Company *see* Duke
Energy Corp.
Southern Recycling Inc., 51 170
Southern States Cooperative
Incorporated, 36 440–42
Southern Sun Hotel Corporation *see*
South African Breweries Ltd.; Sun
International Hotels Ltd.
Southern Union Company, 27 424–26
Southern Water plc, *see* Scottish Power
plc.
Southern Wine and Spirits of America,
Inc., 84 371–375
Southgate Medical Laboratory System, 26
391
Southington Savings Bank, 55 52
The Southland Corporation, II 660–61;
7 490–92 (upd.) *see also* 7-Eleven, Inc.
Southland Mobilcom Inc., 15 196
Southland Royalty Co., 10 190
Southmark Corp., 11 483; 33 398
Southport, Inc., 44 203
Southtrust Corporation, 11 455–57 *see
also* Wachovia Corp.
Southwest Airlines Co., 6 119–21; 24
452–55 (upd.); 71 343–47 (upd.)
Southwest Convenience Stores, LLC, 26
368
Southwest Gas Corporation, 19 410–12

Southwest Property Trust Inc., 52 370
Southwest Sports Group, 51 371, 374
Southwest Water Company, 47 370–73
Southwestern Bell Corporation, V
328–30 *see also* SBC Communications
Inc.
Southwestern Bell Publications, 26 520
Southwestern Electric Power Co., 21
468–70
Southwestern Explosives, Inc., 76 34
Southwestern Gas Pipeline, *see* Mitchell
Energy and Development Corp.
Southwestern Public Service Company,
6 579–81
Southwire Company, Inc., 8 478–80; 23
444–47 (upd.)
Souza Cruz S.A., 65 322–24
Souza Pinto Industria e Comercio de
Artefatos de Borracha Ltda., 71 393
Soviba, 70 322
Sovintel, 59 209, 211
Sovion NV *see* Vion Food Group NV.
Sovran Financial, 10 425–26
Sovran Self Storage, Inc., 66 299–301
SovTransavto, 6 410
Soyco Foods, Inc., 58 137
SP Alpargatas *see* Sao Paulo Alpargatas
S.A.
SP Pharmaceuticals, LLC, 50 123
SP Reifenwerke, V 253
SP Tyres, V 253
Space Control GmbH, 28 243–44
Space Craft Inc., *see* SCI Systems, Inc.
Space Systems Corporation *see* Orbital
Sciences Corp.
Space Systems/Loral, *see* Loral Corp.
Spacehab, Inc., 37 364–66
Spacelabs Medical, Inc., 71 348–50
Spacesaver Corporation, 57 208–09
Spaghetti Warehouse, Inc., 25 436–38
Spago *see* The Wolfgang Puck Food
Company, Inc.
Spalding, Inc., 23 449; 54 73
Spanco Yarns, 62 375
Spangler Candy Company, 44 392–95
Spanish Broadcasting System, Inc., 41
383–86
Spanish International Communications
Corp. *see* Univision Communications
Inc.
Spansion Inc., 80 352–55
Spanx, Inc., 89 423–27
SPAO, 39 184
Spar Aerospace Limited, 32 435–37
SPAR Handels AG, 35 398–401
SpareBank 1 Gruppen, 69 177, 179
Spark Networks, Inc., 91 437–40
Sparkassen-Finanzgruppe *see* Deutscher
Sparkassen- und Giroverband (DSGV).
Sparks-Withington Company *see* Sparton
Corp.
Sparrow Records, 22 194
Sparta Surgical Corporation, 33 456
Spartan Communications, 38 308–09
Spartan Industries, Inc., 45 15
Spartan Insurance Co., 26 486
Spartan Motors Inc., 14 457–59

The Thomson Corporation, 8 525–28; 34 435–40 (upd.); 77 433–39 (upd.)

Thomson International, 37 143

THOMSON multimedia S.A., II 116–17; 42 377–80 (upd.)

Thomson-Ramo-Woolridge see TRW Inc.

Thona Group see Hexagon AB

Thonet Industries Inc., see Shelby Williams Industries, Inc.

Thor Industries Inc., 39 391–94; 92 365–370 (upd.)

Thorn Apple Valley, Inc., 7 523–25; 22 508–11 (upd.)

Thorn EMI plc, I 531–32 see also EMI plc; Thorn plc.

Thorn plc, 24 484–87

Thornhill Inc, 64 217

Thornton Baker see Grant Thornton International.

Thorntons plc, 46 424–26

Thorpe Park, 55 378

Thorsen Realtors, 21 96

Thos. & Wm. Molson & Company see The Molson Companies Ltd.

ThoughtWorks Inc., 90 413–16

Thousand Trails, Inc., 33 397–99

THQ, Inc., 39 395–97; 92 371–375 (upd.)

Threads for Life, 49 244

Threadz, 25 300

Three-Diamond Company see Mitsubishi Shokai.

The 3DO Company, 43 426–30

3 Guys, V 35

Three Ring Asia Pacific Beer Co., Ltd., 49 418

Three Score, 23 100

365 Media Group plc, 89 441–44

3 Suisses International, 12 281

3Com Corporation, 11 518–21; 34 441–45 (upd.) see also Palm, Inc.

3D Planet SpA, 41 409

3dfx Interactive Inc., 54 269–71

3Dlabs, 57 78, 80

3i Group PLC, 73 338–40

3M Company, 61 365–70 (upd.)

360 Youth Inc., 55 15

360networks inc., 46 268

Threshold Entertainment, 25 270

Thrift Drug, V 92

Thrift Mart, 16 65

Thriftimart Inc., 12 153

Thriftway Food Drug, 21 530

Thriftway Foods, 74 365

Thrifty Corporation, 55 58

Thrifty PayLess, Inc., 12 477–79 see also Rite Aid Corp.

Thrifty Rent-A-Car see Dollar Thrifty Automotive Group, Inc.

Thrustmaster S.A., 41 190

Thummel Schutze & Partner, 28 141

Thunder Bay Press, 34 3–5

Thüringer Schokoladewerk GmbH, 53 315

Thyssengas, 38 406–07

ThyssenKrupp AG, IV 221–23; 28 452–60 (upd.); 87 425–438 (upd.)

TI see Texas Instruments.

TI Group plc, 17 480–83

TIAA-CREF see Teachers Insurance and Annuity Association-College Retirement Equities Fund.

Tianjin Automobile Industry Group, 21 164

Tianjin Bohai Brewing Company, 21 230; 50 202

Tianjin Paper Net, 62 350

Tibbett & Britten Group plc, 32 449–52

TIBCO Software Inc., 79 411–14

Tiber Construction Company, 16 286

TIC Holdings Inc., 92 376–379

Tichenor Media System Inc., 35 220

Ticketmaster, 13 508–10; 37 381–84 (upd.); 76 349–53 (upd.)

Ticketron, 37 381–82

TicketsWest.com, 59 410, 412

Ticor Title Insurance Co., see Alleghany Corp.

Tidewater Inc., 11 522–24; 37 385–88 (upd.)

Tidewater Utilities, Inc., 45 275, 277

TIE see Transport International Express.

Tien Wah Press (Pte.) Ltd., IV 600

Tierco Group, Inc., see Premier Parks, Inc.

Tierney & Partners, 23 480

Tiffany & Co., 14 500–03; 78 396–401 (upd.)

TIG Holdings, Inc., 26 486–88

Tiger Aspect Productions Ltd., 72 348–50

Tiger International, Inc., see FedEx Corp.

TigerDirect, Inc., 52 342–44

Tigon Corporation, 41 288

Tiki Corp., 69 365

Tilcon Capaldi, Inc., 64 98

Tilcon-Connecticut Inc., 80 373–76

Tilia Inc., 62 363–65

Tilley Endurables, Inc., 67 364–66

Tillinghast, Nelson & Warren Inc., 32 459

Tillotson Corp., 15 488–90

TIM see Telecom Italia Mobile S.p.A.

Tim Horton's Restaurants see TDL Group Ltd.; Wendy's Inc.

Timber Lodge Steakhouse, Inc., 73 341–43

The Timberland Company, 13 511–14; 54 375–79 (upd.)

Timberline Software Corporation, 15 491–93

TIMCO see Triad International Maintenance Corp.

Time Industries, 26 445

Time-Life Books, Inc. see AOL Time Warner Inc.

Time Life Music, 44 242

Time Out Group Ltd., 68 371–73

Time Saver Stores, Inc., see Dillon Companies Inc.

Time Warner Inc., IV 673–76; 7 526–30 (upd.) see also AOL Time Warner Inc.

Timeplex, see Ascom AG.

Times Fiber Communications, Inc., 40 35–36

The Times Mirror Company, IV 677–78; 17 484–86 (upd.) see also Tribune Co.

Times Publishing Group, 54 116, 118

Timeshare Resale Brokers Inc. see ILX Resorts Inc.

TIMET see Titanium Metals Corp.

Timex Corporation, 7 531–33; 25 479–82 (upd.)

The Timken Company, 8 529–31; 42 381–85 (upd.)

Tioga Gas Plant Inc., 55 20

Tioxide Group plc, 44 117, 119

Tip Top Tailors, 29 162

TIPC Network see Gateway 2000.

Tiphook PLC, 13 530

Tiscali SpA, 48 396–99

TISCO see Tata Iron & Steel Company Ltd.

Tishman Speyer Properties, L.P., 47 403–06

Tissue Technologies, Inc., see Palomar Medical Technologies, Inc.

Titan Acquisition Corporation, 51 34, 36

Titan Cement Company S.A., 64 379–81

The Titan Corporation, 36 475–78

Titan International, Inc., 89 445–49

Titan Sports, Inc., 52 192

Titanium Metals Corporation, 21 489–92

Titleist see Acushnet Co.

Title Insurance Company of America see LandAmerica Financial Group, Inc.

Titmuss Sainer Dechert see Dechert.

TiVo Inc., 75 373–75

Tivoli Audio, 48 85

Tivoli Systems, Inc., 14 392

TJ International, Inc., 19 444–47

The TJX Companies, Inc., V 197–98; 19 448–50 (upd.); 57 366–69 (upd.)

TKR Cable Co., 15 264

TKT see Transkaryotic Therapies Inc.

TL Enterprises, Inc., 56 5

TLC Beatrice International Holdings, Inc., 22 512–15

TLC Gift Company, 26 375

TLO, 25 82

TMNI International Inc., 70 275

TMP Worldwide Inc., 30 458–60 see also Monster Worldwide Inc.

TMS, Inc., 7 358

TMS Marketing, 26 440

TMT see Trailer Marine Transport.

TMW Capital Inc., 48 286

TN Technologies Inc., 23 479

TNI Funding I Inc., 70 275

TNT Crust, Inc., 23 203

TNT Freightways Corporation, 14 504–06

TNT Grading Inc., 50 348

TNT Limited, V 523–25

TNT Post Group N.V., 27 471–76 (upd.); 30 461–63 (upd.) see also TPG N.V.

Toa Tanker Co. Ltd., IV 555

Tobacco Group PLC, 30 231

Tobias, 16 239

Tube Forming, Inc., **23** 517

Tube Service Co., *see* Reliance Steel & Aluminum Co.

Tubed Chemicals Corporation, *see* McCormick & Company, Inc.

Tuborg, *see* Carlsberg A/S.

Tubos de Acero de Mexico, S.A. (TAMSA), 41 404–06

Tuboscope, **42** 420

Tucker, Lynch & Coldwell *see* CB Commercial Real Estate Services Group, Inc.

Tucker Rocky Distributing, **76** 235

TUCO, Inc., *see* Cabot Corp.

Tucows Inc., 78 411–14

Tucson Electric Power Company, 6 588–91

Tuesday Morning Corporation, 18 529–31; **70** 331–33 (upd.)

TUF *see* Thai Union Frozen Products PCL.

Tuff Stuff Publications, **23** 101

TUI *see* Touristik Union International GmbH. and Company K.G.

TUI Group GmbH, 42 283; **44** 432–35

TUJA, *see* AHL Services, Inc.

Tulip Ltd., 89 454–57

Tullow Oil plc, 83 420–423

Tully's Coffee Corporation, 51 384–86

Tultex Corporation, 13 531–33

Tumaro's Gourmet Tortillas, 85 430–33

Tumbleweed, Inc., 33 412–14; **80** 377–81 (upd.)

Tunisair *see* Société Tunisienne de l'Air-Tunisair.

Tupolev Aviation and Scientific Technical Complex, 24 58–60

Tupperware Brands Corporation, 28 478–81; **78** 415–20 (upd.)

Turbine Engine Asset Management LLC, **28** 5

TurboChef Technologies, Inc., 83 424-427

TurboLinux Inc., **45** 363

Turk Telecom, **63** 378, 380

Turkish Airlines Inc. (Türk Hava Yollari A.O.), 72 351–53

Turkish Petroleum Co. *see* Türkiye Petrolleri Anonim Ortakliği.

Turkiye Is Bankasi A.S., 61 377–80

Türkiye Petrolleri Anonim Ortakliği, IV 562–64

Turner Broadcasting System, Inc., II 166–68; **6** 171–73 (upd.); **66** 331–34 (upd.)

Turner Construction Company, 66 335–38

The Turner Corporation, 8 538–40; **23** 485–88 (upd.)

Turnstone Systems, **44** 426

TURPAS *see* Türkiye Petrolleri Anonim Ortakliği

Turtle Wax, Inc., 15 506–09; **93** 465–70 (upd.)

Tuscarora Inc., 29 483–85

The Tussauds Group, 55 376–78

Tutogen Medical, Inc., 68 378–80

Tutor Time Learning Centers Inc., **76** 238, 241

Tutt Bryant Industries PLY Ltd., **26** 231

Tuttle, Oglebay and Company *see* Oglebay Norton Co.

Tuttle Publishing, 86 403–06

TV Azteca, S.A. de C.V., 39 398–401

TV Guide, Inc., 43 431–34 (upd.)

TVA *see* Tennessee Valley Authority.

TVE *see* Television Española, S.A.

TVH Acquisition Corp., *see* Home Insurance Co.

TVI, Inc., 15 510–12

TVN Entertainment Corporation, **32** 239

TVSN Ltd., **64** 185

TVT Records *see* Tee Vee Toons, Inc.

TW Services, Inc., II 679–80

TWA *see* Trans World Airlines; Transcontinental & Western Airways.

TWC *see* The Weather Channel, Inc.

Tweco Co., *see* Thermadyne Holding Corp.

Tweedy, Browne Company L.L.C. *see* Affiliated Managers Group, Inc.

Tweeter Home Entertainment Group, Inc., 30 464–66

Twentieth Century Fox Film Corporation, II 169–71; **25** 490–94 (upd.)

"21" International Holdings, **17** 182

21 Invest International Holdings Ltd., **14** 322

21st Century Food Products *see* Hain Food Group, Inc.

21st Century Mortgage, *see* American Homestar Corp.

21st Century Oncology *see* Radiation Therapy Services, Inc.

21st Century Telecom Services, Inc. *see* RCN Corp.

Twenty-third Publications, **49** 48

24 Hour Fitness Worldwide, Inc., 71 363–65

24/7 Real Media, Inc., **49** 421–24

TWI *see* Trans World International.

Twin City Wholesale Drug Company, **14** 147

Twin Disc, Inc., 21 502–04

Twin Hill Acquisition Company, Inc., **48** 286

Twinings Tea, **41** 31

Twinlab Corporation, 34 458–61

II-VI Incorporated, 69 353–55

2ndhead Oy, **51** 328

21st Century Mortgage, **41** 18, 20

TWW Plc, **26** 62

TXEN, Inc., *see* Nichols Research Corp.

TxPort Inc., *see* Acme-Cleveland Corp.

Ty Inc., 33 415–17; **86** 407–11 (upd.)

Tyco International Ltd., III 643–46; **28** 482–87 (upd.); **63** 400–06 (upd.)

Tyco Submarine Systems Ltd., **32** 217

Tyco Toys, Inc., 12 494–97 *see also* Mattel, Inc.

Tyler Corporation, 23 489–91

Tyndale House Publishers, Inc., 57 391–94

Tyndall's Formal Wear, **60** 5

Tyrolean Airways, **33** 50

Tyskie Brewery, **24** 450

Tyson Foods, Inc., II 584–85; **14** 514–16 (upd.); **50** 491–95 (upd.)

U

U.B. TUFF., **67** 339

U.C.L.A.F *see* Roussel-Uclaf.

U-Haul International Inc. *see* Amerco.

U.S. *see also* US.

U.S. Aggregates, Inc., 42 390–92

U.S. Appliances, **26** 336

U.S. Army Corps of Engineers, 91 491–95

U.S. Bancorp, 14 527–29; **36** 489–95 (upd.)

U.S. Bank of Washington, *see* U.S. Bancorp.

U.S. Banknote Company, **30** 43

U.S. Bearings Company *see* Federal-Mogul Corp.

U.S. Billing, Inc. *see* Billing Concepts Corp.

U.S. Bioscience, Inc., **35** 286, 288

U.S. Borax, Inc., 42 393–96

U.S. Brass, *see* Eljer Industries, Inc.

U.S. Can Corporation, 30 474–76

U.S. Cellular Corporation, 31 449–52 (upd.); **88** 408–13 (upd.)

U.S. Computer of North America Inc., **43** 368

U.S. Delivery Systems, Inc., 22 531–33 *see also* Velocity Express Corp.

U.S. Foodservice, 26 503–06

U.S. Generating Company, **26** 373

U.S. Graphite *see* Wickes Inc.

U.S. Healthcare, Inc., 6 194–96

U.S. Home Corporation, 8 541–43; **78** 421–26 (upd.)

U.S. Industries, Inc., **23** 296; **76** 185, 204, 206

U.S. Intec, **22** 229

U.S. International Reinsurance, *see* Home Insurance Co.

U.S. Investigations Services Inc., **35** 44

U.S. Journal Training, Inc., **72** 172

U.S. Lawns, **31** 182, 184

U.S. Lock Corporation, **28** 50–52

U.S. Long Distance Corp. *see* Billing Concepts Corp.

U.S. News & World Report Inc., 30 477–80; **89** 458–63 (upd.)

U.S. Office Products Company, 25 500–02

U.S. Physical Therapy, Inc., 65 345–48

U.S. Plywood Corp *see* United States Plywood Corp.

U.S. Premium Beef LLC, 91 487–90

U.S. RingBinder Corp., *see* General Binding Corp.

U.S. Robotics Corporation, 9 514–15; **66** 339–41 (upd.)

U.S. Satellite Broadcasting Company, Inc., 20 505–07 *see also* DIRECTV, Inc.

U.S. Shoe Corporation, **43** 98; **44** 365

U.S. Software Inc., **29** 479

Warburtons Ltd., **89** 487–90

Ward's Communications, **22** 441

Wards *see* Circuit City Stores, Inc.

Waremart *see* WinCo Foods.

WARF *see* Wisconsin Alumni Research Foundation.

Warman International *see* Weir Group PLC.

The Warnaco Group Inc., **12** 521–23; **46** 450–54 (upd.) *see also* Authentic Fitness Corp.

Warner Chilcott Limited, **85** 446–49

Warner Communications Inc., **II** 175–77 *see also* AOL Time Warner Inc.

Warner Electric, **58** 67

Warner-Lambert Co., **I** 710–12; **10** 549–52 (upd.) *see also* Pfizer Inc.

Warner Music Group Corporation, **90** 432–37 (upd.)

Warner Roadshow Film Distributors Greece SA, **58** 359

Warners' Stellian Inc., **67** 384–87

Warrantech Corporation, **53** 357–59

Warrell Corporation, **68** 396–98

Warren Apparel Group Ltd., **39** 257

Warren Bancorp Inc., **55** 52

Warren Frozen Foods, Inc., **61** 174

Warren, Gorham & Lamont, *see* The Thomson Corp.

Warren Petroleum, *see* Dynegy Inc.

Warrick Industries, **31** 338

Warrington Products Ltd. *see* Canstar Sports Inc.

Warwick International Ltd., *see* Sequa Corp.

Warwick Valley Telephone Company, **55** 382–84

Wasatch Gas Co., **6** 568

Wascana Energy Inc., **13** 556–58

Washburn Graphics Inc., **23** 100

The Washington Companies, **33** 442–45

Washington Federal, Inc., **17** 525–27

Washington Football, Inc., **35** 462–65

Washington Gas Light Company, **19** 485–88

Washington Inventory Service, **30** 239

Washington Mutual, Inc., **17** 528–31; **93** 483–89 (upd.)

Washington National Corporation, **12** 524–26

Washington Natural Gas Company, **9** 539–41 *see also* Puget Sound Energy Inc.

The Washington Post Company, **IV** 688–90; **20** 515–18 (upd.)

Washington Public Power Supply System, **50** 102

Washington Railway and Electric Company, **6** 552–53

Washington Scientific Industries, Inc., **17** 532–34

Washington Sports Clubs *see* Town Sports International, Inc.

Washington Steel Corp., *see* Lukens Inc.

Washington Water Power Company, **6** 595–98 *see also* Avista Corp.

Washtenaw Gas Company *see* MCN Corp.

Wassall Plc, **18** 548–50

Waste Connections, Inc., **46** 455–57

Waste Control Specialists LLC, *see* alhi, Inc.

Waste Holdings, Inc., **41** 413–15

Waste Management, Inc., **V** 752–54

Water Pik Technologies, Inc., **34** 498–501; **83** 450-453 (upd.)

The Waterbury Companies, *see* Talley Industries, Inc.

Waterford Foods Plc, **59** 206

Waterford Wedgwood plc, **12** 527–29; **34** 493–97 (upd.)

Waterhouse Investor Services, Inc., **18** 551–53

Waterman Marine Corporation, *see* International Shipholding Corporation, Inc.

The Waterman Pen Company *see* BIC Corp.

Watermark Paddlesports Inc., **76** 119

Waterpark Management Inc., **73** 231

WaterPro Supplies Corporation *see* Eastern Enterprises.

Waters Corporation, **43** 453–57

Waterstone's, **42** 444 *see also* HMV Group plc.

Watkins-Johnson Company, **15** 528–30

Watsco Inc., **52** 397–400

Watson & Philip *see* Alldays plc.

Watson Group, **55** 52

Watson-Haas Lumber Company, **33** 257

Watson-Marlow Bredel, **59** 384

Watson Pharmaceuticals Inc., **16** 527–29; **56** 373–76 (upd.)

Watson Wyatt Worldwide, **42** 427–30

Watt & Shand, **16** 61; **50** 107

Watt AG, **6** 491

The Watt Stopper, **21** 348, 350

Wattie Industries, **52** 141

Wattie's Ltd., **7** 576–78

Watts Industries, Inc., **19** 489–91

Watts of Lydney Group Ltd., **71** 391–93

Watts/Silverstein, Inc., **24** 96

Waukesha Engine Servicenter, **6** 441

Wausau Sulphate Fibre Co. *see* Mosinee Paper Corp.

Wausau-Mosinee Paper Corporation, **60** 328–31 (upd.)

Waverly, Inc., **16** 530–32

Waverly Pharmaceutical Limited, **11** 208

Wawa Inc., **17** 535–37; **78** 449–52 (upd.)

The Wawanesa Mutual Insurance Company, **68** 399–401

Waxman Industries, Inc., **9** 542–44

Wayfinder Group Inc., **51** 265

Waymaker Oy, **55** 289

Wayne Home Equipment *see* Scott Fetzer Co.

WAZ Media Group, **82** 419–24

WB *see* Warner Communications Inc.

WBI Holdings, Inc., **42** 249, 253

WCI Holdings Corporation, **V** 223; **41** 94

WCM Beteilingungs- und Grundbesitz AG, **58** 202, 205

WCPS Direct, Inc., **53** 359

WCRS Group plc *see* Aegis Group plc.

WD-40 Company, **18** 554–57; **87** 455–460 (upd.)

We Energies *see* Wisconsin Energy Corp.

WearGuard, *see* Aramark Corp.

The Weather Channel Companies, **52** 401–04 *see also* Landmark Communications, Inc.

Weatherford International, Inc., **39** 416–18

Weaver Popcorn Company, Inc., **89** 491–93

Webb Corbett and Beswick, **38** 402

Webber Oil Company, **61** 384–86

WeBco International LLC, **26** 530

Webco Securities, Inc., **37** 225

Weber, **16** 488

Weber Aircraft Inc., **41** 369

Weber et Broutin France, **66** 363–65

Weber Metal, **30** 283–84

Weber-Stephen Products Co., **40** 458–60

WebEx Communications, Inc., **81** 419–23

WebLogic Inc., **36** 81

WebMD Corporation, **65** 357–60

WebTrends Corporation, **76** 189

Webvan Group Inc., **38** 223

Weddingpages, Inc. *see* The Knot, Inc.

Wedgwood *see* Waterford Wedgewood Holdings PLC.

Weeres Industries Corporation, **52** 405–07

Weetabix Limited, **61** 387–89

Weg S.A., **78** 453–56

Wegener NV, **53** 360–62

Wegert Verwaltungs-GmbH and Co. Beteiligungs-KG, **24** 270

Wegmans Food Markets, Inc., **9** 545–46; **41** 416–18 (upd.)

Weichenwerk Brandenburg GmbH, **53** 352

Weider Health and Fitness, Inc., **38** 238

Weider Nutrition International, Inc., **29** 498–501

Weight Watchers Gourmet Food Co., **43** 218

Weight Watchers International Inc., **12** 530–32; **33** 446–49 (upd.); **73** 379–83 (upd.)

Weil Ceramics & Glass, **52** 148

Weil, Gotshal & Manges LLP, **55** 385–87

Weiner's Stores, Inc., **33** 450–53

Wieden + Kennedy, **75** 403–05

Wienerberger AG, **70** 361–63

Weingut Robert Weil, **65** 328, 330

The Weir Group PLC, **85** 450–53

Weirton Steel Corporation, **IV** 236–38; **26** 527–30 (upd.)

Weis Markets, Inc., **15** 531–33; **84** 422–426 (upd.)

The Weitz Company, Inc., **42** 431–34

Welbilt Corp., **19** 492–94; *see also* Enodis plc.

Welborn Transport Co., **39** 64, 65

Welch Engineering Ltd. *see* Swales & Associates, Inc.

Zero First Co Ltd., **62** 245

Zero Plus Dialing, Inc. *see* Billing
Concepts Corp.

Zetor s.p., **21** 175

Zeus Components, Inc., *see* Arrow
Electronics, Inc.

Zexel Valeo Compressor USA Inc. *see*
Valeo.

ZF Friedrichshafen AG, 48 447–51

Zhenjiang Zhengmao Hitachi Zosen
Machinery Co. Ltd., **53** 173

Zhong Yue Highsonic Electron Company,
62 150

Zhongbei Building Material Products
Company, **26** 510

Zhongde Brewery, **49** 417

Zicam LLC *see* Matrixx Initiatives, Inc.

Ziebart International Corporation, 30
499–501; 66 379–82 **(upd.)**

The Ziegler Companies, Inc., 24
541–45; 63 442–48 **(upd.)**

Ziff Davis Media Inc., 12 560–63; **36**
521–26 (upd.); 73 397–403 **(upd.)**

Zignago Vetro S.p.A., **67** 210–12

Zila, Inc., 46 466–69

Zildjian *see* Avedis Zildjian Co.

Zilkha & Company, **12** 72

ZiLOG, Inc., 15 543–45; **72** 377–80
(upd.)

Zimmer Holdings, Inc., 45 455–57

Zinc Products Company, **30** 39

Zindart Ltd., 60 370–72

**Zingerman's Community of Businesses,
68** 406–08

Zinifex Ltd., 85 474–77

Zinsser *see* William Zinsser & Company,
Inc.

Zio's Italian Kitchens *see* Mazzio's Corp.

Zion Foods, **23** 408

**Zion's Cooperative Mercantile
Institution, 33** 471–74

Zions Bancorporation, 12 564–66; **53**
375–78 **(upd.)**

Zipcar, Inc., 92 429–32

Zippo Manufacturing Company, 18
565–68; **71** 394–99 **(upd.)**

Zipps Drive-Thru, Inc., *see* Rally's.

Zodiac S.A., 36 527–30

Zolfo Cooper LLC, **57** 219

Zoll Foods, **55** 366

Zoloto Mining Ltd., **38** 231

Zoltek Companies, Inc., 37 427–30

Zomba Records Ltd., 52 428–31

Zondervan Corporation, 24 546–49; **71**
400–04 **(upd.)**

Zones, Inc., 67 395–97

Zoom Technologies, Inc., 18 569–71; **53**
379–82 **(upd.)**

Zoran Corporation, 77 489–92

Zotos International, Inc., *see* Shiseido
Company, Ltd.

ZPT Radom, **23** 427

Zuari Cement, **40** 107, 109

Zuellig Group N.A., Inc., **46** 226

Zuffa L.L.C., 89 503–07

Zuivelcooperatie De Seven Provincien UA,
59 194

Zuka Juice, **47** 201

Zumiez, Inc., 77 493–96

Zumtobel AG, 50 544–48

Zurich Financial Services, III 410–12;
42 448–53 **(upd.); 93** 502–10 **(upd.)**

Zurich Insurance Group, **15** 257

Zvezda Design Bureau, **61** 197

Zweckform Büro-Produkte G.m.b.H., **49**
38

Zycad Corp., **11** 489–91; **69** 340–41

Zycon Corporation, *see* Hadco Corp.

Zygo Corporation, 42 454–57

ZymoGenetics Inc., **61** 266

Zytec Corporation, 19 513–15 *see also*
Artesyn Technologies Inc.

Index to Industries

Accounting

American Institute of Certified Public Accountants (AICPA), 44
Andersen, 29 (upd.); 68 (upd.)
Automatic Data Processing, Inc., III; 9 (upd.); 47 (upd.)
CROSSMARK, 79
Deloitte Touche Tohmatsu International, 9; 29 (upd.)
Ernst & Young, 9; 29 (upd.)
FTI Consulting, Inc., 77
Grant Thornton International, 57
Huron Consulting Group Inc., 87
KPMG International, 33 (upd.)
L.S. Starrett Co., 13
McLane Company, Inc., 13
NCO Group, Inc., 42
Paychex, Inc., 15; 46 (upd.)
PKF International 78
Plante & Moran, LLP, 71
PRG-Schultz International, Inc., 73
PricewaterhouseCoopers, 9; 29 (upd.)
Resources Connection, Inc., 81
Robert Wood Johnson Foundation, 35
Saffery Champness, 80
Schenck Business Solutions, 88
StarTek, Inc., 79
Travelzoo Inc., 79
Univision Communications Inc., 24; 83 (upd.)

Advertising & Other Business Services

ABM Industries Incorporated, 25 (upd.)
AchieveGlobal Inc., 90
Ackerley Communications, Inc., 9
ACNielsen Corporation, 13; 38 (upd.)

Acosta Sales and Marketing Company, Inc., 77
Acsys, Inc., 44
Adecco S.A., 36 (upd.)
Adia S.A., 6
Administaff, Inc., 52
The Advertising Council, Inc., 76
The Advisory Board Company, 80
Advo, Inc., 6; 53 (upd.)
Aegis Group plc, 6
Affiliated Computer Services, Inc., 61
AHL Services, Inc., 27
Alloy, Inc., 55
Amdocs Ltd., 47
American Building Maintenance Industries, Inc., 6
American Library Association, 86
The American Society of Composers, Authors and Publishers (ASCAP), 29
Amey Plc, 47
Analysts International Corporation, 36
aQuantive, Inc., 81
The Arbitron Company, 38
Ariba, Inc., 57
Armor Holdings, Inc., 27
Asatsu-DK Inc., 82
Ashtead Group plc, 34
The Associated Press, 13
Avalon Correctional Services, Inc., 75
Bain & Company, 55
Barrett Business Services, Inc., 16
Barton Protective Services Inc., 53
Bates Worldwide, Inc., 14; 33 (upd.)
Bearings, Inc., 13
Berlitz International, Inc., 13
Bernard Hodes Group Inc., 86
Bernstein-Rein, 92
Big Flower Press Holdings, Inc., 21
Billing Concepts, Inc., 26; 72 (upd.)

The BISYS Group, Inc., 73
Boron, LePore & Associates, Inc., 45
The Boston Consulting Group, 58
Bozell Worldwide Inc., 25
BrandPartners Group, Inc., 58
Bright Horizons Family Solutions, Inc., 31
Broadcast Music Inc., 23; 90 (upd.)
Buck Consultants, Inc., 55
Bureau Veritas SA, 55
Burke, Inc., 88
Burns International Services Corporation, 13; 41 (upd.)
Cambridge Technology Partners, Inc., 36
Campbell-Ewald Advertising, 86
Campbell-Mithun-Esty, Inc., 16
Cannon Design, 63
Capita Group PLC, 69
Cardtronics, Inc., 93
Career Education Corporation, 45
Carmichael Lynch Inc., 28
Cash Systems, Inc., 93
Cazenove Group plc, 72
CCC Information Services Group Inc., 74
CDI Corporation, 6; 54 (upd.)
Central Parking Corporation, 18
Century Business Services, Inc., 52
Chancellor Beacon Academies, Inc., 53
ChartHouse International Learning Corporation, 49
Chiat/Day Inc. Advertising, 11
Chicago Board of Trade, 41
Chisholm-Mingo Group, Inc., 41
Christie's International plc, 15; 39 (upd.)
Cintas Corporation, 21
CMG Worldwide, Inc., 89
COMFORCE Corporation, 40
Command Security Corporation, 57
Computer Learning Centers, Inc., 26
Concentra Inc., 71

Aerospace

Airlines

TAP—Air Portugal Transportes Aéreos
Portugueses S.A., 46
TAROM S.A., 64
Texas Air Corporation, I
Thai Airways International Public
Company Limited, 6; 27 (upd.)
Tower Air, Inc., 28
Trans World Airlines, Inc., I; 12 (upd.);
35 (upd.)
TransBrasil S/A Linhas Aéreas, 31
Transportes Aereos Portugueses, S.A., 6
Turkish Airlines Inc. (Türk Hava Yollari
A.O.), 72
TV Guide, Inc., 43 (upd.)
UAL Corporation, 34 (upd.)
United Airlines, I; 6 (upd.)
US Airways Group, Inc., I; 6 (upd.); 28
(upd.); 52 (upd.)
VARIG S.A. (Viação Aérea
Rio-Grandense), 6; 29 (upd.)
Virgin Group Ltd., 12; 32 (upd.); 89
(upd.)
Volga-Dnepr Group, 82
WestJet Airlines Ltd., 38

Automotive

AB Volvo, I; 7 (upd.); 26 (upd.); 67
(upd.)
Accubuilt, Inc., 74
Adam Opel AG, 7; 21 (upd.); 61 (upd.)
ADESA, Inc., 71
Advance Auto Parts, Inc., 57
Aftermarket Technology Corp., 83
Aisin Seiki Co., Ltd., 48 (upd.)
Alamo Rent A Car, Inc., 6; 24 (upd.); 84
(upd.)
Alfa Romeo, 13; 36 (upd.)
Alvis Plc, 47
America's Car-Mart, Inc., 64
American Motors Corporation, I
Applied Power Inc., 32 (upd.)
Arnold Clark Automobiles Ltd., 60
ArvinMeritor, Inc., 8; 54 (upd.)
Asbury Automotive Group Inc., 60
ASC, Inc., 55
Autobacs Seven Company Ltd., 76
Autocam Corporation, 51
Autoliv, Inc., 65
Automobiles Citroen, 7
Automobili Lamborghini Holding S.p.A.,
13; 34 (upd.); 91 (upd.)
AutoNation, Inc., 50
AutoTrader.com, L.L.C., 91
AVTOVAZ Joint Stock Company, 65
Bajaj Auto Limited, 39
Bayerische Motoren Werke AG, I; 11
(upd.); 38 (upd.)
Belron International Ltd., 76
Bendix Corporation, I
Blue Bird Corporation, 35
Bombardier Inc., 42 (upd.)
BorgWarner Inc., 14; 32 (upd.); 85 (upd.)
The Budd Company, 8
Canadian Tire Corporation, Limited, 71
(upd.)
CarMax, Inc., 55
CARQUEST Corporation, 29
Caterpillar Inc., 63 (upd.)

Checker Motors Corp., 89
China Automotive Systems Inc., 87
Chrysler Corporation, I; 11 (upd.)
Commercial Vehicle Group, Inc., 81
CNH Global N.V., 38 (upd.)
Consorcio G Grupo Dina, S.A. de C.V.,
36
Crown Equipment Corporation, 15; 93
(upd.)
CSK Auto Corporation, 38
Cummins Engine Company, Inc., I; 12
(upd.); 40 (upd.)
Custom Chrome, Inc., 16
Daihatsu Motor Company, Ltd., 7; 21
(upd.)
Daimler-Benz A.G., I; 15 (upd.)
DaimlerChrysler AG, 34 (upd.); 64 (upd.)
Dana Corporation, I; 10 (upd.)
Danaher Corporation, 77 (upd.)
Deere & Company, 42 (upd.)
Delphi Automotive Systems Corporation,
45
Directed Electronics, Inc., 87
Discount Tire Company Inc., 84
Don Massey Cadillac, Inc., 37
Donaldson Company, Inc., 49 (upd.)
Douglas & Lomason Company, 16
Dräxlmaier Group, 90
DriveTime Automotive Group Inc., 68
(upd.)
Ducati Motor Holding SpA, 30; 86 (upd.)
Eaton Corporation, I; 10 (upd.); 67
(upd.)
Echlin Inc., I; 11 (upd.)
Edelbrock Corporation, 37
Faurecia S.A., 70
Federal-Mogul Corporation, I; 10 (upd.);
26 (upd.)
Ferrara Fire Apparatus, Inc., 84
Ferrari S.p.A., 13; 36 (upd.)
Fiat SpA, I; 11 (upd.); 50 (upd.)
FinishMaster, Inc., 24
Ford Motor Company, I; 11 (upd.); 36
(upd.); 64 (upd.)
Ford Motor Company, S.A. de C.V., 20
Fruehauf Corporation, I
General Motors Corporation, I; 10 (upd.);
36 (upd.); 64 (upd.)
Gentex Corporation, 26
Genuine Parts Company, 9; 45 (upd.)
GKN plc, III; 38 (upd.); 89 (upd.)
Group 1 Automotive, Inc., 52
Grupo Ficosa International, 90
Guardian Industries Corp., 87
Harley-Davidson Inc., 7; 25 (upd.)
Hastings Manufacturing Company, 56
Hayes Lemmerz International, Inc., 27
Hendrick Motorsports, Inc., 89
The Hertz Corporation, 33 (upd.)
Hino Motors, Ltd., 7; 21 (upd.)
Holden Ltd., 62
Holley Performance Products Inc., 52
Hometown Auto Retailers, Inc., 44
Honda Motor Company Limited (Honda
Giken Kogyo Kabushiki Kaisha), I; 10
(upd.); 29 (upd.)
Hyundai Group, 56 (upd.)
Insurance Auto Auctions, Inc., 23

Isuzu Motors, Ltd., 9; 23 (upd.); 57
(upd.)
INTERMET Corporation, 77 (upd.)
Jardine Cycle & Carriage Ltd., 73
Kawasaki Heavy Industries, Ltd., 63
(upd.)
Kelsey-Hayes Group of Companies, 7; 27
(upd.)
Key Safety Systems, Inc., 63
Kia Motors Corporation, 12; 29 (upd.)
Kwik-Fit Holdings plc, 54
Lazy Days RV Center, Inc., 69
Lear Corporation, 71 (upd.)
Lear Seating Corporation, 16
Les Schwab Tire Centers, 50
Lithia Motors, Inc., 41
LKQ Corporation, 71
Lookers plc, 71
Lotus Cars Ltd., 14
Lund International Holdings, Inc., 40
Mack Trucks, Inc., I; 22 (upd.); 61 (upd.)
The Major Automotive Companies, Inc.,
45
Marcopolo S.A., 79
Masland Corporation, 17
Mazda Motor Corporation, 9; 23 (upd.);
63 (upd.)
Mel Farr Automotive Group, 20
Metso Corporation, 30 (upd.)
Midas Inc., 10; 56 (upd.)
Mitsubishi Motors Corporation, 9; 23
(upd.); 57 (upd.)
Monaco Coach Corporation, 31
Monro Muffler Brake, Inc., 24
Montupet S.A., 63
National R.V. Holdings, Inc., 32
Navistar International Corporation, I; 10
(upd.)
New Flyer Industries Inc. 78
Nissan Motor Company Ltd., I; 11
(upd.); 34 (upd.); 92 (upd.)
O'Reilly Automotive, Inc., 26; 78 (upd.)
Officine Alfieri Maserati S.p.A., 13
Oshkosh Truck Corporation, 7
Paccar Inc., I
PACCAR Inc., 26 (upd.)
Park-Ohio Holdings Corp., 17; 85 (upd.)
Pennzoil-Quaker State Company, IV; 20
(upd.); 50 (upd.)
Penske Corporation, V; 19 (upd.); 84
(upd.)
The Pep Boys—Manny, Moe & Jack, 11;
36 (upd.); 81 (upd.)
Perusahaan Otomobil Nasional Bhd., 62
Peterbilt Motors Company, 89
Peugeot S.A., I
Piaggio & C. S.p.A., 20
Pirelli & C. S.p.A., 75 (upd.)
Porsche AG, 13; 31 (upd.)
PSA Peugeot Citroen S.A., 28 (upd.)
R&B, Inc., 51
Randon S.A., 79
Red McCombs Automotive Group, 91
Regie Nationale des Usines Renault, I
Renault Argentina S.A., 67
Renault S.A., 26 (upd.); 74 (upd.)
Repco Corporation Ltd., 74
Republic Industries, Inc., 26

Bio-Technology

Chemicals

Construction

Electrical & Electronics

Financial Services: Banks

Financial Services: Excluding Banks

Food Products

Food Services & Retailers

Santa Barbara Restaurant Group, Inc., 37
Sbarro, Inc., 16; 64 (upd.)
Schlotzsky's, Inc., 36
Schultz Sav-O Stores, Inc., 21
The Schwan Food Company, 26 (upd.);
  83 (upd.)
Seaway Food Town, Inc., 15
Second Harvest, 29
See's Candies, Inc., 30
Seneca Foods Corporation, 17
Service America Corp., 7
SFI Group plc, 51
Shaw's Supermarkets, Inc., 56
Shells Seafood Restaurants, Inc., 43
Shoney's, Inc., 7; 23 (upd.)
ShowBiz Pizza Time, Inc., 13
Skyline Chili, Inc., 62
Smart & Final, Inc., 16
Smith's Food & Drug Centers, Inc., 8; 57
  (upd.)
Sobeys Inc., 80
Sodexho SA, 29; 91 (upd.)
Somerfield plc, 47 (upd.)
Sonic Corporation, 14; 37 (upd.)
The Southland Corporation, II; 7 (upd.)
Spaghetti Warehouse, Inc., 25
SPAR Handels AG, 35
Spartan Stores Inc., 8
Starbucks Corporation, 77 (upd.)
Stater Bros. Holdings Inc., 64
The Steak n Shake Company, 41
Steinberg Incorporated, II
Stew Leonard's, 56
The Stop & Shop Supermarket Company,
  II; 68 (upd.)
Subway, 32
Super Food Services, Inc., 15
Supermarkets General Holdings
  Corporation, II
Supervalu Inc., II; 18 (upd.); 50 (upd.)
SWH Corporation, 70
SYSCO Corporation, II; 24 (upd.); 75
  (upd.)
Taco Bell Corporation, 7; 21 (upd.); 74
  (upd.)
Taco Cabana, Inc., 23; 72 (upd.)
Taco John's International, Inc., 15; 63
  (upd.)
Tchibo GmbH, 82
TelePizza S.A., 33
Tesco PLC, II
Texas Roadhouse, Inc., 69
Thomas & Howard Company, Inc., 90
Timber Lodge Steakhouse, Inc., 73
Tops Markets LLC, 60
Total Entertainment Restaurant
  Corporation, 46
Toupargel-Agrigel S.A., 76
Trader Joe's Company, 13; 50 (upd.)
Travel Ports of America, Inc., 17
Tree of Life, Inc., 29
Triarc Companies, Inc., 34 (upd.)
Tubby's, Inc., 53
Tully's Coffee Corporation, 51
Tumbleweed, Inc., 33; 80 (upd.)
TW Services, Inc., II
Ukrop's Super Market's, Inc., 39
Unified Grocers, Inc., 93

Unique Casual Restaurants, Inc., 27
United Dairy Farmers, Inc., 74
United Natural Foods, Inc., 32; 76 (upd.)
Uno Restaurant Holdings Corporation,
  18; 70 (upd.)
Uwajimaya, Inc., 60
Vail Resorts, Inc., 43 (upd.)
VICORP Restaurants, Inc., 12; 48 (upd.)
Victory Refrigeration, Inc., 82
Village Super Market, Inc., 7
The Vons Companies, Incorporated, 7; 28
  (upd.)
W. H. Braum, Inc., 80
Waffle House Inc., 14; 60 (upd.)
Wakefern Food Corporation, 33
Waldbaum, Inc., 19
Wall Street Deli, Inc., 33
Wawa Inc., 17; 78 (upd.)
Wegmans Food Markets, Inc., 9; 41
  (upd.)
Weis Markets, Inc., 15
Wendy's International, Inc., 8; 23 (upd.);
  47 (upd.)
The WesterN SizzliN Corporation, 60
Wetterau Incorporated, II
White Castle Management Company, 12;
  36 (upd.); 85 (upd.)
White Rose, Inc., 24
Whittard of Chelsea Plc, 61
Whole Foods Market, Inc., 50 (upd.)
Wild Oats Markets, Inc., 19; 41 (upd.)
Winchell's Donut Houses Operating
  Company, L.P., 60
WinCo Foods Inc., 60
Winn-Dixie Stores, Inc., II; 21 (upd.); 59
  (upd.)
Wm. Morrison Supermarkets PLC, 38
Wolfgang Puck Worldwide, Inc., 26, 70
  (upd.)
Worldwide Restaurant Concepts, Inc., 47
Yoshinoya D & C Company Ltd., 88
Young & Co.'s Brewery, P.L.C., 38
Yucaipa Cos., 17
Yum! Brands Inc., 58
Zingerman's Community of Businesses,
  68

Health & Personal Care Products
Abaxis, Inc., 83
Abbott Laboratories, I; 11 (upd.); 40
  (upd.); 93 (upd.)
Advanced Medical Optics, Inc., 79
Advanced Neuromodulation Systems, Inc.,
  73
Akorn, Inc., 32
ALARIS Medical Systems, Inc., 65
Alberto-Culver Company, 8; 36 (upd.); 91
  (upd.)
Alco Health Services Corporation, III
Alès Groupe, 81
Allergan, Inc., 10; 30 (upd.); 77 (upd.)
American Oriental Bioengineering Inc., 93
American Safety Razor Company, 20
American Stores Company, 22 (upd.)
Amway Corporation, III; 13 (upd.)
AngioDynamics, Inc., 81
ArthroCare Corporation, 73

Artsana SpA, 92
Atkins Nutritionals, Inc., 58
Aveda Corporation, 24
Avon Products, Inc., III; 19 (upd.); 46
  (upd.)
Bally Total Fitness Holding Corp., 25
Bare Escentuals, Inc., 91
Bausch & Lomb Inc., 7; 25 (upd.)
Baxter International Inc., I; 10 (upd.)
BeautiControl Cosmetics, Inc., 21
Becton, Dickinson & Company, I; 11
  (upd.)
Beiersdorf AG, 29
Big B, Inc., 17
Bindley Western Industries, Inc., 9
Biolase Technology, Inc., 87
Biomet, Inc., 10; 93 (upd.)
Biosite Incorporated, 73
Block Drug Company, Inc., 8; 27 (upd.)
The Body Shop International plc, 53
  (upd.)
Boiron S.A., 73
Bolton Group B.V., 86
The Boots Company PLC, 24 (upd.)
Boston Scientific Corporation, 77 (upd.)
Bristol-Myers Squibb Company, III; 9
  (upd.)
Bronner Brothers Inc., 92
C.R. Bard Inc., 9
Candela Corporation, 48
Cantel Medical Corporation, 80
Cardinal Health, Inc., 18; 50 (upd.)
Carl Zeiss AG, III; 34 (upd.); 91 (upd.)
Carson, Inc., 31
Carter-Wallace, Inc., 8
Caswell-Massey Co. Ltd., 51
CCA Industries, Inc., 53
Chattem, Inc., 17; 88 (upd.)
Chesebrough-Pond's USA, Inc., 8
Chronimed Inc., 26
Church & Dwight Co., Inc., 68 (upd.)
Cintas Corporation, 51 (upd.)
The Clorox Company, III; 22 (upd.); 81
  (upd.)
CNS, Inc., 20
Colgate-Palmolive Company, III; 14
  (upd.); 35 (upd.)
Combe Inc., 72
Conair Corp., 17
CONMED Corporation, 87
Connetics Corporation, 70
Cordis Corp., 19
Cosmair, Inc., 8
Coty, Inc., 36
Covidien Ltd., 91
Cybex International, Inc., 49
Cytyc Corporation, 69
Dade Behring Holdings Inc., 71
Dalli-Werke GmbH & Co. KG, 86
Datascope Corporation, 39
Del Laboratories, Inc., 28
Deltec, Inc., 56
Dentsply International Inc., 10
DEP Corporation, 20
DePuy, Inc., 30
DHB Industries Inc., 85
Diagnostic Products Corporation, 73
The Dial Corp., 23 (upd.)

Health Care Services

Hotels

Manor Care, Inc., 25 (upd.)
The Marcus Corporation, 21
Marriott International, Inc., III; 21
  (upd.); 83 (upd.)
McMenamins Pubs and Breweries, 65
Millennium & Copthorne Hotels plc, 71
Mirage Resorts, Incorporated, 6; 28 (upd.)
Monarch Casino & Resort, Inc., 65
Morgans Hotel Group Company, 80
Motel 6, 13; 56 (upd.)
MTR Gaming Group, Inc., 75
MWH Preservation Limited Partnership,
  65
NH Hoteles S.A., 79
Omni Hotels Corp., 12
Paradores de Turismo de Espana S.A., 73
Park Corp., 22
Players International, Inc., 22
Preussag AG, 42 (upd.)
Prime Hospitality Corporation, 52
Promus Companies, Inc., 9
Real Turismo, S.A. de C.V., 50
Red Roof Inns, Inc., 18
Resorts International, Inc., 12
The Ritz-Carlton Hotel Company, L.L.C.,
  9; 29 (upd.); 71 (upd.)
Riviera Holdings Corporation, 75
Sandals Resorts International, 65
Santa Fe Gaming Corporation, 19
The SAS Group, 34 (upd.)
SFI Group plc, 51
Shangri-La Asia Ltd., 71
Showboat, Inc., 19
Sol Meliá S.A., 71
Sonesta International Hotels Corporation,
  44
Starwood Hotels & Resorts Worldwide,
  Inc., 54
Sun International Hotels Limited, 26
Sunburst Hospitality Corporation, 26
Super 8 Motels, Inc., 83
Thistle Hotels PLC, 54
Trusthouse Forte PLC, III
Vail Resorts, Inc., 43 (upd.)
WestCoast Hospitality Corporation, 59
Westin Hotels and Resorts Worldwide, 9;
  29 (upd.)
Whitbread PLC, 52 (upd.)
Young & Co.'s Brewery, P.L.C., 38

Information Technology

A.B. Watley Group Inc., 45
AccuWeather, Inc., 73
Acxiom Corporation, 35
Adaptec, Inc., 31
Adobe Systems Incorporated, 10; 33
  (upd.)
Advanced Micro Devices, Inc., 6
Agence France-Presse, 34
Agilent Technologies, Inc., 38; 93 (upd.)
Akamai Technologies, Inc., 71
Aldus Corporation, 10
Allen Systems Group, Inc., 59
AltaVista Company, 43
Altiris, Inc., 65
Amdahl Corporation, III; 14 (upd.); 40
  (upd.)
Amdocs Ltd., 47

America Online, Inc., 10; 26 (upd.)
American Business Information, Inc., 18
American Management Systems, Inc., 11
American Software Inc., 25
AMICAS, Inc., 69
Amstrad PLC, III
Analex Corporation, 74
Analytic Sciences Corporation, 10
Analytical Surveys, Inc., 33
Anker BV, 53
Ansoft Corporation, 63
Anteon Corporation, 57
AOL Time Warner Inc., 57 (upd.)
Apollo Group, Inc., 24
Apple Computer, Inc., III; 6 (upd.); 77
  (upd.)
aQuantive, Inc., 81
The Arbitron Company, 38
Ariba, Inc., 57
Asanté Technologies, Inc., 20
Ascential Software Corporation, 59
AsiaInfo Holdings, Inc., 43
ASK Group, Inc., 9
Ask Jeeves, Inc., 65
ASML Holding N.V., 50
The Associated Press, 73 (upd.)
AST Research Inc., 9
At Home Corporation, 43
AT&T Bell Laboratories, Inc., 13
AT&T Corporation, 29 (upd.)
AT&T Istel Ltd., 14
Atos Origin S.A., 69
Attachmate Corporation, 56
Autodesk, Inc., 10; 89 (upd.)
Autologic Information International, Inc.,
  20
Automatic Data Processing, Inc., III; 9
  (upd.); 47 (upd.)
Autotote Corporation, 20
Avantium Technologies BV, 79
Avid Technology Inc., 38
Avocent Corporation, 65
Aydin Corp., 19
Baan Company, 25
Baltimore Technologies Plc, 42
Bankrate, Inc., 83
Banyan Systems Inc., 25
Battelle Memorial Institute, Inc., 10
BBN Corp., 19
BEA Systems, Inc., 36
Bell and Howell Company, 9; 29 (upd.)
Bell Industries, Inc., 47
Billing Concepts, Inc., 26; 72 (upd.)
Blackbaud, Inc., 85
Blackboard Inc., 89
Blizzard Entertainment 78
Bloomberg L.P., 21
Blue Martini Software, Inc., 59
BMC Software, Inc., 55
Boole & Babbage, Inc., 25
Booz Allen & Hamilton Inc., 10
Borland International, Inc., 9
Bowne & Co., Inc., 23
Brite Voice Systems, Inc., 20
Broderbund Software, 13; 29 (upd.)
BTG, Inc., 45
Bull S.A., 43 (upd.)
Business Objects S.A., 25

C-Cube Microsystems, Inc., 37
CACI International Inc., 21; 72 (upd.)
Cadence Design Systems, Inc., 11
Caere Corporation, 20
Cahners Business Information, 43
CalComp Inc., 13
Cambridge Technology Partners, Inc., 36
Candle Corporation, 64
Canon Inc., III
Cap Gemini Ernst & Young, 37
Captaris, Inc., 89
CareerBuilder, Inc., 93
Caribiner International, Inc., 24
Catalina Marketing Corporation, 18
CDC Corporation, 71
CDW Computer Centers, Inc., 16
Cerner Corporation, 16
CheckFree Corporation, 81
Cheyenne Software, Inc., 12
CHIPS and Technologies, Inc., 9
Ciber, Inc., 18
Cincom Systems Inc., 15
Cirrus Logic, Incorporated, 11
Cisco-Linksys LLC, 86
Cisco Systems, Inc., 11; 77 (upd.)
Citizen Watch Co., Ltd., III; 21 (upd.);
  81 (upd.)
Citrix Systems, Inc., 44
CMGI, Inc., 76
CNET Networks, Inc., 47
Cogent Communications Group, Inc., 55
Cognizant Technology Solutions
  Corporation, 59
Cognos Inc., 44
Commodore International Ltd., 7
Compagnie des Machines Bull S.A., III
Compaq Computer Corporation, III; 6
  (upd.); 26 (upd.)
Complete Business Solutions, Inc., 31
CompuAdd Computer Corporation, 11
CompuCom Systems, Inc., 10
CompUSA, Inc., 35 (upd.)
CompuServe Interactive Services, Inc., 10;
  27 (upd.)
Computer Associates International, Inc.,
  6; 49 (upd.)
Computer Data Systems, Inc., 14
Computer Sciences Corporation, 6
Computervision Corporation, 10
Compuware Corporation, 10; 30 (upd.);
  66 (upd.)
Comshare Inc., 23
Conner Peripherals, Inc., 6
Control Data Corporation, III
Control Data Systems, Inc., 10
Corbis Corporation, 31
Corel Corporation, 15; 33 (upd.); 76
  (upd.)
Corporate Software Inc., 9
CoStar Group, Inc., 73
craigslist, inc., 89
Cray Research, Inc., III
Credence Systems Corporation, 90
CSX Corporation, 79 (upd.)
CTG, Inc., 11
Cybermedia, Inc., 25
Dairyland Healthcare Solutions, 73
Dassault Systèmes S.A., 25

Insurance

China Life Insurance Company Limited, 65

ChoicePoint Inc., 65

The Chubb Corporation, III; 14 (upd.); 37 (upd.)

CIGNA Corporation, III; 22 (upd.); 45 (upd.)

Cincinnati Financial Corporation, 16; 44 (upd.)

CNA Financial Corporation, III; 38 (upd.)

Commercial Union PLC, III

Connecticut Mutual Life Insurance Company, III

Conseco Inc., 10; 33 (upd.)

The Continental Corporation, III

Crawford & Company, 87

Debeka Krankenversicherungsverein auf Gegenseitigkeit, 72

The Doctors' Company, 55

Empire Blue Cross and Blue Shield, III

Enbridge Inc., 43

Endurance Specialty Holdings Ltd., 85

Engle Homes, Inc., 46

The Equitable Life Assurance Society of the United States Fireman's Fund Insurance Company, III

ERGO Versicherungsgruppe AG, 44

Erie Indemnity Company, 35

Fairfax Financial Holdings Limited, 57

Farm Family Holdings, Inc., 39

Farmers Insurance Group of Companies, 25

Federal Deposit Insurance Corporation, 93

Fidelity National Financial Inc., 54

The First American Corporation, 52

First Executive Corporation, III

Foundation Health Corporation, 12

Gainsco, Inc., 22

GEICO Corporation, 10; 40 (upd.)

General Accident PLC, III

General Re Corporation, III; 24 (upd.)

Gerling-Konzern Versicherungs-Beteiligungs-Aktiengesellschaft, 51

GraceKennedy Ltd., 92

Great-West Lifeco Inc., III

Groupama S.A., 76

Gryphon Holdings, Inc., 21

Guardian Financial Services, 64 (upd.)

Guardian Royal Exchange Plc, 11

Harleysville Group Inc., 37

HDI (Haftpflichtverband der Deutschen Industrie Versicherung auf Gegenseitigkeit V.a.G.), 53

HealthExtras, Inc., 75

HealthMarkets, Inc., 88 (upd.)

Hilb, Rogal & Hobbs Company, 77

The Home Insurance Company, III

Horace Mann Educators Corporation, 22; 90 (upd.)

Household International, Inc., 21 (upd.)

Hub International Limited, 89

HUK-Coburg, 58

Irish Life & Permanent Plc, 59

Jackson National Life Insurance Company, 8

Jefferson-Pilot Corporation, 11; 29 (upd.)

John Hancock Financial Services, Inc., III; 42 (upd.)

Johnson & Higgins, 14

Kaiser Foundation Health Plan, Inc., 53

Kemper Corporation, III; 15 (upd.)

LandAmerica Financial Group, Inc., 85

Legal & General Group plc, III; 24 (upd.)

The Liberty Corporation, 22

Liberty Mutual Holding Company, 59

LifeWise Health Plan of Oregon, Inc., 90

Lincoln National Corporation, III; 25 (upd.)

Lloyd's, 74 (upd.)

Lloyd's of London, III; 22 (upd.)

The Loewen Group Inc., 40 (upd.)

Lutheran Brotherhood, 31

Manulife Financial Corporation, 85

Marsh & McLennan Companies, Inc., III; 45 (upd.)

Massachusetts Mutual Life Insurance Company, III; 53 (upd.)

MBIA Inc., 73

The Meiji Mutual Life Insurance Company, III

Mercury General Corporation, 25

Metropolitan Life Insurance Company, III; 52 (upd.)

MGIC Investment Corp., 52

The Midland Company, 65

Millea Holdings Inc., 64 (upd.)

Mitsui Marine and Fire Insurance Company, Limited, III

Mitsui Mutual Life Insurance Company, III; 39 (upd.)

Modern Woodmen of America, 66

Munich Re (Münchener Rückversicherungs-Gesellschaft Aktiengesellschaft in München), III; 46 (upd.)

The Mutual Benefit Life Insurance Company, III

The Mutual Life Insurance Company of New York, III

National Medical Health Card Systems, Inc., 79

Nationale-Nederlanden N.V., III

The Navigators Group, Inc., 92

New England Mutual Life Insurance Company, III

New York Life Insurance Company, III; 45 (upd.)

Nippon Life Insurance Company, III; 60 (upd.)

Northwestern Mutual Life Insurance Company, III; 45 (upd.)

NYMAGIC, Inc., 41

Ohio Casualty Corp., 11

Old Republic International Corporation, 11; 58 (upd.)

Oregon Dental Service Health Plan, Inc., 51

Palmer & Cay, Inc., 69

Pan-American Life Insurance Company, 48

PartnerRe Ltd., 83

The Paul Revere Corporation, 12

Pennsylvania Blue Shield, III

The PMI Group, Inc., 49

Preserver Group, Inc., 44

Principal Mutual Life Insurance Company, III

The Progressive Corporation, 11; 29 (upd.)

Provident Life and Accident Insurance Company of America, III

Prudential Financial Inc., III; 30 (upd.); 82 (upd.)

Prudential plc, III; 48 (upd.)

Radian Group Inc., 42

The Regence Group, 74

Reliance Group Holdings, Inc., III

Riunione Adriatica di Sicurtà SpA, III

Royal & Sun Alliance Insurance Group plc, 55 (upd.)

Royal Insurance Holdings PLC, III

SAFECO Corporaton, III

The St. Paul Travelers Companies, Inc. III; 22 (upd.); 79 (upd.)

SCOR S.A., 20

Skandia Insurance Company, Ltd., 50

StanCorp Financial Group, Inc., 56

The Standard Life Assurance Company, III

State Auto Financial Corporation, 77

State Farm Mutual Automobile Insurance Company, III; 51 (upd.)

State Financial Services Corporation, 51

Stewart Information Services Corporation 78

Sumitomo Life Insurance Company, III; 60 (upd.)

The Sumitomo Marine and Fire Insurance Company, Limited, III

Sun Alliance Group PLC, III

Sun Life Financial Inc., 85

SunAmerica Inc., 11

Suncorp-Metway Ltd., 91

Suramericana de Inversiones S.A., 88

Svenska Handelsbanken AB, 50 (upd.)

The Swett & Crawford Group Inc., 84

Swiss Reinsurance Company (Schweizerische Rückversicherungs-Gesellschaft), III; 46 (upd.)

Teachers Insurance and Annuity Association-College Retirement Equities Fund, III; 45 (upd.)

Texas Industries, Inc., 8

TIG Holdings, Inc., 26

The Tokio Marine and Fire Insurance Co., Ltd., III

Torchmark Corporation, 9; 33 (upd.)

Transatlantic Holdings, Inc., 11

The Travelers Corporation, III

UICI, 33

Union des Assurances de Pans, III

United National Group, Ltd., 63

Unitrin Inc., 16; 78 (upd.)

UNUM Corp., 13

UnumProvident Corporation, 52 (upd.)

USAA, 10

USF&G Corporation, III

Victoria Group, 44 (upd.)

VICTORIA Holding AG, III

Vision Service Plan Inc., 77

W.R. Berkley Corporation, 15; 74 (upd.)

Materials

Florida Rock Industries, Inc., 46
Foamex International Inc., 17
Formica Corporation, 13
GAF Corporation, 22 (upd.)
The Geon Company, 11
Giant Cement Holding, Inc., 23
Gibraltar Steel Corporation, 37
Granite Rock Company, 26
Groupe Sidel S.A., 21
Harbison-Walker Refractories Company, 24
Harrisons & Crosfield plc, III
Heidelberger Zement AG, 31
Hexcel Corporation, 28
Holderbank Financière Glaris Ltd., III
Holnam Inc., 39 (upd.)
Holt and Bugbee Company, 66
Homasote Company, 72
Howmet Corp., 12
Huttig Building Products, Inc., 73
Ibstock Brick Ltd., 14; 37 (upd.)
Imerys S.A., 40 (upd.)
Imperial Industries, Inc., 81
Internacional de Ceramica, S.A. de C.V., 53
International Shipbreaking Ltd. L.L.C., 67
Joseph T. Ryerson & Son, Inc., 15
Lafarge Coppée S.A., III
Lafarge Corporation, 28
Lehigh Portland Cement Company, 23
Manville Corporation, III; 7 (upd.)
Material Sciences Corporation, 63
Matsushita Electric Works, Ltd., III; 7 (upd.)
McJunkin Corporation, 63
Medusa Corporation, 24
Mitsubishi Materials Corporation, III
Nevamar Company, 82
Nippon Sheet Glass Company, Limited, III
North Pacific Group, Inc., 61
Nuplex Industries Ltd., 92
OmniSource Corporation, 14
Onoda Cement Co., Ltd., III
Otor S.A., 77
Owens-Corning Fiberglass Corporation, III
Pacific Clay Products Inc., 88
Pilkington Group Limited, III; 34 (upd.); 87 (upd.)
Pioneer International Limited, III
PolyOne Corporation, 87 (upd.)
PPG Industries, Inc., III; 22 (upd.); 81 (upd.)
Redland plc, III
Rinker Group Ltd., 65
RMC Group p.l.c., III
Rock of Ages Corporation, 37
Rogers Corporation, 80 (upd.)
Royal Group Technologies Limited, 73
The Rugby Group plc, 31
Schuff Steel Company, 26
Sekisui Chemical Co., Ltd., III; 72 (upd.)
Severstal Joint Stock Company, 65
Shaw Industries, 9
The Sherwin-Williams Company, III; 13 (upd.); 89 (upd.)

The Siam Cement Public Company Limited, 56
SIG plc, 71
Simplex Technologies Inc., 21
Siskin Steel & Supply Company, 70
Solutia Inc., 52
Sommer-Allibert S.A., 19
Southdown, Inc., 14
Spartech Corporation, 19; 76 (upd.)
Ssangyong Cement Industrial Co., Ltd., III; 61 (upd.)
Steel Technologies Inc., 63
Sun Distributors L.P., 12
Symyx Technologies, Inc., 77
Tarmac plc, III, 28 (upd.)
Tilcon-Connecticut Inc., 80
TOTO LTD., III; 28 (upd.)
Toyo Sash Co., Ltd., III
Tuscarora Inc., 29
U.S. Aggregates, Inc., 42
Ube Industries, Ltd., III
United States Steel Corporation, 50 (upd.)
USG Corporation, III; 26 (upd.); 81 (upd.)
Usinas Siderúrgicas de Minas Gerais S.A., 77
Vicat S.A., 70
voestalpine AG, 57 (upd.)
Vulcan Materials Company, 7; 52 (upd.)
Wacker-Chemie GmbH, 35
Walter Industries, Inc., III
Waxman Industries, Inc., 9
Weber et Broutin France, 66
Wienerberger AG, 70
Wolseley plc, 64
ZERO Corporation, 17; 88 (upd.)
Zoltek Companies, Inc., 37

Mining & Metals

A.M. Castle & Co., 25
Acindar Industria Argentina de Aceros S.A., 87
Aggregate Industries plc, 36
Agnico-Eagle Mines Limited, 71
Aktiebolaget SKF, III; 38 (upd.); 89 (upd.)
Alcan Aluminium Limited, IV; 31 (upd.)
Alcoa Inc., 56 (upd.)
Alleghany Corporation, 10
Allegheny Ludlum Corporation, 8
Alliance Resource Partners, L.P., 81
Alrosa Company Ltd., 62
Altos Hornos de México, S.A. de C.V., 42
Aluminum Company of America, IV; 20 (upd.)
AMAX Inc., IV
AMCOL International Corporation, 59 (upd.)
Amsted Industries Incorporated, 7
Anglo American Corporation of South Africa Limited, IV; 16 (upd.)
Anglo American PLC, 50 (upd.)
Aquarius Platinum Ltd., 63
ARBED S.A., IV; 22 (upd.)
Arcelor Gent, 80
Arch Mineral Corporation, 7
Armco Inc., IV
ASARCO Incorporated, IV

Ashanti Goldfields Company Limited, 43
Atchison Casting Corporation, 39
Barrick Gold Corporation, 34
Battle Mountain Gold Company, 23
Benguet Corporation, 58
Bethlehem Steel Corporation, IV; 7 (upd.); 27 (upd.)
BHP Billiton, 67 (upd.)
Birmingham Steel Corporation, 13; 40 (upd.)
Boart Longyear Company, 26
Bodycote International PLC, 63
Boliden AB, 80
Boral Limited, 43 (upd.)
Boral Limited, 43 (upd.)
British Coal Corporation, IV
British Steel plc, IV; 19 (upd.)
Broken Hill Proprietary Company Ltd., IV, 22 (upd.)
Brush Engineered Materials Inc., 67
Brush Wellman Inc., 14
Buderus AG, 37
Cameco Corporation, 77
Caparo Group Ltd., 90
Carpenter Technology Corporation, 13
Chaparral Steel Co., 13
China Shenhua Energy Company Limited, 83
Christensen Boyles Corporation, 26
Cleveland-Cliffs Inc., 13; 62 (upd.)
Coal India Ltd., IV; 44 (upd.)
Cockerill Sambre Group, IV; 26 (upd.)
Coeur d'Alene Mines Corporation, 20
Cold Spring Granite Company Inc., 16; 67 (upd.)
Cominco Ltd., 37
Commercial Metals Company, 15; 42 (upd.)
Companhia Siderúrgica Nacional, 76
Companhia Vale do Rio Doce, IV; 43 (upd.)
Compañia de Minas Buenaventura S.A.A., 93
CONSOL Energy Inc., 59
Corporacion Nacional del Cobre de Chile, 40
Corus Group plc, 49 (upd.)
CRA Limited, IV
Cyprus Amax Minerals Company, 21
Cyprus Minerals Company, 7
Daido Steel Co., Ltd., IV
De Beers Consolidated Mines Limited/De Beers Centenary AG, IV; 7 (upd.); 28 (upd.)
Degussa Group, IV
Diavik Diamond Mines Inc., 85
Dofasco Inc., IV; 24 (upd.)
Dynatec Corporation, 87
Earle M. Jorgensen Company, 82
Echo Bay Mines Ltd., IV; 38 (upd.)
Engelhard Corporation, IV
Eramet, 73
Fansteel Inc., 19
Fluor Corporation, 34 (upd.)
Freeport-McMoRan Copper & Gold, Inc., IV; 7 (upd.); 57 (upd.)
Fried. Krupp GmbH, IV
Gencor Ltd., IV, 22 (upd.)

Publishing & Printing

Retail & Wholesale

AVA AG (Allgemeine Handelsgesellschaft der Verbraucher AG), 33
Aveda Corporation, 24
Aviall, Inc., 73
Aviation Sales Company, 41
AWB Ltd., 56
B. Dalton Bookseller Inc., 25
Babbage's, Inc., 10
Baby Superstore, Inc., 15
Baccarat, 24
Bachman's Inc., 22
Bailey Nurseries, Inc., 57
Ball Horticultural Company 78
Banana Republic Inc., 25
Bare Escentuals, Inc., 91
Barnes & Noble, Inc., 10; 30 (upd.); 75 (upd.)
Barnett Inc., 28
Barney's, Inc., 28
Barrett-Jackson Auction Company L.L.C., 88
Bass Pro Shops, Inc., 42
Baumax AG, 75
Beacon Roofing Supply, Inc., 75
Bear Creek Corporation, 38
Bearings, Inc., 13
bebe stores, inc., 31
Bed Bath & Beyond Inc., 13; 41 (upd.)
Belk Stores Services, Inc., V; 19 (upd.)
Belk, Inc., 72 (upd.)
Ben Bridge Jeweler, Inc., 60
Benetton Group S.p.A., 67 (upd.)
Bergdorf Goodman Inc., 52
Bergen Brunswig Corporation, V; 13 (upd.)
Bernard Chaus, Inc., 27
Best Buy Co., Inc., 9; 23 (upd.); 63 (upd.)
Bestseller A/S, 90
Bhs plc, 17
Big A Drug Stores Inc., 79
Big Dog Holdings, Inc., 45
Big 5 Sporting Goods Corporation, 55
The Big Food Group plc, 68 (upd.)
Big Lots, Inc., 50
Big O Tires, Inc., 20
Birkenstock Footprint Sandals, Inc., 42 (upd.)
Birthdays Ltd., 70
Black Box Corporation, 20
Blacks Leisure Group plc, 39
Blair Corporation, 25; 31 (upd.)
Blokker Holding B.V., 84
Bloomingdale's Inc., 12
Blue Nile Inc., 61
Blue Square Israel Ltd., 41
Bluefly, Inc., 60
Blyth Industries, Inc., 18
The Body Shop International PLC, 11
The Bombay Company, Inc., 10; 71 (upd.)
The Bon Marché, Inc., 23
The Bon-Ton Stores, Inc., 16; 50 (upd.)
Booker Cash & Carry Ltd., 68 (upd.)
Books-A-Million, Inc., 14; 41 (upd.)
Bookspan, 86
The Boots Company PLC, V; 24 (upd.)
Borders Group, Inc., 15; 43 (upd.)

Boscov's Department Store, Inc., 31
Bozzuto's, Inc., 13
Bradlees Discount Department Store Company, 12
Brambles Industries Limited, 42
Bricorama S.A., 68
Brioni Roman Style S.p.A., 67
Brodart Company, 84
Broder Bros. Co., 38
Bronner Display & Sign Advertising, Inc., 82
Brooks Brothers Inc., 22
Brookstone, Inc., 18
Brown Shoe Company, Inc., 68 (upd.)
Brunswick Corporation, 77 (upd.)
The Buckle, Inc., 18
Buhrmann NV, 41
Build-A-Bear Workshop Inc., 62
Building Materials Holding Corporation, 52
Burdines, Inc., 60
Burlington Coat Factory Warehouse Corporation, 10; 60 (upd.)
Burt's Bees, Inc., 58
The Burton Group plc, V
Buttrey Food & Drug Stores Co., 18
buy.com, Inc., 46
C&A, V; 40 (upd.)
C&J Clark International Ltd., 52
Cabela's Inc., 26; 68 (upd.)
Cablevision Electronic Instruments, Inc., 32
Cache Incorporated, 30
Cactus S.A., 90
Caldor Inc., 12
Calloway's Nursery, Inc., 51
Camaïeu S.A., 72
Camelot Music, Inc., 26
Campeau Corporation, V
Campo Electronics, Appliances & Computers, Inc., 16
Car Toys, Inc., 67
The Carphone Warehouse Group PLC, 83
Carrefour SA, 10; 27 (upd.); 64 (upd.)
Carson Pirie Scott & Company, 15
Carter Hawley Hale Stores, Inc., V
Carter Lumber Company, 45
Cartier Monde, 29
Casas Bahia Comercial Ltda., 75
Casey's General Stores, Inc., 19; 83 (upd.)
Castro Model Ltd., 86
Casual Corner Group, Inc., 43
Casual Male Retail Group, Inc., 52
Catherines Stores Corporation, 15
Cato Corporation, 14
CDW Computer Centers, Inc., 16
Celebrate Express, Inc., 70
Celebrity, Inc., 22
CellStar Corporation, 83
Cencosud S.A., 69
Central European Distribution Corporation, 75
Central Garden & Pet Company, 23
Cenveo Inc., 71 (upd.)
Chadwick's of Boston, Ltd., 29
Charlotte Russe Holding, Inc., 35; 90 (upd.)
Charming Shoppes, Inc., 38

Chas. Levy Company LLC, 60
ChevronTexaco Corporation, 47 (upd.)
Chiasso Inc., 53
The Children's Place Retail Stores, Inc., 37; 86 (upd.)
Christian Dior S.A., 49 (upd.)
Christopher & Banks Corporation, 42
Cifra, S.A. de C.V., 12
The Circle K Company, 20 (upd.)
Circuit City Stores, Inc., 9; 29 (upd.); 65 (upd.)
Clare Rose Inc., 68
Clinton Cards plc, 39
The Clothestime, Inc., 20
CML Group, Inc., 10
Co-operative Group (CWS) Ltd., 51
Coach, Inc., 45 (upd.)
Coborn's, Inc., 30
Coinmach Laundry Corporation, 20
Coldwater Creek Inc., 21; 74 (upd.)
Cole National Corporation, 13; 76 (upd.)
Cole's Quality Foods, Inc., 68
Coles Group Limited, V; 20 (upd.); 85 (upd.)
Collectors Universe, Inc., 48
Columbia House Company, 69
Comdisco, Inc., 9
Compagnie Financière Sucres et Denrées S.A., 60
Companhia Brasileira de Distribuiçao, 76
CompUSA, Inc., 10
Computerland Corp., 13
Concepts Direct, Inc., 39
Conn's, Inc., 67
The Container Store, 36
Controladora Comercial Mexicana, S.A. de C.V., 36
CoolSavings, Inc., 77
Coop Schweiz Genossenschaftsverband, 48
Coppel, S.A. de C.V., 82
Corby Distilleries Limited, 14
Corporate Express, Inc., 22; 47 (upd.)
Cortefiel S.A., 64
The Cosmetic Center, Inc., 22
Cost Plus, Inc., 27
Costco Wholesale Corporation, V; 43 (upd.)
Cotter & Company, V
County Seat Stores Inc., 9
Courts Plc, 45
CPI Corp., 38
Crate and Barrel, 9
Croscill, Inc., 42
CROSSMARK, 79
Crowley, Milner & Company, 19
Crown Books Corporation, 21
Cumberland Farms, Inc., 17; 84 (upd.)
CVS Corporation, 45 (upd.)
Daffy's Inc., 26
The Daiei, Inc., V; 17 (upd.); 41 (upd.)
The Daimaru, Inc., V; 42 (upd.)
Dairy Mart Convenience Stores, Inc., 25 (upd.)
Daisytek International Corporation, 18
Damark International, Inc., 18
Dart Group Corporation, 16
Darty S.A., 27
David Jones Ltd., 60

Rubber & Tires

Telecommunications

Hungarian Telephone and Cable Corp., 75
IDB Communications Group, Inc., 11
IDT Corporation, 34
Illinois Bell Telephone Company, 14
Indiana Bell Telephone Company, Incorporated, 14
PT Indosat Tbk, 93
Infineon Technologies AG, 50
Infinity Broadcasting Corporation, 11
InfoSonics Corporation, 81
InterDigital Communications Corporation, 61
Iowa Telecommunications Services, Inc., 85
IXC Communications, Inc., 29
Jacor Communications, Inc., 23
Jones Intercable, Inc., 21
j2 Global Communications, Inc., 75
Koninklijke PTT Nederland NV, V
Landmark Communications, Inc., 55 (upd.)
LCC International, Inc., 84
LCI International, Inc., 16
LDDS-Metro Communications, Inc., 8
Leap Wireless International, Inc., 69
Level 3 Communications, Inc., 67
LIN Broadcasting Corp., 9
Lincoln Telephone & Telegraph Company, 14
LodgeNet Entertainment Corporation, 28
Loral Space & Communications Ltd., 54 (upd.)
MacNeil/Lehrer Productions, 87
Magyar Telekom Rt. 78
Manitoba Telecom Services, Inc., 61
Mannesmann AG, 38
MasTec, Inc., 19; 55 (upd.)
McCaw Cellular Communications, Inc., 6
MCI WorldCom, Inc., V; 27 (upd.)
McLeodUSA Incorporated, 32
Mediacom Communications Corporation, 69
Mercury Communications, Ltd., 7
Metrocall, Inc., 41
Metromedia Companies, 14
Métropole Télévision, 33
Métropole Télévision S.A., 76 (upd.)
MFS Communications Company, Inc., 11
Michigan Bell Telephone Co., 14
MIH Limited, 31
MITRE Corporation, 26
Mobile Telecommunications Technologies Corp., 18
Mobile TeleSystems OJSC, 59
Modern Times Group AB, 36
The Montana Power Company, 44 (upd.)
Motorola, Inc., II; 11 (upd.); 34 (upd.); 93 (upd.)
Multimedia, Inc., 11
National Broadcasting Company, Inc., 28 (upd.)
National Grid USA, 51 (upd.)
National Weather Service, 91
NCR Corporation, III; 6 (upd.); 30 (upd.); 90 (upd.)
NetCom Systems AB, 26
NeuStar, Inc., 81

Nevada Bell Telephone Company, 14
New Valley Corporation, 17
Nexans SA, 54
Nexstar Broadcasting Group, Inc., 73
Nextel Communications, Inc., 27 (upd.)
Nippon Telegraph and Telephone Corporation, V; 51 (upd.)
Nokia Corporation, 77 (upd.)
Norstan, Inc., 16
Nortel Networks Corporation, 36 (upd.)
Northern Telecom Limited, V
NTL Inc., 65
NTN Buzztime, Inc., 86
NYNEX Corporation, V
Octel Messaging, 14; 41 (upd.)
Ohio Bell Telephone Company, 14
Olivetti S.p.A., 34 (upd.)
Orange S.A., 84
Österreichische Post- und Telegraphenverwaltung, V
Pacific Internet Limited, 87
Pacific Telecom, Inc., 6
Pacific Telesis Group, V
Paging Network Inc., 11
PanAmSat Corporation, 46
Paxson Communications Corporation, 33
The Phoenix Media/Communications Group, 91
PictureTel Corp., 10; 27 (upd.)
Portugal Telecom SGPS S.A., 69
Posti- ja Telelaitos, 6
Price Communications Corporation, 42
ProSiebenSat.1 Media AG, 54
Publishing and Broadcasting Limited, 54
Qatar Telecom QSA, 87
QUALCOMM Incorporated, 20; 47 (upd.)
QVC Network Inc., 9
Qwest Communications International, Inc., 37
RCN Corporation, 70
Regent Communications, Inc., 87
Research in Motion Ltd., 54
RMH Teleservices, Inc., 42
Rochester Telephone Corporation, 6
Rogers Communications Inc., 30 (upd.)
Royal KPN N.V., 30
Rural Cellular Corporation, 43
Saga Communications, Inc., 27
Sawtek Inc., 43 (upd.)
SBC Communications Inc., 32 (upd.)
Schweizerische Post-, Telefon- und Telegrafen-Betriebe, V
Scientific-Atlanta, Inc., 6; 45 (upd.)
Seat Pagine Gialle S.p.A., 47
Securicor Plc, 45
Shenandoah Telecommunications Company, 89
Sinclair Broadcast Group, Inc., 25
Sirius Satellite Radio, Inc., 69
Sirti S.p.A., 76
Società Finanziaria Telefonica per Azioni, V
Softbank Corporation, 77 (upd.)
Sonera Corporation, 50
Southern New England Telecommunications Corporation, 6
Southwestern Bell Corporation, V

Spanish Broadcasting System, Inc., 41
Spelling Entertainment, 35 (upd.)
Sprint Corporation, 9; 46 (upd.)
StarHub Ltd., 77
StrataCom, Inc., 16
Swedish Telecom, V
Swisscom AG, 58
Sycamore Networks, Inc., 45
SynOptics Communications, Inc., 10
T-Netix, Inc., 46
Talk America Holdings, Inc., 70
TDC A/S, 63
Tekelec, 83
Telcordia Technologies, Inc., 59
Tele Norte Leste Participações S.A., 80
Telecom Argentina S.A., 63
Telecom Australia, 6
Telecom Corporation of New Zealand Limited, 54
Telecom Eireann, 7
Telecom Italia Mobile S.p.A., 63
Telecom Italia S.p.A., 43
Telefonaktiebolaget LM Ericsson, V; 46 (upd.)
Telefónica de Argentina S.A., 61
Telefónica S.A., V; 46 (upd.)
Telefonos de Mexico S.A. de C.V., 14; 63 (upd.)
Telekom Malaysia Bhd, 76
Telekomunikacja Polska SA, 50
Telenor ASA, 69
Telephone and Data Systems, Inc., 9
Télévision Française 1, 23
TeliaSonera AB, 57 (upd.)
Tellabs, Inc., 11; 40 (upd.)
Telstra Corporation Limited, 50
Thomas Crosbie Holdings Limited, 81
Tiscali SpA, 48
The Titan Corporation, 36
Tollgrade Communications, Inc., 44
TV Azteca, S.A. de C.V., 39
U.S. Satellite Broadcasting Company, Inc., 20
U S West, Inc., V; 25 (upd.)
U.S. Cellular Corporation, 9; 31 (upd.); 88 (upd.)
UFA TV & Film Produktion GmbH, 80
United Pan-Europe Communications NV, 47
United Telecommunications, Inc., V
United Video Satellite Group, 18
Univision Communications Inc., 24; 83 (upd.)
USA Interactive, Inc., 47 (upd.)
UTStarcom, Inc., 77
Verizon Communications Inc. 43 (upd.); 78 (upd.)
ViaSat, Inc., 54
Vivendi Universal S.A., 46 (upd.)
Vodafone Group Plc, 11; 36 (upd.); 75 (upd.)
Vonage Holdings Corp., 81
The Walt Disney Company, II; 6 (upd.); 30 (upd.); 63 (upd.)
Wanadoo S.A., 75
Watkins-Johnson Company, 15
The Weather Channel Companies, 52
West Corporation, 42

The Leslie Fay Company, Inc., 8; 39 (upd.)
Levi Strauss & Co., V; 16 (upd.)
Liz Claiborne, Inc., 8
London Fog Industries, Inc., 29
Lost Arrow Inc., 22
Maidenform, Inc., 20; 59 (upd.)
Malden Mills Industries, Inc., 16
Maples Industries, Inc., 83
Mariella Burani Fashion Group, 92
Marzotto S.p.A., 20; 67 (upd.)
Milliken & Co., V; 17 (upd.); 82 (upd.)
Miroglio SpA, 86
Mitsubishi Rayon Co., Ltd., V
Mossimo, Inc., 27
Mothercare plc, 17; 78 (upd.)
Movie Star Inc., 17
Mulberry Group PLC, 71
Naf Naf SA, 44
Nautica Enterprises, Inc., 18; 44 (upd.)
New Balance Athletic Shoe, Inc., 25; 68 (upd.)
NIKE, Inc., V; 8 (upd.); 75 (upd.)
Nine West Group, Inc., 39 (upd.)
Nitches, Inc., 53
The North Face Inc., 18; 78 (upd.)
Oakley, Inc., 18
Ormat Technologies, Inc., 87
OshKosh B'Gosh, Inc., 9; 42 (upd.)
Oxford Industries, Inc., 8; 84 (upd.)
Pacific Sunwear of California, Inc., 28
Peek & Cloppenburg KG, 46
Pendleton Woolen Mills, Inc., 42
Pentland Group plc, 20
Perry Ellis International, Inc., 41
Phat Fashions LLC, 49
Phoenix Footwear Group, Inc., 70
Pillowtex Corporation, 19; 41 (upd.)
Plains Cotton Cooperative Association, 57
Pluma, Inc., 27
Polo/Ralph Lauren Corporation, 12; 62 (upd.)
Pomare Ltd., 88
Prada Holding B.V., 45
PremiumWear, Inc., 30
Puma AG Rudolf Dassler Sport, 35
Quaker Fabric Corp., 19
Quiksilver, Inc., 18; 79 (upd.)
R.G. Barry Corporation, 17; 44 (upd.)
Rack Room Shoes, Inc., 84
Raymond Ltd., 77
Recreational Equipment, Inc., 18
Red Wing Shoe Company, Inc., 9; 30 (upd.); 83 (upd.)
Reebok International Ltd., V; 9 (upd.); 26 (upd.)
Reliance Industries Ltd., 81
Rieter Holding AG, 42
Robert Talbott Inc., 88
Rocawear Apparel LLC, 77
Rollerblade, Inc., 15
Royal Ten Cate N.V., 68
Russell Corporation, 8; 30 (upd.); 82 (upd.)
St. John Knits, Inc., 14
Salant Corporation, 51 (upd.)
Salvatore Ferragamo Italia S.p.A., 62
Sao Paulo Alpargatas S.A., 75

Saucony Inc., 35; 86 (upd.)
Schott Brothers, Inc., 67
Seattle Pacific Industries, Inc., 92
Shaw Industries, Inc., 40 (upd.)
Shelby Williams Industries, Inc., 14
Shoe Pavilion, Inc., 84
Skechers U.S.A. Inc., 31; 88 (upd.)
Sole Technology Inc., 93
Sophus Berendsen A/S, 49
Spanx, Inc., 89
Springs Global US, Inc., V; 19 (upd.); 90 (upd.)
Starter Corp., 12
Stefanel SpA, 63
Steiner Corporation (Alsco), 53
Steven Madden, Ltd., 37
Stirling Group plc, 62
Stoddard International plc, 72
Stone Manufacturing Company, 14; 43 (upd.)
Stride Rite Corporation, 8; 37 (upd.); 86 (upd.)
Stussy, Inc., 55
Sun Sportswear, Inc., 17
Superior Uniform Group, Inc., 30
Tag-It Pacific, Inc., 85
The Talbots, Inc., 11; 31 (upd.); 88 (upd.)
Tamfelt Oyj Abp, 62
Tarrant Apparel Group, 62
Ted Baker plc, 86
Teijin Limited, V
Thanulux Public Company Limited, 86
Thomaston Mills, Inc., 27
Tilley Endurables, Inc., 67
The Timberland Company, 13; 54 (upd.)
Tommy Hilfiger Corporation, 20; 53 (upd.)
Too, Inc., 61
Toray Industries, Inc., V
True Religion Apparel, Inc., 79
Tultex Corporation, 13
Under Armour Performance Apparel, 61
Unifi, Inc., 12; 62 (upd.)
United Merchants & Manufacturers, Inc., 13
United Retail Group Inc., 33
Unitika Ltd., V
Umbro plc, 88
Vans, Inc., 16; 47 (upd.)
Varsity Spirit Corp., 15
VF Corporation, V; 17 (upd.); 54 (upd.)
Vicunha Têxtil S.A. 78
Volcom, Inc., 77
Walton Monroe Mills, Inc., 8
The Warnaco Group Inc., 12; 46 (upd.)
Wellco Enterprises, Inc., 84
Wellman, Inc., 8; 52 (upd.)
West Point-Pepperell, Inc., 8
WestPoint Stevens Inc., 16
Weyco Group, Incorporated, 32
Williamson-Dickie Manufacturing Company, 14
Wolverine World Wide, Inc., 16; 59 (upd.)
Woolrich Inc., 62

Zara International, Inc., 83

Tobacco
Altadis S.A., 72 (upd.)
American Brands, Inc., V
B.A.T. Industries PLC, 22 (upd.)
British American Tobacco PLC, 50 (upd.)
Brooke Group Ltd., 15
Brown & Williamson Tobacco Corporation, 14; 33 (upd.)
Culbro Corporation, 15
Dibrell Brothers, Incorporated, 12
DIMON Inc., 27
800-JR Cigar, Inc., 27
Gallaher Group Plc, V; 19 (upd.); 49 (upd.)
General Cigar Holdings, Inc., 66 (upd.)
Holt's Cigar Holdings, Inc., 42
House of Prince A/S, 80
Imasco Limited, V
Imperial Tobacco Group PLC, 50
Japan Tobacco Incorporated, V
KT&G Corporation, 62
Nobleza Piccardo SAICF, 64
North Atlantic Trading Company Inc., 65
Philip Morris Companies Inc., V; 18 (upd.)
R.J. Reynolds Tobacco Holdings, Inc., 30 (upd.)
RJR Nabisco Holdings Corp., V
Rothmans UK Holdings Limited, V; 19 (upd.)
Seita, 23
Souza Cruz S.A., 65
Standard Commercial Corporation, 13; 62 (upd.)
Swedish Match AB, 12; 39 (upd.); 92 (upd.)
Swisher International Group Inc., 23
Tabacalera, S.A., V; 17 (upd.)
Taiwan Tobacco & Liquor Corporation, 75
Universal Corporation, V; 48 (upd.)
UST Inc., 9; 50 (upd.)
Vector Group Ltd., 35 (upd.)

Transport Services
Abertis Infraestructuras, S.A., 65
The Adams Express Company, 86
Aegean Marine Petroleum Network Inc., 89
Aéroports de Paris, 33
Air Express International Corporation, 13
Air Partner PLC, 93
Air T, Inc., 86
Airborne Freight Corporation, 6; 34 (upd.)
Alamo Rent A Car, Inc., 6; 24 (upd.); 84 (upd.)
Alaska Railroad Corporation, 60
Alexander & Baldwin, Inc., 10, 40 (upd.)
Allied Worldwide, Inc., 49
AMCOL International Corporation, 59 (upd.)
Amerco, 6
AMERCO, 67 (upd.)
American Classic Voyages Company, 27
American President Companies Ltd., 6

Waste Services

Geographic Index

Germany

Nepal

Netherlands

The Ritz-Carlton Hotel Company, L.L.C., 9; 29 (upd.); 71 (upd.)
The Rival Company, 19
River Oaks Furniture, Inc., 43
River Ranch Fresh Foods LLC, 88
Riverwood International Corporation, 11; 48 (upd.)
Riviana Foods Inc., 27
Riviera Holdings Corporation, 75
Riviera Tool Company, 89
RJR Nabisco Holdings Corp., V
RMH Teleservices, Inc., 42
Roadhouse Grill, Inc., 22
Roadmaster Industries, Inc., 16
Roadway Express, Inc., V; 25 (upd.)
Roanoke Electric Steel Corporation, 45
Robbins & Myers Inc., 15
Robins, Kaplan, Miller & Ciresi L.L.P., 89
Roberds Inc., 19
Robert Half International Inc., 18; 70 (upd.)
Robert Mondavi Corporation, 15; 50 (upd.)
Robert Talbott Inc., 88
Robert W. Baird & Co. Incorporated, 67
Robert Wood Johnson Foundation, 35
Roberts Pharmaceutical Corporation, 16
Robertson-Ceco Corporation, 19
Robinson Helicopter Company, 51
Rocawear Apparel LLC, 77
Roche Bioscience, 11; 14 (upd.)
Rochester Gas and Electric Corporation, 6
Rochester Telephone Corporation, 6
Rock Bottom Restaurants, Inc., 25; 68 (upd.)
Rock-It Cargo USA, Inc., 86
Rock of Ages Corporation, 37
Rock-Tenn Company, 13; 59 (upd.)
The Rockefeller Foundation, 34
Rockefeller Group International Inc., 58
Rockford Corporation, 43
Rockford Products Corporation, 55
RockShox, Inc., 26
Rockwell Automation, 43 (upd.)
Rockwell International Corporation, I; 11 (upd.)
Rockwell Medical Technologies, Inc., 88
Rocky Mountain Chocolate Factory, Inc., 73
Rocky Shoes & Boots, Inc., 26
Rodale, Inc., 23; 47 (upd.)
ROFIN-SINAR Technologies Inc., 81
Rogers Corporation, 61; 80 (upd.)
Rohm and Haas Company, I; 26 (upd.); 77 (upd.)
ROHN Industries, Inc., 22
Rohr Incorporated, 9
Roll International Corporation, 37
Rollerblade, Inc., 15; 34 (upd.)
Rollins, Inc., 11
Rolls-Royce Allison, 29 (upd.)
Roly Poly Franchise Systems LLC, 83
Romacorp, Inc., 58
Roman Meal Company, 84
Ron Tonkin Chevrolet Company, 55
Ronco Corporation, 15; 80 (upd.)
Rooms To Go Inc., 28
Rooney Brothers Co., 25

Roper Industries, Inc., 15; 50 (upd.)
Ropes & Gray, 40
Rorer Group, I
Rosauers Supermarkets, Inc., 90
Rose Acre Farms, Inc., 60
Rose Art Industries, 58
Rose's Stores, Inc., 13
Roseburg Forest Products Company, 58
Rosemount Inc., 15
Rosenbluth International Inc., 14
Rosetta Stone Inc., 93
Ross Stores, Inc., 17; 43 (upd.)
Rotary International, 31
Roto-Rooter, Inc., 15; 61 (upd.)
The Rottlund Company, Inc., 28
Rouge Steel Company, 8
Rounder Records Corporation 79
Roundy's Inc., 14; 58 (upd.)
The Rouse Company, 15; 63 (upd.)
Rowan Companies, Inc., 43
Roy Anderson Corporation, 75
Roy F. Weston, Inc., 33
Royal Appliance Manufacturing Company, 15
Royal Caribbean Cruises Ltd., 22; 74 (upd.)
Royal Crown Company, Inc., 23
RPC, Inc., 91
RPM International Inc., 8; 36 (upd.); 91 (upd.)
RSA Security Inc., 46
RTM Restaurant Group, 58
Rubbermaid Incorporated, III; 20 (upd.)
Rubio's Restaurants, Inc., 35
Ruby Tuesday, Inc., 18; 71 (upd.)
Ruiz Food Products, Inc., 53
Rural Cellular Corporation, 43
Rural/Metro Corporation, 28
Rush Communications, 33
Rush Enterprises, Inc., 64
Russ Berrie and Company, Inc., 12; 82 (upd.)
Russell Corporation, 8; 30 (upd.); 82 (upd.)
Russell Reynolds Associates Inc., 38
Russell Stover Candies Inc., 12; 91 (upd.)
Rust International Inc., 11
Ruth's Chris Steak House, 28; 88 (upd.)
RWD Technologies, Inc., 76
Ryan Beck & Co., Inc., 66
Ryan's Restaurant Group, Inc., 15; 68 (upd.)
Ryder System, Inc., V; 24 (upd.)
Ryerson Tull, Inc., 40 (upd.)
Ryko Corporation, 83
The Ryland Group, Inc., 8; 37 (upd.)
S&C Electric Company, 15
S&D Coffee, Inc., 84
S&K Famous Brands, Inc., 23
S-K-I Limited, 15
S.C. Johnson & Son, Inc., III; 28 (upd.); 89 (upd.)
Saatchi & Saatchi, 42 (upd.)
Sabratek Corporation, 29
SABRE Group Holdings, Inc., 26
Sabre Holdings Corporation, 74 (upd.)
Safe Flight Instrument Corporation, 71
SAFECO Corporaton, III

Safeguard Scientifics, Inc., 10
Safelite Glass Corp., 19
Safeskin Corporation, 18
Safety Components International, Inc., 63
Safety 1st, Inc., 24
Safety-Kleen Systems Inc., 8; 82 (upd.)
Safeway Inc., II; 24 (upd.); 85 (upd.)
Saga Communications, Inc., 27
The St. Joe Company, 31
St. Joe Paper Company, 8
St. John Knits, Inc., 14
St. Jude Medical, Inc., 11; 43 (upd.)
St. Louis Music, Inc., 48
St. Mary Land & Exploration Company, 63
St. Paul Bank for Cooperatives, 8
The St. Paul Travelers Companies, Inc. III; 22 (upd.); 79 (upd.)
Saks Inc., 24; 41 (upd.)
Salant Corporation, 12; 51 (upd.)
salesforce.com, Inc. 79
Salick Health Care, Inc., 53
Salix Pharmaceuticals, Ltd., 93
Sally Beauty Company, Inc., 60
Salomon Inc., II; 13 (upd.)
Salt River Project, 19
Salton, Inc., 30; 88 (upd.)
The Salvation Army USA, 32
Sam Ash Music Corporation, 30
Sam Levin Inc., 80
Sam's Club, 40
Samsonite Corporation, 13; 43 (upd.)
Samuel Cabot Inc., 53
Samuels Jewelers Incorporated, 30
San Diego Gas & Electric Company, V
San Diego Padres Baseball Club LP 78
Sanborn Map Company Inc., 82
Sandals Resorts International, 65
Sanders Morris Harris Group Inc., 70
Sanderson Farms, Inc., 15
Sandia National Laboratories, 49
Sanford L.P., 82
Santa Barbara Restaurant Group, Inc., 37
The Santa Cruz Operation, Inc., 38
Santa Fe Gaming Corporation, 19
Santa Fe International Corporation, 38
Santa Fe Pacific Corporation, V
Sara Lee Corporation, II; 15 (upd.); 54 (upd.)
Sarnoff Corporation, 57
Sarris Candies Inc., 86
SAS Institute Inc., 10; 78 (upd.)
Saturn Corporation, 7; 21 (upd.); 80 (upd.)
Saucony Inc., 35; 86 (upd.)
Sauder Woodworking Company, 12; 35 (upd.)
Sauer-Danfoss Inc., 61
Saul Ewing LLP, 74
Savannah Foods & Industries, Inc., 7
Sawtek Inc., 43 (upd.)
Sbarro, Inc., 16; 64 (upd.)
SBC Communications Inc., 32 (upd.)
SBS Technologies, Inc., 25
SCANA Corporation, 6; 56 (upd.)
ScanSource, Inc., 29; 74 (upd.)
SCB Computer Technology, Inc., 29
SCEcorp, V

Utah Medical Products, Inc., 36
Utah Power and Light Company, 27
UtiliCorp United Inc., 6
UTStarcom, Inc., 77
Utz Quality Foods, Inc., 72
UUNET, 38
Uwajimaya, Inc., 60
Vail Resorts, Inc., 11; 43 (upd.)
Valassis Communications, Inc., 8; 37 (upd.); 76 (upd.)
Valero Energy Corporation, 7; 71 (upd.)
Valhi, Inc., 19
Vallen Corporation, 45
Valley Media Inc., 35
Valley National Gases, Inc., 85
Valley Proteins, Inc., 91
ValleyCrest Companies, 81 (upd.)
Valmont Industries, Inc., 19
The Valspar Corporation, 8; 32 (upd.); 77 (upd.)
Value City Department Stores, Inc., 38
Value Line, Inc., 16; 73 (upd.)
Value Merchants Inc., 13
ValueClick, Inc., 49
ValueVision International, Inc., 22
Van Camp Seafood Company, Inc., 7
Van's Aircraft, Inc., 65
Vance Publishing Corporation, 64
The Vanguard Group, Inc., 14; 34 (upd.)
Vanguard Health Systems Inc., 70
Vans, Inc., 16; 47 (upd.)
Varco International, Inc., 42
Vari-Lite International, Inc., 35
Varian, Inc., 12; 48 (upd.)
Variety Wholesalers, Inc., 73
Variflex, Inc., 51
Varlen Corporation, 16
Varsity Spirit Corp., 15
VASCO Data Security International, Inc. 79
Vastar Resources, Inc., 24
VCA Antech, Inc., 58
VECO International, Inc., 7
Vector Group Ltd., 35 (upd.)
Veeco Instruments Inc., 32
Veit Companies, 43; 92 (upd.)
Velocity Express Corporation, 49
Venator Group Inc., 35 (upd.)
Vencor, Inc., 16
Venetian Casino Resort, LLC, 47
Ventana Medical Systems, Inc., 75
Ventura Foods LLC, 90
Venture Stores Inc., 12
VeraSun Energy Corporation, 87
Verbatim Corporation, 14; 74 (upd.)
Veridian Corporation, 54
VeriFone Holdings, Inc., 18; 76 (upd.)
Verint Systems Inc., 73
VeriSign, Inc., 47
Veritas Software Corporation, 45
Verity Inc., 68
Verizon Communications, 43 (upd.); 78 (upd.)
Vermeer Manufacturing Company, 17
The Vermont Country Store, 93
Vermont Pure Holdings, Ltd., 51
The Vermont Teddy Bear Co., Inc., 36
Vertex Pharmaceuticals Incorporated, 83

Vertis Communications, 84
Vertrue Inc., 77
VF Corporation, V; 17 (upd.); 54 (upd.)
VHA Inc., 53
Viacom Inc., 7; 23 (upd.); 67 (upd.)
Viad Corp., 73
ViaSat, Inc., 54
Viasoft Inc., 27
VIASYS Healthcare, Inc., 52
Viasystems Group, Inc., 67
Viatech Continental Can Company, Inc., 25 (upd.)
Vicon Industries, Inc., 44
VICORP Restaurants, Inc., 12; 48 (upd.)
Victory Refrigeration, Inc., 82
Videojet Technologies, Inc., 90
Vienna Sausage Manufacturing Co., 14
Viewpoint International, Inc., 66
ViewSonic Corporation, 72
Viking Office Products, Inc., 10
Viking Range Corporation, 66
Village Super Market, Inc., 7
Village Voice Media, Inc., 38
Vinson & Elkins L.L.P., 30
Vintage Petroleum, Inc., 42
Vinton Studios, 63
Virbac Corporation, 74
Virco Manufacturing Corporation, 17
Visa International, 9; 26 (upd.)
Vishay Intertechnology, Inc., 21; 80 (upd.)
Vision Service Plan Inc., 77
Viskase Companies, Inc., 55
Vista Bakery, Inc., 56
Vista Chemical Company, I
Vistana, Inc., 22
VISX, Incorporated, 30
Vita Plus Corporation, 60
Vital Images, Inc., 85
Vitalink Pharmacy Services, Inc., 15
Vitamin Shoppe Industries, Inc., 60
Vitesse Semiconductor Corporation, 32
Vitro Corp., 10
Vivra, Inc., 18
Vlasic Foods International Inc., 25
VLSI Technology, Inc., 16
VMware, Inc., 90
Volcom, Inc., 77
Volt Information Sciences Inc., 26
Volunteers of America, Inc., 66
Von Maur Inc., 64
Vonage Holdings Corp., 81
The Vons Companies, Incorporated, 7; 28 (upd.)
Vornado Realty Trust, 20
Vought Aircraft Industries, Inc., 49
Vulcan Materials Company, 7; 52 (upd.)
W. Atlee Burpee & Co., 27
W.A. Whitney Company, 53
W.B Doner & Co., 56
W.C. Bradley Co., 69
W. H. Braum, Inc., 80
W.H. Brady Co., 17
W.L. Gore & Associates, Inc., 14; 60 (upd.)
W.P. Carey & Co. LLC, 49
W.R. Berkley Corporation, 15; 74 (upd.)
W.R. Grace & Company, I; 50 (upd.)

W.W. Grainger, Inc., V; 26 (upd.); 68 (upd.)
W.W. Norton & Company, Inc., 28
Waban Inc., 13
Wabash National Corp., 13
Wabtec Corporation, 40
Wachovia Bank of Georgia, N.A., 16
Wachovia Bank of South Carolina, N.A., 16
Wachovia Corporation, 12; 46 (upd.)
Wachtell, Lipton, Rosen & Katz, 47
The Wackenhut Corporation, 14; 63 (upd.)
Waddell & Reed, Inc., 22
Waffle House Inc., 14; 60 (upd.)
Wagers Inc. (Idaho Candy Company), 86
Waggener Edstrom, 42
Wah Chang, 82
Wahl Clipper Corporation, 86
Wakefern Food Corporation, 33
Wal-Mart Stores, Inc., V; 8 (upd.); 26 (upd.); 63 (upd.)
Walbridge Aldinger Co., 38
Walbro Corporation, 13
Waldbaum, Inc., 19
Waldenbooks, 17; 86 (upd.)
Walgreen Co., V; 20 (upd.); 65 (upd.)
Walker Manufacturing Company, 19
Wall Drug Store, Inc., 40
Wall Street Deli, Inc., 33
Wallace Computer Services, Inc., 36
Walsworth Publishing Co. 78
The Walt Disney Company, II; 6 (upd.); 30 (upd.); 63 (upd.)
Walter Industries, Inc., II; 22 (upd.); 72 (upd.)
Walton Monroe Mills, Inc., 8
Wang Laboratories, Inc., III; 6 (upd.)
The Warnaco Group Inc., 12; 46 (upd.)
Warner Communications Inc., II
Warner Music Group Corporation, 90 (upd.)
Warner-Lambert Co., I; 10 (upd.)
Warners' Stellian Inc., 67
Warrantech Corporation, 53
Warrell Corporation, 68
Warwick Valley Telephone Company, 55
The Washington Companies, 33
Washington Federal, Inc., 17
Washington Football, Inc., 35
Washington Gas Light Company, 19
Washington Mutual, Inc., 17; 93 (upd.)
Washington National Corporation, 12
Washington Natural Gas Company, 9
The Washington Post Company, IV; 20 (upd.)
Washington Scientific Industries, Inc., 17
Washington Water Power Company, 6
Waste Connections, Inc., 46
Waste Holdings, Inc., 41
Waste Management, Inc., V
Water Pik Technologies, Inc., 34; 83 (upd.)
Waterhouse Investor Services, Inc., 18
Waters Corporation, 43
Watkins-Johnson Company, 15
Watsco Inc., 52